BUSINESS AND POLITICS
UNDER
THE PERSIAN EMPIRE

BUSINESS AND POLITICS UNDER THE PERSIAN EMPIRE

The Financial Dealings of
Marduk-nāṣir-apli of the House of Egibi
(521–487 B.C.E.)

by

KATHLEEN ABRAHAM

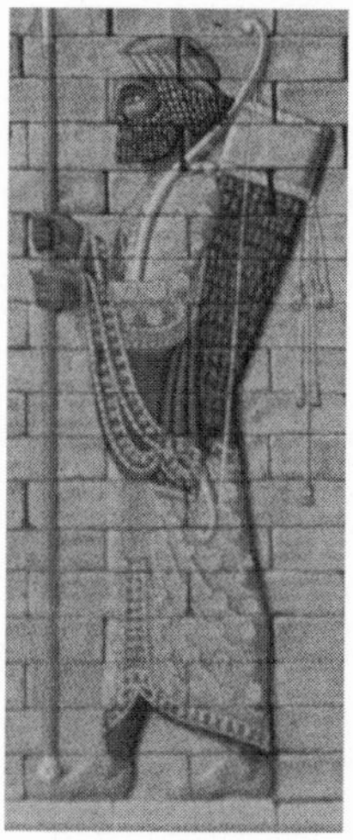

CDL PRESS
2004

Library of Congress Cataloging-in-Publication Data

Abraham, Kathleen
Business and politics under the Persian Empire : the financial dealings of marduk-nasir-apli of the House of Egibi (521–487 B.C.E.) / by Kathleen Abraham.
p. cm.
Includes bibliographical references and index.
ISBN 1-883053-811.
1. Family-owned business enterprises—Iran—History. 2. Business and politics—Iran—History. 3. Marduk-nasir-apli. 4. Finance—Iran—History. I. Title.

HD62.25.A27 2004
338.7'0935–dc22 2003060279

Published by CDL Press, P.O. Box 34454, Bethesda, MD 20827;
E-Mail: cdlpress@erols.com; website: www.cdlpress.com; Fax: 253-484-5542

ISBN 1-883053-811

Dedicated to My Parents

Acknowledgments

I am deeply indebted to Dr. Cornelia Wunsch for sharing with me the unpublished Egibi texts she identified among the thousands of tablets in the British Museum. In the autumn of 1994 she gave me a list of museum numbers and generously put at my disposal her preliminary transcriptions of the texts. In the course of time she shared with me many improved readings, and kindly provided collations of a number of the Strassmaier texts, which I have gratefully incorporated here. It is a very great pleasure to express my profound gratitude to her for her generosity and help in initiating this work and bringing it to completion. Needless to say that the responsibility for faults of any kind is mine alone.

During my stays in the Students' Room at the British Museum I greatly benefitted from the assistance of Dr. C.B.F. Walker, Keeper of the Western Asiatic Antiquities, and from occasional discussions with distinguished scholars who were working on Neo-Babylonian archival texts in the Students' Room at the same time: Professor Karlheinz Kessler, Professor Erle Leichty, Professor Michael Jursa and Professor Ran Zadok. I would also like to express my gratitude to Christopher and Marie-Christine Walker for their hospitality while staying in London. I am indebted to the Trustees for permission to publish tablets from the British Museum.

Financial support for my research on the Egibi archive was provided by a research assistantship in the "Mesopotamian History and Environment Project" at the Katholieke Universiteit Leuven (Belgium) for the years 1993–1995; a postdoctoral fellowship at the Ben Gurion University of the Negev (Israel) granted by the Council for Higher Education (Israel) in 1995–1997; and the Alon Fellowship awarded by the same Council for Higher Education in 1999–2002.

My special appreciation goes to Professor K. Van Lerberghe, of the Katholieke Universiteit Leuven, for introducing me to the world of Sumer and Akkad while I was his graduate student in 1981–1985, and for his ceaseless and generous help after I left Belgium and started my academic career in Israel. For his many efforts on my behalf I am happy to take this opportunity to thank him here.

A special note of thanks must also be offered here to my colleagues at the Bar Ilan University who were ever ready to listen to problems and give useful suggestions; to my friends in Jerusalem who were ever ready to grant practical help, from babysitting to catering; and to my eleven-year-old son, Jonathan, for his humor and patience.

Finally, I cannot adequately express here my gratitude to my parents for their unstinting love and support. They guided me in all my academic and non-academic endeavors with patience and sensitivity. This book is a testament to their constant encouragement and to their dedication to my research.

TABLE OF CONTENTS

ABBREVIATIONS

a.m.	*ana muḫḫi*
Dar	Darius
Dupl.	Duplicate
G.o.B.	governor of Babylon (*šākin ṭēmi*)
IMB	Itti-Marduk-balāṭu/Nabû-aḫḫē-iddin//Egibi
imper.	imperative (grammar)
Ir.	Iranian (= Persian)
Le. E.	Left edge of the tablet
lit.	literally
Lo. E.	Lower edge of the tablet
MBU	Madānu-bēla-uṣur (slave of MNA)
MNA	Marduk-nāṣir-apli/Itti-Marduk-balāṭu//Egibi
NAB	Nabû-aḫḫē-bulliṭ/Itti-Marduk-balāṭu//Egibi
NAI	Nabû-aḫḫē-iddin//Šulaya//Egibi
NB	Neo-Babylonian
Nbn	Nabonidus
o.b.o.	on behalf of
Obv.	Obverse side of the tablet
perf.	perfect (grammar)
PN	Personal name
pret.	preterite (grammar)
rd.	read
Rev.	Reverse side of the tablet
Ri. Ed.	Right edge of the tablet
U. E.	Upper edge of the tablet
wr.	written

Text Sigla

Amherst	see s.v. Ungnad, *AfO* 19
AcSum 19	see s.v. Zadok
AfO 38/39	see s.v. MacGinnis
AfO 42/43	see s.v. Wunsch
AION 77	see s.v. Stolper
AuOr 15	see s.v. Wunsch
AUWE 8/1	see s.v. Kessler
b	= Bertin. Unpublished copies of tablets in the British Museum made by Bertin and preserved in the British Museum.
BaM 21	see s.v. Stolper
BE 9	see s.v. Hilprecht
Bēl-rēmanni	see s.v. Jursa
BM	= tablets from the British Museum, either unpublished or published in the current book
BOR 1	see s.v. Pinches
BOR 2	see s.v. Pinches
Borsippa	see s.v. Joannès
BRM 1	see s.v. Clay
BRU 6	see s.v. San-Nicolò
Camb	see s.v. Strassmaier
CM 3	see s.v. Wunsch
CM 20	see s.v. Wunsch
CT 4	see s.v. Pinches
CT 22	see s.v. Thompson
CT 51, 55–57	see s.v. Pinches
CTMMA 3	see s.v. Spar-Von Dassow
Cyr	see s.v. Strassmaier
Dar	see s.v. Strassmaier
Ebabbar	see s.v. Bongenaar
Fs. Diakonoff	see s.v. Gurney
GCCI 2	see s.v. Doughtery
Iraq 55	see s.v. MacGinnis
Istanbul Murašû	see s.v. Donbaz-Stolper

JCS 53	see s.v. Stolper
Landwirtschaft	see s.v. Jursa
Liv	see s.v. Strassmaier
MHEO 2	see s.v. Biggs
NABU 1995/77	see s.v. Beaulieu - Stolper
NbBU	see s.v. Ebeling
Nbk	see s.v. Strassmaier
Nbn	see s.v. Strassmaier
NRVU	see s.v. San-Nicolo - Ungnad
OECT 10	see s.v. McEwan
OLA 65	see s.v. Abraham and s.v. Zadok
OLP 28	see s.v. Abraham
OrAnt 25	see s.v. Frame
SCT	see s.v. Gordon
TCL 12–13	see s.v. Contenau
TÉBR	see s.v. Joannès
Tempelzehnt	see s.v. Jursa
TUM 2/3	see s.v. Krückmann or s.v. Joannès, *Borsippa*
VS 3–6	see s.v. Ungnad
WZKM 86	see s.v. Weszeli
WZKM 87	see s.v. Weszeli - Baker
YOS 6	see s.v. Dougherty
YOS 7	see s.v. Tremayne
YOS 17	see s.v. Weisberg

SYMBOLS

Babylonian dates are cited in this form: day (in Arabic numerals)/month (in Roman numerals)/regnal year (in Arabic numerals) king's name; Intercalary months are cited as follows: vi(a) = First Ulūl, vi(b) = Second Ulūl, xii(a) = First Addar, and xii(b) = Second Addar.

+	Join.
( )	In the translation, addition to provide a clearer meaning.
/	After a personal name a single slash indicates filiation, to be read "son of" or "daughter of" preceding the name of a father.
//	After a personal name a double slash indicates filiation, to be read "descendant of" preceding the name of an ancestor. Between the (publication) numbers of two tablets a double slash indicates that the texts on the tablets are duplicates.
< >	Text is emended; enclosed sign(s) were left out by the scribe. They are to be added to the transliteration and translation.
{ }	Text is emended; enclosed sign(s) were superfluously added by the scribe. They are to be deleted in the transliteration and translation.
x	Illegible sign or reading uncertain.
$x^{!}$	Text is emended; sign on the tablet is corrected in the transliteration.
$x^{?}$ or (?)	Transliteration or translation of the sign or word is uncertain.
italics	In the translation, the meaning of the word in italics is uncertain.
[x x]	Document broken; space exists for x number of signs in brackets.
[...]	Document broken; text is not restored, space exists for an unknown number of signs.
⸢ ⸣	Document damaged; sign(s) are partially preserved—in particular, upper part of sign(s) is damaged.
[ ]	Document damaged; lower part of sign(s) is damaged.

BIBLIOGRAPHY AND BIBLIOGRAPHICAL ABBREVIATIONS

Abraham, K.

Eretz Israel 27 — "Property and Ownership in the Egibi Family," (in Hebrew) *Eretz Israel* 27 (2002): 1–9.

NABU 1997 — "TCL 13 193: Šušan and Bāṣ," *NABU* 1997/53.

OLA 65 — "The End of Marduk-nāṣir-apli's Career as Businessman and Scribe: New Evidence from Unpublished Egibi Texts from the British Museum," *OLA* 65 (1995): 1–9.

OLP 28 — "Šušan in the Egibi Texts from the Time of Marduk-nāṣir-apli," *OLP* 28 (1997): 55–85.

AHw — W. von Soden, *Akkadisches Handwörterbuch*. Wiesbaden 1959–1981.

Baker, H.D.

BiOr 55 — "Review of C. Wunsch, *Iddin-Marduk*," *BiOr* 55 (1998): 197–204.

Private Archives — *Private Archives from Late 7th - Early 5th Century BC Babylon: their Composition and their Prosopography* [unpublished Ph.D. dissertation, University of Oxford, 1998]. (unavailable to me).

Bass, G.F.

"Sea and River Craft in the Ancient Near East," in: J. Sasson (ed.), *Civilizations of the Ancient Near East* III. Peabody 1995. Pp. 1421–22.

Beaulieu, P.-A.

JNES 52 — "An Episode in the Fall of Babylon to the Persians," *JNES* 52 (1993): 241–61.

MOS Studies 2 — "A Finger in Every Pie: The Institutional Connections of a Family of Entrepreneurs in Neo-Babylonian Larsa," in: A.C.V.M. Bongenaar (ed.), *Interdependency of Institutions and Private Entrepreneurs*. Proceedings of the Second MOS Symposium, Leiden 1998. (PIHANS 87). Istanbul 2000. Pp. 43–72.

YOS 19 — *Legal and Administrative Texts from the Reign of Nabonidus*. (Yale Oriental Series. Babylonian Texts 19). New Haven 2000.

Beaulieu, P.-A. - M.W. Stolper

NABU 1995 — "Two More Achaemenid Texts from Uruk are to be added to those edited in Bagh.Mitt. 21 (1990) 559–621," *NABU* 1995/77.

Biggs R.D.

MHEO 2 — "Šušan in Babylonia," in: H. Gasche e.a. (eds.), *Cinquante-deux reflections sur le Proche-orient ancien offertes en hommage à Léon de Meijer*. (Mesopotamian History and Environment. Occasional Publications 2) Leuven 1994. Pp. 299–304.

Bogaert, R.

L'origine antique de la banque de dépôt. Leiden 1966.

Bongenaar, A.C.V.M.

Ebabbar — *The Neo-Babylonian Ebabbar Temple at Sippar: Its Administration and its Prosopography*. (PIHANS 80). Istanbul 1997.

"Money" — "Money in the Neo-Babylonian Institutions," in: J.G. Dercksen (ed.), *Trade and Finance in Ancient Mesopotamia*. Proceedings of the First MOS Symposium, Leiden 1997. (PIHANS 84). Istanbul 1999. Pp. 159–74.

MOS Studies 2 — "Private Archives in Neo-Babylonian Sippar and their Institutional Connections," in: A.C.V.M. Bongenaar (ed.), *Interdependency of Institutions and Private Entrepreneurs*. Proceedings of the Second MOS Symposium, Leiden 1998 (PIHANS 87). Istanbul 2000. Pp. 73–94.

Briant, P.

Histoire de l'empire Perse. De Cyrus à Alexandre. Paris 1996.

Brinkman, J.A.

"The Akkadian Words for 'Ionia' and 'Ionian'," in: E.F. Sutton, Jr. (ed.), *Daidalikon, Studies in memory of Raymond V. Schoder, S.J.*, Wauconda 1989. Pp. 53–71.

Bruschweiler, F.

RA 83 — "Un Échange de Terrains entre Nabuchodonozor II et un inconnu dans la région de Sippar," *RA* 83 (1989): 158–60.

CAD — *The Assyrian Dictionary of the Oriental Institute of the University of Chicago. Chicago 1956-*.

Cardascia, G.

Murašû — *Les archives des Murašû, une famille d'hommes d'affaires à l'époque perse (455–403 av. J.-C.)*. Paris 1951.

Clay, A.T.

BE 9 — *Business Documents of Murashu, Sons of Nippur Dated in the Reign of Artaxerxes I (464–424 B.C.)*. (The Babylonian Expedition of the University of Pennsylvania. Series A, Cuneiform Texts 9). Philadelphia 1898.

BRM 1 — *Babylonian Business Transactions of the 1st Millennium B.C.* (Babylonian Records in the Library of J. Pierpont Morgan 1). New York 1912.

Cocquerillat, D.

Palmeraies — *Palmeraies et cultures de l'Éanna d'Uruk (559–520).* (Ausgrabungen der deutschen Forschungsgemeinschaft in Uruk-Warka 8). Berlin 1968.

RA 78 — "Compléments aux *Palmeraies et cultures de l'Éanna d'Uruk* (II)," *RA* 78 (1984): 49–70.

RA 79 — "Compléments aux *Palmeraies et cultures de l'Éanna d'Uruk* (IV)," *RA* 79 (1985): 51–59.

Cole, St.W.

Governor's Archive — *Nippur IV. The Early Neo-Babylonian Governor's Archive from Nippur.* (Oriental Institute, Publications 114). Chicago 1996.

Contenau, G.

TCL 12/13 — *Contrats néo-babyloniens I: de Téglath-phalasar III à Nabonide. II: achéménides et séleucides.* (Textes cunéiformes. Musée du Louvre, Département des antiquités orientales 12/13). Paris 1927–29.

Dandamaev, M.A.

"Bagasarū" — "Bagasarū ganzabara," in: M. Mayrhofer e.a. (eds.), *Studien zur Sprachwissenschaft und Kulturkunde, Gedenkschrift für Wilhelm Brandenstein* (1898–1967). Innsbruck 1968. Pp. 235–39.

"Connections" — "Connections Between Elam and Babylonia in the Achaemenid Period," (Vth International Congress of Iranian Art and Archaeology. Tehran-Isfahan-Shiraz, 11th–18th April 1968, Volume 1), pp. 258–64.

Iranians — *Iranians in Achaemenid Babylonia.* (Columbia Lectures on Iranian Studies 6). Costa Mesa - New York 1992.

Slavery — *Slavery in Babylonia from Nabopolassar to Alexander the Great (626–331 BC).* DeKalb, Ill. 1984.

Von Dassow, E.

CTMMA 3 — see s.v. Spar, I.-Von Dassow, E.

Fs. Levine — "Introducing the Witnesses in Neo-Babylonian Documents," in: R. Chazan, W. W. Hallo and L. H. Schiffman (eds.), *Ki Baruch Hu. Ancient Near Eastern, Biblical, and Judaic Studies in Honor of Baruch A. Levine.* Winona Lake 1999. Pp. 3–22.

Donbaz, V. - M.W. Stolper

Istanbul Murašû Texts. (PIHANS 79). Istanbul 1997.

Dougherty, R.Ph.,

GCCI 2 — *Goucher College Cuneiform Inscriptions.* Volume 2. New York 1923–1933.

YOS 6 — *Records from Erech, Time of Nabonides (555–538 B.C.).* (Yale Oriental Series 6). New York 1920.

Van Driel, G.

BiOr 43 — "Neo-Babylonian Texts from the Louvre," *BiOr* 43 (1986): 5–20.

BSA 4 — "Neo-Babylonian Agriculture. I. Introductory Remarks. II. Rivers, Canals and Land: Irrigation," *BSA* 4 (1988): 121–59.

"Entrepreneurs" — "Agricultural Entrepreneurs in Mesopotamia," in: H. Klengel-J. Renger (eds.), *Landwirtschaft im Alten Orient* (BBVO 18). Berlin 1999. Pp. 213–23.

JEOL 29 — "The Rise of the House of Egibi. Nabû-aḫḫē-iddina," *JEOL* 29 (1985–86): 50–67.

JESHO 32 — "The Murašûs in Context," *JESHO* 32 (1989): 203–29.

MOS Studies 2 — "Capital Formation and Investment in an Institutional Context in Ancient Mesopotamia," in: J.G. Dercksen (ed.), *Trade and Finance in Ancient Mesopotamia*. Proceedings of the First MOS Symposium, Leiden 1997. (PIHANS 84). Istanbul 1999. Pp. 25–42.

Phoenix 31 — "De opkomst van een nieuwbabylonische familie: de Egibi's," *Phoenix* 31/2 (1985, [1986]): 33–47.

Durand, J.-M.

TBER — *Textes babyloniens d'époque récente*. (Études assyriologiques 6). Paris 1981.

Ebeling, E.

NbBU — *Neubabylonische Briefe aus Uruk. I.* Berlin 1930.

NbBr — *Neubabylonische Briefe.* (Abhandlungen der Bayerischen Akademie der Wissenschaften, phil.-hist. Klasse N.F. 30). München 1949.

Ellis, Marie de Jong

Agriculture and the State in Ancient Mesopotamia: An Introduction to the Problems of Land Tenure. (Occasional Publications of the Babylonian Fund 1). Philadelphia 1976.

Fales, F.M.

"Rivers" — "Rivers in Neo-Assyrian Geography," in: M. Liverani (ed.), *Neo-Assyrian Geography*. Roma 1995. Pp. 203–15.

Šulmu — "River Transport in Neo-Assyrian Letters," in: J. Zablocka-S. Zawadzki (eds.), *Šulmu IV. Everyday Life in the Ancient Near East.* Poznan 1993. Pp. 79–92.

Frame, G.

OrAnt 25 — "Some Neo-Babylonian and Persian Documents Involving Boats," *Oriens Antiquus* 25 (1986): 29–50.

Freydank, H.

SWU — *Spätbabylonische Wirtschaftstexte aus Uruk.* Berlin 1971.

Gehlken, E.

AUWE 5 — *Uruk. Spätbabylonische Wirtschaftstexte aus dem Eanna-Archiv. I.* (Ausgrabungen in Uruk-Warka. Endberichte 5). Mainz 1990.

NABU 1994 — "Bemerkungen zur Grammatik des Spätbabylonischen," *NABU* 1994/89.

Di Gennaro, T.

AION 55 — "Lo šāpiru nell'Ebabbara neo-babilonese e achemenide," *AION* 55 (1995), 380–405.

George, A.

House Most High. The Temples of Ancient Mesopotamia. Winona Lake 1993.

Gordon, C.H.

Smith College Tablets; 110 Cuneiform Texts Selected from the College Collection. Northampton 1952.

Gurney, O.R.

Fs. Diakonoff — "Three Contracts from Babylon," in: M.A. Dandamaev et al. (eds.), *Societies and Languages of the Ancient Near East. Studies in Honour of I.M. Diakonoff.* Warminster 1982. Pp. 120–29.

Holt, I.L.

AJSL 27 — "Tablets from the R. Campbell Thompson Collection in Haskell Oriental Museum, the University of Chicago," *AJSL* 27 (1911): 193–232.

Joannès, F.

Borsippa — *Archives de Borsippa. La Famille Ea-ilûta-bâni. Étude d'un lot d'archives familiales en Babylonie du VIIIe au Ve siècle av. J.-C.* (École Pratique des Hautes Études Section 6, Sciences historiques et philologiques 2, Hautes Études Orientales 25). Geneva 1989.

"Métaux précieux" — "Métaux précieux et moyens de paiement en Babylonie achéménide et hellénistique," *Transeuphratène* 8 (1994): 137–44.

MOS Studies 2 — "Relations entre intérêts privés et biens des sanctuaires à l'époque néo-babylonienne," in: J.G. Dercksen (ed.), *Trade and Finance in Ancient Mesopotamia.* Proceedings of the First MOS Symposium, Leiden 1997. (PIHANS 84). Istanbul 1999. Pp. 25–42.

"Pouvoirs locaux" — "Pouvoirs locaux et organisations du territoire en Babylonie achéménide," *Transeuphratène* 3 (1990): 173–89.

RA 89(1) — "Les phénomènes de fin d'archives en Mésopotamie: Présentation," *RA* 89 (1995): 1–2.

RA 89(2) — "L'extinction des archives cunéiformes dans la seconde partie de l'époque perse," *RA* 89 (1995): 139–47.

TÉBR — *Textes économiques de la Babylonie récente. Étude des textes de TBER.* (Études assyriologiques, Édition Recherche sur les civilisations 5). Paris 1982.

Jursa, M.

AfO 42/43 — "Review of C. Wunsch, *Iddin-Marduk*," *AfO* 42/43 (1995–96): 255–62.

Bēl-rēmanni — *Das Archiv des Bēl-rēmanni.* (PIHANS 86). Istanbul 1999.

Iraq 59 — "Neu- und spätbabylonische Texte aus den Sammlungen der Birmingham Museums und Art Gallery," *Iraq* 59 (1997): 97–174.

Landwirtschaft — *Die Landwirtschaft in Sippar in neubabylonischer Zeit.* (AfO Beiheft 25). Vienna 1995.

NABU 1995 — "Zu *NABU* 1995/4," *NABU* 1995/61.

Tempelzehnt — *Der Tempelzehnt in Babylonien vom siebenten bis dritten Jahrhundert v. Chr.* (AOAT 254). Münster 1998.

Kent, R.G.

Old Persian Grammar, Texts, Lexicon. (*AOS* 33). New Haven 1953².

Kessler, K.

AUWE 8/1 — *Uruk. Urkunden aus Privathäusern. Die Wohnhäuser westlich des Eanna-Tempelbereichs. Teil I: Die Archive der Söhne des Bēl-ušallim, des Nabû-ušallim und des Bēl-supê-muḫur.* (Ausgrabungen in Uruk-Warka. Endberichte 8/1). Mainz 1991.

AUWE 8/2 — *Uruk. Urkunden aus Privathäusern. Die Wohnhäuser westlich des Eanna-Tempelbereichs. Teil I: Das Archiv des Egibi-Hauses und verstreute Texte.* (Ausgrabungen in Uruk-Warka. Endberichte 8/2). (forthcoming).

Koch, H.

AMI 19 — "Die Achämenidische Poststrasse von Persepolis nach Susa," *AMI* 19 (1986): 134–47.

Kohler, J. - F.E. Peiser

BRL — *Aus dem Babylonischen Rechtsleben.* 4 Vols. Leipzig 1890–1898.

Kratylos — = Kritische Berichts- und Rezensionsorgan für Indogermanische und Allgemeine Sprachwissenschaft, Wiesbaden.

Krauss, S.

Talmudische Archäologie II. Hildesheim 1966.

Krecher, J.

Egibi — *Das Geschäftshaus Egibi in Babylon in neubabylonischer und achämenidischer Zeit.* (unpublished; Habilitationsschrift, Universität Münster, 1970).

Krückmann, O.

TUM 2/3 — *Neubabylonische Rechts- und Verwaltungstexte.* (Texte und Materialien der Frau Professor Hilprecht Collection ... Jena 2/3). Leipzig 1935.

Kümmel, H.M.

Familie, Beruf und Amt im spätbabylonischen Uruk. Prosopographische Untersuchungen zu Berufsgruppen des 6. Jahrhunderts v. Chr. in Uruk. (Abhandlungen der Deutschen Orient-Gesellschaft 20). Berlin 1979.

Lambert, W.G.

JCS 11 — "Ancestors, Authors, and Canonicity," *JCS* 11 (1957): 1–14, 112.

Landsberger, B.

JNES 8 — "Jahreszeiten im Sumerisch-Akkadischen," *JNES* 8 (1949): 248–97.

Date Palm — *The Date Palm and its By-products according to the Cuneiform Sources.* (AfO Beiheft 17). Graz 1967.

Lanz, H.

Ḫarrānu — *Die neubabylonische ḫarrânu-Geschäftsunternehmen.* (Münchener Universitätsschriften, Juristische Fakultät. Abhandlungen zur rechtswissenschaftlichen Grundlagenforschung 18). Berlin 1976.

MacGinnis, J.

AoF 26 — "Additional Prebend Texts from the British Museum," *AoF* 26 (1999): 3–12.

AfO 38/39 — "Neo-Babylonian Prebend Texts from the British Museum," *AfO* 38/39 (1991–92): 74–100.

Iraq 55 — "Two Achaemenid Tablets from the Fitzwilliam Museum, Cambridge," *Iraq* 55 (1993): 149–53.

Letter Orders — *Letter Orders from Sippar and the Administration of the Ebabbara in the Late-Babylonian Period.* Poznan 1995.

WZKM 88 — "BM 64707 and *rikis qabli* in the Ebabbara," *WZKM* 88 (1998): 177–83.

ZA 84 — "The Royal Establishment at Sippar in the 6th Century B.C.," *ZA* 84 (1994): 198–219.

McEwan, G.J.P.

OECT 10 — *Late Babylonian Texts in the Ashmolean Museum.* (Oxford Editions of Cuneiform Texts 10). Oxford 1984.

Millard, A.R. - M. Jursa

AfO 44/45 — "Ein neubabylonischer Brief aus Jerusalem," *AfO* 44/45 (1997–1998): 163–64.

Oelsner, J.

AoF 4 — "Erwägungen zum Gesellschaftsaufbau Babyloniens von der neubabylonischen bis zur achämenidischen Zeit (7.–4. Jh. v.u. Z.)," *AoF* 4 (1976): 131–49.

AoF 12 — "Eine Urkunde des Egibi-Archivs über Vermietung eines Sklaven," *AoF* 12 (1985): 365–67.

Oppenheim, L.

JAOS 61 — "Idiomatic Accadian (Lexicographical Researches)," *JAOS* 61 (1941): 251–71.

Letters — *Letters from Mesopotamia. Official, Business and Private Letters on Clay Tablets from Two Millennia.* Chicago 1967.

Mietrecht — *Untersuchungen zum babylonischen Mietrecht.* (WZKM Beiheft 2). Vienna 1936.

OrNS 9 — "Deux notes de lexicographie accadienne," *OrNS* 9 (1940): 219–22.

Parker, R.A.- W.A. Dubberstein

Chronology — *Babylonian Chronology 626 B.C.-A.D. 75.* (Brown University Studies 19). Providence 1956.

Peiser, F.E.

BV — *Babylonische Verträge des Berliner Museums in Autographie, Transcription und Übersetzung*. Berlin 1890.

Petschow, H.H.

Pfandrecht — *Neubabylonisches Pfandrecht*. (Abhandlungen der Sächsischen Akademie der Wissenschaften, phil.-hist. Kl. 48.1). Berlin 1956.

Pinches, Th.G.

BOR 1 — "Tablets Referring to the Apprenticeship of Slaves at Babylon," *BOR* 1 (1887): 81–85, 88ff.

BOR 2 — "A Babylonian Dower-Contract," *BOR* 2 (1887): 1–8.

CT 4 — *Cuneiform Texts from Babylonian Tablets in the British Museum*. Volume 4. London 1898.

CT 51, 55–57 — *Cuneiform Texts from Babylonian Tablets in the British Museum*. Volume 51 (ed. by C.B.F. Walker), London 1972; Volumes 55–57 (ed. by I.L. Finkel), London 1982.

Peek — *Inscribed Babylonian Tablets in the Possession of Sir Henry Peek, Bart.* London 1888.

Powell, M.A.

"Money" — "Money in Mesopotamia," *JESHO* 39 (1996): 211–44.

Ries, G.

Bodenpachtformulare — *Die neubabylonischen Bodenpachtformulare*. (Münchener Universitätsschriften, Juristische Fakultät. Abhandlungen zur rechtswissenschaftlichen Grundlagenforschung 16). Berlin 1976.

Rimalt, E.S.

AfO 9 — "Zur Lautlehre des Neubabylonischen," *AfO* 9 (1933–34): 124–26

Römer, W.H.Ph.

AOAT 232 — "Beiträge zum Lexikon des Sumerischen [4]. Termini für Schiffe und Schiffahrt, Schiffsteile und Schiffszubehör - vor allem in sumerischen 'literarischen' Texten -," *AOAT* 232 (1993): 343–95.

Roth, M.T.

AOAT 252 — "fTašmētu-damqat and Daughters," in: J. Marzahn-H. Neumann (eds.), *Assyriologica et Semitica. Festschrift für Joachim Oelsner*. (AOAT 252). Münster 2000. Pp. 387–400.

Sack, R.

Cuneiform Documents from the Chaldean and Persian Periods. Selingsgrove-London-Toronto 1994.

Salonen, A.

Nautica — *Nautica Babyloniaca. Eine lexikalische und kulturgeschichtliche Untersuchung*. (Studia Orientalia 11/1). Helsinki 1942.

Wasserfahrzeuge — *Die Wasserfahrzeuge in Babylonien*. (Studia Orientalia 8/4). Helsinki 1939.

Salonen, E.

Über das Erwerbsleben im Alten Mesopotamien. Untersuchungen zu den Akkadischen Berufsnamen. I. (Studia Orientalia 41). Helsinki 1970.

San-Nicolò, M.

Lehrvertrag — *Der neubabylonische Lehrvertrag in rechtsvergleichender Betrachtung.* (Sitzungsberichte der Bayerischen Akademie der Wissenschaften, phil.-hist. Klasse 3). München 1950.

San-Nicolò, M. - H.H. Petschow

BRU 6 — *Babylonische Rechtsurkunden aus dem 6. Jahrhundert v. Chr.* (Abhandlungen der Bayerischen Akademie der Wissenschaften, phil.-hist. Klasse N.F. 51). München 1960.

San-Nicolò, M. - A. Ungnad

NRV — *Neubabylonische Rechts- und Verwaltungsurkunden. I: Rechts- und Wirtschaftsurkunden der Berliner Museen aus vorhellenistischer Zeit.* Leipzig 1935.

NRVU — = *NRV*

Schmitt, R.

"Review of Dandamaev, *Iranians*," *Kratylos* 39 (1994): 82–89.

Shiff, L.B.

Nūr-Sîn — *The Nūr-Sîn Archive: Private Entrepreneurship in Babylon (603–507 B.C.)*, (Ph.D. dissertation, University of Pennsylvania, 1987). Ann Arbor Microfilm Copy 1989.

Spar, I - E. Von Dassow

CTMMA 3 — *Cuneiform Texts in the Metropolitan Museum of Art. Vol. 3: Private Archive Texts from the First Millennium B.C.* New York-Turnhout 2000.

Van der Spek, R. J.

BiOr 51 — Review of D. Weisberg, *The Late Babylonian Texts of the Oriental Institute Collection*, *BiOr* 51 (1994): 600–606.

Stol, M.

RLA 7 — "Lugal-Marada," *RLA* 7 (1987–90): 148–49.

Stolper, M.W.

AION 77 — *Late Achaemenid, Early Macedonian and Early Seleucid Records of Deposit and Related Texts.* (Annali dell'Istituto Universitario Orientale di Napoli, Supplemento n. 77/4). Naples 1995.

AMI 23 — "Tobits in Reverse: More Babylonians in Ecbatana," *AMI* 23 (1990): 161–76.

BaM — "Late Achaemenid Legal Texts from Uruk and Larsa," *BaM* 21 (1990): 559–622.

BiMes "Three Iranian Loanwords in Late Babylonian Texts," in: L.D. Levine-T.C. Young, Jr. (eds.), *Mountains and Lowlands: Essays in the Archaeology of Greater Mesopotamia.* (Bibliotheca Mesopotamica 7). Malibu 1977. Pp. 251–66.

Entrepreneurs *Entrepreneurs and Empire. The Murašû Archive, the Murašû Firm, and Persian Rule in Babylonia.* (PIHANS 54). Istanbul 1985.

JAOS 116 "A Paper Chase after the Aramaic on TCL 13 193," *JAOS* 116 (1996): 517–21.

JCS 53 "Fifth Century Nippur: Texts of the Murašûs and from their Surroundings," *JCS* 53 (2001): 83–132.

JNES 48 "The Governor of Babylon and Across-the-river in 486 B.C," *JNES* 48 (1989): 274–82.

RLA 8 "Militärkolonisten," *RLA* 8 (1993–1997): 205–7.

Strassmaier, J.N.

Cyr *Inschriften von Cyrus, König von Babylon (538–529).* (Babylonische Texte 7). Leipzig 1890.

Dar *Inschriften von Darius, König von Babylon (521–485).* (Babylonische Texte 10–12). Leipzig 1897.

Liv "Die babylonische Inschriften im Museum zu Liverpool nebst anderen aus der Zeit von Nebukadnezzar bis Darius," in: *Actes du sixième congrès international des Orientalistes tenu en 1883 à Leide. Deuxième partie.* Leiden 1885. Pp. 569–624 and Appendix 1–176.

Nbk *Inschriften von Nabuchodonosor, König von Babylon (604–561 v. Chr.).* (Babylonische Texte 5–6). Leipzig 1889.

Nbn *Inschriften von Nabonidus, König von Babylon (555–538 v. Chr.).* (Babylonische Texte 1–4). Leipzig 1889.

ZA 3 "Arsaciden-Inschriften," *ZA* 3 (1888): 143–58.

Streck, M.P.

RLA 9 "Ninurta/Ningirsu. A," *RLA* 9 (1998–2001): 512–22.

ZuZ *Zahl und Zeit. Grammatik der Numeralia und des Verbalsystems im spätbabylonischen.* (Cuneiform Monographs 5). Groningen 1995.

Tallqvist, K.L.

NbN *Neubabylonisches Namenbuch zu den Geschäftsurkunden aus der Zeit des Šamaš-šum-ukīn bis Xerxes.* (Annales Academiae Scientiarum Fennicae, Serie B, 32/II). Helsingfors. 1905.

Tavernier, J.

NABU 2000 "On Some Iranian Names in Late Babylonian Sources," *NABU* 2000/47.

Thompson, R.C.

CT 22 *Cuneiform Texts from Babylonian Tablets in the British Museum.* (CT 22). London 1906.

Tremayne, A.

YOS 7 *Records from Erech, Time of Cyrus and Cambyses (538–521 B.C.).* (Yale Oriental Series. Babylonian Texts 7). New York 1925.

Ungnad, A.

AfO 19 "Neubabylonische Privaturkunden aus der Sammlung Amherst," *AfO* 19 (1959–60): 74–82.

VS 3–6 *Vorderasiatische Schriftdenkmäler der Königlichen Museen zu Berlin.* Volumes 3–6. Leipzig 1907–1908.

Vargyas P.

"Silver and Money" "Silver and Money in Achaemenid and Hellenistic Babylonia," In: J. Marzahn-H. Neumann (eds.), *Assyriologica et Semitica. Festschrift für Joachim Oelsner.* (AOAT 252). Münster 2000. Pp. 513–22.

Waerzeggers, C.

AfO 46/47 "The Records of Inṣabtu from the Naggāru Family," *AfO* 46/47 (1999–2000): 183–200.

Weisberg, D.B.

Guild Structure *Guild Structure and Political Allegiance in Early Achaemenid Mesopotamia.* (YNER 1). New Haven-London 1967.

Texts from the OI *The Late Babylonian Texts of the Oriental Institute Collection.* (Bibliotheca Mesopotamica 24). Malibu 1991.

YOS 17 *Texts from the Time of Nebuchadnezzar.* (Yale Oriental Series, Babylonian Texts 17). New Haven-London 1980.

Weszeli, M.

WZKM 86 "Eseleien," *WZKM* 86 (1996): 461–78.

NABU 1996 "Zu BM 85367 und BM 85576," *NABU* 1996/20.

Weszeli, M. - H.D. Baker

WZKM 87 "Eseleien II," *WZKM* 87 (1997): 231–47.

Wiggerman, F.A.M.

RLA 9 "Nergal. A," *RLA* 9 (1998–2001): 215–23.

Wunsch, C.

AfO 42/43 "Die Frauen der Familie Egibi," *AfO* 42/43 (1995–96): 32–63.

AOAT 252 "Die Richter des Nabonid," in: J. Marzahn-H. Neumann (eds.), *Assyriologica et Semitica. Festschrift für Joachim Oelsner.* (AOAT 252). Münster 2000. Pp. 557–98.

AuOr 15 "Neu-und spätbabylonische Urkunden aus dem Museum von Montserrat," *AuOr* 15 (1997): 139–94.

Babylon-Kolloquium "Neubabylonische Urkunden: die Geschäftsurkunden der Familie Egibi," In: J. Renger (ed.), *Babylon: Focus mesopotamischer Geschichte … 2. Internationales Kolloquium der Deutschen Orient-Gesellschaft, 24–26 März 1998 in Berlin.* Saarbrücken 1999. Pp. 343–64.

CM 3 *Die Urkunden des babylonischen Geschäftsmannes Iddin-Marduk. Zum Handel mit Naturalien im 6. Jahrhundert v. Chr.* (Cuneiform Monographs 3a and b). Groningen 1993.

CM 20	*Das Egibi-Archiv* I. *Die Felder und Gärten*. (Cuneiform Monographs 20a and b). Groningen 2000.
MOS Studies 2	"Neubabylonische Geschäftsleute und ihre Beziehungen zu Palast- und Tempelverwaltungen: Das Beispiel der Familie Egibi," in: A.C.V.M. Bongenaar (ed.), *Interdependency of Institutions and Private Entrepreneurs*. Proceedings of the Second MOS Symposium, Leiden 1998. (PIHANS 87). Istanbul 2000. Pp. 95–118.
"Real Estate"	"The Egibi Family's Real Estate in Babylon (6th Century BC)." In: M. Hudson-B. Levine (eds.), *Land Tenure and Urbanization in the Ancient Near East*. Cambridge, Mass. 1999. Pp. 391–413.

Zadok, R.

Assur 4/3	*Assyrians in Chaldean and Achaemenian Babylonia* (Monographic Journals of the Near East. Assur 4/3). Malibu 1984.
BiOr 41	"Assyro-Babylonian Lexical and Onomastic Notes," *BiOr* 41 (1984): 33–46.
IOS 18	"Notes on Borsippean Documentation of the Eighth-Fifth Centuries B.C.," *IOS* 18 (1998): 249–96.
Iran 14	"On the Connections between Iran and Babylonia in the Sixth Century B.C.," *Iran* 14 (1976): 61–78.
NABU 1997/7	"Some Iranian Anthroponyms and Toponymns," *NABU* 1997/7.
NABU 1997/11	"Two N/LB Documents from the British Museum," *NABU* 1997/11.
OLA 28	*The Pre-hellenistic-Israelite Anthroponomy and Prosopography*. (OLA 28). Leuven 1988.
OLA 65	"Foreigners and Foreign Linguistic Material in Mesopotamia and Egypt," in: K. Van Lerberghe and A. Schoors (eds.), *Immigration and Emigration within the Ancient Near East. Festschrift E. Lipinski*. (OLA 65). Leuven 1995. Pp. 431–47.
RGTC 8	*Geographical Names according to New- and Late-Babylonian Texts*. (Répertoire géographique des textes cunéiformes). Wiesbaden 1985.
West Semites	*On West Semites in Babylonia during the Chaldean and Achaemenian Periods. An Onomastic Study*. Jerusalem 1978.
ZDMG 31	"Arabians in Mesopotamia during the Late-Assyrian, Chaldean, Achaemenian and Hellenistic Periods Chiefly According to the Cuneiform Sources," *ZDMG* 31 (1981): 42–84.

Zadok, R. and T. Zadok

AcSum 19	"A Late-Babylonian Boat Rental," *AcSum* 19 (1997): 267–69.

Zawadzki, St.

AMI 27	"The First Persian Journey of Itti-Marduk-balāṭu," *AMI* 27 (1994): 123–26.

PREFACE

The Egibi archive from Babylon is a corpus of texts reassembled through modern research from tablets housed in different museums and in a few private collections. The archaeological provenance of the tablets is unknown since they were not found *in situ*, but reached the museums and private collections via the antiquities market. The tablets that make up the Egibi archive are not only dispersed over more than one museum, they are often inventoried in different collections within the same museum, which makes the reconstruction of the Egibi archive especially difficult. Most of the tablets are currently in the British Museum and were acquired in the late 1870s and 1880s. The identification of these tablets, dispersed over various collections within the British museum, as belonging to the Egibis started already in the late nineteenth century. Its methodology has since been fixed and refined, not in the least thanks to Dr. Cornelia Wunsch's intensive research on the archive in recent years. Thus, the identification of a tablet of the British Museum as belonging to the Egibi archive is based on its inventory number, as well as prosopographic, chronological, and geographical data contained in the tablet's text.

The first aim of this study is to assemble and edit those texts from the Egibi archive that pertain to Marduk-nāṣir-apli's (=MNA's) institutional connections. The inclusion of a text in the present study is based on two criteria: (1) it must belong to MNA's archive and (2) it must have an institutional background.

I have defined a text as belonging to MNA's archive when it mentions MNA among the contractants, the witnesses, or as the scribe of the text. Occasionally, I have included a text that does not mention MNA explicitly, but belongs to his archive for other reasons:[1] the text is dated within the timespan of MNA's life, falls within his geographical horizon, is registered in one of the museum's collections that is known for its Egibi material, and deals with men and issues that can firmly be connected to MNA and his business.

1. E.g., BM 30274, BM 30446, BM 30651 and BM 30853.

A text has an institutional background when it mentions men holding positions in one of the big institutions or assets owned or nominally due to one of the big institutions.

On the basis of these criteria I have been able to assemble a dossier of 144 texts taken from the corpus of published Egibi texts as well as from the unpublished texts that Dr. Cornelia Wunsch generously made available to me in preliminary transliteration. They are edited in the second part of this study. It includes the re-edition of fifty-eight texts that were previously published but usually in hand copy only and sometimes in need of collation,[2] and the publication of more than eighty new texts from the British Museum.[3]

All 144 texts are transliterated, translated, and provided with philological and text-critical notes. I also made hand copies, at least of those new texts from the British Museum for which there is no copy available either in published form or in the form of a Bertin copy.[4] The collection of Bertin copies remains unpublished, but may be consulted in the British Museum. It consists of over 3000 copies of Neo-Babylonian economic texts preserved in the British Museum that were made by Bertin at the end of the nineteenth century. They are made ready for publication by Professor Leichty.[5] At the head of each text and before its transliteration and translation, I give a summary description of its main information, thus specifying the date on which it was written, the place where it was written, and its content. In addition, I specify the museum number of previously published texts. For new texts from the British Museum I specify

---

2. Earlier published texts re-edited in Part Two of the present book are No. 16 and Nos. 88–144. These are texts previously published by Abraham, *OLA* 65; Contenau, *TCL* 13; Ebeling, *CT* 22; McEwan, *OECT* 10; and Strassmaier, *Darius*.

3. Part two of the present volume includes eighty-seven tablets from the British Museum published for the first time (viz. Nos. 1–15, Nos. 17–87 and No. 125). Most of them contain completely new texts, others contain new information to previously known texts. Thus, one tablet is a join to a previously published text (No. 125 joins Dar 453^{+}) and significantly adds to its understanding, and five other tablets are duplicates of previously published texts (No. 31 = BM 30980 // BRM 1 81; No. 65 = BM 31977 // Dar 472; No. 78 = BM 33936 // Liv 25; No. 81 = BM 33962 // Dar 509; and No. 84 = BM 41442 // BOR 1, 83). They are published in the present volume because the original tablet of the earlier published text is either lost (Liv 25), unknown (BOR 1, 83), fragmentary (Dar 472) or not in the British Museum (BRM 1 81), so that the duplicate from the British Museum is an important new source for verifying the reading of the text or completing it, at least in the former three cases (that of Liv 25, BOR 1, 83 and Dar 472). Moreover, the publication of duplicate texts is important when trying to determine which of the two tablets, either the earlier published one or the new one from the British Museum, was the original and which the copy (cf. comment to Dar 509; more on this matter at Jursa, *Bēl-rēmanni*, 13–19). Finally, two unpublished tablets from the British Museum, viz. BM 31278 and BM 41443, belong to MNA's archive and pertain to his institutional connections but are not included in part two of this volume because the first one is too fragmentary and the second one will be published by Wunsch in her forthcoming book on the Egibis' slaves.

4. For copies of previously published texts I refer to the texts' *editio princeps*.

5. Cf. Wunsch, *Felder* 1, n. 9.

whether or not there exists an unpublished copy in the collection of copies made by Bertin (abbreviated b).

The texts edited in this study's second part are arranged alphabetically (b, BM, CT, Dar, OECT and TCL), and by number. Accordingly, a text referred to as BM 30325 precedes one referred to as Dar 105, and the latter precedes, for instance, Dar 138. As for the system used to refer to the texts, the following should be noted. Previously unpublished texts from the British Museum are referred to by the abbreviations BM followed by the tablet's inventory number. Note that texts referred to by the siglum b (+ number) are tablets preserved in the British Museum, the number of which is unknown[6] but of which a copy was made by Bertin at the end of the nineteenth century. The number following the b refers to the number of Bertin's copy. Previously published texts from the British Museum and from other museums are referred to by their commonly accepted abbreviations followed by the publication number of the text. Accordingly, CT 22 (+ text-number) refers to letters from the British Museum published by Ebeling; Dar (+ text-number) refers to texts from Darius' time published by Strassmaier; OECT 10 (+ text-number) refers to texts from the Ashmolean Museum in Oxford published by McEwan; and TCL 13 (+ text-number) refers to texts from the Louvre published by Contenau.

I have given each text published or re-edited in this volume a new number, which it gets in addition to its museum inventory number or *editio princeps* number, e.g., b. 2800 has become No. 1 in my edition, BM 30233 has become No. 2, BM 30235 has become No. 3 etc. I do not use these new numbers when I myself refer to the texts in the course of my study. In future studies, however, the new numbering system may be useful to refer to the publication or re-edition of a text in the present volume. For example, BM 30233 may be referred to in the future as: BM 30233 = Abraham, *Business and Politics* No. 2.

Besides the copies, transliterations, translations, and commentary, part two of the present volume contains two descriptive catalogues, viz. one that catalogues the texts chronologically, the other one that arranges them thematically.

The second aim of this study is to investigate MNA's institutional connections by addressing the following three issues: the scope of MNA's institutional connections, their source, and their effect on his business.

The first issue is the scope of MNA's institutional connections, i.e., his contacts with state and temple representatives and his dealings with state and temple assets. Regarding the former, the major question to be dealt with concerns the role played by these official representatives in MNA's business. Were the officials with whom he met and who appear in his archive doing business with him, either directly or through their agents? Or were they only present as witnesses while MNA was doing business with private persons, thus passively controlling this private business and giving their tacit consent? As for his dealings with institutional assets, the question arises regarding the level of MNA's

6. So that the tablet can no longer be consulted.

control over them. In particular, we would like to know whether he derived income from them and what he gave in return? MNA may also have been appointed by one of the institutions to act on its behalf so that the margin of profit that he could derive from his institutional connections was rather limited.

The second issue to be investigated centers on two questions. How were the official contacts established and how did they develop in the course of time? Were they established, for instance, in the course of MNA's commodity trade, or did they develop independently from the latter? Were these one-time encounters with specific men that did not last when, for instance, these men were replaced in their office? Or were these long-lasting relations with certain departments in the state and temple administration that gained in stability and diversity as the years went by regardless, at least to some extent, of who worked in the specific department or stood at its head? Had MNA to become part of the state or temple administration in order to gain access to the resources that they owned or controlled, or could he remain an outsider and still enjoy access?

The third issue to be investigated is that of the role played by MNA's institutional contacts in his business in general, and his trade in commodities in particular. Were they an integral part of it and beneficial to it, or in any other way auxiliary to its good functioning? To which degree, indeed, did MNA's trade in commodities, for instance, depend on good relations with the state and the temples?

The study of MNA's institutional connections is primarily based on the information that is provided by the texts from his archive (re)edited in the second part of the present volume. Additional information from other contemporary private archives on links between the owners of the archives and one or more of the big institutions is occasionally used in order to put MNA in perspective. It is, however, a matter that should be further investigated.

In order to deal with the above-mentioned questions I subdivided the discussion below according to the nature of the transaction in which MNA was involved and the role he played in it. Thus, I make the following basic distinctions. The first one is the distinction between the two major institutions of the Babylonian economy in the early Persian period: the state (including the military) and the temple. Accordingly, Chapter Two deals with MNA's connections with representatives of the state and the military establishment as well as with his dealings with state-owned or state-controlled assets. Chapter Three deals with his connections with various temples. Each of these two major chapters is further subdivided along the following principles. The chapter on MNA and the state (i.e., chapter two) is further split up depending on the kind of state-owned or state-controlled asset with which MNA was dealing. The assets in question were taxes in the broad sense (2.1, 2.2, 2.3, and 2.4), boats (2.5), and field rent (2.6). When he was dealing with taxes I further distinguish according to the role played by MNA: payer (2.1 and 2.2), provider of credit (2.3), or receiver (2.4). The chapter on MNA and the temple (i.e., Chapter Three) is arranged according to the temple with which he maintained contacts so as to highlight the continuity of his contacts and their diversity. It soon became clear that several texts fall into more than one category. Some of them, indeed, deal with taxes as well as with boats, e.g., when the taxes in question were those payable by boats passing by bridges; they are, accordingly, discussed in the chapter on taxes as well as in that on boats. Other texts mention state officials as well as temples, e.g., when the officials in question were appointed by the king to represent state interests in the temple. Whenever a temple is mentioned, the text is discussed at length in Chapter Three.

The third aim of this study is to contribute to the prosopography of the Neo-Babylonian and early Persian periods by including a detailed name index with separate entries for first name, patronymy and surname, including a specification of the names' spellings.[7] It was standard practice in the Neo-Babylonian period to identify contracting parties, witnesses, and the scribe of the document not only by their personal name, but by their full filiation as follows: "PN_1, son (or daughter) of PN_2, descendant of PN_3."[8] This stereotype formula has often been schematically abbreviated in the present study as $PN_1/PN_2//PN_3$. It means that PN_1 is the individual's personal name, PN_2 is his father's name (patronymy), and PN_3 is his surname.[9] Not all individuals had surnames so that one may find PN_1/PN_2, i.e., "PN_1 son of PN_2." Whenever the text has only PN_1 *mār* (DUMU, A) PN_2, PN_2 is consistently identified as the surname of PN_1, and accordingly schematically rendered as $PN_1//PN_2$, i.e., "PN_1 descendant of PN_2."

The practice of referring to individuals by personal name, patronymy, and surname makes it possible to identify the same individual or members of his family in more than one tablet provided that one can make use of a detailed name index. Consequently, I have listed a person for which the text gives an affiliation two or three times in my index: under the person's first name, under his father's name, and under his family's name if the latter is being provided by the text. For example: Bēl-erība/Kalbaya//Šumu-libši is listed first s.v. Bēl-erība (as the son of Kalbaya descendant of Šumu-libši); secondly s.v. Kalbaya (as the father of Bēl-erība descendant of Šumu-libši); and thirdly s.v. Šumu-libši (as the ancestor of Bēl-erība son of Kalbaya).

Finally, a few remarks regarding transliteration and transcription of the names. I have not capitalized personal names in the transliterations,[10] and their transcription is idealized rather than phonetic because the rules of Neo-Babylonian phonetics are often a point of contention. Thus, they are transcribed

7. For a prosopography of the Neo-Babylonian texts known before 1905, including those of the Egibi-archive, see Tallqvist, *NbN*. It goes without saying that in this field renewed research is much in need. It is, therefore, to be hoped that Baker's Babylon-prosopography will soon be published (Baker, *Private Archives*; unavailable to me).

8. In Akkadian: PN_1 A-*šú šá* PN_2 A PN_3; or PN_1 DUMU(-*šú*) *šá* PN_2 DUMU (or A) PN_3. For daughters the Akkadian has DUMU.MÍ-*šú* instead of A-, DUMU-*šú*.

9. The names of eponymous ancestors or ancestral professions usually functioned as surnames.

10. The same holds for the transliteration of geographic names and names of divinities.

with classic Babylonian case endings on nouns though the writing of case endings in the Neo-Babylonian period was arbitrary, most likely due to the fact that they were no longer pronounced. For example, a name written ^{md}AG-NUMUN-DÙ is transcribed Nabû-zēra-ibni, even if its pronunciation may have been closer to Nabû-zēr-ibni than to Nabû-zēra-ibni as is suggested by spellings such as ^{md}AG-*ze-er-ib-ni*. Hypocoristic names of the Ca-a type (e.g., ^{m}*kal-ba-a*) have consistently been transcribed with a final -aya, rather than a final diphthong -ay or a final contracted diphthong -â. Furthermore, the logogramic spelling of many Neo-Babylonian personal names causes much confusion, and certain choices have had to be made. A name containing the logogram MU, for instance, can be read in different ways, depending on one's interpretation of the logogram as being either the verb *nadānu* "give" or the noun *šumu* "name." Accordingly, one has to decide whether one reads a name written ^{m}MU-MU as Šuma-iddin or as Nādin-šumi, since both readings are possible. Similarly, one has to decide whether one reads ^{m}MU-URU$_{3}$ (= Šuma-uṣur), or ^{m}MU-ŠEŠ (= Nādin-aḫi). These are only a few examples of logograms whose reading is ambiguous.[11] The logogramic spelling of many names causes several other problems of interpretation. Thus, logogramic spellings for verbs do not give us the exact grammatical form of the verb, unless the scribe has added phonetic complements to the logogram. For example, should the logogram MU = *nadānu* in the name ^{m}MU-MU be read Šuma-*iddin* or Šuma-*nādin*, *Nādin*-šumi or *Iddin*-šumi? Similarly, is a name written ^{m}SIG$_{15}$-^{d}IŠKUR to be read as being Mudammiq-Adad or Udammiq-Adad and one written ^{m}KAR-^{d}EN as being Mušēzib-Bēl or Ušēzib-Bēl? Finally, confusion may arise regarding the interpretation of an /a/-sign at the end of a name: should one read ^{m}MU-*a* (i.e., Iddinaya) or ^{m}MU-A (i.e., Iddin-, Nādin-apli)?[12] The former seems more likely in view of spellings such as ^{m}SU-*a* for ^{m}*eri-ba-a* (hence, = Erībaya, rather than Erība-apli), ^{m}DÙ-*a* for ^{m}*ib-na-a* (= Ibnaya), and ^{m}UR-*a* for ^{m}*kal-ba-a* (= Kalbaya).

Consequently, I have decided to add to each name in the index its spellings instead of just listing the name in its standardized transcription. It saves the reader from having to go to each text reference and having to assemble the different spellings. Moreover, the name accompanied by its spellings enables the reader to easily verify the transcription of the name as given in the index.

---

11. An additional problematic spelling is ^{m}MU-A for which five different interpretations exist: Nādin-apli, Iddin-apli (^{m}MU-A), Nādnaya, Iddinaya and Šumaya (^{m}MU-*a*).

12. For the problematic ^{m}SUM.NA-*a* = ^{m}SUM.NA-A = ^{m}SUM-*na-a*, see Gehlken, *AUWE* 5.

Part One

The Egibi Family

1.1. *The Egibi Family*

The name Egibi is attested as a family name in Babylonia from the late eighth century B.C.E. onward.[13] Two main branches are known of this family, each with its own set of texts. One branch of the family was active in the south, mainly in and around Uruk. The archive of this Uruk branch, which contains several hundred tablets—most of which are still unpublished—records the legal and economic activities of three generations over a period of sixty-five years (555–490 B.C.E.). The other branch of the Egibi family was active in the north, mainly in and around Babylon, for five generations, spanning more than one hundred twenty years (606–482 B.C.E.). A link between the Babylon and Uruk branches cannot be established.

The Egibis in Babylon were a family of *nouveaux riches*. They did not belong to the traditional urban elite of the capital, which derived its wealth from urban real estate and from its position in the temple or royal administration. Originally, members of the Egibi family neither owned any real estate in the city or its environs nor held positions in the temple or palace. Nevertheless, in less than two generations, the family succeeded in climbing the social ladder and in buying land and slaves. These first two generations laid a firm foundation for success in business and for the accumulation of wealth by the generations to come. The third and fourth generations of Egibis were among the wealthiest families in Babylon. The rise of the Egibi family in Babylon, therefore, is an example of outsiders making their way in an economy that was still basically dominated by the temple, the crown, and the traditional urban land-owning elite.

---

13. For the spelling and the origin of the name Egibi, see Lambert, *JCS* 11, 1–14 and 112; and Wunsch, *Felder* 1, 1 n. 3. For the publication of the texts from the Uruk branch of Egibis, see the forthcoming study by Kessler, *AUWE* 8/2. For a genealogical chart of the Babylon branch of Egibis and their relatives, see Wunsch, *Felder* 1, 12–13 and *AfO* 42/43, 34; also Von Dassow, CTMMA 3, 91. On the rise of the Egibi family in the economy and society of Babylon, see Van Driel, *JEOL* 29, 50–67 and *idem*, *Phoenix* 31/2, 33–47; also Abraham, *Eretz Israel* 27 (in Hebrew with English abstract).

The Egibis are exemplary for an entire shift in Babylonian society of the late seventh and sixth centuries. Other Babylonian families became rich in much the same way. Contemporary smaller archives, e.g., from families in Larsa and Borsippa, as well as information about other businessmen in the Egibi archive, show that many individuals from the urban middle and upper classes accumulated wealth in ways similar to those of the Egibis. They were busy in commodity trade, invested in real estate, participated in the agricultural management of land that belonged to others, lent money, traded in slaves internationally, and were involved in politics. The difference between them and the Egibis lies in the degree of their economic success and the amount of wealth they accumulated.

1.2. *The Egibi Archive*[14]

The Egibi archive from Babylon in its present form is one of the most important family archives from the Neo-Babylonian and early Achaemenid periods because of its longevity, its size, and the diversity of subjects it touches upon. It contains title deeds pertaining to the family's real estate, legal documents pertaining to the family's diverse economic activities such as field lease and house rental contracts, slave sales, promissory notes, receipts, quittances, legal documents of a more family-oriented nature, such as inheritance divisions and marriage contracts, and the family's business correspondence. Originally, it may have contained 2500 to 3000 tablets. Today, there are approximately 1700 documents preserved from the archive, which are dated from the late seventh to the early fifth centuries B.C.E. The earliest text dates from the end of Nabupolassar's reign (606 B.C.E.), the latest one from the beginning of Xerxes' reign (482 B.C.E.). During this period of one hundred and twenty-four years the archive was handed down from father to son over five generations. Today, we name the generations after the person who managed the family business and administered its archive. Accordingly, there is the generation of: (1) Šulaya, (2) Nabû-aḫḫē-iddin (=NAI), (3) Itti-Marduk-balāṭu (=IMB), (4) Marduk-nāṣir-apli (=MNA), and (5) Nidinti-Bēl.

It is clear that the 1700 preserved documents from the Egibi's private archive can represent no more than a fragment of the business transactions that the family concluded over those five generations. Even for those periods for

---

14. For a reconstruction of the Egibi archive and a description of the main traits of their business firm on the basis of the texts known till 1970, see Krecher, *Egibi*. For a detailed history of the discovery of the Egibi texts from Babylon, their dispersion over various museums and private collections, the criteria for reassembling the archive in modern times, an up-to-date survey of the study of the archive's contents and its archival character and composition, see Wunsch, *Felder* 1, 1–12 (in German). For a brief, but comprehensive English survey of the main characteristics of the Egibi archive, see Von Dassow, CTMMA 3, 83–92; also note Von Dassow's clear presentation on the reconstruction and content of Neo-Babylonian private archives in general at pp. xiv–xix (with extensive bibliography). On the end of the Babylon-Egibi archive and other contemporary archives, see esp. Joannès, *RA* 89(1): 1–2, and *idem*, *RA* 89(2): 139–47.

which we have relatively many documents, there are no more than four documents per month. What we have, therefore, is a segment of a professionally conducted business in the private sphere, other segments of which remain hidden. The information provided by the archive on the Egibis' business and family affairs is incomplete for two reasons. First, not every transaction needed to be recorded in a written document. Second, not every transaction that was written in antiquity has come to us: some documents were taken out by the Egibis on purpose and kept apart from the main archive, whereas others may just have been lost in the ruins of their house(s). As a matter of fact, the Egibi archive in its present form, i.e., the part that has survived, is a "dead archive." In other words, it is an inactive archive of texts that were taken out from the main archive because they were no longer relevant for current affairs. The active archive is not preserved, at least not for the earlier generations. The sorted-out group of "irrelevant" texts, which make up the present so-called Egibi archive, was preserved and stored separately by the Egibis in sealed jars. They were kept because they might have been needed for future reference, e.g., to prove title to property to be sold or pledged or in legal disputes. This process of sorting and reorganizing archive documents must have occurred for each generation of Egibis.

The archive ends in 482 B.C.E., i.e., the year in which Šamaš-erība ascended to the throne in Babylon and which coincides with the fourth year of Xerxes' reign over Babylonia. We can see a remarkable decrease in the number of documents for the last thirteen years of the archive, for which there are only fifteen texts (27 Dar – 4 Xer), whereas previously there was an average of fifteen texts per year (viz. between 1–26 Dar). The reason for this decrease lies, first and foremost, with the practice of taking out outdated texts from the archive. It may, in addition, be the result of a certain stagnation in business activity and a decrease in wealth when Nidinti-Bēl ran the family business. We do not know whether this was due to Nidinti-Bēl's lack of business acumen, to political instability after Darius' death, or to a combination of both. In previous generations, however, the Egibis successfully survived similar political upheavals. As it is, the Egibi archive was not the only one to come to an end at the beginning of the fifth century, a situation that needs to be addressed in a broader context.

1.3. *The Egibi Business Firm*[15]

The backbone of the Egibi business was the trade in commodities. The Egibis purchased large quantities of grain, dates, onions, and wool in the countryside

15. For a detailed description of the kind of commodity trade in which the Egibis were involved, see Wunsch, *Iddin-Marduk* 1, 21–56; and the reviews on this study by Jursa, *AfO* 42/43, 255–62 and Baker, *BiOr* 55, 197–204. On the Babylon-Egibi's land policy, see Wunsch, *Felder* 2 (in German; for a summary version in English, see *idem*, "Real Estate"). On their houses, see Wunsch's forthcoming study *Das Egibi-Archiv II. Die Häuser*. For the international connections of the Egibis from Babylon, see Zadok, *Iran* 14, 61–78; Zawadzki, *AMI* 27, 123–26; Stolper, *AMI* 23, 170–71; and Abraham, *OLP* 28, 55–85; and the forthcoming study

around Babylon, transporting the goods by boat to the markets in the capital. Upon arrival in the capital, the goods were sold to representatives of the crown and the temple to feed their ever-growing number of dependents. Indeed, during the reigns of Nebuchadnezzar and Nabunaid, Babylonia experienced an unprecedented economic boom. The kings undertook enormous building projects in the capital. Thus, many craftsmen, artisans, and other state-controlled workers—among them a large number of foreigners—were brought to the capital. They worked for the state, but did not have the means to feed themselves, since they did not own land to farm or lease out, at least not in the proximity of the capital. Consequently, they had to be fed by the palace, which distributed food rations to its dependents. This situation created a growing demand for agricultural products to be shipped from the countryside to the capital. Šulaya, the first attested generation of Egibis in Babylon, seized upon this new demand and started trading in commodities. The following generations continued and diversified this business of commodity trade. Its general outline is sufficiently known, but not every stage is equally well documented for each generation.

Besides this commodity trade, members of the Egibi family were active in real estate investment, the trade in slaves, and various industrial, agricultural, and financial ventures, especially in the later generations. The major thrusts of these various economic activities may be summarized as follows. First, the Egibis purchased land by investing the wealth they were accumulating through their business ventures, careful to acquire well-located and connected plots of good-quality land. In addition, they invested in the cultivation and exploitation of the land so that it would produce the highest profits. Second, they set up workshops to process raw materials into finished goods in houses that they either rented or owned for their slaves and menials. Third, they traded in slaves,

---

of F. Joannès - C. Wunsch, *Les voyages d'Itti-Marduk-balāṭu*. On the employment of their slaves in agriculture and specialized crafts, see Dandamaev, *Slavery*, 345–71; Krecher, *Egibi*, 39 (§ 21) 62–65 (§ 26) and 98–100 (§ 31); and Wunsch, *Iddin-Marduk* 1, 42–50; further note that Wunsch is preparing a study on the Egibis' slaves. On their contributions to the wool and beer industries, see Wunsch, *Felder* 1, 100 (beer); 102 and nn. 21f. (wool); and Lanz, *Ḫarrānu*, 142, 155–62 (beer). On loans granted by the Egibis and similar financial transactions, see Bogaert, *Banque*, 105–18 and Oelsner, *AoF* 4; also Wunsch, *Felder* 1, 5 esp. n. 18 and pp. 14f. For their institutional connections (including their political ones), see Wunsch, *MOS Studies* 2, 95–118. For the institutional connections of other families in Babylonia in the Neo-Babylonian and early Persian periods, see esp. Beaulieu, *MOS Studies* 2, 43–72 (private archive of a family of *nouveaux riches* from Larsa); also Bongenaar, *MOS Studies* 2, (private archives of families from the traditional urban elite of Sippar); Jursa, *Bēl-rēmanni* (private archive from Sippar); Kessler, *AUWE* 8/1; and Joannès, *Borsippa*. On private entrepreneurship in the Neo-Babylonian and Persian periods, see, in general, Stolper, *Entrepreneurs* and Van Driel, *JESHO* 32, 203–29; and in particular with regard to the collection of field rent and taxes from institutional land: Cocquerillat, *Palmeraies*, 37ff.; Jursa, *Landwirtschaft*, 85ff.; *idem*, *Tempelzehnt*, 19–36; and Van Driel, "Entrepreneurs." On the Egibi women and those women's dowries, see Wunsch, *AfO* 42/43 and several articles by M.T. Roth, cited by Wunsch, *Felder* 1, 8 n. 42, to which one may add Roth's recent article in *AOAT* 252, 387–99.

for which they travelled to Iran. Fourth, they partook in the cultivation and agricultural management of land that belonged to others, as, for instance, land owned by the Esagil temple in Šaḫrīnu or land owned by absentee landowners such as Bagasarū, the king's treasurer, who owned land along the Rab-kāṣir canal. The Egibis invested in the collection of rent (e.g., *šibšu, imittu*) and taxes (e.g., tithes) from such land.[16] Their senior slaves specialized in the organization of manpower, draft animals, and implements for the cultivation of the land. Other menials belonging to the Egibi household performed the physical work of plowing, sowing, and harvesting. Last but not least, they lent silver. Long-term loans were interest-bearing, at a standard rate of twenty percent per year and were secured by pledges of real estate or slaves. Probably, one reason for their providing credit to others was to gain control of the borrowers' real estate and so enjoy its income. In particular, the Egibis provided credit to persons who had to pay taxes to the state, who had to outfit soldiers and workers, or who wished to escape performing forced labor in the public sector or supplying equipment by paying instead.

The Egibis maintained good political connections, often marrying the daughters of wealthy businessmen. These connections and marriages greatly contributed to the success of their business.

Consequently, by carefully combining business and politics, the Egibis succeeded in having "a finger in every pie" in the private and public sectors of the Babylonian economy. As a matter of fact, they gradually gained a foothold in the state-controlled economy, the temple economy, the military establishment, and the international slave-trade with Persia.

1.4. *The Fourth Generation of Egibis in Babylon and Its Institutional Connections*

Marduk-nāṣir-apli (henceforth MNA)—nicknamed Šir(ik)ku[17]—son of Itti-Marduk-balāṭu (*alias* Iddinaya) belonged to the fourth generation of Egibis. He may have been born as early as 551/550 B.C.E. (= 5 Nbn) but not later than 543/542 B.C.E. (= 13 Nbn). MNA was the eldest of six children born to Itti-Marduk-balāṭu and Nuptaya/Iddin-Marduk//Nūr-Sîn between 551/550 and 530 B.C.E.[18] He was married to Amat-Bāba/Kalbaya//Nabaya by the end of Darius'

---

16. Neo-Babylonian temples frequently leased the collection of certain parts of their field rent as well as the collection of tithes to private entrepreneurs in an attempt to guarantee a fixed sum of revenue in advance. The entrepreneur had to pay a fixed sum of silver to the temple for the right to collect the institution's income from field rent or tithes. The difference between that sum and the sum actually collected represented the entrepreneur's profit or loss.

17. Also Šišku or Šiški. Rarely also Širiktu. Exceptional are Rikki (Dar 76) and Šikku (BM 30772). For the use of nicknames by members of the Egibi family, see Wunsch, *Iddin-Marduk* 1, xiii, 15 n. 64 and p. 82f. with n. 311.

18. I.e., between 5 Nbn - 0 Camb: Wunsch, *AfO* 43/44, 37–39, esp. nn. 41 and 47, on the basis of evidence from IMB's testament (*CM* 3b 260, dated in Cyrus' accession year) and Iddin-Marduk's testament (*AfO* 42/43 No. 2, dated in Cambyses' accession year).

first year.[19] When his father suddenly died in 522/521 B.C.E. (= 8 Camb), being the eldest son, MNA assumed control over family and business affairs. He led the family firm for thirty-five years (1–35 Dar).[20] In the later years of Darius' reign, his son, Nidinti-Bēl, seems to have gradually taken over the management of the business firm.[21] The family lived in Babylon, where MNA owned several houses. Most of his activities were concentrated in this city and its surroundings (Šaḫrīnu, Litāmu, Šuppatu e.a.). Sometimes he travelled to other major cities in Babylonia and beyond on business (Borsippa, Dilbat, Ḫursagkalamma, and Uruk in Babylonia; and Šušan, capital of Persia), owning houses in some of these other cities (see Dar 379, e.g., Ḫursagkalamma and Borsippa).

The fourth generation is the generation for which there is the largest amount of texts. In 1970, Krecher counted approximately 280 texts, most of which were published by Strassmaier.[22] Today, I know of at least forty-nine other legal documents in which MNA appears in the operative section, viz. as one of the contracting parties or in similar functions, and which gradually have

19. About MNA's marriage we hear for the first time in a document from the end of Darius' first year according to which he bought land from his father-in-law next to land that belonged to his wife's dowry (= Dar 26, more at Wunsch, *AfO* 42/43, 42f.).

20. Camb 341, dated on 18/xi/6 Camb, i.e., before IMB's death, regulates the silver debt owed by one Marduk-šāpik-zēri to IMB. In a side clause we hear about another silver debt by the same man, but owed to MNA and his brothers. Accordingly, MNA must have been involved in the family's business while his father was still alive, e.g., contracting loans in his own name. The earliest document in which MNA appears as one of the main contracting parties is Dar 15, dated on [-]/iii/1 Dar. He is attested alive for the last time in Tašrīt of Darius' thirty-fifth year (BM 30591; 27/vii/35 Dar) in a matter concerning the payment for transport costs. In Darius' thirty-third year he still rented a house (BM 31273 = b 2749, unpublished; 18/x/33 Dar), but after that he left several internal issues to his son to be settled, such as the transfer of silver to his brother for the payment of their taxes and of property to his daughter for her dowry (see next note).

21. In Darius' twenty-third year, for instance, Nidinti-Bēl assisted his father as scribe (Weszeli, *WZKM* 86 No. 1 = BM 30913; 19/8/23 Dar). Eleven years later he transferred silver to his uncle for the *rikis qabli* of his father, although the latter was still alive (BM 33928, published in the present volume; 28/ii/35[!] Dar). Shortly afterward, he paid the dowry of one of his sisters from property that MNA, their father (who was still alive), had assigned for this purpose (Wunsch, *AfO* 42/43 No. 7 = BM 33934; 23/ix/34 Dar). In those years Nidinti-Bēl also contracted several deals in his own name as evidenced by some twenty documents dated between 26 Dar and 0 Šamaš-erība, which are mostly unpublished. Accordingly, in those years Nidinti-Bēl dealt with the following issues: the delivery of agricultural products (BM 30440 = b 2617, 26 Dar; BM 33549 = b 2633, 27 Dar; BM 33969 = b 2826, 20[+] Dar), draft animals (BM 32865 = b 2641, 27 Dar; BM 33974 = b 3016, date broken), houses (BM 30782 = b 2709, 32 Dar; BM 31355 = b 2725, [33 or 34 Dar]; BM 31824 = b 2555, 35 Dar; BM 33966 = b 2748, 36 Dar; BM 41453 = b 2820, [36] Dar; BM 33980 = b 2851, 1 Xer; BM 33979, 1 Xer; BM 34547 = b 1013, published by Strassmaier, *ZA* 3, 157f., 0 Šamaš-erība), a boat (BM 31690[+], = No. 56 in the present volume), and the dowries of his wife and sisters (for the texts see Wunsch, *AfO* 42/43 Nos. 7, 10–13), e.a. (BM 31467, [3]4[?] Dar; BM 31800, date broken).

22. Krecher, *Egibi*, 66–100; and 251–349.

been published since 1970.[23] Moreover, there are still more than one hundred unpublished tablets in the British Museum from MNA's time,[24] eighty-eight of which are published in the present volume.[25] Not only are there more texts than for any previous generation, but the texts are more varied, since they contain records on transactions for which there is no evidence from previous generations or for which the information is too scarce to achieve a coherent reconstruction of the facts.

A relatively high level of institutional involvement characterizes the texts from MNA's time. This is apparent from two characteristics: (1) the frequent occurrence of men bearing official titles among the witnesses and/or contractants, and (2) the high amount of texts dealing with assets of a non-private origin (=institutional assets), such as income from taxes or from crown and temple land. Over 140 texts in MNA's archive display either one of these characteristics or both. They show that MNA frequently met with the authorities or their dependent workers and often dealt with assets of high economic value that were either controlled and owned by one of the big public institutions or nominally due to them.

Officials active in various sectors of the Babylonian economy and on various administrative levels frequently occur in texts from MNA's time. Thus, we encounter city governors (*šākin ṭēmi*), district governors (*pāḫātu, bēl pīḫāti, mašennu, mār abarakku*(?)), courtiers (*ša rēš-šarri*), overseers and commanders (*rab kāri, rēš ṣābê, rab ḫanšê, rab dūri, ša bīt ipri*(?), *šaknu*), clerks and secretaries (*sepīru* and *šāpiru*), the king's treasurer (*rab kāṣir, ganzabaru*), the king's representatives in temples (*qīpu, bēl piqitti, bēl pīḫāti*), the temple's chief administrator (*šatammu*), and other administrators (*qīpānu*). We also encounter these officials' deputies (*šanû*) and messengers (*mār šipri*). These officials, as well as their

23. These texts are: twenty-four texts pertaining to MNA's landed real estate (published by Wunsch, *Felder*; for a list of these twenty-four texts, see *Felder* 2, 308f. s.v. Marduk-nāṣir-apli [23 BM-texts], and p. 343 s.v. Širik [1 BM-text]). Three texts pertaining to his wife's dowry and four pertaining to his daughters' dowries (BM-texts; published by Roth and Wunsch; details at Wunsch, *AfO* 42/43 Nos. 4a, 4b–9). Five texts published by Abraham, *OLP* 28, 75–85 and *OLA* 65, 2–3 and 9 (BM-texts). Seven texts published by Von Dassow as CTMMA 3 Nos. 65–70 and No. 129; perhaps also CTMMA 3 Nos. 71–73 unless these three texts belong to the time of MNA's father. Six more texts dispersed over different publications: OECT 10 152 and OECT 10 234; Biggs, *MHEO* 2, p. 299–304 (one text from a private collection); MacGinnis, *Iraq* 55, p. 149–53 (E.36.1904); Weszeli, *WZKM* 86 No. 1 = BM 30913; and Weszeli-Baker, *WZKM* 87 No. 10 = BM 30740. Further note that MNA is mentioned among the inheritors in his father's testament and in that of his father-in-law (BM-texts; for these testaments see n. 18). For a bibliography of all Egibi-texts, see Wunsch *Felder* 1, notes 11–14 and notes 37–39; and *idem*, *Babylon-Kolloquium*, 361ff.

24. Oded Tammuz has kindly notified me of an Egibi text in the Israel Museum in Jerusalem. It is a receipt of silver by MNA from Darius' sixth year. I intend to publish the tablet in the Festschrift in honour of Prof. J. Klein to appear in the series *Bar-Ilan Studies of Assyriology*.

25. S.v. Nos. 1–87 and No. 125.

deputies and messengers, occur among the witnesses or as contractants together with MNA or his slaves.

In addition, MNA frequently met with men who worked for the temple or the state in non-administrative functions. Among them were temple farmers, prebendaries, and craftsmen (*ikkaru ša Nergal, ērib bīti, mubannû, ušparu ša Lugal-Marada,* ^{lú}DÍM), and the workers, hirelings, and soldiers who worked for governors and other officials (*agru, ṣābū, mār sīsî, malāḫu, maṣṣār abulli, šādidu, šadû*(?), and *urāšu;* indirectly also *dalû, nukarribu, qēmêtu,* and *zargaya*).

Finally, texts from MNA's time show that he had access to economically important assets of non-private origin. They were either owned by one of the big public institutions or nominally due to them. Thus, he had access to state and temple income from taxes, corvée-workers, soldiers, land and prebends; in particular, he had access to state-owned boats, officially organized (boat) transports, and state-controlled boat-related facilities, such as quays, bridges, and harbors.

MARDUK-NĀṢIR-APLI AND THE STATE

2.1. *Payments of Taxes and Tolls by Marduk-nāṣir-apli (MNA)*

The first group of texts pertaining to MNA's relation to the state are fifteen compulsory contributions of various kinds to state revenue that were paid by MNA on his own account or on the account of his house(hold).[26] Most of the these texts are formulated as tax receipts from the point of view of the receiver: PN *ina qātē* MNA *maḫir* "PN has received (it) from MNA." The taxes thus received from MNA are named by various technical terms, such as *rikis qabli, nidintu ša* ^{lú}*qašti, miksu,* and *gimru.*

The table below gives a schematic presentation of the main features of the fifteen tax receipts. Thus, it contains details on the texts' date and place of execution and on the tax payments recorded on them: their content, purpose, receiver, and origin.

TABLE 1

Tax Payments by MNA on His Own Behalf or on Behalf of His House(hold)

T.	Payment: of	for
1.	1 mina of silver, med-⅛	*kum rikis qabli u ṣidēti* till end xii/36 Dar
2.	[x] mina(s), orig. 6 minas of silver	[(*kum/ina*) *r*]*ikis qabli* from i/2 till end xii/3 Dar
3.	3⅓ mina + 5 sh. of silver, med-⅛	*rikis qabli ana alāku ana pān šarri*
4.	(1 mina of silver?)[27]	*nidintu ša* ^{lú}*qašti*
5.	*miksu*	letting a loaded boat pass beyond the quay

26. Tax payments by MNA on his own account or on the account of his house(hold): BM 30629, BM 33928, Dar 156 and Dar 206 (*rikis qabli* and similar duties); BM 30747, BM 31347 and Dar 268 (*miksu*); BM 30591, BM 30639, BM 31393, BM 31572, BM 31786, BM 32891, BM 33112 and BRM 1 81 (*gimru*).

27. The text (BM 30629) does not explicitly say how much MNA paid to Gūzānu/Nabû-zēru-līšir//Gaḫal, but if the latter did not come to MNA to settle the matter with him, he was to pay one mina of silver. I, therefore, assume that one mina was the original amount of silver that MNA gave to the said Gūzānu.

6.	*miksu*	letting a loaded boat pass beyond the quay	
7.	*miksu*	a loaded boat	
8–15.	*gimru*	transporting crops	
	to	by (*ina qātē*)	(due) from
1.	Nabû-aḫḫē-bulliṭ, MNA's brother	Nidinti-Bēl	MNA[28]
2.	Marduk-bēlšunu, agent of the G.o.B	MNA	MNA's house[29]
3.	Bēl-iddin, agent of Murašû	MNA	-
4.	Gūzānu	MNA	-
5.	Nabû-bullissu, overseer of the quay	MNA	-
6.	Kulbibi, overseer of the quay	MNA	-
7.	Nergal-ušallim	MNA	-
8–15	clerks in the service of the G.o.B.	MNA	-

T. = *Texts*: 1 = BM 33928 (Babylon, 28/ii/35[!]); 2 = Dar 206 (Babylon, -/vi[b]/3[!]); 3 = Dar 156 (Babylon, 24/i/5); 4 = BM 30629 (Ḫursagkalamma, 12/vii/6); 5 = BM 31347 ([-], 20/ix/[-]); 6 = Dar 268 (Babylon, 18/iv/⌈10⌉); 7 = BM 30747 (no place, no date); 8–15 = BM 30591 (Babylon, 27/vii/35), BM 30639 (Babylon, 28/vii/25), BM 31393 (Babylon, [-]/viii/25), BM 31572 (Babylon, 7/iv/25 or 26), BM 31786 (Babylon, [-]/[-]/⌈25⌉), BM 32891 (Babylon, 11/iv/[-]), BM 33112 (Babylon, 17/v/25) and BRM 1 81 (Babylon, 4/viii/26).

ABBREVIATIONS: G.o.B. = governor of Babylon; med-⅛ = of medium-quality with a percentage of one-eighth alloy; o.b.o. = on behalf of; orig. = originally; sh. = shekels.

NAMES: Bēl-iddin = ~/Itti-Marduk-balāṭu//Aḫu-bani; Gūzānu = ~/Nabû-zēru-līšir//Gaḫal; Kulbibi = ~/Bēl-kāṣir//Eppeš-ilī; Marduk-bēlšunu = ~/Arad-Marduk, Arad-Marduk/Kittiya//Šangû-Ea; Murašû = ~/Marduk-šuma-iddin//Ilu-tillatī; Nabû-aḫḫē-bulliṭ = ~/Itti-Marduk-balāṭu//Egibi; Nabû-bullissu = ~/Nabû-[mukīn-zēri//Ea-ṣalam-ilī (?)]; Nergal-ušallim = ~/Arrabi; Nidinti-Bēl = ~/MNA//Egibi.

The taxes were levied in Babylon by low-ranking officials, agents of the governor of Babylon or clerks in the governor's service during the entire reign of Darius.[30] On four occasions, however, the taxes paid by MNA were received by private persons who do not seem to have been connected to the central administration in any way.[31] Most tax payments took place between 3–10 and 25–26 Dar. Two of the three payments of *miksu*, for instance, mention Darius' tenth year, and seven of the eight payments of *gimru* date from Darius' twenty-fifth and twenty-sixth years. The eighth text shows that MNA continued paying *gimru* as late as Darius' thirty-fifth year. The remaining five texts are dispersed over thirty-two years, between Darius' third and thirty-fifth years. In other

28. BM 33928: 4–5, *ana mala zitti ša MNA*.

29. Dar 206: 7, [*u*]⌈*ltu*⌉ *bīt MNA*.

30. The tax receipts were issued in Babylon, except for BM 30629 (Ḫursagkalamma), BM 31347 (broken) and BM 30747 (not specified).

31. For taxes received by private persons, see BM 30629 (*nidintu ša* [lú]*qašti*), BM 30747 (*miksu*), BM 33928 and Dar 156 (*rikis qabli*).

words, tax payments were not limited to a specific period of MNA's active life as a businessman, but covered the entire period and continued when his son took over his affairs.

The taxes which MNA paid were taxes of a logistic nature, such as the *rikis qabli*-tax, or transport-related obligatory payments, such as the *miksu* boat-toll. In other words, MNA had to contribute to the equipment of soldiers and corvée-workers and had to pay for his use of the state-controlled waterway infrastructure.

It is remarkable that there is not a single occurrence of MNA paying the more common taxes to the state, such as the *ilku* or *qēmi šarri*.[32] The Egibi archive contains several payments of the *ilku* from MNA's time, but the latter was not the payer; he was the one who received the *ilku* payments. MNA probably was subject to the payment of *ilku* or *qēmi šarri*, but the evidence, for whatever reason, is lacking from the archive. Jursa, however, suggests regarding the texts in which MNA received *ilku*—or at least some of them—as proof that MNA, like all other citizens of Babylonia from the same social class, was subject to the payment of *ilku*.[33] This proposal is based on the parallel with the contemporary Bēl-rēmanni archive from Sippar. Accordingly, MNA must have belonged to a tax-unit like Bēl-rēmanni. As a member of such a unit he was subject to the payment of *ilku* and could be appointed head of the unit, who was responsible for the collection of payments from the members of his unit. MNA's receipts of *ilku*, therefore, or at least some of them, may have been part of his collection of payments from members of his unit. Thus, MNA's receipts of *ilku* might prove that MNA had to pay *ilku*, if these receipts were indeed receipts from fellow taxpayers. This matter, however, needs a thorough investigation into the level of acquaintance between MNA and the men from whom he received *ilku* as well as analysis of their socio-economic background.[34]

There is very little evidence that MNA performed corvée-work or paid a sum of silver instead of actually performing the work. In fact, only three texts deal with such matters. Dar 158 concerns the performance of *kanšu* for the king, for which MNA hired the services of Bulṭaya; Dar 411 deals with the performance of maintenance or construction works (*dullu*) at the king's canal to Elam, for which MNA paid silver to Tattanu. In neither case is it made clear who was subject to the performance of these services on behalf of the state. It may have been MNA, but the latter may as well have been a contractor organizing the workforce needed for the works on behalf of the authorities[35] The third text that might refer to corvée incumbent on MNA is CTMMA 3 69, but since the

---

32. TCL 13 198 (discussed below at § 2.3) is a payment of *ilku* by MNA but paid on behalf of a third party and not on his own behalf.

33. Jursa, *Bēl-rēmanni*, 105.

34. This issue will be fully investigated in § 2.4.5.2 (p. 77ff.).

35. More on Dar 411 and Dar 158 at § 2.2.2.

nature of the *dullu*-work assignment mentioned in it is not specified, it cannot be decided whether it was compulsory work for the state or not.

The lack of evidence noted above stands in sharp contrast to evidence from earlier texts in the Egibi archive and other Neo-Babylonian private archives. Iddin-Marduk, MNA's maternal grandfather, for instance, paid for *urāšu*-workmen and for the performance of specific work assignments (*dullu*) in the public sector to the crown.[36] The Murašû's from Nippur, Bēl-rēmanni from Sippar, and members of the Ea-ilūta-bāni family in Borsippa paid taxes (*ilku*) to the state on various occasions. The Murašû archive contains almost a hundred such payments.[37]

Three major questions are raised by the texts:[38]

(1) Did MNA pay on his own behalf or on behalf of a third party in the texts under consideration?

(2) Why were some of the taxes, especially those for outfitting soldiers and corvée-workers, paid to private persons, rather than to representatives of the state?

(3) Were taxes incumbent on MNA's house or on members of his household?

2.1.1. *Rikis Qabli and Similar Duties*

The *rikis qabli* was a tax levied by the Neo-Babylonian and Persian kings to raise money to outfit soldiers and corvée-workers.[39] MNA and his house(hold) were subject to the payment of this tax, having paid this and similar taxes on four different occasions.[40] In Dar 156, for instance, he had to equip the men who had "to go before the king." In BM 33928, he had to supply equipment in general

36. Wunsch, *Iddin-Marduk* 1, 55 and n. 214.

37. Cardascia, *Murašû*; Jursa, *Bēl-rēmanni*, 99ff.; and Joannès, *Borsippa*, 151ff.

38. Tax payments by MNA on his own account are an aspect of MNA that was relatively unknown till now. Although we knew from four previously published texts (Dar 268 [*miksu*], BM 30591 [= Abraham, *OLA* 65; *gimru*], BRM 1 81 [*gimru*] and Dar 156 [*rikis qabli*]) that MNA was subject to the payment of *miksu*, *gimru*, and *rikis qabli* to the state, eleven currently published texts throw new light on the extent of the phenomenon and its nature. Eleven of the fifteen texts are published for the first time in the present volume. These are the BM-texts mentioned above in note 26, except for BM 30591 (= Abraham, *OLA* 65).

39. On payments for equipment (*rikis qabli*) paid by private men directly to those who had to serve in the king's army or to members of their family when the king's man himself was absent, see Jursa, *Iraq* 59, 128 (at No. 47) and Stolper, *JCS* 53, 123–27 (at No. 13). On the equipment of men sent out by the Ebabbar on military and non-military expeditions, including serving with the king, more at Bongenaar, *Ebabbar*, n. 65, p. 131, n. 143, and p. 392; and MacGinnis, *WZKM* 88, 177–83.

40. The texts are in chronological order: Dar 206 (Babylon, vi(b)/3! Dar); Dar 156 (Babylon, 24/i/5 Dar); BM 30629 (Ḫursagkalamma, 12/vii/6 Dar); and BM 33928 (Babylon, 28/ii/35! Dar).

(*rikis qabli*), provide for travel provisions (*ṣidēti*), and pay for the *kīnayātu*.[41] His house(hold) was charged with similar duties, as is evident from Dar 206, which records the transfer of silver for equipment (*rikis qabli*) "from the house of MNA."[42] MNA always chose to pay a sum of silver instead of actually providing for the equipment or travel provisions. In addition, he paid silver for the *nidintu ša* [lú]*qašti* (BM 30629). Unfortunately the term is a hapax. As its name indicates, the payment in question was somehow related to archers ([lú]*qaštu*). It may, therefore, have consisted of active military service as an archer or be an obligation to contribute to the equipping of archers, such as the obligation to provide for a bow.[43]

Presumably MNA paid for the equipment and travel provisions because it was his duty vis-à-vis the state to do so, although the texts are not always clear in this respect. Actually, only one text specifies that the *rikis qabli* that was being paid for was "the share due from" MNA.[44] With respect to the other texts, we have to rely on a negative *argumentum a silentio*, to wit, the fact that MNA's payments were not "on behalf of (*ana muḫḫi*) so-and-so." If the payments were not on behalf of a third party, they must have been on his own behalf. This is further supported by the fact that when he paid taxes on behalf of third parties and expected a reimbursement or at least some kind of *quid pro quo*, the texts always specify that the tax was "due from (*ša*) so-and-so" and paid by MNA "on behalf of (*ana muḫḫi*) so-and-so." The lack of these elements in the texts under consideration, therefore, is meaningful and sufficient ground for the assumption formulated above.

In addition, MNA occasionally may have paid *rikis qabli* on behalf of his "house" rather than on his own behalf. In Dar 206, for instance, he transferred silver from his house to an agent of the governor of Babylon in order to cover the costs of the *rikis qabli* of Darius' second and third years. MNA may actually have paid for the *rikis qabli* that was due from his house in this specific case, rather than for his own *rikis qabli*. However, this remains to be proved. Moreover, it is not clear whether Dar 206 refers to the taxation of a piece of real estate or rather to the taxation of members of the same household, since the word "house" can be taken in either meaning.

One text makes clear that MNA did not bear the burden of these taxes alone, but belonged to a group of individuals who contributed collectively. Indeed, in BM 33928, he contributed together with other members of his family.[45] His

---

41. For *kīnayātu* in BM 33928: 11, see commentary *ad hoc*.

42. A separate paragraph is dedicated to the interpretation of this text, see below § 2.1.2.

43. For *nidintu ša* [lú]*qašti* in BM 30629: 5, see commentary *ad hoc*. For active military service of archers and their need for bows, see, for instance, *Bēl-rēmanni*, 182 = BM 42432 from Sippar (9/xii/18 Dar, cf. Jursa, *Bēl-rēmanni*, 104 and n. 439).

44. BM 33928: 4–5, *ana mala zitti ša MNA*. Note that in Dar 206 the silver for the equipment was taken "from the house of MNA," (and hence, due from it?); for the meaning of this expression, see more at § 2.1.2.

45. Cf. Jursa, *Bēl-rēmanni*, 99ff. on the organization of members of the same family, social

share was paid by his son, Nidinti-Bēl, to Nabû-aḫḫē-bulliṭ, who was MNA's brother and Nidinti-Bēl's uncle. Nabû-aḫḫē-bulliṭ, who received his brother's share according to BM 33928, also received payments for *rikis qabli* from more remote members of the Egibi family.[46] Thus, he received silver for the *rikis qabli* from Nabû-zēra-ibni, who belonged to the Itti-Nabû-balāṭu branch of the Egibi family (BM 31528). The receipt was witnessed by Puršû, brother of Nabû-aḫḫē-bulliṭ and MNA, and written down by Nidinti-Bēl, son of MNA.

Remarkably, MNA's contributions to army and state logistics were received by private persons without official title:

Nabû-aḫḫē-bulliṭ, MNA's brother (BM 33928);

Marduk-bēlšunu/Arad-Marduk//Šangû-Ea (Dar 206);

Bēl-iddin/Itti-Marduk-balāṭu//Aḫu-bani, who was sent by one Murašû/Marduk-šuma-iddin//Ilu-tillatī (Dar 156); and

Gūzānu/Nabû-zēru-līšir//Gaḫal (BM 30629).

Some of these men may have had to serve as soldiers or corvée-workers and MNA may have had to pay for their equipment. This may have been the case for Bēl-iddin and Gūzānu.[47] Perhaps some were agents of men in charge of these soldiers and workers, viz. Marduk-bēlšunu, agent of the governor of Babylon.[48] Still others, like, for instance, Nabû-aḫḫē-bulliṭ, MNA's brother, seem to have been in charge of collecting state-due payments from members of their family, as was pointed out above.[49]

Bēl-iddin/Itti-Marduk-balāṭu//Aḫu-bani, who received money for (his?) equipment from MNA in Dar 156, may have been one of his employees. In fact, he and his brother are known from three other texts that link them to MNA's commodity trade, in general, and his trade at the Uraš gate south of Babylon, in particular. In one of them, Bēl-iddin witnessed a case concerning MNA's purchase of land at the Uraš gate in Litamu and of a house in Ḫursagkalamma.[50]

---

standing and profession in tax-units ("bows"). The parallel evidence from MNA's archive is discussed in § 2.4.3, § 2.4.4, and p. 78ff.

46. Perhaps Nabû-aḫḫē-bulliṭ had been appointed head of the family in matters concerning taxes.

47. Further note that Bēl-iddin received the money for (his?) equipment "by oral order of Murašû/Marduk-šuma-iddin//Ilu-tillatī"; this Murašû may have been Bēl-iddin's commander or work supervisor.

48. For details, see at the discussion of Dar 206 below.

49. Interestingly, Nabû-aḫḫē-bulliṭ collected these payments before the end of the tax-year, on one occasion, and almost a year and a half after the end of the tax-year, on another occasion. More on the timing of the *rikis qabli* payments, below at p. 25.

50. Dar 469 = *CM* 20b 222: 18 (29/i/[19$^{(+)}$]. More on its list of witnesses below at n. 52. Bēl-iddin further witnessed one of MNA's promissory notes that were drafted in Šušan in Darius' sixteenth year: Dar 437 (l. 17: Bēl-iddin/Balāṭu//⸢Aḫu⸣-[bani]); among the witnesses in this and other promissory notes from Šušan we also find three secretaries of the Esagil temple and several other important men. The location of Šušan is disputed: it was

Moreover, he was not the only man in Dar 156 to take an interest in MNA's real estate purchases in this area south of Babylon. Marduk-ēṭir/Mūrānu//Egibi and Marduk-zēra-ibni/Bēl-aḫḫē-iddin//Nappaḫu, first and third witnesses in Dar 156, had similar interests.[51] The recurrence of the three men's names in a text concerning *rikis qabli* and in texts concerning real estate south of Babylon suggests that these two matters were somehow related.[52] The area at the Uraš gate south of Babylon played an important role in MNA's commodity trade.[53] That real estate may have served as places where the crops in which MNA traded were processed or transshipped and made ready for transport. In the light of MNA's trade at the Uraš gate, the link between *rikis qabli* and the Uraš gate may be explained as follows. The men who worked for MNA at the Uraš gate collecting, transshipping, and transporting his crops had to serve in the king's army or in state-sponsored construction works. MNA was responsible for their being fitted out for their service obligations.[54] Bēl-iddin/Itti-Marduk-balāṭu//Aḫu-bani was one of these men who received money for his equip-

---

either the capital of Elam, or a port of economic significance in northern Babylonia (details in Abraham, *OLP* 28, 55–75 and 81). Bēl-iddin's brother may have been present when three men promised to deliver part of the agricultural income from their bow-fief land to MNA in the course of Darius' fourteenth year (Dar 351: 16, [^{m}…]-nu/Balāṭu//Aḫu-bani). The land was located along the Piqūdu canal; hence, it was located near the Uraš gate, and more specifically, in the vicinity of Litamu (Wunsch, *Felder* 2, 155ff.).

51. For Marduk-ēṭir/Mūrānu//Egibi, first witness in Dar 156, see Dar 152: 33 = *CM* 20b 181: 21. For Marduk-zēra-ibni/Bēl-aḫḫē-iddin//Nappaḫu, third witness in Dar 156, see Dar 290 = *CM* 20b 190: 10 (on Dar 290, see also below n. 179). Marduk-zēra-ibni recurs when one of MNA's houses in Babylon was rented out to Arad-Bēl/Kalbaya//Šumu-libši (Camb 182; on the house rent, see also Dar 271 and Dar 424); when MNA settled his debts with Anu-mukīn-apli after MNA's house in Šu'anna, which had been sold to this Anu-mukīn-apli, had been successfully claimed by the Esagil temple (BM 33935: 18); finally, he occurs among the witnesses in Camb 341 and Dar 325.

52. A link between the collection of *rikis qabli* and the area at the Uraš gate south of Babylon is fully supported by evidence from Dar 469 (= *CM* 20b 222). It records a transaction concerning real estate in the said area. Its list of witnesses is of special importance, because several of the men listed recur in texts concerning *rikis qabli*. It shows that some men were interested in matters concerning *rikis qabli*, on the one hand, and the area at the Uraš gate, on the other hand. Consequently, these matters may well have been related to each other (cf. the evidence gathered at n. 605 regarding *CM* 20b 206 and Dar 571 = *CM* 20b 207). For Bēl-iddin, first witness in Dar 469, also see Dar 156 (receipt of *rikis qabli*). For Bēl-eṭēru (-ēṭir)/Nabû-bēlšunu//Šamaš-[mu…], sixth witness in Dar 469, also see Dar 481 Rev. 8′–9′ (read ^{md}EN-*e-ṭè-ru* A-*šú šá* ^{md}AG-EN-*šú-nu* A ^{md}UTU$^{!}$ (for IM)-*mu*-⌜x-x⌝; written on the same day and recording a receipt of *rikis qabli*). On the second witness in Dar 469 and his connections with the collection of *ilku* and boat transports, see more at p. 109 s.v. Tattannu.

53. Wunsch, *Felder* 2, 167.

54. We know that MNA's men in Šaḫrīnu had to pay for equipment (*rikis qabli*) and eventually depended on MNA for the credit. This is clear from the group of texts in which Rīmūt-Bēl and Nabû-makû-uṣur figure (§ 2.6.2). Also cf. Jursa, *Landwirtschaft*, 103ff. (BRM 1 101): the farmer-general had to guarantee that the temple workmen at his disposal met their non-agrarian obligations vis-à-vis the temple, such as *urāšu*-corvée and military service.

ment from MNA, as recorded in Dar 156. His receipt of the money was witnessed by men working in the same trade and geographical area as him.

J. Krecher claims that Bēl-iddin, who received MNA's payment for *rikis qabli* in Dar 156, had been hired by MNA "to go before the king," i.e., to do MNA's military service. The silver that he received from MNA was in remuneration of going before the king instead of MNA.[55] This opinion, however, is based on what I consider to be a misunderstanding of the term *rikis qabli*. The expression *qabla rakāsu* means "gird oneself, equip, get ready" and *rikis qabli*, which is derived from it, refers to the equipment.[56] Accordingly, *rikis qabli* does not refer to any active military service such as "going before the king" but to the duty to equip those performing active military service.[57] Bēl-iddin, who received silver "*rikis qabli* for going before the king," did not receive the silver "for going before the king" but "(for financing) the equipment of those who were going before the king." As pointed out above, he may actually have been one of these men, as Krecher claims, but nothing in the text supports Krecher's claim that he was serving instead of MNA. MNA's duty was to equip those doing army service, not to serve in the king's army himself.

The above-mentioned texts, as well as additional ones from the time of MNA, provide insight into the amount of silver that was paid by individuals for their *rikis qabli* and similar duties. The silver value of the "contribution of the archer" that MNA paid in Darius' sixth year was one mina (BM 30629). MNA's son, however, paid half this sum for his father's *rikis qabli* toward the end of Darius' reign. Indeed, the one mina that he eventually paid covered the *rikis qabli* of the current as well as the next year (BM 33928). The *rikis qabli* for Darius' second and third years amounted to six minas, but in this particular case it was taken from an entire house(hold) and not just from one person or his close relatives (Dar 206). The *rikis qabli* for going before the king in Darius' fifth year seems to have been particularly expensive. MNA paid more than three minas for it (Dar 156). The *rikis qabli* for Darius' twenty-third year payable by Nabû-zēra-ibni to MNA's brother amounted to at least one mina; that of the following two years and a half was also more than one mina (BM 31528). Additional

55. Krecher, *Egibi*, 88 and 96–97. Similar cases of MNA hiring substitutes are found in Dar 154 (to go to Elam), Dar 572 (to go to Elam) and Dar 411 (to work, *dullu*) according to Krecher; cf. opinion adduced by Von Dassow, CTMMA 3, 137. For a similar, but more reserved opinion regarding Dar 154 and Dar 156, see Van Driel, *JESHO* 32, 210. According to Wunsch, *MOS Studies* 2, 112 n. 50, Murašû may have hired Bēl-iddin to perform his *rikis qabli*-duty, and ordered MNA to take care of the matter.

56. *CAD* Q, 11 s.v. *qablu* A "hips, loins, waist," and s.v. mng. 2–3′ *qabla rakāsu* "to gird, equip"; *CAD* R, 97 s.v. *rakāsu* mng. 3e) *qabla* (*qabli*) *rakāsu*, "to gird oneself, to get ready"; and *CAD* R, 345 s.v. *rikis qabli* "equipment of a soldier and the payment made in lieu of it."

57. Cf. Dar 308: 12, *rikis qabli ša ana* ^{kur}*Elam*^{ki}; and Dar 164: 12–13 = Dar 167: 12–13, *rikis qabli ša šanat* 5^{kam} *ša ana alāku ša* ^{uru}*šeladu*: the duty to equip the men who had to go Elam, respectively Šeladu. On military service in the Neo-Babylonian period see Joannès, *TÉBR*, 19f., Stolper, *RLA* 8, 205–7 s.v. Militärkolonisten; *idem*, *JCS* 53, 123ff. (*ṣāb šarri*); and Jursa, *NABU* 1995/61(i.a. *allāku*).

evidence on the amounts of silver that individuals paid for their *rikis qabli* may be obtained from those texts in which MNA or his slave lent silver for the payment of *rikis qabli*. The amounts of borrowed silver were variable and may have been part of the sum total rather than the entire sum that was needed for the *rikis qabli*. Thus, Bēl-iddin/Nabû-zēra-ušabši borrowed half a mina of marked silver from MNA's slave "to equip (the men who had) to go to Elam" in Darius' eleventh year.[58] Nabû-makû-uṣur/Nabû-apla-iddin needed half a mina and an additional fifty shekels "to equip (the men who had) to go to Šeladu" in Darius' fifth year, and Rīmūt-Bēl/Šuma-ukīn, his brother, borrowed two minas for the same purpose. The latter also borrowed more than three minas of silver for corvée-work on dams, which was part of the same *rikis qabli*-duty. In total, these two brothers borrowed the considerable amount of seven minas and seventeen and a half shekels of silver for the *rikis qabli* of Darius' fifth year.[59] As can be seen, the evidence from MNA's archive gives us some insight into the amounts of silver that were paid or lent for *rikis qabli*, but does not give us a unified picture in this respect.

Apparently, there was no fixed timetable for the payment of *rikis qabli*: the payments usually occurred in time, viz. before the end of the year, but could also be largely overdue.[60] Nidinti-Bēl, for instance, paid on behalf of his father for the *rikis qabli* "till the end of Darius' thirty-sixth year" as early as the second month of Darius' thirty-fifth year.[61] This was, most likely, a payment for two years, i.e., Darius' thirty-fifth and thirty-sixth years, paid at the very beginning of the first year, rather than a payment for Darius' thirty-sixth year paid in advance. By way of comparison, we may cite the example from Dar 206, which concerns the *rikis qabli* of Darius' second and third years paid in the sixth month of Darius' second year.[62] In contrast, MNA's brother received silver for the *rikis qabli* of Darius' twenty-fourth year almost one and a half years after the end of that year.[63] The text in question, moreover, refers to an outstanding debt for *rikis qabli* of Darius' twenty-third year. Had he paid for the *rikis qabli* of members of his family in advance and was he now recuperating his silver?

---

58. Dar 308.

59. Dar 164 (half a mina borrowed by Nabû-makû-uṣur in addition to a previous loan of fifty shekels; silver borrowed for his *rikis qabli*); Dar 167 (fifty shekels borrowed by Rīmūt-Bēl in addition to a previous loan of one mina and ten shekels; silver borrowed for Nabû-makû-uṣur's *rikis qabli*). The fifty shekels in Dar 164 and Dar 167 may actually refer to the same loan; and BM 33972: 18–19 (loan of 3 5/6 minas and 7½ shekels of silver).

60. Two instances are inconclusive: BM 30629, dated 12/vii/6 Dar, does not specify for which (part of the) year MNA paid for "the contribution of the archer." The same holds for MNA's *rikis qabli* payment in Dar 156, dated 24/i/5 Dar.

61. BM 33928, dated 28/ii/35[!] Dar.

62. Further cf. Dar 481: *rikis qabli* for Darius' eighteenth and nineteenth years paid in Nisan of Darius' nineteenth year. For an advance payment of *rikis qabli*, see Dar 220 (6/ii/7 Dar): *rikis qabli* for Darius' eighth year is paid at the beginning of his seventh year.

63. BM 31528, dated 26/v/26 Dar.

One wonders whether MNA had to serve as a soldier in addition to providing for a soldier's equipment? The evidence from the archive is not conclusive in this respect. We have already pointed out that the expression "contribution of the archer" in BM 30629 may have implied active military service as an archer, but as long as there is no other attestation of this expression the matter remains undecided. We have noted that Dar 156 has been interpreted by some as referring to MNA's duty to serve in the king's army. However, this interpretation of the text is based on a misunderstanding of the term *rikis qabli* in the expression *rikis qabli ana alāki ana pān šarri*. Two other texts from the archive have been cited to support the claim that MNA had to perform active military service, for which he hired substitutes: Dar 154 and Dar 572. We need to examine these texts more closely. At the beginning of Nisan of Darius' fifth year MNA hired someone to go to Elam on his behalf (Dar 154). The hireling received a salary (*idu*) and had to join the chariot of the governor of Babylon. A third party, who also acted as scribe, guaranteed that the hireling fulfilled his obligation.[64] The reason for this journey to Elam, however, is not explicitly stated. It may have been of a military nature, viz. a march of charioteers to Elam organized by the governor of Babylon in which MNA had to participate, but for which he hired a substitute.[65] However, the motives behind the journey to Elam may have been commercial. We know that MNA had commercial interests in Persia that he had inherited from his father. He may have relied on his acquaintance with the governor of Babylon to seek protection for his men on their business trips to Elam. The governor may even have granted this protection and have allowed MNA's men to join his chariot after MNA had taken care of the recruitment of the charioteers on the governor's behalf. From a letter sent to him by the governor we know that MNA took care of such matters.[66] According to this letter MNA had to settle a dispute with the commander-of-the-fortress in Babylon and have the governor's charioteers ready. Therefore, the governor may well have remunerated MNA for his assistance in the recruitment of his charioteers by allowing MNA's men "to join the governor's chariot," i.e., to travel to Elam under the protection of the governor's troops.[67]

The third and last text that contains a reference to MNA's duty to serve in the army, according to Krecher, is Dar 572. At the end of Darius' twenty-third year MNA paid for the salaries and rations of three men to Nergal-ēṭir. These men either had already left for Elam or were about to go. Krecher assumes that

---

64. For this person, namely (N)apsān/Nergal-uballiṭ//Mudammiq-Adad, see also Dar 509: 20–21. The only other person in Dar 154 who is known from other texts is the brother of the second witness: he bought a plot of land in Bīt-Ḫabḫuru from the Egibis (Liv 33 = *CM* 20b 32: 6, 10).

65. So, Krecher, *Egibi*, 78, who interprets Dar 572 and Dar 156 in the same sense.

66. CT 22 74. For details see § 2.4.2.1.

67. For a possibly similar case, see p. 95 and n. 379.

MNA paid for their salaries and rations because they went (or were going) on his behalf, i.e., instead of him. However, we see nothing in the text to support this assumption, at least not in what is currently preserved of the text.[68]

2.1.2. *Rikis Qabli from the House of MNA*

Dar 206, written in Babylon in the middle of Darius' third year, records the transfer of silver from the house of MNA to an agent of the governor of Babylon. The governor needed the six minas of silver to cover equipment costs for Darius' second and third years. Originally, the governor had ordered Arad-Marduk/Kittiya//Šangû-Ea to get the money for this equipment from the house of MNA. Accordingly, the silver "had been given by order of Bēl-apla-iddin, governor of Babylon, to Arad-Marduk from the house of MNA."[69] It appears, however, that part of the silver had not been transferred to Arad-Marduk, notwithstanding the governor's order. This unpaid portion was transferred eventually by MNA to Marduk-bēlšunu, son of Arad-Marduk, in the middle of Darius' third year, as recorded in the text under consideration.

Dar 206 is a relatively well-preserved text, but its interpretation is hampered by its laconic formulation and its enigmatic reference to the house of MNA. One problem is that it does not explicitly state whose *rikis qabli*-duty was at stake. It does not say, for instance, whether it was the *rikis qabli* "due from (*ša*) so-and-so" or "the share due from (*ana mala zitti ša*) so-and-so."[70] All we know is that it was paid for two years, due to Arad-Marduk, and given to the latter by order of the governor of Babylon "from the house of MNA."[71] The latter idiom may imply that the *rikis qabli* was also due from this house, but such an interpretation needs further proof. The idiom is enigmatic in still another way: What was meant by "house of MNA"? The word "house" (*bītu*) may refer to a family, i.e., a group of persons sharing a common ancestry. In that case Dar 206 may be interpreted in light of BM 33928 and other texts from the Neo-Babylonian and early Persian periods that show that members of the same family were often taxed collectively. However, "the house of MNA" may refer also to a household, i.e., a "house" engaged in domestic production and other economic activities, or it may refer to a building, i.e., a piece of real estate. When interpreted as household or building, the question arises whether it was possible in the Neo-Babylonian and early Persian periods to tax a household for its economic activities or a building for its economic value.

Our understanding of Dar 206 is enhanced through prosopographic research, which attempts to trace a person through multiple texts in an archive. With regard to Dar 206, Marduk-bēlšunu/Arad-Marduk//Šangû-Ea, the man

68. Dar 572 will be discussed in detail in the light of other texts from the archive that deal with similar matters, below at § 2.2.1.

69. Dar 206: 5–8.

70. This information should have been given in Dar 206: 2.

71. Dar 206: 2b–8.

who received the silver from MNA's house, occurs in ten other texts of the archive.[72] From *CM* 20b 99 and TCL 13 185, for instance, we learn that he had been trained as a scribe. He wrote one of MNA's credit notes for *imittu*-dates in Darius' second year and the document recording MNA's payment to Nabû-šuma-ukīn in Darius' seventh year, which may have been a payment for taxes on behalf of a third party. In Dar 334 he was about to receive fifteen shekels of silver and fifteen bundles of onions from one Iddinaya/Arad-Bēl in the course of Darius' twelfth year. The reason for Iddinaya's debt to Marduk-bēlšunu is not specified. Noteworthy, however, is that this Iddinaya, who owed the onions and silver to Marduk-bēlšunu, was one of MNA's plowmen. He plowed bow-fief land on behalf of MNA and, if he was the same as Iddinaya/Ardiya, he also dealt with payments from bow-tax units together with MBU.[73] Perhaps his debt to Marduk-bēlšunu is somehow related to these bow(fief)-related activities.

The fourth text in which Marduk-bēlšunu occurs is Dar 318. One Nabû-ittannu/Nabû-zēru-līšir//Nūr-Papsukkal owed half a mina of silver and thirty-eight *kor* of barley to Marduk-bēlšunu in the same year that the above-mentioned Iddinaya/Arad-Bēl owed him fifteen shekels of silver and fifteen bundles of onions. Again the *causa debendi* is not specified. Moreover, the debtor is otherwise unattested. Noteworthy, however, is that the silver and barley had to be paid "according to the measure of MNA (and) at the river in Til Gula." The reference to MNA's measure shows that MNA was somehow involved in Nabû-ittannu's debt to Marduk-bēlšunu. Furthermore, the reference to the riverine area around Til Gula suggests a link between this debt and the Egibis' commodity trade, esp. the transport of state income by boat, which was an essential part of this trade. We know, for instance, that MBU transported agricultural income from taxes that had been collected in and around Til Gula on behalf of Iddin-Marduk, MNA's maternal grandfather.[74] He, no doubt, continued this activity when he became MNA's slave. Nabû-ittannu mentioned in Dar 318 may well have organized similar transports on behalf of MNA in the same area. Was the barley that he owed to Marduk-bēlšunu according to Dar 318 agricultural income from taxes or rent? Had MNA bought (part of) this barley or rights to (part of) this barley from the man in charge of its collection, *in casu* Marduk-bēlšunu, agent of the governor of Babylon? Did Nabû-ittannu supervise the transport of MNA's barley from Til Gula? If so, he had to measure the barley according to MNA's standard and bring it to Marduk-bēlšunu at the river so that it could be transported from Til Gula.

The interpretation of Dar 318 as a payment for some transport related matter by one of MNA's employees to Marduk-bēlšunu, agent of the governor

72. *CM* 20b 99, Dar 268, Dar 318, Dar 321//TCL 13 190 (= *CM* 20b 202), CTMMA 3 67, Dar 331 (= *CM* 20b 80), Dar 334, Dar 450, E.37.1904 (= *Iraq* 55 No. 2) and TCL 13 185 dated between Darius' second and seventeenth years. On this person, also see at Table 7.

73. For Iddinaya's bow(fief)-related activities, see Dar 307, Dar 400, Dar 430, BM 31026, and the discussion below at p. 76f.

74. Wunsch, *Iddin Marduk* 1, 47f.: CT 22 80, CT 22 81 and BRM 1 65.

of Babylon, is further supported by the fifth attestation of Marduk-bēlšunu in MNA's archive. According to Dar 268, he witnessed MNA's toll payment at the quay in Bīt-Ir'anni for a boat loaded with seventy *kor* of barley in Darius' tenth year. Clearly, Marduk-bēlšunu kept an eye on barley transports by boat that were organized by MNA and his men. Between Darius' tenth and twelfth years, Marduk-bēlšunu attended to several promises made by MNA's leaseholders to dig MNA's fields, return his spades, and pay him rent (CTMMA 3 67, Dar 321, and Dar 331).[75] The last attested encounter between Marduk-bēlšunu and MNA or one of his employees seems to have been of a different nature (Dar 450). Toward the end of Darius' seventeenth year—the year in which MNA experienced financial difficulties[76]—Marduk-bēlšunu paid off MNA's silver debt to Nabû-bāni-aḫi/Marduk-nāṣir//Adad-šammê. Perhaps Marduk-bēl-šunu had assumed warranty for one of MNA's private debts, and been called upon by the creditor to pay. Fourteen years of working together in the levying of taxes, the collection of crops, and the transport of these taxes and crops[77] may have created bonds of friendship between Marduk-bēlšunu and MNA, to the extent that the former was ready to stand surety for the latter in his private affairs. The matter, however, remains undecided. Finally, in E.37.1904 Marduk-bēlšunu witnessed MNA's brother's purchase of a slave; among the witnesses we find several men who recur in texts from MNA's time who have an outspoken institutional background and are discussed in this volume.[78]

This information about Marduk-bēlšunu enhances our understanding of Dar 206. Dar 334 and Dar 318 show that Marduk-bēlšunu collected payments from men who worked for MNA either as plowmen or as commercial agents in Til Gula; Dar 206 shows that he also collected payments from the House of MNA. I suggest that these three texts refer to the same kind of activity, viz. the collection of payments by Marduk-bēlšunu from members of MNA's household. He collected these payments either from the head of the household, MNA (Dar 206), or from its individual members (Dar 318 and Dar 334). Quite likely, men who worked for MNA were attached to his household by virtue of their work and thus were considered members of his house.[79] The payments that

---

75. Dar 321 is a duplicate of TCL 13 190, = *CM* 20b 202. Dar 331 = *CM* 20b 80.

76. See below at p. 153.

77. Dar 206 (levy of taxes), TCL 13 185 (levy of taxes?), Dar 334 (collection of crops and silver), Dar 318 (collection of crops and silver, and probably also the transport of the crops from Til Gula), and Dar 268 (transport of crops by boat past the quay of Bīt-Ir'anni).

78. This applies to the following witnesses of E.37.1904 (= *Iraq* 55 No. 2): Šellibi/Šaddinnu//Ašlāku, Nidintu/Bēl-kāṣir (if //Itinnu), Nidintu/Damqiya//Nādin-še'i, Rīmūt-Bēl/Ardiya//Itinnu, Nabû-bullissu/Iddin-Nabû//Dābibī; and the scribe Bēl-iddin/Lâbāši//Bābūtu. Probably also the witness in E.37.1904: 24: ^md^AG^!^-⸢*ú-ṣur-šú*⸣^?!^ (against MacGinnis' reading ^m^*ši-ṣa-*⸢*šá-ma-mu*⸣)/Mušēzib-Marduk//⸢Nappāḫu⸣^!^. Moreover, Šuma-iddin/Šāpik-zēri//Nabaya, the seller of the slave, is attested among the witnesses in Dar 541.

79. Note that the term *nīšū bīti* (lit., "people of the house") refers to slaves and other men attached as personnel to specific households (*CAD* N_2, 287f. s.v. *nišū* mng. 3; and for the

Marduk-bēlšunu collected from MNA and his men were for taxes (Dar 206). Some of the payments, however, seem to have taken place within the context of MNA's trade in commodities (Dar 334) and more, in particular, within the context of the transport of commodities for MNA's trade from Til Gula (Dar 318). As a matter of fact, Marduk-bēlšunu took a special interest in boat transports that were organized by MNA and his men (Dar 268).

The taxation of the members of MNA's household who were employed in his commodity trade was not an isolated phenomenon.[80] In Darius' fifth year, i.e., approximately two years after Dar 206, we meet with an analogous case. It concerns the *rikis qabli* that was due from two men, Rīmūt-Bēl and Nabû-makû-uṣur. These men worked for MNA in Šaḫrīnu, collecting large amounts of crops, no doubt from institutional land. They had to deliver these crops to MNA in his house. In addition, they had to pay *rikis qabli*. Since they could not meet their *rikis qabli* obligations, they turned to MNA for financial assistance.[81] MNA lent them the silver that they needed for their *rikis qabli*. It was, no doubt, a similar situation that led MNA to pay for the *rikis qabli* of his house(hold) in Dar 206. Accordingly, when it became clear by the middle of Darius' third year that the house of MNA had not paid the full six minas of silver that was due from its members for the *rikis qabli* of the current and previous year, MNA interfered personally. He paid the outstanding debt on behalf of his house(hold). As a matter of fact, Dar 156 may have been an additional example of MNA taking care of the *rikis qabli* of members of his household, as was argued above.[82] It is remarkable that all these cases took place in the early years of Darius' reign, to wit, his third and his fifth year. Finally, we should raise at least the possibility, even if it cannot be proved beyond doubt, that Gūzānu, the baker, whom MNA assisted in paying *ilku* and meeting his obligations vis-à-vis the commander-of-the-fortress, was another of MNA's employees and a member of his household.[83] Gūzānu's case, however, dates from Darius' twenty-sixth and twenty-seventh years.

We should look more closely at several texts from Babylon and Uruk in which men seem to have been taxed because of the house in which they lived (and worked?). In a letter from MNA's archive (BM 31416), the sender of the letter informs MNA that he had taken care of Bēl-iddin's *ilku*-tax and that MNA should not sue Bēl-iddin in this matter.[84] Bēl-iddin, for whom no affiliation is given, is described as "a man from Babylon who lives in the house of Bēl-zēra-

---

workmen of the Ebabbar temple being called, i.a., *nišū bīti*, see Bongenaar, *Ebabbar*, 296 and *passim*).

80. For possible parallels from the time of MNA's father, see Wunsch, *MOS Studies* 2, 105 n. 28.

81. Dar 164, Dar 167 and BM 33972 discussed in § 2.3 and § 2.6.2.

82. Discussed in § 2.1.1.

83. TCL 13 198 and BM 31226 discussed in § 2.3.

84. BM 31416: 9b–15. In lines 16–20 the sender of the letter asked MNA to send something (*šupur*), but the content of these lines remains unclear.

iddin in Bīt-Ḫaḫḫuru."[85] In another text this Bēl-iddin is said to "belong to the house of the man from Babylon."[86] It seems, therefore, that the taxation of Bēl-iddin was linked to two related facts: that he belonged to a group of men from the city of Babylon and that he dwelled in a specific house. Were these men Babylonians (temporarily) residing in Bīt-Ḫaḫḫuru? Two other texts from Babylon point in the same direction, viz. the taxation of persons according to their actual place of residence. Dar 158 refers to the performance of the *kanšu*-service for the king, which seems to have been incumbent upon a group of Babylonians and that may well have been organized by MNA.[87] The second text, which does not belong to the Egibi archive, is an unpublished receipt of silver from four persons who had to pay "*rikis qabli* that is ⸢according to?⸣ the Babylonians." Zadok notes that "both the parties and the witnesses seem to be Borsippeans."[88]

The taxation of men according to their place of residence is also attested in two late-Achaemenid texts from Uruk. The first text records the division of a house, its furniture, and immediate surroundings among three brothers. It states that the three brothers "are occupants each of his own share, (but) they will(?) discharge obligations to the crown jointly."[89] From this clause it follows that the obligations to the crown (*ilku*) were incumbent on the house, so that in case the house was occupied by three different persons, each of these persons had to pay his share of the *ilku*. The second text from Uruk records the receipt of *ilku* for one year from "craftsmen, silver workers who are in Uruk and the surroundings of Uruk."[90] The parallelism between BM 31416 and the latter text from Uruk is striking. In both texts city-dwellers identified in socio-economic (^{lú}*mār Bābili*) or professional (^{lú}*ummānū*) terms were subject to pay the *ilku*.

Based on the taxation of "houses" from Babylon and Uruk in the Persian period, taxes seem to have been levied on houses because of their residents and the use they made of those houses. Probably, the houses were taxed because their occupants performed their trade in them.[91] They may have been work-

85. BM 31416: 6–9a, ^{lú}*mār Bābili*^{ki} *ša ina bīt Bēl-zēra-iddin ša ina* ^{uru}*Bīt-Ḫaḫḫuru ašbi*.

86. BM 30651: 3b–4, *Bēl-iddin* [(x)] *ša bīt mār Bābili*^{ki}. For a discussion of BM 30651, see p. 80f. and p. 90f.

87. Dar 158: 2–3, *ina eleppi ša MNA ša kanšu*, and line 10, ^{lú}*Bābilaya*^{meš} *ša ina eleppi*⸢*šu*?⸣. On Dar 158 also see at § 2.2.2. On MNA hiring professional sailors to sail his boats more at p. 98ff.

88. BM 22024 (cited by Zadok, *IOS* 18, 272): *rikis qabli šá* ⸢*ki-i*⸣ LÚ? TIN.TIR.KI.MEŠ.

89. PN$_1$, PN$_2$, *ù* PN$_3$ *man-nu i-na* ḪA.LA-*šú ú-šu-uz-zu il-ki šá* LUGAL *it-ti a-ḫa-meš il-li*(sic)-*ka-a*, NBCT 1029 Rev.: 7′–9′, published by Beaulieu-Stolper, *NABU* 1995/77.

90. Stolper, *BaM* 21 No. 17. This and the previously cited text from Uruk were quoted by Jursa, *Bēl-rēmanni*, 103, to support his suggestion that wealthy citizens, such as Bēl-rēmanni, were taxed for their urban property, especially their houses.

91. Were such residents, subject to certain taxes, called *aššābu*? For this word, see Jursa, *Bēl-rēmanni*, n. 437. Was the man called Gūzānu *áš-šá-bi* in a text from IBM's time (CTMMA 3 64) such a resident?

shops for the processing of raw materials.[92] Alternatively, the houses may have functioned as depots for agricultural produce in the process of transshipment. In other words, it is possible that taxes had to be paid on a house when it was used for industrial purposes, for instance, when occupied by craftsmen, or when it was used for other economic purposes, for instance, when used as a depot or place of transshipment. Accordingly, Bēl-iddin may have had to pay taxes because he "lived (and worked?) in the house of Bēl-zēra-iddin in Bīt-Ḫaḫḫuru."[93] Similarly, the craftsmen in the text from Uruk had to pay because they "were (working?) in Uruk and its surroundings" and MNA had to pay for his "house" because it was occupied by his servants and employees who were engaged in agricultural and commercial activities on his behalf.[94] If the payments from these house(hold)s were delayed for one reason or another, as in Dar 206, the owner of the house and head of the household were held responsible.

2.1.3. *Miksu and Gimru*

MNA had to pay the state for his use of canals and their related infrastructure. Thus, he paid a toll (*miksu*) to the official in charge of the quay (lú*rab kāri*) in order to have his boats pass through (*šūtuqu*). Most of these *miksu*-payments took place in Darius' tenth year.[95] The payments for "transport costs" (*gimru*) to clerks (lú*sepīru*) in the service of the governor of Babylon in Darius' twenty-fifth and twenty-sixth years are to be understood in the same way. These were, no doubt, obligatory payments to the state in return for access to the waterway infrastructure, such as canals, quays, storehouses, containers, boats, and sailors.[96] Clearly, the transport of agricultural produce by boats was only possible after paying one's dues to the state. The full extent of MNA's involvement in the transport business, however, will be examined in § 2.5.

At this point of the discussion it suffices to point out two general characteristics of the *miksu-* and *gimru*-payments. First, these payments were individual and *ad hoc*. They differ in this respect from the payments for *rikis qabli*

---

92. For houses used as workshops, e.g., Dar 280.

93. In this context it should be pointed out that Bēl-iddin of BM 31416 may have been the same Bēl-iddin after whom a bow was named (Bēl-iddin/Nabû-zēra-ušabši, details at § 2.4.3.1); this bow consisted of menials, as will be argued below on p. 72ff. In other words, Bēl-iddin of BM 31416 may have been a person of servile status with permanent residence in Babylon, but actually living in the house of someone else in Bīt-Ḫaḫḫuru.

94. It was probably for this reason that men as MNA kept staff lists. Such lists recorded the names of the men whom they employed, and the place or house in which they lived (*ašib, ašbū*). Cf. Wunsch, *MOS Studies* 2, 113.

95. This is the case for Dar 268, which is dated in iv/10 Dar, and for BM 30747, which is not dated, but refers to the *miksu* for a boat loaded with onions of Darius' tenth year. The date in the third text regarding *miksu* is, unfortunately, broken off (BM 31347). Most likely, MNA continued paying tolls after Darius' tenth year.

96. Bongenaar, *Ebabbar*, 39.

and similar needs of a logistic nature, which were often paid by a group and for longer periods of time in advance. *Miksu* and *gimru*, on the other hand, were paid by MNA on his own behalf rather than in conjunction with other individuals. Moreover, they were paid whenever the need arose during transport, rather than a year or so in advance. *Miksu*, for instance, was paid when boats needed to pass a bridge or quay. *Gimru* was paid under similar circumstances, particularly when crops had to be transported for storage or sale after the harvest.[97] Second, for *miksu* and *gimru* the texts do not specify the means of payment or the amount.[98] Instead, they specify the load of the boat for which *miksu* or *gimru* was paid.[99] A similar situation is attested in those texts from the archive that record the receipt of *ilku*. It is never indicated how much silver was paid as *ilku*, but it is always specified for which part of the year *ilku* was being paid.[100] In contrast, when payments were made for duties that were specifically related to army or state logistics, such as payments for *rikis qabli*, the exact amount of silver was noted, as well as the exact period of time that was covered by the payment.[101]

2.2. *Payments by MNA for the Salaries and Rations of Soldiers and Corvée-Workers*

MNA paid salaries and rations to men who went to Elam and other places to work in state-sponsored projects, such as the construction of the king's canal (Dar 411), the transport of goods by boat to Babylon (Dar 158), or other projects the nature of which is not specified in the texts (Dar 552, Dar 572, Dar 573, and BM 31203). The question raised by these texts is: Why did MNA pay for the salaries and rations of these men and was he obliged to do so? It has been posited that MNA had to go to Elam to work at the king's canal, but hired substitutes; his payments of salaries and rations were meant to reimburse his substitutes.[102] This interpretation will be challenged in the discussion of the texts below.

---

97. This conclusion is based on the months in which the *gimru*-texts were written: between Dûzu and Araḫsamna (iv–viii). For details, see below at the chapter on MNA and boats (esp. § 2.5.2 and § 2.5.3).

98. An exception is BM 31393, which specifies how much barley was paid for *gimru*. Cf. BM 30591: MNA promises to pay 24.3.2 *kor* of barley for *gimru* to a courtier.

99. On the load of boats in texts from the time of MNA, see below on p. 101f. According to BM 31347 the *miksu* amounted to three percent of the boat's load because for each *kor* one *sūtu* had to be paid.

100. There are three exceptions to this rule. Details below at the discussion of the *ilku*-receipts in § 2.4.4 (esp. p. 68).

101. See at § 2.1.1.

102. For the bibliographical references, see at note 55. For the system at work as documented in texts from the Murašû archive and similar private archives, see Jursa, *Iraq* 59, 128 (at No. 47); Stolper, *RLA* 8, 206 and recently *idem*, *JCS* 53, 123ff.

2.2.1. *The Men of Nergal-ēṭir/Kalbaya//Šumu-libši and those of the Governor of Kish*

At the end of Darius' twenty-second year and again the next year, MNA was urged to transfer silver that was "with him" to Nergal-ēṭir for his men for their salaries and rations.[103] Nergal-ēṭir is mentioned with full affiliation in these texts so that he can be identified as the brother of Bēl-erība/Kalbaya//Šumu-libši, commander-of-fifty. Nergal-ēṭir, however, does not bear any official title in the texts under consideration. According to Dar 552, which was drafted in Babylon on the first of Ṭebēt of Darius' twenty-second year, two men were to appear before MNA within two months with a letter (*šipirtu*) from Nergal-ēṭir. The letter authorized the men to collect from MNA the twenty-one shekels "that were with" him. Exactly one year later the same thing happened again, as can be seen from Dar 573, which is dated on the first of Ṭebēt of Darius' twenty-third year. This time two brothers were to go to MNA in another two months with a letter issued by Nergal-ēṭir enabling them to collect the ten shekels of silver "that were with MNA." The previous day, on the thirtieth of Kislīm of Darius' twenty-third year, Nergal-ēṭir himself appeared before MNA (Dar 572). He came to collect payment for the salary and rations of three men who went or were about to go to Elam for three months.[104] They may have served under the command of Nergal-ēṭir or that of his brother, Bēl-erība, who—according to BM 30274—was a commander-of-fifty. The four men who were sent to MNA according to Dar 552 and Dar 573, most likely were also going to Elam (or had just returned from there), and the silver they received from MNA was probably for their salaries and rations as in Dar 572.

A similar case is recorded in BM 31203, written in Babylon on the fourth of Araḫsamna.[105] In the latter text Amur-qannu received "flour, his rations from the first of Araḫsamna till the first of Kislīm" from someone who delivered this flour "on behalf of MNA." BM 31203, therefore, appears to be another case of a man being sent to MNA to obtain what was needed to cover expenses of rations or salaries. BM 31203, however, does not say by whom Amur-qannu had been sent, whereas the previous documents explicitly referred to Nergal-eṭir as the one who had sent his men.

Two of the above-mentioned texts state that the silver for the salaries and rations paid by MNA was "with MNA" (*ina pān MNA*). This suggests that the silver that MNA had to pay for salaries and rations came from somewhere else and was at his disposal, at least temporarily, till its transfer to the men of Nergal-ēṭir.[106] Unfortunately, the texts do no inform us from where MNA got the silver

---

103. Dar 552 (Babylon, 1/x/22 Dar), Dar 572 ([-], 30/ix/23 Dar), and Dar 573 (Pāni-abul-Enlil, 1/x/23 Dar). For possibly similar cases, see Liv 25, Dar 544, and TCL 13 193 briefly discussed below and in more detail in § 2.7.1.

104. It is not clear from the text whether the men had already gone to Elam or were at the point of going.

105. The year is broken off.

106. On the expression *ina pān* more at n. 144.

that was "with him."[107] However, the fact that this silver was transferred by MNA toward the end of the year, viz. between the end of Kislīm and the first of Ṭebēt, to finance salaries and rations may help clarify this matter. This was the time of the year when there was a shortage of barley in the storehouses and the state needed extra silver to pay rations and salaries to its subjects. It succeeded in doing so by selling its crops, i.e., its income from taxes and field rent to entrepreneurs like MNA before the harvest.[108] Liblut/Mušēzib-Marduk, district-governor of Šaḫrīnu, for instance, sold dates to MNA and the latter transferred five minas, "the price for the dates," to Libluṭ's brother a few days before the end of Darius' twelfth year (Dar 338).[109] Similarly, the silver that MNA transferred to Nergal-ēṭir and his men in Kislīm and Ṭebēt according to Dar 552, Dar 572, and Dar 573 may have been the price to be paid by MNA for his right to state income from taxes and/or field rent. Nergal-ēṭir needed the silver so that he could pay salaries and rations to his men (Dar 572); usually he ordered MNA by letter (*šipirtu*) to pay it to the men whose salaries and rations were at stake (Dar 552, Dar 573).[110]

Finally, we should mention four texts that may imply circumstances similar to the ones described in the four texts discussed above.[111] In one of the texts, viz. Liv 25, MNA was urged by Zababa-iddin/Etellu//Aḫḫū, the governor of Kish, to transfer a large amount of silver to Nabû-uballissu. The previous year he had been urged to transfer a smaller amount of silver to Tattanu in the presence of Zababa-iddin/Etellu, who was, most likely, the same man as Zababa-iddin/Etellu//Aḫḫū, governor of Kish (Dar 411). In the latter case, viz. the one recorded in Dar 411, the silver was needed to finance the works at the king's canal to Elam. Were Nabû-uballissu and Tattanu, who were to collect the silver from MNA by the end of the year, working at the king's canal under the supervision of the governor of Kish? Had the latter sold state income from either taxes or field rent to MNA in order to raise the silver he needed for these works and had he ordered MNA to pay the price for his rights to this state income directly to the men working for him? Significantly, Dar 411 urges MNA to transfer the silver by the end of Darius' fifteenth year, and Liv 25 is dated at the end of Darius' sixteenth year. As was explained above, this was the time of

107. Krecher, *Egibi*, 342, 344 and 345 suggests that MNA borrowed the silver from Nergal-ēṭir, either directly (Dar 572) or through his middlemen (viz. Tabnêa and Ubār in Dar 573; Nabû-iddin, Zitti-Nabû and Sūqaya in Dar 572, and Nabû-natan and Aḫūšunu in Dar 552).

108. These entrepreneurs must have been able to convert the crops thus purchased into silver through their trade in commodities.

109. Dar 338 will be discussed in length in § 2.6.1.

110. Cf. MacGinnis, *Letter Orders* (*passim*, esp. p. 20) regarding letters that were sent to rent-farmers of the Ebabbar temple ordering them to pay barley or dates as food rations or prebendary income directly to the temple personnel instead of bringing the crops to the storehouses.

111. Liv 25, Dar 411, Dar 544, and TCL 13 193. On Liv 25, Dar 544, and TCL 13 193, also see at § 2.7.1. On Dar 411, also see at § 2.2.2.

the year when the state needed extra silver to pay its subjects and it succeeded doing so by selling its income from taxes and/or field rent to private entrepreneurs. Two additional cases of MNA being urged to transfer silver to the authorities before the end of the year for salaries and rations may be found in Dar 544 and TCL 13 193.[112] These texts concern relatively large amounts of silver payable by MNA by the end of the year to representatives of the state. One of the texts, viz. Dar 544, is, moreover, witnessed by Bēl-erība/Kalbaya//Šumu-libši, a man in charge of a contingent of fifty workers or soldiers and frequently attested in documents concerning workers or soldiers. The latter two texts, however, do not explicitly refer to salaries, rations, or state-sponsored construction works.

2.2.2. *Men Doing kanšu- and dullu-Service*

There is very little evidence, if any, that MNA performed corvée-work, paid a sum of silver instead of actually performing the work, or hired someone to do the work on his behalf. In fact, only three texts deal with such matters. Dar 158 (Babylon, 7/iii/⸢5⸣), in my opinion, deals with the performance of *kanšu* for the king, as is evident from line 3, for which I suggest the reading *šá ka-an-šú šá* ⸢LUGAL⸣. The service in question consisted of transporting goods, mostly processed ones, such as oil and flour, by boat to Babylon. MNA hired Bulṭaya/Ḫabaṣīru//Rē'i-alpi to sail the boat against the payment of a monthly salary. On the seventh of Simān an agreement was reached between MNA and Bulṭaya regarding the latter's salary and job assignment. Bulṭaya also acknowledges that he previously received part of his salary, ten shekels, which amounted to the salary for five weeks. It is not clear, however, whether this was an advance payment or rather the payment of outstanding salary.[113] It is also not clear from the text who had to perform the said *kanšu*-service for the king—MNA, Bulṭaya, or an unnamed third party. If it was MNA, he hired Bulṭaya as a substitute and paid him his salary. It is more likely, however, that MNA was not subject to the *kanšu*-service obligation, but rather in charge of its organization. He had to organize the boat transport and accordingly recruited men, some of whom, such as Bulṭaya, were entitled to a salary in remuneration of their participation in the boat transport. The Babylonians who were on the boat according to line 10 may actually have been the group of men who were subject to the performance of the *kanšu*-service.[114]

According to Dar 411,[115] the second text from the archive that deals with service obligations, MNA owed at least one and a half minas of silver to Tattannu/Rīmūt in Araḫsamna of Darius' fifteenth year. The silver "had been

---

112. Details at § 2.7.1.

113. On Dar 158, see also § 2.5.3 (p. 98ff. on MNA hiring professional sailors to sail his boats).

114. Dar 158: 10, ^{lú}*Bābilaya*^{meš} *ša ina eleppi*⸢*šu*?⸣. See also at p. 31.

115. On Dar 411, see already above at p. 35f.

given for work (*dullu*) at the king's canal to Elam."[116] The debt was payable in Babylon before the end of the year. The agreement was reached at the place where the canal maintenance or construction works were being carried out. Were the works in question some kind of corvée, i.e., compulsory service in one of the state-sponsored building projects in far-off places? Did MNA have to contribute to these works and had he borrowed silver from Tattannu in order to meet this obligation? It would be one of the rare examples from the archive showing that MNA was subject to compulsory work in the public sector. It is, therefore, more likely that MNA had been in charge of the organization of the works and, within this context, he recruited men, paid their salaries etc. He may have organized these works on behalf of the governor of Kish, if the man named Zababa-iddin//Etellu, who is listed in Dar 411 as first witness, is to be identified with Zababa-iddin/Etellu//Aḫḫū, governor of Kish according to Liv 25.[117]

The third text that might refer to corvée incumbent on MNA, CTMMA 3 69, records MNA's hiring out of a slave and stipulates that the person receiving the slave is obliged to perform "the work (*dullu*) of MNA's house."[118] The nature of this work is not specified.[119] It may have been work for the state (i.e., corvée) to which MNA's house(hold) was subject,[120] but it may also have been work for MNA privately, i.e., in MNA's private business firm.

2.3. *Financial Assistance Granted by MNA and MBU, His Slave, to Taxpayers*

Several texts from the archive show that MNA and MBU often provided the money that private persons needed to meet their obligations vis-à-vis the state.[121] Thus, MNA helped Rīmūt-Bēl/Šuma-ukīn and Nabû-makû-uṣur, his brother, with their *rikis qabli*-duty in Darius' fifth year; he helped Bēl-nādin-

116. According to Dar 411 MNA owed two minas of silver for unspecified reasons and "in addition, there was a previous debt of one and a half mina that had been given for work at the king's canal to Elam."

117. On the levying of taxes by the governors of major Babylonian cities, e.g., the governor of Babylon, in order to pay rations and salaries to the men under their command who had to go to Elam or perform *urāšu*-work, see, e.g., *Bēl-rēmanni*, 151 = BM 42352 and the evidence collected by Jursa, *Bēl-rēmanni*, 100 n. 412, 105, 109 and 109 n. 458. Cf. Bongenaar, *Ebabbar*, 37–38, on the royal resident in the Ebabbar temple looking for men to go with him to Elam for the performance of work.

118. CTMMA 3 69: 23–24, *dul-lu šá* É MNA PN *ip-pu-uš*.

119. The work he has hired MNA's slave to do is not specified either, though the slave's qualification as a tailor is suggestive.

120. If so, CTMMA 3 69 (*dullu* from the House of MNA) would be similar to Dar 206 (*rikis qabli* from the House of MNA, discussed above at § 2.1.2).

121. Dar 164, Dar 167 and BM 33972 (Rīmūt-Bēl/Šuma-ukīn and his brother); Dar 213, TCL 13 185 and b 2800 (Bēl-nādin-apli/Bēl-uballiṭ//Paḫāru and his brothers); BM 31226 and TCL 13 198 (Gūzānu/Ḫambaqu//Mandidi); and Dar 308 and BM 31026 (Bēl-iddin/Nabû-zēra-ušabši).

apli/Bēl-uballiṭ//Paḫāru and his brothers with their payments to (Nabû-) Šuma-ukīn (a representative of the state?) in the following two years. He also helped Gūzānu/Ḫambaqu//Mandidi with his *ilku* in Darius' twenty-seventh year and with his obligations vis-à-vis the commander-of-the-fortress the previous year. Similarly, MBU helped Bēl-iddin/Nabû-zēra-ušabši with his *rikis qabli* of Darius' eleventh or twelfth year and with what he owed as a member of a bow-unit in Darius' fifteenth year. The ways in which MNA and MBU helped these men will be discussed below.

Rīmūt-Bēl/Šuma-ukīn and Nabû-makû-uṣur, his brother, borrowed silver from MNA in the course of Darius' fifth year in order to meet the(ir) *rikis qabli*-duty for that year (Dar 164, Dar 167, and BM 33972). They had to provide the equipment of the men who were to go to Šeladu, on the one hand, and pay for work on dams, on the other. Thus, Nabû-makû-uṣur needed eighty shekels to equip the men who had to go to Šeladu, borrowing this silver from MNA. Rīmūt-Bēl borrowed an additional two minas from MNA for the same purpose, namely to cover the costs of his brother's *rikis qabli*-duty. Rīmūt-Bēl also borrowed more than three minas of silver for corvée-work on dams, which was part of the(ir) *rikis qabli*-duty in Darius' fifth year. All the silver had to be paid back in Nisan of Darius' sixth year, which was the time of the year when onions were harvested.[122] In fact, it had to be paid back together with the onions that the two brothers owed to MNA. It is, therefore, very likely that the silver that Rīmūt-Bēl and Nabû-makû-uṣur borrowed for the(ir) *rikis qabli* was repayable in onions. If so, MNA had actually "reserved" part of his debtors' onion harvest by granting the loan. Moreover, the two brothers secured their debt to MNA by pledging some of their fields and granting MNA access to part of their onion harvest, viz. that part that was due to them from lease. In this way, MNA had gained considerable control over his debtors' future harvest.[123]

Bēl-iddin/Nabû-zēra-ušabši borrowed silver from MBU, MNA's slave, in order to meet his *rikis qabli*-duty of Darius' eleventh or twelfth year (Dar 308).[124] He had to equip the men on their way to Elam and needed half a mina of silver, which he, accordingly, borrowed from MBU. The silver had to be paid back in Tašrīt of Darius' twelfth year and, since this coincided with the next date harvest, the silver was, most likely, repayable in dates. Bēl-iddin had approximately one year to pay his debt in silver or dates without having to pay interest. The repayment of the debt was secured by a pledge of real estate.

---

122. On the harvesting of onions during the first months of the year, see Wunsch, *Iddin-Marduk* 1, 21f. n. 91.

123. For a full discussion of all debts that Rīmūt-Bēl/Šuma-ukīn and his brother owed to MNA and the ways in which they secured these debts, see § 2.6.2.

124. The text does not say for which year Bēl-iddin had to pay *rikis qabli*, but it was either for the current year, namely Darius' eleventh year, or the next one. Anyway, it had to be paid back in Tašrīt of Darius' twelfth year, i.e., within a year from the day on which Dar 308 was written.

Clearly, lending silver to taxpayers was a lucrative business for two reasons. First, MNA and MBU succeeded in "reserving" part of the indebted taxpayers' future harvest for their own benefit by stipulating that the loans were payable in those months of the year that coincided with the harvest of specific crops. Second, they gained access to real estate that belonged to the indebted taxpayers by seizing it as security for the repayment of their silver.

There were alternative ways to lending silver in order to help out taxpayers, as can be seen in three cases from the archive. First, there is an additional case of financial assistance granted by MBU to Bēl-iddin/Nabû-zēra-ušabši. We already saw how Bēl-iddin borrowed silver from MBU in order to pay for his *rikis qabli*. A few years later he again turned to MBU for assistance, asking him to pay the authorities on his behalf. In BM 31026 MBU pays silver that was "due from the bow-unit of Bēl-iddin/Nabû-zēra-ušabši for the rations of the *zargaya*-(work)men of Darius' fifteenth year" to a messenger of a low-ranking official. MBU paid the silver to this messenger "on behalf of Bēl-iddin."

Second, there is the case of MNA's financial assistance to Gūzānu/Ḫambaqu//Mandidi as recorded in BM 31226 and TCL 13 198. In these texts, from Darius' twenty-sixth and twenty-seventh years, MNA delivers a hireling to an agent of the commander-of-the-fortress and pays *ilku* to an agent of the royal administration. MNA delivered the hireling and paid for the *ilku* "on behalf of Gūzānu." The agent of the royal administration, who received MNA's payment for *ilku*, was Šamaš-iddin/Arad-Marduk//Dēkû. True, the latter does not bear an official title so that he does not represent the royal administration, at least not formally. However, official representation at the trans-action recorded in TCL 13 198 is clear from the list of witnesses. The first witness, Bēl-erība/Kalbaya//Šumu-libši, is attested elsewhere as "commander-of-fifty (corvée-workers or soldiers)."[125] His interests in the collection of taxes, in general, and the recruitment of soldiers and workers, in particular, is well known from other texts in the archive.[126] He is listed, for instance, among the witnesses in BM 31226, mentioned above. The second witness is Nergal-ēṭir, brother of Bēl-erība. He is not attested with an official title, but we know that he administered the collection of silver that was needed to pay salaries and rations to the men who had to go to Elam. In fact, he issued written orders (*šipirtu*) that he gave to these men so that they could go and collect the silver for their salaries and rations from MNA.[127] Consequently, Šamaš-iddin, who collected *ilku* from MNA while Bēl-erība and Nergal-ēṭir were present as witnesses, represented the state. He may have been one of the men who served under Bēl-erība and Nergal-ēṭir and was appointed by them to collect *ilku*. Had he been hired by Gūzānu/Ḫambaqu//Mandidi to serve on his behalf so that the *ilku* paid to him by Gūzānu through MNA's intermediary was meant to cover his costs?

---

125. BM 30274: 6, [lú]*rab ḫanšê*.

126. On Bēl-erība/Kalbaya//Šumu-libši, his brothers and their relationship with MNA, see Table 7 and n. 195.

127. Dar 552, Dar 572 and Dar 573. For details see above at § 2.2.1.

Third, there is the case of MNA's financial assistance to Bēl-nādin-apli/Bēl-uballiṭ//Paḫāru and his brothers in Darius' sixth and seventh years. These men owed silver to Nabû-šuma-ukīn (*alias* Šuma-ukīn)/Bēl-ēṭir//Šangû-Nanaya. MNA paid half a mina of silver to Nabû-šuma-ukīn "on behalf of Bēl-nādin-apli" in Ṭebēt of Darius' sixth year (Dar 213). Probably a month later, Bēl-nādin-apli and his brothers received from MNA [x] minas of silver "in addition to half the mina of silver that had (already) been given to Šuma-ukīn/Bēl-ēṭir//Šangû-Nanaya" (b 2800).[128] The silver that the three brothers thus received was, no doubt, to be transferred to Šuma-ukīn just like half the mina "that had (already) been given to Šuma-ukīn." A year later, MNA paid two minas of silver to Nabû-šuma-ukīn, and this payment was again somehow related to "Bēl-nādin-apli [and] his [brothers]" (TCL 13 185). The texts show that MNA either paid (Nabû-)Šuma-ukīn on behalf of the brothers, or that the latter paid (Nabû-)Šuma-ukīn on their own behalf, but only after they had raised the money that they needed from MNA. In either case, MNA mediated between the brothers and (Nabû-)Šuma-ukīn by providing the money that the former owed to the latter.[129]

MNA's and MBU's activity as middlemen between taxpayers and the authorities was beneficial for the state, but raises the question of reimbursement. The benefits for the state are obvious: the credit that MNA and MBU made available to taxpayers assured the state of its income and, in particular, of cash income rather than crop income. The silver that was needed to pay for the rations of the *zargaya*-(work)men in Darius' fifteenth year, for instance, was received in the middle of the year. Similarly, the commander-of-the-fortress received the hireling who had to serve till the end of the year at the beginning of Tašrīt; Šamaš-iddin/Arad-Marduk/Dekû received the *ilku* for two years at the beginning of the second year; and Nabû-šuma-ukīn/Bēl-ēṭir//Šangû-Nanaya received his (tax-)silver from MNA before the end of the year, viz. between Kislīm and Šabāṭ. These were the months of the year when cash was much in demand by the state. It was the end of the year, before the barley harvest, when storehouses were emptying so that salaries often had to be paid in silver.

The benefits for MNA and MBU, who provided for the credit, however, are less obvious. How were MNA and MBU remunerated for the silver that they

---

128. The date of b 2800 is partly broken: 6/xi/[-] Dar. For the reconstruction 6/xi/[6 Dar] see commentary *ad hoc*.

129. In none of the three texts do we find an explanation for the transfer of silver from MNA to (Nabû-)Šuma-ukīn. However, it may be safely assumed that the transfer was tax-related, especially in view of BM 31533 (1/xii/25 Dar), where Šuma-ukīn occurs as supervising the collection of *ilku* (note the considerable time-gap of eighteen years that exists between BM 31533, on the one hand, and the three texts currently under consideration, on the other hand). Moreover, Dar 213 is actually structured and formulated like an *ilku*-receipt, except that the word *ilku* does not explicitly occur. Further note the reference to a register (GIŠ.DA) in TCL 13 185: 13–15. On such registers, see more in § 3.5.3 (esp. p. 167ff.). On (Nabû-)Šuma-ukīn, also see below at p. 82f. and n. 331.

paid to the authorities or their agents on behalf of Bēl-iddin, Gūzānu, and Bēl-nādin-apli and his brothers? The texts do not tell us, but we may gain some insight into this matter from other texts of the archive. Bēl-nādin-apli and his brothers, for instance, sold one of their slaves to MNA at the end of Kislīm of Darius' sixth year (Dar 212). This sale may have been in repayment of their debt or part of it. Instead of paying their debt in silver, they "sold" a slave to MNA, or in other words, repaid their debt (or part of it) *in natura.* As for Gūzānu, we do not know how he reimbursed MNA for his financial help between Tašrīt of Darius' twenty-sixth and Nisan of Darius' twenty-seventh year, but we know that when MNA needed someone to train his slave as a baker in Addar of Darius' twenty-sixth year, Gūzānu agreed to do so.[130] Finally, we do not know how Bēl-iddin reimbursed MBU for his financial help in Darius' fifteenth year, but we know that MBU administered Bēl-iddin's unit (= "bow"), and had access to the agricultural produce of Bēl-iddin's fields for several years afterward.[131]

Consequently, it is clear that MNA and MBU granted financial assistance to men whom they knew well. In most cases their acquaintance with these men reached beyond the administration of their taxes. Bēl-iddin, for instance, belonged to a unit managed by MBU for several years; the latter may even have been a member of the unit himself.[132] Rīmūt-Bēl and his brother worked in MNA's commodity trade for several years,[133] and Gūzānu may have been a baker in MNA's service. These close relationships between MNA and MBU, on the one hand, and the men whom they helped out with the payment of their taxes, on the other hand, were, no doubt, mutually beneficial.

2.4. *Collection of Taxes, Tolls and Men for Compulsory Service by MNA and MBU*

We are now coming to the fourth aspect of MNA's involvement in the tax system of the early Persian period:[134] his receipt of taxes, tolls, and men for compulsory service from individuals or groups of individuals. This aspect is illustrated by three kinds of texts. First, four texts show that MNA was entitled to collect payments at and for bridges in Darius' twenty-fifth and twenty-sixth years.[135] Second, several texts show how MNA recruited men for compulsory service for the governor of Babylon or the commander-of-the-fortress between Darius' twenty-fourth and twenty-sixth years. He had also recruited corvée-

130. BM 41442.

131. The complex relationship between MBU, on the one hand, and Bēl-iddin, his family and members of his bow-unit, on the other hand, will be addressed in § 2.4.3.1 and § 2.4.5.1.

132. Arguments adduced at p. 74ff.

133. For the labor relationship among Rīmūt-Bēl/Šuma-ukīn, his brother, and MNA, see § 2.6.2.

134. Previously discussed aspects were: tax-payments by MNA (§ 2.1), transfers of silver by MNA for the salaries and rations of state-dependent workers and soldiers (§ 2.2 and probably also § 2.7), and financial assistance granted by MNA and MBU to taxpayers (§ 2.3).

135. The collection of payments at a bridge (or for a bridge) by MNA: TCL 13 196, BM 30366 and BM 31227. Probably also BM 41443 (for the publication of this text, see n. 145).

workers or hirelings to tow boats for the governor of Babylon in the two previous years.[136] Third, there is plenty of evidence that MNA was involved in the collection of the king's flour, *pānāt qašti* and taxes in general (*ilku*) from individuals or corporate entities ("bows"). The texts in question are mostly dated between Darius' twenty-fourth and twenty-sixth years, but MNA's involvement in the collection of taxes from bow-units, for instance, goes back at least to Darius' twelfth year.[137] His slave, MBU, also collected taxes, to wit from members of the same tax-unit, as is evidenced by a group of six texts that center on Bēl-iddin, members of his family, and his unit ("bow") and are dated between Darius' eleventh and seventeenth years.[138]

The texts discussed in this chapter evidence a kind of activity hardly attested in the published texts from MNA's archive. As a matter of fact, most of the texts that will be adduced below are new texts from the British Museum that, in the present study, are being published for the first time. They allow us to fully assess the little evidence that was hitherto available on MNA's involvement in the collection of taxes *et alia*. We knew, for instance, that MNA occasionally assisted Gūzānu, governor of Babylon, in the collection of payments from boats passing a bridge in Babylon,[139] and in the recruiting of soldiers from the governor's chariot-fief.[140] The new texts from the British Museum show that MNA's involvement in the exploitation of bridges and the recruitment of soldiers was not a once-only event, but that it occurred at regular intervals in the later years of Darius' reign. Moreover, it included the recruitment of corvée-workers, mostly for towing boats, in addition to the recruitment of soldiers. Furthermore, we knew that MNA occasionally received taxes (*ilku*) in his own name. It now appears that he did so, not just twice,[141] but on sixteen different occasions within three successive years. Finally, we knew that MBU,

---

136. The recruitment of men for compulsory service by MNA: CT 22 74, BM 30795, BM 31226 and BM 31438 (soldiers and/or workers); BM 30764 and BM 31118 (*urāšu* "corvée-workers"); and BM 31188, BM 31449 and BM 32932 (*agru* "hirelings"). Two additional texts about compulsory service do not mention MNA, but belong to his archive for prosopographic reasons: BM 30446 and BM 30274.

137. The collection of *ilku*, (the king's) flour (*qēmi*) and *pānāt qašti* from individuals by MNA (fifteen texts): BM 30235, BM 30243, BM 30261, BM 30297, BM 30366, BM 30772, BM 30819, BM 31227, BM 31322, BM 31517, BM 31533, BM 33926, BM 41607, CTMMA 3 68 and TCL 13 197. The collection of *ilku*, silver, and flour from groups of individuals ("bow-units") by MNA (three texts): BM 30589 (*ilku*), BM 31798 (silver), and BM 33954 (flour). One fragmentary letter about *ilku*: BM 31416. In total: eighteen tax-receipts by MNA and one letter.

138. The collection of silver from a bow-unit by MBU (one text): Dar 430. This text is to be discussed within its dossier, to wit the so-called Bēl-iddin dossier, which consists of Dar 430 and five other texts, namely Dar 308, Dar 400, Dar 452, Dar 459 and BM 31026 (it does not include Dar 438; more at n. 216).

139. TCL 13 196.

140. CT 22 74.

141. TCL 13 197 (published in 1929) and CTMMA 3 68 (published only very recently, in 2000, and consequently not included in previous studies on the Egibis).

his slave, received silver from a bow-unit that was named after a Bēl-iddin,[142] but there had been no evidence that MNA himself dealt with tax income from such tax-units.

The texts raise certain questions on MNA's and MBU's roles in the collection of taxes and conscripts for the Persian state. Why did they collect these taxes and conscripts. Were they actually entitled to them or did they have to transfer them to the state? Below, we shall discuss the involvement of MNA and his slave MBU in the collection of taxes, workers, and soldiers by examining the evidence on (1) the collection of payments at and for bridges; (2) the recruitment of soldiers and workers; (3) the collection of taxes from members of the same tax-unit ("bow"); and (4) the collection of taxes in general (*ilku*), including the occasional collection of flour (*qēmi*) and *pānāt qašti*, from individuals or groups of individuals ("bows").[143]

2.4.1. *Collection of Payments at or for Bridges (irbi ša gišri, ilki ... ša gišri)*

TCL 13 196 deals with the collection of payments (*isīrtu*) from boats passing the bridge of Babylon and its harbor in Darius' twenty-sixth year. The collection of payments seems to have been the prerogative of the governor of Babylon (*bīt qīptu*). In reality, however, it was organized by MNA, who may have bought or leased the right to collect the payments in exchange for the advance payment of a fixed amount of silver to the governor. As it was, the income from "the collection ... is at the disposal of MNA" (*isīrtu ... ša ina pān MNA*).[144] MNA, however, did not perform the collection by himself, but worked together with several other men who were guardians at the bridge, with whom (*itti*) he shared the "income from the bridge" (*irbi ša gišri*). Moreover, he and one of these co-shareholders, Mūrānu/Nabû-mukīn-apli, decided to seek the help of two additional men to organize the collection of the payments. Thus, Bēl-asûa/Nergal-uballiṭ//Mudammiq-Adad and Ubār/Bēl-aḫḫē-erība//Maṣṣār-elep-rukūbi were granted a right to a portion of the income against the payment of fifteen shekels a month. They had to organize the collection of payments, take care of the bookkeeping, and inform MNA and the guardians in case something unexpected occurred at the bridge.

Accurate bookkeeping at the bridge may have been a complex matter. No doubt, the governor of Babylon wanted to know how much had been collected

142. Dar 430.

143. BM 30366 and BM 31227 are discussed in paragraphs one and four because they concern the collection of *ilku* for a bridge. BM 30589 is discussed in paragraphs three and four because it concerns the collection of *ilku* from a "bow-unit."

144. For the idiom *ina pān* in the phrase *isīrtu/usertu ... ša ina pān MNA*, see commentary at TCL 13 196: 3. For the expression *ina pān* in boat rentals, see § 2.5.3, esp. n. 391. For its occurrence in texts concerning the cultivation of crops on land that is held on contract, see n. 556 (Dar 315 and BM 32930), and cf. the similar expression *īpuš* "he contracted" in BM 33972: 20 (n. 489). For *ina pān* in Dar 552 and Dar 573 concerning silver charged against MNA, see p. 34f., and cf. *kaspu ša ina pān* in BM 30854.

each month so that the income could be fairly divided among the shareholders. Another text from the archive sheds further light on this issue. BM 41443, dated a few months prior to TCL 13 196, mentions a silver debt of MNA to an otherwise unknown person named Mušēzib, and refers in this context to a "register of the bridge."[145] The two minas and ten shekels of silver that MNA owed to this Mušēzib was that "which had been given on MNA's behalf for the register of the bridge." The situation to which the text refers seems to have been as follows. MNA had to transfer a certain amount of silver to an unnamed individual for registration in the bridge accounts. A certain Mušēzib transferred the silver "on behalf of MNA" so that MNA now owed him the silver. He secured the payment of his silver debt to Mušēzib by pledging a slave. The pledge is witnessed, among others, by Nidintu/Kalbaya//Suḫaya, who also witnessed TCL 13 196 and, in general, witnessed several of MNA's boat-related transactions.[146] BM 41443 clearly proves the existence of a register that kept track of the collection of payments from boats at bridges. Moreover, it shows that MNA had to transfer the silver that he had collected at the bridge, or part of it, for registration in this register.

In addition, MNA collected payments for construction work at bridges. In Araḫsamna of Darius' twenty-sixth year, MNA received payment for *ilki ša* DI-*pi ša gišri* of the current year (BM 30366). This income was apparently needed to make some additions to the bridge, as is suggested by the term *ṭīpu* (wr. DI-*pi*) "addition." The previous year, MNA received payment for *ilki ... ša i-da-šú ša gišri Bābili ša ina qātē Bēl-ēṭir*? (BM 31227). Unfortunately, the meaning of the expression *idāšu ša gišri* is unclear.[147] It may refer to the collection of rent at a bridge or perhaps the text should be emended to read: *ú-ra-šú ša gišri*. In the latter case, the payment that MNA received from one Bēl-asûa/Nabû-iddin//Bābūtu would be for corvée-work (*urāšu*) at the bridge—we know that people had to pay for corvée-work at bridges and quays.[148] In any case, it is clear from these two *ilku*-receipts that MNA was intimately involved in the exploitation of bridges and the surrounding harbor, i.a., the bridge and harbor that stood under the supervision of the governor of Babylon, as well as the bridge for which a certain Bēl-ēṭir? was responsible.[149]

---

145. BM 41443: 16–17, KÙ.BABBAR *šá a-na* GIŠ.ŠID *šá* ^{giš}*gi-ši-ri a-na muḫ-ḫi* MNA SUM.NA. The text will be published by C. Wunsch in her book on the slaves of the Egibi family. The obverse of the tablet has already been published from a cast as RTC 20A (= AJSL 27 221). BM 41443 is dated on 8/iii/26 Dar.

146. For Nidintu/Kalbaya//Suḫaya, see p. 52f., Table 7 no. 23, and esp. n. 437. Further note the presence of Passasu/Mušēzib-Marduk//Arad-Nergal among the witnesses. His brother, Ibnaya, witnessed BM 30446, the recruitment of boat-towers in Darius' twenty-fourth year.

147. See commentary at BM 31227: 4.

148. L 4270 from Borsippa (*urāšu ša kāri*) and BM 74601 from Sippar (cited by Jursa, *Bēl-rēmanni*, n. 412: *urāšu ša gišri*).

149. For *ina qāt*(*ē*) "under the responsibility of," cf. *CAD* Q, 192 mng. 7a-2'-b'.

2.4.2. *The Recruitment of Soldiers and Workers by MNA*

Five texts in MNA's archive deal with the recruitment of men for compulsory service between Darius' twenty-fourth and twenty-sixth years.[150] The first text reveals that MNA recruited charioteers and other soldiers for the governor of Babylon. The second one records the recruitment of one of these soldiers, the charioteer Libluṭ/Itti-Nabû-balāṭu, by someone else, but with MNA being present. The following two texts indicate that MNA arranged for the service of men who had been called up by hiring substitutes for them. Thus, he arranged for the service of a baker who had been called up by the commander-of-the-fortress. Similarly, he arranged for the service of the sons of Kalbaya//Suḫaya who had been called up by Šuma-uṣur/Šamaš-ēṭir. The fifth and last text is a fragmentary letter about MNA's collection of equipment and workers. The first four texts belong to a larger group of texts that document the cooperation in various matters between MNA and some of the conscripts mentioned in these texts. Therefore, they need to be studied together. Accordingly, I have assembled three dossiers, each of which focuses on one or two conscripts and their relationship with MNA: (1) the dossier of the charioteer Libluṭ, who is attested in nine legal documents and one letter between Darius' twelfth and twenty-sixth years[151]; (2) a smaller dossier of the baker Gūzānu, which consists of three texts dated between Darius' twenty-sixth and twenty-seventh years[152]—one of these texts mentions Gūzānu's companion Šūzubu from the butcher's family; (3) the dossier regarding the sons of Kalbaya//Suḫaya with Nidintu, one of the sons, as the main protagonist; he is attested among the witnesses in six texts concerning boats from MNA's time.[153]

As documented by at least four texts from Darius' twenty-fourth year,[154] MNA recruited boat-towers and hirelings for the governor of Babylon in addition to recruiting soldiers. Two of these texts document MNA's receipt of

---

150. CT 22 74 (not dated), BM 30795 (26/x/26 Dar), BM 31226 (9/vii/26 Dar), BM 31449 ([-]/[-]/23^{+} Dar), and BM 31438 (not dated).

151. The recruitment of the charioteer Libluṭ/Itti-Nabû-balāṭu//Sīsî is dealt with in the letter CT 22 74 (not dated) and in BM 30795 (26/x/26 Dar). He also occurs among the witnesses in the following eight legal documents, cited in chronological order: BM 33954 (25/iv/12 Dar), Dar 384 (= *CM* 20b 194, 27/viii/[14$^{?}$]), Dar 401 (29/v/15 Dar), BM 41434//BOR 2, 3f. (= Wunsch, *Felder* 1, 174f.; 5/iii/16 Dar), Dar 448 (3/iv/17 Dar), BM 31226 (9/vii/26 Dar), Liv 20 (8/x/26 Dar), and BM 31449 ([-]/[-]/20^{+} Dar). Finally, does Libluṭ also occur in Dar 483 (18/iv/19 Dar), to wit under the name Libluṭ/Iqūpu//Sīsî?

152. The recruitment of Gūzānu and Šūzubu is recorded in BM 31226 (9/vii/26 Dar). Gūzānu also occurs in BM 41442 (15/xii/26 Dar) and TCL 13 198 (11/i/27 Dar).

153. The recruitment of the sons of Kalbaya//Suḫaya is recorded in BM 31449 ([-]/[-]/23^{+} Dar). Nidintu, one of the sons, also occurs in BM 30370 (3–9/v/26 Dar), BM 30961 (12/vi/26 Dar), TCL 13 196 (1/vii/26 Dar), BM 30994 (5/vii/26 Dar) and OECT 10 234 (20^{+}/[-]/26 Dar). For Ardiya/^{m}KAR-*e-a* (emend and read Kalbaya?)//Suḫaya, more at BM 30446: 11.

154. BM 32932 (18/vii/24 Dar), BM 31188 (25/[-]/24 Dar), BM 30764 (23/iii/25 Dar), BM 31118 (4/[-]/25 Dar).

boat-towers from the governor's workforce. The other two texts record his receipt of hirelings to tow boats and do similar kinds of jobs. These hirelings may have originated from the same workforce. A fifth text is a list of men who were drafted to tow boats; it does not mention MNA explicitly, but is linked to his archive on the basis of prosopographic evidence.[155] These five texts regarding the recruitment of boat-towers and hirelings are grouped in a separate, fourth dossier. The analysis of these four dossiers should reveal how and why MNA recruited soldiers, boat-towers, and other workers for state officials.

2.4.2.1. *The Recruitment of the Charioteer Liblut/Itti-Nabû-balāṭu*

CT 22 74 is a letter from Gūzānu to Širku, containing three major parts[156]: (1) a complaint by Gūzānu about Širku's mismanagement, including bitter accusations of conspiracy with the commander-of-the-fortress; (2) practical arrangements on solving the problem with the commander-of-the-fortress; (3) statement on the extent of Širku's authority in military affairs in order to avoid problems in the future.

The letter begins with a complaint by Gūzānu to Širku. The former blames the latter for deceiving him, conspiring with the commander-of-the-fortress, and eventually transferring troops from Gūzānu's chariot-fief to the hands of the commander.[157] Gūzānu claims that Širku deceived him when he wrote that Gūzānu was not to worry about Libluṭ, the other charioteers, and the auxiliaries. According to Širku's reports, these troops were enlisted with Gūzānu and should serve under his command. However, when the commander-of-the-fortress came, he withheld the troops from Gūzānu, claiming that they belonged to him. Gūzānu further claims that Širku went as far as conspiring with the commander. According to Gūzānu, the commander gained control of Gūzānu's troops because Širku personally transferred these troops to him, instead of keeping them available for Gūzānu.

Having fired all his accusations at Širku, Gūzānu then turns to the practical side of the matter. Širku should not go after Libluṭ and the other soldiers for two reasons.[158] First, they had already left by boat in the direction of Danipinu. Second, it was important not to enter into a direct confrontation with the commander. Apparently, Gūzānu did not want to give the commander or any other person a pretext for blaming him for interference with the commander's troops. Going after Libluṭ and taking away the soldiers from him could be used against Gūzānu. He clearly wanted to maintain his reputation and that of his soldiers in the commander's eyes.

155. BM 30446 (4/vii/24 Dar).

156. CT 22 74: 3–14 (=first part); 15–26 (=second part); 26–31(=third part).

157. CT 22 74: 3–12 (= accusation of deceit); 12–13 (= accusation of conspiracy) and 13–14 (accusation of troop transfer).

158. CT 22 74: 15–17 (the soldiers left) and 18–22 (no confrontation with the commander).

Gūzānu ordered Širku to avoid the commander and to go directly to the representative of the crown.[159] Indeed, he should go and talk with Atkal-ana-mār-Esagil, who has no official title in the letter under consideration, but is attested as administrator of the crown under Cambyses' reign and later.[160] They should talk about the possibility of mustering other soldiers instead of the ones who were no longer available to Gūzānu. In other words, Gūzānu wanted to solve his problem with the commander by asking the crown to place other soldiers at his disposal.

At the end of the letter Gūzānu defined the limits of Širku's access to military personnel in clear terms in order to avoid problems like the one described above.[161] It is made clear to Širku which soldiers he could have and which soldiers he could not have. Accordingly, Širku was allowed access to the guards at the gate, the charioteers, and the soldiers from Bīt-Dakkuru residing in Babylon.[162] He was barred access to the troops of the royal household and those of Gūzānu's chariot-fief.[163] The latter included the chief-charioteer Libluṭ, other charioteers under his command, auxiliary troops, and private soldiers.

One problem for our understanding of letters is that persons are usually called by their first names without patronymy, so that it is extremely difficult to identify them and link the letters to a specific archive. In CT 22 74 five individuals are mentioned: (1) Gūzānu, holder of a chariot-fief and sender of the letter; (2) Širku, the addressee, who receives orders from Gūzānu to act on his behalf in a matter concerning his charioteers; (3) the commander-of-the-fortress, who had laid a claim to Gūzānu's charioteers; (4) Atkal-ana-mār-Esagil, to whom Širku should appeal; and (5) Libluṭ, who is called the "charioteer" (*mār* [lú]*sīsê*), head of a group of charioteers, auxiliary troops and private soldiers, who were enlisted with Gūzānu.

I suggest identifying Širku with MNA, Libluṭ with Libluṭ/Itti-Nabû-balāṭu//Sīsî, and Gūzānu with Gūzānu/Nabû-šuma-ukīn//Ša-nāšīšu on the basis of several observations. First, Širku from CT 22 74 may have been the same person as MNA since in texts from his archive he is often called by his nickname Širku. Second, the charioteer Libluṭ may have been the same person as Libluṭ/Itti-Nabû-balāṭu from the charioteer-family (//Sīsî) since a person's family name often reflects this person's occupation. Thus, we find weavers with the family name Išparu, oil-pressers with the family name Ṣāḫit-ginê, barley-

159. CT 22 74: 22–24.

160. Jursa, *Landwirtschaft*,145f. (commentary at line 8f.).

161. BM 30274 throws further light on how such problems could be solved. Indeed, the latter text is a written statement handed out to a certain Ardiya by his commander that he has fulfilled his duties and is released from further service for the next three and a half months. If someone like MNA tried to get hold of Ardiya and recruit him for compulsory service, he could show the written statement from his commander. A similar discharge of service is Stolper, *JCS* 53 No. 13 (= A. 34117) from the Murašû archive.

162. CT 22 74: 28–31.

163. CT 22 74: 26–27 and 31–32.

measurers with the family name Mādidu, and chief temple administrators of the Ebabbar temple with the family name Šangû-Sippar.[164] Third, Gūzānu from CT 22 74 may have been the same person as Gūzānu/Nabû-šuma-ukīn//Ša-nāšīšu, who was governor of Babylon between the years iv/25 Dar and [-]/28 Dar.[165] I suggest this for two reasons. First, this governor, his father, and brothers often occur in texts from the time of MNA; they worked together with MNA and his son in various matters, such as the collection of taxes, the transport of goods by boat, and the recruitment of workers.[166] Moreover, Gūzānu or his father, MNA, and the charioteer Libluṭ/Itti-Nabû-balāṭu appear together in two other texts in the archive, BM 30795 and BM 33954.

The closest parallel to CT 22 74 is found in BM 30795, according to which Libluṭ/Itti-Nabû-balāṭu//Sī<sî>, together with Rīmūt/Marduk-ušallim//P[aḫā]ru, and a group of workers called ^{lú}*šá-da-e-ti* were enlisted to do service under Gūzānu/Na[bû-šuma-ukīn]//Ša-nāšīšu, governor of Babylon.[167] The text in question records the receipt of said persons with the registers of their enlistment in Ṭebēt of Darius' twenty-sixth year.[168] Due to the fragmentary state of the text it is unclear who acknowledged the receipt, but it is important to note that MNA was among the witnesses. His presence at the transaction confirms his relinquishment of claims on the charioteer Libluṭ/Itti-Nabû-balāṭu and the other persons mentioned in the text. This, of course, reminds us of the dispute between Gūzānu and Širku (=MNA) regarding the latter's access to Libluṭ and the other soldiers enlisted to do service with Gūzānu, as related in CT 22 74. It shows that the dispute between Širku and Gūzānu about Libluṭ and the other soldiers, as recorded in CT 22 74, was not an isolated case.

Our understanding of CT 22 74 is further enhanced by the evidence found in BM 33954. This text indicates that the acquaintance between MNA and the charioteer Libluṭ/Itti-Nabû-balāṭu goes back to the years when Gūzānu's father governed Babylon. This text, dated to Darius' twelfth year, deals with the king's income of flour from a group of exorcists. The administration of flour collection was the responsibility of Nabû-šuma-ukīn//Ša-nāšīšu, governor of Babylon, but was actually organized by MNA. Libluṭ/[Itti]-Nabû-balāṭu//Sīsî witnessed the transaction. Moreover, he may have assumed warranty for the punctual delivery of the flour to MNA if one accepts that he is the same person as the Libluṭ who is mentioned without any further affiliation in lines 13–14 of the text under consideration.

---

164. Examples from the Ebabbar archive, see Bongenaar, *Ebabbar*, 311 n. 289.

165. Bongenaar, *Ebabbar*, 9.

166. See index s.v. Nabû-šuma-ukīn (governor of Babylon) and his four sons Gūzānu (governor of Babylon), Ina-Esagil-lilbur (governor of Babylon), Basiya, and Marduk-nāṣir-apli.

167. See commentary at BM 30795: 4.

168. See commentary at BM 30795: 5.

The charioteer Libluṭ/Itti-Nabû-balāṭu is found among the witnesses in nine documents, including BM 33954 mentioned above, from MNA's archive.[169] They show that he followed MNA's business and family affairs for fourteen years, from Darius' twelfth till the end of Darius' twenty-sixth year. Three of these documents have an institutional background. Thus, he witnessed MNA's deliveries of hirelings (BM 31449 and BM 31226) and his anticipated receipt of flour from the bow-unit of exorcists in the name of Nabû-šuma-ukīn//Ša-nāšīšu, governor of Babylon (BM 33954). The other six documents from MNA's archive that Libluṭ witnessed have no explicit link with taxes or the royal administration, but such a link should be seriously considered in at least some of the cases. One of the texts in question, for instance, regards MNA's debt of a large sum of silver, fifty minas, to a member of the prominent Šigûa family (Liv 20).[170] The repayment of the debt was secured by the pledge of a house in which Marduk-ēṭir/Nabû-šuma-iškun//Šumu-libši lived. This tenant took over the credit from the said member of the Šigûa family at some point in time. Liv 20 records MNA's payment of a small part of the debt to Marduk-ēṭir on the eighth of Ṭebēt of Darius' twenty-sixth year and his promise to pay the remainder within a few days. As said, this payment and promise were witnessed by, among others, Libluṭ from the Charioteer family; another witness was Rīmūt/Marduk-ušallim//Paḫāru. Libluṭ and Rīmūt were drafted together that same month to serve with the governor of Babylon.[171] Two and a half months prior to MNA's payment to Marduk-ēṭir the latter wrote the receipt of MNA's payment for transport costs to an agent of the governor of Babylon.[172] The evidence collected above cannot be worked into a coherent narrative. However, it is clear that its protagonists, viz. MNA, Libluṭ, Rīmūt, Marduk-ēṭir, the governor of Babylon, and members of prominent families kept meeting to discuss matters that must, therefore, have been interrelated in one way or another. In view of these scattered pieces of evidence, we cannot exclude the possibility that the large silver debt to a member of the Šigûa family, as recorded in Liv 20, had something to do with the collection of taxes or conscripts by MNA.[173]

169. Consequently, there are ten texts in total that mention the charioteer Libluṭ/Itti-Nabû-balāṭu: the letter CT 22 74 and nine legal documents. See also n. 151.

170. The details of this debt are recorded in Dar 519 (14/i/21 Dar), cf. Petschow, *Pfandrecht*, 172 and Krecher, *Egibi*, 338. For the house that was pledged to secure the repayment of the debt, see also Dar 499 and Krecher, *Egibi*, 334. On the Šigûa family, see Kümmel, *Familie*, 133, 151 and 117 n. 64. One of its members who is mentioned several times in texts from MNA's time in matters related to the Esagil temple is Šaddinnu/Madānu-aḫḫē-iddin. Šaddinnu's brothers (Marduk-nāṣir, Nabû-nādin-aḫi and Šamaš-mukīn-apli), uncles (Kalbaya and Arad-Nergal), father (Madānu-aḫḫē-iddin), and grandfather (Gimillu) are well attested in texts from Uruk; one of his brothers was a scribe in Eanna and overseer of the brewer's prebend; their father was also overseer of this prebend.

171. BM 30795 (26/x/26 Dar).

172. BRM 1 81 (4/viii/26 Dar).

173. Four more texts from MNA's archive were witnessed by Libluṭ, but the information

In summary, MNA was responsible for the recruitment of the charioteer Libluṭ/Itti-Nabû-balāṭu on behalf of Gūzānu, governor of Babylon. Libluṭ and the governors of Babylon met on three occasions between Darius' twelfth and twenty-sixth years.[174] The matter of Libluṭ's service with Gūzānu was the main issue on the occasion of at least two of these encounters.[175] The third encounter, which was chronologically the first one, shows that the labor relation between MNA and Libluṭ predated Gūzānu's governorship. In fact, it went back to the years when Gūzānu's father governed Babylon. Their relationship seems to have concentrated on matters of state-income, in general, and compulsory service, in particular.[176]

2.4.2.2. *The Recruitment of Gūzānu, the Baker, and Šūzubu of the Butcher's Family*

The commander-of-the-fortress needed not only the services of Libluṭ and his charioteers, but also those of Gūzānu/Ḫambaqu//Mandidi and Šūzubu/Uballissu-Marduk//Ṭābiḫu. They asked MNA to hire someone else to serve in their stead. Accordingly, MNA delivered a hireling to an agent of the commander-of-the-fortress in Babylon on behalf of Gūzānu and Šūzubu in Tašrīt of Darius' twenty-sixth year (BM 31226). The hireling had to serve for six months.[177] The commander's agent acknowledged his receipt of the hireling. At the very end of the document it is said that "he was (thus)[?] paid off with regard to their flour-tax of the twenty-sixth (i.e., current) year." The flour-tax was either the original obligation that was due from Gūzānu and Šūzubu and that they met by sending a hireling, or it was an additional obligation. Though we do not know why Gūzānu and Šūzubu had to serve with the said commander, it may have been related to Gūzānu's profession of baker[178] and Šūzubu's

provided by these texts is too limited to establish a connection between the subject matters of these texts and state income. The four texts in question are: Dar 401: a promissory note regarding a silver debt of ½ mina and 5½ shekels of silver; owed by Ardiya/Lâbāši//Eppeš-ilī to MNA; Dar 448: a promissory note regarding a date and barley debt, owed by Ubār/Arad-Bēl//Eppeš-ilī to MNA; Dar 384 = *CM* 20b 194: a promissory note according to which two of MNA's slaves promised to clear their receipt of dates in the accounts of MNA's brother and show the quittance to MNA; and BM 41434//BOR 2, 3f.: a transfer of rights in a plot of land and slaves by MNA to his wife. The location of the land in question is noteworthy because it is loosely related to the collection of *rikis qabli* and to the royal administration (for details see Wunsch, *Felder* 1, 174f. and esp. n. 364).

174. BM 33954, BM 30795 and CT 22 74.

175. CT 22 74 and BM 30795. The labor relation between MNA and the governors of Babylon, however, reached beyond matters of recruitment (details at § 2.1.1 regarding Dar 154, § 2.1.2, § 2.4.1, § 2.4.2.3, § 2.4.3.3, and § 2.5; summary at p. 135).

176. CT 22 74, BM 30795, BM 31449 and BM 31226 (compulsory service); BM 33954 (state income from a bow-unit); Liv 20 (a matter of state income?!); and Dar 401, Dar 448, Dar 384 = *CM* 20b 194 and BM 41434//BOR 2, 3f. (matters of uncertain background).

177. See commentary at BM 31226: 4.

178. We know that Gūzānu/Ḫambaqu//Mandidi was a professional baker from BM 41442

relations with the Butcher's family.[179] The army, no doubt, needed bakers and butchers to prepare food for the soldiers, especially during campaigns. Interestingly, the receipt was witnessed by Libluṭ, the charioteer, Bēl-erība/Kalbaya//Šumu-libši, a commander-of-fifty, a man who is otherwise known from MNA's temple and boat-related transactions, and Nabû-šuma-iddin and his brother.[180] Half a year later MNA paid for Gūzānu's *ilku*-tax (TCL 13 198), paying the *ilku* of the current year and the previous year. The payment was received by Šamaš-iddin/Arad-Marduk//Dēkû and witnessed by, among others, the above-mentioned Bēl-erība, commander-of-fifty, and his brother. Clearly, Gūzānu's contributions to state income were a matter of concern to several men with similar institutional connections: the commander-of-the-fortress in Babylon, a charioteer of the governor of Babylon, and a commander-of-fifty and his brother.

where he agreed to train MNA's slave in the baker's profession. Does Nbn 670 (1/xii/12 Nbn), which is almost fifty years older than the ones mentioned above, also refer to the same person? In line 5 of the text a Gūzānu appears, without affiliation but labelled "the baker" (^{m}*gu-za-nu* LÚ.⸢MU⸣), and in line 3 an Adad-⸢ērеš$^{?}$⸣ (^{md}IM-⸢KAM$^{?}$⸣) perhaps appears. Can the former be identified with Gūzānu/Ḫambaqu//Mandidi, the baker? Can the latter be identified with Addu-ērеš, commander-of-the-fortress ($^{md!}$*ad-du*-KAM LÚ.GAL BÀD, BM 31226: 6), with whom Gūzānu/Ḫambaqu//Mandidi had to serve according to BM 31226 (9/vii/26 Dar)?

179. As for Šūzubu/Uballissu-Marduk, he may have been trained as butcher, as is suggested by his family name, Ṭābiḫu. Šūzubu is attested among the witnesses in Dar 571 (= *CM* 20b 207, see more at n. 605). For Šamaš-ēṭir/Bulluṭaya (*alias* Uballissu-Marduk?)//Ṭābiḫu) the brother of this Šūzubu, see Dar 290 (= *CM* 20b 190 and *Felder* 2, 166; dated 21/xii/10 Dar). MNA delivered *šibšu*-barley to him from a field in Litamu. Some of the witnesses in Dar 290 recur in texts discussed in this book: Marduk-zēra-ibni/Bēl-aḫḫē-iddin//Nappāḫu, second witness in Dar 290 recurs in Dar 156 (perhaps also in BM 33935: 18–19, see commentary *ad hoc*); and Mūrānu/Mušallim-Marduk//Atkuppu, third witness in Dar 290 recurs in Dar 334 and Dar 450. Consequently, Dar 290 may have had an institutional background. Had Šamaš-ēṭir to perform corvée-work or military service like his brother Šūzubu and did MNA provide for his barley-rations in Dar 290 (cf. BM 31203)? In this respect it is worth noting that Šamaš-ēṭir received MNA's barley "in accordance with the register (GIŠ.DA) of Nabû-šuma-uṣur." The register may have kept track of the barley needed by Nabû-šuma-uṣur for the rations of Šamaš-ēṭir and other conscripts, perhaps including himself (more on registers recording the income of barley and its distribution to conscripts at the discussion of BM 30446 on p. 53ff. and that of registers on p. 166ff.). Unfortunately, Nabû-šuma-uṣur, the owner of the register in Dar 290, is cited by his first name only so that it is difficult to trace him in other texts. Was he the man with whom Šamaš-ēṭir had to serve and who held the register of Šamaš-ēṭir's enlistment? Was he the same as Nabû-šuma-uṣur/Marduk(-šuma)-ibni//Ile''i-Marduk who held a register regarding payments for the equipment of the men serving in the king's army (Dar 220, see n. 445)?

180. Libluṭ, Bēl-erība, Nabû-šuma-iddin, and Zēriya, his brother, are four of the six witnesses listed in BM 31226. On Libluṭ/Itti-Nabû-balāṭu//Sīsî, the charioteer, see § 2.4.2.1; on Bēl-erība/Kalbaya//Šumu-libši, the commander-of-fifty, see Table 7 and p. 53ff. (esp. n. 195); on Nabû-šuma-iddin/Šāpik-zēri//Dēkû and his father, see Dar 455 and BM 31347 (details at Table 7).

2.4.2.3. *The Recruitment of the Sons of Kalbaya//Suḫaya*

BM 31449, which was drafted in Babylon between Darius' twenty-third and twenty-ninth years, records the delivery by MNA of one or more persons identified as hireling(s). It is clear that the text concerns the hirelings themselves and not just something belonging to them, such as their salary: the text starts with LÚ.ḪUN.GÁ and there is nothing before the LÚ-sign. These hirelings were delivered by MNA on behalf of Nidintu/Kalbaya//Suḫaya and his brothers to Šuma-uṣur/Šamaš-ēṭir. They were to serve, so it seems, for one month, or for a few days a month for several months. Unfortunately, the text does not say, at least not in its present state of preservation, what kind of service they were to perform and for whom.[181]

The hireling(s) that Nidintu and his brothers had to deliver was possibly to transport people and/or equipment by boat on behalf of a commander-of-fifty, viz. Bēl-erība/Kalbaya//Šumu-libši. This conclusion is based upon four observations. First, Nidintu/Kalbaya//Suḫaya, on whose behalf MNA delivered the hireling(s), had a general interest in boats and boat transports; as such he often appears among the witnesses in texts concerning these matters. Thus, he was present when MNA bought three boats in Darius' twenty-sixth year and dealt with the exploitation of a bridge that same year.[182] Hence, there seems to have been a link between the hireling(s) of Nidintu and his brothers, on the one hand, and the organization of boat transports, on the other. Second, Ardiya/Kalbaya$^{?!}$//Suḫaya, brother of Nidintu, actually towed boats for the state in Darius' twenty-fourth year.[183] If he himself had to tow boats for the state, he may as well have hired someone to tow them for him and his brothers. Remarkably, Bēl-erība/Kalbaya//Šumu-libši, the commander-of-fifty, was

181. This was probably written in the broken part of line 1. Note that BM 31449 is formulated and structured in much the same way as the receipts of state-due income, such as the receipts of corvée-workers and *ilku* that we will analyze below (§ 2.4.2.4, esp. p. 56 and § 2.4.4, esp. p. 64ff.): *ilku*/^{lú}*šadādu*/^{lú}*agru* - period of time - *ša* PN_1 - PN_2 - *ina qātē* MNA - *ana muḫḫi* PN_1 - *māḫir*. Accordingly, the particle *ša*, in BM 31449: 4, is to be taken in the meaning "due from," in other words the hireling was due from Nidintu/Kalbaya//Suḫaya and his brothers.

182. Nidintu/Kalbaya//Suḫaya witnessed BM 30370, BM 30961, OECT 10 234 (boat purchases); TCL 13 196 and BM 41443 (exploitation of a bridge; for the publication of this text, see n. 145). See at Table 7. He also witnessed BM 30994 (about LÚ.DÍM). Moreover, he and his brothers had to deliver a hireling or hirelings for a work assignment the nature of which is unknown in BM 31449. Finally, Nidintu may have been present when MNA paid for the transport costs to an agent of the governor of Babylon and barley for unspecified reasons to another royal official (BM 31786 and BM 31138). The uncertainty in those two cases derives from the fact that the witness Nidintu/Kalbaya(//[...]) in these texts could have been either the above-mentioned Nidintu, descendant of Suḫaya, or Nidintu/Kalbaya//Šuma-ukīn, brother of the commander-of-fifty. Both Nidintus are well attested as witnesses in texts from the time of MNA (details at Table 7).

183. If one reads Ardiya/^{m}*kal*$^{!}$(KAR)-*ba*$^{!}$(E)-*a*//Suḫaya in BM 30446: 11 (more at comment to this line).

present on both these occasions.[184] Third, the delivery of the hireling(s) was, as said, witnessed by a commander-of-fifty, who knew Nidintu from several boat-related transactions and was, in fact, much interested in such transactions. He and Nidintu, for instance, witnessed MNA's purchase of three boats.[185] The commander also witnessed two boat rentals and a payment for transport costs to the governor of Babylon.[186] Moreover, he acted as a scribe at the recruitment of boat-towers on the latter's behalf.[187] This is not surprising since the commander himself was entitled to the services of boat-towers and other workers.[188] Hence, it is very likely that his interest in hirelings in BM 31449 was based on a similar right, to wit, a right to the service of these hirelings for boat transports. In other words, it is very likely that the delivery of the hireling(s) in BM 31449 had something to do with boat-related services on behalf of the state. Finally, there is the fact that Libluṭ/Itti-Nabû-balāṭu//Sīsê, a charioteer in the service of the governor of Babylon, occurs among the witnesses at the delivery of the hireling(s).[189] He was present when MNA collected flour from exorcists on behalf of this governor and hired soldiers for the commander-of-the-fortress.[190] Clearly, the kind of transactions that Libluṭ attended usually concerned the collection of taxes and the recruitment of soldiers. Accordingly, the delivery of the hireling(s) was just another of these transactions concerned with state income from taxes or services that Libluṭ attended.

2.4.2.4. *The Recruitment of Corvée-workers (urāšu)*

The recruitment of men to tow boats for the state is the main issue in BM 30446 from Darius' twenty-fourth year. The text records the receipt of six boat-towers and mentions the receipt of a register (*itti* GIŠ.ŠID). The men were listed by name and full affiliation. There is no mention of any salary for the boat-towers, indicating that their recruitment was, no doubt, compulsory. The register that was transmitted together with the boat-towers, in all likelihood, contained the men's names and other details of their recruitment since they were drafted "according to this register." By means of such registers the royal administration kept record of who had to do public service and when he had to do so. It may also have contained details on the distribution of food rations to the servicemen. This may explain the reference to the "house of the food allowances" in line 5

184. He was, apparently, the scribe of BM 30446 ([Bēl-erība]/Kalbaya//Šumu-libši); and among the witnesses in BM 31449.

185. BM 30370 and BM 30961.

186. BM 30490 and BM 30270 (boat rentals); and BM 32891 (transport costs).

187. BM 30795.

188. BM 30446; perhaps also BM 31188, more at n. 207.

189. CT 22 74.

190. For a full description of all texts in which Libluṭ occurs, see p. 45ff.

of our text.[191] Analogous registers existed for the recruitment of charioteers, ^{lú}*šá-da-e-ti*-workers, and temple-prebendaries.[192]

Strictly speaking, BM 30446 does not belong to MNA's archive because MNA is not mentioned in it.[193] However, it was written by a scribe who is well attested in texts from his archive: [...]/Kalbaya//Šumu-libši. This was, no doubt, Bēl-erība/Kalbaya//Šumu-libši.[194] The latter followed MNA's business affairs very closely, especially those that were related to taxes, draftees, and boat transports, by writing four agreements for him and being present as a witness at eleven others.[195] Bēl-erība's interest in these state-related matters is easily explained. Bēl-erība was a commander-of-fifty and was entitled to the services of corvée-workers. In Dûzu of Darius' twenty-fourth year, for instance, he released a man from further compulsory service with him for the next three and a half months (BM 30274). The man's service was related to work in or at boats. Moreover, Bēl-erība may well have recruited his men—or some of them—from the governor's pool of forced laborers. This may explain Bēl-erība's presence at the recruitment of soldiers and workers for the governor of Babylon and it may indicate that he relinquished his rights to the recruited men for the governor's advantage.[196] His interest in the governor's men, especially

191. See commentary at BM 30446: 5. Probably, cf. Dar 290 (= *CM* 20b 190; see n. 179).

192. More on registers in § 3.5.3.

193. Unlike BM 30795, which is very similar to the text under consideration and regards the recruitment of soldiers and/or workers for the governor of Babylon. In BM 30795 MNA is among the witnesses and his presence implies his relinquishment of rights to the recruited men.

194. Theoretically, it could have been any of his brothers, either Nergal-ēṭir, Nidintu, or Arad-Bēl, but, *de facto*, only Bēl-erība is known to have been a scribe.

195. Cf. Table 7 s.v. Name no. 4. Accordingly, he is attested in eighteen texts from MNA's time between Darius' twenty-second and twenty-seventh years as either scribe, witness, or contractant. As said, he wrote BM 30446. In addition, he wrote BM 30795 (26/x/26 Dar), the document regarding the recruitment of Liblut, Rīmūt, and the LÚ *šá-da-e-ti* for the governor of Babylon that was witnessed by MNA; two boat rentals by MNA (BM 30490 and BM 30270, 5–6/xii/26 Dar) and one payment for transport costs by MNA to the governor of Babylon (BM 32891, 11/iv/[26] Dar). Bēl-erība witnessed twelve documents from MNA's archive. Accordingly, he witnessed agreements regarding the delivery of (hired) soldiers and (other) hirelings by MNA (BM 31226, 9/vii/26 Dar; and BM 31449, [-]/[-]/23+ Dar); MNA's receipt of *ilku* for a bridge (BM 30366, 7/viii/26 Dar); another of MNA's *ilku*-receipts (TCL 13 197, 27/viii/26 Dar); his receipt of, among others, a contribution for the *fittings of an archer* (BM 30772, 20/xii/26 Dar); the payment of *ilku* by MNA on behalf of a third party (TCL 13 198, 11/i/27 Dar); the transfer of silver by MNA to a courtier (Dar 544, 12/iv/22+ Dar) and Bēl-erība's brother (Dar 552, 1/x/22 Dar); the delivery of barley by MNA for the rations of the boatmen of the governor of Babylon (BM 30256, 2/vii/24 Dar); the purchase of boats by MNA (BM 30370, 3–9/v/26 Dar; and BM 30961, 12/vi/26 Dar); and the training of MNA's slave as a baker (BM 41442, 15/xii/26 Dar). Finally, Bēl-erība occurs in BM 30274 (13/iv/24 Dar) as contractant, on which more below.

196. BM 30795. The men in question were the charioteer Liblut, a certain Rīmūt and a group of workers called LÚ *šá-da-e-ti*.

those that could handle boats,[197] may also explain why he was present when MNA paid the governor for a boat transport and for barley-rations for the men on the boat.[198]

There are additional links between BM 30446 and texts from MNA's archive so that its attribution to this archive cannot be doubted. Indeed, three persons among the witnesses in BM 30446 are known from texts from MNA's archive. The first, Kāṣir/Tattannu—probably from the Eppeš-ilī family—witnessed two payments for transport costs by MNA to agents of the governor at the date harvest in Darius' twenty-fifth year.[199] Accordingly, he seems to have been a person involved in the transport of crops by boat after the harvest, and his interest in the recruitment of boat-towers, as recorded in BM 30446, is thus obvious. The same holds for the two sons of Mušēzib-Marduk//Arad-Nergal. Ibnaya, one of them, witnessed the text under consideration; Passasu, his brother, witnessed a debt of MNA that resulted from MNA's exploitation of bridges in Darius' twenty-sixth year.[200] The attestations of Kāṣir/Tattannu and the sons of Mušēzib-Marduk//Arad-Nergal show that the recurrence of men in texts about the recruitment of soldiers and workers, on the one hand, and boat-related transactions, on the other, was not an isolated phenomenon.[201] The third person that is known from MNA's archive and who also occurs in BM 30446 is Mūrānu/Marduk-nāṣir, who probably belonged to the Aḫu-bani family. He paid *ilku* for Darius' twenty-fifth and twenty-sixth years to MNA.[202] His presence among the witnesses at a tax-related transaction—as the recruitment of corvée-workers is—then, is not surprising. As a matter of fact, persons found in MNA's *ilku*-receipts frequently reoccur in his boat-related transactions.[203] This shows that there existed a generic link between both kinds of transactions.

The examination of the witness list of BM 30446 reveals an interesting characteristic of MNA's business. MNA's various economic activities frequently attracted the same people's attention. Thus, the same men occur among the witnesses, scribes, or contractants regardless of whether MNA was recruiting men, organizing the work at bridges, participating in boat transports, or collecting taxes. No doubt, there was a shared common interest in all these

---

197. Is LÚ *šá-da-e-ti* in BM 30795: 10 a misspelling for [lú]*šādidē* "boat-towers"? See commentary at BM 31393: 4.

198. BM 32891 (transport costs) and BM 30256 (rations for boatmen). Moreover, one text seems to confirm the above assumption that Bēl-erība had access to the pool of forced laborers of the governor of Babylon. The text in question is BM 31188. It records the recruitment of a corvée-worker to tow boats for the governor. Previously, this corvée worker had served with a man named Bēl-erība [...] (BM 31188: 4). Should one read Bēl-erība/[Kalbaya//Šumu-libši]? More at note 207 and commentary at BM 31188: 4.

199. BM 30639: 12–13 and BM 31393: 15, dated vii–viii/25 Dar.

200. BM 41443 (see n. 145).

201. Cf., for instance, the witnesses of BM 30274, BM 30795, BM 31226: details at Table 7, esp. p. 112f.

202. BM 31517 and TCL 13 197.

203. Details at Table 7, esp. p. 112f.

transactions, which explains the recurrence of the same men at these miscellaneous transactions.

If necessary, MNA himself recruited corvée-workers to tow boats in Darius' twenty-fourth and twenty-fifth years. Thus, he received "[one c]orvée worker to tow (boats) to the quay" on one occasion (BM 31188) and "one man to tow (boats) to the quay" on another in the course of Darius' twenty-fourth year (BM 32932).[204] These men fell under the administrative responsibility of (*ša qātē*) the governor of Babylon. The same applies to the hirelings that MNA received the next year (BM 30764 and BM 31118).[205] These hirelings were not explicitly "under the authority of the governor of Babylon," but the texts in question leave little doubt in this respect, since they were formulated in exactly the same way as the receipts of boat-towers from the governor's pool of forced laborers. Table 2 below shows the similarity among the four texts.

TABLE 2: Recruitment of Men to Tow Boats

	Text	*Period of Service*	*ša*	*i.q.*	*a.m.*
1	"a hireling to tow (boats)"	6 days a month,[206] till the end of viii/ 25 Dar	PN_1	PN_2	PN_1
2	"⌈a hireling⌉ (to tow boats ?)"	6 days a month, from i/25 till the end of vi/25 Dar	PN_3	PN_3	-
3	"[one c]orvée-worker to tow (boats) to the quay, under the authority of the governor of Babylon"	2 months 2 days	?	PN_4	PN_5
4	"one man to tow (boats) to the quay, under the authority of the governor of Babylon"	2 months (1)2 days	PN_6	PN_7	PN_6

TEXTS: No. 1 = BM 30764; 2 = BM 31118; 3 = BM 31188; and 4 = BM 32932.
ABBREVIATIONS: i.q. = *ina qātē*; a.m. = *ana muḫḫi*.
NAMES: PN_1 = Marduk/Nabû-uṣuršu//Šumu-libši; PN_2 = Nāšibu//Lā-qīpu; PN_3 = Bēl-iddin/Zēriya//Rab-banê; PN_4 = Bēl-uballiṭ/Iddin-Nabû//Bā'iru; PN_5 = Bēl-[...]/Zēriya//MU-[...]; PN_6 = Ḫabaṣīru/Mušēzib-Marduk//Dēkû; and PN_7 = Bēl-iddin/Šuma-iddin//Andaḫar.

---

204. BM 31188, dated 25/[-]/24 Dar: [*ištēn* ^{lú}*u*]*rāšu šadādu ša kāri*; and BM 32932, dated 18/vii/24 Dar: *ištēn* ^{lú}*šadādu ša kāri*. Note that BM 32932 is dated two weeks after BM 30446, which regulated the recruitment of boat-towers, but does not mention MNA.

205. BM 30764 records MNA's receipt of "a hireling to tow (boats)" (^{lú}*agru* ^{lú}*šadīdu*); and BM 31118 his receipt of "a hireling," ($^{[lú]}$⌈*agru*⌉), probably for the same or similar purposes (see commentary *ad hoc* line 1).

206. Since BM 30764 is dated on 23/iii/25 Dar, a period of service ending in viii/25 Dar makes for a five-month period. Cf. BM 31118: from i/25 till the end of vi/25 Dar amounts to six months.

The boat-towers in the four texts under consideration, whether or not they were hired by the person who delivered them, were state property and due to the governor of Babylon. Nevertheless, not the governor, but MNA received the (hired) corvée boat-towers. He also received the register that regulated the compulsory service of one of these men for the month Dûzu.[207] Remarkably, MNA received the men on his own behalf; he did not act "by order of the governor" to receive them in the latter's name.[208] As it is, his right to their service was limited in time; the men were available for a little bit more than two months or for six days a month over a period of approximately half a year.

2.4.2.5. *The Recruitment of Workers* (LÚ.ERIN$_2$.MEŠ)

A fragmentary letter, BM 31438, seems to refer to MNA's collection of funds for equipment (*rikis qabli*) and his recruitment of men. The letter refers to MNA in the third person, so that he was neither the sender nor the recipient of the letter in question. He is said to have come to collect the payments for the *rikis qabli*. He seems to have paid his own share and the recipient of the letter is then urged to pay his share "so that he (MNA) could recruit the men."[209] Moreover, the district governor (LÚ.EN.NAM) had been informed of a problem that seems to have arisen concerning the *šá-di-i*. Perhaps the *šá-di-i* are related to the kind of workers or soldiers called ^{lú}*šá-di-e-ti*, who were to serve with the governor of Babylon together with Libluṭ/Itti-Nabû-balāṭu, the charioteer, and Rīmūt/ Marduk-ušallim//P[aḫā]ru?[210] Possibly these *šá-di-i* or ^{lú}*šá-di-e-ti* were boat-towers (^{lú}*šadīdu*).

2.4.3. *Collection of Payments from Bow-Units* (^{giš}*qaštu*)

In order to facilitate the collection of taxes, the royal administration set up socially homogeneous tax-units of ten people, called "group of ten" (*ešertu*) or "bow of so-and-so" (^{giš}*qaštu ša* PN).[211] Accordingly, members of the same social class were organized in groups of ten, which often included members of the same family, profession, or both. The group was headed by a person who was a *primus inter pares* and after whom the bow-unit was named. He may have been

---

207. BM 31188: 3–5, *adi lē'i maḫrî ša* ^{iti}*Dûzu* ⸢x x⸣ *Bēl-*⸢*erība*⸣ *mār* [...] *ša šanat* 24^{kam} *Darius*. The text is partly broken at this place so that it is not clear whether it refers to the corvée of Dûzu that was to be performed by Bēl-⸢erība⸣/[Zēriya//MU-...], or the corvée that was to be performed for Bēl-⸢erība⸣/[Kalbaya//Šumu-libši]. See more at the commentary at BM 31188: 4.

208. For a similar *argumentum a silentio*, see above p. 21.

209. The recruitment of the men is referred to by the verb *esēru*: LÚ.ERIN$_2$.MEŠ *līsir* (BM 31438 Rev. 2).

210. According to BM 30795.

211. Idea put forward and defended by Jursa, *Bēl-rēmanni*, 99–110. The term *ḫišāru* may also have referred to a group of "ten" (*Ibidem*, n. 440).

identical with the official known as *rab ešerti*.[212] One person, probably the head of the group, collected from its members the silver that was needed to meet the group's obligations. When the obligations included active service, such as going to Elam to work, the group could hire workmen to do the work and pay them from the silver collected from its members.[213] The function of collector rotated among the members of the group.

A well-documented example of such a group of ten is the bow-unit that was named after Bēl-rēmanni of Sippar. It included free citizens (*mār banê*), prebendaries in the Ebabbar, and members of families who held administrative functions in the Ebabbar and belonged to the urban elite of Sippar. These people were Bēl-rēmanni's relatives, friends, colleagues, business partners, and perhaps also neighbors. They frequently appear in texts from his archive. Jursa suggests that this socially homogeneous group of wealthy citizens was taxed by the state because of its members' urban wealth (esp. houses?).[214]

Texts from the time of MNA contain additional information on "bows" and the collection of taxes from these corporate entities.[215] The archive mentions four such bow-units. Table 3 below summarizes the information given by the texts on these bow-units: the name of the bow-unit, the amount of silver or flour that was paid on account of the bow-unit, the names of the persons who paid the silver or flour, the names of those who received these contributions, and the ultimate destination of the silver collected.

2.4.3.1. *MBU and the "Bow-unit of Bēl-iddin/Nabû-zēra-ušabši"*[216]

Bēl-iddin, son of Nabû-zēra-ušabši, was a member of the "bow-unit of Bēl-iddin," a tax-unit named for him. He or members of his family are attested together with MBU, MNA's senior slave, in six texts between the second half of Darius' eleventh and the end of his seventeenth year.[217] One of these texts deals

---

212. For *rab qašti* and *bēl ḫanšê* in this context, see Jursa, *Bēl-rēmanni*, 104.

213. For examples from MNA's archive on men hired to serve the state, see, e.g., BM 30764, BM 31118, BM 31226, and BM 31449; perhaps also BM 30853: 1–5. See also discussion at Dar 154 and the texts discussed at § 2.2. Such hirelings may also have been called "substitutes" (*kutallû*), e.g., Dar 430.

214. Jursa, *Bēl-rēmanni*, 103.

215. The present chapter discusses only those texts that refer to "bow-units" (^{giš}*qaštu*). On the collection of *ilku* and *rikis qabli* from members of the same family and/or profession but without mentioning "bow-units," see § 2.1.1. and § 2.4.4.

216. On Bēl-iddin and his obligations vis-à-vis the state, see already Van Driel, *JESHO* 32, 211f., who based his study on the following texts: Dar 308, Dar 400, Dar 438, Dar 452, and Dar 459. Collation of the texts showed that Bēl-iddin's wife was called ^{f}Qunnabi (not ^{f}Qunnatu): Dar 400: 8, ^{f}*qu-un-na-bi**; Dar 452: *passim*, ^{f}*qu-un-na-bi*; and Dar 459: 8, ^{f}*qu-⸢un*-na*-bi**⸣. Consequently, Dar 438, which mentions one ^{f}*qu-un-na-tu*$_4$, should be excluded from the discussion. Furthermore, I found a new text that can be added to the group of texts regarding Bēl-iddin and his obligations: BM 31026. For parallels to the case of Bēl-iddin from the Egibi archive, see Wunsch, *MOS Studies* 2, 111f.

217. Dar 308 (26/vii/11 Dar; a loan of silver), BM 31026 (3/v/15 Dar; a payment on account

with silver borrowed by Bēl-iddin from MBU to pay for his *rikis qabli* and the pledge of real estate to secure the repayment of the silver. Two other texts deal with payments on account of the bow-unit of Bēl-iddin. The three remaining texts deal with debts of the wife and son of Bēl-iddin to MBU, some of which were originally due from Bēl-iddin himself.

TABLE 3
Tax Income from Bow-Units in Texts from the Time of MNA

Bow-unit	*amount*	*paid by*
0	⅓ mina of silver, med-⅛	MBU and Iddinaya/Ardiya, on account of Bēl-iddin
1b	½ mina of silver, marked	PN$_1$ and PN$_2$, messengers of PN$_3$, deputy of the menials; includes the contributions of PN$_4$ and PN$_5$.
2	⅔ mina of silver, med-⅛	Iqūpu, brother of Bēl-erība.
3	5.2.5 kor of flour	PN$_6$, on account of Bazūzu and his nine administrators
4	[x] shekels of silver (a partial payment)	PN$_7$

	received by	*for*
1a	PN$_8$, messenger of PN$_9$, deputy	*kurummāte ša* ^{lú}*zargaya ša šanat* 15^{kam}
1b	MBU and Iddinaya/ Ardiya	*kumu kutallûtu ša šanat* 16^{kam}
2	MNA	PN$_{10}$ ^{lú}*sepīru ša* ^{lú}*rēšē*^{meš} *ša muḫḫi kurummmāte ša ekalli ešši*
3	MNA	-
4	MNA	-

Bow-units: No. 1a = "Bow-unit of Bēl-iddin/Nabû-zēra-ušabši" (Text: BM 31026); 1b = Idem (Text: Dar 430); No. 2 = "Bow-unit of Bēl-erība/Nādin//Lūṣi-ana-nūr-Marduk and ^{lú}DI-*pa-ni-šú*" (Text: BM 30589); No. 3 = "Bow-unit of Bazūzu and his ⌜nine⌝ administrators of the scribal$^{!}$ school." This bow-unit is one third of the "bow-unit of the exorcists"(Text: BM 33954); and No. 4 = "Bow-unit [of] Bēl-iddin/Tāqiš//[…]" (Text: BM 31798).

Names: PN$_1$ = Nergal-aḫa-iddin/Nabû-aḫḫē-bulliṭ; PN$_2$ = Nabû-nipšaru/Iqīšaya; PN$_3$ = [Amur]ru-šarra-kīni; PN$_4$ = Madānu-⌜iddin⌝; PN$_5$ = Iddinaya […], messenger of ^{f}Saggaya/ Ea-kīni <><> Iddinaya; PN$_6$ = Libluṭ/Murašû//Sîn-tabni; PN$_7$ = Bēl-iddin/Tāqiš//[…]; PN$_8$ = Nabû-uṣuršu/Rīmūt; PN$_9$ = Amurru-šarra-uṣur$^{!}$; PN$_{10}$ = Bēl-erība (no affiliation).

In the first half of Darius' eleventh year, Bēl-iddin needed silver to meet his *rikis qabli* obligation. He had to supply equipment for the men who were to go to Elam. He borrowed half a mina of silver from MBU—the terms of repayment are regulated in a document from the second half of the year (Dar 308). Bēl-iddin also owed thirty *kor* of dates to MBU in addition to half the mina of silver. He had one year, viz. till the next date harvest, to pay off his debts without incurring interest on the silver. In order to secure the repayment of the silver and dates, Bēl-iddin pledged a grain field and a date grove to MBU; the grain field was located in the vicinity of Šaḫrīnu;[218] no precise location is given for the date grove.

In Ab of Darius' fifteenth year, MBU and Iddinaya/Ardiya paid a sum of silver that was "due from the bow-unit of Bēl-iddin" (BM 31026). This silver was needed to finance the food rations of the [lú]*zargaya*-(work)men in Darius' fifteenth year. It was received by a low-ranking official, "a deputy," who sent his messenger to collect the silver.[219] The silver, however, was not the contribution from MBU and Iddinaya but from Bēl-iddin: it was received "on behalf of Bēl-iddin."[220]

On the same day that MBU and Iddinaya paid for Bēl-iddin's obligations of the current year to the said deputy, Bēl-iddin's wife settled her debts of the previous two years with MBU (Dar 400). She delivered 34.2.3 *kor* of dates to MBU: 16 *kor* from Darius' thirteenth and 18.2.3. *kor* from Darius' fourteenth year. These dates were the produce of a palm-grove that was located within the boundaries of Ḫaṣirātu and two sectors of which belonged to Bēl-iddin. The text does not inform us on how Bēl-iddin's wife became indebted to MBU, nor on how the latter became entitled to the dates from Bēl-iddin's palm-grove. However, we may safely assume that MBU had gained access to Bēl-iddin's palm-grove in Ḫaṣirātu in the same way in which he had gained access to Bēl-iddin's real estate in the vicinity of Šaḫrīnu, as related in Dar 308. Accordingly, we may assume that all these plots of land had been pledged to MBU by Bēl-iddin to secure the repayment of his debts. Some of these debts were the result of loans taken from MBU to meet his *rikis qabli* obligation (e.g., Dar 308),

---

of Bēl-iddin's bow-unit, cf. Dar 430), Dar 400 (3/v/15 Dar; a debt of Bēl-iddin's wife), Dar 430 (30/vi/16 Dar; cf. BM 31026), Dar 452 (22/x/17 Dar; debts of Bēl-iddin's wife and son), and Dar 459 (7/xii/17 Dar; *idem*). Some of the texts were written by the same scribe (Iddin-Nergal/Gimillu//Nappāḫu: Dar 400, Dar 430, Dar 452 and Dar 459), or witnessed by the same persons (e.g., Niqūdu/Nergal-iddin//Nūr-zana in Dar 308, Dar 430, Dar 452 and Dar 459; and Kuṣuraya/Arabbi in Dar 400 and Dar 452). For Iddinaya/Ardiya, first witness in Dar 400, see also BM 31026 and Dar 430, and he may be identified with Iddinaya/Arad-Bēl (see more on this identification in § 2.4.5.1). For Bēl-iddin/Gūzānu//Ea-ṣalam-ilī, sixth witness in Dar 400, see also BM 31976, dated twelve years later (fragmentary text from Šaḫrīnu about two calves, MBU, the farmer of Nergal and the messenger of the *mār abarakku* official). The other witnesses in the Bēl-iddin texts are otherwise unknown.

218. See commentary at Dar 308: 9 (*⸢kap/šaḫ⸣-ri-i-ni*).

219. This messenger, Nabû-uṣuršu/Rīmūt, also wrote the tablet.

220. BM 31026: 6b–11, (silver) ... *ina qātē MBU u Iddinaya/Ardiya ana muḫḫi Bēl-iddin eṭir*.

whereas others may have resulted from advance payments made by MBU on behalf of Bēl-iddin for obligations related to Bēl-iddin's bow-unit (e.g., BM 31026).[221]

A year later, in Ulūl of Darius' sixteenth year, MBU and Iddinaya collected silver from members of the bow-unit of Bēl-iddin (Dar 430). The silver was needed to hire a reservist on behalf of the bow-unit to do service in Darius' sixteenth year.[222] It was collected from Nergal-aḫa-iddin/Nabû-aḫḫē-uballiṭ and Nabû-nipšaru/Iqīšaya, who had been sent by the deputy of the menials, and it included contributions from one Madānu-iddin and the wife of one Iddinaya. She had sent her contribution by means of a messenger who happened to bear the same name as her husband, i.e., Iddinaya.

Bēl-iddin's family remained indebted to MBU at least till the end of Darius' seventeenth year, as appears from two texts (Dar 452 and Dar 459). In Ṭebēt Bēl-iddin's wife and son paid off part of Bēl-iddin's debts to MBU. A month and a half later, they promised to pay a small debt of barley within two months. The text, however, makes clear that several other debts, in their own name as well as in the name of Bēl-iddin, remained unsettled. The reason for the debts is not specified, but in the light of the previously discussed texts, a connection with Bēl-iddin's bow-unit and *rikis qabli* is most likely. These were debts, like the one in Dar 400, that resulted from situations as described in Dar 308 and BM 31026.

In summary, the Bēl-iddin texts show that MBU assisted Bēl-iddin in meeting his obligations vis-à-vis the state and his bow-unit, that he got hold of Bēl-iddin's real estate as collateral for the debts that Bēl-iddin accrued in this manner, and that these debts were transferred to Bēl-iddin's wife and son, probably after his death.

2.4.3.2. *MNA and the "Bow-unit of Bēl-erība and* ^{lú}DI-*pa-ni-šú"*

BM 30589 mentions the "bow-unit of Bēl-erība, son of Nādin, descendant of Lūṣi-ana-nūr-Marduk, and his *administrators*?"[223] The text is dated in Simān of Darius' twenty-sixth year and records MNA's receipt of silver for the *ilku* of the previous year. The silver was paid "on behalf of" the bow-unit of Bēl-erība by Iqūpu, who is explicitly identified as the brother of Bēl-erība. In other words, MNA received silver from the member of a bow-unit to which this member's brother and his administrators? also belonged. Unfortunately, Bēl-erība and

---

221. It is not clear from Dar 400 why Bēl-iddin's wife and not Bēl-iddin himself paid MBU. Bēl-iddin may either have died or gone away to Elam. In the following years his wife and son were held responsible for his "bow"-related debts. Note that Iddinaya/Ardiya, who worked together with MBU in the tax administration of Bēl-iddin's bow-unit according to BM 31026 and Dar 430, is the first witness in Dar 400.

222. According to Van Driel, *JESHO* 32, 211f., the silver was collected to pay for a substitute (*kumu kutallûtu*): assuming that Bēl-iddin had died, someone else had to be found to take Bēl-iddin's place.

223. ^{lú}*qīpānišu* (wr. ^{lú}DI-*pa-ni-šú*), "his administrators." On *qīpānu* (pl. of *qīpu*), see commentary at BM 33954: 5.

Iqūpu from the Lūṣi-ana-nūr-Marduk family are otherwise unknown. Consequently, the details of their relationship with MNA as well as the nature of their bow-unit remain unknown. The silver from this bow-unit was needed to finance the rations that were issued by the New Palace in Darius' twenty-fifth year.[224]

2.4.3.3. *MNA and the "Bow-unit of the Exorcists"*

The third bow-unit that occurs in texts from the time of MNA is that of the exorcists (BM 33954). It fell within the administrative responsibility of the governor of Babylon, and (tax) income from it was "property of the king."[225] The bow-unit of the exorcists had been divided into three sub-units. BM 33954 deals with the contribution of one of these sub-units for Darius' eleventh or twelfth year. This sub-unit, called "the bow-unit of Bazūzu and his nine administrators (*qīpānu*) of the scribal[!] school," was headed by Bazūzu. It consisted of ten people, including Bazūzu, all of whom were administrative officials in the service of the scribal school. It no doubt counted among them men of learning such as scribes and exorcists. The taxation of a group of *qīpānu* is attested also in Sippar, where *ilku* was due from "Ḫabaṣīru/Mušēzib-Marduk//Šangû-Ištar-Bābili *ù qí-pa-ni-šú*."[226] Ḫabaṣīru, who headed the group from Sippar, was a member of a prominent family in Sippar and owned prebends in the Ebabbar temple.

Bazūzu and his men had to deliver wheat meal and barley meal for the king on behalf of their bow-unit to the governor of Babylon; MNA was in charge of its collection.[227] Libluṭ/Murašû//Sîn-tabni promised him to deliver the flour, and the date of delivery was set. A Libluṭ and a Kuššaya assumed warranty for the delivery of the flour. Whereas the latter is unknown, the former was, no doubt, Libluṭ/Itti-Nabû-balāṭu//Sīsî; he is mentioned with full affiliation among the witnesses in the text under consideration. This Libluṭ was one of the governor's charioteers and well known to MNA.[228]

---

224. More on this at p. 83.

225. BM 33954: 2–3, *makkūr šarri ša* [giš]*qašti ša* [lú]*āšipū*[meš] *ša ina qātē Nabû-šuma-ukīn* [lú]*šākin ṭēmi Bābili*.

226. Jursa, *Bēl-rēmanni*, 102 n. 427 and 106 n. 447 (SCT 95). See also BM 30589 (if we read *qí*[!](DI)*-pa-ni-šú*, in line 5, see above at § 2.4.3.2 and commentary *ad hoc*), the unpublished BM 31466 and perhaps also BM 30261 (see commentary at line 1). The latter three texts are from Babylon.

227. If Širku in Dar 244: 2 (wr. [m]*ši-rik-tú*) was actually MNA, we have another example of MNA taking care of the collection of the "king's property," *in casu* 240 *kor* of barley (cf. Wunsch, *MOS Studies* 2, n. 29). The barley in question was collected by one of Širku's (i.e., MNA's?) slaves from Marduk-šuma-iddin, the ..., at the king's harbor and turned over to a third party named Arad-Bēl-ṣarbi/Nūrêa. The slave had to enter the barley in the accounts of the latter and give the receipt to Iqūpu/Bēl-[...], agent of the *mašennu*. Dar 244 was written in Babylon on 26/xii/8 Dar. Its witnesses and scribe are not attested in the texts from MNA's archive. Dar 244 was re-edited by Stolper, *BiMes* 7, 254–56.

228. For the nature of their relationship, see § 2.4.2.1. Also note the presence of Rīmūt/

2.4.3.4. *MNA and the "Bow-unit of Bēl-iddin/Tāqiš"*

The fourth and last bow-unit in texts from the time of MNA is the "bow-unit of Bēl-iddin/Tāqiš//[...]" (BM 31798). The text records MNA's receipt of silver from Bēl-iddin, head of this bow-unit. The payment took place in Dûzu, but the year in which it took place is, unfortunately, broken off. Interestingly, this was only a partial payment. Indeed, the silver that Bēl-iddin paid was "from (*ina*) the bow-unit," which means that it was only part of the sum that had to be paid by members of the unit.[229] Another interesting feature of this text is the presence of three witnesses who are otherwise well attested in texts concerning boats and boat-related expenses. It suggests that there was a vital link between MNA's dealings with tax-income and his dealings with boats and boat-transports.[230]

2.4.4. *The Collection of ilku from Individuals and Groups of Individuals*

As mentioned earlier, there is not a single attestation of MNA's paying *ilku* on his own account, but there is considerable evidence of his receiving such taxes. The only text in which *ilku* is received from MNA concerns *ilku* that was due from Gūzānu/Ḫambaqu//Mandidi and paid by MNA "on behalf of" this Gūzānu.[231] All other texts from the time of MNA that mention *ilku* have MNA as the receiver or collector of the *ilku* rather than its payer. Thus, there are sixteen receipts of *ilku* by MNA[232] and one fragmentary letter addressed to MNA about *ilku*.[233] They were written either in Darius' fifteenth year or between his twenty-fourth and twenty-sixth years, mostly in Šaḫrīnu and occasionally in Šabīlu and Bāb-bitāqu. Fourteen of these sixteen *ilku* receipts are new texts from the British Museum. They reveal an interesting aspect of MNA's involvement in the collection of taxes that until now could not be fully assessed. A closer look at the texts should determine the exact role played by MNA in the collection of this state revenue. Table 4 is a schematic presentation of these texts in chronological order.

Marduk-ušallim(//Paḫāru) among the witnesses in BM 33954. He must have been another of the governor's charioteers, because he was enlisted to do service with the governor of Babylon together with Libluṭ/Itti-Nabû-balāṭu//Sīsî according to BM 30795 (both persons also mentioned in witness list of Liv 20).

229. See more at n. 246.

230. A similar link existed among MNA's *ilku*-receipts, his recruitment of men for compulsory service, and his boat-related transactions. See above at the discussion of BM 30446; additional examples are adduced in Table 7 and discussed on p. 112ff.

231. TCL 13 198.

232. Fourteen new texts from the British Museum: BM 30235, BM 30243, BM 30261, BM 30297, BM 30366, BM 30589 (*ilku* from a bow-unit, hence, discussed in the previous chapter), BM 30772, BM 30819, BM 31227, BM 31322, BM 31517, BM 31533, BM 33926, BM 41607; and in addition, the previously published receipts CTMMA 3 68 and TCL 13 197.

233. BM 31416.

TABLE 4
Schematic Presentation of the *ilku* Receipts and the Letter about *ilku* from MNA's Archive

T.	DATE	$	PERIOD	*ilku ša* PN_1		*ina qātē* PN_2	*a*
1	17/iv/15	✔	- 1/iv?/15	Nabû-ittannu+ Bēl-zēri/[...], Nidinti-Bēl + Balāṭu/[...]	≠	Mukkêa/ [...]// Bēl-eṭēru	-
2	8/iv/24	-	- End xii/24	Rīmūt-Bēl/ Mušēzib-Bēl// Nannaya		Rīmūt-Bēl	-
3	6/viii/24	-	i/24! - End xii 24	Nabû-ittannu/ Bēl-šuma-iškun// Suḫaya		Nabû-ittannu	-
4	16/iv/25	-	i/25 - End xii/25	Nabû-bullissu/ Nabû-ittannu// Sippê(a)	≠	Nabû-ittannu	-
5	7/viii/25	✔	i/25 - End xii/25	Bēl-ušallim + Bēl- ēṭir/Bēl-iqīša// Šangû-Ea	≠	Rīmūt/ Kalbaya	✔
6	1/xii/25	-	- End xii/25	Aplaya + Iddin-Nabû/ Bazūzu//Ašlāku, [...]–Nabû/ Itti-Marduk-balāṭu		Aplaya/ Bazūzu// Ašlāku	-
7	5?/xii/25	-	i/25 - End xii/25	Barsiya/Marduk-šuma-uṣur// Bābūtu		Barsiya	-
8	12/xii/25	-	- End xii/25	Amurru-aḫa-uṣur/Šuma-iddin		Amurru-aḫa-uṣur	-
9	4/[-]/25	-	- End xii/25	Bēl-asûa/ Nabû-iddin// Bābūtu		Bēl-asûa	-
10	25/[-]/25	-	i/25 - End xii/25	Mūrānu/ Marduk-nāṣir// Aḫu-bani and half the *ilku* of / Nuḫšaya		Mūrānu/ Marduk-nāṣir //Aḫu-bani	-

11	5/i/26	-	i/25 - End xii/25	Tattannu/ Nabû-balāssu-iqbu//Bābūtu	≠	Iddin-Nabû/ Aḫḫē-iddin-Marduk	✔
12	20/iii/26	✔	i/25 - End xii/25	Bēl-erība/Nādin // Lūṣi-ana-nūr-Marduk *u* LÚ DI-*pa-ni-šú*	≠	Iqūpu, brother of Bēl-erība	-
13	13/iv/2[6$^{?}$]	-	- End xii/26	Rīmūt-Bēl/ Baniya//Itinnu *ù* DI-*pi-ni-šú*	≠	Nabû-ittannu/ Baniya// Itinnu	-
14	7/viii/26	-	iv/26 - End iii/27	Nabû-nādin-aḫi/ Aplaya	≠	Iddinaya/ Qīštiya	✔
15	27/viii/26	-	i/25 - End xii/26	Mūrānu/ Marduk-nāṣir// Aḫu-bani	≠	Rē'ûšunu-Marduk/ Bēl-apla-uṣur //[...]-aya	✔
16	20/xii/26	-	ix/25 - End i/27	Dummuqu/ Balāṭu//Gaḫul	≠	Nabû-iddin/ Iqūpu// Etel-pî	✔
17	-	-	-	Bēl-iddin ^{lú}*mār Bābili*^{ki} *ša ina bīt* PN *ša ina* ^{uru}*Ḫaḫḫuru ašbi*	-	-	-

Cf. TCL 13 198: dated 11/i/27; period: i/26 - end xii/27; *ilku ša* Gūzānu/Ḫambaqu//Mandidi; paid by MNA on behalf of Gūzānu.

T. = *Texts*: 1 = BM 33926; 2 = BM 41607; 3 = BM 30297; 4 = BM 31322; 5 = BM 30243; 6 = BM 31533; 7 = BM 30819; 8 = CTMMA 3 68; 9 = BM 31227; 10 = BM 31517; 11 = BM 30235, 12 = BM 30589; 13 = BM 30261; 14 = BM 30366; 15 = TCL 13 197; 16 = BM 30772; 17 = BM 31416 (not a receipt, but a letter).

ABBREVIATIONS: *a* = *ana muḫḫi* PN_1, i.e., paid on behalf of PN_1; period = period of the year for which *ilku* was paid; $ = specification of the amount of silver received; ≠ = the person from whom the *ilku* was due is not the same as the one who paid for it.

The *ilku*-receipts from MNA's archive have a uniform structure and formulary.[234] The operative section of the receipts reads: *ilki ša* PN ... MNA *ina qātē* PN *maḫir*, "*ilku* (due) from PN ... MNA has received (it) from PN." All receipts indicate the period of the year for which *ilku* was paid: *ilki ša* PN (*ultu* ...) *adi* (*qīt*) ..., "*ilku* from PN (from ...) till (the end of) ... ."[235] The amount of silver thus received is seldom indicated.[236] Four texts further specify the content of the *ilku*, thus adding, for instance, that it was "*ilku* from PN for additions? to the bridge."[237] When the person from whom *ilku* was due was not the one who made the payment,[238] there is an explicit statement to clarify the situation. In such cases, indeed, the phrase *ana muḫḫi* PN_1 is often inserted before the verb *maḫir*, thus clarifying that the person who paid, namely PN_2, did so on behalf of someone else, namely PN_1. The receipt of *ilku* is occasionally followed by a separate clause on the receipt of *pānāt qašti* or *qēmi* (*šarri*).[239] After the operative section with the statement(s) of receipt, follow the list of witnesses, the name of the scribe, and the place and date of execution. A statement regarding copies of the receipt being taken by each party may be found either at the very end of the document or immediately before the list of witnesses.

Ilku could be paid for various reasons. Texts from outside the Egibi archive show that *ilku* was paid "for (going to) Elam," "for transporting *upiyāta*-contributions (and) for corvée-work at the quay," "for half of the corvée-work," "(for meeting the obligations) of a third of one bow-unit," and in return for a fief.[240] The texts from the time of MNA described above add interesting new

234. Receipts for *ilku* and related taxes from contemporary Borsippa and Sippar are similar in their basic structure, formula and content to the *ilku* receipts from the time of MNA (Joannès, *Borsippa*, 155f., e.g., A 118; Jursa, *Bēl-rēmanni*, 99, e.g., *Bēl-rēmanni*, 210f. = BM 42577). The *ilku*-receipts from the Murašû archive, however, are significantly different, in content as well as in formula. See Cardascia, *Murašû*, 99: the obligation to pay *ilku* was linked to the possession of a fief, the amount of silver that was paid was always specified, and the Murašûs acted as middlemen between the fiefholders, who were subject to the *ilku*-tax, on the one hand, and the foreman (*šaknu*) of the fiefholders, who had to collect the tax before its transfer to the state, on the other hand.

235. The formula either follows the opening statement *ilki ša* PN_1 (BM 30261, BM 30243, BM 30297, BM 30366, BM 30772, BM 30819, BM 31517, BM 33926 and CTMMA 3 68), or is placed immediately after *ilki*, thus breaking up the phrase *ilki ša* PN_1 (BM 30235; BM 30589; BM 31227; BM 31322; BM 31533; BM 41607; TCL 13 197). Other elements may stand between *ilki* and *ša* PN: a specification of the nature of the *ilku* (BM 30366, BM 30589 and BM 31227), or the phrase [*ina našpar*]*tu* PN_x (BM 31533).

236. BM 30243, BM 30589, and BM 33926.

237. BM 30366 (*ilki ša ṭīpi ša gišri ša* PN). See also BM 30772, BM 31227 and BM 30589. Details below.

238. This is indicated as follows in the Table: *ilki ša* $PN_1 \neq$ *ina qātē* PN_2 (see s.v. BM 30235, BM 30243, BM 30261, BM 30366, BM 30589, BM 30772, BM 31322, BM 33926, TCL 13 197; and cf. TCL 13 198).

239. BM 30261, BM 30366, BM 30297 and TCL 13 197. Details below.

240. *Ilki ša* ^{kur}*Elam*^{ki} (*Bēl-rēmanni*, 133 = BM 42302); *ilki mala zitti ša zebēli ša upiyāta ša urāšu ša*

examples. *Ilku* was paid "for corvée-work$^{?!}$ at the bridge in Babylon under the supervision of PN," "for additions$^{?}$ to a bridge," "for ... (and) fittings for the archer," and "on account of the bow-unit [of] PN and his administrators$^{?}$... for Bēl-erība, clerk of the commissioners who are (appointed) over the (administration of the) rations of the New Palace."[241]

Some of the *ilku*-receipts refer to *pānāt qašti* and *qēmi* (*šarri*), but it is not clear whether the latter two payments were in addition to the former or only a further specification of its content. Joannès argues that the *pānāt qašti* and *qēmi šarri* taxes were a part of the *ilku* and not an addition to it.[242] In his opinion, *ilku* is to be understood as a collective term for various service obligations and state-due taxes, among which are also *pānāt qašti* and *qēmi šarri*. Nevertheless, the texts from MNA's archive suggest a different interpretation. A closer look at the structure and formulation of the texts will help clarify the issue:

Sequence of the Clauses and their Formulary in:

BM 30261:	*ilku ... eṭir*	copy clause[243]	*pānāt* ^{giš}*qašti eṭir*	witnesses etc.
BM 30366:	*ilku ... maḫir*	copy clause	*pānāt* ^{giš}[*qašti*] *maḫir*	witnesses etc.
TCL 13 197:	*ilku ... maḫir*	⌜*qēmi*⌝ *ša*$^{!}$ PN ... *maḫir*	copy clause	witnesses etc.
BM 30297:	*ilku ... maḫir*	*qēmišu gammar ... maḫir*	witnesses etc	copy-clause

As can be seen, the *ilku*, *pānāt qašti* and *qēmi* (*šarri*) are mentioned in different parts of the contract and each payment has its own verb of receipt (*maḫir*, *eṭir*). Consequently, they appear as three separate payments: the *ilku* as the main one, and the other two as additional, but distinct payments. The fact that the so-called copy-clause may be inserted between the receipt of the *ilku* and the

---

kāri (L 4720 = *Borsippa*, 257); *ilki ša mišil* ^{lú}*urāšu* (Nbn 962, cited by Jursa, *Bēl-rēmanni*, n. 412); and *ilki šalšu* 1 ^{giš}*qašti* (BM 64049, unpublished, cited by Jursa, *Bēl-rēmanni*, 100).

241. *Ilki ... ša urāšu*$^{?!}$ *ša gišir Bābili*^{ki} *ša ina qātē* PN (BM 31227; cf. Sippar text BM 74601 cited by Jursa, *Bēl-rēmanni*, n. 412); *ilki ša ṭīpi*$^{?}$ *ša gišri* (BM 30366); [*il*]*ki*! DI-*pi šá* GIM (= *ṭīpi ša* $^{<\text{giš}>}$*qašti*$^{?}$) *ú-na-at* ^{lú}*qašti* (BM 30772); and *ilki ... ana muḫḫi* ^{giš}*qašti* [*ša*] PN *u* ^{lú}DI(*qí*$^{?}$)*-pa-ni-šú ... maḫir kaspi ana Bēl-erība* ^{lú}*sepīru ša* ^{lú}*rēšī*^{meš} *ša muḫḫi kurummāte ša ekalli ešš*[*u* (x x)] (BM 30589).

242. See Joannès, *Borsippa*, 151ff. Joannès's opinion is mainly based on the evidence from L 4720 = *Borsippa*, 257 (*ilki mala zittišu ša zebēli ša upiyāta ša* ^{lú}*urāšu ša kāri u pānāt qašti u ḫišāru*). In my opinion, however, the text L 4720 lists three different taxes and uses the conjunction *u* to link between them: the *ilku*, ..., *u pānāt qašti u ḫišāru*, i.e., the *ilku*-tax, the *pānāt qašti*-tax and the *ḫišāru*-tax. As for the *ilku*-tax, the text further specifies its content; it is the *ilku* "of (=*ša*) transporting *upiyāta*, (and) of (=*ša*) corvée-work at the quay." Accordingly, L 4720 refers to the obligation to pay *ilku*, and (*u*) to *pānāt qašti u ḫišārū* "the duty of the bow and ten-men," i.e., the duties of men who are organized in "bow-units" and other "groups of ten." For a plausible interpretation of the word *ḫišāru*, see Jursa, *Bēl-rēmanni*, n. 440.

243. The so-called copy clause is the clause stating that "They have taken one (copy of the document) each" (*ištēnā* (*šaṭāru*) *ilteqû*).

receipt of *pānāt qašti* or *qēmi* (*šarri*) further stresses the distinctiveness of the taxes. This clause is typically the final clause of the operative section of Neo-Babylonian legal documents. Accordingly, it is usually found after the main transaction and before the list of witnesses, or at the very end of the document.

The amount of silver that was paid for the *ilku*-tax is specified in only three receipts. Thus, four persons paid one hundred and twenty shekels of marked silver for one year.[244] Bēl-erība and his *administrators*? paid forty shekels of medium-quality silver with a one-eighth percentage of alloy for one year; and two brothers paid twenty-one shekels of the same quality for one year.[245] We cannot determine from this evidence how much one person had to pay annually as *ilku*, because the texts do not afford a uniform picture in this respect. Indeed, the quality of the silver differs from one text to another, as well as the amount of people involved in each case. The fact that most texts do not specify how much exactly had been paid for the *ilku* does not mean that all persons had to pay the same sum, so that there was no need to specify its amount in the text. It is more likely that there was no fixed or standard rate for the *ilku*, and that the amount due depended on personal, professional, and social variables.

It is possible that the texts specified the amount of silver that was paid for the *ilku*-tax when the payment was overdue or when it was a payment from part of the group, not the entire group.[246] It is, indeed, remarkable that two of the three receipts with specification of the amount concerned overdue payments.[247] The only other *ilku* text recording a delayed payment is BM 30235, and the amount is not specified, but in this case there was only a five-day, hence negligible delay. Moreover, the three receipts that contain a specification of the amount of silver that was paid as *ilku*, concern the *ilku* from individuals who belonged to the same group, so that the exact amount paid may have been specified in these cases in order to avoid discussion among the members of the group about who paid what.

By way of comparison, we may adduce evidence from Borsippa, Sippar, and Nippur. In the texts from Borsippa and Sippar the amount paid for *ilku* or similar duties was usually not indicated.[248] A few striking exceptions are a case

---

244. BM 33926. In fact, the text is slightly damaged where the amount of silver is given, and it is not excluded that one has to read one mina instead of two minas. See commentary *ad hoc*.

245. BM 30589 and BM 30243.

246. Possibly, also when it concerned a payment for only part of the year rather than one full year, but since no such payments are known from the MNA texts (all payments were for a full year and for the entire *ilku* and not part of it; except for BM 31517, see more at n. 255), this cannot be proven. For a partial payment from a "bow-unit," see BM 31798: the text specified the amount of silver paid. See also the evidence from Borsippa and Sippar adduced below.

247. BM 33926 and BM 30589. In BM 30243, where the amount of silver paid for the *ilku* is specified, but the payment was in time, the other explanation may apply.

248. E.g., *Ilku*-payments from Borsippa: L 4720 (= *Borsippa*, 257) and A 118 (= *Borsippa*, 279f.).

of *ilku* for only one month and at least two cases of a payment for taxes from only part of the group that was subject to the payment.[249] This evidence seems to confirm the contention formulated above that the need to specify the amount arose particularly when the payment was partial, i.e., when it concerned either only part of the year or part of the group. In Nippur the situation was different. In the Murašû texts the amount was almost always specified and varied between ten shekels and seventeen minas, depending on the kind of land for which the *ilku* was being paid.

The *ilku* receipts from MNA's time always specify for which year *ilku* was being paid. This is done by means of the formula "from ... till ...," or its shorter version: "till ...." In most cases the *ilku* was paid for one year. There are two examples of *ilku* being paid for two years and one example of *ilku* for sixteen months.[250] The fiscal year was usually counted from Nisan till the end of Addar; two texts counted from Dûzu till the end of Simān,[251] and one from Kislīm till the end of Nisan more than a year later.[252] Counting *ilku* for one year, from Nisan till the end of Addar, as is the case in most texts from the Egibi archive, was standard practice in the Murašû texts from the late Persian period.[253] Counting *ilku* from Dûzu till the end of Simān, as in BM 30366 and BM 33926, is unparalleled in contemporary texts; it is close to, though not identical with, the practice known from Borsippa, where the tax-year started in Simān.[254] It

---

Cf. payments for *urāšu* and similar duties in the texts from Borsippa cited by Joannès, *Borsippa*, 155–56. For evidence from Sippar, see Jursa, *Bēl-rēmanni*, 197 = BM 42548 (^{giš}*qaštu*).

249. L 1643 (*Borsippa*, 241f.), Borsippa: *ilku* for one month (cf. Joannès, *Borsippa*, 156). BM 64049 (unpublished, cf. Jursa, *Bēl-rēmanni*, 100, 105f., 109), Sippar: payment for *ilku* by one-third of the group (*ša šalšu* 1 ^{giš}*qašti*); *Bēl-rēmanni*, 151 = BM 42352, Sippar: payment for ^{giš}*qaštu* by certain members of the group (*mala zitti*), explicitly excluding others ([*elat z*]*itti*, lines 11–12); and probably also VS 4 126 = (*Bēl-rēmanni*, 262): *pas'adu*, *pūt zitti* of PN, i.e., the share of one specific person. Other exceptions are TUM 2/3 218 (*urāšu*, Joannès, *idem*, 158), and *Bēl-rēmanni*, 210f. = BM 42577 (*ilku* [of P]N): these two receipts, however, are very fragmentary. Read in *Bēl-rēmanni*, 210f. (= BM 42577): 2, *pūt*/*mala zitti* and compare to *Bēl-rēmanni*, 151 (= BM 42352) and VS 4 126 (= *Bēl-rēmanni*, 262)?

250. TCL 13 197 and TCL 13 198 (two years); BM 30772 (sixteen months). BM 30772 is unique among the *ilku* receipts from the time of MNA for two reasons. First, it counts sixteen months instead of just one year. Second, it starts counting from Kislīm instead of starting from Nisan or Dûzu.

251. BM 30366 ("from Dûzu year 26 till the end of Simān year 27") and BM 33926 ("till the first of Dûzu year 15").

252. BM 30772 (*ilku* for sixteen months), which, as pointed out above (see note 250), is exceptional among the *ilku* receipts in more than one way.

253. See Cardascia, *Murašû*, 100f. See also BM 64049 from Sippar (*ilku* for Darius' fourteenth year), cited by Jursa, *Bēl-rēmanni*, 105f.; and Stolper, *BaM* 21 No. 17 (*ilku* for Artaxerxes' eighth year).

254. E.g., NRVU 569: receipt of payment for specific work-assignments "from the first of Simān of Darius' thirty-second year till the end of Ayyar of Darius' thirty-third year." Probably also in L 4720 (= *Borsippa*, 257), where various obligatory public services were

seems to have been possible to pay in installments,[255] although annual payments appear to have been the rule in Babylon at the time of MNA.

The payments of *ilku* to MNA were usually on time, i.e., before the end of the tax-year. Accordingly, MNA collected the *ilku* for Darius' twenty-fifth year after four months, eight months, or at the very end of the year.[256] Taxes for Darius' twenty-fourth and twenty-sixth years were collected according to a similar pattern, i.e., collection in the fourth and the eighth month, or toward the end of the year.[257] When viewed in terms of agriculture, it follows from the evidence adduced above that *ilku* was usually paid either a month or so after the barley harvest or at the end of the date harvest.[258] Consequently, it is very likely that the *ilku* was paid in freshly harvested barley or dates rather than in silver. In other words, the payments of *ilku* to MNA were probably payments *in natura* rather than cash payments.

Payment of the *ilku* to MNA, however, could also be overdue, from a few days to several months.[259] In the case of overdue payments from the part of the

---

accounted for "from <Simān>$^{?}$ of Darius' twenty-first year till the end of Ayyar of Darius' twenty-fifth year."

255. BM 31517 records the payment of *ilku* "from Nisan of the twenty-fifth year of King Darius till the end of Addar of the twenty-fifth year," but in addition refers to "half the *ilku*" (*mišil ilki*). This may be compared to the expression *mišil šattišu ša šanat* 20[+$^{?.kam}$] in a text from the Bēl-rēmanni archive (*Bēl-rēmanni*, 197 = BM 42548: 3) from approximately the same time (3/vi/20[+$^{?}$] Dar). Similar cases are attested in contemporary Borsippa. Thus, in Borsippa payments for *urāšu* and *pānāt qašti* could be either "from Simān till the end of Araḫsamna" (= first half of the year), or "from Kislīm till the end of Ayyar" (= second half of the year), e.g., TUM 2/3 220–22. A standard counting unit of six months may have been in use for the collection of taxes in Borsippa after Darius' twenty-ninth year (Joannès, *Borsippa*, 151). Indeed, the evidence from the years Dar 29–34 shows that taxes were collected for a half year, one and a half year, or two and a half years. It was also possible to pay taxes on a monthly basis in Borsippa (e.g., TCL 13 173 = *Borsippa*, 316 and *Borsippa*, 241f. = L 1643), but there is no evidence of this practice from MNA's archive.

256. Payments for the *ilku* of Darius' twenty-fifth year made in time are: BM 31322 (16/iv/25), BM 30243 (7/viii/25), BM 31533 (1/xii/25), BM 30819 (5$^{?}$/xii/25) and CTMMA 3 68 (12/xii/25). The month in BM 31227 and BM 31517 is, unfortunately, broken off, but these were payments for the *ilku* of Darius' 25th year made in that same year. For overdue payments, see below.

257. Payments for the *ilku* of Darius' twenty-fourth year made in time are: BM 41607 (8/iv/24) and BM 30297 (6/viii/24). For the *ilku* of Darius' twenty-sixth year, see BM 30261 (13/iv/2[6], unless one has to read year 2[7] and the payment was, accordingly, overdue; see below). For the *ilku* of Darius' twenty-fifth and twenty-sixth years, see TCL 13 197 (27/viii/26); and for that of the following two years, see TCL 13 198 (11/i/27 Dar, i.e., at the beginning of the second year). Similarly, in BM 30366, where *ilku* is paid after four months; and BM 30772, where *ilku* is paid at the very end of the seventeen-month period.

258. Barley was harvested in late Nisan–Ayyar (i–ii); dates in Tašrīt–Araḫsamna (vii–viii), cf. Landsberger, *JNES* 8, 248–97; and Cocquerillat, *Palmeraies*, 28f., 33f. and 62f.

259. The taxpayer was five days overdue in BM 30235 (5/i), seventeen days in BM 33926 (17/iv$^{?}$), and three months in BM 30589 (20/iii). If BM 30261 is to be dated in Darius' twenty-seventh year, the payment was four months overdue (13/iv).

taxpayer, the debt to MNA, however, was converted into silver and the exact amount to be paid was specified in the text.[260] One finds a parallel for this practice of converting overdue tax payments into silver in a contemporary text from Sippar. According to *Bēl-rēmanni*, 251f. (= BM 79128), a certain Nidintu borrowed silver to pay for various taxes. In Simān his creditor agreed that the debt be paid in dates in another four months. Thus, Nidintu had time till the end of the date harvest in Araḫsamna to pay his debt. Apparently, he had been unable to pay in Simān, i.e., after the barley harvest, and was granted additional time till Araḫsamna, i.e., after the date harvest. However, in case Nidinti did not pay his debt by then, his debt would be converted into a debt of silver.[261]

A similar timetable for the collection of *ilku* and analogous taxes seems to have been in effect in other cities in Babylonia during the Neo-Babylonian and Persian periods. Indeed, receipts from Borsippa, Sippar, Uruk, and Nippur show that taxes, when collected for one year or more, were usually paid on time, with a clear preference for payment in the second half of the year.[262] Overdue payments were not uncommon.[263] There are, however, two remarkable differences between the texts from MNA's time and some texts from outside Babylon. The first difference concerns the existence of advance payments in the texts from Nippur and Borsippa, whereas such payments are not attested in the text from MNA's time.[264] The second difference regards interim payments and their

260. See above (p. 68) on the specification of the amount of silver that had to be paid on account of the *ilku* when the payment was overdue.

261. *Bēl-rēmanni*, 251f. (= BM 79128): 26f. (commentary *ad hoc*). It should be further noted that *Bēl-rēmanni*, 251f. regards a late reimbursement: the taxes for which Nidintu had borrowed silver were those of Darius' seventeenth year, whereas the text is dated in Darius' nineteenth year.

262. From Sippar: *pasa'du* for Darius' ninth year paid on 6/xii/9 Dar (VS 4 126 = *Bēl-rēmanni*, 262). From Borsippa: *urāšu* for one and a half years paid after one year (TUM 2/3 220, *urāšu* and *pānāt qašti*) or two months before the end of the period (TUM 2/3 222); *urāšu* for two and a half years collected four and a half months before the end of the period (TUM 2/3 221); and *urāšu* for two months paid a week before the end of the second month (TCL 13 173 = *Borsippa*, 316). From Uruk: *ilku* for Artaxerxes' eighth year was paid on 12+/xi/⌜8⌝ Artaxerxes, i.e., toward the end of the tax-year. From Nippur, see Cardascia, *Murašû*, Table on p. 101 n. 3: Usually between Tašrīt and Araḫsamna.

263. From Borsippa: *ilku* together with other taxes till the end of Ayyar paid two months overdue (L 4720 = *Borsippa*, 257); *urāšu* for one year paid nine months overdue (NRVU 569). From Nippur (See Cardascia, *Ibidem*): delays from a few days up to six months (e.g., taxes for the fifth year paid on 23/v/6, and taxes for the fourth year paid on 10/vi/5). From Sippar: ^{giš}*qaštu* for Darius' seventeenth year paid in the course of Darius's twentieth year (*Bēl-rēmanni*, 151 = BM 42352).

264. In Nippur, advance payments for yearly taxes: the "royal army tax (*ṣāb šarri*)" for the sixth year was paid on 20/xii/5 and a tax for the seventh year was paid on 14/xii/6. In Borsippa, advance payments for monthly taxes or services: the *ilku* for Ab was paid five weeks in advance (*Borsippa*, 241f. = L 1643, 23/iii/9 Dar). Cf. Dar 220 from Babylon (dated 6/ii/7 Dar; Egibi-related text, but not part of the main Egibi archive): *rikis qabli* for Darius' eighth year paid in the beginning of Darius' seventh year.

timetable. In Borsippa certain taxes, *urāšu* in particular, could be paid in six-month installments. When this was the case, payment could not be delayed and occurred as soon as a few days and not later than one and a half months after the beginning of the first month.[265]

Generally speaking, the role of MNA in the sixteen *ilku* receipts under consideration is that of a receiver. MNA is the subject of the verb *maḫir / eṭir*, and thus the receiver of the payment. This is remarkable because we know that *ilku* and similar taxes were, in origin at least, nominally due to the crown. These were taxes the income of which had to go to the royal treasury, to finance the salaries of its dependents and the rations of its soldiers and workers in far-off places such as Elam. In BM 30589, for instance,[266] *ilku* was levied to finance the rations of the New Palace and registered in the accounts of Bēl-erība "clerk of the commissioners who (were appointed) over the (administration of the) rations of the New Palace."

2.4.5. *Role of MNA and MBU in the Collection of State Income from Taxes and Services*[267]

The texts discussed above, in which MNA and MBU collected taxes, tolls, and men for compulsory service raise questions on the role that MNA and MBU played in the Babylonian tax system in the early Persian period. MNA and MBU seem to have been entitled, at least to some degree, to the state's income from taxes, corvée, and conscription, because they were the persons who received this state income in the first instance. In fact, they did not act "by order of" or "as proxy for" any state official,[268] so that we may conclude that they received it in their own name.[269] However, we need to examine the reason MNA and MBU received this state income and the extent to which they could use it for their own benefit. This is especially complex in those cases in which the texts explicitly say that the taxes or conscripts that MNA received were nominally

---

265. Details at n. 255 and n. 262. This information from Borsippa on part-time payments might help in reconstructing *Bēl-rēmanni*, 197 = BM 42548 from Sippar. The latter text records the receipt of *ilku* for half a year on 3/vi. Unfortunately, the text does not say whether this relates to *ilku* for the first or the second half of the year, and the year in question is, moreover, partly broken. Nevertheless, *Bēl-rēmanni*, 197 = BM 42548 may well record the payment of *ilku* for the second half of Darius' 20[+]th year on 3/vi/20[+], i.e., payment after three days, in view of the parallels from Borsippa.

266. Additional examples may be found at Jursa, *Bēl-rēmanni*, 106–9 with literature.

267. Previous (partial) assessments of MNA's role in the Persian tax system at Van Driel, *JESHO* 32, 211f., Wunsch, *MOS Studies 2*, 111ff., and Jursa, *Bēl-rēmanni*, 105. They point out that MNA may have acted as a tax-farmer who collected taxes after paying a fixed amount of silver to the state (*Steuerpacht*), or as a "banker" who gave taxpayers the credit they needed to pay for their taxes (*Zwischenfinanzierung*).

268. BM 31533 seems to be an exception (see below p. 82f.).

269. For the use of such arguments *a silentio*, see above p. 21 and p. 57.

due to the state.[270] Did MNA and MBU have to transfer what they collected to the state or could they use it for their own purposes, and if so, on which basis did the state relinquish its rights over this income to MNA or MBU? MNA's and MBU's role in the collection of state income from compulsory payments and services was, no doubt, complex and variable from case to case.

2.4.5.1. *The Role of MBU*

We start with MBU and his role in the collection of taxes from private persons, *in casu* Bēl-iddin and members of his bow-unit. As pointed out above, six texts document the relationship between MBU and Bēl-iddin between Darius' eleventh and seventeenth year.[271] According to these texts, MBU lent silver to Bēl-iddin to pay for his *rikis qabli* (Dar 308), paid the taxes that Bēl-iddin owed on account of his bow-unit (BM 31026), and collected silver from members of this bow-unit (Dar 430). Bēl-iddin's family remained indebted to MBU at least till Darius' seventeenth year (Dar 400, Dar 452 and Dar 459).

Clearly, MBU used his skills and his resources to manage the personal financial affairs of Bēl-iddin. Thus, he helped Bēl-iddin pay his taxes. His assistance to Bēl-iddin took two forms. He either lent silver to Bēl-iddin to pay for his *rikis qabli* (Dar 308) or made an advance payment on Bēl-iddin's behalf (BM 31026). In the latter case, we must assume that he later recuperated the silver from Bēl-iddin, although this stage is not explicitly attested.

MBU's financial management of Bēl-iddin's affairs turned out to be a lucrative business. As a result of his loan and advance payment, he gained access to real estate that belonged to Bēl-iddin, his debtor. According to Dar 308, MBU had access to his debtor's grain field in the vicinity of Šaḫrīnu, as well as one of his palm-groves in the course of Darius' eleventh year. According to Dar 400, MBU was entitled to the produce from two sectors of a palm-grove in Ḫaṣirātu in the course of Darius' thirteenth and fourteenth years. Finally, in Darius' seventeenth year MBU was entitled to barley and dates from Bēl-iddin's family (Dar 452 and Dar 459). Clearly, MBU's interest in granting credit to Bēl-iddin lay in the possibility of gaining control of his debtor's resources through pledge and of using his debtor's agricultural yields (probably manpower as well) for his own benefit. The indebted tenant of the fields and his family were now obliged to deliver part of the harvest to MBU, and may also have been obliged to fulfil certain work assignments for him.

MBU also used his skills and resources to manage the financial affairs of the bow-unit to which Bēl-iddin belonged. Thus, he managed the collection of taxes from members of Bēl-iddin's bow-unit on behalf of the state in Darius' sixteenth year. In this function he is attested in Dar 430. In the latter text he received silver from two men who had been sent to him by the deputy of the menials with the

270. TCL 13 196 (*bīt qīpti ša* PN, governor of Babylon), BM 33954 (*makkūr šarri* and *ša ina qātē* PN, governor of Babylon), BM 30589 (*ana* PN, state official [*nadnu*]), BM 31188 and BM 32932 (*ša qātē ša* PN, governor of Babylon).

271. Details at § 2.4.3.1.

contributions of several bow-members. The silver that MBU thus received was needed to hire someone who could serve on behalf of the bow-unit of Bēl-iddin.

MBU may actually have belonged to the bow-unit of Bēl-iddin, which he managed. In order to verify this matter the social composition of this bow-unit needs analyzing in more detail. Was it a unit of wealthy citizens, comparable to the bow-unit of Bēl-rēmanni of Sippar? It would, of course, be rather surprising if it turned out that Bēl-iddin's bow-unit was one of wealthy citizens, whereas MBU, who financially assisted these members and managed their unit, was only a slave. In other words, MBU could only be a member of the bow-unit of Bēl-iddin if this unit consisted of a group of persons of servile status.

Two elements in the Bēl-iddin texts allow us to obtain an insight into the socio-economic structure of Bēl-iddin's bow-unit.[272] The first element is the fact that Bēl-iddin turned to a slave for financial assistance. Hence, he could hardly have been a wealthy citizen. If he were a wealthy citizen, albeit temporarily in need of credit, he would have turned to his fellow wealthy citizens for assistance rather than to a slave.[273] Moreover, he remained in debt for a relatively long period of time. His debts, which dated from Darius' eleventh year, or perhaps even earlier, were still partly unpaid at the end of Darius' seventeenth year. This prolonged inability of Bēl-iddin and his family to settle their debts confirms their fundamentally poor financial situation.

The second decisive element in determining the socio-economic structure of Bēl-iddin's bow-unit is the repeated occurrence of a deputy of menials in connection with taxes from this unit.[274] In Dar 430 the deputy of the menials sent his messenger to MBU and Iddinaya in order to give them the silver that had been collected from several bow-members. In BM 31026 another deputy sent his messenger to MBU and Iddinaya in order to collect from them the silver that was due from Bēl-iddin and his bow-unit for the rations of the *zargaya*-(work)men. It appears, therefore, that the deputy of the menials was responsible for collecting contributions from the menials under his supervision. He may have been a menial himself, temporary head of the group and responsible for the collection of contributions from the other menials. In Darius' fifteenth year one Amurru-šarra-uṣur functioned as deputy, whereas a year later one Amurru-šarra-kīni had taken over the job.[275] This accords with the theory put

272. Note that neither Bēl-iddin nor his father are attested in texts other than the ones discussed above (but also see at n. 93). It is, therefore, difficult to get a clear idea of Bēl-iddin's social status, profession, or connections with the Egibi family.

273. Bēl-iddin borrowed silver from MBU and not from MNA. The texts from MNA's archive generally distinguish between a person's debts to MNA and those to MBU (e.g., Bēl-upaḫḫir/Nergal-iddin and his debts to MNA, NAB and MBU, in Dar 509 and related texts). It is true that at some point after Darius' twentieth year MBU's credits were "inherited" by MNA, his master.

274. Dar 430: 7, ^{lú}*šanû ša* ^{lú}*kinattu*; cf. "deputy" (^{lú}*šanû*) in BM 31026: 6.

275. Amurru-šarra-uṣur is the "deputy" in BM 31026; Amurru-šarra-kīni is the "deputy of the menials" in Dar 430.

forward by M. Jursa, according to which the role of collector rotated among the members of the bow-unit.

The two facts adduced above allow for the following conclusions regarding the socio-economic status of the "bow-unit of Bēl-iddin." It was a group of menials, or persons "of servile status attached to a household, doing agricultural and other work under supervision."[276] The unit was supervised by a deputy who acted as temporary head of the group and may have been a menial himself. Tax-related affairs were managed by MBU and Iddinaya/Ardiya, his colleague. Several of the bow-members are known by name. Thus, we know two deputies by name, Amurru-šarra-uṣur and Amurra-šarra-kīni; the two persons sent by these deputies, Nergal-aḫa-iddin/Nabû-aḫḫē-bulliṭ and Nabû-nipšaru/Iqīšaya; Madānu-iddin, whose contribution of a few shekels of silver was handed over by the deputy of the menials to MBU and Iddinaya/Ardiya; and a certain Iddinaya, whose wife ᶠSaggaya was in charge of his contributions to the unit and sent her messenger (also named Iddinaya) to the deputy with her husband's contribution of five or so shekels.[277] It would seem that MBU and Iddinaya/Ardiya were also members of the bow-unit of Bēl-iddin (see below) so that the total of bow-members known by name amounts to eight.

This bow-unit was, therefore, very different in its socio-economic structure from that of wealthy citizens and prebendaries to which Bēl-rēmanni belonged. The organization of workmen and specialized craftsmen in tax-units, however, is not an isolated phenomenon. Two analogous examples may be cited from other places. A late Achaemenid text from Uruk records the payment of half a mina of silver by three persons to the head of their unit. The unit in question consisted of "craftsmen, silver workers who are in Uruk and the surroundings of Uruk."[278] The head of the unit was also chief craftsman. Half the mina that he collected from his fellow craftsmen was half the sum that the unit had to pay for the *ilku*-tax of one year. Similarly, we hear about ten handicraftsmen from Sippar who had to perform the *kanšu*-service, and five *ērib bīti* from Sippar who received dates for their *kanšu*-donkeys.[279]

The above conclusion is further supported by prosopographic evidence. A closer look at the eight individuals who were mentioned in connection with the bow-unit of Bēl-iddin reveals that three of them were, indeed, persons of servile status and, moreover, attached to the household of MNA.

---

276. *CAD* K s.v. *kinattu*.

277. The example of ᶠSaggaya taking care of her husband's bow-tax is, of course, interesting because it clarifies the occurrence of ᶠQunnabi, wife of Bēl-iddin in Dar 400, Dar 452, and Dar 459. When a man who belonged to a bow-unit was absent for one reason or another (death, journey abroad?), his wife had to take care that his share of the bow-related taxes was being paid.

278. Stolper, *BaM* 21 No. 17.

279. Jursa, *Bēl-rēmanni*, 100 (Nbn 237 and *Bēl-rēmanni*, 147 = BM 42347).

The first person to consider in this respect is Iddinaya/Ardiya. As pointed out above, he worked together with MBU in the tax administration of the bow-unit of Bēl-iddin. Thus, he and MBU paid silver to the deputy of the menials on behalf of Bēl-iddin.[280] On the same day he witnessed the receipt of dates by MBU from Bēl-iddin's wife.[281] One year later he and MBU received silver from members of the bow-unit of Bēl-iddin.[282] I suggest that we identify this Iddinaya/Ardiya from the Bēl-iddin texts with Iddinaya/Arad-Bēl, plowman in the service of MNA. Iddinaya/Arad-Bēl occurs in Dar 307, a fragmentary text dated in the middle of Darius' eleventh year. The text refers to arable land that belonged to the bow-fief of Nergal-nāṣir and "had been given to Iddinaya, son of Arad-Bēl."[283] Unfortunately, the laconic formulation of the text does not reveal the terms of the noted land transfer. However, it seems that the land had been given to Iddinaya/Arad-Bēl in order to be plowed, since the text refers to a plow team of MNA[284] in juxtaposition to the transfer of the land to Iddinaya/Arad-Bēl. If this interpretation of the evidence in Dar 307 is correct, Iddinaya/Arad-Bēl was one of MNA's menials who plowed bow-fief land.[285] Consequently, he could have been a member of a bow-unit like the one of Bēl-iddin, which consisted of menials or persons of servile status attached to a household, doing agricultural and other work under supervision.[286] Actually, he is attested in three texts concerning this unit, in which he is called the son of Ardiya.[287] Ardiya is just a shorter form of Arad-Bēl and it refers, no doubt, to the same person. In short, Iddinaya/Arad-Bēl (Ardiya) was one of MNA's plowmen and a member of the bow-unit of Bēl-iddin. He worked together with MNA's slave in the financial administration of the(ir) unit.[288]

The bow-unit of Bēl-iddin included two other menials from MNA's household, MBU and his son Madānu-iddin. MBU was one of MNA's senior slaves and, as shown above, financial manager of Bēl-iddin's unit. If Iddinaya/Ardiya (Arad-Bēl) was a member of the bow-unit of Bēl-iddin, as we argued above, his partner in the financial management of this unit, MBU, must have been a member as well. This is not surprising, taking into account that MBU was a slave and thus fit to be a member of a group of menials. The same holds for one of MBU's sons, Madānu-iddin. A man with the same name is mentioned in

---

280. BM 31026.

281. Dar 400.

282. Dar 430.

283. Dar 307: 3, *ša ana … nadnu*.

284. Dar 307: 4, *ša ina* ^{giš}*epinni ša MNA*.

285. For MNA's access to bow-fief land, further see Dar 351.

286. See above for the arguments to support this description of the bow-unit of Bēl-iddin.

287. Namely in Dar 430 and BM 31026. Note also this person's presence among the witnesses in Dar 400.

288. Iddinaya/Arad-Bēl further occurs in Dar 334, dated in Araḫsamna of Darius' twelfth year. Details at § 2.1.2 (n. 73).

Dar 430: 11. He contributed a few shekels of silver to Bēl-iddin's bow-unit, which its deputy handed over to MBU and Iddinaya/Ardiya. I suggest identifying this Madānu-iddin with his namesake, who is attested as one of MBU's sons.

2.4.5.2. *The Role of MNA: Member of a Tax-unit, Tax Collector, or Entrepreneur?*

We now proceed with examining the role of MNA in the collection of taxes and conscripts from individuals or groups of individuals. The evidence adduced above shows that MNA's involvement in these matters was well established and many-faceted. Indeed, it had started in Darius' twelfth year, or perhaps even earlier,[289] evolved over several years—until at least the end of Darius' twenty-sixth year—and concerned different types of state income. Moreover, this activity is one of the better-documented aspects of MNA's business affairs (eighteen tax-receipts, four receipts of conscripts, three letters and TCL 13 196).[290] This was the core of the evidence, which is elaborated upon by other texts from the archive that prove to be related to these twenty-six core texts in terms of either prosopography or subject matter. On the basis of this evidence we can established the reason MNA collected these taxes and conscripts, and the expected benefits from his involvement in the Babylonian tax system of the early Persian period.

In some cases, MNA could use part of his collections for his own benefit, albeit we do not know all the details of the arrangement between MNA and the representatives of the state.[291] Thus, he could lease out his share of what he collected from the boats that made use of the governor's bridge and harbor to a third party and collect on the lease. Similarly, MNA could utilize the services of the men whom he recruited, at least for a certain period of time, although they belonged to the governor's pool of forced laborers.

It is not clear, however, on what basis the governor relinquished part of his rights to this income from boats and the corvée. Probably, MNA paid fixed amounts of silver on a monthly or yearly basis to the governor in advance for the right to collect payments from the passing boats. The difference between those sums and the sum actually collected represented MNA's profit (or loss) from his (tax-farming) deal with the governor.[292] MNA tried to enhance his

289. BM 33954.

290. The eighteen receipts of taxes by MNA are: fifteen receipts of *ilku* from individuals (BM 30235, BM 30243, BM 30261, BM 30297, BM 30366, BM 30772, BM 30819, BM 31227, BM 31322, BM 31517, BM 31533, BM 33926, BM 41607, CTMMA 3 68 and TCL 13 197); and three receipts of tax income from bow-units (BM 30589 [*ilku*], BM 31798 [silver] and BM 33954 [flour]). The four receipts of conscripts are: BM 31188, BM 32932, BM 30764 and BM 31118. The three letters are: BM 31416 (about *ilku*), CT 22 74, and BM 31438 (about conscripts).

291. TCL 13 196 (concerning the collection of payments from boats at the bridge and harbor of the governor of Babylon) and the texts in which MNA received men from the governor's pool of forced laborers (BM 31188 and BM 32932; probably also BM 30764 and BM 31118).

292. More on MNA's tax and rent farming deals, at n. 325.

profits by (sub)leasing his share and collecting on the lease. Had MNA also paid a lump sum to the governor of Babylon for the right to collect men for compulsory service such as towing boats? Or, had the governor struck a different deal with MNA, viz. one that stipulated that MNA should assist the governor in recruiting corvée-workers in return for being granted limited access to the men's (towing) services? In any case, his involvement in the exploitation of the governor's bridge and harbor, on the one hand, and in the recruitment of the governor's corvée-workers, on the other hand, were only part of a complex labor relationship between MNA and Gūzānu, governor of Babylon. This relationship was not limited to the area of tax-collection, but included various boat-related issues as well, and goes back to the governorship of Gūzānu's predecessors.[293] MNA's cooperation with the governors of Babylon was, no doubt, mutually beneficial.

In most cases, however, MNA's right to the taxes that he collected is less obvious. It is particularly difficult to assess his role in the Babylonian tax system in the eighteen cases in which he received *ilku* and similar payments from individuals or members of bow-units. Was MNA to benefit from the *ilku* that he received? Could he keep the flour that the members of the bow-unit of the exorcists had to deliver to him, even when this flour was nominally "property of the king" and due from a unit that fell within the governor's administrative authority?

Several possibilities are to be considered when assessing MNA's role in the collection of *ilku* and similar payments from individuals or groups of individuals. First, he may have been a member of a tax-unit, who paid taxes, on the one hand, and occasionally collected them from fellow members in his tax-unit before this income was transferred to the state, on the other.[294] Second, he may have been a tax collector who received taxes in the name of the state, but was not in any specific way related to the people from whom he received the taxes. Third, he may have been a private entrepreneur who, like the Murašûs, acted as middleman between the taxpayer and the state.[295] These middlemen provided the individual taxpayer with the credit that he needed to pay off his taxes to the state or, alternatively, made advance payments on the taxpayer's behalf to the royal administration and later recuperated the borrowed silver. The eighteen tax-receipts would, then, reflect this last stage of reimbursement. Private contractors could also pay the state in advance for all taxes of a specific year and later recuperate the invested silver from the individual taxpayers. The eighteen tax-receipts would, then, reflect this second stage, namely the tax-farmer's recuperation of his invested capital.

---

293. See already above at n. 175.

294. Cf. MBU's role in the collection of taxes from the bow-unit of Bēl-iddin/Nabû-zēra-ušabši, as was argued above.

295. On private entrepreneurship in Babylonia in the first millennium B.C.E., see Stolper, *Entrepreneurs*, and Van Driel, "Entrepreneurs."

We start the examination with an attempt to identify the persons from whom MNA collected the *ilku* and similar payments. As said, taxes were often collected from men who were organized in socially homogeneous groups by a member of the group. The role of tax collector rotated among the members of the group. MNA may, therefore, have been appointed tax collector on behalf of his tax-unit, at least from Darius' twenty-fourth to twenty-sixth years. In such a case, his receipts of *ilku* in those years are to be understood as tax collections by MNA from fellow bow-members. Consequently, it is particularly important to investigate if the persons from whom MNA collected taxes constituted a socially homogeneous group and if they were in any way related to him, either business-wise, socially, or personally.

The persons from whom MNA collected *ilku* contributed either individually or together with members of their family, profession or place of residence.[296] The person who was subject to pay *ilku* is introduced in the texts by means of the particle *ša*, literally "of," but in the specific context under discussion should be paraphrased "(which) is due from."[297] As can be seen from Table 4 above (s.v. column *ilku ša* PN_1), the *ilku* was not necessarily imposed on one individual; it could be a burden shared by two or more persons.[298] It could be shared, for instance, by two brothers, two sets of two brothers, or two brothers and a third person.[299] *Ilku* could also be levied upon persons who were tied by profession, as for instance, when collected from "PN and his administrators."[300] Finally, *ilku* could be levied from a group of people from the same city or house(hold), as for instance, when collected from "Bēl-iddin, a man from Babylon who lives in the house of Bēl-zēra-iddin in Bīt-Ḫaḫḫuru."[301]

Frequently, the person who was subject to the payment of *ilku* did not pay himself, but had a third party pay.[302] Thus, he could send his father or brother to pay.[303] However, in most cases the actual payer was in no apparent way related to the person on whose behalf he paid. Perhaps the person who paid the *ilku* was a colleague assisting fellow bow-members.[304] Usually, it is explicitly

---

296. Cf. the evidence on the collection of *rikis qabli* that was adduced above in § 2.1.1 and § 2.1.2.

297. More elaborate formulations are found in a few texts: *ilki gabbi … mala zitti ša* PN, "the entire *ilku* … in so much as it is the share due from PN" (BM 31322; cf. BM 41607); and *ilki … ana muḫḫi* ^{giš}*qašti* [*ša*] PN *u* ^{lú}DI-*pa-ni-šú*, "the *ilku* … on behalf of the bow-unit [of] PN and his *administrators*$^{?}$" (BM 30589; read ^{lú}*qīpānišu* for ^{lú}DI-*pa-ni-šú*$^{?}$).

298. BM 31517, BM 31533, BM 30589, BM 30261, BM 33926, and BM 30243.

299. BM 30243 (two brothers), BM 33926 (two sets of two brothers), and BM 31533 (two brothers and a third person). The situation in BM 31517 is not clear.

300. BM 30261 and BM 30589. For the reading ^{lú}*qīpānišu*$^{!}$ in these texts, see discussions at BM 30261: 2.

301. BM 31416: 5–9.

302. This is highlighted in Table 4 by means of the symbol ≠.

303. BM 31322 (father), BM 30589 and BM 30261 (brothers). Cf. BM 33928 (§ 2.1.1).

304. Probably, cf. MBU in the Bēl-iddin texts discussed above.

stated that the payment was "on behalf of" so-and-so.[305] Sometimes, however, this element is lacking, to wit in those cases in which a father or a brother paid on behalf of the family. On those occasions it was apparently less important to state who paid on whose behalf, because the matter could easily be arranged within the family. In the five instances in which *ilku* was received on behalf of several persons, the actual payer was one of the persons involved, a brother, or someone whom I cannot relate to the original taxpayers.[306]

Very little is known about the persons from whom MNA collected *ilku*. Of the twenty-four taxpayers listed in the Table above only Bēl-iddin ("the man from Babylon who lives in the house of Bēl-zēra-iddin in Bīt-Ḫaḫḫuru") and Aplaya/Bazūzu/Ašlāku (who lived in Šabīlu) are known from other texts from MNA's archive.[307] According to BM 30651, they paid silver to a servant of the governor of Babylon for unknown reasons. This text is an undated list of quantities of silver that refers to Bēl-iddin and Aplaya/Bazūzu/Ašlāku in the following brief way: "[x]+one minas of white silver from Bēl-iddin of the house of the Babylonian," and "two minas of white silver from Aplaya in Šabīlu."[308] The text does not provide any background information as to the reason for the transfers of silver from Bēl-iddin of Babylon and Aplaya of Šabīlu, but in view of BM 31416 and BM 31533, these were probably additional payments for their taxes.

Similarly, the persons who acted as payers on behalf of others are barely known from other texts of the archive. Nabû-ittannu/Baniya//Itinnu, who paid *ilku* to MNA for his brother in Darius' twenty-sixth year,[309] was indebted to Nabû-aḫḫē-bulliṭ, MNA's brother, for unknown reasons in the previous year.[310] The brother of Nabû-iddin/Iqūpu//Etel-pî, who paid MNA for

305. *ana muḫḫi*. See above Table 4 s.v. column *a* (= *ana muḫḫi*).

306. BM 31517 and BM 31533 (one of the persons from whom *ilku* was due; head of the unit?); BM 30261 and BM 30589 (a brother); BM 33926 and BM 30243 (a person, at first sight unrelated to the persons who had to pay *ilku*).

307. BM 31416 (Bēl-iddin) and BM 31533 (Aplaya/Bazūzu//Ašlāku; drafted in Šabīlu).

308. BM 30651: 3–4 (Bēl-iddin), and BM 30651: 7–8 (2 *manê kaspu peṣû ina qātē Aplaya ša ina Šabīlu*). True, Aplaya in BM 30651 is cited by his first name only, so that it is difficult to establish his identity. However, in my opinion, Aplaya, who paid two minas of white silver in Šabīlu according to BM 30651, was probably the same person as Aplaya/Bazūzu//Ašlāku, who paid *ilku* to MNA according to BM 31533, because the latter payment also took place in Šabīlu (BM 31533 was drafted in Šabīlu). In fact, I know of only three texts from the Neo-Babylonian period that mention this place (Nbk 191, BM 30819 and BM 31533). They are all three from the time of MNA. Two of them concerned *ilku* and were, moreover, written by the same scribe in the same week (BM 30819 and BM 31533). This shows that the place was important in terms of the collection of *ilku*, at least from MNA's point of view. Consequently, the "...silver (paid) in Šabīlu" according to BM 30651 may have been silver paid for *ilku*. For the interpretation of BM 30651 as a list of income that belonged to the governor of Babylon (BM 30651 Rev. 3′–4′, [*ina n*]*ašpartu ša* ^{lú}*šākin ṭēmi Arad-Bunene* ^{lú}*arad* ^{lú}*šākin ṭēmi* "Arad-Bunene, servant of the governor [(received) by o]rder of the governor"), see on p. 90.

309. BM 30261. For the date of BM 30261, see commentary on line 15 and above at n. 257.

310. He had to pay his debt no later than Ulūl of the twenty-fifth year (BM 30541, dated [-]/

someone else's *ilku*,[311] occurs among the witnesses in one of MNA's debt settlements[312] —this document concerns MNA's debt to Šaddinnu, a debt that resulted from MNA's purchase of the right to collect field rent (*šibšu)* from the property of Bēl.

Thus, the persons from whom MNA collected *ilku* did not belong to his group of acquaintances.[313] They did not trade with him, nor did they borrow silver from him, lend him silver, or were in any other way involved in MNA's business affairs. They were not present as witnesses when MNA concluded transactions related to his trade in commodities or promised to meet certain obligations vis-à-vis his business partners or the authorities. They were not his neighbors, because we do not find them in any document regarding MNA's houses or land. In short, they were not linked with MNA in any way other than for the purpose of tax payments. The only occasion when he met with them was when taxes were to be collected. Even the two individuals who are attested in more than one text in the archive occur always in connection with taxes. Bēl-iddin, for instance, was a Babylonian who lived in someone else's house. Once he paid *ilku* to MNA and once he paid silver to Arad-Bunene, the governor's servant. Aplaya/Bazūzu//Ašlāku lived in Šabīlu. Once he paid *ilku* to MNA, and once he paid silver to this same Arad-Bunene.

In addition to collecting *ilku*, MNA occasionally collected taxes from bow-units, although he did not belong to these units. We have seen above that MNA collected silver from the "bow-unit of Bēl-erība and LÚ.DI-*pa-ni-šú* (his administrators?)" and from the "bow-unit of Bēl-iddin/Tāqiš," as well as flour from one-third of the "bow-unit of the exorcists."[314] The individuals from whom he actually received the silver and flour, however, are otherwise unknown. Indeed, Bazūzu, Libluṭ/Murašû//Sîn-tabni, Bēl-iddin/Tāqiš, Bēl-erība/Nādin//Lūṣi-ana-nūr-Marduk and his brother Iqūpu do not occur in any other text from MNA's time. Consequently, if MNA had been a member of their units, which were, for the most part, groups of professionals, such as exorcists, scribes, and administrators, we would know them from other texts of the archive as business partners, neighbors, witnesses, surety, or scribes.

In conclusion, it is very unlikely that MNA acted as head of his unit when he collected *ilku* from various persons, silver from the bow-units of Bēl-erība and Bēl-iddin, and flour from the bow-unit of the exorcists. He was, basically,

---

[-]/⌜25⌝ Dar). The *causa debendi* is not known. Was it tax related, in view of Nabû-ittannu's *ilku*-related payment to MNA in BM 30261? Remarkably, two (perhaps three) of the witnesses in BM 30541 are well known from MNA's boat-related transactions; see more at Table 7 s.v. Bēl-asûa, Šullumaya, and Šulum-Bābili.

311. BM 30772.

312. Dar 472, dated 3/x/18 Dar.

313. In contrast, the men who witnessed MNA's collection of taxes are well known from his archive. Details at Table 7.

314. BM 30589, BM 31798, and BM 33954.

unrelated to the persons from whom he collected *ilku* and an outsider to the bow-units from which he collected silver and flour. Accordingly, the situation reflected in the Bēl-rēmanni archive regarding the system of tax collection only partly applies to MNA's archive. On the one hand, there is ample evidence from the archive that people were organized into corporate entities for the purpose of tax collection. On the other hand, MNA is not attested as a member of any of these groups, unlike Bēl-rēmanni from Sippar. Consequently, MNA's role in the collection of *ilku* and taxes from bow-units is to be sought elsewhere.

In a few cases MNA, when receiving *ilku*, seems to have acted as assistant tax collector on behalf of the state. In BM 31533, for instance, MNA received *ilku* from Aplaya/Bazūzu/Ašlāku, his brother, and a third person for Darius' twenty-fifth year "[as prox]y for Šuma-ukīn, son of Bēl-ēṭir."[315] Šuma-ukīn does not bear an official title, but must have represented the interests of the state when he ordered MNA to collect *ilku* from Aplaya and the others. We know, for instance, that this same Aplaya also paid silver (for taxes?) to Arad-Bunene, the governor's servant.[316] Šuma-ukīn/Bēl-ēṭir may, therefore, have been another agent of the governor of Babylon who was charged with the collection of taxes on the governor's behalf.[317] Unfortunately, we do not know whether MNA could keep part of what he received from Aplaya and the others for his own use, or had to transfer all of it to Šuma-ukīn. Anyway, MNA and Šuma-ukīn worked together for several years, and their cooperation, especially in the field of tax collection,[318] must have been mutually beneficial. In the same light we should probably interpret BM 33954.[319] As we have seen above, BM 33954 records the agreement that MNA reached with representatives of the bow-unit of the exorcists regarding their delivery of flour for Darius' eleventh or twelfth year. This flour was "property of the king" and nominally due to Nabû-šuma-ukīn, governor of Babylon, under whose administrative authority the unit in question fell. Was MNA helping the governor out with his collection of the king's flour? We know that MNA assisted this governor's son with the recruitment of soldiers when this son, Gūzānu, had become governor in his father's place.[320] However, MNA may have been collecting the king's flour for his own benefit after he had paid off the governor of Babylon, to whom the flour was nominally due. MNA probably struck similar deals with Gūzānu, Nabû-šuma-ukīn's son, when the latter became governor of Babylon, regarding the collection of payments from boats at a bridge and harbor for which Gūzānu was

---

315. If one accepts the following reconstruction of BM 31533: 4, [*ina na-áš-pu*]*r*?-*tú* ᵐMU-GIN.

316. BM 30651: 7–8 and Rev.: 3′–4′.

317. On Šuma-ukīn/Bēl-ēṭir, see also b 2800; his full name was Nabû-šuma-ukīn/Bēl-ēṭir// Šangû-Nannaya according to Dar 213 and TCL 13 185. More on this person and his relationship with MNA at p. 40 and n. 331.

318. Dar 213, TCL 13 185 and b. 2800.

319. Perhaps also Dar 244, see above at n. 227.

320. CT 22 74 and § 2.4.2.1. More on MNA's assistance to the governors of Babylon at n. 67.

responsible.[321] MNA's cooperation with the governors of Babylon, whatever the details of their deals may have been, proved to be beneficial when MNA needed to transport his crops to the market.[322]

In most cases, MNA received *ilku* from the taxpayers after he had intervened with the authorities on their behalf and paid for their *ilku*: their payments of *ilku* to MNA were actual reimbursement payments. We know that MNA granted loans to taxpayers or made advance payments to the authorities on their behalf.[323] As a result of these and similar activities the taxpayers became indebted to MNA or had to remunerate him for his financial assistance. Iqūpu's *ilku*-payment to MNA in BM 30589, for instance, is a clear example of such a reimbursement. This Iqūpu belonged to a bow-unit named after his brother Bēl-erība. The bow-unit of Bēl-erība had to pay *ilku* for the rations of the New Palace in Darius' twenty-fifth year. A payment in cash ("silver") had already been received by the clerk of the office that issued the rations of the New Palace and the register that kept track of these matters was in his possession. BM 30589, however, does not record this receipt of *ilku*-silver by the clerk in question. It refers to the clerk's receipt as an accomplished fact and does so in a clause that is added to the operative section of the contract. This clause gives the necessary background information to understand the operative section,[324] which records the receipt of *ilku* by MNA from a member of the bow-unit of Bēl-erība on the twentieth of Simān of Darius' twenty-sixth year. It thus becomes clear that the payment of *ilku* to MNA was in essence a reimbursement payment. It was a reimbursement of MNA for his earlier payment in cash to the clerk responsible for the rations of the New Palace. Accordingly, MNA must have made an advance payment for the *ilku* of Darius' twenty-fifth year to the aforementioned clerk on account of the bow-unit of Bēl-erība, and was reimbursed by a member of this unit on the twentieth of Simān of Darius' twenty-sixth year.

Eventually, it appears that more than twenty other taxpayers, in addition to Iqūpu and Bēl-erība, paid *ilku* to MNA rather than to a representative of the state. Had MNA intervened on behalf of each of these taxpayers and paid for each of them individually to the state? It is more likely that he had made a one-time, all-inclusive payment to the state, viz. for the *ilku*-tax of Darius' twenty-

---

321. TCL 13 196. See above at p. 77f.

322. For details, see § 2.5 (esp. p. 113ff.).

323. For the evidence, see above at § 2.3.

324. BM 30589: 8–11 (*kaspu ana PN* [lú]*sepīri ...* [*nadnu*] [giš]*lē'û ittišu*). Similar explanatory clauses, which clarify the transaction that is recorded in the main part of the document, are typically found in promissory notes. They contain a description of the *causa debendi*. Whereas the main part of the promissory note states that on such-and-such date the debtor will pay his debt, the additional clause explains the reason the debt had been contracted, e.g., "Silver that has been given (SUM-*nu*, SUM.NA) for *rikis qabli*" (e.g., Dar 308, Dar 164, Dar 167, and BM 33972; a nice parallel from Sippar is, for instance, *Bēl-rēmanni*, 133 = BM 42302; also cf. Dar 541, re-edited in the present study: about a loan that had been contracted to pay off one's creditor).

fourth, twenty-fifth, and twenty-sixth years, and had thus acquired the right to collect *ilku* for his own benefit in those years. In other words, taxpayers paid their *ilku* to MNA because the latter had bought the right to this state income from the state against the advance payment of a fixed amount of silver. The first stage of this tax-farming venture, namely MNA's purchase of the *ilku* from a representative of the state, is not documented. However, we know that MNA occasionally bought the right to collect income from taxes or field rent by paying a fixed amount of silver to state representatives. Thus, he bought the right to collect field rent from the crown's representative in the Esagil temple in Darius' tenth and eleventh years. He may also have bought the right to collect toll from the governor of Babylon in Darius' twenty-sixth year, and taxes or field rent from the district governor of Šaḫrīnu in Darius' twelfth year.[325] The second stage of MNA's tax-farming venture, viz. the recuperation of his expenses from the individual taxpayers, is documented by the bulk of his *ilku* receipts.

MNA's entrepreneurial activities in the collection of taxes were profitable for all three sides involved. From the point of view of the state, his entrepreneurship warranted that the state had its income, and more particularly had cash income rather than crop income, so that it could pay salaries to its dependents and finance state-sponsored projects in Elam.[326] From MNA's point of view, the purchase of tax-income was profitable in so far that he was able to recuperate his expenses within the tax-year, at least in most cases. As we have seen above, MNA received *ilku*, i.e., was compensated for his (cash) payments of the *ilku* tax, probably *in natura*, in the fourth month after the barley had been harvested, in the eighth month at the time of the date harvest, or toward the end of the year; there were relatively few overdue payments, and if they occurred, MNA was usually compensated in cash rather than *in natura*. From the taxpayer's point of view, the arrangement was acceptable in so far that it enabled him to wait for the harvest to pay his dues to the state.

2.5. *Payments for Boats and Boat-Related Expenses by MNA to State Officials*

MNA frequently met with state officials when dealing with boats and boat transports. We have already seen that he had to pay the state for his use of the state-controlled canals and transport facilities.[327] Thus he paid a toll (*miksu*) to the overseer of the quay and transport costs (*gimru*) to the governor of Babylon

325. Dar 315 (lease, § 3.1.1); TCL 13 196 (toll, § 2.4.1 and p. 77) and Dar 338 (taxes or lease, § 2.6.1). Several other texts from MNA's archive are, most likely, to be interpreted in the light of similar tax or rent farming deals. Accordingly, they record transactions that may have resulted from such deals or are related to them in other ways. For such texts, see § 2.5.2 (*gimru*-texts, p. 93ff.), § 2.6.2 (Rīmūt-Bēl texts, n. 494), § 2.7.1 (TCL 13 193, Liv 25 and Dar 544; n. 529) and § 3.1.3 (Dar 359).

326. Cf. above at p. 40f. on the benefits of MNA's entrepreneurial enterprises.

327. Above at § 2.1.3.

or his agents. These payments gave his boats, which were loaded with barley, onions, and dates, the right of passage and covered various other costs that resulted from the transport of the crops by boat.

The organization of boat transports, however, was more complex than the *miksu-* and *gimru-*payments suggest. In fact, a corpus of thirty-one texts documents MNA's involvement in the organization of boat transports. It includes the three *miksu* and the eight *gimru*-texts, as well as twenty other ones.[328] They show him paying toll and transport costs to officials; renting or purchasing boats, mostly from officials; acquiring men to tow, sail, and unload? the boats, usually by hiring them; and paying for the rations of boatmen or for various other expenses related to boats, such as cables and containers.[329]

The thirty-one texts are dated between Darius' fourth and thirty-fifth years, and it appears, therefore, that the organization of boat transports was not an isolated phenomenon, but an activity that may have been essential to MNA's business and that of his son. Consequently, it is important to have a closer look at these texts in order to examine the role played by the boat-related transactions in the Egibi's business in general. In particular, three issues are to be addressed: (1) the scope of the phenomenon or the level of MNA's involvement in the boat and transport business; (2) the relationship of his boat-related transactions to MNA's other business transactions; and (3) the level of official involvement in MNA's boat-related transactions and the nature of this involvement.

---

328. List of the thirty-one boat-related texts in MNA's archive in numerical order: BM 30256, BM 30270, BM 30370, BM 30490, BM 30591, BM 30639, BM 30747, BM 30764, BM 30799, BM 30853, BM 30961, BM 31118, BM 31138, BM 31188, BM 31347, BM 31393, BM 31554, BM 31572, BM 31690⁺, BM 31786, BM 31891, BM 32891, BM 32932, BM 33112, BRM 1 81, Dar 138, Dar 158, Dar 215, Dar 268, Dar 576 and OECT 10 234. For the connection between BM 31138 and boats, see the arguments adduced below on p. 111f. For a chronological classification of the texts, see below Table 6. For a thematical classification of the texts, see the following footnote and Table 8. Two texts from MNA's archive are not included, although they record transactions that are related to boats. They are not included because MNA is not directly involved in the recorded transactions. Rather, he is just the scribe (BM 32873) or a guarantor at a boat sale (BM 32883). For the texts regarding MNA's collection of payments at and for bridges, see above at § 2.4.1 (TCL 13 196, BM 30366, BM 31227 and BM 41443). They are not included in the now following discussion because they regard MNA's income from boat-related transactions and not his boat-related expenses.

329. Cf. Table 8. *Miksu*: BM 30747; BM 31347; Dar 268. *Gimru*: BM 30591; BM 30639; BM 31786; BM 33112; BM 31572; BM 32891; BM 31393; BRM 1 81. Boat rentals: BM 30853: 5b–8a; 25–27; 30–32; 37b–38; BM 31554; Dar 576; Dar 138; BM 31891; BM 31690⁺; BM 30799; BM 30270; and BM 30490. Boat purchases: OECT 10 234 and BM 30370 (with BM 30961 recording the receipt of the purchase price). Hire of professional sailors: Dar 158 and Dar 215. Acquisition of boat-towers: BM 30764; BM 31118; BM 31188; BM 32932; and probably also BM 30853: 1–5a. Payment for unloading? (*napālu*) boats: BM 30853: 23–24. Payment for cables: BM 30853: 16–18. Payment for the purchase of vessels to transport beer by boat: BM 30853: 21–22. Payment for the rations (*kurummātu*) of technical personnel (probably in return for the right to join officially organized transports): BM 30256; BM 30853: 12b–15; and 19–20. Payment for additional (boat-related) expenses: BM 30853: 8b–9 (garments = rations?); 10–12a; 28–29; 33–35; 35–37a and BM 31138.

2.5.1. *BM 30853 and Related Texts*

BM 30853 is an excellent point of venture to examine what one needed to set up a transport by boat and how this could be obtained. It is an undated list of fifteen different payments in silver and one payment in barley. The Table below gives a schematic presentation of the payments in question.

TABLE 5: Schematic Presentation of the Payments Listed in BM 30853

LINES	PAYMENT OF:	FOR:	TO:
1–2a	silver	hirelings	Šullumu, overseer [...]
2b–5a	silver	garments for hirelings	(*idem*?),[330] in the presence of the governor
5b–8a	silver	hiring of two boats	Bēl-ikṣur, (harbor) master and his workers
8b–9	silver		Bēl-ikṣur, (harbor) master
10–12a	silver	barley	the house of Artasunu, by oral order of the governor
12b–15	silver	barley	Nidinti-Bēl-damqat, by written order of the governor
16–18	silver	boat cables	Nidinti-Bēl-damqat, by written order of the governor
19–20	silver	food rations of boat-towers	(*idem*?)
21–22	silver	beer vessels transported by boat	(*idem*?), by oral order of the governor
23–24	barley	unloading? (*napālu*) of boats	Šuma-ukīn, by oral order of the governor
25–27	silver	hiring of a boat	(*idem*?)
28–29	silver	(unclear)	Gūzu-{ina}-Bēl-aṣbat

330. When the recipient of the silver is not explicitly mentioned, I assume that it was the same person (*idem*) as previously mentioned. More at commentary to BM 30853: 2b–5a.

30–32	silver	hiring of boats	(*idem*?), by oral order of the governor
33–35	silver		Arad-Bunene, in the presence of Napurtu and Bānûnu
35–37a	silver		the governor
37b–38	silver	hiring of a boat loaded with flour	(*idem*?)

The silver and barley were paid to low-ranking superintendents (^{lú}*rab*, ^{lú}*rēš*), and to an unnamed governor of Babylon or his agents. Accordingly, some payments were made directly to the governor himself; others were made in his presence (*ina izuzzu*). Normally, however, the governor sent someone, by written or oral order, to collect the payments on his account. The persons who received these orders are called by their first name only, but can often be identified with persons from MNA's archive, notwithstanding the limited information we have about them. Nidinti-Bēl-damqat and Arad-Bunene, for instance, are known from other texts as servants of the governor of Babylon.[331] BM 30853 also records payments to the overseer (^{lú}*rab*) Šullumu and the headman (^{lú}*rēš*) Bēl-ikṣur. The latter was responsible for the harbor and its workmen, and is known in this function from at least one other text from MNA's archive.[332]

The payments in BM 30853 were for boats, boat equipment, or other expenses related to boats and the transport of goods by boat. Thus, there are four payments for boat rentals, one for boat cables, one for vessels to transport beer by boat, one for men to tow boats, and one for unloading[?] boats. In two instances silver was paid for hirelings or their clothing, and in two other ones for barley. It is very likely that the said expenses for hirelings and barley were, in one way or another, related to boats just like all the other expenses recorded in BM 30853. Accordingly, the hirelings in question may have been acquired to tow boats, and the barley may have been dispensed as food rations for sailors or boat towers. The latter is confirmed by the fact that the man who received the barley in lines 12b–15 is known from another text as receiving barley from MNA

331. See BM 30256: 3–4 (Nidinti-Bēl-damqat) and BM 30651 Rev.: 4' (Arad-Bunene). The other two persons who received orders from the governor of Babylon, Artasunu and Šuma-ukīn, cannot be traced in other documents, unless Šuma-ukīn can be identified with Šuma-ukīn (*alias* Nabû-šuma-ukīn)/Bēl-ēṭir//Šangû-Nannaya (for this person, see above at p. 40 and p. 82f.).

332. BM 31554: 3. Perhaps cf. Bēl-kiṣuršu in BM 41453: 2–3 (details below).

for the food rations of sailors.[333] Finally, there are four payments in BM 30853 for which no specific reason is given, or for which the reason is unclear, so that their link with boats remains undecided. One of these payments, viz. the one in lines 8b–9, however, was a payment to the harbor-master, to whom another payment was made to cover expenses of a boat rental (5b–8a). It is, therefore, very likely that the payment in lines 8b–9 was also related to boat expenses. In short, it appears that BM 30853 is a list of expenses that are all, in one way or another, related to boats.

There is no doubt that BM 30853 belonged to MNA, even though he is not explicitly named in the text,[334] because of the close parallels between this text and at least two other ones from MNA's archive.[335] These texts mention persons and expenses that are also met with in BM 30853, but, unlike BM 30853, they explicitly link these persons and expenses to MNA.[336] A closer look at the texts in question and a comparison with the parallel evidence from BM 30853 will prove, beyond reasonable doubt, that BM 30853 belongs to MNA's archive.

The first text from this archive to which BM 30853 can be linked is BM 30256 (Babylon, 2/vii/24 Dar), because of Nidintu-Bēl-damqat, the governor of Babylon and the transport of beer by boat mentioned in it. According to BM 30853 Nidinti-Bēl-damqat received silver for barley (12b–15), boat cables (16–18), food rations of boat-towers (19–20), and vessels to transport beer by boat (21–22). All receipts were on the account of the governor of Babylon and seem to have taken place on the twenty-sixth of Araḫsamna.[337] The evidence on Nidinti-Bēl-damqat in BM 30256 is very similar to that in BM 30853: it links him to boats, beer, and the governor of Babylon in much the same way as in BM 30853. Indeed, according to BM 30256, Nidinti-Bēl-damqat was a servant of Ina-Esagil-lilbur, the governor of Babylon, and he acted on the governor's orders. Thus, he received barley from MNA for the food rations of his boatmen in Tašrīt of Darius' twenty-fourth year. The men were on a boat transporting beer to Dūr-(Kuri)galzu. In view of this evidence it is most likely that Nidinti-Bēl-damqat in BM 30853 and in BM 30256 must have been the same person. This person organized boat transports in the name of Ina-Esagil-lilbur, governor of Babylon, in Tašrīt of Darius' twenty-fourth year and probably also in Araḫsamna of the

---

333. BM 30256.

334. Nor is anybody else identified as the owner of the list.

335. BM 30256 and BM 31554; perhaps also BM 41453. Close parallels also exist between BM 30853 and BM 30651, but the latter does not explicitly mention MNA. Details below.

336. This is the case of the following persons and expenses mentioned in BM 30853: Nidinti-Bēl-damqat (12b–18), Bēl-ikṣur (5b–8a), Marduk//Paḫāru (35–37), Arad-Bunene, Napurtu (alias Napištu) and Bānûnu (33–35), the expense for the transport of beer in vessels by boat (21–22), the expense of ninety shekels by Marduk//Paḫāru to the governor (35–37), and the expense of silver to Arad-Bunene (33–35).

337. BM 30853 is to be dated in Tašrīt-Araḫsamna of Darius' twenty-fourth year or any other year during Ina-Esagil-lilbur's term of office as governor of Babylon (22–24 Dar). For the date of BM 30853, see discussion *ad hoc*.

same year; it included at least one transport of beer in vessels. For the costs of these transports, such as the costs for the rations of the men on the boat and those who had to tow the boats, Nidinti-Bēl-damqat received barley and silver from MNA. In return, MNA must have been entitled to join these transports.[338] MNA's payments for cables and beer vessels may well have served the same purpose, namely, to join the transports organized by Nidinti-Bēl-damqat against participation in the costs.[339] The latter, however, may also have been independent payments. In that case, MNA paid for cables and vessels because he needed this equipment for his own boat transports.

The second text from MNA's archive to which BM 30853 can be linked is BM 31554 (Babylon, 11 or 21/x/23 Dar), because of Bēl-ikṣur and the rental of a boat mentioned in it. According to BM 30853 Bēl-ikṣur was a "master" who had "harbor workers" at his disposal, hence a harbor-master. On the twenty-fifth of Tašrīt he received silver for the rental of two boats (5b–8a). Three days later he received silver for an unspecified reason (8b–9). According to BM 31554 he was the son of Rīmūt and bore the title "head of the workers," which is similar to the title of Bēl-ikṣur in BM 30853. In Kislīm of Darius' twenty-third year he received silver for the rental of a boat from MNA. He acted on behalf of Basiya/Nabû-šuma-ukīn//Ša-nāšīšu, who was the brother of the governor of Babylon. The evidence from BM 30853: 5b–9 and BM 31554 shows that Bēl-ikṣur, son of Rīmūt, was an official appointed over the harbor and its workers, rented out boats to MNA in Kislīm of Darius' twenty-third year and probably also in Tašrīt of the same year, and at least once acted on behalf of the governor's brother. This Bēl-ikṣur/Rīmūt may also be the person attested in BM 41453 under the slightly different name Bēl-kiṣuršu/Rīmūt//LÚ.⌜x⌝.[340] According to this text, Nidintu, son of MNA, ordered Bēl-kiṣuršu to rent out a small house and a loft at the harbor to Nidintu/Bēl-aḫḫē-erība.

---

338. The payments by MNA were not repayments of debts nor payments for something that MNA had to pay, as for instance, a tax or compulsory service to the state. This is clear from the way the receipt of these payments is formulated in BM 30256 and BM 30853: 12b–22. Indeed, the silver that MNA paid is never called "due from MNA," nor are any terms for "tax," such as *ilku* or *rikis qabli*, used in the texts. We, therefore, expect MNA to have paid the silver in return for a service rendered to him, such as the right to join the transport. Note the presence of Bēl-erība/Kalbaya//Šumu-libši among the witnesses in BM 30256: he was a commander-of-fifty (BM 30274) and took a special interest in matters concerning taxes, draftees, and boat transports.

339. It is probably in the same light that one should interpret the unpublished text BM 31323 from the time of Itti-Marduk-balāṭu, MNA's father (cf. Wunsch, *MOS Studies 2*, n. 28). According to it someone promised under oath to deliver vessels (*dannūtu*) to Itti-Marduk-balāṭu. These vessels had to be given to the governor of Babylon. Did the governor need these vessels to transport (or store) beer? Did Itti-Marduk-balāṭu participate in these transports?

340. Note that the text mentioning Bēl-kiṣuršu/Rīmūt//LÚ.⌜x⌝ is from the end of Darius' reign (BM 41453, dated 19/[-]/[35 or 36?] Dar), whereas the texts concerning his namesake Bēl-ikṣur/Rīmūt are dated approximately a decade earlier (BM 31554, 11 or 21/x/23 [Dar]; for the date of BM 30853, see above at n. 337).

Third, interesting links exist between BM 30853 and BM 30651 (undated). The texts have five persons in common: Nidinti-Bēl-damqat, Marduk//Paḫāru, Arad-Bunene, Napurtu (*alias* Napištu), and Bānûnu. Furthermore, the texts are very close in content, as becomes clear from a comparison of the following two passages. First, one should compare BM 30651: 9–10[341] with BM 30853: 35–37.[342] These lines in either text mention exactly the same amount of silver, to wit, one and a half minas of white silver (i.e., ninety shekels). According to BM 30853, this amount of silver "of Marduk//Paḫāru had been given to the governor," whereas according to BM 30651 the silver "(had been received)$^{?}$ from (*ina qātē*) Marduk//Paḫāru." In other words, an amount of ninety shekels of white silver due from Marduk//Paḫāru had been given to the governor. BM 30853 recorded the expense of this silver from Marduk//Paḫāru's (and MNA's?!) perspective, whereas BM 30651 recorded the income of this silver from the governor's point of view. This conclusion is confirmed by the second parallel between BM 30651 and BM 30853, i.e., between BM 30651 Rev.: 2′–6′[343] and BM 30853: 33–35.[344] The latter passage refers to the payment of silver "to Arad-Bunene, in the presence of Napurtu and Bānûnu," whereas the passage in BM 30651 refers to the receipt of this silver by "Arad-Bunene, the governor's servant, in the presence of Napištu and Bānûnu [by writt]en order of the governor." BM 30651, therefore, was a list of income for the governor; BM 30853, a list of expenses by MNA.

In summary, BM 30853, BM 30256 and BM 31554 record tens of boat-related expenses of MNA to state officials and their agents under the governorship of Ina-Esagil-lilbur (22–24 Dar). MNA rented boats from Bēl-ikṣur, harbor-master, in Kislīm of Darius' twenty-third year, and in Tašrīt of the same or the following year.[345] He participated in the costs for a boat transport of beer that was organized by Nidintu-Bēl-damqat, the slave of Ina-Esagil-lilbur, in the beginning of Tašrīt of Darius' twenty-fourth year. Thus, he paid barley for the food rations of the sailors on the boat.[346] In addition, he paid for the food rations of the boat-towers and some extra barley, but it is not clear whether these expenses relate to the same transport or to another one that was organized by Nidintu-Bēl-damqat in the governor's name.[347] MNA may also have paid for the boat cables and the beer vessels, unless these expenses were unrelated to Nidintu-

---

341. BM 30651: 9–10, 1½ MA.NA KÙ.BABBAR UD-*ú ina* ŠU.II ^{m}*mar-duk* A LÚ.BAḪAR$_2$.

342. BM 30853: 35b–37, 1½ MA.NA KÙ.BABBAR UD-*ú šá* ^{m}*mar-duk* A LÚ.BAḪAR$_2$ *šá a-na* LÚ.GAR-UŠ$_4$ SUM.NA.

343. BM 30651 Rev.: 2′–6′, [1 MA.NA 10] GÍN KÙ.BABBAR UD-*ú* [*ina na*]*-áš-par-tu$_4$ šá* LÚ.GAR-UŠ$_4$ ^{m}ÌR-^{d}*bu-ne-ne* LÚ.ÌR LÚ.GAR-UŠ$_4$ *ina* GUB-*zu* ^{m}*na-piš-tu$_4$ ù* ^{m}*ba-nu-nu*.

344. BM 30853: 33–35, 1 MA.NA 10 GÍN KÙ.BABBAR UD-*ú šá a-na* ^{m}ÌR-^{d}*bu-ne-ne* SUM.NA *ina* GUB-*zu šá* ^{m}*na-pur-tu ù* ^{m}*ba-nu-nu*.

345. BM 31554 and BM 30853: 5b–8a; cf. 8b–9 (boat rentals).

346. BM 30256 (barley for the rations of the boatmen).

347. BM 30853, 19–20 (silver for the rations of the boat-towers) and 12b–15 (silver for barley).

Bēl-damqat's transports.[348] Under the governorship of Ina-Esagil-lilbur, MNA also acquired hirelings, probably to sail or tow boats, from an overseer and paid for their garments (i.e., maintenance?) in the presence of the governor; rented boats from the governor or his agents; and paid the governor or his representatives for unloading? the boats and for some additional unspecified boat-related matters.[349]

2.5.2. *The gimru-Texts*

Under the governorship of Gūzānu, Ina-Esagil-lilbur's brother, MNA paid for transport costs in general (*gimru*) on seven different occasions.[350] Ten years later he paid once more for *gimru*.[351] It shows that payments for *gimru* were not restricted to two specific years in MNA's career, but continued till the very end of his life. The term *gimru* means "expenses," and refers to the total of expenses that someone incurs in the course of a specific activity. Thus, it may refer to expenses for the food rations of administrators and workmen (*gimir kurummāti*). In most cases, however, it refers to expenses for the transport of goods, in particular boat transports.[352] Bongenaar has shown that in the Neo-Babylonian period the generic term *gimru* included payments for (1) hiring boats, (2) transporting of agricultural produce to the storehouse (*kalakku*), (3) loading of agricultural produce from the storehouse into the boat, (4) leasing containers (*makkanu*), (5) wages for hirelings, (6) the official in charge of the quay (lú*rab kāri*), and (7) exit dues (*muṣānē*).[353]

MNA paid *gimru* on a monthly basis in the summer and autumn in Darius' twenty-fifth and twenty-sixth years. Similarly, he promised to pay in the autumn of Darius' thirty-fifth year. The *gimru*-texts are dated as follows: BM 31572 (7/iv/25 Dar); BM 33112 (17/v/25 Dar); BM 31786 ([-]/[vi?]/25 Dar); BM 30639 (28/vii/25 Dar); BM 31393 ([-]/viii/25 Dar); BM 32891 (11/iv/[26?] Dar); BRM 1 81 (4/viii/26 Dar); and BM 30591 (27/vii/35 Dar). I have dated BM 31786 to the sixth month because it creates an unbroken chain of payments for transport costs for each month between the fourth and the eighth months of Darius' twenty-fifth year. Similarly, I have dated BM 32891 to Darius' twenty-sixth—not to his twenty-fifth year—because another text is already dated in the fourth month of that year. Consequently, MNA paid each month between June (iv/25 Dar) and November (viii/25 Dar) of the year 497 B.C.E. In the next year he paid once in June (iv/26 Dar) and once in November (viii/26 Dar). It is probably by accident that the payments for July–October 496 B.C.E. (v–vii/26

348. BM 30853: 16–18 (silver for cables) and 21–22 (silver for beer vessels).

349. BM 30853 *passim*. Details at Table 5.

350. Payments by MNA for *gimru*: BM 30639; BRM 1 81; BM 31786; BM 33112; BM 31572; BM 32891; BM 31393. All dated between Darius' twenty-fifth and twenty-sixth years.

351. Promise by MNA to pay for *gimru*: BM 30591, dated in Darius' thirty-fifth year.

352. *CAD* G, 77–78 s.v. *gimru* mng. 3.

353. Bongenaar, *Ebabbar*, 39.

Dar) are not preserved. There were no payments between December 497 B.C.E. (ix/25 Dar) and May 496 B.C.E. (iii/26 Dar), i.e., in winter and spring.

MNA paid *gimru* to clerks (^{lú}*sepīru*) whose administrative responsibilities were very carefully described in the texts. Some of them bore the additional title "courtier" (*ša-rēš šarri*).[354] They were appointed over groups of royal workers, and occasionally also over ethnic groups. Accordingly, we find "the clerk of the gardeners and the water-drawers,"[355] "the clerk of the specialized craftsmen$^{?}$,"[356] "the clerk of the *female flour millers*$^{?}$,"[357] "the clerk of the commissioners,"[358] "[the clerk$^{?}$] of the ^{lú}*šá-di-e*^{meš},"[359] and "the clerk of the courtiers."[360] Three clerks were either foreigners themselves or were appointed over foreigners. Bazbaka, the clerk of the specialized craftsmen$^{?}$, for instance, was also appointed over the Ionians,[361] and the clerk of the ^{lú}*šá-di-e*^{meš} was "a man from Imbuka" with the Iranian name Rušund/pāta.[362] The clerk of the *female flour millers*$^{?}$ also bore an Iranian name, Mamûzu.[363] The clerks received their orders from the governor of Babylon and, as said, some of them bore the additional title "courtier" (*ša-rēš šarri*). Their employees worked for the New Palace, the Grand Palace, or both.[364] It is, therefore, obvious that the clerks and the groups of men over whom they were appointed were subjects of the crown. In this respect it is also worth noting that one of the *gimru*-texts was witnessed by representatives of the crown. The list of witnesses of BM 30591, indeed, refers to "Bagadāta/Mitrāta; Bēl-ušallim, a courtier; (and) Mamûzu/Ṭābiya." True, only Bēl-ušallim bears an official title. However, the other two have Iranian names, viz. Bagadāta/Mitrāta and Mamûzu, and may, therefore, have been officials in the central administration. Mamûzu, in fact, is known to have been a clerk in the office of the governor of Babylon cashing payments for *gimru* from, a.o., MNA.[365]

---

354. BM 31572, BRM 1 81 and probably also BM 31393. Also BM 30591: MNA's promise to pay *gimru* to a courtier, but without further specification of this courtier's area of administrative responsibility. For the title LÚ.SAG-LUGAL, *ša-rēš šarri* "courtier," see Bongenaar, *Ebabbar*, 99ff. with bibliography.

355. BM 30639: 3–4, LÚ *si-pir-ri šá* LÚ.NU.GIŠ.KIRI$_6$.MEŠ *u* LÚ *da-li-e*.MEŠ.

356. BM 32891: 4–5, [LÚ *s*]*i-pi-ri šá um-ma-nu*, either "clerk of the specialized craftsmen" or "clerk of the troops/bowmen." See commentary *ad hoc*.

357. BM 33112: 5, LÚ *si-pi-ri šá qí-me-e-*⌜tu_4⌝. See commentary *ad hoc*.

358. BM 31572: 4–5, LÚ *si-pir-ri* [*šá*] LÚ.SAG.MEŠ; and BRM 1 81: 2–3, LÚ *si-pir šá* LÚ.SAG.MEŠ.

359. BM 31393: 3–4, LÚ.S[AG$^{?}$ ...] *šá* LÚ *šá-di-e*.MEŠ. See commentary *ad hoc*.

360. BM 31786: 3–4, LÚ *si-p*[*i*(*r*)*-ri šá*] LÚ.SAG-LUGAL.MEŠ.

361. BM 32891: 5, LÚ.[x x] LÚ *ia-ma-*⌜*na*⌝*-a-a*. See commentary *ad hoc*.

362. BM 31393: 3. On LÚ *im-bu-ku-a-a*, see commentary *ad hoc*.

363. BM 33112. Mamûzu recurs among the witnesses together with the Iranian Bagadāta/Mitrāta at MNA's promise to pay *gimru* ten years later (BM 30591).

364. BM 31572 (*ša ekalli ešši*), BM 31786 (*ša ekalli rabî*), and BM 30639 (*ša ekalli rabî u ešši*). Probably also BM 31393 (*šá* LÚ.⌜NAM⌝$^{?}$, "of the dist[rict governor]$^{?}$").

365. BM 33112.

Most *gimru*-payments covered the costs for the transport of crops from institutional land in Tâmti.[366] From the texts we learn that irrigated farmland in this place was leased out and that local governors administrated the collection of rental. BM 32891, for instance, records MNA's payment for the transport of "barley [(from) the fi]xed rent that is due to Bēl-itta[n]nu [and] Šumaya?, district governors, from irrigated farmland in Tâmti."[367] Other texts refer to the transport of barley "fro[m] irrigated farmland in Tâmti"[368] or "from the fixed rent due to Bēl-ittannu."[369] BRM 1 81 refers to the transport of dates, but does not specify their origin. However, since the clerk who received MNA's payment for this transport also received payments for barley transports from Tâmti,[370] the dates in BRM 1 81 most likely originated from the same place. The transported barley in BM 33112 originated "from the estate" and was the "fixed rent due to Iddin-Bēl [and] Tanda."[371] It probably originated from the estate of the crown rather than from that of one of the temples. As stated, the crown's interests are also well-represented in BM 30591 where "Bēl-ušallim, the courtier" and "Mamûzu/Ṭābiya," the clerk of the *female flour millers*?, attended MNA's promise to pay for the *gimru* of goods the origin of which, however, is not further specified. In my opinion, not only the barley in BM 33112, but all the crops for the transport of which MNA paid, including those from the leased fields in Tâmti, seem to have been grown on crown land. This would explain the involvement of district governors, courtiers, the governor of Babylon, and the many clerks of the palace administration in the exploitation of the land in general and the transport of its crops in particular. Consequently, it appears that the crown owned irrigated farmland in Tâmti and that MNA was financially responsible for the transport of its harvest in summer and autumn.

It is not immediately clear why MNA paid for the transport of crops from fields that fell under the administrative responsibility of local governors in Tâmti to clerks in the service of the governor of Babylon. Admittedly, *gimru*-payments are frequently mentioned in conjunction with the lease of private and institutional land. Accordingly, private leaseholders paid the rent from their

366. The texts do not tell us where the crops were transported to. In this respect the *gimru*-texts significantly differ from private arrangements for transport between leaseholders and landowners (see n. 372). Most likely, the crops for which MNA had paid were taken to places where they could be stored or sold. In this respect, Babylon was a very likely port of destination since in the capital there was a constant need for crops to feed the many state-dependent workers living there.

367. BM 32891: 1–3. Similar in BM 31572: 2–3, which regards the transport of barley or dates "from Tâmti, which are under the administrative authority of Bēl-[ittannu? and m...], [the dis]trict governors!," see commentary *ad hoc*.

368. BM 30639: 1–2, *ša ul*[*tu*] garim*tam-tì*.

369. BM 31393: 2; also BM 31786: 2, without explicitly mentioning Tâmti, or the official title of Bēl-ittannu.

370. See BM 31572.

371. BM 33112: 1–2.

harvest and covered all expenses related to the transport of this harvest to the city or any other place agreed upon.[372] Temple farmers, temple gardeners, prebendary farmers, and large-scale leaseholders of temple land delivered part of the harvest as rent (*imittu/sūtu*), covered the costs for transport of the crops, and paid for specific administrative fees.[373] Similarly, farmer-generals of temple land paid lease (*sūtu*), *šibšu*, administrative fees ("rations"), ceremonial presents to specific functionaries, and probably also transport costs.[374]

Consequently, MNA may have paid transport costs because of a lease arrangement between him and the governors of Tâmti or the governor of Babylon. The agreement would have provided for MNA to pay rent from the crops that he grew on institutional land in Tâmti, on the one hand, and for transport of the crops, probably to the capital, on the other. In return, he was entitled to the agricultural surplus of the land. However, he is not attested as leaseholder or farmer-general of institutional land in Tâmti. Moreover, there was clearly more at stake when he paid for the transport of crops from Tâmti than merely carrying out the terms of a lease agreement with representatives of the state. As will be discussed below, the crops and their surplus were an integral part of MNA's trade in commodities, and the need for their transport was the logical outcome of this trade rather than the result of a lease agreement.

In fact, it is more likely that MNA had bought the crops from the governors of Tâmti after they had collected it from their leaseholders as part of his trade in commodities, and subsequently needed transport for the crops. Alternatively, he may have collected the crops himself after he bought the right to do so from the said governors against the payment of a fixed amount of silver in advance. From other texts in the archive we know that MNA occasionally bought agricultural income from rent and/or taxes, or the right to collect the income himself, from local functionaries in the royal administration, as for instance, in the cases recorded in Dar 338 and Dar 315.[375] The crops that he acquired in this way were, no doubt, part of those crops in which he traded and on which he built his fortune. MNA's trade in commodities, indeed, consisted of buying crops in the countryside and selling them at the markets in the capital or wherever they were in demand. The crops in which he traded, however, needed transporting from the fields to the markets. For this transport he needed boats, boat equipment, and men to sail, tow, load and unload the boats. In

372. The port of destination is always meticulously noted down in the contract (e.g,. NRVU 421).

373. Jursa, *Landwirtschaft*, 138ff.; 151 at line 1f. (*suluppū lā gamrūtu, suluppū gamrūtu*); 153 and 157 (i.a. CT 56 693), 166–67 (CT 56 482), and 210 (Cyr 180, costs for transport borne by the temple).

374. Moreover, the farmer-general had to guarantee that the temple workmen at his disposal met their non-agrarian obligations vis-à-vis the temple, such as *urāšu*-corvée and military service, e.g., BRM 1 101 and Jursa, *Landwirtschaft*, 103ff.

375. See n. 325.

addition, he needed access to quays, canals, and storehouses. The equipment and manpower were expensive, especially since they were usually not needed the whole year around, but only after the harvest.[376] Access to the waterway infrastructure was not free, but controlled by the state. We have seen, for instance, that MNA had to pay a toll (*miksu*) to the overseer of the quay for his boats' access to bridges and quays; furthermore, he had to rent boats, hire boat-towers, etc.[377] It now appears that he occasionally made monthly payments for all these expenses to clerks in the governor's service, in addition to making individual payments for each commodity whenever the need arose. These monthly, all-inclusive payments were called *gimru*.

Unfortunately, the *gimru*-texts do not tell us who actually organized the transports for which MNA paid. Were they organized by the governor of Babylon and his clerks and joined by MNA against participation in the costs? *Gimru* was then paid in return for the right to join officially organized transports on a monthly basis. No doubt by virtue of his office, the governor had easy access to the expensive resources that were necessary for the transport of various commodities. Moreover, we know that MNA occasionally joined both waterway and overland transports.[378] It must have been a profitable deal for MNA, since he did not have to invest in all the necessary equipment and men, nor bear all the risk, but only to pay his share in the expenses of the transport. Alternatively, MNA himself may have warranted the transport of the crops for his trade, so that *gimru* was paid in return for access to the state-controlled resources and facilities during a one-month period. In either case, the governor's clerks, who received MNA's payments for the transport of the crops, may have provided for the transport or the access to transport facilities in exchange for MNA's services in the collection of the crops from the farmers. In other words, their assistance in the transport of the crops may have been in response to MNA's assistance in the collection of rent and taxes on behalf of the state, in general, and from crown land in Tâmti, in particular.[379]

---

376. Bongenaar, *Ebabbar*, 39, cites several texts that show that the costs for the transport of flour for the temple amounted to one-third of the original amount of flour that was transported.

377. Thirty-one texts from the archive document this aspect of MNA's business (see above at n. 328). The *gimru*-payments were discussed above, and so were the boat-related expenses recorded in BM 30853, BM 30256, and BM 31554. The other texts will be discussed below in § 2.5.3.

378. In BM 30256, for instance, MNA paid for the rations of the boatmen in a transport that was organized by the governor of Babylon through his servant. For details, see above, p. 88f. at the discussion of BM 30256 and BM 30853: 12b–22. With respect to overland journeys organized by the governor of Babylon, see Dar 154 and the discussion on p. 26.

379. For MNA's assistance in the collection of the king's flour, toll from passing-by boats, soldiers, and corvée-workers on behalf of the governor of Babylon, see BM 33954, TCL 13 196, CT 22 74 and several other texts discussed in § 2.4. In particular, note the possible connection between CT 22 74 and Dar 154, i.e., between MNA's assistance in recruiting the governor's charioteers, on the one hand, and his right to join the governor's chariot on the

Finally, we should investigate the reason that the texts pay so much attention to the administrative responsibilities of the clerks who received the *gimru*-payments from MNA. One wonders about the relevance of this detailed information for the transaction itself. It would have sufficed to state that so-and-so "courtier" or "clerk" received payment by order of the governor of Babylon. Instead the texts describe the administrative responsibilities of each receiving clerk in much detail, thus distinguishing, for instance, between clerks responsible for gardeners and water-drawers of the Grand and New Palace and clerks responsible for courtiers of the New Palace.

The link between the clerks and the transport becomes clear if we assume that the transported crops, and perhaps also the income from the costs of transport, were needed by the clerks in question to pay rations to the men in their offices. It was in their interest that the crops be properly transported to the capital because they needed the crops and/or the income from the transport to feed the agricultural workmen, (crafts)men, administrative personnel, and foreigners under their responsibility—similar to the use of income from taxes to finance the food rations of civil servants. In BM 30589, for instance, the *ilku*-silver from a "bow" was transferred to the "clerk of the commissioners responsible for the (administration of the) rations of the New Palace."[380] Consequently, MNA's concern for an orderly transport of the crops is only one side of the coin. Other parties were interested in the efficient transport of crops from the fields to the capital. The texts, therefore, provide detailed information on these other parties as well.

2.5.3. *Excursus: MNA and the Transport of Goods by Boat*

The previously discussed texts[381] reveal an important characteristic of MNA's involvement in the organization of boat transports, to wit his dependence on state officials, in general, and on the governors of Babylon, in particular. He depended on state representatives to gain access to the resources and facilities that he needed to transport the crops for his trade, such as access to boats, towers, cables, and containers. His acquaintance with the governor of Babylon, in particular, enabled him to obtain these resources and facilities in the most economical way and occasionally to join transports that were organized by the governor's slave against participation in the costs. Moreover, the governor's clerks, who received MNA's payment for the transport of the crops, may also have provided for cheap transport or easy access to transport facilities in exchange for MNA's services in the collection of the crops from the farmers.

---

way to Elam (in remuneration of his assistance?!), on the other hand (more at p. 26). On the cooperation between MNA and the governors of Babylon, see above at n. 175 and below at p. 135 for a summary.

380. BM 30589: 8–11. Additional examples (from Sippar) in Jursa, *Bēl-rēmanni*, 107–9.

381. The eight *gimru*-texts as well as BM 30853, BM 30256, and BM 31554.

The texts discussed above, however, do not reflect the full scope of MNA's involvement in the transport business. The boats that he, according to BM 30853 and BM 31554, rented from the harbor-master and the governor of Babylon, for instance, account for only six out of fourteen boats that he or his son rented between Darius' fourth and thirty-first years. Consequently, we need to take into account all other texts from MNA's archive that record transactions regarding boats and boat transports in order to understand the full extent of his involvement. A matter that demands special attention is the degree to which MNA depended on the governor of Babylon or other officials for the successful management of his boat transports, on the one hand, and on private business relations, on the other. Finally, we shall examine the role the boat-related transactions played in his business and how these transactions contributed to the family's fortune and economic stability.

MNA and his son frequently rented boats. The archive contains six contracts recording the renting of boats: five by MNA and one by his son; two receipts of silver from MNA for the renting of two boats, and a document listing, among others, four different issues of silver for the renting of six boats.[382] The rents did not always take effect on the day that the contract was concluded. Three boat rentals contain a clause specifying that "from day such-and-such the boat would be at MNA's disposal."[383] In one case, the rent was to take effect the next day, and in the two other cases MNA or his son had to wait from a few days up to two weeks before they could use the rented boats.[384] Remarkably, the documents do not specify for how long MNA was entitled to rent the boats. Clearly, it was more important to write down when the rental started than when it ended. This is confirmed by the evidence on the rental of boats from other Neo Babylonian archives.[385]

In most cases, MNA paid one-third mina of white, medium-quality silver as rent for one boat.[386] Although the texts do not specify the term of the rental, the amount of one-third mina, i.e., twenty shekels, suggests rent on a yearly

382. Boat rentals: BM 30270, BM 30490, BM 30799, BM 31690^{+}, BM 31891, and Dar 138. Receipts of boat rent: BM 31554 and Dar 576. Additional document regarding boat rentals: BM 30853. Cf. n. 329.

383. BM 30799: Le. E., [*ultu*] *ūm* 11^{kam} *ša* ^{iti}*Ulūl*$^{?}$ *eleppu ina* [*pān*] *MNA*. Cf. Dar 138: 18 and BM 31690^{+}: 10–11.

384. BM 31690^{+} (the next day); Dar 138 (after five days); and BM 30799 (after two weeks).

385. E.g., BRU 6 39, *Fs. Diakonoff* 124ff. Nos. 2–3, Nbn 782 (on the next day); *AcSum* 19, 267–69 (= BM 15434), *OrAnt* 25 No. 6, BRU 6 36 and BRU 6 41 (on the same day); CT 4 44a (the following week); and BRU 6 34, BRU 6 35, NRVU 146, YOS 6 215, *OrAnt* 25 No. 5 (within a few days, cf. Wunsch, *AuOr* 15 No. 26 (= MM 914): but relevant passage is partly broken). More examples at Joannès, *TÉBR*, 328f.

386. BM 30270, BM 30490, BM 31891, and Dar 576. Amount uncertain in BM 30799 (l. 5) and broken off in BM 31554 (l. 1). Different sums of white silver are mentioned in BM 30853, see more below. Rent could also be paid in dates (thus in BM 31690^{+} and Dar 138), on which see more below.

basis.[387] Indeed, boat rentals from the Neo-Babylonian period show that the cost of hiring a boat for one month varied between three and fifteen shekels; for one year it varied between fifteen and twenty-six shekels; and hiring on a daily basis varied between half a shekel and one shekel a day.[388] Relatively large amounts of white silver were paid for the boats that MNA rented from state officials in BM 30853. He paid thirty-five shekels for one boat (ll. 37b–38), eighty-six shekels for two boats (5b–8), eighty shekels for several boats (30–32) and the extraordinarily high sum of one hundred and twenty shekels for one boat (25–27). The latter boat had to sail from Bāb-Nār-Kabarri to Šušan. Perhaps this involved a long-distance transport—assuming that this Šušan was the capital of Elam—in which the risks of losing the boat were above average, and for which, perhaps, a specific kind of boat or boat equipment was required. Rent could also be paid in dates, which was always reckoned on a daily basis. Thus, MNA paid approximately forty liters of dates for a boat with a capacity of sixty-three thousand liters, and almost five times this amount for a boat whose capacity is not given.[389] No doubt, the boat's loading capacity played a role in determining the rental rate.

MNA rented the boats from professional sailors, but they were not the owners of the boats.[390] The boat rental contracts clearly distinguish between ownership rights and rights of possession of the boat. It was "the boat of PN_1 that was at PN_2's disposal for plying the boatman's trade."[391] The latter must, therefore, have been a man trained in the boatman's trade, in other words, a professional sailor; one of them actually bears the title lú*malāḫu*.[392] The texts from MNA's archive do not specify the conditions for the sailors' disposal of the boats that they had rented out, but three texts from outside the archive shed some light on this matter. These sailors obtained boats by paying the owner an annual compensation (*maddattu*) of fifteen, twenty, or twenty-six shekels of silver in return for free access to the boat.[393] They had to maintain it and sail it for two months, but otherwise they were free to do with the boat as they

387. In CT 4 44a, for instance, the rent for a whole year was twenty shekels, which is exactly the amount that MNA paid for his rented boats. Other examples of boats rented for one year are discussed at Frame, *OrAnt* 25, 33f.; also *OLA* 65, 446f. (= BM 85367, published by Zadok but see collations by Weszeli, *NABU* 1996/20).

388. For examples or lists of prices, see Salonen, *Nautica*, 53–54; Beaulieu, *JNES* 52, 246–47; Joannès, *TÉBR*, 329; Frame, *OrAnt* 25, 33 n. 5; and Gurney, *Fs. Diakonoff*, 126.

389. BM 31690+ (0.1.0.4 *kor* of dates per day) and Dar 138 (1.0.3 *kor* of dates per day).

390. In the Neo-Babylonian period boats could also be rented directly from the owner, e.g., CT 4 44a, BRU 6 34, BRU 6 35, BRU 6 39 and perhaps also BRU 6 36.

391. E.g., BM 30270: 1–3, *eleppu ša* PN_1 *ša ina pān* PN_2 *ana* lú*malaḫūtu*. For *ina pān* and *ana malaḫūtu*, see commentary *ad hoc*. On the expression *ina pān* in other texts from MNA's time, see n. 144.

392. BM 30490: 16.

393. CT 4 44a, *OrAnt* 25 No. 4 and *Fs. Diakonoff* 124ff. No. 2. Consequently, one should not label these texts as simple "hire of a boat."

pleased, so that they could rent it out to third parties and receive the rent.[394] This created a triangular relationship among owner, sailor, and boat tenant and we find clear examples of such a relationship in the boat rentals from MNA's archive. BM 31690⁺, for instance, regards a boat that belonged to Nabū-ēṭir-napšāte but had been given to Aplaya for plying the boatman's trade and was subsequently let by this Aplaya to MNA's son for rent. By repeating Aplaya's name twice it is made clear that he had the boat at his disposal (*ina pān Aplaya*) and rented it out to MNA (*Aplaya ana idišu … iddin*).[395] The other boat rentals from MNA's archive and the receipts of rent money are less clearly formulated in this respect, but were, no doubt, based on the same triangular relationship.[396]

In addition to rent, MNA had to pay for the maintenance of the professional sailor who rented the boat to him. In BM 31891, for instance, he rented a boat "for one-third mina of white, medium-quality silver (in rent) and thirty-six liters of flour in maintenance."[397] MNA paid for maintenance in three more cases, but we do not know the amount paid.[398] Remarkably, there is no payment for maintenance in the two cases in which rent was paid in dates on a daily basis. It may have been included in the rent. As it is, the payments were not for the boat's maintenance, but for that of the sailor. Indeed, two texts make clear that the sailor received payment from MNA for "the rent of the boat and his maintenance" and "for the rent of his boat in addition to (payment for) his maintenance."[399] If the maintenance of the boat were at stake, the possessive pronoun should have been feminine (i.e., *kurummātiša*), since in Akkadian the word for boat is feminine.[400] Moreover, the tenant's obligation to pay for the maintenance of the sailors or men on the rented boat is attested also in texts from outside MNA's archive. The boat-tenant in TUM 2/3 34, for instance, had to pay "three liters of flour a day for the rations of the men who performed the

394. *Fs. Diakonoff* 124ff. No. 2: *eleppa ina kārišunu ukattamū ušursudū* as well as *ina eleppi illakū*; and *OrAnt* 25 No. 4: *eleppa ukattamū ušarsadū*. The boatmen in CT 4 44a seem to have enjoyed better conditions: the boat was already covered (*kuttumu šursudu*) and if it leaked, the owner had to pay the repair costs.

395. BM 31690⁺: 2 (*ina pān*) and 3. Similar clearly formulated examples from outside MNA's archive are, for instance, NRVU 147: 1–5 and *OLA* 65, 446f. = BM 85367: 1–8.

396. The other boat rentals do not repeat the name of the person who had the boat at his disposal before the verb "he gave it for rent" (*ana idišu iddin*). Thus, for instance, BM 30270: 1–7, *eleppu ša* PN$_1$ *ša ina pān* PN$_2$ *ana malaḫūti eleppa ana idišu … iddin*); cf. BM 30490, BM 30799, BM 31891 and Dar 138. In the two receipts of boat rent (BM 31554 and Dar 576) we assume that the receivers were not the owners of the boat, but the persons who had the boat at their disposal, as in the boat rental contracts.

397. BM 31891: 4–5, *ana ⅓ manê kaspu peṣû nuḫḫutu u 1 pān qīme kurummātu*.

398. Thus in BM 30270 and BM 30490. In BM 30799 we find a fragmentary reference to "maintenance" (*kurummātu*) at the end of the contract after the date (l. 19: KURU[M$_6$ …]).

399. BM 30270: 8 (*idi eleppi u kurummātišu*); and BM 30490: 8 (*idi eleppišu adi kurummātišu*).

400. It is true that the Neo-Babylonian dialect no longer rigidly distinguishes between *-šu* (masculine pronoun) and *-ša* (feminine pronoun), and sometimes speaks about *ištēn eleppu* rather than *ištēt eleppu* (e.g., BM 31347: 1, 5). Nevertheless, it is remarkable that the texts

trade of boatman."[401] Consequently, MNA rented not only boats, but also the professional services of the sailor (and his men) on the boats.

As a matter of fact, it did not suffice to rent or buy[402] boats; one also needed the men to sail, tow, and dock the boats, such as experienced sailors (^{lú}*malāḫu*), boat-towers (^{lú}*šadādu*), and men to unload$^{?}$ the boats (*ana napāli*). These professionals could be obtained in various ways. First, their services could be hired. We saw above that it was possible to rent a boat together with the man on the boat. In that case the hirer had to pay for the man's maintenance in addition to paying rent for the boat.[403] The services of these boatmen, however, could also be hired separately. Bulṭaya/Ḫabāṣiru//Rē'i-alpi, for instance, was engaged twice by MNA, once on a monthly basis for eight shekels a month and once on a yearly basis for one-third$^{?}$ mina of marked silver a year.[404] The first time he had to sail a boat to Babylon.[405] He started working on the first of Ayyar of Darius' fifth year and received his first salary five weeks later, on the seventh of Sīmān.[406] He was hired a second time toward the end of the year, but received his salary on the twentieth of Kislīm of the next year, i.e., more than eleven months later.[407] The kind of job he had to fulfil is not specified in this second case, but was, no doubt, related to the transport of crops by boat as in the previous one. In this respect, it should be noted that Bulṭaya's receipts of salary

---

under consideration are firm in their use of *-šu* in the expression *eleppu u kurummātišu*; if the boat's maintenance was at stake, some texts would have had *kurummātišu*, and others *kurummātiša*.

401. *kurummāt* ^{lú}*malaḫūtu*, Joannès, *TÉBR*, 329; also Salonen, *Nautica*, 57–61. For the expression *kurummāt* ^{lú}*malaḫūtu*, see further TÉBR No. 90 and the administrative record Nbn 1129, which lists the issue of dates from the storehouse (*ultu kalak*[*ki*], line 1) for the rations of individuals and groups of professionals; amongst others the list mentions "rations for the obla[tes]" (PAD.ḪI.A LÚ *ši-ra-k*[*u* ...], line 7), and "[rations for] (the men who perform) the trade of boatman" ([PAD.ḪI.A] LÚ *má-laḫ*$_{x}$*-ú-tú*, line 11). Also compare similar expressions in letters and administrative records that mention payments for rent and *kurummātu ša* ^{lú}*malāḫu* (NbBU 238), *kurummātu ša* ^{lú}*malāḫū*^{meš} *u* ^{lú}*agrū*^{meš} (TCL 12 74 and TCL 12 232), and *kurummātu ša* 30 ^{lú}*ṣābē*$^{\text{[meš]}}$ (NbBU 119; cf. NbBU 168: 19–20). For *kiskir* ^{lú}*malāḫūtu* (e.g., Nbn 968), see Bongenaar, *Ebabbar*, 288 n. 249.

402. MNA bought two boats in Darius' twenty-sixth year: OECT 10 234, and BM 30370 (with BM 30961 recording the receipt of the purchase price).

403. Cf. the hirelings (^{lú}*agrū*^{meš}) mentioned in TCL 12 74 and TCL 12 232 from outside MNA's archive quoted above. Also NbBU 71: a letter about a boat that was held up at the quay and for which half a shekel of silver per day had to be paid for its rent (*idi* ^{giš}*eleppi*) in addition to (*u*) one shekel per day for the salary of the hirelings on the boat (*idi* ^{lú}*agrū*^{meš}).

404. Dar 158 and Dar 215. It is not possible to compare the salaries, because we do not know the quality of the silver in Dar 158.

405. Apparently, Bulṭaya had to sail the boat with a team of Babylonians who were performing their *kanšu* service in it. MNA seems to have been in charge of this *kanšu*-boat transport. See above at p. 19, 30ff., and § 2.2.2.

406. See commentary at Dar 158: 20–22.

407. See commentary at Dar 215: 2, 4b–6.

were witnessed by, i.a., two men who knew him and his employer from the latter's transactions with boats, crops from institutional land in Šaḫrīnu and real estate in Litamu.[408] These three kinds of transactions were probably interrelated and Bulṭaya may, therefore, have worked for MNA in the transshipment of these crops and their transport by boat from Šaḫrīnu and Litamu to the markets.

Second, some skilled workers could be obtained from the state's pool of forced laborers. As we have seen above, in the section on the recruitment of corvée-workers, MNA was able to contact some of these workers and have them tow boats on his behalf for a limited period of time.[409] Among them were also hirelings, i.e., men hired by the person who had to tow for the governor of Babylon in order to tow on his behalf.

Third, the services of professional sailors, as well as other services, could be obtained from state officials against payment. Thus, MNA occasionally paid the agents of the governor of Babylon for services of various kinds. He paid for the service of docking[?] boats at the harbor (*ana napāli*) to Šuma-ukīn, who received this payment on the account of the governor of Babylon. He also paid for hirelings to Šullumu, overseer [of the …], who received this payment, as well as MNA's payment for the hirelings' clothing, "in the presence of the governor of Babylon." Consequently, the hirelings may well have belonged to the latter's pool of forced laborers. At other times MNA paid for the right to join a boat transport organized by the governor's servant against participation in the costs for the rations of the men on the boat. Frequently, he paid for the right to use canals, bridges, quays and other infrastructure to quay overseers or clerks in the service of the governor of Babylon.[410]

MNA used his boats to transport agricultural products, especially freshly harvested crops.[411] Many texts refer to the load or loading capacity of the boats in question. The boats for which MNA paid tolls (*miksu*), for instance, were loaded with 70 *kor* of barley, 330 *kor* of mainly dates, and an unspecified amount

---

408. The two men in question are Ea-apla-iddin/Mušēzib-Marduk//Ṭābiḫ-kāri (Dar 158) and Rīmūt-Bēl/Ardiya//Itinnu (Dar 215). The former was present when Bulṭaya was hired by MNA to sail a boat (Dar 158) and when MNA rented a boat (BM 30799). He also owned land in Litamu that he sold to MNA (Dar 217 = *CM* 20b 183; Wunsch, *Felder* 2, 161ff., esp. 163 and n. 339; note the presence of Bulṭaya and Rīmūt-Bēl among the witnesses!). On Rīmūt-Bēl, see more at p. 172 (esp. n. 685).

409. BM 31118, BM 30764, BM 31188, and BM 32932. For a discussion of these texts, see above at § 2.4.2.4.

410. Payments for dockers[?] (BM 30853: 23–24), hirelings (BM 30853: 1–5), rations of boatmen (BM 30256, cf. BM 30853: 12b–15; and 19–20), and access to waterways and their infrastructure (*miksu*- and *gimru*-payments).

411. This was a common use of boats in the Neo-Babylonian period, e.g., the rent of boats "to transport barley to Ālu-Šamaš" (*idi* [giš]*eleppāti*[meš] *ša uṭṭāti ana Ālu-Šamaš uqarrubūni*, Nbn 862; cf. formulation in BM 30853: 31–32), or "to transport straw" (*ana qurrubu ša tibni*, BRU 6 39). Similarly, a boat may be defined in terms of the goods that it transported as "a boat of straw" (*eleppu ša tibni*, Nbk 282), or "a boat of flour" (*eleppu ša qīme*, NbBU 66 and BM 30853:

of onions.[412] The boats for which he had to pay transport costs were loaded with 50, 100, and 200 *kor* of barley, 316 *kor* of dates, 30+ *kor* probably of dates, 400$^?$ *kor* of barley or dates, and additional unknown amounts of barley.[413] Some of the boats that he rented were loaded with barley or flour. Thus, he paid "for the rent of the boats, which (are)$^?$ with Ipriya (and)$^?$ transport(ed) barley," and "for the rental of a boat (for the transport) of flour."[414] Moreover, the person who rented his boat to MNA's son had to guarantee that it could carry 350 *kor* of dates.[415]

It may be inferred from the month in which the texts were written that the boats were mainly used to transport freshly harvested crops. As a matter of fact, the texts recording boat-related transactions are dated in a well-defined period of the year. The Table below, which arranges the texts in a chronological order, shows that MNA concluded transactions regarding boats and their paraphernalia almost exclusively between June (Simān) and November (Araḫsamna).[416] As for the years in which he was active in the transport business, two periods stand out: (1) Darius' fourth to tenth years (518–511 B.C.E.) and (2) Darius' twenty-third to twenty-sixth years (498–495 B.C.E.).[417]

---

38). This was no doubt another way for saying, briefly, that the boat was fit to transport barley etc. More at Salonen, *Nautica*, 29–33. Cf. Römer, *AOAT* 232, 361–66, for older evidence, especially from Sumerian literary sources.

412. Dar 268 (70 *kor*); BM 31347 (330 *kor*); and BM 30747 (unspecified; this text has more than one unique feature. It is witnessed, but not dated; nor does it specify where it was drafted or the name of the scribe who wrote it. Moreover, the payment for *miksu* recorded in it is not received by the overseer of the quay but by Nergal-ušallim, son of Arrabbi, without official title. See more at p. 146.).

413. BM 30639 (50 and 100 *kor*); BM 33112 (200 *kor*); BRM 1 81 (316 *kor*); BM 31393 (30 [+ x] *kor*); BM 31572 (400$^?$ *kor*); BM 31786 and BM 32891 (unknown amounts).

414. BM 30853: 30–32 and 38.

415. BM 31690$^+$: *pūt šūlû ša* 350 *kor suluppī* PN *naši*. Cf. BRU 6 35: *pūt šūlû ša* 150 *kor uṭṭātī* PN *naši*. If it later turned out that the boat carried less than what had originally been agreed upon, the parties had to agree on a financial compensation: TCL 12 121 and *OrAnt* 25 No. 5. Hence the *pūt šūlû*-clause was more than just a guarantee for loading the boat (against San Nicolò, *BRU* 6, 51 at line 9); it guaranteed the loading capacity of the boat. This is the reason that Neo-Babylonian boat rentals often specify the boat's loading capacity, e.g., the rent of "a boat for 3 cows and 24 sheep" (Nbn 401), "a boat that carries 30 *kor*" (*eleppu ša* 3 *kor idikku*, *OrAnt* 25 No. 5), and "a boat that carries 150 *kor*" (*eleppu ša* 150 *kor idikku*, TCL 12 121).

416. In addition, there are four texts dated in January (Ṭebēt), two in March (Addar), and four of which the month is broken off.

417. Cf. the boat-related texts in which MNA was only indirectly involved: BM 32873 (16/xii/26 Dar, scribe) and BM 32883 (10/i/10 Dar, guarantor); and the texts regarding MNA's income from boat- or bridge-related taxes (discussed above at § 2.4.1): BM 31227 (4/[-]/25 Dar), BM 41443 (8/iii/26 Dar), TCL 13 196 (1/vii/26 Dar), and BM 30366 (7/viii/26 Dar).

TABLE 6: Chronological List of MNA's Boat-Related Transactions

TEXT:	DATE:	(JULIAN CALENDAR:)
BM 30799	26/v/4[?] Dar	2 Sept. 518[?] B.C.E.
Dar 138	1 or 9/x/4 Dar	2 or 10 Jan. 517 B.C.E.
Dar 158	7/iii/5 Dar	3 June 517 B.C.E.
Dar 215	20/x/6 Dar	29 Jan. 515 B.C.E.
Dar 268	18/iv/⸢10⸣ Dar	19 July 512 B.C.E.
BM 30747	no date[418]	April 512 – March 511 B.C.E.
BM 31554	11 or 21/x/23 Dar	12 (or 22) Jan. 498 B.C.E.
Dar 576	22/x/23 Dar	23 Jan. 498 B.C.E.
BM 30256	2/vii/24 Dar	25 Sep. 498 B.C.E.
BM 32932	18/vii/24 Dar	11 Oct. 498 B.C.E.
BM 31188	25/[-]/24 Dar	April 498 – March 497 B.C.E.
BM 31138	19/iii/25 Dar	4 July 497 B.C.E.
BM 30764	23/iii/25 Dar	8 July 497 B.C.E.
BM 31572	7/iv/25 (or 26 Dar)	21 July 497 B.C.E. or 11 July 496 B.C.E.
BM 33112	17/v/25 Dar	30 Aug. 497 B.C.E.
BM 30639	28/vii/25 Dar	8 Nov. 497 B.C.E.
BM 31393	[-]/viii/25 Dar	Nov.– Dec. 497 B.C.E.
BM 31118	4/[-]/25 Dar	April 497 – March 496 B.C.E.
BM 31786	[-]/[-]/25 Dar	April 497 – March 496 B.C.E. [419]
BM 32891	11/iv/[26 Dar]	15 July [496 B.C.E.][420]
BM 30370	3–9/v/26 Dar	5–11 Aug. 496 B.C.E.
BM 31891	7/vi/[26 Dar][421]	8 Sept. [496 B.C.E.]
BM 30961	12/vi/26 Dar	13 Sept. 496 B.C.E.
BRM 1 81	4/viii/26 Dar	3 Nov. 496 B.C.E.
BM 30490	5/xii/⸢26⸣ Dar	2 Mar. 495 B.C.E.
BM 30270	6/xii/26 Dar	3 Mar. 495 B.C.E.
OECT 10 234	⸢20+⸣/[-]/26 Dar	April 496 – March 495
BM 31690+	18/viii/31 Dar	23 Nov. 491 B.C.E.
BM 30591	27/vii/35 Dar	19 Oct. 487 B.C.E.
BM 30853	no date	about expenses in the months of Oct. – Nov.
BM 31347	20/ix/[-] Dar	second half of Dec. – beginning of Jan.

418. The text is not dated but refers to crops of Darius' tenth year.

419. Probably month iv, as was argued above at p. 91.

420. Or: [25] Dar, hence 25 July [497 B.C.E.]. More at p. 91.

421. The other two texts regarding MNA's journeys to Birtu-ša-ṣērūa are dated in Darius' twenty-sixth year (BM 30490 and BM 30270 dated on 5 and 6/xii/26 Dar).

The period between June (Simān) and November (Araḫsamna), which may be called the "transport season," was the period in which freshly harvested crops were transported from the fields to storehouses for storage and to markets for distribution. Barley was harvested in Nisan–Ayyar (between March and May), onions in Ayyar (April–May), and dates in Tašrīt-Araḫsamna (between September and November). Accordingly, MNA started doing business with boats at the end of the barley and onion harvests, especially from July (end Šimān) onward, after the crops had been bundled and made ready for transport. He continued transporting these crops for several months and when, by the end of the summer, all the barley and onions had been transported, he turned to transporting the freshly harvested dates in autumn.[422] As pointed out above, in some cases MNA may not have transported the goods himself but had the governor's clerks and servants take care of the transport against participation in the costs. The texts do not tell us to where MNA transported the goods. Most likely, the crops were taken to places where they could be stored or sold. In this respect, Babylon was a very likely port of destination, since in the capital there was a constant need of crops to feed the many state-dependent workers living there.

Outside the "transport season," namely early in March (Addar), MNA rented boats to transport goods to a military stronghold in the countryside known as Birtu-ša-ṣērūa (*alias* Birīššārū'a). Three boat rentals mention this place as the port of destination. MNA was to sail to (*ana*) Birtu-ša-ṣērūa, or more precisely till (*adi*) Birtu-ša-ṣērūa and not beyond its fortress (*birta ul itteq*).[423] The place was clearly a fortified settlement in the countryside, named after the fortress (*birtu*) by which it was dominated. Quite likely, MNA needed the boats to travel to Birtu-ša-ṣērūa and to unload cargo at its fortress, rather than to pick up the harvest from the surrounding fields. This interpretation is based on three arguments. First, he rented the boats with which he was to sail to the said place before the harvest season. Two boats he rented at the end of the winter before the barley harvest. The third boat he rented at the end of the summer before the date harvest. It is, therefore, unlikely that the boats were sent to Birtu-ša-ṣērūa to pick up the harvest, because the crops had not yet been gathered in. Second, the boats arrived at the fortress loaded with cargo. This is clear from BM 30490, which states that "he should *unload*? the boat at the fortress," if one accepts the interpretation of the verb *napālu* as "unload."[424] The other two texts are less explicit in this respect, but the fact that the boats were loaded upon their arrival

422. There is one payment for transport costs that does not fit this pattern, BM 30639, because it is dated in November, but refers to the transport of barley. It may have been a late payment for a barley transport that took place earlier in the year. Actually, lines 8–9 seem to refer to such an earlier transport: "there is a previou[s] register regarding the costs for the transport of fifty *kor* of barley … that he has (already) [r]eceived."

423. BM 30270 (6/xii/26 Dar), BM 30490 (5/xii/26 Dar) and BM 31891 (7/vi/[26] Dar).

424. BM 30490: 26–27: *eleppa ina birtu ša ṣērū'a inappal*, see commentary *ad hoc*.

in Birtu-ša-ṣērūa may be inferred from another clause, viz. the one preventing the boats from sailing beyond the fortress.[425] This clause was meant to reduce the risk of loss. The need for such a clause becomes obvious if we assume that the boats were loaded with cargo. Indeed, it was more urgent to prevent the loss of a loaded boat than that of an unloaded one. Consequently, all three boats that were sent to Birtu-ša-ṣērūa were loaded with cargo and needed to be unloaded at the fortress even in those two cases that lack an explicit clause on unloading the boats. The goods unloaded at the fortress were most likely needed to either feed or equip the soldiers stationed there. In this respect they very likely carried beer or flour to bake bread, rather than raw materials such as freshly harvested dates or barley, which still needed to be processed.[426] In short, if the boats were to arrive in Birtu-ša-ṣērūa to pick up crops that had been gathered in from the surrounding fields, the boats should have been empty upon arrival and the texts should have been dated after harvest time.[427]

The four texts dated in January (Ṭebēt) were probably not directly related to the transport of agricultural produce from the fields to the capital,[428] or they reflect special circumstances. The boat rented on the ninth of Ṭebēt, for instance, was not immediately available (Dar 138). Similarly, the person who received his salary on the twentieth of Ṭebēt had been hired for a year and his work-assignment was, therefore, not limited to the "transport season" (Dar 215). Furthermore, the rent paid in Ṭebēt of Darius' twenty-third year may have been late payments for boats that were hired earlier in the year during the "transport-season" (BM 31554 and Dar 576).

It is further characteristic of MNA's transactions concerning boats and boat transports that they were witnessed and written by a limited group of persons.

---

425. BM 30490: 10b–17; BM 30270: 9b–12; and BM 31891: end Obverse + Left Edge.

426. Was MNA transporting the king's flour that he helped collect on behalf of the governor of Babylon according to BM 33954?

427. I know of one other boat rental from the Neo-Babylonian period that stated where the boat was to go. The contract in question is TUM 2/3 34. The boat in this case had to go "from the quay of Šaṭir (IM^{ki}) till the quay of the Fortress." The village of Šaṭir is known to have been a place in the countryside where military colonists had been settled. From there the boat had to sail to the Fortress. This boat transport, therefore, is very similar in background to the boat transports to the Fortress of Birtu-ša-ṣērūa from MNA's archive. Another of MNA's boats sailed from Bāb-Nār-Kabarru to Šušan (BM 30853: 25–27). The reason of this boat transport, however, is unknown.

428. They may have been linked to MNA's involvement in the production of beer (bibliography below at n. 632). We know that he transported beer in vessels by boat (BM 30853: 12–15 and BM 30256). Boats were used to transport various commodities in the Neo-Babylonian period. For a list of these commodities + text references, see Salonen, *Nautica*, 29–33; and add, the use of boats in the Neo-Babylonian period to transport divine statues (e.g., Beaulieu, *JNES* 52, 245ff.), sacrificial sheep (*OrAnt* 25 No. 6 and Nbn 401, both dated in Nisan), and sheep to be shorn (Nbk 296, receipt of rent *ana* [*idi*] *eleppi ša ana gi-iz-zi illiku*, "for a boat that went to (the place of) shearing"; and Nbn 856 regarding a payment *ana eleppi ša gi-zi*).

Indeed, many texts share witnesses or were written by the same scribe. The Table below illustrates this point.[429]

TABLE 7: Witnesses and Scribes in MNA's Boat-Related Transactions

	Name:	*Attested in Boat-Related Texts as:*		*Attested in Other Texts as:*	
1.	Ardiya	W	in BM 32883	W	in BM 30629 (silver for *nidintu ša* lú*qašti*)
		S	in Dar 215	W	in Dar 338 (commercial venture in Šaḫrīnu)
				W	in BM 31018 (silver for Šaddinnu, *šibšu*-related?)
				W	in E.36.1904 (rent in barley for Darius' tenth year)
				W	in *CM* 20b 232 (*imittu* for MNA; ti[thes] not yet paid)
				W	in Dar 273 (real estate at the Uraš gate) and *passim* in MNA's land transactions
2.	Bēl-asûa	C	in TCL 13 196	W	in BM 30541 (!), (probably *ilku*-related)
		W	in BM 31891 (!)		
		W	in BM 31347 (?)		
		W	in BM 32873		
3.	Bēl-iddin	W	in BM 31572	W	in BM 31951 (silver due to MNA)
		W	in BM 31690+		
		W	in BM 32891		
4.	Bēl-erība	S	in BM 30270 (!)	C	in BM 30274 (recruitment of a soldier for Bēl-erība)
		S	in BM 30490 (//)	S	in BM 30446 (recruitment of boat-towers)
		S	in BM 32891 [//]	S	in BM 30795 (recruitment of workers for the governor)
		W	in BM 30256	W	in BM 30366 (*ilku*, related to the exploitation of a bridge)
		W	in BM 30370 (!)	W	in BM 30772 (*ilku*)
		W	in BM 30961	W	in TCL 13 197 (*ilku*)
				W	in TCL 13 198 (*ilku*)

429. The Table includes TCL 13 196 regarding MNA's income from a bridge, and the two texts regarding boats in which he was only a guarantor (BM 32883) or the scribe of the document (BM 32873). The occurrence of persons in these texts who are also mentioned in the texts regarding MNA's expenses for boats confirms that the group of persons dealing with boats in general was a closed group of acquaintances.

			W	in Dar 544 (silver for a courtier and clerk)
			W	in Dar 552 (silver for Bēl-erība's brother)
			W	in BM 31226 (a hireling for the military commander)
			W	in BM 31449 (a hireling/hirelings)
			W	in BM 41442 (baker apprenticeship)
5. Bulṭaya	W	in BM 30270		
	W	in BM 30490		
6. Ea-apla-iddin	W	in BM 30799	S	in Dar 213 [/], (transfer of tax$^{?}$ silver by MNA)
	W	in Dar 158		
7. Erībaya	W	in BM 30490	C	in Dar 296 (Bagasarū-text)
8. Ḫabaṣīru	W	in BM 30270		
	W	in BM 30490		
9. Ḫašdaya	W	in BM 30270		
	W	in BM 30490		
10. Kāṣir	W	in BM 30639	W	in BM 30446 (//), (recruitment of boat-towers)
	W	in BM 31393		
11. Marduk	W	in BM 31572	W	in BM 31322 (*ilku*)
	W	in BM 31786 [//]	W	in BM 31517 (*ilku*)
	W	in BM 30764	W	in BM 31798 (^{giš}*qaštu*)
			W	in BM 31138 (//), (barley for a courtier and clerk)
12. Marduk-bēlšunu				
	W	in Dar 268	C	in Dar 206 (//), (*rikis qabli*)
			C	in Dar 318 (crops from MNA's employee in Til Gula)
			C	in Dar 334 (crops from MNA's employee)
			C	in Dar 450 (silver debt of MNA)
			S	in TCL 13 185 (transfer of tax$^{?}$ silver by MNA)
			W	in *Iraq* 55 No. 2 (slave sale by MNA's brother)
13. Murašû	W	in BM 32883	W	in Dar 455 (silver for Bēl-iddin, temple-related)
	W	in Dar 268		
14. Nabû-apla-iddin				
	C	in BM 30370		

	C	in BM 30961		
	S	in BM 31891		
15. Nabû-bullissu	S	in BM 30764	S	in BM 31517 (*ilku*)
	S	in BM 31347 (?)		
	C	in BM 31347 (?)		
16. Nabû-ittannu	W	in BM 31554	C	in Dar 220 (*rikis qabli*, not from MNA's archive)
			C	in Dar 481 (*rikis qabli*, not from MNA's archive)
17. Nabû-šuma-iddin				
	W	in BM 31347 (?)	W	in BM 31226 (a hireling for the military commander)
			W	in Dar 455 (silver for Bēl-iddin, temple-related)
18. Nabû-uballiṭ	S	in BM 31393 [//]		
	S	in BM 30639		
19. Nergal-šuma-ibni				
	W	in BRM 1 81	W	in BM 30366 (*ilku*, related to the exploitation of a bridge)
20. Nergal-ušallim				
	W	in Dar 268	W	in BM 41449 (thieves in the city of the *qīpu*)
			W	in Dar 345 (prebend-related)
			W	in Dar 182 (wool for the temple of Lugal-Marada)
			W	in Dar 213 (transfer of tax? silver by MNA)
			W	in Dar 338 (commercial venture in Šaḫrīnu)
21. Nidinti-Bēl	W	in BRM 1 81	W	in BM 41607 (*ilku*)
			S	in Dar 572 (salaries and rations for corvée-workers)
			S	in Dar 338 (commercial venture in Šaḫrīnu)
			W	in BM 31058 (crops from institutional land in Šaḫrīnu)
			W	in Dar 310 (Rīmūt-Bēl text)
			S	in BM 31018 (silver for Šaddinnu, *šibšu*-related?)
22. Nidintu/Ardiya				
	W	in BM 30639	W	in BM 31138: //Rab-līmi, (barley for a courtier and clerk)

	W	in BM 31393	C	in Dar 577 (//), (silver for the governor of Babylon)
23. Nidintu/Kalbaya				
	W	in BM 30370	C	in BM 31449 (a hireling/hirelings)
	W	in OECT 10 234: [Nidintu]	W	in BM 30994 (silver debt to MNA, about ^{lú}DÍM)
	W	in BM 30961	W	? In BM 31138 (//), (barley for a courtier and clerk)
	W	in TCL 13 196		
	W	in BM 41443 [430]		
	W	? in BM 31786 [//]		
24. Rīmūt-Bēl	W	in Dar 215	W	in Dar 182 (wool for the temple of Lugal-Marada)
	S	? in BM 30747	W	in b 2800 (transfer of tax$^{?}$ silver from MNA)
			W	in BM 41442 (baker apprenticeship)
			W	in Dar 296 (Bagasarū-text)
			W	in BM 31058 (crops from institutional land in Šaḫrīnu)
			W	in *Iraq* 55 No. 1 (rent in barley for Darius' tenth year)
			W	in Dar 318 (crops from MNA's employee in Til Gula)
			W	in Dar 217 and Dar 273 (real estate at the Uraš gate)
25. Šullumaya	W	in BM 31572	W	in BM 41607: [Šullumaya], (*ilku*)
	W	in BM 32891	W	in BM 31798 (^{giš}*qaštu*)
			W	? in BM 30541 (reads Šullumu/Nabû-aḫa-iddin, not Šullumaya/Nabû-nādin-aḫi//Nabaya), (probably *ilku*-related)
			W	in Dar 542 (Bagasarū-text)
26. Šulum-Bābili	W	in BM 31891 (//)	W	in BM 30541(!), (probably *ilku*-related)
	W	in BM 32873 (!)		
27. Tattannu	W	in BM 30764	W	in BM 30235 (*ilku*)
	W	in BM 31393	W	in BM 31517 (*ilku*)
	W	in BM 31572	W	in BM 31798 (^{giš}*qaštu*)
	W	in BM 31786 [//]	W	? in BM 31138: Tattannu/[...], (barley for a courtier)
	W	in BM 32891	W	in Dar 469 (real estate at the Uraš gate)

430. For the publication of this text, see n. 145.

NAMES: 1 = Ardiya/Dādiya//Nabaya; 2 = Bēl-asûa/Nergal-uballiṭ//Mudammiq-Adad; 3 = Bēl-iddin/Iddin-Nabû//Dābibī; 4 = Bēl-erība/Kalbaya//Šumu-libši (commander-of-fifty); 5 = Bulṭaya/Šamaš-(zēra)-ibni; 6 = Ea-apla-iddin/Mušēzib-Marduk//Ṭābiḫ-kāri; 7 = Erībaya/Ša-Nabû-šu; 8 = Ḫabaṣīru/Šaddinnu; 9 = Ḫašdaya/Bēl-balāssu-iqbi; 10 = Kāṣir/Tattannu//Eppeš-ilī; 11 = Marduk/Gūzānu//Kaṣṣidakku; 12 = Marduk-bēlšunu/Arad-Marduk//Šangû-Ea; 13 = Murašû/Nabû-aḫḫē-iddin (*alias* Uššaya)//Arad-Nanna or Nanna-utu; 14 = Nabû-apla-iddin/Lâbāši//Nūr-Papsukkal; 15 = Nabû-bullissu/Nabû-mukīn-zēri//Ea-ṣalam-ilī; 16 = Nabû-ittannu/Mušēzib-Marduk//Egibi; 17 = Nabû-šuma-iddin/Šāpik-zēri//Dēkû; 18 = Nabû-uballiṭ//Bēl-apla-uṣur; 19 = Nergal-šuma-ibni/Šullumu; 20 = Nergal-ušallim (*alias* Šullumu)/Mušēzib-Marduk//Nappāḫu; 21 = Nidinti-Bēl/Nabû-dāmiq-ilī (*alias* Damqiya)//Nādin-še'i; 22 = Nidintu/Ardiya//Rab-šušši (*alias* Rab-līmi?); 23 = Nidintu/Kalbaya//Suḫaya; 24 = Rīmūt-Bēl/Ardiya//Itinnu; 25 = Šullumaya/Nabû-nādin-aḫi//Nabaya; 26 = Šulum-Bābili/Tabnêa//Mudammiq-Adad; 27 = Tattannu/Nabû-kāṣir//Dābibī.

ABBREVIATIONS: W = witness; S = scribe; C = contractant; (!) = reading of part of the person's name is emended; ? = identification of the person in the text in question is doubtful; (?) = reading of part of the person's name is doubtful due to its fragmentary state of preservation, but the identification of the person in question is certain; (//) = the text does not give the person's family name (which hampers the identification of the person in question to some degree); [/] = the person's patronymy is broken off; [//] = the person's family name is broken off.

The Table also shows that the same person could be among the witnesses in one contract and be the scribe of another. Bēl-erība/Kalbaya//Šumu-libši, for instance, wrote two boat rentals and one payment of transport costs for MNA; he was present as a witness when MNA bought a boat, paid for it, and paid for the rations of the governor's boatmen.[431] Similarly, Ardiya/Dādiya//Nabaya wrote MNA's rental of the services of the sailor Bulṭaya and witnessed the sale of a boat for which MNA assumed warranty.[432] Furthermore, some of the persons who were MNA's business partners in one contract assisted him as witness or scribe in another. Nabû-apla-iddin/Lâbāši/Nūr-Papsukkal, for instance, sold his boat to MNA in the beginning of Ab of Darius' twenty-sixth year and acknowledged his receipt of the purchase price the next month. A few days prior to this receipt, he assisted MNA in one of his boat rentals. Indeed, he wrote the rental agreement for him so that MNA could use the rented boat to sail to Birtu-ša-ṣērūa.[433] Bēl-asûa/Nergal-uballiṭ//Mudammiq-Adad is another example of someone who assisted MNA in his boat-related transactions in more than one way.[434] He leased the right to collect tolls from boats at a bridge from

431. On Bēl-erība/Kalbaya/Šumu-libši, also see above at n. 195.

432. Ardiya/Dādiya//Nabaya wrote Dar 215 (labor contract) and witnessed BM 32883 (sale of a boat). He frequently witnessed MNA's transactions involving real estate and field-rent (details below on p. 114 n. 456 and at Table 7).

433. Nabû-apla-iddin/Lâbāši//Nūr-Papsukkal was one of the contracting parties in BM 30370 (boat purchase), BM 30961 (receipt of the purchase price) and the scribe of BM 31891 (boat rental).

434. The third example is less conclusive. It regards Nabû-bullissu/Nabû-mukīn-zēri//Ea-ṣalam-ilī. He acted as scribe when MNA received a boat-tower (BM 30764), and probably

MNA and a third party. He also assisted MNA as witness when the latter rented a boat and paid a toll. Finally, he witnessed a transaction that seems to have involved an exchange of boats for which MNA acted as scribe.[435]

The fact that some persons are firmly associated with boat-related transactions is helpful to determine the reason for the payment recorded in BM 31138. According to this document, MNA delivered barley to a courtier and clerk. The reason for the delivery is not specified. However, the list of witnesses of BM 31138 throws an interesting light on this matter. First, the document is witnessed by Marduk/Gūzānu//Kaṣṣidakku, who was also present as witness when MNA paid transport costs to the governor of Babylon and acquired a hireling to tow boats.[436] Nidintu/Kalbaya is also among the witnesses in BM 31138. He most likely belonged to the Suḫaya family and assisted MNA as witness when the latter bought boats, paid for the purchase price, leased his right to collect tolls at a bridge that belonged to the governor of Babylon to two individuals, and settled a debt that was somehow related to the exploitation of bridges.[437] BM 31138 is further witnessed by a man named Nidintu/Ardiya//Rab-līmi, who may be identified with Nidintu/Ardiya//Rab-šušši, if one accepts that Rab-līmi and Rab-šušši are variants of the same family name.[438] The latter witnessed MNA's payments for transport costs to the governor of Babylon as well as another payment of an unknown background to the same governor. His brother witnessed one of MNA's boat rentals.[439] Finally, there is Tattannu, who occurs as first witness in BM 31138. He should be identified with

---

also when he paid tolls, although in the latter case only the scribe's first name is preserved (BM 31347: 16, "The scribe, Nabû-bullissu, son of [...]"). He may well have been the overseer of the quay in Bīt-ṭāb-Bēl who received the payment for toll from MNA (BM 31347: 7–8, "Nabû-bullissu, son of Nabû-[mukīn-zēri descendant of Ea-ṣalām-ilī?]").

435. Bēl-asûa/Nergal-uballiṭ//Mudammiq-Adad is attested in the following boat-related transactions: TCL 13 196 (lease of a share in the right to collect payments at a bridge), BM 31891 (boat rental, //mTUM-dIŠKUR), BM 31347 (*miksu*, Bē[l-...]/Nergal-uballiṭ [...]), and BM 32873 (exchange?). For his occurrence in a tax-related text (BM 30541), see below.

436. Marduk/Gūzānu//Kaṣṣidakku witnessed the following boat-related transactions: BM 31572 and BM 31786 (*gimru*); and BM 30764 (boat-tower). For his occurrence in texts related to taxes (BM 31798, giš*qaštu*; BM 31322 and BM 31517, *ilku*), see below.

437. Nidintu/Kalbaya//Suḫaya witnessed the following boat-related transactions: OECT 10 234 ([...]/Kalbaya//Suḫaya) and BM 30370 (boat purchases); BM 30961 (receipt purchase price); TCL 13 196 (lease of a share in the right to collect payments at a bridge); and BM 41443 (silver debt of MNA that is related to the exploitation of a bridge). He also occurs in texts that are not related to boats (on which see more below): BM 30994 (silver debt to MNA that is related to the lúDÍM) and BM 31449 (he and his brothers had to deliver a hireling or hirelings for a work assignment the nature of which is specified in the broken part of line 1). He or his namesake from the Šumu-libši family witnessed BM 31786 (*gimru*, Nidintu/Kalbaya//[...]) and BM 31138 (barley delivery by MNA to a courtier; Nidintu/Kalbaya).

438. Note that Nidintu/Ardiya//Rab-šušši is attested between vii/25 Dar (BM 30639) and viii/25 Dar (BM 31393); Nidintu/Ardiya//Rab-līmi is attested in iii/25 Dar (BM 31118).

439. Nidintu/Ardiya//Rab-šušši witnessed the following boat-related transactions: BM 30639 and BM 31393 (*gimru*). He is probably also attested in Dar 577 (payment of unknown

Tattannu/Nabû-kāṣir//Dābibī, who witnessed four payments for transport costs and MNA's acquisition of a boat-tower.[440] One of his brothers is second witness in BM 31138; another brother witnessed one of MNA's boat rentals (Dar 138). In short, BM 31138 is witnessed by men who are well known from MNA's archive as witnesses in boat-related transactions. Consequently, the transaction recorded in BM 31138 was, in all likelihood, another such transaction. Accordingly, the barley that MNA paid to the courtier should be considered another payment for either transport costs or food rations of boatmen.[441]

Several of the men who attended MNA's transactions regarding boats and boat transports, especially those regarding tolls and *gimru*, also attended his receipts of taxes (*ilku*, ^{giš}*qaštu*), or were involved in the recruitment of soldiers and workers and in the financing of their equipment (*rikis qabli*).[442] Marduk/Gūzānu//Kaṣṣidakku, for instance, saw MNA paying *gimru* and receiving taxes from individuals and tax-units. Marduk-bēlšunu/Arad-Marduk//Šangû-Ea saw MNA paying boat tolls and received from him *rikis qabli*. Similarly, Kāṣir/Tattannu//Eppeš-ilī was present when MNA paid for transport costs to the governor of Babylon, and also when men were recruited to tow boats. Bēl-erība/Kalbaya//Šumu-libši, however, is the most elaborate instance of a man who was directly or indirectly related to boats, the collection of *ilku*, and the recruitment of manpower. This Bēl-erība was himself a commander-of-fifty and entitled to the service of workers and soldiers. Accordingly, he is often mentioned in this context, either by himself or with MNA.[443] Moreover, he was present at several tax-related issues. Thus, he was present when MNA received *ilku*, paid *ilku*, owed silver to a courtier, paid silver for the salary and rations of the men of Nergal-ēṭir, Bēl-erība's brother, delivered a hireling to the commander-of-the-fortress and (an)other hireling(s) to Šuma-uṣur/Šamaš-ēṭir, and sent his slave to learn the baker's profession. Additional examples of men who witnessed both MNA's boat-related transactions and his receipts of taxes are: Ardiya/Dādiya//Nabaya, Nabû-bullissu/Nabû-mukīn-zēri//Ea-ṣalam-ilī, Nabû-šuma-iddin/Šāpik-zēri//Dēkû, Nergal-šuma-ibni/Šullumu, Nidinti-Bēl/Nabû-dāmiq-ilī//Nādin-še'i, Šullumaya/Nabû-nādin-aḫi// Nabaya, and Tattannu/Nabû-kāṣir//Dābibī.[444]

---

background to the governor of Babylon; boat-related?). His brother witnessed Dar 138 (boat rental).

440. Tattannu/Nabû-kāṣir//Dābibī witnessed the following boat-related transactions: BM 31393, BM 31572, BM 31786, and BM 32891 (*gimru*); and BM 30764 (boat tower). He also witnessed several tax-related transactions (BM 30235, BM 31517, and BM 31798; details below), and the last-minute cancellation of MNA's sale of land in Litamu (Dar 469 = *CM* 20b 222, see above at n. 50).

441. The two men, Muššê and Nabû-rē'ušunu, who are mentioned in BM 31138 in connection with the barley that MNA delivered, may have been the boatmen in question.

442. Also see at the discussion of BM 30446 (p. 55) and BM 31798 (p. 63).

443. BM 30274 and BM 30466 (Bēl-erība alone); and BM 30795 (together with MNA).

444. If the silver mentioned in Dar 213, b 2800, and BM 30541 originated from taxes, the

A link between the levying of taxes, the recruitment of soldiers or workers, and boat transports is further confirmed by the example of Nabû-ittannu/Mušēzib-Marduk//Egibi. Two documents show that this man had to serve in the king's army, but hired Marduk-šuma-uṣur to serve on his behalf; he paid for his substitute's army equipment in Darius' eighth, eighteenth and nineteenth years.[445] Interestingly, he witnessed MNA's renting of a boat from Bēl-ikṣur/Rīmūt, who was a harbor-master with workers (or soldiers, lúṣābūmeš) under his command.[446] Perhaps Nabû-ittannu was one of his workers/soldiers.

In addition, some of the men who witnessed MNA's boat business appear again when MNA dealt with temple-related matters. When MNA delivered wool to the temple of Lugal-Marada, for instance, Nergal-ušallim (*alias* Šullumu)/Mušēzib-Marduk//Nappāḫu and Rīmūt-Bēl/Ardiya//Itinnu witnessed the delivery.[447] When one of MNA's creditors pressed him to pay a debt in which also three secretaries of the Esagil temple were involved, Nabû-šuma-iddin/Šāpik-zēri//Dēkû and Murašû/Nabû-aḫḫē-iddin//Nanna-utu are among the witnesses.[448] These four men, viz. Nergal-ušallim, Rīmūt-Bēl, Nabû-šuma-iddin and Murašû, are well known as witnesses from MNA's boat-related transactions. They also took an interest in some of MNA's real estate transactions[449] and commercial deals involving taxes, hired soldiers, and crops.[450]

Finally, the composition of the witnesses in MNA's boat-related transactions confirms the close link between this business and his trade in com-

---

following persons may be added to the list of persons witnessing MNA's boat-related transactions and those related to taxes: Bēl-asûa, Ea-apla-iddin, Nergal-ušallim, Rīmūt-Bēl, and Šulum-Bābili.

445. Dar 481: "Silver (for) the equipment of Nabû-šuma-uṣur/Marduk-ibni//Ile''i-Marduk, the king's man (serving on behalf)? of Nabû-ittannu/Mušēzib-Marduk//Egibi in Darius' eighteenth and nineteenth year: Nabû-šuma-uṣur has received (it) from Nabû-ittannu." Cf. Dar 220: "Ten shekels of medium-quality silver in addition to a register regarding half a mina of medium-quality silver from the *rikis qabli* duty of the eighth year: Nabû-šuma-uṣur/Marduk-šuma-ibni//Ile''i-Marduk has received (them) from Nabû-ittannu [...]." Cf. Wunsch, *MOS Studies* 2, n. 50 and Stolper, *JCS* 53, nn. 56–57. For Nabû-šuma-uṣur serving in the king's army and keeping record of payments for (his) equipment or rations, perhaps also see Dar 290 (= *CM* 20b 190)? For the latter text, see n. 179.

446. BM 31554. On this Bēl-ikṣur/Rīmūt, who is also attested in BM 30853 and perhaps also in BM 41453 (s.v. Bēl-kiṣuršu/Rīmūt//LÚ.⸢x⸣), see more at p. 89.

447. Nergal-ušallim was present at additional temple-related transactions, viz. BM 41449 (undertaking to deliver the thieves from the city of the *qīpu* to MNA's house) and Dar 345 (promise by a prebendholder to pay his debt to MNA's brother).

448. For the debt to which Dar 455 refers, see Dar 437 and discussion at § 3.1.4.

449. For the presence of Nabû-šuma-iddin, Marduk-šuma-iddin, his brother, Murašû, and Rīmūt-Bēl in some of MNA's real estate transactions, see Dar 217 (= *CM* 20b 183), Dar 265 (= *CM* 20b 13), Dar 273 (= *CM* 20b 191), and Dar 386 (= *CM* 20b 219); probably also Dar 270 (= *CM* 20b 108: Murašû/Uššaya, if Uššaya = Nabû-aḫḫē-iddin//Nanna-utu, Arad-Nanna).

450. For details, see at Table 7 s.v. Nabû-šuma-iddin, Nergal-ušallim, and Rīmūt-Bēl.

modities in and around Šaḫrīnu.[451] First, several of the men we will encounter in the Rīmūt-Bēl and Bagasarū-texts recur in MNA's boat-related texts. Erībaya/Ša-Nabû-šū, for instance, Bagasarū's majordomo, also witnessed MNA's rental of a boat from a canal inspector. A similar case is that of Šullumaya/Nabû-nādin-aḫi//Nabaya, who occurs in one Bagasarū text as well as in two payments for boat transports.[452] The link between MNA's commodity trade and his business with boats is further illustrated by the instance of Nidinti-Bēl/Nabû-dāmiq-ilī (*alias* Damqiya)//Nādin-še'i. He was well-acquainted with MNA's dealings with crops from (institutional) land in Šaḫrīnu, because he wrote or witnessed several of the transactions regarding these crops, but he also witnessed one of MNA's payments for transport costs to the governor of Babylon.[453] An analogous case is that of Rīmūt-Bēl/Ardiya //Itinnu.[454] Similarly, two of the witnesses at MNA's purchase of dates from the governor in Šaḫrīnu, as well as the scribe of the document recording this purchase, recur in boat-related transactions.[455] Finally, we should pay attention to the fact that some of the men who witnessed transactions regarding real estate at the Uraš gate in Litamu recur when MNA concluded boat-related transactions. Tattannu/Nabû-kāṣir//Dābibī, Rīmūt-Bēl/Ardiya//Itinnu and Ardiya/Dādiya//Nabaya are clear examples of this phenomenon.[456]

In addition to this limited group of witnesses and scribes, MNA relied mainly on his acquaintance with state officials, in general, and the governor of Babylon, in particular, in order to obtain the boats, equipment and manpower necessary to run his transport business. The Table below specifies the provider and the origin of each commodity that he acquired to run his transport business. The person from whom he acquired the commodity is listed under the heading "provider." Thus, the professional sailor who rented out someone else's boat to MNA is a "provider," and so is the person who provided a man to tow boats

451. A direct link between MNA's commodity trade and his business with boats was already pointed out above with regard to the *gimru*-texts (§ 2.5.2). Further see below at p. 146 (link between MNA's commodity trade with crops from the land of Bēl in Šaḫrīnu and BM 30747, a payment for the boat toll); and n. 516 (link between Bagasarū-texts and BM 31347, a payment for the boat toll).

452. Erībaya: Dar 296 (Bagasarū) and BM 30490 (boat rental). Šullumaya (see n. 518): Dar 542 (Bagasarū); BM 31572 and BM 32891 (*gimru*).

453. For Nidinti-Bēl/Nabû-dāmiq-ilī (*alias* Damqiya)//Nādin-še'i, see: BM 31018, Dar 338, BM 31058 and Dar 310 (commodity trade in Šaḫrīnu); and BRM 1 81 (*gimru*). Further note his presence at transactions regarding taxes, salaries, and rations (BM 41607 and Dar 572).

454. Rīmūt-Bēl/Ardiya//Itinnu: Dar 215 (hire of a sailor), Dar 296 (Bagasarū), BM 31058 and Dar 318 (commodity trade in and around Šaḫrīnu).

455. See Table 7 s.v. Ardiya, Nergal-ušallim and Nidinti-Bēl (all attested in Dar 338 = purchase of dates from the governor of Šaḫrīnu).

456. Tattannu in Dar 469 = *CM* 20b 222 (Uraš gate) and several boat-related texts. Rīmūt-Bēl in Dar 217 = *CM* 20b 183, Dar 273 = *CM* 20b 191 (Uraš gate), and Dar 215 (hire of a sailor). Ardiya in Dar 273 = *CM* 20b 191 (Uraš gate), Dar 215 and BM 32883 (boat-related).

to MNA by order of the governor of Babylon. The person "behind the scene," who owned the commodity or supervised the transaction by giving orders, is listed under the heading "origin."

TABLE 8: The Contractants in MNA's Boat-Related Transactions

T.	PROVIDER:	ORIGIN:
Boats for Rent		
1	Bēl-ikṣur, (harbor)master	
2	(governor of Babylon)	
3	(Šuma-ukīn)	(governor of Babylon)
4	(Gūzu-Bēl-aṣbat)	governor of Babylon
5	[...]-ittannu/Niqūdu + Bēl-ikṣur/Rīmūt, head of the (harbor) workmen	Basiya/Nabû-šuma-ukīn// Ša-nāšīšu (= brother of the governor of Babylon)
6	Nabû-zēra-iqīša//Erēšu	Balāṭu, canal inspector
7	Kīnaya	Arad-Šamaš?, clerk of ?
8	Šamaš-iddin/Bēl-iddin	Iddin-Nabû
9	Gula-zēra-ibni/Zēr-Bābili//Nappāḫu	[m ...]-uṣuršu?
10	Niqūdu/PN + Kalbi-Bāba/Iddinaya	Iddin-Bēl, slave of Barz[iya]?
11	Aplaya/Iddinaya	Nabû-ēṭir-napšāte/Ḫaddaya
12	Aḫu-atbû/Kalbaya + Nabû-ittannu/ Iddin-Nabû	
Boats for Sale		
13	Nabû-apla-iddin/Lâbāši// Nūr-Papsukkal	
14	Kidinnu/Rīmūt	
Professional Sailors (15), Towers (16–19), Hirelings (20–21), and Dockers? (22)		
15	Bulṭaya/Ḫabaṣīru//Rē'i-alpi	
16	Nāšibu//Lā-qīpu, o.b.o. Marduk/ Nabû-uṣuršu//Šumu-libši	
17	Bēl-iddin/Zēriya//Rab-banê	
18	Bēl-uballiṭ/Iddin-Nabû//Bā'iru, o.b.o. Bēl-[...]/Zēriya//MU-[...]	governor of Babylon
19	Bēl-iddin/Šuma-iddin//Andaḫar, o.b.o. Ḫabaṣīru/Mušēzib-Marduk// Dēkû	governor of Babylon
20	Šullumu, overseer [...]	
21	(Šullumu, overseer [...])	governor of Babylon
22	Šuma-ukīn	governor of Babylon
Boat Equipment (Cables and Containers)		
23	Nidinti-Bēl-damqat, the governor's slave	governor of Babylon
24	(Nidinti-Bēl-damqat, the governor's slave)	governor of Babylon

Additional (Boat-Related) Services		
25	Bēl-ikṣur, (harbor) master	
26	Gūzu-Bēl-aṣbat	
27	governor of Babylon	
28	Arad-Bunene (the governor's slave)	Napurtu and Bānûnu
29	house of Artasunu	governor of Babylon
30	(? Muššê/Inziya + Nabû-re'ûšunu/ Nabû-balāssu-iqbi)	Iddin-Nabû, courtier and clerk
Right to Use the Waterways and Their Infrastructure		
31	Kulbibi/Bēl-kāṣir//Eppeš-ilī, overseer of the quay of Bīt-Ir'anni	
32	Nabû-bullissu/Nabû-[mukīn-zēri// Ea-ṣalam-ilī (?)], overseer of the quay of Bīt-ṭāb-Bēl	
33	Nergal-ušallim/Arrabi	
34	various clerks and courtiers	governor of Babylon
Right to Join Officially Organized Transports		
35	Nidinti-Bēl-damqat, the governor's slave	governor of Babylon
36	(Nidinti-Bēl-damqat, the governor's slave)	(governor of Babylon)

T. = *Text References*: 1 = BM 30853: 5b–8; 2 = BM 30853: 37b–38; 3 = BM 30853: 25–27; 4 = BM 30853: 30–32; 5 = BM 31554; 6 = BM 30490; 7 = BM 30799; 8 = BM 30270; 9 = Dar 138; 10 = BM 31891; 11 = BM 31690+; 12 = Dar 576; 13 = BM 30370 and BM 30961; 14 = OECT 10 234; 15 = Dar 158 and Dar 215; 16 = BM 30764; 17 = BM 31118; 18 = BM 31188; 19 = BM 32932; 20 = BM 30853: 1–2; 21 = BM 30853: 2–5; 22 = BM 30853: 23–24; 23 = BM 30853: 16–18; 24 = BM 30853: 21–22; 25 = BM 30853: 8–9; 26 = BM 30853: 28–29; 27 = BM 30853: 35–37a; 28 = BM 30853: 33–35; 29 = BM 30853: 10–12a; 30 = BM 31138; 31= Dar 268; 32 = BM 31347; 33 = BM 30747; 34 = 8 *gimru*-texts; 35 = BM 30256, cf. BM 30853: 12b–15; 36 = BM 30853: 19–20.

ABBREVIATIONS: o.b.o. = on behalf of (*ana muḫḫi*). Round Brackets: The use of round brackets in the Table means that the information in question is not explicitly mentioned in the relevant passage of BM 30853, but may be inferred from the general structure of the text or from other texts. For this matter I refer to the detailed analysis of BM 30853 above (§ 2.5.1).

When MNA needed boats, he rented them from state officials, either directly or through the intermediary of men in the officials' service. Direct rentals from state officials, however, seem to have been rare. MNA once rented boats from the harbor-master and once from the governor of Babylon (T. 1–2). Usually, he rented the state-owned boats from men who had them at their disposal for sailing or similar purposes. Accordingly, the governor's boats were rented to MNA by Šuma-ukīn and Gūzu-Bēl-aṣbat (T. 3–4). These men received their orders from the governor, and were, probably, his slaves or minor officials in his service. This is further supported by the fact that they are cited without affiliation, as was common for slaves and officials. Similarly, the boat of the governor's brother was made available to MNA through the intermediary of the harbor-master (T. 5). The canal inspector's boat and the boat of an unknown clerk were rented to MNA through the intermediary of their sailors (T. 6–7). Finally, we may assume a similar arrangement for the boats that he rented from Šamaš-iddin (T. 8), Gula-zēra-ibni (T. 9), Niqūdu, Kalbi-Bāba (T. 10), and Aplaya (T. 11). The boats that these five men rented to him were owned by others, who are cited by first name only.[457] As said, it was typical for officials to be cited in this way so that Iddin-Nabû, [ᵐ...]-*uṣuršu*? and Barz[iya]?, whose boats were rented to MNA, may have been state officials.[458] The five men who actually rented these boats to MNA must have been men in their service. Consequently, the aforementioned cases T. 8–11 are, in all likelihood, additional examples of state-owned boats rented to MNA by sailors in the service of the state.[459] Occasionally, he bought rather than rented boats, but the sellers are practically unknown (T. 13–14). Our only additional information about Nabû-apla-iddin/Lâbāši//Nūr-Papsukkal, who sold his boat to MNA, is that he was trained as a scribe.[460]

When MNA needed men to sail, tow, or dock the boats, he either hired them or obtained them from the governor's pool of (forced) laborers. Professional sailors were usually hired together with the boats that they rented out or in a separate agreement (T. 15). In the former case, the rent contracts state that MNA had to pay for the rent of the boat and "his maintenance," i.e., the sailor's (and probably also his men's) maintenance. Towers and dockers were obtained, in one way or another, from the governor's pool of forced laborers. One way to obtain these men was by recruiting them from the individuals who had to provide the governor with such men as part of their obligations vis-à-vis the state (T. 16–19). In return for his assistance in their recruitment, MNA enjoyed their services. However, his rights over this state property were limited in time to a little more than two months a year or to six days a month for approximately half a year. Another way to get towers and dockers from the governor's workforce was to pay the governor's agents for their services (T. 20–22). In this way MNA also acquired boat equipment (T. 23–24). Additional utilities needed to run a transport company were provided against payment in silver to MNA by the same officials who rented their boats to him (T. 25–27) or by their slaves and agents (T. 28–29; probably also T. 30, payment in barley).

Furthermore, MNA needed to get the necessary permits to transport his goods by boat. For the use of canals, bridges, and quays he paid the toll (*miksu*) on the spot (T. 31–33). He could also make a single payment to cover all costs to the authorities and thus acquire some kind of one-month pass, unless one interprets these all-inclusive payments as payments for gaining access to officially organized transports (T. 34).

---

457. Except for Nabû-ēṭir-napšāte/Ḫaddaya in T. 11.

458. Slaves were also cited by their first names only, but since the men in question were the owners of the boats, slaves are less likely candidates.

459. The two men in T. 12 were probably sailors; it is not clear who owned the boats.

460. He wrote BM 31891, the rental of a boat by MNA.

Finally, MNA used his connections with the governor of Babylon to gain access to transports that were organized by the latter against participation in the costs. He had to cover the expenses for the rations. Thus, he delivered barley for the rations of the men who sailed the boats and paid silver for the rations of the men who towed the boats (T. 35 and T. 36). In all instances MNA paid the slave of the governor. His payments for cables and vessels to the same individual, as well as his monthly payments for transport costs in general to clerks in the governor's service, may have served the same purpose (T. 23–24 and T. 34). These may have been payments in return for the right to join officially organized transports.

2.6. *Cultivation and Collection of Crops for State Officials by MNA and His Men*

It appears that MNA collected state income not only from taxes but also from field rent. Several texts indicate that MNA had access to crops from fields in and around Šaḫrīnu that were managed by state officials and in specific cases may also have been privately owned by these officials. As a rule, the crops were due to these state officials as rent, since they are usually described in terms of *imittu* and *šibšu*. In reality, the crops were delivered by the tenant farmers to MNA. The latter subsequently transferred part of the crops to agents of the state officials by means of his slaves, according to some of the texts. The legal basis for MNA's right to these crops is not given by the texts, except in one case where MNA had obviously bought the crops from the state official.

Twelve texts from Šaḫrīnu and its surroundings provide the details.[461] One text concerns dates from Šaḫrīnu to which MNA was entitled after he purchased them from the local governor in Darius' twelfth year (§ 2.6.1). Second, the Rīmūt-Bēl dossier consists of seven texts concerning crops from Šaḫrīnu that Rīmūt-Bēl, Nabû-makû-uṣur, and Kīnaya had to deliver to MNA's house. The texts were written in Šaḫrīnu and in Babylon between Darius' fourth and eleventh years. They are strictly private in character. No officials or officially owned land is mentioned. Nevertheless, several elements in the texts, first and foremost the fact that such large amounts of crops were at stake, suggest that the crops in question were derived from institutional rather than from privately owned land (§ 2.6.2). Finally, the Bagasarū dossier consists of four texts concerning crops that were due to Bagasarū, the king's treasurer, from the lease of fields along the Rab-kāṣir canal. The crops were apparently grown by MNA's tenants and slaves, who had to transfer one third of them to Bagasarū. The other two thirds were, no doubt, for MNA. The texts were drafted in Babylon, Bīt-rab-kāṣir, and Bīt-ṭāb-Bēl; the latter two villages were connected to Šaḫrīnu through the Tupašu canal.[462] They date between Darius' fourth and twenty-first years (§ 2.6.3).

---

461. Dar 338 (§ 2.6.1); Dar 144, Dar 164, Dar 167, Dar 310, BM 31058, BM 31718, BM 33972 (§ 2.6.2); and Dar 105, Dar 296, Dar 527, and Dar 542 (§ 2.6.3).

462. On the location of Bīt-rab-kāṣir, see Wunsch, *Felder* 1, 174 and n. 363 with literature. On

2.6.1. *The Purchase of Dates from the District Governor of Šaḫrīnu*

In Darius' twelfth year MNA purchased dates from Libluṭ/Mušēzib-Marduk, "the district governor ([lú]*paḫātu*) of Šaḫrīnu," and transferred five minas of silver, "the price of the dates," to Libluṭ (Dar 338). The transfer occurred a few days before the end of the year. MNA sent his brother to pay the silver to Nabû-uṣuršu, Libluṭ's brother. The core of Dar 338 deals with the transfer of the original deed of quittance, which only Libluṭ could issue, to MNA. The text does not tell us where those dates came from. Nevertheless, we may safely assume that they were grown on institutional land in Šaḫrīnu that fell under the administrative authority of Libluṭ. The assumed link between the dates and institutional land in Šaḫrīnu is based on the fact that Libluṭ, who sold the dates, is specifically identified as "district governor of Šaḫrīnu." This title was added to Libluṭ's name in order to highlight the fact that he held the dates in his capacity as district governor of Šaḫrīnu. In other words, these were not privately owned dates from Libluṭ's own land, but state income from institutional land in Šaḫrīnu due to Libluṭ, the local governor. Part of this state income, which may have been income from taxes, lease, or both, was sold to MNA.[463]

The institutional origin of the crops in Dar 338 was, no doubt, the reason Šullumu/Mušēzib-Marduk//Nappāḫu attended the transaction. This man was a brother of Libluṭ/Mušēzib-Marduk and Nabû-uṣuršu/Mušēzib-Marduk, who are mentioned in the main portion of the text.[464] Interestingly, Šullumu was frequently present as a witness when MNA dealt with institutional issues, especially those related to temple property.[465] In fact, he is attested among the witnesses in four other documents from MNA's archive.[466] In two of them he bore his full name, Nergal-ušallim. Under this name we find him among the witnesses in BM 41449 and Dar 182. Thus, he was present when Arad-Bēl promised to hand over the thieves who had been caught in the city of the king's resident (*qīpu*) to the house of MNA and when MNA delivered wool to a weaver

---

the location of Bīt-ṭāb-Bēl, Zadok, *RGTC*, 108. It was located in the vicinity of Šaḫrīnu, as goes forth from a text such as Dar 541, which was issued in Bīt-ṭāb-Bēl but obliged the debtor to pay his debt "in the house of MNA in Šaḫrīnu."

463. If Libluṭ/Mušēzib-Marduk in *Bēl-rēmanni*, 151 = BM 42352: 18 (Sippar, 15/[-]/20 Dar; Jursa, *Bēl-rēmanni*, 151–52) is the same person as Libluṭ/Mušēzib-Marduk, district governor of Šaḫrīnu in Dar 338, it follows that this Libluṭ also kept an eye on the collection of tax-silver on behalf of the governor of Babylon. Indeed, he went to Sippar in Darius' twentieth year to witness a payment of silver by members of a bow-unit. This silver was needed to finance works in Elam in Darius' seventeenth year, which were supervised by the governor of Babylon.

464. Consequently, Libluṭ and Nabû-uṣuršu are to be identified as descendants of Nappāḫu. On the identification of their father, see n. 469.

465. Hence, was the land under the administrative authority of the local governor of Šaḫ-rīnu, on which dates were grown (Dar 338), temple-owned land?

466. On this person, also see Table 7.

of the god Lugal-Marada.[467] Further, he is attested under his abbreviated name, Šullumu, among the witnesses in Dar 338, as we pointed out above, and in two other texts, viz. Dar 268 and Dar 345. Thus, he was present when MNA paid the toll for a boat to the overseer of the quay of Bīt-Ir'anni[468] and when Bēl-upaḫḫir/Nergal-iddin arranged the repayment of his debts with NAB.[469] The said Bēl-upaḫḫir and probably also his brother Aplaya were holders of a prebend. Aplaya/Nergal-iddin, for instance, held the prestigious prebend of temple-enterer and pledged part of his prebendary income to MNA as security for his debts.[470] In short, Šullumu (*alias* Nergal-ušallim)/Mušēzib-Marduk//Nappāḫu was clearly interested in temple-related matters: the safety of the king's resident in the temple, a delivery of wool to the temple of Lugal-Marada, and the financial situation of some prebendaries. He also kept track of the transport of agricultural produce past Bīt-Ir'anni. Consequently, the deal recorded in Dar 338 and witnessed by this Šullumu may also have been temple-related or at least related to one of the big institutions, since this was the type of issue with which Šullumu was usually involved.

We should also briefly mention the area of interest of the scribe of Dar 338, because it further highlights the institutional background of the text. Nidinti-Bēl from the Nādin-še'i family was the son of Nabû-damiq-ilī (*alias* Damqiya). He witnessed or wrote several of MNA's documents that concerned crops from institutional land in Šaḫrīnu. He wrote, for instance, the receipt of silver paid by MNA to Šaddinnu for the right to collect *šibšu*-onions from temple land in Šaḫrīnu.[471] In addition, he was present when MNA received *ilku*, paid *gimru*, and paid for the salaries of Nergal-ēṭir's men.[472] One of his brothers is listed as

---

467. BM 41449 (thieves) and Dar 182 (weaver).

468. The overseer of the quay in Bīt-Ir'anni was Kulbibi/Bēl-kāṣir/(Ea-)eppeš-ilī (Dar 268). Three of his brothers are attested in other texts of MNA's archive: Nidinti, a priest in Bāṣ occurs in TCL 13 193 (= text concerning MNA's debt to the governor of Kiš), Mušēzib-Bēl in Dar 296 (one of the Bagasarū-texts), and Bēl-uballiṭ in Dar 73. Their father and uncle maintained business links with the Ea-ilūta-bāni family in Borsippa. Details in Abraham, *NABU* 1997/53: 47–48.

469. Dar 268 (toll) and Dar 345 (Bēl-upaḫḫir/Nergal-iddin). Another agreement between the same Bēl-upaḫḫir, who was also known under the shorter name of Puḫḫuru, and NAB was witnessed by Mušēzib-Marduk/Marduk-šuma-ibni//Nappāḫu (Dar 369): was he the father of Šullumu/Mušēzib-Marduk//Nappāḫu? If he was, Šullumu and his brothers belonged to that branch of the Nappāḫu family for which there exists some 250 tablets (details at Von Dassow, CTMMA 3, 195f.). However, we cannot be sure because there was also a Mušēzib-Marduk//Nappāḫu, son of Marduk-ēṭir (see texts from the time of Iddin-Marduk at Wunsch, *Iddin-Marduk*). Among the witnesses in Dar 369 we also find Aplaya/Nergal-iddin, brother of the debtor.

470. BM 30965.

471. BM 31018. Other texts that concern crops from institutional land (temple land?) in Šaḫrīnu and were witnessed by Nidinti-Bēl/Damqiya (*alias* Nabû-damiq-ilī)//Nādin-še'i: Dar 310 (see n. 495) and BM 31058 (see p. 126f.). More on this person at Table 7.

472. He wrote BM 41607 (*ilku*) and Dar 572 (salaries); and he witnessed BRM 1 81 (*gimru*).

first witness when the earlier mentioned Aplaya/Nergal-iddin pledged part of his prebendary income to MNA; another of Nidinti-Bēl's brothers helped MNA out when he bought a boat and needed someone to write the sale contract.[473] Nidinti-Bēl and his brothers are additional examples of the earlier-noted phenomenon in which the same individuals often recur in documents from MNA's time that deal with various, apparently unrelated issues, such as the collection of agricultural income from institutional land, *ilku*, and boats.

Unfortunately, we do not know whether the dates that Libluṭ sold to MNA had already been harvested. The purchase took place in the middle of Addar, i.e., approximately three and a half months after the date harvest. MNA may have bought dates that the governor had previously collected. Or, more likely, the dates were still to be collected from the field at the next harvest, so that MNA did not just purchase income from taxes and/or rent, but more specifically paid for the right to collect this income in the future. In that case we may call him a tax-farmer or rent-farmer, i.e., a person who bought the right to collect taxes and/or rent and in return annually paid the state a fixed amount.[474] If so, he needed men in the countryside to keep an eye on the cultivation and harvesting of the crops on his behalf. In this light we should probably interpret the Rīmūt-Bēl and Bagasarū-texts discussed below.

Dar 338 clearly shows that such sales of state income, or of rights to state income, to private entrepreneurs was beneficial from the viewpoint of the state. Indeed, it enabled the state to convert crops into cash or to receive cash instead of crops and thus have cash available at the end of the year (Addar), the period of the year when there was a shortage of barley in the storehouses because it fell just before the barley harvest. In such cases the state often needed silver to pay rations and salaries to its subjects. It succeeded in doing so through the kind of sales described above. Occasionally, the authorities ordered MNA to pay the silver, the price for his right to state income directly to the men whose salaries or rations were to be paid from this income.[475]

2.6.2. *Excursus: Large Amounts of Crops from Men in Šaḫrīnu*

The following group of seven texts deals with the obligation of Rīmūt-Bēl/Šuma-ukīn, Nabû-makû-uṣur/Nabû-apla-iddin, his brother,[476] and Kīnaya/Atkal-Šamaš to deliver 254 bundles of onions, 550.8.3 *kor* of dates and 21.3.5 *kor* of barley to MNA in the course of Darius' fifth and sixth years. In addition,

473. BM 30965 and BM 30961.

474. On MNA's tax and rent farming deals, also see at n. 325.

475. Evidence discussed in § 2.2.1.

476. Rīmūt-Bēl was the son of Šuma-ukīn. Nabû-makû-uṣur was the son of Nabû-apla-iddin. They held real estate in common (Dar 144: 8–10 and BM 33972: 22–24), but there is no apparent family link between them because they are the sons of different fathers. Nevertheless, Nabû-makû-uṣur is called "his (i.e., Rīmūt-Bēl's) brother" in Dar 144: 10. Were they the sons of the same mother, but of different fathers (hence, half-brothers)?

Rīmūt-Bēl and his brother owed him a little more than seven minas of silver that they had borrowed to pay for *rikis qabli*. Rīmūt-Bēl also owed sixteen minas of marked silver to Nabû-uṣuršu/Gūzānu, but relied on his surety and MNA to settle this matter in Darius' eleventh year. Rīmūt-Bēl and his brother pledged some of their private land as security for their debts, and allowed MNA to collect part of their income from lease in repayment of their debts. The details of these debts and the ways in which they were secured are recounted in seven documents dated between Darius' fourth and eleventh years.[477]

MNA's connections with Rīmūt-Bēl and Nabû-makû-uṣur are well documented. On the twenty-fifth of Šabāṭ of Darius' fourth year Rīmūt-Bēl owed 297.3.0 *kor* of dates and 11.2.3. *kor* of barley to MNA (Dar 144). The crops were to be delivered at the next harvest "in the house of MNA in Šaḫrīnu"; the barley was due in Ayyar of Darius' fifth year, and the dates in Tašrīt of the same year. Five or six months later, in Ab of Darius' fifth year,[478] he owed fifty shekels of silver and fifty bundles of onions in addition to the earlier mentioned dates and barley and a silver debt of one mina and ten shekels (Dar 167).[479] The onions and the silver were due by the next onion harvest, namely, in Nisan of Darius' sixth year. At about the same time there is a record of another debt of Rīmūt-Bēl to MNA (BM 33972).[480] This time he owed 3⅚ minas and 7½ shekels of silver, 130 bundles of onions and two *kor* of barley. The silver and the onions were due in Nisan of Darius' sixth year, the barley in Ayyar. At the same time, Nabû-makû-uṣur, Rīmūt-Bēl's brother, owed similar large amounts of dates, barley, silver and onions to MNA. On the first of Ab of Darius' fifth year he owed him 245.3.0 *kor* of dates, 8.1.2 *kor* of barley, 80 shekels of silver,[481] and 74 bundles of onions[482] (Dar 164). Part of this large debt was paid off later, but we do not know when exactly because the date is broken off (BM 31718). We hear again about Rīmūt-Bēl in Darius' eleventh year, when he owed the large sum of sixteen minas of marked silver to Nabû-uṣuršu/Gūzānu (Dar 310). Half of this indebted silver, however, had been paid off by Nīryahu/Bēl-zēra-ibni, who had assumed warranty for Rīmūt-Bēl and Kīnaya/Dannu-aḫḫēšu-ibni, his co-debtor. MNA remunerated Nīryahu for his interference on behalf of Rīmūt-Bēl and Kīnaya, and paid him back the eight minas of marked silver.

Some parts of the debts were secured by real estate pledges. Cultivated plots of land, which the debtors held in common, secured all their barley and

---

477. Rīmūt-Bēl and Nabû-makû-uṣur: Dar 144 (Šaḫrīnu, 25/xi/4 Dar), Dar 164 (*idem*, 1/v/5 Dar), Dar 167 (*idem*, [1?]/v/[5?] Dar), BM 33972 (*idem*, between 5 Dar and i/6 Dar), BM 31718 ([-]), and Dar 310 (Babylon, 9/xi/11 Dar); Kīnaya/Atkal-Šamaš//⸢PN⸣: BM 31058 (Babylon, 18/i/[-] Dar).

478. The date of Dar 167 is mostly broken but was, most likely, [1?]/v/[5?] Dar.

479. The barley that was due in Ayyar had not been paid back by Ab. In other words, Rīmūt-Bēl had not met the deadline stipulated in Dar 144, at least not the one regarding the barley.

480. The date of BM 33972 (ll. 29ff.) is broken.

481. Namely, the present debt of half a mina and a previous debt of 50 shekels.

482. Namely the present debt of 30 bundles, and a previous debt of 44 bundles.

date debts, a minor part of their onion debts, and most of their silver debts. The land, consisting of orchards and grain fields, was located along the Borsippa canal and extended up to Royal Street.[483] Usually, it was referred to simply as "the orchards and grain fields" of either Rīmūt-Bēl or Nabû-makû-uṣur, without specification of its precise location or the fact that it was held in common. The latter fact, however, cannot be doubted because whenever Rīmūt-Bēl used the land as security pledge, Nabû-makû-uṣur was among the witnesses, and vice versa.[484]

Other parts of the debt, especially the onion debts, were secured by granting MNA access to his debtors' lease income. In Dar 164 and Dar 167 MNA's right to this income is formulated as follows "he will take the full amount (of silver and onions) due to him from the *šibšu*(-crops) on his field."[485] A fuller version of this formula is found in BM 33972, viz. "MNA will take the full amount of onions from the *šibšu*-onions on his field that Madānu-bēla-uṣur contracted (to cultivate/manage)."[486] The expression *šibšu eqlišu* "his (income from the) *šibšu* field rent" refers to the debtor's right to collect rent from a field in his possession. It cannot refer to the debtor's obligation to pay rent. Debts are not secured by obligations, but by titles. Accordingly, MNA was to obtain full satisfaction for his claim on two hundred and ten bundles of onions and eighty shekels of silver by collecting *šibšu* field rent instead of his debtor. As for the location of the field from which MNA was to collect *šibšu*, BM 33972 informs us that "the upper sector belongs to Rīmūt-Bēl; the low[er] sector, which is located next to the house of the canal inspector, is shared with Nabû-māku-uṣur."[487] It is not clear whether this was one of the debtors' privately owned fields, or rather a field of one of the big institutions or of an absentee landowner, the agricultural management of which was left to Rīmūt-Bēl and his brother.[488]

---

483. Consequently, the land must have been in the vicinity of Šaḫrīnu, which was, in fact, located along the Borsippa canal, southwest from Babylon (Wunsch, *Felder* 1, 174 and n. 360). For the proximity of Borsippa and Šaḫrīnu, see also Dar 261: a document comparable to the Rīmūt-Bēl texts in so far that it concerned the delivery of crops in MNA's house in Šaḫrīnu, but note that Dar 261 was drafted in Borsippa.

484. Dar 164, Dar 167 and BM 33972. The absence of Nabû-makû-uṣur from the list of witnesses in Dar 144 is, therefore, exceptional.

485. Dar 164: 6 and Dar 167: 6, *ina šibšu eqlišu išallim*. For a translation of this formula, see also *CAD* $Š_2$, 386. The term *šibšu* refers to a kind of lease payment. It was a part of the harvest paid by leaseholders to the owner of the land. It was typically levied on the produce grown under and between palm trees, such as barley and paid in sesame or barley; more at Jursa, *Landwirtschaft*, 82f. and 191f.; and Von Dassow, CTMMA 3, xxi, with literature.

486. BM 33972: 20–21, *ina šibšu eqlišu ša šūmī ša MBU īpuš šūmī MNA išallim.*

487. BM 33972: 22–23.

488. According to Wunsch, *Iddin Marduk*, 51, the expression *ina šikittišu* (*ša šūmi*) *išallim*, which is similar to the expression *ina šibšu eqlišu išallim*, implies private ownership. For the possibility of absentee landowners in and around Šaḫrīnu, see the parallel of Bagasarū, discussed below (§ 2.6.3). When considering the possibility that the field to which Rīmūt-

MNA took precautionary measures to guarantee his access to his debtors' *šibšu*. Indeed, he arranged for his slave to cultivate the crops from which the *šibšu* was to be collected. The slave actually worked under contract (*īpuš*).[489] This situation is reminiscent of Dar 315.[490] In the latter case, MNA arranged for his farmers to grow the onions on the land of Bēl in Šaḫrīnu and to collect the *šibšu* for him. In Dar 315 he also appointed a man to supervise the work on the fields from which he was to collect the *šibšu* and remunerated him with a share in the *šibšu*. Thus, he arranged with Marduk-nāṣir/Marduk-ušallim to supervise the cultivation and harvesting of onions on the land of Bēl in Šaḫrīnu in return for a one-third share in the profits.

There was, however, more at stake than just guaranteeing his access to his debtors' lease income. In fact, MNA aimed to control the outcome of the harvest when he sent his slave to work his debtor's fields. In fact, it was important for MNA that the fields in question yield as many crops as possible because the lease that had to be paid from this yield was proportional and not fixed. Indeed, the lease in question is called *šibšu* in the texts, and this shows that it constituted a proportion of the harvest and not a fixed amount.[491] This proportion was usually one-third or one-fourth of the harvest.[492] Consequently, the more crops harvested, the more income from the lease. Under such circumstances it is understandable that MNA took the steps described above. He aimed to build a safety net in order to maximize his profits.

The texts do not tell us from whose land Rīmūt-Bēl and Nabû-makû-uṣur had to collect such large amounts of crops, nor why they had to deliver the crops to the house of MNA in Šaḫrīnu. Several elements in the texts, however, suggest a link among the crops, institutional land, and MNA's trade in commodities. First, there is the fact that the texts were written in Šaḫrīnu and refer to MNA's house in Šaḫrīnu as the place where the crops had to be delivered. This Šaḫrīnu and its surroundings played an important role in MNA's commodity trade; it was one of the places from where MNA obtained crops for his trade.[493] In fact, we know that MNA bought up large amounts of crops that were grown in Šaḫrīnu from the local authorities. Thus he bought dates from the king's governor in Šaḫrīnu (Dar 338) and onions that were grown on the land of Bēl

---

Bēl and Nabû-makû-uṣur granted MNA access was institutional rather than private property, one should note the fact that it was located "next to the house of the canal inspector (*mašennu*)." This kind of official was not only in charge of irrigation and canals, but also administered crown and temple lands in the crown's interest (Jursa, *Landwirtschaft*, 181f.).

489. BM 33972: 20 and commentary *ad hoc*.

490. For Dar 315 and related texts, see § 3.1.

491. On the different kinds of lease payments in the Neo-Babylonian period, see bibliography cited above at n. 485.

492. M. deJ. Ellis, *Agriculture and the State*, 132ff.

493. He "inherited" this commodity trade in and around Šaḫrīnu from Iddin-Marduk, his maternal grandfather, details below.

in Šaḫrīnu from the king's governor in the Esagil (= Bēl's temple, Dar 315). Similarly, he may have bought the crops that Rīmūt-Bēl and Nabû-makû-uṣur had to bring to his house in Šaḫrīnu from one of the king's representatives in the area.[494] It is, therefore, not surprising to find among the witnesses in the Rīmūt-Bēl texts men who also witnessed MNA's purchases of dates and onions from the king's representatives in Šaḫrīnu.[495]

Second, there is the fact that very large amounts of crops were at stake. Such amounts could hardly have been needed for private use. Moreover, they could hardly have been grown on privately owned land. In other words, Rīmūt-Bēl and Nabû-makû-uṣur were not to deliver crops that they grew on their own land. Rather, they were to deliver crops that had been grown on institutional land in Šaḫrīnu. We know that Bēl's temple, i.e., the Esagil, for instance, owned large tracks of land in Šaḫrīnu, and the crops that Rīmūṭ-Bēl and his brother had to deliver to MNA may have derived from this land. The Esagil temple, however, was not the only landowner in the area in and around Šaḫrīnu. Texts from the time of Cambyses, for instance, show that the temples of Nabû and Nergal also derived income from this area, as, for instance, income from tithes.[496] Moreover, high officials in the royal administration, such as Bagasarū, seem to have held land in this area as well, which they probably leased out against the payment of *šibšu*-lease. It is noteworthy that one of the men who acted as a scribe for MNA in his dealings with Rīmūt-Bēl and Nabû-makû-uṣur also acted as scribe in his dealings with Bagasarū.[497] Additional prosopographical links between the Rīmūt-Bēl and Bagasarū texts can be pointed out. Marduk-iqīšanni/Bēl-aḫa-ušabši//Bēl-eṭēru, for instance, witnessed two Rīmūt-Bēl texts, Dar 164 and Dar 167. His son, Iddin-Nabû witnessed one of the Bagasarū texts, Dar 527.[498]

Rīmūt-Bēl, Nabû-makû-uṣur, and MNA probably worked together in the latter's commodity trade on the following terms: MNA provided for the credit, and Rīmūt-Bēl and his brother had to organize the work on the fields. Accordingly, they had to collect the crops from the fields and punctually deliver them to MNA. This part of the agreement was described in Dar 144, Dar 164,

494. He may also have bought crops from local governors in Tâmti and subsequently arranged for their transport (more at § 2.5.2, esp. p. 93ff.). More on MNA's tax and rent farming deals at n. 325.

495. E.g., Nabû-uṣuršu/Mušēzib-Marduk(//Nappāḫu), a witness in Dar 164 and Dar 167 who is also attested in Dar 338 (for details on this man and his family's institutional connections, see discussion of Dar 338 above); and Nidinti-Bēl/Damqiya//Nādin-še'i, a witness in Dar 310, who is also attested in Dar 338, BM 31018 (*šibšu* from the land of Bēl?), BRM 1 81 (*gimru*), e.a. On Nidinti-Bēl/Damqiya (*alias* Nabû-dāmiq-ilī)//Nādin-še'i in texts from the time of MNA, especially in those with institutional background, see more at p. 120f. esp. n. 471.

496. Wunsch, *Iddin-Marduk* 1, n. 240; and *idem*, *MOS Studies* 2, 110 (Dar 533).

497. For the scribe Bēl-ibni/Nergal-zēra-ibni//Šangû-Nanaya, see below at p. 130.

498. Also see below, at p. 130.

Dar 167, and BM 33972. In addition, they had to make sure that the silver, the purchase price of the crops, reached the person from whom MNA had presumably bought the crops. This part of the agreement was probably described in Dar 310, if one accepts that the debt between Rīmūt-Bēl and Nabû-uṣuršu/Gūzānu, described in this text, was due to MNA's prior purchase of crops from the latter. MNA proceeded very carefully. He secured his claim to the crops by real estate pledges and a claim on his debtors' lease income. Moreover, MNA put his slave in charge of the cultivation of the crops from which he was to collect his debtors' lease in order to maximize his profits. Finally, the transfer of MNA's silver to Nabû-uṣuršu/Gūzānu was guaranteed by Nīryahu, who stood surety for Rīmūt-Bēl and Kīnaya/Dannu-aḫḫēšu-ibni, MNA's employees.

We do not know how much the two brothers may have gained from their work agreement with MNA since the texts deal only with the brothers' obligations and not with their rights. Nevertheless, their situation may be compared to that of Marduk-nāṣir/Marduk-ušallim, as described in Dar 315.[499] Accordingly, they may have been shareholders in the profits that MNA expected to make. Furthermore, their familiarity with MNA enabled the brothers to obtain credit when needed, as for instance, when they had to pay for their *rikis qabli* obligations. Clearly, the relationship between MNA and the two brothers reached beyond their joint commercial enterprise and the safety net that MNA built to secure the successful outcome of this enterprise.

The relationship between MNA and Kīnaya/Atkal-Šamaš, on the other hand, is less well known, but must have been similar to that among MNA, Rīmūt-Bēl, and Nabû-makû-uṣur. As a matter of fact, Kīnaya knew Rīmūt-Bēl because the latter was present when the former promised to deliver 8.2.3. *kor* of dates to MNA (BM 31058). He must, therefore, have been working in the same business as Rīmūt-Bēl, viz. the collection of crops from institutional land in Šaḫrīnu on behalf of MNA. As said, other men, such as Marduk-nāṣir/Marduk-ušallim, also worked in this business.[500] It is, therefore, not surprising to find men such as Nidinti-Bēl/Damqiya//Nādin-še'i among the witnesses in BM 31058. He followed MNA's commodity trade in Šaḫrīnu very closely because he witnessed BM 31058 and witnessed or wrote several other contracts concerning MNA's trade in Šaḫrīnu.[501] Further, the presence of Rīmūt-Bēl/Ardiya//Itinnu among the witnesses in BM 31058 is noteworthy. His presence at seven other documents from the time of MNA for over twenty years shows that he was

499. Dar 315 and related texts (discussed in § 3.1.1). For comparable cases, see probably also Dar 261 (cf. n. 483) and the texts discussed in § 3.2.1. No doubt, a thorough examination of all texts from MNA's archive that were issued in Šaḫrīnu would reveal additional aspects of his commodity trade in that area.

500. See previous note (n. 499).

501. Dar 310, Dar 338 and BM 31018 (see already above on p. 120f.). Another man who seems to have kept a close track of MNA's commercial deals in Šaḫrīnu is Kalbaya, MNA's adoptive brother; he witnessed Dar 338 and BM 31058.

loosely involved in matters that concerned Bagasarū's income from land in Bīt-rab-kāṣir, real estate at the Uraš gate, temple property, boats, and probably also state income from taxes.[502] His presence in BM 31058, therefore, confirms the institutional and commercial background of Kīnaya's debt to MNA.

2.6.3. *Crops of Bagasarū from Land along the Rab-kāṣir Canal*

A case similar to the one referred to in the Rīmūt-Bēl texts is the one relating to Bagasarū. It is an additional example of MNA growing crops with the help of local (tenant) farmers and his senior slaves on land in the vicinity of Šaḫrīnu that did not belong to him. The location of the land, as described in the texts, suggests that it belonged to Bagasarū, the "king's treasurer" (*lúrab kāṣir*, *lúganzabaru*).[503] The case of Bagasarū, however, is remarkable in so far that MNA had access to his crops for more than fifteen years.[504]

The texts mention dates, onions, barley, wheat, and cress that were grown on land along the Rab-kāṣir canal, i.e., "the canal of the king's treasurer" (*Nār-lúrab-kāṣir*). The texts were written in Babylon, the village Bīt-ṭāb-Bēl, or a village named "The House of the King's Treasurer" (*Bīt-rab-kāṣir*). The land is, therefore, to be located somewhere between these villages and not far from Babylon. The name of the latter village, as well as that of its canal, suggests a strong link between the land and the office of treasurer of the king. Several possibilities for interpretation exist. The king's treasurer may have owned land in this area that he probably received from the king in remuneration of his services to the crown.[505] Or, he may have been appointed by the king to manage the cultivation of crops on land that the king owned in this area.[506] In the latter case the king's treasurer was entitled to the produce of the land, be it only within the limits of his office. He was not to derive personal benefit from the produce of the land because it belonged to the king, in principle at least.

The nature of the relationship between the parties involved in the cultivation of crops on this land may be illuminated by having a closer look at the texts.[507] Dar 527, dated in Tašrīt of Darius' twenty-first year, records the

502. On Rīmūt-Bēl/Ardiya//Itinnu in texts from the time of MNA, see more in Table 7 and at p. 172 (esp. n. 685).

503. On the title *rab kāṣir*, more at Bongenaar, *Ebabbar*, 136f.

504. Dar 105 (Bīt-rab-kāṣir, 5/i/4 Dar); Dar 296 (Babylon, 18/i/11 Dar); Dar 527 (Bīt-ṭāb-Bēl, 17/vii/21 Dar; and Dar 542?, 20/iii/22 Dar). For previous discussions of the texts, Wunsch, *Felder* 1, 175 (+ bibliography).

505. Note that a text from the time of Cambyses seems to refer to landowners in and around Šaḫrīnu (such as Bagasarū?) as *bēl eqlēti* "holders (=owners?) of the (crown's?) fields" (CT 22 78: 19, discussed in Wunsch, *Iddin-Marduk* 1, 46–47). Apparently, these men did not live on the land they held but relied on their majordomos and on private contractors for its cultivation.

506. So Wunsch, *Felder* 1, 175.

507. Note that Van Driel, "Entrepreneurs," 215 and 222, considers the Bagasarū-case an example of the third type of agricultural entrepreneurship whereby the entrepreneur "takes

promise made by Bēl-aḫa-ittannu / Aḫḫē-iddin to deliver sixty *kor* of dates from land along the Rab-kāṣir canal to MNA. He had to measure the dates in MNA's standard and deliver them in one single payment at the entrepot toward the end of the harvest. In addition, he had to pay the usual by-products of the date harvest, such as baskets and fibres. It is clear that Bēl-aḫa-ittannu was a tenant farmer, because he had to deliver the dates and their by-products in payment of lease (*imittu*). He may have leased the land from Bagasarū, who appears to have been its holder or even its owner as we have explained above, but *de facto*, he had to deliver his lease to MNA. Indeed, his dates were "the harvest of the field that (is located) at the Rab-kāṣir canal, due to MNA and his brothers."[508] Nevertheless, MNA was not entitled to the entire harvest from this land: "one-third of it is the share of Bagasarū, the king's treasurer."[509] The basis of MNA's rights to two thirds of the lease from Bagasarū's land along the Rab-kāṣir canal is not specified in the texts.

The transfer of Bagasarū's share in the harvest is the subject of two other texts in MNA's archive. It was a matter that fell within the responsibility of those among MNA's slaves who had the necessary business know-how. In Dar 542, for instance, Šēpāt-Bēl-aṣbat, MNA's slave, transferred Bagasarū's share in the date-harvest of Darius' twenty-first year. The transfer took place in Simān of the next year, i.e., almost six months after the harvest. Bagasarū's share was received by one of his slaves, who acted as proxy of Bagasarū's majordomo. This strongly suggests that Bagasarū was more of an absentee landowner than a man actually in charge of the cultivation of his land. He had a majordomo and slaves who looked after his land. A similar situation is recorded in Dar 105, but this time it concerned *šibšu*-onions rather than *imittu*-dates. The onions were transferred on the fifth of Nisan, i.e., at the end of the harvest. They were received by a slave of Bagasarū, who acted as proxy for another of Bagasarū's slaves. It is not clear who delivered the onions, but it may have been the two men, [...]-šarra-uṣur and Talimmu, mentioned in line 6, or their agents. Unfortunately, the text is almost completely broken after their names.[510] Nor is it clear whether or how MNA was involved in the transfer.

---

the lease of assets or rights belonging to large estates, 'property' of high officials or members of the royal family."

508. Dar 527: 1–2, ⸢*ebūr*⸣ *eqli* ⸢*ša*⸣ [(...)] ⸢*Nār*$^{?}$⸣-^{lú}*rab-kāṣir ša MNA u aḫḫēšu*. For the origin of the crops, further see Dar 105, written in Bīt-rab-kāṣir and concerning onions from Bagasarū's field; and Dar 296: 1–2, barley, wheat and cress "harvest of the eleventh year from Bagasarū's field, the Treasur[er]" (*ša šanat* 11^{kam} *ebūr eqli ša Bagasarū* ^{lú}*ganzabaru*), written in Babylon.

509. Dar 527: 4–5, *šá ina lìb-bi šal-šú* ḪA.LA *šá* ^{m}*ba-ak-ka-su-ru-ú* LÚ *gan-za-ba-ru*. Cf. Dar 542: 1–2, "*imittu*-dates of King Darius' twenty-first year from a field, Bagasarū's share that (is shared) with MNA and his brothers" (*suluppū imitti eqli ša šanat* 21^{kam} *Darius šarri zitti ša Bagasarū ša itti MNA u aḫḫēšu*); and Dar 105: 1–2, "seventy bundles of *šibšu*-onions from a field, the one-third share of Bagasarū, the king's treasurer" (70 *pittī ša šūmī šibšu eqli zitti šalšu ša Bagasarū* ^{lú}*rab kāṣir*).

510. Are we to restore the name [Bīt-Ir'anni]-šarra-uṣur in line 6 and interpret Dar 105 in the

The transfer of the harvest of Bagasarū's land to those entitled to it or to parts of it was a complicated issue because different people on various levels were involved in this matter. As we have seen above, it involved (MNA's?) tenant farmers who grew the onions and dates on the land along the Rab-kāṣir canal, MNA's slaves who were responsible for the transfer of Bagasarū's share from the harvest of this land, Bagasarū's slaves, who actually received the share, Bagasarū's majordomo, who supervised their receipt, and Bagasarū himself, who seems to have lived in Babylon but who was the ultimate beneficiary of the dates and onions. Under such circumstances problems could easily arise in the course of the transfer. Dar 296, for instance, discusses such a problematic situation. It concerned the harvest of Darius' eleventh year from Bagasarū's land. This harvest had to be transferred to a man named Nidintu, majordomo of Iqīša. Unfortunately, neither Nidintu nor Iqīša is cited by his full name, and so they are, in fact, otherwise unknown. Moreover, we do not know why they were entitled to Bagasarū's crops from Darius' eleventh year. Were they intended for Bagasarū?[511] Nidintu seems to have asked Erībaya, Bagasarū's majordomo, for the reason that the crops from Bagasarū's land had not been transferred to him. Erībaya, however, shifts the responsibility for the irregularities to two other men, viz. Arad-Bāba/Mušēzib-Marduk//Ašlāku and Šellibi/Iddin-Nabû.[512] He claims that he gave the barley, wheat, and cress to these two men, but that they then failed to clear their receipt in Nidintu's accounts. The men actually confirm their receipt of the crops from Erībaya. Eventually, Arad-Bāba and Šellibi were given another month to settle the matter. Interestingly, MNA assumed warranty for Arad-Bāba. In other words, MNA promised to see after the proper conclusion of the transfer of Bagasarū's crops from Arad-Bāba to Nidintu. Arad-Bāba, therefore, was most likely one of the men who worked for MNA in the cultivation of crops on land along the Rab-kāṣir canal and the transfer of part of these crops to Bagasarū.[513] Other such men

---

light of CT 22 80? According to this letter from the time of Cambyses, Bīt-Ir'anni- šarra-uṣur, a local governor (LÚ.NAM; in Bīt-Ir'anni?), allowed Iddin-Marduk to collect three hundred *kor* of dates (from lease?) and their by-products from the area "between the rivers" or from Bīt-ṭāb-Bēl. The dates and by-products were due from the gardeners and their collection was organized by MBU, who at that time was the slave of Iddin-Marduk. Details in Wunsch, *Iddin-Marduk* 1, 47–48.

511. So Krecher, *Egibi*, 288.

512. For Arad-Bāba, see next note. For Šellibi/Iddin-Nabû(//Nappāḫu) and the Nappāḫu archive, more at Von Dassow, CTMMA 3, 195f. (especially text no. 98).

513. For Arad-Bāba/Mušēzib-Marduk//Ašlāku, see also Dar 466 (= *CM* 20b 221), Dar 571 (= *CM* 20b 207), and discussion by Wunsch, *Felder* 1, 167f. He was, most likely, the same man as Arad-Bāba//Ašlāku, who wrote several documents for MNA, i.a. Dar 466, BM 31793 (sale of a prebend), BM 33112 (*gimru*), BM 30243 (*ilku*-receipt), BM 30436 (= b 2535, unpublished, cf. n. 689), and the unpublished BM 31788 (= b 2638; Babylon, 11/i/27 Dar). The latter text records the partial payment of a silver debt by MNA to Mūrānu/Nabû-zēra-iddin//Ašlāku). It is witnessed by Mūrānu/Šaddinnu//Ašlāku, Nergal-ēṭir/Kalbaya//Šumulibši, Ša-Bēl-atta/Marduk-šuma-ibni//Egibi, and Nidinti/Mūrānu. The first three wit-

were, as we have seen above, Bēl-aḫa-ittannu/Aḫḫē-iddin (in Dar 527), Šēpāt-Bēl-aṣbat, MNA's slave (in Dar 542), and perhaps also (the men of?) [...]-šarra-uṣur and Talimmu (in Dar 105).

Interestingly, the Bagasarū-texts, which were adduced above, were written and witnessed by men who knew MNA from comparable ventures in nearby places. Some of these men, for instance, knew MNA from his agricultural ventures in Šaḫrīnu. This holds for the scribe of Dar 105 (Bēl-ibni/Nergal-zēra-ibni//Šangû-Nanaya)[514] and one of the witnesses in Dar 527 (Iddin-Nabû/Marduk-(i)qīšanni//Bēl-eṭēru). Bēl-ibni and the father of Iddin-Nabû recur in two texts concerning MNA's collection of crops from institutional land in Šaḫrīnu. The two texts in question are Dar 164 and Dar 167, written in Šaḫrīnu on the first of Ab of Darius' fifth year and belong to the Rīmūt-Bēl dossier discussed above. They were written by Bēl-ibni/Nergal-zēra-ibni//Šangû-Nanaya, who, as we have pointed out, also wrote Dar 105. In addition, Dar 164 and Dar 167 were witnessed by Marduk-iqīšanni/Bēl-aḫa-ušabši//Bēl-eṭēru, no doubt the father of Iddin-Nabû, whom we previously found among the witnesses in Dar 527. Furthermore, some of the men in the Bagasarū-texts knew MNA from his commercial ventures in other parts of Babylonia. This is clear from the case of Mušēzib-Bēl/Bēl-kāṣir//Ea-eppeš-ilī and members of his family.[515] Mušēzib-Bēl witnessed Dar 296 concerning the transfer of Bagasarū's harvest. He had a brother who was a priest in Bāṣ and witnessed MNA's large silver debt to the governor of Kiš in Šušan in Darius' sixteenth year (TCL 13 193). Another of his brothers was the overseer of the quay in Bīt-Ir'anni, who received tolls from MNA in Darius' tenth year (Dar 268).

Some of the men mentioned in the Bagasarū-texts knew MNA from his boat transports and/or dealings with state income from taxes.[516] We have already pointed out that one of the witnesses in Dar 296 had a brother who was the overseer of the quay in Bīt-Ir'anni and to whom MNA paid tolls (Dar 268). Another example is Erībaya/Ša-Nabû-šū, Bagasarū's majordomo, who should have transferred the harvest from Bagasarū's field to one Nidintu in Darius' eleventh year. He was also present fifteen years later when MNA rented a boat

---

nesses in BM 31788 are well known from several texts published in this book. MNA's silver debt to the said Mūrānu must, therefore, have had an institutional background. Another part of the debt is paid back on 2/xii/28 Dar according to BM 30924 = b 2654, unpublished. Finally, Arad-Bāba//Ašlāku was also among the witnesses in the text from MNA's archive drafted in Šušan and published by Biggs, *MHEO* 2, p. 299ff.

514. In fact, this scribe also worked for Iddin-Marduk, MNA's grandfather, in his commodity trade in Šaḫrīnu (Camb 167 = *CM* 3b 333 and Camb 218 = *CM* 3b 337). Details below on p. 131f.

515. See already above at n. 468.

516. As was already pointed out above at the discussion of MNA's boat-related transactions (§ 2.5, esp. p. 113f.). This is not surprising when we take into consideration that the crops from Bagasarū's land, to which MNA was entitled, had to be transported from Bīt-rab-kāṣir and Bīt-ṭāb-Bēl to Babylon. This aspect of MNA's business is actually attested in BM 31347.

from the sailor of the *mašennu* in order to sail to Birtu-ša-ṣērūa.[517] A third example is that of Šullumaya/Nabû-nādin-aḫi//Nabaya. He is attested in one text concerning Bagasarū, two texts concerning taxes collected by MNA, and two texts concerning transport costs paid by MNA to the governor of Babylon.[518] The most elaborate case, however, is that of Rīmūt-Bēl/Ardiya//Itinnu, who witnessed Dar 296 in Darius' eleventh year. His presence in seven other documents from the time of MNA that span twenty years shows that he was loosely involved in matters that concerned MNA's commodity trade in Šaḫrīnu, temple property, boats, real estate at the Uraš gate in Litamu, and probably also state income from taxes.[519]

Finally, we should point out the origins of MNA's interest in crops from Bīt-rab-kāṣir and Bīt-ṭāb-Bēl in the vicinity of Šaḫrīnu. As a matter of fact, these go back to Cambyses' reign when Iddin-Marduk, MNA's maternal grandfather, established a flourishing business in crops from this area. Texts from the Iddin-Marduk archive, indeed, show how Iddin-Marduk manoeuvred to control the agricultural and tax management of institutional land in and around Šaḫrīnu in order to get hold of large amounts of crops. These crops were subsequently transported from Šaḫrīnu and its surroundings to Babylon, where they could be traded at a favorable price. Iddin-Marduk, however, left the daily management of this commodity trade in the hands of his business-slaves, among them Nergal-rēṣūa and MBU.[520] The latter, for instance, operated in Šaḫrīnu, the area "between the rivers," and the village Bīt-ṭāb-Bēl. He had farmers (*ikkarātu*) and gardeners (*nukaribbū*) at his disposal, as well as other agricultural workers who had to deliver barley, onions, and dates to him. He saw to it that these men received barley for seeds and rations, and silver for other expenses. In view of the Rīmūt-Bēl texts, according to which MNA's employees in Šaḫrīnu had to meet non-agrarian obligations such as *rikis qabli*, it is possible that MBU's other expenses included payments for his workers' *rikis qabli*. MBU corresponded

---

It records MNA's payment of tolls to the overseer of the quay of Bīt-ṭāb-Bēl so that his "boat [...] loaded with ... dates (and) ... barley ... pass beyond the quay of Bīt-ṭ[āb-Bēl]" (BM 31347: 1–3). For a similar case, see discussion of BM 30747 at p. 146.

517. For Erībaya/Ša-Nabû-šū see Dar 296 (18/i/11 Dar, Bagasarū) and BM 30490 (5/xii/26 Dar, boat rental).

518. For Šullumaya/Nabû-nādin-aḫi//Nabaya, see Dar 542 (Bagasarū); BM 31798 and BM 41607 (taxes; perhaps also BM 30541); and BM 31572 and BM 32891 (transport costs). On this person, more at Table 7. His brother, Bēl-iddin/Nabû-nādin-aḫi//Nabaya occurs in another Bagasarū-text, viz. Dar 527 (for Bēl-iddin, also see Dar 571=*CM* 20b 207; on Dar 571 see below at n. 605. Bēl-iddin occurs perhaps also in the fragmentary debt-note published in AOAT 252: 48–49, written in Bīt-ṭāb-Bēl).

519. On Rīmūt-Bēl/Ardiya//Itinnu in texts from the time of MNA, see more at Table 7 and p. 172 (esp. n. 685).

520. E.g., Nbn 280 (= *CM* 3b 149), Cyr 12 (= *CM* 3b 263), Camb 167 (= *CM* 3b 333), Camb 53 (= *CM* 3b 321) and Camb 54 (= *CM* 3b 322) (Nergal-rēṣūa); Camb 218 (= *CM* 3b 337, MBU). These and other documents, as well as several related letters from CT 22 have been discussed in detail by Wunsch, *Iddin-Marduk* 1, 43–55.

with Bīt-Ir'anni-šarra-uṣur, the king's local governor, regarding these matters. Nergal-rēṣūa corresponded with the *bēl piqitti* of Bīt-ṭāb-Bēl regarding similar matters. In addition, MBU had to take care of the collection of tithes for the temple of Nergal and the collection of *šibšu*-lease from the fields of (absentee-) landowners who had apparently left the agricultural management of their fields to private entrepreneurs and their manpower.

MBU, no doubt, continued to supervise the commodity trade in Šaḫrīnu and its surroundings when he became MNA's slave. Thus, he organized the delivery of crops in the house of MNA in Šaḫrīnu.[521] MBU, however, was not the only man who continued to work in Šaḫrīnu after the take-over of affairs by MNA. Indeed, Bēl-ibni/Nergal-zēra-ibni//Šangû-Nanaya, one of the scribes who worked with MBU in the days of Iddin-Marduk, also continued his work when MNA assumed control of the business. He wrote two texts for Iddin-Marduk and three for MNA, all of which concerned crops from land in and around Šaḫrīnu that were due to either Iddin-Marduk or MNA.[522] When MBU died at about Darius' twentieth year,[523] Madānu(-apla)-iddin, one of MBU's sons, continued his father's work in Šaḫrīnu.[524] Other slaves from MNA's house were active in similar ventures in the vicinity of Šaḫrīnu, e.g., Šēpāt-Bēl-aṣbat, who took care of MNA's interests in the agricultural management of Bagasarū's landed estate in Bīt-rab-kāṣir.[525]

2.7. *Payments by MNA to State Officials for Unspecified Reasons*

The five texts adduced below deal with silver that was either owed by MNA or transferred to state officials by him for reasons that are not specified in the texts.[526] They are dated between Darius' sixteenth and twenty-sixth years. The information provided by these texts is very elementary. As a rule, they do not inform us on the origin of the silver that MNA had to give to the authorities, the reason for which he had to give it, or the use that the authorities were to make of it. Accordingly, they refer to silver that was "owed by MNA" (*ina muḫḫi* MNA) to the governor of Kish or received by courtiers from MNA (*ina qātē* MNA), but do not specify, for instance, the cause of MNA's indebtedness or the reason of his payment. A closer look at the texts may throw some light on these matters.

---

521. See BM 33972 and other Rīmūt-Bēl texts discussed above; cf. Dar 261 (Kāṣir/Šulaya had to deliver dates and barley to MBU in the house of MNA in Šaḫrīnu).

522. Camb 167 (= *CM* 3b 333) and Camb 218 (= *CM* 3b 337): Iddin-Marduk; Dar 164, Dar 167 and Dar 105: MNA. See also above p. 130.

523. See at commentary to Dar 509: 3.

524. Dar 541 and BM 31976. Details at § 3.2.1.

525. Nabû-ayyālu was another of MNA's slaves who was employed in Šaḫrīnu, e.g., Dar 243, Dar 349 and Dar 561.

526. TCL 13 193 (Šušan, 10/xii^{b}/16 Dar), Liv 25 (Šušan, 3/xii^{a}/[16] Dar), Dar 544 (Babylon, 12/iv/22$^{?}$ Dar), BM 31138 (Babylon, 19/iii/25 Dar), and BM 31036 (Babylon, 18/xii/26 Dar).

2.7.1. *Silver Debts by MNA to State Officials*

Three texts from the archive record MNA's promise to pay the silver that he owed to some state officials.[527] According to TCL 13 193, MNA owed a large amount of silver, to wit forty-five minas, to a courtier named Šarru-dūrī/Edra. While staying in Šušan, in Addar of Darius' sixteenth year, he promised to settle the debt in Simān upon his return to Babylon. He made a similar promise to Zababa-iddin, governor of Kish, regarding a debt of twenty-three minas of silver, during this same stay in Šušan (Liv 25).[528] MNA's debts stirred the interest of several prominent persons of the civil and temple administration, among them two of the king's representatives in the Esagil temple, a priest from Bāṣ, and fifteen judges. These men were present at the sealing of the two texts that contained MNA's promises to pay his debts. The cause of the debts, however, is not specified, which is in accordance with Neo- and Late-Babylonian notary practice. Accordingly, we cannot know for sure why MNA owed such a large amount of silver to Šarru-dūrī, the courtier, and Zababa-iddin, the governor of Kish.

The debts in TCL 13 193 and Liv 25 may have resulted from a purchase of state income by MNA from the above-mentioned state officials, similar to his purchase of dates from the district governor of Šaḫrīnu as recorded in Dar 338.[529] This may explain the impressive lists of witnesses of the texts under consideration. Accordingly, MNA may have purchased the right to collect taxes or rent instead of the state and still had to transfer (part of) the purchase price to the state representatives from whom he bought the right. Was he to collect the taxes or rent from state-owned land in Šušan? Was this income from taxes or rent needed by the governor of Kish to finance the digging of the king's canal to Elam?[530]

The third text that records a debt of silver by MNA to state officials is Dar 544 from Darius' twenty-second year. On the twelfth of Dûzu MNA promised to pay nine minas of white silver before the end of the year to Nabû-[...], who was a "courtier (and) clerk." The silver was owed by MNA to the said courtier for unspecified reasons. The document was witnessed, among others, by Bēl-erība/Kalbaya//Šumu-libši and his presence strongly suggests that the debt had to do with the recruitment and maintenance of soldiers or workers on behalf of the state. It may have been another case of MNA being urged to

527. TCL 13 193, Liv 25, and Dar 544. For these texts, also see above at § 2.2.1.

528. The first part of the text describes the debt as one between MNA and Nabû-uballissu (ll. 1–3). From the second part of the text, however, it becomes clear that the ultimate creditor of MNA was not Nabû-uballissu, but the governor of Kish (ll. 7–9). Nabû-uballissu had been sent by MNA to reach only an interim agreement with the governor regarding the debt (ll. 6–10).

529. More on Dar 338 at § 2.6.1. MNA may also have purchased rights to state income from bridge tolls, more at TCL 13 196 (§ 2.4.1); for his purchase of temple income from field rent, see Dar 315 (§ 3.1.1). On MNA's tax and rent farming deals, also see at n. 325.

530. For the link between Liv 25 and Dar 411, more at § 2.2.1 (p. 35f.).

transfer (tax-)silver to the authorities before the end of the year so that they could pay the salaries and rations of the men under their responsibility.[531]

If the above interpretation of the texts is accepted, MNA's silver debts to state officials were integral parts of his commercial ventures with state income. These and similar texts from the archive show that MNA purchased state income, converted it into cash, and was obliged to transfer the silver to state officials, such as the district governor of Šaḫrīnu, the governor of Kish, and courtiers. These men needed the silver to finance state-sponsored projects under their authority, such as the digging of canals and the payment of salaries and rations to their dependents. Occasionally, the authorities ordered MNA to transfer the silver directly to the men whose salaries and rations were derived from the state income that MNA had purchased, as we have seen in the texts discussed above in § 2.2.1.

2.7.2. *Payments of Barley and Dates by MNA to Courtiers*[532]

In the spring of Darius' twenty-fifth and twenty-sixth years MNA transferred small amounts of barley and dates to two courtiers for unspecified reasons. BM 31138, for instance, records the receipt of three *kor* of barley from MNA in Simān of Darius' twenty-fifth year. It is not clear who collected the barley from MNA but he or they obviously did so "by order of Iddin-Nabû, courtier (and) clerk."[533] Eleven months later Bēl-ušallim/Ina-Nabû-ultarraḫ, a courtier, received fifteen *kor* of dates from MNA (BM 31036). He collected the dates "by order of Gūzānu, governor of Babylon." These payments of barley and dates by MNA to courtiers were probably payments for boat transports or rations for boatmen.[534] In addition to the dates, Bēl-ušallim received a register that accounted for his receipt of at least two-third minas of silver from MNA.[535]The dates and register were previously "in the hands of" Iqūpu/Nādin//Gaḫul-Marduk.[536]

2.8. *Summary: MNA and the State*

The state officials with whom MNA conducted business had access to economically vital assets: land, water, skilled workers, and expensive equipment (e.g., boats). Accordingly, we found among them city governors (*šākin ṭēmi*),

---

531. For similar cases, more at § 2.2.1.

532. For the title LÚ.SAG-LUGAL, *ša-rēš šarri* "courtier," see Bongenaar, *Ebabbar*, 99ff. with bibliography.

533. BM 31138: 4–5, *ina qibi ša Iddin-Nabû* ^{lú}*ša-rēš šarri* ^{lú}*sepīri*. See commentary to line 7 *ad hoc*.

534. Cf. BM 30256, BM 30853: 12–24, and the eight *gimru*-texts. Details at § 2.5.

535. On this register, more at p. 168.

536. For this Iqūpu, probably cf. Dar 571 (= *CM* 20b 207. On Dar 571, see also n. 605). Was he one of MNA's employees transshipping and transporting crops from the countryside for MNA's trade?

inspectors of rural areas like Šaḫrīnu (*pāḫātu*), the king's treasurer (*rab kāṣir, ganzabaru*), overseers of quays (*rab kāri*), canal inspectors (*mašennu;* ^lú^*mār abarakku*?), harbor-masters (*rēš ṣābê* = *ṣābêšu ša bīt kāri*), commanders of fortresses (*rab dūri*) and of contingents of fifty (soldiers or workers, *rab ḫanšê*), courtiers (*ša-rēš šarri*), and clerks in the king's palaces (*sepīru ... ša ekalli eššil rabî*). They were appointed by the king to control the said assets and drew payments from them on behalf of the royal treasury.

MNA's relationship with the governors of Babylon is the best-documented one and may serve as an example of his business relations in general, and his official ones in particular. It is characterized by three facts: its continuity in time, its comprehensiveness, and its reciprocity. It, no doubt, went back to similar well-established relations of his father's. The evidence from MNA's time shows him paying for the *rikis qabli* of men living and working in his house to an agent of Bēl-apla-iddin, governor of Babylon, in Darius' third year. He collected the king's flour from a group of exorcists on behalf of Nabû-šuma-ukīn//Ša-nāšišu, who governed Babylon at about Darius' twelfth year. Cooperation continued in the second half of Darius' reign during the governorship of Nabû-šuma-ukīn's sons, Ina-Esagil-lilbur and Gūzānu. In those years MNA assisted the governors in more than one way, but also obtained from them the boats, equipment, men and permits needed for the transport of beer, flour, and crops for his trade. Thus, he recruited men to tow boats for Ina-Esagil-lilbur and assisted Gūzānu in the exploitation of his chariot-fief and of one of his bridges. The workers whom he hired to dig and maintain the king's canal to Elam may also have been for a city governor, viz. the governor of Kish, but this cannot be proved. He was entitled to some of the income from the bridge that he helped exploit and to part of the tower-service of the men whom he helped recruit. He may also have organized Gūzānu's expedition by chariot to Elam and help organize several of his boat transports from Tâmti to the capital in return for the right to use the expedition and transports for his own purposes.

MNA had similar, long-term relations with other state officials. He worked with the king's treasurer for fifteen years, with a harbor-master for a little more than a decade,[537] and with a commander-of-fifty for only five years but very intensively, i.e., meeting him sixteen times. In particular, he had established relations with men who had access to large tracks of, no doubt, institutional land in and around Šaḫrīnu. We have mentioned his fifteen-year relationship with the king's treasurer, who possessed land along the Rab-kāṣir canal, but was, most likely, residing in the capital, leaving the management of his land to his majordomo, his slaves, and to private entrepreneurs such as MNA. Similarly, he worked for seven years with Rīmūt-Bēl and his brother in the exploitation of (institutional) land in Šaḫrīnu that was held by these men under unknown conditions.

---

537. If Bēl-ikṣur/Rīmūt in BM 30853 and *CM* 20b 158 is the same as Bēl-kiṣuršu/Rīmūt//LÚ.⸢x⸣ in BM 41453.

MNA also included members of these officials' families in his network of official relations. A clear example at stake is his relationship with the Ša-nāšišu family. Nabû-šuma-ukīn and two of his sons, Ina-Esagil-lilbur and Gūzānu, were governors of Babylon: the first between 22–24 Dar, the second between 25–28 Dar. MNA conducted business with the three of them during their respective governorships. In addition, he did business with another of Nabû-šuma-ukīn's son, Basiya, who does not seem to have fulfilled any official position. A similar case is that of MNA's relations with the sons of Kalbaya//Šumu-libši. One of them, Bēl-erība, was a commander-of-fifty, and his brother, Nergal-ēṭir, though not having an official title, dealt with the recruitment of men who had to go to Elam. MNA did business with each of the brothers separately. Two other sons of Kalbaya//Šumu-libši, Nidintu and Arad-Bēl, occasionally acted as witnesses for MNA. Similarly, he conducted business with the king's inspector in Šaḫrīnu. One of the inspector's brothers participated in the transaction as a messenger; another of his brothers was present as witness and is, furthermore, attested among the witnesses at several other business transactions from MNA's time. The same applies to his relationship with members of the (Ea-) Eppeš-ilī family. Kulbibi/Bēl-kāṣir was the overseer of the quay in Bīt-Ir'anni and MNA paid tolls to him, and three of Kulbibi's brothers are found as witnesses in other texts from MNA's business archive.

It should also be pointed out in this context that MNA may have tried to gain a foothold in the economy of other Babylonian cities through the family connections of several of the officials whom he originally knew from Babylon. Note, for instance, that the governors of Babylon from the Ša-nāšišu family had strong connections with Sippar. Ina-Esagil-lilbur and Gūzānu, for instance, started their careers as temple administrators (*šangû*) of Sippar before being promoted to the office of governor in Babylon.[538] Ina-Esagil-lilbur returned to Sippar to take up the chief administration (*šatammu*) of the Ebabbar temple after Gūzānu, his brother, succeeded him as governor of Babylon. The inspector of Šaḫrīnu, Libluṭ/Mušēzib-Marduk(//Nappāḫu) also seems to have travelled between Babylon and Sippar, since he appears in texts from Babylon and perhaps also once in a text from Sippar with a governor of Babylon. Finally, Kulbibi/Bēl-kāṣir//(Ea-)Eppeš-ilī, the overseer of the quay in Bīt-Ir'anni, had a brother who was a priest in Bāṣ and with whom MNA was acquainted as well; their father and uncle had business connections with the Ea-ilûta-bāni family of Borsippa.

The tendency to limit his business contacts to a few men and their families also applies to his contacts of a private nature. First, he limited these contacts to men trained in certain professions with whom he worked intensively over

538. Details at Bongenaar, *Ebabbar*, 15f.; see also *ibidem*, 473 regarding Babylon-based descendants of the Ša-nāšīšu family; add to this list Bēl-iddin/Tabnēa//Ša-nāšīšu, witness in Dar 573, and perhaps also Tabnēa/Marduk-šuma-ibni//Ša-nāšīšu in *CM* 20b 81 and *CM* 20b 78.

several years. A clear example of this strategy is his relationship with the charioteer Liblut̩/Itti-Nabû-balāṭu, with whom he met eleven times in fourteen years. Similar intensive relations with other professionals are those with the worker (boat-tower?) Nidintu/Kalbaya//Suḫaya (seven meetings between 23⁺–26 Dar), the baker Gūzānu/Ḫambaqu//Mandidi (three meetings in half a year), and the sailor Bulṭaya/Ḫabaṣīru//Rē'i-alpi (two meetings in half a year). Second, MNA relied only on his most experienced slaves in the management of his affairs outside the capital. The management of his commodity trade in Šaḫrīnu, for instance, was left in the hands of MBU, who had been working in this area since the days of Iddin-Marduk, Madānu(-apla)-iddin (i.e., MBU's son), Nabû-ayyālu, and Šēpāt-Bēl-aṣbat. Finally, he often called up the same men as witness or scribe to assist him in matters of a related nature as a means to limit the group of men participating in his business. Consequently, we often found the same men among the witnesses and scribes when MNA was recruiting men, organizing the work at bridges, participating in boat transports, levying taxes, buying crops from the state or the temple, or collecting crops from institutional land. Some of these witnesses and scribes occasionally took part in MNA's business in a more direct way, viz. by concluding contracts with him. The prosopographic evidence collected throughout this book adequately proves this point. Therefore, it suffices to refer to only some of the more outspoken examples, as for instance, Bēl-asûa/Nergal-uballiṭ//Mudammiq-Adad, Rīmūt-Bēl/Ardiya//Itinnu, Ardiya/Dādiya//Nabaya, and the sons of Nabû-dāmiq-ilī (*alias* Damqiya)/Nādin-še'i.

MNA met with the above-mentioned officials for various reasons. The most obvious reason for any citizen in any period of history to come in direct contact with the authorities is when one has to pay taxes, and MNA was no exception to this rule. He paid his own taxes or those of his house(hold)[539] on least at fifteen different occasions between Darius' third and thirty-fifth years, especially between 3–10 and 25–26 Dar. The evidence gathered from these texts may be summarized in the following four points. First, MNA did not pay taxes of a more general kind like *ilku*, at least not on his own behalf. Rather, he paid for duties that were specifically related to either army and state logistics, like *rikis qabli*, or boat transports, like *miksu*. Second, there is no evidence that MNA had to perform corvée or paid instead of doing the work, nor is there conclusive proof that he had to serve in the army, e.g., as an archer or a charioteer. The evidence on MNA hiring men to serve or work in his stead is equally controversial. Third, MNA is not attested as a member or head of a tax-unit ("bow-of-so-and-so"). Nevertheless, when he paid *rikis qabli* he did so together with his

539. The clearest case is that of MNA's payment of *rikis qabli* for his house (Dar 206). The fact that MNA's employees were subject to the payment of taxes (*i.c. rikis qabli*) is clearly evidenced by the Rīmūt-Bēl texts; three other cases are less certain: (1) MNA's payment of *ilku* for Gūzānu/Ḫambaqu//Mandidi as recorded in TCL 13 198 belongs here if the latter was indeed employed (as baker?) in MNA's household; (2) the case recorded in Dar 156; (3) and the short reference to *dullu*-work of the house of MNA in CTMMA 3 69.

brother and his son. Moreover, members of his household, especially those working in his trade in Šaḫrīnu, and probably some of his business-slaves, were grouped for tax purposes into units called the "bow of Bēl-iddin" and "the house of MNA." Fourth, the men who took receipt of MNA's taxes were either representatives of the central administration in Babylon or private persons without an official title, whose relation to the central administration is, therefore, often a matter of speculation. They may have been men subject to the performance of military service or corvée-work and entitled to MNA's tax-silver to buy equipment and travel provisions.

In addition, MNA regularly met with the authorities in the course of his trade in commodities because many of the assets needed for his trade, especially the access to land and water, were controlled by the state.[540] Thus, he met with the king's representatives in the countryside and those in the temple when he bought crops from crown and temple land. Similarly, he met with overseers of quays when he paid tolls for the boats that transported his crops. He may as well have tried to sell his crops to officials residing in the capital (e.g., the governor of Babylon and the commander-of-the-fortress), who, no doubt, needed these crops to feed state-employed workers and soldiers, especially those in the king's palaces and the capital's fortress. The big institutions may also have been a ready market for goods other than crops in which MNA seems to have traded, such as beer, flour, and wool. This may especially apply to officials moving troops of workers and soldiers to Elam (e.g., the governor of Babylon, the commander-of-fifty and his brother).

Moreover, MNA was involved in various transactions with institutional assets that were only loosely related to his trade in commodities. This regards most of his transactions involving taxes, state-controlled bridges, state-owned boats, corvée-workers, and soldiers. It appears from the texts recording these transactions that MNA was economically active as an entrepreneur in the Babylonian tax system of the early Persian period, the exploitation of institutional land, and the transport business.

(1A) TAXES AND TOLLS

Most frequently, MNA dealt with state income from taxes and tolls, and occasionally with temple income from tithes. Tens of texts from his archive deal with these matters and reveal the full scope of his involvement in the Babylonian tax system of the early Persian period. It appears from these texts that MNA not only paid his own taxes, those of his household, and those of men who worked in his trade, but occasionally those of men who were not related to his household or trade in any apparent way, such as Bēl-nādin-apli/Bēl-uballiṭ//Paḫāru and his brothers. Moreover, he frequently received taxes, notwithstanding the fact that these were nominally due to the state.

---

540. Further note that he must have met with officials in the course of the management of his real estate, because some of his land was encumbered with taxes, viz. the *gugallûtu*-tax, e.g., CTMMA 3 67 and Dar 123 (= *CM* 20b 215).

Primarily, MNA and his slave assisted state representatives in levying taxes before the end of the year. Accordingly, they collected taxes by order of these representatives or with their silent consent. We saw that MNA collected the *ilku*-tax "[as prox]y for Šuma-ukīn" and obligatory payments from either bows or boats at bridges "that were under the administrative responsibility (*ša qātē* or *bīt qīpti*) of the governor of Babylon."[541] We do not always know whether MNA could keep some of what he collected for his own use, or had to transfer all of it to the authorities, but he cooperated with the men under whose command he collected the taxes for several years and, no doubt, derived benefits from this close cooperation in one way or another. Similarly, MBU collected silver from members of the bow of Bēl-iddin, so that they were able to hire someone to serve on their behalf and meet their service obligation of Darius' sixteenth year.

The relationship among the three parties involved in the collection of taxes, namely MNA or MBU, the taxpayer, and the state, was usually more complex. As a matter of fact, MNA or MBU frequently mediated between taxpayers, on the one hand, and representatives of the state, on the other, rather than merely collecting taxes on the state's behalf. Their role as middlemen could take three concrete forms. First, they made advance payments in cash to state representatives on behalf of specific taxpayers (e.g., Gūzānu/Ḫambaqu//Mandidi; Bēl-iddin in BM 31026; and probably also Bēl-nādin-apli and his brothers in Dar 213 and TCL 13 185). It is not always clear how MNA and MBU were reimbursed, but men such as Gūzānu/Ḫambaqu//Mandidi may have been employed in MNA's trade or household on a more or less permanent basis and compensated him with their work. Second, MNA often paid a lump sum to the public treasury and was subsequently entitled to all proceeds and profits from the levy of taxes (mainly *ilku*). He concluded tax-farming deals of this kind with the governor of Babylon regarding the collection of *ilku* in Darius' twenty-fourth and twenty-sixth years and probably also regarding the collection of bridge tolls in Darius' twenty-sixth year. He seems to have concluded a similar deal with the Esagil temple regarding the collection of tithes at about Darius' thirteenth year. MNA recuperated most of his expenses from the individual taxpayers after the harvest, as is clear from his receipts of *ilku*. In this manner he gained control over the agricultural yields of these taxpayers. It was, no doubt, also one of the ways in which he acquired the commodities that he needed for his trade, and this shows the likely link that existed between his dealings with taxes and his main business, the trade in commodities. Third, MNA or MBU occasionally provided taxpayers with the credit to pay their dues to the state (e.g., Rīmūt-Bēl/Šuma-ukīn and his brother; Bēl-iddin in Dar 308; and probably also Bēl-nādin-apli and his brothers in b. 2800). This proved to be a profitable investment of their capital since it provided them with access to

541. BM 31533 (Šuma-ukīn/Bēl-ēṭir), BM 33954 (Bow of the exorcists) and TCL 13 196 (the governor's bridge), unless the latter text implies a tax-farming deal between MNA and the governor of Babylon (see below).

their debtor's resources. Thus, MNA and MBU gained access to their debtors' real estate and future harvests; MNA also acquired a slave from one of his debtors, apparently through a pledge sale.

(1B) CORVÉE-WORKERS AND CONSCRIPTS

Texts from MNA's archive frequently mention various kinds of corvée-workers and soldiers, such as men who had to tow boats, sail them or do other boat-related jobs, dig and maintain canals, serve with the commander-of-the-fortress in Babylon, go to Elam with a commander-of-fifty or his brother, and lead the governor's chariot, i.a. to Elam. Occasionally, the service obligation incumbent on these men is described in technical terms as *urāšu*-corvée, *kanšu*-service, or *dullu*-work assignment.

MNA met with the workers and conscripts and dealt with matters related to their obligatory state or army service, in various entrepreneurial ventures. First, he assisted the authorities in recruiting men for various service obligations, and he seems to have been entitled to their services, at least for limited periods of time, in remuneration of his assistance. Thus, he recruited men who had to tow boats for the governor of Babylon as part of their *urāšu*-service obligation in Darius' twenty-fourth and twenty-fifth years. They belonged to the governor's pool of corvée-workers (*ša qātē*), but were at MNA's disposal for approximately two months. He may also have recruited the (*šadê*?-)workers and financed their equipment (*rikis qabli*) for an inspector (*bēl pīḫāti*) about which, unfortunately, very little is known. In addition, MNA recruited soldiers, especially charioteers, for the governor of Babylon and the commander-of-the-fortress in Babylon. He had a very close relationship over the years with one of these charioteers, Libluṭ/Itti-Nabû-balāṭu. The same holds for his relationship with Gūzānu/Ḫambaqu//Mandidi, who served with the commander-of-the-fortress.

Second, MNA hired men for state-sponsored projects in addition to the above-mentioned recruitments of men who had to perform compulsory service apparently without salary. Thus, he organized the royal *kanšu*-service in Darius' fifth year and accordingly hired a sailor to help transport goods to Babylon for the king. The same man was hired again later that year by MNA, but this time he may have served MNA rather than the king. Ten years later, MNA organized the *dullu*-service: he hired a man to help dig and maintain the king's canal to Elam. He may also have hired the men who had to perform service with Šuma-uṣur/Šamaš-ēṭir at about Darius' twenty-third year.

Finally, MNA's assistance in matters of state manpower was not limited to the above-mentioned recruitments and hire of labor. He also assisted in paying rations and salaries to subjects of the state, especially at the end of the year, i.e., when there was a shortage of barley in the storehouses and the state needed extra silver to pay for the maintenance of its subjects. Thus, he gave silver to the men of Nergal-ēṭir who were to go to Elam, either under the command of Nergal-ēṭir or, more likely, under that of his brother, Bēl-erība, who was a commander-of-fifty. MNA's silver covered the men's rations and salaries for three months. Similarly, MNA gave flour for one month to Amur-qannu, but it is not clear where and with whom this man had to serve. His payments for transportation costs to various clerks in Babylon may have had the same purpose, viz. to help them pay rations and salaries to those men under their responsibility. The clerks were in charge of the king's agricultural (gardeners, water-drawers), technical (specialized craftsmen, female flour-millers$^{?}$), and administrative (commissioners, courtiers) personnel, as well as a group of Ionians and a category of workers called ^{lú}*šá-di-e*^{meš}. Most probably, they had to take care of the rations and salaries of these state-dependent workers, and depended on MNA's silver and transport service to meet this task.

(2) CROPS FROM INSTITUTIONAL LAND

MNA was directly involved in the cultivation of crops on institutional land, their harvesting, transshipment, processing, and transport. These activities were firmly integrated into his trade in commodities, but, unfortunately, not everyone of them is equally well-documented. Moreover, it cannot always be determined whether the crops to which he had access were state-income from field rent (e.g., *šibšu, sūtu*, e.a.), or agricultural surplus; nor is it always clear whether MNA leased the land from which he collected crops or had access to it under different terms.

His involvement in the exploitation of institutional land was broadly based and well established. First, it was not limited to one kind of land or crop, but included dates, barley, wheat, onions, and cress from state-owned land (including bow-fiefs[542]), temple-owned land[543] and (royal?) land owned or at least managed by state officials such as the inspector of Šaḫrīnu and the king's treasurer.

Second, it was characterized by various transactions of a commercial as well as an agricultural nature. Indeed, MNA not only bought crops that had been grown on institutional land and were usually collected by the institutions in the form of (*šibšu*-)rent, but he also sought ways to be directly involved in their actual cultivation and harvesting. He may have leased the land for this purpose. He may also have concluded other kinds of contracts with the landowners granting him some control over the agricultural management of their land. As it was, the daily organization of these agricultural issues he left to his plowmen, his senior slaves such as MBU, Madānu(-apla)-iddin, Šēpāt-Bēl-aṣbat and Nabû-ayyālu, and local men like Rīmūt-Bēl/Šuma-ukīn, Nabû-makû-uṣur, Kīnaya/Atkal-Šamaš Bēl-aḫa-ittannu/Aḫḫē-iddin, Arad-Bāba/Mušēzib-Marduk//Ašlāku, Šellibi/Iddin-Nabû and, no doubt, many other men from Šaḫrīnu. The same men coordinated, in all likelihood, the crops' transshipment, transport, and processing. In this way MNA succeeded in building a safety net

542. Dar 307 and Dar 351.

543. More on MNA's involvement in the exploitation of temple-owned land below in chapter 3.

around his commercial dealings and in maximizing his profits. The safety net was extremely important in view of the fact that these deals concerned crops from land that MNA did not own himself.

Third, his commercial and agricultural enterprises with crops from institutional land were geographically and chronologically diverse, because they took place during the entire reign of Darius and in different parts of the countryside around Babylon.[544] At the same time, they were focussed. Indeed, one may discern an attempt to concentrate activities in the rural and riverine area south of the capital: in and around Litamu at the Uraš gate and in Šaḫrīnu and the surrounding villages (i.a., Til-Gula, Bīt-ṭabi-Bēl and Bīt-rab-kāṣir) along the Borsippa canal and the Rab-kāṣir canal. MNA also concentrated on the landed estate of one or two major temples, to wit the Esagil temple and the temple of Nergal, and on long-term relations with a few officials, like Šaddinnu and Bagasarū.

(3) WATERWAY INFRASTRUCTURE

MNA was preoccupied with easy access to the waterway infrastructure, which was heavily controlled by the state but essential to his trade. Thus he sought access to boats, quays, bridges, and harbors. The full scope of his involvement in the boat and transport business is revealed by thirty-one texts that are dated mainly between Darius' fourth and tenth years, and again from Darius' twenty-third year onward. They reveal a variety of boat-related activities in which he directly participated, ranging from paying the state its dues for his use of canals, quays, bridges, and harbors, to finding the most economical way of obtaining the boats, equipment, and manpower that were needed for the transport of the crops in which he traded, including beer and flour.

MNA's entrepreneurship in this area seems to have led to the establishment of a transport company. It specialized in transporting raw materials, such as freshly harvested crops, and processed goods, such as beer and flour. In the harvest season he transported the freshly harvested crops from fields in the countryside, probably to places where they could be stored or sold, i.a. the capital. Outside the harvest season he transported other goods, probably beer, flour, and equipment, to military strongholds in the countryside. Running the company included renting boats, paying transportation costs, acquiring men to sail, tow, and dock the boats, and paying for various other expenses such as taxes, food rations, and equipment. A rather limited group of persons assisted him in this business.

---

544. It may have gone as far as Šušan in the vicinity of Borsippa, if MNA's debts in Dar 437 and TCL 13 193 indeed resulted from a commercial transaction regarding institutional income from Šušan to be located in the vicinity of Borsippa.

Marduk-nāṣir-apli and the Temple

3.1. *MNA and the Esagil Temple*

MNA's relationship with the Esagil temple, which was the temple of the god Marduk (*alias* Bēl) in Babylon, is well documented. First, several texts refer to "the land of Bēl in Šaḫrīnu," the temple's income from the lease of this land, and MNA's access to this income.[545] Second, there are sporadic references in texts from MNA's time to land owned by the Esagil temple in the countryside south of Babylon other than its land in Šaḫrīnu.[546] Third, there is sporadic evidence on the Esagil's income from land other than its income from leases, such as income from tithes.[547] Finally, four texts from MNA's time imply connections with the Esagil temple but leave us largely in the dark as to the nature of these connections.[548]

The texts that document MNA's relations with the Esagil temple are dated between Darius' eleventh and thirty-first years and were drafted in Šaḫrīnu, Babylon, or small settlements south of Babylon. The discussion below focusses on the nature of MNA's relations with the Esagil temple, in general, and the ways in which MNA acquired rights to the temple's income from land, in particular.

3.1.1. *Onions and Dates from the Land of Bēl in Šaḫrīnu (makkūr Bēl)*

Dar 315, written in Šaḫrīnu on the twenty-first of Addar of Darius' eleventh year, grants Marduk-nāṣir/Marduk-ušallim a share in the profits of a deal that MNA and his brother closed with Šaddinnu/Madānu-aḫḫē-iddin//Šigûa. It

545. Dar 315 (which is to be discussed in the light of seven other related texts: BM 30747, BM 31018, BM 31278 [unpubl.], BM 33122, BM 33959, Dar 453^{+}, and Dar 472), Dar 342, and BM 30233.

546. Dar 390 (written in a place called "the field of Bēl" adjacent to Ālu-ša-Libbālaya); also Dar 389 = *CM* 20b 192 (written in Ālu-ša-Kīnaya) which does not explicitly refer to the Esagil temple, but except for this is very similar to Dar 390 in terms of subject matter and persons involved.

547. Dar 359. Tithes, but no temple, may also be mentioned in *CM* 20b 232: 10b–11.

548. BM 33935, Liv 25, Dar 437, and TCL 13 193.

was a deal about the right to *šibšu*-onions, i.e., the right to that part of the onion harvest that had to be paid as lease. *Šibšu*-lease usually constituted between one-third and one-fourth of the harvest.[549] This lease-related matter did not concern only the Egibi-brothers, Marduk-nāṣir, and Šaddinnu, but also the temple of Bēl, the crown's governor in the temple, and the tenant farmers who grew the onions on the temple's land on behalf of the Egibi brothers. These institutions and individuals were part of the deal in the following ways. The temple of Bēl owned the land on which the onions in question were grown, and was, accordingly, the ultimate claimant to all proceeds of the onion harvest.[550] Part of the harvest, however, had to be paid to the crown. Bēl-iddin, the "(king's) governor in the Esagil-temple," was responsible for the collection of this part of the harvest from the land of Bēl in Šaḫrīnu for the royal treasury.[551] In practice, he had delegated his powers to Šaddinnu. Indeed, the latter was his rent-farmer, or as the Akkadian expression goes "in charge of the revenues that are due to Bēl-iddin."[552] It meant that Šaddinnu had bought the right to collect those rent and rent-related revenues from the land of Bēl in Šaḫrīnu that were due to Bēl-iddin. Šaddinnu subsequently sold the right to part of this income, viz. that part that was to be derived from the collection of *šibšu*-lease in Darius' tenth and eleventh years, to MNA and NAB.[553] The latter paid forty-two and a half minas of marked silver for this right to part of the temple's onion harvest.

---

549. See more at n. 492.

550. Dar 315: 1–2, see more at commentary to Dar 315: 1.

551. Bēl-iddin (no affiliation, but see n. 552) bears the title LÚ.EN.NAM-*é-sag-gìl* = ^{lú}*bēl pīḫāt Esagil* (Dar 315: 7). We know from the Ebabbar and Murašû archives that the royal treasury collected its revenues from temple land either directly through its appointed officials, such as local governors (*pīḫātu/pāḫātu*) and canal inspectors (*mašennu*), or indirectly through contractors called *ša muḫḫi sūti* (more at Stolper, *Entrepreneurs,* 42–43). Remarkably, appointed officials and contractors were often the same person (e.g., Lâbâši/Nergal-iddin in the Sippar area, Jursa, *Landwirtschaft,* 111 n. 218; and Bēl-ittannu in the Nippur area, Stolper, *Entrepreneurs,* 39 n. 9 and *idem, MOS Studies 2,* 88).

552. Dar 315: 6–7, *ša <muḫḫi> sūti ša Bēl-iddin.* For a different opinion, see Wunsch, *MOS Studies* 2, 108 and n. 35: Šaddinnu was not a rent-farmer but an agent of Bēl-iddin who was the one farming the right to the temple's income from rent. Further note that E.36.1904 (= *Iraq* 55 No. 1; Babylon, 10/xii/10 Dar) may reflect a similar situation. It concerns 23 *kor* of barley, the rent of Darius' tenth year owed to a man called Bēl-iddin/Mušēzib-Marduk//Ēṭiru (ll. 1–2: 23 *kor uṭṭātu sūtu ša šanat* 10^{kam} *Darius šar Bābili ša Bēl-iddin*) from MNA (*ša ina pān MNA*). Was he the same as Bēl-iddin, the "(king's) governor in the Esagil-temple" responsible for the collection of rent in onions from the land of Bēl in Šaḫrīnu in Darius' tenth and eleventh years according to Dar 315? The Bēl-iddin of Dar 315 (unfortunately, without affiliation) delegated (*in casu* leased) his power to collect rent in onions from MNA to Šaddinnu/Madānu-aḫḫē-iddin//Šigûa, who, accordingly was called *ša <muḫḫi> sūti ša Bēl-iddin* (l. 7); the Bēl-iddin of E.36.1904 (/Mušēzib-Marduk//Ēṭiru) delegated his power to collect rent in barley to Mušēzib-Bēl/Apkallu//Ašlāku who, accordingly, received it *ina našparti ša Bēl-iddin* (l. 6).

553. Dar 315: 1, 3b–6, 8, *šibšu ... ša ina pān* ^{lú}*errēšē ša MNA u NAB ša ina qātē Šaddinnu ša <muḫḫi> sūti ša Bēl-iddin ... ana 42½ manê kaspa ša ginnu imḫurū.*

As a consequence of their deal with Šaddinnu, the two brothers were now empowered to all proceeds of the collection of the *šibšu*-lease, including profits (*utru*). More crops at harvest meant more income from lease and, hence, more profit for MNA and his brother. The two brothers, however, agreed to entitle one Marduk-nāṣir/Marduk-ušallim to part of the profits.[554]

Most likely, MNA and his brother agreed to grant this Marduk-nāṣir a share in the proceeds of the onion-harvest in return for his assistance in the collection of the onions from the farmers in the fields in Šaḫrīnu. It seems, therefore, that MNA and his brother had invested the capital, to wit forty-two and a half minas of silver, whereas Marduk-nāṣir was to invest in the organization of the work on the fields.[555] With this arrangement MNA and his brother did not have to travel from Babylon to Šaḫrīnu at harvest time in order to supervise their farmers. In this respect it is noteworthy that Dar 315 was written a month or so before the onion harvest. Onions were harvested in Ayyar, and Dar 315 was written at the end of Addar.

Clearly, the Egibi brothers did not content themselves with the mere purchase of part of the temple's onion harvest, but tried to control the actual cultivation and harvesting of the onions. We have seen that they hired someone to supervise the work on the fields at harvest time and granted this person a share in the proceeds from the harvest. In addition, they put their own farmers on the land on which the crops were grown. These "tenant farmers of MNA and Nabû-aḫḫē-bulliṭ held the onions"[556] from the property of Bēl in Šaḫrīnu from which MNA was to collect the *šibšu*. There is no determining whether MNA also leased part of the temple land on which the onions were grown[557] or only contracted for his farmers to work the land.[558]

---

554. Dar 315: 9–11 (*šalšu zittu ina utur*). Cf. Dar 359: 6, profits (*utru*) from a commercial deal with the tithes of Bēl.

555. Cf. Wunsch, *MOS Studies* 2, 108. It was for similar reasons that MNA's senior slave, MBU, was stationed in Šaḫrīnu. For a similar labor relation between MNA and other agricultural workers, see his relation with Rīmūt-Bēl/Šuma-ukīn and Nabû-makû-uṣur, discussed above in § 2.6.2 (esp. p. 125f.).

556. Dar 315: 3–4, *ša ina pān* ^{lú}*errēšē ša MNA u NAB*. For the expression *ina pān*, referring to land held on contract, see commentary at Dar 315: 3 (including a comparison with BM 32930: 11–13 and E.36.1904), and cf. the similar expression *īpuš* in BM 33972: 20 (*īpuš*, n. 489). On the expression *ina pān* in texts from MNA's archive, more at BM 30270: 1 and n. 144.

557. MNA may, indeed, have leased temple land (as farmer-general?) and subsequently subleased parts of it to small peasants, who thus became "tenant farmers of MNA and NAB." So, apparently, Van Driel, *JESHO* 32, 215. (Further note *idem*, *MOS Studies* 1, 37ff.: Mesopotamian temples frequently tried to attract tenants, *errēšu*, from outside the institution to bring fallow land under cultivation, by i.a. leasing out their land). According to Wunsch, *Felder* 1, 52 n. 205, however, the farmers in Dar 315 were not private peasants, but temple farmers whom MNA obtained together with the land that he (we assume) leased from the temple.

558. Cf. BM 33972: 20 (above at n. 489).

MNA had to find an economical way to transport the onions to the markets, probably in the capital, where he expected to make additional profits from their sale. This transport is dealt with in BM 30747. In this undated text MNA paid a toll (*miksu*) for a boat that was loaded with "onions of Darius' tenth year." This refers, no doubt, to the onions from the land of Bēl in Šaḫrīnu, part of which MNA and his brother had purchased from Šaddinnu according to Dar 315. It is, therefore, not surprising to find Marduk-nāṣir/Marduk-ušallim among the witnesses in BM 30747. He was the person with whom MNA had contracted to supervise the harvesting of the onions in return for a share in the profits. He must have supervised their transport as well, otherwise he would have had no special reason to attend MNA's toll payment as recorded in BM 30747. It should further be pointed out that this payment was made to Nergal-ušallim/Arrabbi and not to the overseer of the quay. This is remarkable, indeed, because MNA always paid tolls to overseers.[559] Moreover, BM 30747 lacks details on when, where, and by whom it was written. These outstanding features strongly suggest that it was an internal arrangement between MNA and one of his employees, *in casu* Nergal-ušallim/Arrabbi, regarding the payment of tolls rather than an official payment of tolls.[560] Nergal-ušallim must have been one of those men who were employed by MNA in Šaḫrīnu to organize the transshipment and transport of crops from the fields to the markets. Most likely, he received silver from MNA so that he could pay the toll to the overseer of the quay whenever the need arose in the course of the crops' transport. BM 30747, being a private agreement between MNA and one of his employees in Šaḫrīnu, was obviously written by MNA himself on the spot and did not need to be dated.[561]

Unfortunately, things did not go as smoothly as MNA and his brother initially may have expected when they concluded their deal with Šaddinnu. A group of texts from the archive in which MNA and Šaddinnu figure enables us to follow events after Addar of Darius' eleventh year. All through the next seven years, till Ṭebēt of Darius' eighteenth year, MNA remained indebted to Šaddinnu because of his deal regarding the *šibšu*-onions of Darius' tenth and eleventh year. The following six texts offer the details.

On the twenty-fourth of Ṭebēt of Darius' seventeenth year, MNA was able to pay off part of the debt in Babylon, and Šaddinnu was to give back the document regarding this debt to MNA (BM 33959). The exact amount of silver paid is, unfortunately, broken off, but the cause of the debt is described in the first two lines of the text: "The d[ebt(s) of x minas of silver, the price of]? the

559. Dar 268 and BM 31347.

560. Unless BM 30747 was an incomplete copy of an original that contained the details on when, where and by whom it was written.

561. The familiarity between the parties in an agreement occasionally led to laconic formulations of the document recording the agreement, e.g., Kessler, *AUWE* 8/1, 104 (No. 6 and No. 67).

onions from Šaḫrīnu, the property of Bē[l, which are in the hands of ᵐ…], [so]n of Bēl-uṣuršu."[562]According to this reconstruction, the indebted silver was the purchase price that MNA had to pay for the right to collect the *šibšu*-onions in Darius' eleventh year. These onions were grown in Šaḫrīnu (*ša Šaḫrīnu*) on fields owned by the Esagil temple (*makkūr Bēl*). They were grown, as we know from Dar 315, by farmers of MNA and his brother, and were probably to be collected from these farmers by men working for the Egibis, such as Marduk-nāṣir/Marduk-ušallim. Accordingly, the son of Bēl-uṣuršu mentioned in the text under consideration at the end of line 2 may have been either one of the farmers or another agent of the Egibi brothers responsible for the collection of the onions from the farmers. On the same day, the parties agreed on the terms for the repayment of the remainder of the debt (Dar 453⁺).[563] The remaining debt of fourteen minas and twenty shekels of silver was divided into two parts: (1) ten and a half minas and five shekels were to bear interest and their repayment was secured by the pledge of a field in Bīt-Ḫaḫḫuru; (2) three minas and forty-five shekels were to be repaid, apparently, as soon as possible and without interest. Eleven months later MNA managed to pay off that part of the remaining debt that did not bear interest (Dar 472). Indeed, on the third of Ṭebēt of Darius' eighteenth year Šaddinnu acknowledged the receipt of three minas and forty-five shekels from the hands of Nidintu/Kabtiya//Ir'anni on behalf of MNA. Nidintu must have been sent by MNA to personally hand over the indebted sum of silver to Šaddinnu in Babylon. Perhaps Nidintu was another of MNA's agricultural employees in Šaḫrīnu and its surroundings, in addition to Marduk-nāṣir (Dar 315), Nergal-ušallim (BM 30747), the son of Bēl-uṣuršu (BM 33959), and the men occurring in the texts discussed in § 2.6.2 and § 2.6.3 above.

The field in Bīt-Ḫaḫḫuru that MNA pledged to Šaddinnu in Ṭebēt of Darius' seventeenth year (Dar 453⁺) was pledged that same year by MNA and his brother to Anu-mukīn-apli, another of MNA's creditors (BM 33122, 9/[-]/17 Dar). Unfortunately, the month in which the latter text was written is broken off. Consequently, we cannot know whether the field was pledged first to Šaddinnu and later that year to Anu-mukīn-apli, or the other way around or perhaps it was pledged to both simultaneously.[564] The pledge of the field to Anu-mukīn-apli was not possible without Šaddinnu's consent. This is clear from his presence among the witnesses in BM 33122. If his presence as a witness meant that he relinquished his rights to the field that had previously been pledged to him so that it could be safely pledged to Anu-mukīn-apli, BM 33122

---

562. For the reconstruction of these lines, which is essentially based on a comparison with Dar 315, see more at the commentary to BM 33959: 1–2.

563. BM 33959 and Dar 453⁺ were written in Babylon on the same day by the same scribe; the texts also share some of the witnesses.

564. For MNA's attempts to simultaneously pledge the same property to different creditors, more at p. 154.

must be dated after Dar 453⁺, i.e., after Ṭebēt, in the months Šabāṭ to Addar. The close connection between both texts is further stressed by the fact that they share several witnesses.

A Šaddinnu without affiliation occurs in two more texts from MNA's archive. In my opinion this Šaddinnu is the same person as Šaddinnu/Madānu-aḫḫē-iddin//Šigûa who, as we have seen, was responsible for the collection of revenues from the fields of the Esagil temple on behalf of the crown, and sold the right to collect part of these revenues to MNA and his brother. The first text is BM 31018. It records the receipt of silver by a messenger of Šaddinnu from MNA in Babylon in Ab of Darius' eleventh year. The messenger Nabû-nādin-aḫi/Nabû-bēl-šumāti//Dēkû had been sent by Šaddinnu to press MNA to pay his debt of ten minas of marked silver. He had been given a written note (*šipirtu*) that officially authorized him to collect the silver from MNA.[565] Probably Šaddinnu's note to MNA dealt with the same kind of commercial deal as Dar 315, viz. the sale of the right to collect the *šibšu*-onions for two years. Apparently, MNA and Šaddinnu were not always living at the same place and used agents to travel between Babylon and Šaḫrīnu. Thus, MNA sent his agent to Šaddinnu in Babylon to pay off part of the debt (Dar 472) and Šaddinnu sent his agent to collect payment from MNA in Babylon (BM 31018). Moreover, if Šaddinnu in BM 31018 is indeed Šaddinnu/Madānu-aḫḫē-iddin//Šigûa, as we claim, the business relations between him and MNA existed already half a year before Dar 315 was written. The second text that mentions a Šaddinnu without affiliation is the undated and fragmentary letter BM 31278, sent by Šaddinnu to Širku. According to line 7 something was given, and the next line refers to rent and rent-related revenues (*sūtu*).[566] Consequently, the Šaddinnu in this letter is most likely the Šaddinnu we met as rent-farmer of Bēl-iddin in Dar 315 and who was in charge of collecting revenues from temple land in the same text and several related ones.

MNA seems to have concluded commercial deals regarding income from the land of Bēl in Šaḫrīnu with other rent-farmers in the area. The evidence derives from a fragmentary text from Darius' twelfth year (Dar 342). It was written in Šaḫrīnu and mentions the "property of Bēl," "seven gardeners," "[a perso]n in charge of the revenues that are due to Iddinaya," and one "Marduk-nā[ṣir-apli]"; it is broken off after this name. Each of these elements has its parallel in Dar 315, but they cannot be woven into a coherent story like that of Dar 315 because the text has too much missing data. Iddinaya, for instance, has no title, unlike Bēl-iddin, who was the "(king's) governor in the Esagil temple" and the gardeners are not called "of MNA and NAB," unlike the tenant farmers in Dar 315.[567] However, we know from Dar 229, for instance, that MNA had gardeners at his disposal, since one of them, Iqūpu, promised under oath to

565. Cf. Dar 552, Dar 572 and Dar 573.

566. BM 31278: 7: *id-din*(?), and line 8: *a-na su-tu*. The text remains unpublished.

567. See more at the commentary to Dar 342 Obv.: 3.

come to MNA in Ṭebēt of Darius' seventh year. The major impediment to our understanding of Dar 342, however, is the lack of a verb that might have clarified the legal nature of the connection among the "property of Bēl," the "gardeners," Iddinaya's rent-farmer, and MNA.

MNA's involvement in the cultivation of crops on the land of Bēl in Šaḫrīnu continued at least till Darius' thirty-first year. At the end of that year he sent two men to deliver fifty *kor* of dates to Nabû-bullissu/Mūrānu//Paḫāru in Babylon. The latter had to clear his receipt in the accounts of the temple of Bēl, and show the proof of clearance to him (BM 30233).[568] The dates are described in the following terms: "dates, a partial payment, property of Bēl in Šaḫrīnu." This probably meant that the dates that MNA delivered had been grown on the land of Bēl in Šaḫrīnu[569] and were delivered by him in partial fulfilment of the obligations that befell someone who farmed temple land. The conditions under which MNA presumably farmed the land of Bēl, however, are not known. Was he a tenant farmer, a farmer-general, the (temporary) holder of prebendary land or the sub-leaseholder of any of these? Consequently, we do not know why he had to deliver these dates to the temple. Were they in payment of lease, lease-related expenses, tithes, or prebendary duties? Moreover, none of the persons mentioned in BM 30233 can be traced in other texts from MNA's archive, further hampering our understanding of the text in question.[570] In any case, MNA's delivery had to be registered in the "register of Bēl" and the proof of registration had to be handed over to MNA.

3.1.2. *The Field of Bēl (eqli ša Bēl)*

On the fifteenth of Šabāṭ of Darius' fourteenth year Šulum-Bābili/Nidintu promised to deliver three *kor* of first-rate barley to MNA in a place called the "Settlement of Marduk-nāṣir-apli" along the Piqūdu canal (Dar 390). The barley had to be paid according to the measure of MNA in Ayyar. The same day Aplaya/[Baniya] promised to deliver six *kor* of the same kind of barley at an unspecified settlement along the Piqūdu canal (Dar 389).[571] The same people

568. According to BM 30233, Nabû-bullissu undertook to clear his receipt of fifty *kor* of dates in the temple accounts "on behalf of Daḫḫūa and Bēl-apla-iddin," who are cited without affiliation and are otherwise unknown. The proof of clearance, however, was to be given to MNA and not to these two persons. In my opinion, it shows that MNA was the one who had to deliver the dates, and the said Daḫḫūa and Bēl-apla-iddin were merely his agents.

569. I.e., "property of Bēl" (*makkūr Bēl*) in the sense of the "landed estate of Bēl." Unless the expression "property of Bēl" is to be understood as "prerogative of Bēl"; in that case the provenance of the dates is not specified, cf. BM 33930.

570. Except for one of the witnesses, Arad-Bāba/Ḫabaṣīru//Ir'anni, who is also found among the witnesses in BM 30784 (unpublished, 19/vi/26 Dar): a credit of one mina of silver held by Bēl-ittannu/Iqīša-Marduk//Bēl-eṭēru against MNA, payable in the next month and with default interest. Unfortunately, this text does not add anything to our understanding of BM 30233.

571. Dar 389 = *CM* 20b 192, and *Felder* 1, 166. For the reconstruction of the name of Aplaya's father, see next footnote.

were present on both occasions that same day.[572] The agreement with Šulum-Bābili was reached in Ālu-ša-Libbālaya ("Village of the Libbālaya"); the one with Aplaya in Ālu-ša-Kīnaya ("Village of Kīnaya").[573] The former locality is further described as "field of Bēl" that, no doubt, meant that it was located in the vicinity of the landed estate of the temple of Bēl. Consequently, this so-called "field of Bēl" must be located in the rural area along the Piqūdu canal; it was surrounded by small settlements such as the "Settlement of Marduk-nāṣir-apli," the "Village of the Libbālaya," and the "Village of Kīnaya."

The texts do not reveal the reason that Šulum-Bābili and Aplaya had to deliver this first-rate barley to MNA. Had they leased some of MNA's private land in the area along the Piqūdu canal and were their deliveries of barley actually payments of lease?[574] It is remarkable though that the barley is not labelled "lease" (e.g., *šibšu, sūtu*), nor is any privately owned land mentioned in the texts. In fact, the only reference to agricultural land in the texts is the reference to the "field of Bēl" in Dar 390. Had MNA taken up a commercial venture with crops from this field of Bēl or other institutional land along the Piqūdu canal that was located in the immediate proximity of the said field, similar to his commercial ventures with onions, barley and dates from the land of Bēl in Šaḫrīnu?[575]

3.1.3. *The Tithes of Bēl (ešrû ša Bēl)*[576]

The venture of leasing the right to part of the Esagil's income from land did not necessarily result in a failure. At least on one occasion MNA succeeded in

---

572. Thus, the first witness in Dar 389 (= *CM* 20b 192) is the scribe of Dar 390; the second witness in Dar 389 is the person who promised to deliver barley in Dar 390; the third and fourth witnesses in Dar 389 were also present as witnesses in Dar 390; and the scribe of Dar 389 witnessed Dar 390. Consequently, it cannot be doubted that Aplaya/[...], who promised to deliver barley in Dar 389, is to be identified with Aplaya/Baniya, first witness in Dar 390.

573. Dar 389 (= *CM* 20b 192) was written in Ālu-ša-Kīnaya, which Wunsch (*Felder* 1, 158 n. 327) suggests locating in or around Litāmu near the Uraš gate. Dar 390 was written in Ālu-ša-Libbālaya, which Wunsch suggests locating in the same area near the Uraš gate (Wunsch, *Felder* 1, 166f.). On MNA's trade in this area, also see at p. 22ff.

574. We know that MNA and his brothers owned several plots of land along the Piqūdu canal, see Wunsch, *Felder*.

575. MNA's commercial ventures with crops from the land of Bēl in Šaḫrīnu: Dar 315 e.a. (onions); Dar 342 and BM 30233 (dates); his commercial ventures with crops from other institutional land in Šaḫrīnu: Rīmūt-Bēl texts (onions, barley, and dates); Bagasarū texts (onions, barley, wheat, and cress); and Dar 338 (dates). For the Rīmūt-Bēl texts, the Bagasarū texts and Dar 338, see § 2.6.

576. Tithes may also be mentioned in *CM* 20b 232: 10b–11. It is a promissory note to deliver dates (*imittu*-lease) and their by-products to MNA, and refers, i.a., to an outstanding debt of tithes; "the ti[thes?] have not been paid." Other leaseholders had to deliver a lamb to MNA in addition to the usual lease payments (Dar 124 = *CM* 20b 25, Dar 126 = *CM* 20b 137 and Dar 267 = *CM* 20b 43: see p. 159 and esp. n. 626).

turning a profit (*utru*) on his deal. Dar 359 implies that he had successfully leased the right to income from the date tithes that were due to the Esagil temple.[577] The proceeds of this deal were invested by MNA in one of his businesses aimed, most likely, at processing the dates into, perhaps, beer. The text was drafted in Ālu-ša-kī-Bēl in Ṭebēt of Darius' thirteenth year.

3.1.4. *Connections of Uncertain Origin with the Esagil Temple*

MNA's debts to the rent-farmer Šaddinnu, described in Dar 315 and related texts, and his debt recorded in BM 30233, were not the only ones that MNA owed to the Esagil temple. As a matter of fact, MNA was indirectly indebted to the Esagil temple on at least four other occasions. The first three date from the end of Darius' sixteenth year, five years after Dar 315. At that time MNA remained in Šušan together with several officials of the Esagil temple, a priest from Bāṣ, and prominent judges; they appear among the witnesses of the promissory notes that he concluded at that place.[578] Thus, three men, each with the title of "secretary (*šāpiru*) of the Esagil," were among the eleven men who witnessed MNA's silver debt of two and two-third minas to a private person named Bēl-iddin/Mušēzib-Marduk//Sîn-nādin-šumi (Dar 437).[579] Similarly, "a courtier, (the king's) supervisor (*bēl piqitti*) in the Esagil" witnessed, together with six judges and a priest from Bāṣ, MNA's silver debt of forty-five minas to a courtier named Šarru-dūrī/Edra' (TCL 13 193).[580] Finally, "the king's resident (*qīpu*) in the Esagil temple" witnessed, together with nine judges, MNA's silver debt of twenty-three minas to the governor of Kiš (Liv 25).[581]

The origin of the debts in Dar 437, TCL 13 193 and Liv 25 is unknown, but the presence of the Esagil officials proves that they did not just concern MNA and some private person or state official, but concerned the temple as well. It was argued above that MNA's debt to the governor of Kiš resulted from his purchase of state income, or rights to state income, from the said governor.[582] This observation should now be further developed in view of the fact that MNA's debt to the governor of Kiš was witnessed by the king's resident in the Esagil temple. I suggest the possibility that MNA's debt to the governor of Kiš resulted from his purchase of the governor's share in the temple's income. In other words, MNA had bought rights in that part of the Esagil's income that was

---

577. Cf. Jursa, *Tempelzehnt*, 81.

578. Abraham, *OLP* 28 and *NABU* 1997/53.

579. Further note that Bēl-iddin/Mušēzib-Marduk//Sîn-nādin-šumi to whom MNA owed the silver in Dar 437 is the first witness in a text about the theft of temple property (BM 41449).

580. Šarru-dūrī is attested on the same day and at the same place among the witnesses in Dar 435 (see n. 590). On TCL 13 193, see already at § 2.7.1.

581. On this text, see already at § 2.7.1.

582. Possibly, to help him out financing the works at the king's canal to Elam. More at § 2.2.1 and § 2.7.1.

due to the king and was to be collected by the governor of Kiš. We know that MNA had bought rights to the Esagil's income from land in a very similar way a few years earlier and that he remained in debt for several years because of this commercial venture.[583] When it became clear that MNA was having problems paying, the king sent his representative in the temple to follow the deal between MNA and the governor of Kiš. MNA's debt to the governor of Kiš must have endangered royal interests in the temple. Hence, the king's supervisor is among the witnesses in TCL 13 193.[584] Other possibilities, however, are to be considered. Thus, MNA's debts to the governor of Kiš, on the one hand, and Bēl-iddin/Mušēzib-Marduk//Sîn-nādin-šumi, on the other hand, may have resulted from his involvement in the cultivation of crops on temple land as a tenant or rent-farmer, as was perhaps the case in BM 30233 or it may have resulted from MNA's involvement in the collection of crops from prebendaries who grew crops on state land, as was probably the case in BM 33930.[585] In the case of Dar 437, in fact, the debt may have resulted from such a prebend-related deal rather than from a lease-related one. Indeed, the three clerks who witnessed the document are known to have played a role in the administration of prebendary income.[586] The same type of clerks received MNA's dates for the offerings of Nergal, according to BM 33930.

We hear again about MNA's debts to the Esagil temple in Darius' seventeenth year when the temple was remunerated with a house in Šu'anna that belonged to MNA (BM 33935).[587] This incident with the temple is mentioned in connection with a large debt of more than one talent of silver that MNA owed to Anu-mukīn-apli. He had tried to settle his large debt in the past, by selling his house in the neighborhood of Šu'anna to Anu-mukīn-apli.[588] The sale,

---

583. Dar 315 and related texts: MNA bought rights in that part of the Esagil's onion harvest that was due to the king's governor in the temple (*bēl pīḫāt Esagil*). In Dar 315 it concerned income from the Esagil's landed estate in Šaḫrīnu. In TCL 13 193 it may have concerned the temple's income from fields in Šušan, if we assume that Šušan, where TCL 13 193 had been drafted, was somewhere in northern Babylon rather than in Elam. Cf. Šušan in the Borsippa texts, Abraham, *OLP* 28, 72.

584. The *bēl piqitti* (TCL 13 193) like the *qīpu* (Liv 25) was a kind of supervisor appointed by the king to safeguard royal interest in the temples. They seem to have belonged to the high administration of the temple and supervised transactions in various areas of the temple's economy, such as transactions concerning the temple's herds and personnel, or the temple's income from land lease, tithes, and prebends (details in Bongenaar, *Ebabbar*, 105 + bibliography; and MacGinnis, *ZA* 84, 205, 207–11).

585. For BM 30233 see above at § 3.1.1. p. 149. For BM 33930, see below at § 3.2.2.

586. On the relation between *šāpiru* and prebendary income, see Bongenaar, *Ebabbar*, Chapter III.1; and on the *šāpiru* in general, see Di Gennaro, *AION* 55, 380–405, esp. 386–88.

587. The year in which BM 33935 was written is broken off, but Darius' seventeenth year is most likely.

588. The practice is well attested whereby insolvent debtors sell property from their belongings, usually to their creditor, as a means to pay for their debt. E.g., the case from the beginning of Neriglissar's reign: a large track of land on the New canal was sold by the *šākin ṭēmi*

however, had become void after the house had been commandeered by the Esagil temple.[589] Consequently, MNA had to find another way to satisfy Anu-mukīn-apli. He sold two fields and ten slaves, and thereby he was able to settle his debt with Anu-mukīn-apli and leave his house in Šu'anna with the temple. It is remarkable that he did not appeal the temple's seizure of his house—it proves that the temple was acting on a sound legal basis. We do not know how it had become entitled to the house, but we may safely assume that the house had been pledged to the temple by MNA for one of his debts. When MNA decided to sell the house to pay off debts to Anu-mukīn-apli, the temple interfered by claiming priority as creditor. It then appropriated the house, thereby, no doubt, covering MNA's debts to the temple.[590]

By the end of Darius' seventeenth year MNA seems to have had economically strained relations with the Esagil temple, which continued into the next year due to his many debts that remained unsettled.[591] In Ṭebēt of that year, Šaddinnu/Madānu-aḫḫē-iddin//Šigûa pressured MNA to pay off his debt by demanding interest and a security pledge.[592] Almost a month later, in Šabāṭ Bēl-iddin/Mušēzib-Marduk//Sîn-nādin-šumi pressured MNA to pay the remainder of his debt by threatening to exact interest; MNA was granted another month and a half before the debt would bear an annual interest of twenty

---

to the Egibis. The former needed the cash in order to pay off his debts to the Esagil temple (details at Wunsch, *Felder* 1, 65ff.).

589. The Esagil's seizure of the house is formulated as follows (l. 8): *a-na* NÍG.GA *é-sag-íl in-nap-lu* "which has (subsequently) been given to the Esagil temple as compensation (for an unsettled debt)."

590. These may have been the debts that MNA owed to Šarru-dūrī according to TCL 13 193. As we have seen, the latter was a courtier but he may have worked with the Esagil temple on behalf of the king. The assumed link between Šarru-dūrī and the Esagil is based on the fact that one of his credit claims, to wit the one held against MNA, was witnessed by a representative of the Esagil, viz. the *ša-rēš šarri bēl piqitti ša Esagil* (TCL 13 193). It shows that MNA's debts to him also concerned the Esagil. When the Esagil temple seized one of MNA's houses in Šu'anna to cover his debts (BM 33935), Šarru-dūrī was not present, but a year earlier Šarru-dūrī had witnessed the sale of a house that was located next to MNA's house in Šu'anna (Dar 435). It was, moreover, on that same day that he pressed MNA to settle his debt with him (TCL 13 193). Clearly, Šarru-dūrī was keeping a close eye on MNA's house in Šu'anna and therefore attended transactions concerning real estate in the vicinity of that house (hence, his presence in Dar 435). Had this house been pledged to him for the debt about which we are informed in TCL 13 193? Possibly, he may have been the one who eventually informed the temple that MNA was trying to sell his house in Šu'anna to one of his creditors. Such a sale would have hurt his rights in the house as well as the rights of the *bēl piqitti* of the Esagil temple in the same house. When the temple heard of MNA's plans, it took the house and turned it into its property. MNA's other creditor, Anu-mukīn-apli, had to be compensated in another way and this matter is taken care of in BM 33935.

591. On MNA's difficulties in that period, which were probably due to the temporary lack of cash after the inheritance division with his brothers in Darius' fourteenth year, more at Wunsch, *Felder* 1, 161 and 166.

592. Dar 453⁺ (24/x/17 Dar).

percent.[593] Ten days later, one of MNA's houses became "the property of the Esagil," no doubt to cover his debts.[594] As said, it is not absolutely clear from the text that debts are being covered, but the temple was clearly losing patience with MNA. By the end of the next year he managed to pay off a(n additional) small part of his debt to Šaddinnu, and it seems that the matter was close to being finally settled.[595] After this date, indeed, we do not hear any more about MNA's debts to the Esagil temple. However, relations with the temple continued till at least Darius' thirty-first year.[596]

It is possible that MNA tried to cheat the Esagil temple on two occasions in the course of Darius' seventeenth year by using property pledged to the temple for purposes that curtailed the temple's rights to the pledged property. In one instance, he tried to pledge a field to his creditor Anu-mukīn-apli that he had also pledged to Šaddinnu.[597] The latter, however, interfered in time. The pledge to Anu-mukīn-apli took place, but the presence of Šaddinnu among the witnesses shows that MNA and Šaddinnu had come to an alternative arrangement. At about the same time we hear that MNA tried to dupe the same two creditors, viz. Anu-mukīn-apli and the Esagil temple, a second time and in much the same way, i.e., by using the same property to satisfy both creditors.[598] In this second instance, he sold a house in which the temple had vested rights to pay off his debts to Anu-mukīn-apli. When the temple learned about it, it seized the house and made it its property. Anu-mukīn-apli was compensated by the sale of other property from MNA's belongings.

3.2. *MNA and the Temple of Nergal*

Whereas MNA's business relations with the Esagil temple are well attested, his relations with the temple of Nergal are far less well documented, but they are apparently of a similar nature. As a matter of fact, there are only two explicit references to this temple in texts from MNA's time. BM 31976 suggests his involvement in the agricultural exploitation of the land of Nergal and BM 33930, suggests his involvement in the temple's income from its prebendaries. The texts are dated between Darius' twenty-seventh and twenty-ninth years.[599]

---

593. Dar 455 (15/xi/17 Dar), regarding the debt mentioned in Dar 437.

594. BM 33935 (25/xi/[17] Dar).

595. Dar 472 (3/x/18 Dar).

596. BM 30233 (7/xii/31 Dar).

597. BM 33122 (9/[xi–xii]$^{?}$/17 Dar, Anu-mukīn-apli) and Dar 453^{+} (24/x/17 Dar, Šaddinnu). I assume that BM 33122 is dated after Dar 453^{+}. Further see at p. 147f.

598. BM 33935 (15/xi/[17]$^{?}$ Dar).

599. For Dar 533, which is not included in the discussion below because it does not mention MNA but which, nevertheless, contains references to several places known from texts from MNA's time, see more at Wunsch, *MOS Studies 2*, 110.

3.2.1. *The Farmer of Nergal (ikkaru ša Nergal)*

A farmer of Nergal occurs in Darius' twenty-seventh year in a text regarding two heifers that was issued in Šaḫrīnu (BM 31976). The two sides to the transaction regarding these calves were Madānu(-apla)-iddin, slave of MNA, on the one hand, and the messenger of an official with the strange title ^{lú}*mār* (DUMU) *a-ba-rak-ku*, together with the said farmer, on the other. The text also refers to a letter sent by Nabû-bullissu/[...], after which it is broken off. The details of the agreement regarding the calves, therefore, are unknown, especially in view of the fact that there is no verb that might have revealed the legal character of the agreement. Was the *mār abarakku* official, like the canal inspector (*mašennu*) and the district governor (*pīḫātu/pāḫātu*),[600] appointed by the king to draw payments from temple land for the royal treasury? Had MNA leased land from this official and were the calves, the slave and the farmer of Nergal part of the resources at his disposal to exploit the land?[601] In that case, the text under consideration, as well as the next one (Dar 541), may be compared to Dar 315 and related texts.[602] Perhaps MNA had purchased the portion of the harvest that was due to this official and his slave was needed to keep an eye on the means and process of production on the spot. In that case, the texts may be compared to the ones discussed above in § 2.6.[603]

Ibnaya/Nergal-zēra-ibni, the farmer of Nergal, is known from one other text of MNA's archive (Dar 541). This text was written in Bīt-ṭāb-Bēl in Simān of Darius' twenty-second year and concerns Ibnaya's debts to Madānu-apla-iddin, slave of MNA. The debts consisted of ten *kor* of barley, ten shekels of silver, and a bowl of roasted butter. The barley was to be delivered "in the house of MNA at Šaḫrīnu according to MNA's measure." Ibnaya is not identified as a farmer of Nergal in this text, but his debt may have had some remote link with the temple of Nergal. Indeed, when he promised to pay his debt, Nabû-uballiṭ/Lūṣi-ana-nūri//Andaḫar showed up.[604] This means that there was some connection with the temple of Nergal, because this Nabû-uballiṭ was a man with clear interests in matters concerning the property of Nergal; he attended MNA's delivery of *makkasu*-dates for the offerings of Nergal seven years later.[605]

600. More at n. 551.

601. The heifers and the farmer of Nergal may have been provided by the *mār abarakku* official together with the land, or MNA may have had to invest in them as well as in other manpower (*in casu* that of his slave).

602. No doubt, a thorough investigation of all texts from MNA's archive on draught animals could bring to light the true nature of these transactions. See the text-material assembled by Wunsch, *MOS Studies 2*, 110–11.

603. For prosopographic links between Dar 541 (the text about Ibnaya/Nergal-zēra-ibni, farmer of Nergal) and some of the texts discussed in § 2.6 (Dar 164 and Dar 167 from the Rīmūt-Bēl dossier, and Dar 296, a Bagasarū text), see below.

604. More on the list of witnesses of Dar 541 below at p. 157f.

605. BM 33930: Nabû-uballiṭ/Lūṣi-ana-nūri//Andaḫar is first witness. For this man, also

The two texts concerning Ibnaya/Nergal-zēra-ibni, viz. BM 31976 and Dar 541, show that this farmer of Nergal worked for MNA together with Madānu(-apla)-iddin, MNA's slave, in and around Šaḫrīnu between Darius' twenty-second and twenty-seventh years. The farmer and the slave seem to have farmed institutional land in that area, probably the land of Nergal,[606] for which heifers were needed, according to BM 31976. They were involved in agricultural works of another kind, viz. the production of butter, according to Dar 541. The conditions under which Ibnaya worked for MNA are unknown, but there are several points of similarity with the working conditions of Rīmūt-Bēl and Nabû-makû-uṣur. First, Rīmūt-Bēl and Nabû-makû-uṣur worked in MNA's commodity trade in Šaḫrīnu together with one of his slaves, *in casu* Madānu-bēla-uṣur. Similarly, Ibnaya, farmer of Nergal, worked in some agriculture-related matters in Šaḫrīnu, and Bīt-ṭāb-Bēl in the vicinity of Šaḫrīnu, together with another of MNA's slaves, Madānu(-apla)-iddin. Second, Rīmūt-Bēl and Nabû-makû-uṣur had to deliver large amounts of onions, barley, and dates "in the house of MNA in Šaḫrīnu." Similarly, Ibnaya had to deliver barley in the same house of MNA in which Rīmūt-Bēl and Nabû-makû-uṣur had delivered their crops eighteen years earlier. Actually, it is possible that Rīmūt-Bēl, Nabû-makû-uṣur, and Ibnaya/Nergal-zēra-ibni met in Šaḫrīnu while working there for MNA. After all, they had to deliver their crops in the same house of MNA and worked with slaves of MNA that belonged to the same family.[607]

---

see BM 32865 (= b 2641, unpublished, Šaḫrīnu, 6/xiib/27 Dar: a settlement between MNA's son and Nabû-zēra-ibni/Itti-Nabû-balāṭu//Egibi concerning cattle belonging to MNA). He is further known from *CM* 20b 206 and Dar 571 (= *CM* 20b 207), according to which he sold a plot of land to MNA in Addar of Darius' twenty-second year. MNA paid the price only ten months later, in Kislīm of Darius' twenty-third year. The land was located in Šaḫrīnu. The low price of the land indicates that it was either a small plot of land or land of minor value in agricultural terms. Consequently, MNA may well have bought the land for reasons other than agricultural ones. He may, for instance, have needed this plot of land in Šaḫrīnu for transshipment of crops (so Wunsch, *Felder* 1, 173–74), storage of agricultural implements, housing of agricultural workers, and/or stalling of draught animals (all within the context of his exploitation of institutional land in Šaḫrīnu). It is further remarkable that this purchase was witnessed by men who recur as witnesses in MNA's dealings with *ilku*, other tax income, military personnel and equipment (cf. the evidence gathered at n. 52). The first witness in Dar 571, for instance, also attended MNA's purchase of dates from the district governor of Šaḫrīnu (Dar 338) and his receipt of *ilku* for "the fittings for an archer" (BM 30772). The third witness attended one of MNA's *ilku* receipts (BM 30243) and one of his *gimru*-payments (BM 33112). He also wrote the document according to which MNA acquired rights to prebendary income (BM 31793). Remarkable is finally the presence of Šūzubu/Uballissu-Marduk//Ṭābiḫu among the witnesses in Dar 571. He was one of the men who had to serve with the commander-of-the-fortress in Babylon and whose service was taken care of by MNA (BM 31226). Why was he interested in MNA's purchase of this land in Šaḫrīnu?

606. On the interests of the temple of Nergal in income from land in or around Šaḫrīnu, see above at n. 496.

607. Rīmūt-Bēl and Nabû-makû-uṣur worked with Madānu-bēla-uṣur. He was the father of Madānu(-apla)-iddin, with whom Ibnaya/Nergal-zēra-ibni worked.

An additional argument to link the above-mentioned texts to the Rīmūt-Bēl texts or similar texts concerning MNA's ventures with crops from Šaḫrīnu comes from the list of witnesses of Dar 541. Its sixth witness, Šuma-iddin/Šāpik-zēri//Nabaya recurs one year later in Šaḫrīnu in a matter concerning the debt of Iddin-Nabû/Marduk-(i)qīšanni//Bēl-eṭēru to Nabû-ayyālu, one of MNA's slaves (Dar 561). Iddin-Nabû witnessed Dar 527, a Bagasarū-text. Iddin-Nabû's father, Marduk-iqīšanni/Bēl-aḫa-ušabši//Bēl-eṭēru, knew Rīmūt-Bēl and his brother; indeed, he is found among the witnesses in two of their documents, Dar 164 and Dar 167.[608] This prosopographic evidence confirms the above suggestion that the Ibnaya, Rīmūt-Bēl, and Bagasarū texts deal with similar issues. They belong to MNA's commodity trade in and around Šaḫrīnu, which he conducted with the help of his senior slaves, such as MBU, Madānu(-apla)-iddin, Šēpāt-Bēl-aṣbat and Nabû-ayyālu, on the one hand, and local men, such as Ibnaya/Nabû-zēra-ibni (farmer of Nergal), Rīmūt-Bēl, Nabû-makû-uṣur, Iddin-Nabû and many others, on the other.[609]

3.2.2. *Dates for the Offerings of Nergal* (*ginê ša Nergal*)

In Simān of Darius' twenty-ninth year MNA delivered twenty-four *kor* of dates "for the offerings of Nergal to Bēl-ruṣūa, the courtier (*ša-rēš šarri*)" (BM 33930). The dates are qualified as *makkasu*-dates, i.e., dates of excellent quality, which were the kind of dates often used in the preparation of offerings in the temple.[610] Bēl-ruṣūa, the royal official who received the dates from MNA, had to clear his receipt in the accounts of "Bēl-bullissu <and>$^{?}$ his colleagues." These men bore the title of LÚ *š*[*á*$^{?}$-*pi*]*r*$^{?}$-*ri*.MEŠ and may thus have been secretaries in the office that took care of the temple's prebendary income. If so, BM 33930 has a clear prebendal background. This impression is further strengthened by the fact that, ultimately, the dates "were given to the foreman of the ^{lú}*mubannê*."[611] These so-called "cooks" had the prebendal duty to arrange the sacrificial table in the temple.[612] Ingredients for the regular offerings, in general, and *makkasu*-dates, in particular, were typically received by the persons responsible for the preparation of food in the temple. In Sippar bakers, brewers, and oil pressers regularly received barley, emmer, sesame, and dates from the temple, from which they had to prepare the offerings.[613]

---

608. See above, p. 125 and n. 498.

609. Cf. above at § 2.6.

610. Landsberger, *Date Palm*, 54f.; *CAD* M/1 s.v. *makkasu* A. It is remarkable, though, that the *makkasu*-dates are measured in the *kor*-system rather than the *mašīḫu*-system because "The occurrence of offer-*mašīḫu*'s in a text always points to issues for offering purposes (i.e., prebendary) as opposed to issues measured in the GUR system, e.g., for the food rations of the craftsmen." Bongenaar, *Ebabbar*, 146; and Jursa, *Landwirtschaft*, 156.

611. BM 33930: 23–24 and commentary *ad hoc*.

612. Hence, ^{lú}*mubannû* is best translated "arrangers-of-the-sacrificial-table," see Bongenaar, *Ebabbar*, 292f.

613. Bongenaar, *Ebabbar*, 143f.

Unfortunately, the provenance of the dates that MNA delivered remains unspecified, but ingredients for the regular offerings, in general, and *makkasu*-dates, in particular, were usually grown on temple land. Texts from the Ebabbar archive from Sippar, for instance, show that the ingredients were grown and delivered by different categories of people. Among them we find temple-farmers and -gardeners *(ikkaru, nukaribbu)*, small tenant farmers (*errēšu*), rent-farmers of large tracks of land (*ša muḫḫi sūti*), prebendary gardeners (*rab-banê*), holders of other prebends such as temple-enterers who received temple land in remuneration of their services in the temple and, finally, temple personnel who received temple land for their maintenance (*bīt ritti*).[614] There is no saying to which of these categories MNA belonged, if he belonged to any of them at all. Was he a rent-farmer, someone who leased land from a temple rent-farmer, a prebend-holder, or a leaseholder of prebendary land? Bēl-rēmanni, for instance, one of Sippar's wealthy citizens and a contemporary of MNA, (sub-) leased temple land from rent-farmers and temple-enterers.[615] Neither of these cases, however, explains why the dates were received by a courtier if we actually assume that MNA farmed temple land and delivered the dates in fulfilment of his duties as (sub-)leaseholder or (temporary) prebend-holder. Indeed, we expect a representative of the temple to receive the proceeds of temple land from its farmers, leaseholders, and prebendaries.

As a matter of fact, it is more likely that the dates for Nergal's offerings had been grown on crown land, but by temple prebendaries rather than dependents of the state. This explains the receipt of the dates by a courtier and their registration with temple secretaries who administered its income from prebends. Indeed, the fact that the dates were received by a courtier indicates that they had been grown on crown land, rather than on temple land, which fell normally outside the authority of royal officials.[616] Furthermore, the likely fact that the dates were registered in the accounts of the office that dealt with the temple's prebendary income indicates that they had been grown by prebendary gardeners or holders of prebendary land, rather than dependents of the crown.[617] A text from the Bēl-rēmanni archive of Sippar throws interesting new light on the possible correlation between crown land and prebendaries. It

614. Jursa, *Landwirtschaft*, 155ff. (delivery of *makkasu*-dates to the temple in general); n. 317 (delivered by temple farmers); 92f., and 109 (by rent-farmers); 63–65 (by *rab-banê*, who had to contribute fruits from their prebendary grove for the meals of the god in addition to the usual rent); 120f., 193, and 196 (on *bīt ritti*); and 231f. (temple land owned by *ērib bīti*'s; see also MacGinnis, *AfO* 38/39, 75 n. 7; *idem*, *AoF* 26, 4; and Bongenaar, *Ebabbar*, 156).

615. Thus, he a leased land from the rent-farmer Lâbāši in Bīr-ili, and land that belonged to the temple-enterer Nidinti-Marduk and his mother Inbaya in Tīl-Gubbi (Jursa, *Bēl-rēmanni*, 90–97).

616. On the presence of courtiers in Neo-Babylonian temples in general, and the Ebabbar in particular, and on the matters with which these courtiers dealt, more at MacGinnis, *ZA* 84 (esp. p. 207f.); and Bongenaar, *Ebabbar*, 99–106.

617. The correctness of this fact depends on the reading of the profession in line 9.

shows that the former could indeed be cultivated by holders of temple prebends. The text in question, *Bēl-rēmanni*, 164 = BM 42371, mentions land that belonged to the king and the crown prince but was cultivated, among others, by prebendary gardeners of Šamaš. These gardeners grew dates on the crown's land "for the [tab]le of [Šamaš]." Had this land been donated by the crown to the temple,[618] or had the crown confiscated temple land? The text from Sippar is dated in Simān of Darius' twenty-third year, i.e., exactly six years before BM 33930.[619]

Consequently, the dates that MNA delivered according to BM 33930 may have been grown by holders of temple prebends on land that they had received from the temple, in which they served, but was administered by the crown for unknown reasons. The temple prebendaries had to deliver part of their crops to the temple for the offerings of Nergal. MNA must have collected these contributions from the temple prebendaries, although this stage is not documented.[620] He subsequently delivered the dates, which he had presumably collected from the temple prebendaries, to the royal official in charge of their transfer to the temple. Bēl-ruṣūa, the receiving royal official in question, must have been one of those officials or *ša-rēš šarri* whom the king appointed to facilitate communication with the temple.[621] Usually, these officials had to make sure that the temple contributed part of its harvest and cattle to the "royal table" (*naptān šarri*) and the "royal allotment" (*šuṣbuttu ša šarri*). In the case under consideration, the courtier took care of another matter: he organized the supply of dates for the regular offerings of Nergal from crown land and was assisted in this matter by MNA. The agreement between Bēl-ruṣūa and MNA provided that the latter bring in the dates and the former transfer them to the temple. If Bēl-ruṣūa failed to clear MNA's delivery in the accounts of Bēl-bullissu <and>[?] his colleagues, he himself had to provide "the property of Nergal" with dates "instead[?] of MNA('s dates)."

3.3. *MNA and the E'igikalamma Temple*

MNA delivered three talents of first-choice wool to a weaver in the temple of the god Lugal-Marada in Darius' fifth year (Dar 182). The weaver acted as proxy

---

618. So Jursa, *Bēl-rēmanni*, 164–65.

619. Name of king broken, but texts from Bēl-rēmanni archive are dated in Darius' I.

620. It was, in fact, not the only encounter between MNA and temple prebendaries. Several other texts of the archive show MNA's involvement with different prebendary offices and property. Furthermore, there is an interesting prosopographic link between BM 33930 and one of these other prebend-related texts from the archive, Dar 405. The scribe who wrote BM 33930, Šuma-uṣur/Nabû-ittannu, also wrote Dar 405. The latter text concerns *imittu*-dates from a palm-grove that had been pledged to MNA by its owner Aplaya/Nergal-iddin; Aplaya was a temple-enterer (BM 30965). For reasons adduced below (p. 163f.), I assume that the palm-grove that he pledged to MNA was part of his prebendary land.

621. E.g., the *ša-rēš šarri bēl piqitti Eanna*, and the evidence collected by MacGinnis, *ZA* 84, 207–11 on courtiers (*ša-rēš šarri*) and their contacts with the temple administration.

for the chief administrator of the temple.[622] The delivery was recorded in Babylon and witnessed by three men. They are known from other texts from MNA's time and, in fact, knew him from his boat transports, collection of *ilku*, commodity trade in the vicinity of Šaḫrīnu, and interest in bakers.[623] It is not clear how these issues were related to MNA's deliver of wool in the E'igi-kalamma temple, but a relation is likely because it is no coincidence that the same men were present when decisions were taken in these matters. There may also have been a relation between Dar 182 and three texts from MNA's archive according to which MNA demanded the delivery of lambs from his lease-holders in addition to their payment of lease in dates.[624] He may have needed the lambs for their wool,[625] unless they were needed for some sacrificial purpose.[626]

3.4. *MNA, MBU, and the Eḫursag Temple*

Dar 405, written in Šaḫrīnu at the beginning of the date harvest of Darius' fifteenth year, deals with *imittu*-dates from a palm-grove in Ḫarru-Urukaya that had been pledged to MBU by its owner Aplaya/Nergal-iddin.[627] MBU leased the grove to a third party, viz. Aplaya/Gimillu.[628] The latter promised to

---

622. The chief administrator of the temple of Lugal-Marada was Nergal-ina-tēšî-ēṭir. If Jursa's identification of Nergal-ina-tēšî-ēṭir is accepted (Jursa, *Bēl-rēmanni*, 107 n. 453), the same official dealt with wool deliveries for the weavers of Marad (Dar 182, 27/viii/5 Dar), and with date deliveries for the female flour-grinders of Babylon (see text from Bēl-rēmanni archive, *Bēl-rēmanni*, 152 = BM 42353, Babylon, 7/v/26 Dar). Note, however, that more than twenty years separate both occurrences.

623. Nergal-ušallim/Mušēzib-Marduk//Nappāḫu (more at p. 119f. and Table 7 s.v. Nergal-ušallim), for instance, first witness in Dar 182, was a brother of the district governor of Šaḫrīnu from whom MNA bought dates in Darius' twelfth year (Dar 338). Nabû-bullissu/Iddin-Nabû//Dābibī, third witness in Dar 182, was also present when MNA paid for part of his debt to Šaddinnu's messenger (BM 31018). He worked with one of MNA's slaves (in the collection of crops from institutional land) in Šaḫrīnu (Dar 243). For the second witness in Dar 182, Rīmūt-Bēl/Ardiya//Itinnu, see Table 7 above and n. 685 below.

624. Dar 124 (=*CM* 20b 25; dated 10/vi/4 Dar), Dar 126 (= *CM* 20b 137; dated 13/vi/4 Dar), and Dar 267 (= *CM* 20b 43; dated 12/ii/10^{+} Dar).

625. In fact, MNA's dealings with lambs and wool may be traced back to his grandfather's wool business under the reign of Cambyses (on this business, see Wunsch, *Iddin-Marduk* 1, 55f. and *MOS Studies* 2, 102f.). Also see below n. 632.

626. Note the likely connection between (some of the) lambs and sacrifices in the month Addar in Dar 124: 12–13 (= *CM* 20b 25): *ištēn <immeru> kalumu babbānu ana ūm* 20^{kam} (erasure) *ša* ^{itu}*Addari inamdin*; and in Dar 126: 23–24 (= *CM* 20b 137): *ištēn <immeru> kal*[*umu a*]*na ūm* 20^{kam} *ša* ^{iti}*Addari inamdim*. In Dar 267 (= *CM* 20b 43) there is no reference to (sacrifices for) the twentieth of Addar: [...] DU *ištēn immeru babbānu ana M*[*NA inamdin*] (l. 16). Further note that the leaseholder of MNA's palm-grove along the New canal in Dar 124 (= *CM* 20b 25) recurs in *CM* 20b 27. This time he did not have to pay a lamb but rather *šibšu*-barley in addition to lease (*imittu*-dates) and the by-products of the date harvest.

627. On Dar 405, also see below at § 3.5.1.

628. Aplaya/Gimillu is also attested in a recently published text (CTMMA 3 83: 7).

pay his lease at the Borsippa canal in the next month. The royal resident (*qīpu*) in the Eḫursag temple came to Šaḫrīnu to witness Aplaya's promise to MBU. His presence among the witnesses in Dar 405 proves that MBU's lease of the palm-grove and his leaseholder's promise to pay rent were a matter of concern to the Eḫursag temple. In order to understand the temple's interest in this private transaction, it should be pointed out that Aplaya/Nergal-iddin, the owner of the palm-grove, was the holder of a temple-enterer's prebend. Indeed, he pledged beer and bread from his prebend to MBU, as we know from a text dated in Darius' twenty-sixth year (BM 30965).[629] Unfortunately, this text does not tell us in which temple Aplaya held his temple-enterer's prebend. Was he a temple-enterer in the Eḫursag temple and had he received the palm-grove in Ḫarru-Urukaya from the Eḫursag temple in remuneration of his services as temple-enterer in that temple? We know that temple-enterers were granted plots of temple land in remuneration of their services in the temple and must have been free to pledge, sell, lease, or bequeath this land like the other temple prebendaries holding temple-owned land. Thus, Aplaya may have received land in Ḫarru-Urukaya from the Eḫursag temple in remuneration of his services as temple-enterer and may subsequently have pledged this land to MBU. In that case it is understandable that the *qīpu* of the Eḫursag temple was present at the lease of this land by MBU to a third party in Darius' fifteenth year. Therefore, it is likely that Aplaya/Nergal-iddin served in the Eḫursag temple. He pledged income from his prebend to MBU on two occasions: a palm-grove in Darius' fifteenth year, and beer and bread in Darius' twenty-sixth year.[630]

3.5. *Prebendary Offices and Property*[631]

It was not surprising to find MNA and his slaves involved in the production and management of a temple's landed property. This was an area of the temple economy that had traditionally been open to outsiders and private entrepreneurship. Private businessmen could lease and sublease temple land, collect rent, taxes, and tithes for the temple, or farm the right to collect this income from the temple.

It is more surprising to find MNA or MBU, his slave, involved in matters of prebendary income, especially in view of the fact that only a restricted group of people enjoyed access to such income. Prebendaries were traditionally either members of the upper-class families of the city, who at the same time held important offices in the temple administration, or specialized craftsmen who belonged to the temple's permanent workforce. The men who performed the

629. More at § 3.5.1. On the relation between Dar 405 and BM 33930, see above n. 620.

630. Dar 405 (pledge of his palm-grove in the presence of the *qīpu* of the Eḫursag temple) and BM 30965 (beer and bread from his *ērib bīti* prebend in a temple whose name is not specified).

631. On the prebendary system in the Neo-Babylonian period, see Von Dassow, CTMMA 3, xxiii–xxiv with bibliography in n. 68; Bongenaar, *Ebabbar*, 140ff and Jursa, *Bēl-rēmanni*, 40ff. including bibliography.

prebendary duties on their behalf, the so-called "performers" (*epišānu*), were usually professionally trained in the profession that was linked to the prebend; they either worked for one of the temples as specialized craftsmen, or were privately owned slaves sent by their masters. Rarely did people from outside the temple succeed in acquiring prebendary rights on a permanent basis.

In consideration of the above criteria, it is unlikely that MNA was the holder of a prebend or that he or his slave acted as "performer" for a prebend-holder. MNA belonged to a family of *nouveaux riches*, rather than the traditional urban elite of Babylon. Moreover, we do not know of any member of his family who held an administrative or prebendary office in one of the temples in or around Babylon; nor was he or any other member of his family, to the best of my knowledge, professionally trained in one of the prebendary crafts, for instance as baker, brewer, weaver, or oil-presser. Their slaves, however, were occasionally trained in some of these professions, but nothing in the texts suggests that these slaves acted as "performers" for prebendaries.[632]

Nevertheless, we find MNA or MBU in six texts about prebendary property and ditto offices, and these are all new texts from the British Museum, so that it is a previously unknown aspect of MNA's business. The texts name MNA and MBU in connection with two prebends, "the prebend of temple-enterers" and "the prebend of [...]."[633] One text refers to "arrangers-of-the-sacrificial-table," but without mentioning their prebend.[634] The references to the ^{lú}DÍM and the bakers (^{lú}*nuḫatimmu*) are probably to be understood in the same sense, viz. as references to persons who were trained in one of the prebendary professions and occasionally held rights to the income derived from the performance of these professions in the temple.[635] However, the bakers may also have been of a secular nature and unrelated to a temple or its prebendary system. The text mentioning the arrangers-of-the-sacrificial-table also refers to a delivery of

---

632. Dandamaev, *Slavery*, 298. Slaves were employed in the Egibi's brewery, e.g., IMB's slavewoman ^{f}Isḫunnatu, who, no doubt continued in this trade after she became MNA's slave (Dandamaev, *idem*, 337; also CTMMA 3 65; cf. the slave Nabû-ayyālu in, a.o., CTMMA 3 71 and 73; on the Egibi's brewery, see also Lanz, *Ḫarrānu*, 142, 155–62; Van Driel, *BiOr* 43, 7 n. 7; and Wunsch, *Felder* 1, 100, esp. regarding *CM* 20b 54). For the training of one of MNA's slaves as a baker, see BM 41442, discussed in § 3.5.4. For Egibi slaves trained as bakers, weavers, stone-cutters, or tailors, see, for instance, Nbk 133 (Šulaya pledges his slave, a baker), Cyr 64 (= *CM* 3b 278), Camb 345 and Cyr 325 (from the time of MNA's grandfather, Iddin-Marduk); and CTMMA 3 69 (^{lú}KAL$^{!}$.KAL = *mukabbû* from MNA's time; on this profession, see more at Bongenaar, *Ebabbar*, 313). Iddin-Marduk may well have needed the textile craftsmen for processing the large amounts of wool that he bought from the crown prince (Wunsch, *Iddin-Marduk* 1, 56; the same may have applied to MNA).

633. BM 30965: 16, ^{giš}*isqu* ^{lú}*ērib bītūti*, and BM 31793: 9, ^{giš}*isqu ša* ⌜x⌝ [...].

634. BM 33930: 23, ^{lú}*mu-ban-ni-e* (see at § 3.2.2). These *mubannû* were not just cooks, but were part of the prebendary system as "arrangers-of-the-sacrificial-table" because they had to arrange MNA's *makkasu*-dates for the offerings of Nergal.

635. BM 30994, ^{giš}*lē'i ša* LÚ.DÍM (= ^{lú}*mubannû* or ^{lú}*itinnu*, on the reading of the logogram, see commentary at BM 30994: 11); BM 41442 and BM 33968 (^{lú}*nuḫatimmu*, wr. LÚ.MU).

commodities for sacrificial purposes, viz. MNA's delivery of *makkasu*-dates that the said arrangers-of-the-sacrificial-table had to prepare for the god.[636] The first-choice lambs that MNA's leaseholders had to deliver may or may not have been destined for sacrificial purposes.[637]

The texts raise two questions. Did MNA acquire a prebend through purchase, pledge or lease? Or, if he did not hold a prebend and was not entitled to a share from the temple income, what was the reason for his or his slave's contacts with temple-enterers, arrangers-of-the-sacrificial-table, LÚ.DÍM, bakers, offering dates and perhaps also sacrificial lambs?

3.5.1. *Pledge of Parts of a Prebend*

Two texts give evidence on the pledge of parts of the same temple-enterer's prebend to MBU, MNA's senior slave.[638] The first text is BM 30965, written in Babylon in Ab of Darius' twenty-sixth year. At this time MBU must have been dead and MNA was collecting his slave's outstanding credit claims.[639] One of these claims was held against Aplaya/Nergal-iddin and Nabû-ittannu/Nūrea. Aplaya declared under oath that he would bring along the sons of Nabû-ittannu/Nūrea, his co-debtor, to MNA in Babylon before the end of the month. They were to settle their debts of silver, dates, and barley that they owed to MBU. The oath came in addition to a written statement by Aplaya: "In addition, there is a previous document that concerns the term of payment, which is with Aplaya, and (which states that) 1 *qa* of bread as well as 1 *qa* of beer, the income from Aplaya's *ērib bīti*-prebend, have been pledged."[640] According to these lines Aplaya had agreed upon the term of repayment and the establishment of a security pledge. In fact, he had pledged a specific amount of bread and beer, most likely, to his original creditor, MBU. This bread and beer were "the income from Aplaya's *ērib bīti*-prebend." In other words, Aplaya occurs in this text as the holder of a prestigious prebend who used income from this prebend to secure the repayment of his debts to MBU.[641] After the latter's death, MNA became entitled to the pledged prebendary income of bread and beer.

The second text that mentions a pledge of property by Aplaya/Nergal-iddin to MBU is Dar 405 (Šaḫrīnu, 4/vii/15 Dar). The property that was pledged, *in casu* a palm-grove, may have been part of Aplaya's prebendary income, although the text does not explicitly say so. The decisive factor in this

636. BM 33930 (§ 3.2.2).

637. Dar 124 = *CM* 20b 25, Dar 126 = *CM* 20b 137 and Dar 267 = *CM* 20b 43. See above at n. 626.

638. BM 30965 and Dar 405. The evidence from Dar 405 is open to discussion (see already § 3.4).

639. See commentary at Dar 509: 3.

640. BM 30965: 14–17.

641. It is remarkable that Aplaya does not have a family name, but was, nevertheless, the holder of a prestigious prebend.

respect is the presence of an official of the Eḫursag temple as first witness. In discussing Dar 405,[642] I suggested that the palm-grove that Aplaya pledged to MBU belonged to the Eḫursag temple and had been given to him in remuneration of his services as temple-enterer in this temple. Consequently, the temple sent its representative to Šaḫrīnu when MBU leased this palm-grove to a third party; some transactions regarding this palm-grove apparently needed the silent approval of the Eḫursag temple. The above assumption and conclusion were based on three facts: (1) Aplaya/Nergal-iddin was a temple-enterer;[643] (2) temple-enterers could be granted plots of temple land in remuneration of their services in the temple; and (3) prebendaries could freely pledge, sell, lease, or bequeath their prebendary properties and its income. To sum up, Aplaya/Nergal-iddin was a temple-enterer, probably in the Eḫursag temple. He pledged parts of his temple-enterer's prebend to MBU on two occasions. First he pledged his prebendary palm-grove (Dar 405) and, probably at about the same time,[644] he pledged bread and beer from his prebendary income; the rights to the latter income were transferred to MNA after MBU's death (BM 30965).

3.5.2. *Sale of a Prebend*

The sale of a prebend is mentioned in one text from MNA's time, written in a place the name of which is broken off, in Ṭebēt of Darius' twenty-seventh or twenty-eighth year (BM 31793). The text in question aimed to settle debts between MNA and his long-standing debtor Bēl-upaḫḫir/Nergal-iddin. The debts were to be settled through the sale of a prebend and the pledge of some real estate. The first eight lines of this text refer to Bēl-upaḫḫir's debts of silver, dates, and probably also barley, his pledge of land to secure the repayment of the dates, and his repayment of part of the silver to MNA. This is clear from the structure of the text, regardless of the fact that there is no verb to express the notion of repayment. The following lines link the repayment of the debt to the sale of a prebend in which MNA is somehow involved. Unfortunately, this part of the text is fragmentary and the verb at the end of line 10 is broken off. The expression *šīm* ^{giš}*isqi* in line 9, however, makes it clear that a prebend had been sold, and the reconstruction of the verb *imḫurū/iddinū* at the end of line 10, therefore, is almost certain. Moreover, the practice is well attested whereby insolvent debtors sell property from their belongings, usually to their creditor, as a means to pay for their debt. MNA, for instance, sold real estate and slaves to his creditor Anu-mukīn-apli in order to pay off his silver debt.[645]

642. Above at § 3.4.

643. As we known from BM 30965.

644. We do not know when exactly the bread and beer were pledged to MBU, but from a text of Darius' twenty-sixth year, viz. BM 30965 currently under consideration, we know that the pledge was still in force.

645. BM 33935 (more at n. 588). The formulation of BM 33935:9–15 served as basis for the reconstruction of BM 31793:8–12.

Bēl-upaḫḫir/Nergal-iddin, the debtor, was well known to MNA, Nabû-aḫḫē-bulliṭ, and MBU, although the reasons for his indebtedness to them are unknown. The history of his debts can be traced back to the beginning of Darius' thirteenth year. At that time Bēl-upaḫḫir, who was also known as Puḫḫuru, owed silver and onions to Nabû-aḫḫē-bulliṭ (Dar 345). A year later we hear about another silver debt between the same persons (Dar 369). The latter text was witnessed by Bēl-upaḫḫir's brother, Aplaya, whom we have met as the holder of an *ērib bīti* prebend. The next time we hear about Bēl-upaḫḫir is in Kislīm of Darius' twentieth year. He was granted another two months to settle the debt of silver, barley, dates, and cattle that he owed to MBU, with MNA, his creditor's boss (Dar 509). However, six years after the ultimatum the debt had still not been repaid, and new debts of silver, dates, and cattle had been contracted (BM 31360). A new ultimatum was set, the tenth of Ṭebēt of the same year. We do not hear about Bēl-upaḫḫir until a year or two after the ultimatum when we learn that he and his son were still, or probably again, in debt with MNA, owing him four minas of silver and at least sixty-six *kor* of dates (BM 31793).[646] This time the problem of repayment was solved as follows: the repayment of the dates was secured by the pledge of a cultivated plot of land in Ṣilimma; the repayment of the silver, or at least of part of it, was made possible by selling a prebend.[647] Similar solutions were applied in CTMMA 3 70 to secure the repayment of Bēl-upaḫḫir's debts to MNA and MBU, viz. the pledge of real estate to MNA and maybe also the sale of a prebend.[648] In sum, two of the sons of Nergal-iddin, viz. Bēl-upaḫḫir and Aplaya, held prebends, and had known MNA, his brother and his senior slave since Darius' thirteenth and fifteenth years, respectively.

This leaves us with the question of the buyer of the prebend. Theoretically, Bēl-upaḫḫir and his son had two options: they could sell the prebend either to their creditor instead of paying the debt in cash or to a third party and use the silver from the sale to pay off their creditor. Consequently, it cannot be taken for granted that MNA was the buyer of the prebend.[649]

---

646. BM 31793 is dated in either Darius' twenty-seventh or twenty-eighth year, i.e., either a year or two after BM 31360.

647. BM 31793: 4–6 (pledge), 6–12 (sale).

648. CTMMA 3 70: 2′–4′ (pledge) and end line 9′ (sale of prebend). I suggest reading the end of line 9′ as follows: … 1 MA.NA KÙ.BABBAR UD-*ú ši-mi*? GIŠ.ŠUB?.BA. Read at the beginning of line 10′: [*š*]*á* LÚ.x? The date of CTMMA 3 70 is broken off, but it does not have to be dated before Dar 509 (against E. Von Dassow, CTMMA 3, 141) because the debts to MBU mentioned in it remained unsettled for at least six years after Dar 509, as we know now from BM 31360 and BM 31793.

649. The content of the concluding lines of the contract is ambiguous and cannot help solve the question of the buyer of the prebend. See commentary at lines 11–12.

3.5.3. *Silver Debts of the* LÚ.DÍM[650]

The LÚ.DÍM are mentioned in connection with a debt of silver in a promissory note from Darius' twenty-sixth year (BM 30994). The debtor, Nabû-kuzub-ilī from the Eppeš-ilī family, promised to pay the fifty shekels of silver that he owed to MNA within two weeks. Five years later, however, he had still to pay part of the debt (BM 32858).[651] If he paid his debt, MNA had to give "the register of the LÚ.DÍM" to him. This register, therefore, must have contained a specification of the duties to which Nabû-kuzub-ilī and probably also his colleague LÚ.DÍM were subject.[652] Upon fulfilment of these duties, *in casu* the payment of fifty shekels of silver,[653] the document stating these duties would become void and could be given to the person who fulfilled them.[654]

The precise nature of the duties of Nabû-kuzub-ilī and the LÚ.DÍM or the ultimate cause of their debt of fifty shekels, are not specified, but some insight may be gained in this issue from internal as well as external evidence. First, we should note the witnesses in BM 30994 and the scribe of BM 32858. The debt of Nabû-kuzub-ilī to MNA was a matter of concern to Nidintu/Kalbaya//Suḫaya, who, accordingly, attended the debtor's promise to pay within two weeks. This Nidintu was a man subject to the performance of compulsory state service, probably towing boats, and witnessed several of MNA's boat-related transactions.[655] At some of them he met Bēl-erība/Kalbaya//Šumu-libši, a commander-of-fifty.[656] Among the witnesses in BM 30994 is also Nidintu/Kalbaya//Šumu-libši,[657] the brother of Bēl-erība, the commander-of-fifty. He is

650. The LÚ.DÍM was either an "arranger-of-the-sacrificial-table" ([lú]*mubannû*), or a "builder" ([lú]*itinnu*). More at the commentary to BM 30994: 11.

651. The partial repayment of the debt recorded in BM 32858 was witnessed by a judge, who also sealed the document, and three other witnesses. The judge and two of the witnesses belonged to the Eppeš-ilī family, to which the debtor Nabû-kuzub-ilī also belonged. It was one of the more prestigious families in Babylon.

652. Cf. *šaṭāru ša* [lú]*nuḫatimmû*," the document of the bakers" (TCL 13 221: 20–21), in fact a declaration made by the bakers who had to bake for the god's meals according to which they assume warranty for the good quality of their products and the continuous performance of their baker's duty. The document containing the declaration was deposited in the temple. More on this document at Weisberg, *Guild Structure* and Kessler, *AUWE* 8/1, 95–98.

653. The silver may also have been paid instead of performing the duties, cf. the payment of silver instead of providing for equipment (*rikis qabli*) or performing work assignments (*ilku, urāšu*).

654. This provision is reminiscent of the well-known practice of returning the original debenture (*u'iltu*) to the debtor upon repayment of the debt. For similar practices regarding someone who had fulfilled his prebendary duties, see Kessler's comment at *AUWE* 8/1 No. 48. This text from Uruk may have been a note of quittance specifying the day at which an unnamed prebend-holder had performed his prebendary duties.

655. On Nidintu/Kalbaya//Suḫaya, see above at n. 182 and at Table 7.

656. BM 30370 and BM 30961.

657. See commentary at BM 30994: 18–19.

known, in particular, from a text regarding the recruitment of workers on behalf of his brother, in which he occurs among the witnesses.[658] It is likely that the attestation of both Nidintus at a transaction regarding the silver debt of the LÚ.DÍM and at transactions regarding boats or the recruitment of workers, often in the companionship of a commander-of-fifty indicates that these matters were somehow interrelated. Otherwise, the men would not have been present at the agreements that bore upon the said debt, boats, and manpower. The existence of a common background is further confirmed by the personal and business interests of the writer of the receipt of part of the silver debt, BM 32858. The scribe in question, Bēl-uballiṭ//Bēl-eṭēru, was one of MNA's cousins and wrote two other documents for him, BM 30772 and BM 30965.[659] He wrote the first document in the presence of Bēl-erība, the commander-of-fifty who came to witness MNA's receipt of "the [*il*]*ku*[!]-tax, addition to the bow[?](-tax), (and) the *fittings for the archer*." The other document that Bēl-uballiṭ wrote for MNA, BM 30965, concerns the debts of the temple-enterer Aplaya/Nergal-iddin to MBU. The recurrence of Bēl-uballiṭ in these cases shows that there was a common ground to the silver debt of the LÚ.DÍM, the payments for taxes, the equipment of archers, the needs of the commander-of-fifty, and the financial situation of the holder of a temple-enterer's prebend.

Second, we should have a look at other registers that are mentioned in texts from MNA's time to see what can be learned from these texts on their nature.[660] If we know more about the registers to which MNA had access, we may better understand the nature of Nabû-kuzub-ilī's debt that was recorded in the "register of the LÚ.DÍM."

Registers, called either [giš]*lē'u* or [giš]*manâtu*,[661] are frequently mentioned in texts from MNA's time in connection with four kinds of state and temple

---

658. BM 30274. Nidintu/Kalbaya//Šumu-libši may also have kept track of payments for transport costs to the governor of Babylon (BM 31786) and deliveries of barley to another royal official for unspecified reasons (BM 31138). The uncertainty in those two cases derives from the fact that the witness Nidintu/Kalbaya(//[...]) in these texts may have been either the above-mentioned Nidintu/Kalbaya, descendant of Šumu-libši, or Nidintu/Kalbaya, descendant of Suḫaya. Both Nidintus are well attested as witnesses in texts from MNA's time.

659. The scribe of BM 32858 (13/vii/31 Dar) was Bēl-uballiṭ//Bēl-eṭēru. The scribe of BM 30772 (20/xii/26 Dar) was Bēl-uballiṭ/Itti-Marduk-balāṭu//Bēl-eṭēru[!]. The scribe of BM 30965 (21/v/26 Dar) was Bēl-uballiṭ/Itti-Nabû-balāṭu//Bēl-eṭēru. In my opinion this was one and the same scribe in the three cases. Moreover, BM 30772 and BM 30965 were not only written by the same scribe, but also share a witness, viz. Ša-Bēl-atta/Marduk-šuma-ibni//Egibi. The scribe in question was MNA's cousin: he was the son of Ina-Esagil-bēlet, MNA's aunt (i.e., MNA's father's sister-in-law). For the land that he owed along the old Cutha canal together with MNA and his brothers, see Dar 316 (= *CM* 20b 159, dated 14/[-]/11 Dar; discussed in detail at Wunsch, *Felder* 1, 133–39). Further note that Bēl-uballiṭ's brother witnessed one of MNA's payments for transport costs, BRM 1 81 (4/viii/26 Dar).

660. E.g., BM 30233, BM 30446, BM 30589, BM 30639, BM 30795, BM 30853, BM 31036, BM 31188, BM 41443, Dar 290 (= *CM* 20b 190) and TCL 13 185.

661. Written GIŠ.DA = [giš]*lē'u* and GIŠ.ŠID = [giš]*manâtu*.

income: state income from taxes or tolls, the governor's income from boats and boat transports, the temple's income from its landed estate, and state income from corvée and army service. The first kind of registers to consider in this respect are those that kept record of the state's income from taxes and tolls. Thus, the clerk of the commissioners of the New Palace had a register in which he recorded the income of silver from *ilku*. He had received the silver in question from MNA and kept the register "with him."[662] At other instances such registers regarding tax-silver were with MNA. Thus, the register that kept track of his payments to Nabû-šuma-ukīn/Bēl-ēṭir//Šangû-Nannaya, paid on behalf of Bēl-nādin-apli and his brothers, was with MNA.[663] These were, most likely, payments for the *ilku* of Bēl-nādin-apli and his brothers, as argued elsewhere.[664] Payments for toll at bridges were also recorded in registers, as we learn from BM 41443, which mentions a "register of the bridge." MNA had to transfer silver to this register, and in view of TCL 13 196, it may have been part of the silver that MNA had collected at the governor's bridge from passing boats.

Second, texts in MNA's archive refer to registers of payments of various kinds to the governor of Babylon. MNA, for instance, gave such a register, viz. the "register on two-third mi[nas (...)] of medium-quality [silver]," together with fifteen *kor* of dates, to Bēl-ušallim/Ina-Nabû-ultarraḫ, courtier in the service of the governor of Babylon.[665] Similar registers and sealed documents, issued by the governor of Babylon, are mentioned in BM 30853. They were the basis of MNA's payments for various boat-related expenses to Nidinti-Bēl-damqat, servant of the governor Ina-Esagil-lilbur. Thus, MNA paid forty shekels of white silver "for barley to Nidinti-Bēl-damqat according to the register and the sealed tablet of the governor," as well as twenty shekels of silver "for four cables to Nidinti-Bēl-damqat according to the (same?) register and sealed tablet."[666] Furthermore, payments to the governor of Babylon for transport costs were equally accounted for in registers. Thus, Ṣillaya/*Bīt-iltammar*!, "clerk of the gardeners and the water-drawers of the Grand Palace and the New Palace" received a "register regarding the costs for the transport of fifty *kor* of barley," by order of Gūzānu, governor of Babylon. He received this register in addition to MNA's "payment for the transport of one hundred *kor* of barley from irrigated farmland in Tâmti."[667]

---

662. BM 30589.

663. TCL 13 185: 13–15, "The register regarding one and a half minas of silver Bēl-nādin-apli gave to MNA." For the relationship among MNA, Bēl-nādin-apli, and (Nabû-)Šuma-ukīn, see p. 40.

664. Indeed, we know from one of MNA's *ilku*-receipts (BM 31533) that (Nabû-)Šuma-ukīn collected *ilku* and relied on MNA to act on his behalf in this tax-related issue. Also see n. 129.

665. BM 31036.

666. BM 30853: 12ff. For the identification of Nidinti-Bēl-damqat, see BM 30256.

667. BM 30639.

Third, one text in MNA's archive refers to "the register of Bēl."[668] It kept track of payments to the temple, and thus recorded, i.a. MNA's delivery of dates in Darius' thirty-first year.[669]

Fourth, registers are also mentioned in MNA's archive in connection with the recruitment of (corvée-)workers and soldiers for state officials. Thus, when MNA received a boat-tower from the governor's pool of forced laborers, he also received "the previ[ous] register regarding (service in the month) Dûzu."[670] In other words, he received the boat-tower together with a register that kept track of who was drafted to tow boats for the governor and when. A similar procedure may be recorded in BM 30446, where six boat-towers were recruited "together with the register [...] of King Darius," and more specifically "according to the (said?) register." This register may have kept track of specific aspects of the boat-towers' recruitment, to wit the distribution of food for their maintenance.[671] Finally, the governor of Babylon had a register in which he kept track of his charioteer Libluṭ/Itti-Nabû-balāṭu, the latter's companion Rīmūt/Marduk-ušallim//Paḫāru and a group of workers or soldiers called ^{lú}*šá-da-e-ti* (=boat-towers?); these men were enlisted to serve with him.[672] The men were either remunerated for their service or their service was compulsory; the register regarding their service was issued either in order to know who served and accordingly to whom to pay a remuneration, or in order to know who served and accordingly whom to release from additional compulsory service. On the basis of such registers, the authorities also knew how much to pay as rations and to whom.

We may gain some insight into the general outline of such recruitment registers by having a look at similar registers from contemporary temple archives.[673] The abundant evidence from the Neo Babylonian temple archives, in fact, throws light on the bookkeeping procedures of a big institution in the Neo-Babylonian period. Thus, various registers, ledgers, and lists were written

668. BM 30233. For the "register of Bēl" in texts from IMB's time, see Wunsch, *MOS Studies 2*, n. 27 (note that the persons who held the register in BM 31395 appear without official title).

669. Cf. the register of Šamaš that kept track of the temple's income in dates from its gardeners, Jursa, *Landwirtschaft*, 39, n. 88 and 157.

670. BM 31188.

671. BM 30446. More at the commentary to BM 30446: 5 and above at p. 53f. In this respect also note the register mentioned in Dar 290 (= *CM* 20b 190; see above at n. 179); it may have kept track of the income of barley and its distribution for the rations of conscripts.

672. BM 30795. On the charioteer Libluṭ and his service with the governor of Babylon, see also CT 22 74.

673. We have to turn to the temple archives due to the absence of palace archives for the Neo-Babylonian period. However, some evidence on the royal administration may be gained from private archives from Sippar and Nippur. We may cite the following three examples. First, fragmentary administrative texts from Sippar contain lists of men belonging to the same bow-unit who had to serve (Jursa, *Bēl-rēmanni*, 101). Second, the administrative text TUM 2/3 242 from Nippur contains a list of fourteen men who served as king's men in the first and second months of the year (Stolper, *JCS* 53, 125f.). Third, *JCS* 53 No. 13 (= A.

by the temple scribes in order to keep track of who had to serve in which part of the temple and/or for which period of the year.[674] Some of these lists concentrate on one individual. They state that these are "the days of PN for one year in the temple X," and continue with a detailed list of the days in question.[675] Other lists concern groups of prebendaries or temple craftsmen. They state that these are "the days of the brewers for Nisan in the temple X,"[676] or "months of the temple-enterers of Šamaš for one year";[677] they continue with specifying the names of the persons and the exact period of service for each person. In addition, there are temple lists that contain only personal names but these texts may have served a similar purpose as the more elaborate staff lists mentioned earlier, to wit to keep track of who was serving in which part of the temple, and/or at which period.[678] Quite likely, the registers of the royal administration to which the texts from MNA's archive refer must have been organized along similar principles because they served similar purposes, viz. to administer the services that some professionally trained persons had to perform for the benefit of the state. The textual evidence from MNA's archive that was adduced above, in fact, showed that the registers of the governor of Babylon, for instance, and probably also that of other officials, contained the names of the men who had to serve or the month in which they served.[679]

To sum up, the debt of Nabû-kuzub-ilī most likely resulted from the fact that he had to perform public service on behalf of the state or pay taxes as a presumed member of the profession of LÚ.DÍM. If we assume that the LÚ.DÍM were prebendary "cooks" (i.e., LÚ.DÍM = [lú]*mubannû*), it follows that Nabû-kuzub-ilī had to serve in a temple rather than for the state. The register of the LÚ.DÍM, which MNA held and to which Nabû-kuzub-ilī was entitled after redeeming his debt was, no doubt, another of these registers listing who had to

34117) is a receipt issued by the agent of "the ... (governor?) of Nippur" to two men after they had fulfilled their king's man-service for the second and third months of the year. The latter text is, therefore, very similar to BM 30274 published in the present volume.

674. Temple scribes also wrote registers ([giš]*lē'u*) in which they kept account of the temple's expenditures of goods (MacGinnis, *Letter Orders*, 22; Bongenaar, *Ebabbar*, 143 regarding Cyr 31; Jursa, *Landwirtschaft*, 157: *lē'u ša tēlītu*). The "register of the prebends" ([giš]*lē'u ša isqāti*), for instance, listed the amounts of crops paid out to the temple's prebendaries in remuneration of their services (MacGinnis, *Letter Orders*, 9). The "register of the *maššartu*" recorded the combined issue of commodities for offerings (*sattukku, ginû, quqqû, sellu*) and prebendary income (*pappasu*) (e.g., the so-called "offering-lists" published by Freydank, *SWU*). The temple's registers could also record expenditures for non-prebendary purposes, such as food rations for craftsmen.

675. E.g., MacGinnis, *AfO* 38/39 No. 4.

676. E.g., NRVU 619. Cf. NRVU 620.

677. E.g., Bongenaar, *Ebabbar*, 153f. = BM 77834.

678. Cf. *ibidem*, 155–56.

679. BM 30795 (the register of the governor of Babylon); BM 31188 (the register of, perhaps, Bēl-erība/[Kalbaya//Šumu-libši]); and BM 30446 (the register of, perhaps, "Bani-šarra-uṣur, of the House of the food allowances").

pay what to which state official/temple, or alternatively, who had to serve when and with which state official/temple. We have seen that MNA had access to such registers in the course of his dealings with state income from taxes and (compulsory) public service. In the case of BM 30994 and BM 32858 the state's/temple's claim concerned a group of professionals called LÚ.DÍM, and silver that was due from them. MNA arranged for the collection of this silver from the LÚ.DÍM, or at least for the collection of the fifty shekels that were due from one of them, Nabû-kuzub-ilī. It was attended by people who kept track of boat- or tax-related issues and some of whom knew Bēl-erība, the commander-of-fifty.[680]

3.5.4. *Bakers at MNA's Disposal*

In Addar of Darius' twenty-sixth year MNA decided to send his slave, Itti-Uraš-pāniya, to Guzānu/Ḫambaqu//Mandidi for a three-months' baker's course (BM 41442).[681] The contract follows the normal pattern of apprenticeship contracts, with fixation of the teacher's salary *in natura* and a compensation for the slave in case the teacher failed to instruct him.[682]

Bakers were, no doubt, in high demand with army commanders, supervisors of state workers, temple officials, and holders of baker prebends. Indeed, they were needed to bake bread from the flour that the king collected from his subjects (*qīme šarri*) to feed his soldiers and dependent workers. The need for bakers was especially urgent during military campaigns and when state (corvée) workers were on a mission in far-off places such as Elam. Bakers were also needed by the temple and its baker prebendaries in order to prepare food for the gods. The evidence from Neo-Babylonian temple archives shows that temple officials occasionally hired persons who had been trained as bakers, including slaves, from outside the temple in order to assist the temple bakers in baking bread for the gods. Holders of the baker prebend did the same in order to meet their prebendary duties and to capitalize on the flour that remained after they had met those duties.

Consequently, MNA must have calculated that a slave trained as a baker was an economic asset. He could hire him out to one of the big institutions, either the palace, the temple, or the military establishment, in return for a compensation (*maddattu*).[683] Alternatively, he could hire him out to a baker prebendary under similar circumstances. In addition, these slaves worked for his own household.

---

680. See above for the occurrence of Nidintu/Kalbaya//Suḫaya, the scribe Bēl-uballiṭ//Bēl-eṭēru and perhaps also Nidintu/Kalbaya//Šumu-libši in BM 30994 and BM 32858.

681. BM 41442, previously published in BOR 1, 83.

682. San Nicolò, *Lehrvertrag*, 14–15.

683. Another of his slaves, Balāṭu, who was a professional tailor ([lú]*mukabbû*), had been hired out to the slave of one Nabû-aḫḫē-bulliṭ//Šigûa, see CTMMA 3 69. On hiring out slaves by the Egibis, see also the text published by Oelsner, *AoF* 12, 365–67; the kind of work this slave had to perform, however, is not specified.

The plan to hire Itti-Uraš-pāniya out to one of the big institutions after his training as a baker explains why men who were affiliated with such institutions took notice of the slave's training. Indeed, the slave's apprenticeship contract was attended by men who either belonged to one of the institutions or kept an eye on transactions regarding these institutions. Thus, we find among the witnesses a man like Bēl-erība/Kalbaya//Šumu-libši. He is known from other texts as a commander-of-fifty and was, accordingly, a member of the (military) establishment. He was interested in boats, taxes and the recruitment of workers, such as men to tow boats, in addition to the training of MNA's slave as a baker.[684] Another of the witnesses to the apprenticeship contract, Rīmūt-Bēl/Ardiya//Itinnu, had known MNA for at least twenty years. He was a man with interests in transactions of a variegated, but not necessarily disconnected nature. Early in Darius' reign he was a witness when MNA delivered wool to the temple of Lugal-Marada and paid out wages to the sailor Bulṭaya/Ḫabaṣīru//Arad-Nergal, and when Nabû-ittannu/Nabû-zēru-līšir//Nūr-Papsukkal promised to pay his debt of silver and barley to Marduk-bēlšunu/Arad-Marduk. In the later years of Darius' reign Rīmūt-Bēl took notice of the fact that MNA sent his slave to a baker's course. In addition, he occasionally took an interest in MNA's commercial transactions with crops from institutional land in Šaḫrīnu and transactions with land in Litamu at the Uraš gate. It is noteworthy that in these commercial and real estate transactions he was accompanied by other men from families with loose connections to state income from taxes, temple property or boats.[685] Noteworthy, furthermore, is the scribe who wrote the apprenticeship contract: Ša-Bēl-atta/Marduk-šuma-ibni//Egibi. He was interested in matters of *ilku*, equipment for archers, boat transports, and temple-enterers. He occasionally met with the above-mentioned commander-of-fifty in matters that concerned both of them, and with a clerk who dealt with matters concerning specialized craftsmen[?] and Ionians. The latter meeting took place when MNA paid for transport costs to this clerk; Ša-Bēl-atta acted as witness and Bēl-erība as scribe.[686] Finally, we should men-

---

684. See Table 7.

685. Rīmūt-Bēl/Ardiya//Itinnu is attested in the following texts from MNA's archive: Dar 182 (wool for the temple of Lugal-Marada), Dar 215 (salary of the sailor Bulṭaya), E.36.1904 (= *Iraq* 55 No. 1; barley, the rent for Darius' tenth year, due from MNA to Bēl-iddin/Mušēzib-Marduk//Ēṭiru, cf. n. 552), Dar 318 (debt to Marduk-bēlšunu/Arad-Marduk), BM 31058 (dates due to MNA; no doubt related to MNA's business with crops from institutional land in Šaḫrīnu because witnessed by, among others, Rīmūt-Bēl/Šuma-ukīn), Dar 296 (crops from Bagasarū's land in Bīt-rab-kāṣir), BM 41442 (baker apprenticeship), Dar 217 (= *CM* 20b 183, also note the presence of the sailor Bulṭaya) and Dar 273 (= *CM* 20b 191, also note that the first and the fifth witnesses, the brothers of the second witness, and the scribe's brother frequently attended transactions concerning boats, taxes or temple affairs; details in Table 7 and in the name index s.v. Murašû/Nabû-aḫḫē-iddin//Nanna-utu, Ardiya/Dādiya//Nabaya, the sons of Mušēzib-Marduk//Nappaḫu, Nabû-šuma-iddin and Zēriya/Šāpik-zēri//Dēkû). The latter two texts regard real estate in Litamu at the Uraš gate.

686. Ša-Bēl-atta, the scribe of BM 41442, and Bēl-erība, commander-of-fifty, are attested

tion the institutional connections of the man who agreed to train MNA's slave as a baker: Gūzānu/Ḫambaqu//Mandidi. The other two documents in which this Gūzānu occurs show that he was subject to the payment of *ilku* and the delivery of a hireling to the commander-of-the-fortress.[687] In either case MNA mediated between him and the persons who took receipt of the *ilku* or the hireling. Gūzānu's obligations to the state, in general, and the commander-of-the-fortress, in particular, were probably related to his profession as a baker, as we explained in a previous section.[688]

The other text, a declaration before witnesses in the month Šabāṭ of Darius' fifteenth year, regarding the LÚ.MU is, unfortunately, very fragmentary, but again shows MNA's interest in having a baker (or bakers) at his disposal for one reason or another (BM 33968).[689] The names of these witnesses are very fragmentarily preserved on the obverse.[690] The person who made the declaration and whose name is altogether lost in the lacuna at the beginning of the obverse[691] undertook to bring a man (or perhaps more than one man).[692] This man was a baker (or that these men were bakers), because the text continues "if [he does not br]ing along$^{?}$ the bak[er(s)] and [does not deliver (him/them)]$^{?}$ to Marduk-nāṣir-apli."[693] If the baker(s) is (/are) not delivered to MNA, two other men should apparently be given to MNA as compensation as had been agreed upon in a previous document.[694] The substitutes, [Iqīša?]-Marduk and Nabû-zēra-ibni/Aššur-uṣur, are known from other texts from MNA's time: they sold draught animals to MNA.[695] Notwithstanding its fragmentary state of preservation, the text clearly shows that MNA had the right to receive baker(s), but we do not know what he intended to do with the baker(s) at his disposal.

---

together in BM 30772 (a payment for *ilku* and equipment for archers) and BM 32891 (a *gimru*-payment to Bazbaku, "[c]lerk of the specialized craftsmen$^{?}$ and ^{lú}[x x] of the Ionians"). Ša-Bēl-atta and Bēl-erība's brother, Nergal-ēṭir, are attested together in the unpublished BM 31788 (cf. n. 513).

687. BM 31226 (hireling) and TCL 13 198 (*ilku*).

688. See above, p. 50f.

689. Further note the occurrence of a Zababa-ēreš/Nergal-iddin, "descendant of LÚ.MU," among the witnesses in BM 30436 (= b 2535, unpublished; Babylon, 17/v/24 Dar), a text according to which [...]-Nabû/Nabû-zēru-līšir//Amēl-Ea undertook under oath to deliver utensils to MNA, written by Arad-Bābu (cf. n. 513) and witnessed, a.o by Arad-Gula/Marduk-šuma-uṣur//Nabaya (see name index).

690. The first witness may have been Bēl-iddin/Mušēzib-Marduk//Ēṭiru, or one of his brothers. On this Bēl-iddin, more at MacGinnis, *Iraq* 55 No. 1.

691. His name may be preserved at the beginning of Reverse line 7′, viz. [...-Mardu]k$^{?}$.

692. BM 33968 Rev.: 1′–3′, [PN (*u* PN] ⸢x⸣ LÚ GAL ⸢x x⸣ *abbak* "I will bring along [PN (and PN)] the ..."

693. BM 33968 Rev.: 3′–5′ (Rev. 3′ *kī* ^{lú}*nuḫatimmu* 4′ [*lā ītaba*]$^{?}$*kamma ana MNA* (no affiliation) 5′ [*lā ittadin*$^{?}$].

694. BM 33968 Rev.: 5′–7′.

695. Details at comment to BM 33968: 11.

3.6. *Summary: MNA and the Temple*

We may now proceed to summarize the main characteristics of MNA's contacts with temple officials and those of his transactions involving temple property.

MNA worked together with temple prebendaries, with low-level temple personnel, such as weavers, farmers, and secretaries, with the king's representatives in the temple, and with private men who had access to temple land. MNA did not work with the upper strata of the temple administration, like the *šatammu* or the *šangû*, at least not directly; the *šatammu* of the E'igikalamma temple, for instance, sent a weaver (*ušparu*) to meet MNA. Similarly, the Esagil temple administration sent three of its secretaries (*šāpiru*) to witness one of MNA's debts. Direct contacts with the temple were usually on a low level, viz. with the said weaver and secretaries or with temple farmers (*ikkaru*). MNA also had contacts with temple prebendaries (e.g., *ērib bīti*; lúDÍM?), but only on a private level. His access to temple property, in fact, was mostly established through deals with the king's representatives in the temple, like the *qīpu*, the *ša-rēš šarri bēl piqitti*, and the *bēl pīḫāti*, or through otherwise unspecified courtiers (*ša-rēš šarri*'s).

His contacts with the temples were usually long-term and concentrated on a few men and their family. Thus, he maintained contact with Nabû-kuzub-ilī/Bēl-rēmanni//Eppeš-ilī for five years (26–31 Dar), and with Aplaya and Bēl-upaḫḫir, sons of Nergal-iddin, for seven or eight years (20–27 or 28 Dar). The former was a lúDÍM and may, therefore, have held a lúDÍM-prebend in one of the temples in or around Babylon; the latter were temple-enterers. For seven years (11–18 Dar) he worked with Šaddinnu/Madānu-aḫḫē-iddin//Šigûa, from whom he rented the right to Bēl's *sibšu*-onions in Šaḫrīnu. Šaddinnu may also have introduced MNA to the urban elite of Uruk. As a matter of fact, he had several family members living in Uruk: his grandfather, father, two uncles, and three brothers. Some of them were well integrated into the prebendary system of the city's main temple.

Furthermore, his contacts with the temples often went back to similar contacts established in previous generations. Accordingly, he usually worked together with those temples with whom his father and grandfathers had been working, viz. the Esagil temple and the temple of Nergal, and thus continued the family's grip on the income of these temples from their landed estate in and around Šaḫrīnu. Nevertheless, he also maintained contacts with temples about which we do not hear in the previous generations, e.g., the E'igikalamma and Eḫursag temples, and tried to gain a foothold in certain areas of the temple economy, e.g., the prebendary system, in which his predecessors did not seem to have tried or succeeded.

MNA was economically active as entrepreneur in several areas of the temple economy. First and foremost, he participated in the agricultural management of temple land, in much the same way as he participated in the agricultural management of state-owned land and land of state officials. Accordingly, he farmed the right to collect rent (*šibšu*) and tithes (*ešrû*) from temple land, and he may have leased and subleased the land as well in order to control the crops' actual cultivation and harvesting. He left the daily organization of the field work to his tenant-farmers (*errēšu*) and to local men such as Marduk-nāṣir/Marduk-ušallim, Šulum-Bābili/Nidintu, and Aplaya/[Baniya]. The same men may have coordinated the crops' transshipment, transport, and processing as well. His rent-farming deals with the temples took place between Darius' eleventh and eighteenth years and mainly concerned the land of Bēl and Nergal in Šaḫrīnu and along the Piqūdu canal.

Remarkably, MNA bought these rights to the Esagil's income from its land from state officials and not, as we might have expected, from temple officials. As a matter of fact, MNA frequently met with officials who worked in the Esagil temple on behalf of the king, such as the king's inspector (*bēl pīḫātu*), his resident (*qīpu*), and his commissioner (*ša-rēš šarri bēl piqitti*). From the king's inspector, for instance, or more exactly, from Šaddinnu, his rent-farmer, he bought the earlier-mentioned right to collect *šibšu*-rent. Unfortunately, very little is known about the nature of the contacts between MNA and the other two officials, the Esagil's *qīpu* and *ša-rēš šarri bēl piqitti*. They only attended two of MNA's debts to state officials, but were not directly involved in the debts themselves. Similarly, we do not know the nature of MNA's relationship with the king's resident in the Eḫursag temple. He appears among the witnesses to a private transaction between MNA's slave and Aplaya, in Darius' fifteenth year; it may well have been prebend-related since Aplaya was the holder of a temple-enterer's prebend.

Only seldom did MNA meet directly with representatives of the temple in matters related to the exploitation of its land. These direct contacts were usually on a low level; moreover, they are often difficult to understand because of the scarcity of the evidence. In Darius' thirty-first year, for instance, MNA delivered dates that had been grown on the land of the Esagil temple to a man who had to enter them in the temple's register; we do not know, however, with whom this man was to meet in the temple in order to enter MNA's dates in the temple's register. Temple farmers are mentioned in one, perhaps two texts from MNA's archive. Thus, the farmer (*ikkaru*) of Nergal worked together with MNA's slave in Šaḫrīnu in a matter concerning heifer calves; he also produced butter that he had to bring to MNA's slave, but he is not labelled "farmer of Nergal" on that occasion. The tenant-farmers (*errēšū*) who grew onions on the land of Bēl on behalf of MNA were probably not temple farmers but private farmers hired by MNA to grow onions on temple land or, alternatively, subleasing plots of temple land from him.

Second, MNA supplied first-quality products, such as wool, dates, and perhaps lambs to the temple, apparently when the latter suffered a temporary shortage. These deliveries were sometimes directly to the temple, e.g., the delivery of first-quality wool to a weaver of the temple of Lugal-Marada in Darius' fifth year. The latter had been sent by the temple's chief administrator (*šatammu*) to take receipt of MNA's wool. His first-quality dates (*makkasu*) for the offerings of Nergal in Darius' twenty-ninth year, in contrast, were first delivered to a courtier (*ša-rēš šarri*) before their arrival in the temple. They may well have been grown on crown land by prebendholders. As it was, the courtier had to clear MNA's sacrificial dates in the accounts of the men who administrated Nergal's prebendary system ([*šāpi*]*ru*). From there they were, no doubt, transferred to the foreman of the arrangers-of-the-sacrificial-table (*šakin mubannê*), whose prebendary duty it was to serve them to the God. It is worth noting that the men who administrated the Esagil's prebendary system (*šāpir Esagil*) are mentioned under similar circumstances, to wit in connection with an obligation of MNA to a courtier, in a text from Darius' sixteenth year. Unfortunately, we do not know whether the first-choice lambs that MNA received from his tenant farmers were to remain with him for their wool, or were to be sent to the temple for sacrifice.

Third, MNA may also have provided the temple with farmers, skilled workers and draught animals when needed. It is probably in this sense that we should understand the earlier-mentioned references to the tenant farmers (*errēšū*) in Dar 315 and the heifers in BM 31976. It might have been for similar reasons that he trained one of his slaves as a baker, viz. to hire him out to one of the temples, unless this baker was meant to be hired out to the commander-of-the-fortress in Babylon or the holder of a baker's prebend; he might also have had to work for MNA in his private household.

Finally, MNA managed to gain some foothold in one of the cornerstones of the Babylonian temple economy, to wit the prebendary system, notwithstanding the fact that this system was usually closed to outsiders. The scope of his involvement in prebendary matters, however, is often difficult to estimate. Thus, it remains uncertain in which temples he sought to gain a foothold, and to which extent he became the holder of a prebend, if he became one at all. Notwithstanding these uncertainties, MNA clearly succeeded in gaining at least temporary rights to prebendary income, i.e., goods received by prebendaries from the temple in remuneration of their services. He gained these rights in a private arrangement with the prebendaries, viz. by lending silver and requiring some of their prebendary income as security for the loan. Thus, his slave lent silver to the temple-enterer Aplaya/Nergal-iddin and received the latter's prebendary bread, beer, and probably also land in pledge. When the slave died, MNA "inherited" the rights to the prebend. In this way he became the temporary holder of part of a temple-enterer's prebend, although it is not clear in which temple; it may have been the Eḫursag. He may even have bought a prebend from this temple-enterer's brother, Bēl-upaḫḫir (*alias* Puḫḫuru), although the latter may also have sold his prebend to someone other than MNA and given MNA, his creditor, the silver from the prebend's sale rather than the prebend itself. In his effort to realize contacts with prebendaries, he seems to have concentrated on one or two families, viz. the sons of Nergal-iddin, one of whom at least held a temple-enterer's prebend. His contacts with these men, as well as those with Nabû-kuzub-ilī from the Eppeš-ilī family, a LÚ.DÍM, were long-term ones.

As can be seen, MNA entered the temple economy through its back door: through the intermediary of the king's representatives in the temple, by long-standing relations on a private basis with individuals and members of their family who had access to temple land or temple prebends, and probably also through his slaves whom he trained in professions that were needed by, i.a., the temple and its prebendaries.

Conclusion

We may now proceed to summarize the answers to the three main questions, which were formulated in the introduction, and conclude this study of MNA's institutional connections. These questions regarded: (1) the scope of MNA's institutional connections: his contacts with state and temple officials and his transactions involving state or temple property; (2) the integration of these contacts and transactions into his business, and (3) the level of interdependence between the private and the public sectors in the exploitation of economically vital assets as reflected in the texts from MNA's archive.

4.1. *The Scope of MNA's Institutional Connections*

MNA limited his official business contacts to long-term relations with a few men and members of their families who had access to economically vital assets, such as land, water, skilled workers, and expensive equipment. He tried to limit his official business contacts in three ways. First, he preferred working with a few officials with control over more than one asset rather than with many officials with limited power. A good relationship with the governor of Babylon, for instance, opened the door to tax income, bridges, boats, boat equipment, tower-men, soldiers (especially charioteers), and transportation. Second, he worked with them on a permanent basis, rather than going after short-term deals. This is evidenced by his steady relationship with the Esagil temple and with several state officials, some of whom held relatively high positions in the central administration in the capital, as for instance, the governors of Babylon with whom he worked together during the entire reign of Darius. He had similar established relations with men who had access to large tracks of, no doubt, institutional land in the countryside, especially temple-owned land in and around Šaḫrīnu, such as Bagasarū (4–21 Dar), Rīmūt-Bēl and his brother (4–11 Dar), and Šaddinnu (11–18 Dar). Third, MNA included members of the officials' families in his network of official relations, thus limiting business to a circle of close relatives. Some of these family members may have opened the door to the economy of Sippar, Uruk, Bāṣ, and Borsippa for MNA. As a matter of fact, the above-mentioned characteristics are typical for most of MNA's business relations, and not only for those of an official nature. The core of these relations consisted of a few, professionally trained, men, including some of his senior slaves, who assisted MNA in all major areas of his business as partner, witness and / or scribe.

He preferred to work with those officials and temples with whom his father and grandfather had been working, often in the same geographical area and in the same kind of business. Accordingly, he continued working with the governors of Babylon, the Esagil temple and the temple of Nergal, in and around Šaḫrīnu and in matters related to his trade in commodities. Nevertheless, he also enlarged his circle of official acquaintances in the royal administration and his temple connections, and diversified his business operations with them.[696]

The institutional connections of his predecessors were partly political in origin.[697] However, there is no saying whether or to what degree MNA was actually involved in politics. For sure, he continued his father's occasional trips to Persia. He travelled several times to Susa, the Persian capital, and it was always in spring, i.e., when the king was known to reside there. Consequently, these journeys were most likely aimed at seeking royal protection for the family business, especially in times of political insecurity.

MNA met with these officials when he had to pay for his own taxes and for those of his house(hold) and in the course of his trade in commodities, but most of his official contacts were the result of his commercial ventures with institutional assets. As we have seen, he was economically active as an entrepreneur in the tax system (i.e., taxes, toll, tithes, corvée-work, and conscription), the exploitation of institutional land, the transport business, and the temple. The full extant of his entrepreneurship in those four areas has been adequately summarized above in § 2.8 and § 3.6.

4.2. *The Internal Coherence of the Egibi Business Firm at MNA's Time: The Trade in Commodities and Affiliated Businesses*

The trade in commodities was the core of MNA's business and the basis of his wealth; his institutional connections were, initially at least, a spin-off of this trade and ancillary to his wealth. For his trade he needed large amounts of crops, access to resources and facilities for their transshipment, processing and

---

696. Unless this intensification is only superficial. The increase of attested cases of institutional connections in MNA's time in comparison to the relatively poor documentation of institutional connections in the previous generations—at least from what has been published till now—may be the result of archival practices rather than of a genuine increase in economic activity on the part of MNA. Moreover, the publication of new texts from the previous generations may change the picture.

697. Nabû-aḫḫē-iddin, MNA's paternal grandfather, for instance, extended his legal and notarial assistance to Neriglissar and when the latter became king he was rewarded for his earlier assistance and loyalty. He was promoted from court-scribe to royal judge a few months after Neriglissar's accession to the throne, and was able to acquire a large plot of land near the capital for a good price thanks to the king's interference on his behalf. Close connections with the retinue of the crown prince continued in the days of Itti-Marduk-balāṭu, MNA's father. The latter also travelled frequently to Persia.

transport, and a market for their distribution. The big institutions and their representatives, however, controlled much of these assets, and MNA had to find an efficient way to get to them to keep his business going. He succeeded in gaining access to the assets needed for his trade through the establishment of a network of stable relations with the authorities, the scope of which was described in detail above.

Some of his institutional connections, however, grew beyond the needs of his trade into profitable businesses of their own, and thus became an additional source of wealth. Hence, there was more at stake in MNA's dealings with institutional assets than meeting those needs. The transport business is a clear example of a business enterprise that was basically ancillary to his trade, but had at the same time an economic potential of its own. We saw that MNA frequently paid for the right to use state-controlled canals, bridges, quays, and harbors. These payments were an integral part of his trade, which demanded, amongst others, the transportation of the commodities in which he traded from the fields in the countryside to the markets in the cities. His organization of boat transports, however, eventually went beyond the needs of his commodity trade. In fact, he used his boats for purposes other than transporting freshly harvested crops from the countryside to the markets. He used them, for instance, to bring supplies to the army in far-off places. Thus, he was able to transform the boat transports that he had to organize after the onion, barley, and date harvests for his main business into a business of its own, which was run at all times of the year. Moreover, he used the contacts that he established in the course of transporting crops for his trade as stepping stones for other deals. Thus, he was able to rent boats from the governor of Babylon and participated in the collection of tolls at the governor's bridge. He also rented boats from harbor masters and canal inspectors. In other words, he was involved in entrepreneurial enterprises with boats and bridges that, no doubt, evolved from the boat transports of his trade.

A development similar to the one described above may have taken place in MNA's dealings with state income from taxes. We saw above that his employees and members of his household, who were active in his trade, were subject to the payment of taxes and the performance of service obligations. MNA was ultimately responsible for their meeting their obligations vis-à-vis the state. Hence, he helped them out in these matters by paying on their behalf or lending them silver. Several of such cases are attested in the early years of Darius' reign (e.g., Rīmūt-Bēl texts and Dar 206). MNA soon discovered that providing credit to taxpayers, in particular his own employees, proved to be a profitable investment of his capital, since it provided him with access to his debtors' labor and income from land. This may have developed into a more systematic involvement in the levy of taxes in the later years of Darius' reign, whereby MNA not only provided credit to individual taxpayers in difficulties, but paid for everybody's taxes in a specific year, and was reimbursed by them after the harvest (see *ilku*-receipts). In other words, occasional payments of taxes on behalf of third parties within the limits of his commodity trade, eventually developed into true commercial ventures with state income from taxes.

MNA's involvement in agricultural matters developed along similar lines. Occasional purchases of crops from state officials and of rights to the temple's field rent within the context of his commodity trade gave rise to additional entrepreneurial ventures. Thus, he did not just buy crops and rights to crops from state officials, but embarked upon more complex commercial and agricultural operations in which he aimed to get hold of the entire process, viz. from the cultivation of the crops in the countryside south of Babylon till their sale on the Babylon market or till their processing into final products (e.g., flour and beer) in his own workshops and their subsequent distribution (e.g., transport of beer and flour).

MNA's business firm is, therefore, characterized by internal coherence, notwithstanding the variety of economic activities upon which it was based. His many official contacts and entrepreneurial activities with institutional assets had a common source, aim and effect. They originated in his commodity trade, derived support and strength from it, and cooperated in its work; often these affiliated activities developed into independent enterprises with their own profits and thus became an additional source of wealth. This internal coherence greatly contributed to the success of his business.

4.3. *Interdependence of Institutions and Private Entrepreneurs as Reflected in the Texts from MNA's Archive*

MNA's entrepreneurship in the four areas outlined above, viz. the tax system, the exploitation of institutional land, transportation, and the temple economy, were valuable to the state and temple economy as they were to his own private business. As a matter of fact, the big institutions were not always self-sufficient. Moreover, they sought ways to maximize the income from their assets, especially their landed estate, i.a. by reducing cost and risks. Occasionally, they needed to convert their vast income in crops from taxes and land into ready cash, and may have struggled with problems of agricultural surplus. Texts from MNA's archive show how he provided answers to these logistic and financial problems, and problems of efficient management.

Indeed, MNA offered credit facilities, (transport) services, goods of superior quality, and his business know-how as well as that of members of his household.[698] His entrepreneurship in the collection of taxes and bridge tolls and in the recruitment of men, for instance, ensured the constant flow of income to the state in terms of silver, crops, equipment, and manpower. His entrepreneurship with crops from institutional land enabled the institutions to save on manpower and draft animals, to shift the risk of a bad harvest to the entre-

---

698. Probably also final products, like beer, flour e.a. The processing of raw materials into final products took place, in all likelihood, in MNA's own workshops (*bīt kāri*) or "houses." This aspect of his business, however, has not been fully investigated in the present study.

preneur, and to convert their agricultural surplus and other agricultural produce into silver.

MNA's entrepreneurship in the transport business, in particular, illustrates how public and private sectors depended on each other in their control over their access to economically vital assets and how their cooperation in these matters was mutually beneficiary. MNA's entrepreneurship enhanced the proper functioning of the transport system that was vital to the state, as it was to MNA's private business. From the latter's point of view it was important to get the crops that he needed for his trade to the markets efficiently and economically. This was done mostly by boat and involved using canals, quays, bridges, and harbors, which were heavily state-controlled. The state for its part was interested in a well-functioning transport system for its own reasons. On the one hand, it was an important source of income in terms of toll. On the other hand, the state had to get its crops from land in the countryside, for instance in Tâmti, to the capital in order to feed its dependent workers and it had to bring supplies to military strongholds outside the capital in order to provide for its soldiers. MNA used his entrepreneurial skills and financial resources in order to assist the state in all these matters. He assisted in collecting tolls at bridges, paid for the transport costs of the crops from Tâmti, and may even have organized the transports on his own account, depending on one's interpretation of the *gimru*-texts. He carried supplies to the army and recruited men who had to tow boats on behalf of the state or perform analogous jobs. In return for his assistance in transporting the crops, he must have enjoyed some rights, such as the right to join officially organized transports or he must have gained easy access to state-controlled resources and facilities for his own transports for one-month periods. In return for his assistance in recruiting boat-towers he was able to exploit the recruited men for his own needs during a pre-set period of time.

The cooperation between MNA and state representatives in the transport business was profitable in still another sense. It enabled the state to maximize the use of its boats and professionals by renting them out to private business men. Whether the men who rented these boats and professionals out to MNA, such as the governor of Babylon for instance, were making some extra money with state-owned assets on their own account, and hence blurred the separation between the private and the public sector, or acted purely in the state's interests, cannot be determined.

As can be seen, MNA's institutional connections, which were one of the cornerstones of his business, were based on the principle of mutual benefit. He assisted the authorities in matters important to them, such as the levying of taxes, the collection of toll at bridges, the recruitment of workers and soldiers, the organization of officially sponsored projects, the supply of goods in general, and the transport of goods to the capital in particular, the conversion of their crops into silver, and the exploitation of their land. They allowed him to use the assets that they controlled and that were essential for his trade, and often provided him with a market for his goods as well as opportunities for additional business deals.

The study of MNA's institutional connections has revealed his position in the society of his time: how he built a network of good relations with a well-defined group of state officials, how he got a foothold in institutional assets including those belonging to temples, how dependent he was on the institutions for his economic activities, and how dependent the institutions were on MNA's goods, services and entrepreneurial skills for the successful management and maintenance of their resources.

The study of MNA's institutional connections has also enhanced our understanding of his economic success. The Egibi firm in MNA's days was professionally managed and based on a variety of institutional connections and economic activities with institutional assets, but at the same time geographically focused, internally coherent, and limited to a selective group of men with extensive economic power or with a sound professional training, with whom MNA maintained long-standing relations on the basis of the principle of mutual benefit. Some of these activities and connections went back to (were inherited from) IMB, his father, and IM, his maternal grandfather. The publication of more new texts from the Egibi archive in previous generations will, no doubt, further illuminate the roots of MNA's successful trade in commodities and of his good relationship with the authorities—in other words, the dynamics of business and politics in the Egibi archive.

Part Two

Catalogue of the Texts

1. *Thematic Catalogue*

Allotment of a share in profits. Background: MNA and his brother bought from Šaddinnu the right to collect the *šibšu*-lease on onions from the property of Bēl for the years Dar 10–11. MNA, his brother and a third person will share in the profits from this deal.	Dar 315
Apprenticeship contract to teach MNA's slave the baker's profession (LÚ.MU-*ú-tu*).	BM 41442
Cultivation of dates on the property of Bēl by seven gardeners. Refers to the collection of lease-related revenues and to MNA. Very fragmentary.	Dar 342
Delivery of a baker (LÚ.MU) to Marduk-nāṣir-apli (= MNA?). Very fragmentary.	BM 33968
Exchange? of boats. MNA is the scribe.	BM 32873
Fixation of interest and pledge of property for a silver debt. Silver due to Šaddinnu from MNA. Background: cf. Dar 315.	Dar 453+
Fixation of interest for a silver debt by MNA.	Dar 455
Ḫarrānu debt-note with MNA's capital being dates from the tithes of Bēl.	Dar 359
Labor contract to go to Elam for MNA by joining the chariot of the governor of Babylon. Receipt of part of the salary.	Dar 154
Labor contract to sail a boat to Babylon for MNA as part of the *kanšu*-service. Receipt of part of the salary.	Dar 158
Lease of a share in the right to collect toll from boats. Leased out by MNA and his co-shareholder to two individuals. The right to collect toll ultimately belonged to (*bīt qīptu ša, irbi ša*) the governor of Babylon.	TCL 13 196

Letter to Širku (= MNA?) concerning soldiers. Sent by Gūzānu (= governor of Babylon?).	CT 22 74
Letter to Širku (= MNA?) concerning the *ilku*-tax.	BM 31416
Letter to Širku (=MNA?) concerning *rikis qabli.*	BM 31438
List of quantities of silver and barley. Expenditures for boats, boat equipment and boat transports. Reference to the governor and persons known from texts of MNA's archive.	BM 30853
List of quantities of silver and personal names. Reference to the governor and persons known from texts of MNA's archive.	BM 30651
List of quantities of silver. Expenditures. Probably related to MNA.	BM 30854
Loan of silver to MNA and his brothers. With interest, mutual surety, and pledge of land.	BM 33122
Note to remind about payments for seeds that were promised to Širku (= MNA?).	BM 30641
Onions from the property of Bēl in Šaḫrīnu. Mentions Šaddinnu and MNA together. Very fragmentary.	BM 33959
Plot of land with a house built on it neighboring MNA's property. Located in Ḫubur street in the neighborhood called Šu'anna within Babylon. Very fragmentary (= sale?).	Dar 435
Plowed field from a bow-fief, and about a plow(-team) of MNA. Very fragmentary.	Dar 307
Promissory note for barley. Transport costs due from MNA to a courtier.	BM 30591
Promissory note to deliver dates (*imittu*-lease) from land at the Rab-kāṣir canal to MNA. One third is due to Bagasarū.	Dar 527
Promissory note to deliver dates (*imittu*-lease) to MNA's slave. Produce from a palm grove held by MNA's slave as pledge. Witnessed by the royal resident in the Eḫursag.	Dar 405
Promissory note to deliver flour to MNA. Property of the king (*makkūr šarri*). Delivery on account of the bow-unit of the exorcists (*ša* ^{giš}*qašti ša* ^{lú}*ašīpū*^{meš}). Administered by (*ša ina qātē*) the governor of Babylon.	BM 33954
Promissory note to pay a debt of barley to MNA.	Dar 390
Promissory note to pay a debt of barley and dates to MNA. Refers to the debtors' bow-fief land.	Dar 351

Promissory note to pay a debt of barley and dates to MNA. Pledge renewal.	Dar 144
Promissory note to pay a debt of barley, silver, and browned ghee to MNA. The silver had been transferred to the debtor to pay off his creditor. Undertaking by MNA to promptly return the promissory note for previous debts to the debtor.	Dar 541
Promissory note to pay a debt of barley to MNA's slave. Reference to additional outstanding debts.	Dar 459
Promissory note to pay a debt of dates to MNA.	BM 31058
Promissory note to pay a debt of silver and barley to Marduk-bēlšunu. Repayment according to the measure of MNA.	Dar 318
Promissory note to pay a debt of silver and dates to MNA's slave. Pledge of land. Silver had been transferred to the debtor to pay for *rikis qabli.*	Dar 308
Promissory note to pay a debt of silver and onions to Marduk-bēlšunu. No mention of MNA (but cf. Dar 318).	Dar 334
Promissory note to pay a debt of silver and onions to MNA. Repayment of the onions is to be obtained from the (debtor's) *šibšu*. Silver had been transferred to the debtor to pay for *rikis qabli*. Reference to an outstanding debt of dates, barley, onions and silver secured by pledge.	Dar 164
Promissory note to pay a debt of silver and onions to MNA. Repayment of the onions is to be obtained from the (debtor's) *šibšu*. Silver had been transferred to the debtor to pay for *rikis qabli*. References to an outstanding debt of dates, onions and silver secured by pledge.	Dar 167
Promissory note to pay a debt of silver and onions to MNA's brother. Fixation of default interest.	Dar 345
Promissory note to pay a debt of silver, barley and onions to MNA. Pledge renewal. Repayment of the onions is to be obtained from the (debtor's) *šibšu*. Silver had been transferred to the debtor to pay for *rikis qabli*. Reference to an outstanding debt of dates and barley secured by pledge.	BM 33972
Promissory note to pay a debt of silver to MNA.	BM 31951
Promissory note to pay a debt of silver to MNA. Undertaking to return the "Register of the LÚ.DÍM" (GIŠ.DA *šá* LÚ.DÍM) to the debtor upon repayment.	BM 30994
Promissory note to pay a debt of silver to MNA's brother.	BM 30541

Promissory note to pay a debt of silver. Due from MNA. Fixation of default interest. Witnessed by clerks of Esagil.	Dar 437
Promissory note to pay a debt of silver. Due from MNA. Pledge of slaves and land.	TCL 13 193
Promissory note to pay a debt of silver. Due from MNA. Part of the silver had been transferred to MNA to pay for work (*dullu*) at a canal.	Dar 411
Promissory note to pay a debt of silver. Due from MNA to the governor of Kish through an intermediary (*ina qibit ša* MNA).	BM 33936
Promissory note to pay a debt of silver. Due from MNA to a courtier.	Dar 544
Receipt of barley from MNA by a (royal) official. Transport costs. By order of (*ina qibi ša*) the governor of Babylon.	BM 33112
Receipt of barley from MNA by a royal official. Transport costs. By order of (*ina qibi ša*) the governor of Babylon.	BM 32891
Receipt of barley from MNA by a royal official. Transport costs. By order of (*ina qibi ša*) the governor of Babylon.	BM 31572
Receipt of barley from MNA by a royal official. Transport costs. By order of (*ina qibi ša*) the governor of Babylon.	BM 31786
Receipt of barley from MNA by a royal official. Transport costs. As proxy for (*ina našparti ša*) the governor of Babylon. Undertaking to register the receipt in the accounts of the governor.	BM 31393
Receipt of barley from MNA. By order of (*ina qibi ša*) a royal official.	BM 31138
Receipt of barley from MNA. For the rations of the boatman. By order of (*ina qibi ša*) the governor of Babylon.	BM 30256
Receipt of a boat-tower by MNA. From the governor's pool of forced laborers ([^{lú}*u*]*rāšu šādadu*). Reference to a register (regulating the forced-labor service) in Dûzu (GIŠ.DA *maḫrīti ša* ^{iti}*Dûzu*).	BM 31188
Receipt of a boat-tower by MNA. From the governor's pool of (forced) laborers (^{lú}*šādadu*).	BM 32932
Receipt of a boat-tower by MNA. Hired for six days a month during five months from Simānu till Araḫsamnu.	BM 30764
Receipt of a hireling (?) by MNA. Hired for six days a month during six months from Nisan till Ulūl.	BM 31118
Receipt of dates and barley by MNA. Partial repayment of a debt. Fragmentary.	BM 31718

Receipt of dates and silver from MNA by a royal official. By order of (*ina qibi*) the governor of Babylon.	BM 31036
Receipt of dates (*imittu*-lease) from a slave of MNA by a slave of Bagasarū.	Dar 542
Receipt of dates by MNA's slave.	Dar 400
Receipt of flour. Paid on behalf of MNA. Rations for one month	BM 31203
Receipt of *ilku*-silver by MNA (*kaspu … ilki*).	BM 33926
Receipt of *ilku*-silver by MNA (*kaspu … ilki*). Payment on account of a bow-unit (*ana muḫḫi* ^{giš}*qašti*).	BM 30589
Receipt of the *ilku*-tax by MNA.	BM 30819
Receipt of the *ilku*-tax by MNA.	BM 31322
Receipt of the *ilku*-tax by MNA.	BM 30243
Receipt of the *ilku*-tax by MNA.	BM 31533
Receipt of the *ilku*-tax by MNA.	BM 31517
Receipt of the *ilku*-tax by MNA.	BM 30235
Receipt of the *ilku*-tax by MNA.	BM 41607
Receipt of the *ilku*-tax by MNA. Tax related to a bridge.	BM 31227
Receipt of the *ilku*-tax (and)$^{?}$ the entire flour-tax by MNA.	BM 30297
Receipt of the *ilku*-tax (and)$^{?}$ the flour-tax by MNA.	TCL 13 197
Receipt of the *ilku*$^{!}$-tax and other contributions such as "fittings for the archer" (*unāt* ^{lú}*qašti*) by MNA.	BM 30772
Receipt of the *ilku*-tax (and)$^{?}$ *pānāt* ^{giš}*qašti* by MNA.	BM 30261
Receipt of the *ilku*-tax (and)$^{?}$ *pānāt* ^{giš}*qašti* by MNA. Tax related to a bridge.	BM 30366
Receipt of the *ilku*-tax from MNA. Paid on behalf of a third party.	TCL 13 198
Receipt of *makkasu*-dates from MNA by a courtier. For the preparation of offerings in the temple of Nergal (*ana ginê ša Nergal*). Reference to the foreman (LÚ.GAR) of the "arrangers-of-the-sacrificial-table" (LÚ *mu-ban-ni-⸢e⸣*).	BM 33930
[Receipt] of onions, *šibšu*-lease from land (along the Rab-kāṣir canal). One third is due to Bagasarū.	Dar 105

Receipt of the *miksu*-toll from MNA.	Dar 268
Receipt of the *miksu*-toll from MNA.	BM 30747
Receipt of the *miksu*-toll from MNA.	BM 31347
Receipt of payment for salaries and rations from MNA.	Dar 572
Receipt of payment for transport costs from MNA by a royal official. By order of (*ina iqbi ša*) the governor of Babylon.	BM 30639
Receipt of payment for transport costs from MNA by a royal official. By order of (*ina qibi ša*) the governor of Babylon.	BM 30980
Receipt of a person (or persons) from MNA. To do service? Person(s) is/are temple-enterer(s) (^{lú}*ērib bīti*).	BM 31449
Receipt of a person from MNA by an agent of the Commander of the Fortress. To serve in the Fortress of Babylon (LÚ.A.GÀR *ana dūr Bābili*^{ki}).	BM 31226
Receipt of persons together with the register of their enlistment (GIŠ.ŠID). To tow boats. No mention of MNA (but cf. BM 30795).	BM 30446
[Receipt] of persons together with the registers of their enlistment (GIŠ.ŠID.MEŠ). To do service? Reference to the governor of Babylon. MNA is witness.	BM 30795
Receipt of silver and barley by MNA's slave. Partial repayment of a debt.	Dar 452
Receipt of silver by MNA. Partial repayment of a debt.	BM 32858
<Receipt> of silver by MNA. Partial repayment of a debt. Reference to the sale of a prebend by the debtors.	BM 31793
Receipt of silver by MNA. Payment from a bow-unit (*ina* $^{<\text{giš}>}$*qašti*).	BM 31789
Receipt of silver by MNA's brother. Payment for *rikis qabli* (*ina rikis qabli*).	BM 31528
Receipt of silver by MNA's slave and Iddinaya. Payment for doing reserve duty in the army (*kumu kutallûtu*). On account of a bow-unit (*ana muḫḫi* ^{giš}*qašti*).	Dar 430
Receipt of silver from MNA.	b 2800
<Receipt> of silver from MNA.	Dar 213
Receipt of silver from MNA.	TCL 13 185

Receipt of silver from MNA by a royal official. Price of the dates. Settled among the brothers of the parties involved. Undertaking by the official to give any document concerning this silver to MNA's brother.	Dar 338
Receipt of silver from MNA. Payment for *rikis qabli*. By order of (*ina qibi ša*) Murašû/Marduk-šuma-iddin//Ilu-tillatī.	Dar 156
Receipt of silver from MNA. Payment for *rikis qabli*. By order of (*ina qibi ša*) the governor of Babylon.	Dar 206
Receipt of silver from MNA. Partial payment of a debt on behalf of two other persons.	Dar 310
Receipt of silver from MNA. Partial repayment of salary.	Dar 215
Receipt of silver from MNA. Purchase price for a boat. Prompt return of the promissory note about the boat to MNA.	BM 30961
Receipt of silver from MNA. Refers to an order (*šipirtu*) issued by Šaddinnu.	BM 31018
Receipt of silver from MNA. Rent for a boat.	Dar 576
Receipt of silver from MNA. Rent for a boat.	BM 31554
Receipt of silver from MNA. Undertaking to pay remainder upon return from Elam. By order of (*ina qibi*) the governor of Babylon.	Dar 577
Receipt of silver from MNA's slave and Iddinaya by the messenger of a deputy. For the rations of a group of workmen (^{lú}*za-ar-ga-a-a*). On account of a bow-unit (*ša* ^{giš}*qašti*).	BM 31026
Receipt of silver from MNA's son paid on behalf of MNA. For military equipment (*rikis qabli*) and travel provisions (*ṣidēti*). Paid to MNA's brother. Reference to a previous settlement of their *qinayātu*-duties.	BM 33928
Receipt of silver paid on behalf of MNA. Partial repayment of a debt.	Dar 450
Receipt of silver paid on behalf of MNA. Payment of a debt due to Šaddinnu.	Dar 472
Receipt of wool from MNA by a weaver of Lugal-Marada. As proxy for (*ina našpartu ša*) the chief administrator of the E'igi-kalamma.	Dar 182
Release from army service for the next three and a half months. Reference to persons known from texts in MNA's archive.	BM 30274
Renting of a boat by MNA.	BM 31891

Renting of a boat by MNA.	BM 30799
Renting of a boat by MNA.	Dar 138
Renting of a boat by MNA and receipt of the rent money.	BM 30270
Renting of a boat by MNA and receipt of the rent money.	BM 30490
Renting of a boat by MNA's son.	BM 31690^{+}
Renting of a small house at the harbor and a loft by MNA's son.	BM 41453
Sale of a boat. MNA assumes warranty on behalf of the seller.	BM 32883
Sale of a boat to MNA and receipt of the purchase price.	BM 30370
Sale of a slave to MNA and receipt of the purchase price.	Dar 212
[Sale] of a boat to MNA and [receipt] of the [purchase] price. Very Fragmentary.	OECT 10 234
Settlement of a silver debt through sale of land and slaves by MNA to his creditor. A previous house sale became void after the house had been seized by the Esagil temple.	BM 33935
Summons to settle a debt of silver. Silver due to MNA's brother.	Dar 369
Summons to settle debts with MNA.	Dar 509
Summons to settle debts with MNA.	BM 31360
Summons to settle the payment of silver for the "contribution of the archer" (*nidintu šá* ^{lú}*qašti*) with MNA.	BM 30629
Summons to transmit crops from the land of Bagasarū, and to arrange for their proper registration.	Dar 296
Two heifers. Mentions the slave of MNA, a messenger of the *aba-rakku*-official (^{lú}*mar a-ba-rak-ku*), and a farmer (^{lú}*ikkaru*) of Nergal. Fragmentary.	BM 31976
Undertaking to transmit an order (*šipirtu*) issued by Nergal-ēṭir to MNA requiring him to pay silver.	Dar 552
Undertaking to transmit an order (*šipirtu*) issued by Nergal-ēṭir to MNA requiring him to pay silver.	Dar 573
Undertaking to bring the thieves in handcuffs to the house of MNA. The thieves had been caught in the city of the resident between the rivers (*ina bīrit nārāti ina āli ša* ^{lú}*qīpi*).	BM 41449
Undertaking to register the receipt of dates from MNA in the accounts of the temple of Bēl (*ina* GIŠ.DA *ša Bēl*).	BM 30233

Undertaking under oath to bring along one's sons. MNA is the scribe. BM 33121

Undertaking under oath to settle debts to MBU with MNA. Reference to the pledge of income from an *ērib bīti* prebend. BM 30965

2. *Chronological Catalogue*

Text	*Day*	*Month*	*Year (Darius)*	*Julian Calendar (B.C.E.)*	*Place*
Dar 206	-	vi(b)	$3^{!}$	Sept.-Oct. 519	Babylon
Dar 105	5	i	4	15 April 518	Bīt-rab-kāṣir
BM 30799	26	v	$4^{?}$	2 Sept. $518^{?}$	broken
Dar 138	9 (or 1)	x	4	10 (or 2) Jan. 517	Babylon
Dar 144	25	xi	4	24 Feb. 517	Šaḫrīnu
Dar 154	15	i	5	13 April 517	Babylon
Dar 156	24	i	5	22 April 517	Babylon
Dar 158	7	iii	5	3 June 517	Babylon
Dar 164	1	v	5	27 July 517	Šaḫrīnu
Dar 167	[$1^{?}$]	v	[$5^{?}$]	[27] July [517]$^{?}$	[Šaḫrīnu]
Dar 182	27	viii	5	19 Nov. 517	Babylon
BM 30629	12	vii	6	24 Oct. 516	Ḫursag-kalamma
Dar 212	26	ix	6	5 Jan. 515	Ḫaḫḫuru-ša-Kalbaya
Dar 213	7	x	6	16 Jan. 515	Babylon
Dar 215	20	x	6	29 Jan. 515	Babylon
b 2800	6	xi	[6]	13 Feb. [515]	Babylon
TCL 13 185	12	xi	7	9 Feb. 514	Babylon
BM 41449	3^{+}	xii(a)	[5 or 8]	21^{+} Feb. 516 or 18^{+} Feb. 513	Babylon
BM 32883	10	i	10	14 April 512	Babylon
Dar 268	18	iv	⸢10⸣	19 July 512	Babylon
Dar 296	18	i	11	11 April 511	Babylon
BM 31018	2	v	11	22 July 511	Babylon
Dar 307	19	vi(b)	11	6 Oct. 511	Babylon

Text	*Day*	*Month*	*Year (Darius)*	*Julian Calendar (B.C.E.)*	*Place*
Dar 308	26	vii	11	12 Nov. 511	Šaḫrīnu
Dar 310	9	xi	11	20 Feb. 510	Babylon
Dar 315	21	xii	11	3 April 510	Šaḫrīnu
Dar 318	16	i	12	28 April 510	Babylon
BM 33954	25	iv?	12	3 Aug.? 510	Babylon
Dar 334	15	viii	12	20 Nov. 510	Babylon
Dar 338	24	xii	12	25 March 509	Babylon
Dar 342	27	[-]	12	April 510 - March 509	Šaḫrīnu
Dar 345	2	i	13	2 April 509	Babylon
Dar 351	25	v	13	21 Aug. 509	Babylon
Dar 359	⸢29⸣	x	13	20 Jan. 508	Ālu-ša-kī-Bēl
Dar 369	15	i	14	4 May 508	Šaḫrīnu
Dar 390	15	xi	14	24 Feb. 507	Ālu-ša-Libbi-ālaya, eqli-ša-Bēl
BM 33926	17	⸢iv⸣	15	22 July 507	Babylon
BM 31026	3	v	15	7 Aug. 507	Šaḫrinu
Dar 400	3	v	15	7 Aug. 507	Šaḫrīnu
Dar 405	4	vii	15	7 Oct. 507	Šaḫrīnu
Dar 411	22	viii	15	24 Nov. 507	Nār-šarri-ša-Elam
BM 33968	[-]	ix	[15]	Feb.-early March 506	Babylon
Dar 430	30	vi	16	15 Sept. 506	Šaḫrīnu
BM 33936	3	xii(a)	[16]	20 Feb. [505]	Šušan
Dar 435+	10	xii(b)	16	27 March 505	Šušan
TCL 13 193	10	xii(b)	16	27 March 505	Šušan

Text	*Day*	*Month*	*Year (Darius)*	*Julian Calendar (B.C.E.)*	*Place*
Dar 437	[-]	[xii$^?$]	16	April 506 - March 505	Šušan
Dar 450	20	x	17	27 Jan. 504	Babylon
Dar 452	22	x	17	29 Jan. 504	Šaḫrīnu
BM 33959	24	x	17	31 Jan. 504	Babylon
Dar 453$^+$	24	x	17	31 Jan. 504	Babylon
Dar 455	15	xi	17	20 Feb. 504	Babylon
Dar 459	7	xii	17	14 March 504	Šaḫrīnu
BM 33122	9	[-]	17	April 505 - March 504	broken
Dar 472	3	x	18	30 Dec. 504	Babylon
Dar 509	8	ix	20	13 Dec. 502	Babylon
Dar 527	17	vii	21	13 Oct. 501	Bīt-ṭāb-Bēl
Dar 541	3	iii	22	23 May 500	Bīt-ṭāb-Bēl
Dar 542	20	iii	22	9 June 500	—
Dar 544	12	iv	22$^?$	30 June 500	Babylon
Dar 552	1	x	22	14 Dec. 500	Babylon
Dar 572	30	ix	23	1 Jan. 498	broken
Dar 573	1	x	23	2 Jan. 498	Pāni-abul-Enlil
BM 31554	11 or 21	x	23	12 or 22 Jan. 498	Babylon
Dar 576	22	x	23	23 Jan. 498	Babylon
Dar 577	[-]	x	23	Jan. 498	Babylon
BM 31449	[-]	[-]	23$^+$	April 498 -	Babylon
BM 41607	8	iv	24	4 July 498	broken
BM 30274	13	iv	24	9 July 498	Babylon
BM 30256	2	vii	24	25 Sept. 498	Babylon

Text	*Day*	*Month*	*Year (Darius)*	*Julian Calendar (B.C.E.)*	*Place*
BM 30446	4	vii	24	27 Sept. 498	broken
BM 32932	18	vii	24	11 Oct. 498	Babylon
BM 30297	6	viii	24	29 Oct. 498	Babylon
BM 31188	25	[-]	24	April 498 - March 497	Babylon
BM 31138	19	iii	25	4 July 497	Babylon
BM 30764	23	iii	25	8 July 497	Babylon
BM 31572	7	iv	25 (or 26)	21 July 497 or 11 July 496	Babylon
BM 31322	16	iv	25	30 July 497	Babylon
BM 33112	17	v	25	30 Aug. 497	Babylon
BM 30639	28	vii	25	8 Nov. 497	Babylon
BM 30243	7	viii	25	17 Nov. 497	Babylon
BM 31393	[-]	viii	25	Nov.-Dec. 497	Babylon
BM 31533	1	xii	25	9 March 496	Šabīlu
BM 30819	5$^?$	xii	25	13$^?$ March 496	Šabīlu
BM 31118	4	[-]	25	April 497 - March 496	Babylon
BM 31227	4	[-]	25	April 497 - March 496	Bāb-Bitāqu
BM 31517	25	[-]	25	April 497 - March 496	Babylon
BM 30541	[-]	[-]	⸢25⸣	April 497 - March 496	Babylon
BM 31786	[-]	[-]	25	April 497 - March 496	Babylon
BM 31951	[-]	[-]	25	April 497 - March 496	Šaḫrīnu
BM 30235	5	i	26	12 April 496	Babylon
BM 31036	18	ii	26	24 May 496	Babylon

Text	*Day*	*Month*	*Year (Darius)*	*Julian Calendar (B.C.E.)*	*Place*
BM 30589	20	iii	26	25 June 496	Babylon
BM 30261	13	iv	2[6$^{?}$]	17 July 496$^{?}$	Babylon
BM 30370	3–9	v	26	5–11 Aug. 496	Babylon
BM 30965	21	v	26	23 Aug. 496	Babylon
BM 31528	26	v	26	28 Aug. 496	Babylon
BM 30961	12	vi	26	13 Sept. 496	Babylon
BM 31667^{+}	12	vi	26	13 Sept. 496	Babylon
TCL 13 196	1	vii	26	1 Oct. 496	Babylon
BM 30994	5	vii	26	5 Oct. 496	Babylon
BM 31722^{+}	5	vii	26	5 Oct. 496	Babylon
BM 31226	9	vii	26	9 Oct. 496	Babylon
BM 30980	4	viii	26	3 Nov. 496	Babylon
BM 30366	7	viii	26	6 Nov. 496	Babylon
TCL 13 197	27	viii	26	26 Nov. 496	Babylon
BM 31360	2	ix	26	30 Nov. 496	broken
BM 30795	26	x	26	23 Jan. 495	Babylon
BM 30490	5	xii	⸢26⸣	2 March 495	Babylon
BM 30270	6	xii	26	3 March 495	Babylon
BM 41442	15	xii	26	12 March 495	Babylon
BM 32873	16	xii	26	13 March 495	Babylon
BM 30772	20	xii	26	17 March 495	Babylon
OECT 10 234	⸢20^{+}⸣	[-]	26	April 496 - March 495	broken
TCL 13 198	11	i	27	7 April 495	Babylon
BM 31976	24	iii	27	18 June 495	Šaḫrīnu
BM 31793	11	x	27 or 28	28 Dec. 495 or 17 Jan. 493	broken

Text	*Day*	*Month*	*Year (Darius)*	*Julian Calendar (B.C.E.)*	*Place*
BM 33930	3	⸢iii⸣	29	4 ⸢June⸣ 493	Šaḫrīnu
BM 32858	13	vii	31	19 Oct. 491	Babylon
BM 31690^{+}	18	viii	31	23 Nov. 491	Babylon
BM 30233	7	xii	31	9 March 490	Babylon
BM 33928	28	ii	35$^{!}$	25 May 487$^{!}$	Babylon
BM 30591	27	vii	35	19 Oct. 487	Babylon
BM 41453	19	[-]	[35 or 36]	27 Dec. 486$^{?}$	broken
BM 31058	18	i	[-]	March - April	Babylon
BM 31798	8 or 9	iv	[-]	June - July	broken
BM 32891	11	iv	[-]	June - July	Babylon
BM 31891	7	vi	[-]	Aug. - Sept.	Babylon
BM 31203	4	viii	[-]	Oct. - Nov.	Babylon
BM 31347	20	ix	[-]	Nov. - Dec.	broken
BM 33935	25	xi	[-]	Jan. - Feb.	Kār Parakki
BM 33121	20^{+}	xii(a)	[-]	Feb. - March	Til-Gula
BM 30641	30	vii	(no year)	Sept. - Oct.	no place
BM 30651	no date				no place
BM 30747	no date (refers to the *miksu* for onions of the 10th year)				no place
BM 30853	no date (between 22–24 Dar, i.e., April 500 - March 497?)				no place
BM 30854	no date				no place
BM 31377	no date				no place
BM 31416	no date				no place
BM 31438	no date				no place
CT 22 74	no date				no place

Text	*Day*	*Month*	*Year (Darius)*	*Julian Calendar (B.C.E.)*	*Place*
BM 33972	broken (between 5 Dar and Nisan 6 Dar, i.e., April 517 - April 516)				Šaḫrīnu
BM 31718	broken				broken

3. *List of Tablets and Texts Published in Present Volume*

Abraham, *OLA* 65	see s.v. BM 30591	BM 31188	No. 39
b 2800	No. 1	BM 31203	No. 40
BM 30233	No. 2	BM 31226	No. 41
BM 30235	No. 3	BM 31227	No. 42
BM 30243	No. 4	BM 31322	No. 43
BM 30256	No. 5	BM 31347	No. 44
BM 30261	No. 6	BM 31360	No. 45
BM 30270	No. 7	BM 31393	No. 46
BM 30274	No. 8	BM 31416	No. 47
BM 30297	No. 9	BM 31438	No. 48
BM 30366	No. 10	BM 31449	No. 49
BM 30370	No. 11	BM 31517	No. 50
BM 30446	No. 12	BM 31528	No. 51
BM 30490	No. 13	BM 31533	No. 52
BM 30541	No. 14	BM 31554	No. 53
BM 30589	No. 15	BM 31572	No. 54
BM 30591	No. 16	BM 31641	No. 55
BM 30629	No. 17	BM 31667	No. 55
BM 30639	No. 18	BM 31690	No. 56
BM 30641	No. 19	BM 31718	No. 57
BM 30651	No. 20	BM 31722	No. 58
BM 30658	No. 56	BM 31786	No. 59
BM 30747	No. 21	BM 31793	No. 60
BM 30764	No. 22	BM 31798	No. 61
BM 30772	No. 23	BM 31891	No. 62
BM 30795	No. 24	BM 31951	No. 63
BM 30799	No. 25	BM 31976	No. 64
BM 30819	No. 26	BM 31977	No. 65
BM 30853	No. 27	BM 32858	No. 66
BM 30854	No. 28	BM 32873	No. 67
BM 30961	No. 29	BM 32883	No. 68
BM 30965	No. 30	BM 32891	No. 69
BM 30980	No. 31	BM 32932	No. 70
BM 30994	No. 32	BM 33112	No. 71
BM 31018	No. 33	BM 33121	No. 72
BM 31026	No. 34	BM 33122	No. 73
BM 31036	No. 35	BM 33926	No. 74
BM 31058	No. 36	BM 33928	No. 75
BM 31118	No. 37	BM 33930	No. 76
BM 31138	No. 38	BM 33935	No. 77
		BM 33936	No. 78

BM 33954	No. 79
BM 33957	see s.v. BM 33928
BM 33959	No. 80
BM 33962	No. 81
BM 33968	No. 82
BM 33972	No. 83
BM 35235	No. 58
BM 41442	No. 84
BM 41449	No. 85
BM 41453	No. 86
BM 41607	No. 87
BOR 1, 83	see s.v. BM 41442
BRM 1 83	see s.v. BM 30980
CT 22 74	No. 88
Dar 105	No. 89
Dar 138	No. 90
Dar 144	No. 91
Dar 154	No. 92
Dar 156	No. 93
Dar 158	No. 94
Dar 164	No. 95
Dar 167	No. 96
Dar 182	No. 97
Dar 206	No. 98
Dar 212	No. 99
Dar 213	No. 100
Dar 215	No. 101
Dar 268	No. 102
Dar 296	No. 103
Dar 307	No. 104
Dar 308	No. 105
Dar 310	No. 106
Dar 315	No. 107
Dar 318	No. 108
Dar 334	No. 109
Dar 338	No. 110
Dar 342	No. 111
Dar 345	No. 112
Dar 351	No. 113
Dar 359	No. 114
Dar 369	No. 115
Dar 390	No. 116
Dar 400	No. 117
Dar 405	No. 118
Dar 411	No. 119
Dar 430	No. 120
Dar 435	No. 121
Dar 437	No. 122
Dar 450	No. 123
Dar 452	No. 124
Dar 453^{+}	No. 125
Dar 455	No. 126
Dar 459	No. 127
Dar 472	No. 128
Dar 509	No. 129
Dar 527	No. 130
Dar 534	see s.v. Dar 542
Dar 541	No. 131
Dar 542	No. 132
Dar 544	No. 133
Dar 552	No. 134
Dar 572	No. 135
Dar 573	No. 136
Dar 576	No. 137
Dar 577	No. 138
Liv 25	see s.v. BM 33936
OECT 10 234	No. 139
Pinches, Peek 18	see s.v. TCL 13 196
TCL 13 185	No. 140
TCL 13 193	No. 141
TCL 13 196	No. 142
TCL 13 197	No. 143
TCL 13 198	No. 144

Text Editions

No. 1

b 2800

Museum No.: unknown (Bertin copy 2800)
Date: 6/xi/[6] Dar (13 February [515] B.C.E.)
Place: Babylon
Content: Receipt of silver from MNA.

Obv.

1 [x] MA.NA KÙ.BABBAR *a-di* ½ MA.NA KÙ.BABBAR
2 *šá a-na* ^{m}MU-GIN A-*šú šá* ^{md}EN-SUR
3 A LÚ.SANGA-^{d}*na-na-a* SUM.NA
4 ^{md}EN-*na-din*-IBILA *ù* ^{md}AG-MU
5 DUMU.MEŠ *šá* ^{md}EN-DIN-*iṭ* A LÚ.BAḪAR$_{2}$
6 *i-na* ŠU.II ^{md}AMAR.UTU-*na-ṣir*-IBILA
7 A-*šú šá* ^{m}KI-^{d}AMAR.UTU-DIN A ^{m}*e-gi-bi*

Lo. E.

8 *i-na ú-ìl-tì-šú-nu maḫ-ru*

Rev.

9 LÚ *mu-kin-nu* ^{m}ÌR-^{d}ME.ME A-*šú šá*
10 ^{md}AMAR.UTU-MU-URU$_{3}$ A ^{m}*na-ba-a-a*
11 ^{m}*ri-mut*-^{d}EN A-*šú šá* ^{m}ÌR-*ia* A LÚ.DÍM
12 ^{md}AG-*bul-liṭ-su* A-*šú šá* ^{m}MU-^{d}AG
13 A ^{m}*da-bi-bi* ^{md}EN-*ú-bal-liṭ*
14 LÚ.DUB.SAR A-*šú šá* ^{md}AG-MU A LÚ.GAL.DÙ
15 TIN.TIR.KI ITI.ZÍZ UD.6.KAM MU.[x.KAM]

U. E.

16 ^{m}*da-ri-ia-muš* LUGAL TIN.TIR.KI
17 LUGAL KUR.KUR

Translation

[x] mina of silver, in addition to half the mina of silver that has (already) been given to Šuma-ukīn, son of Bēl-ēṭir, descendant of Šangû-Nanaya: Bēl-nādin-apli and Nabû-iddin, sons of Bēl-uballiṭ, descendant of Paḫāru, have received (it) from MNA$_1$ from the debts owed by them (to Šuma-ukīn).

Witnesses:
Arad-Ninurta/Marduk-šuma-uṣur//Nabaya
Rīmūt-Bēl/Ardiya//Itinnu
Nabû-bullissu/Iddin-Nabû//Dābibī
The scribe: Bēl-uballiṭ/Nabû-iddin//Rab-banê
(Place + Date).

Comment

L. 1–3: This previous transfer of half a mina of silver is actually recorded in Dar 213 (re-edited below). A year later MNA paid an additional two minas to the same Šuma-ukīn for the account of Bēl-nādin-apli and his brothers (TCL 13 185). Since the text under consideration does not refer back to the two minas of TCL 13 185, but only to half the mina of Dar 213 it is to be dated after the latter and before the former text (see also commentary at line 15 below).

L. 15: The year in which b 2800 was drafted is broken off (6/xi/[-] Dar), but it can be reconstructed on the basis of a comparison with Dar 213 (7/x/6 Dar) and TCL 13 185 (12/xi/7 Dar), which deal with the same or a similar matter as is dealt with in b 2800. As a matter of fact, b 2800 was written after Dar 213 and before TCL 13 185 for reasons explained at the commentary to lines 1–3. Consequently, its date can be reconstructed as: 6/xi/[6] Dar.

No. 2

BM 30233
Copy: Bertin copy 2702
Date: 7/xii/31 Dar (9 March 490 B.C.E.)
Place: Babylon
Content: Undertaking to register the receipt of dates from MNA in the accounts of the temple of Bēl (*ina* GIŠ.DA *ša Bēl*).

Obv.

1 ⸢50⸣ GUR ZÚ.LUM.MA *la ga-ma-ru-tu*$_4$
2 NÍG.GA ^{d}EN *šá* URU *šá-ḫar-ri-in-nu*
3 ^{md}AG-*bul-liṭ-su* DUMU *šá* ^{m}*mu-ra-nu*
4 DUMU LÚ.BAḪAR$_2$ *i-na* GIŠ.DA *šá* ^{d}EN
5 *a-na muḫ-ḫi* ^{m}*da-aḫ-ḫu-ú-a*
6 *u* ^{md}EN-IBILA-MU *a-di-i qí-it*
7 *šá* ITI.ŠE *ina* GIŠ.DA *ú-šá-az-za*<*-az*>*-ma*

8 *a-na* ^{m}*ši-rik* A-*šú šá* ^{m}MU-*a*
9 A ^{m}*e-gì-bi ú-kal-lam*

REV.

10 LÚ *mu-kin-nu* ^{md}EN-EDURU-URU$_3$ A-*šú šá*
11 ^{md}EN-ŠEŠ.MEŠ-MU A ^{m}GAL-1-*ba-ni-e*
12 ^{m}ÌR<-^{d}>KÁ A-*šú šá* ^{m}*ḫa-ba-ṣi-ru*
13 A ^{m}*ir-a-ni* ^{md}EN-EDURU-MU A-*šú šá* {^{m}}
14 ^{m}*pa-da-a* ^{m}KI-^{d}AMAR.UTU-DIN A-*šú šá*
15 ^{md}EN-NUMUN
16 ^{md}AG-EN-*šú-nu* LÚ.UMBISAG A-*šú šá* ^{md}AG-*na-din*-ŠEŠ
17 A LÚ.ŠITIM TIN.TIR.KI ITI.ŠE UD.7.KAM

LE. E.

18 MU.31.KAM ^{m}*da-a-ri-ia-muš*
19 [LUGAL] TIN.TIR.KI *u* KUR.KUR

TRANSLATION

Nabû-bullissu, son of Mūrānu, descendant of Paḫāru will register the (receipt of) fifty *kor* of dates (from)$^{?}$ the property of Bēl in Šaḫrīnu, in partial payment, in the register of Bēl for the account of Daḫḫûa and Bēl-apla-iddin by the end of Addar; and he will show (the receipt) to MNA$_2$.

Witnesses:
Bēl-apla-uṣur/Bēl-aḫḫē-iddin//Rab-banê
Arad-Bāba/Ḫabaṣīru//Ir'anni
Bēl-apla-iddin/Padā
Itti-Marduk-balāṭu/Bēl-zēri
The scribe: Nabû-bēlšunu/Nabû-nādin-aḫi//Itinnu
(Place + Date)

COMMENT

L. 4: LÚ.BAḪAR$_2$ is written LÚ.DUG.<QA>.BUR.

L. 4–9: For the "clearance formula," see Stolper, *Entrepreneurs*, 33 n. 119 (with bibliography); Von Dassow, CTMMA 3, 203; Weszeli-Baker, *WZKM* 87, 234–36; and Stolper's response to the latter in *JCS* 53, 120.

L. 5: The name Daḫḫûa (or read Ṭaḫḫûa? mng. unknown) may be spelled with a single ḫ (Tallqvist, *NbN*, 52 and Bongenaar, *Ebabbar*, 386), or a double one (Stolper, *JCS* 53 No. 9: 3; CTMMA 3 127: 5 and CTMMA 3 128: 5).

L. 11: The writing ^{m}GAL-1-*ba-ni-e*, with the use of the 1-sign, for Rab-banê is peculiar.

L. 14: The name ^{m}*pa-da-a* probably consists of the Iranian element **pāta* "protected," and is attested in one other Babylonian document from the late period, viz. a late-Achaemenid record of deposit from Babylon (Stolper, *AION* 77 No. 1: 11, Nabû-balāssu-iqbi DUMU *šá* ^{m}*pa-da-a*). The Iranian element **pāta*, however, frequently occurs in compound names in the Neo- and Late Babylonian periods, as for instance, in the name Bagapāta (wr. *-pa-da* or *-pa-a-tú*; refs. at Dandamaev, *Iranians*, 59 no. 95). In my opinion, ^{m}*pa-da-a* does, most likely, not reflect the West Semitic root P-D-Y "to redeem," because Babylonian names containing this root (in the Qal perfect 3 m. sg.) are differently spelled, viz. ^{m}*pa-da*(-ʾ) rather than ^{m}*pa-da-a* as in the case under consideration. See, for instance, the spellings of the compound name Pedayah, viz. ^{m}*pa-da*(-ʾ*-ia*)*-a-ma*, and that of its hypocoristicon, viz. Padiya, spelled ^{m}*pa-di-ia* (Zadok, *West Semites*, 86f. and 256; and *idem*, *OLA* 28, 30, 31 n. 60, 98 and 99 n. 74).

L. 15: Two-thirds of this line are empty, i.e., the scribe started a new line to write his name and the date formula.

No. 3

BM 30235
Copy: Bertin copy 2620
Date: 5/i/26 Dar (12 April 496 B.C.E.)
Place: Babylon
Content: Receipt of the *ilku*-tax by MNA.

OBV.

1 *il-ki šá* TA ITI.BÁR MU.25.KAM
2 EN TIL ITI.ŠE MU.25.KAM
3 ^{m}*da-ri-ia-muš* LUGAL TIN.TIR.KI *u* KUR.KUR
4 *šá* ^{m}*ta-at-tan-nu* A-*šú šá* ^{md}AG-DIN-*su*-E A ^{m}*ba-bu-tu*
5 ^{m}*ši-iš-ki* A-*šú šá* ^{m}SUM.NA-*a* A ^{m}*e-gì-bi*
6 *ina* ŠU.II ^{m}MU-^{d}AG A-*šú šá* ^{m}ŠEŠ.MEŠ-MU-^{d}AMAR.UTU
7 *a-na muḫ-ḫi* ^{m}*ta-at-tan-nu*
8 *ma-ḫi-ir*

REV.

9 LÚ *mu-kin*$_{7}$ ^{m}*ta-at-tan-nu* A-*šú šá* ^{md}AG-KÁD
10 A ^{m}*da-bi-bi*
11 ^{md}U.GUR-MU A-*šú šá* ^{md}AG-*it-tan-nu*
12 ^{m}*šu-lum*-TIN.TIR.KI A-*šú šá* ^{md}AG-NUMUN-MU
13 ^{m}*ḫaš-šá-da-a-a* A-*šú šá* ^{md}EN-MU
14 LÚ.UMBISAG ^{m}NÍG.BA-*ia* A-*šú šá* ^{m}*ni-din-tu*$_{4}$ A LÚ.SANGA-BÁR
15 TIN.TIR.KI ITI.BÁR UD.5.KAM
16 MU.26.KAM ^{m}*da-ri-ia-muš*

U. E.

17 LUGAL TIN.TIR.KI *u* KUR.KUR.MEŠ

Translation

The *ilku*-tax from Nisan of the twenty-fifth year till the end of Addar of the twenty-fifth year of Darius, king of Babylon and the lands, is due from Tattannu, son of Nabû-balāssu-iqbi, descendant of Bābūtu: MNA_2 has received (it) from Iddin-Nabû, son of Aḫḫē-iddin-Marduk, for Tattannu's account.

Witnesses:
Tattannu/Nabû-kāṣir//Dābibī
Nergal-iddin/Nabû-ittannu
Šulum-Bābili/Nabû-zēra-iddin(//Ir'anni?)
Ḫašdaya/Bēl-iddin
The scribe: Qīštiya/Nidintu//Šangû-parakki
(Place + Date).

Comment

L. 12: If this Šulum-Bābili, son of Nabû-zēra-iddin, belonged to the Ir'anni family, we find him among the witnesses in *Bēl-rēmanni*, 151 = BM 42352. The latter text was written in Sippar in Darius' 20th year and belongs to the Bēl-rēmanni archive. It records the receipt of silver for works on a canal in Elam due from Bēl-rēmanni and another person, paid for the account of their bow. The works fell under the administrative authority of the governor of Babylon, who is, however, not cited by name. The reference to the governor links this Sippar text to Babylon so that the occurrence of men known from the Babylon texts is not surprising. The men from Babylon mentioned in *Bēl-rēmanni*, 151 are: the unnamed governor of Babylon, Šulum-Bābili/Nabû-zēra-iddin//Ir'anni and probably also Libluṭ/Mušēzib-Marduk. The latter may be identified with Libluṭ/Mušēzib-Marduk(//Nappāḫu?), district governor of Šaḫrīnu according to Dar 338 (re-edited below).

No. 4

BM 30243
Copy: Bertin copy 2572
Date: 7/viii/25 Dar (17 November 497 B.C.E.)
Place: Babylon
Content: Receipt of the *ilku*-tax by MNA.

OBV.

1 ⅓ MA.NA 1$^{!}$ GÍN KÙ.BABBAR UD-*ú šá ina* 1 GÍN *bit-qa nu-*⸢*uḫ-ḫu*⸣-[*tu*]
2 *il-ki šá* ^{md}EN-GI *ù* ^{md}EN-KAR-*ir* DUMU.MEŠ *šá*
3 ^{md}EN-BA-*šá* DUMU LÚ.SANGA-^{d}IDIM *šá* TA ITI.BÁR MU.25.KAM
4 *a-di* TIL ITI.ŠE MU.25.KAM ^{m}*da-a-ri-ia-muš*
5 LUGAL ^{m}*ši-iš-ki* DUMU-*šú šá* ^{m}SUM.NA-*a* DUMU ^{m}*e-gi-bi*
6 ⸢*i-na*⸣ *qá-at* ^{m}*ri-mu-tu* A-*šú šá* ^{m}*kal-ba-a*
7 [*ana muḫ*]-*ḫi* ^{md}EN-GI *ù* ^{md}EN-KAR-*ir*
8 [*ma*]-*ḫi-ir* 1-*en*.TA.ÀM TI-*ú*

REV.

9 LÚ *mu-kin-nu* ^{md}EN-*ka-ṣir* A-*šú šá* ^{m}*nu-um-mu-*⸢*ru*⸣
10 A ^{m}*da-bi-bi* ^{md}EN-*ki-šìr* A-*šú šá* ^{md}AG-A-MU
11 A LÚ.SANGA-^{d}IDIM ^{md}AG-*ku-ṣur-šú* A-*šú šá* ^{md}AMAR.UTU-SUR
12 ^{m}*na-din* A-*šú šá* ^{m}*zu-ba-a-ta-i-li*
13 ^{m}ÌR-^{d}*ba-ba*$_{6}$ DUB.SAR DUMU LÚ.AZLAG
14 TIN.TIR.KI ITI.APIN UD.7.KAM MU.25.KAM
15 ^{m}*da-a-ri-ia-muš* LUGAL TIN.TIR.KI
16 LUGAL KUR.KUR

TRANSLATION

One-third mina and one$^{!}$ shekel of white, medium-qualit[y] silver, of which one-eighth is alloy, the *ilku*-tax from Nisan of the twenty-fifth year till the end of Addar of the twenty-fifth year of King Darius, are due from Bēl-ušallim and Bēl-ēṭir, sons of Bēl-iqīša, descendant of Šangû-Ea: MNA$_{2}$ [has] received (it) from Rīmūt, son of Kalbaya, [for the ac]count of Bēl-ušallim and Bēl-ēṭir. They have taken one (copy of the document) each.

Witnesses:
Bēl-kāṣir/Nummuru//Dābibī
Bēl-kēšir/Nabû-apla-iddin//Šangû-Ea
Nabû-kuṣuršu/Marduk-ēṭir
Nādin/Zubbât-ili
The scribe: Arad-Bāba//Ašlāku
(Place + Date).

COMMENT

L. 1: The beginning of the line actually reads ⅓ MA.NA GÍN. In order to read ⅓ MA.NA 1$^{!}$ GÍN one has to add a vertical wedge to the GÍN.

No. 5

BM 30256
Copy: Bertin copy 2537
Date: 2/vii/24 Dar (25 September 498 B.C.E.)
Place: Babylon
Content: Receipt of barley from MNA. For the rations of the boatman. By order of (*ina qibi ša*) the governor of Babylon.

OBV.

1 3 GUR ŠE.BAR *ina qí-bi šá*
2 ^{m}*ina-é-sag-íl-li-bir*
3 LÚ.UŠ$_4$-GAR TIN.TIR.KI ^{m}*ni-din-tu$_4$*-^{d}EN-*dam-qát*
4 LÚ *qal-la šá* ^{m}*ina-é-sag-íl-li-bir ina* ŠU.II
5 ^{m}*šiš-ki* A-*šú šá* ^{m}MU-*a* A ^{m}*e-gì-bi*
6 *ma-ḫi-ir* ŠE.BAR *šá a-na* KURUM$_6$.ḪI.A
7 *šá* LÚ.MÁ-LAḪ$_4$.MEŠ *šá ina lìb-bi* GIŠ.MÁ
8 ⸢*šá*⸣ KAŠ.ḪI.A *šá a-na* URU.KUR.TI {URU.KUR.TI}
9 ⸢*il*⸣-*la-ku* SUM.NA-*tu$_4$*

REV.

10 LÚ *mu-kin-nu* ^{m}EN-*šú-nu* A-*šú šá*
11 ^{m}*lib-luṭ* ^{m}ÌR-*ia* A-*šú šá*
12 ^{md}AG-KAR-*ir* ^{m}*ap-la-a* A-*šú šá* ^{m}*ba-zu-zu*
13 A ^{m}*ba-bu-tu* ^{md}EN-SU A-*šú šá*
14 ^{m}*kal-ba-a* A ^{m}MU-*líb-šú*
15 ^{m}*ú-bar* A-*šú šá* ^{md}EN-MU A ^{md}IDIM-*pat-ta-nu*
16 LÚ.UMBISAG ^{md}EN-*it-tan-nu* A-*šú šá*
17 ^{m}MU-^{d}EN TIN.TIR.KI ITI.DU$_6$
18 ⸢UD⸣.2.KAM MU.24.KAM
19 [^{m}*d*]*a-ri-ia-muš* LUGAL E.KI
20 [LUGAL] KUR.KUR.MEŠ

TRANSLATION

By order of Ina-Esagil-lilbur, governor of Babylon, Nidinti-Bēl-damqat, a slave of Ina-Esagil-lilbur, has received three *kor* of barley from MNA$_2$. It is the barley that has been given for the rations of the boatmen who are on the boat (loaded) with beer that will sail to Dūr-(Kuri)galzu {Dūr-(Kuri)galzu}.

Witnesses:
Bēlšunu/Libluṭ
Ardiya/Nabû-ēṭir
Aplaya/Bazūzu//Bābūtu
Bēl-erība/Kalbaya//Šumu-libši
Ubār/Bēl-iddin//Ea-pattannu
The scribe: Bēl-ittannu/Iddin-Bēl
(Place + Date).

Comment

L. 3: The title "governor of Babylon" is usually spelled LÚ.GAR-UŠ$_4$ TIN.TIR.KI, but our text reads either LÚ.UŠ$_4$-GAR TIN.TIR.KI or LÚ.<GAR->UŠ$_4$ *šá* TIN.TIR.KI. For another scribal error in the same text, see the dittography URU.KUR.TI in line 8 below.

L. 6: ŠE.BAR refers back to the previously mentioned three *kor*, although it is not complemented by the anaphoric a_4 or *a'*. If it were another amount of barley, it would have been introduced in an *elat*-clause. Cf. BM 33930: 23–24.

L. 8: For URU.KUR.TI = Dūr-Galzu, Dūr-Kurigalzu, see Zadok, *RGTC* 8, 121 s.v. Dūr-galzu, and Jursa, *Tempelzehnt* No. 7: 15′ (= BM 61184; translation and commentary on p. 25–27). New evidence on this place may be found in *OrAnt* 25 No. 7 (25/ix/18 Nbp = 2 December 608 B.C.E.). The text is an account of dates that had been loaded onto three boats. The total amount of dates is summed up in lines 7–8: "[I]n total 1073 measuring containers of dates *šá* URU.KUR.BAD at the disposal of PN$_1$ and PN$_2$." Frame notes with regard to URU.KUR.BAD that "the exact reading is uncertain," but that this place "likely lay in the general area of Uruk." However, in view of the occurrence of URU.KUR.TI in BM 30256 in a context that is very similar to the one of *OrAnt* 25 No. 7, to wit the transport of agricultural produce by boat, perhaps Frame's reading should be corrected from UTU.KUR.BAD to URU.KUR.TI.

No. 6

BM 30261
Copy: Bertin copy 2836
Date: 13/iv/2[6$^?$] Dar (17 July 496$^?$ B.C.E.)
Place: Babylon
Content: Receipt of the *ilku*-tax (and)$^?$ *pānāt* ^{giš}*qašti* by MNA.

Obv.

1 [*i*]*l-ki šá* ^{m}*ri-mut-*^{d}EN A-*šú šá* ^{m}DÙ-*iá*
2 A LÚ.ŠITIM *ù* DI-*pi-ni-šú šá a-di-i qí-it*
3 ITI.ŠE MU 26.KAM ^{m}*da-ri-ia-muš* LUGAL
4 ^{m}*ši-ir-ku* A-*šú šá* ^{m}MU-*a* A ^{m}*e-gì-bi*
5 *ina* ŠU.II ^{md}AG-*it-tan-nu* A-*šú šá* ^{m}DÙ-*iá* A LÚ.ŠITIM
6 *e-ṭi-ir* 1-*en*.TA.ÀM *il-qu-ú*
7 *pa-na-at* GIŠ.BAN *e-ṭi-ir*

Rev.

8 LÚ *mu-kin-nu* ^{md}30-DINGIR A-*šú šá* ^{m}DÙ-*iá*$^?$ A ^{m}[…]
9 ^{m}KAR-^{d}EN A-*šú šá* ^{md}UTU-PAB A ^{md}AG-⸢BA-x⸣
10 ^{md}AMAR.UTU-PAB A-*šú* <*šá*> ^{md}IDIM-MU A ^{m}MU.MEŠ
11 ^{m}KI-^{d}AG-PAB A-*šú šá*$^!$ ^{md}IDIM-MU A ^{m}DÙ-*eš*-DINGIR
12 ^{m}*ki-di-nu* A-*šú šá*$^!$ ^{m}*ba-la-ṭu* A ^{m}DÙ-*eš*-DINGIR

13 ^{md}AG-ŠEŠ.MEŠ-MU A-*šú šá* ^{md}AG-DA A ^{m}*da-bi-bi*

14 ^{m}*ni-din-tu*$_{4}$-^{d}EN LÚ.UMBISAG A-*šú šá* ^{md}EN-MU A ^{m}[x-x]-*e*/KAL$^{?}$

15 TIN.TIR.KI ITI.ŠU UD.13.KAM MU.20+[...]

LE. E.

16 ^{m}*da-ri-ia-muš* LUGAL E.KI *u* [KUR.KUR]

TRANSLATION

The *ilku*-tax till the end of Addar of the twenty-sixth year of King Darius is due from Rīmūt-Bēl, son of Baniya, descendant of Itinnu, and his ...: MNA$_2$ has been paid by Nabû-ittannu, son of Baniya, descendant of Itinnu. They have taken one (copy of the document) each. He has (also)$^{?}$ been paid the *pānāt* ^{giš}*qašti*.

Witnesses:
Sîn-ilī/Baniya//[^{m}...]
Mušēzib-Bēl/Šamaš-nāṣir//Nabû-⸢BA-x⸣
Marduk-nāṣir/Ea-iddin//Šumāti
Itti-Nabû-nāṣir/Ea-iddin//Eppeš-ilī
Kidinnu/Balāṭu//Eppeš-ilī
Nabû-aḫḫē-iddin/Nabû-ile''i/Dābibī
The scribe: Nidinti-Bēl/Bēl-iddin//^{m}[x-x]-*e*/KAL$^{?}$
(Place + Date).

COMMENT

L. 2: The DI-sign in DI-*pi-ni-šú* is clear. It has two horizontal wedges between the upper and lower *Winkelhaken*, whereas for a KI-sign we need four such horizontal wedges (see, for instance, the KI at the end of the line in *qí-it*). Is this the same word as the problematic LÚ DI-*pa-ni-šú* in BM 30589: 5? The latter document records the receipt of silver that was paid for *ilki* ... *ana muḫḫi* ^{giš}*qašti* [*ša*] PN *u* LÚ DI-*pa-ni-šú*, "the *ilku*-tax ..., on account of the bow [of] PN and his LÚ DI-*pani*" (ll. 2–5). Are (LÚ) DI-*pa*/*pi-ni-šú* in the text under consideration and BM 30589 misspellings for *qīpānīšu* "his administrators"? Such an emended reading is likely in view of the parallel on the collection of *ilku* from "PN *ù qí-pa-ni-šú*" from Sippar (SCT 95 cited by Jursa, *Bēl-rēmanni*, n. 427 and n. 447; cf. BM 31466 from Babylon but unpublished) and the fact that also MNA collected taxes from such corporate professional entities, viz. in BM 33954. In the latter text MNA collected flour from the "bow of the exorcists" and "the bow of Bazūzu and his nine administrators of the scribal school" (ll. 4–5, wr. ⸢9 LÚ$^{?}$⸣ *qí-pa-ni-šú*; cf. line 11, written LÚ *qí-*{*pi*}*-pa-ni-šú*). More on ^{lú}*qīpānu* at BM 33954: 5. It is less likely that there would be a link with the equally enigmatic expressions *il-ki šá* DI-*pi šá giš-ri* (BM 30366: 1), [*il*]-DI(read -*ki*) DI-*pi šá* GIM (BM 30772: 1), and KÙ.BABBAR *šá* DI-*pi šá* GIŠ.BAN (NRVU 551: 1).

L. 3: The number 6 is written with horizontal wedges.

L. 11–12: The scribe wrote only the upper part of the *šá*-signs with their double head, leaving the long vertical tail unnoted. The formula A-*šú šá* of lines 9, 10, 11 and 12 are written one underneath the other.

L. 15: BM 30261 records the payment of *ilku* "till the end of Addar of Darius' twenty-sixth year" (ll. 2–3). Hence, it was probably written in the year 2[6]. Further note that all *ilku*-receipts from MNA's time are dated between iv/24 Dar and xii/26 Dar (except for one receipt from Darius' fifteenth year). For the details see Table 4 in the present volume.

No. 7

BM 30270
Copy: Bertin copy 2602
Date: 6/xii/26 Dar (3 March 495 B.C.E.)
Place: Babylon
Content: Renting of a boat by MNA and receipt of the rent money.

OBV.

1 GIŠ.MÁ *šá* ^{m}MU-^{d}AG *šá ina* IGI
2 ^{md}UTU-MU A-*šú šá* ^{md}EN-MU *a-na*
3 LÚ *ma-la-ḫu-tu* GIŠ.MÁ *a-na i-di-šú*
4 *a-di bi-iš-*tu_4 *šá* EDIN-*ú-a*
5 *a-na* ⅓ MA.NA KÙ.BABBAR UD-*ú nu-uḫ-ḫu-tu*
6 *a-na* ^{m}*ši-rik* A-*šú šá* ^{m}SUM.NA-*a*
7 A ^{m}*e-gì-bi id-din* KÙ.BABBAR-*a'*
8 ⅓ MA.NA *i-di* GIŠ.MÁ *u* $KURUM_6$.ḪI.A-*šú*
9 *e-*[*ṭir*] GIŠ.MÁ *bir-*tu_4

LO. E.

10 *ul i-te-qu ki-i* ⸢GIŠ.MÁ⸣
11 *i-te-qu* 5 MA.NA KÙ.BABBAR

REV.

12 *ina-ad-din* 1-*en*.TA.ÀM TI-⸢*ú*⸣
13 LÚ *mu-kin-nu* ^{m}⸢*ḫa*⸣*-ba-ṣi-ru*
14 A-*šú šá* ^{m}*šad-din-nu* ^{m}⸢*ḫaš*⸣*-da-a-a*
15 A-*šú šá* ^{md}AG-DIN-*su*-E ^{m}*bul-ṭa-a*
16 A-*šú šá* ^{md}UTU-*ib-ni*
17 *u* LÚ.UMBISAG ^{md}EN-SU A-*šú šá* ^{m}*ap-la-a*
18 A ^{m}MU-*líb-ši* E.KI ITI.ŠE

U. E.

19 UD.6.KAM MU.26.KAM
20 ^{m}*da-ri-iá-muš* LUGAL E.KI
21 *u* KUR.KUR

Translation

The boat belonging to Iddin-Nabû, which is at the disposal of Šamaš-iddin, son of Bēl-iddin, for sailing: he has rented the boat out to MNA_2 for one-third mina of white, medium-quality silver (in order to sail) till Bištu-ša-ṣēru'a. He has been paid this one-third mina of silver, (for) the rent of the boat as well as (for) his maintenance. The boat should not pass the fortified settlement; if ⸢the boat⸣ passes it, he (= MNA) shall pay five minas of silver. They have taken one (copy of the document) each.

Witnesses:
Ḫabaṣīru/Šaddinnu
⸢Ḫaš⸣daya/Nabû-balāssu-iqbi
Bulṭaya/Šamaš(-zēra)-ibni
And the scribe: Bēl-erība/Aplaya (= Kalbaya[!?])//Šumu-libši
(Place and Date).

Comment

L. 1: The idiom *ša ina pān* means "which is at the disposal of," viz. "which is held on contract." It refers to commodities or silver that someone held on a contractual basis for his own profit, but that he did not own and hence had to return to its owner in due time. It implies the transfer of the commodity or silver from A (owner) to B (contractor), yet the act of transfer is not in fact recorded. The commodity or silver was made available to B for various reasons, although in most cases they are not specified in the texts. A boat, for instance, may have been put at his disposal "for sailing" (*ana malaḫūtu*, BM 30270 e.a.). Land may have been made available to him for cultivation (e.g., Dar 315: 3 and BM 32930: 13; cf. the idiom *ša … īpuš* in BM 33972: 20), and bridges for collecting tolls (e.g., TCL 13 196: 3). The person to whom the boat, land, or bridge was made available could use it for his own purposes, at least to some degree, and/or derive income from it. He could, for instance, rent the boat or lease the bridge to a third party; he could use the silver of A that was at his disposal to pay his creditor, buy commodities etc. (for *ina pān* credit documents, more at Petschow, *Pfandrecht*, 9f and 50f.; Shiff, *Nūr-Sîn*, 88 n. 75; and, e.g., BM 30854 and Dar 552 in the present volume). For the expression *ina pān*, also see Gehlken, *AUWE* 5, 14.

L. 2–3: The idiom *ana malaḫūtu* here and in other Neo-Babylonian boat rentals means "for plying the boatman's trade" (*CAD* M_1, 153). Syntactically it belongs to *ina pān* and not to *ana idišu iddin*. It usually stands after *ina pān*, but may also stand before it as, for instance, in BM 31891: 2 (cf. NRVU 147 and *Fs. Diakonoff* 124ff. No. 3). It gives the reason that the boat was made available to so-and-so; it does not give the reason that the boat was rented to MNA. One should, therefore, not translate "boat belonging to Iddin-Nabû, which is at the disposal of Šamaš-iddin, he (= Šamaš-iddin) rented it to MNA for sailing," but rather "boat belonging to Iddin-Nabû, which is at the disposal of Šamaš-iddin for sailing, he rented it to MNA." Cf.

Oppenheim, *Mietrecht*, 48–50; Salonen, *Nautica*, 57. Different, Wunsch, *AuOr 15*, 178 "haben sie zur Schiffahrt [zur Miete ... gegeben]."

L. 3: The signs *i-di-šú* are very much squeezed, but the formula *ana idīšu nadānu* or *ana idī* X *nadānu*, "to give for rent/for the rent of X" is well attested in Neo-Babylonian rental contracts in general, and boat rentals in particular (cf. Oppenheim, *Mietrecht*; San Nicolò-Petschow, *BRu* 6, 43ff. and 48ff.; and San-Nicolò-Ungnad, *NRV*, 154ff.). It is possible that when the scribe impressed the A while writing *ap-la-a* in line 17 on the reverse, extremely close to the *i-di-šú* of line 3 on the obverse, the signs of the obverse were squeezed together, and may even have been written over. This may explain why the DI and the ŠÚ of *i-di-šú* are not clear.

L. 4: *bi-iš-tu*$_4$ *šá* EDIN-*ú-a*, = (lit.) "the fortified settlement of the plain," is the name of a place called either Bištu/Birtu-ša-ṣēru'a (cf. Zadok, *RGTC* 8, 78 s.v. Bištu-ša-Šerū'a), or Birišsarū'a (URU *bi-ri-iš-šá-ru-ú-a* in BM 31891: 4, 7). The name of the place is twice spelled etymologically *bi-iš-tu*$_4$ *šá* EDIN-*ú-a* (BM 30270: 4; BM 30490: 11 and 13, cf. *bir-tu*$_4$ *šá* EDIN-*ú-a* in line 26), and once phonetically, Birišsarū'a (URU *bi-ri-iš-šá-ru-ú-a* in BM 31891). The place in question must have been named after the fortress by which it was dominated. Our text explicitly states that the boat that had to sail to Bištu-ša-ṣēru'a should not sail past the fortress (*bir-tu*$_4$, line 9).

L. 13–16: The three witnesses mentioned in these lines also occur as the first three witnesses in BM 30490, which had been written the previous day, probably by the same scribe (see below at lines 17–18). Note that Bulṭaya/Šamaš-ibni in BM 30270 equals Bulṭaya/Šamaš-zēra-ibni in BM 30490: 20–21. BM 30490 has the name of a fourth witness after Bulṭaya/Šamaš-zēra-ibni, to wit Er(ī)baya$^?$/Ša-Nabû-šū (ll. 21–22), but this person is not attested in BM 30270; instead, there is a large empty space of approximately two lines after the name of the last witness in line 16 and the name of the scribe in line 17. The scribe may originally have planned to write the names of four witnesses for which he left an empty space of six lines (starting with line 13), but the fourth witness may not have turned up, so that the last two lines were left empty. If this is indeed so, it would mean that the scribe wrote his name, and perhaps also the date formula following his name, before filling in the names of the witnesses. More likely, however, the empty space after the last witness in line 16 and before the name of the scribe in line 17 is to be compared to BM 31118: 13 and several similar cases in BM 30366: 12, BM 30819: 14, BM 31036: 12, BM 31227: 13, BM 31793: 17, BM 32883: 17 e.a.

L. 17–18: This boat rental agreement was written by Bēl-erība/^{m}*ap-la-a*//Šumu-libši, whereas a person with the same surname but slightly different patronymy, viz. Bēl-erība/^{m}*kal-ba-a*//Šumu-libši, wrote at least three other texts pertaining to boats and boat transports from MNA's archive. The same person also witnessed eleven other texts from MNA's archive in matters such as rations for boatmen, payments for (the maintenance of?) bridges, and boat sales (for details see index s.v. Bēl-erība). He is, moreover, known to have been in charge of a contingent of fifty soldiers (BM 30274). In view of this evidence, one is tempted to equate the scribe of BM 30270 with this frequently attested Bēl-erība/Kalbaya//Šumu-libši. The *-ap-* of Aplaya, however, is clearly there, and though the signs *-la-a* are written on the edge and hence a little less clear, still one can hardly doubt the *-la-a*. Did Bēl-erība when writing BM 30270, or rather the junior scribe who copied his tablet, mess up some signs, so that he wrote AP instead of KAL and LA instead of BA? With respect to this scribe's writing skills, note his organization of the text on the tablet. He wrote on the obverse, lower edge, reverse and upper edge; on the right edge he wrote as follows: *-ḫu-tu* (l. 5), *-a* (l. 6), A-*šú* (l. 8), *-a* (l. 15), and *-la-a* (l. 17). He left one line empty at the end of the list of witnesses (see comment above at lines 13–16).

No. 8

BM 30274
Copy: Bertin copy 2540
Date: 13/iv/24 Dar (9 July 498 B.C.E.)
Place: Babylon
Content: Release from army service for the next three and a half months. Reference to persons known from texts in MNA's archive.

OBV.

1 TA ITI.GU$_4$ MU.24.KAM
2 ^{m}*da-ri-ia-muš* LUGAL ^{m}ÌR-*ia*
3 DUMU *šá* ^{m}IDIM-*ia* A ^{md}*é-a*-DÙ-*eš*-DINGIR
4 ITI *u$_4$-mu*.MEŠ *u dul-lu ina* GIŠ.MÁ-GUR$_8$ DUMU A LUGAL
5 *it-ti* ^{md}EN-SU DUMU *šá* ^{m}UR-*a*
6 DUMU ^{m}MU-*líb-ši* LÚ.GAL *ḫa-an-še-e-šú*
7 *i-te-pu-uš* (erasure)

LO. E.

8 *a-di* TIL ITI.DU$_6$ MU.24.KAM
9 ^{m}*da-ri-ia-muš* ^{md}EN-SU *a-na* UGU
10 x *dul-lu a-na* ^{m}ÌR-*ia ul i-di-ik-ku*

REV.

11 LÚ *mu-kin-nu* ^{m}MU-^{d}AMAR.UTU DUMU *šá*
12 ^{md}AMAR.UTU-SU DUMU ^{m}*bi-ib-bu-ú-a*
13 ^{md}EN-DIN$^{!}$-*iṭ* DUMU *šá* ^{md}AG-URU$_3$-*šú*
14 ^{m}*ni-din-tu$_4$* DUMU *šá* ^{m}UR-*a* DUMU ^{m}MU-*líb-ši*
15 LÚ.UMBISAG ^{md}EN-SUR DUMU *šá* ^{md}EN-MU TIN.TIR.KI
16 ITI.ŠU UD.13.KAM MU.24.KAM
17 ^{m}*da-ri-ia-muš* LUGAL TIN.TIR.KI
18 *u* KUR.KUR.MEŠ

U. E.

19 1-*en*.TA.ÀM {il} TI-*ú*

TRANSLATION

Since Ayyar of the twenty-fourth year of King Darius, Ardiya, son of Kabtiya, descendant of Ea-eppeš-ilī, has performed <x>? days (of service)? (per) month and the work at the *makurru*-boat ... for Bēl-erība, son of Kalbaya, descendant of Šumu-libši, his commander-of-fifty (erasure). Till the end of Tašrīt of the twenty-fourth year of Darius, Bēl-erība cannot call up Ardiya for the x (corvée-) work.

Witnesses:
Iddin-Marduk/Marduk-erība//Bibbûa
Bēl-uballiṭ?/Nabû-uṣuršu
Nidintu/Kalbaya//Šumu-libši (Bēl-erība's brother)
The scribe: Bēl-ēṭir/Bēl-iddin
(Place + Date).

COMMENT

L. 4: I suggest understanding ITI u_4-*mu*.MEŠ as follows: "(per) month <x> days (of service)." A similar situation is described in BM 31188: 3.

L. 5: The preposition *itti* here refers to being enlisted "with" someone to do (military) service, cf. the use of *itti* in *Libluṭ mār* lú*sīsî u* lú*tašlīšū*meš *it-ti-ka šá-aṭ-ru* "Libluṭ, the charioteer, and the auxiliary troops are enlisted with you (to do service)" (CT 22 74: 5–7); and *kaspu ... ša ana* giš*[qa]šti*! *ša* PN_1 *ša ana* PN_2 *ša itti bēl ḫanšê annê* "Silver ... (paid) for the bow(-tax) that is due to PN_1 for (the account of) PN_2, who is (enlisted) with this commander-of-fifty (soldiers)" (*Bēl-rēmanni*, 251f. = BM 79128).

L. 9–10: The last two signs of line 9 are written in very small script to fit them in the little space available at the end of the line. In fact, the scribe started writing them at the very end of the tablet's lower edge; he then continued writing on the lower part of the right edge. The next line, viz. line 10, is also written in very small script; its signs are squeezed between the tablet's lower edge and its reverse side. There seems to be a sign before the DUL, but it is "overshadowed" by the *Personenkeil* of the preceding line and hard to identify. It does not resemble a *šá*.

L. 13: The scribe wrote mdEN-BA-*iṭ*.

No. 9

BM 30297
Copy: Bertin copy 2542
Date: 6/viii/24 Dar (29 October 498 B.C.E.)
Place: Babylon
Content: Receipt of the *ilku*-tax (and)$^?$ the entire flour-tax by MNA.

OBV.

1 *il-ki šá* ^{md}AG-*it-tan-nu* DUMU
2 *šá* ^{md}EN-MU-GAR-*un* DUMU ^{m}*su-ḫa-a-a*
3 *šá ul*<-*tu*> ITI.BÁR *šá* MU.24$^!$.KAM
4 *a-di qí-it šá* ITI.ŠE *šá* MU.24.KAM
5 ^{m}*da-ri-iá-muš* LUGAL ^{m}*ši-iš-ku*
6 DUMU *šá* ^{m}SUM.NA-*a* DUMU ^{m}*e-gi-*[*bi*]
7 *ina* ŠU.II ^{md}[AG]-*it-tan-nu ma-*[*ḫi*]-[*ir*]

LO. E.

8 *qí-me-šú gam-mar šá* MU.24.[KAM]
9 ^{m}*ši-iš-ku ina* ŠU.II ^{md}AG-*it-t*[*an-nu*]

REV.

10 *ma-ḫi-ir* LÚ *mu-kin*$_7$ ^{m}x-[...]
11 DUMU *šá* ^{md}AMAR.UTU-*na-ṣir* A ^{m}⸢*lib*$^?$⸣-*l*[*uṭ*]$^?$
12 ^{md}EN-MU DUMU *šá* ^{md}AG-A-MU
13 A LÚ.SANGA-^{d}*gu-la* ^{m}⸢DU$_{10}$⸣.GA-*ia*
14 DUMU *šá* ^{m}*lá*$^?$-*aq*$^?$-*qu-un-nu-šú*
15 LÚ.UMBISAG ^{m}*eri-ba-a* DUMU *šá* ^{m}*ib-na-a*
16 E.KI ITI.APIN UD.6.KAM
17 MU.24.KAM ^{m}*da-ri-iá-muš*

U. E.

18 LUGAL E.KI LUGAL KUR.KUR 1-*en*.TA.ÀM
19 *il-te-qu-ú*

TRANSLATION

The *ilku*-tax fro<m> Nisan of the twenty-fourth$^!$ year till the end of Addar of the twenty-fourth year of King Darius is due from Nabû-ittannu, son of Bēl-šuma-iškun, descendant of Suḫaya: MNA$_2$ has receiv[ed] (it) from [Nabû]-ittannu. MNA$_2$ has (also)$^?$ received from Nabû-itt[annu] his entire flour(-tax) for the twenty-four[th] year.

Witnesses:
MU(or Ina-tēšê)-[...]/Marduk-nāṣir//⸢Lib⸣[luṭ]$^?$
Bēl-iddin/Nabû-apla-iddin//Šangû-Gula
Ṭābiya/*Laqqunnušu*$^?$
The scribe: Erībaya/Ibnaya
(Place + Date).

They have taken one (copy of the document) each.

COMMENT

L. 3: With regard to the number 24, only two of the three upper wedges are clearly visible. The third one is very faint.

L. 10: It is not certain whether the name of the first witness starts with MU or *ina*-SÙḪ.

L. 14: The first sign may also be read ME (instead of LÁ) and the second one TUQ (instead of AQ).

No. 10

	BM 30366
Copy:	Bertin copy 2616
Date:	7/viii/26 Dar (6 November 496 B.C.E.)
Place:	Babylon
Content:	Receipt of the *ilku*-tax (and)$^{?}$ *pānāt* ^{giš}*qašti* by MNA. Tax related to a bridge.

OBV.

1 *il-ki šá* DI-*pi šá giš-ri šá* ^{md}AG-*na-din*-ŠEŠ
2 DUMU *šá* ^{m}A-*a šá ul-tu* ITI.ŠU MU.26.KAM
3 ^{m}*da-ri-iá-muš* LUGAL E.KI *u* KUR.KUR *a-di qí-it*
4 ITI.SIG$_4$ MU.27.KAM ^{m}*šìr-ku* DUMU *šá* ^{m}SUM.NA-*a*
5 A ^{m}*e-gì-bi ina* ŠU.II ^{m}⸢SUM.NA-*a*⸣ DUMU *šá* ^{m}NÍG.BA-*ia*
6 *a-na muḫ-ḫi* ^{md}AG-⸢*na*⸣-[*din*-ŠEŠ DUMU *šá*] ^{m}A-*a*
7 *ma-ḫi-ir* 1-*en*.ÀM [*il-te-qu*]-⸢*ú*⸣
8 *pa-na-at* GIŠ.[BAN] *ma-ḫi-ir*

REV.

9 LÚ *mu-kin-nu* ^{md}EN-A-MU DUMU *šá* ^{md}AMAR.UTU-MU-MU
10 A LÚ.SANGA-^{d}*gu-la* ^{md}EN-SU DUMU *šá* ^{m}*kal-ba-a*
11 A ^{m}MU-*líb-ši* ^{md}U.GUR-MU-DÙ DUMU *šá*
12 ^{m}*šul-lu-mu*
13 ^{md}AG-ŠEŠ-*it-tan-nu* LÚ.UMBISAG DUMU *šá* ^{m}KAR-^{d}EN
14 A LÚ.GAL-*a-šá*-^{d}MAŠ TIN.TIR.KI ITI.APIN
15 UD.7.KAM MU.26.KAM ^{m}*da-ri-iá-muš*

U. E.

16 LUGAL E.KI *u* KUR.KUR

TRANSLATION

The *ilku*-tax for the … of the bridge from Dûzu of the twenty-sixth year of Darius, king of Babylon and the lands, till the end of Simān of the twenty-seventh year is due from Nabû-nādin-aḫi, son of Aplaya: MNA$_2$ has received (it) from ⸢Iddinaya⸣, son of Qīštiya, for the account of Nabû-nā[din-aḫi, son of] Aplaya. They [have taken] one (a copy of the deed) each.

He has (also)$^{?}$ received the *pānāt* ^{giš}[*qašti*].

Witnesses:

Bēl-apla-iddin/Marduk-šuma-iddin//Šangû-Gula

Bēl-erība/Kalbaya//Šumu-libši

Nergal-šuma-ibni/Šullumu

The scribe: Nabû-aḫa-ittannu/Mušēzib-Bēl//Rabâ-ša-Ninurta

(Place + Date).

COMMENT

L. 1: Should DI-*pi* be read *ṭi-pi*? The *ṭīpu ša gišru* may refer to some additional construction to a bridge, like, for instance, planking (see *AHw*, 1392 s.v. *ṭīpu* "Belag; Auflage, Umschlag; Addition," and the examples cited s.v. *ṭepû* G 3 with regard to additions to houses or canals). Some interesting new examples will be made available by C. Wunsch in her book on the houses of the Egibi family, e.g., two house sales describing the plots of land that had been put up for sale as follows: GI.MEŠ DI-*pi pa-na-at ma-ḫi-ri šá* SILA BÀD *im-gur-*^{d}*En-líl* (BM 45561: 4–5), and GI.MEŠ DI-*pi šá* SILA BÀD *im-gur-*^{d}*en-líl* (BM 45416: 12). The same word is probably found in BM 30772: 1, [*il*]-*ki*$^{!}$(=DI) DI-*pi šá* GIM, and in NRVU 551: 1, *kaspu ša* DI-*pi ša* ^{giš}*qašti* (cf. Joannès, *TÉBR*, 22 "L'argent du supplément sur les (*bît*) *qašti*"). It is not clear whether there is any relationship with the enigmatic (LÚ) DI-*pa*/*pi-ni* in BM 30261 and BM 30589 (see discussion at BM 30261: 2). BM 30366 is not the only text from the archive in which MNA collects *ilku* in connection with a bridge (see also BM 31227); two other texts from his archive further prove that he was intensively involved in the exploitation of bridges (TCL 13 196 and BM 41443).

L. 12: The second half of the line is empty. After this line there follow two empty lines before the scribe started writing his name in line 13, cf. BM 30819: 14, BM 31036: 12, BM 31227: 13, BM 31793: 17, BM 32883: 17 e.a.; probably also BM 30270: 16–17; cf. also BM 31118: 13.

No. 11

BM 30370
Copy: Bertin copy 2615
Date: 3–9/v/26 Dar (5–11 August 496 B.C.E.)
Place: Babylon
Content: Sale of a boat to MNA and receipt of the purchase price.

OBV.

1 GIŠ.MÁ *šá* 6½ KÙŠ *ina muḫ-ḫi šá-bur-ru*
2 *rap-šú* 20 *ina* 1 KÙŠ *šu-bat me-e-šú šá* ^{md}AG-A-MU
3 A-*šú šá* ^{m}*la-a-ba-ši* A ^{m}ZALAG$_2$-^{d}PAP.SUKKAL
4 *a-na* 4 MA.NA KÙ.BABBAR 10 GÍN KÙ.BABBAR *šá ina* 1 GÍN *bit-qa*
5 *šá la gìn-nu šá ḫal-la iṣ-ṣur a-na*
6 ^{m}*ši-rik-ki* A-*šú šá* ^{m}SUM.NA-*a* A ^{m}*e-gi-bi*
7 *id-din pu-ut* LÚ *uš*$^{!}$*-ku-ú-tu šá* GIŠ.MÁ
8 ^{md}AG-A-MU *na-ši* KÙ.BABBAR-*a*$_4$
9 4 MA.NA 10 GÍN UD-*ú* ŠÁM GIŠ.MÁ-*šú*
10 ^{md}AG-A-MU *ina* ŠU.II ^{m}*ši-rik-ki e-ṭir*

REV.

11 LÚ *mu-kin-nu* ^{m}*ni-din-tu*$_4$ A-*šú šá* ^{m}*kal-ba-a*
12 A ^{m}*su-ḫa-a-a* ^{m}*lib-luṭ* A-*šú šá* ^{md}U.GUR-MU
13 A ^{m}LÚ.AZLAG ^{m}*ap-la-a* LÚ.SIPA-LUGAL
14 A-*šú šá* ^{m}*šá-pi-*^{d}TU.TU ^{md}EN-SU
15 A-*šú šá* ^{m}*kal-ba-a* A ^{m}MU-LU-RU-ŠÚ
16 ^{m}ÌR-^{d}MAŠ A-*šú šá* ^{md}EN-KÁD
17 LÚ.UMBISAG ^{md}AMAR.UTU-MU-MU A-*šú šá* ^{md}AG-MU
18 A ^{m}*de-ki-i* TIN.TIR.KI ITI.NE UD.[x].KAM
19 MU.26.KAM ^{m}*da-ar-'i-*⸢*šú*⸣

U. E.

20 LUGAL E.KI *u* KUR.KUR
21 GIŠ.MÁ *ku-tu-ut-*[*mu*] *su-ú ru-kub*$^{?}$*-bi* [(x)]
22 *šá-ḫa-li-e* ⸢*šu*$^{?}$⸣*-lu-ú*

TRANSLATION

The boat belonging to Nabû-apla-iddin, son of Lâbāši, descendant of Nūr-Papsukkal, which is six and a half cubits wide at its beam, (and) with a *keel*$^{?}$ of twenty cubits: he has sold (it) to MNA$_2$ for four minas and ten shekels of unmarked silver, of which one-eighth is alloy, *ša ḫalla iṣṣur*. For the *uškûtu* of the boat Nabû-apla-iddin assumes warranty. These four minas and ten shekels of white silver, the price of his boat, Nabû-apla-iddin has been paid by MNA$_2$.

Witnesses:
Nidintu/Kalbaya//Suḫaya
Libluṭ/Nergal-iddin//Ašlāku

Aplaya/Ša-pî-Marduk, the shepherd of the king
Bēl-erība/Kalbaya//Šumu[!]-libši[!] (wr. [m]MU-LU-RU-ŠÚ)
Arad-Ninurta/Bēl-kāṣir
The scribe: Marduk-šuma-iddin/Nabû-iddin//Dēkû
(Place + Date).

The boat is covered with reed mats, a cargo[?] boat[?] loaded with cress[!].

Comment

L. 2: For the expression *šubat mêšu* see *CAD* $\check{S}_3$, 176 s.v. *šubtu* mng. 2d "keel (?)." Note that the only example cited by the *CAD* is actually the text under consideration.

L. 2–3: Nabû-apla-iddin/Lâbāši//Nūr-Papsukkal, the seller of the boat, wrote a month later the document for one of MNA's boat rentals (BM 31891). He may possibly be linked to the Borsippa archives, if Nabû-bullissu/Lâbāši-Marduk//Nūr-Papsukkal was indeed his brother. This Nabû-bullissu lent money to a descendant of the famous Ea-ilûta-bāni family from Borsippa in Darius' twenty-eighth year (TUM 2/3 62 = *Borsippa*, 45f.).

L. 5: The silver is unmarked *šá ḫal-la iṣ-ṣur*. The meaning of the latter idiom is unknown (cf. *CAD* Ḫ, 43 s.v. *ḫalla*).

L. 7: The *-uš* is badly written: there is only one small vertical instead of two inside the sign and it is written immediately after the upper *Winkelhaken*, rather than in front of it. For what seem to be scribal errors, more at line 15.

L. 7–8: For a discussion on the formula *pūt uškûtu … naši*, esp. when used in the context of boat sales, see San Nicolò, *BRu* 6, 42–43 (regarding YBT 7 173). The formula is also found in BM 32883: 7, where MNA assumed warranty for the *uškûtu* of the boat being sold, and in BM 32873: 8–9 regarding the exchange of boats.

L. 9–10: Although this document states that MNA had paid the price for the boat, only a month later the matter was finally settled (see BM 30961).

L. 15: The signs [m]MU-LU-RU-ŠÚ are fairly clear, although we expect [m]MU-*líb*/*lib-ši*/*šú*, since Bēl-erība/Kalbaya//Šumu-libši is well known from MNA's archive, as scribe and witness, especially in the context of boats, boat transports and boat-towers; see more at the discussion of BM 30270: 17–18. Is this tablet actually a copy of the original and was the scribe copying signs that he did not always understand, thereby turning an original *-líb-* into -LU-RU- (l. 15), and an original *šaḫ-* into ŠA-ḪA- in line 22? Further note his awkward spellings of Darius' name in line 19 and of *kutummu* in line 21.

L. 16: There is an empty space of one line separating the list of witnesses from the name of the scribe and the date-formula.

L. 18: There are at least three wedges (wr. on the right edge), but the lower part of the number is broken off. Consequently, the number was either 3 or any number between 3 and 9.

L. 21–22: The scribe had still to write these two lines, but was clearly running out of space. There was actually enough space left for one more line (= line 21); the next line had to be squeezed between the tablet's upper edge and the beginning of its obverse. I suggest understanding these lines as follows. The spelling *ku-tu-ut-mu* probably stands for *kutummu* "covered" (*CAD* K, 612 s.v. *kutummu*), and *su-ú* may be derived from *sû* "reed mat" (for the use of reed mats in covering boats, see Römer, *AOAT* 232, 394 s.v. § B.IV.b.7 with bibliography). *Ru-kub-bi* seems to refer to a cargo-boat (*CAD* R, 409 s.v. *rukūbu* mng. 1-a); *šaḫ*$^{!}$ (ŠÁ ḪA, cf. line 15)*-li-e* most likely stands for *šaḫlû* "cress"; and the verb at the end of line 22 is probably derived from *šūlû* (Š of *elû*) "to load onto a ship" (for this verb cf. San Nicolò-Petschow, *BRu* 6, 49f. No. 35; and BM 31690^{+}). In short, lines 21–22 may possibly refer to a cargo boat that is covered with reed mats and loaded with cress.

No. 12

BM 30446
Copy: Bertin copy 2532
Date: 4/vii/24 Dar (27 September 498 B.C.E.)
Place: broken
Content: Receipt of persons together with the register of their enlistment (GIŠ.ŠID). To tow boats. No mention of MNA (but cf. BM 30795).

OBV.

1 ^{m}⸢*lib-luṭ* A-*šú šá*⸣ ^{m}*na-din* A ^{m}MU-[…]
2 ^{m}⸢TU-^{d}AMAR.UTU⸣ A-*šú šá* ^{md}EN-DIN-*iṭ* A ^{md}AG-⸢URU$_3$$^{?}$-*šú*⸣
3 *it-ti* GIŠ.ŠID *šá* x x x [x x (x)]
4 *šá* ^{m}⸢*da-ri*⸣-*muš* LUGAL *šá ina* ŠU.II
5 ^{m}⸢*ba-ni*⸣-LUGAL-URU$_3$ *šá* É *ip-ru*
6 *a-ki-*⸢*i*$^{!}$⸣ GIŠ.ŠID *e-ṭir-ú-*⸢*tu*$^{?}$⸣
7 *al-la-a'* ^{m}*nu-úr-*^{d}30

REV.

8 ⸢A-*šú*⸣ *šá* ^{m}ÌR-^{d}EN A ^{m}LÚ.SANGA-^{d}*gu-la*
9 ^{m}*ku-ṣur-a* A-*šú šá* ^{m}*li-ši-ru*
10 ^{md}UTU-MU A-*šú šá* ^{md}EN-ŠEŠ.MEŠ-MU
11 A ^{m}*ir-a-ni* ^{m}ÌR-*iá* A-*šú šá* ^{m}KAR-*e-a*
12 A ^{m}*su-ḫa-a-a* PAP 6 *šá-da-de-e*
13 *a-di* ^{m}*lib-luṭ u* ^{m}TU-^{d}AMAR.UTU
14 ⸢x x⸣-*ra-tu*$_4$ *a-di m/ba-d/ki-le-e*
15 ⸢*ma*⸣-*ḫi-ir* LÚ *mu-kin-nu* ^{m}*ka-ṣi-ru*
16 ⸢A-*šú*⸣ *šá* ^{m}*ta-tan-nu* ^{m}*ib-na*<-*a*>A-*šú šá* ^{m}*mu-še-zib-*^{d}AMAR.UTU
17 ⸢A⸣ ^{m}⸢ÌR⸣-^{d}GIR$_4$.<KÙ> ^{m}*mu-ra-nu* A-*šú šá* ^{md}AMAR.UTU-PAB

U. E.

18 […] A-*šú šá* ^{m}*kal-ba-a* A ^{m}MU-⸢*líb-ši*⸣

19 […] ITI.DU$_6$ UD.4.⸢KAM⸣ ⸢MU⸣.24.<KAM>

LE. E.

20 ^{m}*da-⸢ri⸣-muš* LUGAL ⸢E.KI⸣

21 *u* KUR.KUR

TRANSLATION

⸢Liblut, son of⸣ Nādin, descendant of MU-[…], [and] ⸢*Erība*$^?$-Marduk⸣, son of Bēl-uballiṭ, descendant of Nabû-⸢uṣuršu$^?$⸣, with the list of x x x [x x (x)] of King Darius, which is in the hands of ⸢Bani⸣-šarra-uṣur, of the House of the food allowances, according to the (said)$^?$ list ⸢have been$^?$⸣ received.

Beyond them:
Nūr-Sîn/Arad-Bēl//Šangû-Gula
Kuṣura(pli)/Līšir
Šamaš-iddin/Bēl-aḫḫē-iddin//Ir'anni
Ardiya/Eṭraya (rd. Kalbaya?)//Suḫaya.

In total six boat-towers including Libluṭ and *Erība*$^?$-Marduk …. he ⸢has⸣ received.

Witnesses:
Kāṣir/Tattannu
Ibna<ya>/Mušēzib-Marduk//⸢Arad⸣-Ner<gal>
Mūrānu/Marduk-nāṣir
The scribe: […]/Kalbaya//Šumu-⸢libši⸣
(Place + Date).

COMMENT

The text does not mention MNA, but is adduced here because of its formulary and structure, which are similar to what is found in BM 30795. Both texts are also linked through their scribe. The other persons mentioned in this text, however, are not known from MNA's archive. The text may well have belonged to MNA's archive, although there is no definite proof for it.

L. 2: ^{m}TU-^{d}AMAR.UTU probably stands for Erība-Marduk. The verbal element, viz. *erība*, is usually written with the SU-sign (SU = *erība* from the verb *riābu*). In the text under consideration the scribe apparently interpreted the verbal form *erība* as derived from *erēbu* (and not, as is the case, from *riābu*), and this explains his use of TU instead of SU.

L. 3: For GIŠ.ŠID = *manâtu* "account tablet," see discussion at BM 30795: 3–4. The signs after GIŠ.ŠID resemble ŠI MI KI, cf. the signs after GIŠ.ŠID.MEŠ in BM 30795: 3.

L. 4: The expression *ina qātē* in the present context means "(entrusted) in the hands of" rather than "(received) from," and may be compared to the expression *ša qātē* "administered by." More at BM 30795: 4b.

L. 5: The expression É *ip-ru* is unique. The *CAD* I, 166ff. s.v. *ipru* (Cf. *AHw*, 385) does not mention a *bīt ipru*, and as for the noun *ipru*, the translations are: (1)

barley ration (distributed by the administration of a temple, palace, etc.), for which, however, there is no example from the Neo-Babylonian period; (2) food allowance for subsistence (among private persons), with a few examples from Neo-Babylonian private contracts; (3) field allotted for subsistence (Old Babylonian only). It is not immediately clear how the expression *ša* É *ipru* is linked to the previous lines. It may refer to the list (GIŠ.ŠID) mentioned in line 3, and specify that it is a list "from the house of the food allowances," i.e., a list keeping track of the distribution of food allowances (*in casu*, to the boat-towers mentioned in the same text). Or, *ša* É *ip-ru* may refer to ⸢Bani⸣-šarra-uṣur, and specify his administrative area, viz., that he was an official appointed "over the house of the food allowances." The name of this person in itself is awkward, because names with the elements *šarra-uṣur* have as their first element either the name of a god (e.g., *Nabû-šarra-uṣur*) or the general *Gabbi-ilī-* (see Tallqvist, *NbN*, 325 s.v. *naṣāru*).

L. 7: *al-la-a'* is the preposition *alla* "beyond" (*CAD* A_1, 350f. s.v. *alla*) with the anaphoric *-a'*.

L. 9: Read either ^{m}*ku-ṣur-a* (cf. Stolper, *Entrepreneurs*, 293 s.v. Kuṣura; Von Dassow, CTMMA 3, lxxix s.v. Kuṣurraya; and Joannès, *Borsippa*, 384 s.v. Kuṣurâ), or ^{m}*ku-ṣur*-A (= Kuṣur-apli, cf. Tallqvist, *NbN*, 93 s.v. *Ku-ṣur(-ra)-aplu*).

L. 11: The name KAR-*e-a* is perhaps a logogramic spelling for the more common syllabic spellings *Eṭ-ra-a* (Jursa, *Landwirtschaft*, 254 s.v. *Eṭrāja*), and *E-ṭi-ra-a* (Dar 480: 1). Less probable is that we have a misspelling of the name Nūrea, comparable to the misspelling found in *CM* 20b 171: 13 ^{m}*dan-e-a* = Nūrea. A third possibility is to consider it a scribal error for ^{m}*kal*$^{!}$(KAR)-*ba*$^{!}$(E)-*a*; the sons of Kalbaya/Suḫaya frequently occur in texts from MNA's time (see index). Nidintu/Kalbaya//Suḫaya, for instance, witnessed several of MNA's boat-related transactions, and the occurrence of Ardiya/^{m}*kal*$^{!}$(KAR)-*ba*$^{!}$(E)-*a*//Suḫaya, his brother, in the text under consideration concerning boat tower-men would, therefore, fit in very well.

L. 14: The first two signs seem to be DI and PAT/SUR (read ⸢*di-pat/sur*⸣-*ra-tu*$_4^{?}$).The line remains enigmatic. For *makallû*, see BM 31690^{+}: 8.

L. 15: It is not clear who was the subject of the verb *maḫir*. It may have been Bani-šarra-uṣur, mentioned in line 5, with whom the towers seem to have been enlisted. Cf. problem in BM 30795: 8.

L. 19: There was no space left on the upper edge for the scribe to write KAM after MU.24.

No. 13

BM 30490
Copy: Bertin copy 2618
Date: 5/xii/⸢26⸣ Dar (2 March 495 B.C.E.)
Place: Babylon
Content: Renting of a boat by MNA and receipt of the rent money.

OBV.

1 GIŠ.MÁ *šá* ^{m}*ba-la-ṭu* DUMU *šá* ^{m}*ina-qí-bi-*[^{d}x x]
2 LÚ *ma-še-e-nu šá ina* IGI ^{md}AG-NUMUN-BA-*š*[*á-an-n*]*i*
3 DUMU *šá* ^{m}*e-re-e-šú a-na* LÚ *ma-la-ḫu-tú*
4 GIŠ.MÁ *a-na i-di-šú a-na* ⅓ MA.NA
5 KÙ.BABBAR UD-*ú nu-uḫ-ḫu-tu a-na*
6 ^{m}*ši-rik* DUMU$^{!}$ *šá* ^{m}MU-*a* A ^{m}*e-gi-bi*
7 *id-din* KÙ.BABBAR-*a*$_{4}$ ⅓ MA.NA UD-*ú*
8 *i-di* GIŠ.MÁ-*šú a-di* KURUM$_{6}$.ḪI.[A]-⸢*šú*⸣
9 *ina* ŠU.II ^{m}*ši-rik* DUMU *šá* ^{m}S[UM].NA-*a*
10 *ma-ḫi-ir e-ṭir* G[IŠ.MÁ]

LO. E.

11 *bi-iš-tu*$_{4}$ *šá* EDIN-*ú-a* {x}$^{?}$
12 *ul i-ti-qu ki-i*

REV.

13 GIŠ.MÁ *bi-iš-*[*t*]*u*$_{4}$ *šá* EDIN-*ú-a*
14 *i-te-qu* 5 MA.[N]A KÙ.BABBAR UD-*ú*
15 ^{m}*ši-rik a-na* ^{md}AG-NUMUN-BA-*šá*
16 LÚ *ma-la-ḫu šá* ^{m}DIN LÚ *ma-še-e-nu*
17 *ina-ad-din* 1-*en*.TA.ÀM TI-*ú*
18 LÚ *mu-kin-nu* ^{m}*ḫa-ba-ṣi-ru*
19 DUMU *šá* ^{m}*šad-di-nu* ^{m}*ḫaš*$^{!}$*-da-a* DUMU *šá*
20 ^{md}AG-DIN-*su*-E ^{m}*bul-ṭa-a* DUMU *šá*
21 ^{md}UTU-NUMUN-*ib-ni* ^{m}*ḫaš-da-a-a* DUMU *šá*
22 ^{m}*šá-*^{d}AG-⸢*šu*$^{!}$*-ú*⸣ *u* LÚ.UMBISAG
23 ^{md}EN-SU DUMU *šá* ^{m}*kal-ba-a*

U. E.

24 E.KI ITI.ŠE UD.5.KAM MU.⸢26⸣.[KAM]$^{?}$
25 ^{m}*da-ri-muš* LUGAL E.KI *u* KUR.<KUR>

LE. E.

26 GIŠ.MÁ *ina bir-tu*$_{4}$ *šá* EDIN-⸢*ú-a*⸣
27 ⸢*i*⸣-*nap-pal*

TRANSLATION

The boat belonging to Balāṭu, son of Ina-qībi-[^{d}...], the canal inspector, which is at the disposal of Nabû-zēra-iqīša[nni], son of Erēšu, for sailing: he has rented the boat out to MNA_2 for one-third mina of white, medium-quality silver. This one-third mina of white silver, (payment for) the rent of his boat, *together with* (payment for) ⸢his⸣ maintenance, he has received from MNA_2; he has been paid off. The b[oat] should not pass Bištu-ša-ṣēru'a; if the boat passes Bištu-ša-ṣēru'a MNA_2 shall pay five minas of white silver to Nabû-zēra-iqīša(nni), the boatman of Balāṭu, the canal inspector. They have taken one (copy of the document) each.

Witnesses:
Ḫabaṣīru/Šaddinnu
Ḫašdaya/Nabû-balāssu-iqbi
Bulṭaya/Šamaš-zēra-⸢ibni⸣
⸢Erība⸣ya/Ša-Nabû-⸢šū⸣
And the scribe: Bēl-erība/Kalbaya(//Šumu-libši)
(Place + Date).

He shall *unload*? the boat in Birtu-ša-ṣēru'a.

COMMENT

L. 1: For this canal inspector, cf. Sippar archives, Jursa, *Landwirtschaft*, 110f., 115, 181f. and n. 362f. His name probably ended with a divine name of two signs at the most; they were written on the right edge that is, unfortunately, broken off at this instance, but one can see how many signs it may have contained from lines 2, 3, and 6 where the following signs were written on the edge: *-š[a-an-n]i* (l. 2), *-ḫu-tú* (l. 3) and *-gi-bi* (l. 6).

L. 2: *-š[a-an-n]i* is written on the right edge, and completely fills it up. It shows how many signs the right edge may contain. The same name is written without the additional *-an-ni* in line 15.

L. 6: The DUMU is written over an A-sign.

L. 8: There follow a few scratches on the edge. I translate *adi* in this specific context as "together with" rather than "including." One-third mina was the standard sum paid by MNA for the boats he rented (cf. BM 30270, BM 31891 and Dar 576), and maintenance costs were paid in addition to it (cf. BM 31891, ⅓ *manû ... u* 1 *pān qīmu kurummātu*; similar in BM 30270).

L. 11: For the place Birtu-ša-ṣēru'a, more at BM 30270: 4. At the end of the line there are a few scratches (cf. line 8), which resemble a KI, but the place Birtu-ša-ṣēru'a was never spelled with a KI.

L. 19: The *-ḫaš* is written over a DINGIR.

L. 22: The *-šu* has only two horizontals.

L. 24: The number 26 is written at the very end of the edge. If the scribe wrote KAM it must have been on the bottom corner of the right edge, but this corner is broken off. Possibly, he did not write the KAM, cf. next line.

L. 25: There was enough space left on the edge to write a second KUR.

L. 27: For *i-nap-pal*, "he will *unload*$^{?}$," G-present of *napālu* "to dig out," more at BM 30853: 24.

No. 14

	BM 30541
Copy:	Bertin copy 2335
Date:	[-]/[-]/⸢25⸣ Dar (497–496 B.C.E.)
Place:	Babylon
Content:	Promissory note to pay a debt of silver to MNA's brother.

OBV.

1 [x MA.NA] KÙ.BABBAR UD-*ú šá ina* 1 GÍN *bit-qa*
2 [...]-*tu šá* ^{md}AG-ŠEŠ.MEŠ-*bul-liṭ*
3 [A-*šú šá* ^{m}KI]-^{d}AMAR.UTU-DIN A ^{m}*e-gi-bi*
4 [*ina muḫ-ḫi*] ^{md}AG-*it-tan-nu* A-*šú šá*
5 [^{m}*ba*]-*ni-ia* A LÚ.ŠITIM
6 [*a-di* ...] ⸢ITI⸣.KIN MU.25.KAM
7 [... M]A.NA UD-⸢*ú*⸣ [...]
8 [*i-nam*]-*din*

REV.

9 [LÚ *mu-ki*]*n-nu* ^{m}*šul-lu-mu* A-*šú* [*šá*]
10 ^{md}AG-ŠEŠ-MU ^{md}EN-⸢A.ZU-*ú-a*⸣
11 A-*šú šá* ^{md}U.GUR-DIN-⸢*iṭ*⸣ A ^{m}*mu*-⸢SIG$_{15}$⸣-^{d}IŠKUR
12 ^{md}UTU-MU A-*šú šá* ^{md}AMAR.UTU-SUR
13 ^{m}*šu-lum*-E.KI A-*šú šá* ^{m}*tab-ni-e-a*
14 [A ^{m}]*mu*-⸢SIG$_{15}$⸣-^{d}IŠKUR
15 $^{[m]d}$AG-*mu-še-ti-iq*-UD.DA
16 [LÚ.UM]BISAG ⸢A-*šú šá* ^{m}SUM.NA-*a* A ^{m}*si-lim-mu*⸣$^{?}$

LE. E.

17 [(x)] ⸢x⸣ E.KI [x x] MU.⸢25⸣.[KAM]
18 [^{m}*da*]-*ri*-[*ia*]-*muš* LUGAL E.[KI]
19 [*u* KUR].KUR

TRANSLATION

[x mina(s)] of white silver, of which one-eighth is alloy, [...] is/are due to Nabû-aḫḫē-bulliṭ [son of Itti]-Marduk-balāṭu, descendant of Egibi, [from] Nabû-ittannu, son of [Ba]niya, descendant of Itinnu. [Until ...] Ulūl of the twenty-fifth year [...] [he will p]ay the [x] ⸢mina(s) of⸣ white [silver, ...].

[Witnes]ses:

Šullumu/Nabû-aḫa-iddin

Bēl-⸢asûa⸣/Nergal-uballiṭ//⸢Mudammiq⸣-Adad

Šamaš-iddin/Marduk-ēṭir
Šulum-Bābili/Tabnêa//⸢Mudammiq⸣-Adad
[The scr]ibe: Nabû-mušētiq-uddê⸢/Iddinaya//Silimmu⸣$^{?}$
(Place + Date).

Comment

L. 2: Probably to be reconstructed as [*nu-uḫ-ḫu*]-*tu*.

L. 10: At the end of the line we probably have to read -A.ZU-*ú-a* rather than -*a-su-ú-a*, because the sign has three rather than four horizontals.

L. 16: The name ^{m}*si-lim-mu* is unique. Its closest parallel is the name ^{m}*si-li-im-mu*, which is found in a text from the Murašû archive, where it is a variant spelling for the name Šillimmu (Stolper, *Entrepreneurs*, 299 s.v. Šillimmu). Names starting with *si-lim-* are frequent in the Neo-Babylonian period, but they have the name of a god or the general *-ilī* as their second element, e.g., ^{m}*si-lim-*^{d}EN (Tallqvist, *NbN*, 180–81).

No. 15

BM 30589
Copy: Bertin copy 2619
Date: 20/iii/26 Dar (25 June 496 B.C.E.)
Place: Babylon
Content: Receipt of *ilku*-silver by MNA (*kaspu … ilki*). Payment for the account of a bow-unit (*ana muḫḫi* ^{giš}*qašti*).

Obv.

1 ⅔ MA.NA KÙ.BABBAR *šá ina* 1 GÍN *bit-qa nu-uḫ-ḫu-tú*
2 *il-ki šá ul-tu* ITI.BÁR MU.25 *a-di* TIL
3 ITI.ŠE MU.⸢25⸣.KAM ^{m}*da-*[*a-ri*]*-ia-muš* LUGAL
4 *a-na* UGU GIŠ.BAN [*šá*] ^{md}EN-SU DUMU *šá* ^{m}*na-din*
5 DUMU ^{m}*lu-uṣ-ana-*ZALAG$_{2}$-^{d}AMAR.UTU *u* LÚ DI-*pa-ni-šú*
6 ^{m}*ši-iš-ki* DUMU *šá* ^{m}SUM.NA-*a* DUMU ^{m}*e-gì-bi*
7 *ina* ŠU.II ^{m}*i-qu-pu* ŠEŠ *šá* ^{md}EN-SU
8 *ma-ḫir* KÙ.BABBAR *a-na* ^{md}EN-SU

Lo. E.

9 LÚ *si-pir-ri šá*$^{!}$ LÚ.SAG.MEŠ

Rev.

10 *šá* UGU KURUM$_{6}$.ḪI.A *šá* É.GAL *eš-š*[*ú* (x x)]
11 GÍD.DA *it-ti-šú*
12 LÚ *mu-kin-nu* ^{m}*ḫaš-da-a* DUMU <*šá*> ^{md}⸢x-x⸣-GIN-A
13 DUMU ^{md}30-*da-ma-qu* ^{m}KA$_{5}$.A
14 DUMU <*šá*> ^{m}EN-*šú-nu* DUMU ^{md}30-*da-ma-qu*
15 ^{md}AG-*na-din-*ŠEŠ DUMU *šá* ^{m}*ri-mut-*^{d}EN
16 DUMU ^{m}DÙ-*eš*-DINGIR ^{md}AMAR.UTU-BA-*šá-an-ni*

17 DUB.SAR DUMU *šá* ^{md}AG-URU$_3$-*šú* DUMU LÚ.Ì.SUR-GI.NA
18 TIN.TIR.KI ITI.SIG$_4$ UD.20.KAM

U. E.

19 MU.26.KAM ^{m}*da-a-ri-ia-muš*
20 LUGAL TIN.TIR.KI *u* KUR.KUR

LE. E.

21 1-*en*.TA.ÀM
22 *il-qu-ú*

TRANSLATION

Two-third minas of medium-quality silver, of which one-eighth is alloy, the *ilku*-tax from Nisan of the twenty-fif<th> year till the end of Addar of the ⸢twenty-fifth⸣ year of King Darius, (paid) for the account of the bow [of] Bēl-erība, son of Nādin, descendant of Lūṣi-ana-nūr-Marduk, and his ...: MNA$_2$ has received (it) from Iqūpu, brother of Bēl-erība. The silver, to Bēl-erība, clerk of! the commissioners who (are appointed) over the (administration of the) rations of the New Palace, [(x x)]. The register is with him.

Witnesses:
Ḫašdaya/⸢Marduk/Nergal⸣-mukīn-apli//Sîn-damāqu
Šellibi/Bēlšunu//Sîn-damāqu
Nabû-nādin-aḫi/Rīmūt-Bēl//Eppeš-ilī
The scribe: Marduk-iqīšanni/Nabû-uṣuršu//Ṣāḫiṭ-ginê
(Place + Date).

They have taken one (copy of the document) each.

COMMENT

L. 5: The DI-sign in DI-*pa-ni-šú* is clear and cannot be read KI, especially when the sign is compared with the KI in line 2. For this word, see above at BM 30261: 2.

L. 10: A verb like SUM.NA (*nadin*/*nadnu* "has been given") may be expected at the end of the line, but is, unfortunately, broken off. This is the type of clause typically found after the operative section of promissory notes. The operative section states that the debtor will pay till such-and-such date, and the additional clause states that the object of the obligation had been transferred (SUM-*nu*, SUM.NA) from the creditor to the debtor for such-and-such a purpose (e.g., Dar 308, Dar 164, Dar 167, BM 33972 and Dar 541). I translate this clause (i.e., *ša ana ... nadnu*) in the context as described above as a relative sentence: "It is the silver that ...." or "The silver is that which ...." The same expression, i.e., *ša ana ... nadnu*, in other contexts may be translated as a main sentence rather than a relative one, e.g., BM 30854: Obv. 1 (with bibliographic reference).

L. 12: The divine name is either Marduk (AMAR.UTU) or Nergal (U.GUR).

No. 16

BM 30591
Copy: Abraham, *OLA* 65 (1995): 9
Date: 27/vii/35 Dar (19 Oct. 487 B.C.E.)
Place: Babylon
Content: Promissory note for barley. Transport costs due from MNA to a courtier.

OBV.

1 24 GUR 3 (PI) 2 (BÁN) ŠE.BAR *šá* ^{m}x-x-MU$^{?}$-NI$^{?}$
2 LÚ.SAG-LUGAL *ina* UGU ^{m}*ši-ir-ku*
3 A-*šú šá* ^{m}SUM.NA-*a* A ^{m}*e-gì-bi*
4 *ina* ITI.NE *i-nam-din*
5 ŠE.BAR *gi-mir* ŠE.BAR ⸢x⸣ [x x]
6 *šá* ^{m}*ši-ir-ku ina* ⸢ŠU$^{?}$⸣ [x x x]

LO. E. (probably erased)

REV.

7 LÚ *mu-kin-*⸢*nu*⸣ [^{m}... A-*šú*]
8 *šá* ^{md}EN-NU[MUN$^{?}$ A ^{m}...]
9 ^{md}DUMU-É-MU A-*šú* ⸢*ša* ^{m}⸣ [...]
10 A LÚ.SANGA-^{d}UTU $^{<m>}$*ba-ga-da-a-ti*
11 ⸢A⸣-*šu šá* ^{m}*mi-ti-ri-a-ta* ^{md}EN-GI
12 LÚ.SAG-LUGAL ^{m}*ma-ú-zu-zu* A-*šú šá*
13 ^{m}DU$_{10}$.GA-*ia u* ^{m}*ši-ir-ku* DUB.SAR

U. E.

14 A ^{m}*e-gì-bi* TIN.TIR.KI ITI.⸢DU$_{6}$⸣

LE. E.

15 UD.27.⸢KAM⸣ MU.35.KAM
16 ^{m}*da-*⸢*ri*⸣*-'i-ia-muš* LUGAL

TRANSLATION

24.3.2 *kor* of barley are due to PN, a courtier, from MNA$_{2}$. In Ab he shall deliver (it). The barley is (for) the transport costs of the barley [...] which MNA$_{2}$ ... [...].

Witnesses:
[PN/]Bēl-zē[ra ...]
Mār-bīti-iddin/[...]//Šangû-Šamaš
Bagadāta/Mitrāta
Bēl-ušallim, a courtier
Mamûzu/Ṭābiya
And the scribe: MNA$_{2}$
(Place + Date).

COMMENT

BM 30591 is a re-used tablet. Its text was written over a previously written text, which was erased but not completely, so that here and there signs remain visible underneath the newly written text. Remnants of previous signs can clearly be seen in lines 1 (*passim*), 2 (before SAG), 5 (underneath ŠE.BAR), 10 (underneath LÚ), 11 (underneath MI), and 13. In the latter line it seems that the scribe started writing LÚ.UMBISAG, but then changed the LÚ into *u* ^{m}*ši-*, and the UMBISAG into *-ir-ku*. Finally, there is the awkwardly written E-sign on the Upper Edge of the tablet: the scribe did not finish writing its two final vertical wedges, but moved his hand a little bit to the right and then wrote the two final vertical wedges, which are, consequently, detached from the beginning of the E-sign.

L. 1: The 4 in the number 24 is written with horizontal wedges. Cf. the 5 in the number 35 in line 15. The name at the end of the line is difficult to read because it is written over other, badly erased signs.

L. 10–11: For the spelling of the name Mitrāta (Ir. *Miθrāta) in Akkadian cuneiform sources, see Dandamaev, *Iranians*, 101 (198): ^{m}*mi-it-ra-a-ta* or ^{m}*mi-it-ra*(*-a*)*-tú*. The spelling with *-ti* in our text (^{m}*mi-ti-ri-a-ta*), instead of *-it*, is, therefore, unusual, but cf. ^{m}*mi-ti-ri-a-ni* for Mitrēn in BM 33121: 12. For the name Bagadāta (Ir. *Bagadāta), cf. *ibidem*, 50ff. (82).

L. 11–12: Was this Bēl-ušallim the same as Bēl-ušallim/Ina-Nabû-ultarraḫ mentioned in BM 31036:4? Both men were courtiers and involved in the collection of *gimru*-payments.

L. 12–13: For Mamûzu/Ṭābiya (wr. ^{m}*ma-ú-zu-zu*), more at BM 33112: 4 (wr. ^{m}*ma-mu-ú-zu*).

L. 14: The month was probably DU_6 although the sign is squeezed at the end of the line. Less likely is the reading KIN instead of DU_6.

L. 15: Although the first *Winkelhaken* of the number 30 is written slightly higher than the two others, it can hardly be doubted that the year in which the text under consideration was written was 35 (not 25). This is the latest attestation of MNA being alive. More at Abraham, *OLA* 65 (1995): 1–9.

No. 17

BM 30629
Copy: Bertin copy 2093
Date: 12/vii/6 Dar (24 October 516 B.C.E.)
Place: Ḫursagkalamma
Content: Summons to settle the payment of silver for the "contribution of the archer" (*nidintu šá* ^{lú}*qašti*) with MNA.

OBV.

1 UD.20.KAM *šá* ITI.DU$_6$ ^{m}*gu-za-nu* A-*šú šá*
2 ^{md}AG-NUMUN-GIŠ A ^{m}*ga-ḫal il-la-kam-*{*am*}*-ma*
3 *ina* TIN.TIR.KI *it-ti* ^{md}AMAR.UTU-*na-ṣir*-IBILA
4 A-*šú šá* ^{m}SUM.NA-*a* A ^{m}*e-gi-bi a-na muḫ-ḫi*
5 KÙ.BABBAR *ni-din-tu*$_4$ *šá* LÚ.BAN *šá* ^{md}AMAR.UTU-*na-ṣir*-A
6 *a-na* ^{m}*gu-za-nu id-din-nu i-dab-bu-ub*
7 *ki-i la it-tal-lak* 1 MA.NA KÙ.BABBAR

LO. E.

8 *i-nam-din*

REV.

9 [LÚ *mu*]-[*kin-nu* ^{m}ÌR-*ia*] A-*šú šá*
10 ^{m}*da-di-*[*ia* A ^{m}][*na-ba*]*-a-a*
11 ^{md}AG-MU-MU [A]-*šú* ⸢*šá*⸣ [^{m}DUB$^{?}$]-NUMUN A LÚ.SIMUG
12 ^{m}*mu-ra-šu-ú* A-*šú šá* ^{m}MU-^{d}AMAR.UTU
13 A ^{m}DÙ-*eš*-DINGIR LÚ.UMBISAG ^{md}UTU-SUM.NA
14 A ^{m}*sag-di-di ḫur-sag-kalam-ma*.KI
15 ITI.DU$_6$ UD.12.KAM MU.6.KAM
16 ^{m}*da-a-ri-mu-uš* LUGAL E.KI

U. E.

17 *u* KUR.KUR

TRANSLATION

On the twentieth of Tašrīt, Gūzānu, son of Nabû-zēru-līšir, descendant of Gaḫal, shall come to {to} Babylon to reach an agreement with MNA$_1$ about the silver, the *contribution of/for the archer*, which MNA$_1$ gave (= paid?) to Gūzānu. If he does not come, he shall pay one mina of silver.

Witne[sses]:
[Ardiya]/Dādi[ya//]Nabaya
Nabû-šuma-iddin/[Šāpik$^{?}$]-zēri//Nappāḫu
Murašû/Iddin-Marduk//Eppeš-ilī
The scribe: Šamaš-iddin//Sagdidi
(Place + Date).

COMMENT

L. 5: The expression *nidinti ša* ^{lú}*qašti* is a hapax and moreover, ambiguous because it may refer to a "gift for the archer" as well as to a "gift from the archer." Cf. the expression *nidinti šarri*, which not only refers to a "Crown grant" (i.e., land granted by the Crown to individuals in return for part of the produce. *CAD* N$_2$, 207 s.v. *nidintu* mng. 2), but also to "gifts for (i.e., due to) the king" (Jursa, *Landwirtschaft*, n. 235). On archers (^{lú}*qaštu* "archer," *CAD* Q, 151 s.v. *qaštu* mng. 2b-2′) serving in the king's army, their equipment and the nature of their service, see Bongenaar, *Ebabbar*, 131; also see BM 30772 below.

No. 18

	BM 30639
Copy:	Bertin copy 2576
Date:	28/vii/25 Dar (8 November 497 B.C.E.)
Place:	Babylon
Content:	Receipt of payment (issued) by a royal official for transport costs due by MNA. By order of (*ina iqbi ša*) the governor of Babylon.

OBV.

1 *gi-mi-ir šá* 1 ME GUR ŠE.BAR *šá ul-*[*tu*]

2 GARIM *tam-tì* ^{m}GIŠ.MI-*a-a* LÚ *si-pir-ri*

3 *šá* LÚ.NU.GIŠ.KIRI$_6$.MEŠ *u* LÚ *da-li-e*.MEŠ

4 *šá* É.GAL GAL-*ú u* É.GAL *eš-šú*

5 [D]UMU *šá* ^{m}É-DINGIR-IL-TAM-GA-BI *ina iq-*[*bi*]

6 *šá* ^{m}*gu-za-nu* LÚ.GAR-UŠ$_4$ TIN.TIR.KI

7 *ina* ŠU.II ^{m}*ši-rik* A-*šú šá* ^{m}MU-*a* [A ^{m}*e-gì-bi*]

8 *ma-ḫi-ir e-lat šá* GÍD.DA IGI-[*ú*]

9 *šá gi-mi-ir šá* 50 GUR ŠE.BAR *šá* [(x x)]

LO. E.

10 ^{md}EN-NIGIN-*ir u* ^{m}*ḫaš-da-a-*⸢*a*?⸣

REV.

11 *šá ina iq-bi šá* ^{m}*gu-za-nu* LÚ.GAR-UŠ$_4$ [TIN.TIR.KI]

12 [*m*]*aḫ-ḫír* LÚ *mu-kin*$^{!}$*-nu* ^{m}*ka-ṣir*

13 [A-*šú*] *šá* ^{m}*ta-at-tan-nu* A ^{m}DÙ-*eš*-DINGIR

14 [^{m}*ni*]-*din-tu*$_4$ DUMU *šá* ^{m}ÌR-*ia* A ^{m}GAL-60-*š*[*i*]

15 $^{[m]d}$AG-URU$_3$-*šú* DUMU *šá* ^{md}AG-ŠEŠ.MEŠ-MU

16 [A] ^{md}30-*tab-ni*

17 ^{md}AG-DIN-*iṭ* DUB.SAR DUMU ^{md}EN-A-URU$_3$

18 TIN.TIR.KI ITI.DU$_6$ UD.28.KAM

19 MU.25.KAM ^{m}*da-a-ri-ia-muš*

U. E.

20 LUGAL TIN.TIR.KI *u* KUR.KUR

TRANSLATION

The costs for the transport of one hundred *kor* of barley fro[m] the irrigated farmland in Tâmti: Ṣillaya, clerk of the gardeners and the water-drawers of the Grand Palace and the New Palace, son of *Bīt-iltammar*$^{!}$, has received (it) from MNA$_2$, by order of Gūzānu, governor of Babylon. In addition, there is a previou[s] register regarding the costs for the transport of fifty *kor* of barley of/from [(...)] Bēl-upaḫḫir and Ḫašdaya, which he has (already) [r]eceived by order of Gūzānu, governor of [Babylon].

Witnesses$^{!}$:
Kāṣir[/]Tattannu//Eppeš-ilī
[Ni]dintu/Ardiya//Rab-šušš[i]
Nabû-uṣuršu/Nabû-aḫḫē-iddin[//]Sîn-tabni
The scribe: Nabû-uballiṭ//Bēl-apla-uṣur
(Place + Date).

COMMENT

L. 2: On Tâmti and the transport of agricultural produce from this place, see more at BM 31572: 2.

L. 5: I suggest reading ^{m}É-DINGIR-*il-tam-mar*$^{!}$(GA-BI). The name Bīt-ilī-iltammar "May he see the House of the Gods," is similar in meaning to names such as Ālu-lūmur (Tallqvist, *NbN*, 5), Bābilu-lūmur (Tallqvist, *NbN*, 17), and Ebabbar-lūmur (Tallqvist, *NbN* 203 s.v. Šulaya(12)). Names beginning with *Bīt-* are rare in the Neo-Babylonian period (Tallqvist, *NbN*, 308–9), and are of two types: the type Bīt-Ir'anni-šarra-uṣur, where *bīt-* is a nominative, and the type Bīta-ukīn-Bāba, where *bīt-* is an accusative. There also exist names such as Nergal-ana-bītišu or Ina-ṣilli-bīt- akītu. I found only one other name in which the element *Bīt-* is followed by DINGIR, viz. in one of the Sippar texts: $^{[m]}$É-DINGIR-*da-la-a'* (BM 61774 Rev.: 6', published in Jursa, *Landwirtschaft* No. 24).

L. 5 and 11: The tablet has clearly *ina iq-bi* both in line 5 and in line 11, whereas the usual formulation is *ina qí-bi* "by order of," cf. BM 31226: 6 (*ina iq-ba*) and BM 33936: 7 (*ina qí-bit*).

L. 10: Should we identify Bēl-upaḫḫir mentioned without affiliation in the text under consideration with Bēl-upaḫḫir/Nergal-iddin? Note that in one of the texts regarding the latter's debts to MNA and his brother, viz. Dar 345, two sons of a man named Ḫašdaya occur among the witnesses, and this may be significant for the identification of Bēl-upaḫḫir in the text under consideration, because he is mentioned together with a man named Ḫašdaya in this text.

No. 19

	BM 30641
Copy:	no Bertin copy
Date:	30/vii (no year)
Place:	no place
Content:	Note to remind about payments for seeds that were promised to Širku (= MNA?)

OBV.

1 10 GÍN KÙ.BABBAR UD-*ú šá*
2 ŠE.GIŠ.Ì ⅓ MA.NA KÙ.BABBAR UD-*ú*
3 *šá* GAZI.SAR-*ia taḫ-si-iḫ*-tu_4
4 *la maš*-tu_4 *šá* ^{m}*ar-rab-bi*
5 AD *šá* ^{md}AG-*bul-liṭ-su*
6 *a-na* ^{m}*ši-ir-ku*

REV.

7 *iq-bu-ú*
8 ITI.DU_6 UD.30.KAM
(Remainder of reverse is empty.)

TRANSLATION

Ten shekels of white silver for the sesame seeds, (and) one-third mina of white silver for the *kasia* seeds. A note not to be forgotten, which Arrabi, father of Nabû-bullissu, promised to Širku. The 30th of Tašrīt.

COMMENT

This text contains a brief reminder regarding the delivery of sesame seeds and *kasia* seeds. The reason for the delivery is not stated. The seeds had been promised by Nabû-bullissu, son of Arrabi, to Širku. We cannot be sure that the latter was actually the Širku whom we know from the Egibi family under his full name of Marduk-nāṣir- apli, son of Itti-Marduk-balāṭu. It should be noted that a Nergal-ušallim, son of Arrabi, is mentioned in relation with onions in BM 30747: he received the *miksu*-toll from Širku//Egibi for a boatload of onions. However, no firm connection can be established between BM 30641 (sesame and *kasia* seeds; Nabû-bullissu/Arrabi) and BM 30747 (onions; Nergal-ušallim/Arrabi).

L. 2: For the nature of the plant *kasia*, see Cocquerillat, *Palmeraies*, 30; and *CAD* K, 248ff. s.v. *kasû*.

L. 3: Note the awkward spelling *taḫ-si-iḫ*-tu_4 for the noun *taḫsistu*. For the usual spelling(s) of this noun in the Neo-Babylonian period, see *AHw*, 1302 s.v. *taḫsistu* mng. 4.

No. 20

BM 30651
Copy: no Bertin copy
Date: no date
Place: no place
Content: List of quantities of silver and personal names. Reference to the governor and persons known from texts of MNA's archive.

OBV.

1 [x MA].NA KÙ.BABBAR UD-*ú nu*$^{?}$-[…]
2 *ina* ŠU.II ^{md}U.GUR-MU [(…)]
3 [x]+1 MA.NA KÙ.BABBAR UD-*ú* ⸢*ina* ŠU.II ^{md}EN-MU⸣
4 *šá* É DUMU TIN.TIR.KI
5 2 MA.NA KÙ.BABBAR UD-*ú ina* ŠU.II ^{md}AG-*it-tan-nu*
6 *u* ^{m}*lib-luṭ šá ina* UGU ÍD *eš-šú e-lu-ú*
7 2 MA.NA KÙ.BABBAR UD-*ú ina* ŠU.II ^{m}*ap-la-a*
8 *šá ina* URU *šá-bi-i-lu*
9 1½ MA.NA KÙ.BABBAR UD-*ú ina* ŠU.II ^{m}*mar-duk* A
10 LÚ.BAḪAR$_{2}$
11 [x]+⸢½⸣ MA.NA KÙ.BABBAR UD-*ú* ^{m}*ni-din-tu-*^{d}EN-*dam-qát*
12 [*ina* Š]U.II ^{m}*ḫaš-da-a-a šá ina* URU *šá-bi-i-lu*
13 [x MA.N]A 5 GÍN KÙ.BABBAR UD-*ú* ^{m}*ni-din-*⸢*tu*$_{4}$-^{d}EN-*dam-qát*⸣
(End of obverse is broken off.)

LO. E. (broken)

REV.

1 [x x x ^{md}]⸢*za-ba*$_{4}$-*ba*$_{4}$-MU-MU⸣
2 [x] GÍN KÙ.BABBAR UD-*ú*
3 [*ina n*]*a-áš-par-tu*$_{4}$ *šá* LÚ.GAR-UŠ$_{4}$
4 ^{m}ÌR-^{d}*bu-ne-ne* LÚ.ÌR LÚ.GAR-UŠ$_{4}$
5 *ina* GUB-*zu* ^{m}*na-piš-tu*$_{4}$
6 *ù* ^{m}*ba-nu-nu*
(End of the text. Remainder of reverse is empty.)

TRANSLATION

[x mi]na(s) of white silver […] from Nergal-MU [(…)].

[x]+one minas of white silver ⸢from Bēl-iddin⸣ of the house of the Babylonian.

Two minas of white silver from Nabû-ittannu and Libluṭ at the Upper New canal.

Two minas of white silver from Aplaya in Šabīlu.

One and a half minas of white silver from Marduk, descendant of Paḫāru.

[x]⸢+a half⸣ minas of white silver: Nidinti-Bēl-damqat [f]rom Ḫašdaya in Šabīlu.

[x mi]nas and five shekels of white silver: Nidinti-Bēl-damqat [...].

[...] ⌜Zababa-šuma-iddin⌝.

[...] shekels of white silver [(which ...) as pro]xy for the governor, Arad-Bunene, the governor's servant, in the presence of Napištu and Bānûnu.

COMMENT

BM 30651 does not mention MNA, but is closely related to four texts from his archive. The payment listed in BM 30651: 3–4 should be compared with Bēl-iddin's payment for *ilku* mentioned in the letter BM 31416. The payment listed in BM 30651: 7–8 is to be compared with the payment for *ilku* from Aplaya/Bazūzu//Ašlāku recorded in BM 31533. The payments listed in BM 30651: 9–10, 11–13 and Rev. 2–6 can be identified with payments by MNA to the governor of Babylon for transactions related to boats in BM 30853 and BM 30256. For a full discussion of these connections, see § 2.5.1.

L. 1: At the end of this line one may read *nu*?-[*uḫ-ḫu-tú*] or *ina* Š[ÁM? ...]. There is enough space for at least three signs.

L. 2: After the MU the surface of the obverse and the right edge of the tablet is damaged. In the damaged part of the obverse there is space for three signs; one or two more signs may have followed on the right edge (cf. lines 5 and 6 where the scribe continued writing on the right edge). However, it is not necessarily so that the text continued after mdU.GUR-MU; it may have been a short line, like lines 4, 8, and 10 of the obverse, and almost all lines of the reverse.

L. 4: At the beginning of the line, before the *šá* there is an empty space (cf. line 8).

L. 8: For the place Šabīlu, see Zadok, *RGTC* 8, 282 (probably not far from Babylon). The place is known from one previously published text (viz. Nbk 195: 18 from the time of MNA's grandfather), and from two texts from MNA's time, published here (viz. BM 30819 and BM 31533). The latter are receipts of *ilku* by MNA. It seems, therefore, that MNA visited Šabīlu for the collection of *ilku* only. This may help clarify the reason for the "silver (payment) from Aplaya (paid) in Šabīlu" as recorded in the text under consideration (ll. 7–8). If the only reason for which MNA travelled to Šabīlu was to collect *ilku* (BM 30819 and BM 31533), the silver from Aplaya in Šabīlu (above, ll. 7–8) may well have been silver for his *ilku*. It should further be noted that the *ilku* that MNA received in Šabīlu according to BM 31533 was paid by one Aplaya/Bazūzu//Ašlāku. He was, most likely, the same as the Aplaya mentioned in lines 7–8 in the text above.

L. 10: The LÚ.BAḪAR$_2$ is written in the middle of the line. Cf. line 8.

No. 21

BM 30747
Copy: no Bertin copy
Date: no date (refers to *miksu* for onions of the tenth year)
Place: no place
Content: Receipt of the *miksu*-toll from MNA.

OBV.

1 ⸢*mi*⸣-*ik-su šá* GIŠ.MÁ *šá* SUM.⸢SAR⸣
2 *šá* MU.10.KAM ^{md}U.GUR-GI A-*šú šá*
3 ^{m}*ar-rab-bi ina* ŠU.II ^{m}*ši-ir-ku*
4 A-*šú šá* ^{m}MU-*a* A ^{m}*e-gì-bi*
5 ⸢*ma*⸣-*ḫi-ir*

REV.

6 LÚ ⸢*mu-kin-nu* ^{md}AG⸣-KAR-ZI$^{!}$.MEŠ A-*šú šá*
7 ^{md}AG-KAD A LÚ.ŠITIM ^{md}UTU-DIN-*iṭ*
8 A-*šú šá* ^{m}NUMUN-*ia* ^{md}AG-*it-tan-nu* A-*šú šá*
9 ^{m}*šu-zu-bu* A ^{m}EGIR-DINGIR.MEŠ ^{m}NÍG.KA-UR
10 A-*šú šá* ^{md}AG-ŠEŠ-URU$_3$ ^{md}AMAR.UTU-PAB A-*šú šá*
11 ^{md}AMAR.UTU-GI ^{md}AG-*it-tan-n*[*u*]
12 A-*šú šá* ^{m}SILA-*a-a* A ^{m}*za-ḫu-šú* ^{m}⸢^{d}⸣[x-x]

U. E.

13 [A-*šú šá*] $^{[m]}$[x]-A ^{m}EN-*šú-nu* A-*šú šá* ^{m}⸢x-x-x⸣
14 [^{m}*r*]*i*$^{?}$-*mut*$^{?}$-x [A-*šú šá*] ⸢^{m}ÌR⸣-*ia* A LÚ ⸢x⸣

RI. E.

15 [(x x)] ⸢x⸣ DINGIR

TRANSLATION

Nergal-ušallim, son of Arrabi, has received the *miksu*-toll from MNA$_2$ for a boat loaded with onions (from the harvest) of the tenth year.

Witnesses:
Nabû-ēṭir-napšāti$^{!}$/Nabû-kāṣir//Itinnu
Šamaš-uballiṭ/Zēriya
Nabû-ittannu/Šūzubu//Arkât-ilī
Lâbāši$^{?}$ (read {NÍG.KA}-TÉŠ?)/Nabû-aḫa-uṣur
Marduk-nāṣir/Marduk-ušallim
Nabû-ittann[u]/Sūqaya//*Zaḫušu*
^{md}[... /^{m}][x]-A
Bēlšunu/^{m}[...]
⸢Rīmūt-Bēl⸣$^{?}$ [/]$^{?}$ Ardiya//⸢Itinnu$^{?}$⸣.

COMMENT

The lower and left edges are well-preserved and uninscribed. The right edge has three or four signs but they are difficult to read. However, these signs do not seem to be part of the date formula. Consequently, I have not been able to identify the scribe of the tablet, nor when and where it was written.

L. 2: For Nabû-bullissu/Arrabi, see BM 30641.

L. 2 and 7: The signs DINGIR and U of line 2 (in ^{md}U.GUR-GI), as well as the DINGIR and UTU of line 7 (in ^{md}UTU-DIN-*iṭ*) are written over an erasure.

L. 9: The signs of the name ^{m}NÍG-KA-UR are clear. The UR-sign may be interpreted UR=TÉŠ=*bâšu*, and may, accordingly, refer to the common name *Lâbāši*. The signs NÍG.KA mean *nikkassu*, but names with this noun are very rare; I know of only two examples from the Neo-Babylonian period, which are both listed in Weisberg, *YOS* 17, 62 s.v. Nikkassu (wr. ^{m}NÍG.ŠID). Another possibility is to link the name with *Nikkaya* (wr. ^{m}*Nik/Ník-ka-a-a*), which is occasionally attested in Babylon as a family name (Tallqvist, *NbN*, 167; Wunsch, *Iddin-Marduk* 1, 151).

L. 12: The name ^{m}*za-ḫu-šú* is unique. The signs *-ḫu-šú* resemble the beginning of a ligature, = ^{d}EN/^{d}AG.

L. 13: The partly broken sign may be a NA or a GIN, and if so, the name in question ($^{[m]}$[x]-A) was either $^{[m]}$[*ki*]$^{?}$-[*na*$^{?}$]-*a*, or $^{[m]}$[GIN$^{?}$]-A (= Mukīn$^{?}$-apli).

L. 14: This line is written at the very top of the tablet, i.e., between the end of the upper edge and the beginning of the obverse.

L. 15: Do we have to read $^{[m]⌜d⌝}$30-DINGIR or $^{[m]}$DÙ-*eš*-DINGIR? These are usually surnames and it is unclear whose it could have been.

No. 22

BM 30764
Copy: Bertin copy 2566
Date: 23/iii/25 Dar (8 July 497 B.C.E.)
Place: Babylon
Content: Receipt of a boat-tower by MNA. Hired for six days a month during five months from July till November.

OBV.

1 LÚ.ḪUN.GÁ LÚ *šá-di-du šá* ITI 6 *u*$_4$-*mu*.MEŠ
2 *šá a-di qí-it* ITI.APIN *šá* MU.25.KAM
3 *šá* ^{m}*mar-duk-a* A-[*šú*] *šá* ^{md}AG-URU$_3$-*šú* A ^{m}MU-*líb-ši*
4 ^{m}*ši-rik* A-*šú šá* ^{m}MU-*a* A ^{m}*e-gi-bi*
5 *ina* ŠU.II ^{m}*na-a-ši-bu* A ^{m}*la-qí-pi*
6 *a-na muḫ-ḫi* ^{m}*mar-duk-a ma-ḫir*
7 1-*en*.TA.ÀM *šá-ṭa-ri il-te-qu-ú*

REV.

8 LÚ *mu-kin-nu* ^{m}*mar-duk-a* A-*šú šá* ^{m}*gu-za-nu*
9 A ^{m}*kàṣ-ṣì-dak-ku* ^{m}*ta-at-tan-nu*
10 A-*šú šá* ^{md}AG-KÀD A ^{m}*da-bi-bi*
11 ^{m}*ap-la-a* A-*šú šá* ^{m}*ni-qu-du* A LÚ.ŠITIM
12 LÚ.UMBISAG ^{md}⌜AG⌝-*bul-liṭ-su* A-*šú šá* ^{md}⌜AG⌝-GIN-NUMUN
13 A ^{md}IDIM-NU-DINGIR TIN.TIR.KI ITI.SIG$_4$
14 UD.23.KAM MU.25.KAM ^{m}*da-a-ri-ia-muš*
15 LUGAL TIN.TIR.KI *u* KUR.KUR

TRANSLATION

A hireling to tow boats for six days a month till the end of Araḫsamna of the twenty-fifth year is due from Marduk, son of Nabû-uṣuršu, descendant of Šumu-libši: MNA$_2$ has received (him) from Nāšibu, descendant of Lā-qīpu, for the account of Marduk. They have taken one (copy of the) document each.

Witnesses:
Marduk/Gūzānu//Kaṣṣidakku
Tattannu/Nabû-kāṣir//Dābibī
Aplaya/Niqūdu//Itinnu
The scribe: ⌜Nabû⌝-bullissu/⌜Nabû⌝-mukīn-zēri//Ea-ṣalam-ilī
(Place + Date).

No. 23

BM 30772
Copy: Bertin copy 2621
Date: 20/xii/26 Dar (17 March 495 B.C.E.)
Place: Babylon
Content: Receipt of the *ilku*$^{!}$-tax and other contributions such as "fittings for the archer" (*unāt* ^{lú}*qašti*) by MNA.

OBV.

1 [*il*]-*ki*$^{!}$ DI-*pi šá* GIM *ú-na-at* LÚ.BAN
2 [x x x] *šá* ^{m}*du-um-mu-qu* DUMU *šá* ^{m}*ba-la-ṭu*
3 A ^{m}*ga-ḫúl šá* TA *šá* ITI.GAN MU.25.KAM
4 *a-di qí-it* ITI *šá* BÁR MU.27.KAM
5 ^{m}*da-a-ri-'i-muš* LUGAL *šá* $^{\langle m \rangle}$*šik-ku* DUMU *šá*
6 ^{m}SUM.NA-*a* A ^{m}*e-gi-bi ina* ŠU.II
7 ^{md}AG-MU DUMU *šá* {*šá*} ^{m}*i-qu-pu* A$^{!}$ ^{m}*e-tel-pi*
8 *a-na muḫ-ḫi* ^{m}*du-um-mu-qu*
9 *ma-ḫi-ir* 1-*en*.ÀM TI-*ú*

REV.

10 LÚ *mu-kin-nu* ^{md}AG-*it-tan-nu* A-*šú šá* ^{m}ÌR-*ia*
11 A ^{md}30-DINGIR ^{m}*šá*-^{d}EN-*at-ta-ia*
12 A-*šú šá* ^{md}AMAR.UTU-MU-DÙ A ^{m}*e-gi-bi*
13 ^{md}EN-SU A-*šú šá* ^{m}*kal-ba-a-a* A ^{m}MU-*líb-ši*
14 ^{md}EN-DIN-*iṭ* LÚ.UMBISAG DUMU *šá* ^{m}KI-^{d}AMAR.UTU-DIN
15 A ^{md}EN-[*e*]-*ṭè-ri*$^{!}$ TIN.TIR.KI ITI.ŠE
16 UD.20.KAM MU.26.KAM ^{m}*da-a-ri-muš*
17 LUGAL E.KI *u* KUR.KUR

TRANSLATION

The [*il*]*ku*$^{!}$-tax, the ..., (and)$^{?}$ the *fittings for the archer* [x x x], from Kislīm of the twenty-fifth year till the end of Nisan of the twenty-seventh year of King Darius, are due from Dummuqu, son of Balāṭu, descendant of Gaḫul: MNA_2 has received (it) from Nabû-iddin, son of {of} Iqūpu, descendant$^{!}$ of Etel-pî, for the account of Dummuqu. They have taken one (copy of the document) each.

Witnesses:
Nabû-ittannu/Ardiya//Sîn-ilī
Ša-Bēl-atta/Marduk-šuma-ibni//Egibi
Bēl-erība/Kalbaya//Šumu-libši
The scribe: Bēl-uballiṭ/Itti-Marduk-balāṭu//Bēl-eṭēru$^{!}$
(Place + Date).

COMMENT

L. 1: The wedges in this line are clearly preserved and each sign can be identified without problem: [x] DI DI PI *šá* GIM *ú-na-at* LÚ.BAN. However, the signs together do not lead to any understandable reading. It seems, therefore, that the text in question is a copy made from the original by a junior scribe, who did not always know what he was copying. The scribe's inexperience can also be seen in line 5 ($^{<m>}$), line 7 ({*ša*}, A$^{!}$) and line 15 (-*ri*$^{!}$). Consequently, I suggest emending some signs in the line under consideration and read [*il*]-*ki*$^{!}$ *ṭi-pi šá* (GIŠ).BAN$^{!?}$ *ú-na-at* LÚ.BAN "the [*il*]*ku*$^{!}$-tax, addition to the bow$^{!?}$(-tax), (and) the fittings for the archer." The emendation *ṭi-pi šá* (GIŠ).BAN$^{!?}$ is based on a comparison with similar expressions in BM 30366:1 (*il-ki šá ṭi-pi šá giš-ri*) and NRVU 551: 1 (*kaspu ša ṭi-pi ša* GIŠ.BAN). Moreover, GIM and BAN are easily confounded because the difference lies in one vertical wedge more or less at the end of the sign (cf. Jursa, *Bēl-rēmanni*, 19 regarding *Bēl-rēmanni*, 251f.: 8, 16 = BM 79128 [^{giš}BAN$^{!}$(GIM)], and VS 4 113 = *Bēl-rēmanni*, 261: 12 [$^{<m>}$*kur-ban*$^{!}$(GIM)-*ni*-]). The expression *unāt* ^{lú}*qašti* is, no doubt, to be compared to the similar expression *unūt tāḫazi* "arms" in the Murašû texts, e.g., BE 10 61 that concerns a payment for wages (*idī*), provisions regarding clothing (*ṣidīt lubuš*), and arms (*unūt tāḫazi*). More at Stolper, *RLA* 8, 205–7 s.v. Militärkolonisten. Fitting out the army is usually expressed by terms such as *rikis qabli* and *pasa'du*, see more at Bongenaar, *Ebabbar*, 131.

L. 5: The *šá* after LUGAL is not taken up in the translation. It seems to be a scribal mistake for a *Personenkeil*.

L. 12–13: Bertin copied lines 12 and 13 as one line: A-*šú šá* ^{md}AMAR.UTU-NUMUN-DÙ A ^{m}MU-*líb-ši*.

L. 15: The sign ḪU is to be corrected to *ri* or *ru*.

No. 24

BM 30795
Copy: Bertin copy 2606
Date: 26/x/26 Dar (23 January 495 B.C.E.)
Place: Babylon
Content: [Receipt] of persons together with the registers of their enlistment (GIŠ.ŠID.MEŠ). To do service? Reference to the governor of Babylon. MNA is a witness.

OBV.

1 ⸢^{m}*ri*⸣-*mut* A-*šú šá* ^{md}AMAR.UTU-GI A ^{m}⸢LÚ⸣.B[AḪA]R$_{2}$
2 [*u*] ^{m}*lib-luṭ* A-*šú šá* ^{m}*it-ti*-^{d}AG-DIN A ^{m}LÚ *si*<-*si-e*>
3 *it-ti* GIŠ.ŠID.MEŠ x x LUGAL
4 ŠÁ BAR RI *ina* ŠU.II ^{m}*gu-za-nu* [A-*šú šá* ^{m}]^{d}A[G-MU-GIN]
5 A ^{m}LÚ *šá-na-ni-šú a-ki-i* ⸢GIŠ$^{?}$⸣[x x x] ⸢x⸣ RAT$^{?}$

6 *il-la-a'* GIŠ ⸢x⸣ ⸢GA$^{?}$⸣ ⸢x⸣ [x x (x)]
7 *ù* GIŠ.ŠID.MEŠ ⸢*ina*⸣ [x x x x (x)]
8 *ina* TIN.TIR.KI *a-na* [x x x x (x)]

LO. E.

9 [L]Ú.GAR-UŠ$_4$ TIN.TIR.KI *i*-⸢x⸣ [(x)]

REV.

10 *u* LÚ *šá-da-e*.MEŠ$^{!}$ *e-ṭir*.ME[Š]
11 LÚ *mu-kin-nu* ^{md}EN-*it-tan-nu* A-*šú šá*
12 ^{md}UTU-MU A LÚ.SANGA-BÁR
13 ^{m}*ši-rik* A-*šú šá* ^{m}MU-*a* A ^{m}*e-gi-bi*
14 ^{md}AG-ŠEŠ-MU A-*šú šá* ^{m}*ba-zu-zu* A$^{!}$ ^{m}*ir-a-ni*
15 ^{m}*ḫaš-da-a-a* A-*šú šá* ^{md}AG-ŠEŠ.MEŠ-[*bul*]-⸢*liṭ*⸣
16 ^{md}EN-*it-tan-nu* A-*šú šá* ^{m}*na-pu-uš-tu*$_4$
17 {^{m}} *u* <LÚ>.UMBISAG ^{md}EN-SU A-*šú šá* ^{m}*kal-ba-a* A ^{m}MU-⸢*líb*⸣-[*ši*]
18 E.KI ITI.AB UD.26.KAM
19 MU.26.KAM ^{m}*da-ri-muš* LUGAL

U. E.

20 TIN.TIR.KI *u* KUR.KUR

TRANSLATION

Rīmūt, son of Marduk-ušallim, descendant of P[aḫā]ru, [and] Libluṭ, son of Itti-Nabû-balāṭu, descendant of Sī<sî>, with the lists, ... (of) the king, *ša* x x, in/from the hands of Gūzānu, [son of] N[abû-šuma-ukīn], descendant of Ša-nāšīšu, according to [...] ⸢x⸣. RAT$^{?}$. Beyond them: the ⸢...⸣ [...] and the lists ⸢in⸣ [...] in Babylon to/for [...], governor of Babylon [...], and the ^{lú}... have been received.

Witnesses:
Bēl-ittannu/Šamaš-iddin//Šangû-parakki
MNA$_2$
Nabû-aḫa-iddin/Bazūzu//Ir'anni
Ḫašdaya/Nabû-aḫḫē-⸢bulliṭ⸣
Bēl-ittannu/Napuštu
And <the> scribe: Bēl-erība/Kalbaya//Šumu-⸢lib⸣[ši]
(Place + Date).

COMMENT

For a text similar in formula and outline, see BM 30446.

L. 1: The end of the line is written on the right edge and reverse of the tablet, and the signs are very much squeezed. One can see ^{m}LÚ.⸢DUG⸣.[QA.BU]R. A person named Rīmūt/Mušallim//Paḫāru is listed by Tallqvist, *NbN*, 176 s.v. Rīmūt(45). He is attested in Liv 20 among the witnesses. Remarkably, he actually occurs there together with Libluṭ/Itti-Nabû-balāṭu/Sīsî. The two of them also occur together in the text under consideration (ll. 1–2).

L. 2: After LÚ *si* nothing more was written, but there is little doubt that we should complete as follows: ᵐLÚ *si*<-*si*-*e*>. For Libluṭ/Itti-Nabû-balāṭu// Sīsî, cf. Tallqvist, *NbN*, 96 s.v. Libluṭ(24) and several texts in the present study.

L. 3: These lines seem to refer to bookkeeping records, "*property*? of the king." In my opinion, GIŠ.ŠID.MEŠ is the logogram for *manâtu* "account tablet" (ŠID=*manû*). For the noun *manâtu* see *CAD* M_1, 208 s.v. *manâtu* B ("bookkeeping, accounting"), and Jursa, *Tempelzehnt*, 79–80 and notes 288–89. For the verb *manû* as a technical term for "to account for" ("verbuchen"), see *ibid.*, n. 282. The word that follows GIŠ.ŠID.MEŠ remains unclear, although the signs are relatively clear. The first sign seems to be either UD or GIŠ (or maybe MA/BA?). The second sign is a clear GA. However, the combination UD.GA / GIŠ.GA does not make sense. Is the UD/GIŠ a scribal error for NÍG, and do we have to read NÍG.GA = *makkūru*? The signs that follow GIŠ.ŠID in the parallel text BM 30446: 3 are equally enigmatic (ŠI MI KI?).

L. 4a: The first three signs of this line are: ŠÁ BAR RI. If read *šá bar-ri* they may refer to the *barru*, a kind of tax known from (late) Achaemenid texts (*CAD* B, 120 s.v. *bāru* A; *AHw*, 108 s.v. *bāru* III; Joannès, *TÉBR*, 21ff.). Alternatively, we may read these signs as follows: *šá-ṭir*!(BAR RI) "registered." Were "Rīmūt/Marduk-ušallim//Paḫāru [and] Libluṭ/Itti-Nabû-balāṭu//Sīsî registered in the lists ... of the king?" The verb *šaṭir*, however, is singular whereas its subject is plural; and *ina* would have been more appropriate than the *itti* of line 3.

L. 4b: Since the overall content of the text is unclear, it is uncertain whether *ina qātē* means "in the hands of," or "(received) from." I prefer the former possibility. Accordingly, Rīmūt, Libluṭ and the registers were "administered by" (*ina qātē* // *ša qātē*) Gūzānu/Nabû-šuma-ukīn//Ša-nāšīšu. This Gūzānu is known from other texts as governor of Babylon. He seems to bear his title of governor in BM 30795 as well, viz., in the fragmentary passage in line 8. On the ambiguity of the expression *ina qātē* also see Gehlken, *AUWE* 5, 15; on the parallel *ina qātē* "(entrusted) in the hands of" and *ša* (*ina*) *qātē* "under the (administrative) control of," also see BM 30446:4, BM 31227: 5b, BM 33954: 3 and cf. CT 22 74: 13. On *ša qātē*, also see Gehlken, *id.*, 101 n. 3.

L. 5: I suggest reconstructing a verb of receipt/quittance at the end of this line. For a reconstruction of this line I rely on the parallel text BM 30446. The latter is basically structured as follows: PN_1 [*u*] PN_2 *itti* GIŠ.ŠID *ša* x x x [x x (x)] *ša Darius šarri ša ina qātē* PN_3 *aki* GIŠ.ŠID *eṭrūtu* (wr. *e-ṭir-ú-*⸢*tú*?⸣), "PN_1 [and] PN_2 with the list of x x x [...] of King Darius that is in the hands of PN_3 according to the (said)? list ⸢have been?⸣ paid." Accordingly, I suggest reading *a-ki-i* ⸢GIŠ?⸣.[ŠID.MEŠ *e-ṭi*]*r-rat*? in line 5 of the text under consideration.

L. 6: For *il-la-a'*, cf. *al-la-a'* in BM 30446: 7.

L. 7–9: At the end of line 9 we expect a verb, possibly a form of *nadānu* or *e'ēlu*. I suggest reconstructing lines 7–9 as follows: (7) *ù* GIŠ.ŠID.MEŠ ⸢*ina*⸣ [*muḫḫi* ...] (8) *ina* TIN.TIR.KI *a-na* [*šūmi Gūzānu*] (9) [L]Ú.GAR-UŠ$_4$ TIN.TIR.KI *i*-⸢*'i*$^{?}$⸣-[-*il*$^{?}$-*li*$^{?}$]; and I translate them as follows: "and he will [(officially) draw up$^{?}$] the registers to [the debit of ...] in Babylon in the [name of Gūzānu], governor of Babylon." For the verb *e'ēlu* "bind," see *CAD* E, 40 s.v. *e'ēlu* mng. 2a-2'. It is usually constructed with *ina muḫḫi* ("to the debit of," examples in the *CAD*), and *ana šūmi* ("in the name of," Von Dassow, CTMMA 3, 203 [with bibliography]). Texts published or re-edited in the present volume that seem to have this verb are (in addition to BM 30795: 9): BM 31416: 18, BM 31718: 5', BM 33959: 4 and Dar 338: 5.

L. 10: For LÚ *šá-da-e*.MEŠ$^{!}$, cf. LÚ *šá-di-e*.MEŠ in BM 31393:4. In the text under consideration, however, there is no MEŠ but a TI.

L. 14: The scribe started writing A-*šú šá*, but then tried to change this into A ^{m}.

No. 25

BM 30799
Copy: no Bertin copy
Date: 26/v/4$^{?}$ Dar (2 September 518$^{?}$ B.C.E.)
Place: broken
Content: Renting of a boat by MNA.

OBV.

1 [GI]Š.MÁ *šá* 6 KÙ[Š ...]
2 [*šá*] ^{m}ÌR-^{d}UTU$^{?}$ ⸢x⸣ [...]
3 LÚ *si-pir-ri šá* ^{m}x x [x x] *na-a'*
4 *šá ina* IGI ^{m}*ki-na-a a-na* LÚ.MÁ.LAḪ$_x$-*ú-tu*
5 ⸢*a*⸣-*na i-di-šú a-na* ⸢x⸣ MA.NA KÙ.BABBAR UD-*ú*
6 ⸢*šá*⸣ *ina* 1 GÍN *bit-qa nu-uḫ-ḫu-tú a-na* ^{md}AMAR.UTU-*na-ṣir*-IBILA
7 ⸢A⸣-*šú šá* ^{m}KI-^{d}AMAR.UTU-DIN A ^{m}*e-gì-bi id-din*
8 ⸢*ki*⸣-*i* GIŠ.MÁ ^{md}AMAR.UTU-*na-ṣir*-IBILA
9 ⸢x⸣ ÍD LIBIR$^{?}$.RA *ul-te-bal* ⸢½⸣
10 MA.NA KÙ.BABBAR UD-*ú a-na* ^{m}ÌR-^{d}[UTU]

LO. E.

11 *i-nam-din*

REV.

12 LÚ *mu-kin-nu* ^{md}*é-a*-IBILA-MU A-*šú šá*
13 ^{m}*mu-še-zib*-^{d}AMAR.UTU A LÚ.GÍR.LÁ-*ka-a-ri*
14 ^{m}*ba-la-ṭu* A-*šú šá* ^{m}DINGIR.MEŠ-*la-ba-a'*
15 ^{m}*um-ma-a* A-*šú šá* ^{md}AMAR.UTU-NUMUN-DÙ LÚ.BAḪAR$_2$
16 *u* LÚ.UMBISAG$^{!}$ ^{m}*li*[*b*]-*l*[*uṭ* A-*šú šá*] ^{md}AG-MU-GIN

17 A ^{m}*ši-g*[*u-ú-a* x x (x) I]TI.NE UD.26.KAM
18 MU.⸢4$^{?}$⸣[.KAM] [Darius LUGAL] E.KI *u* KUR.KUR
19 KURU[M$_6$ … ^{md}AM]AR.UTU-*na-ṣir*-IBILA
20 A-⸢*šú šá*⸣ […] ÁŠ$^{?}$

LE. E.

21 [TA] UD.11.KAM *šá* ITI.KIN$^{?}$ GIŠ.MÁ *ina* [IGI]
22 $^{[md]}$AMAR.UTU-*na-ṣir*-IBILA

TRANSLATION

[The b]oat belonging to Arad-Šamaš$^{?}$, […] clerk of ^{m}…, which is six cubits [wide at its beam]$^{?}$ (and) at the disposal of Kīnaya for sailing: he has rented (it) out to MNA$_1$ for ⸢x⸣ mina(s) of white, medium-quality silver, of which one-eighth is alloy. If MNA$_1$ has the boat … the old$^{?}$ canal, he will give to Arad-[Šamaš$^{?}$] ⸢a half⸣ mina of white silver.

Witnesses:
Ea-apla-iddin/Mušēzib-Marduk//Ṭābiḫ-kāri
Balāṭu/Ilī-laba
Ummaya/Marduk-zēra-ibni//Paḫāru
The scribe: Libl[uṭ]/Nabû-šuma-ukīn//Šig[ûa]
(Place + Date).

[His$^{?}$] mainten[ance …] MNA$_1$ [has paid to$^{?}$ …]
[From] the eleventh of Ulūl$^{?}$ the boat will be at the [disposal] of MNA$_1$.

COMMENT

L. 1: In the second half of this line one should probably read *ina muḫ-ḫi šá-bur-ru rap-šú*, cf. e.g., BM 30370: 1–2.

L. 3: Arad-Šamaš$^{?}$ seems to have been a clerk of an ethnic group, if the ending *-na-a'* in the name ^{m}x-x-[x-x]-*na-a'* is understood as a gentilic ending. Cf. Bazbaka, "c[lerk] of the Ionians" in BM 32891: 4–5, ^{m}*ba-az-ba-ka* [LÚ *s*]*i-pi-ri šá um-ma-nu u* LÚ.[*si-pir*]$^{?}$ LÚ *ia-ma-*⸢*na*⸣*-a-a*.

L. 5: We expect an amount of silver, perhaps one-third mina because this sum often occurs in boat rental agreements (cf. BM 31891, 30490 and 30270). However, the sign in question does not really look like a number.

L. 7: There is an erasure at the beginning of the line, i.e., between the *-šú* and the *-šá*.

L. 9a: Should we read at the beginning of the line [*a-d*]*i* or ⸢*šá*⸣? I could see two verticals and there is probably nothing between them, so that a DI-sign is less likely. There is something on top of the first vertical: either two small verticals on the top of a ŠÁ-sign or the *Winkelhaken* on top of the first vertical in a DI-sign.

L. 9b: The verb *ul-te-bal* is a perf. of *šūbulu* (Š of *abālu*) for which the *CAD* lists the following meanings "to send; to have carry away" (*CAD* A$_1$, 24ff. s.v. *abālu* A mng. 9). When interpreted in this sense, the clause of lines 10–12 may have provided that if MNA was careless and "let the Old$^{?}$ canal carry away the boat" (cf. *ibid.*, 27 mng. 9-b), he had to pay. Less likely is to equate *šūbulu* (Š-stem) with *ubbulu* (D-stem), meaning "to load (a boat); to have (a boat) carry a load" (for examples from Sumerian texts, see *ibid.*, 11 s.v. *abālu* A lex.; *CAD* E, 90–91 s.v. *eleppu* lex.; and Römer, *AOAT* 232, 361 s.v. § B.III.1.a.2). When taken in this meaning, the clause in question provided that if MNA used the boat to transport merchandise (i.e., "if he made the boat carry a load," *kī eleppa ultebal*), perhaps "to$^{?}$ the Old$^{?}$ canal," he had to pay (extra?).

L. 14: The name Ilī-laba probably contains the West-Semitic noun *lb'* "lion" (Zadok, *West Semites*, 295), and cf. the name ^{md}*tam-meš-la-ba-a-a* in Cole, *Governor's Archive*, No. 59: 16, 19.

L. 15: The name Ummaya probably contains the Old Iranian element Ama- (Ir.), also attested in the name Amadātu (wr. ^{m}*am-ma-*..., as well as ^{m}*um-ma-*...).

No. 26

BM 30819
Copy: Bertin copy 2575
Date: 5$^{?}$/xii/25 Dar (13$^{?}$ March 496 B.C.E.)
Place: Šabīlu
Content: Receipt of the *ilku*-tax by MNA.

OBV.

1 *il-ki šá* ^{m}*bar-si-a-a* A-*šú šá*
2 ^{md}AMAR.UTU-MU-URU$_{3}$ A ^{m}*ba-bu-tu*
3 *šá ul-tu* ITI.BÁR *šá* MU.25.KAM
4 *a-di-i qí-it šá* ITI.ŠE *šá* MU.25.KAM
5 ^{m}*da-a-ri-maš* LUGAL E.KI *u* KUR.KUR.MEŠ
6 ^{m}*ši-rik-tu*$_{4}$ A-*šú šá* ^{m}SUM.NA-*a*
7 A ^{m}*e-gi-bi ina* ŠU.II
8 (erasure) ^{m}*bar-si-a-a ma-ḫi-*⸢*ir*⸣

LO. E.

9 1-*en-a*.TA-*na-a' šá-ṭa-ri*
10 *il-te-qu-ú*

REV.

11 LÚ *mu-kin-nu* ^{md}EN-MU A-*šú šá* ^{m}*ba-*⸢*si*⸣*-a*
12 A ^{md}EN-*e-ṭè-ru* ^{m}*mu-ra-nu*
13 A-*šú šá* ^{md}AG-MU-MU ^{m}*ni-din-tu*$_{4}$-^{d}EN
14 ^{m}MU-^{d}EN
15 ^{md}AMAR.UTU-DÙ-NUMUN LÚ.UMBISAG A-*šú šá* ^{md}AG-MU-GIŠ A ^{m}DIN
16 URU *šá-bi-il* ITI.ŠE UD.⸢5$^{?}$.KAM⸣
17 MU.25.KAM ^{m}*da-a-ri-*[*muš*$^{?}$]

18 LUGAL E.KI *u* KUR.KUR.MEŠ

LE. E.

19 ^{m}*šul-lu-ma-a* A-*šú šá* ^{m}*kal-*[*ba-a*]

TRANSLATION

The *ilku*-tax from Nisan of the twenty-fifth year till the end of Addar of the twenty-fifth year of Darius, king of Babylon and the lands, is due from Barsiya, son of Marduk-šuma-uṣur, descendant of Bābūtu: MNA$_2$ has received (it) from Barsiya. They have taken one (copy of the) document each.

Witnesses:
Bēl-iddin/Basiya//Bēl-eṭēru
Mūrānu/Nabû-šuma-iddin
Nidinti-Bēl
Iddin-Bēl
The scribe: Marduk-bāni-zēri/Nabû-šumu-līšir//Balāṭu
(Place + Date).
Šullumaya/Kalbaya(//Nabaya)

COMMENT

L. 1: The name ^{m}*bar-si-a-a* is unique. The BAR-sign can be read *bar*, *mas*, *pár*, and the same name may, accordingly, be read ^{m}*bar/mas/pár-si-a-a*.

L. 11: The sign read as *-si-* is very much squeezed, and a reading *-ba-* is not excluded. In Dar 542: 13, however, a Bēl-iddin/^{m}*ba-si-ia* occurs, and he may, therefore, have been the same person as the one mentioned in lines 11–12 of the text under consideration (Bēl-iddin/^{m}*ba-*⸢*si*⸣*-a*//Bēl-eṭēru). The name Basiya is usually spelled with *-ia/iá* at the end (Tallqvist, *NbN* 23 s.v. *Ba-si-ia/iá*; cf. ^{m}*ba-as-si-ia*, Stolper, *Entrepreneurs*, 287), but for a spelling with *-a*, cf. Nbk 31: 13 ^{m}*ba-si-a*.

L. 14: This line is written over an erasure: ^{m}*ni-din* is still visible underneath ^{m}MU-^{d}EN. After ^{d}EN some remnants of one or two signs are still visible. The second half of the line is empty, and after this line follows an empty space of several lines before the name of the scribe in line 15, cf. BM 30366: 12, BM 31036: 12, BM 31227: 13, BM 31793: 17, BM 32883: 17, BM 41442: 15, e.a.; probably also BM 30270: 16–17; cf. also BM 31118: 13.

L. 16: This line is written over an erasure: underneath the sign ITI one can see remnants of badly erased signs. Moreover, the sign UD is written remarkably lower than the previous ŠE. A similar phenomenon is found in the next line, where ^{m}*da-a-ri-*[*muš*$^{?}$] is written lower than the previous signs on the same line. The tablet was written on the fifth rather than on the seventh of Addar; indeed, the sixth wedge is possibly a crack rather than a wedge, and the seventh wedge, which is found underneath line 16, i.e., in between lines 16 and 17, is possibly the prolongation of the fifth wedge rather than an independent wedge.

L. 19: This line, which is found on the left edge of the tablet, is written in a direction different from the one which is usually found on left edges, because it can be read while holding the obverse side of the tablet facing up, whereas one usually reads the left edge with the tablet's reverse facing up. A similar phenomenon is attested in BM 31891; see also the peculiarities of the left edge of BM 32858.

No. 27

BM 30853
Copy: no Bertin copy
Date: no date (between 22–24 Dar?)
Place: no place
Content: List of quantities of silver and barley. Expenditures for boats, boat equipment and boat transports. Reference to the governor and persons known from texts of MNA's archive.

OBV.

1 [(x MA.NA) x GÍ]N KÙ.BABBAR UD-*ú šá a-na* ^{m}*šul-lu-mu*
2 LÚ.GAL [x *a*]-*na* LÚ.ḪUN.GÁ.MEŠ SUM.NA ITI.DU$_{6}$ UD.25.KAM
3 ⅔ MA.NA 1½ GÍN KÙ.BABBAR UD-*ú* 6 GÍN KÙ.BABBAR UD-*ú*
4 ŠÁM TÚG.KUR.RA *ina* GUB-*zu šá* LÚ.GAR-UŠ$_{4}$ *a-na*
5 LÚ.ḪUN.GÁ.MEŠ SUM.NA ITI.DU$_{6}$ UD.25.KAM
6 1⅓ MA.NA 6 GÍN KÙ.BABBAR *i-di* 2-TA GIŠ.MÁ.MEŠ
7 *šá a-na* ^{md}EN-*ik-ṣur* LÚ.SAG *ù* LÚ.ERIN$_{2}$.MEŠ-*šú*
8 *šá* É *kar*$^{!}$-*ri* SUM.NA ITI.DU$_{6}$ UD.28.KAM
9 5 GÍN KÙ.BABBAR UD-*ú šá a-na* ^{md}EN-*ik-ṣur* LÚ.SAG SUM.NA
10 ⅔ MA.NA 1½ GÍN KÙ.BABBAR UD-*ú* ŠÁM 6.2.3 GUR ŠE.BAR
11 *šá ina qí-bi šá* LÚ.GAR-UŠ$_{4}$ *a-na* É ^{m}*ar-ta-su-nu*
12 SUM.NA ITI.DU$_{6}$ UD.26.KAM
13 ⅔ MA.NA KÙ.BABBAR UD-*ú šá a-na* ^{m}*ni-din-tu*$_{4}$-^{d}EN-*dam-qát*
14 *a-na* ŠE.BAR *a-ki-i* GÍD.DA *ù* NA$_{4}$.KIŠIB
15 *šá* LÚ.GAR-UŠ$_{4}$ SUM.NA
16 ⅓ MA.NA KÙ.BABBAR *šá a-na* 4-TA
17 *ḫal-li-ip-tu*$_{4}$ *a-na* ^{m}*ni-din-tu*$_{4}$-^{d}EN-*dam-qát*
18 *a-ki-i* GÍD.DA *u* NA$_{4}$.KIŠIB SUM.NA
19 ⅓ MA.NA KÙ.BABBAR *šá a-na* KURUM$_{6}$.ḪI.A *šá* LÚ *šá-di-di-e*
20 *šá a-di* KÁ ÍD *ka-bar-ri* SUM.NA

REV.

21 10 GÍN KÙ.BABBAR UD-*ú* ŠÁM 10 DÚG *dan-nu-*⸢*tu*⸣ [*šá*] KAŠ
22 *šá ina qí-bi šá* LÚ.GAR-UŠ$_{4}$ *a-na* GIŠ.MÁ.MEŠ *šá* KAŠ.S[A]G SUM.NA
23 8.2.3 GUR ŠE.BAR *šá ina qí-bi šá* LÚ.GAR-UŠ$_{4}$
24 *a-na na-pa-lu šá* GIŠ.MÁ.MEŠ *a-na* ^{m}MU-GIN ⸢SUM⸣.NA
25 2 MA.NA KÙ.BABBAR UD-*ú šá i-di* GIŠ.MÁ *šá ul-tu*

26 KÁ ÍD *ka-bar-ri a-di* URU *šu-šá-an šá* MI-IK-DU
27 *ina lìb-bi i-*⸢*lu*⸣*-ú* SUM.NA
28 12½ GÍN KÙ.BABBAR UD-*ú* ⸢2⸣ PI *qí-me a-na*
29 *na-še-e šá kan-ka*? *a-na* ^{m}*gu-ú-zu-*{*ina*}-^{d}EN-*aṣ-bat* SUM.NA
30 1⅓ MA.NA KÙ.BABBAR UD-*ú šá ina qí-bi šá* LÚ.GAR-UŠ$_4$
31 *a-na i-di* GIŠ.MÁ.MEŠ ⸢*šá*⸣ KI ^{m}*ip-ri-ia*
32 ŠE.BAR *ú-qàr-ri-ba-nu* SUM.NA
33 1 MA.NA 10 GÍN KÙ.BABBAR UD-*ú šá a-na* ^{m}ÌR-^{d}*bu-ne-ne*
34 SUM.NA *ina* GUB-*zu šá* ^{m}*na-pur-tu ù*
35 ^{m}*ba-nu-nu* 1½ MA.NA KÙ.BABBAR UD-*ú*
36 *šá* ^{m}*mar-duk* A LÚ.BAḪAR$_2$ *šá a-na*
37 LÚ.GAR-UŠ$_4$ SUM.NA ½ MA.NA 5 GÍN KÙ.BABBAR UD-*ú*
38 [*šá a*]-*na i-di* GIŠ.MÁ *šá qí-me* SUM.NA
(End of the text; there is a blank area left on the reverse.)

TRANSLATION

(1–2a)[(…) x she]kels of white silver have been given to Šullumu, the overseer […] [f]or the hirelings. (2b–5a)On the twenty-fifth of Tašrīt, forty-one and a half shekels of white silver, (and another) six shekels of white silver, the price of the garments for the hirelings, have been given in the presence of the governor. (5b–8a)On the twenty-fifth of Tašrīt, eighty-six shekels of silver, the rent for two boats, have been given to Bēl-ikṣur, the (harbor)master, and to his workmen at the harbor! house. (8b–9)On the twenty-eighth of Tašrīt, five shekels of white silver have been given to Bēl-ikṣur, the (harbor)master. (10–12a)Forty-one and a half shekels of white silver, the price of 6.2.3 *kor* of barley, have been given by order of the governor to the House of Artasunu. (12b–15)On the twenty-sixth, forty shekels of white silver have been given according to the register and the sealed tablet of the governor to Nidinti-Bēl-damqat for the barley. (16–18)Twenty shekels of silver have been given according to the (same?) register and sealed tablet to Nidinti-Bēl-damqat for four cables. (19–20)Twenty shekels of silver have been given for the rations of the men who tow(ed) (the boats) as far as Bāb Kabarri. (21–22)Ten shekels of white silver, the price of ten beer jars, have been given by order of the governor for the boats that (transport) beer. (23–24)8.2.3 *kor* of barley have been given by order of the governor to Šuma-ukīn for *unloading* the boats. (25–27)One hundred and twenty shekels of white silver have been given as rent for the boat that (sailed) from Bāb Kabarri till Šušan, (and) on which …. (28–29)Twelve and a half shekels of white silver ⸢2⸣ *pān* of flour …, have been given to Gūzu-{ina}-Bēl-aṣbat. (30–32)Eighty shekels of white silver have been given by order of the governor for the rent of the boats, ⸢which (are)?⸣ with Ipriya (and)? transport(ed) barley. (33–35)Seventy shekels of white silver have been given to Arad-Bunene, in the presence of Napuštu and Bānûnu. (35–37a)Ninety shekels of white silver due from Marduk, descendant of Paḫāru, have been given to the governor. (37b–38)Thirty-five shekels of white silver have been given for the rent of the boat (loaded) with flour.

COMMENT

BM 30853 is not dated, but it lists expenses that occurred "on the twenty-fifth of Tašrīt" (ll. 2b and 5b), "the twenty-eighth of Tašrīt" (l. 8b) and "the twenty-sixth" (l. 12b). In the latter case the month is not specified. I assume that BM 30853 listed the expenses chronologically, thus starting with the twenty-fifth of Tašrīt in lines 2b and 5b and continuing with the twenty-eighth of the same month in line 8b. Consequently, the "twenty-sixth" in line 12b must have been the twenty-sixth of the next month, i.e., Araḫsamna. The year to which BM 30853 relates is nowhere indicated. However, it was most likely Darius' twenty-fourth year or any other year during Ina-Esagil-lilbur's term of office as governor of Babylon (22–24 Dar). This assumption is based on evidence from BM 30256 that, as explained above in § 2.5.1, mentions persons and situations that have their exact parallel in BM 30853. BM 30256 was dated on the second of Tašrīt in Darius' twenty-fourth year during the governorship of Ina-Esagil-lilbur.

L. 1–2a: The preposition *ana* is ambivalent: (1) meaning "for" it specifies the reason for which the silver has been given, or in other words, the kind of expense; (2) meaning "to" it specifies the direction of the payment, or in other words, the person who received the silver. Most probably lines 1–2 are to be understood as follows: silver is given "to PN" (*ana* PN) "for (expenses related to) the hirelings" (*ana* ^{lú}*agrī*^{meš}). In other words, PN paid for the hirelings, probably their wages or food allowances, and is now refunded for this expense. Similar cases are found in lines 12b–15, 16–18, 23–24, and 28–29.

L. 2b–5a: These lines record the issue of silver to purchase clothing to be distributed to the hirelings in payment of their salary (cf. Bongenaar, *Ebabbar*, 39–40: the TÚG.KUR.RA garment was commonly given by the temple to workmen for their maintenance, besides barley and dates).

The recipient of the silver issued in these lines is not named, but it was obviously Šullumu. He was mentioned as the recipient in the previous lines, and there was no need, from the point of view of the text, to repeat his name in lines 2b–5a. A new recipient is introduced by name in line 7, Bēl-ikṣur. Cf. BM 30853: 12b–18 (recipient is Nidinti-Bēl-damqat), 19–22 (recipient is not named, hence *idem*), 23–24 (new recipient: Šuma-ukīn); BM 30853: 23–24 (recipient is Šuma-ukīn), 25–27 (recipient is not named, hence *idem*), 28–29 (new recipient: Gūzu-{ina}-Bēl-aṣbat); BM 30853: 28–29 (recipient is Gūzu-{ina}-Bēl-aṣbat), 30–32 (recipient is not named, hence *idem*); 33–35 (recipient is Arad-Bunene); and BM 30853: 35–37a (recipient is the governor), 37b–38 (recipient is not named, hence *idem*).

L. 6: Probably, read KÙ.BABBAR <UD-*ú*>, cf. the white silver paid as boat rental in lines 25–27, 30–32, 37b–38 and cf. other boat rental agreements from MNA's archive.

L. 7–8a: I suggest reading *bīt kar*$^{!}$*-ri*: the sign with its four horizontal and four vertical wedges can be either Ú or KAR. Since the upper part of the last vertical at the right end of the sign does not have the clear double head that characterizes the KAR-sign, the sign resembles more Ú than KAR. Nevertheless, I suggest reading *bīt kar*$^{!}$*-ri* and comparing the information contained in lines 5–8a with similar information in BM 31554 and BM 41453. Accordingly, one should identify Bēl-ikṣur, the headman (LÚ.SAG) who had harbor workmen at his disposal (LÚ.ERIN$_2$.MEŠ-*šú šá* É *kar*$^{!}$*-ri*) according to BM 30853: 5–8a, with Bēl-ikṣur (alias Bēl-kiṣuršu)/Rīmūt, known from these two texts. In BM 31554: 3 he bears the title ⸢LÚ.SAG.ERIN$_2$⸣.MEŠ, and in BM 41453 he has no official title, but rents a small harbor house (É *kar-ri*) and a loft (*rugbu*) by order of MNA's son. On the basis of this evidence, I suggest reconstructing his official title as follows: *rēš ṣābê ša bīt kāri*, "master of the harbor workers." In other words, he was a harbormaster and had harbor workers under his command.

L. 11: Names with the Iranian element *Ar-ta-* are frequent in the Neo-Babylonian and Persian periods (Tallqvist, *NbN*, 16; Stolper, *Entrepreneurs*, 286; Donbaz-Stolper, *Istanbul Murašû*, 160; Dandamaev, *Iranians*, 35ff.). The name *Ar-ta-su-nu*, however, is unique, unless we have to emend and read *Ar-ta-ba*$^{!}$*-nu* (Ir. *Rtabānu or *Rtapāna, Schmitt, *Kratylos* 39, 84). For the latter name, see Amherst 258: 4 (= *AfO* 19, 80f.).

L. 13: For the meaning of *ḫaliptu*, see Jursa, *Tempelzehnt*, 113.

L. 21: Cf. a text from the time of MNA's father, according to which he took care of jars for the governor of Babylon (BM 31323; quoted by Wunsch, *MOS Studies* 2, n. 28).

L. 24: The form spelled *ana na-pa-lu*, with the PA-sign, which cannot be read *-ba-*, shows that *na-pa-lu* is derived from *napālu* "to dig out; to tear down" (viz. G-infinitive after *ana*). This verb is normally not attested in connection with boats (*CAD* N$_1$, 272ff. s.v. *napālu* A), except for its occurrence in the text under consideration, one other text published in the present volume (viz. BM 30490: 27, *i-nab/p-b/pal*), and a Middle Babylonian letter cited by the *CAD* N$_1$, 275 s.v. *napālu* A mng. 2b-2′, but categorized as meaning "obscure." In my opinion, "digging out; or tearing down" boats refers to one of the three following situations. First, it may refer to "hauling up" boats when said of a sunken boat. For this situation, see e.g., *SAA* 1 119 where the verb used is *šūlû* (more at Römer, *AOAT* 232, 369). Second, it may refer to "taking apart" boats when said of those which were made of inflated skins, beams, and branches dismounted upon arrival. For a description of this practice, see Fales, "Rivers," 212f.; Bass, *CANE* III, 1403 and 1421f.; and Briant, *Histoire*, 392f. Third, *napālu* may refer to "unloading" boats. Usually, this activity is expressed by verbs like *(ultu eleppi) našû* and *šurūqu* (Salonen, *Nautica*, 90f.) However, taking into account that "loading" a boat is expressed, i.a. by the verb *šurkubu*, which literally means "to mount, put together" (*CAD* R, 89f. s.v. *rakābu* mng. 8), the opposite action, viz. "unloading," may well be expressed by a verb like *napālu*, which literally means "to tear down, take apart." This may be compared to Aramaic where the verb *prq* "to take apart" is used to refer to unloading cargo, i.a. from boats (Krauss, *Talmudische Archäologie* II, 343). In my opinion, the third possibility is the most appropriate to the specific context of the three texts mentioned above. If so, MNA paid "for unloading" (*ana napālu*, BM 30853: 24) boats, and rented a boat whose sailor "had to unload the boat at the Fortress" (*eleppa ina birti ... inappal*, BM 30490: 26f.). According to the Middle Babylonian letter men "shall unload the barley from the Sealand from the eighteen boats together with the earlier and the later ones that (already) have arrived (*uṭṭeta ša* GN 18 *eleppāti itti panâti u arkâti ikšudāni i-na-ap-pa-*lu_4)."

L. 26–27: If *i-lu-ú* is derived from the verb *elû*, it is either a masculine plural form or a masculine singular with the subjunctive ending. Being a masculine form, the boat mentioned in line 25 is probably not its subject, so that it is not about a boat "going upstream" (*CAD* E, 119 s.v. *elû* mng. 1c–3′). It may have been about "the boat ... on which (*ša ... ina libbi*) ... will arrive/arrived" (*ibid.*, 117 s.v. *elû* mng. 1a-2′); or: "the boat ... on which ... will board/boarded" (*ibid.*, 118 s.v. *elû* mng. 1b-2′; the examples cited by the *CAD*, however, have *ana libbi*). The MI-IK-DU at the beginning of the subordinate sentence is enigmatic. It might be the subject of the verb *elû*.

L. 28–29: Several questions remain unsolved in these lines. First, there is the nature of the relation between the silver and the flour. The text very laconically says that there is "silver (and)$^?$ 2 *pān* of flour." Or, was it "silver (for the purchase of)$^?$ 2 *pān* of flour," although in that case we expect the noun *šīmu* (ŠÁM) "price," as in lines 4 and 21. Second, there is the enigmatic *ana našê ša kanka* (or rd. *kan-nak*$^?$). It reminds one of the known formula of proxy, *ana našê ṣibûti ša* PN *kanik* "sealed upon the wish of PN." For this formula, see recently Waerzeggers, *AfO* 46/47, 194–97.

L. 29: For the name ^{m}*Gu-ú-zu-*{*ina*}-^{d}EN-*aṣ-bat* cf. *CAD* G, 147 s.v. *gūzu*.

L. 36: *ša* in *ša Marduk* probably means "due from" rather than "belonging to," because of the parallel passage in BM 30651: 9–10, where exactly the same amount of silver "(had been received)$^?$ from Marduk//Paḫāru (*ina qātē*)." More at p. 90.

No. 28

BM 30854
Copy: no Bertin copy
Date: no date
Place: no place
Content: List of quantities of silver. Expenditures. Probably related to MNA.

OBV.

1 1 MA.NA 2½ GÍN KÙ.BABBAR ŠÁM 50 DÚG *dan-*˹*na-tu*˺
2 *šá a-na* ^{m}*na-pu-uš-tu*$_{4}$ *u* ^{m}DI.KU$_{5}$-^{d}˹AMAR.UTU SUM˺-*nu-u'*
3 5/6 MA.NA 5 GÍN KÙ.BABBAR *i-di* É.MEŠ
4 16 GÍN KÙ.BABBAR ŠÁM *ši-ka-ri šá la-pa-*˹*ni*˺
5 ˹URU˺ *bar-sip* TU DI? NU Ú A NA [x] A'
(lower half of obverse broken off.)

REV.

1' ˹*a*˺-[*n*]*a*? ˹x˺ [...]
2' 15 GÍN KÙ.BABBAR *u* UR$_{5}$.˹RA-*šú* ^{m}x x x˺ [(x)]
3' 1 ME GUR ZÚ.LUM.MA *šá ina* IGI KÁ.GAL *šá* E.K[I]
4' ZÚ.LUM.MA *šá in-ṭu-ú*
5' 14 GUR ZÚ.LUM.MA *šá* URU *dil-bat*!.KI
6' [⅓] GÍN KÙ.BABBAR *u* UR$_{5}$.RA-*šú šá ina* IGI
7' ˹^{m}IDIM˺-*iá* A-*šú šá* ^{m}GI-^{d}AMAR.UTU

LE. E.

8' [...] IGI? *šá* ^{md}EN-*qa*-[...]
9' [...]-*šá-a'*

TRANSLATION

Sixty-two and a half shekels of silver, the price of fifty jars, were given to Napuštu and Dayyān-˹Marduk˺.

Fifty-five shekels of silver, the rent of the buildings. Sixteen shekels of silver, the price of the beer that from Borsippa .... [...] Fifteen shekels of silver and its interest, ˹^{m}x-x-x˺. One hundred *kor* of dates that are at the gate of Babylon. Dates that are lost/missing. Fourteen *kor* of dates from Dilbat. [Twenty shekels] of silver and its interest, which are charged against ˹Kabtiya˺, son of Mušallim-Marduk. [... which are ch]arged against? Bēl-qa[...] [(...) have been iss]ued?.

COMMENT

Obv. L. 1 end: The *-na* is written on the right edge; the *-tu* is on the reverse.

Obv. L. 2: The clause "*ša ana ... nadnu*" is not necessarily to be translated as a relative clause. On the problem, see Gehlken, *NABU* 1994/89 s.v. 2).

Obv. L. 3 end: The -AMAR.UTU SUM- are written on the right edge; the *-nu-u'* are on the reverse.

Obv. L. 5: We expect the KI-sign after URU *bar-sip*, but the sign is rather a TU. The sign after TU resembles a DI or, perhaps a RU. It is followed by clearly written NU Ú A NA. There follows a sign of which only the upper two verticals are preserved. The last sign on this line is a clear -'. For *lapāni* see *AHw*, 534 s.v. *lapān*(*i*) mng. 2.

Rev. L. 3′ end: the .KI immediately touches upon the *-ni* of Obv. L. 4.

Rev. L. 4′: For *in-ṭu-ú* see *CAD* M$_1$, 431 s.v. *maṭû* mng. 1a–7′ "which are missing," or "which are lost."

Rev. L. 6′, 8′: For silver of PN$_1$ being put at the disposal of PN$_2$ (*kaspu ša* PN$_1$ *ša ina pān* PN$_2$), i.e., charged against PN$_2$, cf. Dar 552 and discussion at BM 30270: 1; on other occurrences of the idiom *ina pān* in texts from MNA's archive, see BM 30270: 1.

Rev. L. 9′: Probably to be read [*na/iš*]-*šá-á* from *našû*.

No. 29

BM 30961 (= Dupl. of BM 31667 + BM 31641)
Copy: Bertin copy 2622
Date: 12/vi/26 Dar (13 September 496 B.C.E.)
Place: Babylon
Content: Receipt of silver from MNA. Purchase price for a boat. Prompt return of the promissory note about the boat to MNA.

OBV.

1 GIŠ.MÁ *šá* ^{md}AG-A-MU DUMU *šá* ^{m}*la-a-ba-ši*
2 DUMU ^{m}ZALAG$_2$-^{d}PAP.SUKKAL *šá a-na* 4 MA.NA 10 GÍN
3 KÙ.BABBAR UD-*ú šá ina* 1 GÍN *bit-qa nu-uḫ-ḫu-tu*
4 ŠÁM GIŠ.MÁ-*šú a-na* ^{m}*ši-iš-ku* DUMU *šá*
5 ^{m}SUM.NA-*a* DUMU ^{m}*e-gì-bi id-din-nu*
6 KÙ.BABBAR *a-ki-i ú-ìl-tì-šú* ^{md}AG-A-MU
7 DUMU *šá* ^{m}*la-a-ba-ši* DUMU ^{m}ZALAG$_2$-^{d}PAP.SUKKAL
8 *ina* ŠU.II ^{m}*ši-iš-ku* DUMU *šá* ^{m}SUM.NA-*a*
9 DUMU ^{m}*e-gi-bi ma-ḫi-ir ú-ìl-t*[*ì*]
10 *šá* GIŠ.MÁ *šá ra-ki-is-tu*$_4$ *ù ka-*[...]
11 *šá ina* IGI ^{m}*ni-qu-du pa-qa-ad*

LO. E.

12 ^{md}AG-A-MU *ki-i ú-tir-ri*

REV.

13 *a-na* ^{m}*ši-iš-ku it-ta-din*
14 LÚ *mu-kin-nu* ^{m}*ni-din-tu*$_4$ DUMU *šá* ^{m}*kal-ba-a*
15 DUMU ^{m}*su-ḫa-a-a* (erasure) ^{md}EN-SU DUMU *šá* ^{m}*kal-ba-a*

16 DUMU ^{m}MU-*líb-ši* ^{md}EN-GI DUMU *šá* ^{md}EN-KÁD
17 ^{md}EN-PAB A-*šú šá* ^{m}⸢SIG$_5$⸣-*iá* A ^{m}*na-din-še-im*
18 ^{m}*mu-ra-nu* A-*šú š*[*á* ^{m}]ÌR-^{d}AMAR.UTU A LÚ.SANGA-^{d}IDIM
19 ^{md}AG-*na-din*-ŠEŠ LÚ.UMBISAG A-*šú šá* ^{m}SIG$_5$-*iá* A ^{m}*na-din-še-im*
20 TIN.TIR.KI ITI.KIN UD.12.KAM MU.26.KAM
21 ^{m}*dar-ri-'i-muš* LUGAL TIN.TIR.KI
22 *u* KUR.KUR.MEŠ

TRANSLATION

The boat belonging to Nabû-apla-iddin, son of Lâbāši, descendant of Nūr-Papsukkal, which he sold to MNA$_2$ for four minas and ten shekels of white, medium-quality silver, of which one-eighth is alloy, the price of his boat: Nabû-apla-iddin, son of Lâbāši, descendant of Nūr-Papsukkal, has received the silver from MNA$_2$ according to the promissory no[te] credited to him. Nabû-apla-iddin has promptly returned the promissory note about the boat, which was packed and s[ealed], and entrusted to Niqūdu, to MNA$_2$.

Witnesses:
Nidintu/Kalbaya//Suḫaya (erasure)
Bēl-erība/Kalbaya/Šumu-libši
Bēl-ušallim/Bēl-kāṣir
Bēl-nāṣir/⸢Damqi⸣ya//Nādin-še'i
Mūrānu/Arad-Marduk//Šangû-Ea
The scribe: Nabû-nādin-aḫi/Damqiya//Nādin-še'i
(Place + Date).

COMMENT

For the document recording the sale of the boat in question, see BM 30370.

L. 10: One should most likely read *ka*-[*ni-ik-tu*$_4$] at the end of the line. For *raksu* "packed," see *CAD* R, 109 s.v. *raksu*, adj., mng. 1f. For the practice of depositing records with third parties, see Stolper, *AION* 77.

L. 11: Since *u'iltu* is a feminine noun (see *rakistu u k*[*aniktu*]), we expect the verb to be *paqdat*. The spelling *pa-qa-ad*, however, suggests a masculine verbal form.

L. 12–13: For the expression PN$_1$ *kī utirri ana* PN$_2$ (= debtor) *ittadin*, "when he returned (it), he gave (it) to PN$_2$," see San Nicolò-Ungnad, *NRV*, 164 s.v. *târu* D. 2; and Stolper, *AMI* 23, 170 n. 21. It refers to the prompt return of the original promissory note that was held by the creditor till payment to the debtor after he paid.

L. 17: All there is of the SIG$_5$ is one of the two front *Winkelhaken* and the closing vertical with the double head.

No. 30

BM 30965
Copy: Bertin copy 2603
Date: 21/v/26 Dar (23 August 496 B.C.E.)
Place: Babylon
Content: Undertaking under oath to settle debts to MBU with MNA. Reference to the pledge of income from an *ērib bīti* prebend to MNA or MBU.

OBV.

1 ^{m}⸢*ap*⸣-*la-a* DUMU *šá* ^{md}U.GUR-SUM.NA
2 *šá* ^{md}AG-*it-tan-nu* MU-*šú ina* ^{d}EN ^{d}AG *u* ^{m}*da-a-ri-ia-muš*
3 LUGAL TIN.TIR.KI LUGAL KUR.MEŠ *a-na* ^{md}AMAR.UTU-*na-ṣir*-EDURU
4 DUMU *šá* ^{m}KI-^{d}AMAR.UTU-DIN DUMU ^{m}*e-gì-bi it-te-me*
5 *ki-i a-di-i qí-it šá* ITI.NE *šá* MU.26.KAM
6 ^{m}*da-a-ri-ia-muš* LUGAL ^{md}AG-*na-din*-ŠEŠ *u* ^{m}MU-^{d}[...]
7 DUMU.MEŠ *šá* ^{md}AG-*it-tan-nu* DUMU *šá* ^{m}ZALAG$_2$-*e-a*
8 *a-na* TIN.TIR.KI *a-na pa-ni-ka ab-ba-kam-ma*
9 *a-ki-i ú-ìl-tì*.MEŠ *šá* KÙ.BABBAR ŠE.BAR [(x)]
10 *ù* ZÚ.LUM.MA *šá* ^{md}DI.KU$_5$-EN-URU$_3$
11 LÚ *qal-li-ka šá ina muḫ-ḫi-ia ù*

LO. E.

12 *ina* UGU ^{md}AG-*it-tan-nu* DUMU *šá* ^{m}ZALAG$_2$-*e-a*
13 *a-na* ^{md}AMAR.UTU-*na-ṣir*-EDURU *ni-iṭ-ṭi-ru*

REV.

14 *e-lat šá-ṭa-ru* IGI-*ú šá a-da-nu*
15 *šá it-ti* ^{m}*ap-la-a ù* 1 SILA$_3$ NINDA.ḪI.A
16 *ù* 1 SILA$_3$ KAŠ SAG GIŠ.ŠUB.BA LÚ.KU$_4$-É-⸢*tú*⸣ [(x)]
17 *šá* ^{m}*ap-la-a maš-ka-nu ṣab-tu* LÚ *mu-kin-nu*
18 ^{m}ÌR-^{d}EN DUMU *šá* ^{m}SIG$_5$-*ia* A ^{m}*na-din-še*-⸢*im*$^{?}$⸣ [(x)]
19 ^{md}EN-*lu-mu-ur* DUMU *šá* ^{md}EN-ŠEŠ.MEŠ-BA-[*šá*]
20 A LÚ.SANGA-^{d}INNIN-TIN.TIR.KI ^{md}AG-NUMUN-DÙ DUM[U *šá*]
21 ^{m}KI-^{d}AG-DIN A ^{m}*e-gi-bi* ^{md}EN-*ki-šìr*
22 DUMU *šá* ^{md}AG-*na-ṣir* A ^{m}EN-*a-a* ^{m}*a-na*-^{d}EN-[*at-k*]*al*
23 DUMU *šá* ^{m}*ki-na-a* ^{m}*šá*-^{d}EN-*at-ta* DUMU *šá* ^{md}AMAR.UTU-MU-DÙ
24 A ^{m}*e-gì-bi* ^{md}EN-DÙ DUMU *šá* ^{m}*gu-za-nu* A ^{m}NUMUN-*a-a*
25 ^{md}EN-DIN-*iṭ* DUB.SAR DUMU *šá* ^{m}KI-^{d}AG-DIN

U. E.

26 ⸢A⸣ ^{md}EN-*e-ṭè-ru* TIN.TIR.KI ITI.NE UD.21.KAM
27 [MU].26.KAM ^{m}*da-ri-ia-muš* LUGAL E.KI *u* KUR.KUR

TRANSLATION

Aplaya, son of Nergal-iddin, whose (second) name is Nabû-ittannu, declared under oath by Bēl, Nabû and Darius, king of Babylon, king of the lands, to MNA_1: "by the end of Ab of the twenty-sixth year of King Darius, I shall bring Nabû-nādin-aḫi and Iddin-^{d}[...], the sons of Nabû-ittannu, son of Nūrea, before you in Babylon, and we shall pay to MNA_1 according to the promissory notes for silver, barley and dates that were due to Madānu-bēla-uṣur, your slave, from me and from Nabû-ittannu, son of Nūrea." In addition, there is a previous document that concerns the term of payment, which is with Aplaya, and (which states that) 1 *qû* of bread as well as 1 *qû* of beer, the income from Aplaya's *ērib bīti*-prebend, have been pledged.

Witnesses:
Arad-Bēl/Damqiya//Nādin-še'i
Bēl-lūmur/Bēl-aḫḫē-iqīša//Šangû-Ištar-Bābili
Nabû-zēra-ibni/Itti-Nabû-balāṭu//Egibi
Bēl-kēšir/Nabû-nāṣir//Bēlaya
Ana-Bēl-a[tk]al/Kīnaya
Ša-Bēl-atta/Marduk-šuma-ibni//Egibi
Bēl-ibni/Gūzānu//Zēriya
The scribe: Bēl-uballiṭ/Itti-Nabû-balāṭu//Bēl-eṭēru
(Place + Date).

COMMENT

L. 2: It is not immediately clear whether the name Nabû-ittannu (l. 2) alludes to Aplaya's full name, i.e., Nabû-(apla)-ittannu, or to a second name of his father, i.e., his father was Nergal-iddin, *alias* Nabû-ittannu. In the text under consideration Aplaya undertakes to settle the debts that exists against him and a man named Nabû-ittannu//Nūrea (l. 12); for that purpose he will bring along the sons of the latter (ll. 5–13). Had Nergal-iddin (*alias* Nabû-ittannu//Nūrea?) a son named Aplaya (l. 1), as well as sons from a different marriage, and were his sons to settle his debts with MNA? Aplaya (son of Nergal-iddin, *alias* Nabû-ittannu//Nūrea) would have taken upon himself to bring all sons of the debtor, including himself, before MNA. On persons bearing two different names (e.g., Marduk-nāṣir-apli = Širku), or whose name was shortened to one of its components (e.g., Nergal-ušallim = Šullumu), see Jursa, *Bēl-rēmanni*, 146 (at line 6, with bibliography). Individuals may have needed certain names in order to be accepted to certain professions. In this respect, it is interesting to note that Aplaya was the owner of an *ērib bīti* prebend. Had he or his father to be named in a certain way, *in casu* Nabû-ittannu, in order to become an *ērib bīti* ("temple-enterer")?

L. 10: On MNA taking care of promissory notes that were held by his slave after Darius' 20th year, see more at Dar 509: 3.

L. 14: For the practice of drawing up documents that state until when a specific obligation is to be met, see for instance, Dar 486: 4, *šaṭāra ša adannu ana eṭēri ittišu išṭurū* "together with it (= the promissory note) they drew up a document concerning the term of payment," and additional examples cited by the *CAD* A_1, 99f. s.v. *adannu* mng. 2–1′ and San Nicolò-Ungnad, *NRV*, 736 s.v. *adannu*.

L. 16: For KAŠ SAG, probably meaning "full-strength beer," see Von Dassow, CTMMA 3, 33 (with bibliography).

No. 31

BM 30980 (= Dupl. of BRM 1 81)
Copy: Bertin copy 2623
Date: 4/viii/26 Dar (3 November 496 B.C.E.)
Place: Babylon
Content: Receipt of payment (issued) by a royal official for transport costs due by MNA. By order of (*ina qibi ša*) the governor of Babylon.

OBV.

1 *gi-mir šá* 3 ME 16 GUR ZÚ.LUM.MA
2 ^{m}*ap-la-a* LÚ.SAG-LUGAL LÚ *si-pir šá*
3 LÚ.SAG.MEŠ *šá* É.GAL *eš-šú ina* ŠU.II
4 ^{m}*ši-ir-ku* DUMU *šá* ^{m}MU-*a* DUMU ^{m}*e-gi-bi*
5 *ina qí-bi šá* {^{m}} ^{m}*gu-za-nu* LÚ.GAR-UŠ$_4$ TIN.TIR.KI
6 *ma-ḫi-ir*

REV.

7 LÚ *mu-kin-nu* ^{md}U.GUR-MU-DÙ DUMU *šá*
8 ^{m}*šul-lu-mu* ^{m}SUM.NA-*a* DUMU *šá* ^{m}NÍG.BA-*ia*
9 ^{m}*ni-din-tu*$_4$ DUMU *šá* ^{md}AMAR.UTU-MU-MU
10 ^{md}EN-*it-tan-*[*nu*] DUMU *šá* ^{m}KI-^{d}AG-DIN
11 DUMU ^{md}EN-*e-ṭe-ru* ^{m}*ni-din-tu*$_4$-^{d}EN
12 DUMU *šá* ^{md}AG-SIG$_5$-DINGIR.MEŠ DUMU ^{m}*na-din-še*
13 ^{md}AMAR.UTU-SUR LÚ.UMBISAG DUMU *šá* ^{md}AG-MU-GAR-*un*
14 DUMU ^{m}MU-*líb-ši* TIN.TIR.KI ITI.APIN
15 UD.4.KAM MU.26.KAM

U. E.

16 ^{m}*da-ri-ia-muš* LUGAL TIN.TIR.KI
17 LUGAL KUR.KUR

TRANSLATION

The costs for the transport of three hundred and sixteen *kor* of dates: Aplaya, courtier (and) clerk of the commissioners of the New Palace, has received (it) from MNA$_2$, by order of Gūzānu, governor of Babylon.

Witnesses:
Nergal-šuma-ibni/Šullumu
Iddinaya/Qīštiya
Nidintu/Marduk-šuma-iddin
Bēl-ittannu/Itti-Nabû-balāṭu//Bēl-eṭēru
Nidinti-Bēl/Nabû-damiq-ilī//Nādin-še'i
The scribe: Marduk-ēṭir/Nabû-šuma-iškun//Šumu-libši
(Place + Date).

COMMENT

L. 2: For this Aplaya, see probably also BM 31572: 4.

L. 5: *ina qí-bi šá* is written over other signs.

No. 32

BM 30994 (= Dupl. of BM 31722 + BM 35235)
Copy: Bertin copy 2608
Date: 5/vii/26 Dar (5 October 496 B.C.E.)
Place: Babylon
Content: Promissory note to pay a debt of silver to MNA. Undertaking to return the "Register of the LÚ.DÍM" (GIŠ.DA *šá* LÚ.DÍM) to the debtor upon repayment.

OBV.

1 50 GÍN KÙ.BABBAR UD-*ú šá ina* 1 GÍN *bit-qa nu-uḫ-ḫu-tú*
2 *šá* ^{md}AMAR.UTU-*na-ṣir*-IBILA DUMU *šá* ^{m}SUM.NA-*a*
3 A ^{m}*e-gi-bi i-na muḫ-ḫi* ^{md}AG-ḪI.LI-DINGIR.MEŠ
4 DUMU *šá* ^{md}EN-*re-man-ni* DUMU ^{m}DÙ-*eš*-DINGIR
5 *a-di* UD.20.KAM *šá* ITI.DU$_{6}$.KÙ *šá* MU.26.KAM
6 ^{m}*da-a-ri-ia-muš* LUGAL KÙ.BABBAR-*a*$_{4}$
7 50 GÍN UD-*ú šá ina* 1 GÍN *bit-qa nu-uḫ-ḫu-tu*
8 ^{md}AG-ḪI.LI-DINGIR.MEŠ *a-na* ^{md}AMAR.UTU-*na-ṣir*-IBILA
9 *i-nam-din u*$_{4}$*-mu šá* KÙ.BABBAR-*a*$_{4}$ 50 GÍN (erase of one sign on the edge)
10 ^{md}AG-ḪI.LI-DINGIR-*ni a-na* ^{md}AMAR.UTU-*na-ṣir*-IBILA
11 *i-nam-din-nu* GÍD.DA *šá* LÚ.DÍM$^{!}$

LO. E.

12 ^{md}AMAR.UTU-*na-ṣir*-IBILA
13 *a-na* ^{md}AG-ḪI.LI-DINGIR.MEŠ *i-nam-din*

REV.

14 LÚ *mu-kin-nu* ^{m}*ḫaš-da-a-a* DUMU *šá* ^{m}*šá*-^{d}AG-*šu-ú*
15 DUMU ^{m}*ši-gu-ú-a* ^{md}EN-*it-tan-nu*
16 DUMU *šá* ^{m}BA-*šá*-^{d}AMAR.UTU DUMU ^{m}UR-^{d}ŠEŠ.KI
17 ^{m}*ni-din-tu*$_{4}$-^{d}EN DUMU *šá* ^{m}*la*$^{!}$*-qí-pi* DUMU LÚ *ir-a-ni*

18 ^{m}*ni-din-*tu_4 DUMU *šá* ^{m}*kal-ba-a* DUMU ^{m}*su-ḫa-a-a*
19 DUMU ^{m}MU-*líb-ši* ^{m}*tab-ni-e-a*
20 DUB.SAR DUMU *šá* ^{m}*ap-la-a* DUMU ^{m}*ga-ḫúl*
21 TIN.TIR.KI ITI.DU_6.KÙ UD.5.KAM MU.26.KAM
22 ^{m}*da-a-ri-ia-muš* LUGAL TIN.TIR.KI
23 *u* KUR.KUR

Translation

Fifty shekels of white, medium-quality silver, of which one-eighth is alloy, are due to MNA_1 from Nabû-kuzub-ilī, son of Bēl-rēmanni, descendant of Eppeš-ilī. By the twentieth of Tašrīt of the twenty-sixth year of King Darius, Nabû-kuzub-ilī shall pay these fifty shekels of white, medium-quality silver, of which one-eighth is alloy, to MNA_1. From the moment Nabû-kuzub-ilī will have paid these fifty shekels to MNA_1, MNA_1 shall give the register of the LÚ.DÍM$^{!}$ to Nabû-kuzub-ilī.

Witnesses:
Ḫašdaya/Ša-Nabû-šū//Šigûa
Bēl-ittannu/Iqīša-Marduk//Kalbi-Nanna
Nidinti-Bēl/Lā-qīpu//Ir'anni
Nidintu/Kalbaya//Suḫaya
<Nidintu/Kalbaya>$^{?}$//Šumu-libši
The scribe: Tabnêa/Aplaya//Gaḫul
(Place + Date).

Comment

BM 30994 and BM 31722^{+} are duplicates. The quality of the latter is generally better than that of the former that has a few strange spellings as well as poorly written signs (see below at lines 10, 11, 14, 17, and 18–19); there is also an erasure at the end of line 9. Further note that the scribe of BM 31722^{+} did not write on the edges (except for *-gi-bi* on the right edge at line 2), and frequently left the last part of the line empty (so in lines 4, 6, 9, 12, 14, 19, 20, and 22). When he finished writing he had still place for one more line on the reverse. For BM 30994, see the line-for-line comment below.

L. 8: The IBILA is written on the reverse (see at lines 15–16).

L. 10: The IBILA is written on the right edge. BM 31722^{+} has -DINGIR.MEŠ, whereas BM 30994 has -DINGIR-*ni*, probably a mistake for -DINGIR.<MEŠ>-*ni* = *ilāni*. The scribe of BM 31722^{+} may have corrected this mistake; cf. lines 11 and 14, where the reading of BM 31772^{+} is generally better than that of BM 30994. If so, the latter is the original, BM 31772^{+} its duplicate copy.

L. 11: The LÚ.DÍM is written with a proper DÍM-sign in BM 31722^{+}, but is badly written in BM 30994. The logogram LÚ.DÍM can be read ^{lú}*mubannû* "temple cook; arranger-of-the-sacrificial-table," or ^{lú}*itinnu* "builder" (bibliography at Bongenaar, *Ebabbar*, 293 n. 252). In my opinion, the LÚ.DÍM in the texts under consideration were arrangers-of-the-sacrificial table because these professionals are mentioned in other texts from the time of MNA (spelled syllabically, e.g., ^{lú}*mu-ban-ni-e*, BM 33930: 23), whereas there is no textual evidence on builders.

L. 14: The scribe wrote ^{m}*šá*-^{d}AG-*šu* (or *ba*)-*ú*. The -*ú* is shorter than usual because the scribe did not have enough space; in fact, the end of the IBILA from line 10 is coming in here.

L. 15–16: These are short lines because they were already partly inscribed, viz. by the IBILA of line 8.

L. 17: The spelling ^{m}NA-*qí-pi* is a mistake for ^{m}*la-qí-pi*, which is found in BM 31722^{+}.

L. 18–19: Were both Nidintu/Kalbaya//Suḫaya and Nidintu/Kalbaya//Šumu-libši present at the transaction? Note that the last third of the line is left empty: it may have been a fully inscribed line had the scribe not forgotten to write Nidintu/Kalbaya. The same strange situation occurs in BM 31722^{+}

No. 33

	BM 31018
Copy:	no Bertin copy
Date:	2/v/11 Dar (22 July 511 B.C.E.)
Place:	Babylon
Content:	Receipt of silver from MNA. Refers to an order (*šipirtu*) issued by Šaddinnu.

OBV.

1 *[ši]-pir-tu*$_4$ *šá* 10 MA.NA KÙ.BABBAR *šá gìn-[nu]*
2 *šá* ^{md}AG-*na-din*-ŠEŠ A-*šú šá* ^{md}AG-⌜EN-MU.MEŠ⌝
3 A ^{m}*de-ki-i a-na pa-ni* ^{m}*ši-ir-ku* A-*šú šá*
4 ^{m}KI-^{d}AMAR.UTU-DIN A ^{m}*e-gì-bi iš-šá-àm*
5 *ina lìb-bi* 5 MA.NA KÙ.BABBAR *šá gìn-nu* ^{md}AG-*na-din*-ŠEŠ
6 A-*šú šá* ^{md}AG-EN-MU.MEŠ A ^{m}*de-ki-i ina* ŠU.II
7 ^{m}*ši-ir-ku* A-*šú šá* ^{m}KI-^{d}AMAR.UTU-DIN A ^{m}*e-gì-bi*
8 *ma-ḫir ši-pir-tu*$_4$ *šá* ^{m}*šad-din-nu*
9 ^{md}AG-*na-din*-ŠEŠ *a-na* ^{m}*ši-ir-ku ul i-d[in]*

REV.

10 LÚ *mu-kin-nu* ^{m}ÌR-*iá* A-*šú šá* ^{m}*da-di-iá*
11 A ^{m}*n[a-b]a-a-a* ^{m}*še-el-li-bi* A-*šú šá* ^{m}*šad-din-nu*
12 A ^{m}LÚ.AZLAG ^{m}MU-MU A-*šú šá* ^{m}x-*iá* A LÚ.ŠITIM
13 ^{m}MU-MU A-*šú šá* ^{m}*šá*-⌜*kin*⌝-MU ^{m}*la-ba-a-ši* A-*šú šá*
14 ^{md}AG-DÙ-⌜ŠEŠ?⌝ [A] ^{m}*ki-din*-^{d}30 ^{md}AG-*bul-liṭ-su*
15 A-*šú* [*šá*] ^{m}MU-⌜^{d}AG⌝ A ^{m}*da-bi-bi* ^{m}*ni-din-tu*$_4$-^{d}EN

16 LÚ.UMBISAG A-*šú šá* ^{md}⸢AG⸣-[*da*]*m*-⸢*iq*⸣-DINGIR A ^{m}*na-din-še-i*[*m*]
17 TIN.TIR.KI ⸢ITI⸣.NE UD.2.KAM MU.11.KAM
18 ^{m}*da-ri-i'-muš* LUGAL E.KI LUGAL KUR.M[EŠ]

TRANSLATION

The [le]tter order for ten minas of mar[ked] silver that Nabû-nādin-aḫi, son of Nabû-⸢bēl-šumāti⸣, descendant of Dēkû, has brought here before MNA$_2$: from it Nabû-nādin-aḫi, son of Nabû-bēl-šumāti, descendant of Dēkû, has received five minas of marked silver from MNA$_2$. Nabû-nādin-aḫi [has] not g[iven] the letter order from Šaddinnu to MNA$_2$.

Witnesses:
Ardiya/Dādiya//Nabaya
Šellibi/Šaddinnu//Ašlāku
Šuma-iddin/[...]-ia//Itinnu
Šuma-iddin/Šākin-šumi
Lâbāši/Nabû-bāni-⸢aḫi$^{?}$⸣//Kidin-Sîn
Nabû-bullissu/⸢Iddin-Nabû⸣//Dābibī
The scribe: Nidinti-Bēl/⸢Nabû⸣-[da]miq-ilī//Nādin-še'i
(Place and Date).

COMMENT

L. 1: *šipirtu* can refer to a letter, as well as to a document that is issued by an official authorizing his deputy to act for him (cf. *CAD* Š$_3$, 65–68 s.v. *šipirtu* A; and MacGinnis, *Letter Orders*, 22 and No. 61). The latter meaning seems to be the case in the text under consideration.

L. 2: It was probably not a letter order "from (*ša*) Nabû-nādin-aḫi," but rather one from someone else "which (*ša*) Nabû-nādin-aḫi brought here (*iššâm*)." In other words, Nabû-nādin-aḫi seems to have acted on behalf of someone else. This is confirmed by lines 8–9 (see below). For the expression *šipirtu našû*, "to bring a letter (order)," cf. Dar 552 (also quoted and translated in *CAD* Š$_3$, 66 s.v. mng. 2a) and Dar 573.

L. 8–9: *šipirtu ša Šaddinnu* means "the letter from (*ša*) Šaddinnu." It seems that Nabû-nādin-aḫi had brought this letter order from Šaddinnu to MNA ordering him to pay ten minas of marked silver. Upon receipt of the letter, MNA paid to Nabû-nādin-aḫi, but he paid only five out of the ten minas of silver that he had to pay according to the letter. Consequently, Nabû-nādin-aḫi did not give (*ul iddin*, wr. *ul i-d*[*in*]) the letter to MNA, but kept it until the full ten minas would be paid.

No. 34

	BM 31026
Copy:	Bertin copy 2318
Date:	3/v/15 Dar (7 August 507 B.C.E.)
Place:	Šaḫrīnu
Content:	Receipt of silver from MNA's slave and Iddinaya by the messenger of a deputy. For the rations of a group of workmen (^{lú}*za-ar-ga-a-a*). For the account of a bow-unit (*ša* ^{giš}*qašti*).

OBV.

1 ⸢⅓⸣ MA.NA KÙ.BABBAR *šá ina* 1 GÍN *bit-qa nu-uḫ<-ḫu>-tú*

2 KURUM$_{6}$.ḪI.A *šá* LÚ *za-ar-ga-a-a šá* MU.15.KAM

3 ^{m}*da-ar-ri-muš-šú* LUGAL *šá* GIŠ.BAN

4 *šá* ^{md}EN-MU A-*šú šá* ^{md}AG-NUMUN-GÁL-*ši*

5 ^{md}AG-*ú-ṣur-šú* A-*šú šá* ^{m}*ri-mut* LÚ.A.KIN

6 *šá* ^{md}KUR.GAL-LUGAL-*ú-ṣu-ur*$^{!}$ LÚ.2-*ú ina* ŠU.II

7 ^{md}DI.KU$_{5}$-EN-URU$_{3}$ LÚ *qal-la šá*

8 $^{[m]d}$AMAR.UTU-*na-ṣir*-IBILA *u* ^{m}MU-*a*

LO. E.

9 [A]-*šú šá* ^{m}ÌR-*iá a-na muḫ-ḫi*

10 ^{md}EN-MU A-*šú šá* ^{md}AG-NUMUN-GÁL-*ši*

REV.

11 ⸢*e*⸣-*ṭi-ir* 1-*en*.TA.ÀM *il-qu-ú*

12 LÚ *mu-kin-nu* ^{md}IŠKUR-LUGAL-URU$_{3}$ A-*šú šá* ^{m}*ri-mut*

13 ^{m}*ki-din*-^{d}AMAR.UTU A-*šú šá* ^{m}*lu<-uṣ-ana>*-ZALAG$_{2}$-^{d}ŠÚ

14 ^{md}AG-*bul-liṭ-su* A-*šú šá* ^{m}KAR-^{d}AMAR.UTU

15 ^{m}KAR-^{d}AMAR.UTU A-*šú šá* ^{md}EN-ŠEŠ-GÁL-*ši* A ^{md}EN-A-URU$_{3}$

16 ^{m}*ki-na-a* A-*šú šá* ^{m}KI-^{d}AMAR.UTU-DIN

17 LÚ.UMBISAG ^{md}AG-*ú-ṣur-šú* A-*šú šá* ^{m}*ri-mut*

18 URU *šaḫ-ri-nu* ITI.NE UD.3.KAM

U. E.

19 MU.15.KAM ^{m}*da-a-ri-muš-šú*

20 LUGAL E.KI *u* KUR.KUR.MEŠ

TRANSLATION

⸢One-third⸣ mina of medium qu<al>ity silver, of which one-eighth is alloy, from the bow of Bēl-iddin, son of Nabû-zēra-ušabši, (for) the rations of the *zargaya*-(work)men of King Darius' fifteenth year: Nabû-uṣuršu, son of Rīmūt, the messenger of Amurru-šarra-uṣur$^{!}$, the deputy, has received (it) from Madānu-bēla-uṣur, a slave of MNA$_{1}$, and Iddinaya, [son] of Ardiya, for the account of Bēl-iddin, son of Nabû-zēra-ušabši. They have taken one (copy of the document) each.

Witnesses:

Adad-šarra-uṣur / Rīmūt
Kidin-Marduk / Lū<ṣi-ana>-nūr-Marduk
Nabû-bullissu / Mušēzib-Marduk
Mušēzib-Marduk / Bēl-aḫa-ušabši / / Bēl-apla-uṣur
Kīnaya / Itti-Marduk-balāṭu
The scribe: Nabû-uṣuršu / Rīmūt
(Place + Date).

Comment

L. 1: For the omission of signs by the scribe, see also below at line 13. For the use of a wrong sign, see below at line 6.

L. 2: The word ^{lú}*za-ar-ga-a-a* is probably derived from the noun *zargû*, which is attested once in a lexical list, and seems to refer to a kind of agricultural worker (^{giš}zar-gi / gú = *za-ar-gu-ú*), so *AHw*, 1515 s.v. *zargû* "ein Korngarbenwender?"; different in *CAD* Z, 67 s.v. *zargû* "(a wooden implement)."

L. 6: The scribe wrote *-ú-ṣu-*DU instead of *-ú-ṣu-ur*.

No. 35

BM 31036
Copy: Bertin copy 2613
Date: 18/ii/26 Dar (24 May 496 B.C.E.)
Place: Babylon
Content: Receipt of dates and silver from MNA by a royal official. By order of (*ina qibi*) the governor of Babylon.

Obv.

1 15 GUR ZÚ.LUM.MA *a-di* GÍD.DA *šá* ⅔ ⸢MA⸣.[NA (...) KÙ.BABBAR]
2 *šá ina* 1 GÍN *bit-qa nu-uḫ-ḫu-tu šá i-na qa-a*[*t*]
3 ^{m}*i-qu-pu* DUMU *šá* ^{m}*na-di-nu* DUMU ^{m}⸢*ga-ḫúl-*^{d}TU.TU⸣
4 ^{md}EN-*ú-šal-lim* LÚ.SAG-LUGAL DUMU *šá* ^{m}*ina-*^{d}AG-*ul-tar-ra-aḫ*
5 *ina* ŠU.II ^{m}*ši-iš-ku* DUMU *šá* ^{m}SUM.NA-*a*
6 DUMU ^{m}*e-gi-bi ina qí-bi* ^{m}*gu-za-nu* {x}
7 LÚ.GAR-UŠ$_4$ TIN.TIR.KI *ma-ḫi-ir* 1-*en*.TA.ÀM
8 *šá-ṭa-ri il-te-qu-ú*

Rev.

9 LÚ *mu-kin-nu* ^{md}EN-KÁD [DUMU *šá* ^{md}A]G-GIN-IBILA DUMU ^{m}*bu-*[*ra-qu*]
10 ^{m}*na*$^{!}$*-pu-uš-tu*$_4$ DUMU *šá* ^{m}EN-*šú-nu* DUMU ^{m}*ga-*⸢*ḫal*⸣
11 [...-S]UR DUMU *šá* ^{m}*la-a-ba-ši* ^{m}*a-za-a'-*⸢*ri-i'*⸣
12 [... *r*]*e-ḫi-e-tu*$_4$
13 ^{md}AG-*ku-ṣur-šú* DUB.SAR DUMU *šá* ^{md}⸢AMAR.UTU$^{?}$⸣-MU-MU DUMU ^{m}E-x
14 TIN.TIR.KI ITI.GU$_4$ UD.18.KAM MU.26.KAM
15 ^{m}*da-a-ri-ia-muš* LUGAL E.KI *u* [...]

TRANSLATION

Fifteen *kor* of dates together with the register on two-third mi[nas (...)] of medium-quality [silver], of which one-eighth is alloy, are in the hands of Iqūpu, son of Nādin, descendant of ⌜Gaḫul-Marduk⌝: Bēl-ušallim, son of Ina-Nabû-ultarraḫ, the courtier, has received (them) from MNA_2, by order of Gūzānu {x}, governor of Babylon. They have taken one (copy of the document) each.

Witnesses:
Bēl-kāṣir[/Na]bû-mukīn-apli//Bu[raqu]
Napuštu/Bēlšunu//Ga⌜ḫal⌝
[m...-ē]ṭir/Lâbāši
Azārī[/... r]ēḫētu
The scribe: Nabû-kuṣuršu/⌜Marduk?⌝-šuma-iddin//mE-x
(Place + Date).

COMMENT

L. 4: For the same courtier Bēl-ušallim/Ina-Nabû-ultarraḫ, see probably BM 31786: 3, where he received barley from MNA in payment for transport costs. In BM 31786 he is cited by first name only, but bears his full official title, lú*ša-rēš šarri* lú*sep*[*īri ša*] lú*ša-rēšī šarri*meš *ša ekalli rabi* [(...)].

L. 6: *ina qí-bi* is written over other signs. At the end of the line there is one horizontal wedge that can be the beginning of a LÚ. Possibly, the scribe started writing LÚ but then decided to continue on the next line.

L. 9: The name of this person is reconstructed on the basis of Dar 298: 12–13.

L. 11: The name m*a-za-a'*-⌜*ri-i'*⌝ is unique.

L. 12: After this line follows one blank line before the scribe started writing his name in line 13, cf. BM 30366: 12, BM 30819: 14, BM 31227: 13, BM 31793: 17, BM 31883: 17, BM 41442: 15, e.a.; probably also BM 30270: 16–17; cf. also BM 31118: 13.

L. 13: The last sign on line 13 resembles a BI, but there are some scratches after the BI, which may have belonged to additional signs.

No. 36

BM 31058
Copy: Bertin copy 3068
Date: 18/i/[-] Dar (March - April)
Place: Babylon
Content: Promissory note to pay a debt of dates to MNA.

OBV.

1 ⸢8⸣ GUR 2 (PI) 3 (BÁN) (erasure) ⸢ZÚ.LUM.MA⸣ *šá* ^{md}AMAR.UTU-PAB-EDURU$^{?}$
2 A-*šú šá* ^{m}KI-^{d}AMAR.UTU-DIN A ^{m}*e-gi-bi*
3 *i-na muḫ-ḫi* ^{m}*ki-na-a* A-*šú šá* ^{m}*at-kal*-^{d}UTU
4 A LÚ$^{?}$ ⸢x x (x)⸣ *šá* ITI.GU_4 ZÚ.LUM.MA-a_4
5 8 GUR 2 (PI) 3 (BÁN) *i-gam-mar-ma* ⸢*a-na*⸣
6 ^{md}AMAR.UTU-*na-ṣir*-EDURU A-*šú šá* ^{m}KI-^{d}AMAR.UTU-DIN
7 A ^{m}*e-gi-bi uṭ-ṭar-ar*
(Two remaining lines of obverse are empty, as well as lower edge.)

REV.

8 LÚ *mu-kin-nu* ^{m}*ni-din-tu$_4$*-^{d}EN A-*šú šá* ^{m}SIG_5-*qí-iá*
9 A ^{m}*na-di-še$^{!}$-e* ^{m}*ri-mut*-^{d}EN A-*šú šá*
10 ^{m}ÌR-*iá* A ^{m}LÚ.DÍM ^{m}GIŠ.GE_6-^{d}EN A-*šú šá*
11 ^{m}EN-*šú-nu* A ^{m}$ZALAG_2$-^{d}30 ^{m}*ri-mut*-^{d}EN
12 A ^{m}MU-GI.NA ^{md}AG-ŠEŠ-*it-tan-nu* A-*šú šá*
13 ^{md}UTU-MU A ^{m}*ki*-x-*šú*-^{d}AG
14 $^{[md]}$[A]G$^{?}$-EDURU-MU DUB.SAR A-*šú šá* ^{md}U.GUR-[x (x)]
15 [A ^{m}NUM]UN-*ú*-⸢*ti*⸣-*iá* TIN.TIR.KI

U. E.

16 [I]TI.BÁR UD.18.KAM M[U.x.KAM]
(Illegible remnants of signs.)

TRANSLATION

8.2.3 *kor* of ⸢dates⸣ are due to MNA_1 from Kīnaya, son of Atkal-Šamaš, descendant of .... In Ayyar he shall pay off in full this (debt of) 8.2.3 *kor* of dates ⸢to⸣ MNA_1.

Witnesses:
Nidinti-Bēl/Damqiya//Nādin-še'i
Rīmūt-Bēl/Ardiya//Itinnu
Ṣilli-Bēl/Bēlšunu//Nūr-Sîn
Rīmūt-Bēl//Šuma-ukīn
Nabû-aḫa-ittannu/Šamaš-iddin//Ki-...-Nabû
The scribe: [Nab]û$^{?}$-apla-iddin/Nergal-[...][//]⸢Zērūtiya⸣
(Place + Date).

Comment

L. 1: Originally, there may have been a different amount of dates at stake. As it is, the scribe erased some of it, and wrote over what he did not erase. The scribe's erasure (of one sign) is still clearly visible after the 3 (BÁN), and remnants of other signs may be seen underneath the ⸢ZÚ.LUM.MA⸣ as follows: LUM is written over the remnants of a ZÚ; MA over that of a LUM; and *šá* over that of a MA.

L. 1 end: The last sign is written on the right edge, and since this edge is very thin the sign in question may have been the short A, rather than the long EDURU.

L. 7–9: Note the following strange spellings *uṭ-ṭar-ar* (the *-ar* is superfluous); ^{m}SIG$_{5}$-*qí-iá* (usually spelled without the *-qí-*); and ^{m}*na-di-še*$^{!}$ (NI)-*e* (with a *-di-* instead of the usual *-din-*).

L. 13: The sign after KI has all the wedges for an EN (one horizontal, two verticals and two *Winkelhaken*), but a name Itti-bēlšu-Nabû does not have real meaning.

L. 17: There are illegible remnants of a few, small signs written on the first third of this line.

No. 37

	BM 31118
Copy:	Bertin copy 2581
Date:	4/[-]/25 Dar (497–496 B.C.E.)
Place:	Babylon
Content:	Receipt of a hireling(?) by MNA. Hired for six days a month during six months from Nisan till Ulūl.

Obv.

1 [x (x)$^{?}$] ⸢x⸣ *šá* ITI 6 *u*$_{4}$-*mu*.⸢MEŠ⸣

2 *šá ul-tu* ITI.⸢BÁR⸣ MU.25.K[AM]

3 *a-di qí-it* ITI.KIN MU.25.KAM

4 *šá* ^{md}EN-MU A-*šú šá* ^{m}NUMUN-*ia* A LÚ.GAL-DÙ

5 ^{m}*ši-rik* A-*šú šá* ^{m}MU-*a* A ^{m}*e-gi-bi*

6 *ina* ŠU.II ^{md}EN-MU *e-ṭir*

7 1-*en*.TA.ÀM *il-qu-ú*

Rev.

8 LÚ *mu-kin-nu* ^{md}30-DINGIR

9 A-*šú šá* ^{m}*ni-qu-du* A ^{m}*aš-gan-du*$_{7}$

10 ^{md}AG-URU$_{3}$-*šú* A-*šú šá* ^{m}*la-ba-ši* A LÚ.⸢x⸣

11 ^{md}UTU-NÍG.BA-*an-ni* A-*šú šá*

12 ^{m}*mi-nu-ú-a-na*-^{d}EN-*da-nu*

13 A LÚ.SANGA-^{d}UTU

14 LÚ.UMBISAG ^{m}*ši-rik* A-*šú šá* ^{m}[MU-*a*]

15 A ^{m}*e-gi-bi* E.[KI ITI.x]

U. E.

16 [UD].4.KAM MU.25.[KAM]

LE. E.

17 ^{m}*da-ri-muš*

18 LUGAL E.KI *u* KUR.KU[R]

TRANSLATION

⸢A hireling⸣ for six days a month, from ⸢Nisan⸣ of the twenty-fif[th] year till the end of Ulūl of the twenty-fifth year, is due from Bēl-iddin, son of Zēriya, descendant of Rab-banê: MNA_2 has received (him) from Bēl-iddin. They have taken one (copy of the document) each.

Witnesses:
Sîn-ilī/Niqūdu//Ašgandu
Nabû-uṣuršu/Lâbāši//⸢Itinnu$^{?}$⸣
Šamaš-iqīšanni/Mīnû-ana-Bēl-dānu//Šangû-Šamaš
The scribe: MNA_2
(Place + Date).

COMMENT

L. 1: The wedges after the initial break seem to be verticals rather than horizontals. If taken as verticals, one may read [LÚ].⸢A.GAR⸣ = *agru* "hireling" (cf. BM 31226: 1). However, it cannot be excluded that one has to read [LÚ.ḪUN].GÁ = *agru* "hireling," although there is very little space at the beginning of the line to fit in both LÚ and ḪUN.

L. 1–3: The MU in lines 1, 2 and 3, the number 20 in line 2 and the number 25 in line 3 are written over other signs.

L. 4–5: The first *šá* in line 4 and the first *Personenkeil* in line 5 are written over other signs.

L. 10: The profession at the end of the line consists of only one sign (probably ŠITIM). It is squeezed on the right edge of the tablet, partly broken, and a little lower than the other signs in the same line because immediately on top of it stands the BI-sign of the end of line 5.

L. 13: This line is half empty. The scribe started a new line in order to write his own name. Thus, he kept his name clearly separated from the list of witnesses. Neo-Babylonian scribes often left one or two empty lines between the end of the list of witnesses and their own name, see BM 30366: 12, BM 30819: 14, BM 31036: 12, BM 31227: 13, BM 31793: 17, BM 32883: 17 e.a.; probably also BM 30270: 16–17.

No. 38

BM 31138
Copy: Bertin copy 2568
Date: 19/iii/25 Dar (4 July 497 B.C.E.)
Place: Babylon
Content: Receipt of barley from MNA. By order of (*ina qibi ša*) a royal official.

OBV.

1 2 GUR ŠE.BAR ^{m}*mu-un-še-e* A-*šú šá*
2 ^{m}*in-zi-ia* 1 GUR ŠE<.BAR>
3 ^{md}AG-SIPA-*šú-nu* A-*šú šá* ^{md}AG-DIN-*su*-E
4 *ina qí-bi šá* ^{m}MU-^{d}AG LÚ.SAG-LUGAL
5 LÚ *si-pir-ri ina* ŠU.II ^{m}*šìr-ki*
6 DUMU *šá* ^{m}SUM.NA-*a* DUMU ^{m}*e-gi-b*[*i*]
7 *ma-ḫi-ra-a'*

REV.

8 LÚ *mu-kin-nu* ^{m}*ta-ta*[*n* ...]
9 ^{md}AG-KÀD DUMU *šá* ^{md}AG-KÀD DUMU ^{m}[...]
10 ^{m}*ni-din-tu*$_{4}$ DUMU *šá* ^{m}*kal-ba-a* ^{m}*ma*[*r*-...]
11 A-*šú šá* ^{m}*gu-za-nu* ^{m}*ni-din-tu*$_{4}$ A-*šú šá*
12 ^{m}ÌR-*ia* A LÚ.GAL-*li-mu*
13 LÚ.UMBISAG ^{m}*šul-lu-mu* A-*šú šá* ^{m}MU-^{d}AG
14 A ^{m}*ka-nik*-KÁ TIN.TIR.KI ITI.SIG$_{4}$
15 UD.20-1-LÁ.KAM MU.25.KAM
16 ^{m}*da-ri-ia-muš* LUGAL E.KI *u* KUR.KUR

TRANSLATION

Two *kor* of barley: Muššê, son of Inziya; one *kor* of bar<ley>: Nabû-re'ûšunu, son of Nabû-balāssu-iqbi. By order of Iddin-Nabû, courtier (and) clerk, (the three *kor* of barley) have been received from MNA$_2$.

Witnesses:
Tatta[nnu] [...]
Nabû-kāṣir/Nabû-kāṣir//[...]
Nidintu/Kalbaya
Ma[rduk]/Gūzānu(//Kaṣṣidakku)
Nidintu/Ardiya//Rab-līmi
The scribe: Šullumu/Iddin-Nabû//Kānik-bābi
(Place + Date).

COMMENT

L. 1: The name ^{m}*mu-un-še-e* is most likely derived from the verb *mašû* A (D participle) "He-who-makes-one-forget(-the-lost-child)," and is thus similar to the name ^{m}*mu-še-en-šá-a* (Š participle), in GCCI 2 292: 4 (cf. *CAD* M_1, 400 s.v. *mašû* A mng. 1e; *AHw*, 632 s.v. *mašû* II Š). A reading ^{m}*mu-un-tir* = *Mutīr* (from the verb *târu*) is less likely; Neo-Babylonian names with the verbal element *mutīr* are of the type (DN-) *Mutīr*(*ri*)-*gimilli* (e.g., Nabû-mutīr-gimilli, Bongenaar, *Ebabbar*, 529; more examples at Tallqvist, *NbN*, 335 s.v. *târu*; Stolper, *Entrepreneurs*, 295; Donbaz-Stolper, *Istanbul Murašû*, 171f.).

L. 2a: The name ^{m}*in-zi-ia* is unique.

L. 2b: There was plenty of space left for the scribe to write BAR.

L. 7: The two amounts of barley (*uṭṭātu*, fem.) mentioned in lines 1–2 are the subject of the verb *maḫrā* (3rd fem. pl.). It is not clear how Muššê and Nabû-re'ûšunu are related to the receipt of the barley.

No. 39

BM 31188
Copy: Bertin copy 2534
Date: 25/[-]/24 Dar (498–97 B.C.E.)
Place: Babylon
Content: Receipt of a boat-tower by MNA. From the governor's pool of forced laborers ([^{lú}*u*]*rāšu šādadu*). Reference to a register (regulating the forced-labor service) in Dûzu (GIŠ.DA *maḫrīti ša* ^{iti}*Dûzu*).

OBV.

1 [1-*en* LÚ *ú*]-*ra-šú šá-da-du šá ka-a-ri*
2 [*šá* ŠU.II] ^{m}*ina-é-sag-ìl-li-bi*[*r*]
3 [LÚ.GAR-UŠ$_4$] TIN.TIR.KI *šá* 2 ITI.MEŠ *u* 2 *u*$_4$-*m*[*u*] *a*-⸢*di-i*⸣
4 GÍD.DA IGI-[*ú*] *šá* ITI.ŠU ⸢x x⸣ ^{md}EN-⸢SU⸣ DUMU [...]
5 *šá* MU.24.KAM ^{m}*da-ri-muš*
6 ⸢LUGAL⸣ E.KI LUGAL KUR.KUR ^{m}*ši-iš-ku* ⸢A-*šú*⸣
7 ⸢*šá*⸣ ^{m}SUM.NA-*a* ⸢A⸣ ^{m}*e-gi-bi ina* ŠU.II
8 ^{md}EN-DIN-*iṭ* A-*šú šá* ^{m}MU-^{d}AG
9 ⸢A⸣ LÚ.ŠU.KU$_6$ *a-na muḫ-ḫi* ^{md}[EN]-[...]

LO. E.

10 [A]-*šú šá* ^{m}*ze-ri-ia* A ^{m}MU-⸢x⸣ [...]
11 *ma-ḫi-ir* (erasure)

REV.

12 (erasure) LÚ *mu-kin-nu*
13 ^{m}*la-a-ba-ši* A-*šú šá* ^{md}AMAR.UTU-NUMUN-DÙ
14 A LÚ.SIPA-ANŠE.KUR.RA ^{md}AG-MU-DÙ
15 A-*šú šá* ^{m}*mu-še-zib*-^{d}EN A ^{md}30-DINGIR.MEŠ
16 ^{m}MU-^{d}AG A-*šú šá* ⸢^{md}EN-NUMUN ^{md}EN-*ik-ṣur*⸣
17 A-*šú šá* ^{m}*šá-du-nu* A LÚ.BAḪAR$_2$

18 ^{md}EN-BA-*šá* LÚ.UMBISAG A-*šú šá* ^{m}*gu-za-nu* E.KI
19 [ITI.x UD].25.KAM MU.24.KAM

U. E.

20 [^{m}*da-ri*]-⸢i'⸣-*muš* LUGAL E.KI
21 [LUGAL] KUR.KUR

LE. E.

22 1-*en*.TA.ÀM *il-qu*-[*ú*]

TRANSLATION

[One for]ced laborer to tow (boats) to the quay, [who is under the administrative authority of] Ina-Esagil-lilbur, [governor] of Babylon, for two months and two day[s] in the twenty-fourth year of Darius, ⸢king⸣ of Babylon, king of the lands, together with a previ[ous] register regarding (service in the month) Dûzu, ⸢x x⸣ Bēl-⸢erība⸣, son of [...]: MNA_2 has received (him and the register) from Bēl-uballiṭ, son of Iddin-Nabû, ⸢descendant⸣ of Bā'iru, for the account of [Bēl]-[...], [son] of Zēriya, descendant of MU-[...]. (erasures).

Witnesses:
Lâbāši/Marduk-zēra-ibni//Rē'i-sīsî
Nabû-šuma-ibni/Mušēzib-Bēl//Sîn-ilī
Iddin-Nabû/⸢Bēl-zēri⸣
⸢Bēl-ikṣur⸣/Šadûnu//Paḫāru
The scribe: Bēl-iqīša/Gūzānu
(Place + Date).

They have taken one (copy of the document) each.

COMMENT

The surface of the tablet is damaged and the signs are squeezed on the tablet. This makes reading it rather difficult, esp. in lines 4–5.

L. 2: The beginning of the line ([*šá* ŠU.II]) is reconstructed on the basis of a comparison with BM 32932: 1–2.

L. 3: Some of the signs at the end of the line may be read in more than one way or are partly broken and hence open to more than one interpretation. The U-sign, for instance, can be read either *u* "and," or as the number 10. The second sign from the end is partly broken and was either *di* or *ki*. Accordingly, the worker whom MNA received had to tow boats for either "two months and (*u*) two days," or "two months twelve days" (cf. BM 32932: 4, *šá* 2 ITI.MEŠ *ù* 12 u_4-*mu*). Furthermore, he had to do the work either "according to (*aki*) a previous register" or "in addition to (*adi*) a previous register."

L. 4: The traces of the two signs are probably to be read ⸢*ina muḫḫi* (UGU)⸣, although they resemble more ⸢MU *šá*⸣ (read <*ana*> ⸢*šumi šá*⸣?). If read *ina muḫḫi*, the boat-tower was "owed by Bēl-erība, son of [...]" (l. 4), and delivered by a man named Bēl-uballiṭ "for the account of (this) [Bēl]-[erība],

[son] of Zēriya, descendant of ^{m}MU-[…]" (ll. 9–10: *ana muḫḫi* [Bēl]-[erība], [son] of Zēriya, descendant of MU-[…]). However, if read <*ana*> *šumi ša*, the boat-tower was probably enlisted "<in the> name of (i.e., with) Bēl-erība"; the latter situation should be compared to BM 30274, where a man named Ardiya had to do service "with (*itti*) Bēl-erība, son of Kalbaya, descendant of Šumu-libši, his commander-of-fifty." In the first case, the affiliation of Bēl-erība at the end of line 4 in the text under consideration is to be reconstructed as follows: son of [Zēriya, descendant of MU-…], on the basis of evidence from lines 9–10. In the second case, Bēl-erība in line 4 was the son of [Kalbaya, descendant of Šumu-libši], on the basis of a comparison with BM 30274: 5–6.

L. 5: The first sign of this line, viz. *šá*, is not written close to the left edge, as it should have been, but slightly more to the right. In fact, this line has been added later by the scribe, and the signs were squeezed in between lines 4 and 6. It was added by the scribe to further specify in which year the worker had to tow boats, and consequently, it should have followed the phrase "for two months and two days" at the end of line 3.

L. 11–12: The second half of line 11 and the first half of line 12 have been erased.

No. 40

BM 31203
Copy: no Bertin copy
Date: 4/viii/[-] (Oct. - Nov.)
Place: Babylon
Content: Receipt of flour. Paid on behalf of MNA. Rations for one month.

OBV.

1 ⸢x GUR⸣ *qí-me* KURUM$_6$.ḪI.A-*su*
2 *šá ul-tu* UD.1.KAM *šá* ⸢ITI⸣.APIN
3 *a-di* UD.1.KAM *šá* ITI.GAN
4 ^{m}*a-*⸢*mur-qa*⸣*-an-nu ina* ŠU.II
5 ^{m}[*n*]*a-di-*[*nu*] A-*šú šá* ^{m}MU-*a*
6 *a-na* ⸢UGU⸣ ^{m}*ši-ir-ku* ⸢A⸣-[*šú šá*]
7 ^{m}MU-*a ma-ḫi-ir*

REV.

8 ⸢LÚ *mu-kin*⸣*-nu* ^{m}ÌR-^{d}*gu-la*
9 ⸢A-*šú šá*⸣ ^{md}U.GUR-MU A ^{m}DÙ-*eš*-DINGIR
10 ⸢^{md}EN-SUR A-*šú šá* ^{md}AG-KAR⸣-ZI.MEŠ
11 A ⸢^{m}BAḪAR$_2$⸣$^{?}$ ⸢x x x⸣$^{?}$
12 ⸢*u* LÚ.UMBISAG⸣ ^{m}ÌR-^{d}*gu-la* A-*šú* [*šá*]
13 ⸢^{m}⸣^{d}AMAR.UTU-MU-URU$_3$ A ^{m}*na-ba-*⸢*a*⸣-[*a*]
14 ⸢E⸣.KI ITI.APIN UD.4.K[AM]
15 (illegible remnants of signs)

U. E.

16 ⸢LUGAL E⸣.KI ⸢LUGAL⸣ KUR.KUR

Translation

Amur-qannu has received from Nādin, son of Iddinaya, ⸢x (x)⸣ flour, his rations from the first of Araḫsamna till the first of Kislīm, (paid) for the ⸢account⸣ of MNA$_2$.

Witnesses:

Arad-Gula/Nergal-iddin//Eppeš-ilī

⸢Bēl-ēṭir/Nabû-ēṭir⸣-napšāti//⸢Paḫāru$^{?}$⸣

⸢And the scribe⸣: Arad-Gula/Marduk-šuma-uṣur//Nabaya

(Place + Date).

Comment

The surface of this tablet is damaged, and hence, often difficult to read.

L. 4: The name ^{m}*a-mur-qa-an-nu* is unique. It seems to contain the verbal element *amur/āmur* (G imper./ pret. 1st sg. of *amāru*) "see/I saw," and a nominal element *qa-nu*. The latter may be the noun *qarnu*, which means "horn; power$^{?}$ (in transferred mng.)" (*CAD* Q, 134–40 s.v. *qarnu*). It occurs in Old Babylonian and Neo-Assyrian names such as *Qa-na-a*-DINGIR and ^{d}*Šá-maš-qa-na-a* (*ibid.*, 140 s.v. mng. 6b; cf. *AHw*, 904 s.v. *qarnu* mng. B-4). For Neo-Babylonian names containing the verb *amāru*, see more at Tallqvist, *NbN*, 305.

L. 10–11: For this person, also see BM 41449: 13. There seem to have followed a few more signs after BAḪAR$_2$, but the last quarter of this line is left empty.

No. 41

BM 31226

Copy: Bertin copy 2612

Date: 9/vii/26 Dar (9 October 496 B.C.E.)

Place: Babylon

Content: Receipt of a person from MNA by an agent of the commander of-the-fortress. To serve in the fortress of Babylon (LÚ.A.GÀR *ana dūr Bābili*^{ki}).

Obv.

1 LÚ.A.GÀR *šá a-na* BÀD TIN.TIR.KI

2 *šá* ^{m}*šu-zu-bu* DUMU *šá* ^{m}*ú-bal-liṭ-su-*^{d}AMAR.UTU

3 A ^{m}GÍR.LÁ *ù* ^{m}*gu-za-nu* DUMU *šá* ^{m}*ḫa-am-ba-qu*

4 *šá a-di-i qí-ti* ITI.ŠE.<2>.KAM *šá* MU.26.KAM A LÚ *man-di-di*

5 ^{md}AMAR.UTU-*re-man-ni* DUMU *šá* ^{md}AMAR.UTU-MU-URU$_3$

6 A LÚ.SANGA-^{d}IŠKUR *ina iq-ba šá* $^{md!}$*ad-du*-KAM LÚ.GAL BÀD *ina* ŠU.II ^{m}*ši-rik-ku/ki*

7 DUMU *šá* ^{m}SUM.NA-*a* A ^{m}*e-gi-bi*
8 *a-na ina* {*muḫ-ḫi*} ^{m}*šu-zu-bu ù*
9 ^{m}*gu-za-nu ma-ḫi-ir* 1-*en-a*.TA.ÀM

LO. E.

10 TI-*ú*

REV.

11 LÚ *mu-kin-nu* ^{md}AG-MU-MU *u* ^{m}NUMUN-*ia*
12 DUMU.MEŠ *šá* ^{m}DUB-NUMUN A ^{m}*de-ku-ú*
13 ^{md}EN-DIN-*iṭ* DUMU *šá* ^{md}AG-KAR-ZI.MEŠ
14 ^{m}*lib-luṭ* DUMU *šá* ^{m}KI-^{d}AG-DIN A LÚ *si-si-i*
15 ^{md}EN-SU DUMU *šá* ^{m}*kal-ba-a* A ^{m}MU-*lìb*$^{?}$(ḪI)-*ši*
16 ^{md}*za-ba*$_{4}$-*ba*$_{4}$-MU DUMU *šá*
17 ^{m}*ni-qu-du* A LÚ.EN.NUN-KÁ.GAL LÚ.UMBISAG
18 ^{md}AG-*it-tan-nu* DUMU *šá* ^{md}IŠKUR-A-MU
19 E.KI ITI.DU$_{6}$ UD.9.KAM MU.26.KAM
20 ^{m}*da-ri-'i-muš* LUGAL E.KI *u* KUR.KUR.MEŠ
21 *qí-me-šú-nu šá* MU.26.KAM

U. E.

22 *e-ṭir*

TRANSLATION

A hireling$^{?}$ for the Citadel of Babylon (to do service) till the end of <Seco>nd Addar of the twenty-sixth year is due from Šūzubu, son of Uballissu-Marduk, descendant of Ṭābiḫu, and Gūzānu, son of Ḫambaqu, descendant of Mandidi: Marduk-rēmanni, son of Marduk-šuma-uṣur, descendant of Šangû-Adad, has received (him) from MNA$_{2}$, for the account of Šūzubu and Gūzānu, by order of Addu-ēreš, commander-of-the-citadel. They have taken one (copy of the document) each.

Witnesses:
Nabû-šuma-iddin and Zēriya/Šāpik-zēri//Dēkû
Bēl-uballiṭ/Nabû-ēṭir-napšāti
Libluṭ/Itti-Nabû-balāṭu//Sīsî
Bēl-erība/Kalbaya//Šumu-libši
Zababa-iddin/Niqūdu//Maṣṣār-abulli
The scribe: Nabû-ittannu/Adad-apla-iddin
(Place + Date).

Their flour(-tax) for the twenty-sixth year has been paid off.

Comment

This is a very densely written tablet, and several lines of the obverse continue on the right edge and even on the reverse side of the tablet.

L. 1: In my opinion the signs A and GÀR are to be read syllabically, viz. [lú]*a-gàr*. It is a syllabic writing of the noun *agru* "hireling." This noun is usually written with the logogram LÚ.ḪUN.GÁ, but syllabic spellings like the one in the text under consideration are attested in BE 9 43: 5, 10 ([lú]*a-gar*, cf. *AHw*, 16 s.v. *agru*), and probably also in BM 31118: 1 ([LÚ].⌜A.GAR⌝).

L. 2: The element -[d]AMAR.UTU is written on the right edge of the tablet.

L. 3–4: The family name of Gūzānu, LÚ *man-di-di*, is written, not at the end of line 3 after the patronymy, where we would normally expect it, but at the end of line 4, where it does not fit contextually. The distribution of the signs over lines 3–4 is as follows: [m]*ḫa-am-* is written on the obverse line 3; *-ba-qu* is written on the right edge of the same line; but LÚ *man-di-di* is written at the end of the next line; in fact, it is squeezed onto the right edge of line 4, beginning underneath the *-qu* of the previous line, and continues onto the reverse of the tablet.

L. 4: BM 31226 was dated at the beginning of Tašrīt (9/vii/26 Dar) and the commander received the hireling "till the end of <Seco>nd Addar of the twenty-sixth year" (l. 4). This equals a period of a little more than six months. I do not think that the phrase "till the end of ... Addar" is a shorter version of the phrase "from the first of Nisan till the end of Addar." It is true that this is the case in the *ilku*-receipts, where the phrase "till the end of Addar" refers to a full year (e.g., BM 41607, BM 31533, CTMMA 3 68, BM 31227, and BM 30261), but it is very unlikely that the hireling in the text under consideration had to serve for such a long period of time.

L. 6: The phrase *ina iq-ba* is a variant of the more common *ina qí-bi* "by order of"; other variants are *ina iq-bi* in BM 30639: 5, 11 and *ina qí-bit* in BM 33936: 7. The DINGIR-sign in [md]*ad-du-* looks more like a MA or BA because it has one horizontal and one vertical wedge, which are deeply impressed in the clay, and two weakly impressed horizontal wedges, which are underneath the other horizontal wedge. The end of the line is very densely written: LÚ.GAL is on the right edge of the tablet, and BÀD *ina* ŠU.II [m]*ši-rik-ku/i* is written on the reverse of the tablet and, in fact, fills up the second half of line 16.

L. 15: The sign resembling ḪI may either be a badly written *-lìb-*, or the beginning of a *-lib-*.

No. 42

BM 31227
Copy: Bertin copy 2569
Date: 4/[-]/25 Dar (497–496 B.C.E.)
Place: Bāb-Bitāqu
Content: Receipt of the *ilku*-tax by MNA. Tax related to a bridge.

OBV.

1 *il-ki šá* ^{md}EN-A.ZU-*ú* A-*šú*
2 *šá* ^{md}AG-MU A ^{m}*ba-bu-tu šá a-di-i*
3 *qí-it* ITI.ŠE *šá* MU.25.KAM ^{m}*da-ri-'i-maš*
4 LUGAL E.KI *u* KUR.KUR *šá i-da-šú*
5 *šá gi-ši-ri* TIN.TIR.KI *šá ina* ŠU.II ^{md}EN-KAR$^{?}$-*ir*
6 ^{m}*šìr-ku* A-*šú šá* ^{m}SUM.NA-*a* A ^{m}*e-gi-bi*
7 [*ina* ŠU].II$^{?}$ ^{md}EN-*a-su-ú ma-ḫi-ir*

LO. E.

8 [1-*e*]*n*.ÀM *il-qu-ú*

REV.

9 [LÚ *mu-kin*]-*nu* ^{m}*eri-ba-a* A-*šú šá*
10 [^{md}...-*mu*]-*še-zib* ^{md}AG-*bul-liṭ-su* A-*šú šá*
11 ^{m}*ḫaš-da-a* ^{m}*šul-lu-ma-a* A-*šú šá*
12 ^{m}*kal-ba-a* A ^{m}*na-ba-a-a*
13 ^{m}*zu-um-bu* A-*šú šá* ^{m}*na-pu-uš-tu*$_{4}$
14 *u* LÚ.UMBISAG ^{m}*šá*-^{d}AG-*i-du-šú* A-*šú šá*
15 ^{m}*la-a-ba-ši* A ^{m}LÚ.SANGA-^{d}IŠKUR
16 URU.KÁ-*bi-ta-qu* I[TI ...]

U. E.

17 UD.4.KAM MU.25.KAM

LE. E.

18 [^{m}*d*]*a-ri-i'-maš*
19 LUGAL E.KI *u* KUR.[KUR]

TRANSLATION

The *ilku*-tax till the end of Addar of the twenty-fifth year of Darius, king of Babylon and the lands, is due from Bēl-asûa, son of Nabû-iddin, descendant of Bābūtu—for the .... of the bridge of Babylon that is the responsibility of Bēl-ēṭir (or -upaḫḫir): MNA$_2$ has received (it) [fro]m$^{?}$ Bēl-asûa. They have taken [one] (copy of the document) each.

The witnesses:
Erībaya/[^{d}...]-mušēzib
Nabû-bullissu/Ḫašdaya
Šullumaya/Kalbaya//Nabaya
Zumbu/Napuštu

The scribe: Ša-Nabû-idūšu/Lâbāši//Šangû-Adad
(Place + Date).

COMMENT

L. 1: The ZU- and SU-signs are not always easy to distinguish from each other. The name Bēl-asûa seems to be written with a ZU in line 1 (cf. Wunsch, *Felder* 2, 281) and with a SU in line 7 (cf. Tallqvist, *NbN*, 27).

L. 4: The word *i-da-šú* seems to be derived from *idū* "hire, wages, rent" (*CAD* I/J, 16–20 s.v. *idū*). However, it is not immediately clear how one should understand the payment of *ilku* ... *ša i-da-šú ša gi-ši-ri*. Does it refer to *ilku* paid "for (*ša*) his rent of the bridge" (but is it possible that taxes were collected from someone's income from rent)? Or did the obligation to pay *ilku* in this case consist of collecting rent from a bridge? In my opinion one should emend the text and read *šá ú*!(I)-*ra*!(DA)-*šú šá gi-ši-ri*; this expression is attested in Sippar (BM 74601, quoted by Jursa, *Bēl-rēmanni*, 100 n. 412). If so, the text refers to *ilku* that consisted of providing an *urāšu*-workmen to work at the bridge. BM 31277 is not the only text from the archive in which MNA is directly involved in the exploitation of bridges (see also BM 30366: 1, *il-ki šá* DI-*pi šá giš-ri*; TCL 13 196 and BM 41443).

L. 5a: Note the spelling *gi-ši-ri* for *gišru* normally spelled *gi-iš-ri/ru*.

L. 5b: The sign may be KAR (= *ēṭir*) or NIGIN (= *upaḫḫir*). This person was in charge of the bridge (*ina qātē* Bēl-ēṭir, -upaḫḫir), and his position is comparable to that of Gūzānu, governor of Babylon, in TCL 13 196 (*bīt qīptu ša* governor). On the expression *ina qātē*, more at BM 30795: 4b.

L. 13: After this line follows one blank line before the scribe started writing his name in line 14, cf. BM 30366: 12, BM 30819: 14, BM 31036: 12, BM 31793: 17, BM 31883: 17, BM 41442: 15, e.a.; probably also BM 30270: 16–17; cf. also BM 31118: 13.

L. 17: The number five is written with horizontal wedges.

No. 43

BM 31322
Copy: Bertin copy 2583
Date: 16/iv/25 Dar (30 July 497 B.C.E.)
Place: Babylon
Content: Receipt of the *ilku*-tax by MNA.

OBV.

1 *il-ki gab-bi šá* TA ITI.BÁR *šá* MU.25.⌜KAM⌝
2 *a-di* TIL ITI.ŠE *šá* MU.25.KAM ᵐ*da-ri-ia-muš* LUGAL
3 ᵐ*ši-iš-ku* DUMU *šá* ᵐMU-*a* A ᵐ*e-gì-bi ma-la* ḪA.LA
4 *šá* ᵐᵈAG-*bul-liṭ-su* DUMU *šá* ᵐᵈAG-*it-tan-nu* A ᵐ*sip-pe-e*
5 ᵐ*ši-iš-ku ina* ŠU.II ᵐᵈAG-*it-tan-nu ma-ḫi-ir*
6 [1]-*en*.TA.ÀM *šá-ṭa-ri* TI-*ú*

REV.

7 LÚ *mu-kin-nu* ᵐ*ni-din-tu*$_4$-ᵈEN DUMU *šá* ᵐᵈ⌜AG⌝-[...]
8 A ᵐ*šá-la-la* ᵐ*mar-duk-a* DUMU *šá* ᵐ*gu-z*[*a-nu*]
9 A ᵐ*kàṣ-ṣì-dak-ku* ᵐ*tat-tan-nu* DUMU *šá* ᵐᵈEN-KÁD
10 A ᵐ*da-bi-bi* ᵐᵈEN-MU DUMU *šá* ᵐŠEŠ-*šú-nu*
11 ᵐMU-*a* DUMU *šá* ᵐᵈEN-SUR A ᵐᵈIŠKUR-*šá-me-e*
12 ᵐ*ku-ṣur-a* LÚ.UMBISAG DUMU *šá* ᵐ*ki-rib-tú* A LÚ.EN.NUN-KÁ.GAL
13 TIN.TIR.KI ITI.ŠU UD.16.KAM MU.25.KAM
14 ᵐ*da-ri-ia-muš* LUGAL TIN.TIR.KI *u* KUR.KUR

TRANSLATION

The entire *ilku*-tax from Nisan of the twenty-fifth year till the end of Addar of the twenty-fifth year of King Darius, - MNA$_2$ -, in so much as it is the share due from Nabû-bullissu, son of Nabû-ittannu, descendant of Sippê(a): MNA$_2$ has received (it) from Nabû-ittannu. They have taken one (copy of) the document each.

Witnesses:
Nidinti-Bēl/⌜Nabû⌝-[...]//Šalāla
Marduk/Gūz[ānu]//Kaṣṣidakku
Tattannu/Bēl (rd. Nabû!)-kāṣir//Dābibī
Bēl-iddin/Aḫūšunu
Iddinnaya/Bēl-ēṭir//Adad-šammê
The scribe: Kuṣura(pli)/Kiribtu//Maṣṣār-abulli
(Place + Date).

COMMENT

Only two-thirds of the obverse are inscribed, and contain the description of the main issue. The lower third part is left empty. The list of witnesses is inscribed on the reverse.

L. 9: Most likely one has to read Nabû$^{!}$-kāṣir rather than Bēl-kāṣir because Tattannu/Nabû-kāṣir//Dābibī is well attested in texts from MNA's time (see index).

L. 12: For the reading of the name Kuṣura(pli), see more at BM 30446: 9.

No. 44

	BM 31347
Copy:	no Bertin copy
Date:	20/ix/[-] Dar (second half of December or beginning of January)
Place:	broken
Content:	Receipt of the *miksu*-toll from MNA.

OBV.

1 [*mi*]-*ik-su šá* 1-*en* GIŠ.MÁ [...]

2 1 ME GUR ZÚ.LUM.MA 50 GUR ŠE.[BAR]

3 *šá ina* UGU *ka-a-ri šá* É-*ṭ*[*a-bi*-^{d}EN]

4 ^{md}AMAR.UTU-PAB-EDURU *ú-še-ti-*⸢*iq*⸣ ⸢x x x x⸣

5 *šá* 1-*en* GIŠ.MÁ *šá* 1 ME 80$^{?}$ ⸢GUR⸣ ZÚ.LUM.MA *šá ina* UG[U *ka-a-ri*]

6 [*šá*] ⸢DU$_{6}$⸣-^{d}*gu-*⸢*la*⸣ ^{md}AMAR.UTU-PAB-EDURU ⸢*ú*⸣-[*še-ti-iq*]

7 $^{[md]}$AG-*bul-liṭ-su* A-*šú šá* ^{md}AG-[...]

8 [LÚ].GAL-*k*[*a*]-*a-ri šá* É-*ṭ*[*a-bi*-^{d}EN]

LO. E.

9 <*i*>-*na qá-ti* $^{m⸢d}$AMAR.UTU⸣-PAB-[EDURU]

REV.

10 A-*šú šá* $^{m⸢}$KI-^{d}AMAR.UTU⸣-DIN A ^{m}*e-gì-bi*

11 *i-na* 1 GUR 1 (BÁN) *mi-ik-su ma-ḫi-*[*ir*]

12 LÚ *mu-kin-nu* ^{md}AG-MU-MU A-*šú š*[*á* ...]

13 ^{m}DUB-NUMUN A LÚ ⸢*de-ki*⸣-*i* ^{md}E[N-...]

14 A-*šú šá* ^{md}U.GUR-DIN-*iṭ* [...]

15 A-*šú šá* ^{m}PA-x-A A LÚ.AN[ŠE...]

16 [LÚ].UMBISAG ^{md}AG-*bul-liṭ-su* A-*šú šá* ^{m}[...]

17 [x x (x)] ITI.[GAN] UD.20.KAM M[U ...]

U. E.

18 [^{m}*d*]*a-*[*ri-ia*]-*mu-uš* LU[GAL ...]

TRANSLATION

The *miksu*-toll for one boat [...] (loaded) with one hundred *kor* of dates (and) fifty *kor* of b[arley], which MNA$_{1}$ made pass beyond the quay of Bīt-ṭ[āb-Bēl], ⸢x x⸣ for one boat (loaded) with one hundred and eighty$^{?}$ *kor* of dates, which MNA$_{1}$ ma[de pass] beyo[nd the quay of] ⸢Til⸣-Gula: Nabû-bullissu, son of

Nabû-[...], overseer of the quay of ⸢Bīt-ṭā⸣[b-Bēl] has receiv[ed] one (*sūt*) per *kor* as *mi*[*k*]*su*-tax from MNA_1.

Witnesses:
Nabû-šuma-iddin/[...]
Šāpik-zēri//Dēkû
Bē[l-...]/Nergal-uballiṭ
[...]/PA-x-A//Amēl-s[īsî]
The scribe: Nabû-bullissu/[...]
(Place + Date).

Comment

L. 1: The wedges after *šá* and before [giš]*eleppu* resemble the EN-sign. Did the scribe intend to write *ša ištēt eleppi* (erroneously spelled *šá* 1-*en* [giš]*eleppu*)? Cf. line 5 where he apparently first wrote 1-*en* and then tried to correct it into 1-*et* by adding a few *Winkelhaken*.

L. 3 and 6: On the place Bīt-ṭāb-Bēl, see Zadok, *RGTC* 8, 108 and the texts cited by Wunsch, *Iddin-Marduk* 1, 155. According to the texts from Iddin-Marduk's (MNA's maternal grandfather) time the *rab kāri* of Bīt-ṭāb-Bēl was appointed over the quay of Bīt-ṭāb-Bēl as well as that of Til-Gula (Wunsch, *id.*, 36). On the identification of the person in question, see more at lines 16–17.

L. 4 and 6: MNA is the subject of the verb *ú-še-ti-iq* so that in this case the person who paid the tax also let the boats pass, whereas in other texts it was the one who received the tax. In Dar 268, for instance, the overseer of the quay, who received the tax from MNA, had to let the boat pass beyond the quay and give it back to MNA (*miksu* ... PN ... *ina qātē MNA ēṭir eleppa* ... PN ... *ú-še-et-te*[*q-ma*] *ana MNA inamdin*). Cf. Camb 272 (= *CM* 3b 347): *ú-še-ti-iq-ma* = *ušetteqma* "he should let pass." The verb *ú-še-ti-iq* in the text under discussion can be either present (*ušetteqma*, cf. Dar 268 and Camb 272) or preterit (*ušētiqma*).

L. 4: There are remnants of approximately three signs. If one reads ⸢*ù mi-ik-su*⸣, which is contextually most appropriate, one has to assume that the scribe wrote these signs in a very squeezed manner. One may see the end of the *ù*, the first *Winkelhaken* of the *mi*-, the lower end of the -*ik*, and one upper horizontal of the -*su*.

L. 11: It is noteworthy that our text does not merely record the receipt of the tax by the overseer, but specifically adds the rate of the tax, viz. 20 percent of the total weight of the transported goods. Accordingly, MNA must have paid sixty-six *kor* in kind, or its equivalent in silver.

L. 12 end: I suggest reconstructing [mDUB-NUMUN]. For Nabû-šuma-iddin/Šāpik-zēri//Dēkû, see Tallqvist, *NbN*, 144/33). Šāpik-zēri himself occurs in the next line.

L. 13–14: The witness mentioned in these lines is probably Bē[l-asûa]/Nergal-uballiṭ, because this person often witnessed transactions regarding boats by MNA (BM 30541: 10; BM 31891: Rev. 4; BM 32873: 12). He belonged to the Mudammiq-Adad family.

L. 16–17: The scribe may have been Nabû-bullissu/Nabû-mukīn-zēri//Ea-ṣalam-ilī, who also wrote BM 31517 (*ilku*-receipt) and BM 30764 (receipt of a boat-tower). Furthermore, one should consider the possibility that this scribe was actually the overseer of the quay to whom MNA paid *miksu* in the present document (rd. in line 7: Nabû-bullissu/Nabû-[mukīn-zēri//Ea-ṣalam-ilī]).

No. 45

BM 31360
Copy: Bertin copy 2605
Date: 2/ix/26 Dar (30 November 496 B.C.E.)
Place: broken
Content: Summons to settle debts with MNA.

OBV.

1 [... 2]6.KAM
2 [^{m}*da-ri-ia-muš*] ⸢LUGAL⸣ [E.KI *u* KUR].KUR ^{md}EN-NIGIN-*ir*
3 [A-*šú šá* ^{m}]⸢^{d}U.GUR-MU *a-na*⸣ [TIN.T]IR.KI *a-na pa-ni*
4 ^{md}AMAR.UTU-*na-ṣir*-IBILA A-*šú šá* ^{m}KI-^{d}AMAR.UTU-DIN A ^{m}*e-gi-bi*
5 *il-la-kam-ma a-na muḫ-ḫi ú-ìl-tì šá* 1 MA.NA [KÙ.BABBAR]
6 UD-*ú nu-uḫ-ḫu-tu šá ina* ⸢1⸣ GÍN *bit-qa* 3 GUR ZÚ.LUM.[MA] ⸢*ù*⸣ GU$_{4}^{?}$
7 *šá* ^{md}AMAR.UTU-*na-ṣir*-IBILA *šá ina muḫ-ḫi-šú ù šá-ṭ*[*a-ru*(.MEŠ)]
8 *šá a-na muḫ-ḫi ú-ìl-tì*.MEŠ *šá* KÙ.BABBAR ŠE.BAR ZÚ.LUM.MA ⸢*ù* GU$_{4}$⸣
9 *šá* ^{md}DI.KU$_{5}$-EN-URU$_{3}$ LÚ *qal-la šá* ^{md}AMAR.UTU-*na-ṣir*-IBILA
10 *šá ina muḫ-ḫi* ^{md}EN-NIGIN-*ir šá* ^{md}AMAR.UTU-*na-ṣir*-IBILA
11 *ul-tu* MU.20$^{!}$.KAM ^{m}*da-ri-ia-muš it-ti*

LO. E.

12 ^{md}EN-NIGIN-*ir iš-ṭu-ru it-ti*
13 ^{md}AMAR.UTU-*na-ṣir*-IBILA *i-dab-bu-ub ki-i*

REV.

14 UD.10.KAM *šá* ITI.AB ^{md}EN-NIGIN-*ir la it-tal-kam-ma*
15 *it-ti* ^{md}AMAR.UTU-*na-ṣir*-IBILA *la id-da-ab-bu*<*-ub*>
16 *a-ki-i ú-ìl-tì*.MEŠ *šá* KÙ.BABBAR ŠE.BAR ZÚ.LUM.MA *ù*
17 GU$_{4}$ *šá* ^{md}AMAR.UTU-*na-ṣir*-IBILA *u* ^{md}DI.KU$_{5}$-EN-URU$_{3}$
18 LÚ *qal-li-šú šá ina muḫ-ḫi* ^{md}EN-NIGIN-*ir a-na* ^{md}AMAR.UTU-*na-ṣir*-[IBILA]
19 *iṭ-ṭi-ir ár-ki a-dan-nu an-na-a* ^{md}EN-NIGIN-*ir a-na*
20 *muḫ-ḫi mim-ma iṭ-ru a-na* ^{md}AMAR.UTU-*na-ṣir*-IBILA

21 [*ul*] *i-šak-kan* LÚ *mu-kin-nu* ^{m}*at-kal*<-*a-na*>-^{d}K[Á] A-*šú šá*
22 [^{md}x]-MU A LÚ.NAGAR ^{md}AG-GIN-NUMUN A-*šú šá* ^{m}*ina*-SÙḪ-SUR
23 [A ^{md}UTU-*a-ba*]-⸢*ri*⸣ ^{m}*ni-qud* A-*šú šá* ^{m}ŠU-^{d}AG A LÚ.SIPA-GU$_{4}$
24 [...] $^{[m]d}$AG-MU-URU$_{3}$ A ^{md}IDIM-*lit-tab-ba-nu*
25 [...]-*a-nu* ^{m}*še-el-li-bi* A-*šú šá*

U. E.

26 [...-*s*]*u-pe-e-mu-ḫur* LÚ.UMBISAG
27 [A LÚ.EN.NU]N-KÁ.GAL
28 [... IT]I.GAN

LE. E.

29 [U]D.2.KAM MU.26.[KAM] [...]
30 LUGAL E.KI *u* K[UR.KUR]

TRANSLATION

[By the tenth of Ṭebēt of the twenty]-sixth [year of Darius], ⸢king⸣ [of Babylon and the La]nds, Bēl-upaḫḫir, [son of] ⸢Nergal-iddin⸣ should come ⸢to⸣ Babylon before MNA$_{1}$ and reach an agreement with MNA$_{1}$ with regard to the debt of one mina of white, medium-quality [silver], of which ⸢one⸣-eighth is alloy, three *kor* of date[s], ⸢and⸣ cattle,? owed by him to MNA$_{1}$; and with regard to the writ[ten agreement(s)] concerning the debts of silver, barley, dates ⸢and cattle⸣ owed by Bēl-upaḫḫir to Madānu-bēla-uṣur, a slave of MNA$_{1}$, which MNA$_{1}$ has concluded with Bēl-upaḫḫir since Darius' twentieth year. If Bēl-upaḫḫir has not shown up and has not reached an agreement with MNA$_{1}$ on the tenth of Ṭebēt, he has to pay off MNA$_{1}$ in agreement with (what is provided for in) the promissory notes for silver, barley, dates and cattle, owed by Bēl-upaḫḫir to MNA$_{1}$ and Madānu-bēla-uṣur, his slave. After that date Bēl-upaḫḫir [cannot] present to MNA$_{1}$ anything about what he might have paid off to MNA$_{1}$.

Witnesses:
Atkal<-ana>-Bā[ba]/[^{m}...]-MU//Nagāru
Nabû-mukīn-zēri/Ina-tēšê-ēṭir//[Šamaš-(a)bā]⸢ri⸣
Niqūdu/Gimil-Nabû//Rē'i-alpi
[^{m}.../]Nabû-šuma-uṣur//Ea-ilūta-bani
[... ^{m}...]-*a-nu*
Šellibi/[...]
The scribe: [... ^{m}...]-suppē-muḫur[//Maṣ]ṣār-abulli
(Place + Date).

COMMENT

L. 1: The beginning of this line most likely reads [*adi ūmi* 10^{kam} *ša* ^{iti}*Ṭebēt šanat* 2]6^{kam}, cf. lines 13–14.

L. 6: The GU_4-sign is squeezed at the end of the line and hence resembles more a DU-sign, i.e., it has the final wedges before rather than after the vertical wedge.

L. 9: On MNA taking care of debts that were owed to his slave after Darius' 20th year, see more at Dar 509: 3.

L. 11–12: The scribe was referring to the agreement that is preserved in Dar 509 and was reached in Darius' twentieth year (8/ix/20 Dar). Although the scribe of BM 31360 wrote MU.21.KAM instead of MU.20.KAM, it is clear that he realized his mistake because he tried to erase the 1. See also line 14.

L. 12–13: The idiom *itti* PN *dabābu* in Neo-Babylonian legal texts means "to plead in court, to litigate against" (*CAD* D, 9 s.v. *dabābu* mng. 4b); in Neo-Babylonian letters it has a more amicable connotation, meaning "to discuss a topic, to come to an agreement with" (mng. 3). In my opinion, this is also the meaning in the text under discussion; Bēl-upaḫḫir, the debtor, is to appear before his creditor (*illikamma*) and to reach an agreement with him (*itti* MNA *idabbub*), rather than appearing in court and pleading against his creditor. If someone had a case to plead in court, it would be MNA and not Bēl-upaḫḫir. The former could claim against his debtor that the debt had not been repaid as had been agreed upon earlier; Bēl-upaḫḫir is the party in fault.

L. 14: According to Dar 509 Bēl-upaḫḫir had to turn up on the tenth of Šabāṭ and he had five days to show the evidence that he had paid off his debts (Dar 509: 1, 7). According to the text under consideration Bēl-upaḫḫir had to show up with the evidence on the tenth of Ṭebēt, which is one month earlier than what was agreed upon in Dar 509. There is no sign in the text that the scribe realized his mistake and tried to correct ITI.AB into ITI.ZÍZ.

L. 22–23: Some erasures are found in this line: at the upper part of the sign NAGAR, and at the end of the sign GIN. The reconstruction of the family name of Nabû-mukīn-zēri/Ina-têšē-ēṭir//Šamaš-abāri is based on a comparison with Dar 325: 9 (cf. Tallqvist, *NbN*, 136 s.v. Nabû-kîn-zîr(9)); he and his brother Bēl-bullissu lived in a rented house in Bīt-Ḫaḫḫuru (Dar 482; cf. *ibid.*, 28 s.v. Bēl-bulliṭsu(6)); their father was MNA's partner in a business venture with capital gained from the tithes of Bēl (Dar 359; note: Šamaš-ina-têšē-ēṭir = Ina-têšē-ēṭir; cf. Tallqvist, *NbN*, 192 s.v. Šamaš(-ina)-ešî-êṭir. The father also occurs in CT 51 55 = *CM* 20b 235); their uncles occur among the witnesses of some of MNA's documents (cf. Tallqvist, *NbN*, 71 s.v. Iddina-Bêl(52); *ibid.*, 190 s.v. Šamaš-êṭir(12); and Wunsch, *Felder* 2, 304 s.v. Kinūnaja).

L. 24: *-lit-tab-ba-nu* is a phonetic spelling for *ilūta-bani*. Cf. *-la-tab-ba-ni* (Tallqvist, *NbN*, 56), and *-at-ta-ba-ni* (Joannès, *Borsippa*, 378).

No. 46

BM 31393
Copy: no Bertin copy
Date: [-]/viii/25 Dar (November-December 497 B.C.E.)
Place: Babylon
Content: Receipt of barley from MNA by a royal official. Transport costs. As proxy for (*ina našparti ša*) the governor of Babylon. Undertaking to register the receipt in the accounts of the governor.

OBV.

1 [3 G]UR 2 PI ŠE.BAR *gi-mir šá* 30 [...]
2 ⸢*šá*⸣ GIŠ.BÁN *šá* ^{md}EN-*it-tan-nu* ^{m}*ru-*[*šu-un-da*/*pa-*(*a*)-*ti*]
3 LÚ *im-bu-ku-a-a* LÚ.S[AG$^{?}$ ...]
4 *šá* LÚ *šá-di-e*.MEŠ *šá* LÚ.⸢x⸣ [(x)] ⸢*ina* ŠU⸣.II [(x)]
5 ^{m}*ši-rik-tu*$_4$ DUMU *šá* ^{m}SUM.NA-*a*
6 DUMU ^{m}*e-gi-bi ina na-áš-par-tu*$_4$
7 *šá* ^{m}*gu-za-nu* LÚ.GAR-UŠ$_4$ TIN.TIR.KI *ma-*[*ḫi-ir*]
8 ŠE.BAR-*a*$_4$ 3 GUR 2 PI ^{m}*ru-šu-u*[*n-da*/*pa-*(*a*)-*t*]*i*
9 *it-ti* ^{m}*gu-za-nu* LÚ.GAR-UŠ$_4$ TIN.TIR.KI
10 *ú-šu-zi-ma a-na* ^{m}*ši-rik-tu*$_4$
11 ⸢*i*⸣*-nam-din*

REV.

12 LÚ *mu-kin-nu* ^{m}*tat-tan-nu* DUMU *šá* ^{md}AG-KÁD
13 DUMU ^{m}*da-bi-bi* ^{m}*ni-din-tu*$_4$
14 DUMU *šá* ^{m}ÌR-*ia* DUMU LÚ.GAL-60-*ši*
15 ^{m}*ka-ṣir* DUMU *šá* ^{m}*ta-at-tan-nu* A ^{m}DÙ-*eš*-DINGIR
16 ^{m}*a-ḫi-ši-tu*$_4$ LÚ *im-bu-*⸢*ku-a-a*⸣
17 ^{md}AG-DIN-*iṭ* LÚ.UMBISAG DUMU ^{m}[...]
18 TIN.TIR.KI ITI.APIN ⸢UD⸣.[x.KAM]
19 MU.25.KAM ^{m}*da-a-ri-iá-*[*muš*]
20 LUGAL E.KI *u* KUR.KUR

TRANSLATION

[3].2.0 *kor* of barley, the costs for the transport of thirty [(+ x) *kor* of barley/dates], ⸢from⸣ the fixed rent due to Bēl-ittannu: Ru[šund/pāta], the man from Imbuka, c[ourtier$^{?}$ (and) clerk$^{?}$] of the ... of the district Gov[ernor]$^{?}$, (and acting) as proxy for Gūzānu, governor of Babylon, has recei[ved] (it) ⸢from⸣ MNA$_2$. Rušund/p[āta] will registe<r> (his receipt of) the 3.2.0 *kor* of barley in the accounts of Gūzānu, governor of Babylon, in favor of MNA$_2$, and give (proof of) it to MNA$_2$.

Witnesses:
Tattannu/Nabû-kāṣir//Dābibī

Nidintu/Ardiya//Rab-šušši
Kāṣir/Tattannu//Eppeš-ilī
Aḫšēti, the man from Imbuka
The scribe: Nabû-uballiṭ//[Bēl-apla-uṣur]
(Place + Date).

COMMENT

The surface of the tablet is very salted, especially so at the end of lines 3–4.

L. 1: For the reconstruction of the end of this line see more at BM 31572: 1. In the text under consideration it was probably dates that had to be transported; the text is dated in Araḫsamna at the time when dates were being harvested (cf. BM 30980).

L. 2: The agricultural products that were being transported originated from fields that were administered by Bēl-ittannu (*ša* ^{giš}*sūtu ša Bēl-ittannu*), see also BM 31786: 2, BM 32891: 2 (*ša* ^{giš}*sūtu ša Bēl-ittannu*) and probably also BM 31572: 2–3 (*ša qātē Bēl-*[*ittannu*], see commentary *ad hoc*). Cf. BM 33112 (^{giš}*su-ú-tu šá Iddin-Bēl* [*u*] *Tanda*). Bēl-ittannu was the district governor of Tâmti (BM 32891; also BM 31572?), and it is, therefore, most likely, that in line 4b of the text under consideration one has to read LÚ.⸢NAM⸣ (or perhaps LÚ.EN.[NAM]), see more below.

L. 2 end and L. 8: The name of the official is either Rušunpāta (Ir. *Rauxšnapāta) or Rušundāta (Ir. *Rauxšnadāta), both Old Iranian names (cf. Dandamaev, *Iranians*, 118 no. 258 and Schmitt, *Kratylos* 39, 86).

L. 3a: On LÚ *im-bu-ku-a-a* see Zadok, *Iran* 14, 66. The two Imbukaens in our text bore Old Iranian names: Rušunp/dāta (ll. 2 and 8) and Aḫšēti (l. 16).

L. 3b: With respect to the official title(s) of Rušund/pāta, I suggest reading LÚ.S[AG-LUGAL LÚ *si-pi*(*r*)*-ri*]. Similar titles were borne by the officials who received payments from MNA for the transport of dates and barley in the other texts (BM 31572: 4; BM 31786: 3; and BM 30980: 2). In the text under consideration, only the beginning of the SAG-sign is preserved, and it may as well be a SI-sign (to be read LÚ *si-*[*pi*(*r*)*-ri* ...]).

L. 4a: The text under consideration seems to refer to a kind of workers (or soldiers?) called ^{lú}*šá-di-e*^{meš}. They occur in two other texts from MNA's time, but with different spellings: *šá-di-i* (without LÚ, BM 31438 Rev.: 5′), and ^{lú}*šá-da-e*$^{\text{meš!}}$ (BM 30795: 10). No attestations from outside the archive are known to me. The three spellings mentioned above may be three deficient spellings for *šaddādu*/*šaddidu*/*šādidu* "boat-tower" (*CAD* Š$_1$, 38, 41f., 47f.; *AHw*, 1123). Hence, probably read in BM 31393 and BM 31438 *šá*<*-da*>*-di-e*/*i* (cf. BM 30446: 12 *šá-da-di-e*) or *šá*<*-di*>*-di-e*/*i* (cf. Cyr 180: 14 *šá-di-di-e*); and in BM 30795 *šá-da*<*-di*>*-e*.

The information provided by these three texts from MNA's archive regarding *šā*(*di*)$^?$*du*-workers may be summarized as follows. First, the governor of Babylon seems to have owned a list with the workers' names;

the list, no doubt, also contained details about their work assignments (BM 30795). Second, MNA took care of their recruitment and of the silver for their equipment. They seem to have been recruited for work under the command of district governors (LÚ.EN.NAM = *bēl pīḫātu*, BM 31438; hence, rd. LÚ.⸢EN⸣-[NAM] or rather LÚ.⸢NAM⸣ in BM 31393: 4b). Third, the matter of their rations was apparently taken care of in Babylon in the office of the governor by a clerk: LÚ.S[AG-LUGAL LÚ *si-pi*(*r*)-*ri*] *šá* LÚ *šá-di-e*.MEŠ *šá* LÚ.⸢NAM⸣, "a cour[tier (and) clerk] (appointed) over (the distribution of rations to) the *šā*(*di*)$^{?}$*du*-workers of the (local) Ins[pector]" (BM 31393: 3–4). MNA assisted him in this matter and paid for the transport of the barley and dates that were needed for these rations.

L. 4b: One should probably read LÚ *šá-di-e*.MEŠ *šá* LÚ.⸢NAM⸣, "*šā*(*di*)$^{?}$*du*-workers belonging to the district gov[ernor]," for two reasons. First, district governors frequently occur in other texts regarding transport costs, viz. in BM 31572 and BM 32891 (LÚ(.EN).NAM.MEŠ). In the latter two texts one Bēl-ittannu was one of the governors (BM 31572, name partly broken). The Bēl-ittannu mentioned in line 2 in the text under consideration (BM 31393) was probably the same person, and one should, therefore, read LÚ.⸢NAM⸣ in line 4b. Second, *šā*(*di*)$^{?}$*du*-workers seem to have worked for such district governors according to BM 31438 (see also above).

L. 16: For ^{m}*a-ḫi-ši-tu*$_{4}$, cf. ^{m}*a-ḫi-še-ti-e* in Amherst 253: 10 (= *AfO* 19, 78). The latter is one of the three possible Akkadian spellings for the Old Iranian name *Āxšētē (so Dandamaev, *Iranians*, 27f.; but differently, Schmitt, *Kratylos* 39, 83f.: ^{m}*a-ḫi-še-ti-e* cannot reflect the Iranian *Xšaita).

L. 17: Nabû-uballiṭ//Bēl-apla-uṣur also wrote BM 30639, another text recording the payment for transport costs by MNA to a royal official. BM 30639 was witnessed by three persons, two of whom are also found in the text under consideration. Moreover, the texts are dated in the same period: BM 30639 is dated on 28/vii/25 Dar, and BM 31393 on [-]/viii/25 Dar.

No. 47

BM 31416
Copy: no Bertin copy
Date: no date
Place: no place
Content: Letter to Širku (= MNA?) concerning the *ilku*-tax.

OBV.

1 [*ṭuppi* ^{m}...]
2 [*a-n*]*a* ^{m}*ši-rik-ki*
3 ⸢ŠEŠ⸣-*iá* ^{d}EN *u* ^{d}AG
4 *šu-lum u* DIN *šá* ŠEŠ-*iá*
5 *liq-bu-ú* ^{md}EN-MU

6 LÚ.DUMU-TIN.TIR.KI
7 *šá ina* É ^{md}EN-NUMUN-MU
8 *šá ina* URU É-*ḫa-ḫu-ru*
9 *áš-bi a-na-ku*
10 *il-ki-šú*
11 [*a*/*i-na*]$^?$ *muḫ-ḫi* [(x x)]

LO. E.

12 ⸢x x⸣ [(x)]

REV.

13 x TA$^?$
14 [*i*]*t-ti*$^?$*-šú*
15 *la ta-dab-ub-bu*
16 *ù pa-ni*
17 *šá* ŠEŠ ⸢x⸣ RI IR SAG ZU
18 *a-na e-il-'*
19 *ki-i šak-nu*
20 *šu-pur*

TRANSLATION

[Letter from ^{m}... to] Širku, my brother. May Bēl and Nabû proclaim health and life for my brother. (Regarding) Bēl-iddin, the man from Babylon, who lives in Bēl-zēra-iddin's house in Bīt-Ḫaḫḫuru: I have/will .... his *ilku* [for the ac]count of$^?$ x x x TA. Do not litigate against$^?$ him; and send ...

COMMENT

L. 12–13: Perhaps read ⸢*áš-lim*⸣, "I paid" on the lower edge (i.e., line 12)? Anyhow, it seems that the sender of the letter wanted to make it clear to Širku that the *ilku* of Bēl-iddin had been taken care of/was being taken care of (ll. 12–13), so that Širku should not litigate against him (ll. 14–15). Should we read in lines 9–13 *anāku ilkišu* [*ana*] *muḫḫi ... elli*$^?$, "(concerning) his *ilku* I take up responsibility for [its payment?]"? On the formula *ana muḫḫi ... elû*, see Wunsch, *Felder* 2, 25 (commentary to line 19f.).

L. 16: The noun *pāni* may be complementary to *šupur* "send before," or *kī šaknu* "when he has planned" (*AHw*, 819 s.v. *pānu*(*m*) I mng. 15; and *CAD* Š$_1$, 138–39 s.v. *šakānu* mng. 5a).

L. 17: This line remains enigmatic. The signs RI and IR are clear. They are followed by either a GA (although there seems to be one vertical wedge too much) or a SAG (but cf. the SAG two lines down). The last sign in this line is written on the edge and upward; it very much resembles a ZU. The one or two verticals before the RI may either be a *Personenkeil* (read ^{m}*ri-ir-ga-zu*, name unknown?) or an A (beginning of a verb in the first person?).

L. 18, 20: The *Winkelhaken* of the -ʼ-sign are very close to each other and it seems that one is lacking. The form *e-il-i'* seems to be the infinitive *e'ēli* "bind." For this verb, more at BM 30795: 7–9. The sender of the letter seems to urge Širku to send (*šupur* "Send!"), probably Bēl-iddin or his proxy, "in order to contract an agreement" (*ana e'ēli*).

No. 48

BM 31438
Copy: no Bertin copy
Date: no date
Place: no place
Content: Letter to Širku (=MNA?) concerning *rikis qabli.*

OBV.

(Opening line(s) lost.)

1′ *ṭè-en-ka ul áš-mu*
2′ MU.AN.NA-a_4 *ul paṭ-ṭír*
3′ ^{m}*ši-iš-ku a-kan-nu*
4′ *ni-is-ḫu ki-i is-su-ḫu*
5′ *ri-kis* $MURUB_4$ *it-tan-nu*
6′ *a-šar* x (x) x *ka*
7′ *ri-kis* $MURUB_4$ *ma-la*
8′ ḪA.LA-*ka in-na*
9′ *u it-ti-šú*

REV.

1 *i-ši-zi-iz-ma*
2 LÚ.$ERIN_2$.MEŠ *li-si-ir*
3 *la tu-uṣ*$^{?}$*-ṣí*$^{?}$*-šú*
4 ^{d}EN *u* ^{d}AG *lu-ú i-du-ú*
5 *ki-i šá-di-i ia-a-nu-ú*
6 *a-na* LÚ.EN.NA[M] *aq-bu-ú*
7 *ina is-qa-a-*tu_4 RI/TAL LA ⸢x⸣ TU
8 [*i-na a*]*-kan-na ta-rak-ka-zu*

TRANSLATION

[...]. I did not receive your order. This (said) year - *it/he has not been released/ solved* (?). Širku is here. After he deducted the expenses he paid for the *rikis qabli.* Give your share of the *rikis qabli according to* your *tablet* (?), and arrange the matter with him so that he can recruit the workers. *You should not leave him* (?). Bēl and Nabû surely know that there is/are no *šá-di-i*. I told (this?) to the district governor. From the allotments (= prebends?) ... ⸢from$^{?}$⸣ [here] *you should* ...

Comment

Obv. L. 1′–2′: The situation described in these lines may be compared to CT 22 74: 27, (the soldiers) *ša ṭēme aškunka puṭṭiršunūti* "about whom I gave you an order, you should allow them to go!" Note the spelling *paṭ-ṭír* for *puṭṭir*.

Obv. L. 3′: Note the spelling ^{m}*ši-iš-ku* instead of the more common ^{m}*ši-iš-ki*.

Obv. L. 4′: For *nisḫu* "expenses," see *CAD* N$_2$, 268 s.v. *nisḫu* A mng. 5b.

Obv. L. 6′: Should we read: *a-šar* GIŠ *ṭup*$^{?}$*-pi*$^{?}$*-ka*? Or, are the last two signs to be read *-rak-ka*, cf. Rev. L. 8 *ta-rak-ka*-ZU?

Rev. L. 3: The *-uṣ* is unusual long; there is a break crossing its horizontal wedge. There is not much visible of the *-ṣí* except for its horizontal wedge and one of its upper *Winkelhaken*.

Rev. L. 5: I suggest interpreting the *šá-di-i* in this letter about *rikis qabli* and workers (LÚ.ERIN$_2$.MEŠ) in the light of the LÚ *šá-di-e*.MEŠ in BM 31393: 4 and the LÚ *šá-da-e*.MEŠ$^{!}$ in BM 30795: 10. More at BM 31393: 4a.

Rev. L. 7: *isqu* may refer to portions of land allotted to individuals or institutions as well as to temple prebends.

No. 49

	BM 31449
Copy:	no Bertin copy
Date:	[-]/[-]/23^{+} Dar (499- B.C.E.)
Place:	Babylon
Content:	Receipt of a hireling from MNA.

Obv.

1 LÚ.ḪUN.GÁ [...]
2 ITI.APIN ⸢MU⸣.20+3[(+x).KAM]
3 ^{m}*da-a-ri-iá-muš* LUGAL
4 *šá* ^{m}*ni-din-tu*$_4$ *u* ŠEŠ.MEŠ-*šú*
5 DUMU.MEŠ *šá* ^{m}*kal-ba-a* A ^{m}*su-ḫa-a-a*
6 ^{m}MU-URU$_3$ A-*šú šá* ^{md}UTU-SUR
7 *ina* ŠU.II ^{m}*ši-rik-ki* DUMU-*šú šá*
8 ^{m}MU-*a* A ^{m}*e-gì-bi*

Rev.

9 ⸢*a*⸣*-na muḫ-ḫi* ^{m}*ni-din-tu*$_4$ *u* [ŠEŠ.MEŠ-*šú*]
10 *ma-ḫir* LÚ *mu-kin-nu* ^{m}*šu-lum*-E.KI
11 DUMU ⸢*šá*⸣ ^{md}AG-ŠEŠ.MEŠ-MU ^{m}*lib-lu-uṭ*
12 A-*šú šá* ^{m}KI-^{d}AG-DIN A ^{m}*si-si-i*
13 ^{md}EN-SU A-*šú šá* ^{m}*kal-ba-a* A ^{m}MU-[*líb-ši*]
14 ^{m}*na-din* A-*šú šá* ^{m}ŠU A ^{m}*e-gì-*[*bi*] [x (x)]$^{?}$
15 ^{md}EN-*it-t*[*an-nu* ...]
16 E.KI IT[I ...]

17 MU.20⁺[...]

LE. E.

18 [LUGAL] E.KI *u* ⌜KUR⌝.KUR

TRANSLATION

A hireling/Hirelings [...] Araḫsamna of the twenty-thi[rd⁺] ⌜year⌝ of King Darius is (/are) due from Nidintu and his brothers, sons of Kalbaya, descendant of Suḫaya: Šuma-uṣur, son of Šamaš-ēṭir has received (him/them) from MNA_2 for the account of Nidintu and [his brothers].

Witnesses:
Šulum-Bābili/Nabû-aḫḫē-iddin
Liblut/Itti-Nabû-balāṭu//Sīsî
Bēl-erība/Kalbaya//Šumu-[libši]
Nādin/Gimillu//Egi[bi]
[The scribe]: Bēl-itt[annu ...]
(Place + Date).

COMMENT

L. 1: It is unclear whether one or more hirelings were meant. The delivery of just one person is usually specified by the use of *ištēn*, but not necessarily so (see, for instance, BM 31118 and BM 31226). It is very unfortunate that the rest of the line is broken, because the broken part may have contained a specification of the kind of work this/these hireling(s) was/were to perform (e.g., LÚ.ḪUN.GÁ(.MEŠ) LÚ *ša-da-di-e*(.MEŠ), cf. BM 30764), the person with whom they had to serve (cf. BM 31226) and/or the period of their service (e.g., "[(for so-many-days a month from month X) till (the end of)] Araḫsamna," cf. BM 30764, BM 31118 and BM 31226).

L. 2: The lower part of the signs is broken. One can see two *Winkelhaken* (= 20), and three horizontals, but below these three horizontals there may have been more wedges. Hence the year may be 23, 25, 26, 27, 28, or 29.

L. 4: The *šá* is to be taken here in the meaning "due from," cf. receipts of payments for *ilku*, boat-towers and other obligatory services, which have the same structure as the text under consideration, to wit: *ilku*/[lú]*šādidu* - period of time - *ša* PN_1 - PN_2 - *ina qātē* PN_3 - *ana muḫḫi* PN_1 - *maḫir*.

No. 50

	BM 31517
Copy:	Bertin copy 2557
Date:	25/[-]/25 Dar (497–496 B.C.E.)
Place:	Babylon
Content:	Receipt of the *ilku*-tax by MNA.

OBV.

1 ⸢*il*⸣-*ki šá* ^{m}*mu-ra-nu* A-*šú šá* ^{md}AMAR.[UTU-PAB]
2 A ^{m}ŠEŠ-*ba-ni ù mi-šil il-ki*
3 A-*šú šá* ^{m}*nu-uḫ-ši-ia šá* TA ITI.BÁR
4 [*šá*] MU.25.KAM ^{m}*da-ri-ia-muš* LUGAL
5 [*a*]-*di qí-it* ITI.ŠE *šá* MU.25.KAM
6 [^{md}AMAR.UTU-PAB]-⸢IBILA⸣ A-*šú šá* ^{m}MU-*a* A ^{m}*e-gi-bi*
7 [*ina* ŠU.II ^{m}]*mu-ra-nu* A-*šú šá* ^{md}AMAR.UTU-PAB
8 [A ^{m}ŠEŠ-*b*]*a-ni ma-ḫir*

LO. E.

9 [1-*en*.TA.À]M *šá-ṭa-ri* TI-*ú*

REV.

10 [LÚ *mu-kin-nu* ^{m}]*mar-duk-a* A-*šú šá* ^{m}*gu-za-nu*
11 [A ^{m}*kàṣ-ṣì-dak-k*]*u* ^{m}SI-PI-*ú-a* A-*šú šá* ^{m}ŠU
12 [A LÚ.EN].NUN-KÁ.GAL ^{m}*ta-at-tan-nu* A-*šú šá*
13 $^{[md]}$AG-KÁD A ^{m}*da-bi-bi* ^{m}*ri-ba-a-ta*
14 A-*šú šá* ^{md}AG-KÁD A LÚ.Ì.DU$_{8}$
15 LÚ.UMBISAG ^{md}AG-*bul-liṭ-su* A-*šú šá* ^{md}AG-GIN-⸢NUMUN⸣
16 A ^{md}IDIM-NU-DINGIR TIN.TIR.KI ITI.⸢x⸣
17 UD.25.KAM MU.25.KAM ^{m}*da-a-r*[*i-ia-muš*]

U. E.

18 LUGAL E.KI *u* KUR.KUR

TRANSLATION

The *ilku*-tax from Nisan [of] the twenty-fifth year of King Darius [t]ill the end of Addar of the twenty-fifth year, which is due from Mūrānu, son of Mar[duk-nāṣir], descendant of Aḫu-bani, and half the *ilku* of (PN)$^{?}$ the son of Nuḫšiya: MNA$_{1}$ has received (it) [from] Mūrānu, son of Marduk-nāṣir, [descendant of Aḫu-b]ani.

[Ea]ch [one] has taken (a copy of) the deed.

[Witnesses]:
Marduk/Gūzānu//[Kaṣṣidakk]u
SI-PI-*ú-a*/Gimillu//[Maṣ]ṣār-abulli
Tattannu/Nabû-kāṣir//Dābibī
Rībâta/Nabû-kāṣir//Atû
The scribe: Nabû-bullissu/Nabû-mukīn-⸢zēri⸣//Ea-ṣalam-ilī

(Place + Date).

Comment

The scribe erred in his description of the facts. He started by referring to the *ilku* owed by Mūrānu (l. 1a) and gave this person's full affiliation: son of Marduk-nāṣir (l. 1b), descendant of Aḫi-bāni (l. 2a) Then he continued by referring to "half the *ilku*" (l. 2b), but it is not clear whose *ilku* this is. It seems to have been the *ilku* of someone whose first name the scribe forgot to write, but whose father was Nuḫšiya (l. 3a). We do not know why Mūrānu paid for Nuḫšiya's son, unless the scribe is wrong, and the only person involved was Mūrānu. The *ilku* for which Mūrānu paid covered the period "from Nisan till the end of Addar of Darius' twenty-fifth year" (ll. 3b–5). Consequently, he paid his own *ilku* for one year "and (in addition to it he paid) half the *ilku* (of the son of Nuḫšiya?)." The additional half part may have been backlogs from the previous year. For a possible identification of this "son (rather descendant?!) of Nuḫšiya," see TCL 13 197: 6 and commentary at line 3 below.

L. 3: The name ^{m}*nu-uḫ-ši-ia* is probably the same name as Nuḫšaya (Tallqvist, *NbN*, 168 s.v. *Nu-uḫ-ša-a-a*, also s.v. *Nu-uḫ-ša-nu* and *Nu-ḫa-šu*. Cf. Nuḫša-Marduk, Joannès, *Borsippa*, 413 and *CAD* N_2, 319 s.v. *nuḫšānu* and *ibid.*, 320 s.v. *nuḫšu* mng. b). Is this "son of Nuḫšaya" to be identified with Rē'ûšunu-Marduk/Bēl-apla-uṣur, descendant of //⌜x-(-x)⌝-*a-a* (read: Nuḫšaya?) mentioned in TCL 13 197: 6? The latter paid Mūrānu's *ilku* of Darius' twenty-sixth year. The Mūrānu of BM 31517 and the one of TCL 13 197, at least, are the same person, so that a connection between both texts is very likely.

L. 6: Bertin's copy has [...]-DIN-*iṭ*, but collation of the tablet has shown that one should read [^{md}AMAR.UTU-PAB]-⌜IBILA⌝.

L. 11: The signs look like ^{m}SI-PI-*ú-a*, but such a name is otherwise unattested. One may perhaps read ^{m}SI.SÁ$^{!}$- = *līšir-*, but then the complementary *-ú-a* does not fit.

No. 51

BM 31528
Copy: Bertin copy 2614
Date: 26/v/26 Dar (28 August 496 B.C.E.)
Place: Babylon
Content: Receipt of silver by MNA's brother. Payment for *rikis qabli* (*ina rikis qabli*).

OBV.

1 1 MA.NA KÙ.BABBAR UD-*ú šá ina* 1 GÍ[N *bit-q*]*a*
2 *ina ri-kis* MURUB$_4$ *šá* TA MU.24.KAM [^{md}AG]-ŠEŠ.MEŠ-*bul-liṭ*
3 DUMU *šá* ^{m}KI-^{d}AMAR.UTU-DIN DUMU ^{m}*e-gi-bi*
4 *ina* ŠU.II ^{md}AG-NUMUN-DÙ DUMU *šá* ^{m}KI-^{d}AG-DIN
5 DUMU ^{m}*e-gì-bi ma-ḫi-ir*
6 *mim-ma i-na ú-ìl-tì šá* [*re-e-ḫi* (*šá*) *r*]*i-kis*
7 *ra-šu-tu šá* ^{md}AG-ŠEŠ.MEŠ-*bul*-[*liṭ*] [*qabli šá* MU 20]+3.KAM

LO. E.

8 *šá ina* UGU ^{md}AG-NUMUN-DÙ
9 ^{md}AG-ŠEŠ.MEŠ-*bul-liṭ*

REV.

10 *ina* ŠU.II ^{md}AG-NUMUN-DÙ *ul ma*-[*ḫir*]
11 *e-lat* IM.GÍD.DA IGI-*ú*
12 *šá* 1 MA.NA KÙ.BABBAR *šá ri-kis* MURUB$_4$
13 *šá* MU.23.KAM 1-*en*.TA.ÀM TI-*ú*
14 LÚ *mu-kin-nu* ^{m}*pur-šu-ú* DUMU *šá* ^{m}SUM.NA-*a* A ^{m}*e-gì-bi*
15 ^{m}ŠEŠ-*šú-nu* DUMU *šá* ^{md}EN-A-MU DUMU ^{md}AG-*ba-nu-nu*
16 ^{md}EN-DIN-*iṭ* DUMU *šá* ^{md}EN-KAR-*ir*
17 DUMU ^{m}*ir-a-ni*
18 ^{m}*ni-din-tu*$_4$-^{d}EN LÚ.UMBISAG DUMU *šá* ^{md}AMAR.UTU-PAB<-A> A ^{m}*e-gì-bi*
19 TIN.TIR.KI ITI.NE UD.26.KAM

U. E.

20 MU.26.KAM ^{m}*da-ri-'i-muš*
21 LUGAL TIN.TIR.KI LUGAL KUR.MEŠ

TRANSLATION

[Nabû]-aḫḫē-bulliṭ, son of Itti-Marduk-balāṭu, descendant of Egibi, has received one mina of white silver, of which one-eigh[th is all]oy, from Nabû-zēra-ibni, son of Itti-Nabû-balāṭu, descendant of Egibi; (it is) part of the *rikis qabli* (incumbent on the latter) since the twenty-fourth year. What remains of the debt, actually [the remainder of the *r*]*ikis* [*qabli* for the twenty]-third [year], which is the credit claim owed to Nabû-aḫḫē-bul[liṭ] by Nabû-zēra-ibni: Nabû-aḫḫē-bulliṭ has not (yet) recei[ved] (it) from Nabû-zēra-ibni. In addition, there is a previous tablet regarding one mina of silver, which is the *rikis qabli* for the twenty-third year.

They have taken one (copy of the document) each.

Witnesses:
Puršû/Iddinaya//Egibi
Aḫūšunu/Bēl-apla-iddin//Nabû-bānûnu
Bēl-uballiṭ/Bēl-ēṭir//Ir'anni
The scribe: Nidinti-Bēl/Marduk-nāṣir<-apli>//Egibi
(Place + Date).

COMMENT

L. 2: Nabû-zēra-ibni had to pay for the *rikis qabli* of almost two and a half years, viz. "since the twenty-fourth year (of Darius' reign)" and probably till 26/v of Darius' twenty-sixth year (= day on which the text in question was dated). We do not know how much he had to pay for these two and a half years, but it was at least one mina of silver.

L. 6–7: The end of line 7 is actually the continuation of the end of line 6. The scribe first wrote that Nabû-zēra-ibni had paid for the *rikis qabli* that was due from him since Darius' twenty-fourth year (ll. 1–5); then he wanted to make it clear that there was still an outstanding debt against Nabû-zēra-ibni, even after he paid for the *rikis qabli* of the last two years and a half (ll. 6–10). In the process of writing these lines about the outstanding debt, he decided to add some details about the cause of the debt, and thus he added the phrase *ša rēḫi ša rikis qabli ša šanat* 23^{kam}, "which is the remainder of the *rikis qabli* for the twenty-third year." However, after finishing writing the main issues, the scribe decided that the issue of the outstanding debt had to be reformulated in a separate clause, and thus he started writing the *elat*-clause (ll. 11–13), in which he not only specified the cause of the outstanding debt, but also its amount. The scribe in question was Nidinti-bēl, MNA's son, probably a junior scribe still learning how to write legal documents.

L. 17: This line is clearly a later addition: it is squeezed in between lines 16 and 18, and its second half is empty. Bertin forgot to copy this line.

No. 52

BM 31533
Copy: Bertin copy 2573
Date: 1/xii/25 Dar (9 March 496 B.C.E.)
Place: Šabīlu
Content: Receipt of the *ilku*-tax by MNA.

OBV.

1 [*il-k*]*i šá* ^{m}*ap-la-a u* ^{m}MU-^{d}AG
2 [DUMU.MEŠ *šá*] ^{m}*ba-zu-zu* A ^{m}LÚ.AZLAG (erasure of KU-sign)
3 [x ^{m}x-^{d}A]G A-*šú šá* ^{m}*it-ti-*^{d}AMAR.UTU-DIN
4 [x x x] ⌜x⌝ *tú* ^{m}MU-GIN A-*šú šá* ^{md}EN-SUR
5 [*a*]-⌜*di*⌝-*i qí-it šá* ITI.ŠE *šá* MU.25.KAM
6 ^{m}*da-a-ri-muš* LUGAL E.KI *u* KUR.KUR.MEŠ
7 ^{m}*ši-rik-tu*$_{4}$ A-*šú šá* ^{m}SUM.NA-*a*
8 A ^{m}*e-gi-bi ina* ŠU.II ^{m}*ap-la-a*
9 [A-*šú*] *šá* ^{m}*ba-zu-zu* A ^{m}LÚ.AZLAG
10 *ma-ḫi-ir*

LO. E.

11 1-*en-a*.TA-*na-a' šá-ṭa-ri il-te-qu-ú*

REV.

12 LÚ *mu-kin-nu* ^{m}*na-din* A-*šú šá* ^{md}AG-NUMUN-URU$_{3}$
13 A ^{m}LÚ.GÍR.LÁ ^{m}*šul-lu-ma-a* A-*šú šá* ^{m}*kal-ba-a*
14 A ^{m}*na-ba-a-a* (erasure of one sign) ^{m}*ḫa-áš-da-a-a*
15 A-*šú šá* ^{m}ŠEŠ-SUM.NA ^{m}DINGIR-NA-A A-*šú šá*
16 ^{m}*na-tan*-DINGIR.MEŠ
17 ^{md}AMAR.UTU-DÙ-NUMUN LÚ.UMBISAG A-*šú šá* ^{md}AG-MU-GIŠ <A> ^{m}DIN$^{!}$
18 URU *šá-bi-il* ITI.ŠE UD.1.KAM
19 [M]U.25.KAM ^{m}*da-a-ri-muš* LUGAL E.KI *u* KUR.KUR.MEŠ

TRANSLATION

The [*ilku*-t]ax [t]ill the end of Addar of the twenty-fifth year of Darius, king of Babylon and the lands, is due from Aplaya and Iddin-Nabû, [sons of] Bazūzu, descendant of Ašlāku (erasure), [...-N]abû, son of Itti-Marduk-balāṭu [x x x] x x Šuma-ukīn, son of Bēl-ēṭir: MNA$_{2}$ has received (it) from Aplaya, [son] of Bazūzu, descendant of Ašlāku.
Each one has taken a (copy of the) deed.

Witnesses:
Nādin/Nabû-zēra-uṣur//Ṭābiḫu
Šullumaya/Kalbaya//Nabaya (erasure)
Ḫašdaya/Aḫa-iddin
DINGIR-NA-A(= *Ilu*(*n*)*naya*?)/Nātan-ilī
The scribe: Marduk-bāni-zēri/Nabû-šumu-līšir<//>Balāṭu$^{!}$

(Place + Date).

COMMENT

L. 3: It is not immediately clear how the son of Itti-Marduk-balāṭu mentioned in this line is related to the recorded receipt of the *ilku*-tax. Probably he was one of the persons who had to pay *ilku* together with the two sons of Bazūzu, and, accordingly, I suggest reading at the beginning of line 3 [*u* ^{m}x-^{d}A]G, "the *ilku*-tax that is due from ...., [and from ^{m}x-N]abû, son of Itti-Marduk-balāṭu."

L. 4: I suggest reconstructing ([*ina na-áš-pu*]*r*$^{?}$-*tú* "[as pro]xy for." The noun *našpartu* (-*par*-) or its variant form *našpaštu* (-*pa-áš*-), however, are never spelled with a -*pur*-.

L.15: The name ^{m}DINGIR-NA-A is unique. It seems to be built on the same pattern as, for instance, ^{m}ŠEŠ-*ú-na-a* (Stolper, *Entrepreneurs*, 284 s.v. Aḫūnā), ^{md}AG-*na-a* (Donbaz-Stolper, *Istanbul Murašû*, 172 s.v. *Nabû-nā*; cf. Tallqvist, *NbN*, 140 s.v. ^{il}*Nabû(-un)-na-a(-a)*, = Nabunnaya). Accordingly, ^{m}DINGIR-*na-a* may be read Ilu(n)naya.

L. 16: The name Natan-ilī is also found in Dar 75: 2, Aḫūa, son of ^{m}*na-da-na*-DINGIR.MEŠ and husband of ^{f}Adīna. The second half of line 16 is empty.

L. 17: It looks as if the scribe corrected a ŠÁ into a DIN.

No. 53

	BM 31554
Copy:	no Bertin copy
Date:	11 or 21/x/23 [Dar] (12 or 22 January 498 B.C.E.)
Place:	Babylon
Content:	Receipt of silver from MNA. Rent for a boat.

OBV.

1 [x MA.N]A KÙ.BABBAR UD-*ú i-di* GIŠ.M[Á ...]
2 [x x -*i*]*t-tan-na* DUMU *šá* ^{m}*ni-qu-du*
3 [x ^{md}]EN-*ik-ṣur* DUMU *šá* ^{m}*ri-mut* LÚ.⸢SAG-ERIN$_2$⸣.MEŠ
4 [*ina* ŠU.II ^{m}]*ši-iš-ku* ⸢DUMU⸣ *šá* ^{m}MU-*a*
5 [A ^{m}*e*]-*gi-bi ina qí-bi* (erasure?)
6 [^{m}x-x]-⸢*ia*⸣ DUMU *šá* ^{md}AG-MU-GIN
7 [DUMU ^{m}*šá-na*]-⸢*ši-šú*⸣ *ma-ḫi-ir-u'*

REV.

8 [LÚ *mu-kin*]-*nu* ^{md}AG-*it-tan-na*
9 ⸢DUMU *šá*⸣ ^{m}*mu-še-zib*-^{d}AMAR.UTU DUMU ^{m}*e-gì-bi*
10 ⸢^{m}*a*⸣-*ḫu*-[*mu*]-*ú-a* DUMU *šá* ^{m}*kal-ba-a*
11 ^{m}*ap-la-a* DUMU *šá* ^{md}AMAR.UTU-MU-URU$_3$
12 ⸢DUMU⸣ ^{m}LÚ.SANGA-BÁR ^{md}EN-MU DUMU *šá* ^{m}

13 *kit-ti-ia* DUMU ^{m}LÚ.BAḪAR$_2$

14 $^{[md]}$EN-ŠEŠ.MEŠ-BA-*šá* LÚ.UMBISAG DUMU *šá* ^{md}AG-⸢ŠEŠ⸣.MEŠ-MU

15 [DUMU ^{m}]⸢*ga-ḫal*⸣ TIN.TIR.KI ITI.AB

U. E.

16 [UD.x]+1.KAM MU.23.KAM

LE. E.

(Broken, but contained the name of the king + title)

TRANSLATION

[x mi]na(s) of white silver, the rent for a boat [...], [which is at the disposal of]$^{?}$ ^{m}[...]-ittannu, son of Niqūdu, [and$^{?}$] Bēl-ikṣur, son of Rīmūt, the ⸢overseer of the workmen⸣: they have received (it) by order of [Bas]⸢iya⸣, son of Nabû-šuma-ukīn, [descendant of Ša-nā]⸢šīšu⸣, [from] MNA$_2$.

[Witn]esses:
Nabû-ittannu/Mušēzib-Marduk//Egibi
Aḫūa/Kalbaya
Aplaya/Marduk-šuma-uṣur//Šangû-parakki
Bēl-iddin/Kittiya//Paḫāru
The scribe: Bēl-aḫḫē-iqīša/Nabû-aḫḫē-iddin[//]⸢Gaḫal⸣
(Place + Date).

COMMENT

L. 2–3: See below at line 7.

L. 6–7: For Basiya/Nabû-šuma-ukīn//Ša-nāšīšu, brother of Ina-Esagil-lilbur and Gūzānu, who both functioned as temple administrators (*šangû*) in Sippar and as governors (*šākin ṭēmi*) in Babylon, see Bongenaar, *Ebabbar*, 470. Basiya does not seem to have held a position in the administration of either city or temple. In the text under consideration he seems to have been the owner of the boat that had been rented out to MNA (see also below at line 7).

L. 7: I understand the spelling *ma-ḫi-ir-u'* as a G stative 3rd masc. pl., = *maḫrū* "they have received." The receivers in question were the son of Niqūdu, mentioned in line 2, and Bēl-ikṣur (read at the beginning of line 3 [*u* ^{md}]EN-*ikṣur*). In my opinion the receivers of the rent were not the owners of the boat, but the men who had the boat at their disposal for plying the boatman's trade. Indeed, the boats that MNA rented were usually rented from such men (e.g., BM 30270). Accordingly, I read at the beginning of line 2 [*ša ina pān*]. The owner of the boat was probably Basiya, who ordered the collection of the rent.

L. 10: There exist various spellings in the Neo-Babylonian archival texts for the names Aḫūa, Aḫḫū, and Aḫḫūtu: e.g., ŠEŠ-*u/ú-tu*, ŠEŠ-*'-tu/ú*, ŠEŠ-*'-ú-tu*, ŠEŠ-*'-ú*(*-a*), ŠEŠ.MEŠ-*ú*(*-tú*), and *A-ḫu-'-ia* (Tallqvist, *NbN*, 302; cf. spellings for the name Aḫiya'ūtu, cited by Joannès, *Borsippa*, 361). As can be seen, these names may be spelled with or without the aleph-sign (ʾ). The spelling with a *-mu-* as in the text under consideration (^{m}*a-ḫu-mu-ú-a* = Aḫūa "My brother") is remarkable, but see also ^{m}*A-ḫu-ma-a* in Cyr 345: 45, and ^{m}ŠEŠ.MEŠ-⸢*mu*⸣-*ú* in BM 33936: 7 (for Aḫḫū). The /m/ was, no doubt, an allograph of /ʾ/ often used in Neo-Babylonian orthography to stress morphophonemic length (e.g., ŠEŠ-*ʾ-tu* = *aḫḫūtu*; Rimalt, *AfO* 9, 125f.; and Reiner, *Linguistic Analysis*, 37f.). I do not think that the /ʾ/ and /m/ in the names under consideration were graphic replacements of the phoneme /w/ (for this phenomenon, see for instance the Neo-Babylonian spellings of the name Darius).

L. 13: Note that the *Personenkeil* for the name Kittiya is written at the end of the previous line.

No. 54

BM 31572
Copy: Bertin copy 2567
Date: 7/iv/25 (or 26) Dar (21 July 497 B.C.E., or 11 July 496 B.C.E.)
Place: Babylon
Content: Receipt of barley from MNA by a royal official. Transport costs. By order of (*ina qibi ša*) the governor of Babylon.

OBV.

1 [x GU]R ŠE.BAR *gi-mir šá* 4 [...]
2 [*šá*]$^{?}$ *ul-tu tam-tì šá* ŠU.II ^{md}EN-[...]
3 [LÚ.N]AM.MEŠ$^{!}$ *ina qí-bi šá* ^{m}*gu-za-nu* LÚ.G[AR-UŠ$_{4}$ TIN.TIR.KI]
4 [^{m}*ap*]-*la-a* LÚ.SAG-LUGAL LÚ *si-pir-ri*
5 [*šá*] LÚ.SAG.MEŠ *šá* É.GAL *eš-šú*
6 [*ina* ŠU].⸢II⸣ ^{m}*ši-ir-ku* DUMU *šá* ^{m}MU-*a* DUMU ^{m}*e-gì-bi*
7 *ma-ḫi-ir*

REV.

8 [LÚ] <*mukinnu*> ^{md}AG-*it-tan-nu* DUMU *šá* ^{m}*ri-mut*-^{d}EN DUMU ^{m}*sip-pe-e-a*
9 ^{m}*mar-duk-a* DUMU *šá* ^{m}*gu-za-nu* DUMU ^{m}*kàṣ-ṣì-dak-ka*
10 $^{m!}$*tat-tan-nu* DUMU *šá* ^{md}AG-KÁD DUMU ^{m}*da-bi-bi*
11 ^{md}EN-MU DUMU *šá* ^{m}MU-^{d}AG DUMU ^{m}*da-bi-bi*
12 $^{[m]}$*mu-ra-nu* DUMU [*šá* ^{m}*šad*]-*din-nu* A LÚ.AZLAG
13 $^{[m]}$*šul-lu-ma-a* ⸢DUMU *šá*⸣ ^{md}AG-*na-din*-ŠEŠ
14 [A] ^{m}*na-ba-a-a*
15 [^{m}*p*]*ur-šu*$^{!}$-*ú* LÚ.UMBISAG DUMU ^{m}*e-gì-bi*$^{!}$
16 ⸢E⸣.KI ITI.ŠU UD.7.KAM MU.[25].[KAM]
17 [^{m}*d*]*a-ri-ʾi-muš* LUGAL E.KI

U. E.

18 *u* KUR.KUR

TRANSLATION

[x *ko*]*r* of barley, the costs for the transport of four [hundred? *kor* of barley/dates] from Tâmti that are under the administrative authority of Bēl-[ittannu? and m...], [the dis]trict governors!: [Ap]laya, courtier (and) clerk [of] the commissioners of the New Palace, has received (it) [fro]m MNA_2, by order of Gūzānu, go[vernor of Babylon].

<Witnesses>:
Nabû-ittannu/Rīmūt-Bēl//Sippêa
Marduk/Gūzānu//Kaṣṣidakku
Tattannu/Nabû-kāṣir//Dābibī
Bēl-iddin/Iddin-Nabû//Dābibī
Mūrānu/Šaddinnu//Ašlāku
Šullumaya/Nabû-nādin-aḫi//Nabaya
The scribe: Puršû!//Egibi!
(Place + Date).

COMMENT

L. 1: The end of the line is, most likely, to be reconstructed as follows: 4 [ME GUR ŠE.BAR/ZÚ.LUM.MA], "four [hundred *kor* of barley/dates]." Cf. BM 30639: 1–2, *gi-mi-ir šá* 1 ME GUR ŠE.BAR *šá ul-*[*tu*] GARIM *tam-tì*; BM 32891: 1–3, *gi-mir* [*šá* ... GUR] ŠE.BAR ... *šá* GARIM *tam-tì*; BM 33112: 1, *gi-mir šá* 2 ME ŠE.BAR; and BM 30980: 1, *gi-mir šá* 3 ME 16 GUR ZÚ.LUM.MA.

L. 2: On the place named Tâmti in Neo-Babylonian documents, see Zadok, *RGTC* 8, 305 s.v. *Tâmtu*(1). The toponym is almost always preceded by the logogram GARIM = *tāmirtu*, the exact meaning of which is still a matter of debate (was it a mere hydrological term, or did it also have an administrative implication?). *AHw*, 1341 s.v. *tawwertum* translates "(Feld-)Flur, Umland, Umgebung"; Van Driel, *BSA* 4, 142–44, interprets the term as meaning "rural district based on a common hydrological feature" and suggests the translation "basin." See also Wunsch, *Felder* 1, 22ff.; Cocquerillat, *Palmeraies*, 27; and Joannès, *TÉBR*, 118. For the transport of agricultural produce from this place under the supervision of the governor of Babylon, see also BM 30639 and BM 32891. At the end of the line I suggest reading Bēl-[ittannu *u* m...], see below.

L. 2–3: The sign after NAM resembles LUGAL, but I do not know of an official with the title LÚ.NAM LUGAL. I suggest emending the sign and read MEŠ (for several other emendations and scribal omissions in this text, see below lines 8, 10 and 15). Accordingly, BM 31572 is about the transport of either barley or dates from a place called Tâmti, where one Bēl-[...] and another person, whose name is lost in the lacuna at the end of line 2, functioned as district governors (LÚ.NAM.MEŠ!). The transport of agricultural produce from Tâmti is also the subject of BM 32891, and from the latter text we get the names of the district governors in question. In the said text MNA paid for the transport of ŠE.BAR [(*šá*) G]IŠ.BÁN *šá* mdEN-*it-ta*[*n*]-*nu* [*u* m]*šu*-⸢*ma*?-*a*?⸣

LÚ.⸢NAM⸣.MEŠ *šá* GARIM *tam-tì*, "barley [(from) the fi]xed rent due to Bēl-itta[n]nu [and] Šu⸢maya?⸣, ⸢district governors⸣, from irrigated farmland in Tâmti" (BM 32891: 2–3). The parallel from BM 32891 enables us to reconstruct *Bēl-*[*ittannu u* ᵐ...] at the end of line 2 in the text under consideration (BM 31572), and to emend LÚ.NAM.MEŠ! in line 3 of the same text. In addition, a comparison between both texts reveals that GIŠ.BÁN *šá Bēl-ittannu* in BM 32891: 2 corresponds to *šá* ŠU.II *Bēl*[*-ittannu*] in BM 31572: 2. The "fixed rent of Bēl-ittannu," therefore, was actually rent due to Bēl-ittannu from irrigated farmland in Tâmti that fell under his administrative authority. The close connection between BM 31572 and BM 32891 is further strengthened by the fact that these texts share three witnesses. Finally, it may be that both texts were written within a time span of four days: BM 31572 is dated 7/iv/25 or 26 Dar, and BM 32891 is dated 11/iv[-] Dar.

L. 4: I propose to read Aplaya ([ᵐ*ap*]*-la-a*) because a person named Aplaya occurs in BM 30980 with the same title and in the same function as in our text. He was a "courtier (and) clerk of the commissioners of the New Palace," and, by order of (*ina qibi*) the governor of Babylon, he received payment for the transport costs from MNA. The LUGAL-sign is written over other signs.

L. 10: It seems that the scribe started writing DINGIR, but forgot the *Personenkeil*. He then added the *Personenkeil*, but did not completely erase the DINGIR-sign. The *Personenkeil* before the name Tattannu, therefore, is written over a partly erased sign.

L. 15: Some signs in this line are written over partly erased signs. The ŠU-sign in ᵐ*pur-šu-ú* has one horizontal in front and hence resembles a LA. The BI-sign in ᵐ*e-gì-bi* has four instead of two *Winkelhaken*.

L. 16: At the beginning of this line one may read either [TIN].⸢TIR⸣.KI or ⸢E⸣.KI. Since only the end of the sign remains, it is not clear whether it was an E or a TIR. The number of the year is either 25 or 26. The lower part of the number is slightly damaged.

No. 55

BM 31667 + BM 31641 (= Dupl. of BM 30961)
Copy: no Bertin copy
Date: 12/vi/26 Dar (13 September 496 B.C.E.)
Place: Babylon
Content: Receipt of silver from MNA. Purchase price for a boat.

OBV.

1 GIŠ.MÁ *šá* ^{md}AG-A-MU DUMU *šá* ^{m}*la-a-ba-ši*
2 DUMU ^{m}ZALAG$_2$-^{d}PAP.SUKKAL *šá a-na* 4 MA.NA 10 GÍN
3 KÙ.BABBAR UD-*ú šá ina* 1 GÍN *bit-qa nu-uḫ-ḫu-tu* ŠÁM GIŠ.MÁ-*šú*
4 *a-na* ^{m}*ši-iš-ku* DUMU *šá* ^{m}SUM.NA-*a* DUMU ^{m}⸢*e*⸣-[*gi-bi*]
5 *id-din-nu* KÙ.BABBAR *a-k*[*i-i*] [*ú*]-*ìl*-[*tì-šú*]
6 ^{md}AG-A-MU DUMU *šá* ^{m}*la*-[*a-ba-ši* DUMU ^{m}ZALAG$_2$-^{d}PAP.SUKKAL]
7 *ina* ŠU.II ^{m}*ši-iš-ku* DUMU [*šá* ^{m}SUM.NA-*a*]
8 DUMU ^{m}*e-gi-bi ma-ḫi*-[*ir ú-ìl-tì*]
9 *šá* GIŠ.MÁ *ra-ki-is-tu*$_4$ ⸢*u*⸣ [...]
10 *šá ina* IGI ^{m}*ni-qu-du pa*-[*qa-ad*]
11 ^{md}AG-A-MU *ki-i u-tir*-[*ri*]

LO. E.

12 *a-na* ^{m}*ši-iš-ku it-t*[*a-din*]

REV.

13 LÚ *mu-kin-nu* ^{m}*ni-din-tu*$_4$ DUMU *šá* ^{m}[*Kalbaya*]
14 DUMU ^{m}*su-ḫa-a-a* ^{md}EN-SU [DUMU *šá Kalbaya*]
15 DUMU ^{m}MU-*líb-ši* ^{md}EN-GI [DUMU *šá Bēl-kāṣir*]
16 ^{md}EN-PAB A-*šú šá* ^{m}SIG$_5$-*iá* A ^{m}*na-din-še*-[*im*]
17 ^{m}*mu-ra-nu* A-*šú šá* ^{m}ÌR-^{d}AMAR.UTU A [*Šangû-Ea*]
18 ⸢^{md}AG-*na*⸣-*din*-[ŠEŠ LÚ.UMBISAG A-*šú šá* ^{m}] SI[G$_5$]-*i*[*a* A ^{m}*n*]*a-din*-[*še*]-*i*[*m*]
19 TIN.TIR.KI ITI.KIN UD.12.KAM MU.26.KAM
20 ^{m}*dar-ri-i'-muš* LUGAL TIN.TIR.KI *u* KUR.KUR.MEŠ

No. 56

BM 31690 + BM 30658
Copy: no Bertin copy
Date: 18/viii/31 Dar (23 November 491 B.C.E.)
Place: Babylon
Content: Renting of a boat by MNA's son.

OBV.

1 GIŠ.MÁ *šá* ^{md}AG-KAR-*ir*-ZI.MEŠ
2 DUMU *šá* ^{m}*ḫa-ad-da-a šá ina pa-ni* ^{m}*ap-la-a*
3 *a-na* LÚ *má-laḫ*$_4$*-ú-tu* ^{m}*ap-la-*[*a*]
4 DUMU *šá* ^{m}SUM.NA-*a a-na i-di-šú*
5 *a-na u*$_4$*-mu* 1 (PI) 4 (SILA$_3$) ZÚ.LUM.MA
6 *a-na* ^{m}*ni-din-tu*$_4$ DUMU *šá* ^{m}*šiš-ki*
7 DUMU ^{m}*e-gi-bi id*<*-din*> 1-*en u*$_4^{!}$*-mu*
8 *ina ma-kal-li-e* ^{m}*ap-la-a*
9 *a-na muḫ-ḫi* ^{m}*ni-din-tu*$_4$

LO. E.

10 *ul i-man-ni ul-tu*

REV.

11 UD 20.1.LÁ.KAM GIŠ.MÁ *ina* IGI ^{m}*ni-din-tu*$_4$
12 1-*en*.TA.ÀM TI-*ú* LÚ *mu-kin-nu*
13 ^{md}EN-MU DUMU ^{m}MU-^{d}AG DUMU ^{m}*da-bi-bi*
14 ^{m}*bul-ṭa-a* DUMU *šá* ^{m}*ba-lat-su* {x} A$^{!}$ ^{m}*mi-ṣir-a-a*
15 ^{m}ÌR-*ia* DUMU *šá* ^{md}AMAR.UTU-LUGAL-*an-ni* {x} A$^{!}$ ^{m}⸢*e-ṭè*⸣*-ru*
16 ^{m}SU-*a* DUMU *šá* ^{md}AG-A-MU A$^{!}$ ^{m}*ba-bu-tu*
17 ^{md}EN-[x] LÚ.UMBISAG DUMU *šá* ^{md}AG-⸢x x x⸣
18 E.KI ITI.APIN UD.18.KAM MU.31.KAM
19 ^{m}*da-ri-ia-a-muš* LUGAL E.KI
20 *u* KUR.KUR

U. E.

21 *pu-ut šu-lu-ú šá* 350 GUR ZÚ.LUM.[MA]
22 ^{m}*ap-la-a na-ši*

LE. E.

23 GIŠ *ma-ši-ḫu šá* É ⸢x x x⸣
24 ^{m}*ap-la-a u-zak-ku*

TRANSLATION

The boat belonging to Nabû-ēṭir-napšāti, son of Ḫaddaya, which is at the disposal of Aplaya for sailing: Aplay[a], son of Iddinaya, has ren<ted> (it) out for 0.1.0.4 *kor* of dates a day to Nidintu, son of MNA$_2$. Each day (that the boat

is) at the mooring place Aplaya shall not reckon on behalf of Nidintu. From the nineteenth onward the boat will be at Nidintu's disposal.
They have taken one (copy of the document) each.

Witnesses:
Bēl-iddin/Iddin-Nabû/Dābibī
Bulṭaya/Balāssu/Miṣiraya
Ardiya/Marduk-šarrāni/Ēṭiru
Erībaya/Nabû-apla-iddin/Bābūtu
The scribe: Bēl-[x]/Nabû-⌜x x x⌝
(Place + Date).

For the loading of three hundred and fifty *kor* of dates Aplaya assumes warranty. The measure of Bīt?-⌜x-x-x⌝ Aplaya will *release*?.

COMMENT

L. 8: On *makallû* "mooring place" see *CAD* M_1, 123 (cf. *AHw*, 588); Salonen, *Nautica*, 38 ("Anlegestelle, Ankerplatz"), and Bruschweiler, *RA* 83: 158–60 ("installation portuaire"). Van Driel, *BSA* 4: 139, points out that in texts describing fields the term rather refers to "the lower end of a field, at the place where it is furthermost from the river or canal from which it derives its irrigation water. ... Some means of drainage lower down the levee."

Le. E.: The signs on the left edge are written parallel to the obverse. The signs after *šá* resemble É/URU MU/I ŠÁ x. The meaning of the expression *mašīḫu zukkû* is unknown to me.

No. 57

BM 31718
Copy: no Bertin copy
Date: broken
Place: broken
Content: Receipt of dates and barley by MNA. Partial repayment of a debt. Fragmentary.

OBV.

(beginning is broken off)

1′ ⌜2 ME?⌝ (erasure)? 45 GUR 3 PI ZÚ.LUM.MA
2′ 8 GUR 1 (PI) 2 (BÁN) ŠE.BAR *šá* mdAMAR.UTU-*na*-[*ṣ*]*ir*-IBILA
3′ DUMU *šá* mKI-dAMAR.UTU-DIN A m*e-gi-bi*
4′ *šá ina muḫ-ḫi* mdAG-*ma-ku-ú-ṣur* A-*šú šá* mdAG-A-M[U]
5′ *e-la-a′ šá ina lìb-bi ú-ìl-tì šá* ⅓ MA.NA [KÙ.BABBAR]
6′ *a-na šu-mu šá* mdDI.KU_5-EN-[URU_3 LÚ] *q*[*al-la*]
7′ *i-na lìb-bi* 58 GUR ⌜*šá*⌝ [x x] [x x x]
8′ [x]+1 GUR ŠE.BAR [x] [...]

LO. E.

9′ *ù* x x [^{md}AMAR.UTU-*na-ṣir*-IBILA]

REV.

10′ [DU]MU *šá* ^{m}KI-^{d}AMA[R.UTU DUMU ^{m}*e-gi-bi*]

11′ *i-na* [Š]U.II ^{md}AG-*ma-*[*ku-ú-ṣur*]

12′ *ma-ḫi-ir* ⸢*1-en*⸣.TA.ÀM *šá-*⸢*ṭa*⸣*-r*[*i*]

13′ *il-te-qu-ú* LÚ *mu-*[*kin*]*-nu* ^{m}KI-⸢^{d}AG⸣-[x-x]

14′ A-*šú šá* ^{m}MU-^{d}AG A ^{md}IDIM-*pat-tan-nu*

15′ ^{m}DU$_{10}$.GA-*ia* A-*šú šá* ^{m}*gi-mil-lu* A ^{m}*ir-a-ni*

16′ ^{md}EN-[*ri-man-ni*] A-*šú šá* ^{m}*kal-*⸢*bi*⸣-^{d}MAŠ$^{?}$ ⸢x⸣ [x]

(Remainder of reverse is broken off.)

LE. E.

17′ LUGAL E.KI LUGAL KUR.KUR

TRANSLATION

[From the promissory notes for … including] ⸢200⸣+45.3.0 *kor* of dates (and) 8.1.2 *kor* of barley owed to MNA$_1$, which were contracted to the debit of Nabû-māku-uṣur, son of Nabû-apla-iddi[n]; in it a debt of one-third mina [of silver (…) was contracted] in the name of Madānu-bēla-[uṣur], s[lave (…)]: from it fifty-eight *kor* ⸢of⸣ […], [x]+one *kor* of barley […], and x x MNA has received from Nabû-mā[ku-uṣur].

They have taken ⸢one⸣ (copy of the) docum[ent] each.

Witnesses:

Itti-⸢Nabû⸣-[…]/Iddin-Nabû//Ea-pattannu

Ṭābiya/Gimillu//Ir'anni

Bēl-[rēmanni]/Kalbi-⸢Ninurta$^{?}$⸣[…]

(Remainder of the list of witnesses and of the scribe, as well as the date formula are broken off).

COMMENT

L. 5′: For the verb *e'ēlu*, more at BM 30795: 7–9.

No. 58

BM 31722 + BM 35235 (= Dupl. of BM 30994)
Copy: Bertin copy 2611
Date: 5/vii/26 Dar (5 October 496 B.C.E.)
Place: Babylon
Content: Promissory note to pay a debt of silver to MNA. Undertaking to return the "Register of the LÚ.DÍM" (GIŠ.DA *šá* LÚ.DÍM) to the debtor upon repayment.

OBV.

1 ⸢50⸣ GÍN KÙ.BABBAR UD-*ú šá ina* 1 GÍN *bit-qa nu-uḫ-ḫu-tú*
2 *šá* ^{md}AMAR.UTU-*na-ṣir*-IBILA DUMU *šá* ^{m}SUM.NA-*a* A ^{m}*e-gi-bi*
3 *i-na muḫ-ḫi* ^{md}AG-ḪI.LI-DINGIR.MEŠ DUMU *šá*
4 ^{md}EN-*re-man-ni* DUMU ^{m}DÙ-*eš*-DINGIR
5 *a-di* UD.20.KAM *šá* ITI.DU$_{6}$.KÙ *šá* MU.26.KAM
6 ^{m}*da-a-ri-ia-muš* LUGAL KÙ.BABBAR-*a*$_{4}$
7 [...] [UD-*ú šá ina* 1 GÍN *bit-qa nu-uḫ-ḫu-tu*]
8 ^{md}AG-ḪI.LI-DINGIR.MEŠ *a-na* ^{md}AMAR.UTU-*na-ṣir*-I[BILA]
9 *i-nam-din u*$_{4}$-*mu šá* KÙ.BABBAR-*a*$_{4}$ 50 GÍN
10 [^{md}AG-HI.L]I-DINGIR.MEŠ *a-na* ^{md}AMAR.UTU-*na-ṣir*-IBILA
11 [*i-nam-di*]*n-nu* GÍD.DA *šá* LÚ.DÍM ^{md}AMAR.UTU-*na-ṣir*-IBILA
12 [*a-n*]*a* ^{md}AG-ḪI.LI-DINGIR.MEŠ *i-nam-din*

REV.

13 LÚ *mu-kin-nu* ^{m}*ḫaš-da-a-a* DUMU *šá* ^{m}*šá*-^{d}AG-⸢*šu-ú*⸣
14 DUMU ^{m}*ši-gu-ú-a* ^{md}EN-*it-tan-nu*
15 DUMU *šá* ^{m}BA-*šá*-^{d}AMAR.UTU [DU]MU ^{m}[UR]-^{d}ŠEŠ.KI
16 ^{m}*ni-din-tu*$_{4}$-^{d}EN DUMU *šá* ^{m}*la*-⸢*qí-pi*⸣ DUMU LÚ *ir-a*-[*ni*]
17 [^{m}*ni-din-tu*$_{4}$] DUMU *šá* ^{m}*kal-ba-a* DUMU ^{m}*su*-⸢*ḫa-a-a*⸣
18 DUMU ^{m}MU-*líb-ši* ^{m}*tab-ni-e-a* DUB.SAR
19 DUMU *šá* ^{m}*ap-la-a* DUMU ^{m}*ga-ḫúl*
20 TIN.TIR.KI ITI.DU$_{6}$.KÙ UD.5.KAM
21 MU.26.KAM ^{m}*da-a-ri-ia-muš* LUGAL TIN.TIR.KI
22 *u* KUR.KUR

TRANSLATION

⸢Fifty⸣ shekels of white, medium-quality silver, of which one-eighth is alloy, are due to MNA$_{1}$ from Nabû-kuzub-ilī, son of Bēl-rēmanni, descendant of Eppeš-ilī. By the twentieth of Tašrīt of the twenty-sixth year of King Darius, Nabû-kuzub-ilī shall pay these [fifty shekels] [of white, medium-quality silver, of which one-eighth is alloy], to MNA$_{1}$. From the moment [Nabû-kuz]ub-ilī [will have pa]id these fifty shekels to MNA$_{1}$, MNA$_{1}$ shall give the register of the LÚ.DÍM [t]o Nabû-kuzub-ilī.

Witnesses:
Ḫašdaya/Ša-Nabû-⸢šū⸣//Šigûa
Bēl-ittannu/Iqīša-Marduk//[Kalbi]-Nanna
Nidinti-Bēl/Lā-⸢qīpu⸣//Ir'a[nni]
[Nidintu]/Kalbaya//Suḫaya
<Nidintu/Kalbaya>$^?$//Šumu-libši
The scribe: Tabnêa/Aplaya//Gaḫul
(Place + Date).

COMMENT

See at BM 30994.

No. 59

	BM 31786
Copy:	Bertin copy 2574
Date:	[-]/[-]/25 Dar (497–496 B.C.E.)
Place:	Babylon
Content:	Receipt of barley from MNA by a royal official. Transport costs. By order of (*ina qibi ša*) the governor of Babylon.

OBV.

1 40 GUR 3 (PI) 2 (BÁN) ŠE.BAR *gi-*[*mir* x GUR]
2 ŠE.BAR *šá* GIŠ.BÁN *šá* ^{md}EN-*it-*⸢*tan*⸣-[*nu*]
3 ^{md}EN-GI LÚ.SAG-LUGAL LÚ *si-p*[*i*(*r*)-*ri šá*]
4 LÚ.SAG-LUGAL.MEŠ *šá* É.GAL *ra-bi* [(...)]
5 *i-na qí-bi šá* ^{m}*gu-za-nu* LÚ.GAR-UŠ$_4$ [TIN.TIR.KI]
6 *ina qa-at* ^{m}*ši-ir-ku* DUMU *šá* ^{m}MU-*a* [A ^{m}*e-gì-bi*]
7 *ma-ḫi-ir* 1-*en*.TA.ÀM TI-[*ú*]

REV.

8 LÚ *mu-kin-nu* ^{md}EN-ŠEŠ.MEŠ-M[U ...]
9 ^{m}*mar-duk-a* DUMU *šá* ^{m}*gu-za-nu* DUMU ^{m}[...]
10 ^{m}*ni-din-tu*$_4$ DUMU *šá* ^{m}*kal-ba-a* DUMU ^{m}[...]
11 ^{md}AG-DIN-*su*-E DUMU *šá* ^{m}MU-^{d}AG
12 ^{md}EN-*it-tan-nu* DUMU *šá* ^{md}⸢AG/EN⸣-[...]
13 ^{m}*ta-at-tan-nu* DUMU *šá* ^{md}AG-⸢x⸣ [(...)]
14 ^{m}*ap-la-a* LÚ.UMBISAG DUMU *šá* ^{md}EN-[...]
15 DUMU ^{md}30-KUR-*nu* TIN.TIR.KI ITI.[...]
16 MU.25.KAM ^{m}*da-a-*[*ri*]-[*muš*]
17 LUGAL [TIN.TIR].[KI] [*u* KUR.KUR]

TRANSLATION

40.3.2 *kor* of barley, the cos[ts for the transport of x *kor*] of barley from the fixed rent due to Bēl-ittan[nu]: Bēl-ušallim, courtier (and) cle[rk of] the courtiers of the Grand Palace [(...)], has received (it) by order of Gūzānu, governor [of Babylon], from MNA_2.
They have take[n] one (copy of the document) each.

Witnesses:
Bēl-aḫḫē-id[din] [...]
Marduk/Gūzānu//[Kaṣṣidakku]
Nidintu/Kalbaya//[...]
Nabû-balāssu-iqbi/Iddin-Nabû
Bēl-ittannu/⸢Nabû/Bēl⸣-[...]
Tattannu/Nabû-⸢kāṣir⸣[(//Dābibī)]
The scribe: Aplaya/Bēl-[...]//Sîn-šadûnu
(Place + Date).

COMMENT

This is an orderly and nicely written tablet.

L. 3: The two *Winkelhaken* after LÚ *si-* may be the beginning of an UD-sign (read *-pir-*) or a PI-sign (read *-pi-*). For the Bēl-ušallim mentioned in this line, who was a courtier in the service of the governor of Babylon, see probably also BM 31036: 4.

L. 4: We may have to read at the end of the line [*u* (É.GAL) *eš-šú*], cf. BM 30639: 4.

L. 9: For the family name of Marduk/Gūzānu, see BM 31572: 9 (another receipt of payment for transport costs).

L. 13: The remnants of the sign after ^{md}AG suggest a reading -⸢*ka*⸣-[*ṣir*] or -⸢KÁD⸣. Tattannu/Nabû-kāṣir//Dābibī is well attested, not only in texts regarding transport costs (BM 31393, BM 31572 and BM 32891), but also in other texts from the time of MNA (Dar 469, BM 31322: $9^?$, BM 30235, BM 31517 and BM 30764).

No. 60

BM 31793
Copy: Bertin copy 2159
Date: 11/x/27 or 28 Dar (28 December 495 B.C.E. or 17 January 493 B.C.E.)
Place: broken
Content: <Receipt> of silver by MNA. Partial repayment of a debt. Reference to the sale of a prebend by the debtors.

OBV.

1 *i-na ú-ìl-tì šá* 4 MA.NA KÙ.BABBAR *šá ina* 1 GÍN *bit-qa*
2 *nu-uḫ-ḫu-tu* 66 GUR ZÚ.LUM.MA *ù* 4 GUR ⸢x x⸣

3 *šá* ^{m}AMAR.UTU-*na-ṣir*-IBILA A-*šú šá* ^{m}KI-^{d}AMAR.UTU-DIN A ^{m}*e-gì-bi*
4 *šá ina muḫ-ḫi* ^{md}EN-NIGIN-*ir* A-*šú šá* ^{md}U.GUR-MU *ù* ŠE.NUMUN-*šú zaq-pi*
5 *šá ina* URU *ṣi-li-im-ma maš-ka-nu ku-um* ⸢66⸣ GUR-a_4
6 *ṣab-tu ina lìb-bi* 1⅔ MA.NA KÙ.BABBAR *šá ina* 1 GÍN *bit*-[*qa*]
7 *nu-uḫ-ḫu-tu ina* SAG.DU *u* UR_5.RA-*šú* [(...)$^{?}$]
8 *ina* ŠU.II ^{m}EN-NIGIN-*ir u* ^{md}EN-x DUMU-*šú ina* U[GU]
9 1⅔ MA.NA ⸢KÙ.BABBAR⸣ ŠÁM GIŠ.ŠUB.BA ⸢*šá*⸣ ⸢x⸣ [...]
10 ⸢*šá*$^{?}$⸣ ^{md}EN-NIGIN-*ir u* ^{m}[^{d}EN-x ...]

LO. E.

11 ^{md}AMAR.UTU-[*na-ṣir*-IBILA]

REV.

12 *it-ti* ^{m}[...]
13 1-*en*.TA.ÀM T[I-*ú* LÚ *mu-kin-nu* ^{m}... A-*šú šá*]
14 ^{m}*lib-luṭ* A LÚ [...]
15 A LÚ.SANGA-^{d}*é-a* ^{m}[...]
16 A ^{md}*é-a*-DÙ-*eš*-DINGIR ^{m}[...]
17 A ^{md}IDIM-*pat-tan-nu* ^{md}⸢AG$^{?}$⸣-[...]
18 ^{m}ÌR-^{d}*ba-*ba_6 DUB.SAR DUMU LÚ.⸢AZLAG⸣ [...]
19 ITI.AB UD.11.KAM MU.⸢27⸣.KAM ^{m}[*da-a*]-⸢*ri-ia-muš*⸣
20 LUGAL [TIN.TIR.KI] LUGAL KUR.KUR

TRANSLATION

From the debt of four minas of medium-quality silver, of which one-eighth is alloy, sixty-six *kor* of dates, and four *kor* ⸢x x⸣, which are due to MNA_1 from Bēl-upaḫḫir, son of Nergal-iddin—and his orchard in Ṣilimma has been pledged for these ⸢sixty-six⸣ *kor*—from it one and two-third minas of medium-quality silver, of which one-eighth is alloy, from the capital and its interest, <(MNA) has received> from Bēl-upaḫḫir and his son Bēl-ibni (or -nāṣir). Ab[out] the one and two-third minas ⸢silver⸣, the price of the prebend of the [...] ⸢which$^{?}$⸣ Bēl-upaḫḫir and [Bēl-ibni (or, -nāṣir) ...], M[NA_1] with ^{m}[...].
They have ta[ken] one (a copy of the document) each.

[Witnesses:]
[.../]Libluṭ//LÚ [...]
[...]//Šangû-Ea
[...]//Ea-eppeš-ilī
[...]//Ea-pattannu
⸢Nabû$^{?}$⸣-[...]
The scribe: Arad-Bāba//⸢Ašlāku⸣
(Place + Date).

COMMENT

L. 2: The signs at the end of the line are unclear. According to BM 31360 and Dar 509 Bēl-upaḫḫir owed silver, barley, dates, and oxen to MNA and his slave.

L. 7–8: The main section of the text under consideration records the receipt of silver in partial payment of a debt. This is clear from the use of the formula *ina u'ilti ša ... ina libbi ...* "from the debt of ..., from it ..." (ll. 1–8a), which characterizes partial payments (cf. e.g., BM 32858; NRVU 349–50, NRVU 360–61, and NRVU 365). Consequently, we expect to find a verb of receipt or quittance, to wit after *ina qātē* PN_1 *u* PN_2 in line 8b, but it is not there. It should have occurred at the end of the *ina u'ilti ša ... ina libbi ...*- formula after *ina qātē* PN_1 *u* PN_2 and before *ina mu[ḫḫi]*. With *ina mu[ḫḫi]* we have a new sentence that deals with the next issue, which is related to the partial payment but still separate from it. Consequently, I assume that the scribe forgot to write the verb of receipt/quittance. Moreover, I suggest reading the name of the receiver, MNA, in the lacuna at the end of line 7.

L. 8b: The name of Bēl-upaḫḫir's son was either ^{md}EN-DÙ(= *-ibni*) or ^{md}EN-PAB(= *-nāṣir*).

L. 8(end)–12: I suggest reading: *ina* U[GU] (9) 1⅔ MA.NA ⌜KÙ.BABBAR⌝ ŠÁM GIŠ.ŠUB.BA ... (10) ⌜*šá*?⌝ ^{md}EN-NIGIN-*ir u* ^{m}[^{d}EN-DÙ/PAB DUMU-*šú im-ḫu-ru-u'*] (11) ^{md}AMAR.UTU-[*na-ṣir*-IBILA] (12) *itti* ^{m}[^{d}EN-NIGIN-*ir u* ^{md}EN-DÙ/PAB DUMU-*šu ul i-dab-bu-ub*], "Ab[out] the one and two-third minas of ⌜silver⌝, the price of the prebend ... ⌜which?⌝ Bēl-upaḫḫir and [Bēl-ibni/nāṣir, his son, sold], M[NA shall not litigate] against B[ēl-upaḫḫir and Bēl-ibni/nāṣir, his son]." This may mean two things. On the one hand, it could mean that MNA is not allowed to raise a claim regarding the amount of 1⅔ minas of indebted silver after he bought the prebend because that part of the debt is to be considered paid off with the acquisition of the prebend. Or, if the prebend had been sold to a third party, it means that MNA is not allowed to claim more than 1⅔ minas from the silver that the debtors gained from the sale of their prebend. Indeed, suppose that Bēl-upaḫḫir and his son succeeded in selling their prebend for more than 1⅔ minas and therefore had cash left from the sale; MNA may want to claim all the money from the sale; in other words, he may require his debtors to pay off their entire debt of 4 minas with the silver they received from the sale, and not just 1⅔ minas. The text then states that MNA is not permitted to raise such a claim: the sale of the prebend covers the repayment of part of the debt only, not the entire debt.

L. 17: After this line follow two empty lines before the scribe started writing his name in line 18, cf. BM 30366: 12, BM 30819: 14, BM 31036: 12, BM 31227: 13, BM 32883: 17 e.a.; probably also BM 30270: 16–17; cf. also BM 31118: 13.

L. 19: The year may be either 27 or 28.

No. 61

BM 31798
Copy: Bertin copy 2783
Date: 8 or 9/iv/[-] Dar (June - July)
Place: broken
Content: Receipt of silver by MNA. Payment from a bow-unit (*ina* $^{\text{<giš>}}$*qašti*).

OBV.

1 [x] GÍN KÙ.BABBAR-*ú i-na* <GIŠ.>BAN [*šá*]
2 ^{md}EN-MU DUMU *šá* ^{m}*ta-qiš* DUMU ^{md}[...]
3 ^{m}*ši-iš-ku* DUMU *šá* SUM.NA-*a* DUMU ^{m}[...]
4 *ina* ŠU.II ^{md}EN-MU DUMU *šá* ^{m}*ta-qiš* DUMU [...]
5 [*ma-ḫ*]*i-ir* 1-*en*.TA.ÀM TI-⸢*ú*⸣
(Remainder of obverse is empty.)

REV.

6 [LÚ *mu-kin*]-*nu* ^{m}*mar-duk-a* DUMU *šá* ^{m}*gu-za-nu*
7 [DUMU LÚ *kàṣ*]-*ṣì-dak-ka* ^{m}*tat-tan-nu* DUMU *šá*
8 [^{md}AG]-KÁD DUMU ^{m}*da-bi-bi* ^{m}*ap-la-a* DUMU *šá*
9 [^{m}*mu*]-*ra-šu-ú* DUMU LÚ.SANGA-BÁR ^{m}*šul-lu-ma-*⸢*a*⸣
10 [DUMU *šá* ^{md}A]G-*na-din*-ŠEŠ DUMU ^{m}*na-ba-a-a*
11 $^{\text{[m]}}$⸢x⸣-^{d}EN$^{?}$ LÚ.UMBISAG DUMU ^{m}*e-gì-*[*bi*]
12 [x x].KI ITI.ŠU UD.8$^{?}$.K[AM ...]
13 [^{m}*da-r*]*i-i'-muš* LUGAL TIN.[TIR.KI]
14 LUGAL KUR.KUR

TRANSLATION

[x] shekels of silver from the <b>ow [of] Bēl-iddin, son of Taqīš, descendant of [...]: MNA$_2$ [has r]eceived (it) from Bēl-iddin, son of Tāqiš, descendant of [...]. They have taken one (copy of the document) each.

Witnesses:
Marduk/Gūzānu//[Kaṣ]ṣidakku
Tattannu/[Nabû]-kāṣir//Dābibī
Aplaya/[Mu]rašû//Šangû-parakki
Šullumaya/[N]abû-nādin-aḫi//Nabaya
The scribe: Iddin-Bēl$^{?}$//Egibi
(Place + Date).

COMMENT

L. 11: A reading ^{m}⸢MU⸣-^{d}EN is possible.

No. 62

BM 31891
Copy: no Bertin copy
Date: 7/vi/[-] Dar (Aug. - Sept.)
Place: Babylon
Content: Renting of a boat by MNA.

OBV.

1 [GIŠ].MÁ *šá* ^{m}MU-^{d}EN LÚ *qal-la šá* ^{m}*bar-*⸢*zi*?-x-x⸣
2 ⸢x⸣ *a-na* LÚ <*ma*>-*laḫ*$_{x}$-*ú-tu ina* ⸢IGI⸣ ^{m}*ni-qu-du* A-*šú šá* $^{\langle m\rangle}$⸢x-x⸣-*iá*?
3 *u* ^{m}*kal-ba*-^{d}KÁ A-*šú šá* ^{m}MU-*a a-na i-di-šú*
4 *a-na* URU *bi-ri-iš-šá-ru-ú-a a-na* ⅓ MA.NA
5 KÙ.BABBAR UD-*ú nu-uḫ-ḫu-tú ù*! 1 PI *qí-me* KURUM$_{6}$.ḪI.[A-*šú*]
6 [*a-na*] ^{m}*ši-ir*<-*ku*> A-*šú šá* ^{m}MU-*a* {x} A ^{m}*e-gi-bi*
7 [x x x (x)] [GI]Š.MÁ URU *bi-ri-iš-šá-*[*ru-ú-a*]
(Remainder of obverse is broken off.)

REV.

1 [LÚ *mu-kin-nu* ...]
2 [...]
3 ^{m}[x x x x (x)] ^{m}⸢DUB?⸣-NUMUN ⸢A?⸣ LÚ.[ŠITIM?]
4 ^{md}EN-[*a-su*]-*ú-a* A-*šú šá* ^{md}U.GUR-*ú-bal-liṭ*
5 A ^{m}TUM-^{d}IŠKUR ^{m}*šu-lum*-TIN.TIR.KI A-*šú šá* ^{m}*tab-ni-e-a*
6 ^{m}MU-^{d}EN A-*šú šá* ^{m}*kal-ba-a*
7 [(*u*) LÚ.DUB.S]AR ^{md}AG-A-MU A-*šú šá* ^{m}*la-ba-a-ši*
8 [A ^{m}ZALAG$_{2}$-^{d}PAP.SU]KKAL TIN.TIR.KI ITI.KIN UD.7.KAM
9 [MU.x.KAM] ^{m}*da-ri-iá-muš* LUGAL E.KI
10 [(...)] *u*? KUR.KUR

LE. E.

1 [*ul i*]-⸢*te*?⸣-*qu ki*?-⸢*i*?⸣ [...]
2 [1-*en*.TA.À]M {x} *il-qu-*[*ú*]

TRANSLATION

[The] boat belonging to Iddin-Bēl, slave of PN, ⸢which?⸣ is at the disposal of Niqūdu, son of $^{\langle m\rangle}$x-x-*iá*, and Kalbi-Bāba, son of Iddinaya, for <sa>iling: [they have ren]ted (it) out [to] MNA$_{2}$ {x} for one-third minas of white, medium-quality silver and! one *pān* of flour for [(his)] maintenance, (in order to sail) to Birišśarūa. [The] boat shall [not] ⸢pass⸣ Biriššarūa; ⸢if?⸣ [...].

[Witnesses]:
[One or two witnesses]
[^{m}.../]⸢Šāpik?⸣-zēri⸢//Itinnu⸣?
Bēl-[as]ûa/Nergal-uballiṭ//Mudammiq!-Adad
Šulum-Bābili/Tabnêa(//Mudammiq-Adad)
Iddin-Bēl/Kalbaya

[(And) the s]cribe: Nabû-apla-iddin/Lâbāši[//Nūr-Pap]sukkal
(Place + Date).

[Each o]ne has taken {x} (a copy).

COMMENT

The scribe of this text does not seem to have been very skillful, as is evident from lines 2, 5 and 6 on the obverse, and from the text on the left edge. He is known from two other texts, dated in August 496 B.C.E., when he sold a boat to MNA (BM 30370 and BM 30961).

Obverse:

L. 1 end: Should we read ^{m}*ri*$^{!}$*-mu*[*t*]-⌜x x⌝ instead of ^{m}*bar-*⌜*zi*$^{?}$-x-x⌝?

L. 2a: The first sign of this line, ⌜x⌝, does not look like a *šá.*

L. 2b: The scribe forgot to write certain signs: <*ma-*>*laḫ*$_{x}$*-ú-tu* and <^{m}>x-x-*iá.*

L. 2(end): As for the reading of this name at the end of the line: the first sign looks like a SAG, the second like a DI, and the third sign is for sure *-iá.*

L. 3: ^{m}*kal-ba-*^{d}KÁ, the signs are clear, but this would be an unusual writing of the name Kalbi-Bāba, since according to Tallqvist (*NbN*, 87) the name is always written with a BI-sign (^{m}*kal-bi-*^{d}KÁ), never with a BA-sign. Still, it is known that in the Neo-Babylonian dialect final short vowels were not pronounced, so that whether one writes -ba or -bi the pronunciation was the same in either case, viz. simply -b.

L. 5: The scribe wrote UGU instead of *ù*.

L. 6: Again, the scribe made several mistakes: he forgot to write the KU in ^{m}*ši-ir*<*-ku*>, and wrote a superfluous sign after ^{m}MU*-a*, marked {x} in the transliteration above (= either *šá*, *a* or the *Personenkeil*).

L. 7f. and left edge: At the beginning of line 7 I suggest reading [*it-ta-din-nu-u'* (*u*)]. From the second half of the line onward the clause starts that prohibits MNA to sail beyond a certain point. The full version of this prohibition can be reconstructed, on the basis of parallels from, e.g., BM 30490: 10b–17a, as follows: (l. 7:) $^{[giš]}$*eleppu* ^{uru}*Biriššārūa* (left edge?!:) [*ul i*]*tteq* ⌜*kī*$^{?}$⌝ [^{giš}*eleppu* ^{uru}*Biriššārūa itteqe* x *manê kaspu* (...) *Širku ana Niqūdu u Kalbi-Bāba inaddin*]$^{?}$, "The boat shall [not pa]ss Biriššarūa; ⌜if$^{?}$⌝ [the boat passes Biriššārū'a, MNA$_{2}$ shall pay x minas of (white, medium-quality) silver to Niqūdu and Kalba-Bāba]$^{?}$." It is not clear, however, where the scribe continued writing after finishing line 7. The obverse is, unfortunately, broken off after this line. The part that is broken is approximately one-third of the obverse, i.e., up to three lines are missing. It seems that the continuation of line 7 is found on the left edge of the tablet, and not only in the lacuna at the end of the obverse. It is not clear why the scribe wrote part of the formulary on the left edge, whereas he seems to have had space left on the obverse.

Reverse:

L. 4–5: The surname of Bēl-asûa/Nergal-uballiṭ is spelled ^{m}TUM-^{d}IŠKUR, which is, no doubt, to be read Mudammiq$^{!}$-Adad, because Bēl-asûa/Nergal-uballiṭ//Mudammiq-Adad is well known from several texts regarding boats from MNA's archive (TCL 13 196, BM 31347, BM 32873, BM 30541).

L. 5: Šulum-Bābili/Tabnêa also belonged to the Mudammiq-Adad family. He occurs, together with Bēl-asûa, in the list of witnesses of BM 32873 and BM 30541.

Left Edge:

The scribe did something strange on the left edge of the tablet: he wrote two lines, but each line is written in a different direction.

L. 1: The first line is written in the direction as expected on the left edge of a tablet, from left to right when holding the reverse up. It contains part of the clause prohibiting to sail beyond a certain point (for details see commentary above at Obverse line 7).

L. 2: The second line on the left edge is written from left to right when holding the obverse up (cf. BM 30819, and see also the peculiarities of the left edge of BM 32858). It contains the statement about handing out copies of the agreement to the parties involved. This clause is usually found either before the list of witnesses or at the very end of the contract.

No. 63

	BM 31951
Copy:	Bertin copy 2578
Date:	[-]/[-]/25 Dar (497–496 B.C.E.)
Place:	Šaḫrīnu
Content:	Promissory note to pay a debt of silver to MNA.

OBV.

1 [... KÙ.BABBAR (*šá*)] *gìn-nu bab-ba-nu-ú šá* ⸢*na-da-nu*⸣
2 [*u ma-ḫa-ri šá*] ^{md}AMAR.UTU-*na-ṣir*-IBILA
3 [DUMU *šá* ^{m}KI-^{d}AMAR.UTU]-DIN DUMU ^{m}*e-gi-bi*
4 [*ina muḫ-ḫi* ^{m}*ni-q*]*u-du* DUMU *šá* ^{md}U.GUR-MU
5 [A ^{m}ZALAG$_{2}$-*za-na* ...] KI/DI *ina* ITI.ZÍZ KÙ.BABBAR-*a*$_{4}$
6 [... *i*]*-gam-mar-ma iṭ-ṭir*
7 [*ú-ìl-tì* I]GI-*tu*$_{4}$ *e-ṭir-tu*$_{4}$ *ši-i*

REV.

8 [LÚ *mu-kin-nu*] ^{m}MU-^{d}EN DUMU *šá* ^{m}*lu*-È-*ana*-ZALAG$_{2}$
9 [A ^{m}*an-da*]-*ḫar* ^{md}EN-MU DUMU *šá* ^{m}MU-^{d}AG
10 [A ^{m}...]-*bi*$^{?}$ ^{m}*lib-luṭ* DUMU *šá* ^{m}[^{d} AMAR.UTU]-SU
11 [A ^{m}...] ^{m}*ap-la-a* DUMU *šá* ^{m}EN-*šú-nu*
12 [...] [^{m}...]-*tu*$_{4}$ DUMU *šá* ^{m}*bul-ṭa-a*

13 [...] [^{m}...]-*la*
14 [...] [^{m}...]-^{d}AMAR.UTU DUB.SAR DUMU *šá*
15 [^{m}... A] ^{m}DÙ-*eš*-DINGIR URU *šaḫ-ri-in-nu*
16 [...] KAM MU.25.KAM

U. E.

17 [...] [^{m}...]-*muš* LUGAL TIN.TIR.[KI]
18 [...] KUR.KUR

Translation

[...] of marked, excellent quality [silver] ⸢used in the country⸣ [is/are due to] MNA$_1$ [from] [Niq]ūdu, son of Nergal-iddin, [descendant of Nūr-zana ...] KI/DI. In Šabāṭ he will pay the full amount of these [...] of silver. [The p]revious [debt] has (already) been paid.

[Witnesses]:
Iddin-Bēl/Lūṣi-ana-nūri//[Anda]ḫar
Bēl-iddin/Iddin-Nabû[//Dābi]bī
Libluṭ/[Marduk]-erība[//^{m}...]
Aplaya/Bēlšunu[//^{m}...]
[^{m}...]-tu/Bulṭaya[//^{m}...]
[^{m}...]-*la* [...]
The scribe: [^{m}...]-Marduk/[^{m}...//]Eppeš-ilī
(Place + Date).

Comment

L. 1: On the qualities of silver and its purity in the Neo-Babylonian period, see Joannès, "Métaux précieux," 137ff.; Powell, "Money," 222–27; Bongenaar, "Money," 172–74, and Vargyas, "Silver and Money," 514–15, 519 and especially notes 6 (on *kaspu ginnu* "minted coins"), 7–8 and 36.

L. 5: Most likely read Niqūdu/Nergal-iddin[//Nūr-zana]. This person was often present in Šaḫrīnu to witness the agreements reached between MNA and Bēl-iddin/Nabû-zēra-ušabši concerning the latter's debts to MBU, MNA's slave (Dar 308, Dar 430, Dar 452 and Dar 459, dated between Darius' eleventh and seventeenth year; on the meaning of the family name, more at Dar 308: 15). These were debts of barley and silver that Bēl-iddin had accrued in the course of paying for his *rikis qabli* and other obligations to which he was subject as a member of a bow. Later, in Darius' twenty-seventh year he witnessed the promise made by Madānu-iddin, MNA's slave, to Nidintu-Bēl, MNA's son, to deliver dates in Babylon (BM 33549 = b 2633, unpublished; Šaḫrīnu, 14/iii/27 Dar). If we can indeed read Niqūdu/Nergal-iddin//Nūr-zana in the text under consideration, it follows that Niqūdu not only witnessed the promises made by others to MNA's slave to pay their debts, but that he himself owed silver to MNA. Note that the silver that he owed was of the same quality as the silver that his friend Bēl-iddin owed to MNA's slave, viz. *ginnu*-marked silver, usually of excellent quality (*babbanu*) and ready for commercial transactions throughout the country (*ša nadāni u maḫāri*). The cause of Niqūdu's indebtedness to MNA is not known. Some of the men who witnessed Niqūdu's debt, however, also witnessed the debt of Nergal's farmer to MNA (Dar 541, Iddin-Bēl/Lūṣi-ana-nūri//Andaḫar) and MNA's payments for the transport of barley from Tâmti (BM 32891 and BM 31572, Bēl-iddin/Iddin-Nabû//Dābibī). Consequently, there may well have been a connection among Niqūdu, Nergal's farmer, and the cultivation of barley on institutional land in Tāmti that went further than sharing witnesses.

L. 7: One should read either *u'ilti* or *rašūtu* in the break at the beginning of the line.

L. 9–10: Bēl-iddin/Iddin-Nabû//Dābibī is known from BM 31572: 11 and BM 32891: 13.

L. 13: The second part of this line is left blank. Moreover, it is followed by a blank line, and only then follows the line with the scribe's name (i.e., line 14).

No. 64

BM 31976
Copy: Bertin copy 2639
Date: 24/iii/27 Dar (18 June 495 B.C.E.)
Place: Šaḫrīnu
Content: About two heifers. Mentions the slave of MNA, a messenger of the *abarakku*-official (^{lú}*mār a-ba-rak-ku*), and a farmer (^{lú}*ikkaru*) of Nergal. Fragmentary.

OBV.

1 2-TA ⸢GU$_{4}$⸣ *bu-ra-ti šá* ^{md}DI.KU$_{5}$-E[N-URU$_{3}$]
2 LÚ.ÌR *šá* ^{m}*ši-rik* A-*šú šá* ^{m}KI-^{d}AMAR.UTU-[DIN]
3 A ^{m}*e-gi-bi šá* ^{m}MU-^{d}EN LÚ.DUMU *šip-ri šá* LÚ *mar*
4 *a-ba-rak-ku u* ^{m}*ib-na-a* LÚ.ENGAR *šá* ^{d}U.GUR DUMU *šá* $^{m⸢d⸣}$U.[GUR]-[x]-DÙ
5 *a-ki-i* [*ši-pir*]-*tú šá* $^{[m]d}$AG-*bul-liṭ-su* A-*šú šá* [...]-*tu*$_{4}$
(Remainder of obverse is broken off.)

REV.

1′ ^{md}UTU-MU A-*šú šá* $^{md⸢}$AMAR.UTU-EN-*šú-nu*⸣
2′ A ^{md}AG-⸢x⸣-NI ^{md}EN-ŠEŠ-MU A-*šú šá* ^{m}ŠU$^{!}$-^{d}UTU
3′ ^{m}ŠEŠ.MEŠ-*šá-a* A-*šú šá* ^{m}*na-din* A ^{m}DÙ-*eš*-DINGIR ^{md}EN-MU
4′ A-*šú šá* ^{m}*gu-za-nu* A ^{md}IDIM-*ṣal-mi*-DINGIR ^{m}ŠU-^{d}UTU A-*šú šá*
5′ ^{md}AG-MU-GIN A ^{m}*ḫu-zu-ú* ^{m}ÌR-^{d}*ba-ba*$_{6}$ A-*šú šá*
6′ ^{m}ŠU-^{d}UTU LÚ.UMBISAG ^{md}AG-MU A-*šú šá* ^{m}*lu-uṣ*<-*a-na*>-ZALAG$_{2}$ [(-...)$^{?}$]
7′ A LÚ.KÙ.DIM URU *šá-ḫi-ri-ni* ITI.SIG$_{4}$ UD.[24].KAM

8′ MU.27.KAM ^{m}*da-ri-mu-šú* LUGAL E.[KI *u* KUR.KUR]

TRANSLATION

Two ⌜heifers⌝ belonging to Madānu-bē[la-uṣur], a slave of MNA_2, which Iddin-Bēl, the messenger of the *mār-abarakku*-official, and Ibnaya, the farmer of Nergal, son of Ner[gal]-[zēra]-ibni, according to the [letter order] of Nabû-bullissu, son of [...]. (Remainder is broken off).

[Witnesses:]
Šamaš-iddin/⌜Marduk-bēlšunu⌝//Nabû-⌜x⌝-NI
Bēl-aḫa-iddin/Gimil$^{!}$-Šamaš
Aḫḫēšaya/Nādin//Eppeš-ilī
Bēl-iddin/Gūzānu//Ea-ṣalam-ilī
Gimil-Šamaš/Nabû-šuma-ukīn//Ḫu(z)zû
Arad-Bāba/Gimil-Šamaš
The scribe: Nabû-iddin/Lūṣi<-ana>-nūri[(-...)$^{?}$] //Kutimmu
(Place + Date).

COMMENT

L. 1: On the occurrence of Madānu-bēla-uṣur in texts dated after Darius' twentieth year, see more at Dar 509: 3. For *burtu* (also *buštu*) "cow, female (heifer) calf," see also Dar 351 and *CAD* B, 334 s.v. *burtu*.

L. 3–4: The reading of the logogram (LÚ.)AGRIG in the Neo-Babylonian period has been much discussed (whether to be read *mašennu* or *abarakku)*, but, in general, scholars have agreed upon the Neo-Babylonian reading (LÚ.) AGRIG = *mašennu* (Jursa, *Landwirtschaft*, 181 and n. 361). However, the remarkable spelling in our text, ^{lú}*mār* (written syllabically with the *mar*-sign!) *a-ba-rak-ku*, seems to raise the issue again.

L. 4: For Ibnaya/Nergal-zēra-ibni, see Dar 541: 4.

L. 5: The theophoric element may also have been Bēl (^{md}EN) instead of Nabû (^{md}AG). The -tu_4 is written on the reverse.

L. 2′a: The sign before the NI is either $ZALAG_2$ or KAL. Should one read Nabû-$ZALAG_2$-*ni* = Nabû-nūrani "Nabû-is-our-Light"? The name as such is not attested, but names such as Nūriya and Nūranu (wr. ^{m}*nu-ra-nu*) are (Tallqvist, *NbN*, 323 for names with the element *nūru* = $ZALAG_2$). The name *Nabû-nūr-ilī* is attested and spelled ^{md}AG-$ZALAG_2$-DINGIR(.MEŠ) (*ibid.*, 142), but this would require an emendation: ^{md}AG-$ZALAG_2$-DINGIR$^{!}$(NI). For another emendation in this text, which is actually supported by additional evidence, see next remark. It is very unlikely that the sign before NI in the name Nabû-x-NI is to be read *dan*(KAL), because the spelling *-dan-ni* for *dannu* "strong" is otherwise unattested in Neo-Babylonian names (*ibid.*, 313).

L. 2′b: Regarding the name of Bēl-aḫa-iddin's father: ^{m}x-^{d}UTU. The sign before ^{d}UTU resembles BA or GIŠ, but for *Iqīša-Šamaš* we expect ^{m}BA-*šá*-^{d}UTU (cf.

Tallqvist, *NbN*, 79–81), not just ^{m}BA-^{d}UTU; as for the element GIŠ = *līšîr*: it is usually the second or third element in Neo-Babylonian names, or it stands alone and is written syllabically (*ibid.*, 97). Consequently, we more likely have to emend and read ^{m}ŠU$^{!}$-^{d}UTU. A Bēl-aḫḫe-iddin/Gimil-Šamaš is actually attested in Dar 272: 3 (^{md}EN-ŠEŠ.MEŠ-MU A-*šú šá* ^{m}*gi-mil-lu*-^{d}UTU). Moreover, among the witnesses in BM 31976 we find another son of Gimil-Šamaš, viz. in lines Rev. 5′–6 (Arad-Bāba), and a Gimil-Šamaš in lines Rev. 4′–5′. The latter was probably the father of Bēl-aḫa-iddin and Arad-Bāba.

L. 5′: The name ^{m}*ḫu-zu-ú* may be a variant spelling of the name Ḫunzû (^{m}*ḫu-un-zu-ú*, Tallqvist, *NbN*, 68).

No. 65

	BM 31977 (= Dupl. of Dar 472)
Copy:	no Bertin copy
Date:	3/x/18 Dar (30 December 504 B.C.E.)
Place:	Babylon
Content:	Receipt of silver paid on behalf of MNA. Payment of a debt due to Šaddinnu.

OBV.

1 [3⅔ MA].NA 5 GÍN KÙ.BABBAR UD-*ú nu-uḫ-ḫu-tu šá ina* 1 ⸢GÍN⸣ [*bit-qa*]
2 [*šá* ^{m}*šad-din-nu*] A-*šú šá* ^{md}DI.KU$_{5}$-ŠEŠ.MEŠ-MU A ^{m}*ši-gu-ú-a*
3 [*i-n*]*a ra-šu-tu-šú šá ina muḫ-ḫi* ^{md}AMAR.UTU-*na-ṣir*-A
4 [A-*šú* šá ^{m}]⸢KI⸣-^{d}AMAR.UTU-[DIN A] ^{m}*e-gì-bi* ⸢*ina* ŠU.II⸣ ^{m}*ni-din-tu*$_{4}$
5 [A-*šú šá* ^{m}]IDIM-*i*[*á* A ^{m}*ir*]-*a-ni a*-⸢*na*⸣ *muḫ-ḫi* [^{md}AMAR.UTU]-⸢*na*⸣-*ṣir*-A
6 ^{m}*šad-din-nu ina* [ŠU]⸢.II⸣ ^{m}⸢*ni-din-tu*$_{4}$ *ma-ḫi*⸣-*ir*
7 1-*en-na*.TA.ÀM *šá-ṭa-r*[*i*] ⸢TI⸣-*ú*
8 LÚ *mu-kin-nu* ^{m}KI-^{d}AG-DIN A-*šú šá* ^{md}AG-NUMUN-BA-*šá*
9 ^{md}EN-DÙ$^{!}$-*iá* A-*šú šá* ^{m}GAR-MU [A] ^{m}*ir-a-ni*
10 [^{m}K]AR-^{d}EN A-*šú šá* ^{md}UTU-ŠEŠ-MU A LÚ.PA<.ŠE.KI>

REV.

11 [^{m}.... A-*š*]*ú šá* ^{m}MU-GIN A ^{md}EN-A-URU$_{3}$
12 [^{m}... A-*šú šá* ^{m}(...-)]EN-*šú-nu* A ^{md}30-KUR-*ú-nu*
13 [^{m}...]⸢-*nu* A-*šú šá*⸣ ^{m}*si-lim*-^{d}EN A ^{md}30-KUR-*nu*
14 $^{[m]}$*la-ba-ši* A-*šú šá* ^{md}AG-DA A ^{m}*da-bi-bi*
15 ^{md}AG-*it-tan-nu* A-*šú šá* ^{md}UTU-NUNUZ-URU$_{3}$ A LÚ.SIMUG
16 ^{md}AG-*bul-liṭ-s*[*u* A]-*šú šá* ^{m}*ni-din-tu*$_{4}$ A LÚ *ka-ník*-KÁ
17 ^{m}*šul-lu-mu* A-*šú šá* ^{m}DUB-NUMUN A ^{m}ZALAG$_{2}$-^{d}ŠÚ
18 ^{md}EN-GI A-*šú šá* ^{md}EN-MU A ^{m}ÌR-^{d}IDIM
19 ^{md}AMAR.UTU-DIN-*su*-E A-*šú šá* ^{m}*i-qu-pu* A ^{m}*e-tel-pi*
20 ^{m}DÙ-NUMUN A-*šú šá* ^{m}DUB-NUMUN A ^{m}LÚ.SANGA-^{d}30
21 [LÚ.UMBISAG] ^{m}KI-⸢^{d}AG⸣-DIN A-*šú šá* ^{md}AMAR.UTU-*re-man-ni* TIN.TIR.KI

Lo. E.

22 ITI.AB UD.3.KAM MU.18.KAM ^{m}*da-ri-ia-m*[*uš*]

23 LUGAL E.KI *u* KUR.KUR.MEŠ

Translation

(For a translation of lines 1–7, see at Dar 472).
Witnesses:
Itti-Nabû-balāṭu/Nabû-zēra-iqīša
Bēl-baniya/Šākin-šumi[//]Ir'anni
[M]ušēzib-Bēl/Šamaš-aḫa-iddin//^{m}Amēl-I<sin>
[^{m}...]/Šuma-ukīn//Bēl-apla-uṣur
[^{m}... /(...-)]Bēlšunu//Sîn-šadûnu
[^{m}...]*nu*/Silim-Bēl//Sîn-šadûnu
Lābâši/Nabû-ile''i//Dābibī
Nabû-ittannu/Šamaš-pir'a-uṣur//Nappāḫu
Nabû-bullissu/Nidintu//Kānik-bābi
Šullumu/Šāpik-zēri//Nūr-Marduk
Bēl-ušallim/Bēl-iddin//Arad-Ea
Marduk-balāssu-iqbi/Iqūpu//Etel-pî
Bāni-zēri//Šāpik-zēri//Šangû-Sîn
[The scribe]: Itti-⸢Nabû⸣-balāṭu/Marduk-rēmanni
(Place + Date).

Comment

L. 5: The end of *-ṣir-* and the -A are written on the right edge.

L. 6–7: The end of line 6 remained uninscribed; in the following line the scribe stretched the TI-*ú* in order to fill up the line till its end.

L. 9: Read ^{md}EN-DÙ$^{!}$(AŠ)-*iá* = Bēl-baniya.

L. 14, 17–18, 20: Occasionally, the scribe left more space blank between words than usual, as may be seen in the following instances: ^{md}AG-DA (blank) A, ^{m}DUB-NUMUN (blank) A, ^{md}EN-MU (blank) A, and [^{m}DÙ-NUMU]N (blank) A-*šú ša*.

L. 21: The .KI is on the right edge.

No. 66

BM 32858
Copy: Bertin copy 2700
Date: 13/vii/31 Dar (19 October 491 B.C.E.)
Place: Babylon
Content: Receipt of silver by MNA. Partial repayment of a debt.

OBV.

1 *ina ú-ìl-tì šá* 50 GÍN KÙ.BABBAR UD-*ú*
2 *šá ina* 1 GÍN *bit-qa šá* ^{md}AMAR.UTU-PAB-ED[URU]
3 DUMU *šá* ^{m}SUM.NA-*a* DUMU ^{m}*e-gi-bi*
4 *šá ina muḫ-ḫi* ^{md}AG-ḪI.LI-DINGIR.MEŠ
5 DUMU *šá* ^{md}EN-*re-man-ni* DUMU ^{m}DÙ-*eš*-DINGIR
6 *ina lìb-bi* ½ MA.NA KÙ.BABBAR UD-*ú*
7 ^{md}AMAR.UTU-PAB-EDURU *ina* ŠU.II
8 ^{md}AG-ḪI.LI-DINGIR.MEŠ *ma-ḫi-ir*
9 1-*en*.TA.ÀM TI-*ú*

REV.

10 *ina ma-ḫar* ^{m}*ḫa-ba-ṣi-ru* DI.KU$_5$
11 (erasure) DUMU ^{m}DÙ-*eš*-DINGIR (erasure)
12 ^{m}MU-^{d}EN DUMU *šá* ^{m}*zu-um-ba-a* A ^{m}DÙ-*eš*-DINGIR
13 ^{md}AG-*ku-ṣur-šú* DUMU *šá* ^{m}*mu-ra-šú-ú* DUMU ^{m}*pap-pa-a-a*
14 ^{md}EN-DIN-*iṭ* DUB.SAR A ^{md}EN-*e*$^{?}$-*ṭè-ru*
15 TIN.TIR.KI ITI.DU$_6$ UD.13.KAM
16 MU.31.KAM ^{m}*da-a-ri-iá-muš*
17 LUGAL TIN.TIR.KI LUGAL KUR.KUR

U. E.

18 ^{m}*bul-ṭa-a* DUMU *šá* ^{m}*ḫa-ba-ṣi-*[*ru*]
19 DUMU ^{m}ÌR-^{d}GIR$_4$-KÙ

LE. E.

20 NA$_4$.KIŠIB / ^{m}*ḫa-ba-ṣi-ru* / LÚ.DI.KU$_5$ / (seal impression)

TRANSLATION

From the debt of fifty shekels of white silver, of which one-eighth is alloy, which is due to MNA$_1$ from Nabû-kuzub-ilī, son of Bēl-rēmanni, descendant of Eppeš-ilī, MNA$_1$ has received half a mina of white silver from Nabû-kuzub-ilī. They have taken one (copy of the document) each.

Under the auspices of Ḫabaṣīru//Eppeš-ilī, the judge
Iddin-Bēl/Zumbaya//Eppeš-ilī
Nabû-kuṣuršu/Murašû//Pappaya
The scribe: Bēl-uballiṭ//Bēl-eṭēru
(Place + Date).
Bulṭaya/Ḫabaṣīru//Arad-Nergal

Seal of Ḫabaṣīru, the judge.

Comment

L. 10: On the formula *ina maḫar,* which introduces the witnesses in this document, see Von Dassow, *Fs. Levine,* 3–22. She notes that it "is preferred for introducing the witnesses to certain types of documents, particularly documents of transactions whose effects are more profound or durable" (p. 18). The use of *ina maḫar* to introduce the witnesses instead of the common *mukinnū* "may reflect the greater weight assigned to the transactions concerned (alienation of real property and alteration of family relationships" (p. 12). Further note Wunsch, *AOAT* 252, 557–98.

L. 11: The line begins with two erased signs, and after the DINGIR there are another three or four erased signs.

L. 13: The family name is written on the right edge of the tablet.

L. 14: The *-ru* is written on the edge of the next line.

L. 20: The text on the left edge is written along the width (and not as usual along the length) of the tablet and hence runs parallel to the text on the reverse. Cf. the peculiarities of the left edge of BM 30819 and BM 31891.

The tablet is sealed. The stamp seal has a figure standing in prayer before a goat-fish and looking to the right. There are some cuneiform signs (probably to be read ^{d}KASKAL.KURxKASKAL.KUR). The tablet has the shape typical of tablets from the Seleucid period.

No. 67

BM 32873
Copy: Bertin copy 2610
Date: 16/xii/26 Dar (13 March 495 B.C.E.)
Place: Babylon
Content: About boats (Exchange$^{?}$ of boats). MNA is the scribe.

Obv.

1 [G]IŠ.MÁ *šá* 6 KÙŠ *ina* UGU *šá-bur-ri rap-šú*
2 *ṭu-bu-ú šá* ⸢*ina*$^{?}$ UGU⸣ *na-bal-kat-tu*$_4$
3 *u* GIŠ.MÁ *šá* 6½ <KÙŠ> *ina* UGU *šá-bur-ri rap-šú*
4 *šá ina giš-ri šá* 1-*et* GIŠ.MÁ *šá* 5 KÙŠ *ina* UGU
5 *šá-bur-ru rap-šú šá* ^{m}*ka-ṣir* DUMU *šá* ^{m}*ip-ri-ia*
6 DUMU ^{md}ŠÚ-AD-*šú* KI *a-*⸢*ḫa*⸣*-meš uš-pi-e*<*-lu*>
7 ^{md}EN-NIGIN-*ir* DUMU *šá* ^{md}KÁ-KAM DUMU ^{m}*mu*-SIG$_5^{?}$-^{d}IŠKUR
8 *pu-ut uš-ku-ú* GIŠ.MÁ *ṭu-ub-bu-ú*
9 *ù* GIŠ.MÁ *šá giš-ri na-ši*

Rev.

10 LÚ *mu-kin-nu* ^{m}*šu-lum*-TIN.TIR.KI DUMU *šá* ^{m}ÌR-^{d}EN

11 DUMU ^{m}DIL-SUR ^{m}*ni-din-tu*$_{4}$ DUMU *šá* ^{md}EN-KÁD DUMU LÚ.ŠITIM
12 ^{md}EN-*a-su-ú-a* DUMU *šá* ^{md}U.GUR-DIN-*iṭ*
13 DUMU ^{m}*mu*-SIG$_{5}$-^{d}IŠKUR ^{m}*šu-lum*-TIN.TIR.KI DUMU *šá*
14 ^{m}*tab-ni-e-a* DUMU ^{m}*mu*-SIG$_{5}^{?}$-^{d}IŠKUR
15 ^{m}BA-*šá-a* DUMU *šá* ^{m}*na-din* DUMU ^{m}*ir-a-ni*
16 ^{m}*ši-ir-ku* DUB.SAR DUMU *šá* ^{m}SUM.NA-*a* DUMU ^{m}*e-gì-bi*
17 TIN.TIR.KI ITI.⸢ŠE⸣ UD.16.KAM MU.26.KAM
18 ^{m}*da-ri-'i-ia-muš* LUGAL TIN.TIR.KI
19 LUGAL KUR.KUR

Translation

[A] boat with a width of six cubits at its beam, which has *run aground*$^{?}$ at the bank, and a boat with a width of six and a half <cubits> at its beam, which is part of a (pontoon-) bridge, - *which/of* -, one boat with a width of five cubits at its beam, which belongs to Kāṣir, son of Ipriya, descendant of Marduk-abušu: with each other <they> have exchang<ed>. Bēl-upaḫḫir, son of Bāba-ēreš, descendant of Mudammiq-Adad, assumes warranty for the *uškûtu* of the *run aground*$^{?}$ boat and the boat of the (pontoon)-bridge.

Witnesses:
Šulum-Bābili/Arad-Bēl//Eda-ēṭir
Nidintu/Bēl-kāṣir//Itinnu
Bēl-asûa/Nergal-uballiṭ//Mudammiq-Adad
Šulum-Bābili/Tabnêa//Mudammiq-Adad
Iqīšaya/Nādin//Ir'anni
The scribe: MNA$_{2}$
(Place + Date)

Comment

The text probably records an exchange of boats between Bēl-upaḫḫir/Bāba-ēreš//Mudammiq-Adad and Kāṣir/Ipriya//Marduk-abušu.

L. 2 and 8: The first boat mentioned in this text was six cubits wide at its beam and is further qualified by the term *ṭubbû* (Lines 1–2: GIŠ.MÁ … *ṭu-bu-ú*, and line 8: GIŠ.MÁ *ṭu-ub-bu-ú*). This form is a D verbal adjective, masc., of the verb *ṭebû*, which in the D-stem means "to submerge, to let sink" (*AHw*, 1383 s.v. *ṭebû* D mng. 1). The verb *ṭebû* is well attested as a nautical term, and the expression *eleppu ṭebī/ūtu*, in particular, refers either to a sinking/sunken boat or to a (loaded) boat with a deep draught draft (*AHw*, 1383 s.v. *ṭēbû*; Salonen, *Nautica*, 98–100 s.v. *ṭb'*; and Id., *Wasserfahrzeuge*, 48–49 s.v. *eleppu ṭebītu/ṭebūtu*; also Römer, *AOAT* 232, 369–70 s.v. § B.III.5.j). In the annals of Sennacherib, for instance, the verb *ṭubbû* refers to the practice of running boats aground for docking at the mooring place (*OIP* 2 118: 11, cited by *CAD* K, 233 s.v. *kāru* A mng. 1c–1' and *CAD* N$_{1}$, 146 s.v. *nēberu* mng. 1-a). Is the expression *eleppu ṭu(-ub)-bu-ú* (D-stem and masc.) a variant of the expression *eleppu ṭebī/ūtu* (G-stem and fem.)? And if so, does it refer to a submerged/sunken boat, one that is loaded with a deep draught draft, or one run aground at the docking place?

L. 2: The noun *nabalkattu* is derived from the verb *nabalkutu* "to cross" and may refer to the device that is used to cross obstacles (mng. 2 in *CAD* N_1, 9 s.v. *nabalkattu* and *AHw*, 694 s.v. *nabalkattum*). Accordingly, it may have the meaning "ladder; ramp," especially when it is used to cross walls or to facilitate the entrance at the city gates (cf. Joannès, *Borsippa*, 130 "rampe d'accès aux portes de la ville"). In the present context of crossing canals by boat, *nabalkattu* probably refers to a bank or ramp along the canal where ships could moor, and such a ramp may have functioned as a kind of landing stage.

L. 4a: The second boat mentioned in this text was part of a pontoon-bridge. For the expression *ša ina gišri*, see more at BM 30961: 10.

L. 4: The second *šá* in this line is problematic: either the scribe forgot to write something (e.g., *ša Bēl-upaḫḫir*, see more below), or the *šá* is a mistake for *u* ("and") or KI (= *itti* "with"). In the preceding lines two boats were introduced, one probably run aground and the other one part of a pontoon-bridge. It is not said whose boats these are, but according to lines 7–8 a man named Bēl-upaḫḫir assumed warranty for the *uškûtu* of these boats. In the second part of line 4 a third boat is introduced, which is said to belong to a man named Kāṣir (ll. 5–6). At the end of line 6 we find the formula typical of exchange documents: "they have exchanged with each other." One wonders who exchanged boats with Kāṣir. It therefore seems that after the second *šá* in line 4 the scribe forgot to write the name of the person who owned the previously described boats and exchanged these boats with the boat belonging to Kāṣir. This person was most likely Bēl-upaḫḫir, who is mentioned in line 7 as the one who assumed warranty for the *uškûtu* of the run aground boat and the pontoon boat. Hence, I suggest reading in line 4 *ša ina gišri ša* <*Bēl-upaḫḫir*>.

L. 6: This line contains the technical term for the exchange: *itti aḫameš ušpellū* (*CAD* $Š_3$, 321 s.v. *šupêlu* mng. 1a-3′, with examples from the Neo-Babylonian period for the exchange of houses, fields and servants; and cf. *ibid.*, 319f. s.v. *šupêltu*, with examples of the exchange of commodities such as barley, dates, and sheep; cf. San Nicolò-Ungnad, *NRV*, 144ff.). The omission of the *-lu-* at the end of the verb is not unusual, cf. the omission of /l/ in some of the spellings of the noun *šupêltu* quoted by *CAD* $Š_3$, 320 s.v. *šupêltu* mng. c): *šu-pe-e-tu*$_4$ *ša uṭṭāti* and *ṭuppi šu-pi-tu*$_4$. The scribe may have forgotten to write the *-lu* because he had reached the end of the tablet. He should have continued writing on the right edge. Was he copying from a tablet where the *-lu* was written on the edge and did he not pay attention to it?

L. 7: It seems that the SIG$_5$ is written over something else (*-dam-iq*?). The DINGIR-sign that follows is badly written, viz. with the horizontal wedge close to the head of the vertical one.

L. 8–9: This kind of guarantee, being one-sided and for the *uškûtu*, is typical of sales (see more at BM 30370: 7–8); in exchange documents, on the other hand, both sides assume warranty for the exchanged objects (San Nicolò-Ungnad, *NRV*, 144).

L. 11: On the reading ^{m}DIL-SUR = Ēda-ēṭir, see Zadok, *NABU* 1997/11 at lines 22, 31; differently, Kessler, *AUWE* 8/1, 99 n. 100.

No. 68

	BM 32883
Copy:	Bertin copy 2175
Date:	10/i/10 Dar (14 April 512 B.C.E.)
Place:	Babylon
Content:	Sale of a boat. MNA assumes warranty on behalf of the seller.

OBV.

1 GIŠ.MÁ *eš-šú ku-ut-tu-mu šá* 7 *ina* [UGU-*šú*]
2 *šá-bu-ru rap-šú šá* ^{md}AG-*ze-er-ib-ni*
3 A-*šú šá* ^{m}KI-^{d}AG-*ba-la-ṭu* A ^{m}*e-gì-bi*
4 *a-na* 8 MA.NA KÙ.BABBAR UD-*ú nu-uḫ-*[*ḫu-tú*]
5 *šá ina* 1 GÍN *bit-qa a-na* ^{md}AMAR.UTU-NÍG.[BA-*an-ni*]
6 DUMU *šá* ^{md}AMAR.UTU-MU-*ú-ṣur* A ^{m}[x x x *i*]*d-din*
7 *pu-ut uš-ku-ú-tu šá* GIŠ.[MÁ ^{md}AMAR.UTU]-⸢*na*⸣-*ṣir*-IBILA
8 A-*šú šá* ^{m}KI-^{d}AMAR.UTU-*ba-la-ṭu* A ^{m}[*e-gì-bi na-š*]*i*
(Remainder of obverse is blank.)

REV.

9 LÚ *mu-kin-nu* ^{md}EN-SUM.NA A-*šú šá* ^{m}*la-a-ba-ši*
10 A ^{m}*ba-bu-tu* ^{m}*kal-ba-a* DUMU-*šú šá* ^{md}AG-ŠEŠ.MEŠ-MU
11 A ^{m}*e-gì-bi* ^{md}EN-DÙ-*uš* DUMU<-*šú*> *šá* ^{md}AG-NUMUN-*li-šìr*
12 A ^{md}*é-a*-DÙ-*eš*-DINGIR ^{md}AG-ŠEŠ.MEŠ-*bul-liṭ*
13 A-*šú šá* ^{m}KI-^{d}AMAR.UTU-*ba-la-ṭu* A ^{m}*e-gi-bi*
14 ^{m}*mu-ra-šu-ú* DUMU-*šú šá* ^{m}*uš-šá-a-a*
15 A ^{md}*na-na-a*-Ú.TU ^{m}SUM.NA-^{d}AG A-*šú šá*
16 ^{m}EN-*šú-nu* A LÚ.BAḪAR$_2$ ^{m}*ar-di-ia* DUMU-*šú šá*
17 ^{m}*da-di-ia* A ^{m}*na-ba-a-a*
18 ^{md}AMAR.UTU-MU-SUM.NA LÚ.UMBISAG DUMU-*šú šá* ^{md}AMAR.UTU-NUMUN-DÙ A ^{m}*e-gì-bi*
19 TIN.TIR.KI ITI.BÁR UD.10.KAM MU.10.KAM
20 ^{m}*da-ri-ia-a-muš* LUGAL TIN.TIR.KI *ù* KUR.KUR

TRANSLATION

A new, covered boat, which is seven (cubits) wide [at its] beam, belonging to Nabû-zēra-ibni, son of Itti-Nabû-balāṭu, descendant of Egibi: he has sold (it) to Marduk-[iqīšanni], son of Marduk-šuma-uṣur, descendant of […], for eight minas of white, medium-quality silver, of which one-eighth is alloy. For the *uškûtu* of the bo[at] MNA_1 [assumes warran]ty.

Witnesses:
Bēl-iddin/Lâbāši//Bābūtu
Kalbaya/Nabû-aḫḫē-iddin//Egibi
Bēl-īpuš/Nabû-zēru-līšir//Ea-eppeš-ilī
Nabû-aḫḫē-bulliṭ/Itti-Marduk-balāṭu//Egibi
Murašû/Uššaya//Nanna-utu
Iddin-Nabû/Bēlšunu//Paḫāru
Ardiya/Dādiya//Nabaya
The scribe: Marduk-šuma-iddin/Marduk-zēra-ibni//Egibi
(Place + Date).

COMMENT

L. 7: For the clause *pūt uškûtu … naši*, see more at BM 30370: 7–8. In our text, however, it was not the seller who assumed warranty, but one of his distant relatives, viz. MNA. The latter was loosely related to the seller through marriage. Indeed, the seller's sister, ᶠŠūqā'ītu/Itti-Nabû-balāṭu//Egibi, was married to Nergal-ēṭir/Itti-Marduk-balāṭu//Egibi, MNA's uncle (Wunsch, *AfO* 42/43, n. 16).

L. 14–15: Tallqvist distinguishes between Murašû/Uššaya (*NbN*, 113 s.v. Murašû(13)) and Murašû/Nabû-aḫḫē-iddin//Nanna-utu (wr. ᵐᵈŠEŠ.KI-Ú/Ù.TU; *ibid.*, s.v. Murašû(8)). These two persons witnessed several documents regarding MNA's agricultural land (cf. Wunsch, *Felder* 2, 312 s.v. Murašû; also in E.36.1904 = MacGinnis, *Iraq* 55 No. 1). However, the occurrence of a Murašû/Uššaya//Nanna-utu in the text under consideration raises the possibility that there was only one Murašû, whose father was called Nabû-aḫḫē-iddin or, alternatively, Uššaya. Moreover, Murašû's family name, Nanna-utu, is also attested under the variant form Arad-Nanna. Indeed, in Dar 268: 10–11 we find among the witnesses ᵐ*mu-ra-šu-ú* A-*šú šá* ᵐᵈAG-ŠEŠ.MEŠ-MU A ᵐ⌜ÌR-ᵈ*na*⌝*-[*na-a*]. Similarly, in the list of witnesses of the unpublished text BM 33931 (Babylon, 13/v/13 Dar; a promissory note with MNA as the debtor), line 15 reads: ᵐ*mu-ra-šu-ú* A-*šú šá* ᵐᵈAG-⌜ŠEŠ-MU⌝ A ᵐÌR-ᵈŠEŠ.KI. In short, Murašû was the son of Nabû-aḫḫē-iddin (*alias* Uššaya), from the Nanna-utu (*alias* Arad-Nanna) family, and is attested in the texts cited by Tallqvist, Wunsch, and MacGinnis (see above), as well as in BM 32883, Dar 268, and BM 33931.

L. 17: This is a short line. After this line follows one empty line before the scribe started writing his name in line 18, cf. BM 30366: 12, BM 30819: 14, BM 31036: 12, BM 31227: 13, BM 31793: 17, BM 41442: 15, e.a.; probably also BM 30270: 16–17; cf. also BM 31118: 13.

No. 69

BM 32891
Copy: Bertin copy 2806
Date: 11/iv/[-] Dar (June - July)
Place: Babylon
Content: Receipt of barley from MNA by a royal official. Transport costs. By order of (*ina qibi ša*) the governor of Babylon.

OBV.

1 [... ŠE].[BAR] *gi-mir*
2 [(*šá*)...] ŠE.BAR [(*šá*) G]IŠ.BÁN *šá* ^{md}EN-*it-ta*[*n*]-*nu*
3 [*u* ^{m}]*šu*-⸢*ma*$^{?}$-*a*$^{?}$⸣ LÚ.⸢NAM⸣.MEŠ *šá* GARIM *tam-tì*
4 ^{m}*ba-az-ba-ka* [LÚ *s*]*i-pi-ri*
5 *šá um-ma-nu u* LÚ.[x x] LÚ *ia-ma*-⸢*na*⸣-*a-a*
6 *ina qí-bi šá* ^{m}*gu*-⸢*za*⸣-[*nu*] ⸢LÚ⸣.GAR-UŠ$_4$ TIN.TIR.KI
7 *ina* ŠU.II ^{m}*ši-iš-ku* DU[MU *šá*] ^{m}SUM.NA-*a*
8 DUMU ^{m}*e-gi*-[*bi ma*]-*ḫi-ir*

REV.

9 LÚ *mu-kin-nu* ^{m}*šá*-^{d}EN-*at-ta*
10 DUMU *šá* ^{md}AMAR.UTU-MU-DÙ A ^{m}*e-gì-bi*
11 ^{m}*tat-tan-nu* DUMU *šá* ^{md}AG-KÁD DUMU ^{m}*da-bi-bi*
12 ^{m}*šul-lu-ma-a* DUMU *šá* ^{md}AG-*na-din*-ŠEŠ (erasure of one sign)
13 DUMU ^{m}*na-ba-a-a* ^{md}EN-MU DUMU *šá*
14 $^{[m]}$MU-^{d}AG DUMU ^{m}*da-bi-bi*
15 $^{[m]}$[MU]-^{d}AG LÚ *ia-ma-na-a-a*
16 [^{m}...-S]U LÚ.UMBISAG DUMU *šá* ^{m}*kal-ba-a*
17 [A ^{m}...] [TIN.TIR].KI ITI.ŠU UD.11.KAM
18 [MU.x.KAM ^{m}*da*]-*a-ri-ia-muš*
19 [LUGAL TIN.TIR.K]I LUGAL KUR.KUR

TRANSLATION

[... bar]ley, the costs for the transport of [...] barley [(from) the fi]xed rent that is due to Bēl-itta[n]nu [and] Šu⸢maya$^{?}$⸣, ⸢district governors⸣, from irrigated farmland in Tâmti: Bazbaka, [c]lerk of the specialized craftsmen$^{?}$ and ^{lú}[x x] of the Ionians, has [re]ceived (it) by order of Gūzā[nu], governor of Babylon, from MNA$_2$.

Witnesses:
Ša-Bēl-atta/Marduk-šuma-ibni//Egibi
Tattannu/Nabû-kāṣir//Dābibī
Šullumaya/Nabû-nādin-aḫi//Nabaya
Bēl-iddin/Iddin-Nabû//Dābibī
[Iddin]-Nabû, the Ionian
The scribe: [Bēl-erī]ba/Kalbaya[//Šumu-libši]

(Place + Date).

Comment

L. 2: For the interpretation of *šá* "due to" in the phrase GIŠ.BÁN *ša Bēl-ittannu*, see discussion at BM 31572: 2.

L. 3: On Tâmti and the transport of agricultural produce from this place, see more at BM 31572: 2–3.

L. 4–5: Bazbaka's first title was "clerk of the specialized craftsmen?" (lú*sepīru ša ummânī*). Or should we read "clerk of the troops" (lú*sepīru ša ummāni*)? The title is otherwise unattested, but it may be compared to the title "chief of the specialized craftsmen?" (lú*rab ummânī*), which is attested in a few texts from Sippar (Bongenaar, *Ebabbar*, 139). Such chiefs were probably state officials employed by the Ebabbar, but the evidence is too scarce to know more about their function (Bongenaar, *ibid.*, 128). In addition, the two titles mentioned above may be variants of the titles lú*rab ummi* and lú*sepīru ša ummi*. If so, they had probably nothing to do with "specialized craftsmen" (*ummânī*), but rather with "troops" (*ummāni*), in general, or "bowmen" (*ummu* in the title *rab ummi* is connected with *ummu* "quiver, bow case"), in particular. If so, it was a military title. For the latter suggestions and the evidence from Sippar and the Murašû archive to support it, see Jursa, *Tempelzehnt*, 68 and n. 240 ("troops"); MacGinnis, *WZKM* 88, 180f.; and Stolper, *JCS* 53, 106f. ("bowmen"). It appears from this evidence that the *rab ummi* equipped temple personnel for (military) service (*rikis qabli*), and that he and his staff (lú*šaknu ša* lú*sepīrī*meš *ša bīt* lú*rab ummi*) managed bow lands, which they leased to the Murašû firm. The lú*sepīru ša ummi* paid tithes to the Ebabbar temple, together with other royal officials, such as the lú(*bēl*) *pīḫāti*, "district governor" (*ibid.*, 67–68). Stolper (p. 107) points out that all holders of the title *rab ummi* "have Babylonian names and none has Iranian names," which may indicate "that the status was provincial, not imperial." Bazbaka, the clerk of the *um-ma-nu* in the text under consideration, however, does not seem to be a Babylonian name. It is a unique name and its meaning and origin are, unfortunately, unknown. Dr. Tavernier suggested to me an Iranian etymology: *Bāzubaga-, "god's arm." For the Babylonian rendering of Iranian -g- with -k-, see the evidence adduced by Hinz, *Altiranisches Sprachgut der Nebenüberlieferungen*, 58. Bazbaka's second title was probably "clerk of the Ionians." Since there is space for no more than one or two signs, I suggest reading LÚ [*si-pir*] (cf. BM 30980: 2), rather than LÚ [*si-pir/pi-ri*]. Alternatively, Bazbaka was a "foreman of the Ionians," in which case LÚ.[GAR (*šá*)] is to be restored.

No. 70

	BM 32932
Copy:	Bertin copy 2541
Date:	18/vii/24 Dar (11 October 498 B.C.E.)
Place:	Babylon
Content:	Receipt of a boat-tower by MNA. From the governor's pool of (forced) laborers (^{lú}*šādadu*).

OBV.

1 ⸢1-*en* LÚ *šá-di-di šá kar*⸣-*ri šá* ŠU.II
2 *šá* ^{m}*ina-é-sag-íl-lil-bir*
3 LÚ.GAR-UŠ$_4$ TIN.TIR.KI {TIN.TIR.KI}
4 *šá* 2 ITI.MEŠ *ù* 12 *u*$_4$-*mu*
5 *a-na ma-la* ḪA.LA *šá* ^{m}*ḫa-ba-ṣi-ru*
6 A-*šú šá* ^{m}KAR-^{d}AMAR.UTU A ^{m}*de-ki-i*
7 *šiš-ki* A-*šú šá* ^{m}SUM.NA-*a* A ^{m}*e-gì-bi*

LO. E.

8 *ina* ŠU.II ^{md}EN-MU A-*šú šá* ^{m}MU-MU

REV.

9 A ^{m}*an-da-ḫar a-na muḫ-ḫi*
10 ^{m}*ḫa-ba-ṣi-ru ma-ḫi-ir*
11 LÚ *mu-kin-nu* ^{m}*mu-še-zib*-^{d}EN A-*šú šá*
12 ^{md}EN-ŠEŠ.MEŠ-SU A ^{m}DA-^{d}AMAR.UTU
13 ^{m}*šul-lu-ma-a* A-*šú šá* ^{md}EN-ŠEŠ.MEŠ-MU A ^{m}*e-gì-bi*
14 ^{md}EN-*it-tan-nu* A-*šú šá* ^{m}ÌR-*ia* A LÚ *ku-tim-mu*
15 ^{m}*ú-ba-na-na* A-*šú šá* ^{md}AG-NUMUN-MU
16 ^{md}EN-*it-tan-nu* DUB.SAR A-*šú šá* ^{m}MU-GIN

U. E.

17 TIN.TIR.KI ITI.DU$_6$ UD.18.KAM
18 MU.24.KAM ^{m}*da-ri-ia-muš* LUGAL

LE. E.

19 1-*en*.TA.ÀM TI-*ú*
20 [^{m}x]-⸢x⸣-*nu* A-*šú šá* ^{md}AG-KAR-ZI.MEŠ [(...)]

TRANSLATION

⸢One man to tow (boats) to the quay⸣ during two months and twelve days, who is under the administrative authority of Ina-Esagil-lilbur, governor of Babylon {Babylon}, in so much as it is the share due from Ḫabaṣīru, son of Mušēzib-Marduk, descendant of Dēkû: MNA$_2$ has received (him) from Bēl-iddin, son of Šuma-iddin, descendant of Andaḫar, for the account of Ḫabaṣīru.

Witnesses:
Mušēzib-Bēl/Bēl-aḫḫē-erība//Ile''i-Marduk
Šullumaya/Bēl-aḫḫē-iddin//Egibi

Bēl-ittannu/Ardiya//Kutimmu
Ubānāna/Nabû-zēra-iddin
The scribe: Bēl-ittannu/Šuma-ukīn
(Place + Date).

They have taken one (copy of the document) each.
[^{m}x]-⸢x⸣-*nu*/Nabû-ēṭir-napšāti [(...)].

COMMENT

L. 3: The second TIN.TIR.KI is written a little bit lower than the preceding signs in the same line.

L. 13: The signs ^{m}*e-gì-bi* are very much squeezed on the tablet. This person is probably to be identified with Šullumu/Bēl-[aḫḫē-iddin]//Egibi known from Dar 514: 13–14 (^{m}*šul-lu-mu* A-*šú šá* ^{md}EN-[...] A ^{m}*e-gì-bi*).

L. 15: The name ^{m}*ú-ba-na-na* is unique. Dr. Tavernier suggested to me understanding it as Iranian in origin (< Ir. *(H)ubānāna-, an *āna*-patronymy reflecting the name *(H)ubānu-, "the good light/ray of light").

No. 71

BM 33112
Copy: Bertin copy 2587
Date: 17/v/25 Dar (30 August 497 B.C.E.)
Place: Babylon
Content: Receipt of barley from MNA by a (royal) official. Transport costs. By order of (*ina qibi ša*) the governor of Babylon.

OBV.

1 20 GUR ŠE.BAR *gi-mir šá* 2 ME ŠE.BAR *šá*
2 NÍG.GA GIŠ *su-ú-tu šá* ^{m}SUM.NA-^{d}EN
3 [*ù*] ^{m}*ta-an-da i-na qí-bi šá* ^{m}*gu-za-nu*
4 [LÚ.GAR-U]Š$_{4}$ TIN.TIR.KI ^{m}*ma-mu-ú-zu* A-*šú šá*
5 [^{m}DU$_{10}$].GA-*ia* LÚ *si-pi-ri šá qí-me-e-*⸢*tu*$_{4}$⸣
6 [*i-n*]*a qá-at* ^{m}*ši-iš-ku* DUMU *šá* ^{m}SUM.NA-*a*
7 [A ^{m}*e*]-*gi-bi ma-ḫi-ir*

REV.

8 [LÚ *mu-kin-nu* ^{m}*m*]*i-nu-ú-a-na-*^{d}EN-*da-a-nu*
9 [A-*šú šá* ^{m}... DU]MU ^{m}MU-*líb-ši*
10 [^{m}...] A-*šú šá* ^{m}*ki-ne-na-a-a*
11 [A ^{m}... ^{m}*š*]*ul-lu-mu* A-*šú šá* ^{m}SÙḪ-SUR
12 [A ^{m}... ^{md}E]N-*it-tan-nu* A-*šú šá* (erasure)
13 [^{m}...]-*nu* A ^{m}*dan-ni-e-a* ^{md}AG-*it-tan-nu*
14 [A]-*šú šá* ^{m}*tab-ni-e-a* DUMU LÚ.SANGA-^{d}MAŠ
15 ^{m}ÌR-^{d}*ba-ba*$_{6}$ LÚ.UMBISAG DUMU LÚ.AZLAG
16 [TIN].TIR.KI ITI.NE UD.17.KAM MU.25.KAM

U. E.

17 ^{m}*da-a-ri-ia-muš* LUGAL TIN.TIR.KI

18 LUGAL KUR.KUR

Translation

Twenty *kor* of barley, the costs for the transport of two hundred *kor* of barley from the estate, the fixed rent of (= due to?) Iddin-Bēl [and] Tanda: Mamûzu, son of [Ṭā]biya, clerk (appointed) over the *female flour millers*, has received (it) by order of Gūzānu, [govern]or of Babylon, [fr]om MNA_2.

[Witnesses]:
Mīnû-ana-Bēl-dānu[/^{m}...]//Šumu-libši
[^{m}...]/Kīnēnaya[//^{m}...]
Šullumu/Tēšê-ēṭir[//^{m}...]
[B]ēl-ittannu/[^{m}...]-*nu*//Dannêa
Nabû-ittannu/Tabnêa//Šangû-Ninurta
The scribe: Arad-Bāba//Ašlāku
(Place + Date).

Comment

L. 2: For the interpretation *šūtu ša* PN "fixed rent of PN" = "fixed rent due to PN," see BM 31572: 2–3 and BM 31891: 2–3.

L. 3: The name ^{m}*ta-an-da* is otherwise unattested.

L. 4: The clerk ^{m}*ma-mu-ú-zu*, son of Ṭābiya, occurs as a witness in BM 30591: 12–13, ^{m}*ma-ú-zu-zu* A-*šú šá* ^{m}DU_{10}.GA-*ia*. The meaning of the name is not known, but the Persian element Vahu- is mostly rendered in Elamite writing as *ma-u-*, e.g., Vahuvaiθa = *hh.ma-u-me-sa*, and Vahučiça *hh.ma-u-zí-iš-šá* (e.g., Koch, *AMI* 19, 136).

L. 5: For the payment of rations to female flour millers (*qēmêtu*), see also *Bēl-rēmanni*, 152 (= BM 42353).

L. 10: The name Kīnēnaya is probably the same as Kīnūnaya, cf. Wunsch, *Felder* 2, 304 s.v. *Kinūnaja*.

L. 11: The signs A-*šú šá* are written over partly erased signs.

No. 72

BM 33121
Copy: Bertin copy 2825
Date: 20^{+}/xii(a)/[-] Dar
Place: Til-Gula
Content: Undertaking under oath to bring along one's sons. MNA is the scribe.

OBV.

1 ^{m}*mi-na-a*-^{d}EN-*da-nu* DUMU *šá* ^{md}AG-MU-URU$_{3}$ DUMU ^{m}[...]
2 *ina* ^{d}EN *u* ^{d}AG *u* ^{m}*da-ri-i'-ia-muš* LUGAL *a*-[*na* (...)]
3 ^{md}AMAR.UTU-*na-ṣir*-A DUMU *šá* ^{md}AG-MU-GIN DUMU ^{m}*šá-n*[*a-ši-šú*]
4 *it-te-me ki-i a-di-i* UD.1.KAM *šá* ITI.ŠE ⸢*ár*⸣-[*ku-ú*]
5 ^{m}*ni-din-tu*$_{4}$ *u* ^{m}KAR-^{d}EN DUMU.MEŠ-*ni*$^{!}$ *šá a-na* [...]
6 *pa-ni* ^{md}AMAR.UTU-*na-ṣir*<-*apli*> *ab-ba-ku*
7 *ḫi-ṭu šá* LUGAL *i-šad-dad ù* [...]
8 *ku-um la ab-ku šá* ^{m}*ni-din-tu*$_{4}$ ⸢*u*⸣ [^{m}KAR-^{d}EN]
9 ^{m}*mi-na-a*-^{d}EN-*dan-nu a*-[...]
10 *i-nam-din*

REV.

11 LÚ *mu-kin-nu* ^{md}⸢x⸣-[...]
12 ^{m}*mi-ti-ri-a-ni* [...]
13 ^{m}*lib-luṭ* LÚ.SAG-LUGAL [...]
14 ^{md}AG-MU-GIN A ^{m}*ib-na-a* ^{m}*ap-la*-[*a* ...]
15 ^{m}*bi-ba-nu* ^{m}MU-^{d}AG A-*šú šá* ^{md}AMAR.UTU$^{?}$-[x]
16 ^{md}EN-KAM DUMU *šá* ^{m}*nu-um-mu-ru* [...]
17 ^{md}AG-GIN-A DUMU *šá* ^{md}AG-⸢MU-MU⸣$^{?}$ [(...)]
18 ^{m}*ši-ir-ku* DUB.SAR DUMU *šá* ^{m}SUM.NA-*a* A [^{m}*e-gi-bi*]
19 DU$_{6}$-^{d}*gu-la* ITI.ŠE IGI-*ú* UD.20^{+}[...]
20 ^{m}*da-ri-'i-ia-muš* LUGAL TIN.TIR.[KI ...]

TRANSLATION

Mīnû-ana-Bēl-dānu, son of Nabû-šuma-uṣur, descendant of [...], declared under oath by Bēl, Nabû and King Darius t[o] Marduk-nāṣir-apli, son of Nabû-šuma-ukīn, descendant of Ša-n[āšīšu]: "By the first of Sec[ond] Addar I shall bring my$^{!}$ sons Nidintu and Mušēzib-Bēl, who for/to [...], before Marduk-nāṣir<-apli>." He will bear the guilt (of a transgression) against the king and [...], Mīnû-ana-Bēl-dānu will give t[o$^{?}$ ...] in compensation for not bringing Nidintu ⸢and⸣ [Mušēzib-Bēl].

Witnesses:
^{md}⸢x⸣-[...]
Mitrēn [...]
Libluṭ, the courtier [/]Nabû-šuma-ukīn//Ibnaya

Apla[ya][/(/)]Bibānu
Iddin-Nabû/Marduk?-[x]
Bēl-ērеš/Nummuru [...]
Nabû-mukīn-apli/Nabû-⌜šuma-iddin⌝? [(...)]
The scribe: MNA_2
(Place + Date).

Comment

L. 5: The subordinated sentence introduced by *šá* toward the end of this line must have contained the background information needed to understand the reason behind the undertaking of Minû-ana-Bēl-dānu to bring his two sons. Unfortunately, the end of the line is broken off. However, the specific use of *abāku* suggests that the sons in question were under some form of obligation toward Marduk-nāṣir-apli. Indeed, when a person swore to bring along someone, it usually concerned (fugitive) slaves, guarantors, or other persons under obligation (see *CAD* A_1, 6ff. s.v. *abāku* mng. 4; *AHw*, 2 s.v. *abāku* G mng. B 1e). In addition, the expression *ḫīṭa šadādu* in line 7 suggests a link with temple property.

L. 7: For the expression *ḫīṭa šadādu*, see *CAD* $Š_1$, 26 s.v. *šadādu* mng. 2h ("to bear guilt, punishment"); *AHw*, 350 s.v. *ḫīṭu* mng. 4c ("Strafe ... sich zuziehen").

L. 12: For the name Mitrēn (Ir. *Miθraina) and the ways in which it is spelled, see more at Dandamaev, *Iranians*, 101f. no. 199; Schmitt, *Kratylos* 39, 86 according to whom the spelling *Mi-it-re/ri-na-'* suggest an Iranian name *Miθrina rather than *Mitraina; and Zadok, *NABU* 1997/7. Additional spellings of the name Mitrēn are listed by Stolper, *Entrepreneurs*, 294: *Mi-it-re-e-na-'* = Mitrēna'; and Donbaz-Stolper, *Istanbul Murašû*, 171: *Mi-it-re-en, Mi-it-ra-ni-'* = Mitrēn. The spelling with *-ti* in our text (wr. ^{m}*mi-ti-ri-a-ni*), instead of *-it*, is, therefore, unusual, but see also ^{m}*mi-ti-ri-a-ta* in BM 30591: 11.

No. 73

	BM 33122
Copy:	no Bertin copy
Date:	9/[-]/17 Dar (505–504 B.C.E.)
Place:	broken
Content:	Loan of silver to MNA and his brothers. With interest, mutual surety, and pledge of land.

Obv.

1 [16⅔ MA.NA 4 GÍN KÙ.BABBAR *pe*]-*ṣu-ú šá ina* 1 GÍN *bit-qa*
2 [... *šá* ^{md}*a-nu*]-⌜*um*⌝-GIN-IBILA DUMU *šá*
3 [^{md}*a-nu-um*-ŠEŠ-MU] ⌜DUMU⌝ ^{md}*é-a-qa-a-lu-i-šem-me*
4 [*ina muḫḫi* ^{m}*ši-ir-ku*] ⌜*ù*⌝ ^{m}*pur-šu-ú* DUMU.MEŠ *šá*
5 [^{m}KI-^{d}AMAR.UTU-DIN] DUMU ^{m}*e-gi-bi šá* ITI *ina muḫ-ḫi* 1 *ma-ni-e*

6 [1 GÍN *ina* UGU KÙ.BABBAR]-*a*$_4$ 16⅔ MA.NA 4 GÍN *ina muḫ-ḫi-šú-nu*
7 [*i-rab-bi* 1-*en pu*]-⸢*ut*⸣ *šá-ni-i na-šu-ú šá qer-bi* KÙ.BABBAR-*a*$_4$
8 [16⅔ MA.NA 4 GÍN] ⸢SAG⸣ *ù* UR$_5$.RA-*šú iṭ-ṭir* ŠE.NUMUN-*šú-nu zaq-pu* UGU
9 [KASKAL.II K]IŠ.KI *šá* ÚS.SA.DU ^{m}SUM.NA-^{d}AG DUMU *šá*
10 [^{m}x(-x)]-*ú-še-zib ù* ÚS.SA.DU ^{md}AG-LUGAL-*ib-ni*
11 [*ù* ŠE.NUMU]N-*šú-nu šá ina* URU É-^{m}*ḫa-aḫ-ḫu-ru šá* ÚS.SA.DU
12 [^{m}ÌR]-^{d}AMAR.UTU DUMU *šá* ^{md}U.GUR-NUMUN-DÙ *ù* ÚS.SA.DU
13 [^{m}x(-x)]-*lu-ṭu* DUMU *šá* ^{m}*šá-du-nu maš-ka-nu šá* ^{md}*a-nu-u*[*m*]-GIN-IBILA
14 LÚ.TUKU-*ú šá-nam-ma ina muḫ-ḫi ul i-šal-laṭ a-di mu*[*ḫ-ḫi* (x x)]
15 ^{md}*a-nu-um*-GIN-IBILA KÙ.BABBAR-*a*$_4$ 16⅔ MA.NA [4 GÍN]
16 *ù* UR$_5$.RA-*šú in-ni-iṭ-ṭe-*[*er-r*]*u*

LO. E.

17 LÚ *mu-kin-nu* ^{m}*eri-ba*-^{d}AMAR.UTU DUMU *šá* ^{md}UTU-MU DUMU ^{m}⸢GAL⸣-[*a-šá*-^{d}MAŠ]

REV.

18 ^{md}EN-DIN-*iṭ* DUMU *šá* ^{m}MU-^{d}AG DUMU ^{m}*da-bi-bi*
19 ^{m}*mu-še-zib*-^{d}AMAR.UTU DUMU *šá* ^{md}AMAR.UTU-*mu-šal-lim* DUMU ^{m}*su-ḫa-a-a*
20 ^{md}AG-*bul-liṭ-su* DUMU <*šá*> ^{m}*šá-kin*-MU DUMU ^{m}*bu-ú-ṣu*
21 ^{m}*ú-bar*{*bar*}-*ru* DUMU *šá* ^{m}*na-di-nu* DUMU LÚ.SANGA-^{d}INNIN-TIN.TIR.KI
22 ^{md}AMAR.UTU-*eri-ba* DUMU *šá* ^{md}AG-NUMUN-GI.NA DUMU ^{m}*ga-ḫal*
23 ^{m}SUM.[NA]-^{d}⸢EN/AG⸣ DUMU *šá* ^{md}EN-DIN$^{!}$-*iṭ*
24 ^{m}*da-d*[*i-ia*] DUMU *šá* ^{md}EN-ŠEŠ.MEŠ-BA-*šá* DUMU ^{md}30-*tab*-[*ni*]-⸢URU$_3^{?}$⸣
25 $^{[md]}$⸢EN/AG-*it-tan*⸣-*nu* DUMU *šá* ^{md}AG-DIN-*su-iq-bi* DUMU ^{md}30-*šá-du-nu*
26 [^{m}x]-SUM.NA DUMU *šá* ^{md}AG-ŠEŠ.MEŠ-MU DUMU ⸢LÚ⸣.Ì.DU$_8$
27 [^{m}*šad-din*]-*nu* DUMU *šá* ^{md}DI.KU$_5$-ŠEŠ.MEŠ-MU DUMU ^{m}⸢*ši*⸣-*gu-ú*-⸢*a*⸣
28 [...] x DUMU *šá* ^{m}ŠEŠ.MEŠ-MU-^{d}AMAR.UTU DUMU LÚ.SANGA-^{d}INNIN-TIN.TIR.KI
29 [^{m}x-x-x]-DU DUMU *šá* ^{m}*i-qu-pu* DUMU ^{m}*e-gi-bi*
30 [^{m}x-x-x]-*nu* DUMU *šá* ^{m}*a-na*-^{d}EN-APIN-*eš* DUMU LÚ *man-di-di*
31 [^{m}x-x-x-x] DUMU *šá* ^{md}AG-IBILA-MU DUMU ^{m}*ba-bu-tu*
32 [^{m}x-x-x-x] DUMU *šá* ^{m}ÌR-*ia* DUMU ^{m}*ḫu-za*$^{?}$-*bi*
33 [^{m}x-x-x-x] DUMU *šá* ^{md}AMAR.UTU-*eri-ba* DUMU LÚ.BUR.GUL
34 [^{m}x-x-x-x] DUMU *šá* ^{m}⸢KAR⸣-^{d}AMAR.UTU DUM[U] ^{m}⸢*ú*-GÁL⸣-*e-a*

U. E.

35 [^{m}*ḫa-ad-da-a* DUB].SAR DUMU *šá* ^{m}*ni-qu-du* DUMU ^{m}*maš-tu*-⸢*ku*$^{?}$⸣
36 [... KI ITI.x U]D.9.KAM MU.17.KAM ^{m}*da-ri-ia-muš*
37 [LUGAL TIN].TIR.KI LUGAL KUR.KUR

LE. E.

NA$_4$.⌜KIŠIB⌝ / ^{m}SU-^{d}AMAR.UTU

RI. E.

NA$_4$.KIŠIB / ^{md}AG-*bul-liṭ-su* (seal impression)

TRANSLATION

[Sixteen minas and forty-four shekels of wh]ite [silver], of which one-eighth is alloy, [... are due to An]u-mukīn-apli, son of [Anu-aḫa-iddin], ⌜descendant of⌝ Ea-qâlu-išemme, [from Širku] ⌜and⌝ Puršû, sons of [Itti-Marduk-balāṭu], descendant of Egibi. [On] these sixteen minas and forty-four shekels [of silver] (interest) [will accrue] against them (at the rate of) [one shekel of silver] per mina per month. [Each one (of the debtors)] assumes warranty for the other. The one who is closest to these [sixteen minas and forty-four shekels] of silver will pay off ⌜the capital⌝ and its interest. Their orchard on the [road to K]iš next to Iddin-Nabû, son of [^{m}...]-ušēzib and next to Nabû-šarra-ibni, [as well as] their [arable lan]d in Bīt-Ḫaḫḫuru next to [Arad]-Marduk, son of Nergal-zēra-ibni and next to [^{m}...]-luṭu, son of Šadûnu, are pledged to Anu-mukīn-apli. No other creditor shall exercise any rights over it unti[l (x x)] Anu-mukīn-apli has received full repayment of these sixteen minas and forty-[four shekels] of silver and its interest.

Witnesses:
Erība-Marduk/Šamaš-iddin//⌜Rabâ⌝-[ša-Ninurta]
Bēl-uballiṭ/Iddin-Nabû//Dābibī
Mušēzib-Marduk/Marduk-mušallim//Suḫaya
Nabû-bullissu/Šākin-šumi//Būṣu
Ubār/Nādin//Šangû-Ištar-Bābili
Marduk-erība/Nabû-zēra-ukīn//Gaḫal
Iddin-^{d}⌜Bēl/Nabû⌝/Bēl-uballiṭ$^{!}$
Dād[iya]/Bēl-aḫḫē-iqīša//Sîn-tabni-⌜uṣur$^{?}$⌝
⌜Bēl/Nabû-ittannu⌝/Nabû-balāssu-iqbi//Sîn-šadûnu
[x]-iddin/Nabû-aḫḫē-iddin//Atû
[Šaddin]nu/Madānu-aḫḫē-iddin//Šigûa
[Bēl-id]din/Aḫḫē-iddin-Marduk//Šangû-Ištar-Bābili
[^{m}...]-DU/Iqūpu//Egibi
[^{m}...]-nu/Ana-Bēl-ēreš//Mandidi
[^{m}...]/Nabû-apla-iddin//Bābūtu
[^{m}...]/Ardiya//Ḫuṣābu
[^{m}...]/Marduk-erība//Purkullu
[^{m}...]/⌜Mušēzib⌝-Marduk//⌜Ušabšêa⌝
[The s]cribe: [Ḫaddaya]/Niqūdu//Maštuk
(Place + Date).
Seal of Erība-Marduk
Seal of Nabû-bullissu

Comment

L. 8–13: On the history of the plots of land that are pledged, see more at Wunsch, *Felder* 1, 59, 92–93, 158–61 and 168. The house in Bīt-Ḫaḫḫuru is also mentioned in Dar 453^{+}: 9–11.

L. 17: For this person, see Tallqvist, *NbN*, 59 s.v. Erba-Marduk(22).

L. 21: Between the father's name and the family name there is an empty space of one to two signs. Cf. lines 23 and 27: an empty space of one sign after the first personal name; also line 32: after the name Ardiya.

L. 23: After the EN/AG-sign there is an empty space; the DIN-sign is written over something else.

L. 28: The first name may end in either an UD or a NA (e.g., [...-^{d}AMAR].UTU, [...-SUM].NA). I suggest reading [^{md}EN-SUM].NA, son of Aḫḫē-iddin-Marduk//Šangû-Ištar-Bābili, because this person is attested in Dar 453^{+}: 22–23, and it is not the only person shared by both texts. Two other persons occur in both BM 33122 and Dar 453^{+}: Šaddinnu/Madānu-aḫḫē-iddin//Šigûa (BM 33122: 27 = Dar 453^{+}: 2), and Ḫaddaya/Niqūdu//Maštuk (BM 33122: 35 = Dar 453^{+}: 21–22).

L. 32: The name ^{m}*ḫu-ṣa*$^{?}$*-bi* is not listed by Tallqvist, *NbN*, but is attested as a family name in Neo-Babylonian texts, see *AHw*, 361 s.v. *ḫuṣābu* mng. 4; further note the attestations listed by Joannès, *Borsippa*, 373f.

L. 34: The name ^{m}⸢*ú*-GÁL⸣-*e-a* (= Uša/ebšêa) is not attested, at least not in this form. In fact, it is a shortened version of names like Bēl-uša/ebši and Nabû-zēra-uša/ebši. (For Neo-Babylonian names with the verb *šubšû*, see Tallqvist, *NbN*, 311).

L. 35: For this person see Dar 453^{+}: 21–22: ^{m}*ḫa-ad-da-a*/Niqūdu//Maštuk.

Le. E. The seal inscription is written upside down on the lower part and runs over the seal impression. The upper part of the left edge is broken off.

Ri. E. The seal inscription is written on the upper part. The lower part of the right edge is damaged.

No. 74

BM 33926
Copy: Bertin copy 2321
Date: 17/⸢iv⸣/15 Dar (22 July 507 B.C.E.)
Place: Babylon
Content: Receipt of *ilku*-silver by MNA (*kaspu … ilki*).

OBV.

1 2$^{?}$ MA.NA KÙ.BABBAR *šá gìn-nu il-ki*
2 *šá* ^{md}AG-*it-tan-nu u* ^{md}EN-NUMUN DUMU.MEŠ *šá* ^{m}[…]
3 ^{m}*ni-din-tu*$_{4}$-^{d}EN *u* ^{m}⸢*ba-la-ṭu*⸣ DUMU.MEŠ *šá* ^{m}[…]
4 *šá a-di* UD.1.KAM *šá* ITI.ŠU$^{?}$ MU.15.KAM
5 ^{m}*ši-ir-*⸢*ku*⸣ DUMU *šá* ^{m}SUM.NA-*a* ⸢A⸣ [^{m}*e-gì-bi*]
6 *ina* ŠU.II ^{m}*muk-ki-e-*⸢*a* DUMU *šá*⸣ [^{m}…]
7 DUMU ^{md}EN-*e-ṭè-ru ma-*[*ḫir*]

LO. E.

8 [1-*en*.T]A.ÀM TI-*ú*

REV.

9 LÚ *mu-kin-nu* ^{md}AMAR.UTU-⸢KAR$^{?}$⸣ DUMU [*šá* ^{m}…]
10 A ^{m}*la-ba-ši* ^{m}MU-^{d}AMAR.UTU A-*šú šá* ^{m}[…]
11 A ^{m}*šá*-MUN.ḪI.<A>-*šú* ^{md}UTU-SU DUMU *šá* ^{m}*ni-*⸢*qu*⸣-[*du*]
12 A LÚ.UŠ.BAR ^{m}MU-^{d}EN DUMU *šá* ^{m}⸢^{d}AMAR.UTU⸣-[…]
13 A LÚ.SANGA-BÁR ^{md}AG-GIN-A A-*šú šá* ^{m}[…]
14 A ^{md}30-[*šá*]-[*du*]-*nu* ^{m}*mu-šeb-š*[*i* …]
15 […] ^{m}*pur-šu-ú* LÚ.U[MBISAG …]
16 TI[N].⸢TIR⸣.KI ITI.⸢ŠU⸣ UD.17.[KAM]
17 ⸢MU⸣.15.KAM ^{m}*da-ri-*⸢*muš*⸣

U. E.

18 [LUGAL] E.KI *u* KUR.KUR

LE. E.

19 ^{md}AG-*it-*⸢*tan-nu*⸣ […]
20 […]

TRANSLATION

Two$^{?}$ minas of marked silver, the *ilku*-tax till the first of Dûzu$^{?}$ of the fifteenth year, are due from Nabû-ittannu and Bēl-zēri, sons of […], [and] from Nidinti-Bēl and ⸢Balāṭu⸣, sons of […]: MNA$_2$ has recei[ved] (it) from Mukkêa, ⸢son of⸣ […], descendant of Bēl-eṭēru. They have taken [one] (copy of the document) each.

Witnesses:
Marduk-⸢ēṭir$^{?}$⸣/[^{m}…]//Lâbāši
Iddin-Marduk/[^{m}…]//Ša-ṭābtīšu
Šamaš-erība/Niqū[du]//Išparu

Iddin-Bēl/⸢Marduk⸣-[...]/Šangû-parakki
Nabû-mukīn-apli/[^{m}...]//Sîn-[ša]dûnu
Mušebši [/...//...]
The scribe: Puršû [/...]
(Place + Date).
Nabû-ittannu/[...].

Comment

The surface of the tablet is badly damaged by salination.

L. 1: It is not absolutely clear whether we have 1 or 2 minas, because the first vertical may just have been a scratch.

L. 3: The personal name at the end of the line has to be short, at the most three signs, because it is already the end of the obverse and the right edge is very thin.

L. 4: The year number (MU.15.KAM) stands at the very end of the obverse and since very little writing space is available on the right edge it is unlikely that the name of Darius followed.

L. 15: The scribe was probably MNA's brother Puršû.

L. 19–20: On the left edge there is approximately 3 cm writing space. The name Nabû-ittannu takes half of the line. Underneath this name there are more signs but they are too squeezed together to be legible.

No. 75

BM 33928 (= Dupl. of BM 33957, unpubl.)
Copy: Bertin copy 2554
Date: 28/ii/35$^{!}$ Dar (25 May 487$^{!}$ B.C.E.)
Place: Babylon
Content: Receipt of silver from MNA's son paid on behalf of MNA. For equipment (*rikis qabli*) and travel provisions (*ṣidēti*). Paid to MNA's brother. Reference to a previous settlement of their *qinayātu*-duties.

Obv.

1 1 MA.NA KÙ.BABBAR *šá ina* 1 GÍN *bit-qa nu-uḫ-ḫu-tu*
2 *ku-um ri-ki-is* MURUB$_4$ *ù ṣi-di-e-ti*
3 *šá a-di qí-it* ITI.ŠE MU.36.KAM
4 ^{m}*da-a-ri-ia-muš* LUGAL *a-na ma-la*
5 ḪA.LA *šá* ^{md}AMAR.UTU-*na-ṣir*-IBILA ⸢DUMU *šá*⸣ ^{m}KI-^{d}AMAR.UTU-DIN
6 DUMU ^{m}*e-gi-bi* AD *šá* ^{m}*ni-din-ti*-^{d}EN
7 ^{md}AG-ŠEŠ.MEŠ-*bul-liṭ* DUMU *šá* ^{m}KI-^{d}AMAR.UTU-DIN
8 DUMU ^{m}*e-gi-bi ina* ŠU.II ^{m}*ni-din-ti*-^{d}EN
9 DUMU *šá* ^{md}AMAR.UTU-*na-ṣir*-IBILA DUMU ^{m}*e-gi-bi*

Lo. E.

10 *ma-ḫi-ir* 1-*en*.TA.ÀM TI-*ú*

11 *qí-na-a-ta-šú-nu šá e-lat an-na-a*

Rev.

12 *it-ti a-ḫa-meš šak-nu*

13 LÚ *mu-kin-nu* ^{md}EN-DIN-*iṭ* DUMU *šá* ^{m}MU-^{d}AG

14 DUMU ^{m}*da-bi-bi* ^{md}AMAR.UTU-NUMUN-DÙ DUMU *šá* ^{md}AG-DIN-*su*-E

15 DUMU ^{md}30-*šá-du-nu* ^{md}EN-*it-tan-nu*

16 DUMU *šá* ^{m}*gu-za-nu* A ^{md}IDIM-*na-ṣir*

17 ^{m}*ni-qu-du* DUMU *šá* ^{md}AG-GI DUMU ^{md}30-*tab-ni*

18 ^{m}*še-el-li-bi* DUMU *šá* ^{m}*ap-la-a*

19 ^{md}EN-A-MU DUB.SAR A-*šú šá* ^{md}AG-KÀD

20 A ^{m}*na-bu-un-na-a-a* TIN.TIR.KI

21 ITI.GU$_4$ UD.28.KAM MU.35$^{!}$.KAM

22 ^{m}*da-a-ri-ia-muš* LUGAL E.KI *u* KUR.KUR

Le. E.

23 ^{m}*ni-din-tu*$_4$-^{d}EN DUMU *šá* ^{md}[AG]-URU$_3$-*šú*

24 DUMU LÚ.ŠITIM

Translation

One mina of medium-quality silver, of which one-eighth is alloy, (paid) instead of (providing for) the equipment of a (military) expedition and the travel provisions, in so much as it is the share due from MNA$_1$, father of Nidinti-Bēl, (for the period) till the end of Addar of the thirty-sixth year of King Darius: Nabû-aḫḫē-bulliṭ, son of Itti-Marduk-balāṭu, descendant of Egibi, has received it from Nidinti-Bēl, son of MNA$_1$. They have taken one (copy of the document) each. They (already) arranged in mutual agreement their *qinayātu*-duty, which is in addition to the aforementioned (*rikis qabli*-duty).

Witnesses:
Bēl-uballiṭ/Iddin-Nabû//Dābibī
Marduk-zēra-ibni/Nabû-balāssu-iqbi//Sîn-šadûnu
Bēl-ittannu/Gūzānu//Ea-nāṣir
Niqūdu/Nabû-ušallim//Sîn-tabni
Šellibi/Aplaya
The scribe: Bēl-apla-iddin/Nabû-kāṣir//Nabunnaya
(Place + Date).
Nidinti-Bēl/[Nabû]-uṣuršu//Itinnu

Comment

BM 33928 and BM 33957 are duplicates. I checked the latter for spelling variations, but did not go into detail regarding the characteristics of the scribe's writing. Note the two following minor deviations in spelling: L. 3: BM 33957 has *a-di-i;* and L. 8: BM 33957 has *i-na*.

L. 11: The first sign may also be a DI (cf. //BM 33957). For *qinayātu* (pl. tantum), see *AHw*, 921, s.v. *qinītu* "Erwerb, ein Opfer"; but the *CAD* adduces the Neo-Babylonian examples s.v. *kīnayātu*: *CAD* K, 379f. "(an additional payment, present, or offering)." For *qinītu* the *CAD* (Q, 254 s.v. *qinītu* A "acquisition, property") gives Neo-Assyrian examples only. The examples cited by the dictionaries for *q/kinayātu* are mostly taken from house rentals and are, hence, less relevant for the case under consideration. For the occurrence of *qinayātu* in connection with a payment for *rikis qabli*, see *Bēl-rēmanni*, 251f. = BM 79128 (Sippar, 2/iv/19 Dar). The text dealt with *rikis qabli* and an additional payment called *qí-na-a-a-ta* (l. 13), which consisted of beer and a lamb.

L. 21: The scribe wrote 25 but in view of the 36th year mentioned in line 3, the 25 in line 21 is clearly to be emended to 35. If so, this would be a clear case of an advance payment: silver for taxes of the 36th year were paid in the second month of the 35th year, unless, of course, we should emend the text even more and read in line 21: MU.36$^{!}$.KAM. The parallel passage in the duplicate tablet BM 33957 is damaged; visible are the lower strokes of a 20 and before that the lower stroke of one of the *Winkelhaken* of the MU.

No. 76

	BM 33930
Copy:	Bertin copy 2626
Date:	3/⸢iii⸣/29 Dar (4 ⸢June⸣ 493 B.C.E.)
Place:	Šaḫrīnu
Content:	Receipt of *makkasu*-dates from MNA by a courtier. For the preparation of offerings in the temple of Nergal (*ana ginê ša Nergal*). Reference to the foreman (LÚ.GAR) of the "arrangers-of-the-sacrificial-table" (LÚ *mu-ban-ni-⸢e⸣*).

OBV.

1 ⸢24⸣ GUR ZÚ.LUM.MA *a-na ma-ak-ka-su*

2 *a-⸢na⸣ gi-ni-e šá* ^{d}U.GUR *ul-tu* UD.1.KAM

3 *šá* ITI.[SIG$_4$] MU.29.KAM *a-di qí<-it>* ITI.KIN *šá* MU.29<.KAM>

4 ^{md}EN-⸢*ru*⸣-*ṣu-ú-a* LÚ.SAG-LUGAL *ina* ŠU.II

5 ^{md}AMAR.U[TU-*n*]*a-ṣir*-IBILA A-*šú šá* ^{m}KI-^{d}AMAR.UTU-DIN

6 A ^{m}*e-g*[*i*]*-bi ma-ḫi-ir* ZÚ.LUM.MA-*a*$_4$

7 24 GUR ^{md}EN-*ru-ṣu-ú-a it-ti*

8 ^{md}⸢EN⸣-*bul-liṭ-su* <*u*>$^{?}$ LÚ ⸢*ki-na*⸣-*at-tu*.MEŠ-*šú*

9 LÚ ⸢x-x⸣-*ri*.ME[Š] ⸢*ú*⸣-*šá-az-zi-ma*

LO. E.

10 ⸢*a*⸣-*na* ^{md}AMAR.UTU-*na-ṣir*-IBILA

11 *i-nam-din*

REV.

12 *ki-i* INA MA *la ul-te-iz-zi ina* ITI.[x]

13 ZÚ.LUM.MA *ku-ú* ZÚ.LUM.MA ^{md}EN-*ru-ṣu-ú-a*

14 *a-na* [UGU$^{?}$] ^{md}AMAR.UTU-*na-ṣir*-IBILA *a-na* NÍG.GA

15 ^{d}U.[GUR *i-nam-d*]*in*

16 LÚ *mu-*⸢*kin*$_7$⸣ ^{md}AG-DIN-*iṭ* A-*šú šá* ^{m}*lu*-È-*ana*-ZALAG$_2$

17 A ^{m}*an-da-ḫar* ^{md}U.GUR-DÙ A-*šú šá* ^{m}KAR-^{d}EN A ^{m}ÌR-^{d}GIR$_4$.KÙ

18 ^{m}EN-*šú-nu* A-*šú šá* ^{m}*la-ba-ši* ^{m}*ba-la-ṭu* A-*šú šá*

19 ^{md}U.GUR-SUR ^{m}MU-^{d}EN A-*šú šá* ^{m}EN-*šú-nu* A ^{md}30-PAB

20 LÚ.UMBISAG ^{m}MU-URU$_3$ A-*šú šá* ^{md}AG-*it-tan-nu*

21 URU *šaḫ-ri-i-ni* ITI.SI[G$_4$] UD.3.KAM MU.29<.KAM>

U. E.

22 ^{m}*da-a-ri-ia-muš* LUGAL E.KI *u* KUR.KUR

23 ZÚ.LUM.MA *šá* LÚ.GAR LÚ *mu-ban-ni-*⸢*e*⸣

24 SUM.NA-*u'*

LE. E.

25 ^{m}*ta-*[*at*]*-tan-nu* A-*šú šá*

26 [x x x (x)]

TRANSLATION

Bēl-ruṣūa, the courtier, has received from MNA$_1$ ⸢twenty-four⸣ *kor* of *makkasu*-dates for (the preparation of) Nergal's offerings (in the period starting) from the first of [Simān] of the twenty-ninth year (and) till the en<d> of Ulūl of the twenty-nin<th> year. Bēl-ruṣūa will registe<r> (the receipt of) these twenty-four *kor* of dates in the accounts of ⸢Bēl⸣-bullissu <and>$^{?}$ his colleagues, the ..., and he will give (proof of it) to MNA$_1$. If he does not registe<r> (the receipt), Bēl-ruṣūa [should gi]ve dates instead of the (aforementioned) dates to the property of Ner[gal] for the [account$^{?}$] of MNA$_1$ in the month [x].

Witnesses:
Nabû-uballiṭ/Lūṣi-ana-nūri//Andaḫar
Nergal-ibni/Mušēzib-Bēl//Arad-Nergal
Bēlšunu/Lâbāši
Balāṭu/Nergal-ēṭir
Iddin-Bēl/Bēlšunu//Sîn-nāṣir
The scribe: Šuma-uṣur/Nabû-ittannu
(Place + Date).

The dates (are those) that the foreman of the arrangers-of-the-sacrificial-table gave.

Tattannu/[...]

Comment

The tablet is very densely written.

L. 1: The number 24 is written [10]+10+4; there is no doubt that the number was 24 because it clearly says so in line 7. For *makkasu*-dates see *AHw*, 589 s.v. *makkasu* mng. C "(gute) Schnittdatteln," and *CAD* M_1, 131f s.v. *makkasu* A "(a choice quality of dates)." For the use of dates of divergent quality in the preparation of the regular offerings, see Bongenaar, *Ebabbar*, 143f., 168f., and 238f.

L. 3: The number 29 is written at the very end of the right edge and on the reverse (MU.20 on Ri. Ed., 9 on Rev.), and there was no place left to write KAM.

L. 9a: I suggest reading LÚ *š[á$^?$-pi]r$^?$-ri*.MEŠ "overseers," because this type of official is known to have supervised prebendary professional groups, such as the bakers, the brewers, the butchers, e.a. (*CAD* $Š_1$, 454f. s.v. *šāpiru* mng. 1a-4'; cf. Bongenaar, *Ebabbar*, 142; and MacGinnis, *Letter Orders*, 127f.). Note that the usual syllabic spelling for *šāpiru* in Neo-Babylonian texts is ^{lú}*šá-pi-ri*, with *-pi-* and not *-pir-*, as is apparently the case in our text.

L. 9b: The verb *ú-šá-az-zi-ma*, no doubt, belongs to the so-called "clearance formula": *ušazzazma ... inamdin*. For the meaning of this formula, see bibliography cited at BM 30233: 4–9. The defective writing *ú-šá-az-zi<-iz>-ma* for *ušazzazma* is not exceptional, cf. the writings *ú-šá-az-zi-ma* and *[ú-šá]-⸢az-zu⸣-ma* (in Donbaz-Stolper, *Istanbul Murašû* Nos. 35 and 37), *ú*-ŠAD-*za-zi* (CT 49 46), *ú<-šá>-za-az-ma* (NRVU 364), and the examples cited by Stolper, *JNES* 48, 287f. See also below at line 12.

L. 12–13: The verb *ul-te-iz-zi* in line 12 is probably another defective spelling, to be read: *ul-te-iz-zi<-iz>* = *ultezziz*, perf. from *šuzzu(z)zu*. These lines deal with the possibility that Bēl-ruṣūa does not clear his receipt of the dates in the accounts of Bēl-bullissu: *ki-i ... la ul-te-iz-zi<-iz>*. The signs INA MA after *kî* do not make sense. Possibly the scribe was a beginner and/or he was copying from an original document, which read *ki-i* ZÚ.LUM.MA *la ul-te-iz-zi<-iz>*, without understanding what he was copying. The supposed inexperience of the scribe might also explain the rather frequent omission of signs in this text.

L.23 On *mubannû* ("arranger-of-the-sacrificial-table") see *AHw*, 665; *CAD* M_2, 158; and Bongenaar, *Ebabbar*, 292ff. I do not know of the existence of a *šaknu* (^{lú}GAR) "foreman" who was appointed over the "arrangers-of-the-sacrificial-table" or over any other group of prebendaries from other Neo-Babylonian texts. Prebendaries were usually supervised by officials who bore the title "chief," *rabu* (^{lú}GAL). For the occurrence of foremen (*šaknu*) who were appointed over groups of bow-fiefholders and collected rents and taxes from these feudatories, see Stolper, *Entrepreneurs*, 82ff. ("fiscal officer"). See also *CAD* $Š_1$, 188–90 s.v. *šaknu*, mng. 3, and discussion section on p. 191.

L. 23–24: In my opinion, this short remark relates to the previously mentioned dates, i.e., the twenty-four *kor* of *makkasu*-dates that MNA delivered for the offerings in the temple of Nergal; it does not refer to some other dates, although the formulation in these lines is, admittedly, laconic (cf. BM 30256: 6–9). If so, MNA previously received the dates from the foreman of the arrangers-of-the-sacrificial-table. The latter may have collected them from a group of prebend-holders over whom he was appointed (cf. the function of foremen appointed over fiefholders, as pointed out in the previous remark).

L. 26: The signs are too squeezed to be legible, but the Tattannu in question may have been the son of Lūṣi-ana-nūri, and the brother of Nabû-uballiṭ mentioned in line 16. A Tattannu/Lūṣi-ana-nūri occurs among the witnesses in Dar 405. The latter text was written by the same scribe as the text under consideration, although fourteen years previously. Moreover, it is linked to temple matters as the text under consideration: it has the *qīpu* of the Eḫursag temple among its witnesses and records the pledge of land to MNA by a man named Aplaya, who was the holder of an *ērib bīti* prebend according to BM 30965.

No. 77

	BM 33935
Copy:	Bertin copy 2809
Date:	25/xi/[-] Dar (December-January)
Place:	URU KAR AN BÁR
Content:	Settlement of a silver debt through sale of land and slaves by MNA to his creditor. A previous house sale became void after the house had been seized by the Esagil temple.

OBV.

1 50 MA.NA 4 GÍN 2-TA ŠU.II.MEŠ KÙ.BABBAR *ina ú-ìl-tì*
2 *šá* 1 GUN 4 MA.NA 14 GÍN KÙ.BABBAR SAG.DU ŠÁM
3 GI.MEŠ É *ép-šú šá ina* KI-*tì šu-an-na*.KI
4 *šá qé-reb* TIN.TIR.KI *šá* ^{md}AMAR.UTU-*na-ṣi-ir*-IBILA
5 DUMU *šá* ^{m}KI-^{d}AMAR.UTU-DIN DUMU ^{m}*e-gì-bi a-na kàs-pi*
6 *a-na* ^{md}60-GIN-IBILA DUMU *šá* ^{md}60-ŠEŠ-MU
7 DUMU ^{md}*é-a*-ME-ŠE.GA *id-di-nu-ú-ma*
8 É *šú-a-ti*$^{!}$ *a-na* NÍG.GA *é-sag-íla in-nap-lu*
9 KÙ.BABBAR-a_4 50 MA.NA 4 GÍN 2-TA ŠU.II.MEŠ
10 *i-na* SAG.DU *u* UR$_5$.RA ^{md}60-GIN-IBILA
11 *ina* ŠU.II ^{md}AMAR.UTU-*na-ṣi-ir-ap-lu ma-ḫi-ir*
12 KÙ.BABBAR ŠÁM 2 GUR ŠE.NUMUN *zaq-pu ù*
13 4 GUR 3 (PI) 2 (BÁN) ŠE.NUMUN A.ŠÀ *mi-ri-šú ù* 10-TA
14 LÚ-*tú šá* ^{md}AMAR.UTU-*na-ṣi-ir*-IBILA *a-na*

15 ^{md}60-GIN-IBILA *id-di-nu* 1-*en-a*.TA.ÀM TI-*ú*

REV.

16 LÚ *mu-kin-nu* ^{m}*id-di-ia* DUMU *šá* ^{m}*šu-la-a* DUMU LÚ.SANGA-^{d}MAŠ

17 ^{m}*ba-ri-ku*-DINGIR DUMU *šá* ^{md}*il-ta-mi-iš-ma-ḫir*

18 ^{md}⸢UTU$^{?}$-KÁD⸣ DUMU *šá* ^{m}*ri-mut* ^{md}AMAR.UTU-MU-DÙ DUMU *šá* ^{m}SUM.NA-*a*

19 DUMU LÚ.SIMUG ^{m}GIN-NUMUN DUMU *šá* ^{m}*šu-la-a* A ^{m}KUR-*i* ^{m}[x]-⸢x⸣ ⸢DUMU$^{?}$⸣

20 $^{[m]}$⸢x⸣-DINGIR ^{m}ŠEŠ-[MU DUMU *šá*] $^{[m]}$[x-x]-⸢*ú*$^{?}$⸣ ^{md}AG-*it*-[x-x(-x)]

21 [x x] ^{md}AM[AR.UTU-… … ^{m}…-*n*]*a-na-a* ^{m}MU-[x]-⸢x⸣-*ú*

22 […] ^{md}AG-ŠEŠ-*it-tan-na*

23 [… -Z]I.MEŠ ^{m}SUM.NA-*a* DUMU *šá* ^{m}SUM.NA-ŠEŠ

24 […] ⸢x⸣ DUMU *šá* ^{md}INNIN-MU-URU$_3$ A ^{m}⸢*ki*⸣-*din*-^{d}AMAR.UTU

25 […]-NUMUN-BA-*šá* A ^{m}KUR-*i* ^{md}UTU-EN-NUMUN

26 [x x] ^{md}60-ŠEŠ-⸢MU⸣ A ^{m}MU-*lib-ši* ^{md}30-*ba-ra-ku*

27 [DUMU] ⸢*šá*$^{?}$⸣ ^{m}EN-MU ^{md}x-PAB DUMU *šá* ^{m}*ri-mut* A ^{m}KUR-*i*

28 ^{md}30-KÁD DUMU *šá* ^{m}MU-^{d}AG ^{m}MU-^{d}AG DUMU *šá* ^{m}DÙ-*ia*

29 [x x x]-GI DUMU *šá* ^{md}AG-ŠEŠ-MU ^{m}KA$_5$.A DUMU *šá* ^{m}*ni-din-ti*

30 [^{md}AG]-⸢KAR⸣-ZI.MEŠ DUB.SAR DUMU *šá* ^{md}INNIN-*tab-ni*-URU$_3$

31 [x x x]-⸢^{d}⸣*na-na-a* URU KAR AN BÁR ITI.ZÍZ UD.25.KAM

32 [MU.x].KAM ^{m}*da-a-ri-ia-a-mu-uš* LUGAL TIN.TIR.KI

33 LUGAL KUR.KUR

LE. E.

TOP

[NA$_4$.KIŠIB ^{md}]*a-nu*<-*um*> / [GIN]-IBILA / [DUMU] *šá* ^{md}60- / [ŠE]Š-MU

MIDDLE

seal impression

BOTTOM

[DU]MU ^{md}*é-a-* / *qa-a-lu-* / *i-šem-me*

TRANSLATION

Fifty minas, four shekels and two-thirds (of a shekel) of silver, part of an initial debt of one talent, four minas and fourteen shekels of silver. (The latter sum is) the price of the plot of land including the house built on it in Babylon's Šu'anna-quarter that MNA sold to Anu-mukīn-apli, son of Anu-aḫa-iddin, descendant of Ea-qâlu-išemme, but that has (subsequently) been given to the Esagil temple as compensation (for an unsettled debt). Anu-mukīn-apli has received these fifty minas, four shekels and two-thirds (of a shekel) of silver, (owed to him) from the capital and the interest, from MNA: it is the value in silver of an orchard of two *kor*, a grain field of 4.3.2 *kor* and ten slaves that MNA gave (= sold?) to Anu-mukīn-apli. They have taken one (copy of the document) each.

Witnesses:
Iddiya/Šulaya//Šangû-Ninurta
Barīk-il/Iltammeš-māḫir
⌜Šamaš$^{?}$-kāṣir⌝/Rīmūt
Marduk-šuma-ibni/Iddinaya//Nappāḫu
Mukīn-zēri/Šulaya//Kurî
[PN]⌜/$^{?}$⌝[x]-DINGIR
Aḫa-[iddin]/^{m}[...]
Nabû-it[tannu$^{?}$][/]Marduk-[...][//][^{m}...]-*na-na-a*
MU-[x]-⌜x⌝-*ú* [...]
[...] Nabû-aḫa-ittannu
[... -na]pšāti
Iddinaya/Nādin-aḫi
[^{m}...]/Ištar-šuma-uṣur//Kidin-Marduk
[^{m}...][/][^{m}...]-zēra-iqīša//Kurî
Šamaš-bēl-zēri[/]Anu-aḫa-⌜iddin⌝//Šumu-libši
Sîn-barak[/]Bēl-iddin
^{md}x-nāṣir(,-uṣur)/Rīmūt//Kurî
Sîn-kāṣir/Iddin-Nabû
Iddin-Nabû/Baniya
[^{m}...]-ušallim/Nabû-aḫa-iddin
Šellibi/Nidintu
The scribe: [Nabû]-⌜ēṭir⌝-napšāti/Ištar-tabni-uṣur[//][x x x]-Nanaya
(Place + Date).
[Seal of] Anu-[mukīn]-apli[/]Anu-[a]ḫa-iddin[/]/Ea-qâlu-išemme

COMMENT

L. 17: The verbal element *maḫir* is very rare in Neo-Babylonian names (see Tallqvist, *NbN*, 321–22), but names with the divine element Iltammeš are common (*ibid.*, 217 s.v. ^{il}ZA.MAL.MAL; additional examples of names with Iltammeš in Jursa, *Landwirtschaft*, 255; Donbaz-Stolper, *Istanbul Murašû*, 168 and Stolper, *Entrepreneurs*, 292).

L. 18: Should we correct the scribe and read Marduk-zēra$^{!}$-ibni (instead of Marduk-šuma-ibni)? A person named Marduk-zēra-ibni/Bēl-aḫḫē-iddin//Nappāḫu is known from Dar 156: 14. Is he the same as the one named Marduk-zēra$^{!}$-ibni/Iddinaya//Nappāḫu in the text under consideration?

L. 19 end –20: The reconstruction as given above seems to me the most likely one for two reasons. First, the remnants at the end of line 19 resemble DUMU. However, it is not followed by *šá* as in the other instances in this text. Second, there is space for one or two signs before DINGIR at the beginning of line 20, and what is visible does not resemble the *Personenkeil*. If it were the *Personenkeil*, lines 19 end – 20 may be interpreted differently, viz. (19) ... A ^{m}KUR-*i* ^{m}[x]-⌜x-x(not DUMU)⌝ (20) [(x)] ^{md}60-ŠEŠ-MU DUMU *šá* .... In the latter case, the name following A KUR-*i* at the end of line 19 is superfluous.

L. 22, 26, 29: Note the following spellings: *-na* (not the usual *-nu*) in ^{md}AG-ŠEŠ-*it-tan-na* (22), *-lib-* (not the usual *-líb-*) in ^{m}MU-*lib-ši* (26), and *-ti* (not the usual *-tu*$_4$) in ^{m}*ni-din-ti* (29).

L. 23: The first sign visible in this line resembles the end of ZI, but it may also have been the end of ŠEŠ (read: [...-ŠE]Š.MEŠ).

L. 25: The name Šamaš-bēl-zēri is strange and otherwise unattested. Common names with the elements Šamaš-bēl- are Šamaš-bēl-ilī and Šamaš-bēla-uṣur.

L. 26: The name Sîn-*ba-ra-ku* contains the West-semitic root B-R-K "to bless": Sîn-barak(a) = "Sîn has blessed" (Zadok, *West Semites*, 79f.).

L. 27: Should we read ^{md}UTU$^{?}$-PAB: there are two *Winkelhaken* but there is no closing vertical? The family name Kurî is well attested in texts from Uruk (Beaulieu, *YOS* 19, 45; Weisberg, *YOS* 17, 45 and *Texts of the OI*, 55).

L. 30: There is one empty line before this line, thus separating the name of the scribe (ll. 30–31) from the list of witnesses.

L. 31: The wedges after URU read AŠ BA A and seem to form one sign, viz. KAR, because they are written close to each other; they are followed by AN BÁR. A place called URU KAR AN BÁR is unknown to me. Should we read instead URU *šu*$^{!}$(AŠ-BA)-*šá*$^{!}$(A)-*an* {BÁR}? The BÁR may stand for the month Nisan, and be a scribal error; the month in which the document was written was Šabāt (ITI.ZÍZ) as goes forth from what follows BÁR.

No. 78

BM 33936 (= Dupl. of Liv 25)
Copy: Abraham, *OLP* 28: 83
Date: 3/xii(a)/[16] Dar (20 February [505] B.C.E.)
Place: Šušan (EREN.KI)
Content: Promissory note to pay a debt of silver. Due from MNA to the governor of Kish through an intermediary (*ina qibit ša* MNA).

OBV.

1 23 MA.NA KÙ.BABBAR *šá ina* 1 GÍN *bit-qa nu-uḫ-ḫu-*[*tu*]
2 *šá* ^{md}AG-*ú-bal-liṭ-su* A-*šú šá* ^{md}AG-*ki-šìr*
3 A ^{m}DIL-SUR *ina* UGU ^{m}*ši-ir-ku* A-*šú šá* ^{m}MU-*a* A ^{m}*e-gi-bi*
4 *ina* ITI.GU$_4$ *ina* TIN.TIR.KI KÙ.BABBAR-*a*$_4$ 23 MA.NA
5 *šá ina* 1 GÍN *bit-qa nu-uḫ-ḫu-tú ina* SAG.DU-*šú*
6 *i-nam-di-in* KÙ.BABBAR-*a*$_4$ 23 MA.NA ^{md}AG-*ú-bal-liṭ-su*
7 *ina qí-bit šá* ^{m}*ši-ir-ku a-na* ^{md}*za-ba*$_4$*-ba*$_4$-MU
8 A-*šú šá* ^{m}*e-tel-lu* A ^{m}ŠEŠ.MEŠ-⸢*mu**⸣-*ú* LÚ.GAR-UŠ$_4$ KIŠ.KI
9 *ra-šu-ú šá* UGU ^{m}*ši-ir-ku* ^{md}AG-*ú-bal-liṭ-su*
10 *it-tad-di-in*

REV.

11 LÚ *mu-kin-nu* ^{m}IGI-^{d}EN-*a-dag-gal* LÚ.TIL.GÍD.DA *é-sag-íla**
12 ^{md}AG-EN-*šú-nu* LÚ.DI.KU$_5$ A ^{m}DA-^{d}AMAR.UTU ^{md}AG-ZI-*tì*-URU$_3$ LÚ.DI.KU$_5$
13 A ^{m}*šá-na-ši-šú* ^{m}*la-a-ba-ši* LÚ.DI.KU$_5$ DUMU ^{m}LÚ.GAL-60-*ši*
14 ^{m}NUMUN-*ia* LÚ.DI.KU$_5$ A-*šú šá* ^{m}*nar-gi-ia*
15 ^{m}KI-^{d}AG-*nu-uḫ-ḫu* LÚ.DI.KU$_5$ A-*šú šá* ^{md}EN-DA
16 ^{md}AG-*it-tan-nu* LÚ.DI.KU$_5$ A-*šú šá* ^{m}*ri-mut*
17 ^{md}AG-DIN-[*iṭ*] A-*šú šá* ^{m}*ni-din-tu*$_4$-^{d}EN ^{md}EN-A-MU
18 A-*šú šá* ^{m}ÌR-^{d}*gu-la* A ^{m}DÙ-*eš*-DINGIR ^{md}AG-KÁD LÚ.DI.KU$_5$
19 A ^{md}30-*tab-nu* ^{m}*ni-din-tu*$_4$ LÚ.DI.KU$_5$ A ^{m}ŠÁ-ŠID-DAK-KU
20 ^{m}MU-^{d}AG LÚ.DI.KU$_5$ A ^{m}*ši-gu-ú-a*
21 ^{m}*ši-ir-ku* DUB.SAR A-*šú šá* ^{m}MU-*a* A [^{m}*e-gi-bi*]
22 EREN.KI ITI.ŠE IGI-*ú* UD.3.KAM [MU].[16.KAM]
23 ^{m}*da-ri-'i-ia-muš* LUGAL T[IN.TIR.KI *u* KUR.KUR]

SEALS:

LO. E.

TOP

NA$_4$.KIŠIB / ^{m}IGI-^{d}EN-*a-dag-gal* / LÚ.TIL.GÍD.DA (= witness 1)

MIDDLE

NA$_4$.KIŠIB / ^{md}AG-EN-*šú-nu* / LÚ.DI.KU$_5$ (= witness 2)

U. E.

TOP

NA$_4$.KIŠIB / ^{m}NUMUN-*ia* / LÚ.DI.KU$_5$ (= witness 5)

MIDDLE

NA$_4$.KIŠIB / ^{m}MU-^{d}AG / LÚ.DI.KU$_5$ (upside down) (= witness 12)

BOTTOM

[NA$_4$.KIŠIB / ^{m}...] / [LÚ].⸢DI⸣.KU$_5$ (upside down)

RI. E.

TOP

LÚ.DI.KU$_5$ / NA$_4$.KIŠIB / ^{m}KI-^{d}AG-*nu-uḫ-ḫu* (= witness 6)

MIDDLE

NA$_4$.KIŠIB ^{md}AG-*it-tan-nu* (= witness 7)

BOTTOM

[NA$_4$.KIŠIB] / ⸢^{m}*ni-din-tu*$_4$⸣ / LÚ.DI.KU$_5$ (upside down) (= witness 11$^{?}$)

LE. E.

NA$_4$.KIŠIB / ^{md}EN-A-MU (= witness 9)

TRANSLATION

Twenty-three minas of medium qualit[y] silver, of which one-eighth is alloy, are due to Nabû-uballissu, son of Nabû-kēšir, descendant of Eda-ēṭir, from MNA_2. He shall pay these twenty-three minas of medium-quality silver, of which one-eighth is alloy, without interest, in Ayyar in Babylon. Nabû-uballissu, by order of MNA_2, Nabû-uballissu has given these twenty-three minas of silver to Zababa-iddin, son of Etellu, descendant of Aḫḫū*, governor of Kiš, creditor of MNA_2.

Witnesses:

1. Pān-Bēl-adaggal, (royal) resident in the Esagil temple
2. Nabû-bēlšunu//Ile''i-Marduk, judge
3. Nabû-napišta-uṣur//Ša-nāšīšû, judge
4. Lâbāši//Rab-šušši, judge
5. Zēriya/Nargiya, judge
6. Itti-Nabû-nuḫḫu/Bēl-ile''i, judge
7. Nabû-ittannu/Rīmūt, judge
8. Nabû-uballiṭ/Nidinti-Bēl
9. Bēl-apla-iddin/Arad-Gula//Eppeš-ilī
10. Nabû-kāṣir//Sîn-tabni, judge
11. Nidintu//Kaṣṣidakku?, judge
12. Iddin-Nabû//Šigûa, judge

The scribe: MNA_2.
(Place + Date).
Seal of Pān-Bēl-adaggal, (royal) resident
Seal of Nabû-bēlšunu, judge
Seal of Zēriya, judge
Seal of Iddin-Nabû, judge
[Seal of m...], ⌜judge⌝
Judge - Seal of Itti-Nabû-nuḫḫu
Seal of Nabû-ittannu
[Seal of] ⌜Nidintu⌝, judge
Seal of Bēl-apla-iddin

Comment

L. 7: For *ina qí-bit* instead of the common *ina qí-bi*, cf. BM 31226: 6 (*ina iqba*) and BM 30639: 5, 11 (*ina iqbi*).

L. 7–8: For one Zababa-iddin/Etellu, with no surname nor official title, see Dar 411: 10–11.

L. 8: For the spelling of the name Aḫḫ(')ū see more at BM 31554: 10.

L. 10: Liv 25 has *it-ta-di-in*.

L. 19: The signs of the name mŠÁ-ŠID-DAK-KU (cf. Liv 25 mŠÁ-ŠID-DAK-KA) are written in a clear way. Was the scribe copying signs from an original without really understanding them? Probably, we should emend as follows: m*kas*!(ŠÀ)-*si*!(ŠID)-*dak-ku*/*ka*. For syllabic spellings of the name *Kaṣṣidakku*, see Tallqvist, *NbN*, 88 s.v. Kas(s)idakku, and *CAD* K, 268 s.v. *kaṣṣidakku* mng. b.

L. 20: Our text has ^{m}MU-^{d}AG, but the duplicate text Liv 25 has ^{m}MU-^{d}EN, and Strassmaier may mistakenly have copied ^{d}EN instead of ^{d}AG.

L. 21: The family name Egibi is reconstructed on the basis of Liv 25, where the name is clearly written.

L. 22: Liv 25 clearly has MU.16.KAM.

No. 79

	BM 33954
Copy:	Bertin copy 2235
Date:	25/iv$^{?}$/12 Dar (3 August$^{?}$ 510 B.C.E.)
Place:	Babylon
Content:	Promissory note to deliver flour to MNA. Property of the king (*makkūr šarri*). Delivery on account of the bow-unit of the exorcists (*ša* ^{giš}*qašti ša* ^{lú}*ašīpū*^{meš}). Administered by (*ša ina qātē*) the governor of Babylon.

OBV.

1 4 GUR ⸢3$^{?}$⸣ (BÁN) *qí-me* ŠE.BAR 1 GUR 2 (PI) 2 (BÁN) *qí-me* GIG.BA

2 NÍG.GA LUGAL *šá* GIŠ.BAN *šá* LÚ *a-ši-pu*.MEŠ

3 *šá ina* ŠU.II ^{md}AG-MU-GIN LÚ.GAR-UŠ$_4$ TIN.TIR.KI

4 *šá* ⅓ TA GIŠ.BAN *šá* ^{m}*ba-zu-zu* (erasure$^{?}$)

5 ⸢9 LÚ$^{?}$⸣ *qí-pa-ni-šú šá* É LÚ.DUB.SAR$^{!}$

6 [^{m}]*lib-luṭ* A-*šú šá* ^{m}*mu-ra-šu-ú*

7 A ^{md}30-*tab-ni a-di-i* UD.29.KAM *šá* ITI.ŠU$^{?}$

8 [MU.12].KAM *qí-me* ŠE.BAR-*a*$_4$ 4 GUR ⸢3$^{?}$⸣ (BÁN)

9 [*q*]*í-me* GIG.BA-*a*$_4$ 1 GUR 2 (PI) 2 (BÁN) *šá* GIŠ.[BAN] M[U$^{?}$.x.KAM]$^{?}$

LO. E.

10 *gam-ri-ma a-na muḫ-ḫi* ^{m}*ba-zu-zu*

REV.

11 *u* LÚ *qí-*{*pi*}*-pa-ni-šú a-na* ^{md}AMAR.UTU-*na-ṣir*-A

12 A-*šú šá* ^{m}KI-^{d}AMAR.UTU-DIN A ^{m}*e-gì-bi iṭ-*[*ṭ*]*ir*

13 *pu-ut e-ṭè-ru šá qí-me* ŠE.BAR *u qí-me* GIG.BA

14 ^{m}*lib-luṭ u* ^{m}*ku-uš-šá-a-a na-šu-ú*

15 LÚ *mu-kin*$_7$ ^{m}ÌR-^{d}EN A-*šú šá* ^{m}*ina*-SÙḪ-SUR DUMU ^{m}*bi-bi* ^{m}*ri-mut* DUMU *šá* ^{md}ŠÚ-⸢GI⸣

16 ^{m}*ri-mut* A-*šú šá* ^{md}AMAR.UTU-BA-*šá-an-ni* A ^{m}DUMU-*si-si-i*

17 ^{md}U.GUR-MU A-*šú šá* ^{m}[x]-⸢SU$^{?}$⸣ A ^{m}NUMUN-*ú-tu-ia*

18 ^{m}*lib-luṭ* A-*šú šá* [^{m}KI]-^{d}AG-DIN A ^{m}DUMU-*si-si-i* ^{m}MU-^{d}AG

19 A-*šú šá* ^{md}UTU-NUMUN-DÙ ⸢A⸣ [LÚ].EN.NUN-KÁ.GAL ^{md}EN-SU

20 A ^{m}*ri-mut*-^{d}⸢*é*⸣-*a* ^{m}*za-ni-e* A ^{m}MU-^{d}⸢AG$^{?}$⸣

21 ^{m}⸢*ina*-SÙḪ-SUR⸣$^{?}$ A-*šú šá* ^{m}MU-MU A ^{md}EN-*e-ṭè-*⸢*ru*⸣

U. E.

22 ^{md}EN-NUMUN-DÙ DUB.SAR A ^{m}*da-bi-bi* TIN.TIR.⸢KI⸣

23 ⸢ITI⸣.[ŠU$^{?}$] UD.25.KAM MU.12.KAM

LE. E.

24 ^{m}*da-ri-iá-muš* LUGAL E.KI *u* KUR.KUR

TRANSLATION

4.0.⸢3$^{?}$⸣ *kor* of barley flour (and) 1.2.2 *kor* of wheat flour from the bow of the exorcists, which is administered by Nabû-šuma-ukīn, governor of Babylon. It is the property of the king. One-third of it is from the bow of Bazūzu (erasure?) (and) his ⸢nine⸣ administrators of the scribal$^{!}$ school. By the twenty-ninth of Dûzu (or Tašrīt) of the [twelfth year] Libluṭ, son of Murašû, descendant of Sîn-tabni, will deliver the full amount of 4.0.⸢3$^{?}$⸣ *kor* of barley flour (and) 1.2.2 *kor* of wheat flour from the [bow(-tax)] [of the eleventh (or twelfth) yea]r, to MNA$_1$, for the account of Bazūzu and his ad{id}ministrators. Libluṭ and Kuššaya assume warranty for the delivery of the barley flour and the wheat flour.

Witnesses:
Arad-Bēl/Ina-tēšê-ēṭir//Bibi (=<Dā>bibī, or =<Kul>bibi?)
Rīmūt/Marduk-⸢ušallim⸣(//Paḫāru)
Rīmūt/Marduk-iqīšanni//Mār-sīsî
Nergal-iddin/[x]-⸢erība$^{?}$⸣//Zērūtiya
Libluṭ/[Itti]-Nabû-balāṭu//Mār-sīsî
Iddin-Nabû/Šamaš-zēra-ibni//Maṣṣār-abulli
Bēl-erība//Rīmūt-Ea
Zanê//Iddin-⸢Nabû$^{?}$⸣
⸢Ina-tēšê-ēṭir⸣$^{?}$/Šuma-iddin//Bēl-eṭēru
The scribe: Bēl-zēra-ibni//Dābibī
(Place + Date).

COMMENT

L. 1: The *-me* in *qí-me* here and *passim* has rather the shape of a LÁ, but the expression KI.LÁ *šuqultu* "weight" does not make sense in the present context.

L. 2: I understand LÚ *a-ši-pu*.MEŠ as referring to the "exorcists" (*āšipū*). A derivation from the word *āšibu* (read the signs LÚ *a-ši-bu*.MEŠ, probably a synonym for *aššābū*), "residents, inhabitants" is less likely. Cf. Jursa, *Bēl-rēmanni*, 103 and notes 78, 437. See also above n. 91.

L. 3: For *ša* (*ina*) *qātē* "administered by," see discussion at BM 30795: 4b.

L. 4: Some signs at the end of this line seem to have been erased. The passage is difficult to read because some signs from the reverse (l. 15) are written right underneath the signs in question, viz. between the end of line 4 and the end of line 5.

L. 5: The *qīpānu* (wr. $^{⸢lú⸣}$*qí-pa-ni-*, pl. of *qīpu*) were administrative officials appointed by the king and responsible for a specific region, city or a temple;

they often formed a collegium (*CAD* Q, 264–68; *AHw*, 922–923). Among them were also professional scribes (MacGinnis, *Letter Orders*, 129; *CAD* Q, 266 s.v. *qīpu* mng. 1e), so that the reference to "administrators of the house of the scribe" in line 5 may be unique, but not unusual. In our text they formed a group of ten men, including Bazūzu, and had to provide the governor of Babylon with the king's flour. Cf. SCT 95 from Sippar, cited by Jursa, *Bēl-rēmanni*, 102 n. 427 and 106 n. 447. For additional examples from MNA's archive, see BM 30261: 2 and BM 30589: 5.

L. 7–8: It is not clear whether we have to read ITI.ŠU (= Dûzu) or ITI.DU$_6$ (= Tašrīt) at the end of line 7. The sign for the month in the date formula on the upper edge is also unclear (see below line 23). The year in line 8 is either 11.KAM or 12.KAM, but the latter is more likely since the text itself is dated in that year.

L. 11: The LÚ *qí pi pa ni šú* in this line is most likely a scribal error for ^{lú}*qīpānīšu* (LÚ *qí-{pi}-pa-ni-šú*), so that we have the same terminology as in line 5. A reading LÚ *qí-pi pa-ni-šú* "the administrators (^{lú}*qīpī*) at his disposal" in line 11 is less likely, because the plural of *qīpu* is either *qīpūtu* or *qīpānu*, not *qīpī*.

L. 12: The TIR-sign has been written over a badly erased sign, which seems to have been IR.

L. 15: The family name ^{m}*bi-bi* is possibly to be emended to either ^{m}*<da->bi-bi* or ^{m}*<kul->bi-bi*. The last sign of this line is very much squeezed and appears on the obverse of the tablet, between lines 4 and 5. There is no saying whether the sign in question is NUMUN, URU$_3$/ŠEŠ or MU.

L. 20: The first name Zanê (^{m}*za-ni-e*) may be compared to the patronymy ^{m}*za-an-ni-e* (Dar 133: 12) and the surname ^{m}*za-an-ni-e-tú* (Peiser, *BV*, 17: 9). Refs. at Tallqvist, *NbN*, 217. According to Tallqvist, *NbN*, 314f., these names contain the same enigmatic element as found in the family name Nūr-zana. Further note the surname ^{m}*za-an-ni-e-a* in YOS 17 21: 16 (Nabû-bēlšunu/Marduk-aḫa-iddin//~). Do these names contain the Iranian element *zani* "skilled, trained" (Dr. Tavernier, personal communication)? More on the name Nūr-zana at Dar 308:15.

L. 21: A person named Iddin-Bēl/Šuma-iddin//Bēl-eṭēru occurs among the witnesses in the promissory note for barley owed by MNA for the rent of Darius' tenth year to Bēl-iddin/Mušēzib-Marduk//Ēṭiru (MacGinnis, *Iraq* 55 No. 1). He may have been the brother of ⸢Ina-tēšê-ēṭir⸣$^{?}$ mentioned in the text under consideration.

L. 23: Only the general outline of the sign is preserved so that it cannot be decided whether to read DU$_6$, KIN, or ŠU because the beginning of that particular sign is broken.

No. 80

BM 33959
Copy: Bertin copy 2382
Date: 24/x/17 Dar (31 January 504 B.C.E.)
Place: Babylon
Content: About onions from the property of Bēl in Šaḫrīnu. Mentions Šaddinnu and MNA together. Very fragmentary.

OBV.

1 ⸢*ú*$^{?}$⸣-[…] SUM.SAR *šá* URU *šá-aḫ-ri-nu*
2 NÍG.⸢GA⸣ ^{d}E[N] […] [A]-[*šú*] ⸢*šá*⸣ ^{md}EN-URU$_3$-*šú šá* MU.11.KAM
3 ^{m}*da*-[*a*]-[*ri-ia-muš* …] ^{md}AMAR.UTU-*na-ṣir*-A
4 [A-*šú šá* ^{m}KI-^{d}AMAR.UTU-DIN A ^{m}*e-gi-b*]*i e-il-li-ti*
5 [… ^{m}]⸢*šad*⸣-*din-nu* A-*šú šá* ^{md}DI.KU$_5$-ŠEŠ.⸢MEŠ⸣<-MU>
6 […] ⸢x⸣ ^{md}AMAR.UTU-*na-ṣir*-A
7 [A-*šú šá* ^{m}KI-^{d}AMAR.UTU-DI]N A ^{m}*e-gì-bi it-te-en-ṭi-ir*
8 […] *ú-ìl-tì i-na-áš-am-ma*
9 [… *i-na*]-*ad-din*

LO. E.

Broken off.

REV.

10 [LÚ *mu-kin-nu* … ^{md}]⸢EN$^{?}$⸣-A-MU
11 […] [^{md}EN]-⸢*it-tan-nu* DUMU *šá*⸣ ^{md}AG-URU$_3$-*šú* DUMU LÚ.SANGA-^{d}IDIM
12 [^{m}…]-⸢x⸣ A-*šú šá* ^{md}IDIM-NUMUN-BA-*šá* A ^{m}*ba-bu-tú*
13 [^{m}KI-^{d}E]N-*lam-mir* A-*šú šá* ^{md}EN-*ki-šìr* A ^{md}30-[…]
14 ^{m}⸢*mu*⸣-*šal-lim*-^{d}AMAR.UTU A-*šú šá* ^{m}*mu-šeb-šú* A ^{md}AG-*na-a-a*
15 ^{m}*mu-še-zib*-^{d}EN A-*šú šá* ^{md}UTU-ŠEŠ-MU A ^{m}LÚ-PA.ŠE.KI
16 ^{md}AG-DIB-UD.DA A-*šú šá* ^{m}MU-^{d}EN A LÚ-PA.ŠE.KI
17 ^{md}EN-SUM.NA DUB.SAR DUMU LÚ.SIPA-ANŠE.KUR.RA
18 [TIN].TIR.KI ITI.AB UD.24.KAM MU.17.KAM
19 [^{m}*da*]-*a-ri-ia-muš* LUGAL E.KI *u* [KUR.KUR]

TRANSLATION

The p[romissory note(s) for] the onions from Šaḫrīnu, (from)$^{?}$ the ⸢property⸣ of B[ēl], […], [so]n ⸢of⸣ Bēl-uṣuršu, of the eleventh year of Da[rius], [which to the debit of] MNA$_1$ had been contracted - […] Šaddinnu, son of Madānu-aḫḫē<-iddin>, have/has been paid off [… b]y$^{?}$ MNA$_1$. […] he will bring up the promissory note and [gi]ve (it) […].

[Witnesses:]
[^{m}…][/]⸢Bēl$^{?}$⸣-apla-iddin […]
[Bēl]-⸢ittannu⸣ ⸢/⸣Nabû-uṣuršu//Šangû-Ea
[^{m}…]/Ea-zēra-iqīša//Bābūtu

[Itti-B]ēl-lāmur/Bēl-kēšir//Sîn-[šadûnu]
Mušallim-Marduk/Mušebši//Nabunnaya
Mušēzib-Bēl/Šamaš-aḫa-iddin//Amēl-Isin
Nabû-mušētiq-uddê/Iddin-Bēl//Amēl-Isin
The scribe: Bēl-iddin//Rē'i-sīsî
(Place + Date).

COMMENT

According to the reconstructions as suggested below, BM 33959 records the quittance of a silver debt that MNA owed to Šaddinnu. The debt originated in MNA's purchase of the right to collect the *šibšu*-rent of Darius' eleventh year from Šaddinnu (see also Dar 453^{+} and Dar 315).

L. 1: I suggest reconstructing ⸢*ú*?⸣-[*ìl-tì*.(MEŠ) *šá* x MA.NA KÙ.BABBAR ŠÁM], "The p[romissory note(s) for x minas of silver, the price of]? the onions." This reconstruction is based on a comparison with Dar 453^{+}: 6–7. In fact, the text under discussion was written on the same day and by the same scribe as Dar 453^{+} and shares many of its witnesses as well as its subject matter.

L. 2: Possibly to be read: NÍG.⸢GA⸣ ^{d}E[N *šá ina* IGI ^{m}... A]-[*šú*] ⸢*šá*⸣ ^{md}EN-URU$_3$-*šú*, "onions, the ⸢property⸣ of Bē[l, which are with ^{m}...], [so]n ⸢of⸣ Bēl-uṣuršu." If so, this son of Bēl-uṣuršu was probably one of the farmers mentioned in Dar 315: 3–4. For the syntax of *makkūr Bēl*, more at Dar 315: 1.

L. 3–4: I suggest reconstructing ^{m}*da*-[*a*]-[*ri-ia-muš šá ina muḫ-ḫi*], "... which to the debit of" on the basis of Dar 453^{+}: 3. The signs at the end of line 4 are difficult to read, but may resemble *e-'?-le?-et?* (= stative form of the verb *e'ēlu*?). Accordingly, lines 1, 3–4 may be translated: "The p[romissory note ...] ... [which] was contracted [to the debit of] MNA." For the verb *e'ēlu*, more at BM 30795: 7–9.

L. 6: I suggest reconstructing [*ina qa-a*]*t*?, "[b]y?." One cannot read [*ina* ŠU].⸢II⸣.

L. 8: I suggest reconstructing [*a-di* UD.x.KAM *šá* ITI.x], "[By the xth of MN]."

L. 9: I suggest reconstructing [*a-na* ^{md}AMAR.UTU-*na-ṣir*-A *i-na*]-*ad-din*, "[He shall gi]ve (it) [to MNA]."

L. 11: This Bēl-ittannu, son of Nabû(-tabtanni)-uṣur(šu), is well attested in the Egibi archive (Wunsch, *Felder* 2, 284).

L. 12: A person named Arad-Nergal/Ea-zēra-iqīša//Bābūtu occurs in Liv 33: 15 (= *CM* 20b 32), and his brother Nabû-kuṣuršu/Ea-zēra-iqīša[//Bābūtu] apparently occurs in Dar 453^{+}: 14. The latter document shares several witnesses with the document under consideration.

L. 13: The use of the LAM-sign is exceptional. The verbal element *-lūmur/līmur* in names such as Itti-Bēl-lū/īmur and Bēl-lūmur is usually written *-lu-(um)-mur/mir, -li-(im)-mur/mir,* or *lum-mir/mur* (cf. Tallqvist, *NbN*, 82 s.v. *Itti-Bêl-limmir* and *Itti-Bêl-lu-mur*, but see p. 305 for names with *lāmur*, wr. *la-mur* in Neo-Assyrian sources). The same person is attested in Dar 453^{+}: 16, where this name is spelled *-lum-mir*.

L. 17: Read PA<.LU> = SIPA. For the same spelling, also see Dar 144: 9.

No. 81

BM 33962 (= Dupl. of Dar 509)
Copy: Bertin copy 2448
Date: 8/ix/20 Dar (13 December 502 B.C.E.)
Place: Babylon
Content: Summons to settle debts with MNA.

OBV.

1 [… ITI].⸢ZÍZ⸣ MU.20.KAM ^{m}*d*[*a-*…]
2 ⸢^{md}EN-NIGIN-*ir*⸣ [A]-*šú ša* ^{md}U.GUR-M[U …]
3 *šá ú-ìl-tì šá* KÙ.BABBAR ŠE.BAR ZÚ.LUM.MA […]
4 LÚ *qal-la šá* ^{md}AMAR.UTU-*na-din*-A A-*šú šá* ^{m}KI-^{d}A[MAR …]
5 *šá ina muḫ-ḫi-šú i-na-áš-šam-ma a-na* ^{md}AMAR.UTU-*n*[*a-*…]
6 A-*šú šá* ^{m}KI-^{d}AMAR.UTU-DIN A ^{m}*e-gi-bi ú-kal-lam ki-i*
7 [U]D.15.KAM *šá* ITI.ZÍZ MU.20.KAM *mim-ma šá e-ṭè-ru*
8 [*š*]*á ú-ìl-tì šá* KÙ.BABBAR ŠE.BAR ZÚ.LUM.MA GU$_4$ *šá* ^{md}DI.KU$_5$-EN-URU$_3$
9 *šá ina muḫ-ḫi-šú a-na* ^{md}AMAR.UTU-*na-din*-A *la uk-tal*-⸢*li*⸣-*mu*
10 *a-ki-i ú-ìl-tì šá* KÙ.BABBAR ŠE.BAR ZÚ.LUM.MA GU$_4$
11 $^{[md]}$⸢DI.KU$_9$⸣-EN-URU$_3$ LÚ *qal-la šá* ^{md}AMAR.UTU-*na-ṣ*[*ir*$^{?}$ …]

LO. E.

12 [*šá ina muḫ-ḫi-šú*] [*a*]-*na* ^{md}AMAR.UTU-*na-din*-A
13 [A-*šú šá* ^{m}KI]-^{d}AMAR.UTU-DIN A ^{m}*e-gi-bi* ⸢x x⸣

REV.

14 [KÙ.BABBAR *šá* ^{md}]DI.KU$_5$-EN-URU$_3$ *iṭ-ṭi-ir*
15 LÚ *mu-kin-nu* ^{m}*ta-at-tan-nu* A-*šú šá* ^{m}SU-^{d}AMAR.UTU A ^{md}AMAR.⸢UTU-I⸣
16 ^{m}*i-qu-pu* A-*šú šá* ^{m}MU-^{d}EN A ^{m}ZALAG$_2$-^{d}30
17 ⸢^{m}*bu-na*⸣-*nu* A-*šú šá* ^{m}*su-qa-a-a* A ^{md}30-*ga-mil*
18 ⸢^{m}NUMUN⸣-*ia* A-*šú šá* ^{m}BA-*šá-a* A ^{m}*š*[*i-gu-ú*]-*a*
19 ^{m}*zu-um-ba-a* A-*šú šá* ^{m}*kur-ban-ni*-^{d}ŠÚ [A ^{m}*bi-ib-bu*]-⸢*ú-a*⸣
20 ^{md}AG-*it-tan-nu* A-*šú šá* ^{md}EN-DIN-*iṭ* A ^{m}LÚ.A.[ZU …]
21 ⸢^{md}AG-MU-MU⸣ ^{m}*nap-sa-an* A-*šú šá* ^{md}U.GUR-DIN-*i*[*ṭ*]
22 [A ^{m}SIG$_{15}$-^{d}IŠKUR] LÚ.UMBISAG A-*šú šá* ^{m}M[U-…]
23 [… UD.8].KAM MU.20.KAM ^{m}*da-a-r*[*i-ia-muš*]
24 [LUGAL] E.KI LUGAL KUR[.KUR]

LE. E.

25 ⸢^{m}*ni-din*⸣-[*tu*$_4$ A-*šu ša* ^{m}*mi*]-⸢*it*⸣-*ra*-⸢*a*⸣-[*ta*]
26 ⸢x x⸣ [(…)]

For a translation and comments, see at Dar 509.

No. 82

BM 33968
Copy: Bertin copy 2823
Date: [-]/ix/[15] Dar (February–early March 506 B.C.E.)
Place: Babylon
Content: About the delivery of a baker (LÚ.M[U]) to Marduk-nāṣir-apli (= MNA?). Very fragmentary.

OBV.

1 [...] ITI.ZÍZ *šá* MU.15.KAM
2 [... L]Ú *mu-kin-nu*.MEŠ
3 [... ^{m}]^{d}EN-DÙ *e*$^{?}$-*pu*$^{?}$-*uš* ⸢x⸣
4 [...]-[UTU$^{?}$] A-*šú šá* ^{md}AG-NUMUN-DÙ ⸢ḪU$^{?}$ x⸣
5 [...] ⸢x⸣ NU
6 [...]-AMAR.UTU
7–9 (lines too fragmentary to be legible)
10 [...] ⸢ x⸣ DU U′ ŠÁ GIŠ [x x + edge]
11 [... ^{m}]⸢BA⸣-^{d}AMAR.UTU [x x (x) + edge]

LO. E.

(almost completely broken off, but seems to have been inscribed.)

REV.

1′ [...]
2′ [...] ⸢x⸣ LÚ GAL ⸢x x⸣
3′ [...] ⸢IQ$^{?}$⸣ *a-ba-ak ki-i* LÚ.M[U (x x)]
4′ [... *la i-ta-ba*]$^{?}$-*ak-kam-ma a-na* ^{md}AMAR.UTU-PAB-EDURU
5′ [... *a-ki*]-*i šá-ṭa-ri maḫ-ru-ú*
6′ [...]-^{d}AMAR.UTU *u* ^{md}AG-NUMUN-DÙ A-*šú šá* ^{md}ŠÁR-AD-URU$_{3}$
7′ [... AMAR.UT]U$^{?}$ *a-na* ^{md}AMAR.UTU-PAB-IBILA *i-nam-din*
8′ [LÚ *mu-kin-nu* ^{m}...] A-*šú šá* ^{m}KAR-^{d}ŠÚ A ^{m}*e-ṭè-ru*
9′ [...] A LÚ.AZLAG ^{m}*id-ra-a*
10′ [...]-MU A-*šú šá* ^{m}*ú-bar* ^{md}EN-SUR A-*šú šá* ^{md}30-⸢MU$^{?}$⸣
11′ [...] A ^{m}DÙ-⸢*eš*⸣-DINGIR ^{md}EN-*iq-bi*
12′ [...] ⸢x A-*šú šá*⸣ ^{m}MU-*a*

U. E.

13′ [LÚ.UMBISAG A] ^{m}*na-din-še-im* E.KI ITI.GAN
14′ [UD.x.KAM MU.x.KAM ^{m}*da-ri-ia*]-*muš* LUGAL E.KI LUGAL KUR.KUR

TRANSLATION

The obverse and the beginning of the reverse are too fragmentary to be translated.

(Rev. 2′ff.) [...] the overseer [...] I will bring. If [he does not br]ing$^{?}$ the bak[er(s)] and to Marduk-nāṣir-apli [does not deliver]$^{?}$, [accor]ding to the previous document [...-Mardu]k[?] will give [Iqīša[?]]-Marduk and Nabû-zēra-ibni, son of Aššur-aba-uṣur, to Marduk-nāṣir-apli.

[Witnesses]:
[m...]/Mušēzib-Marduk//Ēṭiru
[...]//Ašlāku
Idrā [...]
[...]-MU/Ubār
Bēl-ēṭir/Sîn-⸢iddin[?]⸣
[...]//Eppeš-ilī
Bēl-iqbi [...]
[The scribe[?]:] [m...]/Iddinaya[//]Nādin-še'i
(Place + Date).

COMMENT

This tablet is very fragmentary. First, it is broken off so that what we have is actually a fragment of a larger tablet, the original size of which is difficult to reconstruct. Currently, it measures 5,3 (W) × 5,8 (L) cm. Second, its surface, especially on the obverse, is badly damaged. However, the signs that are preserved are usually fairly legible.

Each line may have contained up to sixteen signs (see, for instance, line 14′), not including the right edge. The latter is preserved completely in Obv. lines 1–7 and Rev. lines 6′–12′, which shows that it was wide enough for two signs (e.g., -AD-URU_3 in line 6′). It is only partly preserved in Rev. lines 4′–5′.

Obverse:

L. 3: The last sign was probably erased.

L. 4: At the beginning after the break there is one upper *Winkelhaken* and a vertical: read -[UTU[?]]. The DÙ is very small and at the very end of the obverse; it is followed by two more signs on the right edge.

L. 11: Does this line refer to Iqīša(BA<-*šá*>)-Marduk(dAMAR.UTU)? Cf. Rev. line 6′. He and Nabû-zēra-ibni/Aššur-aba-uṣur sold draught animals to MNA as we know from Dar 392 (also see at the comment to Dar 351 below); Iqīša-Marduk may have been Nabû-zēra-ibni's son.

Reverse:

L. 2′: The two signs after LÚ.GAL are very difficult to read. They do not resemble LÚ.MU; the first one may be DI or KI.

L. 3′: With LÚ.M[U] the scribe reached the obverse's end. He may have continued writing on the right edge (cf. lines 6′, 7′, 8′, and 11′), but may as well have continued on the next line (cf. lines 5′, 10′ and 12′).

L. 5′: I suggest restoring [*la it-ta-din*], "If [he does not give]."

L. 6′: For Nabû-zēra-ibni/Aššur-aba-uṣur, also see Dar 351 (below) and Dar 392. For Iqīša-Marduk, who was perhaps his son, see Dar 392 and above at line 11. For the reading of ^{d}ŠÁR = Aššur in personal names, see Zadok, *Assur* 4/3, 3–8.

L. 12′–13′: I suggest reconstructing the beginning of line 13′ as: [LÚ.UMBISAG], although the space available allows for more signs. Several members of the Nādin-še'i family acted as scribes for members of the Egibi family (see index), and a person named ^{m}[.../]Iddinaya//Nādin-še'i is attested as witness in the unpublished deed BM 31383: 10 = b 2778, and its duplicate BM 31935 = b 2786; Babylon, 21/v/[-] Dar). It contains MNA's promise to pay the dates that he owed to Bēl-kāṣir/Bēl-ēṭir//Ir'anni to the latter "in Ayyar at the river in Babylon according to the measure of Bēl-ēṭir" (ll. 1–6). The list of witnesses that follows this promise mentions, among others, a man named ^{m}⸢x⸣-[...] $^{[m]}$SUM.NA-*a* A ^{m}*na-din-še-im* (ll. 9–10).

No. 83

	BM 33972
Copy:	Bertin copy 3065
Date:	broken (between 5 Dar and Nisan 6 Dar, i.e., 517–April 516 B.C.E.)
Place:	Šaḫrīnu
Content:	Promissory note to pay a debt of silver, barley and onions to MNA. Pledge renewal. Repayment of the onions is to be obtained from the (debtor's) *šibšu*. Silver had been transferred to the debtor to pay for *rikis qabli*. Reference to an outstanding debt of dates and barley secured by pledge.

OBV.

1 3⸢5/6 MA.NA⸣ [x] ⸢7½⸣ G[ÍN KÙ.BABBAR 2 GUR ŠE.BAR *ù*]
2 1 ME 30 *pít-ti šá* SUM.SAR *š*[*á* MNA]
3 DUMU-*šú šá* ^{m}*it-ti*-^{d}AMAR.UTU-DIN A ^{m}[*e-gi-bi ina* UGU]
4 ^{m}*ri-mut*-^{d}EN DUMU-*šú šá* ^{m}MU-GIN *ina* ITI.B[ÁR]
5 *šá* MU.6.KAM KÙ.BABBAR-*a'* 3 5/6 MA.NA 7½ GÍN
6 1 ME 30 *pít-ti šá* SUM.SAR *i-nam-din ina* ITI.GU$_4$
7 *šá* MU.6.KAM 2 GUR ŠE.BAR *ga-mir-tu*$_4$ *ina muḫ-ḫi* 1-*et*
8 *rit-tu*$_4$ *ina ma-ši-ḫu ša* ^{md}AMAR.UTU-*na*-PAB-A *i-nam-din*
9 A.ŠÀ.MEŠ *gab-bi zaq-pu u pi-i šul-pu ul-tu*
10 ÍD *bar-sip*.KI *a-di muḫ-ḫi* KASKAL.II LUGAL É *maš-ka-nu*
11 IGI-*ú maš-ka-nu šá* ^{md}AMAR.UTU-*na*-PAB-A LÚ.TUKU-*ú šá-nam-ma*
12 *ina muḫ-ḫi ul i-šal-laṭ a-di muḫ-ḫi* ^{md}AMAR.UTU-*na*-PAB-A

LO. E.

13 [LÚ].TUKU-*ú-šú i-šal-lim-mu e-lat ú-ìl-tì*
14 IGI-*ti šá* 2 ME 97 GUR 3 PI

REV.

15 ZÚ.LUM.MA 11 GUR 2 (PI) 3 (BÁN) ŠE.BAR *ra-šu-tú*

16 *šá* ^{md}AMAR.UTU-*na*-PAB-A *šá ina muḫ-ḫi* ^{m}*ri-mut*-^{d}EN
17 *šá* A.ŠÀ.MEŠ-*šú gab-bi zaq-pu u pi-i šul-pu* <*šá*>
18 *maš-ka-nu ṣab-tú* KÙ.BABBAR *ša a-na dul-lu šá mu-še-ši-ni-tu*$_4$
19 *ri-ki-is qab-lu šá* MU.5.KAM SUM-*nu*
20 *ina šib-šú* A.ŠÀ-*šú šá* SUM.SAR *šá* ^{md}DI.KU$_5$-EN-PAB *i-pu-uš*
21 SUM.SAR ^{md}AMAR.UTU-*na*-PAB-A *i-šal-lim*

LE. E.

22 KÁ *e-le-nu-ú šá* ^{m}*ri-mut*-^{d}EN KÁ *šu*-⸢*pa*⸣-[*lu*]
23 *šá* ÚS.SA.DU É LÚ.AGRIG ḪA.LA-*šú šá* KI [(x)]
24 ^{md}AG-*ma-a-ku*-URU$_3$

REV.

25 LÚ *mu-kin-nu* ^{m}*la-ba-ši* A-*šú šá* ^{md}AG-DÙ-ŠEŠ A ^{m}EZENxKASKAL-^{d}30
26 ^{md}AG-ŠEŠ$^{!}$.MEŠ$^{!}$<-*bul*->*liṭ* A-*šú šá* ^{m}*na-din* A LÚ.ŠU.KU$_6$ ^{md}AG-*ma-a*-⸢*ku*-URU$_3$⸣
27 A-*šú šá* ^{md}AG-A-MU ^{md}KÁ-⸢DÙ⸣ A-*šú šá* ^{md}AG-⸢x⸣ [...]
28 ^{md}EN-DÙ A-*šú šá* ^{md}U.GUR-N[UMUN- ...]
29 [URU] *šaḫ-ri-nu* ITI.[...]
(Remainder of reverse is broken off.)

TRANSLATION

Three and ⸢five-sixth⸣ minas (and) ⸢seven and a half⸣ she[kels of silver, two *kor* of barley and] one hundred and thirty bundles of onions [are due t]o MNA [from] Rīmūt-Bēl, son of Šuma-ukīn. In Ni[san] of the sixth year he will deliver these three and five-sixth minas and seven and a half shekels of silver, and these one hundred and thirty bundles of onions. In Ayyar of the sixth year he will deliver the full amount of two *kor* of barley, in one installment according to MNA$_1$'s measure. All the previously pledged fields, the ones planted with trees as well as the grain fields, from the Borsippa canal to the Royal Street, are pledged (anew) to MNA$_1$. No other creditor shall exercise any rights over these until MNA$_1$ has received full repayment of his credit claim. In addition, there is a previous debt of 297.3.0 *kor* of dates and 11.2.3 *kor* of barley owed by Rīmūt-Bēl to MNA$_1$, <for which> all his (previously mentioned?) fields, the ones planted with trees as well as the grain fields, have been pledged. It is the silver that has been given for work at the dams, (payment for) the *rikis qabli* of the fifth year. MNA$_1$ will receive full repayment of the onions from the *šibšu*-onions on his (= the debtor's) field that Madānu-bēla-uṣur contracted (to cultivate/ manage). The upper sector belongs to Rīmūt-Bēl; the low[er] sector, which is located next to the house of the canal inspector, is shared with Nabû-māku-uṣur.

Witnesses:
Lâbāši/Nabû-bāni-aḫi//Kidin-Sîn
Nabû-aḫḫē$^{!}$<-bulliṭ>/Nādin//Bā'iru
Nabû-māku-⸢uṣur⸣/Nabû-apla-iddin

Bāba-⸢ibni⸣/Nabû-[...]
[The scribe]: Bēl-ibni/Nergal-zē[ra-ibni//Šangû-Nanaya].

Comment

L. 20–21: Cf. Dar 164: 6, Dar 167: 6 and *CAD* Š$_1$, 218 s.v. *šalāmu* mng. 6b. I suggest interpreting *epēšu* in the light of the noun *ēpišānu* "contractor" (lit. "performer," i.e., the person who contracted to perform the work connected with a prebend instead of the prebendary himself, or who contracted to repair and do maintenance works for someone else; hence "contractor;" more at Bongenaar, *Ebabbar*, 167 and 263f.). MBU may have contracted to (physically) cultivate the field (*eqlam epēšu*, *AHw*, 226 s.v. *epēšu* mng. I.8.c and e: "bearbeiten, bebauen"; *CAD* E, s.v. *epēšu*, 230 mng. 2f-5′: "to cultivate"), or he may have taken up its agricultural management rather than doing the physical work of cultivation, cf. Jursa's remark (*Bēl-rēmanni*, 151) on *epēšu* in BM 42352: 6 "wahrscheinlich nicht '(Arbeit physisch) verrichten', sondern 'betreiben, durchführen' im Sinne von 'finanzieren'."

L. 28: The scribe's name is reconstructed on the basis of Dar 164, whose subject matter is very closely related to that of the text under consideration. For this person in several texts from the time of Itti-Marduk-balāṭu//Egibi, see Tallqvist, *NbN*, 31 s.v. Bēl-ibni (28).

No. 84

BM 41442 (= Dupl. of *AJSL* 27 221//BOR 1, 83)
Copy: Bertin copy 2604
Date: 15/xii/26 Dar (12 March 495 B.C.E.)
Place: Babylon
Content: Apprenticeship contract to teach MNA's slave the baker's profession (LÚ.MU-*ú-tu*).

Obv.

1 ^{md}AMAR.UTU-PAB-*ap-lu* DUMU *šá* ^{m}KI-^{d}AMAR.UTU-DIN DUMU ^{m}*e-gì-bi*
2 *i-na ḫu-ud lìb-bi-šú* ^{m}KI-^{d}URAŠ-IGI-*ia*
3 LÚ *qal-la-šú a-na la-ma-a-du* LÚ.MU-*ú-tu*
4 *a-di ṭup-pi ù ṭup-pi ù* 3.ITI.MEŠ *a-na*
5 ^{m}*gu-za-nu* DUMU *šá* ^{m}*ḫa-am-ba-qu* DUMU LÚ *man-di-di*
6 *id-din* LÚ.MU-*ú-tu dul-lu qa-ti-šú gab-bi ú-lam-mad-su*
7 *ki-i ul-tam-mi-du-šú* 1-*et* TÚG *ú-za-ri* ^{md}AMAR.UTU-PAB-*ap-lu*
8 *a-na* ^{m}*gu-za-nu i-nam-din ki-i la ul-tam-mi-du-šú*
9 u_4-*mu* 3 SILA$_3$ ŠE.BAR *man-da-at šá* ^{m}KI-^{d}URAŠ-IGI-*ia*
10 ^{m}*gu-za-nu a-na* ^{md}AMAR.UTU-*na-ṣir-ap-lu*
11 *i-nam-din* 1-*en*.TA.ÀM *šá-ṭa-ri*
12 TI-*ú*

REV.

13 LÚ *mu-kin-nu* ^{m}*ri-mut*-^{d}EN DUMU *šá* ^{m}ÌR-*ia* DUMU LÚ.⸢ŠITIM⸣

14 ^{m}*iṣ-ṣu-ur* DUMU *šá* ^{md}AG-MU-MU DUMU ^{m}DÙ-*eš*-DINGIR

15 ^{md}EN-SU DUMU *šá* ^{m}*kal-ba-a* DUMU ^{m}MU-*líb-ši*

16 ^{m}*šá*-^{d}EN-*at-ta* LÚ.DUB.SAR DUMU *šá* ^{md}AMAR.UTU-MU-DÙ

17 DUMU ^{m}*e-gi-bi* TIN.TIR.KI ITI.ŠE UD.15.KAM

18 MU.26.KAM ^{m}*da-a-ri-ia-muš* LUGAL TIN.TIR.KI

19 LUGAL KUR.KUR

TRANSLATION

MNA$_1$ has voluntarily given his slave Itti-Uraš-pāniya to Gūzānu, son of Ḫambaqu, descendant of Mandidi, in order to learn the baker's profession until further notice but for (at least) three months. He shall teach him all the skills of his baker's profession. If he has taught him, MNA$_1$ shall give to Gūzānu an *uzāru*-garment; if he has not taught him, Gūzānu shall give to MNA$_1$ three *qû* of barley for each day as compensation for Itti-Uraš-pāniya. They have taken one (copy of the) document each.

Witnesses:
Rīmūt-Bēl/Ardiya//⸢Itinnu⸣
Iṣṣūr/Nabû-šuma-iddin//Eppeš-ilī
Bēl-erība/Kalbaya//Šumu-libši
The scribe: Ša-Bēl-atta/Marduk-šuma-ibni//Egibi
(Place + Date).

COMMENT

L. 4: The term of the contract was as was agreed upon "for an indeterminate length of time (*adi ṭuppi u ṭuppi*), but (*u*) (at least for) three months." For the expression *adi ṭuppi u/ana ṭuppi*, see *AHw*, 1394 s.v. *ṭuppi* mng. 5; Von Dassow, CTMMA 3, 242f. ("for an indeterminate time"), Wunsch, *Iddin-Marduk* 2, 4 ("Von 'Termin' bis 'Termin'"), and Stolper, *JCS* 53, 107 and 125 n. 57 "(and) until further notice."

L. 7: For ^{túg}*uzāru*, see *AHw*, 1447 s.v. *uzāru*; and Kessler, *AUWE* 8/1, 176 (paid as *qīštu*).

L. 14: Iṣṣūr's brothers are known from documents from the time of Cyrus and Darius (Tallqvist, *NbN*, 94 s.v. Lâbāši(48); *ibid.*, 154 s.v. Nabû-zēra-iqīša(15); and *ibid.*, 45 s.v. Bēl-uballiṭ(66)). Interesting in this respect is the presence of Lâbāši among the witnesses in MM 595 (= Wunsch, *AuOr* 15 No. 18: 14) from Darius' reign. The latter document records the lease of private land. The leaseholder had to deliver fresh vegetables (*mašqu* = vegetables; or perhaps pieces of meat: Bongenaar, *Ebabbar*, n. 255) on the fourth and the fifteenth of Ab, as well as 1100 pomegranates and to pay eight shekels for dates. Wunsch (*Id.*, p. 172) notes that the text probably had a cultic background even when it concerned the lease of private land, and this for two reasons. First, the fixation of specific days on which the vegetables (or meat?) had to be delivered and, second, the fact that vegetables (or meat?) are known to have been part of deliveries made in the context of prebends (viz. *mubannû*, "arrangers-of-the-sacrificial-table"). If so, the lease contract recorded in *AuOr* 15 No. 18 and the apprenticeship contract recorded in BM 41442 may be linked to (prebendary) professionals, viz. arrangers-of-the-sacrificial-table (*AuOr* 15 No. 18) and bakers (BM 41442). It is therefore interesting to find a son of Nabû-šuma-iddin from the Eppeš-ilī family among the witnesses in the said lease contract and another of his sons in the present apprenticeship contract. These men may have been professional bakers and/or arrangers-of-the-sacrificial-table, and therefore present at transactions involving bakers and vegetables for the sacrificial table.

L. 15: After this line follows one empty line before the scribe started writing his name in line 18, cf. BM 30366: 12, BM 30819: 14, BM 31036: 12, BM 31227: 13, BM 31793: 17, BM 32883: 17, e.a.; probably also BM 30270: 16–17; cf. also BM 31118: 13.

L. 19: LUGAL KUR KUR is written in middle of the line. Remainder of this line, as well as the remainder of the reverse, is empty, i.e., some two lines. The scribe occasionally used the right edge of the tablet to write one sign and thus finish the sentence. In general, the edges of the tablet are uninscribed.

No. 85

BM 41449
Copy: Bertin copy 2833
Date: 3^{+}/xii(a)/[5 or 8] Dar (21^{+} Feb. 516 B.C.E. or 18^{+} Feb. 513 B.C.E.)
Place: Babylon
Content: Undertaking to bring the thieves in handcuffs to the house of MNA. The thieves had been caught in the city of the resident between the rivers (*ina birīt nārāti ina āli ša* ^{lú}*qīpi*).

OBV.

1 UD.1.KAM *šá* ITI.SIG$_4$ *šá* MU.⸢x⸣.[KAM …]
2 LUGAL TIN.TIR.KI LUGAL KUR.KUR ^{m}ÌR-⸢^{d}EN⸣ [A-*šú šá* ^{m} …]
3 A ^{m}*e-ṭè-ru* LÚ *sa-a-ri*.MEŠ *šá ni-i*[*k-* …]
4 *i-na bi-rit* ÍD.MEŠ *ina* URU *šá* LÚ *qí-pi*
5 *a-na* É ^{md}AMAR.UTU-*na-ṣir*-IBILA *ik-si-*⸢x⸣
6 *ib-ba-kam-ma a-na* ^{md}AMAR.UTU-*na-ṣir*-IBILA
7 *i-nam-din e-lat ra-šu-tu šá* ^{md}AMAR.UTU-*na-ṣir*-IBILA
8 *šá ina muḫ-ḫi* ^{m}ÌR-^{d}EN

REV.

9 LÚ *mu-kin-nu* ^{md}EN-MU A-*šú šá* ^{m}*mu-še-zib-*^{d}AMAR.UTU A ^{md}30-*na-din-*MU
10 ^{m}*na-di-nu* A-*šú šá* ^{m}ÌR-^{d}*gu-la* A ^{m}*lul-tam-mar-*^{d}IŠKUR

11 ^{m}*la-a-ba-ši* A-*šú šá* ^{md}AG-DÙ-ŠEŠ A ^{m}*ki-din*-^{d}30
12 ^{md}U.GUR-GI A-*šú šá* ^{m}*mu-še-zib*-^{d}AMAR.UTU A LÚ.SIMUG
13 ^{md}EN-KAR-*ir* A-*šú šá* ^{md}AG-KAR-ZI.MEŠ ⌜A LÚ.BAḪAR$_2$⌝
14 ^{md}AG-DIN-*su-iq-bi* LÚ.UMBISAG <A> $^{m⌜}$x⌝-[...]
15 TIN.TIR.KI ITI.ŠE IGI-*ú* UD.3+[...]
16 ^{m}*da-ri-'i-mu-uš* [...]

TRANSLATION

On the first of Simān of the [xth year of Darius], king of Babylon, king of the lands, shall Arad-⌜Bēl⌝, [son of ^{m}...], descendant of Ēṭiru, bring the thieves, who *ni-i*[*k*...], to the house of Marduk-nāṣir-apli, after having arrested (them) between the rivers in the city of the resident; and he shall hand (them) over to Marduk-nāṣir-apli. In addition, there is the credit claim owed to Marduk-nāṣir-apli by Arad-Bēl.

Witnesses:
Bēl-iddin/Mušēzib-Marduk//Sîn-nādin-šumi
Nādin/Arad-Gula//Lultammar-Adad
Lâbāši/Nabû-bāni-aḫi//Kidin-Sîn
Nergal-ušallim/Mušēzib-Marduk//Nappāḫu
Bēl-ēṭir/Nabû-ēṭir-napšāti//⌜Paḫāru⌝
The scribe: Nabû-balāssu-iqbi<//> ^{m}[...]
(Place + Date).

COMMENT

L. 1: At the end of the line it looks as if there was a vertical wedge so that the number of the year can be between one and nine. Most likely, we should read "on the first of Simān of the [6th (or 9th) year of Darius]," in view of line 15 (more below).

L. 2: Is Arad-Bēl/[...]/Ēṭiru to be identified with Ardiya/Marduk-šarrāni//Ēṭiru, who witnessed BM 31690^{+}? It would be another example of a person witnessing MNA's boat-related as well as temple-related transactions, cf. Table 7 and the discussion following it.

L. 4: The expression "city of the resident" is otherwise unattested, but it probably refers to the quarter(s) of the temple domain (or the city?) that were under the *qīpu*'s responsibility. For the conception of the temple as a city, see also the expression *qabalti āli*, which was "the designation for the complex of buildings (...) in Sippar that belonged to the Ebabbar temple: the shrines of the gods, the storehouses, the workshops and the accommodation for the (sacrificial) animals" (Bongenaar, *Ebabbar*, 423). The thieves, therefore, may have stolen property from "the city of the resident," i.e., from the temple. Theft of temple property by individuals seems to have been a relatively common phenomenon in the Neo-Babylonian period, see for instance YOS 7 10 and several other examples from the Eanna archive (cf. Joannès, *MOS Studies* 2, 29ff. on theft and other illicit appropriations of temple property by individuals). For *birītu* "in-between terrain, peninsula, wall," see *CAD* B, 252 s.v. *birītu*, *AHw*, 128 s.v. *birītu* mng. 3, and Wunsch, *Felder* 1, 71–72.

L. 5: It is syntactically difficult to interpret *ana bīt Marduk-nāṣir-apli* as complementary to *iksi*⌜*šu*⌝ because we do not expect the preposition *ana* with the verb "to put in fetters, to arrest." Consequently, I think that *ana bīt Marduk-nāṣir-apli* is complementary to the verb of the next sentence, *ibbakamma* (l. 6), so that one should translate "to the house of MNA he shall bring."

L. 5–7: The last sign of line 5 looks like a *šu*, but a *ma* is not excluded. In either case there is a problem. Since there was more than one thief, the pronominal suffix should have been -*šunu* rather than -*šu* "the thieves ... he arrested them (*iksišunu*)." If we read *iksīma* "he arrested and" it is remarkable that the following two verbs are in the present-future (*iparras*) "he shall bring them along and give them to Marduk-nāṣir-apli." The connection between *iksima* and the two other verbs (*ibbakamma ... inamdin*), therefore, is probably one of logical subordination, so that one should translate as follows: "the thieves, who *ni-i*[*k*-...], having put (them) in fetters he shall bring along to the house of Marduk-nāṣir-apli (*ibbakamma*) and hand over to Marduk-nāṣir-apli (*inamdin*)."

L. 14: The scribe's family name may have started with a ḪAR-sign.

L. 15: The text under consideration was written in the month First Addar. The year in which it was written is broken off, but it must have been between Darius' first and ninth years (see line 1 above). Most likely, it was either Darius' fifth or eighth year because these were the only leap years in the first nine years of Darius' reign.

No. 86

BM 41453
Copy: Bertin copy 2820. The text will be published with a copy by Wunsch, *Häuser*.
Date: 19/[-]/[35 or 36$^{?}$] Dar (27 December 486 B.C.E.?)
Place: broken
Content: Renting of a small house at the harbor and a loft by MNA's son.

OBV.

1 [É *kar-ri*] ⸢*u*⸣ *rug*$^{!}$*-bu šá ina* UGU [*b/pur*]*-ra-ku*
2 *šá* ^{m}*ni-din-tu*$_{4}$ DUMU *šá* ^{m}*ši-iš-ki* ^{md}EN*-ki-ṣur-šú*
3 DUMU *šá* ^{m}*ri-mut* DUMU LÚ ⸢x⸣ *ina na-áš-par-tu*$_{4}$
4 *šá* ^{m}*ni-din-tu*$_{4}$ *a-na i-di* É *a-na u*$_{4}$*-mu*
5 4 SILA$_{3}$ NINDA.ḪI.A 1 SILA$_{3}$ 5 *šá* GIŠ.BÁN.MEŠ *bab*$^{!}$*-ba-nu-ú*
6 *a-na* ^{m}*ni-din-tu*$_{4}$ DUMU *šá* ^{md}EN-ŠEŠ.MEŠ-SU
7 *id-din baṭ-lu šá* NINDA.ḪI.A*-a*$_{4}$ 4 SILA$_{3}$ *šá i-di* ⸢*kar*⸣-[*ri*]
8 *u rug-bu* ^{m}*ni-din-tu*$_{4}$ *ul i-šak-kan*

LO. E.

9 *ul-tu* UD.20.KAM *šá* ITI.GAN {UD.20}
10 4 SILA$_{3}$ NINDA.ḪI.A *i-di kar-ri u ru*[*g-bu*]

REV.

11 *i-nam-din a-di qí-it* ITI.[x *šá*]
12 MU.36.KAM É *kar-ri u rug-bu ina* IGI
13 ^{m}*ni-din-tu*$_{4}$ 1*-en*.TA.ÀM TI*-ú*
14 LÚ *mu-kin-nu* ^{m}*ni-din-tu*$_{4}$ DUMU *šá* ^{md}EN-MU
15 [DUMU ^{m}*dan-ni-e-a*] ^{m}*ni-din-tu*$_{4}$ DUMU *šá* ^{m}ŠU
16 [...] [x] <m>*šá*-^{d}AG-ARḪUŠ*-šú*
17 [...] A
18 [... ^{m}...] ⸢DUMU *šá*⸣ ^{m}*ni-din-tu*$_{4}$-^{d}EN
19 [...] UD.19.KAM

U. E.

20 [...] ^{m}*da-ri-iá-muš*
21 [...].KI *u* KUR.KUR

TRANSLATION

[(Regarding) the house at the harbor] ⸢and⸣ the loft$^{!}$ that are at the ..., (and) which is (in the possession)$^{?}$ of Nidintu, son of Širku: Bēl-kiṣuršu, son of Rīmūt, descendant of ⸢x⸣, (acting) as proxy for Nidintu, has paid rent for the building(s), (to wit) four *qû* of bread (and) one *qû* five ... of outstanding$^{!}$ quality per day, to Nidintu, son of Bēl-aḫḫē-erība. Nidintu shall not make an interruption in this (delivery of) four *qû* of bread, which is the rent for (the house at) the har[bor] and the loft. Until the twentieth of Kislīm {the twentieth} he shall deliver four *qû* of bread as rent for (the house at) the harbor and the lo[ft]. Until the end of [month x] of the thirty-sixth year the house at the harbor and the loft will be at Nidintu's disposal. They have taken one (copy of the document) each.

Witnesses:
Nidintu/Bēl-iddin//[Dannêa]
Nidintu/Gimillu[...]
Ša-Nabû-rēmūšu [...]
[The scribe:] [^{m}...]/Nidinti-Bēl
(Place + Date).

COMMENT

L. 1: For the meaning of *rugbu* see *CAD* R, 402ff. s.v. *rugbu* and *AHw*, 993. For the *bīt kāri* being a small house in the harbor area of the city that was rented to slaves and workmen (e.g., *bīt kāri ša* LÚ.MU), mostly for payment in kind, see *CAD* K, 238f. s.v. *kāru* A in *bīt kāri* mng. 3; and *AHw*, 451b s.v. *kāru* mng. 1c). On the renting of such buildings, see Oppenheim, *Mietrecht*, 55ff. on the renting of *rugbu* and *ibid.*, 63ff. on the renting of *bīt kāri*. The rented buildings are located at what should probably be read BUR RA KU but the meaning of which remains unknown (cf. *rugbu ša ina muḫḫi a-su-up-pu* in NRVU 788).

L. 3: For Bēl-kiṣuršu (*alias* Bēl-ikṣur?), son of Rīmūt, see probably also BM 30853: 6–8 and BM 31554: 3.

L. 4: The *idi bīti* no doubt refers to the rent for the *bīt kāri u rugbu* (see line 12).

L. 5: The signs are *qa-pa*(perhaps *ba-* or *ma-*)*nu-ú*. Should we read *bab*!*-ba-nu-ú*? It is not clear what was qualified as being of "excellent quality." For a similar problem, see TCL 13 187: 4–5, where the rent for a workshop amounted to 3 SILA$_3$ KURUM$_6$.ḪI.A 1 SILA$_3$ 6 *bab-ba-nu-ú* a day.

L. 6: There is a slight possibility that Nidintu/Bēl-aḫḫē-erība was the brother of Ubār/Bēl-aḫḫē-erība who was hired by MNA to collect tolls from boats sailing past a bridge (TCL 13 196), in other words, it is possible that the two sons of Bēl-aḫḫē-erība were employed in MNA's boat business.

L. 14–15: This witness's father was the scribe of a text that was drafted in Uruk but that mentions the *šākin ṭēmi* of Babylon (Sack, *Cuneiform Documents* No. 8, dated 5 Camb.)

No. 87

BM 41607
Copy: Bertin copy 2548
Date: 8/iv/24 Dar (4 July 498 B.C.E.)
Place: broken
Content: Receipt of the *ilku*-tax by MNA.

OBV.

1 [*i*]*l-ki šá a-di qí-it* ITI.ŠE *šá* MU.24.KAM
2 [^{m}*da*]*-ri-iá-a-muš* LUGAL E.KI *u* KUR.KUR
3 [*ma-l*]*a* ḪA.LA *šá* ^{m}*ri-mut-*^{d}EN A-*šú šá*
4 [^{m}*mu-š*]*e-zib-*^{d}EN A ^{m}*na-an-na-a-a*
5 [^{m}*šìr*]*-ku* A-*šú šá* ^{m}MU-*a* A ^{m}*e-gi-bi*
6 [*ina* ŠU.II] [^{m}][*r*]*i-mut-*^{d}EN *ma-ḫi-ir*
7 [*ištēnâ* (*šaṭāri*)] TI<-*ú*>

REV.

8 [LÚ *mu-kin-nu* ^{m}...] A-*šú šá*
9 [...]-*ši*
10 [...]-*šu-ú*
11 [...]-*ru* A-*šú šá*
12 [...]-⸢x-x A⸣ ^{m}DÙ-*eš*-DINGIR
13 [...] A-*šú šá* ^{md}AG-*na-din*-ŠEŠ A ^{m}*na-ba-a-a*
14 [LÚ.UMBISAG ^{m}*ni-din-*tu_4 -^{d}E]N A-*šú šá* ^{m}SIG$_5$-*iá* A ^{m}*na-din-še-im*
15 [...] ITI.ŠU UD.8.KAM

U. E.

16 MU.24.KAM ^{m}*da-ri-iá-a-muš*
17 LUGAL E.KI *u* KUR.KUR

TRANSLATION

The *ilku*-tax till the end of Addar of the twenty-fourth year of Darius, king of Babylon and the lands, [in so much] as it is the share due from Rīmūt-Bēl, son of [Muš]ēzib-Bēl, descendant of Nannaya: MNA$_2$ has received (it) [from] Rīmūt-Bēl. They have take<n> [one] (copy of the document) [each].

[Witnesses:]
[^{m}...]/[...]-ši
[...]-šu
[...]-ru/[...]//Eppeš-ilī
[Šullumaya?]/Nabû-nādin-aḫi//Nabaya
[The scribe: Nidinti-Bē]l/Damqiya//Nādin-še'i
(Place + Date).

COMMENT

L. 4: The family name Nannaya is written over other signs but is, nevertheless, clearly there.

L. 6–7: There is one blank line between lines 6 and 7.

Reverse: Much of the left side of the reverse is broken off so that three quarters of the first four lines and one fourth of the other lines are lacking.

No. 88

	CT 22 74
Museum No.:	BM 33077
Date:	no date
Place:	no place
Content:	Letter to Širku (= MNA?) concerning soldiers. Sent by Gūzānu (= governor of Babylon?).

OBV.

1 IM ^{m}*gu-za-nu a-na* ^{m}*ši-ir-ku*
2 ŠEŠ-*ia* ^{d}EN *u* ^{d}AG *šu-lum u* DIN *šá* ŠEŠ-*ia*
3 *liq-bu-ú ina* TIN.TIR.KI *u*$_{4}$*-mu-us-su*
4 *pi-ir-ṣa-tu*$_{4}$ *it-ti-ia ta-dab-bu-ub*
5 *ta-qab-ba-a um-ma* ^{m}*lib-lu-ṭu*
6 DUMU LÚ *si-si-i ù* LÚ *taš-li-šú*.MEŠ-*ka*
7 *it-ti-ka šá-aṭ-ru u* LÚ.GAL-BÀD
8 *ki-i il-li-ku ina ku-ta-al-li-ia*
9 ^{m}*lib-lu-ṭu u* DUMU.MEŠ LÚ *si-si-i*
10 *gab-bi uk-ti-il um-ma at-tu-ú-a*
11 *iš-šú-nu ù* LÚ *taš-li-šú*.MEŠ *šá it-ti-ia*
12 *i-ta-bak at-ta pi-ia it-ti-šú*
13 *šá-ak-na-a-ta u* NÍG.KA$_{9}$-*su*
14 *a-na muḫ-ḫi-ia ina* ŠU.II-*šú tat-ta-šú*
15 *en-na* ^{m}*lib-lu-ṭu* DUMU LÚ *si-si-i*
16 *ina* SAG.DU GIŠ.MÁ.MEŠ *šá-k*[*a*$^{?}$]-⸢*na*$^{?}$⸣
17 *a-na* URU *da-ni-pi-nu-ma*
18 *ù* LÚ.DUMU.⸢MEŠ LÚ⸣ *si-si-i*
19 LÚ *taš-li-*[*šú*.MEŠ] *u* LÚ.ERIN$_{2}$.MEŠ DUMU.DÙ.MEŠ
20 *ina* ŠU.II-*šú la tu-maš-šar pi-*⸢*ir-ki*⸣$^{?}$
21 *a-na* LÚ.GAL-BÀD *it-ti* LÚ.ERIN$_{2}$.MEŠ-*ia*
22 *la i-dab-bu-ub at-ta a-na*
23 ^{m}*at-kal-a-na*-DUMU-*é-sag-gil a-na muḫ-ḫi*
24 *qí-bi* LÚ.ERIN$_{2}$.MEŠ *ku-um* LÚ.ERIN$_{2}$.MEŠ *in-na-áš-šú*
25 *ba-ga-ni-i'* ^{m}*da-ri-ia-a-muš* LUGAL
26 *ina muḫ-ḫi-ka* LÚ.ERIN$_{2}$.MEŠ *šá ga-ar-du*

27 *šá ṭè-e-me áš-ku-nu-ka pu-uṭ-ṭi-ir-šú-nu-tu*
28 *a-mir* LÚ.EN.NUN-KÁ.GAL.MEŠ LÚ.DUMU.MEŠ *si-si-i*
29 *gab-bi ina pa-ni-ka ù* LÚ.ERIN$_2$.MEŠ
30 *šá* É-*da-ku-ru šá ina* TIN.TIR.KI *áš-bu-u'*
31 *ina pa-ni-ka it-ti* LÚ.ERIN$_2$.MEŠ
32 *šá* É-GIŠ.GIGIR-*ia la ta-dab-bu-ub*

Translation

(1)Letter from Gūzānu to Širku, my brother. (2–3)May Bēl and Nabû grant my brother peace and life. (3–5)In Babylon you told me lies every day, you kept saying as follows: (5–7)"Libluṭ, the charioteer, and your auxiliaries are enlisted with you (to do service)." (7–8)Yet, when the commander-of-the-fortress came, (8–10)he withheld Libluṭ and all the (other) charioteers from me, saying: (10–11)"They belong to me!," (11–12)and even my auxiliaries he took along! (12–14)And you -, you made common cause with him and transferred my (military) resources to him. (15–17)Libluṭ, the charioteer, has now been appointed at the head of a fleet (to go) to Danipinu, (18–20)but you must not (try to) release the charioteers, the auxiliaries, or the soldiers of the *mār bānē* from his hands. (20–22)He must not raise improper claims against my soldiers with the commander-of-the-fortress. (22–24)As for you, talk about this with Atkal-ana-mār-Esagil. (24)Muster (other) soldiers instead of the soldiers (which the commander withheld from me). (25–26)The royal dignity? of Darius burdens you. (26)The soldiers of the *gardu*-workers, (27)about whom I gave you an order, you must allow to go. (28–29)Realize that the guards at the gates and all the charioteers are (already) at your disposal, (29–31)and that the troops from Bīt-Dakkuru who are stationed in Babylon are (also) at your disposal, (31–32)so you must not interfere with the troops of my chariot-fief.

Comment

For a translation of the text with philological notes, see Ebeling, *NbBr*, No. 74; important philological notes also at Oppenheim, *JAOS* 61, 261ff. and Id., *OrNS* 9, 222; for a translation, also see Oppenheim, *Letters*, 143; and Joannès, *TÉBR*, 24 and "Pouvoirs locaux," n. 60. Some grammatical issues have been discussed by Streck, *ZuZ*, 52 (§ 39b), 117 (§ 17b), and 173 (§ 38b).

L. 3: Joannès, "Pouvoirs locaux," understands *ina Bābili* as an expression of time and not of place ("Tous les jours, depuis Babylone, tu me racontes des mensonges").

L. 6: The *tašlišu* was the third man, i.e., the third fighter on a chariot (*AHw*, 1339 s.v. *tašlīšu*; cf. quotations from our text in *CAD* Ṣ, 54 s.v. *ṣābu* and S, 335 s.v. *sīsû* in *mār sīsî*). He may well have been the shield bearer (*CAD* Š$_1$, 235 s.v. *šaṭāru* mng 3a-4').

L. 7b–10a: For the expression *ana/ina kutalli kullu*, "to withhold from," which is similar to the expression *ana/ina kutalli šakānu*, see Oppenheim's commentary and *CAD* K, 511 s.v. *kullu* mng 1e-5′ ("to hold back, to detain)." Cf. *CAD* K, 606 s.v. *kutallu* mng. 5c ("instead of me he kept PN and the chariot drivers") and *CAD* S, 335 s.v. *sīsû* in *mār sīsê* ("he withheld from my reserves"). Ebeling and Joannès give a different translation for lines 7b–10a because they divide the sentences in a different way: "alors que le Chef de la Citadelle, lorsqu'il est parti derrière moi (*kī illiku ina kutalliya*), a laissé sur place (*uktīl*) Libluṭ et tous les cavaliers" (so Joannès in "Pouvoirs locaux"; similar in *TÉBR*, viz. "Mais le commandant de forteresse, lorsqu'il est venu après moi, a réquisitionné Liblûṭu et les servants de cavalerie tous ensemble"; and cf. Ebeling's "aber der Festungskommandant hielt, nachdem er nach mir gekommen war, den Libluṭ und die Pferdeleute alle fest"). All translations bring out the fact that the charioteers were held back by the commander-of-the-fortress instead of being placed at Gūzānu's disposal.

L. 10–11: For *at-tu-ú-a iš-šú-nu*, see Oppenheim, *OrNS* 9, 222.

L. 12–13: The idiom *pû šakānu* can have the neutral meaning "to bespeak; to be in understanding": *AHw*, 873 s.v. *pû* I mng. D 1d "in meinen Namen bist du mit ihm verabredet"; cf. Joannès, "Pouvoirs locaux:" "Quant à toi, tu t'arrange avec lui en mon nom" and Ebeling, according to whom Širku had been appointed as Gūzānu's spokesman (cf. Joannès, *TÉBR*, "Quant à toi qui avais été placé auprès de lui comme défenseur de mes intérêts"). However, the idiom *pû šakānu itti* can also have the pejorative meaning of "to make common cause with": see Oppenheim's commentary, and *CAD* $Š_1$, 148 s.v. *šakānu itti* ("but you made common cause (?) with him"); note that our text is not cited at *CAD* $Š_1$, 140–41 s.v. *šakānu* mng. 5a (idiomatic phrases, *pû itti* "to conspire, make common cause with"). The difference in translation reflects a difference in interpretation of the relation between Gūzānu and Širku: either Gūzānu is reminding Širku that he and the commander-of-the-fortress are to be in understanding (*AHw* and Joannès), or he is accusing Širku of having hurt Gūzānu's interest by having conspired with the commander-of-the-fortress (*CAD* $Š_1$) or by having deceived Gūzānu about the commander's real intentions (Oppenheim). The same differences in interpretation are reflected in the divergent translations of lines 13–14.

L. 13–14: The main verb of these lines is *tat-ta-šú* = *tatta(dna)šu* "you gave to him." This verb is complemented by the adverbial expression *ina qātē*, which in the present context means "(entrusted) into the hands of" (cf. *CAD* $Š_1$, 148 s.v. *šakānu itti*; on the expression *ina qātē*, more at BM 30795: 4b). The direct object of *tatta(dna)šu* is the last word of line 13, which is to be read NÍG.KA_9-*su* = *nikkassu*, "asset"; it is further qualified by *ana muḫḫiya* "for my account": *nikkassu ana muḫḫiya* refers to "the assets for my account = my assets" (cf. *CAD* $Š_1$, 148 s.v. *šakānu itti*, "but you made common cause(?) with him and transferred my assets to him"). The transfer of Gūzānu's assets to the commander by Širku was part of the conspiracy about which we heard in the previous lines. For a different interpretation, see Joannès,

"Pouvoirs locaux." Širku had to defend Gūzānu's interests (ll. 12–13) "en récupérant d'entre ses mains (le produit des obligations) qu'il m'impose!" (ll. 13–14). In other words, he had to reclaim the charioteers so that they could be transferred to the person to whom they were due, probably Atkal-ana-mār-Esagil. The differences are the following: *ina qātēšu* "from his hands," *tatta(dna)šu* "you should take back," *šá-kàs-su* (end line 13) = *šakāssu* from *šakānu*, together with *ana muḫḫi* "to impose an obligation" (cf. Ebeling).

L. 19: For the translation of *ṣābē mār bānê*, see *CAD* Ṣ, 54 s.v. *ṣābu* "free soldiers" and *CAD* S, 335 s.v. *sīsû* in *mār sīsî* "private soldiers." Recently, Stolper, *JCS* 53, 127, has suggested reading LÚ.ERIN$_2$.MEŠ LUGAL$^{!?}$, "the king's$^?$ men," instead of DUMU DÙ.MEŠ.

L. 20: In the present context *ina qātēšu* means "from his hands" (so also Joannès, "Pouvoirs locaux," "et que tu ne libères pas de ses mains"). In other words, Libluṭ has been appointed head of a fleet by the commander- of-the-citadel so that it is not advisable to try to release the charioteers and the auxiliaries from his hands. But differently Ebeling, Oppenheim, Joannès, *TÉBR* ("tu ne vas pas les lui abandonner") and *CAD* S, 335 s.v. *sīsû* in *mār sīsî* "so you must not release … to his command"; and *CAD* Ṣ, 54 s.v. *ṣābu* "you must not leave to him …." In their opinion, Širku should try to get hold of the other men, viz. those who are not on the boat together with Libluṭ, and thus release them from under Libluṭ's command.

L. 20b–22: Translation as given by Stolper, *JCS* 53, 127. Libluṭ, or more in general, people, should not reproach Gūzānu's men before the commander-of-the-citadel (so Oppenheim and Ebeling); or, they should not blame Gūzānu's men for things for which the commander-of-the-citadel was to be blamed (Joannès).

L. 23: For *Atkal-ana-mār-Esagil,* who was an administrator of the Crown during Cambyses reign and later, see Jursa, *Landwirtschaft*, 146 and n. 292. According to Joannès, *TÉBR*, 25, Gūzānu had to transfer some of his charioteers to this Atkal-ana-mār-Esagil, but was unable to do so since the commander-of-the-fortress had withheld them from him. Gūzānu had ordered Širku to take care of this matter and meet this obligation to the Crown. Consequently, Širku was "burdened by the royal dignity of Darius" (ll. 25–26).

L. 25–26: For *bagani* see *CAD* B, 28 s.v. *bagani* "curse(?)." The implications of this sentence are not clear.

L. 26: On the *gardu*-workers and state-controlled labor, see Dandamaev, *Slavery*, 568ff.; Id., *AoF* 22, 34–36 ("workmen of the royal household"); and Stolper, *Entrepreneurs*, 55–59 with bibliography.

L. 31–32: For the translation of *itti … lā tadabbub* "do not interfere with …," see *CAD* D, 10 s.v. *dabābu* mng. 5b and cf. *CAD* S, 335 s.v. *sīsû* in *mār sīsî*.

No. 89

	Dar 105
Museum No.:	BM 41603
Date:	5/i/4 Dar (15 April 518 B.C.E.)
Place:	Bīt-rab-kāṣir
Content:	[Receipt] of onions, *šibšu*-lease from land (along the Rab-kāṣir canal). One third is due to Bagasarū.

OBV.

1 70 *pít-ti šá* SUM.SAR *šib-šú* A.ŠÀ
2 ḪA.LA *šal-šú šá* ^{m}*ba-ag-sa-ru-ú*
3 LÚ.GAL *ka-ṣir* ^{md}EN-KAR-*ir* LÚ *qal-la*
4 [*šá* ^{m}*ba-a*]*g-sa-ru-ú ina na-áš-par-ti*
5 [*ša* ^{m}x]-⸢x⸣-*ia* LÚ *qa*[*l-l*]*a šá* ^{m}*ba-ag-sa-ru-ú*
6 [*ina* ŠU.II ^{md}x-x-LU]GAL-URU$_{3}$ ⸢*ù*⸣ ^{m}*ta-lim-mu*
7 [x x x x x] A $^{m?}$⸢x x⸣ ^{m}*ḫa-an-zi-ri*
(Remainder of obverse (one line?) and Lo. E. are broken off.)

REV.

1′ [...] ⸢^{d}EN$^{?}$⸣ A-*šú šá*
2′ [x x x] A LÚ ŠU.KU$_{6}$
3′ [x x x] x ^{m}*ta-at-tan-nu* A-*šú šá* ^{m}KAR-^{d}EN
4′ [^{m}*šá-p*]*i-i-kal-bi* A-*šú šá* ^{m}*áḫ-ia-li-du*
5′ *u* LÚ.UMBISAG ^{md}EN-DÙ A-*šú šá* ^{md}U.GUR-NUMUN-DÙ
6′ A LÚ.SANGA-^{d}*na-na-a* É-GAL-*ka-ṣir*
7′ ITI.BÁR UD.5.KAM MU.4.KAM
8′ ^{m}*da-ri-ʼa-muš* LUGAL TIN.TIN.KI
9′ *u* KUR.KUR

TRANSLATION

Seventy bundles of onions, the *šibšu*-lease from the field (along the Rab-kāṣir canal). It is the one-third share of Bagasarū, the Treasurer. Bēl-ēṭir, a slave [of Ba]gasarū, (and) proxy [for ^{m}...]-ia, a(nother) slave of Bagasarū, [has received (them) from (?) ^{md}...-ša]rra-uṣur ⸢and⸣ Talīmu [...] Ḫāziri [...].

[Witnesses:]

[...]//Bā'iru

Tattannu/Mušēzib-Bēl

[Ša-p]î-kalbi/Aḫ-yalīd

And the scribe: Bēl-ibni/Nergal-zēra-ibni//Šangû-Nanaya

(Place + Date).

COMMENT

L. 1: A.ŠÀ is the last word written on this line. Hence, the field in question is not further described. A similar situation is found in Dar 542, concerning

Bagasarū's share in *imittu*-dates from the harvest of Darius' twenty-first year. However, from Dar 527 we know that the land from which MNA, his brothers and Bagasarū derived income was located along the Rab-kāṣir canal. Further note that in Dar 296 the land is called "land of Bagasarū" (l. 2).

L. 2: For the Old Iranian name Bagasarū (Ir. *Bagasravā), see Dandamaev, *Iranians*, 60ff. (no. 98).

L. 7: On the name Ḫāziru (wr. ^{m}*ḫa-an-zi-ri*), see Tallqvist, *NbN*, 316 s.v. *ḫṣr*; *CAD* Ḫ, 166 s.v *ḫāziru*; and *AHw*, 339 s.v. *ḫāziru*.

L. 3′: I could see no other sign after ^{d}EN.

L. 4′: For names like ^{m}*áḫ-ia-li-du* in texts from the Neo-Babylonian period, see Zadok, *West Semites*, 279f. n. 2. The verbal element *ia-li-du* is derived from the West semitic root Y-L-D "to bear, bring forth, beget" and seems to be a passive *qatīl* formation ("begotten"); on the latter formation, see Zadok, *Id.*, 122ff.

L. 5′: The scribe left one line empty before writing his name.

No. 90

	Dar 138
Museum No.:	BM 31316
Date:	9 (or 1)/x/4 Dar (10 or 2 January 517 B.C.E.)
Place:	Babylon
Content:	Renting of a boat by MNA.

OBV.

1 GIŠ.MÁ *šá* $^{m⸢d}$x⸣-*ú-ṣur*$^{!}$(GU)-*šú* ⸢A$^{?}$⸣ [(-*šu šá*) ...]

2 *šá ina* IGI ^{md}*gu-la**-NUMUN-DÙ

3 A-*šú šá* ^{m}NUMUN-TIN.TIR.KI <A> LÚ.⸢SIMUG⸣

4 *a-na* ⸢*i*⸣-*di-šú a-na* u_4-⸢*mu*⸣*

5 1 GUR 3* (BÁN) ZÚ.LUM.MA *a-na*

6 ^{md}AMAR.UTU-*na-ṣir*-A A-*šú šá*

7 $^{m⸢}$KI⸣*-^{d}AMAR.UTU-⸢DIN⸣* A ^{m}*e-gi-bi* [*id-din*]

LO. E.

8 *e-lat* 1-*me* 50 GUR ZÚ.⸢LUM⸣.[MA]

9 *a-na* ⸢x x x *id-di-in*⸣$^{?}$

REV.

10 LÚ *mu-kin-nu* ^{md}AG-ŠEŠ.MEŠ-⸢*bul-liṭ*⸣

11 A-*šú šá* ^{md}AG-KÁD A ^{m}*da-bi-bi*

12 ^{m}MU-^{d}EN A-*šú šá* ^{md}AMAR.UTU-SU

13 A ^{m}*ba-la-ṭu* LÚ.UMBISAG ^{md}ŠÚ-GIN-A

14 A-*šú šá* ^{m}DÙ-*ia* A LÚ.GAL-60-*ši*

15 TIN.TIR.KI ITI.AB <UD>.9.KAM

16 ⸢MU⸣.4.KAM ^{m}*da-ri-'a-uš*

U. E.

17 ⸢LUGAL⸣ TIN.TIR.KI LUGAL KUR.KUR

18 TA UD.⸢14⸣*.KAM GIŠ.MÁ *ina* IGI-*šú*

Translation

The boat belonging to ^{m}[…]-*uṣuršu*$^{?}$ [(…)], which is at the disposal of Gula-zēra-ibni, son of Zēr-Bābili, <descendant of> ⸢Nappāḫu⸣: [he has given it] for rent to MNA$_1$ for 1.0.3 *kor* of dates per day. In addition, ⸢*he gave* 150 *kor* of dates for ….⸣$^{?}$.

Witnesses:
Nabû-aḫḫē-bulliṭ/Nabû-kāṣir//Dābibī
Iddin-Bēl/Marduk-erība//Balāṭu
The scribe: Marduk-mukīn-apli/Baniya//Rab-šušši
(Place + Date).

From the ⸢fourteenth⸣ the boat will be at his disposal.

Comment

L. 1: Collation of the tablet has not lead to any solution for this line. Is the name in question to be read ^{m}⸢x⸣-*ú-šal-lim* or ^{m}⸢x⸣-*ú-ṣur*$^{!}$(GU)-*šú*? The sign before the break resembles ⸢UD⸣.

L. 7: Most likely, *id-din* was written on the right edge.

L. 9: Collation of the tablet has not lead to any solution for this line. It does not refer to a payment for "maintenance" (KURUM$_6$.ḪI.A) for two reasons. First, the signs after *a-na* do not resemble KURUM$_6$.ḪI.A; and second, the amount of 150 *kor* is far too high (cf. the small amount paid for maintenance in the boat rental BM 31891). Does the 150 *kor* refer to a load of dates to be transported by the boat: *a-na qurrubu/šūlu*? And should we read *id-di-in* at the end of the line? One may see the three *Winkelhaken* of the *id-* (copied as ŠÁ by Strassmaier), the *di-* except for its closing vertical (copied as ŠE by Strassmaier), and most of the *-in*.

L. 18: Boats were sometimes rented on a specific day but made available a few days later only, even up to two weeks later. In BM 31690^{+}, for instance, the boat is rented on the eighteenth of Araḫsamna and will be available on the next day (l. 11); in BM 30799 the boat is rented on the twenty-sixth of Ab but not available before the eleventh of Ulūl, i.e., two weeks later (l. 10). In the case under consideration, the boat was rented on the ninth and available five days later.

No. 91

	Dar 144
Museum No.:	BM 32877
Date:	25/xi/4 Dar (24 February 517 B.C.E.)
Place:	Šaḫrīnu
Content:	Promissory note to pay a debt of barley and dates to MNA. Pledge renewal.

OBV.

2-ME 97 GUR 3 PI ZÚ.LUM.MA 11 GUR 2 (PI) 3 (BÁN)
ŠE.BAR *šá* ^{md}AMAR.UTU-PAB-A A-*šú šá* ^{m}KI-^{d}AMAR.UTU-DIN
A ^{m}*e-gi-bi ina muḫ-ḫi* ^{m}*ri-mut*-^{d}EN A-*šú šá* ^{m}MU*-GIN
ina ITI.GU$_4$ MU.5.KAM 11 GUR 2 (PI) 3 (BÁN) ŠE.BAR *i-nam-din*
ina ITI.DU$_6$ MU.5.KAM 2-ME 90 GUR 7 GUR 3 PI
ZÚ.LUM.MA *ina* GIŠ *ma-ši-ḫu šá* ^{md}AMAR.UTU-PAB-A
ina É ^{md}AMAR.UTU-PAB-A *ina* UGU 1-*en*^{sic} *rit-tu*$_4$
i-nam-din ŠÀ.A^{sic}-*šú zaq-pu ù pi-i šul-pu*
šá muḫ-ḫi ÍD *bár*<-*si*>*pa* KI ḪA.LA-*šú šá* KI
^{md}AG-*ma-a-ku*-PAB ŠEŠ-*šú* É *maš-ka-nu* IGI-*ú*
šá ^{md}AMAR.UTU-PAB-A *maš-ka-nu šá* ^{md}ŠÚ-PAB-⸢A⸣
LÚ.TUKU-*ú šá-nam-ma ina muḫ-ḫi ul i-šal-laṭ*

REV.

a-di ^{md}ŠÚ-PAB-A LÚ.TUKU-*ú-su i-šal-lim*
LÚ *mu-kin-nu* ^{md}AG-ŠEŠ.MEŠ-DIN A-*šú šá* ^{m}*na-din*
A LÚ.ŠU.KU$_6$ ^{m}*kal-bi*-^{d}KÁ A-*šú šá* ^{md}AG-*ú-nam-mir*
A LÚ.SIPA-ANŠE.KUR.RA ^{m}EN-*šú-nu* A-*šú šá*
^{m}*ki-i*-^{d}AG ^{md}EN-MU A-*šú šá* ^{md}AG-DIN-*su*-E
A ^{m}*e-gi-bi* ^{m}*gu-za-nu* A-*šú šá* ^{md}AG-BE-DIN
LÚ.UMBISAG ^{md}U.GUR-MU-DÙ A LÚ.SANGA-^{d}*e*^{sic}-*a*
URU *šá-ḫa-ri-nu* ITI.ZÍZ UD.25.KAM
MU.4.KAM ^{m}*da-ri-muš* LUGAL E.KI
LUGAL KUR.KUR

TRANSLATION

297.3.0 *kor* of dates (and) 11.2.3 *kor* of barley are due to MNA$_1$ from Rīmūt-Bēl, son of Šuma*-ukīn. In Ayyar of the fifth year he will deliver the 11.2.3 *kor* of barley. In Tašrīt of the fifth year he will deliver the 297.3.0 *kor* of dates in one installment in MNA$_1$'s house according to MNA$_1$'s measure. His orchard and grain field at the Bor<sip>pa canal, his part (of the land) that he (shares) with Nabû-māku-uṣur, his brother, the pledge previously held by MNA$_1$ is (still) pledged to MNA$_1$. No other creditor shall exercise any rights over it until MNA$_1$ has received full repayment of his credit claim.

Witnesses:

Nabû-aḫḫē-bulliṭ/Nādin//Bā'iru
Kalbi-Bāba/Nabû-unammir//Rē'i-sīsî
Bēlšunu/Kī-Nabû
Bēl-iddin/Nabû-balāssu-iqbi//Egibi
Gūzānu/Nabû-mīta-uballiṭ
The scribe: Nergal-šuma-ibni//Šangû-Ea
(Place + Date).

COMMENT

The text has several scribal peculiarities, or rather errors (indicated by ^{sic}). Moreover, some signs in the first two lines were written over other signs: the number ninety in line 1 (hence, Strassmaier's copy has 60+(4×10)), the *šá* after ŠE.BAR in line 2, and the -DIN at the end of line 2. There is an erasure between the -PAB-A and A in line 2.

L. 8: The scribe wrote ŠÀ A-*šú zaqpu u pī šulpu*. This is most likely a scribal error for A.ŠÀ-*šú zaqpu u pī šulpu*. Cultivated plots of land along the Borsippa canal were pledged to MNA by he same debtor according to BM 33972: 9–10 (wr. A.ŠÀ.MEŠ-*šú gabbi zaqpu u pī šulpu ultu* ^{id}*Barsip*^{ki} *adi muḫḫi ḫarrān šarri*), and a similar plot of land for which, however, no location is given, is pledged according to Dar 167: 10–11 (wr. A.ŠÀ-*šú zaqpu u pī šulpu*).

L. 9: SIPA is written with the PA-sign only. Cf. spelling in BM 33959: 17. For a clear SIPA-sign see below, line 16.

L. 19: The scribe left two lines empty before writing his name. The name of the god Ea is written with the *e*-sign and not with the *é*-sign as usual.

No. 92

	Dar 154
Museum No.:	BM 32851
Date:	15/i/5 Dar (13 April 517 B.C.E.)
Place:	Babylon
Content:	Labor contract to go to Elam for MNA by joining the chariot of the governor of Babylon. Receipt of part of the salary.

OBV.

1 ^{m}*ku-ṣur-ra-a* A-*šú ša* ^{m}DÙ-*iá* A ^{m}DÙ-*a-šá**-DINGIR*-*iá**
2 *a-na i-di-šú it-ti* LÚ.ERIN$_2$.MEŠ *šá* GIŠ.GIGIR
3 *šá* ^{md}EN-A-MU LÚ.GAR-UŠ$_4$ E.KI *a-na* URU.KUR.ELAM.MA.KI
4 *a-na {ina} muḫ-ḫi* ^{m}*ši-ir-ku* A-*šú šá* ^{m}SUM.NA-*a* A ^{m}*e-gi-bi*
5 *il-lak-ku* 50* GÍN KÙ.BABBAR *šá ina** 1 GÍN *bit-qa*
6 ^{m}*ku-ṣur-ra-a i-di-šú a-di qí-it* ITI.DU$_6$
7 *ina* ŠU.II ^{m}*ši-ir-ku ma-ḫi-ir* 1-*en-a*.TA
8 *šá-ṭa-ri* <*il*>*-qu-ú pu-ut* ^{m}*ku-ṣur-ra-a*
9 ^{m}⸢*nap*⸣**-sa-nu** A-*šú šá* ^{md}U.GUR-DIN-*iṭ*

10 *na-ši*

Rev.

11 LÚ *mu-kin-nu* ^{md}AMAR.UTU-MU-URU$_{3}$ A-*šú šá* ^{m}*kur-ban-ni*-^{d}AMAR.UTU

12 A LÚ.SIPA<-ANŠE>.KUR.RA ^{m}MU-^{d}AG A-*šú šá* ^{m}EN-*šú-nu*

13 A LÚ.GÍR.LÁ-*kar-ri* ^{md}EN-*it-tan-nu* A-*šú šá* ^{m}KI-^{d}AG-DIN

14 A ^{m}*ma-la-ḫu* ^{m}*ap-sa-nu* LÚ.UMBISAG A-*šú šá*

15 ^{md}U.GUR-DIN-*iṭ* A ^{m}SIG$_{15}$-^{d}IŠKUR TIN.TIR.KI ITI.BÁR

16 UD.15.KAM MU.5.KAM ^{m}*da-ri-mu*<*-uš*>

17 LUGAL TIN.TIR.KI LUGAL KUR.KUR

Translation

Kuṣuraya, son of Baniya, descendant of Banâ-ša-iliya*, shall go to Elam for his salary on {at} behalf of MNA$_2$, together with the men of the chariot of Bēl-apla-iddin, governor of Babylon. Kuṣuraya has received from MNA$_2$ fifty* shekels of silver, of which one-eighth is alloy, his salary through the end of Tašrīt. They <have ta>ken one (copy of the) document each. ⸢Napsān⸣, son of Nergal-uballiṭ, assumes warranty for Kuṣuraya.

Witnesses:
Marduk-šuma-uṣur/Kurbanni-Marduk//Rē'i<-sī>sî
Iddin-Nabû/Bēlšunu//Ṭābiḫ-kāri
Bēl-ittannu/Itti-Nabû-balāṭu//Malāḫu
The scribe: (N)apsān*/Nergal-uballiṭ//Mudammiq-Adad
(Place + Date).

Comment

L. 9: The name Napsānu, wr. ^{m}*nap-sa-nu,* is spelled ^{m}*ap-sa-nu* in line 14. In Dar 509: 20 the same person occurs again, and his name is spelled ^{m}*nap-sa-an.* It is of West-Semitic origin (Zadok, *West Semites*, 113f. and 157f.), and also attested in the Murašû archive: ^{m}*na-ap-sa-an* or ^{m}*nap-sa-an*, son of Nadbiya.

No. 93

	Dar 156
Museum No.:	BM 30451
Date:	24/i/5 Dar (22 April 517 B.C.E.)
Place:	Babylon
Content:	Receipt of silver from MNA. Payment for *rikis qabli*. By order of (*ina qibi ša*) Murašû/Marduk-šuma-iddin//Ilu-tillatī.

Obv.

1 ⅓ MA.NA 5 GÍN KÙ.BABBAR *šá ina* 1 GÍN *bit-qa*

2 *nu-uḫ-ḫu-tu e-lat* 3 MA.NA KÙ.BABBAR *maḫ-ru-ú*

3 *šá ina* 1 GÍN *bit-qa nu-uḫ-ḫu-tu* ^{md}EN-MU

4 A-*šú šá* ^{m}KI-^{d}AMAR.UTU-DIN A ^{m}ŠEŠ-*ba-ni*

5 *ina* ŠU.II ^{md}AMAR.UTU-*na-ṣir*-IBILA A-*šú šá*
6 ^{m}KI-^{d}AMAR.UTU-DIN A ^{m}*e-gi-bi ina qí-bi*
7 *šá* ^{m}*mu-ra-šu-ú* A-*šú šá* ^{md}AMAR.UTU-MU-MU

LO. E.

8 A ^{m}DINGIR-KASKAL+KUR-*ú ri-kis* MURUB$_4$-*šú**
9 *a-na a-la-ku a-na pa-ni* LUGAL

REV.

10 *ma-ḫi-ir* LÚ *mu-kin-nu* ^{md}AMAR.UTU-KAR-*ir*
11 A-*šú šá* ^{m}*mu-ra-nu* A ^{m}*e-gi-bi*
12 ^{md}EN-DIN-*iṭ* A-*šú šá* ^{m}*ki-rib-tú* A ^{m}ZALAG$_2$-^{d}30
13 ^{md}AMAR.UTU-NUMUN-DÙ A-*šú šá* ^{md}EN-ŠEŠ.MEŠ-MU
14 A LÚ.SIMUG ^{m}ÌR-^{d}*ba-ba*$_6$ DUB.SAR
15 A-*šú šá* ^{md}U.GUR-*ú-še-zib* A ^{m}*e-gì-bi*
16 TIN.TIR.KI ITI.BÁR UD.24.KAM

U. E.

17 MU.5.KAM ^{m}*da-ri-ia-mu*[*š*]
18 LUGAL E.KI LUGAL KUR.KUR

TRANSLATION

One-third mina and five shekels of medium-quality silver, of which one-eighth is alloy, besides the previous three minas of medium-quality silver, of which one-eighth is alloy: Bēl-iddin, son of Itti-Marduk-balāṭu, descendant of Aḫu-bani, has received (it) by order of Murašû, son of Marduk-šuma-iddin, descendant of Ilu-tillatī from MNA$_1$. (Paid for) His *rikis qabli* for going before the king.

Witnesses:
Marduk-ēṭir/Mūrānu//Egibi
Bēl-uballiṭ/Kiribtu//Nūr-Sîn
Marduk-zēra-ibni/Bēl-aḫḫē-iddin//Nappāḫu
The scribe: Arad-Bāba/Nergal-ušēzib//Egibi
(Place + Date).

COMMENT

L. 2: The *maḫ*- is written on the right edge; the following two signs, viz. *-ru-ú* are on the reverse.

L. 8: For the reading of surname ^{m}DINGIR-KASKAL+KUR-*ú*, more at Bongenaar, *Ebabbar*, 464f. He prefers reading Balīḫu (i.e., ^{md}KASKAL+KUR-*ú*).

No. 94

	Dar 158
Museum No.:	BM 30787
Date:	7/iii/⸢5⸣ Dar (3 June 517 B.C.E.)
Place:	Babylon
Content:	Labor contract to sail a boat to Babylon for MNA as part of the *kanšu*-service. Receipt of part of the salary.

OBV.

1 ^{m}⸢*bul**-*ṭa**⸣-*a* A-*šú šá* ^{m}*ḫa**-⸢*ba**⸣-*ṣi**-*ru* A LÚ.⸢SIPA*-GU$_{4}$*⸣

2 *a-na i-di-šú a-na* ITI 8 GÍN KÙ.BABBAR *ina* GIŠ*.MÁ*

3 *šá* ^{md}AMAR.UTU-*na-ṣir*-IBILA *šá ka-an-šú šá* ⸢LUGAL⸣*

4 ⸢*ina lìb*⸣-*bi a-na i-di-šú il-lak* ITI 1 (PI) 1 (BÁN) 3 SILA$_{3}$ KI.LÁ (or *qí-me*)

5 *šá** LUGAL* *saḫ-li-e u šam-ni* ^{md}AMAR.UTU-*na-ṣir*-IBILA

6 *a-na* ^{m}*bul-ṭa-a i-nam-din* ^{m}*bul-ṭa-a it-ti*

7 GIŠ.MÁ *il-lak u* GIŠ.MÁ *a-di-i* TIN.TIR.[KI]

8 *ul ú* ⸢*x x*⸣ *ri* ⸢x x x⸣ *šá* (erasure) ⸢x x⸣ [...]

9 [(x)] *x kal la* ⸢x x x x x⸣ [...]

10 [L]Ú.TIN.TIR.KI.MEŠ *šá ina* GIŠ.MÁ-⸢*šú*?⸣ [...]

LO. E.

11 [*ul*]-⸢*tu*⸣ UD.10.KAM *šá* ITI.SIG$_{4}$ ^{m}[...]

12 ⸢*i*⸣-*n*[*am-din*] LÚ *mu-kin-nu* ^{md}*é**-[...]

REV.

13 A-*šú šá* ^{m}*mu-še-zib*-^{d}AMAR.UTU A LÚ.GÍR.LÁ -⸢*ka*⸣-[*a-ri*]

14 ^{m}ÌR-^{d}*gu-la* A-*šú šá* ^{md}AMAR.UTU-MU-U[RU$_{3}$]

15 A ^{m}*na-ba-a-a* ^{md}AG-*it-tan-nu* A-*šú šá*

16 ^{md}AG-ZI-URU$_{3}$ A ^{md}30-*da-ma-qu* LÚ.UM[BISAG]

17 ^{m}*gi-mil-lu*-^{d}UTU A-*šú šá* ^{m}*šul-lu-mu* A ^{m}*na-din*

18 E.KI ITI.SIG$_{4}$ UD.7.KAM MU.⸢5⸣.KAM

19 ^{m}*da-a-ri-muš* LUGAL E.KI *u* KUR.KUR ⸢*e-lat*⸣

20 10 GÍN KÙ.BABBAR *ina i-di-šú* ^{m}⸢*bul**-*ṭa**-*a** *ina** ŠU.II*⸣

21 ^{md}AMAR.UTU-*na-ṣir*-IBILA *ma-ḫir*

22 [1-*e*]*n*.TA.ÀM {*a'*} *il-qu-ú*

TRANSLATION

Bulṭaya, son of Ḫabaṣīru, descendant of ⸢Rē'i-alpi⸣ shall sail for a monthly salary of eight shekels in ⸢the boat⸣ of Marduk-nāṣir-apli, which is (part of) his (MNA's?) *kanšu* service for the ⸢king⸣. Each month Marduk-nāṣir-apli shall give to Bulṭaya 0.1.1.3 *kor* royal *flour*, cress and oil. Bulṭaya shall go with the boat, and he shall not ... the boat until Babylon, and ... [...] the Babylonians who are in ⸢his?⸣ boat [...] [fr]⸢om⸣ the tenth of Simān ^{m}[...] shall g[ive].

Witnesses:

E[a-apla-iddin]/Mušēzib-Marduk//Ṭābiḫ-[kāri]

Arad-Gula/Marduk-šuma-uṣur//Nabaya
Nabû-ittannu/Nabû-napišta-uṣur//Sîn-damāqu
The ⸢scribe⸣: Gimil-Šamaš/Šullumu//Nādin
(Place + Date).

⸢In addition: Bulṭaya⸣ has (already) received ten shekels from his salary ⸢from⸣ Marduk-nāṣir-apli. They have taken [one] (copy of the document) each.

COMMENT

L. 1: Strassmaier's copy gives a different name, but collation of the tablet as well as the parallel from Dar 215 leave no doubt about the reading as given above.

L. 3a: The text refers to one Marduk-nāṣir-apli, but does not give his father's name nor his family name. This was, no doubt, MNA: he hired Bulṭaya a second time according to Dar 215.

L. 3b: On the *kanšu*-service, which consisted of joining a "donkey caravan in the service of the palace, to which teams of ten men were attached" (*CAD* K, 158 s.v. *kanšu*), see more at Jursa, *Bēl-rēmanni*, 53 and 100. The present text shows that it may also consist of joining a boat transport. For a different reading of this passage, viz. *šá-ka-an-šú ša* [... *išakkan*] (G inf. + pron. suffix 3rd masc. sg. from *šakānu*), see Peiser, *BRL* 3, 45.

L. 4–5: Should one read KI.LÁ *šá* LUGAL "royal weight" or *qí-me šá* LUGAL "the king's flour"? Moreover, were the flour (*qīmu*?), cress (*saḫlû*), and oil (*šamnu*) given to Bulṭaya for his maintenance in addition to his salary? Or were these commodities given to him in order to be transported? In the latter case the *kanšu*-service obligation consisted of transporting the king's flour and other bulk goods by boat for the palace (cf. the service obligation of *zebēlu ša upiyātu*, Joannès, *Borsippa*, 153).

L. 7b–8a: In these and the following lines we expect precautionary measures against non-fulfilment of the assigned job by Bulṭaya, e.g., if he should stop working (e.g., *baṭālu*, *marāṣu*, *matû*, cf. Oppenheim, *Mietrecht*, 48–50), a specification of the route that Bulṭaya had to follow, or the ultimate destination of his voyage. The exact reading of these lines, however, remains enigmatic, even after collation of the text. The signs at the beginning of line 8 resemble *ú ma/ba/šu pi ri/tal*, and should most likely be read *ú-ma-ši*$^{!?}$*-ri* as suggested by Peiser, *Id.*, i.e., from the verb *muššuru*. If so, it is stipulated in lines 7b–8 that "he shall not leave (the boat) until (he reaches) Babylon." This makes sense, but the ending in *-ri* is unexpected because the verb is not final weak, and we contextually need *umaššar* in the present rather than *umaššir* in the preterite. A less likely, alternative reading is: *ú-šab*$^{!?}$*-ṭal*, derived from the verb *baṭālu*, which means to "stop, interrupt an activity, to cease regular deliveries, to come to an end (said of supplies)"; *šubṭulu* "to discontinue, to interrupt." Hence, "he shall not stop (the boat) until (he reaches) Babylon." In either case, whether one reads *ú-ma-ši-ri* or *ú-šab-ṭal*, lines 7b–8a secure that the boat sails without interruption as far as Babylon.

L. 8b: I suggest reading ⸢*u dul*?*-lu*?⸣ *šá* (erasure of one sign) ⸢*ku*?*-ut*?⸣-[*tu-mu*] "and the work of co[vering (the boat) …]," D inf. of *katāmu*.

L. 9: I have no solution for the reading of this line. The first visible sign may be interpreted as a TA (so Strassmaier), or the end of a LI. It is followed by a clear KAL and LA. Is *ta-kal-la* derived from the verb *kalû* "detain" and does it relate to the boat, which "is not to be delayed" (N pres. 3rd fem. sg., *la takkalla*)? The verb *kalû* is in fact frequently used with respect to boats being stopped, detained or delayed, see *CAD* K, 100 s.v. mng. 2e. See also at TCL 13 196: 15. Less likely the verb *ta-kal-la* relates to ⸢*dullu*?⸣ *ku*[*ttumu*]? (see reconstruction of line 8b above), "⸢the work?⸣ of co[vering?]" the boat that is "to be done without delay." The end of the line is relatively well preserved, but unclear to me.

L. 12–13: For this person, cf. Wunsch, *Felder* 2, 289 s.v. Ea-apla-iddin; he also witnessed MNA's renting of a boat recorded in BM 30799 of the previous year.

L. 20–22: These ten shekels of silver that Bulṭaya received from MNA amount to a five-weeks' salary because Bulṭaya had been hired for eight shekels a month (see line 2). Consequently, Bulṭaya must have started working for MNA on the first of Ayyar, i.e., five weeks prior to the date of Dar 158.

L. 22: The ÀM is written over an *-a'* and followed by an *-a'*.

No. 95

	Dar 164
Museum No.:	BM 41428
Date:	1/v/5 Dar (27 July 517 B.C.E.)
Place:	Šaḫrīnu
Content:	Promissory note to pay a debt of silver and onions to MNA. Repayment of the onions is to be obtained from the (debtor's) *šibšu*. Silver had been transferred to the debtor to pay for *rikis qabli*. Reference to an outstanding debt of dates, barley, onions and silver secured by pledge.

OBV.

1 ½ MA.NA KÙ.BABBAR 30 *pít-ti šá* SUM.SAR *šá*
2 ^{md}AMAR.UTU-*na*-PAB-A A-*šú šá* ^{m}KI-^{d}AMAR.UTU-DIN
3 A ^{m}*e-gì-bi ina muḫ-ḫi* ^{md}AG-*ma-a-ku*-URU$_3$ A-*šú šá*
4 ^{md}AG-A-MU *ina* ITI.BÁR *šá* MU.6.KAM KÙ.BABBAR-*a'*
5 ½ MA.NA 30 *pít-ti šá* SUM.SAR *i-nam-din*
6 *ina šib-šú* A.ŠÀ-*šú i-šal-lim e-lat ú-ìl-tì* IGI-*ti*
7 *šá* 2-ME 45 GUR 3 PI ZÚ.LUM.MA
8 8 GUR 1 (PI) 2 (BÁN) ŠE.BAR *u ú-ìl-tì šá* 50 GÍN KÙ.BABBAR *ù* ⸢44⸣ *pít-ti* ⸢(*šá*) SUM.SAR⸣
9 *ra-šu-tú šá* ^{md}AMAR.UTU-*na*-PAB-A *šá muḫ-ḫi*

LO. E.

10 ^{md}AG-*ma-a-ku*-URU$_3$ *šá* A.ŠÀ.MEŠ-*šú zaq-pu*

11 *u pi-i šul-pu maš-ka-nu ṣab-tú*

REV.

12 KÙ.BABBAR *šá a-na ri-ki-*⸢*is*⸣ *qab-lu šá* MU.5.KAM

13 *šá a-na a-la-ku* [*šá* URU *še*]-*e-la-du*

14 *a-na* ^{md}AG-*ma-a-ku*-[URU$_3$ SUM]-*nu* LÚ *mu-kin-nu*

15 ^{md}AMAR.UTU-BA-*šá-an-ni* [A-*šú šá* ^{md}E]N-PAB-GÁL-*ši*

16 A ^{md}EN-*e-ṭe-ri* ^{md}⸢EN⸣*-[x (x)] A-*šú šá* ^{md}AG-NUMUN-⸢x⸣

17 ^{md}AG-URU$_3$-*šú* A-*šú šá* ^{m}KAR-^{d}AMAR.UTU ^{m}*ri-mut*-^{d}EN

18 A-*šú šá* ^{m}MU-GIN

19 LÚ.UMBISAG ^{md}EN-DÙ A-*šú šá* ^{md}U.GUR-NUMUN-DÙ

20 A LÚ.SANGA-^{d}*na-na-a* URU *šaḫ-ri-nu* ITI.NE

21 UD.1.KAM MU.5.KAM ^{m}*da-ri-'i-muš*

22 LUGAL TIN.TIR.KI *u* KUR.MEŠ

TRANSLATION

Half a mina of silver (and) thirty bundles of onions are due to MNA$_1$ from Nabû-māku-uṣur, son of Nabû-apla-iddin. In Nisan of the sixth year he will pay half this mina of silver (and) these thirty bundles of onions. He (= MNA) will receive full repayment from the *šibšu*(-crops) on his (= the debtor's) field. In addition, there is a previous debt of 245.3.0 *kor* of dates (and) 8.1.2 *kor* of barley, as well as a debt of fifty shekels of silver and ⸢forty-four⸣ bundles of ⸢onions⸣, the credit claims owed to MNA$_1$ by Nabû-māku-uṣur, for which his orchards and grain fields have been taken as pledge. The (indebted) silver is that which has been given to Nabû-māku-uṣur (to pay) for the *rikis qabli* (of the men who have) to go to [Š]eladu in (Darius') fifth year.

Witnesses:
Marduk-iqīšanni[/]Bēl-aḫa-ušabši//Bēl-eṭēru
⸢Bēl⸣-[...]/Nabû-zēra-⸢x⸣
Nabû-uṣuršu/Mušēzib-Marduk
Rīmūt-Bēl/Šuma-ukīn
The scribe: Bēl-ibni/Nergal-zēra-ibni//Šangû-Nanaya
(Place + Date).

COMMENT

L. 2, 9: The verbal element *nāṣir* in the name Marduk-nāṣir-apli is spelled ^{md}AMAR-UTU-*na*-PAB-A; probably to be transliterated as follows: ^{md}AMAR-UTU-{*na*}-PAB-A. Cf. Dar 167: 2.

L. 8: The signs at the end of the line are very much squeezed and it is not clear whether the scribe wrote *šá* SUM.SAR, or left out the *šá* to save space for writing SUM.SAR.

L. 16: Collation showed that one should read ^{md}⸢EN⸣-[MU] A-*šú šá* ^{md}AG-NUMUN-⸢MU$^{?}$⸣, so that this line refers to the man who is listed as first witness in Dar 167. The second witness in Dar 167 = first witness in Dar 164; the third witness in Dar 167 = third witness in Dar 164; and Dar 167 and Dar 164 were written by the same scribe.

No. 96

	Dar 167
Museum No.:	BM 41451
Date:	[1$^{?}$]/v/[5$^{?}$] Dar ([27] July [517] B.C.E.)
Place:	[Šaḫrīnu]
Content:	Promissory note to pay a debt of silver and onions to MNA. Repayment of the onions is to be obtained from the (debtor's) *šibšu*. Silver had been transferred to the debtor to pay for *rikis qabli*. Reference to an outstanding debt of dates, onions and silver secured by pledge.

OBV.

1 50 (erasure)* GÍN KÙ.BABBAR 50 [*pít-ti šá*]

2 SUM.SAR *šá* ^{md}AMAR.UTU-*na*-PAB-A A-*šú šá* ^{m}K[I-^{d}AMAR.UTU-DIN]

3 *ina muḫ-ḫi* ^{m}*ri-mut*-^{d}EN A-*šú šá* ^{m}MU-GIN

4 *ina* ITI.BÁR *šá* MU.6.KAM KÙ.BABBAR-*a'* 50 GÍN

5 50 *pít-ti šá* SUM.SAR *i-nam-din*

6 *ina šib-šú* A.ŠÀ-*šú i-šal-lim e-lat ú-ìl-tì*

7 *ra-šu-tu* IGI-*ti šá* ⸢2-ME 97* GUR 3 (PI)⸣

8 ZÚ.LUM.MA 11 GUR 2 (PI) 3 (BÁN) ŠE.BAR *u e-lat*

9 *ú-ìl-tì šá* 1 MA.NA 10 GÍN KÙ.BABBAR

REV.

10 *šá muḫ-ḫi* ^{m}*ri-mut*-^{d}EN *šá* A.ŠÀ-*šú*

11 *zaq-pu* [*u*] *pi-i šul-pu maš-ka-nu ṣab-tú*

12 KÙ.BABBAR *šá a-na* [*ri*]-*ki-is qab-lu*$^{!}$(BA) *šá* MU.5.KAM ⸢*šá*⸣ [*a-na a-la-ku*]

13 *šá* URU *še-e-l*[*a-du*] *a-na* ^{md}AG-*ma-a-ku*-URU$_3$ SUM-*nu*

14 LÚ *mu-kin-nu* ^{md}EN-MU

15 A-*šú šá* ^{md}AG-⸢NUMUN-MU⸣ ^{md}AMAR.UTU-BA-*šá-an-ni* [A-*šú šá*] ^{m}[^{d}EN-PAB-G]ÁL*-*ši*

16 A ^{md}EN-*e-ṭe-ri* ^{md}AG-URU$_3$-*šú* A-*šú* [*šá* ^{m}KAR-^{d}AMAR].UTU

17 ^{md}AG-*ma-a-ku*-URU$_3$ A-*šú šá* ^{md}AG-A-[MU]

18 LÚ.UMBISAG ^{md}EN-DÙ ⸢A⸣-[*šú šá* ^{md}U.GUR-NUMUN.DÙ]

19 A LÚ.SANGA-^{d}*na-na*-[*a* URU *šaḫ-ri-nu*]

20 ITI.NE UD.[1$^{?}$.KAM MU.5$^{?}$.KAM]

21 $^{[m]}$*da-ri-'i*-[*muš* …]

Translation

Fifty shekels of silver and fifty [bundles of] onions are due to MNA_1 from Rīmūt-Bēl, son of Šuma-ukīn. In Nisan of the sixth year he will pay these fifty shekels of silver (and) these fifty bundles of onions. He (= MNA) will receive full repayment from the *šibšu*(-crops) on his (= the debtor's) field. In addition, there is a previous debt of ⌜297!.3.0⌝ *kor* of dates (and) 11.2.3 *kor* of barley, as well as a debt of one mina (and) ten shekels of silver, charged against Rīmūt-Bēl, for which his orchard and grain field have been taken! as pledge. The (indebted) silver is that which has been given to Nabû-māku-uṣur (to pay) for the *rikis qabli* (of the men who have) [to go to] Šel[adu] in (Darius') fifth year.

Witnesses:
Bēl-iddin/Nabû-⌜zēra-iddin⌝
Marduk-iqīšanni/Bē[l-aḫa-u]šabši//Bēl-eṭēru
Nabû-uṣuršu/[Mušēzib-Mar]duk
Nabû-māku-uṣur/Nabû-apla-[iddin]
The scribe: Bēl-ibni/[Nergal-zēra-ibni]//Šangû-Nana[ya]
(Place + Date).

Comment

The reconstructions in lines 12, and 15–20 are based on the parallel passages in Dar 164, which was written by the same scribe, and probably on the same day and in the same place as the text under consideration.

L. 2: On the transliteration of the name Marduk-nāṣir-apli in this line, see at Dar 164: 2. The name Itti-Marduk-balāṭu could not have fitted on the obverse; the scribe must have written part of it on the edge, which is, unfortunately, broken off.

L. 10–11: The grain field and orchard (A.ŠÀ *zaqpu u pī šulpu*) for which, unfortunately, no location is given, was, no doubt, part of the land along the Borsippa canal that the same debtors had pledged to MNA according to Dar 144: 8–10, BM 33972: 9–10 and Dar 164: 10–11.

L. 15: I read ^{md}AG-⌜NUMUN (not MU)-MU⌝ in view of Dar 164: 16.

No. 97

Dar 182
Museum No.: BM 30683
Date: 27/viii/5 Dar (19 November 517 B.C.E.)
Place: Babylon
Content: Receipt of wool from MNA by a weaver of Lugal-Marada. As proxy for (*ina našpartu ša*) the chief administrator of the E'igikalamma.

OBV.

1 3 GÚ.UN SÍK.ḪI.A *bab-ba-ni-tu*$_4$
2 ^{md}AG-*it-tan-nu* A-*šú šá* ^{m}*tab-ni-e-a* LÚ.UŠ.BAR
3 *šá* $^{\ulcorner d* \urcorner}$LUGAL-$^{d!*}$AMAR$^{!*}$-DA$^{!*}$ *ina na-áš-par-tu*$_4$ *šá*
4 ^{md}U.GUR-*ina*-SÙḪ$^{!}$-SUR LÚ.ŠÀ.TAM *é-igi-kalam-ma*
5 *ina* ŠU.II ^{m}*ši-ir-ku* {A-*šú šá* ^{m}*ši-ri-ku*}
6 A-*šú šá* ^{m}MU-*a* A ^{m}*e-gì-bi ma-ḫir*

REV.

7 LÚ *mu-kin-nu* ^{md}U.GUR-GI A-*šú šá*
8 ^{m}KAR-^{d}AMAR.UTU A LÚ.SIMUG ^{m}*ri-mut*-^{d}EN
9 A-*šú šá* ^{m}ÌR-*ia* A LÚ.ŠITIM ^{md}AG-*bul-liṭ-su*
10 <A-*šú šá*> ^{m}MU-^{d}AG A ^{m}*da-bi-bi*
11 LÚ.UMBISAG ^{m}*šad-din-nu* A-*šú šá* ^{md}EN-ŠEŠ.MEŠ-BA-*šá*
12 TIN.TIR.KI ITI.APIN UD.27.KAM
13 MU.5.KAM ^{m}*da-ri-'i-muš*
14 LUGAL E.KI LUGAL KUR.KUR

TRANSLATION

Three talents of first-rate wool: Nabû-ittannu, son of Tabnêa, the weaver of Lugal-Marada$^{!}$, (acting) as proxy for Nergal-ina-tēšê$^{!}$-ēṭir, the chief administrator of the E'igikalamma temple, has received (it) from MNA$_2$.

Witnesses:
Nergal-ušallim/Mušēzib-Marduk//Nappāḫu
Rīmūt-Bēl/Ardiya//Itinnu
Nabû-bullissu</>Iddin-Nabû//Dābibī
The scribe: Šaddinnu/Bēl-aḫḫē-iqīša
(Place + Date).

COMMENT

There are several scribal errors (see at lines 3, 4, 5 and 10).

L. 3: No doubt, the divine name mentioned in this line is Lugal-Marada, in view of the temple that is mentioned at the end of the next line (viz., E'igikalamma). The E'igikalamma temple, indeed, is commonly identified as the temple of Lugal-Marada in Marad (Stol, *RLA* 7, s.v. 148 s.v. Lugal-

Marada). Lugal-Marada was the local manifestation of Nergal in Marad, but some late lists of divine names identify Lugal-Marada with Ninurta (Stol, *Id.*; Wiggermann, *RLA* 9, 222 s.v. Nergal.A; and Streck, *RLA* 9, 518; there is also evidence for an identification of the E'igikalamma temple with "the house of Ninurta," details at George, *House Most High*, 104 no. 520). However, something went wrong when the scribe had to write this divine name, which is normally spelled ^{d}LUGAL-AMAR.DA or ^{d}LUGAL-*ma-rad-da*. He must have started to write the name, but then decided to start over again and overwrote what he had previously written (cf. next line). The result is a confusing mixture of wedges after *šá* ^{d}LUGAL, some of which are more deeply impressed than others. This confusion is not reflected in Strassmaier's copy.

L. 4: After ^{m}U.GUR-*ina* the scribe wrote ŠÀ.TAM, then realized that he had still to finish the personal name, so that he tried to turn the ŠÀ.TAM into a ŠÙḪ. For a possible identification of Nergal-ina-tēšê-ēṭir, see Jursa, *Bēl-rēmanni*, n. 453.

No. 98

	Dar 206
Museum No.:	BM 31187
Date:	vi(b)/3$^{!}$ Dar (September-October 519 B.C.E.)
Place:	Babylon
Content:	Receipt of silver from MNA. Payment for *rikis qabli*. By order of (*ina qibi ša*) the governor of Babylon.

OBV.

1 [x M]A.NA KÙ.BABBAR *ri-iḫ-*tu_4 6 MA.NA KÙ.BABBAR
2 [(*kum, ina*)$^{?}$ *r*]*i-kis** $MURUB_4$ *šá ul-tu-ú** ITI.BÁR
3 MU.2.KAM *a-di qí-it* ITI.ŠE MU.3.KAM ^{m}*da-ri-'i-uš*
4 LUGAL E.KI LUGAL KUR.KUR *šá* ^{m}ÌR-^{d}AMAR.UTU A-*šú šá*
5 ^{m}*kit-ti-iá* A LÚ.SANGA-^{d}IDIM *šá ina qí-bi*
6 *šá* ^{md}EN-*ap-lu*-MU LÚ.GAR-$UŠ_4$-*ba-bi-i-li*
7 [*u*]*l*-⸢*tu*⸣-*ú* É ^{md}AMAR.UTU-*na-ṣir*-IBILA
8 [*a-n*]*a* ^{m}ÌR-^{d}⸢AMAR.UTU⸣ SUM.NA ^{md}AMAR.UTU-E[N-*šú-nu*]
9 [A-*šú*] *šá* ^{m}ÌR-^{d}⸢AMAR.UTU⸣ *ina qá-at*

LO. E.

10 $^{[m]d}$AMAR.UTU-*na-ṣir-ap-lu* A-*šú** *š*[*á**]
11 [^{m}KI-^{d}A]MAR.UTU-DIN A ^{m}*e-gi-bi*

REV.

12 [*ma*]-*ḫir*
13 LÚ *mu-kin-nu* ^{md}AG-DÙ-NUMUN A-*šú šá* ^{m}$ZALAG_2$-*e-a*
14 A LÚ.SANGA-^{d}*na-na-a* ^{md}AG-*mu-še-ti-iq*-UD.DA
15 A-*šú šá* ^{m}*šu-la-a* A ^{m}*tu-na-a*

16 ^{md}EN-MU A-*šú šá* ^{md}AG-*na-din-ip-ri*
17 A ^{md}IDIM-DINGIR-*ú-tu*-DÙ
18 ^{md}AG-*bul-liṭ-su* LÚ.UMBISAG A-*šú šá*
19 ^{md}EN-ŠEŠ.MEŠ-BA-*šá* A ^{m}*na-din-še***-e*
20 E.KI ITI.KIN*.2.KAM MU.3$^{!*}$.KAM
21 ^{m}*da-ri-'i-uš* LUGAL E.KI LUGAL KUR.KUR

TRANSLATION

[x m]inas of silver, the remainder of six minas of silver, (payment for) the [*r*]*ikis qabli* duty from Nisan of the second year until the end of Addar of the third year of Darius, king of Babylon, king of the lands, (which) were due to Arad-Marduk, son of Kittiya, descendant of Šangû-Ea, (and) which have been given by order of Bēl-apla-iddin, governor of Babylon, [t]o Arad-⸢Marduk⸣ [f]⸢rom⸣ the House of MNA$_1$: Marduk-b[ēlšunu, son] of Arad-⸢Marduk⸣, [has re]ceived (it) from MNA$_1$.

Witnesses:
Nabû-bāni-zēri/Nūrea//Šangû-Nanaya
Nabû-mušētiq-uddê/Šulaya//Tunaya
Bēl-iddin/Nabû-nādin-ipri//Ea-ilūta-bani
The scribe: Nabû-bullissu/Bēl-aḫḫē-iqīša//Nādin-še'i
(Place + Date).

COMMENT

L. 2: At the beginning of the line there is very little space, so that a reconstruction *ina* is more likely than *kum*. The KIS-sign is stretched out horizontally and may have been written by an unexperienced scribe or by a scribe who did not know which sign he was copying.

L. 15: For the name Tunaya, more at Zadok, *Iran* 14, 67.

L. 19: The *še* is written over a *ni*.

L. 20: The month is KIN*.2.KAM, so that no day is given. As far as the year is concerned, one must read 3 at the end of line 20, notwithstanding the fact that there seem to be five or six wedges rather than three. Indeed, Darius' fifth and sixth years are not known as intercalary years (at least not as having an intercalary Ulūl), whereas for Darius' third year an intercalary Ulūl is attested in another source (cf. Parker-Dubberstein, *Chronology*, 7 and 30). The figure 3 was probably written over the remnants of a horizontal wedge, which gives the impression that there was a second row of wedges beneath the three wedges of the figure 3.

No. 99

Dar 212
Museum No.: BM 30927
Date: 26/ix/6 Dar (5 January 515 B.C.E.)
Place: Ḫaḫḫuru-ša-Kalbaya
Content: Sale of a slave to MNA and receipt of the purchase price.

OBV.

1 ^{md}EN-*na-din*-IBILA ^{md}AG-MU *u* ^{m}I-^{d}EN
2 DUMU.MEŠ *šá* ^{md}EN-DIN-*iṭ* A LÚ.BAḪAR$_2$
3 *ina ḫu-ud lìb-bi-šú-nu* ^{md}AG-*si-il-lim*
4 LÚ *qal-la-šú-nu a-na* 4 MA.NA 10 GÍN KÙ.BABBAR UD-*ú*
5 *nu-uḫ-ḫu-tu šá ina* 1 GÍN *bit-qa a-na* ŠÁM *ḫa-ri-iṣ*
6 *a-na* ^{md}AMAR.UTU-*na-ṣir*-IBILA A-*šú šá* ^{m}KI-^{d}AMAR.UTU-DIN
7 A ^{m}*e-gi-bi id-din-nu-'u pu-ut si-hi-ú**
8 *pa-qir-ra-nu* LÚ.ÌR-LUGAL-*ú-tu* LÚ.DUMU-DÙ-*ú-tu*
9 *u* LÚ *šu-šá-an-nu-tu šá ina muḫ-ḫi* ^{md}AG-*sil-lim*
10 *il-la-'a* ^{md}EN-*na-din*-IBILA ^{md}AG-MU
11 *u** ^{m}I-^{d}EN *na-šu-ú* KÙ.BABBAR-*a'* 4 MA.NA 10 GÍN

REV.

12 *ši-i-mu* ^{md}AG-*sil-lim* LÚ *qal-la-šú-nu*
13 ^{md}EN-*na-din*-A ^{md}AG-MU *u* ^{m}I-^{d}EN
14 *ina* ŠU.II ^{md}AMAR.UTU-*na-ṣir*-IBILA *e-ṭi-ru-u'*
15 LÚ *mu-kin-ni* ^{md}AG-MU-GAR-*un* A-*šú šá* ^{m}ÌR-^{d}ME.ME
16 A LÚ.ŠU.KU$_6$ ^{m}ÌR-^{d}*gu-la* A-*šú šá* ^{md}AMAR.UTU-MU-URU$_3$*
17 A ^{m}*na-ba-a-a* ^{md}U.GUR-MU A-*šú šá* ^{m}*ba-ni-ia*
18 A ^{m}*šá-na-ši-šú* ^{m}*ni-din-tu$_4$*-^{d}EN A-*šú šá* ^{md}AG-*ka-ṣir*
19 A LÚ.BAḪAR$_2$ ^{md}*mu-še-zib*-^{d}AMAR.UTU LÚ.UMBISAG A-*šú šá*
20 ^{md}UTU-*ú*-SIG$_5$-*iq* A ^{m}*šá*-MUN.ḪI.A-*šú*
21 URU *ḫa-aḫ-ḫu-ru* URU *šá*-^{m}{*šá*}-*kal-ba-a* ITI.GAN UD.26.KAM

LE. E.

22 MU.6.KAM ^{m}*da-ri-ia-a-muš*
23 LUGAL TIN.TIR.KI LUGAL KUR.KUR

TRANSLATION

Bēl-nādin-apli, Nabû-iddin and Nā'id-Bēl, sons of Bēl-uballiṭ, descendant of Paḫāru, have voluntarily sold their slave Nabû-silim for four minas and ten shekels of white medium-quality silver, of which one-eighth is alloy, as its full price, to MNA$_1$. Bēl-nādin-apli, Nabû-iddin and Nā'id-Bēl assume guaranty against any challenger (of the legality of the sale), any claimant (to a right of ownership), (and suit claiming) the status of royal slave, *mār bānê* or *šušānu*, which arise over Nabû-silim. Bēl-nādin-apli, Nabû-iddin and Na'id-Bēl have been paid those four minas and ten shekels of silver, the price for their slave Nabû-silim, by MNA$_1$.

Witnesses:
Nabû-šuma-iškun/Arad-Ninurta//Bā'iru
Arad-Gula/Marduk-šuma-uṣur//Nabaya
Nergal-iddin/Baniya//Ša-nāšīšu
Nidinti-Bēl/Nabû-kāṣir//Paḫāru
The scribe: Mušēzib-Marduk/Šamaš-udammiq//Ša-ṭābtišu
(Place + Date).

Comment

L. 7: Note the spelling *si-ḫi-ú* (not *si-ḫi-i*).

L. 15: Note the spelling LÚ *mu-kin-ni* (not LÚ *mu-kin-nu*).

No. 100

Dar 213
Museum No.: BM 77848
Date: 7/x/6 Dar (16 January 515 B.C.E.)
Place: Babylon
Content: <Receipt> of silver from MNA.

Obv.

1 ½ MA.NA KÙ.BABBAR *šá ina* 1 GÍN [*bit-qa*]
2 *nu-uḫ-ḫu-tu* ^{md}AG-MU-GIN DUMU-*šú*
3 *šá* ^{md}EN-SUR A LÚ.SANGA-^{d}*na-na-a*
4 *ina* ŠU.II ^{md}AMAR.UTU-*na-ṣir*-A
5 A-*šú šá* ^{m}KI-^{d}AMAR.UTU-DIN A ^{m}*e-gì-bi*

Lo. E.

6 *a-na muḫ-ḫi* ^{md}EN-*na-din*-A
7 A<-*šú šá*> ^{md}EN-DIN-*iṭ* A LÚ.BAḪAR$_2$ <*ma-ḫir*>

Rev.

8 LÚ *mu-kin-nu* ^{md}U.GUR-*ú-še-zib*
9 A-*šú šá* ^{m}*nad-na-a* A ^{m}MU-*líb-ši*
10 ^{m}*šul-lu-mu* A<-*šú šá*> ^{m}KAR-^{d}AMAR.UTU
11 A LÚ.SIMUG ^{m}⸢*lib*{-A}⸣-*luṭ* A<-*šú šá*> ^{md}AMAR.UTU-MU-DÙ
12 A LÚ.SANGA-^{d}MAŠ ^{md}IDIM-A-MU
13 DUB.SAR A LÚ.GÍR.LÁ-KAR

U. E.

14 TIN.TIR.KI ITI.AB UD.7.KAM
15 MU.6.KAM ^{m}*da-ri-ia-muš*
16 LUGAL E.KI LUGAL KUR.KUR

Translation

Half a mina of medium-quality silver of which one-eighth [is alloy]: Nabû-šuma-ukīn, son of Bēl-ēṭir, descendant of Šangû-Nanaya <has received (it)> from MNA$_1$, for the account of Bēl-nādin-apli, <son of> Bēl-uballiṭ, descendant of Paḫāru.

Witnesses:
Nergal-ušēzib/Nadnaya//Šumu-libši
Šullumu</>Mušēzib-Marduk//Nappāḫu
Libluṭ</>Marduk-šuma-ibni//Šangû-Ninurta
The scribe: Ea-apla-iddin//Ṭābiḫ-kāri
(Place + Date).

Comment

This transfer of half a mina of silver from MNA to Nabû-šuma-ukīn (*alias* Šuma-ukīn)/Bēl-ēṭir//Šangû-Nanaya is also mentioned in b 2800: 1–3; analogous transfers are mentioned in TCL 13 185.

No. 101

	Dar 215
Museum No.:	BM 32931
Date:	20/x/6 Dar (29 January 515 B.C.E.)
Place:	Babylon
Content:	Receipt of silver from MNA. Partial payment of salary.

Obv.

1 ^{m}*bul-ṭa-a* A-*šú šá* ^{m}*ḫa-ba-ṣi-ru* A LÚ.SIPA-GU$_4$
2 *a-na i-di a-na* MU-*an-na* ⸢⅓⸣ MA.NA KÙ.BABBAR *šá gìn-nu*
3 *ina pa-ni* ^{md}AMAR.UTU-PAB-A A-*šú šá* ^{m}KI-^{d}AMAR.UTU-DIN
4 A ^{m}*e-gì-bi ú-šu-zi-iz ul-tu*
5 UD.1.KAM *šá* ITI.ZÍZ ^{m}*bul-ṭa-a ina pa-ni*
6 ^{md}AMAR.UTU-PAB-EDURU* *ú-šu-zi-iz*
7 ⅓ MA.NA KÙ.BABBAR *šá* ^{m}*bul-ṭa-a ina* ŠU.II
8 ^{md}AMAR.UTU-PAB-EDURU* *ma-ḫi-ir*

Rev.

9 LÚ *mu-kin-nu* ^{m}*ri-mut-*^{d}EN A-*šú šá*
10 ^{m}ÌR-*ia* A LÚ.ŠITIM ^{m}*ḫa-aḫ-ḫu-ru*
11 A-*šú šá* ^{md}AG-KAR-ZI.MEŠ A ^{m}*dan-ni-e-a*
12 LÚ.UMBISAG ^{m}ÌR-*ia* A-*šú šá* ^{m}*da-di-ia*
13 A ^{m}*na-ba-a-a* E.KI ITI.AB
14 UD.20.KAM MU.6.KAM ^{m}*da-ri-'i-muš*
15 LUGAL E.KI LUGAL KUR.KUR

Translation

Bulṭaya, son of Ḫabaṣīru, descendant of Rē'i-alpi, has been put at the disposal of MNA_1 for a yearly salary of ⸢one-third?⸣ mina of marked silver. From the first of Šabāṭ Bulṭaya has been at the disposal of MNA_1. (The) one-third mina of silver {*of*} Bulṭaya has received from MNA_1.

Witnesses:
Rīmūt-Bēl/Ardiya//Itinnu
Ḫaḫḫuru/Nabû-ēṭir-napšāti//Dannêa
The scribe: Ardiya/Dādiya//Nabaya
(Place + Date).

Comment

L. 2: Strassmaier read ½ MA.NA, but the sign in question is partly damaged. I did not see the horizontal wedge that should have cut through the vertical one to make ½; actually, I saw a sign the shape of which much resembles the ⅓ of line 7. This sum, viz. Bulṭaya's salary, seems to be lower than the one that Bulṭaya received a year and a half ago from MNA, although we cannot be sure because the comparison is hampered by the fact that Dar 158 does not specify the quality of the silver. Previously, Bulṭaya received eight shekels a month for sailing a boat to Babylon (Dar 158: 2), and now he is to receive a little more than one-and-a-half shekels of marked silver a month ("⸢⅓?⸣ mina per year," line 2) for an unspecified kind of job.

L. 4b–6: On the formula *ana idīšu ina pāni* PN *šuzzuzu* in labor contracts to refer to the rent of a person, see Kessler, *AUWE* 8/1, 115ff. (including bibliography). In the text under consideration Bulṭaya "had been put at the disposal" (*ú-šu-zi-iz*, = *ušezziz*/*ušziz*, Š pret.; cf. TCL 13 173 = *Borsippa*, 316: 3–5, *ina pān* PN *ú-šu-zu*) of MNA "since the first of Šabāṭ." It should be noted that Dar 215 is dated in the month that precedes Šabāṭ (ll. 13–14). The "first of Šabāṭ," therefore, probably refers to the previous year, Darius' 5th year. If so, Bulṭaya had been working for almost a year, i.e., from the first of Šabāṭ (= month xi) of Darius' 5th year till the twentieth of the Ṭebēt (= month x) of Darius' 6th year (the day on which the text under consideration was written). However, he had not received his salary. In the present document he received the one-third mina that had been agreed upon as the salary for one year. For a different opinion, see Peiser, *BRL* 3, 46: Bulṭaya has put himself (*ušziz*, line 4) at the disposal of MNA, i.e., from the first of Šabāṭ he puts himself (*ušziz*, line 6) at the disposal of MNA. These translations largely disregard the fact that *ú-šu-zi-iz* reflects a preterit-form, but for the rest leave the text fairly comprehensible, viz. it is a text recording a labor contract between MNA and Bulṭaya according to which the latter is to start working in ten days from the day on which the contract was concluded—there are ten days between the twentieth of Ṭebēt and the first of Šabāṭ. He received an advance payment for a full year.

No. 102

Dar 268 (Re-edited by Abraham, *NABU* 1997/53)
Museum No.: BM 30543
Date: 18/iv/⸢10⸣ Dar (19 July 512 B.C.E.)
Place: Babylon
Content: Receipt of the *miksu*-toll from MNA.

OBV.

1 *mi-ik-su šá* 70 GUR ŠE.BAR
2 ^{m}*kul-bi-bi* A-*šú šá* ^{md}EN-KÁD
3 A ^{m}DÙ-*eš*-DINGIR LÚ.GAL-*ka-ri šá* É
4 ^{m}*ir-a-ni ina* ŠU.II ^{m}*ši-iš-ki** A-*šú*
5 *šá* ^{m}SUM.NA-*a* A ^{m}*e-gi-bi*
6 *e-ṭir* GIŠ*.MÁ* *šá* 70 GUR ŠE.BAR
7 [^{m}*kul*]*-*bi-bi ina muḫ-ḫi ka-ri šá* É
8 [^{m}*ir-a*]-⸢*ni*⸣* *ú**-*še**-*et**-*te*[*q**-*ma*]

LO. E.

9 [*a*]-⸢*na*⸣ ^{m}*ši-iš-ki** *i*-⸢*nam*⸣*-*din**

REV.

10 LÚ *mu-kin-nu* ^{m}*mu-ra-šu-ú*
11 A-*šú šá* ^{md}AG-ŠEŠ.MEŠ-MU A ^{m}⸢ÌR-^{d}*na*⸣*-[*na-a*]
12 ^{md}AG-*mu*-⸢SIG$_{15}$⸣ A-*šú šá* ^{md}AG-ZI.MEŠ-URU$_{3}$
13 A ^{m}*e-gì-bi* ^{m}SILA-*a-a* A-*šú šá* ^{m}A-*a*
14 A ^{m}*de-ki-i* ^{md}AMAR.UTU-EN-*šú-nu*
15 A-*šú šá* ^{m}ÌR-^{d}AMAR.UTU A LÚ.SANGA-^{d}IDIM
16 ^{m}*šul-lu-mu* A-*šú šá* ^{m}KAR-^{d}AMAR.UTU
17 A LÚ.SIMUG ^{m}NÍG.BA-*iá* A-*šú šá*

U. E.

18 ^{m}MU-^{d}AG A ^{m}⸢*zu-x-i u* LÚ$^{?}$⸣.[UMBISAG]
19 ^{md}AG-URU$_{3}$-*šú* A LÚ.⸢BAḪAR$_{2}$⸣

LE. E.

20 E.KI ITI.ŠU UD.18.[KAM]
*21 [MU].⸢10⸣.KAM⸣ ^{m}*da-ri*-⸢*ia*⸣-*m*[*uš*]
*22 [...]$^{?}$

TRANSLATION

The *miksu*-toll on seventy *kor* of barley: Kulbibi, son of Bēl-kāṣir, descendant of Eppeš-ilī, overseer of the quay of Bīt-Ir'anni, has received (it) from MNA$_{2}$. [Kul]bibi shall let the boat pass (loaded) with seventy *kor* of barley beyond the quay of Bīt-[Ir'ann]i, [and] he shall give (it) to MNA$_{2}$.

Witnesses:
Murašû/Nabû-aḫḫē-iddin//⸢Arad⸣-Na[nna]
Nabû-⸢mudammiq⸣/Nabû-napšāti-uṣur//Egibi

Sūqaya/Aplaya//Dēkû
Marduk-bēlšunu/Arad-Marduk//Šangû-Ea
Šullumu/Mušēzib-Marduk//Nappāḫu
Qīštiya/Iddin-Nabû//⸢PN⸣
And [the scribe]: Nabû-uṣuršu//⸢Paḫāru⸣
(Place + Date).

COMMENT

L. 7: ^{m}NUMUN- as copied by Strassmaier is no longer visible on the tablet. The name ^{m}NUMUN-*bi-bi* is probably to be read ^{m}*kul-bi-bi* (so Wunsch, *Felder* 2, 305).

L. 11: More on this Murašû at BM 32883: 14–15.

L. 20–22 (Left Edge): At the time Strassmaier copied the tablet the signs on the left edge must have been better preserved than today. The MU as copied by Strassmaier, for instance, is no longer visible on the tablet. Neither did I see the signs LUGAL E.KI u KUR.KUR, which, according to Strassmaier's copy, were written on the left edge.

No. 103

	Dar 296
Museum No.:	BM 30926
Date:	18/i/11 Dar (11 April 511 B.C.E.)
Place:	Babylon
Content:	Summons to transmit crops from the land of Bagasarū, and to arrange for their proper registration.

OBV.

1 ⸢1-ME 70⸣ GUR ŠE.BAR 4 GUR GIG.BA 4 GUR *saḫ-li-e* [(x x x)]*
2 *šá* MU.11*.KAM BURU$_{14}$ A.ŠÀ *šá* ^{m}*ba-ga-'a-sa-ru-ú* LÚ *gan-za-*⸢*ba*⸣-[*ru*]
3 ^{m}*ni-din-tu*$_{4}$ LÚ.GAL É *šá* ^{m}BA-*šá-a iq-bu-ú um-ma* ^{m}⸢SU⸣-[*a* (x x)]*
4 LÚ.GAL É *ina muḫ-ḫi-iá ul-taz-zi-iz* ŠE.BAR-*a*$_{4}$ 1-ME 70 GUR
5 ^{m}ÌR-^{d}KÁ *u* ^{m}*še-el-li-bi i-da-ḫar-in-ni ù*
6 4 GUR GIG.BA 4 GUR *saḫ-li-e a-na e-lat a-na* ^{m}*še-el-li-bi*
7 *at-ta-din* ^{m}ÌR-^{d}*ba-ba*$_{6}$ A-*šú-šá* ^{m}KAR-^{d}AMAR.UTU A LÚ.AZLAG *u* ^{m}*še-el-li-bi*
8 A-*šú-šá* ^{m}MU-^{d}AG *e-li rama-ni-šú-nu ú-kin-nu-u' um-ma* ŠE.BAR-*a*$_{4}$
9 1-ME 70 GUR *ina* ŠU.II ^{m}*eri-ba-a ni-it-ta-ši u* ^{m}*še-*{*ḫu*}*-el-li-bi*
10 *e-li rama-ni-šú ú-kin um-ma* 4 GUR GIG.BA 4 GUR *saḫ-li-e*
11 *a-na-ka a-na e-lat* ^{m}ÌR-^{d}*ba-ba*$_{6}$ *ina* ŠU.II ^{m}SU-*a at-ta-ḫar*$^{!}$
12 *a-di* UD.20.KAM *šá* ITI.GU$_{4}$ 1-ME 70 GUR ŠE.BAR ^{m}ÌR-^{d}*b*[*a-ba*$_{6}$]

LO. E.

*13 *u* ^{m}*še-el-li-bi ina pa-ni* ^{m}*ni-din-tu*$_{4}$ *ú-šá-*⸢*ad*⸣$^{?*}$-[x x]

REV.

14 *a-na* ^{m}*eri-ba-a i-nam-din-nu-u'* *ù* 4 GUR GIG.BA ⸢4⸣ [GUR *saḫ-li-e*]

15 ^{m}*še-el-li-bi a-na e-lat-šú i-na muḫ-ḫi* ^{m}*ni-din-tu*$_{4}$ *ú-šá-az-za-a*[*z-ma*]

16 *a-na* ^{m}SU-*a* A-*šú-šá* ^{m}*šá*-^{d}AG-*šu-ú i-nam-din* ^{md}AMAR.UTU-*na-ṣir*-A A-*šú-šá*

17 ^{m}KI-^{d}AMAR.UTU-DIN *pu-ut* GÌR.II *šá* ^{m}ÌR-^{d}KÁ *na-ši* ^{m}*šu-lum*-TIN.TIR.KI A-*šú-šá*

18 ^{md}EN-ŠEŠ-MU *pu-ut* GÌR.II *šá* ^{m}*še-el-li-bi na-ši* LÚ *mu-kin-nu*

19 ^{md}AMAR.UTU-*na-ṣir*-A A-*šú-šá* ^{m}KI-^{d}AMAR.UTU-DIN A ^{m}*e-gi-bi* ^{m}KAR-^{d}EN A-*šú-šá*

20 ^{md}EN-KÁD A ^{md}IDIM-DÙ-*uš*-DINGIR ^{md}AG-KAR-ZI.MEŠ A-*šú-šá* ^{m}*ni-qu-du*

21 A ^{m}*mu*-SIG$_{5}$-*iq*-^{d}IŠKUR ^{m}*bul-luṭ*$^{?!}$(TAR)-*a-a* A-*šú-šá* ^{m}*ú-bar* ^{m}*pir-'u* A-*šú-šá* ^{m}*šá-du-nu*

22 ^{m}*mu-ra-nu* A-*šú-šá* ^{m}KAR-^{d}AMAR.UTU A LÚ.AZLAG ^{m}*ni-din-tu*$_{4}$ A-*šú-šá* ^{md}EN-MU A LÚ.AZLAG

23 ^{m}*ri-mut*-^{d}EN A-*šú-šá* ^{m}ÌR-*iá* A LÚ.ŠITIM ^{md}EN-SU A-*šú-šá* ^{md}AG-*re-man-ni*

24 ^{md}AG-*bul-liṭ-su* A-*šú-šá* ^{m}EN-*šú-nu* ^{m}ŠEŠ-*lu-mur* A-*šú-šá* ^{md}LUM.LUM-ŠEŠ.[MEŠ-MU]

25 ^{md}AG-*bul-liṭ-su* DUB.SAR A-*šú-šá* ^{md}AG-MU-*ú-kin* A ^{m}*la-ku*[*p-pu-ru*]

U. E.

*26 TIN.TIR.KI ITI.BÁR UD.18.KAM MU.11.KAM ^{m}*da-ri-ia*-[(*a*)-*muš*]

27 LUGAL E.KI LUGAL KUR.KUR

TRANSLATION

(Regarding) ⸢one hundred and seventy⸣ *kor* of barley, four *kor* of wheat, (and) four *kor* of cress, the harvest of the eleventh year from Bagasarū's field, the treasur[er], Nidintu, majordomo of Iqīša said as follows: "⸢Erībaya⸣, (Bagasarū's) majordomo, has registered (them) in my accounts(, saying): 'Arad-Bāba and Šellibi received these one hundred and seventy *kor* of barley from me; also the four *kor* of wheat (and) the four *kor* of cress I have given, but to Šellibi only'." Arad-Bāba, son of Mušēzib-Marduk, descendant of Ašlāku, and Šellibi, son of Iddin-Nabû testified on their own account (saying) as follows: "We have received these one hundred and seventy *kor* of barley;" and Šellibi testified on his own account (saying) as follows: "Only I, - Arad-Bāba not included -, have received the four *kor* of wheat (and) the four *kor* of cress from Erībaya." By the twentieth of Ayyar Arad-B[āba] and Šellibi shall trans[mit$^{?}$] the one hundred and seventy *kor* of barley before Nidintu and give (proof of it) to Erībaya; and Šellibi alone shall register the four *kor* of wheat (and) ⸢the four⸣ [*kor* of cress] in the accounts of Nidintu, [and] give (proof of it) to Erībaya, son of Ša-Nabû-šū. MNA$_{1}$ assumed warranty for Arad-Bāba. Šulum-Bābili, son of Bēl-aḫa-iddin assumed warranty for Šellibi.

Witnesses:

MNA$_1$
Mušēzib-Bēl/Bēl-kāṣir//Ea-eppeš-ilī
Nabû-ēṭir-napšāti/Niqūdu//Mudammiq-Adad
Bulṭaya[!]/Ubār
Pir'u/Šadûnu
Mūrānu/Mušēzib-Marduk//Ašlāku
Nidintu/Bēl-iddin//Ašlāku
Rīmūt-Bēl/Ardiya//Itinnu
Bēl-erība/Nabû-rēmanni
Nabû-bullissu/Bēlšunu
Aḫa-lūmur/^{d}LUM-LUM-aḫḫē-⸢iddin⸣
The scribe: Nabû-bullissu/Nabû-šuma-ukīn//Laku[ppuru]
(Place + Date).

COMMENT

The principal parties are Nidintu, majordomo of Iqīša and Erībaya, majordomo of Bagasarū. The issue is the transporting of crops from Bagasarū's land by the latter to the former, and the proper registration of this transaction in the accounts of Nidintu. Problems arose due to the fact that the transmission of the crops took place through agents, viz. Arad-Bāba and Šellibi. They received the crops from Erībaya, and apparently should have transferred them to Nidintu and given proof of the transaction to Erībaya. The agents did not deny their receipt of the crops. In fact, they admit and confirm it in lines 7–11. If so, they had no alibi and were, accordingly, obliged to "trans[mit?] the one hundred and seventy *kor* of barley before Nidintu by the twentieth of Ayyar, [and] give (proof of it) to Erībaya; and as for Šellibi, he should register the four *kor* of wheat and ⸢four⸣ [*kor* of cress] in the accounts of Nidintu, [and] give (proof of it) to Erībaya, son of Ša-Nabû-šu" (ll. 12–16). Clearly, the responsibility was borne by these two men only. MNA assumed warranty that Arad-Bēl meet his obligation; another person did the same for Šellibi. MNA was also present as first witness. As far as Erībaya was concerned, he was free from any charge. Nidintu explicitly discharged him of any responsibility declaring that "⸢Erībaya⸣, the majordomo, has registered (the crops) in my accounts" (ll. 3–4a). We have to assume that in the following lines (viz. ll. 4b–7), Nidintu is quoting Erībaya's words: "(He told me as follows:) The one hundred and seventy *kor* of barley Arad-Bāba and Šellibi have received from me and the four *kor* of wheat and four *kor* of cress I have given to Šellibi." Arad-Bāba and Šellibi actually confirm their receipt of the crops from the hands of Erībaya in the following lines (ll. 7–11).

L. 2: The year is Darius' eleventh year (MU.11.KAM). Strassmaier copied MU.10.KAM. The *Winkelhaken* (=10) and the vertical (=1) are, indeed, written very close to each other, which gives the impression that there is only a *Winkelhaken*. Cf. the way the scribe wrote 11 in line 26.

L. 3: For *rab bīti*, "majordomo," see Bongenaar, *Ebabbar*, 135–36. The end of the line and the right edge are broken off, and the last visible sign may have been SU (so Strassmaier), but it is fragmentary. I assume that ⸢Erībaya⸣ was Bagasarū's majordomo. Eleven years later, a man named Piššaya bore the title of Bagasarū's majordomo (Dar 542).

L. 4: *ina muḫḫi* is most probably a variant of *itti* in this context. So Weszeli-Baker, *WZKM* 87, 235. For the formula *šuzzuzu-ma nadānu*, see BM 30233: 4–9.

L. 8: For *eli ramānišu ukīn* "he testified against himself," i.e., he proved the charges against him and he convicted himself, see Von Dassow, *Fs. Levine*, 9f.

L. 11: The sign at the end of the line resembles ŠI (not DIN as copied by Strassmaier). Should we read *at-ta-ši* (from the verb *našû*) or *at-ta-ḫar*$^{!}$ (from the verb *maḫāru*, cf. line 5)?

L. 13: I suggest to read *ú-šá-*⸢*ad*⸣-[*gil-ma*] at the end of the line.

L. 24: The signs at the end of the line are hardly visible.

No. 104

	Dar 307
Museum No.:	BM 31433
Date:	19/vi(b)/11 Dar (6 October 511 B.C.E.)
Place:	Babylon
Content:	About a plowed field from a bow-fief, and about a plow (team) of MNA. Very fragmentary.

OBV.

1 ŠE.NUMUN *ma-a-a-ri di*$^{!}$*-ku-ú-tu*
2 *šá i-na* É GIŠ.BAN *šá* ^{md}U.GUR-*na-ṣir*
3 *šá a-na* ^{m}SUM.NA-*a* DUMU *šá* ^{m}ÌR-^{d}EN SUM.NA
4 *šá i-na* GIŠ*.APIN *šá* ^{md}AMAR.UTU-*na-ṣir*<-A>
5 [A*-*šú šá* ^{m}][SUM.NA]-*a* A ^{m}*e-gì-bi*
6 [...]-*an-na* [...]
(Remainder is broken off.)

REV.

7 [x x x (x)] ^{md}AG-MU-MU DUMU *šá* ^{md}AG-EN-MU.MEŠ
8 A LÚ.SANGA-^{d}IŠKUR ^{m}ÌR-^{d}EN DUMU *šá* ^{m}*kal-ba-a*
9 A ^{m}MU-*líb-ši* ^{md}UTU-MU DUMU *šá* ^{m}DUB-NUMUN A LÚ.NAGAR
10 ^{m}*zab-di-ia* DUMU *šá* ^{md}AG-DA ^{m}*ta-at-tan-nu* DUMU *šá* ^{md}EN-MU
11 ^{md}EN-DIN-*iṭ* DUB.SAR DUMU *šá* ^{md}AG-MU A LÚ.GAL-DÙ
12 TIN.TIR.KI ITI.KIN.2.KAM UD.20-1-LÁ.KAM
13 MU.11.KAM ^{m}*da-ri-ia-muš*

U. E.

*14 LUGAL TIN.TIR.KI LUGAL KUR.KUR

TRANSLATION

Arable land broken up by the *ma(y)yāru*-plow that is part of the bow-fief of Nergal-nāṣir, that has been given to Iddinaya, son of Arad-Bēl, (and) that ... the plow (team) of MNA_1 [...].

[Witnesses]:

Nabû-šuma-iddin/Nabû-bēl-šumāti//Šangû-Adad

Arad-Bēl/Kalbaya//Šumu-libši

Šamaš-iddin/Šāpik-zēri//Nagāru

Zabdiya/Nabû-ile''i

Tattannu/Bēl-iddin

The scribe: Bēl-uballiṭ/Nabû-iddin//Rab-banê

(Place + Date).

COMMENT

L. 1: For *ma(y)yāru* and *dekû*, see Jursa, *Landwirtschaft*, 140–41.

L. 4: Strassmaier copied *šá i-na* É APIN, but collation of the tablet has shown that one should read GIŠ instead of É, even with the area between the two horizontals of the GIŠ being slightly damaged. Moreover, the idiom GIŠ.APIN = *epinnu* is well known. It was the technical term for a team of plowmen (see Jursa, *Landwirtschaft*, 9 and index s.v. Pflug(team); also *CAD* E, 237 s.v. *epinnu* mng. b-4′ "personnel of the plow"). The two signs before GIŠ.APIN are written in a careless way. Strassmaier copied *i-na* and that is what they actually look like. Consequently, the phrase *ša ina epinni ša* MNA may be translated "that by the plow (team) of MNA," and the verb to be completed in the break in line 6 may have been something like "[has been cultivated]."

L. 4 end: There was still enough space at the end of the line to write A, without having to use the right edge.

L. 5: In view of the space available at the beginning of the line A-*šú šá* is more likely than DUMU *šá*, although the scribe never used the former.

L. 6: After *-la* there may have followed at least three more signs.

L. 11: The two signs LÚ.GAL are written very closely to each other. Did the scribe squeeze these signs in order to fit the surname LÚ.GAL-DÙ on the reverse, without having to use the right edge?

No. 105

Dar 308
Museum No.: BM 31027
Date: 26/vii/11 Dar (12 November 511 B.C.E.)
Place: Šaḫrīnu
Content: Promissory note to pay a debt of silver and dates to MNA's slave. Pledge of land. Silver had been transferred to the debtor to pay for *rikis qabli*.

OBV.

1 30 GUR ZÚ.LUM.MA ½ MA.NA KÙ.BABBAR *šá gìn-nu*
2 *šá* ^{md}DI.KU$_5$-EN-URU$_3$ LÚ *qal-la šá* ^{md}AMAR.UTU-PAB-A
3 A ^{m}*e-gi-bi ina muḫ-ḫi* ^{md}EN-MU A-*šú šá*
4 ^{md}AG-NUMUN-GÁL-*ši ina* ITI.DU$_6$ *šá* MU.12.KAM
5 ZÚ.LUM.MA-*a*$_4$ 30 GUR *ina ma-ši-ḫu šá* 1 PI
6 *ina muḫ-ḫi* 1-*et rit-tu*$_4$ *ina* URU *šá-ḫa-ri-nu*
7 *i-nam-din* KÙ.BABBAR-*a*$_4$ ½ MA.NA *šá gìn-nu*
8 *ina* ITI.DU$_6$ *šá* MU.12.KAM *ina* SAG.DU-*šú*

LO. E.

9 *i-nam-din* A.ŠÀ *šá* ⸢x*⸣ *-ri-i-ni pi-i šul-pu u* GIŠ.GIŠIMMAR
10 *maš-ka-nu šá* ^{md}DI.KU$_5$-EN-URU$_3$ *a-di*
11 *muḫ-ḫi šá* KÙ.BABBAR-*šú u* ZÚ.LUM.MA-*šú i-šal-li-mu*

REV.

12 KÙ.BABBAR *ri-kiš* MURUB$_4$ *šá a-na* KUR.ELAM.KI ⸢SUM-*nu**⸣
13 LÚ *mu-kin-nu* ^{md}U.GUR-MU A-*šú šá* ^{md}AMAR.UTU-SUR
14 A ^{m}NUMUN-*a-a* ^{m}*ni-qu-du* A-*šú šá* ^{md}U.GUR-MU
15 A ^{m}ZALAG$_2$-*za-nu* ^{m}*ba-la-ṭu* A-*šú šá* ^{md}AG-DÙ-NUMUN
16 A ^{m}LÚ.EN.NUN-KÁ.GAL ^{md}EN-KÁD A-*šú šá* ^{m}DÙ-*iá*
17 A ^{m}ÌR-^{d}GIR$_4$.KÙ ^{m}ÌR-*ia* A-*šú šá*
18 ^{md}AG-EN-MU.MEŠ A ^{m}*al-la-a* ^{md}AG-ŠEŠ-PAB
19 LÚ.UMBISAG A ^{m}KAR-^{d}AMAR.UTU URU *šá-ḫa-ri-nu*
20 ITI.DU$_6$ UD.26.KAM MU.11.KAM
21 ^{m}*da-ri-mu-šú* LUGAL E.KI *u* KUR.MEŠ

TRANSLATION

Thirty *kor* of dates (and) half a mina of marked silver are due to Madānu-bēla-uṣur, a slave of MNA$_1$, from Bēl-iddin, son of Nabû-zēra-ušabši. In Tašrīt of the twelfth year he will deliver these thirty *kor* of dates in one installment in Šaḫrīnu according to the *pān*-measure. Half the mina of marked silver he will pay without interest in Tašrīt of the twelfth year. The grain field and palm grove of ⸢…⸣rīnu are pledged to Madānu-bēla-uṣur until he has received full repayment of his silver and his dates. The silver is that which has been given (to Bēl-iddin to go) to Elam, (his) *rikis qabli* duty.

Witnesses:
Nergal-iddin/Marduk-ēṭir//Zēriya
Niqūdu/Nergal-iddin/Nūr-zana
Balāṭu/Nabû-bāni-zēri//Maṣṣār-abulli
Bēl-kāṣir/Baniya//Arad-Nergal
Ardiya/Nabû-bēl-šumāti//Allaya
The scribe: Nabû-aḫa-uṣur//Mušēzib-Marduk
(Place + Date).

COMMENT

L. 9: The sign ⸢x⸣ in ⸢x⸣-*ri-i-ni* resembles a KAP. For the fields of Kaprīnu in the vicinity of Šaḫrīnu, see Dar 438: 6 and Zadok, *RGTC* 8, 193, wr. ^{garim}*kap-ri-ni/nu* or *kap-pa-ri-in-ni*. There is a slight possibility that the sign in question is a badly written ŠAḪ, but in this respect it should be pointed out that the scribe of Dar 308 wrote ^{uru}*šá-ḫa-* rather than *šaḫ-* when spelling the place name Šaḫrīnu (see lines 6 and 19).

L. 15: Niqūdu's family name may be transliterated either ^{m}ZALAG$_2$-*za-nu*, or ^{m}*zab-za-nu*, but the meaning of the name remains enigmatic in either case. A noun *zabzanu*, for instance, is not attested to the best of my knowledge. When reading ^{m}ZALAG$_2$-*za-nu*, the first element stands for the noun *nūru*, "light"; the second element, however, is problematic. It is spelled in different ways: -*za-nu* (in the text under consideration), -*za-na* (Dar 430: 17, perhaps also in BM 31951: 5, -*z*]*a*$^?$-*na*$^?$), and -*za*$^!$(ŠÁ)-*na* (Dar 459: 12). Is it a verbal adjective from *zanānu* (i.e., *zannu* = "provided with"; *CAD* Z, 46, s.v. *zannu* (or *zānu*), "(mng. uncert.)"; *AHw*, 1510 s.v. *zannu* I "ausgestattet"). Or should we understand the form as follows: *za*(-ʾ)-*nu*/*na* = *za'in*/*zân* (from the verb *za'ānu*), "to be decorated with" (*CAD* Z, 47f. s.v. *zânu* mng. a-1′-b′; and *AHw*, 1499f. s.v. *za'ānu*)? If not Akkadian, the element *za-nu*/*na* may be Iranian in origin. Dr. Jan Tavernier suggested to me interpreting Nūr-zana as a composite name. Accordingly, it may consist of the Akkadian *nūr* = "light of," and the Iranian *dana* "kind, sort, species," hence meaning "Light of the human race." For Old Iranian nouns containing the element *dana*, see, for instance, *paruzana* "having many (kinds of) men," and *vispazana* "containing all (kinds of) men" (Kent, *Old Persian Grammar*, 211). Finally, note that Tallqvist, *NbN*, 314f., links the family name Nūr-zana with the rare names ^{m}*za-an-ni-e* (patronymy) and ^{m}*za-an-ni-e-tú* (family name), but for these names, probably see under Zanê (BM 33954: 20).

L. 18: The name ^{m}*Al-la-a* is unique. It is probably a hypocoristicon of a name like ^{m}*Al-la-*^{d}*Bēl-īnīya* "(Upon whom) if not upon Bēl are my eyes (directed)," cf. *CAD* A$_1$, 352 s.v. *alla* prep. mng. b-2′.

No. 106

Dar 310
Museum No.: BM 30223
Date: 9/xi/11 Dar (20 February 510 B.C.E.)
Place: Babylon
Content: Receipt of silver from MNA. Partial payment of a debt on behalf of two other persons.

OBV.

1 *ina ú-ìl-tì šá* 16 MA.NA KÙ.BABBAR *šá gìn-nu šá* ^{md}AG-URU$_3$-*šú*
2 A-*šú šá* ^{m}*gu-za-nu šá ina* UGU ^{m}*ri-mut*-^{d}EN A-*šú šá*
3 ^{m}MU-GI.NA *u* ^{m}*ki-na-a* A-*šú šá* ^{m}*dan-nu*-ŠEŠ.MEŠ-*šú*-DÙ
4 *e-li-tu*$_4$ *u* ^{m}*ni-ri-ia-a-ma* A-*šú šá* ^{md}EN-NUMUN-DÙ
5 *pu-ut e-ṭè-ru na-šu-ú ina lìb-bi* 8 MA.NA KÙ.BABBAR *šá gìn-nu*
6 ^{m}*ni-ri-ia-a-ma* A-*šú šá* ^{md}EN-NUMUN-DÙ *ina* ŠU.II
7 ^{md}AMAR.UTU-PAB-A A-*šú šá* ^{m}KI-^{d}AMAR.UTU-DIN A ^{m}*e-gì-bi*
8 *a-na* UGU ^{m}*ri-mut*-^{d}EN *u* ^{m}GIN-A *ma-ḫi-ir*
9 1-*en*.TA.ÀM *il-qu-ú*

REV.

10 LÚ *mu-kin-nu* ^{m}ÌR-*ia* A-*šú šá* ^{m}*da-di*-⸢*iá*⸣ [A x x x (x)]*
11 ^{m}UR-A A-*šú šá* ^{md}AG-ŠEŠ.MEŠ-MU A ^{m}*e-gì-bi*
12 ^{m}*bi-ba-nu* A-*šú šá* ^{md}IGI.DU-LUGAL-URU$_3$ ^{m}*ni*-[x-x-x]*
13 A-*šú šá* ^{m}SIG$_5$-*ia* A ^{m}*na-din-še-im* ^{md}EN-BA-*šá* A-⸢*šú šá*⸣
14 ^{m}NUMUN-*tú* ^{md}*nin-urta*-DIN-*iṭ* A-*šú šá* ^{m}EN-*šú-nu*
15 ⸢^{m}*ni*⸣-*din-tu*$_4$ A-*šú šá* ^{md}30-ŠEŠ-MU ^{md}AG-*bul-liṭ-su*
16 A-*šú šá* ^{m}ÌR-^{d}AMAR.UTU A LÚ.SANGA-^{d}IDIM
17 ^{md}EN-DIN-*iṭ* LÚ.UMBISAG A-*šú šá* ^{md}AG-KAR-ZI.MEŠ
18 A LÚ.AD.KID TIN.TIR.KI ITI.ZÍZ UD.9.KAM MU.11.KAM
19 ^{m}*da-ri-ia-muš* LUGAL TIN.TIR.KI *u* KUR.KUR

TRANSLATION

From the promissory note for sixteen minas of marked silver belonging to Nabû-uṣuršu, son of Gūzānu, which was issued to the debit of Rīmūt-Bēl, son of Šuma-ukīn and Kīnaya, son of Dannu-aḫḫēšu-ibni, and for the payment of which Nīryahu, son of Bēl-zēra-ibni assumed warranty: from it eight minas of marked silver Nīryahu, son of Bēl-zēra-ibni, has received from MNA$_1$ for the account of Rīmūt-Bēl and Kīnaya. They have taken one (copy of the document) each.

Witnesses:
Ardiya/Dādiya[//Nabaya]
Kalbaya/Nabû-aḫḫē-iddin//Egibi
Bibānu/Nergal-šarra-uṣur
Ni[dinti-Bēl]/Damqiya//Nādin-še'i

Bēl-iqīša/Zērūtu
Ninurta-uballiṭ/Bēlšunu
Nidintu/Sîn-aḫa-iddin
Nabû-bullissu/Arad-Marduk//Šangû-Ea
The scribe: Bēl-uballiṭ/Nabû-ēṭir-napšāti//Atkuppu
(Place + Date).

COMMENT

L. 3. The name *Dannu-aḫḫēšu-ibni* is unique. Names with *dannu* are of the type DN-*dannu* or *Dannu*-DN. Names with *-aḫa-ibni* (not *-aḫḫēšu-ibni* as in the present case) have a divine name as their first element, e.g., Marduk-, Nabû-, Nergal-aḫa-ibni (Tallqvist, *NbN*, 309f. s.v. *banû*).

No. 107

	Dar 315
Museum No.:	BM 30721
Date:	21/xii/11 Dar (3 April 510 B.C.E.)
Place:	Šaḫrīnu
Content:	Allotment of a share in profits. Background: MNA and his brother bought from Šaddinnu the right to collect the *šibšu*-lease on onions from the property of Bēl for the years Dar 10–11. MNA, his brother and a third person will share in the profits from this deal.

OBV.

1 *šib-šú šá* SUM.SAR NÍG.GA ^{d}EN *šá* URU *šaḫ-ri-nu a-di* ⸢x x (x)⸣
2 *šá* MU.10.KAM *ù* MU.11.KAM ^{m}*da-a-ri-muš*
3 LUGAL TIN.TIR.KI *u* KUR.KUR *šá ina* IGI LÚ *er-re-še-e šá*
4 ^{md}AMAR.UTU-*na-ṣir*-IBILA *ù* ^{md}AG-ŠEŠ.MEŠ-*bul-liṭ*
5 DUMU.MEŠ *šá* ^{m}KI-^{d}AMAR.UTU-DIN A ^{m}*e-gi-bi šá ina* ŠU.II
6 ^{m}*šad-din-nu* A-*šú šá* ^{md}DI.KU$_5$-ŠEŠ.MEŠ-MU A ^{m}*ši-gu-ú-a*
7 *šá* GIŠ.BÁN *šá* ^{md}EN-MU LÚ.EN.NAM-*é-sag-ìl*
8 *a-na* 42½ MA.NA KÙ.BABBAR *šá gìn-nu im-ḫu-ru-u'*
9 *šal-šú* ḪA.LA *i-na ú-tur* ^{md}AMAR.UTU-*na-ṣir* A-*šú*
10 *šá* ^{md}AMAR.UTU-GI *it-ti* ^{md}AMAR.UTU-*na-ṣir*-IBILA
11 [*u* ^{md}AG-ŠEŠ.MEŠ-*bul-liṭ ik-kal*]

LO. E.

12 (Broken off.)

REV.

13* ⸢*ú**-*še**-*ṣu**-*ú**⸣
14 LÚ *mu-kin-nu* ^{m}SUM.NA-*a* A-*šú šá* ^{m}*na-di-nu* A ^{m}DÙ-*eš*-DINGIR
15 ^{md}AG-ŠEŠ.MEŠ-*bul-liṭ* A-*šú šá* ^{m}*na-di-nu* A LÚ.ŠU.KU$_6$
16 ^{md}U.GUR-*ina*-SÙḪ-KAR-*ir* A-*šú šá* ^{md}AG-DÙ-ŠEŠ A ^{m}*ir-a-nu*

17 ^{md}AG-*na-ṣir* A-*šú šá* ^{m}DÙ-*ia* A ^{m}ÌR-^{d}GIR$_4$.KÙ
18 LÚ.UMBISAG ^{md}AG-ZI-*tì*-URU$_3$ A-*šú šá* ^{md}UTU-GIN-A A ^{m}EN-*ba-ni*
19 URU *šaḫ-ri-nu* ITI.ŠE UD.21.KAM MU.11.KAM
20 ^{m}*da-a-ri-muš* LUGAL TIN.TIR.KI *u* KUR.KUR
21 1-*en*.TA.ÀM *il-te-qu-ú*

Translation

(Regarding) the *šibšu*-lease in onions (from) the property of Bēl in Šaḫrīnu, including ⌜x x (x)⌝ of the tenth and eleventh year of Darius, king of Babylon and the lands, which are with the farmers of MNA$_1$ and Nabû-aḫḫē-bulliṭ, sons of Itti-Marduk-balāṭu, descendant of Egibi, who bought (them) for forty-two and a half minas of marked silver from Šaddinnu, son of Madānu-aḫḫē-iddin, descendant of Šigûa, official in charge of the lease (administration) of Bēl-iddin, the (king's) governor in the Esagil temple. Marduk-nāṣir, son of Marduk-ušallim [will enjoy] a one-third share from the profits together with MNA$_1$ [and Nabû-aḫḫē-bulliṭ]; [...] *they will let out.*

Witnesses:
Iddinaya/Nādin//Eppeš-ilī
Nabû-aḫḫē-bulliṭ/Nādin//Bā'iru
Nergal-ina-tēšê-ēṭir/Nabû-bāni-aḫi//Ir'anni
Nabû-nāṣir/Baniya//Arad-Nergal
The scribe: Nabû-napišta-uṣur/Šamaš-mukīn-apli//Bēl-bani
(Place + Date).

They have taken one (copy of the document) each.

Comment

L. 1: The expression "property of Bēl" (*makkūr Bēl*) can be an apposition to the onions as well as to the *šibšu* and is therefore ambiguous (cf. BM 33959: 1–2). If the "property of Bēl" qualifies the onions, it follows that the onions were grown on fields belonging to the temple of Bēl ("property" in the sense of real estate). Line 1 is then to be translated: "The *šibšu*-lease in onions (from) the property (i.e., real estate) of Bēl in Šaḫrīnu." On the other hand, if the "property of Bēl" qualifies the *šibšu* and not the onions, it follows that the income from the *šibšu* was the prerogative of the temple of Bēl ("property" in the sense of asset). Line 1 is then to be translated: "The *šibšu*-lease in onions, property (i.e., asset) of Bēl" (cf. *CAD* Š$_2$, 386 s.v. *šibšu* mng. f-2': "tax on garlic (owed to) the exchequer of Bēl"). In the latter case the ownership of the fields on which the onions were grown is not explicitly stated, but only implied. However, we know that the Esagil temple in fact owned large tracks of land in Šaḫrīnu on which onions were grown (Wunsch, *Iddin-Marduk*). As it is, the temple of Bēl appears in Dar 315 as the ultimate rightholder to the *šibšu* that was collected from the harvest of its land in Šaḫrīnu. Further note Petschow's (*Pfandrecht*, n. 406) comment on Neo-Babylonian *makkūru*: it does not express the abstract concept of ownership (for which there are only circumventory expressions in Akkadian, e.g., Object *ša* PN), but rather refers to concrete "goods, effects, property" (cf. Ungnad, *NRV* Glossar, s.v. *makkuru* "Besitztum als Tempelgut," and Ries, *Bodenpacht*, n. 243).

L. 1 end: At the end of the line there are remnants of two or three signs, but they are too fragmentary to be legible.

L. 3: For the idiom *ša ina pān*, more at BM 30270: 1. Strictly speaking, it was the land of Bēl "which was (put) at the disposal of the farmers," and not the onions. The farmers had the land at their disposal (i.e., held it on contract), and grew onions on it; hence the free translation given above "onions ... which are with the farmers." Cf. BM 32930: 11–13: "In addition, (Bēl-ēṭir owes) barley, the re[mainder] of the *šibšu*-rent for Ayyar of the seventh year from (the produce of) the field that is at Bēl-ēṭir's disposal (*šibšu eqli ... ša ina pān Bēl-ēṭir*)." The field that Bēl-ēṭir had at his disposal and from the income of which he had to pay *šibšu* in barley to MNA was most likely institutional land rather than MNA's private land. In other words, Bēl-ēṭir cultivated barley on (institutional) land under contract on behalf of MNA. This is, then, very similar to the situation described in Dar 315 (and probably also E.36.1904 discussed in n.552 above) according to which farmers grew *šibšu*-onions on behalf of MNA on the land of Bēl that was put at their disposal (*ina pān*). And cf. BM 33972: 20, according to which MBU grew *šibšu*-onions together with Rīmūt-Bēl and his brother for MNA on institutional land that he held on contract (*ša īpuš*).

L. 7: The expression *ša sūti* is understood here as an abbreviated form of the well-known title *ša* (*ina*) *muḫḫi sūti*, "in charge of rents / revenues (from land held on contract)." For this title, see Stolper, *Entrepreneurs*, 40–45; *JCS* 53, 117, 119; and Van Driel, *JESHO* 32, 215–16.

L. 12–14: The end of the operative section is, unfortunately, broken off, so that we do not know much about the arrangement between the Egibi brothers and Marduk-nāṣir, except that the latter had the right to a one-third share in the profits. The operative section is separated from the list of witnesses by one empty line, viz. between lines 13–14.

No. 108

Dar 318
Museum No.: BM 30838
Date: 16/i/12 Dar (28 April 510 B.C.E.)
Place: Babylon
Content: Promissory note to pay a debt of silver and barley to Marduk-bēlšunu. Repayment according to the measure of MNA.

OBV.

1 ½ MA.NA KÙ.BABBAR *šá ina* 1 GÍN *bit-qa* ˹*nu-uḫ-ḫu-tú*˺
2 38 GUR ŠE.BAR *šá* ^{md}AMAR.UTU-EN-*šú-nu* A-*šú šá*
3 ^{m}ÌR-^{d}AMAR.UTU A LÚ.SANGA-^{d}IDIM *ina muḫ-ḫi*
4 ^{md}AG-*it-tan-nu* A-*šú šá* ^{md}AG-NUMUN-SI.SÁ
5 A ^{m}*nu-úr*-^{d}PAP.SUKKAL *ina* URU.DU$_{6}$-^{d}ME.ME
6 [*ina mu*]*ḫ-ḫi* ÍD *ina* UGU 1-*et rit-tu*$_{4}$
7 [*ina* (GIŠ.)*m*]*a-ši-ḫu šá* ^{md}AMAR.UTU-PAB-A
8 [(...) *i-na*]*m-din i-na šap-liš ka-a-ri*
9 *i-nam-din*

REV.

10 [LÚ *m*]*u-kin-nu* ^{m}*da-di-ia* A-*šú šá* ^{m}KAR-^{d}˹AMAR.UTU˺
11 [A ^{m}]*ni*-˹x(-x)˺-*nu* ^{md}AG-GIN-EDURU A-*šú šá* ^{md}AG-MU-GIN
12 [A] ^{m}*ḫa-di-e-ri-eš* ^{m}*ri-mut*-^{d}EN A-*šú šá*
13 $^{[m]}$ÌR-*ia* A LÚ.ŠITIM ^{m}*ap-la-a*
14 A-*šú šá* ^{m}*ba-la-ṭu* A ^{m}LÚ.ŠU.KU$_{6}$
15 ^{md}EN-*it-tan-nu* DUB.SAR A-*šú šá* ^{md}AG-PAB-*šú*
16 A LÚ.SANGA-^{d}IDIM TIN.TIR.KI ITI.BÁR
17 UD.16.KAM MU.12.KAM ^{m}*da-ri-ia-muš*
18 LUGAL E.KI LUGAL KUR.KUR

TRANSLATION

Half a mina of ˹medium-quality˺ silver, of which one-eighth is alloy, (and) thirty-eight *kor* of barley are due to Marduk-bēlšunu, son of Arad-Marduk, descendant of Šangû-Ea, from Nabû-ittannu, son of Nabû-zēru-līšir, descendant of Nūr-Papsukkal. He [will del]iver (it) in one installment [a]t the river in Til-Gula [according to] Marduk-nāṣir-apli's measure. At the lower embankment he will deliver (it).

[W]itnesses:
Dādiya/Mušēzib-Marduk[//]$^{[m]}$Ni-x(-x)-nu
Nabû-mukīn-apli/Nabû-šuma-ukīn[//]Ḫadi-eriš
Rīmūt-Bēl/Ardiya//Itinnu
Aplaya/Balāṭu//Bā'iru
The scribe: Bēl-ittannu/Nabû-uṣuršu
(Place + Date).

COMMENT

L. 11: The sign after the *ni-* resembles ḪU or RI.

L. 12: The name Ḫadi-eriš, "He(the child)-is-happy-and-jubilates" (*CAD* Ḫ, 27 s.v. *ḫadû* mng. 3) is attested here and in Dar 377: 5[!].

No. 109

	Dar 334
Museum No.:	BM 30864
Date:	15/viii/12 Dar (20 November 510 B.C.E.)
Place:	Babylon
Content:	Promissory note to pay a debt of silver and onions to Marduk-bēlšunu. No mention of MNA (but cf. Dar 318).

OBV.

1 15 GÍN KÙ.BABBAR *šá gìn-nu šá na-da-nu u ma-*⸢*ḫa*⸣*-r*[*i*]

2 *ù* 15 *pi-i-tu*$_4$ *šá* SUM.SAR *šá*

3 ^{md}AMAR.UTU-EN-*šú-nu* A-*šú šá* ^{m}ÌR-^{d}AMAR.UTU

4 A LÚ.SANGA-^{d}IDIM *ina* UGU ^{m}SUM.NA-*a* A-*šú šá*

5 ^{m}ÌR-^{d}EN *ina* ITI.BÁR KÙ.BABBAR-*a*$_4$

6 15 GÍN *ina* SAG.DU-*šú u pi-i-tu*$_4$*-a*$_4$

7 15 *ina-an-din*

REV.

8 LÚ *mu-kin-nu* ^{m}*ni-qu-du* A-*šú šá* [x x x x]

9 A ^{m}*tu-na-a* ^{m}KA$_5$.A A-*šú šá* ^{m}*šad-din-nu*

10 A LÚ.AZLAG ^{m}BA-*šá-a* A-*šú šá* ^{md}AG-GIN-A

11 A ^{md}IDIM-*pat-ta-nu* ^{m}*mu-ra-nu* A-*šú šá*

12 ^{m}GI-^{d}AMAR.UTU A LÚ.AD.KID ^{md}EN-DIN-*iṭ*

13 LÚ.UMBISAG A-*šú šá* ^{md}AG-KAR-ZI.MEŠ A LÚ.AD.KID

14 TIN.TIR.KI ITI.APIN UD.15.KAM MU.12.KAM

15 ^{m}*da-ri-ia-muš* LUGAL TIN.TIR.KI

16 *u* KUR.KUR

TRANSLATION

Fifteen shekels of marked silver used in the country and fifteen bundles of onions are due to Marduk-bēlšunu, son of Arad-Marduk, descendant of Šangû-Ea, from Iddinnaya, son of Arad-Bēl. In Nisan he will pay the fifteen shekels of silver, without interest, and (deliver) the fifteen bundles.

Witnesses:

Niqūdu/[^{m}...]//Tunaya

Šellibi/Šaddinnu//Ašlāku

Iqīšaya/Nabû-mukīn-apli//Ea-pattannu

Mūrānu/Mušallim-Marduk//Atkuppu

The scribe: Bēl-uballiṭ/Nabû-ēṭir-napšāti//Atkuppu
(Place + Date).

No. 110

	Dar 338
Museum No.:	BM 30154
Date:	24/xii/12 Dar (25 March 509 B.C.E.)
Place:	Babylon
Content:	Receipt of silver from MNA by a royal official. Price of the dates. Settled among the brothers of the parties involved. Undertaking by the official to give any document concerning this silver to MNA's brother.

OBV.

1 5 MA.NA KÙ.BABBAR *šá ina* 1 GÍN *bit-qa nu-uḫ-ḫu-tú*

2 *šá* ^{md}AMAR.UTU-PAB*-A A-*šú šá* ^{m}KI-^{d}AMAR.UTU-DIN A ^{m}*e-gì-bi*

3 ŠÁM ZÚ.LUM.MA *ú-ìl-tì šá ina muḫ-ḫi* ^{m}*lib-luṭ* A-*šú šá*

4 ^{m}KAR-^{d}AMAR.UTU LÚ *pa-ḫa-tu*$_4$ *šá* URU *šaḫ*$^{!}$-*ri-in-nu*

5 ⸢*i*⸣*-*li-lu u*$^{?*}$ ^{md}AG-URU$_3$-*šú* A-*šú šá* ^{m}KAR-^{d}AMAR.UTU ŠEŠ-*šú*

6 *it-ti-šú iš-pu-ru um-ma* KÙ.BABBAR-*a*$_4$ 5 MA.NA UD-*ú*

7 *ina* ŠU.II ^{md}AG-URU$_3$-*šú šu-bu-lu* KÙ.BABBAR-*a*$_4$ 5 MA.NA UD-*ú nu*-⸢*uḫ-ḫu-tú*⸣

8 ^{md}AG-URU$_3$-*šú ina na-áš-par-tu*$_4$ ^{m}*lib-luṭ* ŠEŠ-*šú*

9 ⸢-⸣* *ina* ŠU.II ^{md}AG-ŠEŠ.MEŠ-*bul-liṭ* A-*šú šá* ^{m}KI-^{d}AMAR.UTU-DIN A ^{m}*e-gì-bi*

10 ŠEŠ-*šú šá* ^{md}AMAR.UTU-PAB-EDURU *ina qí-bi šá* ^{md}AMAR.UTU-PAB-EDURU

LO. E.

11 *ma-ḫir a-di-i** UD.15.KAM *šá* ITI.NE

12 [MU].13.KAM ^{m}*da-ri-'i-muš šá-ṭa-ri šá* KÙ.BABBAR<-*a*$_4$>

REV.

13 [5 MA].NA UD-*ú nu-uḫ-ḫu-tú* SAG.DU [*ú-ìl*]-*ti*

14 ⸢*šá**⸣ [^{m}*li*]*b-luṭ* LÚ *pa-ḫa-tu*$_4$ *šá šaḫ*$^{!}$-*ri-in-nu* ⸢ŠEŠ-*šú* x⸣ x

15 *šá* KÙ.BABBAR-*a*$_4$ 5 MA.NA *ina* ŠU.II-*šú ma-ḫir i-na-áš-šá-am-ma*

16 *a-na* ^{md}AG-ŠEŠ.MEŠ-*bul-liṭ* ŠEŠ-*šú šá* ^{md}AMAR.UTU-PAB-EDURU *ina* ⸢URU *šaḫ*$^{!}$-*ri-in-nu*⸣

17 *i-nam-din* LÚ *mu-kin-nu* ^{m}*kal-ba-a* ⸢A-*šú šá* ^{md}AG-ŠEŠ.MEŠ-MU⸣

18 A ^{m}*e-gì-bi* ^{md}AMAR.UTU-PAB A-*šú šá* ^{md}⸢AMAR.UTU-KAR⸣ A ^{md}30-⸢SIG$_5$-*iq*⸣

19 ^{m}ÌR-*iá* A-*šú šá* ^{m}*da-di-iá* A ^{m}*na-ba-a-a* ^{md}AG-*it-tan-nu*

20 A-*šú šá* ^{m}ÌR-*iá* A ^{md}30-DINGIR ^{md}EN-DIN-*iṭ* A-*šú šá* ^{md}AMAR.UTU-MU-DÙ

21 ^{m}*šul-lu-mu* A-*šú šá* ^{m}KAR-^{d}AMAR.UTU A LÚ.SIMUG ^{m}*ba-si-iá* A-*šú šá*

22 ^{m}*su-qa-a-a** A ^{m}*ba-si-iá* ^{md}UTU-DIN-*iṭ* A-*šú šá* ^{md}AG-NUMUN-GIŠ

23 A LÚ.SANGA-^{d}UTU ^{m}*ni-din-tu$_4$*-^{d}EN LÚ.UMBISAG A-*šú šá* ^{m}⸢*dam**-*qi**-*ia*⸣

24 A ^{m}*na-din-še-e* E.KI ITI.ŠE UD.24.KAM MU.12.KAM

25 ^{m}*da-ri-'i-muš* LUGAL E.KI LUGAL KUR.KUR

TRANSLATION

(1–2a)Five minas of medium-quality silver, of which one-eighth is alloy, of (read: are due from?) MNA$_1$, the price of the dates. (2b–7a)Libluț, son of Mušēzib-Marduk, district governor of Šaḫrīnu ⸢contracted[!]⸣ a promissory note to <his[?]> debit ⸢and[?]⸣ sent Nabû-uṣuršu, son of Mušēzib-Marduk, his brother with it; it (reads) as follows: "Send the five minas of white silver through Nabû-uṣuršu." Nabû-uṣuršu, (acting) as proxy for his brother Libluț, has received these five minas of white, medium-quality silver from the hands of Nabû-aḫḫē-bulliț, son of Itti-Marduk-balāṭu, son of Egibi, brother of MNA$_1$, (who acted) by order of MNA$_1$. (Any) document about <these> [five] minas of white, medium-quality silver, the capital sum, [(and more in particular,) the promis]sory note ⸢credited to[!]⸣ [Lib]luț, district governor of Šaḫrīnu: ⸢his brother x RI⸣, who received the five minas of silver from him, shall bring (it) and give (it) to Nabû-aḫḫē-bulliț, brother of MNA$_1$, in Šaḫrīnu, by the fifteenth of Ab of the thirteenth year of Darius.

Witnesses:
Kalbaya/Nabû-aḫḫē-iddin//Egibi
Marduk-nāṣir/⸢Marduk-ušēzib⸣//Sîn-⸢mudammiq⸣
Ardiya/Dādiya//Nabaya
Nabû-ittannu/Ardiya//Sîn-ilī
Bēl-uballiț/Marduk-šuma-ibni
Šullumu/Mušēzib-Marduk//Nappāḫu
Basiya/Sūqaya//Basiya
Šamaš-uballiț/Nabû-zēru-līšir//Šangû-Šamaš
The scribe: Nidinti-Bēl/⸢Damqiya⸣//Nādin-še'i
(Place + Date).

COMMENT

L. 2: The PAB cannot be doubted. Strassmaier mistakenly took cracks in the clay for remnants of signs, and accordingly read GIN instead of PAB. For cracks interpreted as wedges, also see lines 5 and 9.

L. 1–3: The five minas of silver are *ša MNA* and the promissory note for these five minas (*u'iltu*) is *ša ina muḫḫi Libluț*. Neo-Babylonian deeds usually introduce the creditor by means of the particle *ša* and the debtor by means of the phrase *ina muḫḫi*: e.g., silver *ša* PN$_1$ *ina muḫḫi* PN$_2$ means (literally) "silver belonging to PN$_1$ (the creditor) is charged against PN$_2$ (the debtor)." Accordingly, in the text under consideration, MNA would be the creditor (*ša MNA*) and Libluț the debtor (*ša ina muḫḫi Libluț*). However, according to lines 7b–11 and 14b–15 Libluț's brother received the silver. He had been sent to act as Libluț's proxy (*ina našparti*, line 8; cf. lines 6–7a). Libluț, therefore, must have been the creditor. MNA sent his brother to pay the silver (*ina qibi*, line 10), and must, therefore, have been the debtor. Consequently, *ša MNA* in line 2 is to be understood "due from MNA" and is similar in meaning to the expression *ša* PN in the *ilku*-receipts; *ina muḫḫi Liblut̩* in line 3, however, remains difficult. Should we emend the text and read *u'iltu ša ina muḫḫi<šu>*, "promissory note that is charged against <him> (=MNA)"?

L. 3–6: The main clause, viz. *u'iltu* .... *umma* ... ("The promissory note ... (states) as follows: ..."), is expanded by two relative clauses, viz. *ša* .... ⸢*ī'ilû*! *u*?⸣ ... *išpuru* (on which more below). In the translation above these three clauses are all rendered as main sentences for reasons of clarity.

L. 4: The scribe wrote ^{lú}*pāḫātu šá* ^{uru}*ḫar-ri-in-ni* in line 4, but ^{lú}*pāḫātu šá ḫar-ri-in-ni* in line 14, and similarly, *ina* ^{uru}*ḫar-ri-in-nu* at the end of line 16. The town in question was, no doubt, Šaḫrīnu. Should we, therefore, read ^{lú}*pāḫātu šá* ^{uru}*<šá->ḫar-ri-in-ni* in line 4 (haplography); similarly, read in line 16 *ina* ^{uru}*<šá->ḫar-ri-in-nu*, and read ^{lú}*pāḫātu* $^{\text{<uru>}}$*šá-ḫar-ri-in-ni* in line 14? Or is the ḪAR-sign in all three cases a badly written ŠAḪ-sign? We encountered a similar problem in Dar 308: 9.

L. 5: Strassmaier copied ⸢x⸣ LI LU, which I suggest reading as follows: ⸢*i**⸣*<-'i>-{li}-lu* (= *ī'ilû*) from the verb *e'ēlu*. For this verb, see at BM 30795: 7–9. It is not clear whether it is followed by a *u* or only a crack in the clay. For cracks interpreted as wedges, see lines 1 and 9.

L. 6: For the expression *itti* ... *šapāru* see *AHw*, 405 s.v. *itti* mng. A-2a "(zusammen) mit ... schicken." Apparently, Liblut̩ sent (*išpuru*) his brother to MNA with the promissory note (*ittišu*) that he had contracted with MNA. This is confirmed by lines 7b–11, in particular by the expression *ina našpartu Liblut̩* in line 8, according to which Nabû-uṣuršu had been sent by his brother to go and collect the silver from MNA.

L. 7: For the meaning of *ina qātē šūbulu*, see *CAD* A_1, 25 s.v. *abālu*. The signs ⸢*uḫ-ḫu-tú*⸣ at the end are written on the reverse in a very small script.

L. 9: There are cracks in the clay at the beginning of the line, but no *šá* (against Strassmaier). For cracks interpreted as wedges, also see lines 1 and 5.

L. 10: MNA, the debtor, had ordered his brother to pay off the debt (*ina qibi*). In this respect it is noteworthy that the text under consideration was written shortly before MNA left for Šušan. Indeed, a month later we find him in Šušan (Dar 346, 22/i/13 Dar). It is therefore likely that before leaving, MNA ordered his brother to take care of some of the more urgent business matters, such as this matter with Liblut̩.

L. 14b: We expect the name of Liblut̩'s brother, viz. Nabû-uṣuršu, to be mentioned explicitly rather than being referred to by a mere "his brother." The end of the line remains enigmatic.

L. 15: The verb *maḫir* lacks the subjunctive ending *-u* (*maḫru*) although it stands in a relative clause after *ša*. Note that the verbs *ī'ilû* and *išpuru* in the relative clause of lines 5–6 are in the subjunctive.

L. 11–17: Once the outstanding debt of five minas was paid, the creditor should no longer have any document with which he could claim this sum. The promissory note for the five minas, in particular, should be invalidated either by physically breaking it, as was usually done, or by handing it over to the debtor, as in the present case (cf. Petschow, *Pfandrecht*, 10–24 and Shiff, *Nūr-Sîn*, 44, and nn. 69–70 at p. 87f.).

No. 111

	Dar 342
Museum No.:	BM 31424
Date:	27/[-]/12 Dar (510–509 B.C.E.)
Place:	Šaḫrīnu
Content:	About the cultivation of dates on the property of Bēl by seven gardeners. Refers to the collection of lease-related revenues and to MNA. Very fragmentary.

OBV.

1 […] NÍG.GA ^{d}EN 7 <LÚ>.NU.GIŠ.K[IRI$_{6}$.(MEŠ)] ⸢x x *šá* x x x⸣
2 […] ⸢x x x x x x⸣ […]
3 […]-*ba/ma-a-a šá* GIŠ.BÁN *šá* ^{m}SUM.NA-*a*
4 […]-*nu* A-*šú šá* ^{md}AG-[…]
5 […] A *a-na* [x x x] GUR$^{?}$
6 […] $^{[md]}$AMAR.UTU-*na-*[*ṣir* …]
7 […] ⸢x x⸣ […]
(Remainder of obverse is broken off.)

REV.

1 $^{[m]d}$AMAR.UTU-MU-URU$_{3}$ A ^{m}*na-ba-a-a*
2 $^{[m]}$SILA-*a-a* A-*šú šá* ^{m}EN-NUMUN A ^{m}*bu-ra*[*q-qa*$^{?}$]
3 $^{[m]}$MU-^{d}AG A-*šú šá* ^{m}DIN-*su* A ^{md}AG-⸢*še**-*e**-*me*⸣
4 [^{m}*t*]*a-qiš*-^{d}*gu-la* DUB.SAR DUMU-*šú šá*
5 [^{m}x(-x)-*b*/*m*]*a-a* ^{m}*im-bu*-IGI-*iá*
6 [URU *šá*]-*aḫ-ri-in**-*nu**⸣

U. E.

7 [ITI x UD].27.KAM MU.12.<KAM>
8 [^{m}*da-a-r*]*i-muš* LUGAL E.KI ⸢x x x⸣

TRANSLATION

The obverse of the tablet is too fragmentary for translation.
The reverse contains the names of the witnesses; among them we find:
Marduk-šuma-uṣur//Nabaya

Sūqaya/Bēl-zēri//Bura[qu]
Iddin-Nabû/Balāssu//Nabû-⌜šeme⌝
The scribe: [T]aqīš-Gula/[^{m}...]m(or b)aya//Imbu-pāniya
(Place + Date).

COMMENT

This is a small tablet the surface of which is very much damaged. Currently, it measures 5,2 (W) × 3,6 (L), and originally it must not have been much wider: the first three lines on the reverse are almost completely preserved, and therefore, shows how much is lacking at the beginning of the other lines.

Obv. L. 1: The GIŠ is written at the end of the line. K[IRI$_6$] followed on the right edge. The scribe continued writing on the tablet's reverse, but the five or so signs that he wrote there (i.e., below ^{m}*im-bu*-IGI-*iá*) are very difficult to read. ⌜IM ŠÁ BA⌝, as copied by Strassmaier, is highly doubtful, except for the ŠÁ. Should we read ⌜*šá* (*ina*) URU *šá-aḫ-ri-nu*⌝?

Obv. L. 3: [...]-*ba/ma-a-a ša sūti ša* PN, cf. Dar 315: 7, PN$_1$ *ša sūti ša* PN$_2$ *bēl pīḫāti Esagil*, "PN$_1$ who is in charge of the lease (administration) of PN$_2$, district governor in Esagil." Accordingly the signs -*b/ma-a-a* at the beginning of the line probably belonged to a personal name.

Obv. L. 6: The Marduk-nā[ṣir-...] mentioned in this line is likely to be identified with Marduk-nāṣir-apli from the Egibi family (MNA), because the persons who witnessed the text under consideration are known from other texts from MNA's archive. For details see below.

Rev. L. 1: The person in question was probably Arad-Gula/Marduk-šuma-uṣur//Nabaya or one of his brothers if he had any (for Arad-Gula, see Wunsch, *Felder* 2, 276).

Rev. L. 2: Sūqaya belonged to the Buraqu family (usually wr. ^{m}*bu-ra-qu/qa*, Tallqvist, *NbN*, 51 s.v. Buraqu; for Sūqaya see Wunsch, *Id.*, 337). There is very little space at the end of the line so that -*qa* is more likely than -*qu*.

Rev. L. 3: This Iddin-Nabû is known from other texts from Babylon, usually as a scribe (Wunsch, *Id.*, 297).

No. 112

	Dar 345
Museum No.:	BM 30745
Date:	2/i/13 Dar (2 April 509 B.C.E.)
Place:	Babylon
Content:	Promissory note to pay a debt of silver and onions to MNA's brother. Fixation of default interest.

OBV.

1 [1 ME 4]0 *pi-ti šá* SUM.SAR *bab-ba-nu-ú*
2 [1] MA.NA KÙ.BABBAR *šá gin-nu šá* ^{md}AG.ŠEŠ.MEŠ-*bul-liṭ*
3 A-*šú šá* ^{m}KI-^{d}AMAR.UTU-DIN A ^{m}*e-gi-bi*
4 *ina muḫ-ḫi* ^{md}EN-NIGIN-*ir* A-*šú šá* ^{md}U.GUR-MU
5 *ina* ITI.BÁR *pi-ti-a*$_4$ 1 ME 40
6 *šá* SUM.SAR *ina-an-din u* KÙ.BABBAR-*a*$_4$ 1 MA.NA *šá gin-nu*
7 *ina* ITI.SIG$_4$ *i-nam-din šá* ITI *ina muḫ-ḫi*
8 [1] MA.NA 1 GÍN KÙ.BABBAR *ḫu-bul-lu*$_4$
9 ⸢*ina muḫ*⸣-*ḫi-šú i-rab-bi e-lat*
10 *ú-ìl-tì* IGI-*tu*$_4$ 1 ME 40 *pi-ti* ⸢SUM.SAR⸣

REV.

11 LÚ *mu-kin-nu* ^{m}*šul-lu-mu* A-*šú šá* ^{m}KAR-^{d}⸢ŠÚ A⸣
12 LÚ.SIMUG ^{md}LUM.LUM-AD-URU$_3$ A-*šú šá*
13 ^{m}*ḫaš-da-a* ^{m}*ri-mut*-^{d}EN A<-*šú šá*> ^{m}MU-^{d}AG
14 <A> LÚ.GAL-DÙ ^{m}MU-^{d}EN A-*šú šá* ^{m}*ni-qu-du*
15 ^{m}KAR-^{d}EN A-*šú šá* ^{m}*ḫaš-da-a* A LÚ.SIMUG$^{?*}$
16 [L]Ú.UMBISAG ^{md}EN-NIGIN-*ir* A-*šu šá* ^{md}U.GUR-MU
17 [TIN.T]IR.KI ITI.BÁR UD.2.KAM
18 [M]U.13.KAM ^{m}*da-ri-i'-mu-šú*
19 LUGAL E.KI LUGAL KUR.KUR

TRANSLATION

One hundred and forty bundles of first-rate onions (and) one mina of marked silver are due to Nabû-aḫḫē-bulliṭ, son of Itti-Marduk-balāṭu, descendant of Egibi, from Bēl-upaḫḫir, son of Nergal-iddin. In Araḫsamna he will deliver these one hundred and forty bundles of onions, and in Simān he will pay the one mina of marked silver. Interest will accrue against him (at the rate of) one shekel of silver per mina per month. In addition, there is a previous debt of one hundred and forty bundles ⸢of onions⸣.

Witnesses:
Šullumu/Mušēzib-⸢Marduk⸣//Nappāḫu
^{d}LUM.LUM-aba-uṣur/Ḫašdaya
Rīmūt-Bēl/Iddin-Nabû<//>Rab-banê
Iddin-Bēl/Niqūdu

Mušēzib-Bēl/Ḫašdaya//Nappāḫu
The scribe: Bēl-upaḫḫir/Nergal-iddin
(Place + Date).

COMMENT

L. 12: The reading of ^{d}LUM.LUM is unknown to me.

L. 13–14: In view of the attestation of a Baqqu/Iddin-Nabû//Rab-banê at the time of Darius (Tallqvist, *NbN*, 22 s.v. *Baqqu*), I suggest reading ^{m}*ri-mut*-^{d}EN A<-*šú šá*> ^{m}MU-^{d}AG <A> LÚ.GAL-DÙ.

L. 15: Strassmaier copied LÚ.I.ŠI, but what he interpreted as I is the beginning of a SIMUG-sign. The very end of the SIMUG-sign, however, resembles ŠI.

No. 113

	Dar 351
Museum No.:	BM 33100
Date:	25/v/13 Dar (21 August 509 B.C.E.)
Place:	Babylon
Content:	Promissory note to pay a debt of barley and dates to MNA. Refers to the debtors' bow-fief land.

OBV.

[2-ME GUR] ZÚ.LUM.MA *ù* 70 GUR ŠE.BAR *šá* ^{md}AMAR.UTU-PAB-EDURU
[A-*šú šá*] ^{m}KI-^{d}AMAR.UTU-DIN A ^{m}*e-gi-bi ina muḫ-ḫi* ^{m}*ni-din-tu*$_{4}$-^{d}EN
[A-*šú šá*] ^{md}AG-MU-MU ^{md}KÁ-KAM DUMU *šá* ^{md}AG-*ri-bi*-URU$_{3}$
[*ù*] ^{md}AG-NUMUN-DÙ DUMU *šá* ^{m}⸢^{d*}ŠÁR*-AD*⸣-URU$_{3}$ *ina* ITI.GU$_{4}$ MU.14.KAM
[ŠE.B]AR-*a*$_{4}$ 70 GUR *ina muḫ-ḫi* 1-*et rit-tu*$_{4}$ *ina muḫ-ḫi maš-kát-tú i*-[*i*]*l**-⸢*i*′⸣
[*ina* I]TI.DU$_{6}$ MU.14.KAM ZÚ.LUM.MA-*a*$_{4}$ 2-ME *ina ḫa-ṣa-ri i-nam-di-in*
[x-*b*]*i* É GIŠ.BAN.MEŠ-*šú-nu šá* 3-TA *uš-ri-e-ti*
[*šá* L]Ú.SIPA-*gi-ni-e* LÚ *ga**-*da-a-a ù* LÚ.DUMU-*dam-qa*
[*šá ina m*]*uḫ-ḫi* ÍD *pi-qu-du a-di muḫ-ḫi ma-ka-li-e*
[...] A ⸢x x⸣ ÍD$^{?}$.MEŠ *šu-a-tì*
[... GU$_{4}$] [*bu-uš*]-*tu*$_{4}$ *um-ma*-[*nu*]

REV.

[x x x x]* ⸢^{m}x-MU⸣ ⸢x x⸣ ^{d}AMAR.UTU-[x x]
[A x x (x)] ^{md}AG-*bul-liṭ-su* DUMU *šá* ^{m}*gi-mil-lu* [(x x)]
[x x]⸢x⸣ ^{m}*gi-mil-lu* DUMU *šá* ^{md}UTU-MU-SI.SÁ
[^{m}x-x]-⸢x⸣-*bu* A-*šú šá* ^{m}*ki-na-a* ^{m}MU-^{d}AMAR.UTU A-*šú šá* ^{md}UTU-*na-ṣir*
[^{m}x x]-*nu* DUMU *šá* ^{m}*ba-la-ṭu* A ^{m}ŠEŠ-*ba-ni* ^{md}AMAR.UTU-MU-URU$_{3}$
[DUMU *šá*] ^{md}AG-GIN-NUMUN A ^{m}LÚ.GAL-DÙ ^{m}MU-^{d}EN A-*šú šá* ^{m}*ib-na-a*
[A LÚ].SANGA$^{!}$-BÁR ^{m}NÍG.BA-^{d}AMAR.UTU DUMU *šá* ^{m}*ri-mut* A ^{m}*da-bi-bi*
[^{m}]^{d}AMAR.UTU-NUMUN-DÙ A-*šú šá* ^{md}EN-MU A ^{m}*da-bi-bi*
[^{m}*lib*]-*luṭ* LÚ.DUB.SAR <A-*šú šá*> ^{m}MU-^{d}AG A ^{m}*e-ṭè-ru* TIN.TIR.K[I]

21 [ITI.N]E UD.25.KAM MU.13.KAM ^{m}*da-ri-ia-m*[*uš*]

22 LUGAL TIN.TIR.KI *u* KUR.KUR

TRANSLATION

[Two hundred *kor*] of dates and seventy *kor* of barley are due to MNA_1 from Nidinti-Bēl, [son of] Nabû-šuma-iddin, Bāba-ēreš, son of Nabû-rībi-uṣur, [and] Nabû-zēra-ibni, son of ⌜Aššur-aba⌝-uṣur. In Ayyar of the fourteenth year he ⌜will bring⌝ these seventy *kor* of [barley] in one installment in front of the storehouse. In Tašrīt of the fourteenth year he will deliver these two hundred *kor* of dates at the entrepot. [It is the in]come$^{?}$ from their bow-fief land of which three-tenths [(*each*) *belong to*] the herdsmen, the *gaṭṭāya*-workers and the Mār-Damqa(-soldiers$^{?}$), [... which is (located) a]long the Piqūdu canal till the mooring place [...], these ⌜x x x⌝ [...] trained heifer.

[Witnesses]:
[PN/]$^{?}$ Marduk-[...]$^{?}$
Nabû-bullissu/Gimillu [...]
Gimillu/Šamaš-šumu-līšir(//Šamaš-(a)bāri?)
[^{m}...]-*bu*/Kīnaya
Iddin-Marduk/Šamaš-nāṣir
[^{m}...]-*nu*/Balāṭu//Aḫu-bani
Marduk-šuma-uṣur[/]Nabû-mukīn-zēri//Rab-banê
Iddin-Bēl/Ibnaya//Šangû$^{!}$-parakki
Qīšti-Marduk/Rīmūt//Dābibī
Marduk-zēra-ibni/Bēl-iddin//Dābibī
The scribe: [Lib]luṭ</>Iddin-Nabû//Ēṭiru
(Place + Date).

COMMENT

A partial payment of the debt is mentioned in Dar 392: 14–15, which deals with the purchase of draught animals by MNA from Nabû-zēra-ibni/Aššur-aba-uṣur and Iqīša-Marduk (his son?). The sellers seem to have tried to balance their debt of two hundred *kor* of dates and seventy *kor* of barley to MNA with their claim against him to pay for the draught animals (Dar 351: 11; cf. Krecher, *Egibi*, 308–9 and Peiser, *BRL* 4, 50–51). For Nabû-zēra-ibni/Aššur-aba-uṣur, see also BM 33968: 6′ concerning the delivery of a baker to MNA (and for Iqīša-Marduk, see probably BM 33968: 11). Another of the debtors in Dar 351, Nidinti-Bēl/Nabû-šuma-iddin, is also known as lessee of MNA in Dar 335 (see below at L. 2).

L. 2: This Nidinti-Bēl, son of Nabû-šuma-iddin, belonged to the Kidin-Sîn family, and is attested with full affiliation in Dar 335: 4 (= *CM* 20b 205). The latter text reveals a complex relationship among Nidinti-Bēl, MNA, and several other persons "regarding the *imittu*-dates from the *ḫanšû*-field of Itti-māku-Bēl/Nabû-zēra-ukīn//Miṣiraya in Dūru-ša-karrabbi" (Dar 335:

1–2). These dates were owed by Nidinti-Bēl to MNA and not to Itti-māku-Bēl, although the latter seems to have been the owner of the land on which the dates had been grown (ll. 3–5), *De facto*, it was one Iddin-Nabû/Nummuru//Aškāpu, who, as an intermediary (?), "received (them) from Nidinti-Bēl upon request of Iddin-Bēl/[ᵐx-x-]-MU//Ea-ibni" (ll. 5–8).

L. 4: For Nabû-zēra-ibni/Aššur-aba-uṣur, also see Dar 392: 1 and BM 33968: 6′ (above).

L. 6: On the Persian etymology of *ḫaṣāru* "enclosure" as the place where crops were to be delivered, more at Stolper, *BiMes 7*, 252–54.

L. 4–6: The text is dated in the summer of Darius' thirteenth year, i.e., after the barley harvest, but before the date harvest. Van Driel, *JESHO* 32, 207, points out that "not only the barley, but also the dates will be delivered in year 14, even though the dates of year 13 had not yet been harvested. The reasons for this long-term contract are not stated."

L. 7a: I suggest reading [*ir*]*bi bīt* ^giš^*qaštišunu*, (the dates and barley) "[are the in]come from their bow-fief."

L. 7b: The noun *uš-ri-e-ti* is derived from *ušurtu* "tenth" (Streck, *Zahl und Zeit*, 34 s.v. § I 29.50), not from *ešrētu* "tithes" (as against *AHw*, 258 s.v. *ešrû* II "tithe"; note that the *CAD* does not cite our text under *ešrētu*, nor under *ešrû* A "tithe," *CAD* E, 368–70; similarly, Jursa, in his work on the temple tithes [*Tempelzehnt*] does not discuss the text under consideration). Accordingly, the bow-fief in question was divided into ten parts, but the text under consideration dealt with the income from three-tenths only, viz., the tenth that belonged to the herdsmen (*rē'i-ginê*), the tenth of the *gaṭṭā'a*-workers, and the tenth of the Mār-Damqa(-soldiers[?]).

L. 8a: Strassmaier's copy has ^lú^*lud-da-a-a*, but one should, no doubt, correct this and read ^lú^*ga-ṭa-a-a*. According to the dictionaries the *gaddā'a* (or *gaddāya*) was a type of official (*CAD* G, 7f. s.v. *gadā'a* and *AHw*, 273 s.v. *gaddāja*), but Zadok (*BiOr* 41, 34 "cane cutter, woodcutter") and Jursa (*Landwirtschaft*, 189 and n. 378) have recently argued that they (read *gaṭṭā'ā*) were a kind of worker.

L. 8b: For LÚ.DUMU *dam-qa* as a family name, see also Dar 379: 31, where a certain Marduk-šuma-iddin/Nabû-nādin-aḫi//LÚ *dam-qa* is mentioned as neighbor of one of the houses that belonged to the Egibis. When used as a title (e.g., in two Sippar texts quoted by Bongenaar, *Ebabbar*, 46) or as a noun (e.g., in the text under consideration and in the Neo-Babylonian letter published by Millard-Jursa, *Afo* 44/45, 163f.), it does probably not merely refer to a person of a good family (against *CAD* M_1, 257–58 s.v. *mār damqa* NB*; and *CAD* D, 70 s.v. *damqu* mng. 3), but it had a specific professional (military?) connotation. *Damqu* can indeed mean "trained" and occurs in this meaning with respect to soldiers (see *CAD* D, 71 s.v. *damqu* mng. 4), esp. in expressions such as ^(lú)^*mār damqi*, which refers to a specific kind of soldier (*CAD* M_1, 258 s.v. **mār damqi*, always wr. LÚ.A.SIG_5, (LÚ.)DUMU.SIG_5, or

LÚ.A.SIG; additional references *passim* in *SAA* text editions, e.g., *SAA* V, 153 "chariot fighter, nobleman," hence, close to the modern "an officer and a gentleman"?), and the Neo-Assyrian LÚ.BAN-*dammaqūte*, who were "expert archers" (*CAD* D, 67 s.v. *dammaqu*).

L. 9: On *makallû* "mooring place," see BM 31690^{+}: 8.

L. 11: For *buštu* (also *burtu*), see above at BM 31976: 1.

L. 12: The reverse starts with line 12 and contains the list of witnesses. Probably, restore at the beginning of the line [LÚ *mu-kin-nu*]. The signs between MU and ^{d}AMAR.UTU do not really resemble DUMU *šá*; moreover, I could not see the lower end of the *Personenkeil* before ^{d}AMAR.UTU. The reconstruction of this line remains doubtful.

L. 16: I suggest reading at the beginning of the line [Bēl-id]din, in view of Bēl-iddin/Balāṭu//⸢Aḫu⸣-[bani] in Dar 437: 17.

L. 18: The surname Šangû-parakki is strangely written [A LÚ]-É-BAR-BÁR. Moreover, [A LÚ] is very little for the amount of space actually available at the beginning of the line.

No. 114

	Dar 359
Museum No.:	BM 30273
Date:	⸢29⸣/x/13 Dar (20 January 508 B.C.E.)
Place:	Ālu-ša-kī-Bēl
Content:	*Ḫarrānu* debt-note with MNA's capital being dates from the tithes of Bēl.

OBV.

1 [51] GUR ZÚ.LUM.MA *šá* ^{md}AMAR.UTU-*na-ṣir*-IBILA
2 A-*šú šá* ^{m}KI-^{d}AMAR.UTU-DIN A ^{m}*e-gi-bi ina muḫ-ḫi*
3 ^{md}UTU-*ina*-SÙḪ-SUR A-*šú šá* ^{md}UTU-MU A ^{md}UTU-*ba-ri*
4 *a-na* KASKAL.II *mim-ma ma-la ina* URU *u* EDIN
5 *ina* UGU ZÚ.<LUM>.MA-*a'* 51 GUR ^{md}UTU-*ina*-SÙḪ-SUR
6 *ip-pu-šu ina ú-tur a-ḫi* ḪA.LA ^{md}ŠÚ*-*na-ṣir*-A
7 *it-ti* ^{md}UTU-*ina*-SÙḪ-SUR *ik-kal*
8 *pu-ut* SAG.DU ZÚ.LUM.MA ^{md}UTU-*ina*-SÙḪ-SUR
9 *na-ši a-di* 3-TA MU.AN.NA.MEŠ [(...)]
10 KI <*a*>-*ḫa*.MEŠ *šak-na-at* ZÚ.LUM.MA
11 *eš-ru-ú šá* ^{d}EN

REV.

12 LÚ *mu-kin*$_{7}$ ^{m}ÌR-^{d}*gu-la* A-*šú šá*
13 ^{md}ŠÚ-MU-URU$_{3}$ A ^{m}*na-ba-a-a* ^{m}KI-^{d}AG-DIN
14 A-*šú šá* ^{m}*mu-ra-nu* A ^{m}DÙ-*eš*-DINGIR ^{md}AG-*bul-liṭ-su*
15 A-*šú šá* ^{m}*gi-mil-lu* A ^{m}*ba-bu-tu* ^{md}UTU-SUR

16 A-*šú šá* ^{md}UTU-MU A ^{md}UTU-*a-ba-ri*
17 ^{md}AG-ŠEŠ-*it-tan-nu* A-*šú šá* ^{md}AG-MU-URU$_3$
18 A LÚ.SANGA-^{d}*na-na**-*a* ^{m}SU-*a* A-*šú šá* ^{md}AG-NUMUN-DÙ
19 ^{m}*gu-za-nu* A-*šú šá* ^{m}*kal-ba-a* A LÚ.SANGA-^{d}*na-na-a*
20 LÚ.UMBISAG ^{md}AMAR.UTU-*re-man-ni* A-*šú šá* ^{md}ŠÚ-DIN-*su*-E
21 A ^{m}*na-ba-a-a* URU-*šá*-^{m}*ki-i*-^{d}EN ITI.AB
22 UD.⸢29⸣.KAM MU.13.KAM ^{m}*da-ri-iá-muš*
23 LUGAL E.KI *u* KUR.KUR

Translation

[Fifty-one] *kor* of dates have been transferred from MNA$_1$ to Šamaš-ina-tēšê-ēṭir, son of Šamaš-iddin, descendant of Šamaš-(a)bāri for a business venture. From all of what Šamaš-ina-tēšê-ēṭir may earn from these fifty-one *kor* of dates, in or out of town, MNA$_1$ will enjoy an equal share in the profit with Šamaš-ina-tēšê-ēṭir. Šamaš-ina-tēšê-ēṭir assumes warranty for the capital amount of the dates. [...] has been jointly invested for up to three years. The dates are the tithes of Bēl.

Witnesses:
Arad-Gula/Marduk-šuma-uṣur//Nabaya
Itti-Nabû-balāṭu/Mūrānu//Eppeš-ilī
Nabû-bullissu/Gimillu//Bābūtu
Šamaš(-ina-tēšê)$^{?}$-ēṭir/Šamaš-iddin//Šamaš-abāri
Nabû-aḫa-ittannu/Nabû-šuma-uṣur//Šangû-Nanaya
Erībaya/Nabû-zēra-ibni
Gūzānu/Kalbaya//Šangû-Nanaya
The scribe: Marduk-rēmanni/Marduk-balāssu-iqbi//Nabaya
(Place + Date).

Comment

L. 1–3: Literally, "... dates belonging to (*ša*) MNA$_1$ that are charged against (*ša ina muḫḫi*) Šamaš-ina-tēšê-ēṭir for a business partnership (*ana ḫarrāni*)."

L. 10–11: Cf. Jursa, *Tempelzehnt*, 81.

L. 22: The day may be 27, 28, or 29.

No. 115

Dar 369
Museum No.: BM 31359
Date: 15/i/14 Dar (4 May 508 B.C.E.)
Place: Šaḫrīnu
Content: Summons to settle a debt of silver. Silver due to MNA's brother.

OBV.

1 [UD.20].KAM *šá* ITI.BÁR *šá* MU.14.KAM
2 [^{m}*da-a*]-*ri-ia-muš* LUGAL ^{m}*pu-uḫ-ḫu-ru* A-*šu šá*
3 ^{md}U.GUR-MU 1 MA.NA KÙ.BABBAR *šá gin-nu ina ra-šu-tú*
4 *šá* ^{md}AG-ŠEŠ.MEŠ-*bul-liṭ šá ina* UGU-*ḫi-šú i-na-áš-am-ma*
5 *a-na* ^{md}AG-ŠEŠ.MEŠ-*bul-liṭ i-na-ad-din ki-i*
6 UD.20.KAM *šá* ITI.BÁR *šá* MU.14.KAM KÙ.BABBAR-a_4
7 1 MA.NA *šá gin-nu* ^{m}*pu-uḫ-ḫu-ru a-na*
8 ^{md}AG-ŠEŠ.MEŠ-*bul-liṭ la it-tan-nu*

LO. E.

9 11 GUR ŠE.BAR *ku-um* KÙ.BABBAR-a_4 1 MA.NA
10 *ina* ITI.GU_4 ^{m}*pu-uḫ-ḫu-ru a-na*

REV.

11 ^{md}AG-ŠEŠ.MEŠ-*bul-liṭ i-na-ad-din*
12 LÚ *mu-kin-nu* ^{m}*ap-la-a* A-*šú šá* ^{md}U.GUR-MU
13 ^{md}AG-A-MU A-*šú šá* ^{m}*a-ra-nu* ^{m}*mu-še-zib*-^{d}AMAR.UTU
14 A-*šú šá* ^{md}AMAR.UTU-MU-DÙ A LÚ.SIMUG ^{md}AG-*bul-liṭ-su*
15 A-*šú šá* ^{m}MU-^{d}EN A ^{md}IDIM-DÙ-*eš*-DINGIR ^{md}AG-*it-tan-nu*
16 A-*šú šá* ^{m}MU-^{d}AG A ^{m}*nu-ḫa-šú* ^{md}AG-KAR-*ir*
17 A-*šú šá* ^{md}AMAR.UTU-GIN-A ^{md}EN-*it-tan-nu* LÚ.UMBISAG
18 [A-*šú š*]*á* ^{md}AG-PAB-*šú* A LÚ.SANGA-^{d}IDIM
19 [UR]U *šá-ḫi-ri-nu* ITI.BÁR UD.15.KAM
20 [MU].14.KAM ^{m}*da-ri-ia-muš*
21 LUGAL E.KI *u* KUR.KUR

TRANSLATION

On the twentieth of Nisan of the fourteenth year of King Darius Puḫḫuru, son of Nergal-iddin, shall bring one mina of marked silver from Nabû-aḫḫē-bulliṭ's credit claim that is charged against him, and he shall give (it) to Nabû-aḫḫē-bulliṭ. If on the twentieth of Nisan of the fourteenth year Puḫḫuru has not paid the one mina of marked silver to Nabû-aḫḫē-bulliṭ, Puḫḫuru shall deliver to Nabû-aḫḫē-bulliṭ eleven *kor* of barley instead of the one mina of silver, in Ayyar.

Witnesses:
Aplaya/Nergal-iddin
Nabû-apla-iddin/Arānu

Mušēzib-Marduk/Marduk-šuma-ibni//Nappāḫu
Nabû-bullissu/Iddin-Bēl//Ea-eppeš-ilī
Nabû-ittannu/Iddin-Nabû//Nuḫāšu
Nabû-ēṭir/Marduk-mukīn-apli
The scribe: Bēl-ittannu/Nabû-uṣuršu//Šangû-Ea
(Place + Date).

COMMENT

The parties involved in this promissory note are cited by their first names only, except for Puḫḫuru, who is identified as the son of Nergal-iddin. The latter was, no doubt, the same man as Bēl-upaḫḫir, son of Nergal-iddin; Nabû-aḫḫē-bulliṭ is to be identified with MNA's brother with the same name. On Bēl-upaḫḫir and his debts to MNA's slave, see also Dar 509, BM 31360, and BM 31793.

L. 13: The name ^{m}*a-ra-nu*, which is the name of Nabû-apla-iddin's father, is a hapax. Tallqvist, *NbN*, 306 derives it from the verb *rē'û* "to herd." He considers it a variant spelling for the common name Ir'anni (usually wr. *ir-a-nu/ni*). However, Ir'anni is typically a family name, whereas ^{m}*a-ra-nu* in the text under consideration appears as a patronymy. Moreover, one expects a spelling *ar-a-nu*, rather than *a-ra-nu* for a name like A/Ir'anni.

No. 116

	Dar 390
Museum No.:	BM 31006
Date:	15/xi/14 Dar (24 February 507 B.C.E.)
Place:	Ālu-ša-Libbi-ālaya, *eqli-ša-Bēl*
Content:	Promissory note to pay a debt of barley to MNA.

OBV.

1 3 GUR ŠE.BAR *bab-ba-ni-tu*$_4$ *šá*
2 ^{md}AMAR.UTU-PAP-A DUMU *šá* ^{m}KI-^{d}AMAR.UTU-DIN
3 [A ^{m}*e-g*]**i-bi ina muḫ-ḫi* ^{m}*šu-lum*-TIN.TIR.KI
4 ⸢DUMU *šá*⸣* ^{m}*ni-din-tu*$_4$ *ina* ITI.GU$_4$ ŠE.BAR-*a*$_4$
5 3 GUR *ina ma-ši-ḫu šá* ^{md}AMAR.UTU-PAP-A
6 *ina* UGU 1-*et rit-tu*$_4$ *ina* URU-*šá*-^{md}AMAR.UTU-PAP-A
7 ⸢*ina muḫ*⸣-*ḫi* ÍD *pi-qu-du ina-ad-din*

REV.

8 LÚ *mu-kin-nu* ^{m}*ap-la-a* DUMU *šá*
9 ^{m}*ba-ni-ia* ^{m}MU-^{d}AG DUMU *šá* ^{m}DIN-*su*
10 A ^{md}PA-*še-e* ^{m}ÌR-^{d}U.GUR <DUMU *šá*>*
11 ^{md}AG-DÙ-ŠEŠ A LÚ.BAḪAR$_2$
12 ^{m}ŠEŠ-MU DUMU *šá* ^{m}MU-MU ^{m}*ú-qu-pu* DUMU ^{m}⸢PAP⸣
13 ^{m}*ú-bar* LÚ.UMBISAG A ^{m}*šá-na-ši-šú* URU-*šá*-

14 *lib-bi*-URU-*a-a* A.ŠÀ-*šá*-^{d}EN ITI.ZÍZ
15 UD.15.KAM MU.14.KAM ^{m}*da-a-r*[*i*]*-*mu*[*š*]*
16 LUGAL TIN.TIR.KI LUGAL KUR.KUR

TRANSLATION

Three *kor* of first-rate barley are due to MNA$_1$ from Šulum-Bābili, ⸢son of⸣ Nidintu. In Ayyar he will deliver these three *kor* of barley in one installment, according to MNA's measure, in Ālu-ša-Marduk-nāṣir-apli along the Piqūdu canal.

Witnesses:
Aplaya/Baniya
Iddin-Nabû/Balāssu//Nabû-šê
Arad-Nergal</>Nabû-bāni-aḫi//Paḫāru
Aḫa-iddin/Šuma-iddin
Iqūpu/⸢Aḫa(-abiya?)⸣.
The scribe: Ubār//Ša-nāšīšu
(Place + Date).

COMMENT

L. 10: The surname Nabû-šeme is well known (Tallqvist, *NbN*, 143). For the spelling *-še-e* (= *šeme*), compare, for instance, the spelling *šu-ú* for *šūmu* and *ku-ú* for *kūm* (examples quoted by Wunsch, *Iddin-Marduk* 2, 77).

L. 10 end: There is enough space on the right edge to write DUMU *šá*, but the scribe must have forgotten about it.

L. 12 end: The scribe did not have much space available to write the name of Iqūpu's father. In fact, he already wrote the end of the DUMU on the right edge, and could add just one more sign, which is the PAP; he could not continue writing on the other side of the tablet, i.e., the obverse, because the -*a*$_4$ of line 4 was taking up its space. There are some wedges visible on the right edge, viz. below the end of the DUMU, and they may have belonged to the name of Iqūpu's father, but the passage in question is illegible. Consequently, we do not know whether ^{m}PAP was Iqūpu's father's full name (PAP = Aḫa, or = Nāṣir?), or an abbreviated form of it (e.g., Nabû-nāṣir, Aḫa-abiya), used by the scribe because of the lack of space. Note that a Iqūpu, son of Aḫa-abiya (wr. ^{m}ŠEŠ-AD-*ia*) occurs in Dar 447: 4 (not Egibi related text) (Babylon, 17 Dar).

L. 13 end: The right edge is left empty. There are, however, a few scratches that Strassmaier took for wedges being part of the name of Iqūpu's father.

L. 15: The end of the line is damaged, and I could not see the *-'i-uš* as copied by Strassmaier. In my opinion, the signs in question are *-r*[*i*]*-mu*[*š*].

No. 117

	Dar 400
Museum No.:	BM 30699
Date:	3/v/15 Dar (7 August 507 B.C.E.)
Place:	Šaḫrīnu
Content:	Receipt of dates by MNA's slave.

OBV.

1 16 GUR ZÚ.LUM.MA MU.13.KAM ^{m}*da-ri-mu-šú*

2 LUGAL ⸢E.KI *u* KUR.KUR.MEŠ⸣ 18 GUR 2 (PI) 3 (BÁN) ZÚ.LUM.MA

3 MU.14.KAM *šá* 2-TA ⸢KÁ.MEŠ⸣ *šá* GARIM *ḫa-ṣi-ra-tu*$_4$

4 *šá* ^{md}EN-MU A-*šú šá* ^{md}AG-NUMUN-GÁL-*ši*

5 PAB 34 GUR 2 (PI) 3 (BÁN) ZÚ.LUM.MA *ina** *ra-šu-tu-šú*

6 SAG.DU *u* UR$_5$.RA ^{md}DI.KU$_5$-EN-URU$_3$

7 LÚ *qal-la šá* ^{md}ŠÚ-PAB-A A ^{m}*e-gi-bi*

8 *ina* ŠU.II ^{f}*qu-un-na-bi** DUMU.MÍ-*su šá* ^{m}⸢ŠEŠ.MEŠ-MU⸣

9 DAM ^{md}EN-MU *ma-ḫir*

REV.

10 LÚ *mu-kin-nu* ^{m}SUM.NA-*a* A-*šú šá* ^{m}ÌR-*iá*

11 ^{m}*ku-ṣur-ra-a* A-*šú šá* ^{m}*ár-bi* ^{md}EN-KÁD

12 A-*šú šá* ^{m}*ḫa-ba-ṣi-ru* ^{m}MU-^{d}EN A-*šú šá*

13 ^{md}U.GUR-MU ^{m}*ni-qud* A-*šú šá* ^{m}MU-^{d}AG

14 A ^{m}DÙ-*eš*-DINGIR ^{md}EN-MU A-*šú šá* ^{m}*gu-za-na*

15 A ^{md}IDIM-*ṣa-lam*-DINGIR LÚ.UMBISAG ^{m}MU-^{d}U.GUR

16 A-*šú šá* ^{m}ŠU A LÚ.SIMUG URU *šaḫ-ri-nu*

17 ITI.NE UD.3.KAM MU.15.KAM

18 ^{m}*da-ri-'i-šú* LUGAL E.KI *u* KUR.KUR

TRANSLATION

Sixteen *kor* of dates of the thirteenth year of Darius, king ⸢of Babylon and the lands⸣, (and) 18.2.3 *kor* of dates of the fourteenth year, from two ⸢sectors⸣ of irrigated farmland in Ḫaṣirātu that belong to Bēl-iddin, son of Nabû-zēra-ušabši—in total 34.2.3 *kor* of dates—: Madānu-bēla-uṣur, a slave of MNA$_1$, has received (these dates), (viz.) the principal amount and the interest from his credit claim, from ^{f}Qunnabi, daughter of ⸢Aḫḫē-iddin⸣, wife of Bēl-iddin.

Witnesses:
Iddinaya/Ardiya
Kuṣuraya/Ar(ra)bi
Bēl-kāṣir/Ḫabaṣīru
Iddin-Bēl/Nergal-iddin
Niqūdu/Iddin-Nabû//Eppeš-ilī
Bēl-iddin/Gūzānu//Ea-ṣalam-ilī
The scribe: Iddin-Nergal/Gimillu//Nappāḫu
(Place + Date).

COMMENT

L. 3 The place ^{garim}Ḫaṣirātu is a hapax (Zadok, *RGTC* 8, 156).

No. 118

Dar 405
Museum No.: BM 30825
Date: 4/vii/15 Dar (7 October 507 B.C.E.)
Place: Šaḫrīnu
Content: Promissory note to deliver dates (*imittu*-lease) to MNA's slave. Produce from a palm grove held by MNA's slave as pledge. Witnessed by the royal resident in the Eḫursag.

OBV.

1 ⸢5⸣ (GUR) 2 (PI) 3 (BÁN) ZÚ.LUM.MA ZAG.LU A.ŠÀ *šá ḫar-ri*
2 LÚ.UNUG.KI-*a-a šá* ^{m}A-*a* A-*šú šá* ^{md}U.GUR-MU
3 ⸢É$^{?}$⸣**maš-ka-nu šá* ^{md}DI.KU$_5$-EN-URU$_3$
4 LÚ *qal-la šá* ^{md}AMAR.UTU-*na-ṣir*-A
5 A ^{m}*e-gi-bi ina muḫ-ḫi* ^{m}A-*a* A-*šú šá*
6 ^{m}*gi-mil-lu ina* ITI.APIN ZÚ.LUM.MA-*a'*
7 5 (GUR) 2 (PI) 3 (BÁN) *gam-ru-tu ina* GIŠ *ma-ši-ḫu*
8 [*šá*]* 1 PI *ina muḫ-ḫi* 1-*et rit-ti*

LO. E.

*9 ⸢*ina*⸣ *muḫ-ḫi* ÍD *bar-sip*.KI

REV.

10 *a-na* ^{md}DI.KU$_5$-EN-URU$_3$ *i-nam-din*
11 LÚ *mu-kin-nu* ^{md}30-LUGAL-*bul-liṭ* LÚ *qí-pi*
12 *šá é-ḫur-sag* ^{m}*bul-lu-ṭu* A-*šú šá* ^{md}UTU-NUMUN-GÁL-*ši*
13 A ^{md}30-*šá-du-nu* ^{m}*ta-at-tan-nu* A-*šú šá*
14 ^{m}*lu*-È-*ana*-ZALAG$_2$ ^{md}EN-SU A-*šú šá* ^{m}DÙ-*ia*
15 LÚ.UMBISAG ^{m}MU-URU$_3$ A-*šú šá* ^{md}AG-*it-tan-nu*
16 URU *šaḫ-ri-i-ni* ITI.DU$_6$ UD.4.KAM
17 MU.15.KAM ^{m}*da-a-ri-ia-muš*
18 LUGAL E.KI *u* KUR.KUR.MEŠ

TRANSLATION

5.2.3 *kor* of dates, the *imittu*-lease from the field in Ḫarru-Urukaya that belongs to Aplaya, son of Nergal-iddin (but) is pledged to Madānu-bēla-uṣur, a slave of MNA$_1$, are due from Aplaya, son of Gimillu. In Araḫsamna he will deliver the full amount of 5.2.3 *kor* of dates to Madānu-bēla-uṣur in one installment according to the *pān*-measure at the Borsippa canal.

Witnesses:
Sîn-šarra-bulliṭ, royal resident (*qīpu*) in the Eḫursag temple
Bulluṭu/Šamaš-zēra-ušabši//Šîn-šadûnu

Tattannu/Lūṣi-ana-nūri
Bēl-erība/Baniya
The scribe: Šuma-uṣur/Nabû-ittannu
(Place + Date).

No. 119

	Dar 411
Museum No.:	BM 30272
Date:	22/viii/15 Dar (24 November 507 B.C.E.)
Place:	Nār-šarri-ša-Elam
Content:	Promissory note to pay a debt of silver. Due from MNA. Part of the silver had been transferred to MNA (the debtor) to pay for work (*dullu*) at a canal.

OBV.

1 2 MA.NA KÙ.BABBAR UD-*ú nu-uḫ-ḫu-tú* <*šá*> *ina* 1 GÍN *bit-qa*
2 *šá la gìn-nu šá* ^{m}*ta-at-tan-nu* A-*šú šá* ^{m}*ri-mut*
3 *ina muḫ-ḫi* ^{m}*ši-ir-ku* A-*šú šá* ^{m}MU-*a*
4 A ^{m}*e-gì-bi ina* ITI.ŠE KÙ.BABBAR-*a*$_{4}$ 2 MA.NA
5 UD-*ú nu-uḫ-ḫu-tú šá ina* 1 GÍN *bit-qa*
6 *šá la gìn-nu ina* E.KI *i-nam-din*
7 *a-di-i ú-ìl-tì* IGI-*tu*$_{4}$
8 *šá* 1½ MA.NA KÙ.BABBAR *šá a-na dul-lu*
9 *šá* ÍD LUGAL *šá* KUR.ELAM.KI SUM.NA

REV.

10 LÚ *mu-kin-nu* ^{md}*za-ba*$_{4}$-*ba*$_{4}$-MU A-[*šú*] [*šá*]*
11 ^{m}*e-tel-lu* ^{m}*ni-din-tu*$_{4}$ A-*šú šá* ^{m}⌜x⌝-[...]
12 A ^{m}*e-gì-bi* ^{m}*ú-bar* A-*šú šá* ^{m}SU-*a*
13 A ^{m}LÚ.ŠITIM ^{md}AG-KAR-ZI.MEŠ A-*šú šá*
14 ^{m}ŠEŠ-*šú-nu* A ^{m}*ar-rab-bi**-*i** ^{m}MU-MU A-*šú šá*
15 ^{md}*za-ba*$_{4}$-*ba*$_{4}$-SU A ^{m}LÚ-*ú* ^{md}AG-MU-GIN
16 A-*šú šá* ^{m}DIN-*su*-^{d}AMAR.UTU LÚ.UMBISAG ^{m}*bul-ṭa-a*
17 A-*šú šá* ^{m}MU-^{d}EN ÍD LUGAL *šá* KUR.ELAM.KI
18 ITI.APIN UD.22.KAM MU.15.KAM
19 ^{m}*da-ri-iá-muš* LUGAL E.KI *u* KUR.KUR

TRANSLATION

Two minas of white, medium-quality silver that is unmarked and of which one-eighth is alloy, are due to Tattannu, son of Rīmūt, from MNA$_{2}$. In Addar he shall pay these two minas of white, medium-quality silver, which is unmarked and of which one-eighth is alloy, in Babylon. This includes the previous debt of one and a half minas of silver that had been given (to pay) for the work at the king's canal to Elam.

Witnesses:
Zababa-iddin/Etellu
Nidintu/[...]//Egibi
Ubār/Erībaya//Itinnu
Nabû-ēṭir-napšāti/Aḫūšunu//Arrabi
Šuma-iddin/Zababa-erība//Amēlu
Nabû-šuma-ukīn/Uballissu-Marduk
The scribe: Bulṭaya/Iddin-Bēl
(Place + Date).

COMMENT

L. 9 end: The NA of SUM.NA is written over something else. There is another SUM.NA between lines 9 and 10 (see Strassmaier's copy).

L. 10 end: With A-[*šú*] [*šá*]* the scribe reached the end of the reverse. The right edge is damaged and could have contained approximately three signs. However, I do not think that the scribe used this space on the right edge to write the name of Zababa-iddin's father. In fact, the scribe used the right edge only in lines 2 (-*mut*), 4 (.NA), and 15 (-GIN), to finish writing what he had begun, but not to start writing a new word. If so, he wrote the name of Zababa-iddin's father on a new line (= line 11). A Zababa-iddin, son of Etellu is known as governor of Kish from BM 33936 ([16] Dar). If this is the same person, he was probably the one in charge of digging the king's canal to Elam. Note that BM 33936 was written in Elam's capital (viz. EREN.KI = Šušan). It concerned a large debt of silver by MNA to Zababa-iddin.

L. 11: This Nidintu from the Egibi family was probably not MNA's son. His father's name does not seem to have started with Marduk-, but rather with Nabû-, or Bēl-.

L. 11 end: In the broken part at the end of the line there could have been one more sign on the reverse, and two on the edge.

No. 120

	Dar 430
Museum No.:	BM 32859
Date:	30/vi/16 Dar (15 September 506 B.C.E.)
Place:	Šaḫrīnu
Content:	Receipt of silver by MNA's slave and Iddinaya. Payment for doing reserve duty in the army (*kumu kutallûtu*). On account of a bow-unit (*ana muḫḫi* ^{giš}*qašti*).

OBV.

1 ½ MA.NA KÙ.BABBAR *šá gìn-nu šá na-da-na u ma-ḫa-ri*
2 *ku-mu* ˹*ku*˺*-tal-la-ú-tu šá* MU.16.KAM
3 ^{m}*da-ri-'i-šú* LUGAL E.KI *u* KUR.KUR.MEŠ *a-na muḫ-ḫi*
4 GIŠ.BAN *šá* ^{md}EN-MU A-*šú šá* ^{md}AG-NUMUN-GÁL-*ši*
5 *ina* ŠU.II ^{md}IGI.DU-ŠEŠ-MU A-*šú šá* ^{md}AG-ŠEŠ.MEŠ-*bul-liṭ*
6 ˹*u**˺ ^{md}AG-*ni-ip-šá-ri* A-*šú šá* ^{m}BA-*šá-ia* LÚ.KIN.GI$_4$.A
7 [*šá* ^{md}KUR].GAL-LUGAL-*ki-i-ni* LÚ.2-*ú šá* LÚ *ki***-na-ta**
8 [^{md}DI.KU$_5$]-EN-PAB LÚ *qal-la šá* ^{md}ŠÚ-*na-ṣir*-A A ^{m}*e-gi-bi*
9 [*u* ^{m}SUM].˹NA˺-*a* A-*šú šá* ^{m}ÌR-*ia ma-ḫir-u'*
10 [*eṭ*$^{?}$*-r*]*a-a-a'* KÙ.BABBAR-*a*$_4$ ½ MA.NA *ina lìb-bi*
11 [x x] GÍN *a-na* UGU-*i'* ^{md}DI.KU$_5$-˹MU˺ [...]

REV.

12 [x x] 5 GÍN *a-na muḫ-ḫi* ^{m}SUM.NA-*a* [...]
13 [LÚ A].˹KIN*˺ *šá* ^{f}*sag-ga-a* DUMU.MÍ-*su šá* ^{md}IDIM-*ki-i-ni*
14 DAM ^{m}MU-*a* LÚ *mu-kin-nu* ^{md}AG-GIN-A
15 A-*šú šá* ^{md}AMAR.UTU-GI ^{md}EN-*it-tan-na* A-*šú šá*
16 ^{m}*kal-ba-a* A ^{m}*ga-ḫal* ^{m}*ni-qu-du* A-*šú šá*
17 ^{md}U.GUR-MU A ^{m}ZALAG$_2$-*za-na* ^{m}*ni-din-tu*$_4$ A-*šú šá*
18 ^{md}AG-GIN-A A LÚ-^{d}IDIM ^{m}*ba-la-ṭu* A-*šú šá*
19 ^{md}UTU-SU
20 LÚ.UMBISAG ^{m}MU-^{d}U.GUR A-*šú šá* ^{m}ŠU A LÚ.SIMUG
21 URU *šaḫ-ri-nu* ITI.KIN UD.30.KAM MU.16.KAM
22 ^{m}*da-ri-'i-šú* LUGAL E.KI *u* KUR.KUR.MEŠ

TRANSLATION

Half a mina of marked silver used in the country, (paid) instead of serving as a reservist in the sixteenth year of Darius, king of Babylon and the lands, on account of the bow of Bēl-iddin, son of Nabû-zēra-ušabši: from Nergal-aḫa-iddin, son of Nabû-aḫḫē-bulliṭ, ˹and˺ Nabû-nipšaru, son of Iqīšaya, messenger [of Amur]ru-šarra-kīni, deputy of the menials, [Madānu]-bēla-uṣur, a slave of MNA$_1$, [and Iddi]naya, son of Ardiya, have received (it); they are [paid] ˹off˺$^{?}$. This half a mina of silver: from it [x x] shekels on account of Madānu-˹iddin˺

[...], [x x] five shekels on account of Iddinaya [...], [the mess]⌜enger⌝ of ᶠSaggaya, daughter of Ea-kīni, wife of Iddinaya.

Witnesses:
Nabû-mukīn-apli/Marduk-ušallim
Bēl-ittannu/Kalbaya//Gaḫal
Niqūdu/Nergal-iddin//Nūr-zana
Nidintu/Nabû-mukīn-apli//Amēl-Ea
Balāṭu/Šamaš-erība
The scribe: Iddin-Nergal/Gimillu//Nappāḫu
(Place + Date).

Comment

L. 2: On *kutallūtu* in general, see *AHw*, 518 s.v. *kutallūtu* "Ersatzmannstellung." The translation above follows the opinion expressed in the *CAD* K, 607 s.v. *kutallūtu* "obligation to serve as a reservist in the royal army." This obligation is incumbent on Bēl-iddin on account of his bow(-tax) and should, therefore, be compared to Bēl-iddin's obligation to pay for "the food provisions for the *zargaya*-(work)men" that he had to pay as part of his bow(-tax) according to BM 31026. For a different opinion, see Van Driel, *JEHSO* 32: 211, according to whom Bēl-iddin had died and a replacement (*kutallūtu*) had to be found for his bow-fief.

L. 6: *-ni-ip-šá-ri* may possibly reflect the Aramaic *mpšr* (and is not related to the Akkadian noun *nību*), so *CAD* N_2, 205 s.v. *nību* A mng. 1.

L. 7: The noun *kinattu* (or *kinātu*) in Neo-Babylonian archival texts usually means "colleague, fellow worker." However, it may also have the specific meaning of "menial," e.g., in the expression *ša ina pān kinatti*. More at *CAD* K, 381f. s.v. *kinattu* and *AHw*, 479f. s.v. *kinattu*.

L. 13: The name ᶠ*sag-ga-a* is unique. Did the scribe mistakenly write *-ga-* instead of *-gìl-*? In fact, the wedges of the GA-sign make up the first part of the GÌL-sign, so that we may have a defective writing of *-gìl-*. Moreover, (E)saggila(ya) is a common name, for men and women alike (see Tallqvist, *NbN*, 60 and 180).

L. 17: For the name Nūr-zana, more at Dar 308: 15.

No. 121

	Dar 435
Museum No.:	BM 31975
Date:	10/xii(b)/16 Dar (27 March 505 B.C.E.)
Place:	Šušan
Content:	About a plot of land with a house built on it neighboring MNA's property. Located in Ḫubur street in the neighborhood called Šu'anna within Babylon. Very fragmentary (= sale?).

OBV.

1 24 GI.MEŠ É *ep-šú* KI-*tì šu-*⸢*ma**⸣*-an*.KI *šá qé-reb* E.KI

2 *šá* DA É ^{md}EN-*eri-ba* A-*šú šá* ^{md}AG-EN-*šú-nu* A ^{m}AD-NU-ZU

3 ^{md}AG-*bul-liṭ-su* A-*šú šá* ^{md}AG-MU-GAR*-*un šá ina su-ú-qu šá ḫu-ur-*[*bi*]

4 *mu-ur-ra-du a-di šá* ^{m}*ši-iš*<-*ki*> A-*šú šá* ^{m}SUM.N[A-*a* ...]

(Remainder of obverse is broken off.)

REV.

1′ A [...]

2′ A-*šú šá* ^{m}⸢*šu*⸣-*ri*-[...]

3′ ^{m}*ḫa-an-ṭu-ú-šú* A-*šú šá* ^{m}⸢*ka-am**⸣-*mu-šú*-DINGIR.MEŠ ^{m}*ri-mu*[*t* (...)]

4′ LÚ.DI.KU$_5$ A-*šú šá* ^{m}SUM.NA-*a* {^{m}} ^{m}*i-qu-pu* A-*šú šá* ^{md}AG-*na-din**-⸢ŠEŠ⸣*

5′ A ^{m}*su-ḫa-a-a* ^{md}AG-ŠEŠ.MEŠ-MU LÚ.UMBISAG A ^{m}*ga-ḫal*

6′ *šu-šá-an* ITI.ŠE DIRIG UD.10.KAM MU.16.KAM ^{m}*da-ri-ia-muš*

7′ LUGAL E.KI LUGAL KUR.MEŠ

U. E.

*TOP

NA$_4$.KIŠIB / ^{m}MU-^{d}AG / LÚ.DI.KU$_5$

MIDDLE

NA$_4$.KIŠIB / ^{m}*ba-si-ia*

BOTTOM

NA$_4$.KIŠIB / ^{m}LUGAL-BÀD

RI. E.

*TOP

NA$_4$.KIŠIB / ^{m}*am-ma-*⸢*da-a-tú* / LÚ.DI.KU$_5$⸣

LE. E.

*TOP

[NA$_4$.KIŠIB] / [^{m}*ri-m*]*ut* / ⸢^{m}SUM.NA⸣-*a* / LÚ.DI.KU$_5$

TRANSLATION

Twenty-four "reeds" of land with a house built on it (located) within Babylon, in the Šu'anna-quarter, in Ḫubur-street, which goes down as far as (the house) of MNA$_2$, next to the house of Bēl-erība, son of Nabû-bēlšunu, descendant of Abī-ul-īde, (and) Nabû-bullissu, son of Nabû-šuma-iškun, [...].

[Witnesses]:
[...]/Šuri-[...]
Ḫanṭušu/Kamūšu-ilū
Rīmūt/Iddinaya, the judge
Iqūpu/Nabû-nādin-⸢aḫi⸣//Suḫaya
The scribe: Nabû-aḫḫē-iddin//Gaḫal
(Place + Date).
Seal of Iddin-Nabû, the judge
Seal of Basiya
Seal of Šarru-dūrī
Seal of Amadātu, the judge
⸢Seal of Rīmūt/Iddinaya⸣, the judge

Comment

For the connection between this text and other texts from the archive that mention Šušan, see Abraham, *NABU* 1997/53 and Id., *OLP* 28, 55–85. On the Aramaic, see Stolper, *JAOS* 116, 517–21.

L. 3: *ḫu-ur-*[*bi*] is a variant spelling for *ḫu-bur*(*-ru*), which is the name of a street in Babylon (cf. *CAD* Ḫ, 220 s.v. *ḫubūru* A). Differently, *AHw*, 358 s.v. *ḫurbu*, relates it to the Aramaic *ḫorbā* "destruction," which is a *hapax* in the text under consideration.

Rev. 2′: Is ᵐ⸢*šu*⸣*-ri-*[...] to be read ᵐ*šu-ri-ni-tu*$_4$? The latter was the family name of one Bēl-dayyānu/Marduk-zēra-ibni (Dar 332: 15 = *CM* 20b 161).

Rev. 3′–5′: The witnesses mentioned in these lines occur also in TCL 13 193: Ḫanṭūšu/Kamūšu-ilū (wr. ᵐ*ka-mu-šu-i-lu*, 33), Rīmūt/Iddinaya//Nappāḫu (34–35), and Iqūpu/Nabû-nādin-aḫi//Suḫaya.

Seals: For the persons who sealed this tablet, see also TCL 13 193: Iddin-Nabû/Nabû-talīm-uṣur (32), Basiya/Šilaya (30), Šarru-dūrī/Edrā (*passim*), Rīmūt/Iddinaya//Nappāḫu (34–35); and Amadātu (wr. ᵐ*am-ma-da-a-tú*), who is probably the same person as Umadātu (wr. ᵐ*um-ma-da-a-tú*), son of Udunātu, in TCL 13 193: 25 and Le. E.

No. 122

	Dar 437
Museum No.:	BM 30488
Date:	[-]/[xii$^{?}$]/16 Dar (April 506 - March 505 B.C.E.)
Place:	Šušan
Content:	Promissory note to pay a debt of silver. Due from MNA. Fixation of default interest. Witnessed by clerks of the Esagil.

OBV.

1 2⅔ MA.NA KÙ.BABBAR *pe-ṣu-ú šá ina* 1 GÍN *bit-qa* ⸢*nu-uḫ*⸣-[*ḫu-tu*]

2 *šá* ^{md}EN-SUM.NA DUMU *šá* ^{m}*mu-še-zib*-^{d}AMAR.UTU DU[MU ^{md}30-*na-din*-MU]

3 *ina muḫ-ḫi* ^{m}*ši-iš-ki* DUMU *šá* ^{m}SUM.NA-*a* DUMU ^{m}[*e-gi-bi*]

4 *i-na* ITI.SIG$_4$ *šá* MU.17.KAM KÙ.BABBAR-*a*$_4$ 2⅔ MA.NA ⸢KÙ.BABBAR⸣ [UD-*ú*]

5 *šá ina* 1 GÍN *bit-qa nu-uḫ-ḫu-tu i-na* KÁ.DINGIR.RA.KI

6 *i-na* SAG.DU-*šú i-na-ad-di-in ki-i i-na* ITI.SIG$_4$

7 *šá* MU.17.KAM KÙ.BABBAR-*a*$_4$ 2⅔ MA.NA *pe-ṣu-ú šá ina* 1 GÍN *bit-qa*

8 [*nu*]-*uḫ-ḫu-tu la it-tan-nu šá* KÙ.BABBAR-*a*$_4$ 2⅔ MA.NA *šá* ITI

9 *ina muḫ-ḫi* 1 *ma-ni-e* 1 GÍN KÙ.BABBAR UR$_5$.RA *ina muḫ-ḫi-šú i-rab-bi*

REV.

10 [LÚ *mu*]-*kin-nu* ^{md}EN-ŠEŠ.MEŠ-SUM.NA LÚ.UGULA-*é-sag-ìl*

11 DUMU *šá* ^{m}*la-a-ba-ši* DUMU LÚ-^{d}*é-a* ^{md}EN-*re-man-ni* LÚ.UGULA-*é-sag-ìl*

12 DUMU *šá* ^{md}AG-MU-GIN DUMU LÚ.GAL-DÙ-^{d}AMAR.UTU ^{m}*ši-iš-ki* LÚ.UGULA-*é-sag-ìl*

13 DUMU *šá* ^{md}AG-GI DUMU LÚ.ŠU.KU$_6$ ^{md}EN-A*-SUM.NA DUMU *šá* ^{m}*ni-qu-du*

14 DUMU ^{m}*aš-gan-du*$_7$ ^{md}EN-A-SUM.NA DUMU *šá* ^{m}*ri-mut*-^{d}EN DUMU LÚ.SIMUG

15 ^{md}AG-MU-GIN DUMU *šá* ^{md}AG-*mu-še-ti-iq*-UD.DA DUMU LÚ IŠ ⸢x⸣ [...]

16 ^{md}EN-SUM.NA DUMU *šá* ^{md}AG-DIN-*su*-E ^{md}AG-A-MU DUMU *šá* [...]

17 DUMU ^{m}*ga-ḫal* ^{md}EN-MU DUMU *šá* ^{m}*ba-la-ṭu* DUMU ^{m}⸢ŠEŠ⸣-[*ba-ni* ^{m}...]

18 ⸢DUMU⸣* *šá* ^{m}*še-el-li-bi* DUMU ^{m}*maš-tuk*.MEŠ ^{m}[...]

19 LÚ.SIPA-ANŠE.KUR.RA ^{m}SUM.NA-ŠEŠ [...]

U. E.

20 ⸢DUMU⸣ ^{m}SIG$_{15}$-^{d}IŠKUR URU *šu-šá-an*.KI [...]

21 MU.16.KAM ^{m}*da*-[*ri-ia-muš*]

LE. E.

*22 LUGAL KÁ.DINGIR.MEŠ.KI LUGAL KUR.KUR

Translation

Two and two-third minas of white, medium-qua[lity] silver, of which one-eighth is alloy, are due to Bēl-iddin, son of Mušēzib-Marduk, descen[dant of Sîn-nādin-šumi], from MNA_2. In Simān of the seventeenth year he will pay these two and two-third minas of ⌜white⌝, medium-quality ⌜silver⌝, of which one-eighth is alloy, without interest in Babylon. If by Simān of the seventeenth year he has not paid these two and two-third minas of white, medium-quality silver of which one-eighth is alloy, interest will accrue against him on these two and two-third minas of silver (at the rate of) one shekel of silver per mina per month.

Witnesses:
Bēl-aḫḫē-iddin/Lâbāši//Amēl-Ea, secretary (*šāpiru*) in the Esagil temple
Bēl-rēmanni/Nabû-šuma-ukīn//Rab-banê-Marduk, secretary (*šāpiru*) in the Esagil temple
Širku/Nabû-ušallim//Bā'iru, secretary (*šāpiru*) in the Esagil temple
Bēl-apla-iddin/Niqūdu//Ašgandu
Bēl-apla-iddin/Rīmūt-Bēl//Nappāḫu
Nabû-šuma-ukīn/Nabû-mušētiq-uddê//LÚ...
Bēl-iddin/Nabû-balāssu-iqbi
Nabû-apla-iddin/[...]//Gaḫal
Bēl-iddin/Balāṭu//⌜Aḫu⌝-[bani]
[Kiribtu-Marduk]/Šellibi//Maštuk
^{m}[...][//]Rē'i-sīsî
[The scribe]: Nādin-aḫi[/...]//Mudammiq-Adad
(Place + Date).

Comment

For the connection between this text and other texts from the archive that mention Šušan, see Abraham, *NABU* 1997/53 and Id., *OLP* 28, 55–85.

L. 13: The A* of ^{md}EN-A*-MU is clearly visible, but it may be that the scribe tried to erase it.

L. 17–18: Line 18 starts with the expression "son of X, descendant of Y," so that the first name of this person whose affiliation is given in line 18 is to be looked for at the end of line 17. Unfortunately, the end of line 17 is broken off. As it is, the person in question can be identified from his attestation in other texts: for Kiribtu(-Marduk)/Šellibi//Maštuk, see Tallqvist, *NbN*, 91 s.v. Kiribtu(12) and Kiribtu-Marduk(1). He occurs among the witnesses in Dar 498 (Babylon, 14/i/20 Dar), a document in which Šamaš-ina-tēšê-ēṭir/Šamaš-iddin//Šamaš-abāri, MNA's partner in the business venture with dates from the tithes of Bēl (Dar 359), promised to deliver dates and barley to MNA in Bīt-Ḫaḫḫuru; this Šamaš-ina-tēšê-ēṭir is further found among the witnesses in CT 51 55 = *CM* 20b 235.

No. 123

Dar 450
Museum No.: BM 30309
Date: 20/x/17 Dar (27 January 504 B.C.E.)
Place: Babylon
Content: Receipt of silver paid on behalf of MNA. Partial payment of a debt.

OBV.

1 ⌜*i-na*⌝* *ú-ìl-tì šá* 6⅔ MA.NA 1 GÍN KÙ.BABBAR
2 *šá ina* 1 GÍN *bit-qa nu-uḫ-ḫu-tu šá* ^{md}AG-DÙ-ŠEŠ
3 DUMU-*šú šá* ^{md}AMAR.UTU-*na-ṣir* DUMU ^{md}IŠKUR-*šam-me-e*
4 *šá ina muḫ-ḫi* ^{md}AMAR.UTU-*na-ṣir*-IBILA DUMU-*šú šá* ^{m}KI-^{d}AMAR.UTU-DIN
5 DUMU ^{m}*e-gi-bi ina lìb-bi* 4 MA.NA KÙ.BABBAR UD-*ú nu-uḫ-ḫu-tú*
6 ^{md}AG-DÙ-ŠEŠ DUMU-*šú šá* ^{md}AMAR.UTU-*na-ṣir* DUMU ^{md}IŠKUR-*šam-me-e*
7 *ina qa-at* ^{md}AMAR.UTU-EN-*šú-nu* DUMU-*šú šá* ^{m}ÌR-^{d}AMAR.UTU
8 DUMU LÚ.SANGA-^{d}IDIM *a-na muḫ-ḫi* ^{md}AMAR.UTU-*na-ṣir*-IBILA
9 DUMU-*šú šá* ^{m}KI-^{d}AMAR.UTU-DIN DUMU ^{m}*e-gi-bi ma-ḫi-ir*

REV.

10 LÚ *mu-kin-nu* ^{md}EN-SUM.NA DUMU-*šú šá* ^{m}SUM.NA-⌜^{d}EN⌝
11 DUMU LÚ.SANGA-^{d}*é-a* ^{m}*mi-nu-ú*-DIŠ-^{d}EN-*da-a**-*nu*
12 DUMU-*šú šá* ^{md}EN-MU DUMU ^{m}*sag-di-di* ^{m}*mu-ra-nu* DUMU-*šú šá*
13 ^{m}*mu-šal-lim*-^{d}ŠÚ DUMU LÚ.AD.KID ^{md}AMAR.UTU-MU-MU DUMU-*šú šá*
14 ^{m}*šul-lu-mu* DUMU LÚ *i-tin-nu* ^{md}EN-*it-tan-nu* DUMU-*šú šá*
15 ^{md}AG-URU$_3$-*šú* A LÚ.GAL-DÙ
16 ^{md}EN-SUM.NA DUB.SAR DUMU ^{md}KÁ*-*ù**-*tu*
17 TIN.TIR.KI ITI.AB UD.20.KAM MU.17.KAM
18 ^{m}*da-a-ri-ia-muš* LUGAL E.KI LUGAL KUR.KUR

*LO. E.

19 NA$_4$.KIŠIB / ^{md}EN-SUM.NA / DUB.SAR + seal impression.

TRANSLATION

From the debt of six and two-third minas and one shekel of medium-quality silver, of which one-eighth is alloy, which are due to Nabû-bāni-aḫi, son of Marduk-nāṣir, descendant of Adad-šammê, from MNA$_1$: from it Nabû-bāni-aḫi, son of Marduk-nāṣir, descendant of Adad-šammê, received four minas of white, medium-quality silver from Marduk-bēlšunu, son of Arad-Marduk, descendant of Šangû-Ea, for the account of MNA$_1$.

Witnesses:
Bēl-iddin/Iddin-⌜Bēl⌝//Šangû-Ea
Mīnû-ana-Bēl-dānu/Bēl-iddin//Sagdidi

Mūrānu/Mušallim-Marduk//Atkuppu
Marduk-šuma-iddin/Šullumu//Itinnu
Bēl-ittannu/Nabû-uṣuršu//Rab-banê
The scribe: Bēl-iddin//Bābūtu[!]
(Place + Date).
Seal of Bēl-iddin, the scribe

COMMENT

The scribe carefully planned the writing of this tablet as is clear from the following four facts: (1) he wrote the contract on the obverse; (2) the list of witnesses who were present at the concluding of this contract are on the reverse; (3) an empty space of at least two lines (i.e., after line 15) separates the list of witnesses from the scribe's name; and (4) the scribe rarely wrote on the right edge (used to write *-ḫu-tu* in line 5 and the end of -IBILA in line 8), and he did not write on the lower edge. In fact, the text of the contract filled up only three-fourths of the obverse; the remaining space including part of the lower edge was used to impress the scribe's seal on the right side and add the seal inscription on the left side (= Lo. E., line 19).

L. 13: It seems that *-lim-*^{d}ŠÚ are written over something else.

L. 14: Note the syllabic writing LÚ *i-tin-nu*. This Marduk-šuma-iddin is attested in two more documents from the Egibi archive, in which his family name is written with the logogram LÚ.ŠITIM (Dar 376: 13 and Dar 379: 82).

L. 16: For the spelling ^{md}KÁ-*ù-tu* = Bābūtu and other spellings of this name, see Tallqvist, *NbN*, 17 s.v. Bābūtu. The scribe, Bēl-iddin(/Lâbāši)/Bābūtu was also the scribe of Dar 402 (= *CM* 20b 110); for additional attestations, see Tallqvist, *NbN*, 33 s.v. Bēl-iddin(81).

No. 124

	Dar 452
Museum No.:	BM 67413
Date:	22/x/17 Dar (29 January 504 B.C.E.)
Place:	Šaḫrīnu
Content:	Receipt of silver and barley by MNA's slave. Partial payment of a debt.

OBV.

1 [*ú-ìl-t*]*ì šá* 35 GUR ZÚ.LUM.M[A (*ù*)]
2 [½ MA.NA] KÙ.BABBAR *šá gìn-nu šá* ^{md}DI.KU$_{5}$-[EN-URU$_{3}$]
3 [LÚ *qal-l*]*a šá* ^{md}AMAR.UTU-*na-ṣir*-A A $^{m⌈}$*e*$^{⌉}$-[*gi-bi*]
4 [*ina muḫ-ḫ*]*i* ^{md}U.GUR-DIN-*iṭ* A-*šú šá* ^{md}EN-[MU]
5 *u* ^{f}*qu-un-na-bi* DUMU.MÍ-*su šá* ^{m}ŠEŠ.[MEŠ-MU]
6 DAM ^{md}EN-MU AMA-*šú* KÙ.BABBAR-*a*$_{4}$ ½ M[A.NA]
7 ^{md}DI.KU$_{5}$-EN-URU$_{3}$ *ina* ŠU.II ^{md}U.GUR-DIN-*iṭ* [A-*šú šá*]

8 ^{md}EN-MU *u* ^{f}*qu-un-na-bi* AMA-*šú ma-*[*ḫir*]
9 *ù* 3 GUR 2 (PI) 3 (BÁN) ŠE.BAR *ina ra-šu-tu šá* ^{md}DI.KU$_5$-[EN-URU$_3$]
10 *šá muḫ-ḫi* ^{md}EN-MU AD *šá* ^{md}U.GUR-DIN-*iṭ*
11 ^{md}DI.KU$_5$-EN-URU$_3$ *ina* ŠU.II ^{md}U.GUR-DIN-*iṭ*
12 *u* ^{f}*qu-un-na-bi* DAM ^{md}EN-[MU]
13 AMA-*šú ma-ḫir* LÚ *mu-kin-nu*

REV.

14 ^{md}IDIM-MU A-*šú šá* ^{md}UTU-MU A ^{m}⌜x⌝-[...]
15 ^{m}*ni-qu-du* A-*šú šá* ^{md}U.GUR-MU A ^{m}*n*[*u**-*úr-za-na*]
16 ^{md}U.GUR-MU A-*šú šá* ^{m}*ri-mut*-^{d}EN [^{m}...]
17 A-*šú šá* ^{m}DÙ-*iá* ^{m}*šul-lu-ma-a* A-*šú šá* ^{m}DIN-*ṭu* [(...)]
18 ^{m}*ku-ṣur-ra-a* A-*šú šá* ^{m}*a-ra-bi* ^{m}*ka-ṣir*
19 A-*šú šá* ^{m}DIN-*ṭu* LÚ.UMBISAG ^{m}MU-^{d}U.GUR A-*šú šá*
20 ^{m}*gi-mil-lu* A LÚ.SIMUG URU *šaḫ-ri-*[*in-nu*]
21 ITI.AB UD.22.KAM MU.17.KAM ^{m}*da-*[*ri-ia-muš*]
22 LUGAL TIN.TIR.KI *u* KUR.KUR.MEŠ 1-*en*.TA.ÀM
23 *il-qu-ú*

TRANSLATION

[A deb]t of thirty-five *kor* of date[s (and) half a mina] of marked silver is owed to Madānu-[bēla-uṣur, the sla]ve of MNA$_1$, [b]y Nergal-uballiṭ, son of Bēl-[iddin], and ^{f}Qunnabi, his mother, daughter of Aḫ[ḫē- iddin], wife of Bēl-iddin. Half the mi[na] of silver Madānu-bēla-uṣur has recei[ved] from Nergal-uballiṭ, [son of] Bēl-iddin, and ^{f}Qunnabi, his mother; and Madānu-bēla-uṣur has (also) received 3.2.3 *kor* of barley from hi[s] credit claim that is charged against Bēl-iddin, father of Nergal-uballiṭ, from Nergal-uballiṭ and his mother ^{f}Qunnabi, wife of Bēl-[iddin].

Witnesses:
Ea-iddin/Šamaš-iddin//⌜x⌝-[...]
Niqūdu/Nergal-iddin//N[ūr-zanu]
Nergal-iddin/Rīmūt-Bēl
[^{m}...]/Baniya
Šullumaya/Balāṭu
Kuṣuraya/Arrabi
Kāṣir/Balāṭu
The scribe: Iddin-Nergal/Gimillu//Nappāḫu
(Place + Date).

They have taken one (copy of the document) each.

COMMENT

L. 9: *ina rašûtu ša Madānu-*[*bēla-uṣur*] was above translated "from hi[s] credit claim" rather than "from Madānu-[bēla-uṣur]'s credit claim for reasons of clarity.

L. 11: There is not enough space at the end of the line for the affiliation of Nergal-uballiṭ.

L. 14: The sign at the end of the line resembles the beginning of either BE or NA.

L. 15: For this Niqūdu and the meaning of his family name, more at Dar 308: 15.

No. 125

Dar 453⁺

Museum No.: BM 31423 (= Dar 453) + BM 31726

Date: 24/x/17 Dar (31 January 504 B.C.E.)

Place: Babylon

Content: Fixation of interest and pledge of property for a silver debt. Silver due to Šaddinnu from MNA. Background: cf. Dar 315.

OBV.

1 10½ MA.NA 5 GÍN KÙ.BABBAR *šá ina* 1 GÍN *bit-qa nu-uḫ-ḫu-tu*

2 *šá* ^{m}*šad-din-nu* DUMU *šá* ^{md}DI.KU$_{5}$-ŠEŠ.MEŠ-SUM.NA DUMU ^{m}*ši-gu-ú-a*

3 ⸢*ina*⸣ UGU ^{md}AMAR.UTU-*na-ṣir*-IBILA DUMU *šá* ^{m}KI-^{d}AMAR.UTU-DIN DUMU ^{m}[*e-gi-bi*]

4 [*šá* IT]I *ina muḫ*-[*ḫi* KÙ.BABBAR-*a*$_{4}$] 10½ MA.NA 5 GÍN

5 *ul-tu* ITI.ZÍZ *i*[*na muḫ-ḫi-šú*] *i-rab-bi* ⸢KÙ.BABBAR⸣ *šu-a-tì*

6 *a-di* 3⅔ MA.NA [5 GÍ]N KÙ.BABBAR <*ri*>-*ḫi*-{*iḫ*}-*it ú-ìl-tì*

7 *šá* ŠÁM SUM.SAR *šá* ⸢MU⸣.11.KAM ^{m}*da-a-ri-ia-muš* LUGAL

8 [*šá*] ^{m}*šad-din-nu* ⸢*šá*⸣ [x x x] ^{md}AMAR.UTU-*na-ṣir*-IBILA

9 [*im-ḫ*]*u-r*[*u-u'* ŠE.NUMUN-*šú šá ina*] ⸢URU⸣ É-^{m}*ḫa-aḫ-ḫu-ru*

10 [*šá* ÚS.SA.DU ^{m}ÌR-AMAR].[UTU] DUMU *šá* ^{md}U.GUR-NUMUN-DÙ$^{!}$

11 [...] ⸢x⸣ ^{m}*šad-din-nu*

LO. E.

12 [... 10½] [M]A.⸢NA⸣ 5 GÍN KÙ.BABBAR *ù* UR.RA$_{5}$-*šú*

13 [*in-n*]*i*-⸢*iṭ*⸣-*ṭi-ru*

REV.

14 [LÚ *mu-kin-nu* ^{m}]^{d}AG-*ku-ṣur-šú* DUMU *šá* ^{md}IDIM-NUMUN-BA-*šá*

15 [DUMU ^{m}*ba-bu-tú*] ^{m}*za-an*-[*zi*]-*ri* DUMU *šá* ^{md}[AG]-A-MU

16 [DUMU] ^{md}IDIM-*pat-t*[*an-nu* ^{m}K]I$^{?}$-^{d}EN-*lum-mir* DUMU *šá*

17 ^{md}EN-*ki*-⸢*šìr*⸣ [A ^{md}30-*šá-du*]-*nu* ^{m}SILIM-*im*-^{d}AMAR.UTU

18 DUMU *šá* ^{m}⸢*mu*⸣-[*šeb-ši* DUMU ^{m}*na-b*]*u-un-na-a-a* ^{md}AG-DIB-UD.DA

19 DUMU *šá* ^{m}MU-^{d}E[N DUMU ^{m}LÚ-PA.ŠE.KI] ^{md}EN-*it-tan-nu* DUMU *šá* ^{md}AG-URU$_{3}$-*šú* DUMU LÚ.SANGA-^{d}IDIM

20 $^{[m]}$KAR-^{d}EN DUMU *šá* [^{md}UTU]-ŠEŠ-MU DUMU LÚ-PA.ŠE.KI

21 [^{m}*gi*]-*mil-lu* DUMU *šá* ^{md}EN-SUM.NA DUMU ^{m}*e-gì-bi* ⸢^{m}⸣*ḫa-ad-da-a*

22 [DUMU *šá* ^{m}]⸢*ni*⸣-*qu-du* DUMU ^{m}*maš-tuk* ^{md}EN-MU DUMU *šá* ^{m}ŠEŠ.MEŠ-MU-^{d}AMAR.UTU

23 DUMU LÚ.SANGA-^{d}INNIN-TIN.TIR.KI ^{m}*ki-din*-A DUMU *šá* ^{md}EN-MU DUMU ^{m}ÌR-^{d}IDIM
24 ^{md}EN-SUM.NA DUB.SAR DUMU LÚ.SIPA-*si-si-i* TIN.TIR.KI
25 ITI.AB UD.24.KAM MU.17.KAM ^{m}*da-a-ri-ia-muš*
U. E.
26 LUGAL TIN.TIR.KI LUGAL KUR.KUR
27 NA$_{4}$.KIŠIB (seal impression) ^{md}EN-SUM.NA DUB.SAR

Translation

Ten and a half minas and five shekels of medium-quality silver, of which one-eighth is alloy, are due to Šaddinnu, son of Madānu-aḫḫē-iddin, descendant of Šigûa, from MNA$_{1}$. On [these] ten and a half minas and five shekels [of silver] (interest) will accrue ag[ainst him] (at the rate of one shekel per mina) [per m]onth from Addar on. The said ⸢silver⸣, together with three minas and forty-[five] shekels of silver, is the <re>mainder of a debt (that resulted) from the purchase of the onions of King Darius' eleventh ⸢year⸣, [which] Šaddinnu, who is in char[ge of the lease (administration)], [so]l[d to] MNA$_{1}$. [His acreage that is in] Bīt-Ḫaḫḫuru [next to Arad-Mar][duk], son of Nergal-zēra-ibni$^{!}$ [(…) is pledged t]o Šaddinnu [till these ten and a half m]⸢inas⸣ and five shekels [of silver] and its interest [will have] been paid off.

[Witnesses]:
Nabû-kuṣuršu/Ea-zēra-iqīša[//Bābūtu]
Zanzīru/[Nabû]-apla-iddin[//]Ea-patt[annu]
[Itt]i$^{?}$-Bēl-lummir/Bēl-kē⸢šir⸣[//Sîn-šadû]nu
Mušallim-Marduk/⸢Mu⸣[šebši][//Nab]unnaya
Nabû-mušētiq-uddê/Iddin-Bē[l][//Amēl-Isin]
Bēl-ittannu/Nabû-uṣuršu//Šangû-Ea
Mušēzib-Bēl/[Šamaš]-aḫa-iddin//Amēl-Isin
[Gi]millu/Bēl-iddin//Egibi
Ḫaddaya[/]Niqūdu//Maštuk
Bēl-iddin/Aḫḫē-iddin-Marduk//Šangû-Ištar-Bābili
Kidin-apli/Bēl-iddin//Arad-Ea
The scribe: Bēl-iddin//Rē'i-sīsî
(Place + Date).
Seal of Bēl-iddin, the scribe

Comment

L. 4–5: These lines contain the clause concerning interest that in its full version should have read: [*šá* IT]I *ina muḫ-*[*ḫi* (1 *ma-ni-e* 1 GÍN *ina* UGU) KÙ.BABBAR-*a*$_{4}$] 10½ MA.NA 5 GÍN *ul-tu* ITI.ZÍZ *i*[*na muḫ-ḫi-šú*] *i-rab-bi*.

L. 6: The amount was 3⅔ MA.NA 5 GÍN, cf. Dar 472.

L. 8–9a: I suggest reading *šá* [GIŠ.BÁN *a-na*] MNA [*imḫ*]*ur*[*u*], on the basis of the parallel in Dar 315: 6–8.

L. 9: For the history of this land in Bīt-Ḫaḫḫuru, see also BM 33122 (esp. lines 8–13), and Wunsch, *Felder* 1, 158–61.

L. 10: The DÙ in ^{md}U.GUR-NUMUN-DÙ$^{!}$ is rather a PAP because it lacks the small vertical wedge in the middle necessary for a DÙ. The emendation, however, cannot be doubted because [Arad]-Marduk/Nergal-zēra-ibni was a neighbor of the Egibis in Bīt-Ḫaḫḫuru according to BM 33122: 12.

L. 11: This line was no doubt added by the scribe at a later stage; in fact, it is squeezed at the very end of the obverse. The spaces between the signs are larger than usual, and the signs of the name Šaddinnu are stretched horizontally to have them fit into the narrow space that was available at the edge of the obverse.

L. 12–13: These lines contain a shortened version of the so-called "*rašû*-clause," which normally reads ^{lú}*rašû šanamma ina muḫḫi ul išallaṭ adi* PN (= creditor) *kasapšu* (amount, *u ḫubullašu*) *inneṭṭiru* (cf. Petschow, *Pfandrecht*, 96ff. and n. 288). It is impossible to fit this entire clause into lines 12–13, and we must, therefore, assume that the scribe used a shortened version of the clause in question (cf. lines 4–5 regarding the interest-clause). In view of the amount of space that is available at the beginning of line 12, I suggest reading (12) [*a-di* KÙ.BABBAR-*šú* 10½ M]A.⸢NA⸣ etc. Clearly, from the end of line 10 onward till the beginning of the list of witnesses on the reverse of the tablet, the scribe made several mistakes.

L. 14–24: For the reconstruction of some of the names in the list of witnesses see BM 33959: 12–16.

No. 126

Dar 455
Museum No.: BM 30863
Date: 15/xi/17 Dar (20 February 504 B.C.E.)
Place: Babylon
Content: Fixation of interest for a silver debt by MNA.

OBV.

50 GÍN KÙ.BABBAR UD-*ú šá ina* 1 GÍN *bit-qa nu-uḫ-ḫu-tu*
šá ^{md}EN-SUM.NA DUMU-*šú šá* ^{m}*mu-še-zib*-^{d}AMAR.UTU
A ^{md}30-*na-din*-MU *ina muḫ-ḫi* ^{md}AMAR.UTU-*na-ṣir*-A
DUMU-*šú šá* ^{m}KI-^{d}AMAR.UTU-DIN DUMU ^{m}*e-gi-bi*
KÙ.BABBAR *ri-ḫi-it ú-ìl-tì šá* 2⅔ MA.NA
⸢*i-na*⸣ UD.1.KAM *šá* ITI.BÁR *šá* MU.18.KAM
šá ITI *a-na* UGU 1 *ma-ni-e* 1 GÍN [KÙ.BABBAR]
ina muḫ-ḫi-šú i-rab-bi

LO. E.

LÚ *mu-kin-nu* ^{md}AMAR.UTU-*mu-bal-liṭ-su*
A-*šú šá* ^{md}AG-⸢KAR⸣-ZI.MEŠ

REV.

11 DUMU* ^{md}30-*tab-ni*-URU$_3$ ^{m}SUM.NA-^{d}AMAR.UTU DUMU-*šú šá*

12 ^{md}AG-GI DUMU ^{md}30-*na-din*-[MU] ^{md}AG-MU-⸢SUM.NA⸣

13 DUMU-*šú šá* ^{m}DUB-NUMUN DUMU ^{m}*de-ki-i* ^{m}*pur-šu-ú*

14 DUMU-*šú šá* ^{m}KI-^{d}AMAR.UTU-DIN DUMU ^{m}*e-gi-bi*

15 ^{m}*mu-ra-šu-ú* DUMU-*šú šá* ^{md}AG-ŠEŠ.MEŠ-MU

16 DUMU ^{md}ŠEŠ.KI-Ú.TU ^{md}AG-*ú-ṣur-šú*

17 DUB.SAR DUMU-*šú šá* ^{m}*kit-ti-ia* A LÚ.SANGA-^{d}IDIM

18 TIN.TIR.KI ITI.ZÍZ UD.15.KAM MU.17.KAM

19 ^{m}*da-a-ri-ia-muš* LUGAL TIN.TIR.KI

20 LUGAL KUR.KUR

U. E.

21 NA$_4$.KIŠIB ^{md}AMAR.UTU<-*mu*>-*bal-liṭ-su* DUB.SAR (there is no seal impression)

TRANSLATION

Fifty shekels of white, medium-quality silver, of which one-eighth is alloy, are due to Bēl-iddin, son of Mušēzib-Marduk, descendant of Sîn-nādin-šumi, from MNA$_1$. The silver is the remainder of a debt of two and two-third minas. From the first of Nisan of the eighteenth year interest will accrue against him (at the rate of) one shekel of silver per mina per month.

Witnesses:
Marduk-muballissu/Nabû-⸢ēṭir⸣-napšāti/Sîn-tabni-uṣur
Iddin-Marduk/Nabû-ušallim//Sîn-[nādin]-šumi
Nabû-šuma-⸢iddin⸣/Šāpik-zēri//Dēkû
Puršû/Itti-Marduk-balāṭu//Egibi
Murašû/Nabû-aḫḫē-iddin//Nanna-utu
The scribe: Nabû-uṣuršu/Kittiya//Šangû-Ea
(Place + Date).
Seal of Marduk<-mu>ballissu, the scribe

COMMENT

For the debt recorded in this text and its likely relation to the Esagil temple, more at Dar 437.

L. 21: The first witness, Marduk-muballissu, sealed the document and the legend on his seal reveals that he was a professional scribe. More on this person and his relationship with MNA as reflected in Dar 469 at Wunsch, *Felder* 1, 165f. However, he did not write the present document, because it is clear from lines 16–17 that Nabû-uṣuršu wrote it.

No. 127

	Dar 459
Museum No.:	BM 33958
Date:	7/xii/17 Dar (14 March 504 B.C.E.)
Place:	Šaḫrīnu
Content:	Promissory note to pay a debt of barley to MNA's slave. Reference to additional outstanding debts.

OBV.

1 ⸢3$^{?}$⸣ (PI) 2 (BÁN) ŠE.BAR *šá* ^{md}DI.KU$_5$-EN-[URU$_3$]
2 LÚ *qal-la šá* ^{md}AMAR.UTU-*na*-⸢*ṣir*⸣-[A A ^{m}*e-gi-bi*]
3 *ina muḫ-ḫi* ^{md}U.GUR-DIN-*iṭ* A-*šú šá* [^{md}EN-MU *u* ^{f}*qu-un-na-bi*]
4 DUMU.MÍ-*su šá* ^{m}ŠEŠ.MEŠ-MU AMA-*šú ina* ITI.GU$_4$ [ŠE.BAR *ga-m*]*ir**-*tu*$_4^{*}$
5 *ina ma-ši-ḫu šá* ^{md}DI.KU$_5$-EN-PAB *ina muḫ-ḫi*
6 1-*et rit-tu*$_4$ *ina* É ^{md}DI.KU$_5$-EN-URU$_3$
7 *i-nam-din-nu-u'* 1-*en pu-ut* 2-*i na-šu-ú šá qe-reb* ŠE.BAR *id-dan e-lat ra-šu-tu* IGI*-*tu*$_4^{*}$
8 *šá ina muḫ-ḫi* ^{md}U.GUR-DIN-*iṭ u* ^{f}*qu*-⸢*un**-*na**-*bi**⸣ {AMA*-*šú**}
9 AMA-*šú u e-lat ra-šu-tu* [(*maḫrītu*) *ša ina muḫḫi*]
10 ^{md}EN-MU AD ^{m}[^{d}U.GUR-DIN-*iṭ*]

REV.

11 LÚ *mu-kin-nu* ^{m}*ni-qu-*[*du* A-*šú šá* ^{md}U.GUR-MU]
12 A ^{m}*nu-úr-za**-*na* ^{md}EN-[...]
13 A-*šú šá* ^{m}*ni-qu-du* A ^{m}LÚ.GAL-⸢DÙ⸣ [(...)]
14 ^{md}EN-*ik-ṣur* A-*šú* šá ^{m}MU-^{d}EN A ^{m}[...]
15 ^{md}U.GUR-MU A-*šú šá* ^{m}EN-*šú-nu*
16 ^{md}EN-MU A-*šú šá* ^{m}KAR-^{d}EN
17 A LÚ.ŠU.KU$_6$
18 LÚ.UMBISAG ^{m}MU-^{d}U.GUR A-*šú šá* ^{m}*gi-mil-lu*
19 A LÚ.SIMUG URU *šaḫ-ri-nu*
20 ITI.ŠE UD.7.KAM MU.17.KAM
21 ^{m}*da-ri-'i-šú* LUGAL E.[KI *u* KUR.KUR]

TRANSLATION

0.⸢3$^{?}$⸣.2 *kor* of barley are due to Madānu-bēla-[uṣur], a slave of MNA$_1$, from Nergal-uballiṭ, son of [Bēl-iddin, and ^{f}Qunnabi], his mother, daughter of Aḫḫē-iddin. In Ayyar they will deliver [the full am]ount of barley in one installment in Madānu-bēla-uṣur's house, according to Madānu-bēla-uṣur's measure. They assume warranty for each other. The one who is closest to the barley shall deliver (it). In addition, there is a previous credit claim charged against Nergal-uballiṭ and ^{f}Qu⸢nnabi⸣, {his mother} his mother, and still another credit claim [charged against] Bēl-iddin, father [of Nergal-uballiṭ].

Witnesses:
Niqū[du/Nergal-iddin]//Nūr-zana
Bēl-[ikṣur]/Niqūdu//Rab-⸢banê⸣ [(...)]
Bēl-ikṣur/Iddin-Bēl//^{m}[...]
Nergal-iddin/Bēlšunu
Bēl-iddin/Mušēzib-Bēl//Bā'iru
The scribe: Iddin-Nergal/Gimillu//Nappāḫu
(Place + Date).

COMMENT

L. 4: The scribe continued writing [ŠE.BAR *ga-m*]*ir-tu*$_4$ on the edge of the tablet, but these signs have not been copied by Strassmaier (cf. lines 7–8).

L. 7–8: The scribe wrote IGI-*tu*$_4$ on a new line on the edge and reverse of the tablet, but this cannot be seen in Strassmaier's copy. The same applies to AMA-*šú* at the end of line 8.

L. 12: For this Niqūdu and his surname Nūr-zana, more at Dar 308: 15. For Bēl-ikṣur/Niqūdu//Rab-banê, see Tallqvist, *NbN* 36 s.v. Bēl-ikṣur(7).

No. 128

Dar 472 (= Dupl. of BM 31977)
Museum No.: BM 31869
Date: 3/x/18 Dar (30 December 504 B.C.E.)
Place: Babylon
Content: Receipt of silver paid on behalf of MNA. Payment of a debt due to Šaddinnu.

OBV.

1 3⅔ MA.NA 5 GÍN KÙ.BABBAR UD-*ú nu-uḫ-ḫu-tu*
2 *šá ina* 1 GÍN *bit-qa šá* ^{m}*šad-din-nu* A-*šú šá* ^{md}DI.KU$_5$-ŠEŠ.MEŠ-MU
3 A ^{m}*ši-gu-ú-a i-na ra-šu-tu-šú šá ina muḫ-ḫi*
4 ^{md}AMAR.UTU-*na-ṣir*-A A-*šú šá* ^{m}KI-^{d}AMAR.UTU-DIN A ^{m}*e-gì-bi*
5 [*ina* ŠU.II] ^{m}*ni-din-tu*$_4$ A-*šú šá* ^{m}IDIM-*iá* A ^{m}*ir-a-nu*! *a-na muḫ-ḫi*
6 [^{md}AMAR.UTU]-⸢*na*⸣-*ṣir*-A ^{m}*šad-din-nu ina* ŠU.II ^{m}*ni-din-tu*$_4$
7 [*ma-ḫi-ir* 1-*en-na*].⸢TA⸣.ÀM *šá-ṭa-ri* TI-*ú*
8 [LÚ *mu-kin-nu* ^{m}KI]-^{d}AG-DIN A-*šú šá* ^{md}AG-NUMUN-BA-*šá*
9 [^{md}EN-DÙ-*iá* A-*šú šá*] ^{m}GAR-MU A ^{m}*ir*-⸢*a*⸣-[*nu*/*i*]
10 [^{m}KAR-^{d}EN A-*šú šá*] ^{md}UTU-ŠEŠ-⸢MU⸣ [A LÚ.PA.ŠE.KI]

LO. E.

?11 [...]

REV.

12 [...]
13 [...]
14 [...]

15 [… SIM]UG
16 […]-KÁ
17 ⸢^{m}*šul-lu-mu* A-*šú šá* ^{m}DUB-NUMUN⸣ A ^{m}ZALAG$_2$-^{d}ŠÚ
18 ^{md}EN-GI A-*šú šá* ^{md}EN-MU A ^{m}ÌR-^{d}IDIM
19 ^{md}AMAR.UTU-DIN-*su*-E A-*šú šá* ^{m}*i-qu-pu* A ^{m}*e-tel-pi*
20 ^{m}DÙ-NUMUN A-*šú šá* ^{m}DUB-NUMUN A ^{m}LÚ.SANGA-^{d}30
21 LÚ.UMBISAG ^{m}KI-^{d}AG-DIN A-*šú šá* ^{md}AMAR.UTU-*re-man-ni* TIN.TIR.KI
22 ITI.AB UD.3.KAM MU.18.KAM ^{m}*da-a-ri-ia-muš*
23 LUGAL E.KI *u* KUR.KUR.MEŠ

Translation

Three minas and forty-five shekels of white, medium-quality silver, of which one-eighth is alloy, are due to Šaddinnu, son of Madānu-aḫḫē-iddin, descendant of Šigûa, from his credit claim that is charged against MNA$_1$: [from the hands of] Nidintu, son of Kabtiya, descendant of Ir'anni, - Šaddinnu [has received (it)] from Nidintu for the account of MNA$_1$. They have taken [one] (copy of the document) each.

(For a complete list of witnesses, see at BM 31977.)

The scribe: Itti-Nabû-balāṭu/Marduk-rēmanni

(Place + Date).

Comment

Dar 472 and BM 31977 differ in the following respects. First, the obverse, the reverse, and the edges of Dar 472 are fully inscribed, whereas BM 31977 has no writing on the edges, except for one line on the lower edge and two signs on the right edge (see at lines 5 and 21). Second, the scribe of Dar 472 left almost no blank space between his signs, whereas the scribe of BM 31977 has nicely spaced signs, and even left relatively large blank spaces in a few cases, as may be seen in lines 14, 17–18, and 20 (for details, see comment at BM 31977). Third, the scribes divided the text differently on the obverse of their tablets. In fact, the scribe of BM 31977 wrote *ina* 1 GÍN *bit-qa* at the end of line 1, and not at the beginning of line 2 as did the scribe of Dar 472. In this way, he could continue writing in a more "relaxed" way, i.e., he did not have to fit as much text in line 2 and the following lines as did the scribe of Dar 472 (see especially in lines 6–7). Moreover, he could leave the edges empty, whereas the one of Dar 472 had to use all space available on the tablet. Finally, there are a few differences in spelling: ^{m}*ir-a-nu* (Dar 472: 5) vs. ^{m}*ir-a-ni* (BM 31977: 5), and ^{m}*da-a-ri-a-muš* (Dar 472: 22) vs. ^{m}*da-ri-ia-muš* (BM 31977: 22).

L. 5: From the duplicate BM 31977 we know that we have to reconstruct [*ina* ŠU.II] at the beginning of this line; remarkably, the same expression is repeated at the end of line 6.

Left Edge: This edge is completely broken off, so that line 11 may have been written on the reverse rather than on the left edge.

No. 129

	Dar 509 (= Dupl. of BM 33962)
Museum No.:	BM 30448
Date:	8/ix/20 Dar (13 December 502 B.C.E.)
Place:	Babylon
Content:	Summons to settle debts with MNA.

OBV.

1 *a-di-i* UD.10.KAM *šá* ITI.⸢ZÍZ⸣ MU.20.<KAM> ^{m}*da-a-ri-iá-muš* LUGAL
2 ^{md}EN-NIGIN-*ir* A-*šú šá* ^{md}U.GUR-MU *mim-mu iṭ*-⸢*ri*⸣*-[x]*
3 *šá ú-ìl-tì šá* KÙ.BABBAR ŠE.BAR ZÚ.LUM.MA *ù* GU$_4$ *šá* ^{md}DI.KU$_5$-EN-URU$_3$
4 LÚ *qal-la šá* ^{md}AMAR.UTU-*na-din*-A A-*šú šá* ^{m}KI-^{d}AMAR.UTU-DIN A ^{m}*e-gì-bi*
5 *šá ina muḫ-ḫi-šú i-na-áš-šam-ma a-na* ^{md}AMAR.UTU-*na-din*-A
6 A-*šú šá* ^{m}KI-^{d}AMAR.UTU-DIN A ^{m}*e-gi-bi ú-kal-lam ki-i*
7 UD.15.KAM *šá* ITI.ZÍZ MU.20.KAM *mim-mu e-ṭè-ru*
8 *šá ú-ìl-tì šá* KÙ.BABBAR ŠE.BAR ZÚ.LUM.MA GU$_4$ *šá* ^{md}DI.KU$_5$-EN-URU$_3$
9 *šá ina muḫ-ḫi-šú a-na* ^{md}AMAR.UTU-*na-din*-A *la uk-tal-li-mu*
10 *a-ki-i ú-ìl-tì*.MEŠ *šá* KÙ.BABBAR ŠE.BAR ZÚ.LUM.MA GU$_4$ *šá* ^{md}DI.KU$_5$-EN-URU$_3$
11 LÚ *qal-la šá* ^{md}AMAR.UTU-*na-ṣir**-A *šá ina muḫ-ḫi-šú a-na*
12 ^{md}AMAR.UTU-*na-din*-A A-*šú šá* ^{m}KI-^{d}AMAR.UTU-DIN A ^{m}*e-gi-bi*
13 [KÙ.BABB]AR *šá* ^{md}DI.KU$_5$-EN-URU$_3$ *iṭ-ṭi-ir*

REV.

14 LÚ *mu-kin-nu* ^{m}*ta-at-tan-nu* A-*šú šá* ^{m}SU-^{d}AMAR.UTU A ^{md}AMAR.UTU-I*
15 ^{m}*i-qu-pu* A-*šú šá* ^{m}MU-^{d}EN A ^{m}ZALAG$_2$-^{d}30 ^{m}*bu-na-nu*
16 A-*šú šá* ^{m}*su-qa-a-a* A ^{md}30-*ga-mil* ^{m}NUMUN-*ia*
17 A-*šú šá* ^{m}BA-*šá-a* A ^{m}*ši-gu-ú-a* ^{m}*zu-um-ba-a*
18 A-*šú šá* ^{m}*kur-ban-ni*-^{d}ŠÚ (erasure) A ^{m}*bi-ib-bu-ú-a*
19 ^{md}AG-*it-tan-nu* A-*šú šá* ^{md}EN-DIN-*iṭ* A ^{m}LÚ.A.ZU
20 ^{m}*šu-lum*-E.KI A-*šú šá* ^{md}AG-MU-MU ^{m}*nap-sa-an*
21 A-*šú šá* ^{md}U.GUR-DIN-*iṭ* A ^{m}SIG$_{15}$-^{d}IŠKUR
22 ^{m}*ni-din-tu*$_4$ A-*šú šá* ^{m}*mi-it-ra-a-ta* ^{m}*mu-še-zib*-^{d}AMAR.UTU
23 LÚ.UMBISAG A-*šú šá* ^{m}MU-GIN TIN.TIR.KI ITI.GAN UD.8.KAM
24 MU.20.KAM ^{m}*da-a-ri-ia-muš* LUGAL TIN.TIR.KI
25 LUGAL KUR.KUR

Translation

Until the tenth of Šabāṭ of King Darius' twentie<th> year can Bēl-upaḫḫir, son of Nergal-iddin, bring (evidence) on whatever he ⸢has⸣ pai[d] of the debt of silver, barley, dates and cattle that he owes to Madānu-bēla-uṣur, a slave of MNA$_1$; and he will show (it) to MNA$_1$. If on the ⸢fifteenth⸣ of Šabāṭ he has not shown to MNA what has been paid of the debt of silver, barley, dates (and) cattle that he owes to Madānu-bēla-uṣur, he will have to pay ⸢the silver⸣ of Madānu-bēla-uṣur to MNA$_1$ according to the promissory notes for silver, barley, dates (and) cattle that he owes to Madānu-bēla-uṣur, slave of MNA$_1$.

Witnesses:
Tattannu/Erība-{x}Marduk//Marduk-nā'id
Iqūpu/Iddin-Bēl//Nūr-Sîn
Būnānu/Sūqaya//Sîn-gamil
Zēriya/Iqīšaya//Šigûa
Zumbaya/Kurbanni-Marduk//Bibbûa
Nabû-ittannu/Bēl-uballiṭ//Asû
Šulum-Bābili/Nabû-šuma-iddin
Napsān/Nergal-uballiṭ//Mudammiq-Adad
Nidintu/Mitrāta
The scribe: Mušēzib-Marduk/Šuma-ukīn(//Bābūtu)
(Place + Date).

Comment

Dar 509 and BM 33962 are duplicates. When trying to determine which was the original and which the copy (or, perhaps they were both copies from a third source?), the following observations are to be made.

1. The scribe who wrote Dar 509 organized his tablet as follows: the lower, upper, and left edges are uninscribed. The right edge is inscribed as follows: LUGAL (l. 1), [x] (l. 2), .KU$_5$-EN-URU$_3$ (l. 3), *-gì-bi* (l. 4), -EN-URU$_3$ (l. 10), and -I* (l. 14; the wedges of the preceding AMAR.UTU are very small to make them fit into the little space available). Some lines are shorter than usual, viz. lines 13, 21, and 25. The witness list, starting in line 15, is separated from the rest of the text by some extra spacing, viz. between lines 14–15. Superfluous wedges, including those due to a scribal correction, are visible in line 11; there is an erasure in line 18.

2. The scribe who wrote BM 33962 organized his tablet as follows: the upper edge is empty, but the lower and the left edges are inscribed. The right edge of the tablet is now broken off in lines 1–5 and lines 21–24, so that we cannot know whether it was inscribed. Where preserved, it is inscribed with only a few signs: *ṣ[ir*-A] (l. 11), (⸢*ú-a*⸣ (l. 19), ⸢-I⸣ (l. 15), and *-mil* (l. 17).

3. The two scribes differed in their spelling habits in the following cases: *mim-mu* (Dar 509: 7) vs. *mim-ma šá* (BM 33962: 7); *ú-ìl-tì*.MEŠ (Dar 509: 10) vs. *ú-ìl-tì* (BM 33962: 10); TIN.TIR.KI (Dar 509: 24) vs. E.KI (BM 33962: 24); and note also <KAM> (Dar 509: 1) vs. KAM (BM 33962: 1).

4. A major difference occurs in line 10. In BM 33962 the line ends with GU$_4$. The scribe could have written two more signs and have continued on the right edge; instead, he left this space empty and continued on the next line with ^{md}DI.KU$_5$-EN-URU$_3$. The scribe of Dar 509 divided the text in a different way: he wrote ^{md}DI.KU$_5$-EN-URU$_3$ at the end of line 10, using all space available, viz. till the end of the right edge. In this way, he could continue writing in a more "relaxed" way (cf. Dar 472), viz. he did not have to fit too many signs on one line (e.g., the short lines 13 and 21), did not have to continue writing on the right edge to finish a word (after line 10 it is, indeed, empty), and could leave more space between the lines (e.g., between lines 14–15). Similarly, he could leave the lower, upper and left edges empty.

5. Another major difference is found in the list of witnesses. Generally, the list of witnesses in both texts is identical, i.e., the same names are listed in the same order. However, there is one remarkable exception, viz. regarding Nidintu/Mitrāta, last witness in Dar 509 (l. 22). He is not found in BM 33962, at least not where we would have expected him, viz. in line 22 at the end of the list. Instead, his name occurs on the left edge of BM 33962. This means that his name was added later. Is Dar 509 a "revised improved edition," putting Nidintu's name were it should have been, viz. among the witnesses? Or, was it the other way around: Nidintu's name was originally listed as last witness, but forgotten by the scribe of BM 33962, who added his name on the left edge when he realized his mistake? This one example confirms how complicated it is to understand the relation between duplicate texts.

6. The scribes erred in writing the personal name of Madānu-bēla-uṣur's owner. They consistently wrote *-na-din-* instead of *-na-ṣir-* (Dar 509: 4, 5, 9, and 12; cf. duplicate BM 33962, where preserved). Only in Dar 509: 11 did the scribe try to correct his mistake: the ṢIR-sign is written over a partly erased *-din-*A; one can still clearly see the double head of the original A-sign after the *ṣir*. The parallel passage in the duplicate is damaged (BM 33962: 11 end, *-d*[*in-*...] or *-ṣ*[*ir-* ...]).

In addition, note that I preferred to translate the clause *u'iltu ša ... ša MBU ša ina muḫḫišu*, which occurs three times in Dar 509 (//BM 33962) as follows: "the debt of ... which he owes to MBU." Literally, it means "the promissory note for .... belonging to MBU, which is charged against him."

Finally, it should be pointed out that Madānu-bēla-uṣur, one of MNA's senior slaves, had probably already died at the time at when this document was drawn up (Wunsch, *Iddin-Marduk* 1, 45–49, esp. n. 189). In this document, as well as in several others, MNA took care of the affairs that had been administered by his slave during his lifetime, but that had not been settled before his death (also BM 30965, BM 31360, BM 31976; and Dar 541: MNA togather with MBU's son).

L. 11: Superfluous wedges are visible at two signs: at *-ṣir**- (explained at line 4 above), and at *ina*.

L. 18: The ŠÚ is written over (an) erased sign(s) (AMAR.UTU?), and is also followed by one erased sign.

L. 22: For the name Mitrāta, see Dandamaev, *Iranians*, 100 (198), and above at BM 30591: 11–12.

No. 130

	Dar 527
Museum No.:	BM 41438
Date:	17/vii/21 Dar (13 October 501 B.C.E.)
Place:	Bīt-ṭāb-Bēl
Content:	Promissory note to deliver dates (*imittu*-lease) from land at the Rab-kāṣir canal to MNA. One third is due to Bagasarū.

OBV.

1 60 GUR ZÚ.LUM.MA ZAG.LU ⸢BURU$_{14}$⸣ A.ŠÀ ⸢*šá*⸣
2 ⸢ÍD$^{?*}$⸣ LÚ.GAL-*ka-ṣir šá* ^{md}AMAR.UTU-PAB-A *ù*
3 ŠEŠ.MEŠ-*šú* DUMU.MEŠ *šá* ^{m}KI-^{d}AMAR.UTU-DIN A ^{m}*e-gì-bi*
4 *šá ina lìb-bi šal-šú* ḪA.LA *šá* ^{m}*ba-ak-ka-su-ru-ú*
5 LÚ *gan-za-ba-ru ina muḫ-ḫi* ^{md}EN-ŠEŠ-*it-tan-nu*
6 A-*šú-šá* ^{m}ŠEŠ.MEŠ-MU *ina* ITI.APIN ZÚ.LUM.MA-*a'*
7 60 GUR *ina* GIŠ *ma-ši-ḫu šá* ^{md}AMAR.UTU-PAB-A
8 *ina muḫ-ḫi* 1-*et* KIŠIB *ina ḫa-ṣa-ru i-nam-din*
9 *it-ti* 1 GUR *bil-*[*tú g*]*i-*⸢*pu*⸣*-ú tu-ḫal-*⸢*la**⸣
10 *man-ga-ga lìb-lìb-bi* 2-TA *da-ri-ku*
11 *i-nam-din*

LO. E.

*12 *sis-sin-nu ul e-ṭir ù* 1-KÙŠ *mis-*[*ḫu*]
13 *šá mu-še-in-ni-e-ti ul ni-iḫ-ḫi-i*[*s*]

REV.

14 LÚ *mu-kin-nu* ^{m}KI-^{d}EN-*lum-mir* A-*šú šá*
15 ^{m}*šá-*^{d}AG-*šu-ú* ^{m}*ḫaš-da-a* A-*šú šá* ^{md}AMAR.UTU-MU-MU
16 A ^{m}LÚ.SANGA-BÁR ^{m}MU-^{d}AG A-*šú šá* ^{md}AMAR.UTU-*qí-šá-an-ni*
17 A ^{m}EN-*e-ṭi-ru* ^{m}MU-^{d}EN A-*šú šá* ^{md}UTU-ŠEŠ-MU
18 ^{md}EN-MU LÚ.UMBISAG A-*šú šá* ^{md}AG-*na-din*-ŠEŠ
19 A ^{m}*na-ba-a-a* É-*ṭa-bi-*^{d}EN ITI.DU$_{6}$ UD.17.KAM
20 MU ⸢21⸣.KAM ^{m}*da-ri-ia-a-muš* LUGAL TIN.TIR.KI
21 LUGAL KUR.KUR

TRANSLATION

Sixty *kor* of *imittu*-dates, the harvest of the field that (is located) ⸢at the⸣ Rab-kāṣir canal, are due to MNA$_{1}$ and his brothers from Bēl-aḫa-ittannu, son of Aḫḫē-iddin. One-third of it is the share of Bagasarū, the Treasurer, (in the harvest). In Araḫsamna he shall deliver these sixty *kor* of dates according to MNA_1's measure, in one installment at the entrepot. For each *kor* he shall give a load of spadices, spathes ⸢and⸣ fibres, the offshoot(s), (and) two *darīku*-containers. The *sissinnu* has not been paid; and not even one cubit of the stre[tch] of the dam assigned to him for work is withdrawn.

Witnesses:
Itti-Bēl-lummir/Ša-Nabû-šū
Ḫašdaya/Marduk-šuma-iddin//Šangû-parakki
Iddin-Nabû/Marduk-(i)qīšanni//Bēl-eṭēru
Iddin-Bēl/Šamaš-aḫa-iddin
The scribe: Bēl-iddin/Nabû-nādin-aḫi//Nabaya
(Place + Date).

COMMENT

L. 9–11: In the translation of the by-products of the date palm (*in casu*: *gipû, tuḫallu, mangaga, liblibbi,* and *darīku*) that the leaseholder had to deliver in addition to the dates I follow Cocquerillat, *Palmeraies*, 31–32 (also Id., *RA* 78, 65 n. 27: *mangaga* does not refer to the spathes but to the bast), and the translations into English by Von Dassow, CTMMA 3, 58. See also Landsberger, *Date Palm*, 42–56 whose translations for *tuḫallu* and *gipû*, however, differ from the translations as given above: he translates *tuḫallu* as "palm-leaf container" (p. 48; cf. *AHw*, 1366 s.v. *tuḫallu*), and *gipû* as "date basket" (p. 55; cf. *CAD* G, 85f. s.v. *gipû* A). For translations of the by-products into English, see also Stolper, *JCS* 53, 114: *tuḫallu*-baskets, *lib*(*lib*)*bi* "fronds," *mangaga* "fibers."

L. 12–13: For *sissinnu* "payment in dates due to the cultivator of a date orchard," see *CAD* S, 326f. s.v. *sissinnu* mng. 5; also see Jursa, *Landwirtschaft*, 126. For *mušannītu* "dam, dike," see *CAD* M_2, 259 s.v. *mušannītu*, Van Driel, *BSA* 4, 136ff. and Jursa, *Landwirtschaft*, 184ff.

L. 18: The scribe left approximately one line empty before he wrote his name.

L. 20: The scribe corrected himself in this line: the 21.KAM is written over what seems to have been a MU.x. The latter was then corrected into 21.KAM and MU was added before it. However, the scribe had to write it (i.e., the MU) on the edge (i.e., the left edge), because there was no place for it on the reverse at the beginning of the line.

No. 131

Dar 541
Museum No.: BM 30822
Date: 3/iii/22 Dar (23 May 500 B.C.E.)
Place: Bīt-ṭāb-Bēl
Content: Promissory note to pay a debt of barley, silver, and browned ghee to MNA. The silver had been transferred to the debtor to pay off his creditor. Undertakings by MNA to promptly return the promissory note for previous debts to the debtor.

OBV.

1 ⸢10⸣ GUR ŠE.BAR 10 GÍN KÙ.BABBAR UD-*ú* ⸢*nu-uḫ*⸣-*ḫu*-⸢*tú*$^{?}$⸣ ⸢1-*en ni-sip*⸣
2 ⸢x⸣ *ni*-⸢x *ḫi-me-tú*⸣ *qu-li-tu*$_4$ *šá* ^{md}AMAR.UTU-*na-ṣir*-A
3 A-*šú šá* ^{m}KI-^{d}AMAR.UTU-DIN A ^{m}*e-gì-bi ina muḫ-ḫi*
4 ^{m}DÙ-*a* A-*šú šá* ^{md}U.GUR-NUMUN-DÙ *ina qí-it*
5 *šá* ITI.SIG$_4$ *šá* MU.22.KAM ^{m}*da-ri-ia-muš*
6 ŠE.BAR-*a*$_4$ 10 GUR *gam*<-*ru*>-*tì ina ma-ši-ḫu*
7 *šá* ^{md}AMAR.UTU-*na-ṣir*-A 1-*et rit-tu*$_4$
8 *ina* URU *šaḫ-ri-i-ni ina* É ^{md}AMAR.UTU-*na-ṣir*-A
9 *i-nam-din* KÙ.BABBAR-*a*$_4$ 10 GÍN UD-*ú nu-uḫ-ḫu*-[*tú*]$^{?*}$
10 1-*en ni-sip šá ḫi-me-tu*$_4$ *qu-li-tu*$_4$
11 *i-nam-din ú-ìl-tì* IGI-*tu*$_4$
12 *šá* 12 GUR ŠE.BAR ⸢*ina*⸣ SAG.DU *ù* 1-*en* x ⸢x⸣
13 ⸢*u*⸣ *ḫi-me-tu*$_4$ *qu-li-tu*$_4$ *šá* ^{md}DI.KU$_5$-⸢IBILA⸣-MU

REV.

14 *šá ina muḫ-ḫi* ^{m}DÙ-*a* ^{md}AMAR.UTU-*na-ṣir*-A
15 *ki-i ú-tir-ri a-na* ^{m}DÙ-*a it-ta-din*
16 KÙ.BABBAR-*a*$_4$ 10 GÍN UD-*ú šá a-na* ^{m}MU-^{d}AG
17 LÚ.TUKU-*ú šá* ^{m}DÙ-*a* SUM.NA LÚ *mu-kin-nu*
18 ^{md}EN-MU A-*šú šá* ^{md}AG-A-MU A ^{m}*ir-a-ni*
19 ^{md}AG-*it-tan-nu* A-*šú šá* ^{m}MU-^{d}AG A ^{m}*ir-a-ni*
20 ^{m}MU-^{d}EN A-*šú šá* ^{m}*lu*-È-*nu-úr* A ^{m}*an-da-ḫar*
21 ^{m}*bi-ba-nu* A-*šú šá* ^{md}EN-A-MU A ^{m}*ga-ḫal*
22 ^{md}AG-DIN-*iṭ* A-*šú šá* ^{m}*lu*-È-*nu-úr*
23 A ^{m}*an-da-ḫar* ^{m}MU-MU A-*šú šá* ^{m}DUB-NUMUN DUMU ^{m}*na-ba-a-a*
24 ^{m}*bul-ṭa-a* A-*šú šá* ^{m}MU-^{d}U.GUR A ^{m}DÙ-*eš*-DINGIR
25 ^{m}*zab-di-ia* A-*šú šá* ^{m}*pa-di-ia* LÚ.UMBISAG
26 ^{md}AG-A-MU A-*šú šá* ^{md}EN-MU A ^{m}*e-gì-bi*
27 URU-É-DU$_{10}$.GA-^{d}EN ITI.SIG$_4$ UD.3.KAM
28 MU.22.KAM ^{m}*da-ri-'i-muš* LUGAL E.KI
29 *u* KUR.KUR

TRANSLATION

⸢Ten⸣ *kor* of barley, ten shekels of white, ⸢medium-quality⸣ silver, {⸢one container⸣} ⸢one⸣ con⸢tainer of⸣ browned ⸢ghee⸣ are due to MNA$_1$ from Ibnaya, son of Nergal-zēra-ibni. At the end of Simān of Darius' twenty-second year he will deliver the f<u>ll ten *kor* of barley in one installment in MNA$_1$'s house in Šaḫrīnu, according to MNA$_1$'s measure. Those ten shekels of white, medium-quality silver (and) the one container of browned ghee he will deliver (immediately?). MNA$_1$ has promptly returned the previous promissory note for twelve *kor* of barley, capital amount, and the one …, and the browned ghee that were owed to Madānu-⸢apla⸣-iddin by Ibnaya, to Ibnaya. The (indebted) ten shekels of white silver are those that have been given to Iddin-Nabû, creditor of Ibnaya.

Witnesses:
Bēl-iddin/Nabû-apla-iddin//Ir'anni
Nabû-ittannu/Iddin-Nabû//Ir'anni
Iddin-Bēl/Lūṣi-(ana)-nūri//Andaḫar
Bibānu/Bēl-apla-iddin//Gaḫal
Nabû-uballiṭ/Lūṣi-(ana)-nūri//Andaḫar
Šuma-iddin/Šāpik-zēri//Nabaya
Bulṭaya/Iddin-Nergal//Eppeš-ilī
Zabdiya/Padiya
The scribe: Nabû-apla-iddin/Bēl-iddin//Egibi
(Place + Date).

COMMENT

L. 1: The signs at the end of the line, i.e., after KÙ.BABBAR UD-*ú*, are very squeezed, and it seems that *-tú* is lacking. The *-sip* is actually on the right edge.

L. 2: Probably, we have again 1-*en ni-sip* at the beginning of the line (dittography with the end of previous line). The wedges of *ḫi-me-tú* are very small and squeezed.

L. 11–15: These lines refer to debts between MNA's slave and Ibnaya, but oblige MNA (and not his slave) to take care of bringing the original promissory note to the debtor. Probably MNA and his slave are taking care of one of the promissory notes that were left by MBU, the slave's father, after his death; cf. Dar 509.

L. 13: The last two signs of this line are at its very end and on the right edge.

L. 25: Zabdiya (Zadok, *West Semites*, 115) and Padiya (*Id.*, *OLA* 28, 30 and 98) are Aramaic names.

L. 29: This line is somehow squeezed on the edge of the tablet's obverse, viz. above the GÍN KÙ.BABBAR of line 1.

No. 132

	Dar 542 (= Dupl. of Dar 534)
Museum No.:	BM 30938
Date:	20/iii/22 Dar (9 June 500 B.C.E.)
Place:	no place
Content:	Receipt of dates (*imittu*-lease) from a slave of MNA by a slave of Bagasarū

OBV.

1 ZÚ.LUM.MA ⸢ZAG.LU A.ŠÀ⸣ *šá* MU.21.KAM

2 ^{m}*da-ri-'i-muš* ⸢LUGAL ḪA⸣.LA *šá* ^{m}*ba-ga-sa-ru-ú*

3 *šá it-ti* ^{md}AMAR.UTU-PAB-A *u* ŠEŠ.MEŠ-*šú*

4 DUMU.MEŠ *šá* ^{m}KI-^{d}AMAR.UTU-DIN DUMU ^{m}*e-gi-bi*

5 ^{md}AG-*gab-bi-i-li-e* LÚ *qal-la*

6 *šá* ^{m}*ba-ga-sa-ru-ú* DUMU *šip-ri* (erasure)

7 *šá* ^{m}*pi-iš-ši-ia* LÚ.GAL É *šá* ^{m}*ba-ga-sa-ru-ú*

8 *ina* ŠU.II ^{m}*še-pát*-^{d}EN-*aṣ-bat* LÚ *qal-la šá* ^{md}AMAR.UTU-PAB-A *ma-ḫi-ir*

LO. E.

9 1-*en*.TA.ÀM TI-*ú*

REV.

10 15 GUR ZÚ.LUM.MA *ina* ŠU.II ^{m}*še-pát*-^{d}EN-⸢*aṣ-bat*⸣

11 LÚ *qal-la šá* ^{md}AMAR.UTU-PAB-A

12 ^{md}AG-*gab-bi-i-li-e*

13 *ma-ḫi-ir* LÚ *mu-kin-nu* ^{md}EN-MU

14 DUMU *šá* ^{m}*ba-si-ia* ^{m}GI-*a* DUMU *šá* (erasure)

15 ^{md}AG-*na-din*-ŠEŠ A ^{m}*na-ba-a-a*

16 ^{m}DIN DUMU *šá* ^{m}ŠEŠ-SUM.NA ^{md}AG-*ku-ṣur-šú*

17 DUMU *šá* ^{md}AMAR.UTU-SUR A $^{[m]}$LÚ.GAL-^{d}*nin-líl*

18 [(*u*) LÚ]*.UMBISAG ^{m}*ni-din-tu*$_{4}$ DUMU *šá* ^{m}*ku-ṣur-a*

U. E.

19 ITI.SIG$_{4}$ UD.20.KAM MU.22.KAM

20 [^{m}*da-ri-ia-muš* LUGAL E.KI] ⸢*u*⸣ KUR.KUR

LE. E.

21 ^{md}AG-*bul-liṭ-su* DUMU *šá* ^{m}[...]

22 A ^{md}EN-[...]

TRANSLATION

The *imittu*-dates of ⸢King⸣ Darius' twenty-first year from the field (along the Rab-kāṣir canal). It is Bagasarū's share (in the harvest) that (is shared) with MNA$_{1}$ and his brothers. Nabû-gabbi-ilī, a slave of Bagasarū, (and) a messenger of Piššiya, Bagasarū's majordomo, has received (them) from Šēpāt-Bēl-aṣbat, a slave of MNA$_{1}$. They have taken one (copy of the document) each. Fifteen kor of dates (is what) Nabû-gabbi-ilī received from Šēpat-Bēl-aṣbat, MNA$_{1}$'s slave.

Witnesses:
Bēl-iddin/Basiya
Šullumaya/Nabû-nādin-aḫi//Nabaya
Balāṭu/Aḫa-iddin
Nabû-kuṣuršu/Marduk-ēṭir//Rabâ(-ša)-Ninlil
The scribe: Nidintu/Kuṣura(pli)
(Date).

COMMENT

The surface of tablet Dar 542 is fully inscribed: obverse, lower edge, reverse, upper edge, and left edge. Every line on the obverse continues onto the right edge, and three of them continue even onto the reverse (*-sa-ru-ú* of line 2, *-sa-ru-ú* of line 7, and AMAR.UTU-PAB-A *ma-ḫi-ir* of line 8). The fact that the scribe used the reverse for lines 7 and 8 obliged him to keep lines 11 and 12 on the reverse shorter than usual. There is a long erasure from the end of line 6 onward, which continues well onto the reverse; because of this erasure, line 13 on the reverse is also kept short. There is another erasure of a few signs at the end of line 14. There are superfluous wedges (probably from scribal corrections) in line 7 (between GAL and É) and line 8 (*passim*). Further note that if the scribe had not stretched out certain signs in lines 3–5 (e.g., ŠEŠ, GI and QAL) he could have written these lines without having to use the right edge.

The first eight lines of this document record the receipt of *imittu*-dates by Bagasarū's slave from MNA's slave, but they do not state how much had been received. The statement of receipt is followed by the statement that each party had taken a copy of the document. The latter is written on the lower edge (l. 9), and usually marks the end of the operative section. It should have been followed by the list of witnesses. However, the reverse starts off with a reference to the receipt of fifteen *kor* of dates (ll. 1–13a), and only then follow the names of the witnesses (ll. 13b–17). Remarkably, it is not described as a payment "in addition to" (*elat*) the previously described payment of *imittu*-dates. Consequently, I consider it as a further specification of the latter. In other words, Bagasarū's slave received *imittu*-dates from MNA's slave (ll. 1–8), *in casu* fifteen *kor* (ll. 10–13).

Interestingly, there exists a duplicate of this text, viz. Dar 534, and the latter does not contain the said specification about the amount of dates received. Indeed, Dar 534 only records the receipt of *imittu*-dates. In other words, it contains the text of Dar 542 up till line 9. Its last sentence (i.e., line 11) is "They have taken one (copy of the document) each." For unknown reasons, the scribe did not continue writing and consequently, Dar 534 does not contain what is found on the reverse, upper edge, and left edge of Dar 542. Accordingly, most of the reverse of Dar 534 is empty. Dar 534 is a word-for-word copy of Dar 542: 1–9, with one spelling variant, viz. in line 7 (*šip-ru* vs. *šip-ri*); it does not follow the same division of lines.

Finally, we do not know where these tablets had been drafted. In line 19 we expect the name of the place where the present document had been drafted before the date formula. Had the scribe forgotten about it?

L. 1: For the location of the field, more at Dar 105: 1.

L. 7: For the name Piššiya, more at Dandamaev, *Iranians*, 114 (no. 247) and Schmitt, *Kratylos* 39, 86 (< Ir. *Pišiya or *Piθriya).

No. 133

	Dar 544
Museum No.:	BM 30661
Date:	12/iv/22$^{?}$ Dar (30 June 500 B.C.E.)
Place:	Babylon
Content:	Promissory note to pay a debt of silver. Due from MNA to a courtier.

OBV.

1 9 GÍN KÙ.BABBAR UD-*ú n*[*u*-...]
2 *šá ina* 1 GÍN *bit-qa šá* ^{md}AG-[...]
3 LÚ.SAG-LUGAL LÚ *si-pir ina mu*[*ḫ-ḫi*]
4 ^{m}*ši-iš-ki* A-*šú šá* ^{m}SUM.NA-⌈*a*⌉
5 A ^{m}*e-gì-bi* UD.12.KAM *šá* ITI.Š[E ...]
6 *i-nam-din*

REV.

7 LÚ *mu-kin-nu* ^{m}*ap-la-a*
8 A-*šú šá* ^{m}MU-^{d}AMAR.UTU A ^{m}LÚ.EN.NUN-KÁ.GAL
9 ^{md}EN-SU A-*šú šá* ^{m}*kal-ba-a* A ^{m}MU-*l*[*íb-ši*]
10 ^{md}EN-SU A-*šú šá* ^{m}KAR-^{d}AMAR.UTU A LÚ.[...]
11 LÚ.UMBISAG ^{m}*la-a-ba-ši* A-*šú šá* ^{m}[...]
12 A LÚ.EN.NUN-KÁ.GAL TIN.TIR.K[I ...]
13 ITI.ŠU UD.12.KAM MU.22$^{?}$.[KAM]
14 ^{m}*da-ri-ia-muš* LUG[AL ...]
15 LUGAL KUR.KUR

TRANSLATION

Nine shekels of white, medium-[quality] silver of which one-eighth is alloy, are due to Nabû-[...], the courtier (and) clerk, from MNA$_2$. On the twelfth of A[ddar MNA$_2$] shall pay (it).

Witnesses:
Aplaya/Iddin-Marduk//Maṣṣār-abulli
Bēl-erība/Kalbaya//Šumu-l[ibši]
Bēl-erība/Mušēzib-Marduk//LÚ [...]
The scribe: Lâbāši/[PN]//Maṣṣār-abulli
(Place + Date).

COMMENT

L. 13: The year is probably 22: MU.21+⸢x⸣.[KAM]

No. 134

	Dar 552
Museum No.:	BM 31142
Date:	1/x/22 Dar (14 December 500 B.C.E.)
Place:	Babylon
Content:	Undertaking to transmit an order (*šipirtu*) issued by Nergal-ēṭir to MNA requiring him to pay silver.

OBV.

1 ⅓ MA.NA 1 GÍN KÙ.BABBAR UD-*ú ina* ⸢x⸣-[x x]
2 *šá* ^{md}AG-*na-ta-nu* DUMU *šá* ^{m}*še-e*[*l-li-bi*]
3 *ù* ^{m}ŠEŠ-*šú-nu* DUMU *šá* ^{md}UTU-*a-a* [(...)]
4 *ina* IGI ^{m}*ši-iš-ki* DUMU *šá* ^{m}MU-*a* DUMU ^{m}⸢*e*⸣-[*gi-bi*]
5 *ina* ITI.BÁR *ši-pir-tu*$_4$ *šá* ^{md}U.GUR-SUR
6 *a-na* IGI ^{m}*ši-iš-ku i-na-áš-am-ma*
7 KÙ.BABBAR-*a*$_4$ ⅓ MA.NA 1 GÍN ^{m}*ši-iš-ku**
8 *a-na* ^{md}AG-*na-ta-nu u* ^{m}ŠEŠ-*šú-nu*
9 *i-nam-din*

REV.

10 LÚ *mu-kin-ni* ^{md}EN-A-MU DUMU *šá* ^{m}DU$_{10}$.GA-*ia*
11 DUMU ^{m}*šá-na*<-*ši*>-*šú* ^{md}AMAR.UTU-KAM DUMU *šá* ^{m}*du-muq*
12 DUMU LÚ.SIMUG ^{md}EN-SU DUMU *šá* ^{m}*kal-ba-a*
13 DUMU ^{m}MU-*líb-ši*
14 ^{md}AG-*ú-ṣur*-ZI-*tì* LÚ.UMBISAG DUMU ^{m}*ga-ḫal*
15 TIN.TIR.KI ITI.AB UD.1.KAM MU.22.KAM
16 ^{m}*da-ri-ia-muš* LUGAL TIN.TIR.KI
17 LUGAL KUR.KUR

TRANSLATION

One-third mina and one shekel of white silver from the sa[lary]? owed to Nabû-natan, son of Šel[libi], and Aḫūšunu, son of Šamšaya, are with MNA$_2$. In the month Nisan he (rd. they?) will bring the order from Nergal-ēṭir before MNA$_2$, and MNA$_2$ shall pay these one-third mina and one shekel of silver to Nabû-natan and Aḫūšunu.

Witnesses:
Bēl-apla-iddin/Ṭābiya//Ša-nā<šī>šu
Marduk-ēreš/Dummuqu//Nappāḫu
Bēl-erība/Kalbaya//Šumu-libši
The scribe: Nabû-uṣur-napišti//Gaḫal
(Place + Date).

Comment

This document is an *ina pān* promissory note. Cf. BM 30854 and discussion at BM 30270 (with bibliography). For a translation of the text under consideration, see also *CAD* $Š_3$, 66 s.v. *šipirtu* "legal document issued by officials authorizing their deputies to act for them."

Dar 552 belongs to a group of three documents that deal with related issues: Dar 552, Dar 573, and Dar 572. The former two are very similar in the information they provide. First, there is a certain amount of silver, viz. 20 shekels in Dar 552 and 10 shekels in Dar 573 (l. 1). Second, this amount is due to two pairs of two men, viz. Nabû-natan/Šellibi and Aḫūšunu/Šamšaya in Dar 552 (ll. 1–3); and Tabnêa/Nabû-ušallim and Ubār, his brother, in Dar 573 (ll. 1–2a). Note that the expression for "due to" is slightly different in the two cases: *šá* in Dar 573: 1, but *ina* ⌜x⌝[…] *šá* in Dar 552: 1–2 (more at comment to this lines). Third, the silver in question is *ina pān* MNA, i.e., "at the disposal of MNA, held on contract by MNA" (Dar 552: 4 = Dar 573: 2b–3). Fourth, MNA promises to give the said silver to the persons mentioned earlier (*ana …. inamdin*) by a certain date (Dar 552: 7–9 = Dar 573: 7b–9).

The more problematic passage in both texts is the stipulation found in Dar 552: 5–6 = Dar 573: 4–7a. It concerns a letter order, which was perhaps issued by Nergal-ēṭir (*šipirtu ša Nergal-ēṭir* in Dar 552: 5, but *šipirtu Nergal-ēṭir* without *šá* in Dar 573: 4b–6a). This order "he (sg.) will bring before MNA" (*ana/ana pāni MNA inaššâmma*, Dar 552: 6 = Dar 573: 6b–7a). The question is: Who was meant by "he"? Was it one of the men to whom the silver was due? If so, he had to bring the letter order issued by Nergal-ēṭir (*šipirtu* (*ša*) *Nergal-ēṭir inaššâmma*); yet, the texts continue by saying that MNA had to hand out the silver to both of them, viz. "to PN_1 and PN_2" (*MNA ana* PN_1 *u* PN_2 *inamdin*), and not just to one of them. Hence, it may be we have to emend and read "they shall bring" (*inaššûma*) instead of the singular "he shall bring" as given by the texts.

Another solution is to consider Nergal-ēṭir the one who had to bring a letter order and receive the silver from MNA. If so, the passage under consideration is to be translated "Nergal-ēṭir shall bring a letter order (from whom?) to MNA and MNA shall give the silver for PN_1 and PN_2 (to Nergal-ēṭir)." In another document from the archive, Nergal-ēṭir indeed appeared before MNA and received from him payment for "the salary and rations …. [of] PN_1, PN_2 and PN_3" (Dar 572).

L. 1: It is not clear what should be read at the end of the line: *ina* ⌜*ú*?⌝-[*ìl-tì*]? or perhaps *ina* ⌜*i*?⌝-[*di*]? in view of Dar 572: 5.

L. 5–6: Cf. Dar 573: 4–7 and Dar 572: 3–5. In the latter two texts Nergal-ēṭir occurs with full affiliation, viz. son of Kalbaya, descendant of Šumu-libši. Bēl-erība, his brother is among the witnesses in the present text. Nergal-ēṭir probably held a position in the royal administration, similar to his brother Bēl-erība's, who was "commander over (a contingent) of fifty (soldiers)" (BM 30274). Was he helping out his brother in organizing an expedition (to Elam?), recruiting men and supplies?

L. 6: The verb *inaššâmma* is in the singular although there are two creditors. It is, therefore, not clear which of the creditors is the subject of the verb (cf. *CAD* Š$_3$, 66 s.v. *šipirtu*). I suggest reading the verb in the plural, notwithstanding its singular form (see comment above).

L. 7–9: According to Dar 572: 5–8 MNA was to pay for salaries and rations. The silver that he pays in the text under consideration, therefore, was most likely to be used to cover similar needs.

No. 135

	Dar 572
Museum No.:	BM 31409
Date:	30/ix/23 Dar (1 January 498 B.C.E.)
Place:	broken
Content:	Receipt of payment for salaries and rations from MNA.

OBV.

1 [x x *šá* ^{md}A]G-SUM.NA *u* ^{m}ḪA.LA-^{d}AG DUMU.MEŠ
2 [*šá* ^{m}x-x(-x)] *u* ^{m}⸢*su-qa*⸣*-a-a* DUMU *šá* ^{m}*kal-ba-a*
3 [x (x) ^{md}U.GUR-KA]R-*ir* DUMU *šá* ^{m}*kal-ba-a* A ^{m}MU-*líb-ši*
4 [x x x ^{m}]*ši-ir-ku* DUMU *šá* ^{m}SUM.NA-*a* A ^{m}*e-gì-bi*
5 [x x x] *i-di ù* KURUM$_6$.ḪI.A *šá* 3 ITI.MEŠ *šá a-di* KUR.ELAM.MA.KI
6 [*šá* ^{m}]^{d}AG-MU ^{m}ḪA.LA-^{d}AG *u* ^{m}*su-qa-a-a*
7 $^{[m]d}$U.GUR-KAR-*ir ina* ŠU.II *šá* ^{m}*ši-ir-ku*
8 *e-ṭi-ir*

REV.

9 [LÚ *m*]*u-kin-nu* ^{md}AMAR.UTU-KAM DUMU *šá*
10 [^{m}*d*]*u-muq-qu* DUMU LÚ.SIMUG ^{md}EN-MU DUMU *šá*
11 [^{m}TIL-*i*]*a* DUMU LÚ.BAḪAR$_2$
12 [^{m}x(-x)]-MU A-*šú šá* ^{md}AMAR.UTU-SUR
13 [^{m}x(-x)]-^{d}EN LÚ.UMBISAG A ^{m}*na-din-še-e*
14 [... ITI].GAN UD.30.KAM MU.23.KAM
15 [^{m}*da-r*]*i-'i-muš* LUGAL E.KI *u* KUR.KUR

TRANSLATION

$^{(1–2)}$[... Na]bû-iddin and Zitti-Nabû, sons of [^{m}...], and ⸢Sūqaya⸣, son of Kalbaya, $^{(3)}$[... Nergal-ē]ṭir, son of Kalbaya, descendant of Šumu-libši, $^{(4)}$[...] MNA$_2$. $^{(5–6)}$[The silver for] the salary and rations [of] Nabû-iddin, Zitti-Nabû and Sūqaya to go to Elam for three months $^{(7–8)}$Nergal-ēṭir received from MNA$_2$.

Witnesses:
Marduk-ēreš/Dummuqu//Nappāḫu
Bēl-iddin/[Gimriy]a//Paḫāru
[...]-iddin/Marduk-ēṭir
The scribe: [Nidinti]-Bēl//Nādin-še'i
(Place + Date).

COMMENT

Dar 572 deals with a matter similar to the one dealt with in Dar 552 and Dar 573 (see comment at Dar 552 above). It concerns the salary and rations for three men travelling to Elam: Nabû-iddin, Zitti-Nabû and Sūqaya (ll. 5–6). Nergal-ēṭir received payment for their salary and rations from MNA (ll. 7–8). In this case it was clearly to Nergal-ēṭir and not to one of the men to whom MNA paid, and it is, therefore, different from the cases described in Dar 552 and Dar 573 where apparently one of the men had to come to MNA with Nergal-ēṭir's letter order and collect the silver from MNA. Further, note that the first four lines of Dar 572 are, unfortunately, fragmentary. They refer to Nergal-ēṭir, MNA, and the three men whose salary and rations were at stake. The problem is that the relation between them cannot be determined for certain, because the pertinent passages, including the main verb, are broken.

L. 1–7: Krecher suggested reconstructing the beginning of these lines as follows: (1) [KÙ.BABBAR *šá* ^{md}A]G-, (3) [*šá* ^{md}U.GUR-], (4) [*a-na muḫ-ḫi* ^{m}], (5) [*a-na*], (6) [*a-na*], (7) [*id-di*(*n*)-*nu*]. According to him, Nergal-ēṭir had paid for the salaries and rations of the three men who went to Elam; his payment had been "on behalf of MNA" (l. 4). In the end MNA reimbursed Nergal-ēṭir for the expenses (ll. 7–8). The problem is that one cannot read [*id-di*(*n*)-*nu*] at the beginning of line 7: there is not enough space available.

L. 5: The scribe wrote *šá a-di* KUR.ELAM.MA.KI on the reverse. Consequently, line 12 on the reverse is a short line.

L. 10–11: For this Bēl-iddin, see also Dar 573: 11–12.

L. 13: There is one empty line before this line.

L. 14: The number 30 is written over vertical wedges. There are two big *Winkelhaken* and a third smaller one, so that the number is, no doubt, 30.

No. 136

	Dar 573
Museum No.:	BM 30453
Date:	1/x/23 Dar (2 January 498 B.C.E.)
Place:	Pāni-abul-Enlil
Content:	Undertaking to transmit an order (*šipirtu*) issued by Nergal-ēṭir to MNA requiring him to pay silver.

OBV.

1 ⸢10⸣ GÍN KÙ.BABBAR *šá* ^{m}*tab*$^{!*}$*-ni-e-a u* $^{<m>*}$*ú-bar*

2 A.MEŠ *šá* ^{md}AG-GI *ina pa-ni* ^{m}*ši-ir-ku*

3 A-*šú šá* ^{m}SUM.NA-*a* A ^{m}*e-*⸢*gì-bi*⸣ {⸢x x⸣}*

4 <*a*>-*di* TIL ⸢ITI⸣.⸢BÁR$^{?}$⸣ *ši-pir-tu*$_{4}$ <*šá*>$^{?}$

5 ^{md}U.GUR-KAR-*ir* A-*šú šá* ^{m}*kal-ba-a*

6 A ^{m}MU-*líb-ši a-na* ^{m}*ši-ir-ku*

*LO. E.

7 *i-na-áš-šam-ma* KÙ.BABBAR-*a*$_{4}$

8 10 GÍN UD-*ú* ^{m}*ši-ir-ku a-na*

REV.

9 ^{m}*tab-ni-e-a u* ^{m}*ú-bar i-nam-din*

10 LÚ *mu-kin-nu* ^{md}EN-A-MU A-*šú šá* ^{m}DU$_{10}$.GA-*ia*

11 A ^{m}*šá-na-ši-šú* ^{md}EN-MU A-*šú šá* ^{m}TIL-*ia*

12 A LÚ.BAḪAR$_{2}$ ^{md}EN-MU A-*šú šá* ^{m}*tab-ni-e-a*

13 A ^{m}*šá-na-ši-šú* ^{m}*ni-din-tu*$_{4}$ LÚ.UMBISAG A-*šú šá*

14 ^{md}AG-GI ^{md}EN-SU [A-*šú šá* x x x]

*U. E.

15 [*p*]*a-ni*-KÁ.GAL-^{d}*en-líl* ITI.AB

16 [UD].1.KAM MU.23.KAM

*LE. E.

17 ^{m}*da-ri-'i-ia-muš* [LUGAL E.KI *u* KUR.KUR]

TRANSLATION

⸢Ten⸣ shekels of silver owed to Tabnêa and Ubār, descendants of Nabû-ušallim, are with MNA$_{2}$. {⸢By the e⸣}$^{!}$ -<B>y the end of ⸢Nisan$^{?}$⸣ he (rd. they) will bring the order <from>$^{?}$ Nergal-ēṭir, son of Kalbaya, descendant of Šumu-libši, before MNA$_{2}$, and MNA$_{2}$ shall pay these ten shekels to Tabnêa and Ubār.

Witnesses:
Bēl-apla-iddin/Ṭābiya//Ša-nāšīšu
Bēl-iddin/Gimriya//Paḫāru
Bēl-iddin/Tabnêa//Ša-nāšīšu
The scribe: Nidintu/Nabû-ušallim
Bēl-erība [...]
(Place + Date).

COMMENT

L. 3: Should we read {⸢*a-di qí*⸣} at the end of the line?

L. 4: The month in question was probably Nisan. Cf. Dar 552: 5, which was drafted exactly one year earlier. Dar 552 has *šipirtu ša*, and should we, therefore, add <*šá*> at the end of the line? There was more than enough space left at the end of the line to write *šá*. More at the comment to Dar 552.

L. 7: For *inaššâmma* (sg.), more at Dar 552: 6.

L. 7–9: According to Dar 572: 5–8 MNA was ordered to finance salaries and rations.

L. 12–13: Was Bēl-iddin/Tabnêa//Ša-nāšīšu a younger brother of Šākin-šumi/Tabnêa//Ša-nāšīšu who was a ^{lú}[*mār šipri*?] *ša* ^{lú}*bēl piqitti ša Esagil* in Nbn 558: 16 (dated 11 Nbn)? On the latter, see also Bongenaar, *Ebabbar*, 473. This would bring the "official" representation at Dar 573 to two; see also line 14. Was Bēl-iddin's father the same as Tabnêa/Marduk-šuma-ibni//Ša-nāšīšu, who leased land from MNA between 2–12 Dar? For this Tabnêa, more at Wunsch, *Felder* 1, 58 and 2, 345 (index).

L. 14: This Bēl-erība was most likely the son of Kalbaya, descendant of Šumu-libši. Cf. his appearance among the witnesses in Dar 552. He was Nergal-eṭir's brother and a commander-of-fifty.

No. 137

	Dar 576
Museum No.:	BM 31427
Date:	22/x/23 Dar (23 January 498 B.C.E.)
Place:	Babylon
Content:	Receipt of silver from MNA. Rent for a boat.

OBV.

1 ⸢⅓ MA.NA KÙ.BABBAR⸣ UD-*ú šá ina* 1 GÍN *bit-qa nu-uḫ-ḫu-tú*

2 ⸢*i-di* GIŠ⸣.MÁ-*šú-nu* ^{m}ŠEŠ-*at-bu-ú* A-*šú šá*

3 ⸢^{m}*kal-ba-a*⸣ *ù* ^{md}AG-*it-tan-nu* A-*šú šá*

4 ^{m}MU-⸢^{d}AG⸣ *ina* ŠU.II ^{m}*ši-rik-ku* A-*šú šá* ^{m}MU-*a*

5 ⸢A⸣ ^{m}[*e-gi-bi* ...]

(Remainder of obverse is broken off.)

REV.

1′ A-*šú šá* ^{m}⸢x⸣-[...]

2′ E.KI ITI.AB UD.22.KAM MU.23.KAM

3′ ^{m}*da-ri-iá-muš* LUGAL E.KI *u* KUR.KUR

TRANSLATION

Aḫu-atbû, son of ⸢Kalbaya⸣, and Nabû-ittannu, son of Iddin-⸢Nabû⸣ [have received] from MNA$_2$ ⸢one-third mina⸣ of white, medium-quality ⸢silver⸣, of which one-eighth is alloy, ⸢the rent⸣ for their boat. (Remainder is broken off). (Place + Date).

COMMENT

The surface of this tablet is very damaged.

L. 1–2: Since the amount of silver is one-third mina, it was most probably a payment for rent, hence read ⸢*i-di*⸣ (maybe wr. *i-na*, but too damaged to see the difference). Indeed, in texts concerning the rent of boats the annual rent usually amounted to one-third mina of silver, cf. e.g., BM 31891, BM 30490 and BM 30270.

No. 138

Dar 577
Museum No.: BM 30720
Date: [-]/x/23 Dar (January 498 B.C.E.)
Place: Babylon
Content: Receipt of silver from MNA. Undertaking to pay remainder upon return from Elam. By order of (*ina qibi*) the governor of Babylon.

OBV.

1 ⸢x⸣ *šá* ^{m}*ni-din-tu*$_4$ DUMU *šá* ^{m}ÌR-*ia* ⸢LÚ$^{?}$⸣ [...]
2 ^{m}*ni-din-tu*$_4$ *a-na* ½ MA.NA KÙ.BABBAR ⸢UD-*ú*⸣
3 *ina qí-bi šá* ^{m}*ina-é-sag-íl-l*[*i-*...]
4 LÚ.GAR-UŠ$_4$ TIN.TIR.KI DUMU *šá* ^{md}AG-[MU-GIN]
5 DUMU ^{m}*šá-na-ši-šú šá* TA ITI.⸢BÁR⸣ [...]
6 ^{m}*da-ri-'i-muš* LUGAL TIN.TIR.KI L[UGAL KUR.KUR.MEŠ]
7 *a-di* TIL ITI.ŠE *šá* MU.24.KAM [...]
8 ^{m}*ši-ir-ku* DUMU *šá* ^{m}SUM.NA-*a* DUMU ^{m}[*e-gi-bi*]

LO. E.

9 ⸢*id*⸣-*din ina* ⸢*lìb*⸣-*bi** 10 GÍN KÙ.BABBAR UD-⸢*ú*⸣

REV.

10 ^{m}*ni-din-tu*$_4$ *ina* ŠU.II ^{m}*ši-iš-ki ma**-*ḫ*[*i**-*ir*]
11 *ù ri-ḫi* ⅓ MA.NA KÙ.BABBAR *ina* E.⸢KI⸣*
12 *šá* TA KUR.ELAM.MA.KI *i-ru-bu* ⸢x⸣ [(...)]
13 *a-na* ^{m}*ni-din-tu*$_4$ *i-nam-din* LÚ ⸢*mu-kin-nu*⸣
14 ^{md}EN-MU DUMU *šá* ^{m}*ba-ni-ia* DUMU ^{m}⸢*na*⸣*-[...]
15 ^{md}AG-*bul-liṭ-su* DUMU *šá* ^{m}SUM.NA-⸢*a*⸣* [...]
16 DUMU *šá* ^{m}*mu-še-zib*-^{d}AG LÚ.UMBISAG ^{md}AG-[...]
17 A-*šú šá* ^{m}*ina*-SÙḪ-SUR TIN.TIR.KI ITI.AB U[D.x.KAM]
18 MU.23.KAM ^{m}*da-ri-'i-muš* LUGAL ⸢E.KI⸣
19 LUGAL KUR.KUR.MEŠ

TRANSLATION

The ⸢x⸣ of Nidintu, son of Ardiya, ⸢the?⸣ [...]: Nidintu ⸢has⸣ given (it) for half a mina of ⸢white⸣ silver [to] MNA_2 from ⸢Nisan⸣ [of the x-th year] of Darius, king of Babylon, K[ing of the Lands] till the end of Addar of the twenty-fourth year [...], by order of Ina-Esagil-li[lbur], governor of Babylon, son of Nabû-[šuma-ukīn], descendant of Ša-nāšīšu. From ⸢this⸣ (sum) Nidintu has re[ceived] ten shekels of white silver from MNA_2, and the remainder (sum) of one-third mina of silver he shall pay to Nidintu in Babylon upon his return from Elam.

⸢Witnesses⸣:
Bēl-iddin/Baniya//⸢Na⸣[baya]
Nabû-bullissu/Iddinaya[//Dābibī]
[...]/Mušēzib-Nabû
The scribe: Nabû-[...]/Ina-tēšê-ēṭir
(Place + Date).

COMMENT

L. 1: It remains unclear what exactly Nidintu gave to MNA. Collation of the tablet shows that there is space for one, maybe two signs at the beginning of line 1. Only the lower part and the end of the sign(s) are clear, and these remnants resemble a BAN-sign (hence, = *qaštu* "bow"?). It is noteworthy that all other texts that mention MNA and Ina-Esagil-lilbur concern boats, boatmen, or men to tow boats. However, a reconstruction GIŠ.MÁ is very unlikely, due to the little space available and the remnants of the sign(s) still visible.

L. 2: Strassmaier copied ⸢UD-*ú*⸣, but these signs are no longer visible on the tablet.

L. 3: The beginning of the LI-sign that Strassmaier copied is no longer visible on the tablet. The verbal element in the name Ina-Esagil-lilbur is usually spelled *-li-bur, lil-bur* or *lil-bir* (cf. Bongenaar, *Ebabbar*, 31).

L. 11: Krecher, *Egibi*, 345f. suggests reading *ina e-r*[*e-bi*] at the end of line 11, and translates lines 11–12 "so bald MNA aus Elam (wieder) 'hereinkommt'." Collation of the tablet, however, showed that one should read *ina* E.⸢KI⸣ at the end of line 11.

L. 12: The translation "when he will return from Elam" (*ša ultu Elam irrubu*) supposes that MNA went to Elam and is soon to arrive in Babylon. For a different opinion, see Dandamaev, "Connections," 259: MNA had sent his commercial agent to Elam for a joint venture with the governor of Babylon; when MNA's man would come back with the silver from Elam, MNA would pay the governor his share of it.

L. 13: Strassmaier copied ⸢*mu-kin-nu*⸣, but I could see only ⸢*mu*⸣-[*kin-nu*].

L. 14: Bēl-iddin/Baniya from the Nabaya family witnessed several of MNA's documents, only one of which has been published (Dar 280, and the unpublished documents BM 30416: 7f. = b 0796, BM 33113: ⸢20⸣ = b 2244 and

BM 31530: ⸢19⸣ = b 2805). Tallqvist, *NbN*, 32 distinguishes between a Bēl-iddin/Baniya//[…], who is attested in our text and in Dar 280 and a Bēl-iddin/Baniya//Nabaya, who is attested in Camb 356 and Dar 492. There is no doubt, however, that this is the one and the same person who acted as a witness for MNA on several occasions. His brother, Marduk-balāssu-iqbi, also frequently witnessed transactions concluded by MNA or wrote them for him, especially those relating to real estate (Wunsch, *Felder* 2, 307), as well as other kinds of transactions (Tallqvist, *NbN*,100).

L. 15: After ^{m}SUM.NA Strassmaier copied the beginning of ^{d}AG or ^{d}EN, but I see an A-sign. The person in question was no doubt Nabû-bullissu/Iddin-Nabû//Dābibī, who frequently occurs in texts from MNA's archive (see Tallqvist, *NbN*, 127 s.v. Nabû-bulliṭsu(24); also in b 2800, BM 31018 and TCL 13 185).

L. 17: Strassmaier copied ⸢E.KI⸣, but these signs are no longer visible on the tablet.

No. 139

OECT 10 234
Museum No.: 1884.100
Date: ⸢20$^{(+?)}$⸣/[-]/26 Dar (April 496 - March 495 B.C.E.)
Place: broken
Content: [Sale] of a boat to MNA and [receipt] of the [purchase] price. Very fragmentary.

OBV.

1′ [GIŠ.MÁ …] ⸢x x x x x x x⸣
2′ [*šá-bu-ru rap*]-⸢*šú*⸣ *šá* ^{m}*ki-din-nu* DUMU *šá* ^{m}*ri-mut*
3′ [DUMU ^{m}x-x(-x) *a-na*] 5/6 MA.NA KÙ.BABBAR *šá ina* 1 GÍN *bit-qa*
4′ [*a-na* ŠÁ]M$^{?}$ *gam-ru-tu a-na*
5′ [^{m}*ši-iš-ku* DUMU *šá* ^{m}SUM].NA-*a* DUMU ^{m}*e-gì-bi id-din*
6′ [KÙ.BABBAR-*a′* 5/6 MA.NA *šá*] *ina* 1 GÍN *bit-qa nu-uḫ-ḫu-tu*
7′ [(…) ^{m}*ki-din*]-*nu ina* ŠU.II ^{m}*ši-iš-ku*
8′ [*ma-ḫir pu-ut u*]*š-ku-tu šá* GIŠ.MÁ

LO. E.

9′ [*na*]-*ši*

REV.

10′ [LÚ *mu-kin-nu* ^{m}x-x-(x)]-⸢x⸣ DUMU *šá* ^{m}*mu-ra-nu* DUMU LÚ.GAL-*ba-ni*-⸢*e*⸣
11′ [^{m}… DUM]U *šá* ^{m}*kal-ba-a* DUMU ^{m}*su-ḫa-a-a*
12′ [^{m}…]-^{d}EN DUMU *šá* ^{m}*ḫa<-ba>-ṣi-ru* DUMU ^{m}*dan-ni-e*
13′ [^{m}…]-⸢x⸣-SUM.NA-A ^{md}AG-GUB.BA
14′ [^{m}…]-⸢*e/dan*⸣-*nu* ^{m}GI-A DUMU *ša* ^{md}AG-MU-DIN-*ṣur*
15′ [$^{m…}$ LÚ].UMBISAG DUMU ^{m}*sag-gil-a-a*

16′ [... UD].⸢20$^{(+?)}$⸣.KAM MU.26.KAM

17′ [...] ⸢x⸣.KI LUGAL K[UR ...]

TRANSLATION

[A boat ... w]⸢ide⸣ [at its beam], belonging to Kidinnu, son of Rīmūt, [descendant of PN, for] five-sixth minas of [medium-quality] silver, of which one-eighth is alloy, [for the] full [price$^{?}$] to MNA$_2$ he gave. [The five-sixth minas of] medium-quality [silver], of which one-eighth is alloy, [(...) Kidin]nu [received] from MNA$_2$. [For the *u*]*škûtu* of the boat [he assumes warran]ty.

[Witnesses]:
[...]/Mūrānu//Rab-banê
[...]/Kalbaya//Suḫaya
[...]-Bēl/Ḫa<ba>ṣīru//Dannê<a>$^{?}$
[... Ner]gal$^{?}$-nādin-apli
Nabû-šuzziz[/...]-*dan-nu*
Mušallim-apli/Nabû-šuma-uṣur$^{?}$
The scribe: [...]//Saggilaya
(Place + Date).

COMMENT

One fourth of the obverse is broken off, so that the beginning of all lines is lost. One should probably reconstruct approximately five signs at the beginning of each line. From what is preserved one may conclude that the tablet originally recorded the sale of a boat. Decisive proof for this contention are the occurrence of *gamrūtu* in line 4′ and *uškûtu* in line 8′.

L. 1′: This line probably contained a description of the boat put up for sale.

L. 4′: This line probably contained the phrase *ana šīmū gamrūtu* "for the full price."

L. 8′: On the guarantee for *uškûtu* in sale contracts, see more at BM 30370: 7–8.

L. 13′: I suggest reading after the break: ... ^{md}U].⸢GUR$^{!}$⸣-SUM.NA-A = [Ner]gal$^{!}$-nādin-apli, although the name as such is unattested. It is similar to names such as Nabû-nādin-apli and Bēl-nādin-apli, where the verbal element *nādin*, however, is spelled either syllabically or with the logogram MU rather than SUM.NA as in the case under consideration.

L. 13′ end: Names with the verbal element *izuzzu*/*šuzzuzu* are rare (Tallqvist, *NbN*, 324).

L. 14′: The name ^{m}GI-A, probably to be read Mušallim-apli, is otherwise unattested. The name of his father is enigmatic. The signs as copied by McEwan are: ^{md}AG-MU-DIN-ṢUR. Should we read Nabû-šuma-*u*$^{!}$-*ṣur*, even if the verbal element -*uṣur* is always written with either the URU$_3$-sign or syllabically -*ú-ṣur*, -*ú-ṣu-ur*/*úr* (Tallqvist, *NbN*, 325 s.v. *naṣāru*), so that the occurrence of -*u* as in the case under consideration is exceptional?

No. 140

	TCL 13 185
Museum No.:	Mnb 1870
Date:	12/xi/7 Dar (9 February 514 B.C.E.)
Place:	Babylon
Content:	Receipt of silver from MNA.

OBV.

1 2 MA.NA KÙ.BABBAR *šá ina* 1 GÍN *bit-qa nu-*[*uḫ-ḫu-tu*]
2 *ri-ḫi-it* 1+[x MA.NA x GÍN KÙ.BABBAR] *ma-la*
3 *šá* ^{md}EN-*na-din*-[A x x] *šú*
4 *šá a-na* 1½ MA.NA ⸢x x x x⸣ [(...)]$^{?}$
5 ^{m}KI-^{d}AMAR.UTU-DIN DUMU ^{m}*e-gi-bi a-na*
6 2½ MA.NA KÙ.BABBAR *i-din-nu-u'* KÙ.BABBAR-*a*$_4$
7 2 MA.NA TUKU-*tú* UR$_5$.RA-*šú* ^{md}AG-MU-GIN
8 [A-*šú šá*] ^{md}EN-KAR-*ir* DUMU LÚ.SANGA-^{d}EN
9 [x x x] ^{md}AMAR.UTU-*na-ṣir*-A
10 [x (x)] *e-ṭe-ru ù ú-ìl-*[*ti*]
11 [*šá* 2]½ MA.NA KÙ.BABBAR *ki-i* ŠAḪ/ŠUL BU
12 *a-na* ^{md}AMAR.UTU-*na-ṣir*-A *it-ta-din*
13 *e-lat* GÍD.DA *šá* 1½ MA.NA KÙ.BABBAR *šá*
14 ^{md}EN-*na-din*-A *a-na* ^{md}AMAR.UTU-*na-ṣir*-A
15 *id-di-nu* LÚ *mu-kin-nu* ^{m}ÌR-^{d}*gu-la*
16 DUMU *šá* ^{md}AMAR.UTU-MU-URU$_3$ A ^{m}*na-ba-a-a*
17 ^{md}AG-*bul-liṭ-su* DUMU *šá* ^{m}SUM.NA-^{d}AG
18 DUMU ^{md}*da-bi-bi* ^{m}⸢SUM$^{?}$.NA$^{?}$⸣-^{d}AG DUMU *šá*
19 ^{m}*ba-la-ṭu* DUMU ^{md}AG-*ú-ṣur*$^{!}$-[*šú*]
20 ^{md}AMAR.UTU-EN-*šú-nu* DUB.SAR DUMU *šá*
21 ^{m}ÌR-^{d}AMAR.UTU DUMU ⸢LÚ$^{?}$.SANGA⸣-^{d}[...]$^{?}$
22 [TIN].TIR.KI ITI.ZÍZ UD.12.KAM
23 MU.7.KAM ^{m}*da-a-ri-ia-*[*muš*]
24 [LU]GAL E.KI LUGAL KUR.KUR

TRANSLATION

Two minas of medium-[quality] silver, of which one-eighth is alloy, remainder of 1+[x minas], in so much as it is what Bēl-nādin-apli [and] his [brothers (?) (owe)] - ... (he/they?) gave-. These two minas of silver, the capital sum and its interest, Nabû-šuma-ukīn, [son of] Bēl-ēṭir, descendant of Šangû-Bēl (read: -Nanaya?), received [from] MNA$_1$. He has promptly returned the promissory note [for x]+½ minas of silver to MNA$_1$. In addition, there is a register regarding one and a half minas of silver that Bēl-nādin-apli gave to MNA.

Witnesses:

Arad-Gula / Marduk-šuma-uṣur / Nabaya
Nabû-bullissu / Iddin-Nabû / / Dābibī
⸢Iddin$^{?}$⸣-Nabû / Balāṭu / / Nabû-uṣuršu$^{!}$
The scribe: Marduk-bēlšunu / Arad-Marduk / / ⸢Šangû$^{?}$⸣-^{d}[Ea]$^{?}$
(Place + Date).

COMMENT

L. 2: Should we read 1+[3$^{?}$ MA.NA] and relate this debt to the price of the slave that Bēl-nādin-apli and his brothers sold to MNA the previous year (see Dar 212)? Its purchase price was four minas and ten shekels.

L. 3: Probably read ^{md}EN-*na-din*-[IBILA *u* ŠEŠ.MEŠ]-*šú*.

L. 4: From the remnants of signs as copied by Contenau we may reconstruct the following reading: ⸢^{m}⸣$^{[d]}$⸢ŠÚ-PAB$^{?}$-A⸣ [A]-⸢*šú*⸣ *šá*. The passage needs collation.

L. 4–6: The formulation in these lines is awkward with its double use of *ana* + amount of silver (*ša ana* 1½ *manê* ⸢*MNA*$^{?}$⸣ *ana* 2½ *manê kaspu iddinu / ū*). Do these sums of silver refer to the sums that MNA paid for the account of Bēl-nādin-apli and his brothers to (Nabû-)Šuma-ukīn over the last year? We know that he paid half a mina of silver according to Dar 213, [x] minas according to b 2800, and two minas according to TCL 13 185: 1. Or is there any link between these sums of 1½ and 2½ minas, i.e., four minas, on the one hand, and the four minas and ten shekels, price of Bēl-nādin-apli's slave sold to MNA (Dar 212), on the other? See also commentary at line 2 above.

L. 8: Read ^{d}*na-na-a* instead of ^{d}EN? For Nabû-šuma-ukīn (*alias* Šuma-ukīn) / Bēl-ēṭir / / Šangû-Nanaya, creditor of Bēl-nādin-apli and his brothers, see Dar 213 and b 2800.

L. 9: Probably read [*ina* ŠU.II] at the beginning of the line.

L. 11–12: At the end of line 11 I suggest emending the text as follows: <*u*>-*tir*$^{!}$(ŠAḪ)-*ri*$^{?!}$(BU). For the expression PN_1 *kī utirri ana* PN_2 (= debtor) *ittadin*, more at BM 30961: 12–13.

No. 141

TCL 13 193 (Re-edited by Abraham, *NABU* 1997/53).
Museum No.: Mnb 1130
Date: 10/xii(b)/16 Dar (27 March 505 B.C.E.)
Place: Šušan
Content: Promissory note to pay a debt of silver. Due from MNA. Pledge of slaves and land.

OBV.

1 45 MA.NA KÙ.BABBAR *šá ina* 1 GÍN *bit-qa nu-uḫ-ḫu-tu*
2 *šá* ^{m}LUGAL-BÀD LÚ.SAG LUGAL DUMU *šá* ^{m}*id-ra***-a'*
3 *ina muḫ-ḫi* ^{m}*ši-rik šá* MU-*šú* 2-*ú* ^{md}AMAR.UTU-*na-ṣir*-A
4 DUMU *šá* ^{m}SUM.NA-*a* DUMU ^{m}*e-gi-bi ina* ITI.SIG$_4$
5 KÙ.BABBAR-*a*$_4$ 45 MA.NA *šá ina* 1 GÍN *bit-qa nu-uḫ-ḫu-tu ina* TIN.TIR.KI
6 *ina* SAG.DU-*šú i-nam-din* ^{md}DI.KU$_5$-EN-URU$_3$ ^{fd}[*na-n*]*a**-*a**-EN-URU$_3$
7 DAM-*šú* ^{md}*za-ba*$_4$-*ba*$_4$-MU ^{md}DI.KU$_5$-MU ^{m}EN-*gab-bi*-^{d}EN-*um*-⸢*mu*⸣
8 ^{m}ŠEŠ-*šú-nu* DUMU.MEŠ-*šú* ^{f}*ḫa-áš-da-a'-i-tu*$_4$ *ù*
9 ^{f}*a-ḫat-su-nu* DUMU.MÍ.MEŠ-*šú* PAP 8 LÚ *a-me-lu-ut-tu*$_4$
10 LÚ.UN.MEŠ É-*šú* ŠE.NUMUN-*šú zaq-pi ù pi-i šul-pu*
11 *gab-bi šá* URU *šup-pa-tu*$_4$ ÚS.SA.DU ^{md}AG-*na-ṣir*
12 DUMU *šá* ^{m}KI-^{d}AG-*lum-mir* DUMU ^{m}*ba-si-ia* ÚS.SA.DU
13 ^{m}*ni-din-ti* (erasure) DUMU *šá* ^{md}AMAR.UTU-SU DUMU ^{m}*e-gì-bi*
14 *maš-ka-nu šá* ^{m}LUGAL-BÀD LÚ.TUKU-*ú šá-nam-ma ina muḫ-ḫi*
15 *ul i-šal-laṭ a-di-i* UGU *šá* ^{m}LUGAL-BÀD KÙ.BABBAR-*šu a*$_4$
16 ⸢45⸣ MA.NA *šá** *ina* 1 GÍN *bit-qa nu-uḫ-ḫu-tu*
17 *i-šal-lim-mu ki-i ina* ITI.SIG$_4$ KÙ.BABBAR-*a*$_4$ 45 MA.NA
18 *šá** *ina* 1 GÍN *bit-qa nu-uḫ-ḫu-tu la it-tan-nu* ^{md}DI.KU$_5$-⸢EN-URU$_3$⸣
19 ⸢*u*⸣* ^{f*d}*na-na-a*-EN-URU$_3$ DAM-*šú* ^{md}*za-ba*$_4$-*ba*$_4$-MU

REV.

20 ^{m}ŠEŠ-*šú-nu* (erasure of one sign) ^{md}DI.KU$_5$-MU ^{m}EN-*gab-bi*-^{d}EN-*um-mu*
21 ^{f}*a-ḫat-su-nu* (erasure of two signs) ^{f}*ḫaš-da*-{⸢*áš*⸣}-*a'-i-tu*$_4$ DUMU.MÍ.MEŠ-*šú*
22 PAP 8 LÚ-*ut-su* LÚ.UN.MEŠ É-*šú u* ŠE.NUMUN-*šú* É *maš-ka-nu šá* ^{m}LUGAL-BÀD
23 *ki-i* ŠÁM *ḫa-ri-iṣ ku-um* KÙ.BABBAR-*a*$_4$ 45 MA.NA
24 *šá ina* 1 GÍN *bit-qa nu-uḫ-ḫu-tu pa-ni* ^{m}LUGAL-BÀD *id-dag-gal*
25 LÚ *mu-kin-nu* ^{m}*um-ma-da-a-tú* LÚ.DI.KU$_5$ DUMU *šá* ^{m}*ú-du-na-a-tú*
26 ^{m}*ap-la-a* LÚ.DI.KU$_5$ DUMU *šá* ^{md}AG-*re-man-ni* ^{m}*man-nu-a-ki-i*-^{d}AG
27 LÚ.SAG LUGAL LÚ.EN *pi-qit-tu*$_4$ *é-sag-íla* ^{m}*ni-din-ti*
28 LÚ.SANGA LAMxKUR.RU.KI DUMU *šá* ^{md}EN-*ka-ṣir* DUMU ^{m}DÙ-*eš*-DINGIR
29 ^{m}*a-bi-a-bu* LÚ.DI.KU$_5$ DUMU *šá* ^{m}*a-ti-ka-am* ^{m}*na-din* DUMU *šá*
30 ^{m}*ḫa-ba-ṣi-ru* ^{m}*ba-si-ia* DUMU *šá* ^{m}*ši-la-a'* ^{m}*mu-ra-nu*
31 DUMU *šá* ^{m}MU-MU DUMU ^{m}AD-NU-ZU ^{m}*a-tar-ba-nu-uš** LÚ.DI.KU$_5$

32 DUMU *šá* ^{m}*ba-ga-da-a-tú* ^{m}MU-^{d}AG LÚ.DI.KU$_{5}$ DUMU *šá* ^{md}AG-*ta-lim*-URU$_{3}$

33 ^{m}*ḫa-an-ṭu-šu* DUMU *šá* ^{m}*ka-mu-šu-i-lu* ^{m}*i-qu-pu* DUMU *šá*

34 ^{md}AG-*na**-⸢*din*-ŠEŠ⸣* {ŠEŠ}* DUMU ^{m}*su-ḫa-a-a* ^{m}*ri-mut* DUMU *šá* ^{m*}SUM.NA-*a*

35 DUMU LÚ.SIMUG ^{m}*su-qa***-a-a* DUMU *šá* ^{m}SU$^{!}$-^{d}AMAR.UTU DUMU LÚ.GAL-DÙ*

36 ^{m}*ni-din-ti*-^{d}EN DUB.SAR DUMU *šá* ^{m}ŠU$^{?}$-^{d}UTU URU* *šu***-šá-an*$^{!*}$ (seal inscription, see below) ITI.ŠE EGIR-*ú*

37 UD.10.KAM MU.16<.KAM> (seal inscription, see below) [^{m}*da*]*-a***-ri-ia-mu-uš*

38 […]* KUR*

U. E.

(1) (written crosswise in comparison to the text on the reverse of the tablet:)
[NA$_{4}$].⸢KIŠIB⸣* / ^{m*}*ni-din-ti* / LÚ.SANGA URU.LAMx⸢KUR.RU⸣.KI, cylinder seal impression (to the right of the inscription)

(2) (written close to and in the same direction as line 36:)
NA$_{4}$.KIŠIB ^{m*}*ba***-s*[*i***-ia*]
stamp seal impression (underneath the inscription)

(3) NA$_{4}$.KIŠIB / ^{m}MU-^{d}AG, stamp seal impression (to the right of the inscription)

(4) (written close to and in the same direction as line 37:)
NA$_{4}$.KIŠIB ^{m}*a-tar-ba-nu-uš** [DUMU *šá*] ^{m}*ba*-⸢*ga*⸣-[*da-a-tú*]
stamp seal impression (underneath the inscription)

RI. E. (parallel to lines 21ff.:)
NA$_{4}^{*}$<.KIŠIB>* ^{m}ŠEŠ-⸢KAM⸣ / LÚ.DI.KU$_{5}$ / DUMU *šá* / ^{m}*ba-ri-ki*-DINGIR / stamp seal impression

LE. E.

(1) [NA$_{4}$.KIŠIB ^{m}]**na***-d*[*in*]$^{?*}$ / stamp seal impression

(2) NA$_{4}$.KIŠIB / ^{m}*um-ma-da-a-tú*, cylinder seal impression with Aramaic inscription.

TRANSLATION

(1–4a)Forty-five minas of medium-quality silver, of which one-eighth is alloy, are due to Šarru-dūrī, son of Idrā, a courtier, from Širku, whose second name is Marduk-nāṣir-apli, son of Iddinaya, descendant of Egibi. (4b–6a)In Simān he will pay these forty-five minas of medium-quality silver, of which one-eight is alloy, without interest in Babylon. (6b–14a)Pledged to Šarru-dūrī are: Madānu-bēla-uṣur, ^{f}[Nan]aya-bēla-uṣur, his wife; Zababa-iddin, Madānu-iddin, Bēl-gabbi-Bēlumma, Aḫūšunu, his sons; ^{f}Ḫašdayītu and ^{f}Aḫāssunu, his daughters. In total: eight slaves, people belonging to his household; (and) his entire orchard and grain field in Šuppātu (located) next to Nabû-nāṣir, son of Itti-Nabû-lummir, descendant of Basiya, (and) next to Nidintu, son of Marduk-erība, descendant of Egibi. (14b–17a)No other creditor shall exercise any rights over these until Šarru-dūrī has received full repayment of these forty-five minas of medium-quality silver, of which one-eighth is alloy. (17b–24)If these forty-five minas of medium-quality silver, of which one-eighth is alloy, have not been given by Simān, then Madānu-⸢bēla-uṣur⸣, and Nanaya-bēla-uṣur, his wife; Zababa-iddin, Aḫūšunu, Madānu-iddin, Bēl-gabbi-Bēlumma, Aḫāssunu, (and) Ḫašdayītu, his children—in total, eight of his slaves, people belonging to his household—as well as his field, (all) pledged to Šarru-dūrī, will belong to Šarru-dūrī for the full price instead of the forty-five minas of medium-quality silver, of which one-eighth is alloy.

(25–35)Witnesses:
Umadātu/Udunātu, a judge
Aplaya/Nabû-rēmanni, a judge
Mannu-aki-Nabû, a courtier and *bēl piqitti* of the Esagil
Nidintu/Bēl-kāṣir//Eppeš-ili, a priest from Bāṣ
Abī-abu/Atikām, a judge
Nādin/Ḫabaṣīru
Basiya/Šilaya
Mūrānu/Šuma-iddin//Abī-ul-īde
Ātarbānuš/Bagadāta, a judge
Iddin-Nabû/Nabû-talîm-uṣur, a judge
Ḫanṭūšu/Kamūšu-ilū
Iqūpu/Nabû-⸢nādin⸣-aḫi//Suḫaya
Rīmūt/Iddinaya//Nappāḫu
Sūqaya/Erība!-Marduk//Rab-banê
(36a)The scribe: Nidinti-Bēl/Gimil?-Šamaš
(36b–38)(Place + Date).
⸢Seal⸣ of Nidintu, priest from Bāṣ
Seal of Bas[iya]
Seal of Iddin-Nabû
Seal of Ātarbānuš[/] Baga[dāta]
Se<al> of Aḫi-⸢ēreš⸣/Barīk-il, a judge
[Seal of] Nād[in]
Seal of Umadātu

Comment

For the seals, see L. Delaporte, *Catalogue des cylindres orientaux, cachets et pierres gravées du Musée du Louvre*. II. *Acquisitions*, Paris, 1923, Planche 130 fig. 5a, 5b (A 797). For the reading of the Aramaic inscription on the left edge of TCL 13 193, see now Stolper, *JAOS* 116. For some of the witnesses, cf. Dar 453+.

L. 5: The phrase *ina* TIN.TIR.KI was added later to the text, on the right edge.

L. 21: There is no erasure at the end of the line as suggested by Contenau's copy.

L. 25: For the Old Iranian names Umadātu (= Amadātu in Dar 435: Rev. 11′; Ir. *Amadāta), and Udunātu (Ir. *Hudānāta), see Tavernier, *NABU* 2000/47).

L. 29–32: For the Old Iranian names Ātarbānuš (Ir. Ātrbānuš), Atikām (Ir. *Atikāma), and Bagadāta (Ir. *Bagadāta), see Dandamaev, *Iranians*, 47 (no. 67), 48 (no. 72), and 50ff. (no. 82).

L. 34: Iqūpu's father was Nabû-*na**-⸢*din*-ŠEŠ⸣* {ŠEŠ}*, i.e., Nabû-nādin-aḫi. The same person is called Nabû-nāṣir in Dar 435: Rev. 4′.

L. 36: The reading of the name of the scribe's father is difficult. It seems that one should read ^{m}ŠU$^{?}$-, rather than ^{m}SU-, because the second vertical wedge in Contenau's copy is actually a break in the tablet.

No. 142

	TCL 13 196 (= Dupl. of Pinches, Peek 18)
Museum No.:	Mnb 1131
Date:	1/vii/26 Dar (1 October 496 B.C.E.)
Place:	Babylon
Content:	Lease of a share in the right to collect tolls from boats. Leased out by MNA and his co-shareholder to two individuals. The right to collect tolls ultimately belonged to (*bīt qīptu ša, irbi ša*) the governor of Babylon.

OBV.

1 ⸢x⸣-*si*$^{!}$-*ir-tu*$_4$ *šá ina muḫ-ḫi gi-iš-ri ù ka-a-ri*
2 *e-ri-du ù e-lu-ú* É *qip-tu*$_4$ *šá* ^{m}*gu-za-nu*
3 LÚ.GAR-UŠ$_4$ TIN.TIR.KI *šá i-na pa-an* ^{m}*ši-ir-ka* A-*šú šá* ^{m}SUM.NA
4 ^{m}*ši-ir-ka* A-*šú šá* ^{m}SUM.NA-*a a-na a-ḫi* ḪA.LA *šá ina ir-bi*
5 *šá gi-iš-ri šá* ^{m}*gu-za-nu* LÚ.GAR-UŠ$_4$ TIN.TIR.KI *šá it-ti*
6 ^{m}*mu-ra-nu* A-*šú šá* ^{md}AG-GIN-IBILA ^{md}AG-*bul-liṭ-su*
7 A-*šú šá* ^{m}*gu-za-nu u* ^{m}*ḫa*-⸢*ri*⸣-*ṣa-nu u* ^{m}*i-qu-pu* ^{md}U.GUR-*ib-ni*
8 LÚ.EN.NUN.MEŠ *gi-iš-ri* ^{m}*ši-ir-ka* A-*šú šá* ^{m}SUM.NA-*a*
9 A ^{m}*e-gi-bi u* ^{m}*mu-ra-nu* A-*šú šá* ^{md}AG-GIN-IBILA
10 A LÚ.EN.NUN-GIŠ.MÁ-U$_5$.KU *a-na su-ú-tu a-na* ITI 15 GÍN KÙ.BABBAR
11 UD-*ú šá ina* 1 GÍN *bit-qa nu-uḫ-ḫu-tú a-na* ^{md}EN-*a-su-ú-a*
12 A-*šú šá* ^{md}U.GUR-DIN-*iṭ* A ^{m}*mu*-SIG$_5$-*iq*-^{d}IŠKUR
13 *ù* ^{m}*ú-ba-ru* A-*šú šá* ^{md}EN-ŠEŠ.MEŠ-SU A LÚ.EN.NUN-GIŠ.MÁ-U$_5$.KU
14 *id-di-nu-u'* GIŠ.MÁ.MEŠ *šá ina muḫ-ḫi gi-iš-ri*
15 *i-ki-il-la-a'* ^{md}EN-*a-su-ú-a u* ^{m}*ú-ba-ru*
16 *is-si-ru-u'* KÙ.BABBAR *ir-bi šá gi-iš-ri*
17 *šá* ITI-*us-su šá* ^{m}*ši-ir-ka u* ^{m}*mu-ra-nu*
18 LÚ.EN.MEŠ ḪA.LA-*šú* ^{md}EN-*a-su-ú-a ù* ^{m}*ú-ba-ru*
19 *šá* ⸢*la*$^{?}$⸣ ^{m}*ši-ir-ka ul i-na-an-di-nu-u'*
20 *na-áš-par-tu*$_4$ *ma-la a-na muḫ-ḫi giš-ri tal-la-ku*
21 ^{md}EN-*a-su-ú-a u* ^{m}*ú*-⸢*bar*⸣ *a-na* ^{m}*šìr-ku*

22 *u* LÚ.EN.NUN.MEŠ *giš-ri ú-kal-la-mu-u'*
23 LÚ *mu-kin-nu* ^{md}AG-*it-tan-nu* A-*šú šá* ^{m}*ar-di-ia* A ^{md}30-DINGIR.⸢MEŠ⸣
24 ^{m}ÌR-^{d}AMAR.UTU A-*šú šá* ^{m}*mu-še-zib-*^{d}EN A ^{m}*sip-pe-e*
25 ^{m}*mu-ra-nu* A-*šú šá* ^{md}EN-SUM.NA A ^{m}*šá-na-ši-šú* ^{md}AG-SIPA-*šú-nu*
26 A-*šú šá* ^{md}AG-MU-URU$_3$ A ^{m}*ka-ník*-KÁ ^{m}*ni-din-tu*$_4$
27 A-*šú šá* ^{m}*kal-ba-a* A ^{m}*su-ḫa-a-a*
28 ^{m}KAR-^{d}AMAR.UTU LÚ.UMBISAG A-*šú šá* ^{m}MU-GI.NA A ^{m}*ba-bu-tu*
29 TIN.TIR.KI ITI.DU$_6$ UD.1.KAM MU.26.KAM ^{m}*da-a-ri-iá-mu*[*š*]
30 LUGAL E.KI LUGAL KUR.KUR 1-*en*.TA.ÀM *il-qu-*⸢*ú*⸣

Translation

The levy (of tolls) at the bridge and the harbor (from boats) going downstream and upstream, the … of Gūzānu, governor of Babylon, which is at the disposal of MNA$_2$. A half share in the income from the bridge of Gūzānu, governor of Babylon, which is (shared) with Mūrānu, son of Nabû-mukīn-apli, Nabû-bullissu, son of Gūzānu, as well as with Ḫarīṣānu, and Iqūpu, (and) Nergal-ibni, guardians of the bridge: MNA$_2$ and Mūrānu, son of Nabû-mukīn-apli, descendant of *Maṣṣār-elep-rukūbi,* have leased (it) to Bēl-asûa, son of Nergal-uballiṭ, descendant of Mudammiq-Adad, and Ubār, son of Bēl-aḫḫē-erība, descendant of *Maṣṣār-elep-rukūbi,* for a monthly payment of fifteen shekels of white, medium-quality silver, of which one-eighth is alloy. Bēl-asûa and Ubār shall demand tolls from the boats that moor at the bridge. Bēl-asûa and Ubār shall not pass on the silver, the monthly income from the bridge that is due to MNA$_2$ and Mūrānu, owners of a share in it, ⸢without (the consent of)$^{?}$⸣ MNA$_2$. Bēl-asûa and Ubār shall show to MNA$_2$ and to the guardians of the bridge any written message that comes concerning the bridge.

Witnesses:
Nabû-ittannu/Ardiya//Sîn-ilī
Arad-Marduk/Mušēzib-Bēl//Sippê
Mūrānu/Bēl-iddin//Ša-nāšīšu
Nabû-rē'ûšunu/Nabû-šuma-uṣur//Kānik-bābi
Nidintu/Kalbaya//Suḫaya
The scribe: Mušēzib-Marduk/Šuma-ukīn//Bābūtu
(Place + Date).

They have taken one (copy of the document) each.

Comment

For a translation of the text, see also Joannès, "Pouvoirs locaux," 186 n. 56. Parts of the text are also translated in the *CAD* (see *CAD* E, 119 s.v. *elû* mng. 1b–3'; Q, 263 s.v. *qīptu* in *bīt qīptu*; G, 108 s.v. *gišru* B; and S, 425 s.v. *sūtu* A mng. 4b).

L. 1: The first word should be read either ˹*ú*˺-*se*$^{!}$(SU)-*er-tu*$_4$, (cf. *AHw*, 1437 s.v. *usertu*, "Einforderung"), or ˹*is*˺-*si*$^{!}$(SU)-*ir-tu*$_4$ (cf. *CAD* I, 197f. s.v. *isīrtu* A "collection of payment").

L. 2: The translation of the expression *bīt qīptu ša Gūzānu* is difficult. Joannès translates "prérogative de Guzânu," i.e., the toll is nominally due to Gūzānu. So probably also *AHw*, 922 s.v. *qīptu* "Vertrauen, Kredit," mng. 5. As a matter of fact, harbors fell within the administrative responsibility of the governors of Babylon (e.g., Bēl-ēṭir/Šamaš-aḫa-iddin *rab kāri ša Gūbaru* in Camb 96: this Gūbaru was probably the governor of Babylon, so Stolper, *JNES* 48, 289). According to the *CAD* Q, 263 s.v. *qīptu* in *bīt qīptu*, the meaning of the expression is unknown, but it must have referred to a location: "(payable) at the *bīt qīptu* belonging to PN, the governor of Babylon...." Cf. Salonen, *Nautica*, 34: *bīt kibtum* "Weizenlager."

L. 3: The collection of payments from boats passing the bridge and harbor that fell within the administrative responsibility of the governor of Babylon was organized by MNA. This is clear from the expression *isīrtu/usertu ša ina muḫḫi gišri u kāri ... ša ina pān MNA*, according to which the bridge and harbor, and hence the income derived from these commodities, were (put) "at the disposal of MNA." For the expression *ina pān*, more at BM 30270: 1. Part of this income from the governor's bridge was subsequently leased by MNA and Mūrānu to two other men for a monthly payment of fifteen shekels (= lines 4–14).

L. 5b–8a: The income from the bridge is shared by six people, viz. MNA and five other persons, who were "guardians of the bridge": Mūrānu/Nabû-mukīn-apli, Nabû-bullissu/Gūzānu, Ḫarīṣānu, Iqūpu, and Nergal-ibni. The way in which the scribe used the particle *u* "and," however, is peculiar, because we expect it to appear only between the last two names in a list of names. For a different view see *CAD* G, 108 s.v. *gišru* B mng. 1b; and S, 425 s.v. *sūtu* A mng. 4b.

L. 10, 13: *Maṣṣār-elep-rukūbi* was probably a family name, cf. *CAD* M$_1$, 343 s.v. *maṣṣāru* mng 1b-4′ and R, 410 s.v. *rukūbu* mng. 1a-2′-b′. Less outspoken in this respect is *AHw*, 621 s.v. *maṣṣāru* mng. 2c, and 994 s.v. *rukūbu* mng. 2b.

L. 15: This line is quoted by *CAD* K, 100 s.v. *kalû* in G., mng. 2e "to stop, detain, delay (a boat)," and translated by *CAD* G, 108 s.v. *gišru* B mng. 1b: "all ships that moor at the bridge." Differently, at *AHw*, 429 s.v. *kalû* in N., mng. 1 "zurückgehalten werden," i.e., "the boats that are stopped at the bridge." The same verb is probably found in Dar 158: 9.

L. 19: *šá* ˹*la*$^{?}$˺ ^{m}*ši-ir-ka* "without (the consent of)$^{?}$ MNA$_2$"; or should we read *šá* ˹ŠU.II˺ ^{m}*ši-ir-ka* "that is due to MNA$_2$"?

No. 143

	TCL 13 197
Museum No.:	Mnb 1821
Date:	27/viii/26 Dar (26 November 496 B.C.E.)
Place:	Babylon
Content:	Receipt of the *ilku*-tax (and)$^{?}$ the flour-tax by MNA.

OBV.

1 [*i*]*l-ki šá ul-tu* ITI.BÁR MU.25.KAM
2 *a-di qí-it* ITI.ŠE MU.26.KAM
3 ^{m}[*da-a*]*-ri-iá-muš* LUGAL *šá* ^{m}*mu-ra-nu* A-*šú šá*
4 ^{md}AMAR.UTU-PAB$^{!}$ A ^{m}ŠEŠ-*ba-ni* ^{m}*ši-iš-ku* [A]-*šú šá*
5 [^{m}S]UM.NA-*a* A ^{m}*e-gì-bi ina* ŠU.II
6 ^{m}SIPA-*šú-nu*-^{d}AMAR.UTU A-*šú šá* ^{md}EN-A-URU$_3$ A ^{m}⸢x(-x)⸣-*a-a*
7 *a-na* UGU ^{m}*mu-ra-nu ma-ḫi-ir*
8 ⸢*qí*⸣*-me šá*$^{!}$ ^{m}*mu-ra-nu* ^{m}⸢*ši-iš-ku*⸣
9 *ina* ŠU.II ^{m}SIPA-*šú-nu*-^{d}AMAR.UTU *a-na* UGU
10 ^{m}*mu-ra-nu ma-ḫi-ir*
11 1.TA.ÀM TI-*ú*
12 LÚ [*mu*]*-kin-nu* ^{md}EN-SU A-*šú šá* ^{m}*šul-*⸢*lu-mu*⸣
13 ^{md}EN-SU A-*šú šá* ^{md}AMAR.UTU-x ^{m}⸢x-x⸣-x A-*šú šá*
14 ^{md}EN-*ú-šal-*⸢*lim*⸣ ^{md}EN-SU A-*šú šá*
15 ^{m}*kal-ba-a* A ^{m}MU-*líb-ši*
16 ^{md}ŠÁR-*ta-ri-bi* A-*šú šá* ^{md}EN-x
17 ^{m}MU-^{d}EN LÚ.UMBISAG A-*šú šá* ^{m}*šá-du-nu* E.KI
18 ⸢ITI⸣.APIN UD.27.KAM MU.26.KAM
19 [^{m}*d*]*a-ri-iá-muš* LUGAL E.KI *u* KUR.KUR

TRANSLATION

The *ilku*-tax from Nisan of the twenty-fifth year till the end of Addar of the twenty-sixth year of King Darius is due from Mūrānu, son of Marduk-nāṣir$^{!}$, descendant of Aḫu-bani. MNA$_2$ has received (it) from Rē'ûšunu-Marduk, son of Bēl-apla-uṣur, descendant of ⸢…-aya⸣, for the account of Mūrānu. ⸢MNA$_2$⸣ has (also)$^{?}$ received the ⸢flour⸣-tax owed by Mūrānu from Re'ûšunu-Marduk for the account of Mūrānu.

Witnesses:
Bēl-erība/Šullumu
Bēl-erība/Marduk-x
⸢*Mušēbši*$^{?}$⸣/Bēl-ušallim
Bēl-erība/Kalbaya//Šumu-libši
Aššur-tarībi/Bēl-x
The scribe: Iddin-Bēl/Šadûnu
(Place + Date).

Comment

L. 1: Is the number of the year 25 (as in Contenau's copy; i.e., a payment for two years, cf. TCL 13 198) or rather 26 (i.e., a payment for one year)?

L. 4: Contenau's copy has DÙ instead of PAB.

L. 6: Should one read ^{m}⸢*na*$^{?}$-*ba*$^{?}$-*a-a*? or ^{m}⸢*nu-uḫ*⸣-*šá-a* and cf. BM 31517: 3?

L. 13: The sign after ^{md}AMAR.UTU may be a bad copy of I (*-nā'id*), KAM (*-ēreš*), MU (*-iddin*) or URU$_3$ (*-nāṣir*). The name that follows has been copied by Contenau as ^{m}⸢KAL⸣-PI: should we read ^{m}⸢*mu-šib*⸣-*ši*?

No. 144

	TCL 13 198
Museum No.:	Mnb 1861
Date:	11/i/27 Dar (7 April 495 B.C.E.)
Place:	Babylon
Content:	Receipt of the *ilku*-tax from MNA. Paid on behalf of a third party.

Obv.

1 *il-ki šá* ^{m}*gu-za-nu* A-*šú šá* ^{m}*ḫa-am-ba-qu*
2 A LÚ *man-di-di šá* TA ITI.BÁR MU.26.KAM
3 EN TIL ITI.ŠE MU.27.KAM ^{m}*da-a-ri-ia-muš*
4 ^{md}UTU-MU A-*šú šá* <m>ÌR-^{d}AMAR.UTU A ^{m}*de-ki-i*
5 *ina* ŠU.II ^{m}*ši*$^{!}$-*iš-ki* A-*šú šá* ^{m}MU-*a* A ^{m}*e-gì-bi*
6 *a-na muḫ-ḫi* ^{m}*gu-za-nu* A-*šú šá* ^{m}*ḫa-am-ba-qu*
7 A ^{m}*man-di-di ma-ḫi-ir* ⸢1-*en*.TA⸣.ÀM
8 TI-*ú*

Rev.

9 LÚ *mu-kin-nu* ^{md}[EN]-SU *u* ^{md}U.GUR-SUR
10 DUMU.MEŠ *šá* ^{m}*kal-ba-a* A ^{m}MU-*líb-ši* ^{m}*i-qu-pu*
11 A-*šú šá* ^{m}*gu-za-nu* A LÚ.ŠU.KU$_6$ ^{md}AG-URU$_3$-*šú*
12 A-*šú šá* ^{md}AG-*it-tan-nu*
13 ^{m}ÌR-^{d}*ba-ba*$_6$ DUB.SAR DUMU LÚ.AZLAG
14 TIN.TIR.KI ITI.BÁR UD.11.KAM MU.27.KAM
15 ^{m}*da-a-ri-ia-muš* LUGAL E.KI LUGAL KUR.KUR

Translation

The *ilku*-tax from Nisan of the twenty-sixth year till the end of Addar of the twenty-seventh year of Darius is due from Gūzānu, son of Ḫambaqu, descendant of Mandidi. Šamaš-iddin, son of Arad-Marduk, descendant of Dēkû, has received (it) from MNA$_2$ on behalf of Gūzānu, son of Ḫambaqu, descendant of Mandidi.

They have taken one (copy of the document) each.

Witnesses:
[Bēl]-erība and Nergal-ēṭir/Kalbaya//Šumu-libši
Iqūpu/Gūzānu//Bā'iru
Nabû-uṣuršu/Nabû-ittannu
The scribe: Arad-Bāba//Ašlāku
(Place + Date).

Part Three

Personal Name Index

Abbreviations

A. = ancestor;
br. = brother;
daugh. = daughter;
desc. = descendant;
^{f} = female personal name;
F. = father;
husb. = husband;
S. = son of;
Svt. = (male or female) servant;
wr. = written.
* = person in question is a witness;
** = person in question is the scribe of the tablet.

A

Abī-abu (^{m}*a-bi-a-bu*)
S. of Atikām TCL 13 193: 29*

Abī-ul-īde (^{m}AD-NU-ZU)
A. of Bēl-erība S. of Nabû-bēlšunu Dar 435: 2
A. of Mūrānu S. of Šuma-iddin TCL 13 193: 31

Adad-apla-iddin (^{md}IŠKUR-A-MU)
F. of Nabû-ittannu BM 31226: 18

Adad-šammê (^{md}IŠKUR-*šá-me-e*, ^{md}IŠKUR-*šam-me-e*)
A. of Iddinaya S. of Bēl-ēṭir BM 31322: 11
A. of Nabû-bāni-aḫi S. of Marduk-nāṣir Dar 450: 3, 6

Adad-šarra-uṣur (^{md}IŠKUR-LUGAL-URU$_{3}$)
S. of Rīmūt BM 31026: 12*

Addu-ēreš (^{md}*ad-du*-KAM)
No affiliation BM 31226: 6 (Official)

Aḫ-yalīd (^{m}*áḫ-ia-li-du*)
F. of Ša-pî-kalbi Dar 105: 4′

Aḫa-iddin (^{m}ŠEŠ-SUM.NA, ^{m}ŠEŠ-MU)
S. of Šuma-iddin Dar 390: 12*
S. of […] BM 33935: 20*
F. of Balāṭu Dar 542: 16
F. of Ḫašdaya BM 31533: 15

Aḫa-lūmur (^{m}ŠEŠ-*lu-mur*)
S. of ^{d}LUM-LUM-aḫḫē-iddin Dar 296: 24*

^{f}Aḫāssunu (^{f}*a-ḫat-su-nu*)
Svt. of MNA (daugh. of MBU) TCL 13 193: 9, 21

Aḫḫē-iddin (^{m}ŠEŠ.MEŠ-MU)
F. of Bēl-aḫa-ittannu Dar 390: 6
F. of ^{f}Qunnabi Dar 400: 8; Dar 452: 5; Dar 459: 4

Aḫḫē-iddin-Marduk (^{m}ŠEŠ.MEŠ-MU-^{d}AMAR.UTU)
F. of Bēl-iddin desc. of Šangû-Ištar-Bābili Dar 453^{+}: 22; BM 33122: 28

F. of Iddin-Nabû BM 30235: 6

Aḫḫēšaya (^{m}ŠEŠ.MEŠ-*šá-a*)
S. of Nādin desc. of Eppeš-ilī BM 31976: Rev. 3′*

Aḫḫū (^{m}ŠEŠ.MEŠ-⸢*mu*⸣-*ú*)
A. of Zababa-iddin S. of Etellu BM 33936: 8

Aḫi-⸢ēreš⸣ (^{m}ŠEŠ-⸢KAM⸣)
S. of Barīk-il TCL 13 193: U. E.

Aḫšēti (^{m}*a-ḫi-ši-tu*$_{4}$)
No affiliation BM 31393: 16*

Aḫu-atbû (^{m}ŠEŠ-*at-bu-ú*)
S. of Kalbaya Dar 576: 2

Aḫu-bani (^{m}ŠEŠ-*ba-ni*)
A. of Bēl-iddin S. of Balāṭu Dar 437: 17 (⸢Aḫu⸣-[bani])
A. of Bēl-iddin S. of Itti-Marduk-balāṭu Dar 156: 4
A. of Mūrānu S. of Marduk-nāṣir BM 31517: 2, 8; TCL 13 197: 4
A. of [...]-*nu* S. of Balāṭu Dar 351: 16

Aḫūa (⸢^{m}*a*⸣-*ḫu*-[*mu*]-*ú-a*)
S. of Kalbaya BM 31554: 10*

Aḫūšunu (^{m}ŠEŠ-*šú-nu*)
S. of Bēl-apla-iddin desc. of Nabû-bānûnu BM 31528: 15*
S. of Šamšaya Dar 552: 3, 8
F. of Bēl-iddin BM 31322: 10
F. of Nabû-ēṭir-napšāti desc. of Arrabi Dar 411: 14
Svt. of MNA (S. of MBU) TCL 13 193: 8, 20

Allaya (^{m}*al-la-a*)
A. of Ardiya S. of Nabû-bēl-šumāti Dar 308: 18

Amadātu (^{m}*am-ma*-⸢*da-a-tú*⸣ Dar 435, ^{m}*um-ma-da-a-tú* TCL 13 193)
S. of Udunātu Dar 435: U.E. (seal; no patronymy !); TCL 13 193: 25*, Le. E. (seal)

Amēl-Ea (LÚ-^{d}*é-a*, LÚ-^{d}IDIM)
A. of Bēl-aḫḫē-iddin S. of Lâbāši Dar 437: 11
A. of Nidintu S. of Nabû-mukīn-apli Dar 430: 18

Amēl-Isin ($^{(m)}$LÚ-PA.ŠE.KI)
A. of Mušēzib-Bēl S. of Šamaš-aḫa-iddin BM 31977 (//Dar 472): 10 (wr. LÚ.PA<.ŠE.KI>); BM 33959: 15; Dar 453^{+}: 20
A. of Nabû-mušētiq-uddê S. of Iddin-Bēl BM 33959: 16; Dar 453^{+}: [18]

Amēl-S[īsî] (LÚ.AN[ŠE...])
A. of [...] S. of PA-x-A BM 31347: 15

Amēlu (^{m}LÚ-*ú*)
A. of Šuma-iddin S. of Zababa-erība Dar 411: 15

Ammaya, see s.v. Ummaya

Amur-qannu (^{m}*a-mur*-⸢*qa*⸣-*an-nu*)
No affiliation BM 31203: 4

Amurru-šarra-kīni ([^{md}KUR].GAL-LUGAL-*ki-i-ni*)
No affiliation Dar 430: 7 (Official)

Amurru-šarra-uṣur (^{md}KUR.GAL-LUGAL-*ú-ṣu*-DU)
No affiliation BM 31026: 6 (Official)

Ana-Bēl-atkal (^{m}*a-na*-^{d}EN-[*at-k*]*al*)
S. of Kīnaya BM 30965: 22*

Ana-Bēl-ēreš (^{m}*a-na*-^{d}EN-APIN-*eš*)
F. of [...]-*nu* desc. of Mandidi BM 33122: 30

Andaḫar (^{m}*an-da-ḫar*)
A. of Bēl-iddin S. of Šuma-iddin BM 32932: 9
A. of Iddin-Bēl S. of Lūṣi-ana-nūri Dar 541: 20; BM 31951: 9
A. of Nabû-uballiṭ S. of Lūṣi-ana-nūri Dar 541: 23; BM 33930: 17

Anu-aḫa-iddin (^{md}60-ŠEŠ-MU)
F. of Anu-mukīn-apli desc. of Ea-qâlu-išemme BM 33935: 6; BM 33122: [3]
F. of Šamaš-bēl-zēri desc. of Šumu-libši BM 33935: 26

Anu-mukīn-apli (^{md}60-GIN-IBILA, ^{md}*a-nu-um*-GIN-IBILA)
S. of Anu-aḫa-iddin desc. of Ea-qâlu-išemme BM 33935: 6, 10, Le. E. (seal); BM 33122: 2, 13, 15

Aplaya (^{m}*ap-la-a*, ^{m}A-*a*)
S. of Baniya Dar 390: 8*
S. of Bazūzu desc. of Ašlāku BM 31533: 1, 8
S. of Bazūzu desc. of Bābūtu BM 30256: 12*
S. of Balāṭu desc. of Bā'iru Dar 318: 13*
S. of Bēlšunu [desc. of ...] BM 31951: 11*

A. of Bulṭaya S. of Ḫabaṣīru BM 32858: 19
A. of Ibnaya S. of Mušēzib-Marduk BM 30446: 17 (wr. ⸢^{m}ÌR⸣-^{d}GIR$_4$.<KÙ>)
A. of Nabû-nāṣir S. of Baniya Dar 315: 17
A. of Nergal-ibni S. of Mušēzib-Bēl BM 33930: 17

Arad-Ninurta (^{m}ÌR-^{d}MAŠ, ^{m}ÌR-^{d}ME.ME)
S. of Bēl-kāṣir BM 30370: 16*
S. of Marduk-šuma-uṣur desc. of Nabaya b 2800: 9*
F. of Nabû-šuma-iškun desc. of Bā'iru Dar 212: 15

Arad-Šamaš$^{?}$ (^{m}ÌR-^{d}UTU$^{?}$)
No affiliation (?) BM 30799: 2, 10 (Official)

Arānu (^{m}*a-ra-nu*)
F. of Nabû-apla-iddin Dar 369: 13

Ardiya (^{m}ÌR-*ia*/*iá*, ^{m}*ar-di-ia*)
S. of Dādiya desc. of Nabaya Dar 338: 19*; Dar 215: 12**; BM 32883: 16*; BM 31018: 10*; BM 30629: [9*]; Dar 310: 10*
S. of Eṭraya desc. of Suḫaya BM 30446: 11
S. of Kabtiya desc. of Ea-eppeš-ilī BM 30274: 2, 10
S. of Marduk-šarrāni desc. of Ēṭiru BM 31690^{+}: 15*
S. of Nabû-bēl-šumāti desc. of Allaya Dar 308: 17*
S. of Nabû-ēṭir BM 30256: 11*
F. of Bēl-ittannu desc. of Kutimmu BM 32932: 14
F. of Iddinaya Dar 400: 10; Dar 430: 9; BM 31026: 9
F. of Nabû-ittannu desc. of Sîn-ilī Dar 338: 20; BM 30772: 10; TCL 13 196: 23
F. of Nidintu desc. of Rab-līmi BM 31138: 12
F. of Nidintu desc. of Rab-šušši BM 30639: 14; BM 31393: 14
F. of Nidintu Dar 577: 1
F. of Rīmūt-Bēl desc. of Itinnu b 2800: 11; BM 30747: ⸢14⸣$^{?}$; BM 31058: 9; BM 41442: 13; Dar 182: 9; Dar 215: 10; Dar 318: 13; Dar 296: 23
F. of [...] desc. of Ḫušābu BM 33122: 32

Arkât-ilī (^{m}EGIR-DINGIR.MEŠ)
A. of Nabû-ittannu S. of Šūzubu BM 30747: 9

Arrabi (^{m}*a-ra-bi*, ^{m}*ár-bi*, ^{m}*ar-rab-bi*)
F. of Kuṣuraya Dar 400: 11; Dar 452: 18
F. of Nabû-bullissu BM 30641: 4
F. of Nergal-ušallim BM 30747: 3
A. of Nabû-ēṭir-napšāti S. of Aḫūšunu Dar 411: 14 (wr. ^{m}*ar-rab-bi-i*)

Artabānu, see s.v. Artasunu

Artasunu (^{m}*ar-ta-su-nu*, read ^{m}*ar-ta-ba*$^{!}$*-nu*?)
No affiliation BM 30853: 11

Asû (^{m}LÚ.A.ZU)
A. of Nabû-ittannu S. of Bēl-uballiṭ Dar 509: 19

Ašgandu (^{m}*aš-gan-du*$_7$)
A. of Bēl-apla-iddin S. of Niqūdu Dar 437: 14
A. of Sîn-ilī S. of Niqūdu BM 31118: 9

Ašlāku ($^{(m)}$LÚ.AZLAG)
A. of Aplaya S. of Bazūzu BM 31533: 2, 9
A. of Arad-Bāba (S. of Mušēzib-Marduk) BM 30243: 13; BM 33112: 15; BM 31793: ⸢18⸣; Dar 296: 7; TCL 13 198: 13
A. of Iddin-Nabû S. of Bazūzu BM 31533: 2
A. of Libluṭ S. of Nergal-iddin BM 30370: 13
A. of Mūrānu S. of Mušēzib-Marduk Dar 296: 22
A. of Mūrānu S. of Šaddinnu BM 31572: 12
A. of Nidintu S. of Bēl-iddin Dar 296: 22
A. of Šellibi S. of Šaddinnu Dar 334: 10; BM 31018: 12
A. of [...] BM 33968: Rev. 9′

Aššur-aba-uṣur
F. of Nabû-zēra-ibni BM 33968: Rev. ⸢6′⸣ (wr. ⸢^{md}ŠÁR-AD⸣$^{?}$-URU$_3$); Dar 351: 4 (wr. ^{m}⸢DIL-SUR-AD$^{!}$⸣-URU$_3$)

Aššur-tarībi (^{md}ŠÁR-*ta-ri-bi*)
S. of Bēl-x TCL 13 197: 16*

Ātarbānuš (^{m}*a-tar-ba-nu-uš*)
S. of Bagadāta TCL 13 193: 31*

Atikām (^{m}*a-ti-ka-am*)
F. of Abī-abu TCL 13 193: 29

Atkal-ana-Bāba (^{m}*at-kal*<*-a-na*>-^{d}K[Á])

F. of [...]-*nu* desc. of Aḫu-bani Dar 351: 16
A. of Iddin-Bēl S. of Marduk-erība Dar 138: 13
A. of Marduk-bāni-zēri S. of Nabû-šumu-līšir BM 30819: 15; BM 31533: 17[!]

Balīḫu (mdKASKAL+KUR-*ú*) see s.v. Ilu-tillatī

Banâ-ša-iliya (mDÙ-*a-šá*-DINGIR-*iá*)
A. of Kuṣuraya S. of Baniya Dar 154: 1

Bāni-šarra-uṣur (m⸢*ba-ni*⸣-LUGAL-URU$_3$)
No affiliation BM 30446: 5 (Official)

Bāni-zēri (mDÙ-NUMUN)
S. of Šāpik-zēri desc. of Šangû-Sîn BM 31977 (//Dar 472): 20*

Baniya (mDÙ-*ia*/*iá*, m*ba-ni-ia*
F. of Aplaya Dar 390: 9
F. of Bēl-erība Dar 405: 14
F. of Bēl-iddin desc. of Na[baya] Dar 577:14
F. of Bēl-kāṣir desc. of Arad-Nergal Dar 308: 16
F. of Iddin-Nabû BM 33935: 28
F. of Kuṣuraya desc. of Banâ-ša-iliya Dar 154: 1
F. of Marduk-mukīn-apli desc. of Rab-šušši Dar 138: 14
F. of Nabû-ittannu desc. of Itinnu BM 30261: 5; BM 30541: 5 (wr. [m*ba*]-*ni-ia*)
F. of Nabû-nāṣir desc. of Arad-Nergal Dar 315: 17
F. of Nergal-iddin desc. of Ša-nāšīšu Dar 212: 17
F. of Rīmūt-Bēl desc. of Itinnu BM 30261: 1
F. of Sîn-ilī desc. of [...] BM 30261: 8
F. of [...] Dar 452: 17

Bānûnu (m*ba-nu-nu*)
No affiliation BM 30853: 35; BM 30651: Rev. 6′

Barīk-il (m*ba-ri-ku*/*ki*-DINGIR)
S. of Iltammeš-māḫir BM 33935: 17*
F. of Aḫi-⸢ēreš⸣ TCL 13 193: U. E.

Barsiya (m*bar-si-a-a*)
S. of Marduk-šuma-uṣur desc. of Bābūtu BM 30819: 1, 8

Barz[iya]? (m*bar*-⸢*zi*?-x-x⸣)
No affiliation BM 31891: 1

Basiya (m*ba-si-ia*/*iá*)
S. of Nabû-šuma-ukīn [desc. of Ša-nā]šīšu BM 31554: 6 (wr. [mx-x]-⸢*ia*⸣)
S. of Sūqaya desc. of Basiya Dar 338: 21*
S. of Šilaya Dar 435: U.E. (seal, no affiliation) TCL 13 193: 30*
F. of Bēl-iddin desc. of Bēl-eṭēru BM 30819: 11 (wr. m*ba*-⸢*si*⸣-*a*); Dar 542: 14 (no desc.)
A. of Basiya S. of Sūqaya Dar 338: 22
A. of Nabû-nāṣir S. of Itti-Nabû-lummir TCL 13 193: 12

Bazbaka (m*ba-az-ba-ka*)
No affiliation BM 32891: 4 (Official)

Bazūzu (m*ba-zu-zu*)
F. of Aplaya desc. of Ašlāku BM 31533: 2
F. of Aplaya desc. of Bābūtu BM 30256: 12
F. of Iddin-Nabû desc. of Ašlāku BM 31533: 2
F. of Nabû-aḫa-iddin desc. of Ir'anni BM 30795: 14
No affiliation BM 33954: 4, 10

Be-[...] (m⸢*be*?⸣-[...] or m⸢*Na*?⸣-[...])
A. of Ea-iddin S. of Šamaš-iddin Dar 452: 14

Bēl-aḫa-iddin (mdEN-ŠEŠ-MU)
S. of Gimil[!]-Šamaš BM 31976: Rev. 2′*
F. of Šulum-Bābili Dar 296: 18

Bēl-aḫa-ittannu (mdEN-ŠEŠ-*it-tan-nu*)
S. of Aḫḫē-iddin Dar 390: 5

Bēl-aḫa-ušabši (mdEN-PAB/ŠEŠ-GÁL-*ši*)
F. of Marduk-iqīšanni desc. of Bēl-eṭēru Dar 164: 15; Dar 167: 15
F. of Mušēzib-Marduk desc. of Bēl-apla-uṣur BM 31026: 15

Bēl-aḫḫē-erība (mdEN-ŠEŠ.MEŠ-SU)
F. of Mušēzib-Bēl desc. of Ile''i-Marduk BM 32932: 12
F. of Nidintu BM 41453: 6
F. of Ubār desc. of Maṣṣār-elep-rukūbi TCL 13 196: 13

Bēl-aḫḫē-iddin (mdEN-ŠEŠ.MEŠ-MU/SUM.NA)
S. of Lâbāši desc. of Amēl-Ea Dar 437: 10* (Official)
S. of [...] BM 31786: 8*

F. of Bēl-apla-uṣur desc. of Rab-banê BM 30233: 11
F. of Marduk-zēra-ibni desc. of Nappāḫu Dar 156: 13
F. of Šamaš-iddin desc. of Ir'anni BM 30446: 10
F. of Šullumaya desc. of Egibi BM 32932: 13

Bēl-aḫḫē-iqīša (^{md}EN-ŠEŠ.MEŠ-BA-*šá*)
S. of Nabû-aḫḫē-iddin//⸢Gaḫal⸣ BM 31554: 14**
F. of Bēl-lūmur desc. of Šangû-Ištar-Bābili BM 30965: 19
F. of Dād[iya] desc. of Sîn-tabni-⸢uṣur$^{?}$⸣ BM 33122: 24
F. of Nabû-bullissu desc. of Nādin-še'i Dar 206: 19
F. of Šaddinnu Dar 182: 11

Bēl-apla-iddin (^{md}EN-A/EDURU/IBILA-MU, ^{md}EN-A-SUM.NA, ^{md}EN-*ap-lu*-MU)
S. of Arad-Gula desc. of Eppeš-ilī BM 33936: 17*; Le.E.*
S. of Marduk-šuma-iddin desc. of Šangû-Gula BM 30366: 9*
S. of Nabû-kāṣir desc. of Nabunnaya BM 33928: 19**
S. of Niqūdu desc. of Ašgandu Dar 437: 13*
S. of Padā BM 30233: 13*
S. of Rīmūt-Bēl desc. of Nappāḫu Dar 437: 14*
S. of Ṭābiya desc. of Ša-nāšīšu Dar 552: 10*; Dar 573: 10*
F. of Aḫūšunu desc. of Nabû-bānûnu BM 31528: 15
F. of Bibānu desc. of Gaḫal Dar 541: 21
[F./A. of] [...] BM 33959: 10* (wr. [^{md}]⸢EN$^{?}$⸣-A-MU)
No affiliation Dar 154: 3; Dar 206: 6 (governor); BM 30233: 6

Bēl-apla-uṣur (^{md}EN-EDURU/A-URU$_3$)
S. of Bēl-aḫḫē-iddin desc. of Rab-banê BM 30233: 10*
F. of Rē'ûšunu-Marduk S. of desc. of ⸢...-aya⸣
A. of Mušēzib-Marduk S. of Bēl-aḫa-ušabši BM 31026: 15
A. of Nabû-uballiṭ BM 30639: 17; BM 31393: [17]?
A. of [...] S. of Šuma-ukīn BM 31977 (// Dar 472): 11

Bēl-asûa (^{md}EN-*a-su-ú-a*, ^{md}EN-*a-su-ú*, ^{md}EN-A.ZU-*ú*(-*a*) BM 31227 and BM 30541)
S. of Nabû-iddin desc. of Bābūtu BM 31227: 1, 7
S. of Nergal-uballiṭ desc. of Mudammiq-Adad BM 30541: 10*; BM 31891: Rev. 4*; BM 32873: 12*; TCL 13 196: 11, 15, 18, 21
S. of Nergal-uballiṭ BM 31347: ⸢13*⸣? (wr. ^{md}E[N-...])

Bēl-balāssu-iqbi (^{md}EN-DIN-*su*-E)
F. of Ḫašdaya BM 30270: 15; BM 30490: 20

Bēl-bani (^{m}EN-*ba-ni*)
A. of Nabû-napišta-uṣur S. of Šamaš-mukīn-apli Dar 315: 18

Bēl-baniya (^{md}EN-DÙ$^{!}$-*iá*)
S. of Šākin-šumi desc. of Ir'anni BM 31977 (// Dar 472): 9

Bēl-bullissu (^{md}⸢EN⸣-*bul-liṭ-su*)
No affiliation BM 33930: 8 (Official)

Bēl-ēreš (^{md}EN-KAM)
S. of Nummuru BM 33121: 16*

Bēl-erība (^{md}EN-SU, ^{md}EN-*eri-ba* Dar 435)
S. of Aplaya (= Kalbaya$^{?!}$) desc. of Šumu-libši BM 30270: 17**
S. of Baniya Dar 405: 14*
S. of Kalbaya desc. of MU-LU-RU-ŠÚ BM 30370: 14*
S. of Kalbaya desc. of Šumu-libši BM 30256: 13*; BM 30274: 5, 9; BM 30366: 10*; BM 30446: [18]**; BM 30490: 23** (no desc.); BM 30772: 13*; BM 30795: 17**; BM 30961: 15* (//BM 31667^{+}: 14*); BM 31226: 15*; BM 31449: 13*; BM 32891: 16** (wr. [^{md}EN-S]U); BM 41442: 15*; Dar 544: 9*; Dar 552: 12*; TCL 13 197: 14*; TCL 13 198: 9*
S. of Marduk-x TCL 13 197: 13 *
S. of Mušēzib-Marduk desc. of LÚ [...] Dar 544: 10*
S. of Nabû-bēlšunu desc. of Abī-ul-īde Dar 435: 2
S. of Nabû-rēmanni Dar 296: 23*
S. of Nādin desc. of Lūṣi-ana-nūr-Marduk BM 30589: 4, 7

S. of Šullumu TCL 13 197: 12*
S. of [...] BM 31188: 4
desc. of Rīmūt-Ea BM 33954: 19*
No affiliation BM 30589: 8 (Official)
Dar 573: 14*

Bēl-eṭēru (^{md}EN-*e-ṭi/ṭè-ru/ri*)
A. of Bēl-iddin S. of Basiya BM 30819: 12
A. of Bēl-ittannu S. of Itti-Nabû-balāṭu BM 30980: 11
A. of Bēl-uballiṭ S. of Itti-Nabû-balāṭu BM 30965: 26
A. of Bēl-uballiṭ S. of Itti-Marduk-balāṭu BM 30772: 15
A. of Bēl-uballiṭ BM 32858: 14
A. of ⸢Ina-tēšê-ēṭir⸣$^{?}$ S. of Šuma-iddin BM 33954: 21
A. of Iqūpu S. of Gūzānu TCL 13 198: 11
A. of Marduk-iqīšanni S. of Bēl-aḫa-ušabši Dar 164: 16; Dar 167: 15
A. of Mukkêa S. of [...] BM 33926: 7

Bēl-ēṭir (^{md}EN-KAR-*ir*, ^{md}EN-SUR)
S. of Bēl-iddin BM 30274: 15**
S. of Bēl-iqīša desc. of Šangû-Ea BM 30243: 2, 7
S. of Nabû-ēṭir-napšāti desc. of Paḫāru BM 31203: ⸢10⸣*; BM 41449: 13*
S. of Sîn-⸢iddin$^{?}$⸣ BM 33968: Rev. 10′*
F. of Bēl-uballiṭ desc. of Ir'anni BM 31528: 16
F. of Iddinaya desc. of Adad-šammê BM 31322: 11
F. of (Nabû-)Šuma-ukīn desc. of Šangû-Nanaya b 2800: 2; BM 31533: 4 (no desc.); Dar 213: 3; TCL 13 185: 8
No affiliation BM 31227: 5 (or -upaḫḫir)
Svt. of Bagasarū Dar 105: 3

Bēl-gabbi-Bēlumma (^{m}EN-*gab-bi*-^{d}EN-*um-mu*)
Svt. of MNA (S. of MBU) TCL 13 193: 7, 20

Bēl-ibni (^{md}EN-DÙ)
S. of Bēl-upaḫḫir BM 31793: 8, [10] (wr. ^{md}EN-x; or read Bēl-nāṣir?)
S. of Gūzānu desc. of Zēriya BM 30965: 24*
S. of Nergal-zēra-ibni desc. of Šangû-Nanaya Dar 105: 5′**; Dar 164: 19**; Dar 167: 18**; S. of Nergal-zē[ra-ibni desc. of Šangû-Nanaya] BM 33972: 28[**]
BM 33968: 3

Bēl-iddin (^{md}EN-MU/SUM.NA)
S. of Aḫḫē-iddin-Marduk desc. of Šangû-Ištar-Bābili Dar 453^{+}: 22*; BM 33122: [28]*
S. of Aḫūšunu BM 31322: 10*
S. of Balāṭu desc. of Aḫu-[bani] Dar 437: 17*
S. of Baniya (desc. of Na[baya] Dar 577:14*)
S. of Basiya desc. of Bēl-eṭēru BM 30819: 11*; Dar 542: 13* (no desc.)
S. of Gimriya desc. of Paḫāru Dar 572: 10*; Dar 573: 11*
S. of Gūzānu desc. of Ea-ṣalam-ilī Dar 400: 14*; BM 31976: Rev. 3′*
S. of Iddin-⸢Bēl⸣ desc. of Šangû-Ea Dar 450: 10*
S. of Iddin-Nabû desc. of Dābibī BM 31572: 11*; BM 31690^{+}: 13*; BM 31951: 9* (desc. broken); BM 32891: 13*
S. of Itti-Marduk-balāṭu desc. of Aḫu-bani Dar 156: 3
S. of Kittiya desc. of Paḫāru BM 31554: 12*
S. of Lâbāši desc. of Bābūtu BM 32883: 9*
S. of Mušēzib-Bēl desc. of Bā'iru Dar 459: 16*
S. of Mušēzib-Marduk desc. of Sîn-nādin-šumi BM 41449: 9*; Dar 437: 2; Dar 455: 2
S. of Nabû-apla-iddin desc. of Ir'anni Dar 541: 18*
S. of Nabû-apla-iddin desc. of Šangû-Gula BM 30297: 12*
S. of Nabû-balāssu-iqbi desc. of Egibi Dar 144: 17*
S. of Nabû-balāssu-iqbi Dar 437: 16*
S. of Nabû-nādin-aḫi desc. of Nabaya Dar 527: 18**
S. of Nabû-nādin-ipri desc. of Ea-ilūta-bani Dar 206: 16*
S. of Nabû-zēra-iddin Dar 164: ⸢16⸣*; Dar 167: 14*

BM 31449: ⸢15⸣[**] (Bēl-itt[annu ...])
No affiliation (GIŠ.BÁN *šá* ~) BM 31393: 2; BM 31786: 2; BM 32891: 2; also BM 31572: 2? (wr. Bēl-[ittannu], Official)

Bēl-kāṣir (^{md}EN-*ka-ṣir*, ^{md}EN-KÁD)
S. of Baniya desc. of Arad-Nergal Dar 308: 16*
S. of Ḫabaṣīru Dar 400: 11*
S. of Nabû-mukīn-apli desc. of Bu[raqu] BM 31036: 9*
S. of Nummuru desc. of Dābibī BM 30243: 9*
F. of Arad-Ninurta BM 30370: 16
F. of Bēl-ušallim BM 30961: 16; BM 31667^{+}: [15]
F. of Kulbibi desc. of Eppeš-ilī Dar 268: 2
F. of Mušēzib-Bēl desc. of Ea-eppeš-ilī Dar 296: 20
F. of Nidintu desc. of Eppeš-ilī TCL 13 193: 28
F. of Nidintu desc. of Itinnu BM 32873: 11
F. of Tattannu desc. of Dābibī BM 31322: 9 (mistake for Nabû-kāṣir?)

Bēl-kēšir (^{md}EN-*ki-šìr*)
S. of Nabû-apla-iddin desc. of Šangû-Ea BM 30243: 10*
S. of Nabû-nāṣir desc. of Bēlaya BM 30965: 21*
F. of Itti-Bēl-lummir/lāmur desc. of Sîn-[šadûnu] BM 33959: 13; Dar 453^{+}: 17

Bēl-kiṣuršu (^{md}EN-*ki-ṣur-šú*, see s.v. Bēl-ikṣur S. of Rīmūt)

Bēl-lūmur (^{md}EN-*lu-mu-ur*)
S. of Bēl-aḫḫē-iqīša desc. of Šangû-Ištar-Bābili BM 30965: 19*

Bēl-nādin-apli (^{md}EN-*na-din*-IBILA/A)
S. of Bēl-uballiṭ desc. of Paḫāru b 2800: 4; Dar 212: 1, 10, 13; Dar 213: 6; no affiliation TCL 13 185: 3, 14

Bēl-nāṣir (^{md}EN-PAB)
S. of Bēl-upaḫḫir BM 31793: 8, [10] (wr. ^{md}EN-x; or read Bēl-ibni?)
S. of Damqiya desc. of Nādin-še'i BM 30961: 17*; BM 31667^{+}: 16*

Bēl-qa-[...] (^{md}EN-*qa*-[...])
BM 30854: Rev. 8′

Bēl-rēmanni (^{md}EN-*re-man-ni*)
S. of Kalbi-⸢Ninurta⸣ BM 31718: ⸢16′⸣*
S. of Nabû-šuma-ukīn desc. of Rab-banê-Marduk Dar 437: 11* (Official)
F. of Nabû-kuzub-ilī desc. of Eppeš-ilī BM 30994: 4 (//BM 31722^{+}: 4); BM 32858: 5

Bēl-ruṣūa (^{md}EN-*ru-ṣu-ú-a*)
BM 33930: 4, 7, 13 (Official)

Bēl-šuma-iškun (^{md}EN-MU-GAR-*un*)
F. of Nabû-ittannu desc. of Suḫaya BM 30297: 2

Bēl-uballiṭ (^{md}EN-DIN-*iṭ*, ^{md}EN-*ú-bal-liṭ* b 2800)
S. of Bēl-ēṭir desc. of Ir'anni BM 31528: 16*
S. of Iddin-Nabû desc. of Bā'iru BM 31188: 8
S. of Iddin-Nabû desc. of Dābibī BM 33122: 18*; BM 33928: 13*
S. of Itti-Marduk-balāṭu desc. of Bēl-eṭēru BM 30772: 14**
S. of Itti-Nabû-balāṭu desc. of Bēl-eṭēru BM 30965: 25**
(S. of Itti-Nabû-balāṭu?) desc. of Bēl-eṭēru BM 32858: 14**
S. of Kiribtu desc. of Nūr-Sîn Dar 156: 12*
S. of Marduk-šuma-ibni Dar 338: 20*
S. of Nabû-ēṭir-napšāti desc. of Atkuppu Dar 310: 17**; Dar 334: 12**
S. of Nabû-ēṭir-napšāti BM 31226: 13*
S. of Nabû-iddin desc. of Rab-banê b 2800: 13**; Dar 307: 11**
S. of Nabû-uṣuršu BM 30274: 13* (wr. ^{md}EN-BA(= DIN$^{!}$)-*iṭ*)
F. of Bēl-nādin-apli desc. of Paḫāru b 2800: 4; Dar 212: 2; Dar 213: 7
F. of Nā'id-Bēl desc. of Paḫāru Dar 212: 2
F. of Nabû-iddin desc. of Paḫāru b 2800: 4; Dar 212: 2
F. of TU-Marduk desc. of Nabû-⸢uṣuršu$^{?}$⸣ BM 30446: 2
F. of Iddin-x BM 33122: 23$^{!}$
F. of Nabû-ittannu desc. of Asû Dar 509: 19

Bēl-upaḫḫir (^{md}EN-NIGIN-*ir*)

S. of Bāba-ēreš desc. of Mudammiq$^{?}$-Adad BM 32873: 7
S. of Nergal-iddin BM 31360: 2, 10, 12, 14, 18, 19; BM 31793: 4, 8, 10; Dar 345: 4, 16**; Dar 509: 2; *alias* Puḫḫuru Dar 369: 2, 7, 10
F. of Bēl-ibni/nāṣir BM 31793: 8, [10]
No affiliation BM 30639: 10

Bēl-uṣuršu (^{md}EN-URU$_3$-*šú*)
F. of [...] BM 33959: 2

Bēl-ušallim (^{md}EN-GI, ^{md}EN-*ú-šal-lim*)
S. of Bēl-iddin desc. of Arad-Ea BM 31977 (//Dar 472): 18*
S. of Bēl-iqīša desc. of Šangû-Ea BM 30243: 7
S. of Bēl-kāṣir BM 30961: 16*; BM 31667^{+}: 15*
S. of Ina-Nabû-ultarraḫ BM 31036: 4 (Official)
F. of ⸢*Mušēbši*$^{?}$⸣ TCL 13 197: 14
No affiliation (Official) BM 30591: 11*; BM 31786: 3

Bēl-zēra-ibni (^{md}EN-NUMUN-DÙ)
desc. of Dābibī BM 33954: 22**

Bēl-zēra-iddin (^{md}EN-NUMUN-MU)
No affiliation BM 31416: 7

Bēl-zē[ra ...] (^{md}EN-NU[MUN]$^{?}$)
F. of [...] BM 30591: 8

Bēl-zēri (^{md}EN-NUMUN)
F. of Iddin-Nabû BM 31188: ⸢16⸣
F. of Itti-Marduk-balāṭu BM 30233: 15
F. of Sūqaya desc. of Buraqu Dar 342: Rev. 2 (wr. ^{m}EN-NUMUN)

Bēl-[...] (^{md}EN-[...])
S. of Bēl-upaḫḫir BM 31793: 8, [10] (wr. ^{md}EN-x, probably read Bēl-ibni, or -nāṣir)
S. of Nabû-⸢x x x⸣ BM 31690^{+}: 17** (wr. Bēl-[x])
S. of Nergal-uballiṭ BM 31347: ⸢13⸣* (wr. ^{md}E[N-...], read Bē[l-asûa]?)
S. of Niqūdu desc. of Rab-⸢banê⸣ Dar 459: 12* (probably read Bēl-[ikṣur])
S. of Zēriya desc. of MU-[...] BM 31188: 9 (wr. ^{md}[EN]-[...])
F. of Aplaya desc. of Sîn-šadûnu BM 31786: 14
F. of Aššur-tarībi TCL 13 197: 16
BM 31572: 2 (Official, probably read Bēl-[ittannu])

Bēlaya (^{m}EN-*a-a*)
A. of Bēl-kēšir S. of Nabû-nāṣir BM 30965: 22

Bēlšunu (^{m}EN-*šú-nu*, ^{md}EN-*šú-nu* BM 30747)
S. of Kī-Nabû Dar 144: 16*
S. of Lâbāši BM 33930: 18*
S. of Libluṭ BM 30256: 10*
S. of [...] BM 30747: 13*
F. of Aplaya BM 31951: 11
F. of Iddin-Bēl desc. of Sîn-nāṣir BM 33930: 19
F. of Iddin-Nabû desc. of Paḫāru BM 32883: 16
F. of Iddin-Nabû desc. of Ṭābiḫ-kāri Dar 154: 12
F. of Nabû-bullissu Dar 296: 24
F. of Napuštu desc. of Gaḫal BM 31036: 10
F. of Nergal-iddin Dar 459: 15
F. of Ninurta-uballiṭ Dar 310: 14
F. of Ṣilli-Bēl desc. of Nūr-Sîn BM 31058: 11
F. of Šellibi desc. of Sîn-damāqu BM 30589: 14
F. of [...] desc. of Sîn-šadûnu BM 31977 (// Dar 472): 12 (wr. [(...-)]EN-*šú-nu*)

Bibānu (^{m}*bi-ba-nu*)
S. of Bēl-apla-iddin desc. of Gaḫal Dar 541: 21*
S. of Nergal-šarra-uṣur Dar 310: 12*
[F./A. of] Aplaya BM 33121: 15

Bibbûa (^{m}*bi-ib-bu-ú-a*)
A. of Iddin-Marduk S. of Marduk-erība BM 30274: 12
A. of Zumbaya S. of Kurbanni-Marduk Dar 509: 18

Bibi (^{m}*bi-bi*)
A. of Arad-Bēl S. of Ina-tēšê-ēṭir BM 33954: 15 (read <Dā>bibī, or = <Kul>bibi?)

Bīt-iltammar$^{!}$ (^{m}É-DINGIR-IL-TAM-GA-BI)
F. of Ṣillaya BM 30639: 5

Bulluṭu (^{m}*bul-lu-ṭu*)
S. of Šamaš-zēra-ušabši desc. of Sîn-šadûnu Dar 405: 12*

Bulṭaya (^{m}*bul-ṭa-a*)

S. of Balāssu desc. of Miṣiraya BM 31690^{+}: 14*
S. of Ḫabaṣīru desc. of Arad-Nergal BM 32858: 18*
S. of Ḫabaṣīru desc. of Rē'i-alpi Dar 158: 1, 6, 20; Dar 215: 1, 5, 7
S. of Iddin-Bēl Dar 411: 16**
S. of Iddin-Nergal desc. of Eppeš-ilī Dar 541: 24*
S. of Šamaš(-zēra)-ibni BM 30270: 15*; BM 30490: 20*
S. of Ubār Dar 296: 21* (wr. ^{m}*bul-luṭ*$^{?!}$(TAR)-*a-a*)
F. of [...]-*tu* BM 31951: 12

Būnānu (^{m}*bu-na-nu*)
S. of Sūqaya desc. of Sîn-gāmil Dar 509: 15*

Buraqu (^{m}*bu-ra*[*q-qu/a*])
A. of Bēl-kāṣir S. of Nabû-mukīn-apli BM 31036: 9 (^{m}*bu*-[...])
A. of Sūqaya S. of Bēl-zēri Dar 342: Rev. 2

Būṣu (^{m}*bu-ú-ṣu*)
A. of Nabû-bullissu S. of Šākin-šumi BM 33122: 20

D

Dābibī (^{m}*da-bi-bi*)
A. of Bēl-iddin S. of Iddin-Nabû BM 31690^{+}: 13; BM 31572: 11; BM 31951: ⸢10⸣ ([...]-*bi*$^{?}$); BM 32891: 14
A. of Bēl-kāṣir S. of Nummuru BM 30243: 10
A. of Bēl-uballiṭ S. of Iddin-Nabû BM 33122: 18; BM 33928: 14
A. of Bēl-zēra-ibni BM 33954: 22
A. of Lâbāši S. of Nabû-ile''i BM 31977 (// Dar 472): 14
A. of Marduk-zēra-ibni S. of Bēl-iddin Dar 351: 19
A. of Nabû-aḫḫē-bulliṭ S. of Nabû-kāṣir Dar 138: 11
A. of Nabû-aḫḫē-iddin S. of Nabû-ile''i BM 30261: 13
A. of Nabû-bullissu S. of Iddin-Nabû b 2800: 13; BM 31018: 15; Dar 182: 10; also Dar 577: [15]?; TCL 13 185: 18
A. of Qīšti-Marduk S. of Rīmūt Dar 351: 18
A. of Tattannu S. of Bēl-kāṣir BM 31322: 10 (probably read Nabû-kāṣir for Bēl-kāṣir)
A. of Tattannu S. of Nabû-kāṣir BM 30235: 10; BM 30764: 10; BM 31393: 13; BM 31517: 13; BM 31572: 10; BM 31786: [13]; BM 31798: 8; BM 32891: 11

Dādiya (^{m}*da-di-ia/iá*)
S. of Bēl-aḫḫē-iqīša desc. of Sîn-tabni-⸢uṣur$^{?}$⸣ BM 33122: 24* (^{m}*da-d*[*i-ia*])
S. of Mušēzib-Marduk desc. of Ni-x(-x)-nu Dar 318: 10*
F. of Ardiya desc. of Nabaya BM 30629: 10; BM 31018: 10; BM 32883: 17; Dar 215: 12; Dar 310: 10; Dar 338: 19

Daḫḫûa (^{m}*da-aḫ-ḫu-ú-a*)
No affiliation BM 30233: 5

Damqiya (^{m}SIG$_5$-*ia/iá*; ^{m}⸢*dam-qi-ia*⸣ Dar 338; ^{m}SIG$_5$-*qí-iá* BM 31058; *alias* Nabû-damiq-ilī desc. of Nādin-še'i)
F. of Arad-Bēl desc. of Nādin-še'i BM 30965: 18
F. of Bēl-nāṣir desc. of Nādin-še'i BM 30961: 17; BM 31667^{+}: 16
F. of Nabû-nādin-aḫi desc. of Nādin-še'i BM 30961: 19; BM 31667^{+}: [18]
F. of Nidinti-Bēl desc. of Nādin-še'i BM 31058: 8; BM 41607: 14; Dar 310: 13; Dar 338: ⸢23⸣

Dannêa (^{m}*dan-ni-e-*(*a*))
A. of Ḫaḫḫuru S. of Nabû-ēṭir-napšāti Dar 215: 11
A. of Nidintu S. of Bēl-iddin BM 41453: [15]
A. of [...]-Bēl S. of Ḫabaṣīru OECT 10 234: 12'

Dayyān-Marduk (^{m}DI.KUD-^{d}⸢AMAR.UTU⸣)
No affiliation BM 30854: 2

Dēkû (^{m}/LÚ *de-ki-i*, ^{m}*de-ku-ú*)
A. of Ḫabaṣīru S. of Mušēzib-Marduk BM 32932: 6
A. of Marduk-šuma-iddin S. of Nabû-iddin BM 30370: 18
A. of Nabû-nādin-aḫi S. of Nabû-bēl-šumāti BM 31018: 3, 6
A. of Nabû-šuma-iddin S. of Šāpik-zēri BM 31226: 12; Dar 455: 13
A. of Sūqaya S. of Aplaya Dar 268: 14

A. of Šamaš-iddin S. of Arad-Marduk TCL 13 198: 4
A. of Šāpik-zēri BM 31347: 13
A. of Zēriya S. of Šāpik-zēri BM 31226: 12

DINGIR-NA-A, see s.v. Ilunnaya

Dummuqu (^{m}*du-um-mu-qu*, ^{m}*du-muq* Dar 552, [^{m}*d*]*u-muq-qu* Dar 572)
S. of Balāṭu desc. of Gaḫul BM 30772: 2, 8
F. of Marduk-ēreš desc. of Nappāḫu Dar 552: 11; Dar 572: 10

E

E-x (^{m}*e*-x)
A. of Nabû-kuṣuršu S. of Marduk$^{?}$-šuma-iddin BM 31036: 13

Ea-apla-iddin (^{md}IDIM-A-MU, ^{md}*é-a*-IBILA-MU)
S. of Mušēzib-Marduk desc. of Ṭābiḫ-kāri BM 30799: 12*; Dar 158: 12* (^{md}*é*-[...]); Dar 213: 12** (no patronymy)

(Ea-)Eppeš-ilī (^{md}*é-a*-DÙ-*eš*-DINGIR, ^{md}IDIM-DÙ-*eš*-DINGIR, ^{m}DÙ-*eš*-DINGIR, ^{md}IDIM-DÙ-*uš*-DINGIR Dar 296)
A. of Aḫḫēšaya S. of Nādin BM 31976: Rev. 3'
A. of Arad-Gula S. of Nergal-iddin BM 31203: 9
A. of Ardiya S. of Kabtiya BM 30274: 3
A. of Bēl-apla-iddin S. of Arad-Gula BM 33936: 18
A. of Bēl-īpuš S. of Nabû-zēru-līšir BM 32883: 12
A. of Bulṭaya S. of Iddin-Nergal Dar 541: 24
A. of Ḫabaṣīru BM 32858: 11
A. of Iddin-Bēl S. of Zumbaya BM 32858: 12
A. of Iddinaya S. of Nādin Dar 315: 14
A. of Iṣṣūr S. of Nabû-šuma-iddin BM 41442: 14
A. of Itti-Nabû-balāṭu S. of Mūrānu Dar 359: 14
A. of Itti-Nabû-nāṣir S. of Ea-iddin BM 30261: 11
A. of Kāṣir S. of Tattannu BM 30639: 13; BM 31393: 15
A. of Kidinnu S. of Balāṭu BM 30261: 12
A. of Kulbibi S. of Bēl-kāṣir Dar 268: 3
A. of Mušēzib-Bēl S. of Bēl-kāṣir Dar 296: 20
A. of Murašû S. of Iddin-Marduk BM 30629: 13
A. of Nabû-bullissu S. of Iddin-Bēl Dar 369: 15
A. of Nabû-kuzub-ilī S. of Bēl-rēmanni BM 30994: 4 (//BM 31722^{+}: 4); BM 32858: 5
A. of Nabû-nādin-aḫi S. of Rīmūt-Bēl BM 30589: 16
A. of Nidintu S. of Bēl-kāṣir TCL 13 193: 28
A. of Niqūdu S. of Iddin-Nabû Dar 400: 14
A. of [...]-Marduk BM 31951: 15
A. of [...]-*ru* S. of [...] BM 41607: 12
A. of [...] BM 33968: Rev. 11'; BM 31793: 16

Ea-iddin (^{md}IDIM-MU)
S. of Šamaš-iddin desc. of Be/Na$^{?}$-[...] Dar 452: 14*
F. of Itti-Nabû-nāṣir desc. of Eppeš-ilī BM 30261: 11
F. of Marduk-nāṣir desc. of Šumāti BM 30261: 10

Ea-ilūta-bani (^{md}IDIM-DINGIR-*ú-tu*-DÙ, ^{md}IDIM-*lit-tab-ba-nu*)
A. of Bēl-iddin S. of Nabû-nādin-ipri Dar 206: 17
A. of [...] [S. of] Nabû-šuma-uṣur BM 31360: 24

Ea-kīni (^{md}IDIM-*ki-i-ni*)
No affiliation Dar 430: 13

Ea-nāṣir (^{md}IDIM-*na-ṣir*)
A. of Bēl-ittannu S. of Gūzānu BM 33928: 16

Ea-pattannu (^{md}IDIM-*pat-ta/tan-nu*)
A. of Itti-⸢Nabû⸣-[...] S. of Iddin-Nabû BM 31718: 14'
A. of Iqīšaya S. of Nabû-mukīn-apli Dar 334: 11
A. of Ubār S. of Bēl-iddin BM 30256: 15
A. of Zanzīru S. of [Nabû]-apla-iddin Dar 453^{+}: 16 (wr. ^{md}IDIM-*pat-t*[*an-nu*])
A. of [...] BM 31793: 17

Ea-qâlu-išemme (^{md}*é-a*-ME-ŠE.GA, ^{md}*é-a-qa-a-lu-i-šem-me*)
A. of Anu-mukīn-apli S. of Anu-aḫa-iddin BM 33122: 3; BM 33935: 7, Le. E. (seal)

Ea-ṣalam-ilī (^{md}IDIM-NU-DINGIR, ^{md}IDIM-*ṣa-lam*-DINGIR, ^{md}IDIM-*ṣal-mi*-DINGIR)
A. of Bēl-iddin S. of Gūzānu BM 31976: Rev. 4′; Dar 400: 15
A. of Nabû-bullissu S. of Nabû-mukīn-zēri BM 30764: 13; BM 31517: 16

Ea-zēra-iqīša (^{md}IDIM-NUMUN-BA-*šá*)
F. of Nabû-kuṣuršu desc. of Bābūtu Dar 453^{+}: 14
F. of [Nabû-kuṣuršu?] desc. of Bābūtu BM 33959: 12

Eda-ēṭir (^{m}DIL-SUR)
A. of Nabû-uballissu S. of Nabû-kēšir BM 33936: 3
A. of Šulum-Bābili S. of Arad-Bēl BM 32873: 11

Egibi (^{m}*e-gi/gì-bi*)
A. of Arad-Bāba S. of Nergal-ušēzib Dar 156: 15
A. of Bēl-iddin S. of Nabû-balāssu-iqbi Dar 144: 18
A. of Gimillu S. of Bēl-iddin Dar 453^{+}: 21
A. of Kalbaya S. of Nabû-aḫḫē-iddin BM 32883: 11; Dar 310: 11; Dar 338: 18
A. of Marduk-ēṭir S. of Mūrānu Dar 156: 11
A. of MNA (*passim*)
A. of Marduk-šuma-iddin S. of Marduk-zēra-ibni BM 32883: 18
A. of Nabû-aḫḫē-bulliṭ (*alias* Puršû), br. of MNA BM 30541: 3; BM 31528: 3, 14; BM 31572: 15; BM 32883: 13; BM 33122: 5; BM 33928: 8; Dar 315: 5; Dar 338: 9; Dar 345: 3; Dar 455: 14
A. of Nabû-apla-iddin S. of Bēl-iddin Dar 541: 26
A. of Nabû-ittannu S. of Mušēzib-Marduk BM 31554: 9
A. of Nabû-mudammiq S. of Nabû-napšāti-uṣur Dar 268: 13
A. of Nabû-zēra-ibni S. of Itti-Nabû-balāṭu BM 31528: 5; BM 32883: 3; BM 30965: 21
A. of Nādin S. of Gimillu BM 31449: 14
A. of Nidinti(-Bēl) S. of MNA BM 33928: 9; BM 31528: 18; BM 31690^{+}: 7
A. of Nidintu S. of Marduk-erība TCL 13 193: 13
A. of Nidintu S. of [...] Dar 411: 12
A. of Ša-Bēl-atta S. of Marduk-šuma-ibni BM 30965: 24; BM 30772: 12; BM 32891: 10; BM 41442: 17
A. of Šullumaya S. of Bēl-aḫḫē-iddin BM 32932: 13
A. of [...]-Bēl$^{?}$ BM 31798: 11
A. of [...]-DU S. of Iqūpu BM 33122: 29

Eppeš-ilī (^{m}DÙ-*eš*-DINGIR, see s.v. Ea-eppeš-ilī)

Erēšu (^{m}*e-re-e-šú*)
F. of Nabû-zēra-iqīša BM 30490: 3

Erība-Marduk (^{m}*eri-ba*-^{d}AMAR.UTU, ^{m}SU-^{d}AMAR.UTU)
S. of Bēl-uballiṭ desc. of Nabû-⌜uṣuršu$^{?}$⌝ BM 30446: 2, 13 (wr. ^{m}TU-^{d}AMAR.UTU)
S. of Šamaš-iddin desc. of ⌜Rabâ⌝-[ša-Ninurta] BM 33122: 17*, Le. E.
F. of Tattannu desc. of Marduk-nā'id Dar 509: 14
F. of Sūqaya desc. of Rab-banê TCL 13 193: 35$^{!}$

Erībaya (^{m}SU-*a*, ^{m}*eri-ba-a*)
S. of Ibnaya BM 30297: 15**
S. of Nabû-apla-iddin desc. of Bābūtu BM 31690^{+}: 16*
S. of Nabû-zēra-ibni Dar 359: 18*
S. of Ša-Nabû-šū BM 30490: 21* ($^{m⌜}$*ir-ba*$^{⌝?}$*-a-a*); Dar 296: 3, 9, 14, 16
S. of [...]-mušēzib BM 31227: 9*
F. of Ubār desc. of Itinnu Dar 411: 12

Etel-pî (^{m}*e-tel-pi*)
A. of Marduk-balāssu-iqbi S. of Iqūpu BM 31977 (//Dar 472): 19
A. of Nabû-iddin S. of Iqūpu BM 30772: 7

Etellu (^{m}*e-tel-lu*)
F. of Zababa-iddin desc. of Aḫḫū BM 33936: 8
F. of Zababa-iddin Dar 411: 11

Ēṭiru (^{m}*e-ṭè-ru*)
A. of Arad-Bēl [S. of ...] BM 41449: 3

A. of Ardiya S. of Marduk-šarrāni BM 31690^{+}: ⸢15⸣ (wr. ^{m}⸢*e-ṭè*⸣-*ru*).

A. of [Lib]luṭ S. of Iddin-Nabû Dar 351: 20

A. of [...] S. of Mušēzib-Marduk BM 33968: Rev. 8′

Eṭraya (^{m}KAR-*e-a*)

F. of Ardiya desc. of Suḫaya BM 30446: 11

G

Gaḫal (^{m}*ga-ḫal*)

A. of Bēl-ittannu S. of Kalbaya Dar 430: 16

A. of Bibānu S. of Bēl-apla-iddin Dar 541: 21

A. of Gūzānu S. of Nabû-zēru-līšir BM 30629: 2

A. of Marduk-erība S. of Nabû-zēra-ukīn BM 33122: 22

A. of Nabû-aḫḫē-iddin Dar 435: Rev. 5′

A. of Nabû-apla-iddin S. of [...] Dar 437: 17

A. of Nabû-uṣur-napišti Dar 552: 14

A. of Napuštu S. of Bēlšunu BM 31036: 10

Gaḫul (^{m}*ga-ḫúl*)

A. of Dummuqu S. of Balāṭu BM 30772: 3

A. of Tabnêa S. of Aplaya BM 30994: 20 (//BM 31722^{+}: 19)

Gaḫul-Marduk (^{m}⸢*ga-ḫúl*-^{d}TU.TU⸣)

A. of Iqūpu S. of Nādin BM 31036: 3

Gimil-Nabû (^{m}ŠU-^{d}AG)

F. of Niqūdu desc. of Rē'i-alpi BM 31360: 23

Gimil-Šamaš (^{m}ŠU-^{d}UTU, ^{m}*gi-mil-lu*-^{d}UTU)

S. of Nabû-šuma-ukīn desc. of Ḫu(z)zû BM 31976: Rev. 4′*

S. of Šullumu desc. of Nādin Dar 158: 17**

F. of Arad-Bāba BM 31976: Rev. 6′

F. of Bēl-aḫa-iddin BM 31976: Rev. 2′

F. of Nidinti-Bēl TCL 13 193: 36* (wr. ^{m}ŠU$^{?}$-^{d}UTU)

Gimillu (^{m}*gi-mil-lu*, ^{m}ŠU)

S. of Bēl-iddin desc. of Egibi Dar 453^{+}: 21*

S. of Šamaš-šumu-līšir Dar 351: 14*

F. of Aplaya Dar 405: 6

F. of Iddin-Nergal desc. of Nappāḫu Dar 400: 16; Dar 430: 20; Dar 452: 20; Dar 459: 18

F. of Nabû-bullissu desc. of Bābūtu Dar 359: 15

F. of Nabû-bullissu (desc. of Bābūtu?) Dar 351: 13

F. of Nādin desc. of Egi[bi] BM 31449: 14

F. of Nidintu BM 41453: 15

F. of SI-PI-ú-a [desc. of Maṣ]ṣār-abulli BM 31517: 11

F. of Ṭābiya desc. of Ir'anni BM 31718: 15′

Gimriya (^{m}TIL-*ia*)

F. of Bēl-iddin desc. of Paḫāru Dar 572: ⸢13⸣ (wr.[^{m}TIL-*i*]*a*); Dar 572; Dar 573: 11

Gula-zēra-ibni (^{md}*gu-la*-NUMUN-DÙ)

S. of Zēr-Bābili <desc. of> ⸢Nappāḫu⸣ Dar 138: 2

Gūzānu (^{m}*gu-za-nu/na*)

S. of Ḫambaqu desc. of Mandidi BM 41442: 5, 8, 10; BM 31226: 3, 9; TCL 13 198: 1, 6

S. of Kalbaya desc. of Šangû-Nanaya Dar 359: 19*

S. of Nabû-mīta-uballiṭ Dar 144: 18*

S. of Nab[û-šuma-ukīn] desc. of Šanāšīšu (governor) BM 30795: 4; also see below s.v. No affiliation

S. of Nabû-zēru-līšir desc. of Gaḫal BM 30629: 1, 6

F. of Bēl-ibni desc. of Zēriya BM 30965: 24

F. of Bēl-iddin desc. of Ea-ṣalam-ilī BM 31976: Rev. 4′; Dar 400: 14

F. of Bēl-iqīša BM 31188: 18

F. of Bēl-ittannu desc. of Ea-nāṣir BM 33928: 16

F. of Iqūpu desc. of Bā'iru TCL 13 198: 11

F. of Marduk desc. of Kaṣṣidakku BM 30764: 8; BM 31138: 11 (no desc.); BM 31322: 8; BM 31517: 10; BM 31572: 9; BM 31786: 9; BM 31798: 6

F. of Ma[r-...] BM 31138: 11 (F. of Marduk desc. of Kaṣṣidakku)

F. of Nabû-bullissu TCL 13 196: 7
No affiliation (governor): BM 30639: 6, 11; BM 30980: 5; BM 31036: 6; BM 31393: 7, 9; BM 31572: 3; BM 31786: 5; BM 32891: 6; BM 33112: 3; CT 22 74: 1 (no title); TCL 13 196: 2, 5

Gūzu-Bēl-aṣbat (^{m}*gu-ú-zu*{*-ina*}-^{d}EN-*aṣ-bat*)
No affiliation BM 30853: 29

Ḫ

Ḫabaṣīru (^{m}*ḫa-ba-ṣi-ru*)
S. of Mušēzib-Marduk desc. of Dēkû BM 32932: 5, 10
S. of Šaddinnu BM 30270: 13*; BM 30490: 18*
F. of Arad-Bāba desc. of Ir'anni BM 30233: 12
F. of Bēl-kāṣir Dar 400: 12
F. of Bulṭaya desc. of Arad-Nergal BM 32858: 18
F. of Bulṭaya desc. of Rē'i-alpi Dar 158: 1; Dar 215: 1
F. of Nādin TCL 13 193: 30
F. of [...]-Bēl desc. of Dannêa OECT 10 234: 12′
desc. of Eppeš-ilī BM 32858: 10*, 20 (seal)

Ḫaddaya (^{m}*ḫa-ad-da-a*)
S. of Niqūdu desc. of Maštuk BM 33122: [35]**; Dar 453^{+}: 21*
F. of Nabû-ēṭir-napšāti BM 31690^{+}: 2

Ḫadi-eriš (^{m}*ḫa-di-e-ri-eš*)
A. of Nabû-mukīn-apli S. of Nabû-šuma-ukīn Dar 318: 12

Ḫaḫḫuru (^{m}*ḫa-aḫ-ḫu-ru*)
S. of Nabû-ēṭir-napšāti desc. of Dannêa Dar 215: 10*

Ḫambaqu (^{m}*ḫa-am-ba-qu*)
F. of Gūzānu desc. of Mandidi BM 31226: 3; BM 41442: 5; TCL 13 198: 1, 6

Ḫanṭušu (^{m}*ḫa-an-ṭu-ú-šú*, ^{m}*ḫa-an-ṭu-šu*)
S. of Kamūšu-ilū Dar 435: Rev. 3′*; TCL 13 193: 33*

Ḫarīṣānu (^{m}*ḫa-*⸢*ri*⸣*-ṣa-nu*)
No affiliation TCL 13 196: 7

Ḫašdaya (^{m}*ḫaš-da-a*, ^{m}*ḫaš(-šá)-da-a-a*, ^{m}*ḫa-áš-da-a-a*)
S. of Aḫa-iddin BM 31533: 14*
S. of Bēl-balāssu-iqbi BM 30270: 14*; BM 30490: 19*
S. of Bēl-iddin BM 30235: 13*
S. of Marduk-šuma-iddin desc. of Šangû-parakki Dar 527: 15*
S. of Nabû-aḫḫē-bulliṭ BM 30795: 15*
S. of Ša-Nabû-šū desc. of Šigûa BM 30994: 14* (//BM 31722^{+}: 13)
S. of ⸢Marduk/Nergal⸣-mukīn-apli desc. of Sîn-damāqu BM 30589: 12*
F. of ^{d}LUM.LUM-aba-uṣur Dar 345: 13
F. of Mušēzib-Bēl desc. of Nappāḫu$^{?}$ Dar 345: 15
F. of Nabû-bullissu BM 31227: 11
No affiliation BM 30639: 10; BM 30651: 12

^{f}Ḫašdayītu (^{f}*ḫa-áš-da-a'-i-tu*$_{4}$, ^{f}*ḫaš-da-*{⸢*áš*⸣}*-a'-i-tu*$_{4}$)
Svt. of MNA (daugh. of MBU) TCL 13 193: 8, 21

Ḫāziri (^{m}*ḫa-an-zi-ri*)
Dar 105: 7

Ḫu(z)zû (^{m}*ḫu-zu-ú*)
A. of Gimil-Šamaš S. of Nabû-šuma-ukīn BM 31976: Rev. 5′

Ḫuṣābu (^{m}*ḫu-za*$^{?}$*-bi*)
A. of [...] S. of Ardiya BM 33122: 32

I

Ibnaya (^{m}*ib-na-a*, ^{m}DÙ*-a*)
S. of Mušēzib-Marduk desc. of ⸢Arad⸣-Ner<gal> BM 30446: 16*
S. of Nergal-zēra-ibni Dar 541: 4, 14, 15, 17; BM 31976: 4
F. of Erībaya BM 30297: 15
F. of Iddin-Bēl desc. of Šangû-parakki Dar 351: 17
A. of Libluṭ S. of Nabû-šuma-ukīn BM 33121: 14

Iddin-^{d}[...] (^{m}MU-^{d}[...])
S. of Nabû-ittannu BM 30965: 6

Iddin-Bēl (^{m}MU/SUM.NA-^{d}EN)
S. of Bēlšunu desc. of Sîn-nāṣir BM 33930: 19*
S. of Ibnaya desc. of Šangû-parakki Dar 351: 17*
S. of Kalbaya BM 31891: Rev. 6*

S. of Lūṣi-ana-nūri desc. of Andaḫar Dar 541: 20*; BM 31951: 8*
S. of Marduk-erība desc. of Balāṭu Dar 138: 12*
S. of ⸢Marduk⸣-[...] desc. of Šangû-parakki BM 33926: 12*
S. of Nergal-iddin Dar 400: 12*
S. of Niqūdu Dar 345: 14*
S. of Šadûnu TCL 13 197: 17**
S. of Šamaš-aḫa-iddin Dar 527: 17*
S. of Zumbaya desc. of Eppeš-ilī BM 32858: 12*
F. of Bēl-iddin desc. of Šangû-Ea Dar 450: 10
F. of Bēl-ikṣur desc. of [...] Dar 459: 14
F. of Bēl-ittannu BM 30256: 17
F. of Bulṭaya Dar 411: 17
F. of Iqūpu desc. of Nūr-Sîn Dar 509: 15
F. of Nabû-bullissu desc. of Ea-eppeš-ilī Dar 369: 15
F. of Nabû-mušētiq-uddê desc. of Amēl-Isin BM 33959: 16; Dar 453^{+}: 19
Svt. of Barz[iya]$^{?}$ BM 31891: 1
No affiliation BM 30819: 14*; BM 31976: 3 (*mār šipri*); BM 33112: 2

Iddin-Marduk (^{m}MU/SUM.NA-^{d}AMAR.UTU)
S. of Marduk-erība desc. of Bibbûa BM 30274: 11*
S. of Nabû-ušallim desc. of Sîn-nādin-šumi Dar 455: 11*
S. of Šamaš-nāṣir Dar 351: 15*
S. of [...] desc. of Ša-ṭābtīšu BM 33926: 10*
F. of Aplaya desc. of Maṣṣār-abulli Dar 544: 8
F. of Murašû desc. of Eppeš-ilī BM 30629: 12

Iddin-Nabû (^{m}MU/SUM.NA-^{d}AG)
S. of Aḫḫē-iddin-Marduk BM 30235: 6
S. of Balāṭu desc. of Nabû-uṣuršu$^{!}$ TCL 13 185: 18* (wr. ⸢^{m}SUM.NA⸣$^{?}$-^{d}AG)
S. of Balāssu desc. of Nabû-šeme Dar 342: Rev. 3*; Dar 390: 9*
S. of Baniya BM 33935: 28*
S. of Bazūzu desc. of Ašlāku BM 31533: 1
S. of Bēlšunu desc. of Paḫāru BM 32883: 15*
S. of Bēlšunu desc. of Ṭābiḫ-kāri Dar 154: 12*
S. of ⸢Bēl-zēri⸣ BM 31188: 16*
S. of Marduk$^{?}$-[...] BM 33121: 15*
S. of Marduk-(i)qīšanni desc. of Bēl-eṭēru Dar 527: 16*
S. of Nabû-talîm-uṣur Dar 435: U.E. (seal, no affiliation); TCL 13 193: 32*
S. of Šamaš-zēra-ibni ⸢desc. of⸣ Maṣṣār-abulli BM 33954: 18*
S. of [...]-ušēzib BM 33122: 9
F. of Bēl-iddin desc. of Dābibī BM 31572: 11; BM 31690^{+}: 13; BM 31951: 9 (desc. broken); BM 32891: 14
F. of Bēl-uballiṭ ⸢desc. of⸣ Bā'iru BM 31188: 8
F. of Bēl-uballiṭ desc. of Dābibī BM 33122: 18; BM 33928: 13
F. of Itti-⸢Nabû⸣-[...] desc. of Ea-pattannu BM 31718: 14'
F. of [Lib]luṭ desc. of Ēṭiru Dar 351: 20
F. of Nabû-balāssu-iqbi BM 31786: 11
F. of Nabû-bullissu desc. of Dābibī b 2800: 12; BM 31018: ⸢15⸣; Dar 182: 10; also Dar 577: 15 *alias* Iddinaya?; TCL 13 185: 17
F. of Nabû-ittannu desc. of Ir'anni Dar 541: 19
F. of Nabû-ittannu desc. of Nuḫāšu Dar 369: 16
F. of Nabû-ittannu Dar 576: 4
F. of Qīštiya desc. of ⸢PN⸣ Dar 268: 18
F. of Rīmūt-Bēl desc. of Rab-banê Dar 345: 13
F. of Sîn-kāṣir BM 33935: 28
F. of Šellibi Dar 296: 8
F. of Šullumu desc. of Kānik-bābi BM 31138: 13
desc. of Šigûa BM 33936: 20*, U.E. (seal); Dar 435: U.E. (seal)
A. of Zanê BM 33954: 20 (^{m}MU-⸢^{d}AG$^{?}$⸣)
No affiliation BM 30270: 1; BM 31138: 4 (Official); BM 32891: 15* (LÚ *ia-ma-na-a-a*); Dar 541: 16

Iddin-Nabû/Bēl (^{m}SUM.[NA]-^{d}⸢AG/EN⸣)
S. of Bēl-uballiṭ$^{!}$ BM 33122: 23*

Iddin-Nergal (^{m}MU-^{d}U.GUR)
S. of Gimillu desc. of Nappāḫu Dar 400: 15**; Dar 430: 20**; Dar 452: 19**; Dar 459: 18**

F. of Bulṭaya desc. of Eppeš-ilī Dar 541: 24

Iddinaya (^{m}MU/SUM.NA-*a*, see also s.v. Itti-Marduk-balāṭu desc. of Egibi)
S. of Arad-Bēl Dar 307: 3; Dar 334: 4
S. of Ardiya BM 31026: 8; Dar 400: 10*; Dar 430: 9
S. of Bēl-ēṭir desc. of Adad-šammê BM 31322: 11*
S. of Nādin desc. of Eppeš-ilī Dar 315: 14*
S. of Nādin-aḫi BM 33935: 23*
S. of Qīštiya BM 30366: 5; BM 30980: 8*
F. of Aplaya BM 31690^{+}: 4
F. of Kalbi-Bāba BM 31891: 3
alias Itti-Marduk-balāṭu, F. of MNA (*passim*)
F. of Marduk-šuma-ibni desc. of Nappāḫu BM 33935: 18
F. of Nabû-bullissu Dar 577: 15 (Iddinaya *alias* Iddin-Nabû desc. of Dābibī?)
F. of Nabû-mušētiq-uddê ⌜desc. of Silimmu⌝ BM 30541: ⌜16⌝
F. of Nādin BM 31203: 5
F. of Puršû desc. of Egibi BM 31528: 14
F. of Rīmūt desc. of Nappāḫu Dar 435: Rev. 4′, U.E. (no desc.); TCL 13 193: 34
[(F. of ...)$^{?}$ desc. of] Nādin-še'i BM 33968: Rev. 12′[**]
No affiliation (or broken) Dar 342: 3; Dar 430: 12, 14 (messenger and husband of ^{f}Šaggaya)

Iddiya (^{m}*id-di-ia*)
S. of Šulaya desc. of Šangû-Ninurta BM 33935: 16*

Idrā (^{m}*id-ra-a/a'*)
F. of Šarru-dūrī TCL 13 193: 2
BM 33968: Rev. 9′*

Ile''i-Marduk (^{m}DA-^{d}AMAR.UTU)
A. of Mušēzib-Bēl S. of Bēl-aḫḫē-erība BM 32932: 12
A. of Nabû-bēlšunu BM 33936: 12

Iltammeš-māḫir (^{md}*il-ta-mi-iš-ma-ḫir*)
F. of Barīk-il BM 33935: 17

Ilī-laba (^{m}DINGIR.MEŠ-*la-ba-a'*)
F. of Balāṭu BM 30799: 14

Ilu-tillatī (^{m}DINGIR-KASKAL+KUR-*ú*)
A. of Murašû S. of Marduk-šuma-iddin Dar 156: 8

Ilunnaya$^{?}$ (^{m}DINGIR-NA-A)
S. of Nātan-ilī BM 31533: 15*

Imbu-pāniya (^{m}*im-bu*-IGI-*iá*)
A. of Taqīš-Gula S. of [...]-m/baya Dar 342: Rev. 5

Ina-Esagil-lilbur (^{m}*ina-é-sag-íl/ìl-li-bir*, ^{m}*ina-é-sag-íl-lil-bir*)
S. of Nabû-[šuma-ukīn] desc. of Ša-nāšīšu (governor) Dar 577: 3.
No affiliation BM 30256: 2, 4; BM 31188: 2; BM 32932: 2

Ina-Nabû-ultarraḫ (^{m}*ina*-^{d}AG-*ul-tar-ra-aḫ*)
F. of Bēl-ušallim BM 31036: 4

Ina-qībi-[...] (^{m}*ina-qí-bi*-[...])
F. of Balāṭu BM 30490: 1

Ina-tēšê-ēṭir (^{m}*ina*-SÙḪ-SUR)
S. of Marduk-nāṣir desc. of ⌜Libluṭ$^{?}$⌝ BM 30297: 1[0]* (= ^{m}*ina*-SÙḪ-[...], or read ^{m}MU-[...]?)
S. of Šuma-iddin desc. of Bēl-eṭēru BM 33954: ⌜21*⌝
F. of Arad-Bēl desc. of Bibi BM 33954: 15
F. of Nabû-mukīn-zēri [desc. of Šamaš-(a)bā]ri BM 31360: 22
F. of Nabû-[...] Dar 577: 17

Inziya (^{m}*in-zi-ia*)
F. of Muššê BM 31138: 2

Ipriya (^{m}*ip-ri-ia*)
F. of Kāṣir desc. of Marduk-abušu BM 32873: 5
No affiliation BM 30853: 31

Iqīša-Marduk (^{m}BA-*šá*-^{d}AMAR.UTU)
F. of Bēl-ittannu desc. of Kalbi-Nanna BM 30994: 16 (//BM 31722^{+}: 15)

Iqīšaya (^{m}BA-*šá-a/ia*)
S. of Nādin desc. of Ir'anni BM 32873: 15*
S. of Nabû-mukīn-apli desc. of Ea-pattannu Dar 334: 10*
F. of Nabû-nipšaru Dar 430: 6
F. of Zēriya desc. of Šigûa Dar 509: 17
No affiliation Dar 296: 3

Iqūpu (^{m}*i-qu-pu*, ^{m}*ú-qu-pu* Dar 390)
S. of Gūzānu desc. of Bā'iru TCL 13 198: 10*

Itti-Nabû-balāṭu (^{m}KI-^{d}AG-DIN, ^{m}*it-ti*-^{d}AG-DIN BM 30795, ^{m}KI-^{d}AG-*ba-la-ṭu* BM 32883)
  S. of Marduk-rēmanni BM 31977 (//Dar 472): 21**
  S. of Mūrānu desc. of Eppeš-ilī Dar 359: 13*
  S. of Nabû-zēra-iqīša BM 31977 (//Dar 472): 8*
  F. of Bēl-uballiṭ desc. of Bēl-eṭēru BM 30965: 25
  F. of Bēl-ittannu desc. of Bēl-eṭēru BM 30980: 10
  F. of Bēl-ittannu desc. of Malāḫu Dar 154: 13
  F. of Libluṭ desc. of (Mār-)Sīsî BM 30795: 2; BM 31226: 14; BM 31449: 12; BM 33954: 18
  F. of Nabû-zēra-ibni desc. of Egibi BM 30965: 21; BM 31528: 4; BM 32883: 3

Itti-Nabû-lummir (^{m}KI-^{d}AG-*lum-mir*)
  F. of Nabû-nāṣir desc. of Basiya TCL 13 193: 12

Itti-Nabû-nāṣir (^{m}KI-^{d}AG-PAB)
  S. of Ea-iddin desc. of Eppeš-ilī BM 30261: 11*

Itti-Nabû-nuḫḫu (^{m}KI-^{d}AG-*nu-uḫ-ḫu*)
  S. of Bēl-ile''i BM 33936: 15*, Ri.E. (Seal)

Itti-⸢Nabû⸣-[...]
  S. of Iddin-Nabû desc. of Ea-pattannu BM 31718: 13′*

Itti-Uraš-pānīya (^{m}KI-^{d}URAŠ-IGI-*ia*)
  Svt. of MNA BM 41442: 2, 9

K

Kabtiya (^{m}IDIM-*ia*/*iá*)
  S. of Mušallim-Marduk BM 30854: Rev. 7′
  F. of Ardiya desc. of Ea-eppeš-ilī BM 30274: 3
  F. of Nidintu desc. of Ir'anni BM 31977 (//Dar 472): 5

Kalbi-Bāba (^{m}*kal-ba*/*bi*-^{d}KÁ)
  S. of Iddinaya BM 31891: 3
  S. of Nabû-unammir desc. of Rē'i-sīsî Dar 144: 15*

Kalbi-Nanna (^{m}UR-^{d}ŠEŠ.KI)
  A. of Bēl-ittannu S. of Iqīša-Marduk BM 30994: 16 (//BM 31722^{+}: 15)

Kalbi-⸢Ninurta⸣ (^{m}*kal*-⸢*bi*⸣-^{d}MAŠ$^{?}$ ⸢x⸣ [x])
  F. of Bēl-[rēmanni] BM 31718: 16′

Kalbaya (^{m}*kal-ba-a*, ^{m}UR-*a* BM 30274, ^{m}*kal-ba-a-a* BM 30772)
  S. of Nabû-aḫḫē-iddin desc. of Egibi BM 32883: 10*; Dar 310: 11*; Dar 338: 17*
  F. of Aḫu-atbû Dar 576: 3
  F. of Aḫūa BM 31554: 10
  F. of Arad-Bēl desc. of Šumu-libši Dar 307: 8
  F. of Bēl-erība desc. of Šumu-libši BM 30256: 14; BM 30274: 5; BM 30366: 10; BM 30446: 18; BM 30490: 23 (no desc.); BM 30772: 13; BM 30795: 17; BM 30961: 15; BM 31226: 15; BM 31449: 13; BM 31667^{+}: [14]; BM 32891: 16; BM 41442: 15; Dar 544: 9; Dar 552: 12; TCL 13 197: 15; TCL 13 198: 10
  F. of Bēl-erība desc. of MU-LU-RU-ŠÚ BM 30370: 15
  F. of Bēl-ittannu desc. of Gaḫal Dar 430: 16
  F. of Gūzānu desc. of Šangû-Nanaya Dar 359: 19
  F. of Iddin-Bēl BM 31891: Rev. 6
  F. of Nergal-ēṭir desc. of Šumu-libši TCL 13 198: 10; Dar 572: 3; Dar 573: 5
  F. of Nidintu BM 31138: 10
  F. of Nidintu desc. of Suḫaya BM 30370: 11; BM 30961: 14; BM 30994: 18 (//BM 31722^{+}: 17); BM 31449: 5; BM 31667^{+}: [13]; OECT 10 234: 11′; TCL 13 196: 27
  F. of Nidintu desc. of Šumu-libši BM 30274: 14; BM 30994: 19 (//BM 31722^{+}: 18)?
  F. of Nidintu desc. of [...] BM 31786: 10
  F. of Rīmūt BM 30243: 6
  F. of Sūqaya Dar 572: 2
  F. of Šullumaya desc. of Nabaya BM 30819: 19 (no desc.); BM 31227: 12; BM 31533: 13

Kamūšu-ilū
  F. of Ḫanṭušu Dar 435: Rev. 3′ (wr. ^{m}⸢*ka-am*⸣-*mu-šú*-DINGIR.MEŠ); TCL 13 193: 33 (wr. ^{m}*ka-mu-šu-i-lu*)

Kānik-bābi (^{m}*ka-nik*/*ník*-KÁ)

A. of Šullumu S. of Iddin-Nabû BM 31138: 14
A. of Nabû-bullissu S. of Nidintu BM 31977 (// Dar 472): 16
A. of Nabû-rē'ûšunu S. of Nabû-šuma-uṣur TCL 13 196: 26

Kāṣir (ᵐ*ka-ṣir*, ᵐ*ka-ṣi-ru* BM 30446)
S. of Balāṭu Dar 452: 18*
S. of Ipriya desc. of Marduk-abušu BM 32873: 5
S. of Tattannu desc. of Eppeš-ilī BM 30639: 12*; BM 31393: 15*
S. of Tattannu BM 30446: 15*

Kaṣṣidakku (ᵐ*kàṣ-ṣì-dak-ka/ku*)
A. of Marduk S. of Gūzānu BM 30764: 9; BM 31322: 9; BM 31517: [11]; BM 31572: 9; BM 31786: [9]; BM 31798: 7 (wr. [LÚ *kàṣ*]-*ṣì-dak-ka*)
A. of Nidintu BM 33936: 19? (wr. ᵐŠÁ-ŠID-DAK-KU)

Kī-Nabû (ᵐ*ki-i*-ᵈAG)
F. of Bēlšunu Dar 144: 17

Ki-...-Nabû (ᵐ*ki*-x-*šú*-ᵈAG)
A. of Nabû-aḫa-ittannu S. of Šamaš-iddin BM 31058: 13

Kidin-apli see s.v. Kidina(pli)

Kidin-Marduk (ᵐ*ki-din*-ᵈAMAR.UTU)
S. of Lūṣi-ana-nūr-Marduk BM 31026: 13*
A. of [...] S. of Ištar-šuma-uṣur BM 33935: 24

Kidin-Sîn (ᵐ*ki-din*-ᵈ30, ᵐEZENxKASKAL-ᵈ30)
A. of Lâbāši S. of Nabû-bāni-aḫi BM 31018: 14; BM 33972: 25; BM 41449: 11

Kidina(pli) (ᵐ*ki-din*-A/*a*)
S. of Bēl-iddin desc. of Arad-Ea Dar 453⁺: 23*

Kidinnu (ᵐ*ki-di/din-nu*)
S. of Balāṭu desc. of Eppeš-ilī BM 30261: 12*
S. of Rīmūt OECT 10 234: 2', 7'

Kīnaya (ᵐ*ki-na-a*)
S. of Atkal-Šamaš desc. of [...] BM 31058: 3
S. of Itti-Marduk-balāṭu BM 31026: 16*
F. of Ana-Bēl-a[tk]al BM 30965: 23
F. of [...]-*bu* Dar 351: 15
No affiliation BM 30799: 4

Kīnēnaya (ᵐ*ki-ne-na-a-a*)
F. of [...] [desc. of ...] BM 33112: 10

Kiribtu (ᵐ*ki-rib-tú*)
F. of Bēl-uballiṭ desc. of Nūr-Sîn Dar 156: 12
F. of Kuṣura(pli) desc. of Maṣṣār-abulli BM 31322: 12

Kiribtu-Marduk (?)
S. of Šellibi desc. of Maštuk Dar 437: [17]*?

Kittiya (ᵐ*kit-ti-ia/iá*)
F. of Arad-Marduk desc. of Šangû-Ea Dar 206: 5
F. of Bēl-iddin desc. of Paḫāru BM 31554: 13
F. of Nabû-uṣuršu desc. of Šangû-Ea Dar 455: 17

Kulbibi (ᵐ*kul-bi-bi*)
S. of Bēl-kāṣir desc. of Eppeš-ilī Dar 268: 2, 7

Kurbanni-Marduk (ᵐ*kur-ban-ni*-ᵈŠÚ/AMAR.UTU)
F. of Marduk-šuma-uṣur desc. of Rē'i-sīsî Dar 154: 11
F. of Zumbaya desc. of Bibbûa Dar 509: 18

Kurî (ᵐKUR-*i*)
A. of Mukīn-zēri S. of Šulaya BM 33935: 19
A. of [...]-PAB S. of Rīmūt BM 33935: 27
A. of [...]-zēra-iqīša BM 33935: 25

Kuššaya (ᵐ*ku-uš-šá-a-a*)
No affiliation BM 33954: 14

Kuṣura(pli) (ᵐ*ku-ṣur*-A/*a*)
S. of Kiribtu desc. of Maṣṣār-abulli BM 31322: 12**
S. of Līšir BM 30446: 9

Kuṣuraya (ᵐ*ku-ṣur-ra-a*)
S. of Arrabi Dar 400: 11*; Dar 452: 18*
S. of Baniya desc. of Banâ-ša-iliya Dar 154: 1, 6, 8
F. of Nidintu Dar 542: 18

Kutimmu (LÚ.KÙ.DIM, LÚ *ku-tim-mu*)
A. of Bēl-ittannu S. of Ardiya BM 32932: 14

A. of Nabû-iddin S. of Lūṣi<-ana>-nūr(i)[(...)$^{?}$] BM 31976: Rev. 7′

L

Lā-qīpu (^{m}*la-qí-pi*)
F. of Nidinti-Bēl desc. of Ir'anni BM 30994: 17 (//BM 31722^{+}: 16)
A. of Nāšibu BM 30764: 5

Lâbāši (^{m}*la*(*-a*)*-ba-ši*, ^{m}*la-ba-a-ši*)
S. of Nabû-aḫa-uṣur BM 30747: 9*? (wr. ^{m}{NÍG.KA-}TÉŠ)
S. of Marduk-zēra-ibni desc. of Rē'i-sīsî BM 31188: 13*
S. of Nabû-bāni-aḫi desc. of Kidin-Sîn BM 31018: 13*; BM 33972: 25*; BM 41449: 11*
S. of Nabû-ile''i desc. of Dābibī BM 31977 (// Dar 472): 14*
S. of [...] desc. of Maṣṣār-abulli Dar 544: 11**
F. of Bēl-aḫḫē-iddin desc. of Amēl-Ea Dar 437: 11
F. of Bēl-iddin desc. of Bābūtu BM 32883: 9
F. of Bēlšunu BM 33930: 18
F. of Nabû-apla-iddin desc. of Nūr-Papsukkal BM 30370: 3; BM 30961: 1, 7; BM 31667^{+}: 1, 6; BM 31891 Rev: 7**
F. of Nabû-uṣuršu desc. of LÚ.˹Itinnu$^{?}$˺ BM 31118: 10
F. of Ša-Nabû-idūšu desc. of Šangû-Adad BM 31227: 15
F. of [...]-*ēṭir* BM 31036: 11
A. of Marduk-˹ēṭir$^{?}$˺ S. [of ...] BM 33926: 10
desc. of Rab-šušši BM 33936: 13*

Lakuppuru (^{m}*la-ku*[*p-pu-ru*])
A. of Nabû-bullissu S. of Nabû-šuma-ukīn Dar 296: 25

Laqqunnušu$^{?}$ (^{m}*lá$^{?}$/me$^{?}$-aq$^{?}$/tuq$^{?}$-qu-un-nu-šú*)
F. of Ṭābiya BM 30297: 14

Libluṭ (^{m}*lib-luṭ*, ^{m}*lib-lu-uṭ/ṭu*)
S. of Iddin-Nabû desc. of Ēṭiru Dar 351: ˹20˺** (wr. ˹^{m}*lib*˺*-luṭ*)
S. of Itti-Nabû-balāṭu desc. of Sīsî BM 30795: 2; BM 31226: 14*; BM 31449: 11*; BM 33954: 14, 18*; CT 22 74: 5, 9, 15
S. of [Marduk]-erība [desc. of ...] BM 31951: 10*
S. of Marduk-šuma-ibni desc. of Šangû-Ninurta Dar 213: 11*
S. of Murašû desc. of Sîn-tabni BM 33954: 6
S. of Mušēzib-Marduk Dar 338: 3, 8, 14 (Official)
S. of Nabû-šuma-ukīn desc. of Ibnaya BM 33121: 13* (Official)
S. of Nabû-šuma-ukīn desc. of Šig[ûa] BM 30799: 16* (wr. ^{m}*li*[*b*]*-l*[*uṭ*])
S. of Nādin desc. of MU-[...] BM 30446: 1, 13
S. of Nergal-iddin desc. of Ašlāku BM 30370: 12*
F. of Bēlšunu BM 30256: 11
F. of [...] desc. of LÚ [...] BM 31793: 14
A. of MU-[...] (or Ina-tēšê-[...]) S. of Marduk-nāṣir BM 30297: 10 (^{m}˹*lib*˺-*l*[*uṭ*]$^{?}$)
No affiliation BM 30651: 6

Līšir (^{m}*li-ši-ru*)
F. of Kuṣura(pli) BM 30446: 9

LÚ [...]
A. of Bēl-erība S. of Mušēzib-Marduk Dar 544: 10
A. of Bēl-kiṣuršu S. of Rīmūt BM 41453: 3 (LÚ.˹x˺)
A. of Nabû-šuma-ukīn S. of Nabû-mušētiq-uddê Dar 437: 15 (LÚ IŠ ˹x˺)
A. of [...] [S. of] Libluṭ BM 31793: 14

Lultammar-Adad (^{m}*lul-tam-mar-*^{d}IŠKUR)
A. of Nādin S. of Arad-Gula BM 41449: 10

LUM.LUM-aba-uṣur (^{md}LUM.LUM-AD-URU$_{3}$)
S. of Ḫašdaya Dar 345: 12*

LUM-LUM-aḫḫē-iddin (^{md}LUM.LUM-ŠEŠ.MEŠ-MU)
F. of Aḫa-lūmur Dar 296: 24

Lūṣi-ana-nūr-Marduk (^{m}*lu-uṣ-ana-*ZALAG$_{2}$-^{d}ŠÚ/AMAR.UTU)
F. of Kidin-Marduk BM 31026: 13*
A. of Bēl-erība S. of Nādin BM 30589: 5

Lūṣi-ana-nūri (^{m}*lu-*È/*uṣ-ana-*ZALAG$_{2}$; ^{m}*lu-*È*-nu-úr* Dar 541)
F. of Iddin-Bēl desc. of Andaḫar BM 31951: 8; Dar 541: 20

F. of Nabû-iddin desc. of Kutimmu BM 31976: Rev. 6′ (wr. Lūṣi<-ana>-nūr(i)[(...)$^{?}$]
F. of Nabû-uballiṭ desc. of Andaḫar BM 33930: 16; Dar 541: 22
F. of Tattannu Dar 405: 14

M

Madānu-aḫḫē-iddin (^{md}DI.KU$_5$-ŠEŠ.MEŠ-MU/SUM.NA)
F. of Šaddinnu desc. of Šigûa BM 31977 (//Dar 472): 2; BM 33122: 27; BM 33959: 5 (wr. Madānu-aḫḫē<-iddin>, and no desc.); Dar 315: 6; Dar 453^{+}: 2

Madānu-apla-iddin (^{md}DI.KU$_5$-⸢IBILA⸣-MU)
No affiliation (=Svt. of MNA?) Dar 430: 11 (wr. ^{md}DI.KU$_5$-⸢MU⸣ [...])
Svt. of MNA Dar 541: 13; TCL 13 193: 7, 20 (wr. ^{md}DI.KU$_5$-MU, S. of MBU)

Madānu-bēla-uṣur (^{md}DI.KU$_5$-EN-URU$_3$/PAB)
Svt. of MNA BM 30965: 10; BM 31026: 7; BM 31360: 9, 17; BM 31718: 6′; BM 31976: 1; Dar 308: 2, 10; Dar 400: 6; Dar 405: 3, 10; Dar 430: 8; Dar 452: 2, 7, 9, 11; Dar 459: 1, 5, 6; Dar 509: 3, 8, 10, 13; TCL 13 193: 6, 18 (husb. of ^{f}Nanaya-bēla-uṣur)
No affiliation (= Svt. of MNA?) BM 33972: 20

Madānu-iddin (see s.v. Madānu-apla-iddin)

Malāḫu (^{m}*ma-la-ḫu*)
A. of Bēl-ittannu S. of Itti-Nabû-balāṭu Dar 154: 14

Mamûzu (^{m}*ma-mu-ú-zu*, ^{m}*ma-ú-zu-zu*)
S. of Ṭābiya BM 30591: 12*; BM 33112: 4 (Official)

Mandidi (LÚ *man-di-di*, ^{m}*man-di-di* TCL 13 198: 7)
A. of Gūzānu S. of Ḫambaqu BM 31226: 4; BM 41442: 5; TCL 13 198: 2, 7
A. of [...]-*nu* S. of Ana-Bēl-ēreš BM 33122: 30

Mannu-aki-Nabû (^{m}*man-nu-a-ki-i*-^{d}AG)
No affiliation (Official) TCL 13 193: 26*

Ma[r-...] (^{m}*ma*[*r*-...], read Marduk S. of Gūzānu desc. of Kaṣṣidakku)
S. of Gūzānu BM 31138: 10*

Mār-bīti-iddin (^{md}DUMU-É-MU)
S. of [...] desc. of Šangû-Šamaš BM 30591: 9*

Mār-sīsî (^{m}DUMU-*si-si-i* BM 33954, see s.v. Sīsî)

Marduk (^{m}*mar-duk-(a)*, ^{md}AMAR.UTU BM 32883)
S. of Gūzānu desc. of Kaṣṣidakku BM 30764: 8*; BM 31138: ⸢10⸣* (no desc.); BM 31322: 8*; BM 31517: 10*; BM 31572: 9*; BM 31786: 9*; BM 31798: 6*
S. of Nabû-uṣuršu desc. of Šumu-libši BM 30764: 3, 6
desc. of Paḫāru BM 30651: 9; BM 30853: 36

Marduk-abušu (^{md}ŠÚ-AD-*šú*)
A. of Kāṣir S. of Ipriya BM 32873: 6

Marduk-balāssu-iqbi (^{md}ŠÚ/AMAR.UTU-DIN-*su*-E)
S. of Iqūpu desc. of Etel-pî BM 31977 (//Dar 472): 19*
F. of Marduk-rēmanni desc. of Nabaya Dar 359: 20

Marduk-bāni-zēri (^{md}AMAR.UTU-DÙ-NUMUN)
S. of Nabû-šumu-līšir desc. of Balāṭu BM 30819: 15**; BM 31533: 17**

Marduk-bēlšunu (^{md}AMAR.UTU-EN-*šú-nu*)
S. of Arad-Marduk desc. of Šangû-Ea Dar 206: 8 (no desc.); Dar 268: 14*; Dar 318: 2; Dar 334: 3; Dar 450: 7; TCL 13 185: 20**
F. of Šamaš-iddin desc. of Nabû-⸢x⸣-NI BM 31976: Rev. ⸢1′⸣

Marduk-ēreš (^{md}AMAR.UTU-KAM)
S. of Dummuqu desc. of Nappāḫu Dar 552: 11*; Dar 572: 9 *

Marduk-erība (^{md}AMAR.UTU-SU, *-eri-ba*)
S. of Nabû-zēra-ukīn desc. of Gaḫal BM 33122: 22*
F. of Iddin-Bēl desc. of Balāṭu Dar 138: 12
F. of Iddin-Marduk desc. of Bibbûa BM 30274: 12
F. of Libluṭ [desc. of ...] BM 31951: 10 (wr. $^{m[d}$AMAR.UTU]-SU)

F. of Nidintu desc. of Egibi TCL 13 193: 13
F. of [...] desc. of Purkullu BM 33122: 33

Marduk-ēṭir (^{md}AMAR.UTU-SUR/KAR, -KAR-*ir* Dar 156)
S. of Mūrānu desc. of Egibi Dar 156: 10*
S. of Nabû-šuma-iškun desc. of Šumu-libši BM 30980: 13**
S. [of ...] desc. of Lâbāši BM 33926: 9*?
F. of Nabû-kuṣuršu desc. of Rabâ-ša-Ninlil BM 30243: 11 (no desc.); Dar 542: 17
F. of Nergal-iddin desc. of Zēriya Dar 308: 13
F. of Šamaš-iddin BM 30541: 12
F. of [...]-iddin Dar 572: 12

Marduk-iqīšanni (^{md}AMAR.UTU-BA-*šá-an-ni*, ^{md}AMAR.UTU-NÍG.[BA-*an-ni*] BM 32883)
S. of Bēl-aḫa-ušabši desc. of Bēl-eṭēru Dar 164: 15*; Dar 167: 15*
S. of Marduk-šuma-uṣur desc. of [...] BM 32883: 5
S. of Nabû-uṣuršu desc. of Ṣāḫiṭ-ginê BM 30589: 16**
F. of Iddin-Nabû desc. of Bēl-eṭēru Dar 527: 16 (wr. ^{md}AMAR.UTU-*qí-šá-an-ni*)
F. of Rīmūt desc. of Mār-sīsî BM 33954: 16

Marduk-muballissu (^{md}AMAR.UTU-*mu-bal-liṭ-su*)
S. of Nabû-ēṭir-napšāti desc. of Sîn-tabni-uṣur Dar 455: 9*, 21 (seal)

Marduk-mukīn-apli (^{md}ŠÚ/AMAR.UTU-GIN-A)
S. of Baniya desc. of Rab-šušši Dar 138: 13**
S. of Itti-Marduk-balāṭu desc. of Egibi Dar 338: 2 (= MNA$_1$?!)
F. of Nabû-ēṭir Dar 369: 17

Marduk-mušallim (^{md}AMAR.UTU-*mu-šal-lim*)
F. of Mušēzib-Marduk desc. of Suḫaya BM 33122: 19

Marduk-nā'id (^{md}AMAR.UTU-I)
A. of Tattannu S. of Erība-Marduk Dar 509: 14

Marduk-nāṣir (^{md}AMAR.UTU-PAB, -*na-ṣir*)
S. of Ea-iddin desc. of Šumāti BM 30261: 10*
S. of Marduk-ušallim BM 30747: 10*; Dar 315: 9
S. of ⌜Marduk-ušēzib⌝ desc. of Sîn-⌜mudammiq⌝ Dar 338: 18*
F. of Mūrānu desc. of Aḫu-bani BM 31517: 1, 7; TCL 13 197: 4 (wr. ^{md}AMAR.UTU-PAB$^{!}$)
F. of Mūrānu BM 30446: 17
F. of Nabû-bāni-aḫi desc. of Adad-šammê Dar 450: 3, 6
F. of MU-[...] (or Ina-tēšê-[...]) desc. of ⌜Libluṭ$^{?}$⌝ BM 30297: 11
Dar 342: 6 ($^{[md]}$AMAR.UTU-*na*-[*ṣir* ...], = MNA?)

Marduk-nāṣir-apli (^{md}AMAR.UTU-*na-ṣir*-IBILA/A)
S. of Nabû-šuma-ukīn desc. of Ša-n[āšīšu] BM 33121: 3, 6
No affiliation BM 41449: 5, 6, 7; Dar 158: 3, 5, 21; Dar 206: 7

Marduk-rēmanni (^{md}AMAR.UTU-*re-man-ni*)
S. of Marduk-balāssu-iqbi desc. of Nabaya Dar 359: 20**
S. of Marduk-šuma-uṣur desc. of Šangû-Adad BM 31226: 5
F. of Itti-Nabû-balāṭu BM 31977 (//Dar 472): 21

Marduk-šarrāni (^{md}AMAR.UTU-*šar-an-ni*)
F. of Ardiya desc. of Ēṭiru BM 31690^{+}: 15

Marduk-šuma-ibni (^{md}AMAR.UTU-MU-DÙ)
S. of Iddinaya desc. of Nappāḫu BM 33935: 18*
F. of Bēl-uballiṭ Dar 338: 20
F. of Libluṭ desc. of Šangû-Ninurta Dar 213: 11
F. of Mušēzib-Marduk desc. of Nappāḫu Dar 369: 14
F. of Ša-Bēl-atta desc. of Egibi BM 30965: 23; BM 30772: 12; BM 32891: 10; BM 41442: 16

Marduk-šuma-iddin (^{md}AMAR.UTU-MU-MU/SUM.NA)
S. of Marduk-zēra-ibni desc. of Egibi BM 32883: 18**
S. of Nabû-iddin desc. of Dēkû BM 30370: 17**

S. of Šullumu desc. of Itinnu Dar 450: 13*
F. of Bēl-apla-iddin desc. of Šangû-Gula BM 30366: 9
F. of Ḫašdaya desc. of Šangû-parakki Dar 527: 15
F. of Murašû desc. of Ilu-tillatī Dar 156: 7
F. of Nabû-kuṣuršu desc. of E-x BM 31036: 13 (^{md}⸢AMAR.UTU$^?$⸣-MU-MU)
F. of Nidintu BM 30980: 9

Marduk-šuma-uṣur (^{md}AMAR.UTU-MU-URU$_3$, ^{md}ŠÚ-MU-URU$_3$ Dar 359, ^{md}AMAR-UTU-MU-*ú-ṣur* BM 32883)
S. of Kurbanni-Marduk desc. of Rē'i-sīsî Dar 154: 11*
S. of Nabû-mukīn-zēri desc. of Rab-banê Dar 351: 16*
F. of Aplaya desc. of Šangû-parakki BM 31554: 11
F. of Arad-Gula desc. of Nabaya BM 31203: 13; Dar 158: 14; Dar 212: 16; Dar 342: Rev. 1; Dar 359: 13; TCL 13 185: 16
F. of Arad-Ninurta desc. of Nabaya b 2800: 10
F. of Barsiya desc. of Bābūtu BM 30819: 2
F. of Marduk-iqīšanni desc. of […] BM 32883: 6
F. of Marduk-rēmanni desc. of Šangû-Adad BM 31226: 5
F. of […] desc. of Nabaya Dar 342: Rev. 1 (s.v. F. of Arad-Gula)

Marduk-ušallim (^{md}ŠÚ/AMAR.UTU-GI)
F. of Marduk-nāṣir BM 30747: 11; Dar 315: 10
F. of Nabû-mukīn-apli Dar 430: 15
F. of Rīmūt desc. of Paḫāru BM 30795: 1; BM 33954: 15 (wr. ^{md}ŠÚ-⸢GI⸣, and no desc.)

Marduk-ušēzib (^{md}⸢AMAR.UTU-KAR⸣)
F. of Marduk-nāṣir desc. of Sîn-⸢mudammiq⸣ Dar 338: ⸢18⸣

Marduk-zēra-ibni (^{md}AMAR.UTU-NUMUN-DÙ)
S. of Bēl-aḫḫē-iddin desc. of Nappāḫu Dar 156: 13*
S. of Bēl-iddin desc. of Dābibī Dar 351: 19*
S. of Nabû-balāssu-iqbi desc. of Sîn-šadûnu BM 33928: 14*
F. of Marduk-šuma-iddin desc. of Egibi BM 32883: 18
F. of Ummaya desc. of Paḫāru BM 30799: 15

Marduk-[…] (^{md}ŠÚ/AMAR.UTU-[…])
F. of Bēl-erība TCL 13 197: 13
F. of Iddin-Bēl desc. of Šangû-parakki BM 33926: ⸢12⸣
F. of Iddin-Nabû BM 33121: 15 (wr. ^{md}AMAR.UTU$^?$-[x])
F. of Nabû-it[tannu desc. of …]-*na-na-a* BM 33935: 21

Maṣṣār-abulli (LÚ.EN.NUN-KÁ.GAL)
A. of Aplaya S. of Iddin-Marduk Dar 544: 8
A. of Balāṭu S. of Nabû-bāni-zēri Dar 308: 16 (^{m}LÚ.EN.NUN-KÁ.GAL)
A. of Iddin-Nabû S. of Šamaš-zēra-ibni BM 33954: 19
A. of Kuṣura(pli) S. of Kiribtu BM 31322: 12
A. of Lâbāši S. of […] Dar 544: 12
A. of SI-PI-*ú-a* S. of Gimillu BM 31517: 12 ([Maṣ]ṣār-abulli)
A. of Zababa-iddin S. of Niqūdu BM 31226: 17
A. of […]-suppē-muḫur BM 31360: 27 ([Maṣ]ṣār-abulli)

Maṣṣār-elep-rukūbi (LÚ.EN.NUN-GIŠ.MÁ-U$_5$.KU)
A. of Mūrānu S. of Nabû-mukīn-apli TCL 13 196: 10
A. of Ubār S. of Bēl-aḫḫē-erība TCL 13 196: 13

Maštuk (^{m}*maš-tuk*(.MEŠ), ^{m}*maš-tu-*⸢*ku*$^?$⸣)
A. of Ḫaddaya S. of Niqūdu BM 33122: 35; Dar 453$^+$: 22
A. of [Kiribtu-Marduk?] S. of Šellibi Dar 437: 18

Metuqqunnušu$^?$ (^{m}*me*$^?$*-tuq*$^?$*-qu-un-nu-šú*), see s.v. *Laqqunnušu*$^?$

Mīnû-ana-Bēl-dānu (^{m}*mi-na-a-*^{d}EN-*da/dan-nu*, ^{m}*mi-nu-ú-a-na-*^{d}EN-*da*(*-a*)*-nu*, ^{m}*mi-nu-ú-*DIŠ-^{d}EN-*da-a-nu*)

S. of Bēl-iddin desc. of Sagdidi Dar 450: 11*
S. of Nabû-šuma-uṣur desc. of [...] BM 33121: 1, 9
[S. of ... desc.] of Šumu-libši BM 33112: 8*
F. of Šamaš-iqīšanni desc. of Šangû-Šamaš BM 31118: 12

Miṣiraya (^{m}*mi-ṣir-a-a*)
A. of Bulṭaya S. of Balāssu BM 31690^{+}: 14

Mitrāta (^{m}*mi-it-ra-a-ta*, ^{m}*mi-ti-ri-a-ta*)
F. of Bagadāta BM 30591: 11
F. of Nidintu Dar 509: 22

Mitrēn (^{m}*mi-ti-ri-a-ni*)
BM 33121: 12*

MNA$_1$ (^{md}AMAR.UTU-*na-ṣir*-A/EDURU/IBILA, ^{md}AMAR.UTU-*na-ṣi-ir-ap-lu*, ^{md}AMAR.UTU-*na*-PAB-A, ^{md}AMAR.UTU-PAB-A/EDURU/IBILA, *-ap-lu*, ^{md}ŠÚ-*na-ṣir*-A, ^{md}ŠÚ-PAB-A, ^{md}AMAR.UTU-*na-din*^{sic}-A Dar 509: 4, 5, 9, 12)
S. of Itti-Marduk-balāṭu (*alias* Iddinaya) desc. of Egibi (*passim*)
F. of Nidinti-Bēl desc. of Egibi BM 31528: 18; BM 33928: 9

MNA$_2$ (^{m}*ši-ir/iš-ku*, ^{m}*ši-iš-ki*, ^{m}*ši-rik(-ki/tu$_4$)*, ^{m}*šìr-ku*, ^{m}*šiš-ki*, ^{m}*ši-rik*$^{!}$*-ku* Dar 576: 4, ^{m}*ši-ri-ku* Dar 182: 5, $^{\langle m \rangle}$*šik-ku* BM 30772: 5, ^{m}*šìr-ki* BM 31138: 5)
S. of Iddinaya (*alias* Itti-Marduk-balāṭu) desc. of Egibi. Attested as contractant: *passim*. Attested as witness or scribe in: BM 30591: 13**; BM 30795: 13*; BM 31118: 14**; BM 32873: 16**; BM 33121: 18**; BM 33936: 21**
F. of Nidintu BM 31690^{+}: 6 (desc. of Egibi); BM 41453: 2

MU-LU-RU-ŠÚ (^{m}MU-LU-RU-ŠÚ, read ^{m}MU-*lìb*$^{!}$*-šú*)
A. of Bēl-erība S. of Kalbaya BM 30370: 15

MU-[...]
S. of Marduk-nāṣir desc. of ⌜Libluṭ$^{?}$⌝ BM 30297: 10* (= ^{m}x-[...], or read Inatēšê-[...]?)
A. of Bēl-[...] S. of Zēriya BM 31188: 10
A. of Libluṭ S. of Nādin BM 30446: 1
BM 33935: 21* (wr. ^{m}MU-[x]-⌜x⌝-*ú*)

Mudammiq-Adad (^{m}(*mu*-)SIG$_{15}$-^{d}IŠKUR, ^{m}*mu*-SIG$_5$(*-iq*)-^{d}IŠKUR)
A. of Bēl-asûa S. of Nergal-uballiṭ BM 30541: 11; BM 31891: Rev. 5 (wr. ^{m}TUM-^{d}IŠKUR); BM 32873: 13; TCL 13 196: 12
A. of Bēl-upaḫḫir S. of Bāba-ēreš BM 32873: 7
A. of Nabû-ēṭir-napšāti S. of Niqūdu Dar 296: 21
A. of Nādin-aḫi Dar 437: 20
A. of Napsān S. of Nergal-uballiṭ Dar 154: 15; Dar 509: 21
A. of Šulum-Bābili S. of Tabnêa BM 30541: 14; BM 32873: 14

Mudammiq$^{?}$-Adad (wr. ^{m}TUM-^{d}IŠKUR, see s.v. Mudammiq-Adad)

Mukīn-zēri (^{m}GIN-NUMUN)
S. of Šulaya desc. of Kurî BM 33935: 19*

Mukkêa (^{m}*muk-ki-e-a*)
S. of [...] desc. of Bēl-eṭēru BM 33926: 6

Mūrānu (^{m}*mu-ra-nu*)
S. of Arad-Marduk desc. of Šangû-Ea BM 30961: 18*; BM 31667^{+}: 17*
S. of Bēl-iddin desc. of Ša-nāšīšu TCL 13 196: 25*
S. of Marduk-nāṣir desc. of Aḫu-bani BM 31517: 1, 7; TCL 13 197: 3, 7, 8, 10
S. of Marduk-nāṣir BM 30446: 17*
S. of Mušallim-Marduk desc. of Atkuppu Dar 334: 11*; Dar 450: 12*
S. of Mušēzib-Marduk desc. of Ašlāku Dar 296: 22*
S. of Nabû-mukīn-apli desc. of Maṣṣār-elep-rukūbi TCL 13 196: 6, 9, 17
S. of Nabû-šuma-iddin BM 30819: 12*
S. of Šaddinnu desc. of Ašlāku BM 31572: 12*
S. of Šuma-iddin desc. of Abī-ul-īde TCL 13 193: 30*
F. of Itti-Nabû-balāṭu desc. of Eppeš-ilī Dar 359: 14
F. of Marduk-ēṭir desc. of Egibi Dar 156: 11
F. of Nabû-bullissu desc. of Paḫāru BM 30233: 3
F. of Šuma-iddin desc. of Abī-ul-īde TCL 13 193: 31

F. of Šullumu (see s.v. F. of Nergal-ušallim)
F. of [...] desc. of Ēṭiru BM 33968: Rev. 8′
F. of [...] desc. of Ušabšêa BM 33122: 34
A. of Nabû-aḫa-uṣur Dar 308: 19

Mušēzib-Nabû (^{m}*mu-še-zib*-^{d}AG)
F. of [...] Dar 577: 16

Muššê (^{m}*mu-un-še-e*)
S. of Inziya BM 31138: 1

N

Na-[...] (^{m}⌜*na*⌝-[...])
A. of Bēl-iddin S. of Baniya Dar 577: 14 (probably read Nabaya)
A. of Ea-iddin S. of Šamaš-iddin Dar 452: 14 (or read ^{m}⌜*be*?⌝-[...])

Nā'id-Bēl (^{m}I-^{d}EN)
S. of Bēl-uballiṭ desc. of Paḫāru Dar 212: 1, 11, 13

Nabaya (^{m}*na-ba-a-a*)
A. of Arad-Gula S. of Marduk-šuma-uṣur BM 31203: 13; Dar 158: 15; Dar 212: 17; Dar 359: 13; TCL 13 185: 16
A. of Arad-Ninurta S. of Marduk-šuma-uṣur b 2800: 10
A. of Ardiya S. of Dādiya BM 30629: 10 BM 31018: 11; BM 32883: 17; Dar 215: 13; Dar 310: [10]; Dar 338: 19
A. of Bēl-iddin S. of Baniya Dar 577: 14 (wr. ^{m}⌜*na*⌝-[...])
A. of Bēl-iddin S. of Nabû-nādin-aḫi Dar 527: 19
A. of Marduk-rēmanni S. of Marduk-balāssu-iqbi Dar 359: 21
A. of Šullumaya S. of Kalbaya BM 31227: 12; BM 31533: 14
A. of Šullumaya S. of Nabû-nādin-aḫi BM 31572: 14; BM 31798: 10; BM 32891: 13; BM 41607: 13 ([Šullumaya]); Dar 542: 15
A. of Šuma-iddin S. of Šāpik-zēri Dar 541: 23
A. of [...] S. of Marduk-šuma-uṣur Dar 342: Rev. 1 (probably s.v. A. of Arad-Gula)
A. of [...] S. of Nabû-nādin-aḫi BM 41607: 13 (see s.v. A. of Šullumaya)

Nabû-aḫa-iddin (^{md}AG-ŠEŠ-MU)
S. of Bazūzu desc. of Ir'anni BM 30795: 14*
F. of Šullumu BM 30541: 10
F. of [...]-ušallim BM 33935: 29

Nabû-aḫa-ittannu (^{md}AG-ŠEŠ-*it-tan-nu*)
S. of Mušēzib-Bēl desc. of Rabâ-ša-Ninurta BM 30366: 13**
S. of Nabû-šuma-uṣur desc. of Šangû-Nanaya Dar 359: 17*
S. of Šamaš-iddin desc. of Ki-...-Nabû BM 31058: 12*
BM 33935: 22* (wr. ^{md}AG-ŠEŠ-*it-tan-na*)

Nabû-aḫa-uṣur (^{md}AG-ŠEŠ-PAB/URU$_{3}$)
F. of NÍG-KA-UR BM 30747: 10
desc. of Mušēzib-Marduk Dar 308: 18**

Nabû-aḫḫē-bulliṭ (^{md}AG.ŠEŠ.MEŠ-*bul-liṭ*, ^{md}AG-ŠEŠ.MEŠ-DIN Dar 144)
S. of Itti-Marduk-balāṭu desc. of Egibi BM 30541: 2; BM 31528: 2, 7, 9; BM 32883: 12*; BM 33928: 7; Dar 315: 4; Dar 338: 9, 16; Dar 345: 2
S. of Nabû-kāṣir desc. of Dābibī Dar 138: 10*
S. of Nādin desc. of Bā'iru BM 33972: 26* (wr. ^{md}AG-ŠEŠ$^{!}$.MEŠ$^{!}$-<*bul*->*liṭ*) ; Dar 144: 14*; Dar 315: 15*
F. of Ḫašdaya BM 30795: 15
F. of Nergal-aḫa-iddin Dar 430: 5
No affiliation Dar 369: 4, 5, 8, 11 (= NAB?)

Nabû-aḫḫē-iddin (^{md}AG-ŠEŠ.MEŠ-MU)
S. of Nabû-ile''i desc. of Dābibī BM 30261: 13*
F. of Kalbaya desc. of Egibi BM 32883: 10 (no desc.); Dar 310: 11; Dar 338: 17
F. of Murašû desc. of Arad-Nanna Dar 268: 11
F. of Murašû desc. of Nanna-utu Dar 455: 15
F. of Nabû-uṣuršu desc. of Sîn-tabni BM 30639: 15
F. of Šulum-Bābili BM 31449: 11
F. of [...]-iddin desc. of Atû BM 33122: 26
desc. of Gaḫal Dar 435: Rev. 5′**

Nabû-apla-iddin (^{md}AG-IBILA/A/EDURU-MU)
S. of Arānu Dar 369: 13*

S. of Bēl-iddin desc. of Egibi Dar 541: 26**
S. of Lâbāši desc. of Nūr-Papsukkal BM 30370: 2, 8, 10; BM 30961: 1, 6, 12; BM 31891: Rev. 7**; BM 31667^{+}: 1, 6, 11
S. of Nergal-[…] desc. of ⸢Zērūtiya⸣ BM 31058: 14** (wr. [^{md}A]G$^{?}$-EDURU-MU)
S. of […] desc. of Gaḫal Dar 437: 16*
F. of Bēl-iddin desc. of Ir'anni Dar 541: 18
F. of Bēl-iddin desc. of Šangû-Gula BM 30297: 12
F. of Bēl-kēšir desc. of Šangû-Ea BM 30243: 10
F. of Erībaya desc. of Bābūtu BM 31690^{+}: 16
F. of Nabû-māku-uṣur BM 31718: 4'; BM 33972: 27; Dar 164: 4; Dar 167: 17
F. of Zanzīru desc. of Ea-pattannu Dar 453^{+}: 15 (^{md}[AG]-A-MU)
F. of […] desc. of Bābūtu BM 33122: 31

Nabû-⸢BA-x⸣ (^{md}AG-⸢BA-x⸣)
A. of Mušēzib-Bēl S. of Šamaš-nāṣir BM 30261: 9

Nabû-balāssu-iqbi (^{md}AG-DIN-*su*-E, *-iq-bi*)
S. of Iddin-Nabû BM 31786: 11*
F. of Bēl-iddin desc. of Egibi Dar 144: 17
F. of Bēl-iddin Dar 437: 16
F. of Bēl/Nabû-ittannu desc. of Sîn-šadûnu BM 33122: 25
F. of Marduk-zēra-ibni desc. of Sîn-šadûnu BM 33928: 14
F. of Nabû-rē'ûšunu BM 31138: 3
F. of Tattannu desc. of Bābūtu BM 30235: 4
desc. of […] BM 41449: 14**

Nabû-bāni-aḫi (^{md}AG-DÙ-ŠEŠ)
S. of Marduk-nāṣir desc. of Adad-šammê Dar 450: 2, 6
F. of Arad-Nergal desc. of Paḫāru Dar 390: 11
F. of Lâbāši desc. of Kidin-Sîn BM 31018: 14 (^{md}AG-DÙ-⸢ŠEŠ$^{?}$⸣); BM 33972: 25; BM 41449: 11
F. of Nergal-ina-tēšê-ēṭir desc. of Ir'anni Dar 315: 16

Nabû-bāni-zēri (^{md}AG-DÙ-NUMUN)
S. of Nūrea desc. of Šangû-Nanaya Dar 206: 13*
F. of Balāṭu desc. of Maṣṣār-abulli Dar 308: 15

Nabû-bānûnu (^{md}AG-*ba-nu-nu*)
A. of Aḫūšunu S. of Bēl-apla-iddin BM 31528: 15

Nabû-bēl-šumāti (^{md}AG-EN-MU.MEŠ)
F. of Ardiya desc. of Allaya Dar 308: 18
F. of Nabû-nādin-aḫi desc. of Dēkû BM 31018: 2, 6
F. of Nabû-šuma-iddin desc. of Šangû-Adad Dar 307: 7

Nabû-bēlšunu (^{md}AG-EN-*šú-nu*)
S. of Nabû-nādin-aḫi desc. of Itinnu BM 30233: 16**
F. of Bēl-erība desc. of Abī-ul-īde Dar 435: 2
desc. of Ile''i-Marduk BM 33936: 12*, Lo.E.*

Nabû-bullissu (^{md}AG-*bul-liṭ-su*)
S. of Arad-Marduk desc. of Šangû-Ea Dar 310: 15*
S. of Arrabi BM 30641: 5
S. of Bēl-aḫḫē-iqīša desc. of Nādin-še'i Dar 206: 18**
S. of Bēlšunu Dar 296: 24*
S. of Gimillu desc. of Bābūtu Dar 359: 14*
S. of Gimillu [desc. of …] Dar 351: 13*
S. of Gūzānu TCL 13 196: 6
S. of Ḫašdaya BM 31227: 10*
S. of Iddin-Bēl desc. of Ea-eppeš-ilī Dar 369: 14*
S. of Iddin-Nabû desc. of Dābibī b 2800: 12*; BM 31018: 14*; Dar 182: 9*; also Dar 577: 15?; TCL 13 185: 17*
S. of Iddinaya [(*alias* Iddin-Nabû) desc. of Dābibī?] Dar 577: 15*
S. of Mūrānu desc. of Paḫāru BM 30233: 3
S. of Mušēzib-Marduk BM 31026: 14*
S. of Nabû-ittannu desc. of Sippê(a) BM 31322: 4
S. of Nabû-mukīn-zēri desc. of Ea-ṣalam-ilī BM 30764: 12**; BM 31517: 15**
S. of Nabû-šuma<-iškun$^{?}$> Dar 435: 3
S. of Nabû-šuma-ukīn desc. of Laku[ppuru] Dar 296: 25**
S. of Nabû-[…] BM 31347: 7 (Official)

S. of Nidintu desc. of Kānik-bābi BM 31977 (// Dar 472): 16*
S. of Šākin-šumi desc. of Būṣu BM 33122: 20*, Ri.E. (Seal)
S. of [...] BM 31347: 16**
F. of [...]-*tu* BM 31976: 5

Nabû-gabbi-ilī (^{md}AG-*gab-bi-i-li-e*)
Svt. of Bagasarū Dar 542: 5

Nabû-damiq-ilī (^{md}AG-SIG$_5$-DINGIR.MEŠ, ^{md}⸢AG⸣-[*da*]*m*-⸢*iq*⸣-DINGIR; *alias* Damqiya)
F. of Nidinti-Bēl desc. of Nādin-še'i BM 30980: 12; BM 31018: 16

Nabû-ēṭir (^{md}AG-KAR-*ir*)
S. of Marduk-mukīn-apli Dar 369: 16*
F. of Ardiya BM 30256: 12

Nabû-ēṭir-napšāti (^{md}AG-KAR(-*ir*)-ZI.MEŠ)
S. of Aḫūšunu desc. of Arrabi Dar 411: 13*
S. of Ḫaddaya BM 31690^{+}: 1
S. of Ištar-tabni-uṣur [desc. of ...]-Nanaya BM 33935: ⸢30⸣**
S. of Nabû-kāṣir desc. of Itinnu BM 30747: 6*
S. of Niqūdu desc. of Mudammiq-Adad Dar 296: 20*
F. of Ḫaḫḫuru desc. of Dannêa Dar 215: 11
F. of Bēl-ēṭir desc. of Paḫāru BM 31203: 10; BM 41449: 13
F. of Bēl-uballiṭ desc. of Atkuppu Dar 310: 17; Dar 334: 13
F. of Bēl-uballiṭ BM 31226: 13
F. of Marduk-muballissu desc. of Sîn-tabni-uṣur Dar 455: 10
F. of [...]-*nu* BM 32932: 20

Nabû-ibni (^{md}AG-DÙ)
S. of Nergal-zēra-[...] BM 33972: 28[**]

Nabû-iddin (^{md}AG-MU, ^{md}AG-SUM.NA Dar 572: 1)
S. of Bēl-uballiṭ desc. of Paḫāru b 2800: 4; Dar 212: 1, 10, 13
S. of Iqūpu desc. of Etel-pî BM 30772: 7
S. of Lūṣi<-ana>-nūri[(...)$^{?}$] desc. of Kutimmu BM 31976 Rev.: 6′**
S. of [...] Dar 572: 1, 6
F. of Bēl-asûa desc. of Bābūtu BM 31227: 2
F. of Bēl-uballiṭ desc. of Rab-banê b 2800: 14; Dar 307: 11
F. of Marduk-šuma-iddin desc. of Dēkû BM 30370: 17

Nabû-ile''i (^{md}AG-DA)
F. of Lâbâši desc. of Dābibī BM 31977 (// Dar 472): 14
F. of Nabû-aḫḫē-iddin desc. of Dābibī BM 30261: 13
F. of Zabdiya Dar 307: 10

Nabû-ittannu (^{md}AG-*it-tan-nu*/*na*)
S. of Adad-apla-iddin BM 31226: 18**
S. of Ardiya desc. of Sîn-ilī BM 30772: 10*; Dar 338: 19*; TCL 13 196: 23*
S. of Baniya desc. of Itinnu BM 30261: 5; BM 30541: 4
S. of Bēl-šuma-iškun desc. of Suḫaya BM 30297: 1, 7, 9
S. of Bēl-uballiṭ desc. of Asû Dar 509: 19*
S. of Iddin-Nabû desc. of Ir'anni Dar 541: 19*
S. of Iddin-Nabû desc. of Nuḫāšu Dar 369: 15*
S. of Iddin-Nabû Dar 576: 3
S. of Marduk-[...] [desc. of ...]-*na-na-a* BM 33935: 20* (wr. ^{md}AG-*it*-[x-x(-x)]
S. of Mušēzib-Marduk desc. of Egibi BM 31554: 8*
S. of Nabû-balāssu-iqbi desc. of Sîn-šadûnu BM 33122: 25* (wr. $^{[md]}$⸢EN/AG-*it-tan*⸣-*nu*)
S. of Nabû-napišta-uṣur desc. of Sîn-damāqu Dar 158: 15*
S. of Nabû-zēru-līšir desc. of Nūr-Papsukkal Dar 318: 4
S. of Nūrea BM 30965: 7, 12 (father of Nabû-nādin-aḫi and Iddin-^{d}[...])
S. of Rīmūt-Bēl desc. of Sippêa BM 31572: 8*
S. of Rīmūt BM 33936: 16*, Ri.E.
S. of Sūqaya desc. of *Zaḫušu* BM 30747: 11*
S. of Šamaš-pir'a-uṣur desc. of Nappāḫu BM 31977 (// Dar 472): 15*
S. of Šūzubu desc. of Arkât-ilī BM 30747: 8*
S. of Tabnêa desc. of Šangû-Ninurta BM 33112: 13*
S. of Tabnêa Dar 182: 2
S. of [...] BM 33926: 2

F. of Nabû-šuma-ukīn desc. of LÚ IŠ ⸢x⸣ Dar 437: 15

Nabû-nādin-aḫi (^{md}AG-*na-din*-ŠEŠ)
S. of Aplaya BM 30366: 1, 6
S. of Damqiya desc. of Nādin-še'i BM 30961: 19**; BM 31667^{+}: 18**
S. of Nabû-bēl-šumāti desc. of Dēkû BM 31018: 2, 5, 9
S. of Nabû-ittannu BM 30965: 6
S. of Rīmūt-Bēl desc. of Eppeš-ilī BM 30589: 15*
F. of Bēl-iddin desc. of Nabaya Dar 527: 18;
F. of Iqūpu desc. of Suḫaya Dar 435: Rev. 4'; TCL 13 193: 34
F. of Nabû-bēlšunu desc. of Itinnu BM 30233: 16
F. of Šullumaya desc. of Nabaya BM 31572: 13; BM 31798: 10; BM 32891: 12; BM 41607: 13 ([Šullumaya]); Dar 542: 15
F. of [...] desc. of Nabaya BM 41607: 13 (see s.v. F. of Šullumaya)

Nabû-nādin-ipri (^{md}AG-*na-din-ip-ri*)
F. of Bēl-iddin desc. of Ea-ilūta-bani Dar 206: 16

Nabû-napišta-uṣur (^{md}AG-ZI(-*tì*)-URU$_{3}$)
S. of Šamaš-mukīn-apli desc. of Bēl-bani Dar 315: 18**
F. of Nabû-ittannu desc. of Sîn-damāqu Dar 158: 16
desc. of Ša-nāšīšu BM 33936: 12*

Nabû-napšāti-uṣur (^{md}AG-ZI.MEŠ-URU$_{3}$)
F. of Nabû-mudammiq desc. of Egibi Dar 268: 12

Nabû-nāṣir (^{md}AG-*na-ṣir*)
S. of Baniya desc. of Arad-Nergal Dar 315: 17*
S. of Itti-Nabû-lummir desc. of Basiya TCL 13 193: 11
F. of Bēl-kēšir desc. of Bēlaya BM 30965: 22

Nabû-natan (^{md}AG-*na-ta-nu*)
S. of Šel[libi] Dar 552: 2, 8

Nabû-nipšaru (^{md}AG-*ni-ip-šá-ri*)
S. of Iqīšaya Dar 430: 6 (*mār šipri*)

Nabû-nūr-ilī (?), see s.v. Nabû-⸢x⸣-NI

Nabû-rēmanni (^{md}AG-*re-man-ni*)
F. of Aplaya TCL 13 193: 26
F. of Bēl-erība Dar 296: 23

Nabû-rē'ûšunu (^{md}AG-SIPA-*šú-nu*)
S. of Nabû-balāssu-iqbi BM 31138: 3
S. of Nabû-šuma-uṣur desc. of Kānik-bābi TCL 13 196: 25*

Nabû-rībi-uṣur (^{md}AG-*ri-bi*-URU$_{3}$)
F. of Bāba-ēreš Dar 351: 3

Nabû-silim (^{md}AG-*si-il-lim*, ^{md}AG-*sil-lim*)
Svt. of Sons of Bēl-uballiṭ//Paḫāru Dar 212: 3, 9, 12

Nabû-šarra-ibni (^{md}AG-LUGAL-*ib-ni*)
No affiliation (?) BM 33122: 10

Nabû-šeme (^{md}AG-⸢*še-e-me*⸣, ^{md}PA-*še-e*)
A. of Iddin-Nabû S. of Balāssu Dar 342: Rev. 3; Dar 390: 10

Nabû-šuma-ibni (^{md}AG-MU-DÙ)
S. of Mušēzib-Bēl desc. of Sîn-ilī BM 31188: 14*
F. of [...] BM 33968: 4

Nabû-šuma-iddin (^{md}AG-MU-MU/SUM.NA)
S. of Nabû-bēl-šumāti desc. of Šangû-Adad Dar 307: 7*
S. of Šāpik-zēri desc. of Dēkû BM 31226: 11*; Dar 455: 12*
S. of [Šāpik$^{?}$]-zēri desc. of Nappāḫu BM 30629: 11*
S. of [...] BM 31347: 12*
F. of Bēl-iddin Dar 167: 15? (wr. ^{md}AG-⸢NUMUN/MU⸣-MU)
F. of Iṣṣūr desc. of Eppeš-ilī BM 41442: 14
F. of Mūrānu BM 30819: 13
F. of Nabû-mukīn-apli BM 33121: 17 (^{md}AG-⸢MU-MU⸣$^{?}$)
F. of Nidinti-Bēl Dar 351: 3
F. of Šulum-Bābili Dar 509: 20

Nabû-šuma-iškun (^{md}AG-MU-GAR-*un*)
S. of Arad-Ninurta desc. of Bā'iru Dar 212: 15*
F. of Marduk-ēṭir desc. of Šumu-libši BM 30980: 13
F. of Nabû-bullissu Dar 435: 3

Nabû-šuma-ukīn (^{md}AG-MU-GIN, ^{md}AG-MU-*ú-kin* Dar 296)
alias Šuma-ukīn, S. of Bēl-ēṭir desc. of Šangû-Nanaya Dar 213: 2; TCL 13 185: 7

Nabû-zēra-ibni (^{md}AG-NUMUN-DÙ, ^{md}AG-*ze-er-ib-ni* BM 32883)
- S. of Itti-Nabû-balāṭu desc. of Egibi BM 30965: 20*; BM 31528: 4, 8, 10; BM 32883: 2
- S. of ⌜Aššur-aba⌝-uṣur BM 33968: Rev. 6′; Dar 351: 4;
- F. of Erībaya Dar 359: 18

Nabû-zēra-iddin (^{md}AG-NUMUN-MU)
- F. of Bēl-iddin Dar 164: 16 (wr. ^{md}AG-NUMUN-⌜x⌝); Dar 167: 15? (wr. ^{md}AG-⌜NUMUN/MU⌝-MU)
- F. of Šulum-Bābili BM 30235: 12
- F. of Ubānāna BM 32932: 15

Nabû-zēra-iqīša (^{md}AG-NUMUN-BA-*šá*)
- S. of Erēšu BM 30490: 2 (wr. Nabû-zēra-iqīš[ann]i), 15
- F. of Itti-Nabû-balāṭu BM 31977 (//Dar 472): 8

Nabû-zēra-ukīn (^{md}AG-NUMUN-GI.NA)
- F. of Marduk-erība desc. of Gaḫal BM 33122: 22

Nabû-zēra-ušabši (^{md}AG-NUMUN-GÁL-*ši*)
- F. of Bēl-iddin BM 31026: 4, 10; Dar 308: 4; Dar 400: 4; Dar 430: 4

Nabû-zēra-uṣur (^{md}AG-NUMUN-URU_3)
- F. of Nādin desc. of Ṭābiḫu BM 31533: 12

Nabû-zēru-līšir (^{md}AG-NUMUN-GIŠ/SI.SÁ, -*li-šìr*)
- F. of Bēl-īpuš desc. of Ea-eppeš-ilī BM 32883: 11
- F. of Gūzānu desc. of Gaḫal BM 30629: 2
- F. of Nabû-ittannu desc. of Nūr-Papsukkal Dar 318: 4
- F. of Šamaš-uballiṭ desc. of Šangû-Šamaš Dar 338: 22

Nabû-[...] (^{md}AG-[...])
- S. of Ina-tēšê-ēṭir Dar 577: 16**
- F. of Bēl-[x] BM 31690^{+}: 17 (wr. ^{md}AG-⌜x-x-x⌝)
- F. of Bāba-⌜ibni⌝ BM 33972: 27 (wr. ^{md}AG-⌜x⌝ [...])
- F. of Nabû-bullissu BM 31347: 7
- F. of Nidinti-Bēl desc. of Šalāla BM 31322: ⌜7⌝
- F. of [...]-*nu* Dar 342: 4
- No affiliation (Official) Dar 544: 2 BM 31793: ⌜17*⌝?

Nabû-⌜x⌝-NI (^{md}AG-⌜x⌝-NI)
- A. of Šamaš-iddin S. of $^{md⌜}$Marduk-bēlšunu⌝ BM 31976: Rev. 2′

Nabû/Bēl-[...] ($^{md⌜}$AG/EN⌝-[...])
- F. of Bēl-ittannu BM 31786: 12

Nabunnaya (^{md}AG-*na-a-a*, ^{m}*na-bu-un-na-a-a*)
- A. of Bēl-apla-iddin S. of Nabû-kāṣir BM 33928: 20
- A. of Mušallim-Marduk S. of Mušebši BM 33959: 14; Dar 453^{+}: 18

Nādin (^{m}*na-din*, ^{m}*na-di-nu*)
- S. of Arad-Gula desc. of Lultammar-Adad BM 41449: 10*
- S. of Gimillu desc. of Egi[bi] BM 31449: 14*
- S. of Ḫabaṣīru TCL 13 193: 29*, Le. E. (seal)
- S. of Iddinaya BM 31203: 5
- S. of Nabû-zēra-uṣur desc. of Ṭābiḫu BM 31533: 12*
- S. of Zubbât-ili BM 30243: 12*
- F. of Aḫḫēšaya desc. of Eppeš-ilī BM 31976: Rev. 3′
- F. of Bēl-erība desc. of Lūṣi-ana-nūr-Marduk BM 30589: 4
- F. of Iddinaya desc. of Eppeš-ilī Dar 315: 14
- F. of Iqīšaya desc. of Ir'anni BM 32873: 15
- F. of Iqūpu desc. of ⌜Gaḫul-Marduk⌝ BM 31036: 3
- F. of Libluṭ desc. of MU-[...] BM 30446: 1
- F. of Nabû-aḫḫē-bulliṭ desc. of Bā'iru BM 33972: 26; Dar 144: 14; Dar 315: 15
- F. of Ubār desc. of Šangû-Ištar-Bābili BM 33122: 21
- A. of Gimil-Šamaš S. of Šullumu Dar 158: 17

Nādin-aḫi (^{m}SUM.NA-ŠEŠ; for ^{m}MU-ŠEŠ, see s.v. Šuma-uṣur)
- F. of Iddinaya BM 33935: 23
- desc. of Mudammiq-Adad Dar 437: 19[**]

Nādin-še'i (^{m}*na-din-še-im*, ^{m}*na-din-še-e*, ^{md}PA-*še-e* Dar 390, ^{m}*na-di-še*$^{!}$-*e* BM 31058)
- A. of Arad-Bēl S. of Damqiya BM 30965: 18
- A. of Bēl-nāṣir S. of Damqiya BM 30961: 17; BM 31667^{+}: 16

Nergal-iddin (^{md}U.GUR-MU, ^{md}U.GUR-SUM.NA BM 30965)
- S. of Baniya desc. of Ša-nāšīšu Dar 212: 17 *
- S. of Bēlšunu Dar 459: 15*
- S. of Marduk-ēṭir desc. of Zēriya Dar 308: 13*
- S. of Nabû-ittannu BM 30235: 11*
- S. of Rīmūt-Bēl Dar 452: 16*
- S. of [...]-⸢erība$^{?}$⸣ desc. of Zērūtiya BM 33954: 17*
- F. of Aplaya BM 30965: 1; Dar 369: 12; Dar 405: 2
- F. of Arad-Gula desc. of Eppeš-ilī BM 31203: 9
- F. of Bēl-upaḫḫir BM 31360: ⸢3⸣; BM 31793: 4; Dar 345: 4, 16; Dar 369: 3 (Puḫḫuru *alias* Bēl-upaḫḫir); Dar 509: 2
- F. of Iddin-Bēl Dar 400: 13
- F. of Libluṭ desc. of Ašlāku BM 30370: 12
- F. of Niqūdu desc. of Nūr-zana Dar 308: 14; Dar 430: 17; Dar 452: 15; Dar 459: [11]
- F. of [Niq]ūdu (desc. of Nūr-zana?) BM 31951: 4
- No affiliation (?) BM 30651: 2

Nergal-ina-tēšê-ēṭir (^{md}U.GUR-*ina*-SÙḪ-KAR-*ir*, ^{md}U.GUR-*ina*-SÙḪ-SUR)
- S. of Nabû-bāni-aḫi desc. of Ir'anni Dar 315: 16*
- No affiliation Dar 182: 4 (Official)

Nergal$^{?}$-nādin-apli ([^{m}U.GU]R$^{?}$-SUM.NA-A) OECT 10 234: 13′*

Nergal-nāṣir (^{md}U.GUR-*na-ṣir*)
- No affiliation Dar 307: 2

Nergal-šarra-uṣur (^{md}IGI.DU-LUGAL-URU$_{3}$)
- F. of Bibānu Dar 310: 12

Nergal-šuma-ibni (^{md}U.GUR-MU-DÙ)
- S. of Šullumu BM 30366: 11*, BM 30980: 7*
- desc. of Šangû-Ea Dar 144: 19**

Nergal-uballiṭ (^{md}U.GUR-DIN-*iṭ*, ^{md}U.GUR-*ú-bal-liṭ* BM 31891)
- S. of Bēl-iddin (husb. of ^{f}Qunnabi) Dar 452: 4, 7, 10, 11; Dar 459: 3, 8, [10]
- F. of Bēl-asûa desc. of Mudammiq-Adad BM 30541: 11; BM 31891: Rev. 4; BM 32873: 12; TCL 13 196: 12
- F. of Bē[l-...] BM 31347: 14 (probably read Bē[l-asûa])
- F. of Napsān desc. of Mudammiq-Adad Dar 154: 9 (no desc.), 15; Dar 509: 21

Nergal-ušallim (^{md}U.GUR-GI)
- S. of Arrabi BM 30747: 2
- *alias* Šullumu, S. of Mušēzib-Marduk desc. of Nappāḫu BM 41449: 12*; Dar 182: 7*

Nergal-ušēzib (^{md}U.GUR-*ú-še-zib*)
- S. of Nadnaya desc. of Šumu-libši Dar 213: 8*
- F. of Arad-Bāba desc. of Egibi Dar 156: 15

Nergal-zēra-ibni (^{md}U.GUR-NUMUN-DÙ)
- F. of Arad-Marduk BM 33122: 12; Dar 453^{+}: 10
- F. of Bēl-ibni desc. of Šangû-Nanaya BM 33972: 28 (wr. ^{md}U.GUR-N[UMUN-DÙ]); Dar 105: 5′; Dar 164: 19; Dar 167: [18]
- F. of Ibnaya BM 31976: 4 (wr. $^{m⸢d⸣}$U.[GUR]-[NUMUN]-DÙ); Dar 541: 4

Nergal-[...]
- F. of [Nab]û$^{?}$-apla-iddin desc. of ⸢Zērūtiya⸣ BM 31058: 14

Nidinti-Bēl (^{m}*ni-din-tu*$_{4}$-^{d}EN, ^{m}*ni-din-ti*-^{d}EN BM 33928)
- S. of Bēl-iddin desc. of [...]-e/KAL$^{?}$ BM 30261: 14**
- S. of Damqiya desc. of Nādin-še'i, see s.v. S. of Nabû-damiq-ilī
- S. of Gimil$^{?}$-Šamaš TCL 13 193: 36**
- S. of Lā-qīpu desc. of Ir'anni BM 30994: 17* (//BM 31722^{+}: 16)
- S. of Nabû-kāṣir desc. of Paḫāru Dar 212: 18*
- S. of Marduk-nāṣir-apli desc. of Egibi BM 31528: 18**; BM 33928: 6, 8
- S. of Nabû-damiq-ilī (*alias* Damqiya) desc. of Nādin-še'i BM 30980: 11*; BM 31018: 15**; BM 31058: 8*; BM 41607: [14]**; Dar 310: 12* (wr. ^{m}*ni*-[x-x-x-]); Dar 338: 23**; Dar 572: ⸢13⸣ ** (no patronymy)

S. of [Nabû]-uṣuršu desc. of Itinnu BM 33928: 23*
[S. of] Nabû-šuma-iddin Dar 351: 2
S. of ⌜Nabû⌝-[...] desc. of Šalāla BM 31322: 7*
S. of [...] BM 33926: 3
F. of Nabû-uballissu BM 33936: 17
F. of [...] BM 41453: 18
No affiliation BM 30819: 13*

Nidinti-Bēl-damqat (^{m}*ni-din-tu*$_4$-^{d}EN-*dam-qát*)
Svt. of Ina-Esagil-lilbur BM 30256: 3
No affiliation BM 30651: 11, 13; BM 30853: 13, 17 (Probably svt. of Ina-Esagil-lilbur)

Nidintu (^{m}*ni-din-tu*$_4$, ^{m}*ni-din-ti* BM 33935, TCL 13 197)
S. of Ardiya desc. of Rab-līmi BM 31138: 11*
S. of Ardiya desc. of Rab-šušši BM 30639: 14*; BM 31393: 13*
S. of Ardiya Dar 577: 1, 2, 10, 13
S. of Bēl-aḫḫē-erība BM 41453: 6
S. of Bēl-kāṣir desc. of Eppeš-ili TCL 13 193: 27*, U. E. (seal)
S. of Bēl-kāṣir desc. of Itinnu BM 32873: 11*
S. of Bēl-iddin desc. of Ašlāku Dar 296: 22*
S. of Bēl-iddin desc. of [Dannêa] BM 41453: 14*
S. of Gimillu [...] BM 41453: 15*
S. of Kabtiya desc. of Ir'anni BM 31977 (//Dar 472): 4, 6
S. of Kalbaya desc. of Šumu-libši BM 30274: 14*; BM 30994: 19* (//BM 31722^{+}: 18)?
S. of Kalbaya desc. of Suḫaya BM 30370: 11*; BM 30961: 14*; BM 30994: 18* (// BM 31722^{+}: 17); BM 31449: 4, 9; BM 31667^{+}: 13*; OECT 10 234: [11']; TCL 13 196: 26*
S. of Kalbaya desc. of [...] BM 31786: 10*
S. of Kalbaya BM 31138: 10*
S. of Kuṣura(pli) Dar 542: 18**
S. of Marduk-erība desc. of Egibi TCL 13 193: 13
S. of Marduk-šuma-iddin BM 30980: 9*
S. of Mīnû-ana-Bēl-dānu BM 33121: 5, 8
S. of Mitrāta Dar 509: 22*
S. of Nabû-mukīn-apli desc. of Amēl-Ea Dar 430: 17*
S. of Nabû-ušallim Dar 573: 13**
S. of Sîn-aḫa-iddin Dar 310: 15*
S. of Širku desc. of Egibi BM 31690^{+}: 6, 9, 11; BM 41453: 2, 4, 8, 13 (no desc.)
S. of [...] desc. of Egibi Dar 411: 11*
F. of Bēl-kāṣir desc. of Eppeš-ili TCL 13 193: 28
F. of Nabû-bullissu desc. of Kānik-bābi BM 31977 (// Dar 472): 16
F. of Qīštiya desc. of Šangû-parakki BM 30235: 14
F. of Šellibi BM 33935: 29
F. of Šulum-Bābili Dar 390: 4
desc. of Kaṣṣidakku$^{?}$ BM 33936: 19*, Ri.E.
No affiliation (majordomo) Dar 296: 3, 13, 15

NÍG.KA-UR (read ^{m}{NÍG.KA-}TÉŠ = *Lâbāši*?)
S. of Nabû-aḫa-uṣur BM 30747: 9

Niqūdu (^{m}*ni-qu-du*, ^{m}*ni-qud*)
S. of Iddin-Nabû desc. of Eppeš-ilī Dar 400: 13*
S. of Gimil-Nabû desc. of Rē'i-alpi BM 31360: 23*
S. of Nabû-ušallim desc. of Sîn-tabni BM 33928: 17*
S. of Nergal-iddin desc. of Nūr-zana Dar 308: 14*; Dar 430: 16*; Dar 452: 15*; Dar 459: 11*
S. of Nergal-iddin BM 31951: 4 (wr. [^{m}*ni-q*]*u-du*)
S. of [...] desc. of Tunaya Dar 334: 8*
S. of [...]-*ia*$^{?}$ BM 31891: 2
F. of Aplaya desc. of Itinnu BM 30764: 11
F. of Bēl-apla-iddin desc. of Ašgandu Dar 437: 13
F. of Bēl-[ikṣur] desc. of Rab-⌜banê⌝ Dar 459: 13
F. of Ḫaddaya desc. of Maštuk Dar 453^{+}: 22; BM 33122: 35
F. of Iddin-Bēl Dar 345: 14
F. of Nabû-ēṭir-napšāti desc. of Mudammiq-Adad Dar 296: 21
F. of Sîn-ilī desc. of Ašgandu BM 31118: 9

F. of Šamaš-erība desc. of Išparu BM 33926: 11(wr. ^{m}*ni*-⸢*qu*⸣-[*du*])
F. of Zababa-iddin desc. of Maṣṣār-abulli BM 31226: 17
F. of [...]-ittannu BM 31554: 2
No affiliation BM 30961: 11; BM 31667^{+}: 10

Ni[...] ($^{[m]}$*ni*-⸢x(-x)⸣-*nu*)
A. of Dādiya S. of Mušēzib-Marduk Dar 318: 11

Ninurta-uballiṭ (^{md}*nin-urta*-DIN-*iṭ*)
S. of Bēlšunu Dar 310: 14*

Nuḫāšu (^{m}*nu-ḫa-šú*)
A. of Nabû-ittannu S. of Iddin-Nabû Dar 369: 16

Nuḫšiya (^{m}*nu-uḫ-ši-ia*)
F. of <PN>$^{?}$ BM 31517: 3

Nummuru (^{m}*nu-um-mu-ru*)
F. of Bēl-ēreš BM 33121: 16
F. of Bēl-kāṣir desc. of Dābibī BM 30243: 9

Nūr-Marduk (^{m}ZALAG$_2$-^{d}ŠÚ)
A. of Šullumu S. of Šāpik-zēri BM 31977 (//Dar 472): 17

Nūr-Papsukkal (^{m}*nu-úr*-^{d}PAP.SUKKAL, ^{m}ZALAG$_2$-^{d}PAP.SUKKAL)
A. of Nabû-apla-iddin S. of Lâ[bāši] BM 30370: 3; BM 30961: 2, 7; BM 31667^{+}: 2, [6]; BM 31891: Rev. 8
A. of Nabû-ittannu S. of Nabû-zēru-līšir Dar 318: 5

Nūr-Sîn (^{m}ZALAG$_2$-^{d}30, ^{m}*nu-úr*-^{d}30)
S. of Arad-Bēl desc. of Šangû-Gula BM 30446: 7
A. of Bēl-uballiṭ S. of Kiribtu Dar 156: 12
A. of Iqūpu S. of Iddin-Bēl Dar 509: 15
A. of Ṣilli-Bēl S. of Bēlšunu BM 31058: 11

Nūr-zana (^{m}*nu-úr-za-na*, ^{m}ZALAG$_2$-*za-na*/*nu*)
A. of Niqūdu S. of Nergal-iddin Dar 308: 15; Dar 430: 17; Dar 452: [15]; Dar 459: 12

Nūrea (^{m}ZALAG$_2$-*e-a*)
F. of Nabû-bāni-zēri desc. of Šangû-Nanaya Dar 206: 13
F. of Nabû-ittannu BM 30965: 7, 12

P

PA-x-A (^{m}PA-x-A)
F. of [...] desc. of Amēl-S[īsî] BM 31347: 15

Padā (^{m}*pa-da-a*)
F. of Bēl-apla-iddin BM 30233: 14

Padiya (^{m}*pa-di-ia*)
F. of Zabdiya Dar 541: 25

Paḫāru (LÚ.BAḪAR$_2$)
A. of Arad-Nergal S. of Nabû-bāni-aḫi Dar 390: 11
A. of Bēl-ēṭir S. of Nabû-ēṭir-napšāti BM 31203: ⸢11⸣ (wr. ^{m}⸢BAḪAR$_2$⸣$^{?}$); BM 41449: ⸢13⸣
A. of Bēl-iddin S. of Gimriya Dar 572: 11; Dar 573: 12
A. of Bēl-iddin S. of Kittiya BM 31554: 13 (wr. ^{m}LÚ.BAḪAR$_2$)
A. of Bēl-nādin-apli S. of Bēl-uballiṭ b 2800: 5; Dar 212: 2; Dar 213: 7
A. of ⸢Bēl-ikṣur⸣ S. of Šadûnu BM 31188: 17
A. of Iddin-Nabû S. of Bēlšunu BM 32883: 16
A. of Marduk BM 30651: 10; BM 30853: 36
A. of Nā'id-Bēl S. of Bēl-uballiṭ Dar 212: 2
A. of Nabû-bullissu S. of Mūrānu BM 30233: 4
A. of Nabû-iddin S. of Bēl-uballiṭ b 2800: 5; Dar 212: 2
A. of Nabû-uṣuršu Dar 268: ⸢19⸣
A. of Nidinti-Bēl S. of Nabû-kāṣir Dar 212: 19
A. of Rīmūt S. of Marduk-ušallim BM 30795: ⸢1⸣
A. of Ummaya S. of Marduk-zēra-ibni BM 30799: 15

Pān-Bēl-adaggal (^{m}IGI-^{d}EN-*a-dag-gal*)
No affiliation BM 33936: 11*, Lo.E.* (Official)

Pappaya (^{m}*pap-pa-a-a*)
A. of Nabû-kuṣuršu S. of Murašû BM 32858: 13

Pir'u (^{m}*pir-'u*)
S. of Šadûnu Dar 296: 21*

Piššiya (^{m}*pi-iš-ši-ia*)

F. of Bēl-ikṣur BM 31554: 3 (Official)
F. of Bēl-kiṣuršu desc. of LÚ ⸢x⸣ BM 41453: 3
F. of Kidinnu OECT 10 234: 2′
F. of Nabû-ittannu BM 33936: 16
F. of Nabû-uṣuršu BM 31026: 5, 17
F. of Qīšti-Marduk desc. of Dābibī Dar 351: 18
F. of ⸢Šamaš$^{?}$-kāṣir⸣ BM 33935: 18
F. of Tattannu Dar 411: 2
F. of [...]-PAB desc. of Kurî BM 33935: 27

Rīmūt-Bēl (^{m}*ri-mut*-^{d}EN)
S. of Ardiya desc. of Itinnu b 2800: 11*; BM 30747: ⸢14⸣*?; BM 31058: 9*; BM 41442: 13*; Dar 182: 8*; Dar 215: 9*; Dar 296: 23*; Dar 318: 12*
S. of Baniya desc. of Itinnu BM 30261: 1
S. of Iddin-Nabû desc. of Rab-banê Dar 345: 13*
S. of [Muš]ēzib-Bēl desc. of Nannaya BM 41607: 3, 6
S. of Šuma-ukīn BM 31058: 11*; BM 33972: 4, 16, 22; Dar 144: 3; Dar 164: 17*; Dar 167: 3, 10;
F. of Bēl-apla-iddin desc. of Nappāḫu Dar 437: 14
F. of Nabû-ittannu desc. of Sippê(a) BM 31572: 8
F. of Nabû-nādin-aḫi desc. of Eppeš-ilī BM 30589: 15
F. of Nergal-iddin Dar 452: 16
desc. of Šuma-ukīn BM 31058: 11*

Rīmūt-Ea (^{m}*ri-mut*-^{d}⸢*é*⸣-*a*)
A. of Bēl-erība BM 33954: 20

Rušund/pāta (^{m}*ru-šu-un-d*[*a*/*pa*$^{?}$-*ti*])
No affiliation BM 31393: 2, 8 (Official)

S

^{f}Saggaya (^{f}*sag-ga-a*)
Daugh. of Ea-kīni (wife of Iddinaya) Dar 430: 13

Sagdidi (^{m}*sag-di-di*)
A. of Mīnû-ana-Bēl-dānu S. of Bēl-iddin Dar 450: 12
A. of Šamaš-iddin BM 30629: 14

Saggilaya (^{m}*sag-gil-a-a*)
A. of [...] OECT 10 234: 15′

Silim-Bēl (^{m}*si-lim*-^{d}EN)
F. of [...] desc. of Sîn-šadûnu BM 31977 (// Dar 472): 13

Silimmu (^{m}⸢*si-lim-mu*⸣)
A. of Nabû-mušētiq-uddê S. of ⸢Iddinaya⸣ BM 30541: ⸢16⸣

SI-PI-*ú-a* (^{m}SI-PI-*ú-a*)
S. of Gimillu desc. of [Maṣ]ṣār-abulli BM 31517: 11*

Sîn-aḫa-iddin (^{md}30-ŠEŠ-MU)
F. of Nidintu Dar 310: 15

Sîn-barak (^{md}30-*ba-ra-ku*)
[S. of]$^{?}$ Bēl-iddin BM 33935: 26*

Sîn-damāqu (^{md}30-*da-ma-qu*)
A. of Ḫašdaya S. of ⸢Marduk/Nergal⸣-mukīn-apli BM 30589: 13
A. of Nabû-ittannu S. of Nabû-napišta-uṣur Dar 158: 16
A. of Šellibi S. of Bēlšunu BM 30589: 13

Sîn-damiq see s.v. Sîn-mudammiq

Sîn-gamil (^{md}30-*ga-mil*)
A. of Būnānu S. of Sūqaya Dar 509: 16

Sîn-iddin (^{md}30-⸢MU$^{?}$⸣)
F. of Bēl-ēṭir BM 33968: Rev. 10′

Sîn-ilī (^{md}30-DINGIR, ^{md}30-DINGIR.MEŠ)
S. of Baniya desc. of [...] BM 30261: 8*
S. of Niqūdu desc. of Ašgandu BM 31118: 8*
A. of Nabû-ittannu S. of Ardiya BM 30772: 11; Dar 338: 20; TCL 13 196: 23
A. of Nabû-šuma-ibni S. of Mušēzib-Bēl BM 31188: 15

Sîn-kāṣir (^{md}30-KÁD)
S. of Iddin-Nabû BM 33935: 28*

Sîn-mudammiq (^{md}30-⸢SIG$_{5}$-*iq*⸣)
A. of Marduk-nāṣir S. of ⸢Marduk-ušēzib⸣ Dar 338: 18

Sîn-nādin-šumi (^{md}30-*na-din*-MU)
A. of Bēl-iddin S. of Mušēzib-Marduk BM 41449: 9; Dar 437: [2]; Dar 455: 3
A. of Iddin-Marduk S. of Nabû-ušallim Dar 455: 12 (wr. ^{md}30-*na-din*-[MU])

Sîn-nāṣir (^{md}30-PAB)
A. of Iddin-Bēl S. of Bēlšunu BM 33930: 19

Sîn-šadûnu (^{md}30-*šá-du-nu*, ^{md}30-KUR/NÍG.DU(-*ú*)-*nu*)
A. of Aplaya S. of Bēl-[...] BM 31786: 15

F. of Ḫašdaya desc. of Šigûa BM 30994: 14 (//BM 31722^{+}: 13)
F. of Itti-Bēl-lummir Dar 527: 15

Ša-nāšīšu (^{m}*šá-na-ši-šú*)
A. of [Bas]iya S. of Nabû-šuma-ukīn BM 31554: ⸢7⸣
A. of Bēl-apla-iddin S. of Ṭābiya Dar 552: 11; Dar 573: 11
A. of Bēl-iddin S. of Tabnêa Dar 573: 13
A. of Gūzānu S. of Nab[û-šuma-ukīn] BM 30795: 5 (wr. ^{m}LÚ *šá-na-ni-šú*)
A. of Ina-Esagil-lilbur S. of Nabû-[šuma-ukīn] Dar 577: 5
A. of Marduk-nāṣir-apli S. of Nabû-šuma-ukīn BM 33121: ⸢3⸣
A. of Mūrānu S. of Bēl-iddin TCL 13 196: 25
A. of Nabû-napišta-uṣur BM 33936: 13
A. of Nergal-iddin S. of Baniya Dar 212: 18
A. of Ubār Dar 390: 13

Ša-pî-kalbi ([^{m}*šá-p*]*i-i-kal-bi*)
S. of Aḫ-yalīd Dar 105: 4′*

Ša-pî-Marduk (^{m}*šá-pi*-^{d}TU.TU)
F. of Aplaya BM 30370: 14

Ša-ṭābtīšu (^{m}*šá*-MUN.ḪI.A-*šú*)
A. of Iddin-Marduk S. of [...] BM 33926: 11
A. of Mušēzib-Marduk S. of Šamaš-udammiq Dar 212: 20

Šaddinnu (^{m}*šad-din-nu*)
S. of Bēl-aḫḫē-iqīša Dar 182: 11**
S. of Madānu-aḫḫē-iddin desc. of Šigûa BM 31977 (//Dar 472): 2, 6; BM 33122: 27*; BM 33959: 5 (no desc.); Dar 315: 6; Dar 453^{+}: 2, 8, 11
F. of Ḫabaṣīru BM 30270: 14; BM 30490: 19 (wr. ^{m}*šad-di-nu*);
F. of Mūrānu desc. of Ašlāku BM 31572: 12
F. of Šellibi desc. of Ašlāku BM 31018: 11; Dar 334: 9
No affiliation BM 31018: 8 (Probably S. of Madānu-aḫḫē-iddin desc. of Šigûa)

Šadûnu (^{m}*šá-du-nu*)
F. of [...]-*lu-ṭu* BM 33122: 13
F. of ⸢Bēl-ikṣur⸣ desc. of Paḫāru BM 31188: 17
F. of Iddin-Bēl TCL 13 197: 17
F. of Pir'u Dar 296: 21

Šākin-šumi (^{m}GAR-MU; ^{m}*šá-kin*-MU)
F. of Bēl-baniya desc. of Ir'anni BM 31977 (//Dar 472): 9
F. of Nabû-bullissu desc. of Būṣu BM 33122: 20
F. of Šuma-iddin BM 31018: 13

Šalāla (^{m}*šá-la-la*)
A. of Nidinti-Bēl S. of ⸢Nabû⸣-[...] BM 31322: 8

Šamaš-(a)bāri (^{md}UTU(-*a*)-*ba-ri*)
A. of Nabû-mukīn-zēri S. of Ina-tēšê-ēṭir BM 31360: 23 ([^{md}UTU-*a-ba*]-⸢*ri*⸣)
A. of Šamaš(-ina-tēšê)$^{?}$-ēṭir S. of Šamaš-iddin Dar 359: 3, 16

Šamaš-aḫa-iddin (^{md}UTU-ŠEŠ-MU)
F. of Iddin-Bēl Dar 527: 17
F. of Mušēzib-Bēl desc. of Amēl-Isin BM 31977 (//Dar 472): 10; BM 33959: 15; Dar 453^{+}: 20

Šamaš-bēl-zēri (^{md}UTU-EN-NUMUN)
S. of Anu-aḫa-⸢iddin⸣ desc. of Šumu-libši BM 33935: 25*

Šamaš-erība (^{md}UTU-SU)
S. of ⸢Niqūdu⸣ desc. of Išparu BM 33926: 11*
F. of Balāṭu Dar 430: 19

Šamaš-ēṭir (^{md}UTU-SUR, also see s.v. Šamaš-ina-tēšê-ēṭir)
F. of Šuma-uṣur BM 31449: 6

Šamaš-ibni (^{md}UTU-*ib-ni*)
alias Šamaš-zēra-ibni, F. of Bulṭaya BM 30270: 16

Šamaš-iddin (^{md}UTU-MU/SUM.NA)
S. of Arad-Marduk desc. of Dēkû TCL 13 198: 4
S. of Bēl-aḫḫē-iddin desc. of Ir'anni BM 30446: 10
S. of Bēl-iddin BM 30270: 2
S. of ⸢Marduk-bēlšunu⸣ desc. of Nabû-⸢x⸣-NI BM 31976: Rev. 1′*
S. of Marduk-ēṭir BM 30541: 12*
S. of Šāpik-zēri desc. of Nagāru Dar 307: 9*
F. of Bēl-ittannu desc. of Šangû-parakki BM 30795: 12
F. of Ea-iddin desc. of Be/Na$^{?}$-[...] Dar 452: 14

A. of Nabû-aḫa-ittannu S. of Nabû-šuma-uṣur Dar 359: 18
A. of Nabû-bāni-zēri S. of Nūrea Dar 206: 14
A. of (Nabû-)Šuma-ukīn S. of Bēl-ēṭir b 2800: 3; Dar 213: 3; TCL 13 185: 8 (read Šangû-Nanaya for Šangû-Bēl)

Šangû-Ninurta (LÚ.SANGA-^{d}MAŠ)
A. of Iddiya S. of Šulaya BM 33935: 16
A. of Libluṭ S. of Marduk-šuma-ibni Dar 213: 12
A. of Nabû-ittannu S. of Tabnêa BM 33112: 14

Šangû-parakki (LÚ.SANGA-BÁR)
A. of Aplaya S. of Marduk-šuma-uṣur BM 31554: 12 (wr. ^{m}LÚ.SANGA-BÁR)
A. of Aplaya S. of Murašû BM 31798: 9
A. of Bēl-ittannu S. of Šamaš-iddin BM 30795: 12
A. of Ḫašdaya S. of Marduk-šuma-iddin Dar 527: 16
A. of Iddin-Bēl S. of Ibnaya Dar 351: 18
A. of Iddin-Bēl S. of ⌈Marduk⌉-[...] BM 33926: 13
A. of Qīštiya S. of Nidintu BM 30235: 14

Šangû-Sîn (^{m}LÚ.SANGA-^{d}30)
A. of Bāni-zēri S. of Šāpik-zēri BM 31977 (//Dar 472): 20

Šangû-Šamaš (LÚ.SANGA-^{d}UTU)
A. of Mār-bīti-iddin S. of [...] BM 30591: 10
A. of Šamaš-uballiṭ S. of Nabû-zēru-līšir Dar 338: 23

Šāpik-zēri (^{m}DUB-NUMUN)
F. of Bāni-zēri desc. of Šangû-Sîn BM 31977 (//Dar 472): 20
F. of Nabû-šuma-iddin desc. of Dēkû BM 31226: 12; Dar 455: 13
F. of Nabû-šuma-iddin desc. of Nappāḫu BM 30629: 11? (^{m}[DUB$^{?}$]-NUMUN)
F. of Šamaš-iddin desc. of Nagāru Dar 307: 9
F. of Šullumu desc. of Nūr-Marduk BM 31977 (//Dar 472): 17
F. of Šuma-iddin desc. of Nabaya Dar 541: 23
F. of Zēriya desc. of Dēkû BM 31226: 12
F. of [...] ⌈desc. of Itinnu⌉$^{?}$ BM 31891: Rev. 3* (^{m}⌈DUB⌉$^{?}$-NUMUN)
desc. of Dēkû BM 31347: 13

Šarru-dūrī (^{m}LUGAL-BÀD)
S. of Edrā Dar 435: U.E. (seal, and no affiliation); TCL 13 193: 2, 14, 15, 22, 24

Šellibi (^{m}*še-el-li-bi*, ^{m}KA$_5$.A)
S. of Aplaya BM 33928: 18*
S. of Bēlšunu desc. of Sîn-damāqu BM 30589: 13*
S. of Iddin-Nabû Dar 296: 5, 6, 7, 8, 9, 13, 15
S. of Nidintu BM 33935: 29*
S. of Šaddinnu desc. of Ašlāku BM 31018: 11*; Dar 334: 9*
S. of [...] BM 31360: 25*
F. of [Kiribtu-Marduk?] desc. of Maštuk Dar 437: 18
F. of Nabû-natan Dar 552: 2

Šēpāt-Bēl-aṣbat (^{m}*še-pát*-^{d}EN-⌈*aṣ-bat*⌉)
Svt. of MNA Dar 542: 8

Šigûa (^{m}*ši-gu-ú-a*)
A. of Ḫašdaya S. of Ša-Nabû-šū BM 30994: 15 (//BM 31722^{+}: 14)
A. of Iddin-Nabû BM 33936: 20
A. of Libluṭ S. of Nabû-šuma-ukīn BM 30799: 17 (wr. ^{m}*ši-g*[*u-ú-a*])
A. of Šaddinnu S. of Madānu-aḫḫē-iddin BM 33122: 27; Dar 315: 6; Dar 453^{+}: 2; BM 31977 (//Dar 472): 3
A. of Zēriya S. of Iqīšaya Dar 509: 17

Šilaya (^{m}*ši-la-a'*)
F. of Basiya TCL 13 193: 30

Širiktu see s.v. Širku

Širku (^{m}*ši-ir-ku*, ^{m}*ši-iš/rik-ki*, ^{m}*šiš-ki*), also see s.v. MNA$_2$
S. of Iddinaya (*alias* Itti-Marduk-balāṭu) desc. of Egibi, see s.v. MNA$_2$
S. of Nabû-ušallim desc. of Bā'iru Dar 437: 12* (Official)
F. of Nidintu desc. of Egibi, see s.v. MNA$_2$
No affiliation (= MNA$_2$?) BM 30641: 6; BM 31438: 3'; BM 31416: 2

Šišku/i see s.v. Širku

Šulaya (^{m}*šu-la-a*)
F. of Iddiya desc. of Šangû-Ninurta BM 33935: 16

F. of Mukīn-zēri desc. of Kurî BM 33935: 19
F. of Nabû-mušētiq-uddê desc. of Tunaya Dar 206: 15

Šullumaya (^{m}*šul-lu-ma-a*, ^{m}GI-*a* Dar 542)
S. of Balāṭu Dar 452: 17*
S. of Bēl-aḫḫē-iddin desc. of Egibi BM 32932: 13*
S. of Kalbaya desc. of Nabaya BM 30819: 19* (no desc.); BM 31227: 11*; BM 31533: 13*
S. of Nabû-nādin-aḫi desc. of Nabaya BM 31572: 13*; BM 31798: 9*; BM 32891: 12*; BM 41607: [13]*; Dar 542: 14*

Šullumu (^{m}*šul-lu-mu*)
S. of Iddin-Nabû desc. of Kānik-bābi BM 31138: 13**
alias Nergal-ušallim, S. of Mušēzib-Marduk desc. of Nappāḫu Dar 213: 10*; Dar 268: 16*; Dar 338: 21*; Dar 345: 11*
S. of Nabû-aḫa-iddin BM 30541: 9*
S. of Šāpik-zēri desc. of Nūr-Marduk BM 31977 (//Dar 472): 17*
S. of Tēšê-ēṭir [desc. of …] BM 33112: 11*
F. of Bēl-erība TCL 13 197: 12
F. of Gimil-Šamaš desc. of Nādin Dar 158: 17
F. of Marduk-šuma-iddin desc. of Itinnu Dar 450: 14
F. of Nergal-šuma-ibni BM 30366: 12
No affiliation BM 30853: 1 (Official)

Šulum-Bābili (^{m}*šu-lum*-E/TIN.TIR.KI)
S. of Arad-Bēl desc. of Eda-ēṭir BM 32873: 10*
S. of Bēl-aḫa-iddin Dar 296: 17
S. of Nabû-aḫḫē-iddin BM 31449: 10*
S. of Nabû-šuma-iddin Dar 509: 20*
S. of Nabû-zēra-iddin BM 30235: 12*
S. of Nidintu Dar 390: 3
S. of Tabnêa desc. of Mudammiq-Adad BM 30541: 13*; BM 32873: 13*; BM 31891: Rev. 5* (no desc.)

Šuma-iddin (^{m}MU-MU)
S. of […]-ia desc. of Itinnu BM 31018: 12*
S. of Šākin-šumi BM 31018: 13*
S. of Šāpik-zēri desc. of Nabaya Dar 541: 23*
S. of Zababa-erība desc. of Amēlu Dar 411: 14*
F. of Aḫa-iddin Dar 390: 12
F. of Bēl-iddin desc. of Andaḫar BM 32932: 8
F. of ⌜Ina-tēšê-ēṭir⌝? desc. of Bēl-eṭēru BM 33954: 21

Šuma-ukīn (^{m}MU-GIN, ^{m}MU-GI.NA)
alias Nabû-šuma-ukīn, S. of Bēl-ēṭir desc. of Šangû-Nanaya b 2800: 2; BM 31533: 4 (no desc.)
F. of Bēl-ittannu BM 32932: 16
F. of Mušēzib-Marduk desc. of Bābūtu Dar 509: 23 (no desc.); TCL 13 196: 28
F. of Rīmūt-Bēl BM 33972: 4; Dar 144: 3; Dar 164: 18; Dar 167: 3
F. of […] desc. of Bēl-apla-uṣur BM 31977 (//Dar 472): 11
A. of Rīmūt-Bēl BM 31058: 12
No affiliation BM 30853: 24

Šuma-uṣur (^{m}MU-URU$_{3}$)
S. of Nabû-ittannu BM 33930: 20**; Dar 405: 15**
S. of Šamaš-ēṭir BM 31449: 6

Šumāti (^{m}MU.MEŠ)
A. of Marduk-nāṣir S. of Ea-iddin BM 30261: 10

Šumaya ($^{[m]}$*šu*-⌜*ma*?-*a*?⌝)
No affiliation BM 32891: 3 (Official)

Šumu-libši (^{m}MU-*líb-ši*, ^{m}MU-*lib-ši* BM 33935, ^{m}MU-*líb-šú* BM 30256)
A. of Arad-Bēl S. of Kalbaya Dar 307: 9
A. of Bēl-erība S. of Aplaya (read Kalbaya?) BM 30270: 18
A. of Bēl-erība S. of Kalbaya BM 30256: 14; BM 30274: 6; BM 30366: 11; BM 30772: 13; BM 30795: 17; BM 30961: 16; BM 31226: 15; BM 31449: ⌜13⌝; BM 31667+: 15; BM 32891: [17]; BM 41442: 15; Dar 544: 9 (wr. ^{m}MU-*l*[*íb-ši*]); Dar 552: 13; TCL 13 197: 15; TCL 13 198: 10
A. of Marduk S. of Nabû-uṣuršu BM 30764: 3
A. of Marduk-ēṭir S. of Nabû-šuma-iškun BM 30980: 14
A. of Mīnû-ana-Bēl-dānu [S. of …] BM 33112: 9

A. of Nergal-ēṭir S. of Kalbaya TCL 13 198: 10; Dar 572: 3; Dar 573: 6
A. of Nergal-ušēzib S. of Nadnaya Dar 213: 9
A. of Nidintu S. of Kalbaya BM 30274: 14; BM 30994: 19 (//BM 31722^{+}: 18)?
A. of Šamaš-bēl-zēri S. of Anu-aḫa-⸢iddin⸣ BM 33935: 26
A. of [...] S. of Kalbaya BM 30446: 18
No affiliation, unless s.v. Nidintu S. of Kalbaya BM 30994: 19 (//BM 31722^{+}: 18)

Šuri-[...] (^{m}⸢*šu*⸣-*ri*-[...])
F. of [...] Dar 435: Rev. 2′

Šūzubu (^{m}*šu-zu-bu*)
S. of Uballissu-Marduk desc. of Ṭābiḫu BM 31226: 2, 8
F. of Nabû-ittannu desc. of Arkât-ilī BM 30747: 9

T

Tabnêa (^{m}*tab-ni-e-a*)
S. of Aplaya desc. of Gaḫul BM 30994: 19** (//BM 31722^{+}: 18)
F. of Bēl-iddin desc. of Ša-nāšīšu Dar 573: 12
F. of Nabû-ittannu Dar 182: 2
F. of Šulum-Bābili desc. of Mudammiq-Adad BM 30541: 13; BM 31891: Rev. 5 (no desc.); BM 32873: 14
desc. of Nabû-ušallim Dar 573: 1, 9

Tālimu (^{m}*ta-lim-mu*)
Dar 105: 6

Tanda (^{m}*ta-an-da*)
No affiliation BM 33112: 3

Taqīš (^{m}*ta-qiš*)
F. of Bēl-iddin desc. of [...] BM 31798: 2, 4

Taqīš-Gula (^{m}[*t*]*a-qiš-*^{d}*gu-la*)
S. of [...]-m/baya desc. of Imbu-pāniya Dar 342 Rev: 4**

Tattannu (^{m}*ta-at-tan-nu*, ^{m}*tat-tan-nu*)
S. of Bēl-iddin Dar 307: 10*
S. of Bēl-kāṣir desc. of Dābibī BM 31322: 9* (probably read Nabû-kāṣir for Bēl-kāṣir)
S. of Erība-Marduk desc. of Marduk-nā'id Dar 509: 14*
S. of Lūṣi-ana-nūri Dar 405: 13*
S. of Mušēzib-Bēl {A} Dar 105: 3′*
S. of Nabû-balāssu-iqbi desc. of Bābūtu BM 30235: 4, 7
S. of Nabû-kāṣir desc. of Dābibī BM 30235: 9*; BM 30764: 9*; BM 31393: 12*; BM 31517: 12*; BM 31572: 10*; BM 31786: 13*; BM 31798: 7*; BM 32891: 11*
S. of Rīmūt Dar 411: 2
S. of [...] BM 33930: 25*
F. of Kāṣir desc. of Eppeš-ilī BM 30639: 13; BM 31393: 15
F. of Kāṣir BM 30446: 16 (^{m}*ta-tan-nu*)
BM 31138: 8* (^{m}*ta-ta*[*n* ...])

Tēšê-ēṭir (^{m}SÙḪ-SUR)
F. of Šullumu [desc. of ...] BM 33112: 11

TU-Marduk (^{m}TU-^{d}AMAR.UTU, = Erība-Marduk?)
S. of Bēl-uballiṭ desc. of Nabû-⸢uṣuršu$^{?}$⸣ BM 30446: 2, 13

TUM-Adad see s.v. Mudammiq$^{?}$-Adad

Tunaya (^{m}*tu-na-a*)
A. of Nabû-mušētiq-uddê S. of Šulaya Dar 206: 15
A. of Niqūdu S. of [...] Dar 334: 9

Ṭ

Ṭābiḫ-kāri (LÚ.GÍR.LÁ-*kar-ri*, *-ka-a-ri*, -KAR Dar 213)
A. of Ea-apla-iddin S. of Mušēzib-Marduk BM 30799: 13; Dar 158: 13; Dar 213: 13 (no patronymy)
A. of Iddin-Nabû S. of Bēlšunu Dar 154: 13

Ṭābiḫu (^{m}(LÚ.)GÍR.LÁ)
A. of Nādin S. of Nabû-zēra-uṣur BM 31533: 13
A. of Šūzubu S. of Uballissu-Marduk BM 31226: 3

Ṭābiya (^{m}DU$_{10}$.GA-*ia*)
S. of Gimillu desc. of Ir'anni BM 31718: 15′*
S. of Metuqqunnušu$^{?}$ BM 30297: 13*
F. of Bēl-apla-iddin desc. of Ša-nāšīšu Dar 552: 10; Dar 573: 10
F. of Mamûzu BM 30591: 13; BM 33112: 5 ([^{m}DU$_{10}$].GA-*ia*)

U

Z

S. of Kurbanni-Marduk desc. of Bibbûa Dar 509: 17*
F. of Iddin-Bēl desc. of Eppeš-ilī BM 32858: 12

Zumbu (^{m}*zu-um-bu*)
S. of Napuštu BM 31227: 13*

Zu[...] (^{m}⸢*zu-x-i*⸣)
A. of Qīštiya S. of Iddin-Nabû Dar 268: 18

1.2 Partially Broken Names

⸢...-aya⸣ (wr. ^{m}⸢x(-x)⸣*-a-a*)
desc. of Rē'ûšunu-Marduk S. of Bēl-apla-uṣur TCL 13 197: 6

[...]-*a-nu*
BM 31360: 25*

[...]-Bēl
S. of Ḫabaṣīru desc. of Dannêa OECT 10 234: 12'* ([...]-^{d}EN)
desc. of Egibi BM 31798: 11** ($^{[m]}$⸢x⸣-^{d}EN$^{?}$)

[...]-*bi* ([^{m}...]-*bi*$^{?}$) (= [Dābi]bī?)
A. of Bēl-iddin S. of Iddin-Nabû BM 31951: 10

[...]-*bu* ([^{m}x-x]-⸢x⸣-*bu*)
S. of Kīnaya Dar 351: 15*

[...]-DINGIR ($^{[m]}$⸢x⸣-DINGIR)
⸢A of⸣$^{?}$ [...] BM 33935: 20

[...]-DU
S. of Iqūpu desc. of Egibi BM 33122: 29*

[...]-*e*/KAL (^{m}[x-x]-*e*/KAL$^{?}$)
A. of Nidinti-Bēl S. of Bēl-iddin BM 30261: 14

[...]-*e*/*dan-nu*
[F./A. of] Nabû-šuzziz OECT 10 234: 14'

[...]-erība$^{?}$ (^{m}[x]-⸢SU$^{?}$⸣)
F. of Nergal-iddin desc. of Zērūtu BM 33954: 17

[...]-ēṭir ([^{m}...-S]UR)
S. of Lâbāši BM 31036: 11*

[...]-*ia*$^{?}$
F. of Niqūdu BM 31891: 2 (<m>⸢x-x⸣-*iá*$^{?}$)
Dar 105: 5 ([^{m}x-x]-*ia*)

[...]-iddin
S. of Marduk-ēṭir Dar 572: 12 *
S. of Nabû-aḫḫē-iddin desc. of Atû BM 33122: 26* ([^{m}x]-SUM.NA)
S. of Ubār BM 33968: Rev. 10'* ([...]-MU)
F. of Atkal<-ana>-Bāba desc. of Nagāru BM 31360: 22 ([^{md}x]-MU)

[...]-ittannu ([^{m}x-x-*i*]*t-tan-na*)
S. of Niqūdu BM 31554: 2

[...]-ia
F. of Šuma-iddin desc. of Itinnu BM 31018: 12 (^{m}⸢x⸣-*iá*)
BM 31951: 13* ([...]-*ia*)

[...]-*lu-ṭu*
S. of Šadûnu BM 33122: 13

[...]-m/baya
F. of Taqīš-Gula desc. of Imbu-pāniya Dar 342: Rev. 5 (wr. [^{m}x(-x)-*m*/*b*]*a-a*)
Dar 342: 3 [$^{m?}$...]-*m*/*ba-a-a*)

[...]-Marduk ([...]-^{d}AMAR.UTU)
S. of [... desc. of] (Ea)-eppeš-ilī BM 31951: 14**
BM 33968: 6

[...]-MU
S. of Ubār BM 33968: 10'*

[...]-mukīn-apli (^{md}⸢x-x⸣-GIN-A)
F. of Ḫašdaya desc. of Sîn-damāqu BM 30589: 12 (read either Marduk-, or Nergal-mukīn-apli)

[...]-mušēzib ([...-*mu*]-*še-zib*)
F. of Erībaya BM 31227: 10

[...]-MU$^{?}$-NI$^{?}$ (^{m}x-x-MU$^{?}$-NI$^{?}$)
No affiliation (Official) BM 30591: 1

[...]-Nabû ([^{m}x-^{d}A]G)
S. of Itti-Marduk-balāṭu BM 31533: 3

[...]-*na-na-a*
A. of Nabû-it[tannu$^{?}$] S. of Marduk-[...] BM 33935: 21 ([^{m}...]-⸢*na*⸣-*na-a*)

[...]-nādin-apli see s.v. Nergal$^{?}$-nādin-apli

[...]-Nanaya
A. of [Nabû]-⸢ēṭir⸣-napšāti S. of Ištar-tabni-uṣur BM 33935: 31 ([x x x]-⸢d⸣*na-na-a*)

[... -na]pšāti ([... -Z]I.MEŠ)
BM 33935: 23*

[...]-*ni-ia*

1.3 Broken Names

1.3.1 First Name Broken

S. of Šuma-ukīn desc. of Bēl-apla-uṣur BM 31977 (// Dar 472): 11*

S. of Šuri-[...] Dar 435: Rev. 2′*

S. of [...]-*ši* BM 41607: 8*

desc. of Ašlāku BM 33968: Rev. 9′ *

desc. of Bā′iru Dar 105: Rev. 2′

desc. of Ea-pattannu BM 31793: 16*

desc. of (Ea-)Eppeš-ilī BM 33968: Rev. 11′*; BM 31793: 15*

[desc. of] Rē′i-sīsî Dar 437: 18*

desc. of Saggilaya OECT 10 234: 15′ **

desc. of Šangû-Ea BM 31793: 14*

⌜desc. of⌝? [x]-DINGIR BM 33935: 19*

1.3.2 Patronomy Broken

F. of Aḫa-iddin BM 33935: 20 (wr. [m][x-x]-⌜*ú*?⌝)

F. of Arad-⌜Bēl⌝ desc. of Ēṭiru BM 41449: 2

F. of ⌜Balāṭu⌝ BM 33926: 2

F. of Bēlšunu BM 30747: 13 (wr. ⌜^{m}x-x⌝-[x])

F. of Bēl-zēri BM 33926: 2

F. of Iddin-Marduk desc. of Ša-ṭābtīšu BM 33926: 10

F. of Iqūpu Dar 390: 12

F. of Lâbāši desc. of Maṣṣār-abulli Dar 544: 11

F. of Mār-bīti-iddin desc. of Šangû-Šamaš BM 30591: 9

F. of Marduk-⌜ēṭir⌝? desc. of Lâbāši BM 33926: 9

F. of Mukkêa desc. of Bēl-eṭēru BM 33926: 7

F. of Nabû-apla-iddin desc. of Gaḫal Dar 437: 16

<F./A. of> Nabû-balāssu-iqbi BM 41449: 14

F. of Nabû-bullissu BM 31347: 16

F. of Nabû-iddin Dar 572: 2

F. of Nabû-ittannu BM 33926: 2

F. of Nabû-mukīn-apli desc. of Sîn-šadûnu BM 33926: 13

F. of Nabû-šuma-iddin BM 31347: 12

F. of Nādin-aḫi desc. of Mudammiq-Adad Dar 437: 19

F. of Nidintu desc. of Egibi Dar 411: 11

F. of Niqūdu desc. of Tunaya Dar 334: 8

F. of Puršû desc. of Egibi BM 33122: 5

F. of Šellibi BM 31360: 26

F. of Tattannu BM 33930: 26

F. of Zitti-Nabû Dar 572: 2

F. of [...]-Marduk desc. of Eppeš-ilī BM 31951: 15

F. of [...]-*ru* desc. of Eppeš-ilī BM 41607: 12

F. of [...] Dar 576: Rev. 1′ (wr. ^{m}⌜x⌝-[...])

1.3.3 Surname Broken

A. of Bēl-iddin S. of Taqīš BM 31798: 2, 4

A. of Bēl-ikṣur S. of Iddin-Bēl Dar 459: 14

A. of Ea-iddin S. of Šamaš-iddin Dar 452: 14

A. of Kīnaya S. of Atkal-Šamaš BM 31058: 4 (wr. ^{m}x-x-x)

A. of Kidinnu S. of Rīmūt OECT 10 234: 3′

A. of Libluṭ S. of [Marduk]-erība BM 31951: 11

A. of Marduk-iqīšanni S. of Marduk-šuma-uṣur BM 32883: 6

A. of Mīnû-ana-Bēl-dānu S. of Nabû-šuma-uṣur BM 33121: 1

<A.> of Nabû-balāssu-iqbi BM 41449: 14

A. of Nabû-kāṣir S. of Nabû-kāṣir BM 31138: 9

A. of Nidintu S. of Kalbaya BM 31786: 10 (= Suḫaya or Šumu-libši)

A. of Sîn-ilī S. of Ibnaya BM 30261: 8

A. of Šullumu S. of Têšē-ēṭir BM 33112: 12

A. of [...] S. of Kīnēnaya BM 33112: 11

Geographical Name Index

Names of Temples and Deities

Bēl (^{d}EN)
makkūr (NÍG.GA) ~: BM 30233: 2; BM 33959: 2 Dar 315: 1; Dar 342: 1 *ešrû ša* ~: Dar 359: 11

E'igikalamma (*é-igi-kalam-ma*)
Dar 182: 4 (*šatammu* ~)

Esagil (*é-sag-íla, é-sag-ìl*)
BM 33935: 8 (*makkūr* ~) BM 33936: 11 (*qīpu* ~) Dar 315: 7 (*bēl pīḫāt* ~); Dar 437: 10, 11, 12 (*šāpir* ~)

Lugal-Marada (⸢^{d*}⸣LUGAL-$^{d!}$AMAR$^{!}$-DA$^{!}$)
Dar 182: 3

Nergal (^{d}U.GUR)
BM 31976: 4 (*ikkaru ša* ~) BM 33930: 2 (*ginê ša* ~); 14f. (*makkūr* ~)

Professions and Officials

abarakku
see s.v. *mār abarakku*

agru (LÚ.A.GÀR, LÚ.ḪUN.GÁ, ⸢LÚ *a-gar*⸣$^{?}$)
BM 30764: 1; BM 30853: 2, 5; BM 31118: ⸢1⸣; BM 31226: 1; BM 31449: 1

āšipu (LÚ *a-ši-pu*)
BM 33954: 2

bēl pīḫāti (LÚ *pa-ḫa-tu*$_4$, LÚ(.EN).NAM)
BM 31393: ⸢4⸣; BM 31438: Rev. 6; BM 31572: 3; BM 32891: 3 (~ ^{garim}*tam-tì*); Dar 315: 7 (~ *é-sag-ìl*); Dar 338: 4, 14 (~ *ša* ^{uru}*Šaḫrīnu*)

dayyānu ((LÚ.)DI.KU$_5$)
BM 33936 *passim*; BM 32858: 10, 20

dalû (LÚ *da-li-e*)
see s.v. *sepīru*

ērib bīti (LÚ.KU$_4$ É)
BM 31449: 1

errēšu (LÚ *er-re-še-e*)
Dar 315: 3

ganzabaru (LÚ *gan-za-ba-ru*)
Dar 296: 2 Dar 527: 5

gardu (*ga-ar-du*)
see s.v. *ṣābū*

gaṭṭāya (LÚ *ga*$^!$*-da-a-a*)
Dar 351: 8

ikkaru ša Nergal (LÚ.ENGAR *šá* ^{d}U.GUR)
BM 31976: 4

Imbuka (LÚ *im-bu-ku-a-a*)
BM 31393: 3

Ionian(s) (LÚ *ia-ma-na-a-a*)
BM 32891: 5 (also see s.v. *sepīru*), 15

kinattu (LÚ ⸢*ki-na*⸣*-at-tu*, LÚ *ki-na-ta*)
BM 33930: 8; Dar 430: 7

LÚ.DÍM (= *mubannû* or *itinnu*)
BM 30994: 11 (//BM 31722^{+}: 11)

LÚ [...]
BM 33930: 9 (LÚ ⸢x-x⸣-*ri*.ME[Š]); Dar 577: 1 (⸢LÚ$^{?}$⸣ [...])

malāḫu (LÚ *ma-la-ḫu*)
BM 30490: 16

mār abarakku (LÚ DUMU *a-ba-rak-ku*)
BM 31976: 3f.

mār Bābili (DUMU/LÚ-TIN.TIR.KI LÚ.DUMU-TIN.TIR.KI)
BM 30651: 4 ([(x)] *ša bīt* ~); BM 31416: 6; Dar 158: 10

mār banê (DUMU.DÙ)
see s.v. *ṣābū*

mār damqa (LÚ.DUMU-*dam-qa*)
Dar 351: 8

mār šipri ((LÚ.)DUMU *šip-ri*, LÚ.A.KIN, LÚ.KIN.GI$_4$.A)
BM 31026: 5; BM 31976: 3; Dar 430: 6, ⸢13⸣; Dar 542: 6

mār sīsî (DUMU LÚ *si-si-i*)
CT 22 74: 6, 9, 15, 18, 28

mašennu (LÚ *ma-še-e-nu*, LÚ.AGRIG)
BM 30490: 2, 16; BM 33972: 23

maṣṣār abulli (LÚ.EN.NUN-KÁ.GAL)
CT 22 74: 28

maṣṣār gišri (LÚ.EN.NUN-*gi-iš-ri*, *-giš-ri*)
TCL 13 196: 8, 22

mubannû (LÚ *mu-ban-ni-*⸢*e*⸣)
see s.v. *šaknu*

mukinnu ([LÚ] *mu-kin-nu*)

BM 33968: 2

nuḫatimmu (LÚ.MU)
BM 33968: Rev. 3′; also see s.v. LÚ.DÍM

nukarribu (LÚ.NU.GIŠ.KIRI$_6$)
Dar 342: Obv. 1 (wr. <LÚ>.NU.GIŠ. K[IRI$_6$]); also see s.v. *sepīru*

pāḫātu, see s.v. *bēl pīḫāti*

qaštu (LÚ.BAN)
BM 30772: 1 (*unāt* ~)

qēmêtu (*qí-me-e-*⸢*tu*$_4$⸣)
see s.v. *sepīru*

qīpānu (usually in ~*šu* "his ~")
BM 30261: 2? (wr. DI-*pi-ni-šú*); BM 30589: 5? (wr. LÚ DI-*pa-ni-šú*); BM 33954: 5 (⸢LÚ$^?$⸣ *qí-pa-ni-šú*), 11 (LÚ *qí-*{*pi*}*-pa-ni-šú*)

qīpu (LÚ.TIL.GÍD.DA)
BM 33936: 11 (~ Esagil)

rab bīti (LÚ.GAL É)
Dar 296: 3, 4; Dar 542: 7

rab dūri (LÚ.GAL BÀD)
BM 31226: 6; CT 22 74: 7, 21

rab ḫanšê (LÚ.GAL *ḫa-an-še-e*)
BM 30274: 6

rab kāri (LÚ.GAL-*ka*(-*a*)-*ri*)
BM 31347: ⸢8⸣; Dar 268: 3

rab kāṣir (LÚ.GAL *ka-ṣir*)
Dar 105: 3; also see s.v. Nār$^?$ Rab-kāṣir

rab […] (LÚ GAL […]/⸢x x⸣)
BM 30853: 2; BM 33968: Rev. 2′

rē'u ginê ([LÚ.]SIPA-*gi-ni-e*)
Dar 351: 8

rēšu (LÚ.SAG)
BM 30853: 7, 9; BM 31393: 3 (LÚ.S[AG$^?$ …]); ~ *ša ekalli eššu* see s.v. *sepīru*; ~ *ša ekalli rabi* see s.v. *sepīru*

sepīru (LÚ *si-pi-ri*, LÚ *si-pir*)
BM 30589: 9f. (~ *ša rēšī ša muḫḫi kurummāti ša ekalli eššī*); BM 30639: 2f. (~ *ša nukarribī u dalê ša ekalli rabi u ekalli eššī*); BM 30799: 3 (~ *ša* ^{m}x x [x x] *na-a'*); BM 30980: 2f. (~ *ša rēšī ša ekalli eššī*); BM 31138: 5; BM 31393: [3]f. (~ *ša šadê ša bēl* [*pīḫāti*]); BM 31572: 4f. (~ [*ša*] *rēšī ša ekalli eššī*); BM 31786: ⸢3f.⸣ (~ [*ša*]-*rēšī ša šarri ša ekalli rabi*; BM 32891: [5] (~ (of) the Ionians)?; BM 32891: 4f. (~ *ša ummânī*); BM 33112: 5 (~ *ša qēmêti*); Dar 544: 3

ṣābū (LÚ.ERIN$_2$.MEŠ)
BM 30853: 7f.; BM 31554: ⸢3⸣; CT 22 74: 21, 24, 29; 19 (~ DUMU.DÙ.MEŠ); 26 (~ *ša gardu*); 31f. (~ *ša* ^{giš}*narkabti*); Dar 154: 2 (~ *ša* ^{giš}*narkabti*)

ša bīt ipri (*ša* É *ip-ru*)
BM 30446: 5

ša bīt mār Bābili
see s.v. *mār Bābili*

ša (*muḫḫi*) *sūti* (*ša* GIŠ.BÁN)
Dar 315: 7; Dar 453: [8]

(*ša*)-*rēš šarri* (LÚ.SAG-LUGAL)
BM 30591: 2, 12; BM 30980: 2; BM 31036: 4; BM 31138: 4; BM 31572: 4; BM 33930: 4; Dar 544: 3

šādidu (LÚ *šá-di-du*/*di*(-*e*))
BM 30853: 19; BM 30764: 1; BM 30446: 12 (wr. *šá-da-de-e*); BM 31188: 1 (wr. *šá-da-du*); BM 32932: 1

šadû
BM 30795: 10 (wr. LÚ *šá-da-e*.MEŠ$^!$); BM 31438: Rev. 5 (wr. *šá-di-i*); BM 31393: 4 (wr. LÚ *šá-di-e*.MEŠ, see s.v. *sepīru*)

šākin ṭēmi (LÚ.GAR-UŠ$_4$)
BM 30651: 3′f.; BM 30853: 4, 11, 15, 22, 23, 30, 37

šākin ṭēmi Bābili (LÚ.GAR-UŠ$_4$ E.KI, -TIN.TIR.KI, -*ba-bi-i-li* Dar 206)
BM 30256: 3; BM 30589: 9, 11; BM 30795: 9; BM 30980: 5; BM 31036: 7; BM 31188: 3; BM 31393: 7, 9; BM 31572: [3]; BM 31786: ⸢5⸣; BM 32891: 6; BM 32932: 3; BM 33112: ⸢4⸣; BM 33954: 3; Dar 154: 3; Dar 206: 6; Dar 577: 4; TCL 13 196: 3, 5

šākin ṭēmi Kiš (LÚ.GAR-UŠ$_4$ KIŠ.KI)
BM 33936: 8

šaknu (LÚ.GAR)
BM 33930: 23 (~ ^{lú} *mubannê*)

šanû (LÚ.2-*ú*)
BM 31026: 6; Dar 430: 7

šāpiru
BM 33930: 9 (LÚ *š*[*á*$^?$-*pi*]*r*$^?$-*ri*.MEŠ); Dar 437: 10, 11, 12 (LÚ.UGULA-*é-sag-ìl*)

šarru (LUGAL)
see s.v. *ḫarrān šarri* and s.v. *makkūr šarri*

šatammu (LÚ.ŠÀ.TAM)
Dar 182: 4 (~ E'igikalamma)

tašlišū (LÚ *taš-li-šú* .MEŠ)
CT 22 74: 6, 11

ummânu (*um-ma-nu*)
see s.v. *sepīru*

urašû ([LÚ *ú*]-*ra-šú*)
BM 31188: 1

ušparu (LÚ.UŠ.BAR)
Dar 182: 2

zargaya (LÚ *za-ar-ga-a-a*)
BM 31026: 2

Texts Cited

Part Four

1. BM 30641

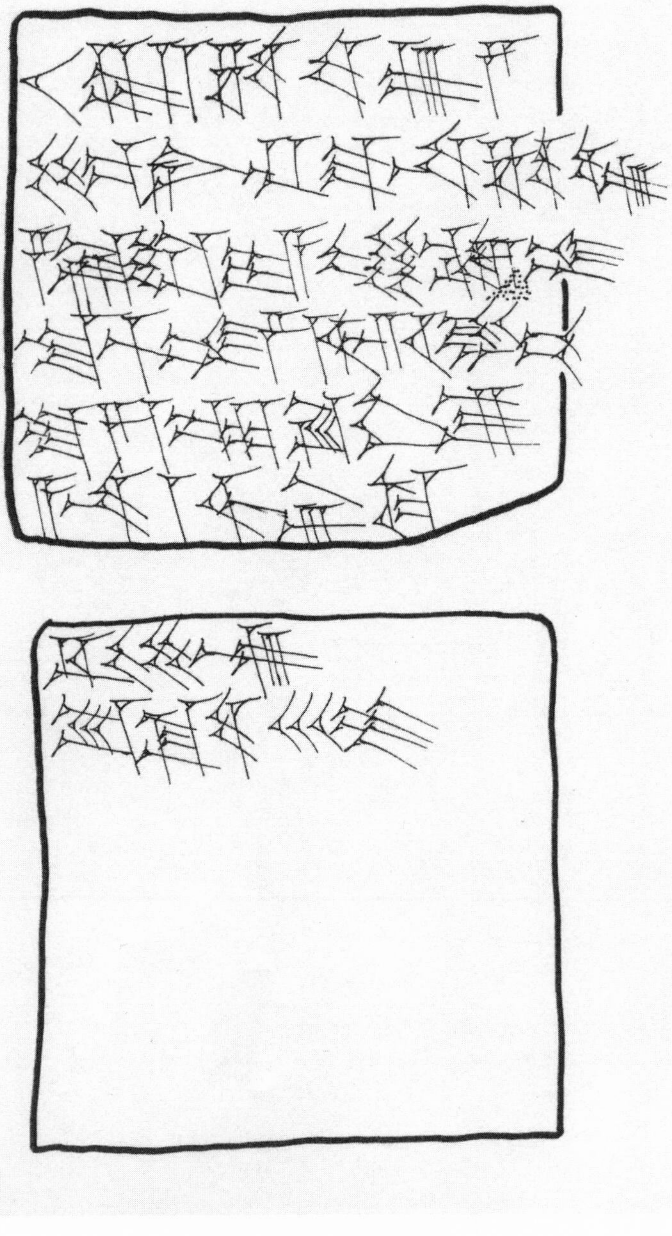

2. BM 30651
Obverse

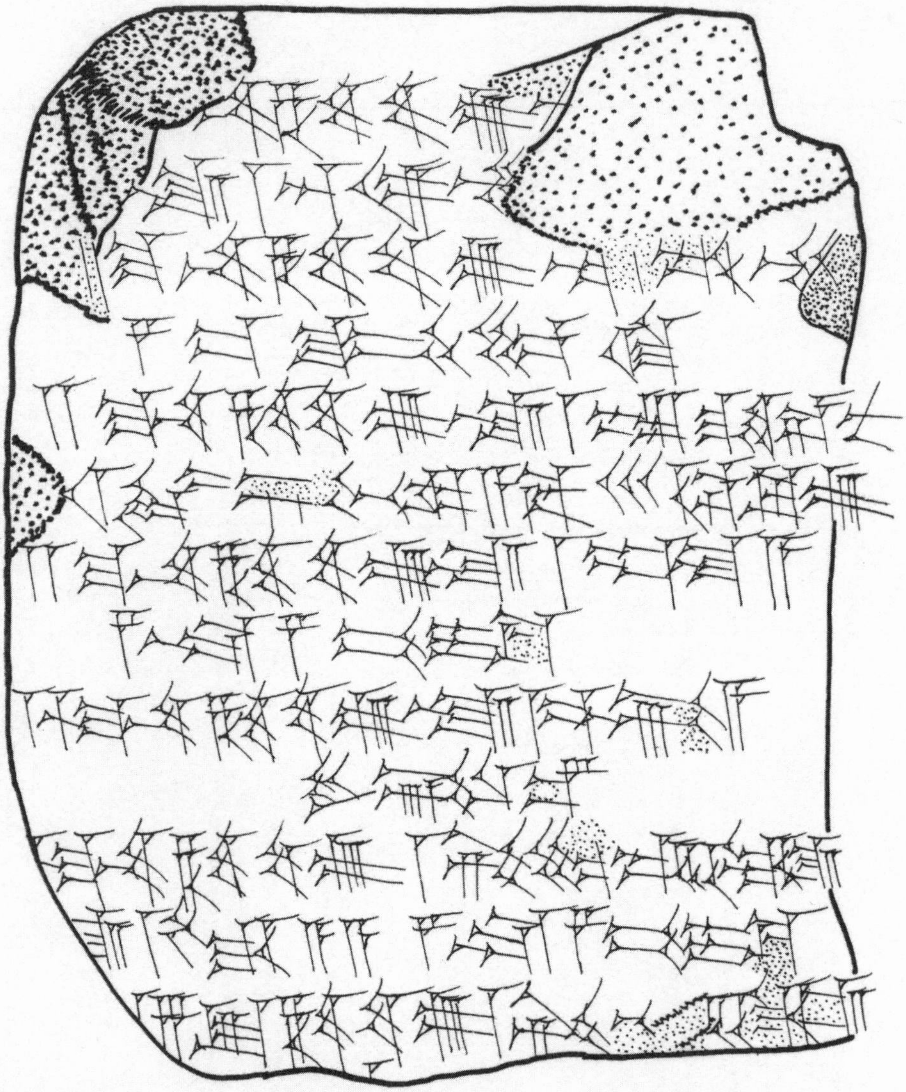

2. BM 30651
Reverse

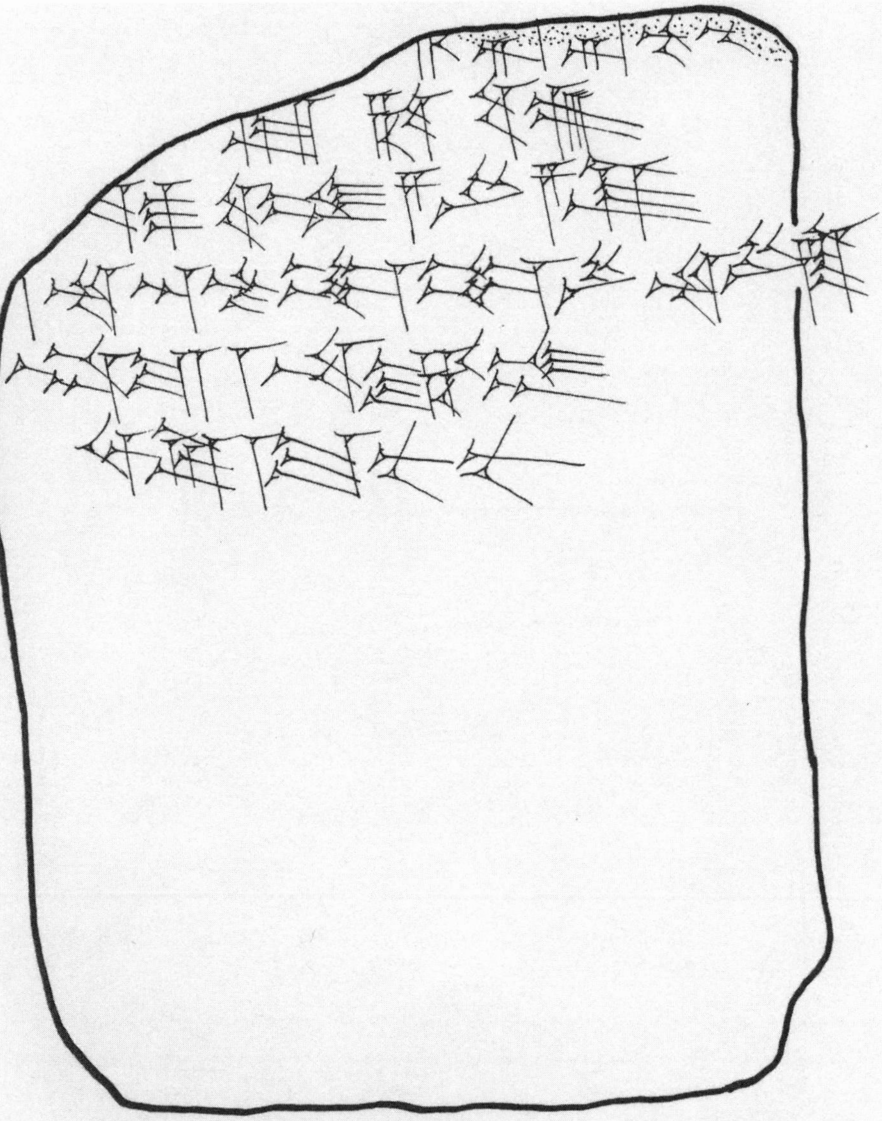

3. BM 30747

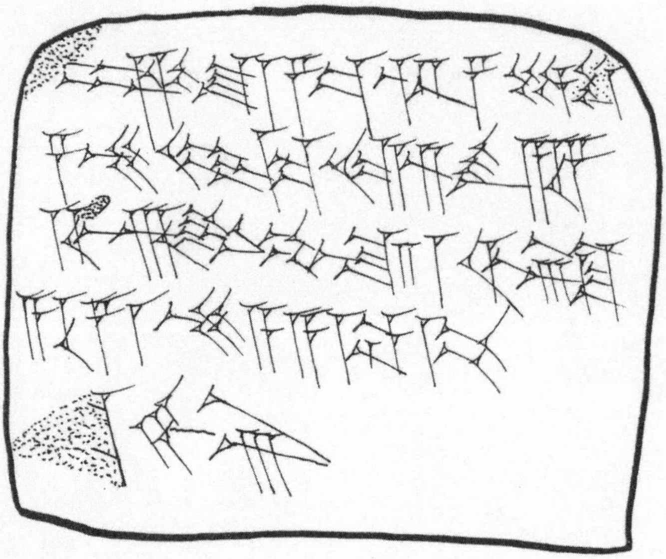

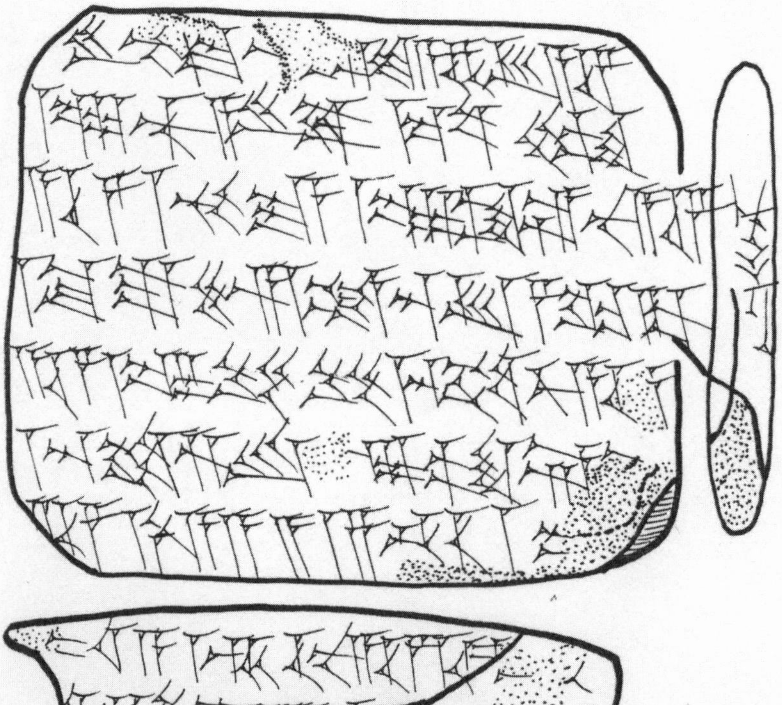

4. BM 30799

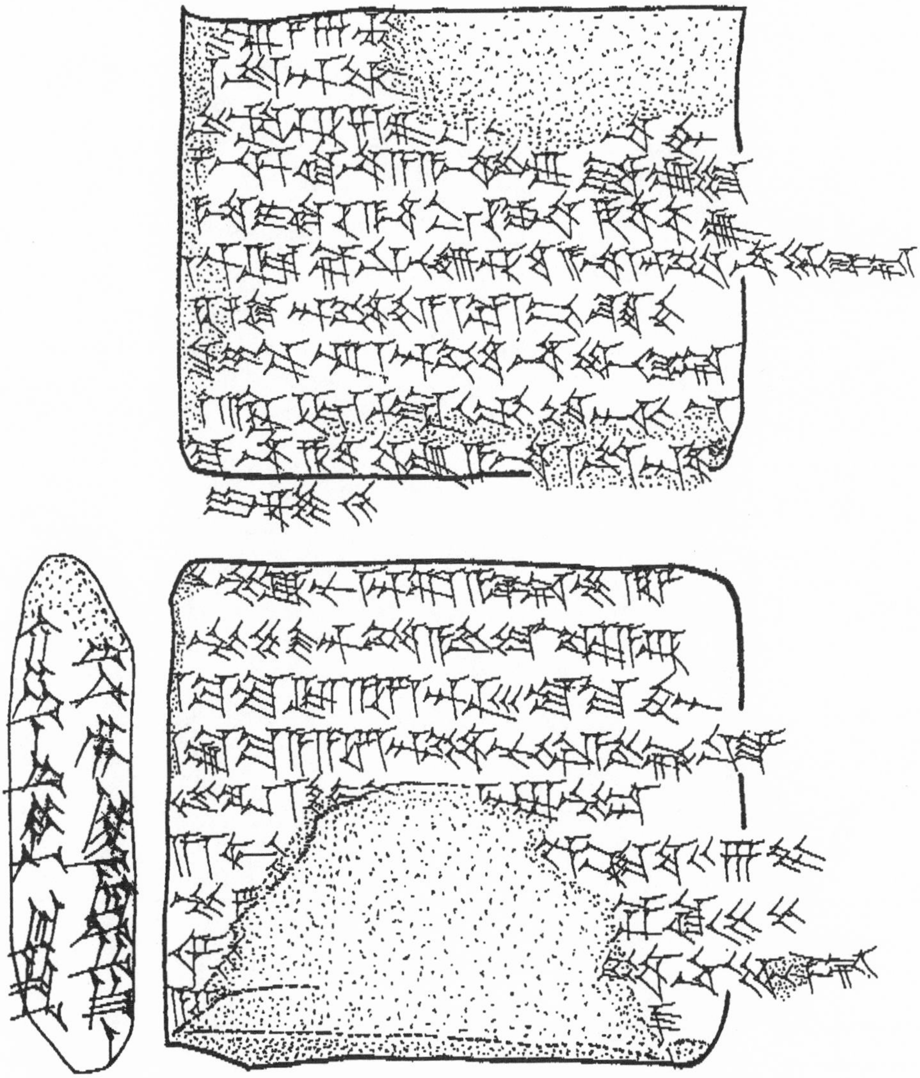

5. BM 30853
Obverse

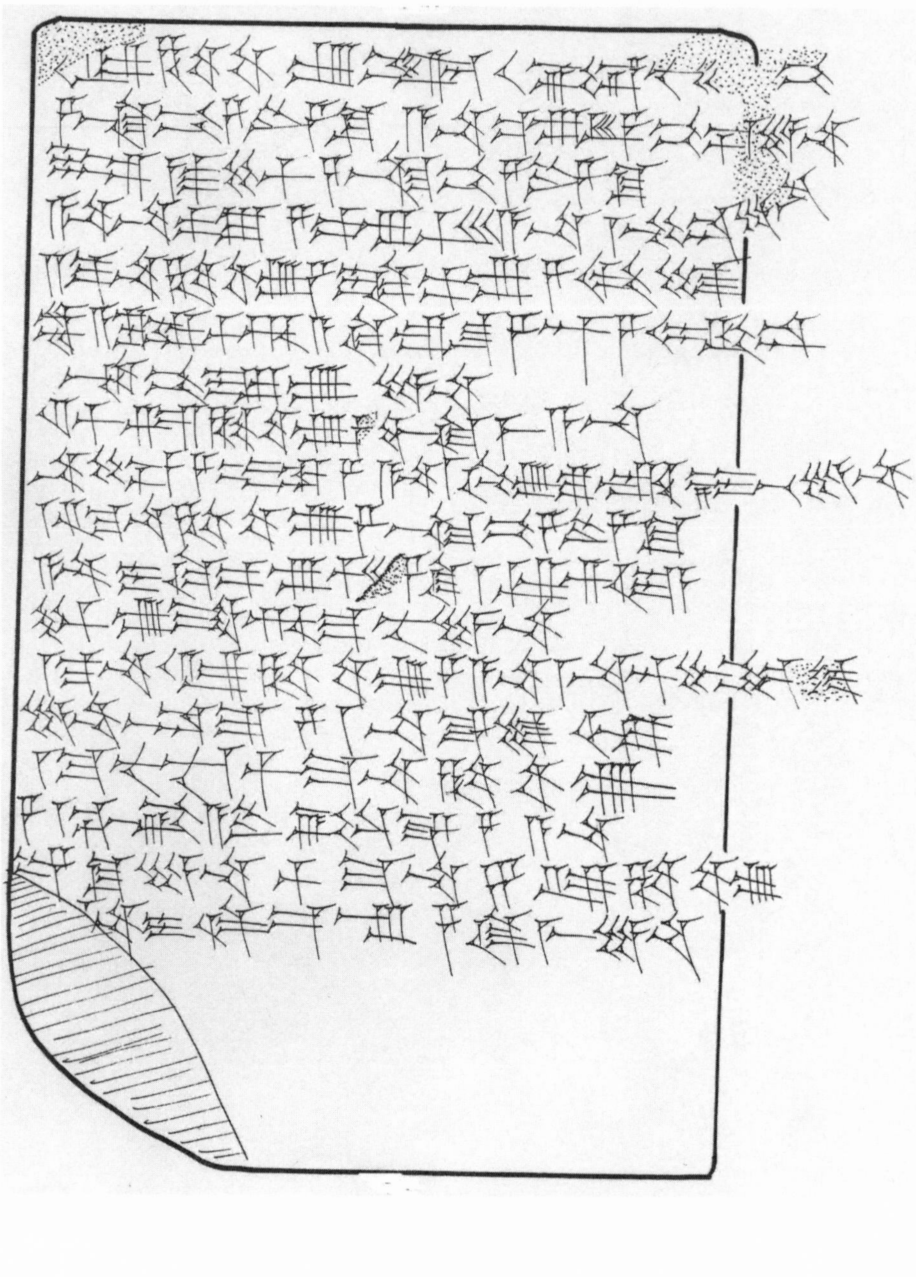

5. BM 30853
Reverse

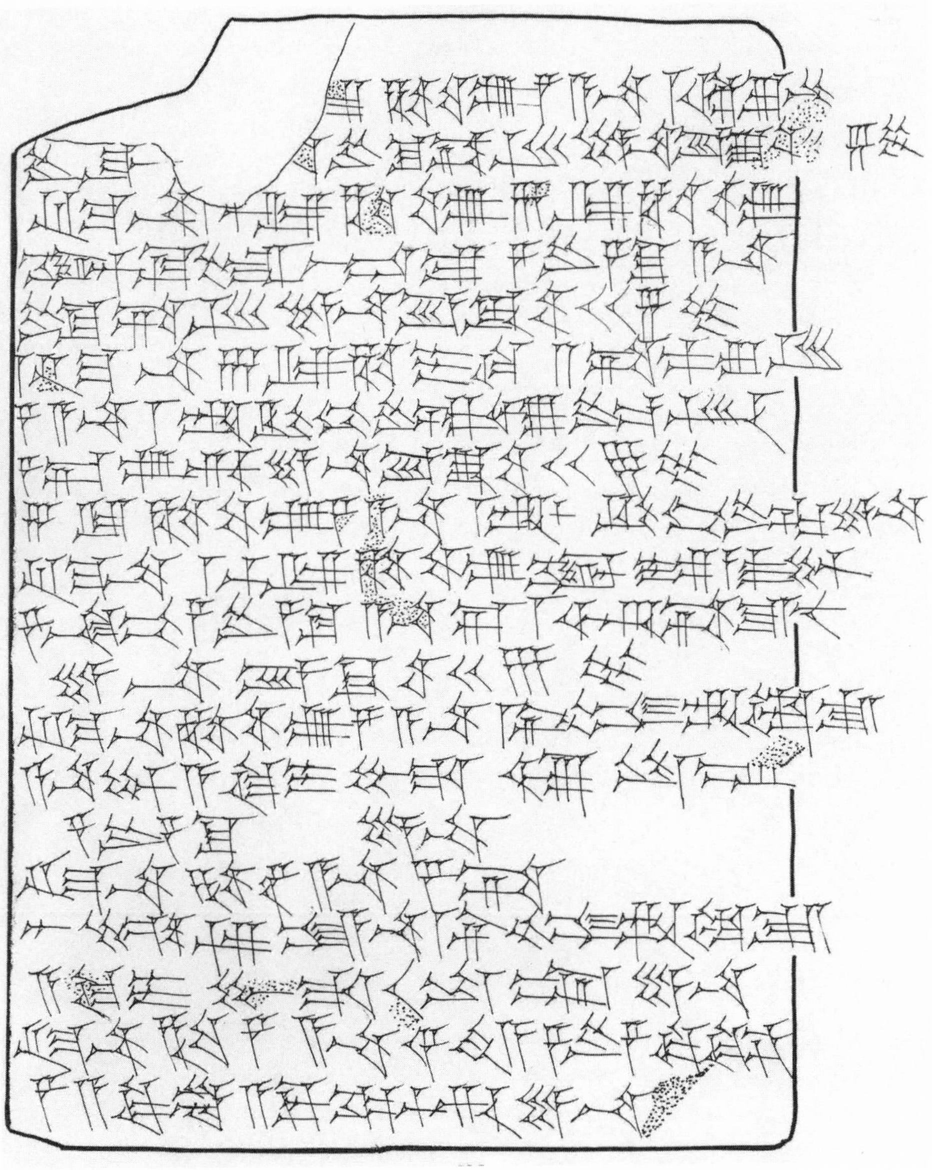

6. BM 30854

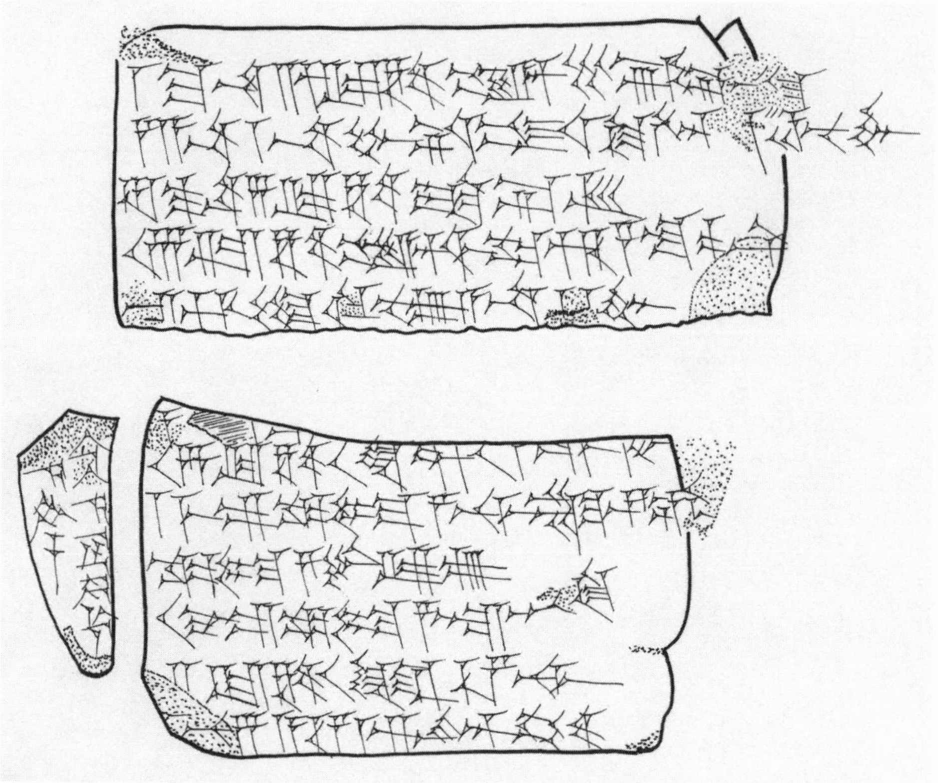

7. BM 31018

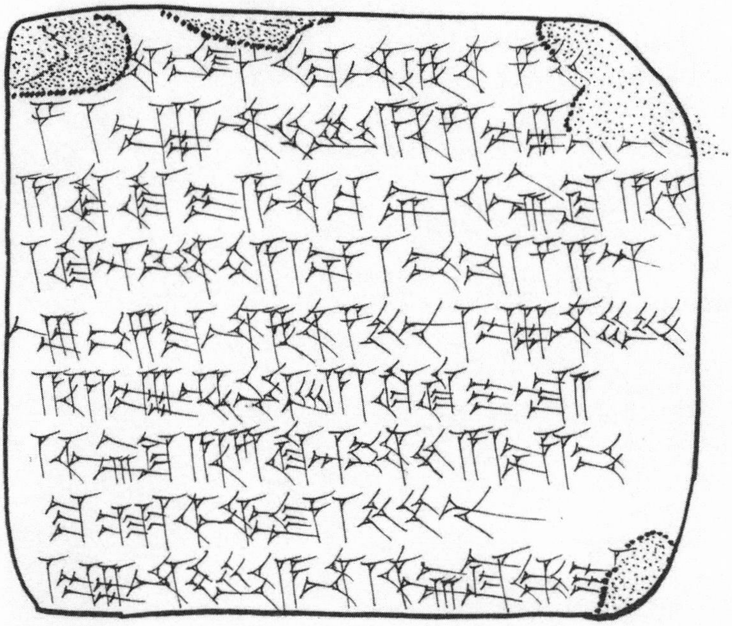

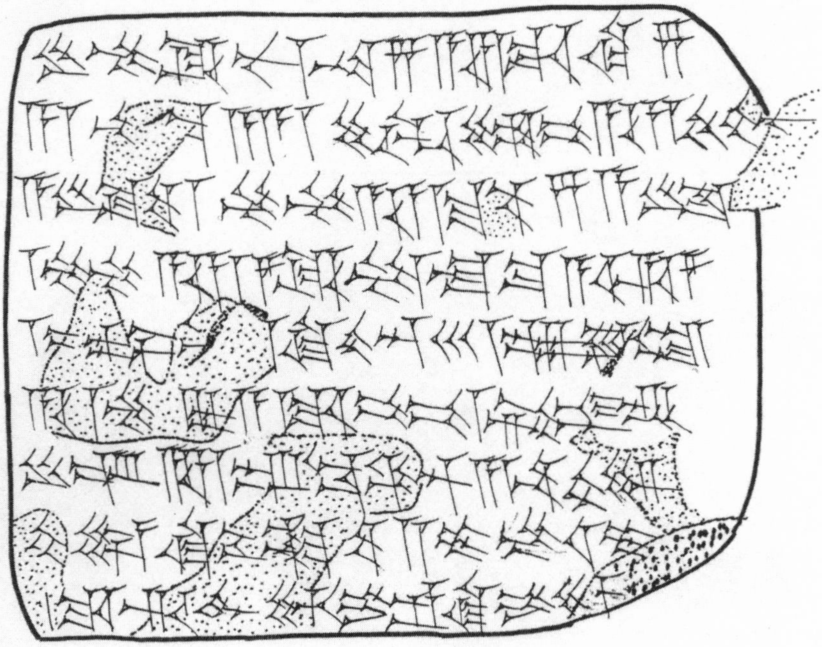

8. BM 31203

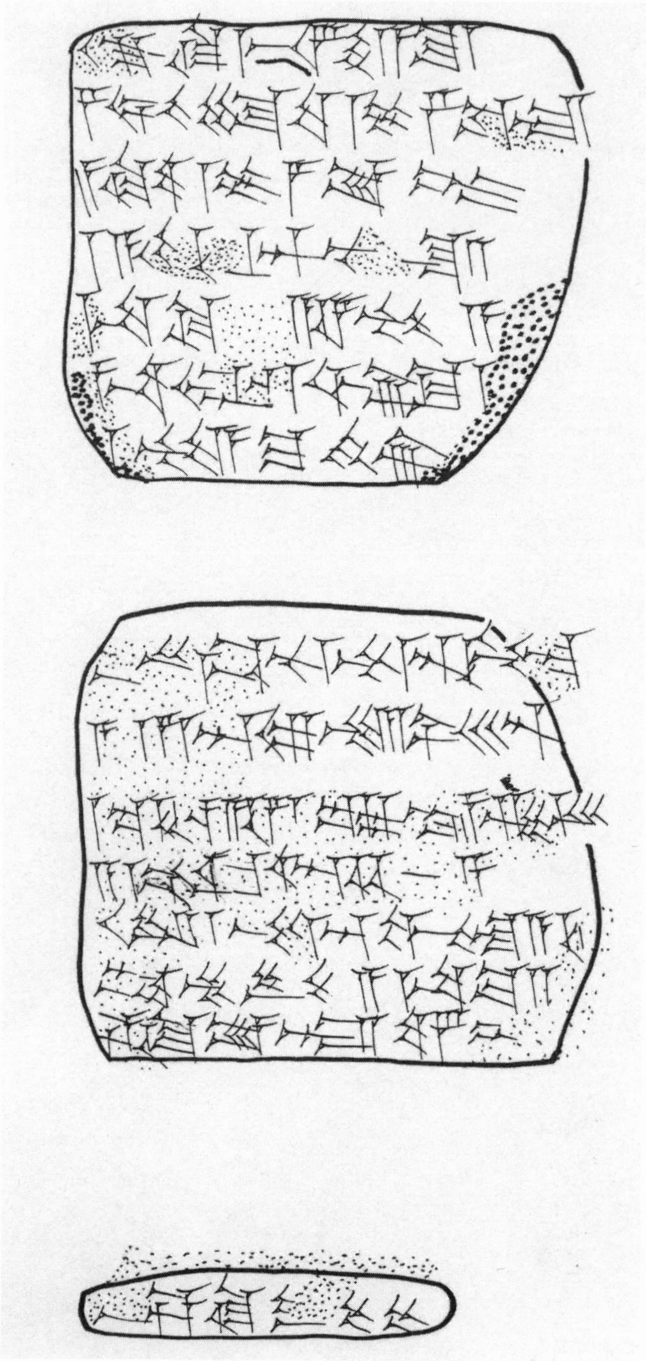

9. BM 31393

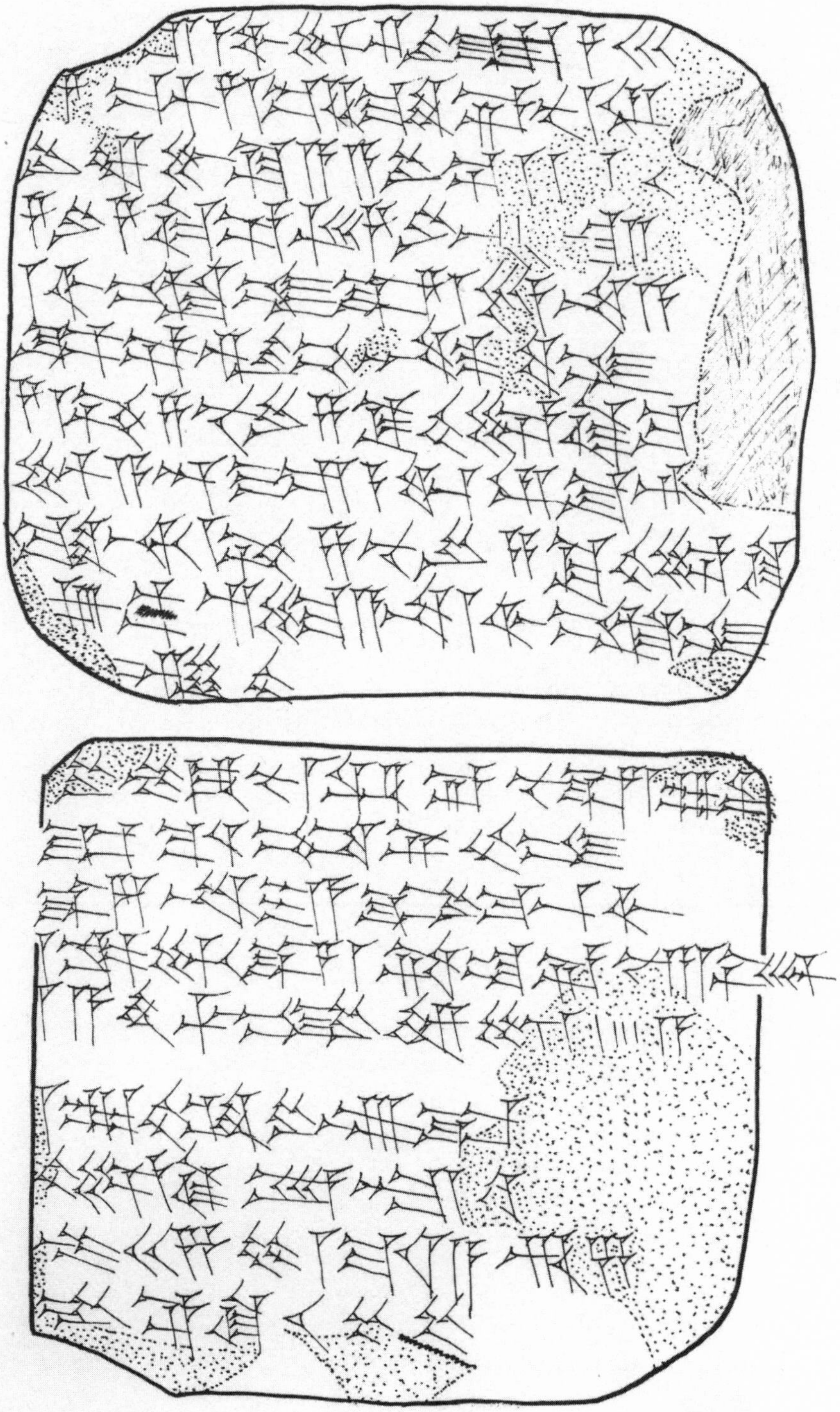

10. BM 31347

11. BM 31416

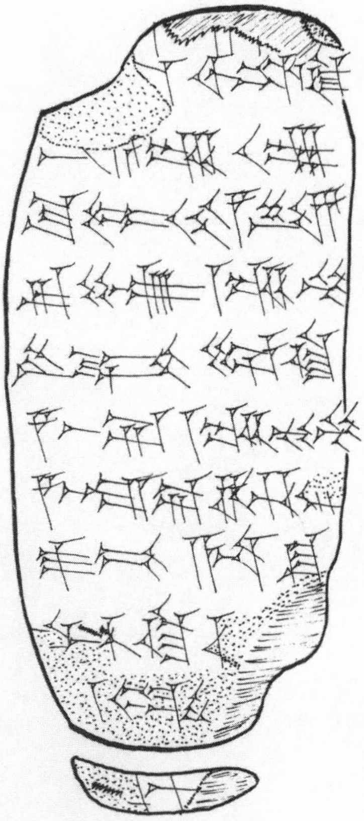

Obverse

Reverse

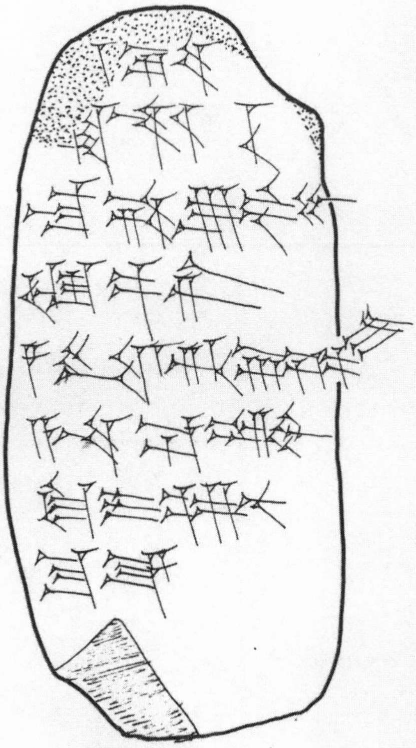

12. BM 31438

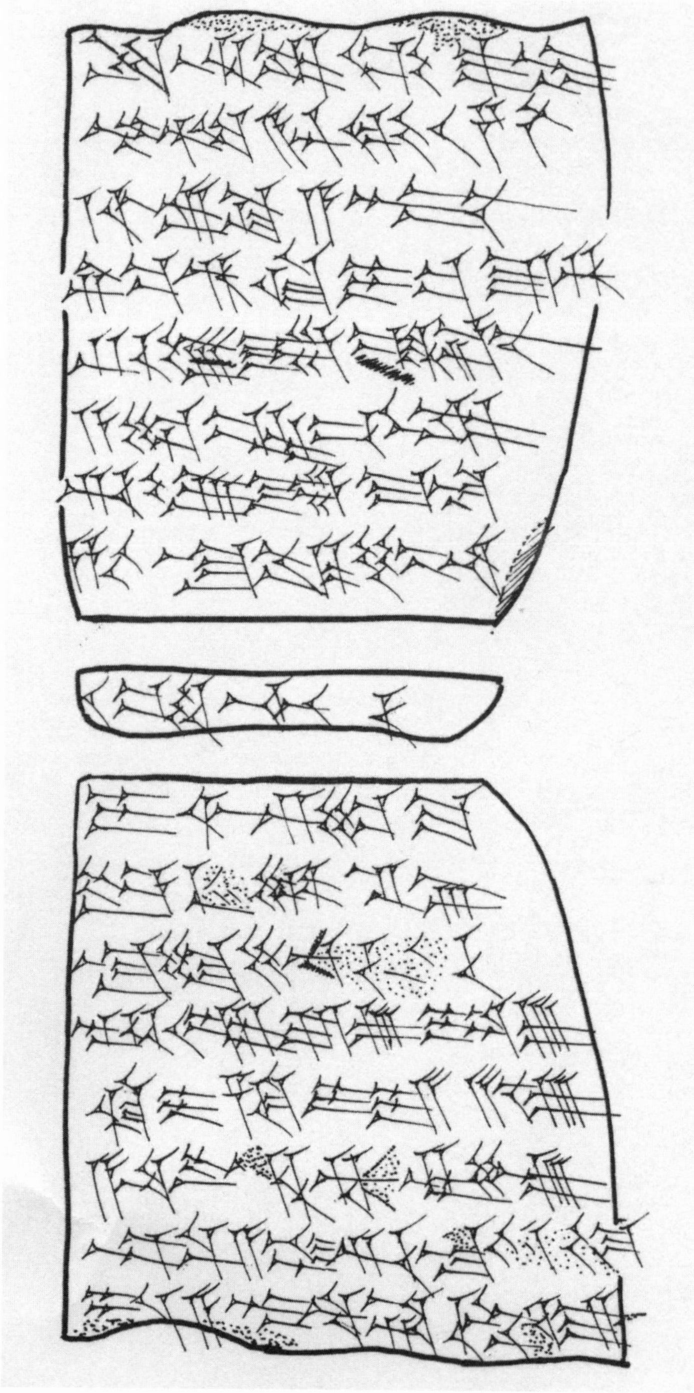

13. BM 31449

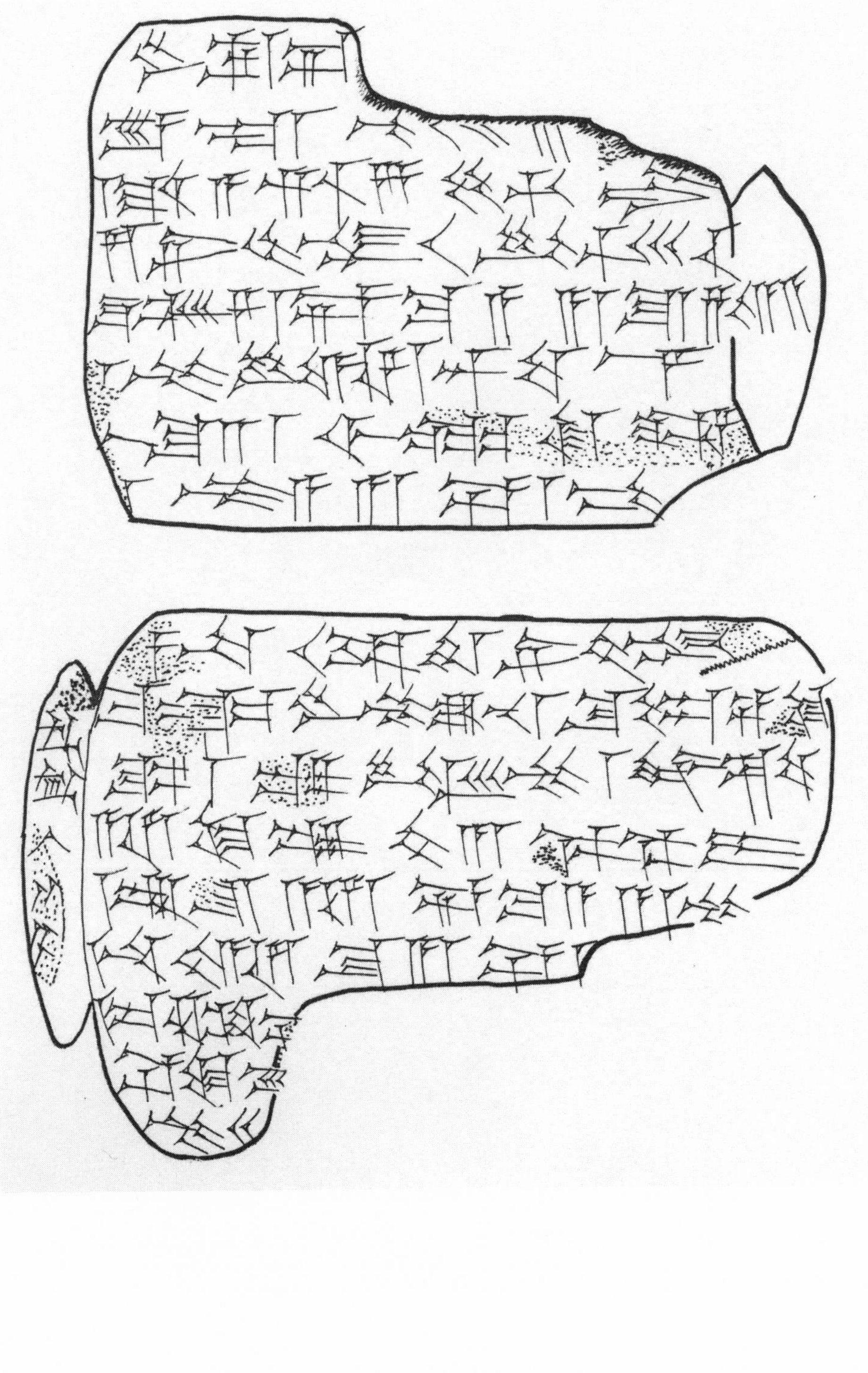

14. BM 31554

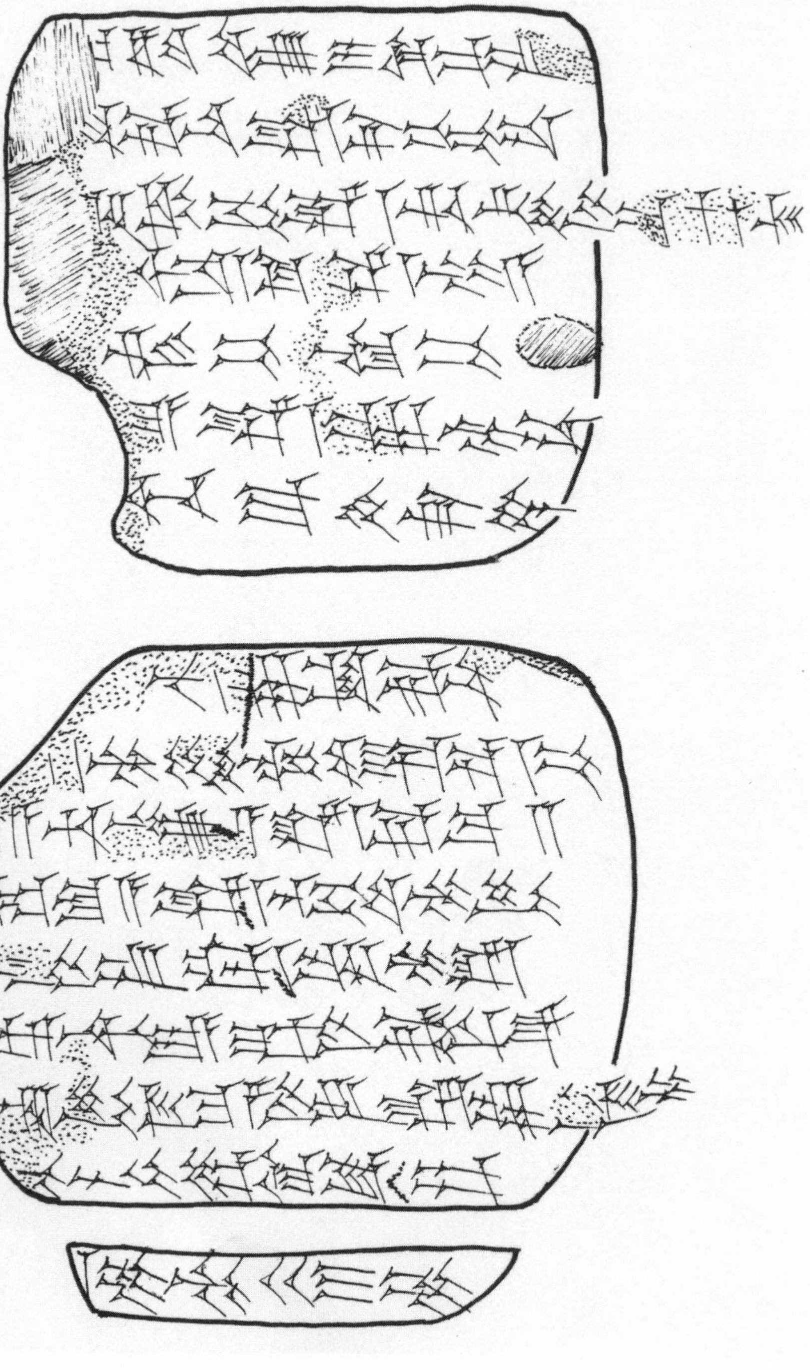

15. BM 31667 + BM 31641

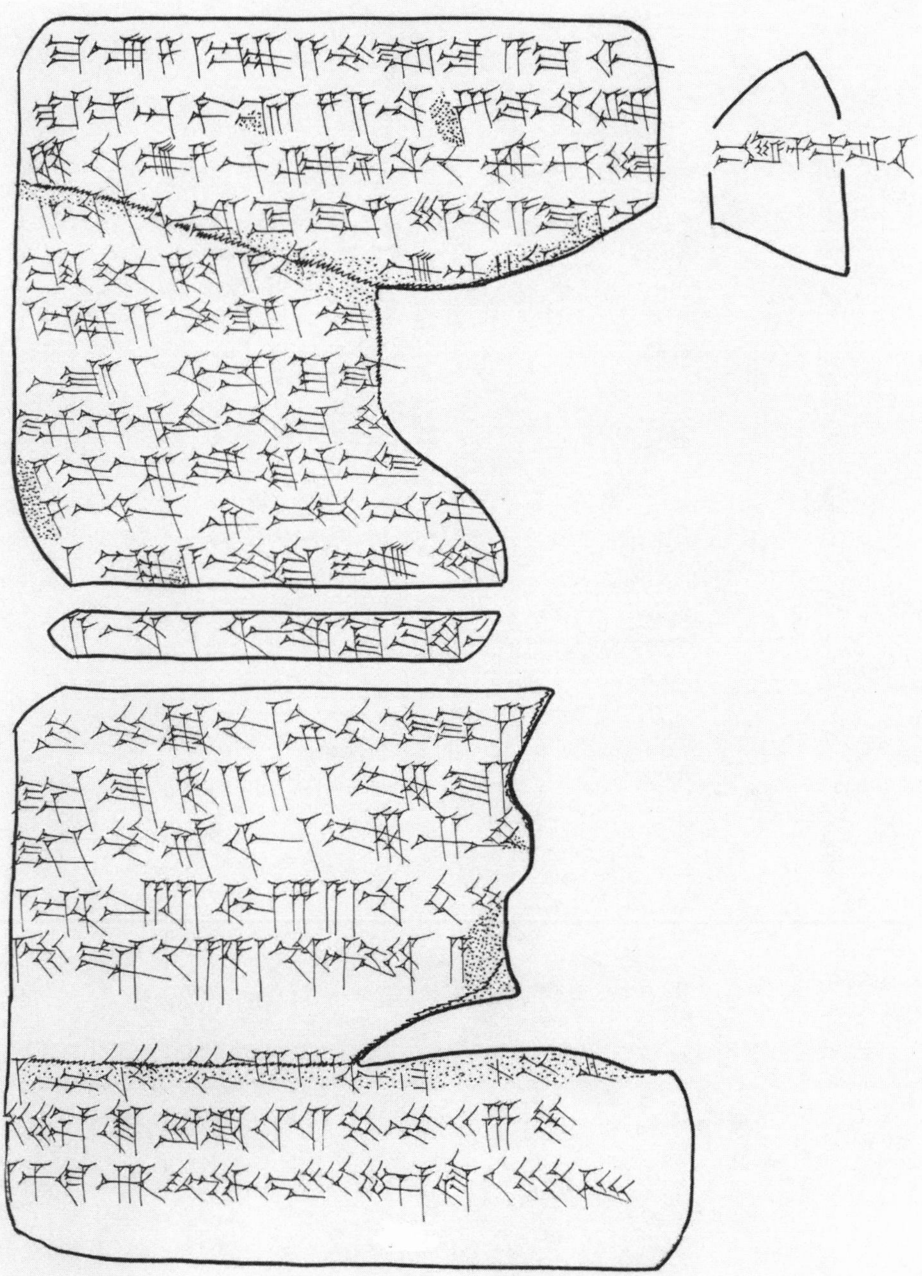

16. BM 31690 + BM 30658

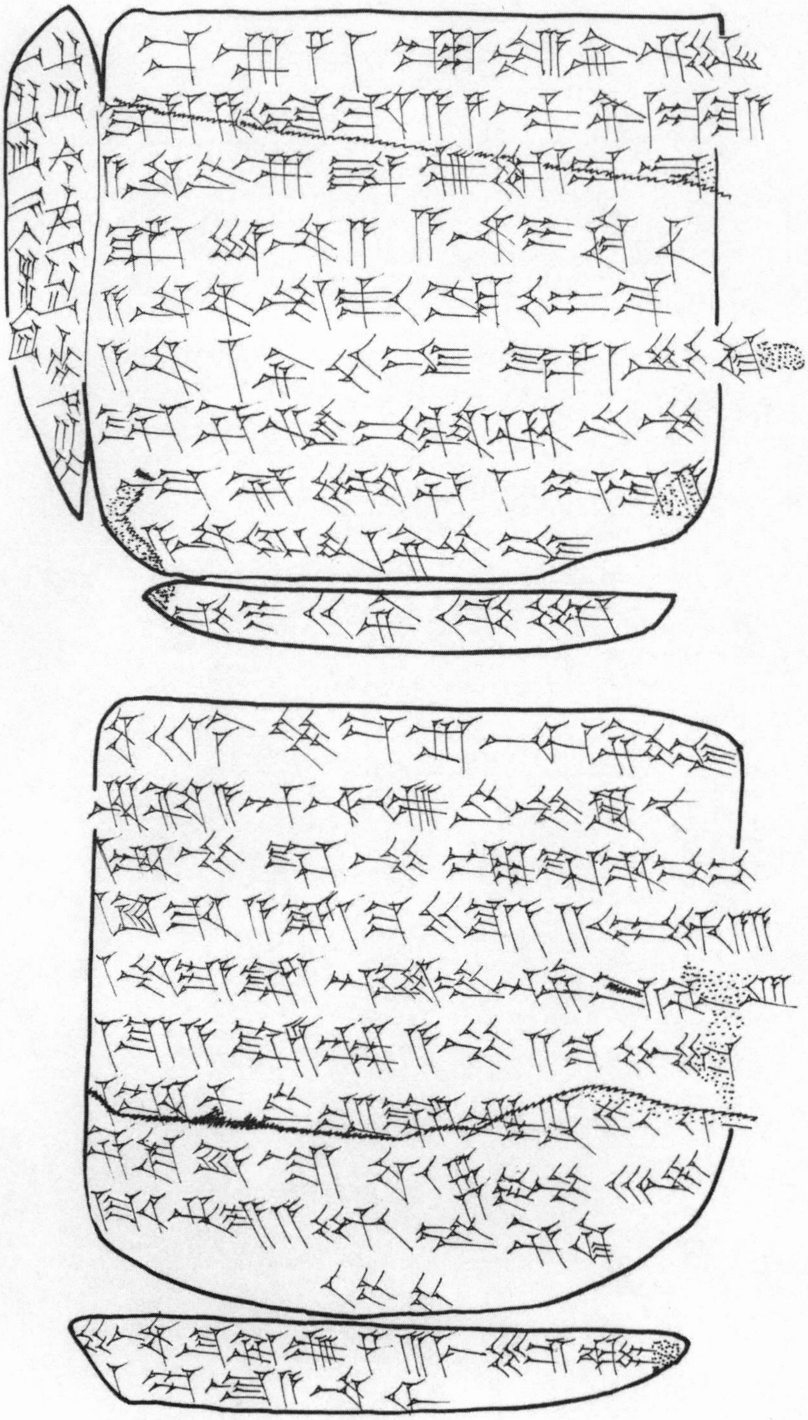

17. BM 31718

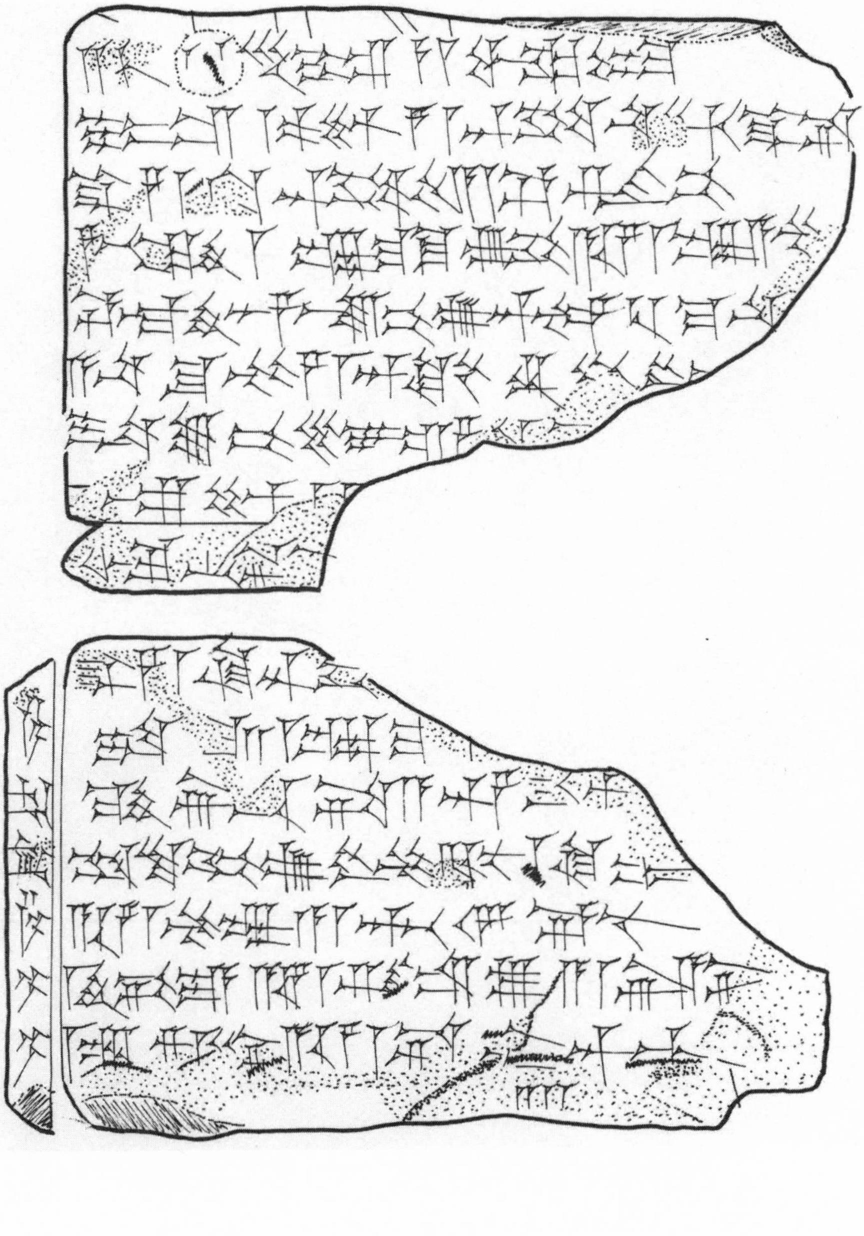

18. BM 31891

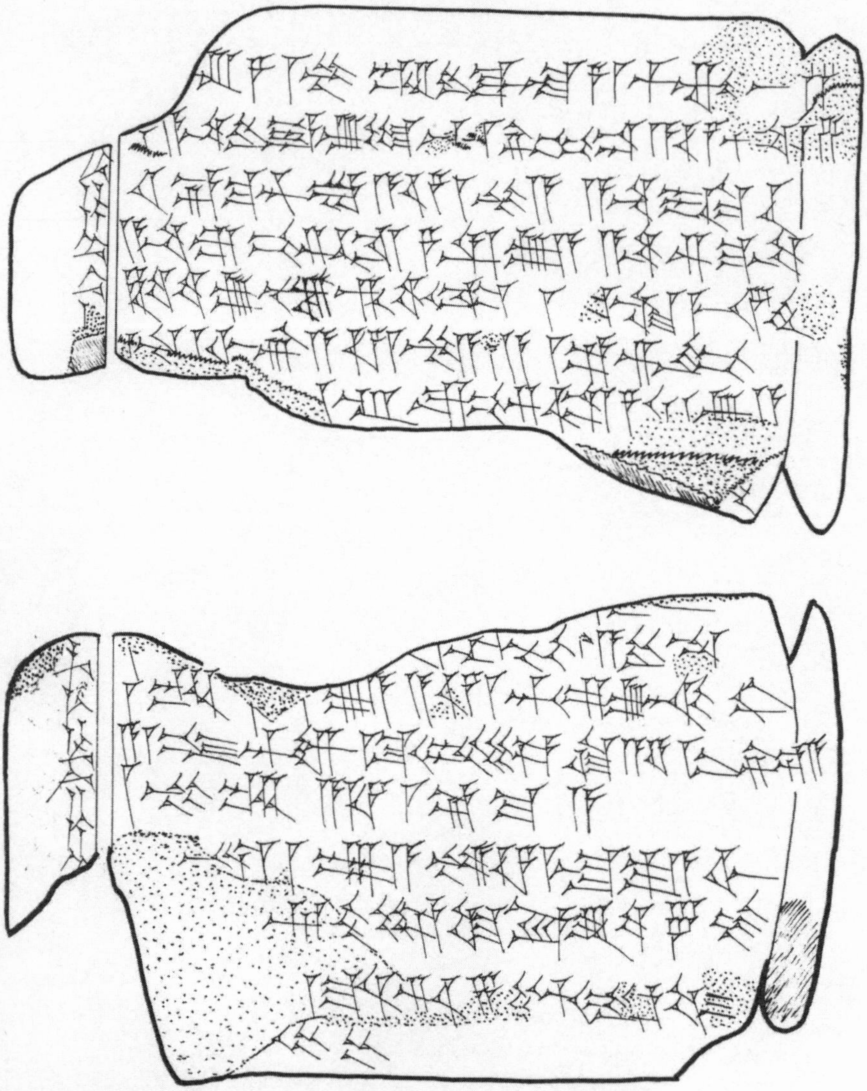

19. BM 33122
Obverse

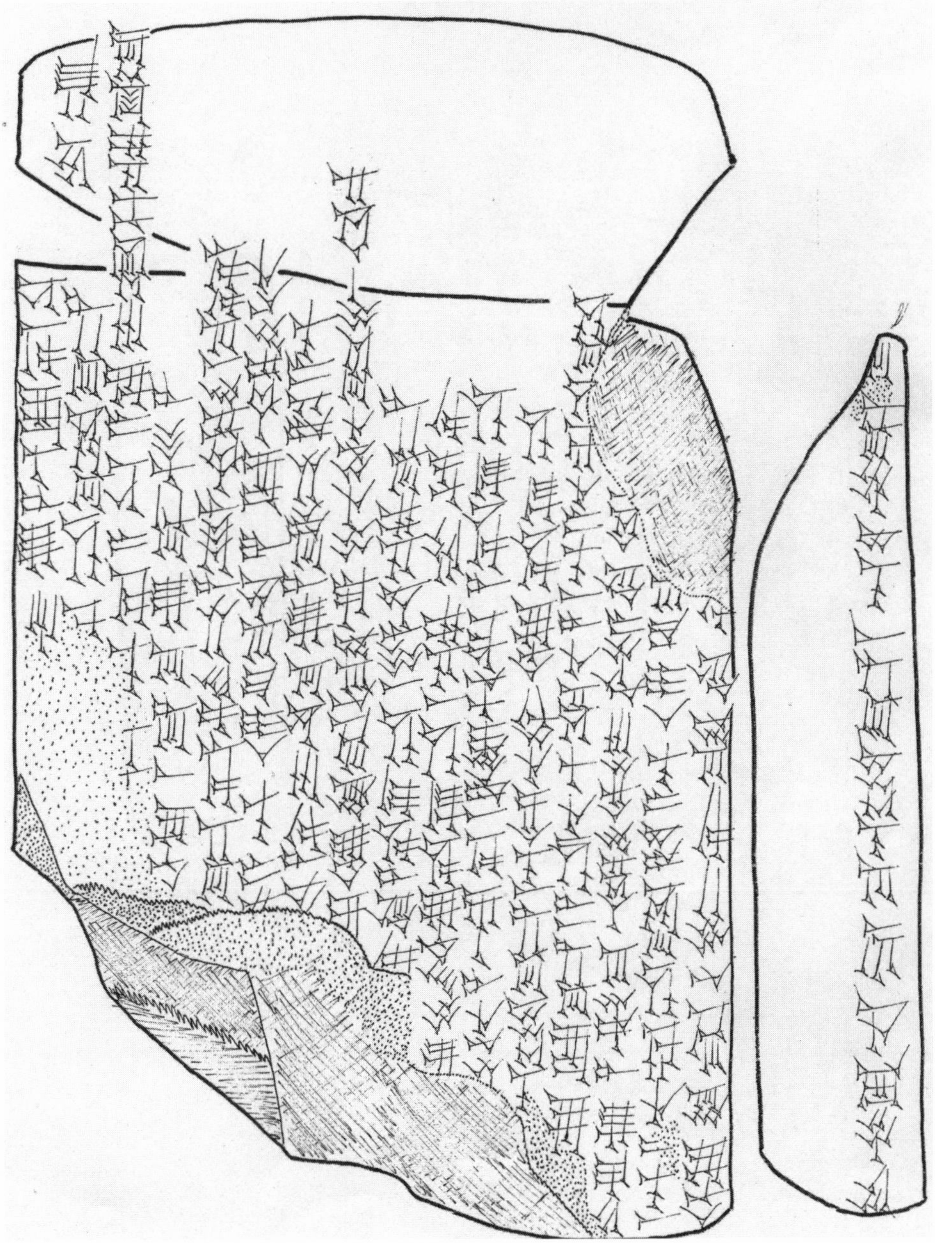

19. BM 33122
Reverse

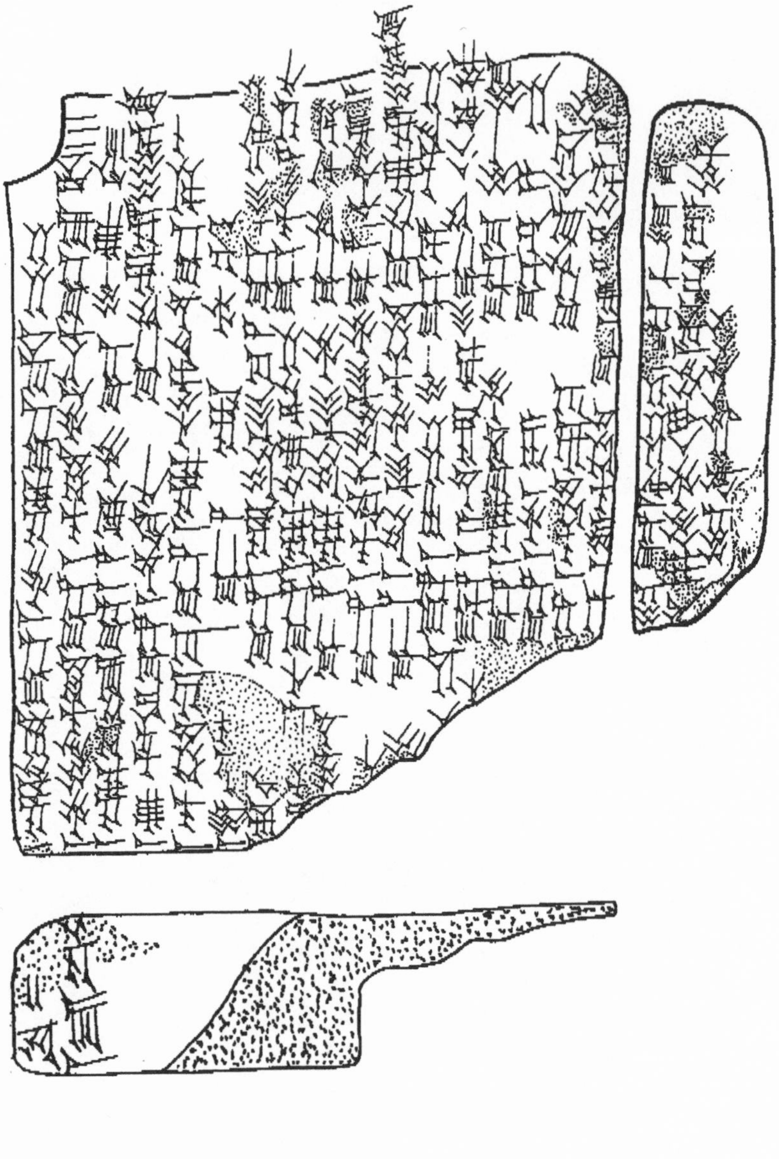